Investment
Valuation

Tools and Techniques for Determining the Value of *Any* Asset

Fourth Edition

ASWATH DAMODARAN
www.damodaran.com

WILEY

Published by John Wiley & Sons, Inc., Hoboken, New Jersey.
Published simultaneously in Canada.

For general information on our other products and services or for technical support, please contact our Customer Care Department within the United States at (800) 762-2974, outside the United States at (317) 572-3993 or fax (317) 572-4002.

Wiley also publishes its books in a variety of electronic formats. Some content that appears in print may not be available in electronic formats. For more information about Wiley products, visit our web site at www.wiley.com.

Library of Congress Cataloging-in-Publication Data:

Damodaran, Aswath.
    Investment valuation : tools and techniques for determining the value of any asset / Aswath Damodaran.—4th ed.
        p. cm.—(Wiley finance series)
    Includes bibliographical references and index.
    ISBN 978-1-394-25460-6 (cloth); ISBN 978-1-394-25461-3 (ebk);
    ISBN 978-1-394-25462-0 (ebk); ISBN 978-1-394-26273-1 (paper);
    ISBN 978-1-394-26274-8 (ebk); ISBN 978-1-394-26275-5 (ebk)
    1. Corporations—Valuation—Mathematical models. I. Title.
    HG4028.V3 D353 2025
    658.15—dc23   2024034300

SKY10091801_112124

I would like to dedicate this book to Michele, whose patience and support made it possible, to my four children—Ryan, Brendan, Kendra, and Kiran—who provided the inspiration, and to my two grandchildren—Noah and Lily—who provided the joy.

Contents

Preface to the Fourth Edition

This is a book about valuation—the valuation of stocks, bonds, options, futures and real assets. It is a fundamental precept of this book that any asset can be valued, albeit imprecisely in some cases. I have attempted to provide a sense of not only the differences between the models used to value different types of assets, but also the common elements in these models.

The past two decades have been eventful ones for those interested in valuation for several reasons. First, the growth of Asian and Latin American markets brought emerging market companies into the forefront, and you will see the increased focus on these companies in this edition. Second, we saw the havoc wreaked by macroeconomic factors on company valuations during the bank crisis of 2008 and the pandemic in 2020, both which shook faith in markets and created new questions in valuation. The lessons I learned about financial fundamentals during these crises about risk-free rates, risk premiums, and cash flow estimation are incorporated into the text. Third, the past decade has seen the surge in platform companies, where the most impressive numbers about these companies are not in their operating metrics, but in the users and subscribers on their platforms. In this edition, we directly confront the question of how to value a subscriber, user, or customer, and use the answer to value these companies. Fourth, I have spent more time in the last decade talking about how valuations are bridges between stories and numbers, and in this edition, I have added a chapter explaining how to build these bridges. Finally, as meme stocks and crypto investments capture the imagination of some in the market, we look at pricing and valuing them.

With each shift, the perennial question arises: "Is valuation still relevant in this market?" and my answer remains unchanged, "Absolutely and more than ever." As technology increasingly makes the printed page an anachronism, I have tried to adapt in many ways. First, this book will be available in e-book format, and hopefully will be just as useful as the print edition (if not more so). Second, every valuation in this book will be put on the website that will accompany this book (www.damodaran.com), as will a significant number of datasets and spreadsheets. In fact, the valuations in the book will be updated online, allowing the book to have a much closer link to real-time valuations.

In the process of presenting and discussing the various aspects of valuation, I have tried to adhere to four basic principles. First, I have attempted to be as comprehensive as possible in covering the range of valuation models that are available to an analyst doing a valuation, while presenting the common elements in these models and providing a framework that can be used to pick the right model for any valuation scenario. Second, the models are presented with real-world examples, warts and all, to capture some of the problems inherent in applying these models. There is the obvious danger that some of these valuations will appear to be hopelessly wrong in hindsight, but this cost is well worth the benefit. Third, in keeping with my belief that valuation models are universal and not market-specific, illustrations from markets outside the United States are interspersed throughout the book. Finally, I have tried to make the book as modular as possible, enabling a reader to pick and choose sections of the book to read, without a significant loss of continuity.

CHAPTER 1

Introduction to Valuation

Every asset, financial as well as real, that is expected to generate cash flows in the future, has a value. The key to successfully investing in and managing these assets lies in understanding not only what the value is, but the sources of the value. It is undeniable that some assets are easier to value than others, and the details of valuation will vary from case to case. Thus, valuing of a real estate property will require different information and follow a different format than valuing a publicly traded stock. What is surprising, however, is not the differences in techniques across assets, but the degree of similarity in the basic principles of valuation.

This chapter lays out a philosophical basis for valuation, together with a discussion of how valuation is or can be used in a variety of frameworks, from portfolio management to corporate finance.

A PHILOSOPHICAL BASIS FOR VALUATION

It was Oscar Wilde who described a cynic as one who "knows the price of everything, but the value of nothing". He could very well have been describing some analysts and many investors, a surprising number of whom subscribe to the "bigger fool" theory of investing, which argues that the value of an asset is irrelevant as long as there is a "bigger fool" around willing to buy the asset from them. While this may provide a basis for some profits, it is a dangerous game to play, since there is no guarantee that such an investor will still be around when the time to sell comes.

A postulate of sound investing is that an investor does not pay more for an asset than it's worth. This statement may seem logical and obvious, but it is forgotten and rediscovered at some time in every generation and in every market. There are many who argue that value is in the eye of the beholder, and that any price can be justified if there are other investors willing to pay that price. That is dangerous, at least as an investment starting point. Perceptions may be all that matter when the investment is a painting or sculpture, but investors do not (and should not) buy most assets for aesthetic or emotional reasons; financial assets are acquired for the cash flows expected on them. Consequently, perceptions of value have to be backed up by reality, which implies that the price paid for any asset should reflect the cash flows it is expected to generate. The models of valuation described in this book attempt to relate value to the level and expected growth of these cash flows.

PRICING VERSUS VALUATION

Financial academics and practitioners use the words "price" and "value" interchangeably, with the former perhaps swayed by their early beliefs in efficient markets, where the two are expected to converge, and the latter by an assumption that these words measure the same things. In Figure 1.1, we draw a distinction between valuation and pricing, and argue that value and price are not only determined by different factors but require different tools. As the book's title indicates, we will examine the details of how to value assets, and we will also look at how best to price those assets in later chapters.

It is true that large numbers of market participants, perhaps even most, are not investors, but instead choose to play the "pricing" game. In that game, winning is defined as buying at a low price and selling at a higher one, taking advantage of shifts in market mood and momentum, with value playing little or no role. Throughout this book, we will classify these participants as traders, and we will hope that they, too, will be able to find use for the pricing portions of this book.

As a final note, we will argue that no matter which side of the investing/pricing divide you fall on, you will benefit by understanding how the other side works. Thus, if you are a true believer in intrinsic value, you will find yourself become better at valuation, if you understand how traders price assets. Conversely, if you are a trader, focused on the pricing process, you will become a better trader, if you learn more about how investors think and value companies.

THE BERMUDA TRIANGLE OF VALUATION

Like all analytical disciplines, valuation has developed its own set of myths over time. This section examines and debunks some of those myths and argues that the biggest challenges to valuation are not technical or mechanical, but come from the way we, as human beings, bring bias into out analyses and deal with uncertainty about the future and from the complexity that has been a by-product of access to data and powerful tools.

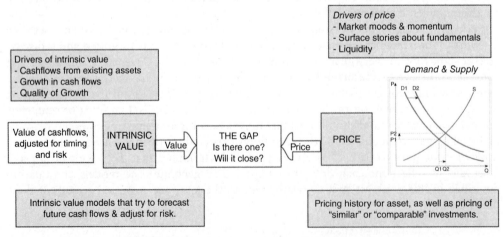

FIGURE 1.1   Value versus Price—The Difference

Bias: The Power of Your Priors

Valuation is neither the science that some of its proponents make it out to be nor the objective search for true value that idealists would like it to become. The models that we use in valuation may be quantitative, but the inputs leave plenty of room for subjective judgments. Thus, the final value that we obtain from these models is colored by the bias that we bring into the process. In fact, in many valuations, the price gets set first and the valuation follows.

The obvious solution is to eliminate all bias before starting on a valuation, but this is easier said than done. Given the exposure we have to external information, analyses, and opinions about a firm, it is unlikely that we embark on most valuations without some bias. In fact, a great deal of bias is subconscious. An investor who picks a company to value almost never does so with a blank slate, since that pick was probably triggered by something he or she heard about the company or read about it. In some cases, the bias can come from what you think about a company's products or its managers. If, like me, you have been an Apple products user for four decades, you will be biased to finding Apple under-valued and Microsoft overvalued before you even look at either company's numbers. Similarly, if you are an investor valuing Tesla in early 2024, it would be impossible for you to separate your views on Tesla from your views on Elon Musk, a man who evokes strong positive and negative reactions.

Can you avoid being biased? We don't think so, but you can be open about these biases, at least with yourself, since that may allow you to counter them, when you estimate numbers for the future. You can also avoid taking strong public positions on the value of a firm before the valuation is complete. In far too many cases, the decision on whether a firm is under- or overvalued precedes the actual valuation,[1] leading to seriously biased analyses. The second is to minimize, prior to the valuation, the stake we have in whether the firm is under- or overvalued.

Institutional concerns play a role in determining the extent of bias in valuation. For instance, it is an acknowledged fact that equity research analysts are more likely to issue buy rather than sell recommendations[2], i.e., they are more likely to find firms to be under-valued than overvalued. This can be traced partly to the difficulties analysts face in obtaining access and collecting information on firms that they have issued sell recommendations on, and partly to pressure that they face from portfolio managers, some whom might have large positions in the stock. In some cases, this trend is exacerbated by the pressure on equity research analysts to deliver investment banking business. Similarly, when bankers are asked to value target companies for mergers and acquisitions, the fact that banking compensation is tied to whether the deal is done and not to whether the deal is favorably priced, will cause target company valuations to be biased upwards. Again, if you do work for these institutions, it may be difficult, if not impossible, to counter those biases, but being aware that they exist is the first step to dealing with them.

As consumers of other people's valuations, the lesson of this section is that when using a valuation done by a third party, the biases of the analyst(s) should be considered before

---

[1] This is most visible in takeovers, where the decision to acquire a firm often seems to precede the valuation of the firm. It should come as no surprise, therefore, that the analysis almost invariably supports the decision.

[2] In most years, buy recommendations outnumber sell recommendations by a margin of 10 to 1. In recent years, this trend has become even stronger.

decisions are made on its basis. For instance, a self-valuation done by a target firm in a takeover is likely to be positively biased. While this does not make the valuation worthless, it suggests that the analysis should be viewed with skepticism.

BIAS IN EQUITY RESEARCH

The lines between equity research and salesmanship blur most in periods that are characterized by "irrational exuberance". In the late 1990s, the extraordinary surge of market values in the companies that comprised the new economy saw many equity research analysts, especially on the sell side, step out of their roles as analysts and become cheerleaders for these stocks. While these analysts might have been well-meaning in their recommendations, the fact that the investment banks that they worked for were leading the charge on initial public offerings from these firms exposed them to charges of bias and worse.

In 2001, the crash in the market values of dot-com stocks and the anguished cries of investors who had lost wealth in the crash created a firestorm of controversy. There were congressional hearings where legislators demanded to know what analysts knew about the companies they recommended and when they knew it, statements from the Securities and Exchange Commission (SEC) about the need for impartiality in equity research, and decisions taken by some investment banks to create at least the appearance of objectivity. Investment banks reinforced created Chinese walls to separate their investment bankers from their equity research analysts. While that technical separation has helped, the real source of bias—the intermingling of banking business, trading, and investment advice—has not been touched.

Should there be government regulation of equity research? It would not be wise, because regulation tends to be heavy-handed and creates side costs that seem quickly to exceed the benefits. A much more effective response can be delivered by portfolio managers and investors. Equity research that is biased should be discounted or, in egregious cases, even ignored. Alternatively, new equity research firms that deliver only investment advice can meet a need for unbiased valuations.

Uncertainty: Feature, Not Bug!

There is a widely held view in valuation that the answer to feeling uncertain about your inputs is to collect more information and do more research. That is not true. Even at the end of the most careful and detailed valuation, there will be uncertainty about the final numbers, colored as they are by assumptions that we make about the future of the company and economy. It is unrealistic to expect or demand certainty in valuation, since cash flows and discount rates are estimated, and those estimates will be wrong, in hindsight, because the real world delivers surprises that cannot be anticipated.

The degree of precision in valuations is likely to vary widely across investments. The valuation of a large and mature company with a long financial history will usually be much more precise than the valuation of a young company in a sector in turmoil. If this latter company happens to operate in an emerging market, with additional disagreement about the future of the market thrown into the mix, the uncertainty is magnified. In Chapter 23, we argue that the difficulties associated with valuation can be related to where a firm is in the life cycle. Mature firms tend to be easier to value than growth firms, and young start-up companies are more difficult to value than companies with established products and markets. The problems are not with the valuation models that we use, though, but with the difficulties we run into in making estimates for the future. Many investors and analysts use the uncertainty about the future or the absence of information to justify not doing full-fledged valuations. In reality, though, the payoff to valuation is greatest in these firms.

There is another aspect of valuation where uncertainty comes into play. After you finish valuing a company, you may be tempted to think that you are done, but it is a work in progress. The value obtained from any valuation model is affected by firm-specific as well as market-wide information, and that value will change as new information is revealed. This information may be specific to the firm, affect an entire sector, or alter expectations for all firms in the market. As examples of firm-specific information, consider earnings reports that firms release on a quarterly basis, which can cause large swings in stock prices and value. On the macro front, inflation rising unexpectedly, as in 2022, and interest rates rising can change valuations across all companies in the market. In 2020, a pandemic that shut the global economy down, altered business valuations dramatically, and so can wars and natural disasters. Put simply, the notion that a well-done intrinsic valuation is timeless and never has to be revisited is delusional. Even the best-done valuation ages quickly and must be updated to reflect current information, and with globalization and business disruption, we would argue that value has become more unstable over time. When analysts change their valuations, they will undoubtedly be asked to justify them, and in some cases the fact that valuations change over time is viewed as a problem. The best response is the one that John Maynard Keynes gave when he was criticized for changing his position on a major economic issue: "When the facts change, I change my mind. And what do you do, sir?"

The biggest damage to valuation comes from how analysts and investors react to uncertainty, not its presence. Instead of facing up to uncertainty and using the statistical, financial, and probabilistic tools that we can use to deal with it in a healthy fashion, the more common responses seem to be denial, i.e., acting as if uncertainty does not exist, or paralysis, where you stop valuing companies during crises, or if the companies are young start-ups, with the excuse that valuation is pointless in the face of uncertainty. We believe that the payoff to doing valuation is greatest when times are darkest, and when uncertainty looms, since even an imprecise valuation is better than not doing valuation at all!

Complexity: Bigger, Not Always Better!

A few decades ago, valuations were simpler because analysts and investors had no choice. Data was limited, and the tools we had to use that data were primitive, and the analyses had to reflect those limitations. As data access has broadened and become more effortless, and the tools that we have become more powerful, it has become easier and easier to build big models, and to resist the temptation to add more detail. Complexity in valuation is now more the rule than the exception, with hundreds of line items and layers of detail.

It may seem obvious that making a model more complete and complex should yield better valuations; but it is not necessarily so. As models become more complex, the number of inputs needed to value a firm tends to increase, bringing with it the potential for input errors. These problems are compounded when models become so complex that they become "black boxes" where analysts feed in numbers at one end and valuations emerge

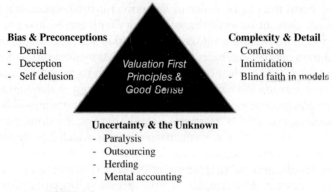

FIGURE 1.2   The Bermuda Triangle of Valuation

from the other. All too often when a valuation fails, the blame gets attached to the model rather than the analyst. The refrain becomes "It was not my fault. The model did it."

There are three important points that need to be made about all valuation. The first is to adhere to the principle of parsimony, which essentially states that you do not use more inputs than you absolutely need to value an asset. The second is to recognize that there is a trade-off between the additional benefits of building in more detail and the estimation costs (and error) with providing the detail. The third is to understand that models don't value companies—*you* do. In a world where the problem that you often face in valuations is not too little information but too much, and separating the information that matters from the information that does not, is almost as important as the valuation models and techniques that you use to value a firm.

In Sum

This section was titled the Bermuda Triangle of Valuation for a simple reason. Just as ships and aircraft are rumored to have disappeared in the mythical section of the Atlantic termed the Bermuda Triangle, analysts and investors valuing companies seem to lose their good sense when confronted with bias, uncertainty and complexity, as can be seen in Figure 1.2.

This phenomenon may also explain why, in our view, having more data and powerful tools has led valuations to become qualitatively "worse" rather than "better" over the last four decades.

MARKET EFFICIENCY

There is no idea in finance more likely to cause a strong negative reaction from investors than the notion of market efficiency. In the early years of finance, as a discipline, it is true that the prevailing wisdom was that markets were efficient, nullifying the reason for active investing and making valuations almost pointless.

Implicit in the act of valuation is the assumption that markets make mistakes and that we can find these mistakes, often using information that tens of thousands of other investors have access. Thus, it seems reasonable to say that those who believe that markets are inefficient should spend their time and resources on valuation, whereas those who believe that markets are efficient should take the market price as the best estimate of value.

This statement, though, does not reflect the internal contradictions in both positions. Those who believe that markets are efficient may still feel that valuation has something to contribute, especially when they are called on to value the effect of a change in the way a firm is run or to understand why market prices change over time. Furthermore, it is not clear how markets would become efficient in the first place, if investors did not attempt to find under- and overvalued stocks and trade on these valuations. In other words, a precondition for market efficiency seems to be the existence of millions of investors who believe that markets are not efficient.

On the other hand, those who believe that markets make mistakes and buy or sell stocks on that basis must believe that ultimately markets will correct these mistakes (i.e., become efficient), because that is how they make their money. This is, therefore, a fairly self-serving definition of inefficiency—markets are inefficient until you take a large position in the stock that you believe to be mispriced, but they become efficient after you take the position.

It is best to approach the issue of market efficiency as a skeptic. Recognize that on the one hand markets make mistakes but, on the other, finding these mistakes requires a combination of skill and luck. This view of markets leads to the following conclusions: First, if something looks too good to be true—a stock looks obviously undervalued or overvalued— it is probably *not* true. Second, when the value from an analysis is significantly different from the market price, start off with the presumption that the market is correct; then you have to convince yourself that this is not the case before you conclude that something is over- or undervalued. This higher standard may lead you to be more cautious in following through on valuations, but given the difficulty of beating the market, this is not an undesirable outcome.

THE ROLE OF VALUATION

Valuation is useful in a wide range of tasks. The role it plays, however, is different in different arenas. The following section lays out the relevance of valuation in portfolio management, in acquisition analysis, and in corporate finance.

Valuation in Portfolio Management

The role that valuation plays in portfolio management is determined in large part by the investment philosophy of the investor. Valuation plays a minimal role in portfolio management for a passive investor, whereas it plays a larger role for an active investor. Even among active investors, the nature and the role of valuation are different for different types of active investment. Market timers should use valuation much less than investors who pick stocks for the long term, and their focus is on market valuation rather than on firm-specific valuation. Among stock pickers, valuation plays a central role in portfolio management for fundamental analysts and a peripheral role for technical analysts.

Fundamental Analysts   The underlying theme in fundamental analysis is that the true value of the firm can be related to its financial characteristics—its growth prospects, risk profile, and cash flows. Any deviation from this true value is a sign that a stock is under- or overvalued. It is a long-term investment strategy, and the assumptions underlying it are:

■ The relationship between value and the underlying financial factors can be measured.
■ The relationship is stable over time.
■ Deviations from the relationship are corrected in a reasonable time period.

Valuation should be the central focus in fundamental analysis. Some analysts use discounted cash flow models to value firms, but there are others who use multiples such as the price-earnings and price–book value ratios. Since investors using this approach hold a large number of undervalued stocks in their portfolios, their hope is that, on average, these portfolios will do better than the market.

Franchise Buyers   The philosophy of a franchise buyer is best expressed by an investor who has been very successful at it—Warren Buffett. "We try to stick to businesses we believe we understand," Mr. Buffett writes.[3] "That means they must be relatively simple and stable in character. If a business is complex and subject to constant change, we're not smart enough to predict future cash flows." Franchise buyers concentrate on a few businesses they understand well and attempt to acquire undervalued firms. Often, as in the case of Mr. Buffett, franchise buyers wield influence on the management of these firms and can change financial and investment policy. As a long-term strategy, the underlying assumptions are that:

■ Investors who understand a business well are in a better position to value it correctly.
■ These undervalued businesses can be acquired without driving the price above the true value, and sometimes at a bargain.

Valuation plays a key role in this philosophy, as franchise buyers are attracted to a particular business because they believe it is undervalued. They are also interested in how much additional value they can create by restructuring the business and running it right.

Chartists   Chartists believe that prices are driven as much by investor psychology, as by any underlying financial variables. The information available from trading—price movements, trading volume, short sales, and so forth—gives an indication of investor psychology and future price movements. The assumptions here are that prices move in predictable patterns, that there are not enough marginal investors taking advantage of these patterns to eliminate them, and that the average investor in the market is driven more by emotion than by rational analysis.

While valuation does not play much of a role in charting, there are ways in which an enterprising chartist can incorporate it into analysis. For instance, valuation can be used to determine support and resistance lines[4] on price charts.

---

[3]This is extracted from Mr. Buffett's letter to stockholders in Berkshire Hathaway for 1993.
[4]On a chart, the support line usually refers to a lower bound below which prices are unlikely to move, and the resistance line refers to the upper bound above which prices are unlikely to venture. While these levels are usually estimated using past prices, the range of values obtained from a valuation model can be used to determine these levels (i.e., the maximum value will become the resistance line and the minimum value will become the support line).

Information Traders   Prices move on information about the firm. Information traders attempt to trade in advance of new information or shortly after it is revealed to financial markets, buying ahead of good news and selling on bad. The underlying assumption is that these traders can anticipate information announcements and gauge the market reaction to them better than the average investor in the market.

For an information trader, the focus is on the relationship between information and changes in value, rather than on value per se. Thus, an information trader may buy stock in even an overvalued firm if he or she believes that the next information announcement is going to cause the price to go up because it contains better than expected news. If there is a relationship between how undervalued or overvalued a company is and how its stock price reacts to new information, then valuation could play a role in investing for an information trader.

Market Timers   Market timers note, with some legitimacy, that the payoff to calling turns in markets is much greater than the returns from stock picking. They argue that it is easier to predict market movements than to select stocks, and that these predictions can be based on factors that are observable.

While valuation of individual stocks may not be of any use to a market timer, market timing strategies can use valuation in at least two ways:

1. The overall market itself can be valued and compared to the current level.
2. A valuation model can be used to value individual stocks, and the results across all stocks are used to determine whether the market is over- or undervalued. For example, as the number of stocks that are overvalued, using a discounted cash flow model, increases relative to the number that are undervalued, there may be reason to believe that the market is overvalued.

Efficient Marketers   Efficient marketers believe that the market price at any point in time represents the best estimate of the true value of the firm, and that any attempt to exploit perceived market efficiencies will cost more than it will make in excess profits. They assume that markets aggregate information quickly and accurately, that marginal investors promptly exploit any inefficiencies, and that any inefficiencies in the market are caused by friction such as transaction costs, and cannot be exploited.

For efficient marketers, valuation is a useful exercise to determine why a stock sells for the price that it does. Since the underlying assumption is that the market price is the best estimate of the true value of the company, the objective becomes determining what assumptions about growth and risk are implied in this market price, rather than on finding under- or overvalued firms.

Valuation in Acquisition Analysis

Valuation should, though it often does not, play a central part in acquisition analysis. The bidding firm or individual has to decide on a fair value for the target firm before making a bid, and the target firm has to determine a reasonable value for itself before deciding to accept or reject the offer.

There are also special factors to consider in takeover valuation. First, the effects of synergy on the combined value of the two firms (target plus bidding firm) have to be considered before a decision is made on the bid. Those who suggest that synergy is impossible to value and should not be considered in quantitative terms are wrong. Second, the effects on value of changing management and restructuring the target firm, i.e., the value of control, will have to be considered in deciding on a fair price. This is of particular concern in hostile takeovers.

Finally, there is a significant problem with bias in takeover valuations. Target firms may be overly optimistic in estimating value, especially when the takeovers are hostile and they are trying to convince their stockholders that the offer prices are too low. Similarly, if the bidding firm has decided for strategic reasons to do an acquisition, there may be strong pressure on the analyst to come up with an estimate of value that backs up the acquisition.

Valuation in Corporate Finance

If the objective in corporate finance is the maximization of firm value,[5] the relationship between financial decisions, corporate strategy, and firm value must be delineated. In recent years, management consulting firms have started offering companies advice on how to increase value. Their suggestions have often provided the basis for the restructuring of these firms.

The value of a firm can be directly related to decisions that it makes—on which projects it takes, on how it finances them, and on its dividend policy. Understanding this relationship is key to making value-increasing decisions and to sensible financial restructuring. In short, it is difficult to see how you can make good corporate finance decisions, without understanding valuation.

CONCLUSION

Valuation plays a key role in many areas of finance—in corporate finance, in mergers and acquisitions, and in portfolio management. The models presented in this book will provide a range of tools that analysts in each of these areas will find useful, but the cautionary note sounded in this chapter bears repeating. Valuation is not an objective exercise, and any preconceptions and biases that an analyst brings to the process will find their way into the value. And even the very best valuation will yield an estimate of the value, with a substantial likelihood of you being wrong in your assessment.

QUESTIONS AND SHORT PROBLEMS

In the problems following, use an equity risk premium of 5.5 percent if none is specified.

1. The value of an investment is:
   a. The present value of the cash flows on the investment.
   b. Determined by investor perceptions about it.
   c. Determined by demand and supply.
   d. Often a subjective estimate, colored by the bias of the analyst.
   e. All of the above.

---

[5]The objective in corporate finance is to maximize the value of the business, and it is difficult, if not impossible, to construct sensible corporate financial policy without an understanding of the drivers of value.

2. There are many who claim that value is based on investor perceptions and perceptions alone, and that cash flows and earnings do not matter. This argument is flawed because:
   a. Value is determined by earnings and cash flows, and investor perceptions do not matter.
   b. Perceptions do matter, but they can change. Value must be based on something more substantial.
   c. Investors are irrational. Therefore, their perceptions should not determine value.
   d. Value is determined by investor perceptions, but it is also determined by the underlying earnings and cash flows. Perceptions must be based on reality.
3. You use a valuation model to arrive at a value of $15 for a stock. The market price of the stock is $25. The difference may be explained by:
   a. A market inefficiency: The market is overvaluing the stock.
   b. The use of the wrong valuation model to value the stock.
   c. Errors in the inputs to the valuation model.
   d. All of the above.

CHAPTER 2

Approaches to Valuation

Analysts use a wide range of models in practice, ranging from the simple to the sophisticated. These models often make very different assumptions, but they do share some common characteristics and can be classified in broader terms. There are several advantages to such a classification: It makes it easier to understand where individual models fit into the big picture, why they provide different results, and when they have fundamental errors in logic.

In general terms, there are three approaches to valuation. The first, intrinsic valuation, relates the value of an asset to the present value (PV) of expected future cash flows on that asset. The second, pricing, estimates what to pay for an asset by looking at the pricing of comparable assets relative to a common variable, such as earnings, cash flows, book value, or sales. The third, contingent claim valuation, uses option pricing models to measure the value of assets that share option characteristics. Some of these assets are traded financial assets like warrants, and some of these options are not traded and are based on real assets, (e.g., projects, patents, and oil reserves). The latter are often called real options. There can be significant differences in outcomes depending on which approach is used. One of the objectives in this book is to explain the reasons for such differences in value across different models, and to help in choosing the right model to use for a specific task.

INTRINSIC VALUATION

In intrinsic valuation, you value an asset or business by looking at its capacity to generate cash flows, and the growth and risk in these cash flows. In the last century, a discounted cash flow valuation (DCF) model has become the most widely used tool for estimating intrinsic value. While intrinsic valuation is only one of the three ways of estimating what an asset is worth and most practitioners in the real-world price assets rather than value them, it is the foundation on which all other approaches are built. To price assets correctly, we need to understand the fundamentals of discounted cash flow valuation. To apply option pricing models to value assets, we often have to begin with a discounted cash flow valuation. This is why so much of this book focuses on discounted cash flow valuation. Anyone who understands its fundamentals will be able to analyze and use the other approaches. This section considers the basis of this approach, a philosophical rationale for discounted cash flow valuation, and an examination of the different sub-approaches to discounted cash flow valuation.

Basis for Discounted Cash Flow Valuation

This approach has its foundation in the present value rule, where the value of any asset is the present value of expected future cash flows on it.

$$\text{Value of Asset} = \frac{E(\text{Cash Flow}_1)}{(1+r)^1} + \frac{E(\text{Cash Flow}_2)}{(1+r)^2} + \cdots + \frac{E(\text{Cash Flow}_n)}{(1+r)^n}$$

where   n = Life of the asset
E (Cash flow$_t$) = Expected Cash flow in period t
r_c = Discount rate reflecting the riskiness of the estimated cash flows

The cash flows will vary from asset to asset—dividends for stocks, coupons (interest) and the face value for bonds, and after-tax cash flows for a project. The discount rate will be a function of the riskiness of the estimated cash flows, with higher rates for riskier assets and lower rates for safer projects.

You can think of discounted cash flow valuation on a continuum. At one end of the spectrum, you have the default-free zero coupon bond, with a guaranteed cash flow in the future. Discounting this cash flow at the riskless rate should yield the value of the bond. A little further up the risk spectrum are corporate bonds, where the cash flows take the form of coupons and there is default risk. These bonds can be valued by discounting the cash flows at an interest rate that reflects the default risk. Moving up the risk ladder, we get to equities in publicly traded companies or private businesses, where there are expected cash flows with substantial uncertainty around the expectations. The value here should be the present value of the expected cash flows at a discount rate that reflects the uncertainty in the expected cashflows.

Underpinnings of Discounted Cash Flow Valuation

In discounted cash flow valuation, we try to estimate the intrinsic value of an asset based on its fundamentals. What is intrinsic value? For lack of a better definition, consider it the value that would be attached to the firm by an unbiased analyst, who not only estimates the expected cash flows for the firm correctly, given the information available at the time, but also attaches the right discount rate to value these cash flows. Hopeless though the task of estimating intrinsic value may seem to be, especially when valuing young companies with substantial uncertainty about the future, making the best estimates that you can and persevering to estimate value can still pay off because markets make mistakes. While market prices can deviate from intrinsic value (estimated based on fundamentals), you are hoping that the two will converge sooner rather than later.

Categorizing Discounted Cash Flow Models

There are literally thousands of discounted cash flow models in existence. Investment banks or consulting firms often claim that their valuation models are better or more sophisticated than those used by their contemporaries. Ultimately, however, discounted cash flow models can vary only a couple of dimensions.

Equity Valuation and Firm Valuation   There are two paths to valuation in a business: The first is to value just the equity stake in the business, while the second is to value the entire business, which includes, besides equity, the other claimholders in the firm (bondholders, preferred

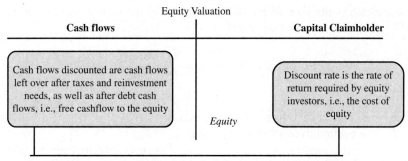

Present Value of cash flows to equity, discounted back at the cost equity, is the value of equity

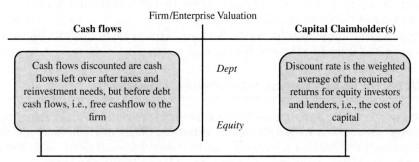

Present Value of cash flows to firm, discounted back at the cost of capital, is the value of the entire firm (business).

FIGURE 2.1 Equity versus Firm Valuation

stockholders). While both approaches discount expected cash flows, the relevant cash flows and discount rates are different under each. Figure 2.1 captures the essence of the two approaches.

The value of equity is obtained by discounting expected cash flows to equity (i.e., the residual cash flows after meeting all expenses, reinvestment needs, tax obligations, and debt cash flows) at the cost of equity (i.e., the rate of return required by equity investors in the firm).

$$\text{Value of Equity} = \sum_{t=1}^{t=\infty} \frac{E(\text{CF to Equity}_t)}{(1 + k_e)^t}$$

where n = Life of the asset
CF to Equity$_t$ = Expected cash flow to equity in period t
k$_e$ = Cost of equity

The dividend discount model is a special case of equity valuation, where the value of equity is the present value of expected future dividends.

The value of the firm is obtained by discounting expected cash flows to the firm (i.e., the residual cash flows after meeting all operating expenses, reinvestment needs, and taxes, but prior to any payments to either debt or equity holders) at the weighted average cost of capital (k_c), which is the cost of the different components of financing used by the firm, weighted by their market value proportions.

$$\text{Value of Firm (Business)} = \sum_{t=1}^{t=\infty} \frac{E(CF \text{ to Firm}_t)}{(1+k_c)^t}$$

where n = Life of the asset
CF to firm$_t$ = Expected cash flow to firm in period t
    k_c = Weighted average cost of capital

While these approaches use different definitions of cash flow and discount rates, they will yield the same estimates of value for equity as long as you are consistent in your assumptions in valuation. The key error to avoid is mismatching cash flows and discount rates, since discounting cash flows to equity at the cost of capital will lead to an upwardly biased estimate of the value of equity, while discounting cash flows to the firm at the cost of equity will yield a downwardly biased estimate of the value of the firm. Illustration 2.1 shows the equivalence of equity and firm valuation.

ILLUSTRATION 2.1: Effects of Mismatching Cash Flows and Discount Rates

Assume that you are analyzing a company with the following cash flows for the next five years. Assume also that the cost of equity is 13.625%, and the firm can borrow long term at 10%. (The tax rate for the firm is 50%.) The current market value of equity is $1,073, and the value of debt outstanding is $800. Table 2.1 summarizes cash flows to equity and the firm for the next five years, with terminal values for both.[1]

TABLE 2.1 Cashflows to Equity and Firm

Year	Cashflow to Equity	Interest (1–t)	Cashflow to Firm
1	$ 50.00	$40	$ 90.00
2	$ 60.00	$40	$ 100.00
3	$ 68.00	$40	$ 108.00
4	$ 76.20	$40	$ 116.20
5	$ 83.49	$40	$ 123.49
Terminal Value	$1603.008		$2363.008

The cost of equity is given as an input and is 13.625%, and the after-tax cost of debt is 5%:

Cost of Debt = Pre − tax cost of debt (1 − tax rate) = 10% (1 − .5) = 5%

Given the market values of equity and debt, we can estimate the cost of capital:

WACC = Cost of Equity [Equity/(Debt + Equity)] + Cost of Debt
[(Debt/(Debt + Equity)]
= 13.625% (1073/1873) + 5% (800/1873) = 9.94%

---

[1]For purposes of this example, take the terminal values as given, rather than computed. We will return to the question of estimating terminal value later in this book.

METHOD 1: DISCOUNT CASH FLOWS TO EQUITY AT COST OF EQUITY TO GET VALUE OF EQUITY

We discount cash flows to equity at the cost of equity:

$$PV\,of\,Equity = 50/1.13625 + 60/1.13625^2 + 68/1.13625^3 + 76.2/1.13625^4$$
$$+ (83.49 + 1603)/1.13625^5 = \$1073$$

METHOD 2: DISCOUNT CASH FLOWS TO FIRM AT COST OF CAPITAL TO GET VALUE OF FIRM

$$PV\,of\,Firm = 90/1.0994 + 100/1.0994^2 + 108/1.0994^3 + 116.2/1.0994^4$$
$$+ (123.49 + 2363)/1.0994^5 = \$1873$$

$$PV\,of\,Equity = PV\,of\,Firm - Market\,Value\,of\,Debt$$
$$= \$1873 - \$800 = \$1,073$$

Note that the value of equity is $1,073 under both approaches. It is easy to make the mistake of discounting cash flows to equity at the cost of capital or the cash flows to the firm at the cost of equity.

ERROR 1: DISCOUNT CASH FLOWS TO EQUITY AT COST OF CAPITAL TO GET TOO HIGH A VALUE FOR EQUITY

$$PV\,of\,Equity = 50/1.0994 + 60/1.0994^2 + 68/1.0994^3 + 76.2/1.0994^4$$
$$+ (83.49 + 1603)/1.0994^5 = \$1248$$

ERROR 2: DISCOUNT CASH FLOWS TO FIRM AT COST OF EQUITY TO GET TOO LOW A VALUE FOR THE FIRM

$$PV\,of\,Firm = 90/1.13625 + 100/1.13625^2 + 108/1.13625^3 + 116.2/1.13625^4$$
$$+ (123.49 + 2363)/1.13625^5 = \$1613$$

$$PV\,of\,Equity = PV\,of\,Firm - Market\,Value\,of\,Debt$$
$$= \$1613 - \$800 = \$813$$

The effects of using the wrong discount rate are clearly visible in the last two calculations (Error 1 and Error 2). When the cost of capital is mistakenly used to discount the cash flows to equity, the value of equity increases by $175 over its true value ($1,073). When the cash flows to the firm are erroneously discounted at the cost of equity, the value of the firm is understated by $260. It must be pointed out, though, that getting the values of equity to agree with the firm and equity valuation approaches can be much more difficult in practice than in this example. We return to this subject in Chapters 14 and 15 and consider the assumptions that we need to make to arrive at this result.

Cost of Capital Versus APV Approaches   In Figure 2.1, we noted that a firm can finance its business using either equity or debt. What are the effects of using debt on value? On the plus side, the tax deductibility of interest expenses provides a tax subsidy or benefit to the firm, which increases with the tax rate faced by the firm on its income. On the minus side, debt does increase the likelihood that the firm will default on its commitments and be forced into bankruptcy. The net effect can be positive, neutral, or negative. In the cost of capital approach, we capture the effects of debt in the discount rate:

Cost of capital = Cost of equity (Proportion of equity used to fund business)
   + Pre − tax cost of debt (1 − tax rate)
   (Proportion of debt used to fund business)

Thus, if the tax benefits of debt exceed its effects on bankruptcy cost, using more debt will lower the cost of capital. The cash flows discounted are pre-debt cash flows and do not include any of the tax benefits of debt (since that would be double counting).

In a variation, called the *adjusted present value (APV) approach*, we separate the effects on value of debt financing from the value of the assets of a business. Thus, we start by valuing the business as if it were all equity funded and assess the effect of debt separately, by first valuing the tax benefits from the debt and then subtracting out the expected bankruptcy costs.

> Value of business = Value of business with 100% equity financing
> + Present value of expected tax benefits from debt
> − Expected bankruptcy costs

While the two approaches take different tacks to evaluating the value added or destroyed by debt, they will provide the same estimate of value, if we are consistent in our assumptions about cash flows and risk. In Chapter 15, we will return to examine these approaches in more detail.

Total Cash Flow versus Excess Cash Flow Models   The conventional discounted cash flow model values an asset by estimating the present value of all cash flows generated by that asset at the appropriate discount rate. In excess return (and excess cash flow) models, only cash flows earned in excess of the required return are viewed as value creating, and the present value of these excess cash flows can be added to the amount invested in the asset to estimate its value. To illustrate, assume that you have an asset in which you invested $100 million and that you expect to generate $12 million in after-tax cash flows in perpetuity. Assume further that the cost of capital on this investment is 10 percent. With a total cash flow model, the value of this asset can be estimated as follows:

$$\text{Value of asset} = \frac{\text{Expected cash flow}}{\text{Cost of capital}} = \frac{\$12 \text{ million}}{.10} = \$120 \text{ million}$$

With an excess return model, we would first compute the excess return made on this asset:

$$\text{Excess return} = \text{Cash flow earned} - \text{Cost of capital} \times \text{Capital invested in asset}$$
$$= \$12 \text{ million} - .10 \times \$100 \text{ million} = \$2 \text{ million}$$

We then add the present value of these excess returns to the investment in the asset:

$$\text{Value of asset} = \text{Present value of excess return} + \text{Investment in asset}$$
$$= \frac{\$2 \text{ million}}{.10} + \$100 \text{ million} = \$120 \text{ million}$$

Note that the answers in the two approaches are equivalent. Why, then, would we want to use an excess return model? By focusing on excess returns, this model brings home the point that it is not earnings per se that create value, but earnings in excess of a required return. Chapter 32 considers special versions of these excess return models. As in this simple example, with consistent assumptions, total cash flow and excess return models are equivalent.

A SIMPLE TEST OF CASH FLOWS

There is a simple test that can be employed to determine whether the cash flows being used in a valuation are cash flows to equity or cash flows to the firm.

- If the cash flows that are being discounted are after interest expenses (and principal payments), they are cash flows to equity and the discount rate used should be the cost of equity.
- If the cash flows that are discounted are before interest expenses and principal payments, they are usually cash flows to the firm.

There are other items that need to be considered when estimating these cash flows, and they are considered in extensive detail in the coming chapters.

In general, cash flows to equity start with net income, which is after interest and principal payments, whereas cash flows to the firm start with operating income or earnings before interest and taxes.

Applicability and Limitations of Discounted Cash Flow Valuation

Discounted cash flow valuation is based on expected future cash flows and discount rates. Given these estimation requirements, this approach is easiest to use for assets (firms) whose cash flows are currently positive and can be estimated with some reliability for future periods, and where a proxy for risk that can be used to obtain discount rates is available. The further we get from this idealized setting, the more difficult (and more useful) discounted cash flow valuation becomes. Here are some scenarios where discounted cash flow valuation might run into trouble and need to be adapted.

Money-Losing Firms   A distressed firm generally has negative earnings and cash flows and expects to lose money for some time in the future. For these firms, estimating future cash flows is difficult to do, since there is a strong probability of bankruptcy. For firms that are expected to fail, discounted cash flow valuation can yield an upwardly biased estimate of value, since the method values the firm as a going concern providing positive cash flows to its investors. Even for firms that are expected to survive, cash flows will have to be estimated until they turn positive, since obtaining a present value of negative cash flows will yield a negative value for equity[2] or for the firm. We will examine these firms in more detail in Chapters 22 and 30.

Cyclical Firms   The earnings and cash flows of cyclical firms tend to follow the economy—rising during economic booms and falling during recessions. If discounted cash flow valuation is used on these firms, expected future cash flows are usually smoothed out, unless the analyst wants to undertake the onerous task of predicting the timing and duration of economic recessions and recoveries. In the depths of a recession many cyclical

---

[2]The protection of limited liability should ensure that no stock will sell for less than zero. The price of such a stock can never be negative.

firms look like troubled firms, with negative earnings and cash flows. Estimating future cash flows then becomes entangled with analyst predictions about when the economy will turn and how strong the upturn will be, with more optimistic analysts arriving at higher estimates of value. This is unavoidable, but the economic biases of the analysts have to be taken into account before using these valuations.

Firms with Unutilized Assets   Discounted cash flow valuation reflects the value of all assets that produce cash flows. If a firm has assets that are unutilized (and hence do not produce any cash flows), the value of these assets will not be reflected in the value obtained from discounting expected future cash flows. The same caveat applies, to a lesser degree, to underutilized assets, since their value will be understated in discounted cash flow valuation. While this is a problem, it is not insurmountable. The value of these assets can always be obtained externally[3] and added to the value obtained from discounted cash flow valuation. Alternatively, the assets can be valued as though they are used optimally.

Firms with Patents or Product Options   Firms sometimes have unutilized patents or licenses that do not produce any current cash flows and are not expected to produce cash flows in the near future, but are valuable, nevertheless. If this is the case, the value obtained from discounting expected cash flows to the firm will understate the true value of the firm. Again, the problem can be overcome by valuing these assets in the open market or by using option pricing models, and then adding the value obtained from discounted cash flow valuation. Chapter 28 examines the use of option pricing models to value patents.

Firms in the Process of Restructuring   Firms in the process of restructuring often sell some of their assets, acquire other assets, and change their capital structure and dividend policy. Some of them also change their ownership structure (going from publicly traded to private status and vice versa) and management compensation schemes. Each of these changes affects future cash flows and the riskiness of the firm. Using historical data for such firms can give a misleading picture of the firm's value. However, these firms can be valued, even in the light of the major changes in investment and financing policy, if future cash flows reflect the expected effects of these changes and the discount rate is adjusted to reflect the new business and financial risk in the firm. Chapter 31 takes a closer look at how value can be altered by changing the way a business is run.

Firms Involved in Acquisitions   There are at least two specific issues relating to acquisitions that need to be considered when using discounted cash flow valuation models to value target firms. The first is the thorny one of whether there is synergy in the merger and how its value can be estimated. To do so will require assumptions about the form the synergy will take and its effect on cash flows. The second, especially in hostile takeovers, is the effect of changing management on cash flows and risk. Again, the effect of the change can and should be incorporated into the estimates of future cash flows and discount rates and hence into value. Chapter 25 looks at the value of synergy and control in acquisitions.

---

[3]If these assets are traded on external markets, the market prices of these assets can be used in the valuation. If not, the cash flows can be projected, assuming full utilization of assets, and the value can be estimated.

Private Firms   The biggest problem in using discounted cash flow valuation models to value private firms is the measurement of risk (to use in estimating discount rates), since most risk/return models require that risk parameters be estimated from historical prices on the asset being analyzed and make assumptions about the profiles of investors in the firm that may not fit private businesses. One solution is to look at the riskiness of comparable firms that are publicly traded. The other is to relate the measure of risk to accounting variables, which are available for the private firm. Chapter 24 looks at adaptations to valuation models that are needed to value private businesses.

The point is not that discounted cash flow valuation cannot be done in these cases, but that we have to be flexible enough to adapt our models. The fact is that valuation is simple for firms with well-defined assets that generate cash flows that can be easily forecasted. The real challenge in valuation is to extend the valuation framework to cover firms that vary to some extent or the other from this idealized framework. Much of this book is spent considering how to value such firms.

PRICING OR RELATIVE VALUATION

While we tend to focus most on intrinsic valuation when discussing valuation, the reality is that much of what passes for valuation in practice is pricing. The decision on how much to pay for most assets, from the house you buy to the stocks you invest in, are based on how similar assets are priced by others in the marketplace. This section begins with a basis for pricing, moves on to consider its underpinnings, and then considers common variants within relative valuation.

Basis for Pricing/Relative Valuation

In pricing, the number attached to an asset is derived from the pricing of comparable assets, standardized using a common variable, such as earnings, cash flows, book value, or revenues. One illustration of this approach is the use of an industry-average price-earnings ratio to price equity in a firm, the assumption being that the other firms in the industry are comparable to the firm being priced and that the market, on average, prices these firms correctly. Another variant is the EV to EBITDA multiple, with firms selling at low multiples of EBITDA relative to comparable firms being considered undervalued. Revenue multiples are also used to price firms, with the average price or enterprise value to sales ratios of firms with similar characteristics being used for comparison. While these multiples are among the most widely used, there are others that also play a role in analysis—Price to book, EV to invested capital, and market value to replacement value (Tobin's Q), to name a few.

Underpinnings of Pricing

Unlike discounted cash flow valuation, which is a search for intrinsic value, relative valuation relies much more on the market being right, at least on average. In other words, we assume that the market is correct in the way it prices stocks on average, but that it makes errors on the pricing of individual stocks. We also assume that a comparison of multiples will allow us to identify these errors, and that these errors will be corrected over time.

The assumption that markets correct their mistakes over time is common to both discounted cash flow and relative valuation, but those who use multiples and comparables to pick stocks argue, with some basis, that errors made in pricing individual stocks in a sector are more noticeable and more likely to be corrected quickly. For instance, they would argue that a software firm that trades at a price-earnings ratio of 10 when the rest of the sector trades at 25 times earnings is clearly underpriced, and that the correction toward the sector average should occur sooner rather than later. Proponents of discounted cash flow valuation would counter that this is small consolation if the entire sector is over-priced by 50 percent.

Categorizing Pricing Models

Analysts and investors are endlessly inventive when it comes to using pricing. Some compare multiples across companies, while others compare the multiple of a company to the multiples it used to trade at in the past.

Fundamentals versus Comparables   In discounted cash flow valuation, the value of a firm is determined by its expected cash flows. Other things remaining equal, higher cash flows, lower risk, and higher growth should yield higher value. Some analysts who use multiples go back to these discounted cash flow models to extract multiples. Other analysts compare multiples across firms or time and make explicit or implicit assumptions about how firms are similar or vary on fundamentals.

Using Fundamentals   The first approach relates pricing multiples to the fundamentals about the firm being valued—growth rates in earnings and cash flows, reinvestment and risk. This approach to estimating multiples is equivalent to using intrinsic valuation, requiring the same information and yielding the same results. Its primary advantage is that it shows the relationship between multiples and firm characteristics and allows us to explore how multiples change as these characteristics change. For instance, what will be the effect of evolving profit margins on the Enterprise Value-sales ratio? What will happen to price-earnings ratios as growth rates decrease? What is the relationship between price–book value ratios and return on equity?

Using Comparable Firms and Peer Groups   The more common approach to using multiples is to compare how a firm is priced with how similar firms are priced by the market or, in some cases, with how the firm was priced in prior periods. As we see in the later chapters, finding similar and comparable firms is often a challenge, and frequently we have to accept firms that are different from the firm being valued on one dimension or the other. When this is the case, we have to either explicitly or implicitly control differences across firms on growth, risk, and cash flow measures. In practice, controlling for these variables can range from the naive (using industry averages) to the sophisticated (multivariate regression models where the relevant variables are identified and controlled for).

Cross-Sectional versus Time Series Comparisons   In most cases, analysts price stocks on a relative basis, by comparing the multiples they are trading at, to the multiples at which other firms in the same business are trading at, contemporaneously. In some cases, however, especially for mature firms with long histories, the comparison is done across time.

Cross-Sectional Comparisons   When we compare the price-earnings ratio of a software firm to the average price-earnings ratio of other software firms, we are pricing the firm, and basing that pricing on cross-sectional comparisons. The conclusions can vary, depending on our assumptions about the firm being priced and the comparable firms. For instance, if we assume that the firm we are pricing is similar to the average firm in the industry, we will conclude that it is cheap if it trades at a multiple that is lower than the average multiple. If, however, we assume that the firm being priced is riskier than the average firm in the industry, we might conclude that the firm should trade at a lower multiple than other firms in the business. In short, you cannot compare firms without making assumptions about their fundamentals.

Comparisons Across Time   If you have a mature firm with a long history, you can compare the multiple it trades at today to the multiple it used to trade at in the past. Thus, Ford Motor Company may be viewed as cheap because it trades at six times earnings, if it has historically traded at 10 times earnings. To make this comparison, however, you must assume that your firm's fundamentals have not changed over time. For instance, you would expect a high-growth firm's price-earnings ratio to drop over time and its expected growth rate to decrease as it becomes larger. Comparing multiples across time can also be complicated by changes in interest rates, the behavior of the overall market, and market disruption. For instance, as interest rates fall below historical norms and the overall market rises, you would expect most companies to trade at much higher multiples of earnings and book value than they have historically. In the case of Ford, the comparison across time can be misleading since the automobile business has been disrupted by electric car makers.

Applicability and Limitations of Multiples

The allure of multiples is that they are simple and easy to relate to. They can be used to obtain estimates of pricing quickly for firms and assets, and are particularly useful when a large number of comparable firms are traded on financial markets, and the market is, on average, pricing these firms correctly. They tend to be more difficult to use to price unique firms with no obvious comparables, with little or no revenues, and with negative earnings.

By the same token, multiples are also easy to misuse and manipulate, especially when comparable firms are used. Given that no two firms are exactly alike in terms of risk and growth, the definition of comparable firms is a subjective one. Consequently, a biased analyst can choose a group of comparable firms to confirm his or her biases about a firm's pricing. Illustration 2.2 shows an example. While this potential for bias exists with discounted cash flow valuation as well, the analyst in DCF valuation is forced to be much more explicit about the assumptions that determine the final value. With multiples, these assumptions are often left unstated.

The other problem with using multiples based on comparable firms is that it builds in errors (overvaluation or undervaluation) that the market might be making in valuing these firms. In Illustration 2.2, for instance, if the market has overvalued all computer software firms, using the average PE ratio of these firms to value an initial public offering will lead to an overvaluation of the IPO. In contrast, discounted cash flow valuation is based on firm-specific growth rates and cash flows, so it is less likely to be influenced by market errors in valuation.

ILLUSTRATION 2.2:   The Potential for Misuse with Comparable Firms

Assume that an analyst is valuing an initial public offering (IPO) of a firm that manufactures computer software. At the same time,[4] the price-earnings multiples of other publicly traded firms manufacturing software are shown in Table 2.2:

TABLE 2.2   PE ratios for software firms

Firm	Multiple
Adobe Systems	23.2
Autodesk	20.4
Broderbund	32.8
Computer Associates	18.0
Lotus Development	24.1
Microsoft	27.4
Novell	30.0
Oracle	37.8
Software Publishing	10.6
System Software	15.7
Average PE ratio	*24.0*

While the average PE ratio using the entire sample is 24, it can be changed markedly by removing a couple of firms from the group. For instance, if the two firms with the lowest PE ratios in the group (Software Publishing and System Software) are eliminated from the sample, the average PE ratio increases to 26.7. If the two firms with the highest PE ratios in the group (Broderbund and Oracle) are removed from the group, the average PE ratio drops to 21.2.

ASSET-BASED VALUATION MODELS

There are some analysts who add a fourth approach to valuation to the three described in this chapter. They argue that you can value the individual assets owned by a firm and aggregate them to arrive at a firm value—asset-based valuation models. In fact, there are several variants on asset-based valuation models. The first is liquidation value, which is obtained by aggregating the estimated sale proceeds of the assets owned by a firm. The second is replacement cost, where you estimate what it would cost you to replace all of the assets that a firm has today. The third is the simplest: use accounting book value as the measure of the value of the assets, with adjustments to the book value made where necessary.

While analysts may use asset-based valuation approaches to estimate value, they are not alternatives to intrinsic valuation and pricing, since both replacement and liquidation values have to be obtained using one or another of these approaches. Ultimately, all models attempt to value assets; the differences arise in how we identify the assets and how we attach value to each asset. In liquidation valuation, we

---

[4]These were the PE ratios for these firms at the end of 1992.

look only at assets in place and estimate how much they are worth based on what similar assets are priced at in the market. In discounted cash flow valuation, we consider all assets and include expected growth potential to arrive at value. The two approaches may, in fact, yield the same values if you have a firm that has no growth potential and the market assessments of value reflect expected cash flows.

CONTINGENT CLAIM VALUATION

Perhaps the most revolutionary development in valuation is the acceptance, at least in some cases, that the value of an asset may be greater than the present value of expected cash flows if the cash flows are contingent on the occurrence or nonoccurrence of an event. This acceptance has largely come about because of the development of option pricing models. While these models were initially used to value traded options, there has been an attempt in recent years to extend the reach of these models into more traditional valuation. There are many who argue that assets such as patents or undeveloped reserves are really options and should be valued as such, rather than with traditional discounted cash flow models.

Basis for Approach

A contingent claim or option is a claim that pays off only under certain contingencies—if the value of the underlying asset exceeds a prespecified value for a call option or is less than a prespecified value for a put option. Much work has been done in the past 50 years in developing models that value options, and these option pricing models can be used to value any assets that have optionlike features.

Figure 2.2 illustrates the payoffs on call and put options as a function of the value of the underlying asset. An option can be valued as a function of the following variables: the current value and the variance in value of the underlying asset, the strike price and the time to expiration of the option, and the riskless interest rate. This was first established by Fischer Black and Myron Scholes in 1972 and has been extended and refined subsequently in numerous variants. While the Black-Scholes option pricing model ignores dividends and assumes that options will not be exercised early, it can be modified to allow for both. A discrete-time variant, the binomial option pricing model, has also been developed to price options.

An asset can be valued as an option if the payoffs are a function of the value of an underlying asset. It can be valued as a call option if, when that value exceeds a prespecified level, the asset is worth the difference. It can be valued as a put option if it gains value as the value of the underlying asset drops below a prespecified level, and if it is worth nothing when the underlying asset's value exceeds that specified level.

Underpinnings of Contingent Claim Valuation

The fundamental premise behind the use of option pricing models is that discounted cash flow models tend to understate the value of assets that provide payoffs that are contingent on the occurrence of an event. As a simple example, consider an undeveloped oil reserve

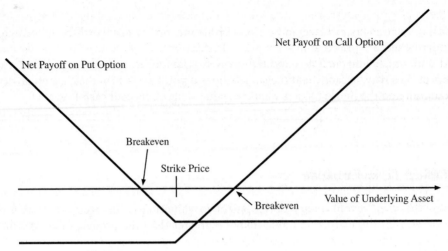

FIGURE 2.2   Payoff Diagram on Call and Put Options

belonging to Petrobras. You could value this reserve based on expectations of oil prices in the future, but this estimate would miss the fact that the oil company will develop this reserve only if oil prices go up, and will not if oil prices decline. An option pricing model would yield a value that incorporates this right.

When we use option pricing models to value assets such as patents and undeveloped natural resource reserves, we are assuming that markets are sophisticated enough to recognize such options and incorporate them into the market price. If the markets do not do so right now, we assume that they will eventually; the payoff to using such models comes about when this correction occurs.

Categorizing Option Pricing Models

The first categorization of options is based on whether the underlying asset is a financial asset or a real asset. Most listed options, whether they be options listed on the Chicago Board Options Exchange or callable fixed income securities, are on financial assets such as stocks and bonds. In contrast, options can be on real assets, such as commodities, real estate, or even investment projects; such options are often called real options.

A second and overlapping categorization is based on whether the underlying asset is traded. The overlap occurs because most financial assets are traded, whereas relatively few real assets are traded. Options on traded assets are generally easier to value, and the inputs to the option pricing models can be obtained from financial markets. Options on nontraded assets are much more difficult to value, since there are no market inputs available on the underlying assets.

Applicability and Limitations of Option Pricing Models

There are several direct examples of securities that are options—LEAPS, which are long-term equity options on traded stocks; contingent value rights, which provide protection to stockholders in companies against stock price declines; and warrants, which are long-term call options issued by firms.

There are other assets that generally are not viewed as options but still share several option characteristics. Equity, for instance, can be viewed as a call option on the value of the underlying firm, with the face value of debt representing the strike price and the term of the debt measuring the life of the option. A patent can be analyzed as a call option on a product, with the investment outlay needed to get the project going considered the strike price and the patent life becoming the time to expiration of the option.

There are limitations in using option pricing models to value long-term options on nontraded assets. The assumptions made about constant variance and dividend yields, which are not seriously contested for short-term options, are much more difficult to defend when options have long lifetimes. When the underlying asset is not traded, the inputs for the value of the underlying asset and the variance in that value cannot be extracted from financial markets and must be estimated. Thus, the final values obtained from these applications of option pricing models have much more estimation error associated with them than the values obtained in their more standard applications (to value short-term traded options).

CONCLUSION

There are three basic, albeit not mutually exclusive, approaches to valuation. The first is intrinsic valuation, most often taking the form of a discounted cash flow valuation, where cash flows are discounted at a risk-adjusted discount rate to arrive at an estimate of value. The analysis can be done purely from the perspective of equity investors by discounting expected cash flows to equity at the cost of equity, or it can be done from the viewpoint of all claimholders in the firm, by discounting expected cash flows to the firm at the weighted average cost of capital. The second is pricing or relative valuation, where the pricing of an asset is based on the pricing of similar assets. The third is contingent claim valuation, where an asset with contingent cash flows is valued using an option pricing model. There should be a place for each among the tools available to any analyst interested in valuation.

QUESTIONS AND SHORT PROBLEMS

In the problems following, use an equity risk premium of 5.5 percent if none is specified.

1. Discounted cash flow valuation is based on the notion that the value of an asset is the present value of the expected cash flows on that asset, discounted at a rate that reflects the riskiness of those cash flows. Specify whether the following statements about discounted cash flow valuation are true or false, assuming that all variables are constant except for the one mentioned:
   a. As the discount rate increases, the value of an asset increases.
      True _____   False _____
   b. As the expected growth rate in cash flows increases, the value of an asset increases.
      True _____   False _____
   c. As the life of an asset is lengthened, the value of that asset increases.
      True _____   False _____

d. As the uncertainty about the expected cash flow increases, the value of an asset increases.
    True _____   False _____
e. An asset with an infinite life (i.e., it is expected to last forever) will have an infinite value.
    True _____   False _____

2. Why might discounted cash flow valuation be difficult to do for the following types of firms?
    a. A private firm, where the owner is planning to sell the firm.
    b. A biotechnology firm with no current products or sales, but with several promising product patents in the pipeline.
    c. A cyclical firm during a recession.
    d. A troubled firm that has made significant losses and is not expected to get out of trouble for a few years.
    e. A firm that is in the process of restructuring, where it is selling some of its assets and changing its financial mix.
    f. A firm that owns a lot of valuable land that is currently unutilized.

3. The following are the projected cash flows to equity and to the firm over the next five years:

Year	CF to Equity	Int (1 – t)	CF to Firm
1	$ 250.00	$ 90.00	$ 340.00
2	$ 262.50	$ 94.50	$ 357.00
3	$ 275.63	$ 99.23	$ 374.85
4	$ 289.41	$104.19	$ 393.59
5	$ 303.88	$109.40	$ 413.27
Terminal Value	$3,946.50		$6,000.00

The firm has a cost of equity of 12% and a cost of capital of 9.94%. Answer the following questions:
    a. What is the value of the equity in this firm?
    b. What is the value of the firm?

4. You are estimating the price-earnings multiple to use to value Paramount Corporation by looking at the average price-earnings multiple of comparable firms. The following are the price-earnings ratios of firms in the entertainment business.

Firm	PE Ratio
Disney (Walt)	22.09
Time Warner	36.00
King World Productions	14.10
New Line Cinema	26.70

    a. What is the average PE ratio?
    b. Would you use all the comparable firms in calculating the average? Why or why not?
    c. What assumptions are you making when you use the industry-average PE ratio to value Paramount Corporation?

CHAPTER 3

Understanding Financial Statements

Financial statements provide the fundamental information that we use to analyze and answer valuation questions. It is important, therefore, that we understand the principles governing these statements by looking at four questions:

1. How valuable are the assets of a firm? The assets of a firm can come in several forms—assets with long lives such as land and buildings, assets with shorter lives such as inventory, and intangible assets that nevertheless produce revenues for the firm such as patents and trademarks.
2. How did the firm raise the funds to finance these assets? In acquiring assets, firms can use the funds of the owners (equity) or borrowed money (debt), and the mix is likely to change as the assets age.
3. How profitable are these assets? A good investment is one that makes a return greater than the cost of funding it. To evaluate whether the investments that a firm has already made are good investments, we need to estimate what returns these investments are producing.
4. How much uncertainty (or risk) is embedded in these assets? While we have not yet directly confronted the issue of risk, estimating how much uncertainty there is in existing investments, and the implications for a firm, is clearly a first step.

This chapter looks at the way accountants would answer these questions, and why the answers might be different when doing valuation. Some of these differences can be traced to the differences in objectives: Accountants try to measure the current standing and immediate past performance of a firm, whereas valuation is much more forward-looking.

THE BASIC ACCOUNTING STATEMENTS

There are three basic accounting statements that summarize information about a firm. The first is the balance sheet, shown in Figure 3.1, which summarizes the assets owned by a firm, the value of these assets, and the mix of financing (debt and equity) used to finance these assets at a point in time.

The next is the income statement, shown in Figure 3.2, which provides information on the revenues and expenses of the firm, and the resulting income made by the firm, during a period. The period can be a quarter (if it is a quarterly income statement) or a year (if it is an annual report).

Finally, there is the statement of cash flows, shown in Figure 3.3, which specifies the sources and uses of cash to the firm from operating, investing, and financing activities during a period. The statement of cash flows can be viewed as an attempt to explain what the cash flows during a period were, and why the cash balance changed during the period.

Assets				Liabilities
Recorded at cost	Non-Cash Current Assets		Current Liabilities	Recorded at cost
Recorded at current value	Cash & Marketable Securities (ST)		Interest-bearing Debt	Recorded as original proceeds
Recorded at original cost, net of depreciation	Property, Plant & Equipment			
Recorded at original cost, updated cost or priced at current market levels	Financial Investments		Accounting Liabilities	Recorded at estimated value
Mostly a plug variable (Goodwill)	Intangible Assets		Shareholder Equity	Summation of accounting history, book value + retained earnings

FIGURE 3.1   The Balance Sheet

	Item	Explanation
Start with	Revenues	Accountant's estimate of the revenues/sales generated by any transactions made the business during the period
Net out	Cost of Goods Sold	Estimated costs that are directly associated with producing the product/service sold by the company
To get	**Gross Profit**	Unit profitability, before covering other indirect costs and financial expenses
Net out	Operating Expenses	Include all expenses associated with operations this year, with no benefits spilling over into future years
To get	**Operating Profit**	Profitability of business/operations
Net out	Financial Expenses	Expenses associated with nonequity financing (debt, for instance)
Add in	Financial Income	Income earned on cash balance and on financial investments (in companies and securities)
To get	**Pretax Profit**	Income to equity investors, prior to taxes
Net out	Taxes	Taxes, based upon taxable income (may not equate to cash taxes paid)
To get	**Net Profit**	Income to equity investors, after taxes

FIGURE 3.2   Income Statement

Cash Flow Effect	Item	Why?
Start with	Net income	Equity Income
Plus	Depreciation and amortization	Add back non-cash items
Plus	Other noncash expenses	
Plus or Minus	Change in accounts receivables	Get to cash to equity
	Change in inventory	from operations
	Change in other current assets	
	Change in accounts payable	
	Change in taxes due	
Equals	**Cash flow from operations**	

Cash Flow Effect	Item	Why?
Minus	Capital expenditures	Investment in operating
Plus	Divestitures of assets	assets
Minus	Cash acquisitions	
Minus	Investments in financial assets	Investment in
Minus	Investments in nonoperating assets	nonoperating assets
Plus	Divestitures of securities & nonoperating assets	
Equals	**Cash flow from investing**	

Action	Item	Why?
Plus	Debt raised	Net Cash from/to debt
Minus	Debt repaid	
Plus	New equity isuances	Net Cash from/to equity
Minus	Dividends paid	Investors
Minus	Stock buybacks	
Equals	**Cash flow from financing**	

FIGURE 3.3   Statement of Cash Flows

ASSET MEASUREMENT AND VALUATION

When analyzing any firm, we want to know the types of assets that it owns, the value of these assets, and the degree of uncertainty about this value. Accounting statements do a reasonably good job of categorizing the assets owned by a firm, a partial job of assessing the value of these assets, and a poor job of reporting uncertainty about asset value. This section begins by looking at the accounting principles underlying asset categorization and measurement, and the limitations of financial statements in providing relevant information about assets.

Accounting Principles Underlying Asset Measurement

An asset is any resource that has the potential either to generate future cash inflows or to reduce future cash outflows. While that is a general definition broad enough to cover almost any kind of asset, accountants add a caveat that for a resource to be an asset, a firm has to have acquired it in a prior transaction and be able to quantify future benefits with reasonable precision. The accounting view of asset value is to a great extent grounded in the notion of historical cost, which is the original cost of the asset, adjusted upward for improvements made to the asset since purchase and downward for the loss in value associated with the aging of the asset. This historical cost is called the book value. While the generally accepted accounting principles (GAAP) for valuing an asset vary across different kinds of assets, three principles underlie the way assets are valued in accounting statements:

1. *An abiding belief in book value as the best estimate of value.* Accounting estimates of asset value begin with the book value, and unless a substantial reason is given to do otherwise, accountants view the historical cost as the best estimate of the value of an asset.
2. *A distrust of market or estimated value.* When a current market value exists for an asset that is different from the book value, accounting convention seems to view this market value with suspicion. The market price of an asset is often viewed as both much too volatile and too easily manipulated to be used as an estimate of value for an asset. This suspicion runs even deeper when a value is estimated for an asset based on expected future cash flows.
3. *A preference for underestimating value rather than overestimating it.* When there is more than one approach to valuing an asset, accounting convention takes the view that the more conservative (lower) estimate of value should be used rather than the less conservative (higher) estimate of value. Thus, when both market and book value are available for an asset, accounting rules often require that you use the lesser of the two numbers.

Measuring Asset Value

The financial statement in which accountants summarize and report asset values is the balance sheet. To examine how asset value is measured, let us begin with the way assets are categorized in the balance sheet. First there are the fixed assets, which include the long-term assets of the firm, such as plant, equipment, land, and buildings. Next, we have the short-term assets of the firm, including inventory (raw materials, work in progress, and finished goods, receivables (summarizing moneys owed to the firm), and cash; these are categorized as current assets. We then have investments in the assets and securities of other firms, which are generally categorized as financial or non-operating investments. Finally, we have what is loosely categorized as intangible assets. These include not only assets such as patents and trademarks that presumably will create future earnings and cash flows, but also uniquely accounting assets such as goodwill that arise because of acquisitions made by the firm.

Fixed Assets   Generally accepted accounting principles (GAAP) in the United States require the valuation of fixed assets at historical cost, adjusted for any estimated loss in value from the aging of these assets. While in theory the adjustments for aging should reflect the loss of earning power of the asset as it ages, in practice they are much more a product of accounting rules and convention, and these adjustments are called depreciation. Depreciation methods can very broadly be categorized into straight line (where the loss in asset value is assumed to be the a constant every year over its lifetime) and accelerated (where the asset loses more value in the earlier years and less in the later years). While tax rules, at least in the United States, have restricted the freedom that firms have on their choices of asset life and depreciation methods, firms continue to have a significant amount of flexibility on these decisions for reporting purposes. Thus, the depreciation that is reported in the annual reports may not be, and generally is not, the same depreciation that is used in the tax statements.

Since fixed assets are valued at book value and are adjusted for depreciation provisions, the value of a fixed asset is strongly influenced by its age, with older assets having lower value, and further by its depreciable life and the depreciation method used. Many firms in the United States use straight-line depreciation for financial reporting while using accelerated depreciation for tax purposes, since firms can report better earnings with the former, at least in the years right after the asset is acquired.[1] In contrast, firms in other countries often use accelerated depreciation for both tax and financial reporting purposes, leading to reported income that is understated relative to that of their U.S. counterparts.

Current Assets   Current assets include inventory, cash, and accounts receivable. It is in this category that accountants are most amenable to the use of market value, especially in valuing marketable securities.

Accounts Receivable   Accounts receivable represent money owed by entities to the firm on the sale of products on credit. When the Home Depot sells products to building contractors and gives them a few weeks to make their payments, it is creating accounts receivable. The accounting convention is for accounts receivable to be recorded as the amount owed to the firm based on the billing at the time of the credit sale. The only major valuation and accounting issue is when the firm has to recognize accounts receivable that are not collectible. Firms can set aside a portion of their income to cover expected bad debts from credit sales, and accounts receivable will be reduced by this reserve. Alternatively, the bad debts can be recognized as they occur, and the firm can reduce the accounts receivable accordingly. There is the danger, however, that absent a decisive declaration of a bad debt, firms may continue to show as accounts receivable amounts that they know are unlikely ever to be collected.

Cash   Cash is one of the few assets for which accountants and financial analysts should agree on value. The value of a cash balance should not be open to estimation error. Having said this, we note that fewer and fewer companies hold cash in the conventional sense (as currency or as demand deposits in banks). Firms often invest the cash in interest-bearing accounts, commercial paper, or in Treasuries so as to earn a return on their investments. In either case, market value can sometimes deviate from book value. While there is minimal default risk in either of these investments, interest rate movements can affect their value. The valuation of marketable securities is examined later in this section.

Inventory   Three basic approaches to valuing inventory are allowed by GAAP: first in, first out (FIFO); last in, first out (LIFO); and weighted average.

1. *First in, first out (FIFO).* Under FIFO, the cost of goods sold is based on the cost of material bought earliest in the period, while the cost of inventory is based on the cost of material bought later in the year. This results in inventory being valued close to

---

[1]Depreciation is treated as an accounting expense. Hence, the use of straight-line depreciation (which is lower than accelerated depreciation in the first few years after an asset is acquired) will result in lower expenses and higher income.

current replacement cost. During periods of inflation, the use of FIFO will result in the lowest estimate of cost of goods sold among the three valuation approaches, and the highest net income.

2. *Last in, first out (LIFO)*. Under LIFO, the cost of goods sold is based on the cost of material bought toward the end of the period, resulting in costs that closely approximate current costs. The inventory, however, is valued based on the cost of materials bought earlier in the year. During periods of inflation, the use of LIFO will result in the highest estimate of cost of goods sold among the three approaches, and the lowest net income.

3. *Weighted average*. Under the weighted average approach, both inventory and the cost of goods sold are based on the average cost of all material bought during the period. When inventory turns over rapidly, this approach will more closely resemble FIFO than LIFO.

Firms often adopt the LIFO approach for its tax benefits during periods of high inflation. The cost of goods sold is then higher because it is based on prices paid toward to the end of the accounting period. This, in turn, will reduce the reported taxable income and net income while increasing cash flows. Studies indicate that larger firms with rising prices for raw materials and labor, more variable inventory growth, and an absence of other tax loss carryforwards are much more likely to adopt the LIFO approach.

Given the income and cash flow effects of inventory valuation methods, it is often difficult to compare the profitability of firms that use different methods. There is, however, one way of adjusting for these differences. Firms that choose the LIFO approach to value inventories have to specify in a footnote the difference in inventory valuation between FIFO and LIFO, and this difference is termed the LIFO reserve. It can be used to adjust the beginning and ending inventories, and consequently the cost of goods sold, and to restate income based on FIFO valuation.

Investments (Financial) and Marketable Securities   In the category of investments and marketable securities, accountants consider investments made by firms in the securities or assets of other firms, as well as other marketable securities, including Treasury bills or bonds. The way in which these assets are valued depends on the way the investment is categorized and the motive behind the investment. In general, an investment in the securities of another firm can be categorized as a *minority passive investment*, a *minority active investment*, or a *majority active investment*, and the accounting rules vary depending on the categorization.

Minority Passive Investments   If the securities or assets owned in another firm represent less than 20 percent of the overall ownership of that firm, an investment is treated as a minority passive investment. These investments have an acquisition value, which represents what the firm originally paid for the securities, and often a market value. Accounting principles require that these assets be subcategorized into one of three groups—investments that will be held to maturity, investments that are available for sale, and trading investments. The valuation principles vary for each.

■ For an investment that will be held to maturity, the valuation is at historical cost or book value, and interest or dividends from this investment are shown in the income statement.

- For an investment that is available for sale, the valuation is at market value, but the unrealized gains or losses are shown as part of the equity in the balance sheet and not in the income statement. Thus, unrealized losses reduce the book value of the equity in the firm, and unrealized gains increase the book value of equity.
- For a trading investment, the valuation is at market value, and the unrealized gains and losses are shown in the income statement.

Firms are allowed an element of discretion in the way they classify investments and, subsequently, in the way they value these assets. This classification ensures that firms such as investment banks and some holding companies, whose assets are primarily securities held in other firms for purposes of trading, revalue the bulk of these assets at market levels each period. This is called marking to market and provides one of the few instances in which market value trumps book value in accounting statements. Note, however, that this mark-to-market ethos did not provide any advance warning in 2008 to investors in financial service firms of the overvaluation of subprime and mortgage-backed securities.

Minority Active Investments If the securities or assets owned in another firm represent between 20 percent and 50 percent of the overall ownership of that firm, an investment is treated as a minority active investment. While these investments have an initial acquisition value, a proportional share (based on ownership proportion) of the net income and losses made by the firm in which the investment was made is used to adjust the acquisition cost. In addition, the dividends received from the investment reduce the acquisition cost. This approach to valuing investments is called the equity approach.

The market value of these investments is not considered until the investment is liquidated, at which point the gain or loss from the sale relative to the adjusted acquisition cost is shown as part of the earnings in that period.

Majority Active Investments If the securities or assets owned in another firm represent more than 50 percent of the overall ownership of that firm, an investment is treated as a majority active investment. In this case, the investment is no longer shown as a financial investment but is instead replaced by the assets and liabilities of the firm in which the investment was made. This approach leads to a consolidation of the balance sheets of the two firms, where the assets and liabilities of the two firms are merged and presented as one balance sheet.[2] The share of the equity in the subsidiary that is owned by other investors is shown as a minority interest on the liability side of the balance sheet. To provide an illustration, assume that Firm A owns 60% of Firm B. Firm A will be required to consolidate 100% of Firm B's revenues, earnings, and assets into its own financial statements and then show a liability (minority interest) reflecting the accounting estimate of value of the 40% of Firm B's equity that does not belong to it. A similar consolidation occurs in the other financial statements of the firm as well, with the statement of cash flows reflecting the cumulated cash inflows and outflows of the combined firm. This is in contrast to the equity approach used for minority active investments, in which only the dividends received on the investment are shown as a cash inflow in the cash flow statement.

---

[2] Firms have evaded the requirements of consolidation by keeping their share of ownership in other firms below 50 percent.

Here again, the market value of this investment is not considered until the ownership stake is liquidated. At that point, the difference between the market price and the net value of the equity stake in the firm is treated as a gain or loss for the period.

Intangible Assets   Intangible assets include a wide array of assets, ranging from patents and trademarks to brand names and great management. Not only has accounting struggled with whether and how to value these intangibles, the rules vary widely across different intangibles.

Patents and Trademarks   Patents and trademarks are valued differently depending on whether they are generated internally or acquired. When patents and trademarks are generated from internal research, the costs incurred in developing the asset are expensed in that period, even though the asset might have a life of several accounting periods. Thus, the intangible asset is often not valued in the balance sheet of the firm. In contrast, when an intangible asset is acquired from an external party, it is treated as an asset.

Intangible assets have to be amortized over their expected lives, with a maximum amortization period of 40 years. The standard practice is to use straight-line amortization. For tax purposes, however, firms are generally not allowed to amortize goodwill or other intangible assets with no specific lifetime, though recent changes in the tax law allow for some flexibility in this regard.

Brand Name, Great Management, and Other True Intangibles   Companies have always derived some or a great deal of their value from assets that have no form to them. General Motors in its formative years benefited from having legendary chief executive officer (CEO) Alfred Sloan, and IBM built its reputation as a technology company from its capacity to improve computing powers and capacity. Many of the stocks in the Nifty Fifty, stocks that soared in the late 1960s, were companies like Polaroid and Eastman Kodak that derived a large portion of their value from their intangible assets.

With the rise of personal computers in the 1980s and the arrival of the internet in the 1990s, intangible assets have come to play an increasing role in determining company value. Consequently, even a cursory check at the largest market cap companies in the world will reveal companies like Microsoft, Apple and Alphabet, all firms that are light on physical assets. That trend has created a crisis in accounting, with almost none of the intangible assets showing up on balance sheets. The accounting rule writers have talked about the need to write new rules to bring intangible assets on to balance sheets, but progress has been slow and uneven, hindered by the unwillingness to change expensing rules. After all, as long as the money spent to create intangible assets, which include research and development (R&D) (technology and drug companies), brand-name advertising (consumer product companies), exploration costs (natural resource firms) and even recruiting and training expenses (consulting firms), are treated as operating expenses, the pathway to creating meaningful values on the balance sheet will be blocked.

As general advice, you should not expect to see accounting estimates of value of most intangible assets, even if they have immense value, and when you do see estimates on balance sheets, you should view them skeptically.

Goodwill   To examine how accounting talks about how goodwill is translating into intangible asset values on balance sheets, we took a look at intangible assets on corporate balance sheets. The good news is that intangible assets have risen as a percent of total assets on accounting balance sheets in the last few decades. The bad news is that almost all of that rise has come from one intangible asset, goodwill, which is more plug variable than asset. After all, goodwill is the by-product of acquisitions. When a firm acquires another firm, the purchase price is first allocated to tangible assets, and the excess price is then allocated to any intangible assets, such as patents or trade names. Any residual becomes goodwill. While accounting principles suggest that goodwill captures the value of any intangibles that are not specifically identifiable, it is really a reflection of the difference between the book value of assets of the acquired firm and the market value paid in the acquisition. This approach is called purchase accounting, and goodwill is amortized over time. Until 2000, firms that did not want to see this charge against their earnings often used an alternative approach called pooling accounting, in which the purchase price never shows up in the balance sheet. Instead, the book values of the two companies involved in the merger were aggregated to create the consolidated balance of the combined firm. The rules on acquisition accounting have changed substantially in the past decade both in the United States and internationally. Not only is purchase accounting required on all acquisitions, but firms are no longer allowed to automatically amortize goodwill over long periods (as they were used to doing). Instead, acquiring firms are required to reassess the values of the acquired entities every year; if the values have dropped since the acquisition, the value of goodwill must be reduced (impaired) to reflect the decline in value. If the acquired firm's values have gone up, though, the goodwill cannot be increased to reflect this change.[3]

ILLUSTRATION 3.1: Asset Values for Raytheon and the Home Depot in Fiscal 2022 (Fiscal 2023)

Table 3.1 summarizes asset values, as measured in the balance sheets of RTX, a conglomerate that was created from combining Raytheon and portions of United Technologies, and the Home Depot, a building supplies retailer, at the end of the 2023 fiscal year (in millions of dollars):

TABLE 3.1 Asset Values for RTX and Home Depot

	RTX	Home Depot
Net fixed assets	$ 15,748	$25,631
Operating Lease Asset	$ 1,638	$ 6,941
Goodwill	$ 53,699	$ 7,444
Net Intangibles	$ 35,399	$ 0
Customer financing	$ 2,392	$ 0
Other assets	$ 4,576	$ 3,958
Total non-current assets	$113,452	$43,974
Cash & Equivalents	$ 6,587	$ 2,757
Accounts receivables	$ 10,838	$ 3,317
Contract Assets	$ 12,139	$ 0
Inventories	$ 11,777	$24,886
Other current assets	$ 7,076	$ 1,511
Total current assets	*$ 48,417*	*$32,471*
Total assets	$161,869	$76,445

[3] Once an acquisition is complete, the difference between market value and book value for the target firm does not automatically become goodwill. Existing assets can be reappraised first to fair value and the difference becomes goodwill.

Before we look at the numbers, it is worth noting that RTX's 2022 fiscal year ended on December 31, 2022, and thus, is a calendar year, whereas Home Depot's 2023 fiscal year ended on January 31, 2023, making it more equivalent to a report for the 2022 calendar year. Looking at the numbers, there are a few points worth making about these asset values:

1. *Goodwill.* Both RTX and Home Depot have large amounts of goodwill on their balance sheets, reflecting acquisitions that each company has made in the past. The goodwill measures the difference between the prices that these companies paid to acquire their targets and the book value of the assets, reassessed to reflect their fair value. Reflecting changes in accounting rules on goodwill 20 years ago, the goodwill is reappraised on an annual basis and impaired, if the assessment is made that too much was paid for the target.
2. *Operating Lease Asset.* Home Depot reports an operating lease asset, reflecting an accounting rule change in 2019 requiring companies to capitalize their operating lease commitments. Home Depot leases most of their stores, and the present value of lease commitments is shown both as a liability and a counter asset. RTX also has lease obligations that have been capitalized, but the amount is much smaller.
3. *Customer financing and accounts receivable.* RTX often provides financing to its customers to acquire its products. Since these contracts tend to run over several years, the present value of the payments due in future years is shown as an asset in the form of customer financing. The current portion of these payments is shown as accounts receivable. The Home Depot provides credit to its customers as well, but all these payments due are shown as accounts receivable since they are all short-term.
4. *Inventories.* RTX offers no specifics on how it values its inventory, while the Home Depot uses the lower of cost (with first-in-first-out) or market value, as determined by the retail inventory approach.
5. *Net Intangibles.* RTX has a large number for net intangibles, reflecting acquisitions of collaboration assets, exclusivity assets, developed technology, and trademarks, and value these assets based upon what they paid to acquire them, net of amortization.
6. *Investments and Acquired Intangibles.* RTX and Home Depot have investments in other businesses, where they retain significant influence and use the equity method to record these investments. RTX also has acquired distribution rights and technology that they record at cost.

Finally, the balance sheet for RTX fails to report the value of a very significant asset, which is the effect of past research and development (R&D) expenses. Since accounting convention requires that these be expensed in the year that they occur and not be capitalized, the research asset does not show up in the balance sheet. Chapter 9 considers how to capitalize research and development expenses and the effects on balance sheets.

MEASURING FINANCING MIX

The second set of questions that we would like to answer and would like accounting statements to shed some light on, relate to the mix of debt and equity used by the firm and the current values of each. The bulk of the information about these questions is provided on the liabilities side of the balance sheet and the footnotes to it.

Accounting Principles Underlying Liability and Equity Measurement

Just as with the measurement of asset value, the accounting categorization of liabilities and equity is governed by a set of fairly rigid principles. The first is a *strict categorization of financing into either a liability or an equity* based on the nature of the obligation. For an obligation to be recognized as a liability, it must meet three requirements:

1. The obligation must be expected to lead to a future cash outflow or the loss of a future cash inflow at some specified or determinable date.

2. The firm cannot avoid the obligation.

3. The transaction giving rise to the obligation has to have already happened.

In keeping with the earlier principle of conservatism in estimating asset value, accountants recognize as liabilities only cash flow obligations that cannot be avoided.

The second principle is that the values of both liabilities and equity in a firm are *better estimated using historical costs* with accounting adjustments, rather than with expected future cash flows or market value. The process by which accountants measure the value of liabilities and equities is inextricably linked to the way they value assets. Since assets are primarily valued at historical cost or at book value, both debt and equity also get measured primarily at book value. The next section examines the accounting measurement of both liabilities and equity.

Measuring the Value of Liabilities and Equities

Accountants categorize liabilities into current liabilities, long-term debt, and long-term liabilities that are not debt or equity. Next, we will examine the way they measure each of these.

Current Liabilities   Under current liabilities are categorized all obligations that the firm has coming due in the next year. These generally include:

- *Accounts payable*, representing credit received from suppliers and other vendors to the firm. The value of accounts payable represents the amounts due to these creditors. For this item, book and market values should be similar.
- *Short-term borrowing*, representing short-term loans (due in less than a year) taken to finance the operations or current asset needs of the business. Here again, the value shown represents the amounts due on such loans, and the book and market values should be similar, unless the default risk of the firm has changed dramatically since it borrowed the money.
- *Short-term portion of long-term borrowing*, representing the portion of the long-term debt or bonds that is coming due in the next year. Here again, the value shown is the actual amount due on these loans, and market and book values should converge as the due date approaches.
- *Other short-term liabilities*, which is a catchall component for any other short-term liabilities that the firm might have, including wages due to its employees and taxes due to the government.

Of all the items in the balance sheet, absent outright fraud, current liabilities should be the one for which the accounting estimates of book value and financial estimates of market value are closest.

Long-Term Debt   Long-term debt for firms can take one of two forms. It can be a long-term loan from a bank or other financial institution, or it can be a long-term bond issued to financial markets, in which case the creditors are the investors in the bond. Accountants measure the value of long-term debt by looking at the present value of payments due on the loan or bond at the time of the borrowing. For bank loans, this will be equal to the nominal value of the loan. With bonds, however, there are three possibilities: When bonds are issued at par value, for instance, the value of the long-term debt is generally measured in terms of the nominal obligation created (i.e., principal due on the borrowing). When bonds are issued at a premium or a discount on par value, the bonds are recorded at the issue price, but the premium or discount is amortized over the life of the bond. As an extreme example, companies that issue zero coupon debt have to record the debt at the issue price, which will be significantly below the principal (face value) due at maturity. The difference between the issue price and the face value is amortized each period and is treated as a noncash interest expense that is tax deductible.

In all these cases, the value of debt is unaffected by changes in interest rates during the life of the loan or bond. Note that as market interest rates rise or fall, the present value of the loan obligations should decrease or increase. This updated market value for debt is not shown on the balance sheet. If debt is retired prior to maturity, the difference between book value and the amount paid at retirement is treated as an extraordinary gain or loss in the income statement.

Finally, companies that have long-term debt denominated in nondomestic currencies must adjust the book value of debt for changes in exchange rates. Since exchange rate changes reflect underlying changes in interest rates, it does imply that this debt is likely to be valued much nearer to market value than is debt in the domestic currency.

Other Long-Term Liabilities   Firms often have long-term obligations that are not captured in the long-term debt item. These include obligations to lessors on assets that firms have leased, to employees in the form of pension fund and health care benefits yet to be paid, and to the government in the form of taxes deferred. In the past two decades, accountants have increasingly moved toward quantifying these liabilities and showing them as long-term liabilities.

Leases   Firms often choose to lease long-term assets rather than buy them. Lease payments create the same kind of obligation that interest payments on debt create, and they must be viewed in a similar light. If a firm is allowed to lease a significant portion of its assets and keep it off its financial statements, a perusal of the statements will give a very misleading view of the company's financial strength. Consequently, accounting rules have been devised to force firms to reveal the extent of their lease obligations on their books.

Until 2019, there were two ways of accounting for leases. In an operating lease, the lessor (or owner) transfers only the right to use the property to the lessee. At the end of the lease period, the lessee returns the property to the lessor. Since the lessee does not assume the risk of ownership, the lease expense is treated as an operating expense in the income statement and the lease does not affect the balance sheet. In a capital lease, the lessee assumes some of the risks of ownership and enjoys some of the benefits. Consequently, the lease, when signed, is recognized both as an asset and as a liability (for the lease payments) on the balance sheet. The firm gets to claim depreciation each year on the asset and also deducts the interest expense component of the lease payment each year. In general, capital leases recognize expenses sooner than equivalent operating leases.

In 2019, both IFRS and GAAP changed the rules on accounting for leases, requiring that almost all leases would be treated as capital leases, following the same process for converting lease commitments into debt and counter-assets. We will cover this lease-to-debt conversion process in a later chapter, and it remains a useful one to understand, since there remain parts of the world where the old lease rules still apply. For firms that have to follow GAAP and IFRS, you should now see lease debt show up on the balance sheet and lease assets show up as long-term assets.

Employee Benefits Employers can provide pension and health care benefits to their employees. In many cases, the obligations created by these benefits are extensive, and a failure by the firm to adequately fund these obligations needs to be revealed in financial statements.

Pension Plans In a pension plan, the firm agrees to provide certain benefits to its employees, either by specifying a defined contribution (wherein a fixed contribution is made to the plan each year by the employer, without any promises as to the benefits that will be delivered in the plan) or a defined benefit (wherein the employer promises to pay a certain benefit to the employee). In the latter case, the employer has to put sufficient money into the plan each period to meet the defined benefits.

Under a defined contribution plan, the firm meets its obligation once it has made the prespecified contribution to the plan. Under a defined benefit plan, the firm's obligations are much more difficult to estimate, since they will be determined by a number of variables, including the benefits that employees are entitled to, the prior contributions made by the employer and the returns they have earned, and the rate of return that the employer expects to make on current contributions. As these variables change, the value of the pension fund assets can be greater than, less than, or equal to pension fund liabilities (which include the present value of promised benefits). A pension fund whose assets exceed its liabilities is an overfunded plan, whereas one whose assets are less than its liabilities is an underfunded plan, and disclosures to that effect have to be included in financial statements, generally in the footnotes.

When a pension fund is overfunded, the firm has several options. It can withdraw the excess assets from the fund, it can discontinue contributions to the plan, or it can continue to make contributions on the assumption that the overfunding is a transitory phenomenon that could well disappear by the next period. When a fund is underfunded, the firm has a liability, though accounting standards require that firms reveal only the excess of accumulated pension fund liability[4] over pension fund assets on the balance sheet.

Health Care Benefits A firm can provide health care benefits in either of two ways—by making a fixed contribution to a health care plan without promising specific benefits (analogous to a defined contribution plan) or by promising specific health benefits and setting aside the funds to provide these benefits (analogous to a defined benefit plan). The accounting for health care benefits is very similar to the accounting for pension obligations.

Deferred Taxes Firms often use different methods of accounting for tax and financial reporting purposes, leading to a question of how tax liabilities should be reported. Since accelerated depreciation and favorable inventory valuation methods for tax accounting purposes lead to a deferral of taxes, the taxes on the income reported in the financial

---

[4]The accumulated pension fund liability does not take into account the projected benefit obligation, where actuarial estimates of future benefits are made. Consequently, it is much smaller than the total pension liabilities.

statements will generally be much greater than the actual tax paid. The same principles of matching expenses to income that underlie accrual accounting suggest that the deferred income tax be recognized in the financial statements. Thus, a company that pays taxes of $55,000 on its taxable income based on its tax accounting, and that would have paid taxes of $75,000 on the income reported in its financial statements, will be forced to recognize the difference ($20,000) as deferred taxes. Since the deferred taxes will be paid in later years, they will be recognized when paid.

It is worth noting that companies that actually pay more in taxes than the taxes they report in the financial statements create an asset called a deferred tax asset. This reflects the fact that the firm's earnings in future periods will be greater, as the firm is given credit for the deferred taxes.

The question of whether the deferred tax liability is really a liability is an interesting one. On one hand, the firm does not owe the amount categorized as deferred taxes to any entity and treating it as a liability makes the firm look riskier than it really is. On the other hand, the firm will eventually have to pay its deferred taxes and treating the amount as a liability seems to be the conservative thing to do.

Preferred Stock   When a company issues preferred stock, it generally creates an obligation to pay a fixed dividend on the stock. Accounting rules have conventionally not viewed preferred stock as debt because the failure to meet preferred dividends does not result in bankruptcy. At the same time, the fact the preferred dividends are cumulative makes them more onerous than common equity. Thus, preferred stock is a hybrid security, sharing some characteristics with equity and some with debt.

Preferred stock is valued on the balance sheet at its original issue price, with any cumulated unpaid dividends added on. Convertible preferred stock is treated similarly, but it is treated as equity on conversion.

Equity   The accounting measure of equity is a historical cost measure. The value of equity shown on the balance sheet reflects the original proceeds received by the firm when it issued the equity, augmented by any earnings made since (or reduced by losses, if any) and reduced by any dividends paid out and buybacks during the period. While these three items go into what we can call the book value of equity, three other points need to be made about this estimate:

1. When companies buy back stock for short periods, with the intent of reissuing the stock or using it to cover option exercises, they are allowed to show the repurchased stock as treasury stock, which reduces the book value of equity. Firms are not allowed to keep treasury stock on the books for extended periods and have to reduce their book value of equity by the value of repurchased stock in the case of stock buybacks. Since these buybacks occur at the current market price, they can result in significant reductions in the book value of equity.
2. Firms that have significant losses over extended periods or carry out massive stock buybacks can end up with negative book values of equity.
3. Relating back to the discussion of marketable securities, any unrealized gain or loss in marketable securities that are classified as available for sale is shown as an increase or a decrease in the book value of equity in the balance sheet.

As part of their financial statements, firms provide a summary of changes in shareholders' equity during the period, where all the changes that occurred to the accounting measure of equity value are summarized.

As a final point on equity, accounting rules still seem to consider preferred stock, with its fixed dividend, as equity or near-equity, largely because preferred dividends can be deferred or cumulated without the risk of default. To the extent that there can still be a loss of control in the firm (as opposed to bankruptcy), we have already argued that preferred stock shares almost as many characteristics with unsecured debt as it does with equity.

ILLUSTRATION 3.2: **Measuring Liabilities and Equity in RTX and the Home Depot in 2022 (Fiscal 2023)**

Table 3.2 summarizes the accounting estimates of liabilities and equity at RTX and the Home Depot for the most recent fiscal year 2023 in millions of dollars:

TABLE 3.2 Liabilities and Equity—Raytheon and Home Depot

	RTX	*Home Depot*
Accounts payable and other liabilities	$ 10,698.00	$ 11,443.00
Accrued employee salaries/compensation	$ 2,491.00	$ 1,991.00
Deferred Revenue	$ 0.00	$ 3,064.00
Taxes payable	$ 0.00	$ 578.00
Short term debt	$ 189.00	$ 1,231.00
Short-term portion of long-term debt	$ 1,283.00	$ 0.00
Contract Liabilities	$ 17,183.00	$ 0.00
Current Lease Debt	$ 0.00	$ 945.00
Other Current Liabilities	$ 14,917.00	$ 3,858.00
Total current liabilities	$ 46,761.00	$ 23,110.00
Accrued Pension Liabilities	$ 2,385.00	$ 0.00
Other long-term liabilities	$ 7,511.00	$ 2,566.00
Deferred income taxes	$ 0.00	$ 1,019.00
Long-term debt	$ 42,355.00	$ 41,962.00
Lease Debt	$ 1,412.00	$ 6,226.00
Total long-term liabilities	$ 53,663.00	$ 51,773.00
Shareholders' equity - par value	$ 0.00	$ 90.00
Additional paid-in capital	$ 37,055.00	$ 12,592.00
Retained earnings	$ 52,154.00	$ 76,896.00
Accrued Losses	−$ 2,419.00	−$ 718.00
Unclaimed ESOP	−$ 15.00	$ 0.00
Treasury Stock	−$ 26,977.00	−$ 87,298.00
Shareholders' equity	$ 59,798.00	$ 1,562.00
Minority interests	$ 1,647.00	$ 0.00
Total Equity	$ 61,445.00	$ 1,562.00
Total liabilities	**$ 161,869.00**	**$ 76,445.00**

Home Depot also has collected revenues in advance of delivering products and services, but it is a far smaller value. RTX's legacy commitments to pay pensions to its employee result in accrued pension liabilities. The changes to the accounting treatment of operating leases, which resulted in a lease asset, also show up as lease liabilities, for both companies, with the Home Depot having more in commitments.

The most striking feature of both balance sheets is the shareholders' equity values. Due to significant buybacks of their own stock (treasury stock), the book equities for both companies have depleted, with Home Depot book equity a fraction of its market value.

MEASURING EARNINGS AND PROFITABILITY

How profitable is a firm? What did it earn on the assets that it invested in? These are fundamental questions we would like financial statements to answer. Accountants use the income statement to provide information about a firm's operating activities over a specific time period. The income statement is designed to measure the earnings from assets in place. This section examines the principles underlying earnings and return measurement in accounting, and the way they are put into practice.

Accounting Principles Underlying Measurement of Earnings and Profitability

Two primary principles underlie the measurement of accounting earnings and profitability. The first is the principle of accrual accounting. In accrual accounting, the revenue from selling a good or service is recognized in the period in which the good is sold or the service is performed (in whole or substantially). A corresponding effort is made on the expense side to match expenses to revenues.[5] This is in contrast to a cash-based system of accounting, where revenues are recognized when payment is received and expenses are recorded when paid.

The second principle is the categorization of expenses into operating, financing, and capital expenses. Operating expenses are expenses that, at least in theory, provide benefits only for the current period; the cost of labor and materials expended to create products that are sold in the current period is a good example. Financing expenses are expenses arising from the nonequity financing used to raise capital for the business; the most common example is interest expenses. Capital expenses are expenses that are expected to generate benefits over multiple periods; for instance, the cost of buying land and buildings is treated as a capital expense.

Operating expenses are subtracted from revenues in the current period to arrive at a measure of operating earnings of the firm. Financing expenses are subtracted from operating earnings to estimate earnings to equity investors or net income. Capital expenses are written off over their useful lives (in terms of generating benefits) as depreciation or amortization.

Measuring Accounting Earnings and Profitability

Since income can be generated from a number of different sources, generally accepted accounting principles (GAAP) require that income statements be classified into four sections—income from continuing operations, income from discontinued operations, extraordinary gains or losses, and adjustments for changes in accounting principles.

---

[5] If a cost (such as an administrative cost) cannot easily be linked with particular revenues, it is usually recognized as an expense in the period in which it is consumed.

Generally accepted accounting principles require the recognition of revenues when the service for which the firm is getting paid has been performed in full or substantially, and the firm has received in return either cash or a receivable that is both observable and measurable. Expenses linked directly to the production of revenues (like labor and materials) are recognized in the same period in which revenues are recognized. Any expenses that are not directly linked to the production of revenues are recognized in the period in which the firm consumes the services. Accounting has resolved one inconsistency that bedeviled it for years, with a change in the way it treats employee options. Unlike the old rules, where these option grants were not treated as expenses when granted but only when exercised; the new rules require that employee options be valued and expensed when granted (with allowances for amortization over periods). Since employee options are part of compensation, which is an operating expense, the new rules make more sense.

While accrual accounting is straightforward in firms that produce goods and sell them, there are special cases where accrual accounting can be complicated by the nature of the product or service being offered. For instance, firms that enter into long-term contracts with their customers are allowed to recognize revenue on the basis of the percentage of the contract that is completed. As the revenue is recognized on a percentage-of-completion basis, a corresponding proportion of the expense is also recognized. When there is considerable uncertainty about the capacity of the buyer of a good or service to pay for it, the firm providing the good or service may recognize the income only when it collects portions of the selling price under the installment method.

Reverting to the discussion of the difference between capital and operating expenses, operating expenses should reflect only those expenses that create revenues in the current period. In practice, however, a number of expenses are classified as operating expenses that do not seem to meet this test. The first is depreciation and amortization. While the notion that capital expenditures should be written off over multiple periods is reasonable, the accounting depreciation that is computed on the original historical cost often bears little resemblance to the actual economic depreciation. The second expense is research and development expenses, which accounting standards classify as operating expenses, but which clearly provide benefits over multiple periods. The rationale used for this classification is that the benefits cannot be counted on or easily quantified and uncertain.

Much of financial analysis is built around the expected future earnings of a firm, and many of these forecasts start with the current earnings. It is therefore important to know how much of these earnings comes from the ongoing operations of the firm, and how much can be attributed to unusual or extraordinary events that are unlikely to recur on a regular basis. From that standpoint, it is useful that firms categorize expenses into operating and nonrecurring expenses, since it is the earnings prior to extraordinary items that should be used in forecasting. Nonrecurring items include:

- *Unusual or infrequent items*, such as gains or losses from the divestiture of an asset or division, and write-offs or restructuring costs. Companies sometimes include such items as part of operating expenses. As an example, Boeing in 1997 took a write-off of $1,400 million to adjust the value of assets it acquired in its acquisition of McDonnell Douglas, and it showed this as part of operating expenses.
- *Extraordinary items*, which are defined as events that are unusual in nature, infrequent in occurrence, and material in impact. Examples include the accounting gain

associated with refinancing high-coupon debt with lower-coupon debt, and gains or losses from marketable securities that are held by the firm.

▨ *Losses associated with discontinued operations*, which measure both the loss from the phaseout period and any estimated loss on sale of the operations. To qualify, however, the operations have to be separable from the firm.

▨ *Gains or losses associated with accounting changes*, which measure earnings changes created by both accounting changes made voluntarily by the firm (such as a change in inventory valuation) and accounting changes mandated by new accounting standards.

ILLUSTRATION 3.3:   Measures of Earnings—RTX and the Home Depot in 2022 (Fiscal 2023)

Table 3.3 summarizes the income statements of RTX and the Home Depot for the 2023 fiscal year, ending in December 2023 for the former and January 2023 for the latter, in millions of dollars:

TABLE 3.3 Measuring Earnings at Raytheon and Home Depot

	RTX	Home Depot
Revenues	$68,920.00	$157,403.00
Cost of Sales	$56,831.00	$104,625.00
Gross Profit	$12,089.00	$ 52,778.00
− S, G & A Expenses	$ 5,809.00	$ 26,284.00
− Depreciation	$ 0.00	$ 2,455.00
− R&D expenses	$ 2,805.00	$ 0.00
+ Other Income	$ 86.00	$ 0.00
Operating income	$ 3,561.00	$ 24,039.00
+ Nonoperating Income	$ 1,780.00	$ 0.00
+ Other Income	$ 0.00	$ 55.00
− Interest expenses	$ 1,505.00	$ 1,617.00
Earnings before taxes	$ 3,836.00	$ 22,477.00
− Income taxes	$ 456.00	$ 5,372.00
Net earnings (Loss)	$ 3,380.00	$ 17,105.00
− Profits due to Minority Interests	$ 185.00	
Net Income/ Loss	$ 3,195.00	

Note that RTX includes $4,211 million in depreciation in its costs of sales, while Home Depot reports depreciation separately. RTX's operating income is reduced by the research and development expense, which is treated as an operating expense by accountants, and we will address this issue in chapter 9. Finally, RTX does have a majority interest in another venture, and it subtracts out the losses on the portion of the venture that does not belong to them (minority interests) to get to its net income.

Measures of Profitability   While the income statement allows us to estimate how profitable a firm is in absolute terms, it is just as important that we gauge the profitability of the firm in terms of percentage returns. Two basic ratios measure profitability. One examines the profitability relative to the capital employed to get a rate of return on investment. This can be done either from the viewpoint of just the equity investors, or by looking at the entire firm. Another examines profitability relative to sales, by estimating a profit margin.

Return on Assets and Return on Capital   The *return on assets* (ROA) of a firm measures its operating efficiency in generating profits from its assets, prior to the effects of financing.

$$\text{Return on assets (after-tax)} = \frac{\text{Earnings before interest \& taxes } (1 - \text{tax rate})}{\text{Total assets}}$$

Earnings before interest and taxes (EBIT) is the accounting measure of operating income from the income statement, and total assets refers to the assets as measured using accounting rules—that is, using book value (BV) for most assets. Alternatively, return on assets can be written as:

$$\text{Return on assets (after-tax)} = \frac{\text{Net income} + \text{Interest expenses } (1 - \text{tax rate})}{\text{Total assets}}$$

By separating the financing effects from the operating effects, the return on assets provides a cleaner measure of the true return on these assets. By dividing by total assets, the return on assets does understate the profitability of firms that have substantial current assets.

ROA can also be computed on a pretax basis with no loss of generality, by using the earnings before interest and taxes and not adjusting for taxes:

$$\text{Pre-tax Return on assets} = \frac{\text{Earnings before interest \& taxes}}{\text{Total assets}}$$

This measure is useful if the firm or division is being evaluated for purchase by an acquirer with a different tax rate.

The problem with total assets is that it includes cash and nonoperating assets, creating noise in the estimate as a measure of operating profitability. A more useful measure of return relates the operating income to the capital invested in the firm, where capital is defined as the sum of the book value of debt and equity, net of cash. This is the return on invested capital (ROC or ROIC) and provides not only a truer measure of return, but one that can be compared to the cost of capital to measure the quality of a firm's investments.

$$\text{Pre-tax ROIC} = \frac{\text{Earnings before interest and taxes}}{(\text{Book Value of Equity} + \text{Book Value of Debt} - \text{Cash})}$$

$$\text{After-tax ROIC} = \frac{\text{Earnings before interest and taxes } (1 - \text{tax rate})}{(\text{Book Value of Equity} + \text{Book Value of Debt} - \text{Cash})}$$

The denominator is generally termed invested capital and measures the book value of operating assets. For both measures, the book value can be measured at the beginning of the period, or as an average of beginning and ending values.

ILLUSTRATION 3.4:　**Estimating Return on Capital—RTX and the Home Depot in Fiscal 2023**

Table 3.4 summarizes the after-tax return on assets and return on capital (ROC) estimates for Raytheon and the Home Depot, using both average and beginning measures of capital in the most recent fiscal years (2023):

TABLE 3.4　Return on Capital for Raytheon and Home Depot

	RTX	Home Depot
After-tax operating income	$ 3,561	$24,039.22
Book value of capital—beginning	$47,618	$34,783
Book value of capital—ending	$46,398	$41,725
Book value of capital—average	$47,008	$38,254
Return on capital (based on average)	7.58%	62.84%
Return on capital (based on beginning)	7.48%	69.11%
Invested Capital at the end of fiscal 2023		
Shareholders' equity	$61,445.00	$ 1,562.00
+ Total Debt	$43,827.00	$43,193.00
+ PV of Lease Obligations	$ 1,412.00	$ 7,171.00
− Cash	$ 6,587.00	$ 2,757.00
− Goodwill	$53,699.00	$ 7,444.00
Invested Capital	$46,398.00	$41,725.00

　　The equation below shows the computation of capital invested, and it is a sum of the book values of equity, all interest-bearing debt and lease debt, net of cash, and goodwill. In computing returns on capital, we use both average and the start-of-the-year capital invested numbers. RTX's numbers reflect its struggles to generate a decent return on capital, but Home Depot's numbers are overstated, because its book equity is deflated by buybacks.

Decomposing Return on (Invested) Capital　The return on capital of a firm can be written as a function of the operating profit margin it has on its sales, and its capital turnover ratio.

$$\text{ROIC} = \frac{\text{Earnings before interest and taxes } (1 - t)}{\text{Sales}}$$
$$\times \frac{\text{Sales}}{\text{Invested Capital}}$$
$$= \text{After-tax Operating Margin} \times \text{Sales to Capital}$$

Thus, a firm can arrive at a high ROC by either increasing its profit margin or utilizing its capital more efficiently to increase sales. There are likely to be competitive constraints and technological constraints on both variables, but a firm still has some freedom within these constraints to choose the mix of profit margin and capital turnover that maximizes its ROC. The return on capital varies widely across firms in different businesses, largely because of differences in profit margins and capital turnover ratios.

mgnroc.xls: **This is a dataset on the web that summarizes the operating margins, turnover ratios, and returns on capital of firms in the United States, as classified by industry.**

Return on Equity While the return on capital measures the profitability of the overall firm, the return on equity (ROE) examines profitability from the perspective of the equity investor, by relating the equity investor's profits (net profit after taxes and interest expenses) to the book value of the equity investment.

$$ROE = \frac{\text{Net Income}}{\text{Book Value of Equity}}$$

Since preferred stockholders have a different type of claim on the firm than do common stockholders, the net income should be estimated after preferred dividends, and the book value should be that of only common equity.

Determinants of Noncash ROE Since the ROE is based on earnings after interest payments, it is affected by the financing mix that the firm uses to fund its projects. In general, a firm that borrows money to finance projects and that earns a ROC on those projects which exceeds the after-tax interest rate it pays on its debt, will be able to increase its ROE by borrowing. The return on equity, not including cash, can be written as follows:[6]

$$ROE = ROIC + \frac{D}{E}[ROIC - i(1 - t)]$$

where   ROIC = EBIT$(1 - t)$/(BV of debt + BV of equity − Cash)

   D/E = BV of debt/BV of equity

      i = Interest expense on debt/BV of debt

      t = Tax rate on ordinary income

The second term captures the benefit of financial leverage.

---

[6]To derive this formula, assume that cash is zero, and replace EBIT $(1 - t)$ with (Net Income + Interest Expense $(1 - t)$)/(D + E) and the interest rate with Interest Expense/Debt in the equation and work through to a solution.

$$\begin{aligned}
ROC + D/E[ROC - i(1 - t)] &= [NI + Int(1 - t)]/(D + E) + D/E\{[NI + Int(1 - t)] \\
&\quad /(D + E) - Int(1 - t)/D\} \\
&= \{[NI + Int(1 - t)]/(D + E)\}(1 + D/E) - Int(1 - t)/E \\
&= NI/E + Int(1 - t)/E - Int(1 - t)/E = NI/E = ROE
\end{aligned}$$

ILLUSTRATION 3.5:   Return on Equity Computations: RTX and the Home Depot in Fiscal 2023

Table 3.5 summarizes the return on equity for RTX and the Home Depot in 2023:

TABLE 3.5   Return on Equity for Raytheon and Home Depot

	RTX	*Home Depot*
Net income	$ 3,195	$17,105
Book value of equity—beginning	$72,632	($ 1,696)
Book value of equity—ending	$59,798	$ 1,562
Book value of equity—average	$66,215	($ 67)
Return on equity (based on average)	4.83%	NA
Return on equity (based on beginning)	4.40%	NA

The results again indicate that RTX had a substandard year in 2023, but Home Depot's book equity problems become an issue again. In fact, the company reported a negative value for shareholder's equity at the end of 2022, making return on equity a meaningless number.

 roe.xls: **This is a dataset on the web that summarizes the returns on equity of firms in the United States, as classified by industry.**

MEASURING RISK

How risky are the investments the firm has made over time? How much risk do equity investors in a firm face? These are two more questions that we would like to find the answers to in the course of an investment analysis. Accounting statements do not really claim to measure or quantify risk in a systematic way, other than to provide footnotes and disclosures where there might be risk embedded in the firm. This section examines some of the ways in which accountants try to assess risk.

Accounting Principles Underlying Risk Measurement

To the extent that accounting statements and ratios do attempt to measure risk, there seem to be two common themes.

The first is that the risk being measured is the risk of default—that is, the risk that a fixed obligation, such as interest or principal due on outstanding debt, will not be met. The broader equity notion of risk, which measures the variance of actual returns around expected returns, does not seem to receive much attention. Thus, an all-equity-financed firm with positive earnings and few or no fixed obligations will generally emerge as a low-risk firm from an accounting standpoint, in spite of the fact that its earnings are unpredictable.

The second theme is that accounting risk measures generally take a static view of risk, by looking at the capacity of a firm at a point in time to meet its obligations. For instance, when ratios are used to assess a firm's risk, the ratios are almost always based on one period's income statement and balance sheet.

Accounting Measures of Risk

Accounting measures of risk can be broadly categorized into two groups. The first is disclosures about potential obligations or losses in values that show up as footnotes on balance sheets, which are designed to alert potential or current investors to the possibility of significant losses. The second measure is ratios that are designed to measure both liquidity and default risk.

Disclosures in Financial Statements   In recent years, the disclosures that firms have to make about future obligations have proliferated. Consider, for instance, the case of contingent liabilities. These refer to potential liabilities that will be incurred under certain contingencies, as is the case, for instance, when a firm is the defendant in a lawsuit. The general rule that has been followed is to ignore contingent liabilities that hedge against risk, since the obligations on the contingent claim will be offset by benefits elsewhere.[7] In recent periods, however, significant losses borne by firms from supposedly hedged derivatives positions (such as options and futures) have led to FASB requirements that these derivatives be disclosed as part of a financial statement. In fact, pension fund and health care obligations have moved from mere footnotes to actual liabilities for firms.

Financial Ratios   Financial statements have long been used as the basis for estimating financial ratios that measure profitability, risk, and leverage. Earlier the section on earnings looked at two of the profitability ratios—return on equity and return on capital. This section looks at some of the financial ratios that are often used to measure the financial risk in a firm.

Short-Term Liquidity Risk   Short-term liquidity risk arises primarily from the need to finance current operations. To the extent that the firm has to make payments to its suppliers before it gets paid for the goods and services it provides, there is a cash shortfall that has to be met, usually through short-term borrowing. Though this financing of working capital needs is done routinely in most firms, financial ratios have been devised to keep track of the extent of the firm's exposure to the risk that it will not be able to meet its short-term obligations. The two ratios most frequently used to measure short-term liquidity risk are the current ratio and the quick ratio.

Current Ratios   The current ratio is the ratio of the firm's current assets (cash, inventory, accounts receivable) to its current liabilities (obligations coming due within the next period).

$$\text{Current Ratio} = \frac{\text{Current Assets}}{\text{Current Liabilities}}$$

---

[7]This assumes that the hedge is set up competently. It is entirely possible that a hedge, if sloppily set up, can end up costing the firm money.

A current ratio below 1, for instance, would indicate that the firm has more obligations coming due in the next year than assets it can expect to turn into cash. That would be an indication of liquidity risk.

While traditional analysis suggests that firms maintain a current ratio of 2 or greater, there is a trade-off here between minimizing liquidity risk and tying up more and more cash in net working capital (Net working capital = Current assets − Current liabilities). In fact, it can be reasonably argued that a very high current ratio is indicative of an unhealthy firm that is having problems reducing its inventory. In recent years, firms have worked at reducing their current ratios and managing their net working capital better.

Reliance on current ratios has to be tempered by a few concerns. First, the ratio can be easily manipulated by firms around the time of financial reporting dates to give the illusion of safety; second, current assets and current liabilities can change by an equal amount, but the effect on the current ratio will depend on its level before the change.[8]

Quick or Acid Test Ratios   The quick or acid test ratio is a variant of the current ratio. It distinguishes current assets that can be converted quickly into cash (e.g., cash and marketable securities) from those that cannot (e.g., inventory and accounts receivable).

$$\text{Quick Ratio} = \frac{\text{Cash} + \text{Marketable Securities}}{\text{Current Liabilities}}$$

The exclusion of accounts receivable and inventory is not a hard-and-fast rule. If there is evidence that either can be converted into cash quickly, it can, in fact, be included as part of the quick ratio.

Turnover Ratios   Turnover ratios measure the efficiency of working capital management by looking at the relationship of accounts receivable and inventory to sales and to the cost of goods sold:

$$\text{Accounts receivable turnover} = \text{Sales/Average Accounts receivable}$$
$$\text{Inventory turnover} = \text{Cost of Goods Sold/Average Inventory}$$

These statistics can be interpreted as measuring the speed with which the firm turns accounts receivable into cash or inventory into sales. These ratios are often expressed in terms of the number of days outstanding:

$$\text{Days of receivables} = \text{365/Accounts receivable turnover}$$
$$\text{Days of inventory} = \text{365/Inventory turnover}$$

A similar pair of statistics can be computed for accounts payable, relative to purchases:

$$\text{Accounts payable turnover} = \text{Purchases/Average Accounts payable}$$
$$\text{Days of payables} = \text{365/Accounts payable turnover}$$

---

[8]If the current assets and current liabilities increase by an equal amount, the current ratio will go down if it was greater than 1 before the increase, and go up if it was less than 1.

Since accounts receivable and inventory are assets, and accounts payable is a liability, these three statistics (standardized in terms of days outstanding) can be combined to get an estimate of how much financing the firm needs to raise to fund working capital needs.

$$\text{Required Financing Period} = \text{Days of receivables} + \text{Days of inventory} \\ - \text{Days of payables}$$

The greater the financing period for a firm, the more it will need short term financing to cover the deficit.

 wcdata.xls: This is a dataset on the web that summarizes working capital ratios for firms in the United States, as classified by industry.

Long-Term Solvency and Default Risk Measures of long-term solvency attempt to examine a firm's capacity to meet interest and principal payments in the long term. Clearly, the profitability ratios discussed earlier in the section are a critical component of this analysis. The ratios specifically designed to measure long-term solvency try to relate profitability to the level of debt payments in order to identify the degree of comfort with which the firm can meet these payments.

Interest Coverage Ratios The interest coverage ratio measures the capacity of the firm to meet interest payments from predebt, pretax earnings.

$$\text{Interest Coverage Ratio} = \frac{\text{Earnings before interest and taxes}}{\text{Interest Expenses}}$$

The higher the interest coverage ratio, the more secure is the firm's capacity to make interest payments from earnings. This argument, however, has to be tempered by the recognition that the amount of earnings before interest and taxes is volatile and can drop significantly if the economy enters a recession. Consequently, two firms can have the same interest coverage ratio but be viewed very differently in terms of risk.

The denominator in the interest coverage ratio can be easily extended to cover other fixed obligations such as lease payments. If this is done, the ratio is called a fixed charges coverage ratio:

$$\text{Fixed Charges Coverage Ratio} = \frac{\text{EBIT} - \text{Fixed charges}}{\text{Fixed Charges}}$$

Finally, this ratio, while stated in terms of earnings, can be restated in terms of cash flows by using earnings before interest, taxes, depreciation, and amortization (EBITDA) in the numerator and cash fixed charges in the denominator.

$$\text{Cash Fixed Charge Ratio} = \frac{\text{EBITDA}}{\text{Cash Fixed Charges}}$$

Both interest coverage and fixed charges coverage ratios are open to the criticism that they do not consider capital expenditures—a cash flow that may be discretionary in the very short term but not in the long term if the firm wants to maintain growth. One way of capturing the extent of this cash flow, relative to operating cash flows, is to compute a ratio of the two:

$$\text{Operating cash flow to capital expenditures} = \frac{\text{Cash flows from Operations}}{\text{Capital Expenditures}}$$

While there are several different definitions of cash flows from operations, the most accounting-centered way comes from the statement of cash flows measure the cash flows from continuing operations to equity investors, before interest, but after taxes and after meeting working capital needs.

$$\text{Equity Cash flows from Operations} = \text{Net Income} + \text{Depreciation}$$
$$- \text{Change in noncash working capital}$$

---

 dbtfund.xls: **This is a dataset online that summarizes the interest coverage ratios for firms in the United States, as classified by industry.**

ILLUSTRATION 3.6:   Interest and Fixed Charges Coverage Ratios: RTX and the Home Depot in Fiscal 2023

Table 3.6 summarizes interest and fixed charges coverage ratios for RTX and the Home Depot in 2023:

TABLE 3.6   Interest and Fixed Charge Coverage: Raytheon and Home Depot

	RTX	Home Depot
EBIT	$3,561	$24,039
Interest expense	$1,505	$ 1,617
Interest coverage ratio	2.37	14.87
EBIT	$3,561	$24,039
Operating lease expenses (Fixed)	$ 463	$ 1,169
Interest expenses	$1,505	$ 1,617
Fixed charges coverage ratio	1.81	8.63
EBITDA	$7,772	$26,494
Cash fixed charges	$1,968	$ 2,786
Cash fixed charges coverage ratio	3.95	9.51
Cash flows from operations	$7,883	$14,615
Capital expenditures	$2,415	$ 3,119
Cash flows/Capital expenditures	3.26	4.69

RTX, based on its operating income in 2023, looks riskier than the Home Depot on all the measures of debt load, with less earnings and cashflows generated, relative to debt payments and fixed charges. For both companies, operating income has ebbed and flowed over the years, and it might make more sense when computing these ratios to look at the average operating income over time.

finratio.xls: **This spreadsheet allows you to compute the interest coverage and fixed charges coverage ratios for a firm based on financial statement data.**

Debt Ratios Interest coverage ratios measure the capacity of the firm to meet interest payments, but do not examine whether it can pay back the principal on outstanding debt. Debt ratios attempt to do this by relating debt to total capital or to equity:

$$\text{Debt to Capital} = \text{Debt}/(\text{Debt} + \text{Equity})$$
$$\text{Debt to Equity} = \text{Debt}/\text{Equity}$$

The first ratio measures debt as a proportion of the total capital of the firm and cannot exceed 100 percent. The second measures debt as a proportion of the book value of equity in the firm and can be easily derived from the first, since:

$$\text{Debt to Equity} = \text{Debt to Capital}/(1 - \text{Debt to Capital})$$

While these ratios presume that capital is raised from only debt and equity, they can be easily adapted to include other sources of financing such as preferred stock. Although preferred stock is sometimes combined with common stock under the equity label, it is better to keep the two sources of financing separate, and to compute the ratio of preferred stock to capital (which will include debt, equity, and preferred stock).

There are two close variants of debt ratios. In the first, only long-term debt is used rather than total debt, with the rationale that short-term debt is transitory and will not affect the long-term solvency of the firm.

$$\text{Long-term Debt to Capital} = \text{Long-term Debt}/(\text{Long-term Debt} + \text{Equity})$$
$$\text{Long-term Debt to Equity} = \text{Long-term Debt}/\text{Equity}$$

Given the ease with which some firms can roll over short-term debt and the willingness of many firms to use short-term financing to fund long-term projects, these variants can provide a misleading picture of the firm's financial leverage risk.

The second variant of debt ratios uses market value (MV) instead of BV, primarily to reflect the fact that some firms have a significantly greater capacity to borrow than their book values indicate.

$$\text{Market Value Debt to Capital} = \text{MV of Debt}/(\text{MV of Debt} + \text{MV of Equity})$$
$$\text{Market Value Debt to Equity} = \text{MV of Debt}/\text{MV of Equity}$$

Many analysts disavow the use of market value in their calculations, contending that market values, in addition to being difficult to get for debt, are volatile and hence unreliable. These contentions are open to debate. It is true that the market value of debt is difficult to get for firms that do not have publicly traded bonds, but the market value of equity not only is easy to obtain, but it also is constantly updated to reflect marketwide and firm-specific changes. Furthermore, using the book value of debt as a proxy for market value in those cases where bonds are not traded does not significantly shift most market value-based debt ratios.[9]

ILLUSTRATION 3.7:   Book Value Debt Ratios and Variants—RTX and the Home Depot

Table 3.7 summarizes different estimates of the debt ratio for Boeing and the Home Depot, in 2023, using book values of debt and equity for both firms:

TABLE 3.7   Debt ratios for Raytheon and Home Depot

	RTX	Home Depot
Long-term debt	$ 42,355	$ 41,962
Short-term debt	$ 1,472	$ 1,231
Long term lease debt	$ 1,412	$ 6,226
Short-term lease debt	$ 0	$ 945
Book value of equity	$ 61,445	$ 1,562
Long-term debt/Equity	71.23%	3085.02%
Long-term debt/(Long-term debt + Equity)	41.60%	96.86%
Total Debt/Equity	73.63%	3224.33%
Total Debt/(Total Debt + Equity)	42.40%	96.99%
Market value of equity	$120,930	$363,720
Total Debt/Equity (Market)	37.41%	13.85%
Total Debt to Capital (Market)	27.22%	12.16%

In 2023, Home Depot's book debt ratios look outlandishly high, but it is because their book equity by the end of 2023 fiscal year was so low (which also affected accounting returns on capital and equity). The contrast, when you use market value is striking, and the Home Depot has a lower debt load than RTX.

 dbtfund.xls: This is a dataset on the web that summarizes the book value debt ratios and market value debt ratios for firms in the United States, as classified by industry.

OTHER ISSUES IN ANALYZING FINANCIAL STATEMENTS

There are significant differences in accounting standards and practices across countries and these differences may color comparisons across companies.

Differences in Accounting Standards and Practices

Differences in accounting standards across countries affect the measurement of earnings. These differences, however, are not so great as they are made out to be by some analysts, and they cannot explain away radical departures from fundamental principles of

---

[9]Deviations in the market value of equity from book value are likely to be much larger than deviations for debt, and are likely to dominate in most debt ratio calculations.

valuation. Choi and Levich, in a 1990 survey of accounting standards across developed markets, note that most countries subscribe to basic accounting notions of consistency, realization, and historical cost principles in preparing accounting statements. As countries increasingly move toward international financial reporting standards (IFRS), it is worth noting that IFRS and U.S. GAAP are more similar than dissimilar on many issues, as can be seen in Table 3.8. It is true that there are areas of differences that remain, and most of these differences can be accounted and adjusted for when comparisons are made between companies in the United States and companies in other financial markets. Statistics such as price-earnings ratios, which use stated and unadjusted earnings, can be misleading when accounting standards vary widely across the companies being compared.

TABLE 3.8 Differences between IFRS and GAAP (in 2023)

	IFRS	GAAP
Rules vs. Principle	More principle-based	More rule-based
Inventory	FIFO or Weighted-average cost. Can be written down if market value drops but can be written up if it rises again	FIFO, LIFO or Weighted-average cost Can be written down if market value drops but cannot be written back up if circumstances change
Fair value	Allowed on any asset that can be fairly valued including property, plant & equipment and intangible assets	Allowed only on marketable securities
Impairment losses	Impairment losses when asset value drops, but reversal allowed, if market value rises again	Impairment losses when asset value drops but no reversals
Intangible assets	Development costs can be capitalized, when future economic benefits become more tangible	Expensed. With software, costs be capitalized once technological feasibility can be demonstrated.
Fixed assets	Initially recorded at cost but can be marked up or down to market value later	Recorded at cost and depreciated
Leases	Leases, include those on some intangible assets, are capitalized.	Leases are capitalized but only on tangible assets
Goodwill	Impaired at the cash-unit level, does not allow for qualitative exceptions and can exceed the value of goodwill	Impaired at reporting unit level, allows for qualitative exceptions and cannot exceed goodwill

CONCLUSION

Financial statements remain the primary source of information for most investors and analysts. There are differences, however, between how accounting and financial analysts approach answering a number of key questions about the firm.

The first question relates to the nature and the value of the assets owned by a firm. Assets can be categorized into investments already made (assets in place) and investments yet to be made (growth assets); accounting statements provide a substantial amount of historical information about the former and very little about the latter. The focus on the original price of assets in place (book value) in accounting statements can lead to significant differences between the stated value of these assets and their market value. With growth assets, accounting rules result in low or no values for assets generated by internal research.

The second issue is the measurement of profitability. The two principles that govern how profits are measured are accrual accounting—in which revenues and expenses are shown in the period in which transactions occur, rather than when the cash is received or paid—and the categorization of expenses into operating, financing, and capital expenses. While operating and financing expenses are shown in income statements, capital expenditures are spread over several time periods and take the form of depreciation and amortization. Accounting standards have finally fixed their miscategorization of operating leases as operating expenses (they are financing expenses) but they still miscategorize research and development expenses as operating expenses (when they are capital expenses).

Financial statements also deal with short-term liquidity risk and long-term default risk, albeit imprecisely. While the emphasis in accounting statements is on examining the risk that firms may be unable to make payments that they have committed to make, there is very little focus on risk to equity investors.

QUESTIONS AND SHORT PROBLEMS

In the problems following, use an equity risk premium of 5.5 percent if none is specified.

Coca-Cola's balance sheet for December 1998 is summarized (in millions of dollars) for problems 1 through 9:

Cash & Near Cash	1648	Accounts Payable	3141
Marketable Securities	159	Short-term Borrowings	4462
Accounts Receivable	1666	Other Short-term liabilities	1037
Other Current Assets	2017	*Current Liabilities*	8640
Current Assets	*6380*	Long-term Borrowings	687
Long-term investments	1863	Other long-term Liabilities	1415
Depreciable Fixed Assets	5486	Noncurrent liabilities	2102
Nondepreciable Fixed Assets	199		
Accumulated Depreciation	2016	Share Capital (Paid-in)	3060
Net Fixed Assets	*3669*	Retained Earnings	5343
Other Assets	7233	Shareholder Equity	8403
Total Assets	**19145**	**Total Liabilities & Equity**	**19145**

1. Consider the assets on Coca-Cola's balance sheet and answer the following questions:
   a. Which assets are likely to be assessed closest to market value? Explain.
   b. Coca-Cola has net fixed assets of $3,669 million. Can you estimate how much Coca-Cola paid for these assets? Is there any way to know the age of these assets?
   c. Coca-Cola seems to have far more invested in current assets than in fixed assets. Is this significant? Explain.
   d. In the early 1980s, Coca-Cola sold off its bottling operations, and the bottlers became independent companies. How would this action have impacted the assets

on Coca-Cola's balance sheet? (The manufacturing plants are most likely to be part of the bottling operations.)

2. Examine the liabilities on Coca-Cola's balance sheet.
   a. How much interest-bearing debt does Coca-Cola have outstanding? (You can assume that other short-term liabilities represent sundry payables, and other long-term liabilities represent health care and pension obligations.)
   b. How much did Coca-Cola obtain in equity capital when it issued stock originally to the financial markets?
   c. Is there any significance to the fact that the retained earnings amount is much larger than the original paid-in capital?
   d. The market value of Coca-Cola's equity is $140 billion. What is the book value of equity in Coca-Cola? Why is there such a large difference between the market value of equity and the book value of equity?
3. Coca-Cola's most valuable asset is its brand name. Where in the balance sheet do you see its value? Is there any way to adjust the balance sheet to reflect the value of this asset?
4. Assume that you have been asked to analyze Coca-Cola's working capital management.
   a. Estimate the net working capital and noncash working capital for Coca-Cola.
   b. Estimate the firm's current ratio.
   c. Estimate the firm's quick ratio.
   d. Would you draw any conclusions about the riskiness of Coca-Cola as a firm by looking at these numbers? Why or why not?

   Coca-Cola's income statements for 1997 and 1998 are summarized (in millions of dollars) for problems 5 through 9:

	1997	1998
Net revenues	$18,868	$18,813
Cost of goods sold	6,015	5,562
Selling, general, and administrative expenses	7,852	8,284
Earnings before interest and taxes	5,001	4,967
Interest expenses	258	277
Nonoperating gains	1,312	508
Income tax expenses	1,926	1,665
Net income	4,129	3,533
Dividends	1,387	1,480

   The following questions relate to Coca-Cola's income statements.

5. How much operating income did Coca-Cola earn, before taxes, in 1998? How does this compare to how much Coca-Cola earned in 1997? What are the reasons for the difference?
6. The biggest expense for Coca-Cola is advertising, which is part of the selling, general, and administrative (G&A) expenses. A large portion of these expenses is designed to build up Coca-Cola's brand name. Should advertising expenses be treated as operating expenses, or are they really capital expenses? If they are to be treated as capital expenses, how would you capitalize them? (Use the capitalization of R&D as a guide.)

7. What effective tax rate did Coca-Cola have in 1998? How does it compare with what the company paid in 1997 as an effective tax rate? What might account for the difference?

8. You have been asked to assess the profitability of Coca-Cola as a firm. To that end, estimate the pretax operating and net margins in 1997 and 1998 for the firm. Are there any conclusions you would draw from the comparisons across the two years?

9. The book value of equity at Coca-Cola in 1997 was $7,274 million. The book value of interest-bearing debt was $3,875 million. Estimate:
   a. The return on equity (beginning of the year) in 1998.
   b. The pretax return on capital (beginning of the year) in 1998.
   c. The after-tax return on capital (beginning of the year) in 1998, using the effective tax rate in 1998.

10. SeeSaw Toys reported that it had a book value of equity of $1.5 billion at the end of 1998 and 100 million shares outstanding. During 1999, it bought back 10 million shares at a market price of $40 per share. The firm also reported a net income of $150 million for 1999, and paid dividends of $50 million. Estimate:
    a. The book value of equity at the end of 1999.
    b. The return on equity, using beginning book value of equity.
    c. The return on equity, using the average book value of equity.

CHAPTER 4

The Basics of Risk

When valuing assets and firms, we need to use discount rates that reflect the riskiness of the cash flows. In particular, the cost of debt has to incorporate a default spread for the default risk in the debt, and the cost of equity has to include a risk premium for equity risk. But how do we measure default and equity risk? More importantly, how do we come up with the default and equity risk premiums?

This chapter lays the foundations for analyzing risk in valuation. It presents alternative models for measuring risk and converting these risk measures into acceptable hurdle rates. It begins with a discussion of equity risk and presents the analysis in three steps. In the first step, risk is defined in statistical terms to be the variance in actual returns around an expected return. The greater this variance, the riskier an investment is perceived to be. The next step, the central one, is to decompose this risk into risk that can be diversified away by investors and risk that cannot. The third step looks at how different risk and return models in finance attempt to measure this nondiversifiable risk. It compares the most widely used model, the capital asset pricing model (CAPM), with other models, explains how and why they diverge in their measures of risk, and the implications for the equity risk premium.

The final part of this chapter considers default risk and how it is measured by ratings agencies. By the end of the chapter, we should have a way of estimating the equity risk and default risk for any firm.

WHAT IS RISK?

Risk, for most of us, refers to the likelihood that in life's games of chance we will receive an outcome that we will not like. For instance, the risk of driving a car too fast is getting a speeding ticket or, worse still, getting into an accident. *Merriam-Webster's Collegiate Dictionary*, in fact, defines the verb to risk as "to expose to hazard or danger". Thus, risk is perceived almost entirely in negative terms.

In finance, our definition of risk is both different and broader. Risk, as we see it, refers to the likelihood that we will receive a return on an investment that is different from the return we expect to make. Thus, risk includes not only the bad outcomes (returns that are lower than expected), but also good outcomes (returns that are higher than expected). In fact, we can refer to the former as downside risk and the latter as upside risk, but we consider both when measuring risk. The spirit of our definition of risk in finance is captured best by the Chinese symbols for risk:

$$危機$$

Loosely defined, the first symbol is the symbol for "danger", while the second is the symbol for "opportunity", making risk a mix of danger and opportunity. It illustrates very clearly the trade-off that every investor and business has to make—between the higher rewards that come with the opportunity and the higher risk that has to be borne as a consequence of the danger.

Much of this chapter can be viewed as an attempt to come up with a model that best measures the danger in any investment, and then attempts to convert this into the opportunity that we would need to compensate for the danger. In finance terms, we term the danger to be "risk" and the opportunity to be "expected return".

What makes the measurement of risk and expected return so challenging is that it can vary depending on whose perspective we adopt. When analyzing the risk of a firm, for instance, we can measure it from the viewpoint of the firm's managers. Alternatively, we can argue that the firm's equity is owned by its stockholders, and that it is their perspective on risk that should matter. A firm's stockholders, many of whom hold the stock as one investment in a larger portfolio, might perceive the risk in the firm very differently from the firm's managers, who might have the bulk of their capital, human and financial, invested in the firm.

We argue that risk in an investment has to be perceived through the eyes of investors in the firm. Since firms often have thousands of investors, often with very different perspectives, it can be asserted that risk has to be measured from the perspective of not just any investor in the stock, but of the marginal investor, defined to be the investor most likely to be trading on the stock and affecting its price. The objective in valuation is to measure the value of an asset to those who will be pricing it. If we want to stay true to this objective, we have to consider the viewpoint of those who set the stock prices, and they are the marginal investors.

EQUITY RISK AND EXPECTED RETURN

To demonstrate how risk is viewed in finance, risk analysis is presented here in three steps: first, defining risk in terms of the distribution of actual returns around an expected return; second, differentiating between risk that is specific to one or a few investments and risk that affects a much wider cross section of investments (in a market where the marginal investor is well diversified, it is only the latter risk, called market risk, that will be rewarded); and third, alternative models for measuring this market risk and the expected returns that go with it.

Defining Risk

Investors who buy an asset expect to earn returns over the time horizon that they hold the asset. Their actual returns over this holding period may be very different from the expected returns, and it is this difference between actual and expected returns that is a source of risk. For example, assume that you are an investor with a one-year time horizon buying a one-year Treasury bill (or any other default-free one-year bond) with a 5 percent expected return. At the end of the one-year holding period, the actual return on this investment will be 5 percent, which is equal to the expected return. The return distribution for this investment is shown in Figure 4.1. This is a riskless investment.

To provide a contrast to the riskless investment, consider an investor who buys stock in a firm, say Boeing. This investor, having done her research, may conclude that she can make an expected return of 30 percent on Boeing over her one-year holding period. The actual return over this period will almost certainly not be equal to 30 percent; it might be much greater or much lower. The distribution of returns on this investment is illustrated in Figure 4.2.

In addition to the expected return, an investor now has to consider the following. First, note that the actual returns, in this case, are different from the expected return. The spread of the actual returns around the expected return is measured by the variance or standard deviation of the distribution; the greater the deviation of the actual returns from the expected return, the greater the variance. Second, the bias toward positive or negative returns is

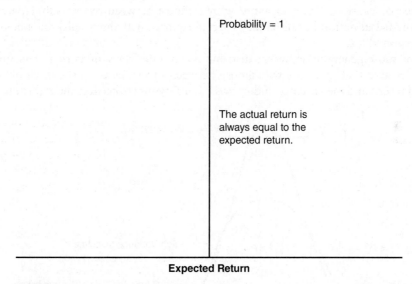

FIGURE 4.1   Probability Distribution of Returns on a Risk-Free Investment

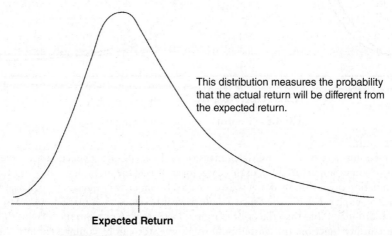

FIGURE 4.2   Return Distribution for Risky Investment

represented by the skewness of the distribution. The distribution in Figure 4.2 is positively skewed, since there is a higher probability of large positive returns than large negative returns. Third, the shape of the tails of the distribution is measured by the kurtosis of the distribution; fatter tails lead to higher kurtosis. In investment terms, this represents the tendency of the price of this investment to jump (up or down from current levels) in either direction.

In the special case where the distribution of returns is normal, investors do not have to worry about skewness and kurtosis, since there is no skewness (normal distributions are symmetric) and a normal distribution is defined to have a kurtosis of zero. Figure 4.3 illustrates the return distributions on two investments with symmetric returns.

When return distributions are normal, the characteristics of any investment can be measured with two variables—the expected return, which represents the opportunity in the investment, and the standard deviation or variance, which represents the danger. In this scenario, a rational investor, faced with a choice between two investments with the same standard deviation but different expected returns, will always pick the one with the higher expected return.

In the more general case, where distributions are neither symmetric nor normal, it is still conceivable that investors will choose between investments on the basis of only the expected return and the variance, if they possess utility functions that allow them to do so.[1]

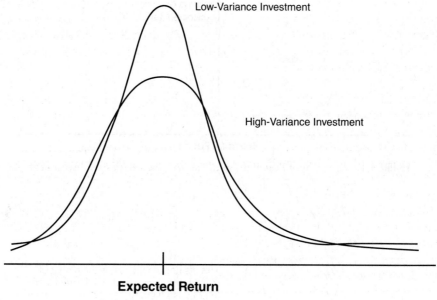

Expected Return

FIGURE 4.3   Return Distribution Comparisons

---

[1]A utility function is a way of summarizing investor preferences into a generic term called "utility" on the basis of some choice variables. In this case, for instance, the investors' utility or satisfaction is stated as a function of wealth. By doing so, we effectively can answer questions such as, "Will investors be twice as happy if they have twice as much wealth? Does each marginal increase in wealth lead to less additional utility than the prior marginal increase?" In one specific form of this function, the quadratic utility function, the entire utility of an investor can be compressed into the expected wealth measure and the standard deviation in that wealth.

It is far more likely, however, that they prefer positive skewed distributions to negatively skewed ones, and distributions with a lower likelihood of jumps (lower kurtosis) over those with a higher likelihood of jumps (higher kurtosis). In this world, investors will trade off the good (higher expected returns and more positive skewness) against the bad (higher variance and kurtosis) in making investments.

In closing, it should be noted that the expected returns and variances that we run into in practice are almost always estimated using past returns rather than future returns. The assumption made when using historical variances is that past return distributions are good indicators of future return distributions. When this assumption is violated, as is the case when the asset's characteristics have changed significantly over time, the historical estimates may not be good measures of risk.

 optvar.xls: This is a dataset on the web that summarizes standard deviations in stock prices in various sectors in the United States.

Diversifiable and Nondiversifiable Risk

Although there are many reasons why actual returns may differ from expected returns, we can group the reasons into two categories: firm-specific and market-wide. The risks that arise from firm-specific actions affect one or a few investments, while the risks arising from market-wide reasons affect many or all investments. This distinction is critical to the way we assess risk in finance.

Components of Risk   When an investor buys stock or takes an equity position in a firm, he or she is exposed to many risks. Some risk may affect only one or a few firms, and this risk is categorized as firm-specific risk. Within this category, we would consider a wide range of risks, starting with the risk that a firm may have misjudged the demand for a product from its customers; we call this project risk. For instance, consider Boeing's investment in a Super Jumbo jet. This investment is based on the assumption that airlines want a larger airplane and are willing to pay a high price for it. If Boeing has misjudged this demand, it will clearly have an impact on Boeing's earnings and value, but it should not have a significant effect on other firms in the market. The risk could also arise from competitors proving to be stronger or weaker than anticipated, called competitive risk. For instance, assume that Boeing and Airbus are competing for an order from Qantas, the Australian airline. The possibility that Airbus may win the bid is a potential source of risk to Boeing and perhaps some of its suppliers, but again, few other firms will be affected by it. Similarly, Disney recently launched new shows on its streaming platform, trying to draw in new subscribers. Whether it succeeds is clearly important to Disney and its competitors, but it is unlikely to have an impact on the rest of the market. In fact, risk measures can be extended to include risks that may affect an entire sector but are restricted to that sector; we call this sector risk. For instance, a cut in the defense budget in the United States will adversely affect all firms in the defense business, including Boeing, but there should be no significant impact on other sectors. What is common across the three risks described—project, competitive, and sector risk—is that they affect only a subset of firms.

There is another group of risks that is much more pervasive and affects many if not all investments. For instance, when interest rates increase, all investments are affected, albeit to different degrees. Similarly, when the economy weakens, all firms feel the effects, though cyclical firms (such as automobiles, steel, and housing) may feel it more. We term this risk market risk.

Finally, there are risks that fall in a gray area, depending on how many assets they affect. For instance, when the dollar strengthens against other currencies, it has a significant impact on the earnings and values of firms with international operations. If most firms in the market have significant international operations, and the exchange rate exposure is in the same direction, it could well be categorized as market risk. If only a few do, it would be closer to firm-specific risk. Figure 4.4 summarizes the spectrum of firm-specific and market risks.

Why Diversification Reduces or Eliminates Firm-Specific Risk: An Intuitive Explanation As an investor, you could invest all your portfolio in one asset. If you do so, you are exposed to both firm-specific and market risk. If, however, you expand your portfolio to include other assets or stocks, you are diversifying, and by doing so you can reduce your exposure to firm-specific risk. There are two reasons why diversification reduces or, at the limit, eliminates firm-specific risk. The first is that each investment in a diversified portfolio is a much smaller percentage of that portfolio than would be the case if you were not diversified. Any action that increases or decreases the value of only that investment or a small group of investments will have only a small impact on your overall portfolio, whereas undiversified investors are much more exposed to changes in the values of the investments in their portfolios. The second reason is that the effects of firm-specific actions on the prices of individual assets in a portfolio can be either positive or negative for each asset for any period. Thus, in very large portfolios this risk will average out to zero and will not affect the overall value of the portfolio.

In contrast, the effects of market-wide movements are likely to be in the same direction for most or all investments in a portfolio, though some assets may be affected more than others. For instance, other things being equal, an increase in interest rates will

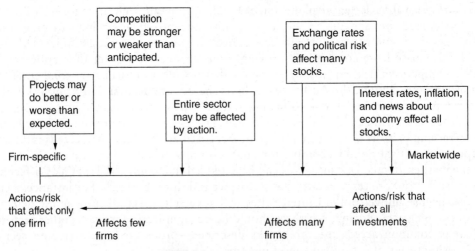

FIGURE 4.4 Breakdown of Risk

lower the values of most assets in a portfolio. Being more diversified does not eliminate this risk.

A Statistical Analysis of Diversification-Reducing Risk   The effects of diversification on risk can be illustrated dramatically by examining the effects of increasing the number of assets in on portfolio variance. The variance in a portfolio is partially determined by the variances of the individual assets in the portfolio and partially by how they move together; the latter is measured statistically with a correlation coefficient or the covariance across investments in the portfolio. It is the covariance term that provides an insight into why diversification will reduce risk and by how much.

Consider a portfolio of two assets. Asset A has an expected return of μ_A and a variance in returns of σ^2_A, while asset B has an expected return of μ_B and a variance in returns of σ^2_B. The correlation in returns between the two assets, which measures how the assets move together, is ρ_{AB}. The expected returns (μ) and variances (σ^2) of two-asset portfolio can be written as a function of these inputs and the proportion of the portfolio going to each asset.

$$\mu_{\text{Portfolio}} = w_A \mu_A + (1 - w_B)\mu_B$$
$$\sigma^2_{\text{Portfolio}} = w^2_A \sigma^2_A + (1 - w_A)^2 \sigma^2_B + 2w_A(1 - w_A)\rho_{AB}\sigma_A\sigma_B$$

where w_A = Proportion of the portfolio in asset A

The last term in the variance formulation is sometimes written in terms of the covariance in returns between the two assets, which is:

$$\sigma_{AB} = \rho_{AB}\sigma_A\sigma_B$$

The savings that accrue from diversification are a function of the correlation coefficient. Other things remaining equal, the higher the correlation in returns between the two assets, the smaller are the potential benefits from diversification. It is worth adding, though, that the benefits of correlation exist even for positively correlated assets and are non-existent only when the correlation is equal to one.

Mean-Variance Models Measuring Market Risk

While most risk and return models in use in finance agree on the first two steps of the risk analysis process (i.e., that risk comes from the distribution of actual returns around the expected return, and that risk should be measured from the perspective of a marginal investor who is well diversified), they part ways when it comes to measuring nondiversifiable or market risk. This section will discuss the different models that exist in finance for measuring market risk and why they differ. It begins with what still is the most widely used model for measuring market risk in finance—the capital asset pricing model (CAPM)—and then discusses the alternatives to this model that have developed over the past two decades. While the discussion will emphasize the differences, it will also look at what the models have in common.

Capital Asset Pricing Model   The risk and return model that has been in use the longest and is still the standard for most practitioners is the capital asset pricing model (CAPM). This section will examine the assumptions on which the model is based, and the measures of market risk that emerge from these assumptions.

WHY IS THE MARGINAL INVESTOR ASSUMED TO BE DIVERSIFIED?

The argument that diversification reduces an investor's exposure to risk is clear both intuitively and statistically, but risk and return models in finance go further. These models look at risk through the eyes of the investor most likely to be trading on the investment at any point in time—the marginal investor. They argue that this investor, who sets prices for investments, is well diversified; thus, the only risk that he or she cares about is the risk added to a diversified portfolio or market risk. This argument can be justified simply. The risk in an investment will always be perceived to be higher for an undiversified investor than for a diversified one, since the latter does not shoulder any firm-specific risk and the former does. If both investors have the same expectations about future earnings and cash flows on an asset, the diversified investor will be willing to pay a higher price for that asset because of his or her perception of lower risk. Consequently, the asset, over time, will end up being held by diversified investors.

This argument is powerful, especially in markets where assets can be traded easily and at low cost. Thus, it works well for a stock traded in developed markets, since investors can become diversified at fairly low cost. In addition, a significant proportion of the trading in developed market stocks is done by institutional investors, who tend to be well diversified. It becomes a more difficult argument to sustain when assets cannot be easily traded, or the costs of trading are high. In these markets, the marginal investor may well be undiversified, and firm-specific risk may therefore continue to matter when looking at individual investments. For instance, real estate in most countries is still held by investors who are undiversified and have the bulk of their wealth tied up in these investments.

Assumptions   While diversification reduces the exposure of investors to firm-specific risk, most investors limit their diversification to holding only a few assets. Even large mutual funds rarely hold more than a few hundred stocks, and many of them hold as few as 10–20. There are two reasons why investors stop diversifying. One is that an investor or mutual fund manager can obtain most of the benefits of diversification from a relatively small portfolio, because the marginal benefits of diversification become smaller as the portfolio gets more diversified. Consequently, these benefits may not cover the marginal costs of diversification, which include transactions and monitoring costs. Another reason for limiting diversification is that many investors (and funds) believe they can find undervalued assets, and thus, choose not to hold those assets that they believe to be fairly valued or overvalued.

The capital asset pricing model assumes that there are no transaction costs, all assets are traded, and investments are infinitely divisible (i.e., you can buy any fraction of a unit of the asset). It also assumes that everyone has access to the same information and that investors, therefore cannot find under- or overvalued assets in the marketplace. By making these assumptions, it allows investors to keep diversifying without additional cost. At the limit, their portfolios will not only include every traded asset in the market, but these assets will be held in proportion to their market value (MV).

The fact that this portfolio includes all traded assets in the market is the reason it is called the market portfolio, which should not be a surprising result, given the benefits of diversification and the absence of transaction costs in the capital asset pricing model. If diversification reduces exposure to firm-specific risk and there are no costs associated with adding more assets to the portfolio, the logical limit to diversification is to hold a small proportion of every traded asset in the economy. If this seems abstract, consider the market portfolio to be an extremely well-diversified mutual fund that holds stocks and real assets. In the CAPM, all investors will hold combinations of the riskier asset and that supremely diversified mutual fund.[2]

Investor Portfolios in the CAPM   If every investor in the market holds the identical market portfolio, how exactly do investors reflect their risk aversion in their investments? In the capital asset pricing model, investors adjust for their risk preferences in their allocation decision, where they decide how much to invest in a riskless asset and how much in the market portfolio. Investors who are risk averse might choose to put much or even all of their wealth in the riskless asset. Investors who want to take more risk will invest the bulk or even all of their wealth in the market portfolio. Investors who invest all their wealth in the market portfolio, and are desirous of taking on still more risk, would do so by borrowing at the riskless rate and investing in the same market portfolio as everyone else.

These results are predicated on two additional assumptions. First, there exists a riskless asset, where the expected returns are known with certainty. Second, investors can lend and borrow at the riskless rate to arrive at their optimal allocations. While lending at the riskless rate can be accomplished fairly simply by buying Treasury bills or bonds, borrowing at the riskless rate might be more difficult for individuals to do. There are variations of the CAPM that allow these assumptions to be relaxed and still arrive at conclusions that are consistent with the model.

Measuring the Market Risk of an Individual Asset   The risk of any asset to an investor is the risk added by that asset to the investor's overall portfolio. In the CAPM world where all investors hold the market portfolio, the risk to an investor of an individual asset will be the risk that this asset adds to the market portfolio. Intuitively, if an asset moves independently of the market portfolio, it will not add much risk to the market portfolio. In other words, most of the risk in this asset is firm-specific and can be diversified away. In contrast, if an asset tends to move up when the market portfolio moves up and down when it moves down, it will add risk to the market portfolio. This asset has more market risk and less firm-specific risk. Statistically, this added risk is measured by the covariance of the asset with the market portfolio.

Measuring the Non-diversifiable Risk   In a world in which investors hold a combination of only two assets—the riskless asset and the market portfolio—the risk of any individual asset will be measured relative to the market portfolio. In particular, the risk of any asset will be the risk it adds to the market portfolio. To arrive at the appropriate measure of this added risk, assume that σ^2_m is the variance of the market portfolio prior to the addition of the new asset and that the variance of the individual asset being added to this portfolio is σ^2_i. The market value portfolio weight on this asset is w_i, and the covariance in returns between the individual asset and the market portfolio is σ_{im}.

---

[2]The significance of introducing the riskless asset into the choice mix and the implications for portfolio choice were first noted in Sharpe (1964) and Lintner (1965). Hence, the model is sometimes called the Sharpe-Lintner model.

The variance of the market portfolio prior to and after the addition of the individual asset can then be written as:

$$\text{Variance prior to asset i added} = \sigma_m^2$$
$$\text{Variance after asset i added} = \sigma_{iii}^2 = w_i^2\sigma_i^2 + (1 - w_i)^2\sigma_m^2 + 2\ w_i\ (1 - w_i)\sigma_{im}$$

The market value weight on any individual asset in the market portfolio should be small, since the market portfolio includes all traded assets in the economy. Consequently, the first term in the equation should approach zero, and the second term should approach σ_m^2, leaving the third term (σ_{im} the covariance) as the measure of the risk added by asset i.

Standardizing Covariances   The covariance is a percentage value, and it is difficult to pass judgment on the relative risk of an investment by looking at this value. In other words, knowing that the covariance of Boeing with the market portfolio is 55 percent does not provide us a clue as to whether Boeing is riskier or safer than the average asset. We therefore standardize the risk measure by dividing the covariance of each asset with the market portfolio by the variance of the market portfolio. This yields a risk measure called the beta of the asset:

$$\text{Beta of asset i} = \frac{\sigma_{im}}{\sigma_m^2}$$

Since the covariance of the market portfolio with itself is its variance, the beta of the market portfolio (and, by extension, the average asset in it) is 1. Assets that are riskier than average (using this measure of risk) will have betas that exceed 1, and assets that are safer than average will have betas that are lower than 1. The riskless asset will have a beta of zero.

Getting Expected Returns   The fact that every investor holds some combination of the riskless asset and the market portfolio leads to the next conclusion, which is that the expected return on an asset is linearly related to the beta of the asset. In particular, the expected return on an asset can be written as a function of the risk-free rate and the beta of that asset:

$$E(R_i) = R_f + \beta_i[E(R_m) - R_f]$$

where $E(R_i)$ = Expected return on asset i

$\quad\quad R_f$ = Risk-free rate

$\quad E(R_m)$ = Expected return on market portfolio

$\quad\quad \beta_i$ = Beta of asset i

To use the capital asset pricing model, we need three inputs. While the next chapter looks at the estimation process in far more detail, each of these inputs is estimated as follows:

- The riskless asset (R_f) is defined to be an asset for which the investor knows the expected return with certainty for the time horizon of the analysis.
- The equity risk premium ($E(R_m) - R_f$) is the premium demanded by investors for investing in the market portfolio, which includes all risky assets in the market, instead of investing in a riskless asset.
- The beta (β_i) defined as the covariance of the asset divided by the market portfolio, measures the risk added by an investment to the market portfolio.

In summary, in the capital asset pricing model all the market risk is captured in one beta measured relative to a market portfolio, which at least in theory should include all traded assets in the marketplace held in proportion to their market value.

Arbitrage Pricing Model   The restrictive assumptions on transaction costs and private information in the capital asset pricing model, and the model's dependence on the market portfolio, have long been viewed with skepticism by both academics and practitioners. Ross (1976) suggested an alternative model for measuring risk called the arbitrage pricing model (APM).

Assumptions   If investors can invest risklessly, and earn more than the riskless rate, they have found an arbitrage opportunity. The premise of the arbitrage pricing model is that investors take advantage of such arbitrage opportunities, and in the process eliminate them. If two portfolios have the same exposure to risk but offer different expected returns, investors will buy the portfolio that has the higher expected returns and sell the portfolio with the lower expected returns, and earn the difference as a riskless profit. To prevent this arbitrage from occurring, the two portfolios have to earn the same expected return.

Like the capital asset pricing model, the arbitrage pricing model begins by breaking risk down into firm-specific and market risk components. As in the capital asset pricing model, firm-specific risk covers information that affects primarily one or a few firms. Market risk affects many or all firms and would include unanticipated changes in a number of economic variables, including gross national product (GNP), inflation, and interest rates. Incorporating both types of risk into a return model, we get:

$$R = E(R) + m + \varepsilon$$

where R is the actual return, E(R) is the expected return, m is the market-wide component of unanticipated risk, and ε is the firm-specific component. Thus, the actual return can be different from the expected return, because of either market risk or firm-specific actions.

Sources of Market-wide Risk   While both the capital asset pricing model and the arbitrage pricing model make a distinction between firm-specific and market-wide risk, they measure market risk differently. The CAPM assumes that market risk is captured in the market portfolio, whereas the arbitrage pricing model allows for multiple sources of market-wide risk and measures the sensitivity of investments to changes in each source. In general, the market component of unanticipated returns can be decomposed into economic factors:

$$R = E(R) + m + \varepsilon$$
$$= R + \left(\beta_1 F_1 + \beta_2 F_2 + \cdots + \beta_n F_n\right) + \varepsilon$$

where β_j = Sensitivity of investment to unanticipated changes in market risk factor j

F_j = Unanticipated changes in market risk factor j

Note that the measure of an investment's sensitivity to any macroeconomic (or market) factor takes the form of a beta, called a factor beta. In fact, this beta has many of the same properties as the market beta in the CAPM.

Effects of Diversification   The benefits of diversification were discussed earlier in the context of the breakdown of risk into market and firm-specific risk. The primary point of that discussion was that diversification eliminates firm-specific risk. The arbitrage pricing model uses the same argument and concludes that the return on a portfolio will not have a firm-specific component of unanticipated returns. The return on a portfolio (Rp) can be written as the sum of two weighted averages—that of the anticipated returns in the portfolio and that of the market factors:

$$R_p = \left(w_1 R_1 + w_2 R_2 + \cdots + w_n R_n\right) + \left(w_1 \beta_{11} + w_2 R\beta_{12} + \cdots + w_n \beta_{1n}\right)F_1$$
$$+ \left(w_1 \beta_{21} + w_2 R\beta_{22} + \cdots + w_n \beta_{2n}\right)F_2 \cdots$$

where w_j = Portfolio weight on asset j (where there are n assets)

   R_j = Expected return on asset j

   β_{ij} = Beta on factor i for asset j

Expected Returns and Betas   The final step in this process is estimating an expected return as a function of the betas just specified. To do this, we should first note that the beta of a portfolio is the weighted average of the betas of the assets in the portfolio. This property, in conjunction with the absence of arbitrage, leads to the conclusion that expected returns should be linearly related to betas. To see why, assume that there is only one factor and three portfolios. Portfolio A has a beta of 2.0 and an expected return of 20 percent; portfolio B has a beta of 1.0 and an expected return of 12 percent; and portfolio C has a beta of 1.5 and an expected return of 14 percent. Note that investors can put half of their wealth in portfolio A and half in portfolio B, and end up with portfolios with a beta of 1.5 and an expected return of 16 percent. Consequently, no investor will choose to hold portfolio C until the prices of assets in that portfolio drop and the expected return increases to 16 percent. By the same rationale, the expected returns of every portfolio should be a linear function of the beta. If they were not, we could combine two other portfolios, one with a higher beta and one with a lower beta, to earn a higher return than the portfolio in question, creating an opportunity for arbitrage. This argument can be extended to multiple factors with the same results. Therefore, the expected return on an asset can be written as:

$$E(R) = R_f + \beta_1\left[E(R_1) - R_f\right] + \beta_2\left[E(R_2) - R_f\right]\ldots+\beta_n\left[E(R_n) - R_f\right]$$

where R_f = Expected return on a zero-beta portfolio

   β_j = Sensitivity of investment to unanticipated changes in market

     risk factor j

   $E(R_j)$ = Expected return on a portfolio with a factor beta of 1 for

     factor j, and zero for all other factors (where j = 1, 2, ..., K factors)

The terms in the brackets can be considered to be risk premiums for each of the factors in the model.

The capital asset pricing model can be considered to be a special case of the arbitrage pricing model, where there is only one economic factor driving market-wide returns, and the market portfolio is the stand-in for the factor.

$$E(R_i) = R_f + \beta_i \left[E(R_m) - R_f \right]$$

The APM in Practice   The arbitrage pricing model requires estimates of each of the factor betas and factor risk premiums in addition to the riskless rate. In practice, these are usually estimated using historical data on asset returns and a factor analysis. Intuitively, in a factor analysis, we examine the historical data looking for common patterns that affect broad groups of assets (rather than just one sector or a few assets). A factor analysis provides two output measures:

1. It specifies the number of common factors that affected the historical return data.
2. It measures the beta of each investment relative to each of the common factors and provides an estimate of the actual risk premium earned by each factor.

The factor analysis does not, however, identify the factors in economic terms. In summary, in the arbitrage pricing model the market risk is measured relative to multiple unspecified macroeconomic variables, with the sensitivity of the investment relative to each factor being measured by a beta. The number of factors, the factor betas, and the factor risk premiums can all be estimated using the factor analysis.

Multifactor Models for Risk and Return   The arbitrage pricing model's failure to identify the factors specifically in the model may be a statistical strength, but it is an intuitive weakness. The solution seems simple: Replace the unidentified statistical factors with specific economic factors, and the resultant model should have an economic basis while still retaining much of the strength of the arbitrage pricing model. That is precisely what multifactor models try to do.

Deriving a Multifactor Model   Multifactor models generally are determined by historical data rather than by economic modeling. Once the number of factors has been identified in the arbitrage pricing model, their behavior over time can be extracted from the data. The behavior of the unnamed factors over time can then be compared to the behavior of macroeconomic variables over that same period, to see whether any of the variables is correlated, over time, with the identified factors.

For instance, Chen, Roll, and Ross (1986) suggest that the following macroeconomic variables are highly correlated with the factors that come out of factor analysis: industrial production, changes in default premium, shifts in the term structure, unanticipated inflation, and changes in the real rate of return. These variables can then be correlated with returns to come up with a model of expected returns, with firm-specific betas calculated relative to each variable.

$$E(R) = R_f + \beta_{GNP}\left[E(R_{GNP}) - R_f\right] + B_{Inf}\left[E(R_{Inf}) - R_f\right] + \cdots + \beta_\delta\left[E(R_\delta) - R_f\right]$$

where β_{GNP} = Beta relative to changes in industrial production

$E(R_{GNP})$ = Expected return on a portfolio with a beta of one on the industrial production factor and zero on all other factors

B_{Inf} = Beta relative to changes in inflation

$E(R_{Inf})$ = Expected return on a portfolio with a beta of one on the inflation factor and zero on all other factors

The costs of going from the arbitrage pricing model to a macroeconomic multifactor model can be traced directly to the errors that can be made in identifying the factors. The economic factors in the model can change over time, as will the risk premium associated with each one. For instance, oil price changes were a significant economic factor driving expected returns in the 1970s but are not as significant in other time periods. Using the wrong factor or missing a significant factor in a multifactor model can lead to inferior estimates of expected return.

ALTERNATIVE MODELS FOR EQUITY RISK

The CAPM, arbitrage pricing model, and multifactor model represent attempts by financial economists to build risk and return models from the mean-variance base established by Harry Markowitz (1991). There are many, though, who believe the basis for the model is flawed and that we should be looking at alternatives, and in this section, we will look at some of them.

Different Return Distributions

From its very beginnings, the mean-variance framework has been controversial. While there have been many who have challenged its applicability, we will consider these challenges in three groups. The first group argues that stock prices, in particular, and investment returns, in general, exhibit too many large values to be drawn from a normal distribution. They argue that the fat tails on stock price distributions lend themselves better to a class of distributions called power law distributions, which exhibit infinite variance and long periods of price dependence. The second group takes issue with the symmetry of the normal distribution and argues for measures that incorporate the asymmetry observed in actual return distributions into risk measures. The third group posits that distributions that allow for price jumps are more realistic, and that risk measures should consider the likelihood and magnitude of price jumps.

Fat Tails and Power Law Distributions   Benoit Mandelbrot, a mathematician who also did pioneering work on the behavior of stock prices, was one of those who took issue with the use of normal and lognormal distributions. He argued, based on his observation of stock and real asset prices, that a power law distribution characterized them better. In a powerlaw distribution, the relationship between two variables, Y and X, can be written as follows:

$$Y = \alpha^X$$

In this equation, α is a constant (constant of proportionality), and k is the power law exponent. Mandelbrot's key point was that the normal and lognormal distributions were best suited for series that exhibited mild and well-behaved randomness, whereas power law distributions were more suited for series that exhibited large movements and what he termed *wild randomness*. Wild randomness occurs when a single observation can affect the population in a disproportionate way; stock and commodity prices exhibit wild randomness. Stock and commodity prices, with their long periods of relatively small movements, punctuated by wild swings in both directions, seem to fit better into the wild randomness group.

What are the consequences for risk measures? If asset prices follow power law distributions, the standard deviation or volatility ceases to be a good risk measure and a good basis for computing probabilities. Assume, for instance, that the standard deviation in annual stock returns is 15 percent and that the average return is 10 percent. Using the normal distribution as the base for probability predictions, this will imply that the stock returns will exceed 40 percent (average plus two standard deviations) only once every 44 years, and 55 percent only (average plus three standard deviations) only once every 740 years. In fact, stock returns will be greater than 85 percent (average plus five standard deviations) only once every 3.5 million years. In reality, stock returns exceed these values far more frequently, a finding consistent with power law distributions, where the probability of larger values declines linearly as a function of the power law exponent. As the value gets doubled, the probability of its occurrence drops by the square of the exponent. Thus, if the exponent in the distribution is 2, the likelihood of returns of 25 percent, 50 percent, and 100 percent can be computed as follows:

Returns will exceed 25 percent: once every 6 years.

Returns will exceed 50 percent: once every 24 years.

Returns will exceed 100 percent: once every 96 years.

Note that as the returns get doubled, the likelihood increases four-fold (the square of the exponent). As the exponent decreases, the likelihood of larger values increases; an exponent between 0 and 2 will yield extreme values more often than a normal distribution. An exponent between 1 and 2 yields power law distributions called stable Paretian distributions, which have infinite variance. In an early study, Fama (1965) estimated the exponent for stocks to be between 1.7 and 1.9, but subsequent studies have found that the exponent is higher in both equity and currency markets.[3]

In practical terms, the power law proponents argue that using measures such as volatility (and its derivatives such as beta) underestimate the risk of large movements. The power law exponents for assets, in their view, provide investors with more realistic risk measures for these assets. Assets with higher exponents are less risky (since extreme values become less common) than assets with lower exponents.

Mandelbrot's challenge to the normal distribution was more than a procedural one. Mandelbrot's world, in contrast to the Gaussian mean-variance one, is a world where prices move jaggedly over time and look as though they have no pattern at a distance, but where

---

[3]In a paper in *Nature* (Gabaix, X., Gopikrishnan, P., Plerou, V., and Stanley, H.E., 2003, *A theory of power law distributions in financial market fluctuations*, Nature 423, 267–70), researchers looked at stock prices on 500 stocks between 1929 and 1987 and concluded that the exponent for stock returns is roughly three.

patterns repeat themselves, when observed closely. In the 1970s, Mandelbrot created a branch of mathematics called *fractal geometry* where processes are not described by conventional statistical or mathematical measures but by fractals; a fractal is a geometric shape that when broken down into smaller parts replicates that shape. To illustrate the concept, he uses the example of the coastline that, from a distance, looks irregular and up close looks roughly the same—fractal patterns repeat themselves. In fractal geometry, higher fractal dimensions translate into more jagged shapes; the rugged Cornish coastline has a fractal dimension of 1.25, whereas the much smoother South African coastline has a fractal dimension of 1.02. Using the same reasoning, stock prices that look random, when observed at longer time intervals, start revealing self-repeating patterns, when observed over shorter time periods. More volatile stocks score higher on measures of fractal dimension, thus making it a measure of risk. With fractal geometry, Mandelbrot was able to explain not only the higher frequency of price jumps (relative to the normal distribution) but also long periods where prices move in the same direction and the resulting price bubbles.

Asymmetric Distributions Intuitively, it should be downside risk that concerns us and not upside risk. In other words, it is not investments that go up significantly that create heartburn and unease, but investments that go down significantly. The mean-variance framework, by weighting both upside volatility and downside movements equally, does not distinguish between the two. With a normal or any other symmetric distribution, the distinction between upside and downside risk is irrelevant because the risks are equivalent. With asymmetric distributions, though, there can be a difference between upside and downside risk. Studies of risk aversion in humans conclude that (1) they are loss averse, that is, they weigh the pain of a loss more than the joy of an equivalent gain; and (2) they value very large positive payoffs—long shots—far more than they should be, given the likelihood of these payoffs.

In practice, return distributions for stocks and most other assets are not symmetric. Instead, asset returns exhibit fat tails (i.e, more jumps) and are more likely to have extreme positive values than extreme negative values (simply because returns are constrained to be no less than −100 percent). As a consequence, the distribution of stock returns has a higher incidence of extreme returns (fat tails or kurtosis) and a tilt toward very large positive returns (positive skewness). Critics of the mean-variance approach argue that it takes too narrow a view of both rewards and risk. In their view, a fuller return measure should consider not just the magnitude of expected returns but also the likelihood of very large positive returns or skewness, and a more complete risk measure should incorporate both variance and the possibility of big jumps (co-kurtosis). Note that even as these approaches deviate from the mean-variance approach in terms of how they define risk, they stay true to the portfolio measure of risk. In other words, it is not the possibility of large positive payoffs (skewness) or big jumps (kurtosis) that they argue should be considered, but only that portion of the skewness (co-skewness) and kurtosis (co-kurtosis) that is market-related and not diversifiable.

Jump Process Models The normal, power law, and asymmetric distributions that form the basis for the models we have discussed in this section are all continuous distributions. Observing the reality that stock prices do jump, there are some who have argued for the use of jump process distributions to derive risk measures.

Press (1967), in one of the earliest papers that attempted to model stock price jumps, argued that stock prices follow a combination of a continuous price distribution and a Poisson distribution, where prices jump at irregular intervals. The key parameters of the

Poisson distribution are the expected size of the price jump (μ), the variance in this value (δ^2), and the likelihood of a price jump in any specified time period (λ), and Press estimated these values for 10 stocks. In subsequent papers, Beckers (1981) and Ball and Torous (1983) suggest ways of refining these estimates. In an attempt to bridge the gap between the CAPM and jump process models, Jarrow and Rosenfeld (1984) derive a version of the capital asset pricing model that includes a jump component that captures the likelihood of market jumps and an individual asset's correlation with these jumps.

While jump process models have gained some traction in option pricing, they have had limited success in equity markets, largely because the parameters of jump process models are difficult to estimate with any degree of precision. Thus, while everyone agrees that stock prices jump, there is little consensus on the best way to measure how often this happens, whether these jumps are diversifiable, and how best to incorporate their effect into risk measures.

Regression or Proxy Models   The conventional models for risk and return in finance (CAPM, arbitrage pricing model, and even multifactor models) start by making assumptions about how investors behave and how markets work to derive models that measure risk and link those measures to expected returns. While these models have the advantage of a foundation in economic theory, they seem to fall short in explaining differences in returns across investments. The reasons for the failure of these models run the gamut: The assumptions made about markets are unrealistic (no transactions costs, perfect information) and investors don't behave rationally (and behavioral finance research provides ample evidence of this).

With proxy models, we essentially give up on building risk and return models from economic theory. Instead, we start with how investments are priced by markets and relate returns earned to observable variables. Rather than talk in abstractions, consider the work done by Fama and French in the early 1990s. Examining returns earned by individual stocks from 1962 to 1990, they concluded that CAPM betas did not explain much of the variation in these returns. They then took a different tack and looked for company-specific variables that did a better job of explaining return differences they pinpointed two variables—the market capitalization of a firm and its price-to-book ratio (the ratio of market cap to accounting book value for equity). Specifically, they concluded that small market cap stocks earned much higher annual returns than large market cap stocks and that low price-to-book ratio stocks earned much higher annual returns than stocks that traded at high price-to-book ratios. Rather than view this as evidence of market inefficiency (which is what prior studies that had found the same phenomena had done), they argued if these stocks earned higher returns over long time periods, they must be riskier than stocks that earned lower returns. In effect, market capitalization and price-to-book ratios were better proxies for risk, according to their reasoning, than betas. In fact, they regressed returns on stocks against the market capitalization of a company and its price-to-book ratio to arrive at the following regression for U.S. stocks:

$$\text{Expected Monthly Return} = 1.77\% + 0.11 \ \ln(\text{Market Capitalization in \$millions})$$
$$+ 0.35 \ \ln\left(\text{Book Value of } \frac{\text{Equity}}{\text{Market}} \text{ Capitalization}\right)$$

In a pure proxy model, you could plug the market capitalization and book-to-market ratio for any company into this regression to get expected monthly returns.

In the two decades since the Fama-French paper brought proxy models to the fore, researchers have probed the data (which has become more detailed and voluminous over time) to find better and additional proxies for risk. Some of the proxies are highlighted here:

■ *Earnings momentum.* Equity research analysts will find vindication in research that seems to indicate that companies that have reported stronger than expected earnings growth in the past earn higher returns than the rest of the market.

■ *Price momentum.* Chartists will smile when they read this, but researchers have concluded that price momentum carries over into future periods. Thus, the expected returns will be higher for stocks that have outperformed markets in recent time periods and lower for stocks that have lagged.

■ *Liquidity.* In a nod to real-world costs, there seems to be clear evidence that stocks that are less liquid (lower trading volume, higher bid-ask spreads) earn higher returns than more liquid stocks.

While the use of pure proxy models by practitioners is rare, they have adapted the findings for these models into their day-to-day use. Many analysts have melded the CAPM with proxy models to create composite or melded models. For instance, many analysts who value small companies derive expected returns for these companies by adding a small cap premium to the CAPM expected return:

$$\text{Expected Return} = \text{Riskfree Rate} + \text{Beta} \times \text{Equity Risk Premium} + \text{Small Cap Premium}$$

The threshold for small capitalization varies across time but is generally set at the bottom decile of publicly traded companies, and the small cap premium itself is estimated by looking at the historical premium earned by small cap stocks over the market. Using the Fama-French findings, the CAPM has been expanded to include market capitalization and price-to-book ratios as additional variables, with the expected return stated as:

$$\text{Expected Return} = \text{Riskfree Rate} + \text{Beta} \times \text{Equity Risk Premium} + \text{Size Beta} \times \text{Small Cap Premium} + \text{Book-to-Market beta} \times \text{Book-to-market Premium}$$

The size and the book-to-market betas are estimated by regressing a stock's returns against the size premium and book-to-market premiums over time; this is analogous to the way we get the market beta, by regressing stock returns against overall market returns.

While the use of proxy and melded models offers a way of adjusting expected returns to reflect market reality, there are three dangers in using these models.

1. *Data mining.* As the amount of data that we have on companies increases and becomes more accessible, it is inevitable that we will find more variables that are related to returns. It is also likely that most of these variables are not proxies for risk, and that the correlation is a function of the time period that we look at. In effect, proxy models are statistical models and not economic models. Thus, there is no easy way to separate the variables that matter from those that do not.

2. *Standard error.* Since proxy models come from looking at historical data, they carry all of the burden of the noise in the data. Stock returns are extremely volatile over

time, and any historical premia that we compute (for market capitalization or any other variable) are going to have significant standard errors. The standard errors on the size and book-to-market betas in the three-factor Fama-French model may be so large that using them in practice creates almost as much noise as it adds in precision.

3. *Pricing error or risk proxy.* For decades, value investors have argued that you should invest in stocks with low PE ratios that trade at low multiples of book value and have high dividend yields, pointing to the fact that you will earn higher returns by doing so. (In fact, a scan of Benjamin Graham's screens from security analysis[4] for cheap companies unearths most of the proxies that you see in use today.) Proxy models incorporate all of these variables into the expected return, and thus render these assets to be fairly priced. Using the circular logic of these models, markets are always efficient because any inefficiency that exists is just another risk proxy that needs to get built into the model.

Non-price–Based Models All of the models that we have described in this chapter, at least so far, have a common feature. They use stock price movements as the basis for measuring risk, with the deviations being in how to break down that risk into components or factors. There are many who take issue with this approach to measuring risk, arguing that the approach is incompatible with intrinsic valuation, where we start with a presumption that markets make mistakes.

For those who are inherently suspicious of any market-price based measure, there is always accounting information that can be used to come up with a measure of risk. In particular, firms that have low debt ratios, high dividends, stable and growing accounting earnings, and large cash holdings should be less risky to equity investors than firms without these characteristics. While the intuition is impeccable, converting it into an expected return can be problematic, but here are some choices:

(a) *Pick one accounting ratio and create scaled risk measures around that ratio.* The median book debt-to-capital ratio, in book value terms, for U.S. companies at the start of 2024 was 25%. If the book debt for the firm you are analyzing is only 20%, that would yield a relative risk measure of 0.8 for the company. The perils of this approach lie in the accounting ratio used, since there are risky firms that may look safe on the basis of that ratio. Thus, technology firms, which tend to have low debt ratios, would look safe on a debt-to-capital metric. An alternative that may have wider reach is to compute the variability in accounting earnings at firms, and then scaling the standard deviation in earnings for a firm to the average standard deviation across the market.

(b) *Compute an accounting beta*: If you want to preserve the diversified investor perspective and measure the risk added to portfolios by firm, you can estimate an accounting beta, by relating changes in accounting earnings at a firm to accounting earnings for the entire market. Firms that have more stable earnings than the rest of the market or whose earnings movements have nothing to do with the rest of the market will have low accounting betas. An extended version of this approach would be to estimate the accounting beta as a function of multiple accounting variables including dividend payout ratios, debt ratios, cash balances and earnings stability for the entire market.

---

[4]Graham, B., 1949, *The Intelligent Investor* (New York: HarperBusiness, reprinted in 2005).

Plugging in the values for an individual company into this regression will yield an accounting beta for the firm. While this approach looks promising, here are some cautionary notes: accounting numbers are smoothed out and can hide risk and are estimated at most four times a year (as opposed to market numbers which get minute by minute updates).

In keeping with Milton Friedman's adage that it takes a model to beat one, it is easy to critique any risk and return model, but it is worth remembering that no matter which model you choose, it comes with limitations. Ultimately, disagreements about how to measure risk and bring it into expected return should not be used as an excuse for measuring risk at all, and using the same expected return (or cost of equity) for all firms or making up rates of return, based upon gut feeling and intuition.

A COMPARATIVE ANALYSIS OF EQUITY RISK MODELS

When faced with the choice of estimating expected returns on equity or cost of equity, we are therefore faced with several choices, ranging from the CAPM to proxy models. Table 4.1 summarizes the different models and presents their pluses and minuses.

The decision must be based as much on theoretical considerations as it will be on pragmatic considerations. The CAPM is the simplest of the models, insofar as it requires only one firm-specific input (the beta), and that input can be estimated readily from public information. To replace the CAPM with an alternative model, whether it be from the mean variance family (arbitrage pricing model or multifactor models), alternative return process families (power, asymmetric, and jump distribution models), or proxy models, we need evidence of substantial improvement in accuracy in future forecasts (and not just in explaining past returns).

TABLE 4.1 Alternative Models for Cost of Equity

Model	Expected Return	Pluses	Minuses
CAPM	$E(R) = Rf + \beta\left(E(R_m) - R_f\right)$	Simple to compute	Does not explain returns on broad segments of market
APM (n statistical factors)	$E(R) = R_f + \sum_{j=1}^{j=n} \beta_j\left(E(R_j) - R_f\right)$	Breaks down market risk into components	Factors are statistical, not economic
Multifactor Model (n macroeconomic factors)	$E(R) = R_f + \sum_{k=1}^{k=n} \beta_k\left(E(R_k) - R_f\right)$	Breaks down market risk into macro risk components	Macro factors change over time.
Proxy	$E(R) = a + bX_1 + cX_2$	Does best at explaining differences in past returns	No economic rationale, backward-looking and subject to data mining
Accounting	$E(R) = Rf + \text{Relative Risk Measure} * \text{Risk Premium}$	Closer to intrinsic value view of risk	Accounting metrics are measured infrequently, and smoothed out.

Ultimately, the survival of the capital asset pricing model as the default model for risk in real-world applications is a testament to both its intuitive appeal and the failure of more complex models to deliver significant improvement in terms of estimating expected returns. We would argue that a judicious use of the capital asset pricing model, without an over reliance on historical data, is still the most effective way of dealing with risk in valuation in most cases. In some sectors (commodities) and segments (closely held companies, illiquid stocks), using other, more complete models will be justified. We will return to the question of how improvements in estimating the inputs to the CAPM can generate far more payoff than switching to more complicated models for cost of equity.

MODELS OF DEFAULT RISK

The risk discussed so far in this chapter relates to cash flows on investments being different from expected cash flows. There are some investments, however, in which the cash flows are promised when the investment is made. This is the case, for instance, when you lend to a business or buy a corporate bond; the borrower may default on interest and principal payments on the borrowing. Generally speaking, borrowers with higher default risk should pay higher interest rates on their borrowing than those with lower default risk. This section examines the measurement of default risk and the relationship of default risk to interest rates on borrowing.

In contrast to the general risk and return models for equity, which evaluate the effects of market risk on expected returns, models of default risk measure the consequences of firm-specific default risk on promised returns. While diversification can be used to explain why firm-specific risk will not be priced into expected returns for equities, the same rationale cannot be applied to securities that have limited upside potential and much greater downside potential from firm-specific events. To see what is meant by limited upside potential, consider investing in the bond issued by a company. The coupons are fixed at the time of the issue, and these coupons represent the promised cash flow on the bond. The best-case scenario for you as an investor is that you receive the promised cash flows; you are not entitled to more than these cash flows even if the company is wildly successful. All other scenarios contain only bad news, though in varying degrees, with the delivered cash flows being less than the promised cash flows. Consequently, the expected return on a corporate bond is likely to reflect the firm-specific default risk of the firm issuing the bond.

Determinants of Default Risk

The default risk of a firm is a function of two variables. The first is the firm's capacity to generate cash flows from operations, and the second is its financial obligations—including interest and principal payments.[5] Firms that generate high cash flows relative to their financial obligations should have lower default risk than do firms that generate low cash flows relative to obligations. Thus, firms with significant existing investments that generate high cash flows will have lower default risk than will firms that do not have such investments.

---

[5] Financial obligation refers to any payment that the firm has legally obligated itself to make, such as interest and principal payments. It does not include discretionary cash flows, such as dividend payments or new capital expenditures, which can be deferred or delayed without legal consequences, though there may be economic consequences.

In addition to the magnitude of a firm's cash flows, the default risk is also affected by the volatility in these cash flows. The more stability there is in cash flows, the lower is the default risk in the firm. Firms that operate in predictable and stable businesses will have lower default risk than will otherwise similar firms that operate in cyclical or volatile businesses.

Most models of default risk use financial ratios to measure the cash flow coverage (i.e., the magnitude of cash flows relative to obligations) and control for industry effects in order to evaluate the variability in cash flows.

Bond Ratings and Interest Rates   The most widely used measure of a firm's default risk is its bond rating, which is generally assigned by an independent ratings agency. The two best known are Standard & Poor's (S&P) and Moody's. Thousands of companies are rated by these two agencies, and their views carry significant weight with financial markets.

The Ratings Process   The process of rating a bond starts when the issuing company requests a rating from a bond ratings agency. The ratings agency then collects information from both publicly available sources, such as financial statements, and the company itself and makes a decision on the rating. If the company disagrees with the rating, it is given the opportunity to present additional information. This process is presented schematically for one ratings agency, Standard & Poor's, in Figure 4.5.

The ratings assigned by these agencies are letter ratings. A rating of AAA from Standard & Poor's and Aaa from Moody's represents the highest rating, granted to firms that are viewed as having the lowest default risk. As the default risk increases, the ratings decline toward D for firms in default (Standard & Poor's). A rating at or above BBB by Standard & Poor's (or Baa by Moody's) is categorized as investment grade, reflecting the view of the ratings agency that there is relatively little default risk in investing in bonds issued by these firms.

Determinants of Bond Ratings   The bond ratings assigned by ratings agencies are primarily based on publicly available information, though private information conveyed by the firm to the ratings agency does play a role. The rating assigned to a company's bonds will depend in large part on financial ratios that measure the capacity of the company to meet debt payments and generate stable and predictable cash flows. While a multitude of financial ratios exist, Table 4.2 summarizes some of the key ratios used to measure default risk.

TABLE 4.2   Definition of Financial Ratios: S&P

Financial Ratio	Definition
EBITDA/Revenues	EBITDA/Revenues
ROIC	ROIC = EBIT/(BV of debt + BV of equity − Cash)
EBIT/Interest expenses	Interest coverage ratio
EBITDA/Interest	EBITDA/Interest expenses
FFO/debt	(Net Income + Depreciation)/Debt
Free operating CF/Debt	Funds from operations/Debt
Discounted CF/Debt	Discounted cash flows/Debt
Debt/EBITDA	BV of Debt/EBITDA
D/(D + E)	BV of Debt/(BV of Debt + BV of equity)

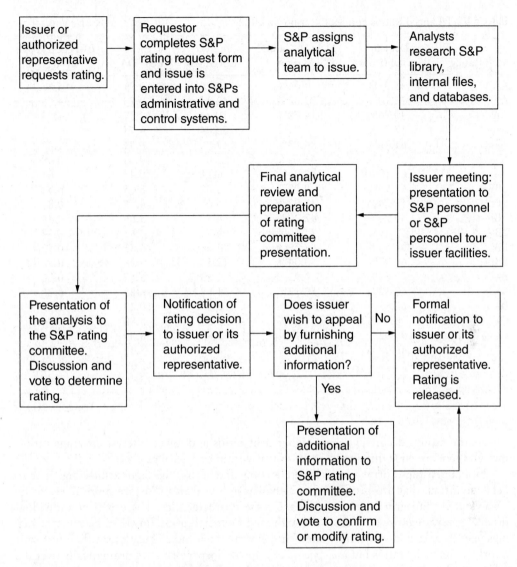

FIGURE 4.5   The Ratings Process

There is a strong relationship between the bond rating a company receives and its performance on these financial ratios. Table 4.3 provides a summary of the median values for some of these ratios[6] from 2022 for different S&P ratings classes for manufacturing firms.

---

[6]See the Standard & Poor's online site (www.standardandpoors.com/ratings/criteria/index.htm).

TABLE 4.3 Financial Ratios and S&P Ratings in 2022

S&P Rating	Debt to Capital (Book)	Debt to Capital (Market)	Interest Coverage	Debt to EBITDA	EBITDA/Fixed Charges
AAA	35.02%	4.04%	42.90	0.91	4.88
AA+	35.10%	3.62%	42.47	0.79	4.58
AA	40.76%	14.78%	10.44	2.07	1.73
AA−	57.75%	26.74%	32.04	4.75	1.05
A+	61.78%	34.83%	12.74	6.81	1.83
A	58.34%	46.74%	10.07	10.05	0.49
A−	68.10%	48.04%	6.14	10.43	0.61
BBB+	63.95%	48.00%	5.00	8.05	0.52
BBB	59.74%	36.07%	6.03	4.77	0.83
BBB−	59.74%	42.28%	4.59	5.86	0.48
BB+	59.89%	35.10%	4.54	3.61	0.74
BB	66.84%	48.29%	2.68	6.83	0.53
BB−	66.97%	43.04%	2.56	5.26	0.52
B+	70.63%	54.92%	1.83	5.57	0.40
B	68.12%	57.92%	1.68	6.85	0.23
B−	63.82%	57.73%	0.47	10.23	0.31
CCC+	70.77%	76.26%	0.61	8.88	0.34
CCC	99.02%	88.71%	0.85	8.09	0.76
CCC−	46.08%	49.02%	0.11	5.42	0.76
CC	52.07%	80.06%	−1.98	−12.09	−0.47
D	118.58%	94.19%	−0.98	15.49	0.66

As the ratings decline, you see higher debt ratios and lower interest coverage ratios, though there are wide differences across firms within each ratings class.

Not surprisingly, firms that generate income and cash flows significantly higher than debt payments, that are profitable, and that have low debt ratios are more likely to be highly rated than firms that do not have these characteristics. There will be individual firms whose ratings are not consistent with their financial ratios, however, because the ratings agency does add subjective judgments into the final mix. Thus, a firm that performs poorly on financial ratios but is expected to improve its performance dramatically over the next period may receive a higher rating than is justified by its current financials. For most firms, however, the financial ratios should provide a reasonable basis for estimating the bond rating.

Bond Ratings and Interest Rates   The interest rate on a corporate bond should be a function of its default risk, which is measured by its rating. If the rating is a good measure of the default risk, higher-rated bonds should be priced to yield lower interest rates than those of lower-rated bonds. In fact, the difference between the interest rate on a bond with default risk and a default-free government bond is the default spread. This default spread will vary by maturity of the bond and can also change from period to period, depending on economic conditions. Chapter 7 considers how best to estimate these default spreads and how they might vary over time.

CONCLUSION

Risk, as defined in finance, is measured based on deviations of actual returns on an investment from its expected returns. There are two types of risk. The first, called equity risk, arises in investments where there are no promised cash flows, but there are expected cash flows. The second, default risk, arises on investments with promised cash flows.

On investments with equity risk, the risk is best measured by looking at the variance of actual returns around the expected returns, with greater variance indicating greater risk. This risk can be broken down into risk that affects one or a few investments, called firm-specific risk, and risk that affects many investments, referred to as market risk. When investors diversify, they can reduce their exposure to firm-specific risk. If we assume that the investors who trade at the margin are well diversified, the risk we should be looking at with equity investments is the nondiversifiable or market risk. The different models of equity risk introduced in this chapter share this objective of measuring market risk, but they differ in the way they do it. In the capital asset pricing model, exposure to market risk is measured by a market beta, which estimates how much risk an individual investment will add to a portfolio that includes all traded assets. The arbitrage pricing model and the multifactor model allow for multiple sources of market risk and estimate betas for an investment relative to each source. Regression or proxy models for risk look for firm characteristics, such as size, that have been correlated with high returns in the past and use these to measure market risk. In all these models, the risk measures are used to estimate the expected return on an equity investment. This expected return can be considered the cost of equity for a company.

On investments with default risk, risk is measured by the likelihood that the promised cash flows might not be delivered. Investments with higher default risk should face higher interest rates, and the premium that we demand over a riskless rate is the default spread. For many U.S. companies, default risk is measured by rating agencies in the form of a bond rating; these ratings determine, in large part, the interest rates at which these firms can borrow. Even in the absence of ratings, interest rates will include a default spread that reflects the lenders' assessments of default risk. These default-risk-adjusted interest rates represent the cost of borrowing or debt for a business.

QUESTIONS AND SHORT PROBLEMS

In the problems following, use an equity risk premium of 5.5 percent if none is specified.

1. The following table lists the stock prices for Microsoft from 1989 to 1998. The company did not pay any dividends during the period.

Year	Price
1989	$1.20
1990	$2.09
1991	$4.64
1992	$5.34

(continued)

(*continued*)

Year	Price
1993	$5.05
1994	$7.64
1995	$10.97
1996	$20.66
1997	$32.31
1998	$69.34

  a. Estimate the average annual return you would have made on your investment.
  b. Estimate the standard deviation and variance in annual returns.
  c. If you were investing in Microsoft today, would you expect the historical standard deviations and variances to continue to hold? Why or why not?

2. Unicom is a regulated utility serving northern Illinois. The following table lists the stock prices and dividends on Unicom from 1989 to 1998.

Year	Price	Dividends
1989	$36.10	$3.00
1990	$33.60	$3.00
1991	$37.80	$3.00
1992	$30.90	$2.30
1993	$26.80	$1.60
1994	$24.80	$1.60
1995	$31.60	$1.60
1996	$28.50	$1.60
1997	$24.25	$1.60
1998	$35.60	$1.60

  a. Estimate the average annual return you would have made on your investment.
  b. Estimate the standard deviation and variance in annual returns.
  c. If you were investing in Unicom today, would you expect the historical standard deviations and variances to continue to hold? Why or why not?

3. The following table summarizes the annual returns you would have made on two companies—Scientific Atlanta, a satellite and data equipment manufacturer, and AT&T, the telecommunications giant—from 1989 to 1998.

Year	Scientific Atlanta	AT&T
1989	80.95%	58.26%
1990	−47.37%	−33.79%
1991	31.00%	29.88%
1992	132.44%	30.35%
1993	32.02%	2.94%
1994	25.37%	−4.29%
1995	−28.57%	28.86%
1996	0.00%	−6.36%
1997	11.67%	48.64%
1998	36.19%	23.55%

    a. Estimate the average annual return and standard deviation in annual returns in each company.

    b. Estimate the covariance and correlation in returns between the two companies.

    c. Estimate the variance of a portfolio composed, in equal parts, of the two investments.

4. You are in a world where there are only two assets, gold and stocks. You are interested in investing your money in one, the other, or both assets. Consequently, you collect the following data on the returns on the two assets over the past six years.

	Gold	Stock Market
Average return	8%	20%
Standard deviation	25%	22%
Correlation	0.4	

    a. If you were constrained to pick just one, which one would you choose?

    b. A friend argues that this is wrong. He says that you are ignoring the big payoffs that you can get on the other asset. How would you go about alleviating his concern?

    c. How would a portfolio composed of equal proportions in gold and stocks do in terms of mean and variance?

    d. You now learn that GPEC (a cartel of gold-producing countries) is going to vary the amount of gold it produces in relation to stock prices in the United States. (GPEC will produce less gold when stock markets are up and more when they are down.) What effect will this have on your portfolio? Explain.

5. You are interested in creating a portfolio of two stocks—Coca-Cola and Texas Utilities. Over the past decade, an investment in Coca-Cola stock would have earned an average annual return of 25%, with a standard deviation in returns of 36%. An investment in Texas Utilities stock would have earned an average annual return of 12%, with a standard deviation of 22%. The correlation in returns across the two stocks is 0.28.

    a. Assuming that the average return and standard deviation, estimated using past returns, will continue to hold in the future, estimate the future average returns and standard deviation of a portfolio composed 60% of Coca-Cola and 40% of Texas Utilities stock.

    b. Now assume that Coca-Cola's international diversification will reduce the correlation to 0.20, while increasing Coca-Cola's standard deviation in returns to 45%. Assuming all of the other numbers remain unchanged, estimate one standard deviation of the portfolio in (a).

6. Assume that you have half your money invested in Times Mirror, the media company, and the other half invested in Unilever, the consumer product company. The expected returns and standard deviations on the two investments are:

	Times Mirror	Unilever
Expected return	14%	18%
Standard deviation	25%	40%

Estimate the variance of the portfolio as a function of the correlation coefficient (start with −1 and increase the correlation to +1 in 0.2 increments).

7. You have been asked to analyze the standard deviation of a portfolio composed of the following three assets:

	Expected Return	Standard Deviation
Sony Corporation	11%	23%
Tesoro Petroleum	9%	27%
Storage Technology	16%	50%

You have also been provided with the correlations across these three investments:

	Sony Corporation	Tesoro Petroleum	Storage Technology
Sony Corporation	1	−0.15	0.2
Tesoro Petroleum	−0.15	1	−0.25
Storage Technology	0.2	−0.25	1

Estimate the variance of a portfolio, equally weighted across all three assets.

8. Assume that the average variance of return for an individual security is 50 and that the average covariance is 10. What is the expected variance of a portfolio of 5, 10, 20, 50, and 100 securities? How many securities need to be held before the risk of a portfolio is only 10% more than the minimum?

9. Assume you have all your wealth (a million dollars) invested in the Vanguard 500 index fund, and that you expect to earn an annual return of 12%, with a standard deviation in returns of 25%. Since you have become more risk averse, you decide to shift $200,000 from the Vanguard 500 index fund to Treasury bills. The T-bill rate is 5%. Estimate the expected return and standard deviation of your new portfolio.

10. Every investor in the capital asset pricing model owns a combination of the market portfolio and a riskless asset. Assume that the standard deviation of the market portfolio is 30% and that the expected return on the portfolio is 15%. What proportion of the following investors' wealth would you suggest investing in the market portfolio and what proportion in the riskless asset? (The riskless asset has an expected return of 5%.)
   a. An investor who desires a portfolio with no standard deviation.
   b. An investor who desires a portfolio with a standard deviation of 15%.
   c. An investor who desires a portfolio with a standard deviation of 30%.
   d. An investor who desires a portfolio with a standard deviation of 45%.
   e. An investor who desires a portfolio with an expected return of 12%.

11. The following table lists returns on the market portfolio and on Scientific Atlanta, each year from 1989 to 1998.

Year	Scientific Atlanta	Market Portfolio
1989	80.95%	31.49%
1990	−47.37%	−3.17%
1991	31.00%	30.57%
1992	132.44%	7.58%
1993	32.02%	10.36%
1994	25.37%	2.55%

Year	Scientific Atlanta	Market Portfolio
1995	-28.57%	37.57%
1996	0.00%	22.68%
1997	11.67%	33.10%
1998	36.19%	28.32%

a. Estimate the covariance in returns between Scientific Atlanta and the market portfolio.
b. Estimate the variances in returns on both investments.
c. Estimate the beta for Scientific Atlanta.

12. United Airlines has a beta of 1.5. The standard deviation in the market portfolio is 22%, and United Airlines has a standard deviation of 66%.
   a. Estimate the correlation between United Airlines and the market portfolio.
   b. What proportion of United Airlines' risk is market risk?

13. You are using the arbitrage pricing model to estimate the expected return on Bethlehem Steel, and have derived the following estimates for the factor betas and risk premium:

Factor	Beta	Risk Premium
1	1.2	2.5%
2	0.6	1.5%
3	1.5	1.0%
4	2.2	0.8%
5	0.5	1.2%

a. Which risk factor is Bethlehem Steel most exposed to? Is there any way, within the arbitrage pricing model, to identify the risk factor?
b. If the risk-free rate is 5%, estimate the expected return on Bethlehem Steel.
c. Now assume that the beta in the capital asset pricing model for Bethlehem Steel is 1.1, and that the risk premium for the market portfolio is 5%. Estimate the expected return using the CAPM.
d. Why are the expected returns different using the two models?

14. You are using the multifactor model to estimate the expected return on Emerson Electric, and have derived the following estimates for the factor betas and risk premiums:

Macro-economic Factor	Measure	Beta	Risk Premia ($R_{factor} - R_f$)
Level of Interest rates	T.bond rate	0.5	1.8%
Term Structure	T.bond rate – T.bill rate	1.4	0.6%
Inflation rate	CPI	1.2	1.5%
Economic Growth	GNP Growth rate	1.8	4.2%

With a riskless rate of 6%, estimate the expected return on Emerson Electric.

15. The following equation is reproduced from the study by Fama and French of returns between 1963 and 1990.

$$Rt = 1.77 - 0.11 \ln(MV) + 0.35 \ln\left(\frac{BV}{MV}\right)$$

where MV is the market value of equity in hundreds of millions of dollars and BV is the book value of equity in hundreds of millions of dollars. The return is a monthly return.

a. Estimate the expected annual return on Lucent Technologies if the market value of its equity is $180 billion and the book value of its equity is $73.5 billion.

b. Lucent Technologies has a beta of 1.55. If the riskless rate is 6% and the risk premium for the market portfolio is 5.5%, estimate the expected return.

c. Why are the expected returns different under the two approaches?

CHAPTER 5

Option Pricing Theory and Models

In general, the value of any asset is the present value of the expected cash flows on that asset. This chapter considers an exception to that rule when it looks at assets with two specific characteristics. First, these assets, derive their value from the values of other assets, making them derivative assets. Second, the cash flows on the assets are contingent on the occurrence of specific events. These assets are called options, and the present value of the expected cash flows on these assets will understate their true value. This chapter describes the cash flow characteristics of options, considers the factors that determine their value, and examines how best to value them.

BASICS OF OPTION PRICING

An option provides the holder with the right to buy or sell a specified quantity of an underlying asset at a fixed price (called a strike price or an exercise price) at or before the expiration date of the option. Since it is a right and not an obligation, the holder can choose not to exercise the right and can allow the option to expire. There are two types of options—call options and put options.

Call and Put Options: Description and Payoff Diagrams

A call option gives the buyer of the option the right to buy the underlying asset at the strike price or the exercise price at any time prior to the expiration date of the option. The buyer pays a price for this right. If at expiration the value of the asset is less than the strike price, the option is not exercised and expires worthless. If, however, the value of the asset is greater than the strike price, the option is exercised—the buyer of the option buys the stock at the exercise price, and the difference between the asset value and the exercise price comprises the gross profit on the investment. The net profit on the investment is the difference between the gross profit and the price paid for the call initially.

A payoff diagram illustrates the cash payoff on an option at expiration. For a call, the net payoff is negative (and equal to the price paid for the call) if the value of the underlying asset is less than the strike price. If the price of the underlying asset exceeds the strike price, the gross payoff is the difference between the value of the underlying asset and the strike price, and the net payoff is the difference between the gross payoff and the price of the call. This is illustrated in Figure 5.1.

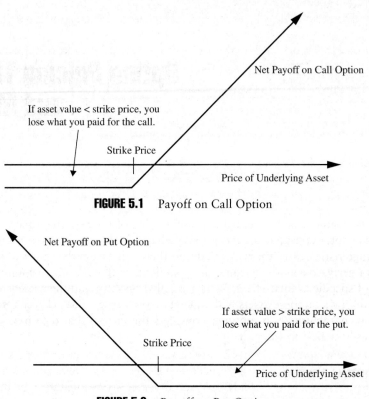

FIGURE 5.1   Payoff on Call Option

FIGURE 5.2   Payoff on Put Option

A put option gives the buyer of the option the right to sell the underlying asset at a fixed price, again called the strike or exercise price, at any time prior to the expiration date of the option. The buyer pays a price for this right. If the price of the underlying asset is greater than the strike price, the option will not be exercised and will expire worthless. But if the price of the underlying asset is less than the strike price, the owner of the put option will exercise the option and sell the stock at the strike price, claiming the difference between the strike price and the market value of the asset as the gross profit. Again, netting out the initial cost paid for the put yields the net profit from the transaction.

A put has a negative gross payoff, if the value of the underlying asset exceeds the strike price and has a gross payoff equal to the difference between the strike price and the value of the underlying asset, if the asset value is less than the strike price. This is summarized in Figure 5.2.

Determinants of Option Value   The value of an option is determined by six variables relating to the underlying asset and financial markets.

1. *Current value of the underlying asset.* Options are assets that derive value from an underlying asset. Consequently, changes in the value of the underlying asset affect the value of the options on that asset. Since calls provide the right to buy the underlying asset at a fixed price, an increase in the value of the asset will increase the value of the calls. Puts, on the other hand, become less valuable as the value of the asset increases.
2. *Variance in value of the underlying asset.* The buyer of an option acquires the right to buy or sell the underlying asset at a fixed price. The higher the variance in the value of

the underlying asset, the greater the value of the option.[1] This is true for both calls and puts. While it may seem counterintuitive that an increase in a risk measure (variance) should increase value, options are different from other securities since buyers of options can never lose more than the price they pay for them; in fact, they have the potential to earn significant returns from large price movements.

3. *Dividends paid on the underlying asset.* The value of the underlying asset can be expected to decrease if dividend payments are made on the asset during the life of the option. Consequently, the value of a call on the asset is a *decreasing* function of the size of expected dividend payments, and the value of a put is an *increasing* function of expected dividend payments. A more intuitive way of thinking about dividend payments, for call options, is as a cost of delaying exercise on in-the-money options. To see why, consider an option on a traded stock. Once a call option is in-the-money (i.e., the holder of the option will make a gross payoff by exercising the option), exercising the call option will provide the holder with the stock and entitle him or her to the dividends on the stock in subsequent periods. Delaying exercise the option will mean that these dividends are forgone.

4. *Strike price of the option.* A key characteristic used to describe an option is the strike price. In the case of calls, where the holder acquires the right to buy at a fixed price, the value of the call will decline as the strike price increases. In the case of puts, where the holder has the right to sell at a fixed price, the value will increase as the strike price increases.

5. *Time to expiration on the option.* Both calls and puts are more valuable the greater the time to expiration. This is because the longer time to expiration provides more time for the value of the underlying asset to move, increasing the value of both types of options. Additionally, in the case of a call, where the buyer has the right to pay a fixed price at expiration, the present value of this fixed price decreases as the life of the option increases, increasing the value of the call.

6. *Riskless interest rate corresponding to life of the option.* Since the buyer of an option pays the price of the option up front, an opportunity cost is involved. This cost will depend on the level of interest rates and the time to expiration of the option. The riskless interest rate also enters into the valuation of options when the present value of the exercise price is calculated, since the exercise price does not have to be paid (received) until expiration on calls (puts). Increases in the interest rate will increase the value of calls and reduce the value of puts.

Table 5.1 summarizes the variables and their predicted effects on call and put prices.

American versus European Options: Variables Relating to Early Exercise

A primary distinction between American and European options is that an American option can be exercised at any time prior to its expiration, while European options can be exercised only at expiration. The possibility of early exercise makes American options more valuable than otherwise similar European options; it also makes them more difficult to value. There is one compensating factor that enables the former to be valued using models

---

[1]Note, though, that higher variance can reduce the value of the underlying asset. As a call option becomes more in-the-money, the more it resembles the underlying asset. For very deep in-the-money call options, higher variance can reduce the value of the option.

TABLE 5.1   Summary of Variables Affecting Call and Put Prices

	Effect On	
Factor	Call Value	Put Value
Increase in underlying asset's value	Increases	Decreases
Increase in variance of underlying asset	Increases	Increases
Increase in strike price	Decreases	Increases
Increase in dividends paid	Decreases	Increases
Increase in time to expiration	Increases	Increases
Increase in interest rates	Increases	Decreases

designed for the latter. In most cases, the time premium associated with the remaining life of an option and transaction costs make early exercise suboptimal. In other words, the holders of in-the-money options generally get much more by selling the options to someone else than by exercising the options.

OPTION PRICING MODELS

Option pricing theory has made vast strides since 1972, when Fischer Black and Myron Scholes published their pathbreaking paper that provided a model for valuing dividend-protected European options. Black and Scholes used a "replicating portfolio"—a portfolio composed of the underlying asset and the risk-free asset that had the same cash flows as the option being valued—and the notion of arbitrage to come up with their final formulation. Although their derivation is mathematically complicated, there is a simpler binomial model for valuing options that draws on the same logic.

Binomial Model

The binomial option pricing model is based on a simple formulation for the asset price process in which the asset, in any time period, can move to one of two possible prices. The general formulation of a stock price process that follows the binomial path is shown in Figure 5.3. In this figure, S is the current stock price; the price moves up to Su with probability p and down to Sd with probability 1 − p in any time period.

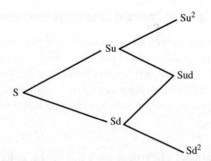

FIGURE 5.3   General Formulation for Binomial Price Path

Creating a Replicating Portfolio   The objective in creating a replicating portfolio is to use a combination of risk-free borrowing/lending and the underlying asset to create the same cash flows as the option being valued. The principles of arbitrage apply then, and the value of the option must be equal to the value of the replicating portfolio. In the case of the general formulation shown in Figure 5.3, where stock prices can move either up to Su or down to Sd in any time period, the replicating portfolio for a call with strike price K will involve borrowing $B and acquiring Δ of the underlying asset, where:

$$\Delta = \frac{C_u - C_d}{S_u - S_d}$$

where C_u = Value of the call if the stock price is S_u
  C_d = Value of the call if the stock price is S_d

In a multiperiod binomial process, the valuation has to proceed iteratively (i.e., starting with the final time period and moving backward in time until the current point in time). The portfolios replicating the option are created at each step and valued, providing the values for the option in that period. The final output from the binomial option pricing model is a statement of the value of the option in terms of the replicating portfolio, composed of Δ shares (option delta) of the underlying asset and risk-free borrowing/lending.

Value of call = Current Value of Underlying asset × Option Delta
× Borrowing needed to replicate the option

ILLUSTRATION 5.1: Binomial Option Valuation

Assume that the objective is to value a call with a strike price of $50, which is expected to expire in two time periods, on an underlying asset whose price currently is $50 and is expected to follow the binomial process laid out in Figure 5.4.

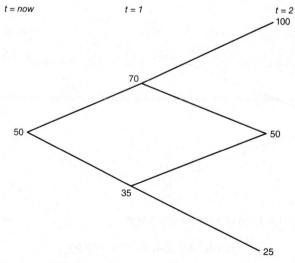

FIGURE 5.4   Binomial Tree for Option Pricing

Now assume that the interest rate is 11%. In addition, define:

$$\Delta = \text{Number of shares in the replicating portfolio}$$
$$B = \text{Dollar borrowing in replicating portfolio}$$

The objective is to combine Δ shares of stock and B dollars of borrowing to replicate the cash flows from the call with a strike price of $40. This can be done iteratively, starting with the last period and working back through the binomial tree.

Step 1: Start with the end nodes and work backward:

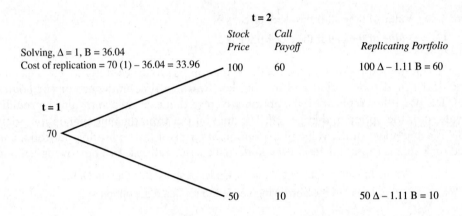

Thus, if the stock price is $70 at $t = 1$, borrowing $45 and buying one share of the stock will give the same cash flows as buying the call. The value of the call at $t = 1$, if the stock price is $70, is therefore:

$$\text{Value of call} = 70\,(1) - 36.04 = 33.96$$

Considering the other leg of the binomial tree at $t = 1$,

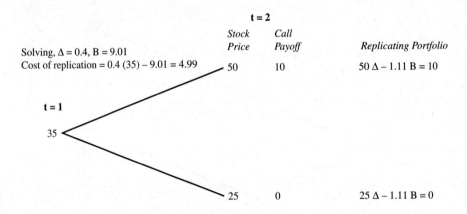

If the stock price is $35 at $t = 1$, then the call is worth $4.99:

$$\text{Value of call} = 35(0.4) - 9.01 = \$4.99$$

Step 2: Move backward to the earlier time period and create a replicating portfolio that will provide the cash flows the option will provide.

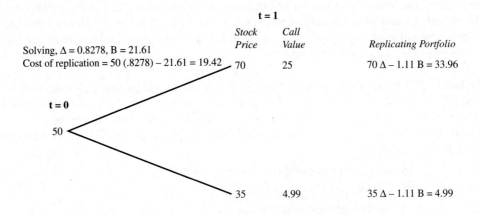

In other words, borrowing $21.61 and buying 0.8278 of a share will provide the same cash flows as a call with a strike price of $40 over the call's lifetime. The value of the call, therefore, has to be the same as the cost of creating this position.

$$\text{Value of call} = \text{Current Stock Price}\left(\frac{5}{7}\right) - \text{Borrowing}$$

$$= 50\left(\frac{5}{7}\right) - 21.61 = \$19.42$$

The Determinants of Value   The binomial model provides insight into the determinants of option value. The value of an option is not determined by the *expected* price of the asset but by its *current* price, which, of course, reflects expectations about the future. This is a direct consequence of arbitrage. If the option value deviates from the value of the replicating portfolio, investors can create an arbitrage position (i.e., one that requires no investment, involves no risk, and delivers positive returns). To illustrate, if the portfolio that replicates the call costs more than the call does in the market, an investor could buy the call, sell the replicating portfolio, and be guaranteed the difference as a profit. The cash flows on the two positions will offset each other, leading to no cash flows in subsequent periods. The call option value also increases as the time to expiration is extended, as the price movements (u and d) increase, and with increases in the interest rate.

While the binomial model provides an intuitive feel for the determinants of option value, it requires a large number of inputs, in terms of expected future prices at each node. As time periods are made shorter in the binomial model, you can make one of two assumptions about asset prices. You can assume that price changes become smaller as periods get shorter; this leads to price changes becoming infinitesimally small as time periods approach zero, leading to a continuous price process. Alternatively, you can assume that price changes stay large even as the period gets shorter; this leads to a jump price process, where prices can jump in any period. This section considers the option pricing models that emerge with each of these assumptions.

Black-Scholes Model

When the price process is continuous (i.e., price changes become smaller as time periods get shorter), the binomial model for pricing options converges on the Black-Scholes model. The model, named after its cocreators, Fischer Black and Myron Scholes, allows us to estimate the value of any option using a small number of inputs, and has been shown to be robust in valuing many listed options.

The Model While the derivation of the Black-Scholes model is far too complicated to present here, it is based on the idea of creating a portfolio of the underlying asset and the riskless asset with the same cash flows, and hence the same cost, as the option being valued. The value of a call option in the Black-Scholes model can be written as a function of the five variables:

$$S = \text{Current value of the underlying asset}$$
$$K = \text{Strike price of the option}$$
$$t = \text{Life to expiration of the option}$$
$$r = \text{Riskless interest rate corresponding to the life of the option}$$
$$\sigma^2 = \text{Variance in the ln(value) of the underlying asset}$$

The value of a call is then:

$$\text{Value of call} = S\, N(d_1) - Ke^{-rt} N(d_2)$$

$$d_1 = \frac{\ln\left(\frac{S}{K}\right) + \left(r + \frac{\sigma^2}{2}\right)t}{\sigma\sqrt{t}}$$

$$d_2 = d_1 - \sigma\sqrt{t}$$

Note that e^{-rt} is the present value factor and reflects the fact that the exercise price on the call option does not have to be paid until expiration, since the model values European options. $N(d_1)$ and $N(d_2)$ are probabilities, estimated by using a cumulative standardized normal distribution, and the values of d_1 and d_2 obtained for an option. The cumulative distribution is shown in Figure 5.5.

In approximate terms, $N(d_2)$ yields the likelihood that an option will generate positive cash flows for its owner at exercise (i.e., that $S > K$ in the case of a call option and that

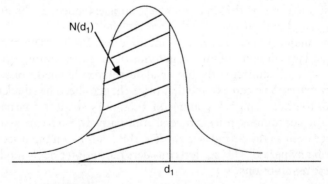

FIGURE 5.5 Cumulative Normal Distribution

K > S in the case of a put option). The portfolio that replicates the call option is created by buying $N(d_1)$ units of the underlying asset and borrowing $Ke^{-rt} N(d_2)$. The portfolio will have the same cash flows as the call option, and thus the same value as the option. $N(d_1)$, which is the number of units of the underlying asset that are needed to create the replicating portfolio, is called the option delta.

A NOTE ON ESTIMATING THE INPUTS TO THE BLACK-SCHOLES MODEL

The Black-Scholes model requires inputs that are consistent on time measurement. There are two places where this affects estimates. The first relates to the fact that the model works in continuous time, rather than discrete time. That is why we use the continuous time version of present value ($\exp^{-rt}$) rather than the discrete version, $(1 + r)^{-t}$. It also means that the inputs such as the riskless rate have to be modified to make them continuous time inputs. For instance, if the one-year Treasury bond rate is 6.2 percent, the risk-free rate that is used in the Black-Scholes model should be 6.15%

$$\text{Continuous Risk free Rate} = \ln(1 + \text{Annual Interest Rate})$$
$$= \ln(1.062) = 0.0615 \text{ or } 6.15\%$$

The second relates to the period over which the inputs are estimated. For instance, the preceding rate is an annual rate. The variance that is entered into the model also must be an annualized variance. The variance, estimated from ln (asset prices), can be annualized easily because variances are linear in time if the serial correlation is zero. Thus, if monthly or weekly prices are used to estimate variance, the variance is annualized by multiplying by 12 or 52, respectively.

ILLUSTRATION 5.2: Valuing an Option Using the Black-Scholes Model

On March 6, 2001, Cisco Systems was trading at $13.62. We will attempt to value a July 2001 call option with a strike price of $15, trading on the CBOE on the same day for $2. The following are the other parameters of the options:

- The annualized standard deviation in Cisco Systems stock price over the previous year was 81%. This standard deviation is estimated using weekly stock prices over the year, and the resulting number was annualized as follows:

    Weekly standard deviation in stock prices = 11.23%

    Annualized standard deviation in stock prices = 11.23% × $\sqrt{52}$ = 81%

- The option expiration date is Friday, July 20, 2001. There are 103 days to expiration, and the annualized Treasury bill rate corresponding to this option life is 4.63%.

The inputs for the Black-Scholes model are as follows:

    Current stock price (S) = $13.62

    Strike price on the option = $15

    Option life = 103/365 = 0.2822

Standard deviation in ln (stock prices) = 81%

Riskless rate = 4.63%

Inputting these numbers into the model, we get:

$$d_1 = \frac{\ln\left(\frac{13.62}{15.00}\right) + \left(.0463 + \frac{.81^2}{2}\right)t}{.81\sqrt{.2822}} = 0.0212$$

$$d_2 = .0212 - .81\sqrt{.2822}$$

Using the normal distribution, we can estimate the $N(d_1)$ and $N(d_2)$:

$$N(d_1) = .5085$$
$$N(d_2) = .3412$$

The value of the call can now be estimated:

$$\text{Value of Call} = 13.62(.5085) - 15\ \exp^{(-.0463)(.2822)}(.3412) = \$1.87$$

Since the call is trading at $2, it is slightly overvalued, assuming that the estimate of standard deviation used is correct.

IMPLIED VOLATILITY

The only input in the Black Scholes on which there can be significant disagreement among investors is the variance. While the variance is often estimated by looking at historical data, the values for options that emerge from using the historical variance can be different from the market prices. For any option, there is some variance at which the estimated value will be equal to the market price. This variance is called an implied variance.

Consider the Cisco option valued in Illustration 5.2. With a standard deviation of 81 percent, the value of the call option with a strike price of $15 was estimated to be $1.87. Since the market price is higher than the calculated value, we tried higher standard deviations, and at a standard deviation 85.40 percent the value of the option is $2 (which is the market price). This is the implied standard deviation or implied volatility.

Model Limitations and Fixes   The Black-Scholes model was designed to value European options that can be exercised only at maturity and whose underlying assets do not pay dividends. In addition, options are valued based on the assumption that option exercise does not affect the value of the underlying asset. In practice, assets do pay dividends, options sometimes get exercised early, and exercising an option can affect the value of the underlying asset. Adjustments exist that, while not perfect, provide partial corrections to the Black-Scholes model.

Dividends   The payment of a dividend reduces the stock price; note that on the ex-dividend day, the stock price generally declines. Consequently, call options become less valuable and put options more valuable as expected dividend payments increase. There are two ways of dealing with dividends in the Black-Scholes model:

1. *Short-term options.* One approach to dealing with dividends is to estimate the present value of expected dividends that will be paid by the underlying asset during the option life and subtract it from the current value of the asset to use as S in the model.

$$\text{Modified Stock Price} = \text{Current Stock Price} - \text{Present value of expected}$$
$$\text{dividends during option life}$$

2. *Long-term options.* Since it becomes less practical to estimate the present value of dividends the longer the option life, an alternate approach can be used. If the dividend yield (y = Dividends/Current value of the asset) on the underlying asset is expected to remain unchanged during the life of the option, the Black-Scholes model can be modified to take dividends into account.

$$\text{Value of call} = Se^{-yt}N(d_1) - Ke^{-rt}N(d_2)$$

$$d_1 = \frac{\ln\left(\frac{S}{K}\right) + \left(r - y + \frac{\sigma^2}{2}\right)t}{\sigma\sqrt{t}}$$

$$d_2 = d_1 - \sigma\sqrt{t}$$

From an intuitive standpoint, the adjustments have two effects. First, the value of the asset is discounted back to the present at the dividend yield to consider the expected drop in asset value resulting from dividend payments. Second, the interest rate is offset by the dividend yield to reflect the lower carrying cost from holding the asset (in the replicating portfolio). The net effect will be a reduction in the value of calls estimated using this model.

ILLUSTRATION 5.3: Valuing a Short-Term Option with Dividend Adjustments—The Black-Scholes Correction

Assume that it is March 6, 2001, and that AT&T is trading at $20.50 a share. Consider a call option on the stock with a strike price of $20, expiring on July 20, 2001. Using past stock prices, the annualized standard deviation in the log of stock prices for AT&T is estimated at 60%. There is one dividend, amounting to $0.15, and it will be paid in 23 days. The riskless rate is 4.63%.

Present value of expected dividend = $0.15/1.0463^{23/365} = $0.15

Dividend-adjusted stock price = $20.50 − $0.15 = $20.35

Time to expiration = 103/365 = 0.2822

Variance in ln (stock prices) = $0.6^2 = 0.36$

Riskless rate = 4.63%

The value from the Black-Scholes model is:

$$d_1 = 0.2551 \qquad N(d_1) = 0.6007$$
$$d_2 = -0.0636 \qquad N(d_2) = 0.4745$$
$$\text{Value of call} = 20.35(0.6007) - 20\ \exp^{(-0.0463)(0.2822)}(0.4746) = \$2.86$$

The call option was trading at $2.60 on that day.

ILLUSTRATION 5.4: Valuing a Long-Term Option with Dividend Adjustments—Primes and Scores

The CBOE offers longer-term call and put options on some stocks. On March 6, 2001, for instance, you could have purchased an AT&T call expiring on January 17, 2003. The stock price for AT&T is $20.50 (as in the previous example). The following is the valuation of a call option with a strike price of $20. Instead of estimating the present value of dividends over the next two years, assume that AT&T's dividend yield will remain 2.51% over this period and that the risk-free rate for a two-year Treasury bond is 4.85%. The inputs to the Black-Scholes model are:

$$d_1 = \frac{\ln\left(\frac{20.50}{20.00}\right) + \left(.0485 - .0251 + \frac{0.6^2}{2}\right)1.8333}{0.6\sqrt{1.8333}} = 0.4894 \quad N(d_1) = 0.6877$$

$$d_2 = 0.4894 - 0.6\sqrt{1.8333} = 0.3230 \qquad\qquad\qquad N(d_2) = 0.3733$$

The value from the Black-Scholes model is:

$$\text{Value of call} = 20.50\, \exp^{(-0.0251)(1.8333)}(0.6877) - 20\, \exp^{(-0.0485)(1.8333)}(0.3733) = \$6.63$$

The call was trading at $5.80 on March 8, 2001.

 optst.xls: **This spreadsheet allows you to estimate the value of a short-term option when the expected dividends during the option life can be estimated.**

 optlt.xls: **This spreadsheet allows you to estimate the value of an option when the underlying asset has a constant dividend yield.**

Early Exercise   The Black-Scholes model was designed to value European options that can be exercised only at expiration. In contrast, most options that we encounter in practice are American options and can be exercised at any time until expiration. As mentioned earlier, the possibility of early exercise makes American options more valuable than otherwise similar European options; it also makes them more difficult to value. In general, though, with traded options, it is almost always better to sell the option to someone else rather than exercise early, since options have a time premium (i.e., they sell for more than their exercise value). There are two exceptions. One occurs when the underlying asset pays large dividends, thus reducing the expected value of the asset. In this case, call options may be exercised *just before an ex-dividend date*, if the time premium on the options is less than the expected decline in asset value as a consequence of the dividend payment. The other exception arises when an investor holds both the underlying asset and *deep in-the-money puts* (i.e., puts with strike prices well above the current price of the underlying asset) on that asset at a time when interest rates are high. In this case, the time premium on the put may be less than the potential gain from exercising the put early and earning interest on the exercise price.

There are two basic ways of dealing with the possibility of early exercise. One is to continue to use the unadjusted Black-Scholes model and to regard the resulting value as a floor or conservative estimate of the true value. The other is to try to adjust the value of the option for the possibility of early exercise. There are two approaches for doing so. One uses the Black-Scholes model to value the option to each potential exercise date. With options on stocks, this basically requires that the investor values options to each ex-dividend day and chooses the maximum of the estimated call values. The second approach is to use a modified version of the binomial model to consider the possibility of early exercise. In this version, the up and the down movements for asset prices in each period can be estimated from the variance.[2]

Approach 1: Pseudo-American Valuation

Step 1: Define when dividends will be paid and how much the dividends will be.

Step 2: Value the call option to each ex-dividend date using the dividend-adjusted approach described earlier, where the stock price is reduced by the present value of expected dividends.

Step 3: Choose the maximum of the call values estimated for each ex-dividend day.

ILLUSTRATION 5.5: Using Pseudo-American Option Valuation to Adjust for Early Exercise

Consider an option with a strike price of $35 on a stock trading at $40. The variance in the ln (stock prices) is 0.05, and the riskless rate is 4%. The option has a remaining life of eight months, and there are three dividends expected during this period:

Expected Dividend	Ex-Dividend Day
$0.80	In 1 month
$0.80	In 4 months
$0.80	In 7 months

The call option is first valued to just before the first ex-dividend date:

$$S = \$40, K = \$35, t = 1/12, \sigma^2 = 0.05, r = 0.04$$

The value from the Black-Scholes model is:

$$\text{Value of call} = \$5.131$$

---

[2]To illustrate, if σ^2 is the variance in ln(stock prices), the up and the down movements in the binomial can be estimated as follows:

$$u = \exp^{(r - \sigma^2)(\frac{1}{m}) + \sqrt{\sigma^2 T/m}}$$

$$d = \exp^{(r - \sigma^2)(\frac{1}{m}) - \sqrt{\sigma^2 T/m}}$$

where u and d are the up and down movements per unit time for the binomial, T is the life of the option, and m is the number of periods within that lifetime.

The call option is then valued to before the second ex-dividend date:

$$\text{Adjusted Stock Price} = \$40 - \$0.80/1.04^{1/12} = \$39.20$$
$$K = \$35, \quad t = 4/12, \quad \sigma^2 = 0.05, \quad r = 0.04$$

The value of the call based on these parameters is:

$$\text{Value of call} = \$5.073$$

The call option is then valued to before the third ex-dividend date:

$$\text{Adjusted Stock Price} = \$40 - \$0.80/1.04^{1/12} - \$0.80/1.04^{4/12} = \$38.41$$
$$K = \$35, \quad t = 7/12, \quad \sigma^2 = 0.05, \quad r = 0.04$$

The value of the call based on these parameters is:

$$\text{Value of call} = \$5.128$$

The call option is then valued to expiration:

$$\text{Adjusted Stock Price} = \$40 - \$0.80/1.04^{1/12} - \$0.80/1.04^{4/12}$$
$$- \$0.80/1.04^{7/12} = \$37.63$$
$$K = \$35, \quad t = 8/12, \quad \sigma^2 = 0.05, \quad r = 0.04$$

The value of the call based on these parameters is:

$$\text{Value of call} = \$4.757$$

Approach 2: Using the Binomial Model The binomial model is much more capable of handling early exercise because it considers the cash flows at each time period, rather than just at expiration. The biggest limitation of the binomial model is determining what stock prices will be at the end of each period, but this can be overcome by using a variant that allows us to estimate the up and the down movements in stock prices from the estimated variance. There are four steps involved:

Step 1: If the variance in ln (stock prices) has been estimated for the Black-Scholes valuation, convert these into inputs for the binomial model:

$$u = \exp^{\sigma\sqrt{dt}} \left(r - \frac{\sigma^2}{2} \right) dt$$
$$d = \exp^{-\sigma\sqrt{dt}} \left(r - \frac{\sigma^2}{2} \right) dt$$

where u and d are the up and the down movements per unit time for the binomial, and dt is the number of periods within each year (or unit time).

Step 2: Specify the period in which the dividends will be paid and make the assumption that the price will drop by the amount of the dividend in that period.

Step 3: Value the call at each node of the tree, allowing for the possibility of early exercise just before ex-dividend dates. There will be early exercise if the remaining time premium on the option is less than the expected drop in option value as a consequence of the dividend payment.

Step 4: Value the call at time 0, using the standard binomial approach.

bstobin.xls: **This spreadsheet allows you to estimate the parameters for a binomial model from the inputs to a Black-Scholes model.**

Impact of Exercise on Underlying Asset Value The Black-Scholes model is based on the assumption that exercising an option does not affect the value of the underlying asset. This may be true for listed options on stocks, but it is not true for some types of options. For instance, the exercise of warrants increases the number of shares outstanding and brings fresh cash into the firm, both of which will affect the stock price.[3] The expected negative impact (dilution) of exercise will decrease the value of warrants, compared to otherwise similar call options. The adjustment for dilution to the stock price is fairly simple in the Black-Scholes valuation. The stock price is adjusted for the expected dilution from the exercise of the options. In the case of warrants, for instance:

$$\text{Dilution Adjusted } S = (Sn_S + Wn_w)/(n_S + n_w)$$

where S = Current value of the stock
n_w = Number of warrants outstanding
W = Value of warrants outstanding
n_S = Number of shares outstanding

When the warrants are exercised, the number of shares outstanding will increase, reducing the stock price. The numerator reflects the market value of equity, including both stocks and warrants outstanding. The reduction in S will reduce the value of the call option.

There is an element of circularity in this analysis since the value of the warrant is needed to estimate the dilution-adjusted S and the dilution-adjusted S is needed to estimate the value of the warrant. This problem can be resolved by starting the process off with an assumed value for the warrant (e.g., the exercise value or the current market price of the warrant). This will yield a value for the warrant, and this estimated value can then be used as an input to re-estimate the warrant's value until there is convergence.

FROM BLACK-SCHOLES TO BINOMIAL

The process of converting the continuous variance in a Black-Scholes model to a binomial tree is a simple one. Assume, for instance, that you have an asset that is trading at $30 currently and that you estimate the annualized standard deviation in the asset value to be 40 percent; the annualized riskless rate is 5 percent. For simplicity, let us assume that the option that you are valuing has a four-year life and that each period is a year. To estimate the prices at the end of each of the four years, we begin by first estimating the up and down movements in the binomial:

(continued)

---

[3]Warrants are call options issued by firms, either as part of management compensation contracts or to raise equity.

(*continued*)

$$u = \exp^{.40\sqrt{1}}\left(.05 - \frac{.4^2}{2}\right) = 1.4477$$

$$d = \exp^{-.40\sqrt{1}}\left(.05 - \frac{.4^2}{2}\right) = 0.6505$$

Based on these estimates, we can obtain the prices at the end of the first node of the tree (the end of the first year):

Up Price = $30(1.4477) = $43.43
Down Price = $30(0.6505) = $19.52

Progressing through the rest of the tree, we obtain the following numbers (in Figure 5.6):

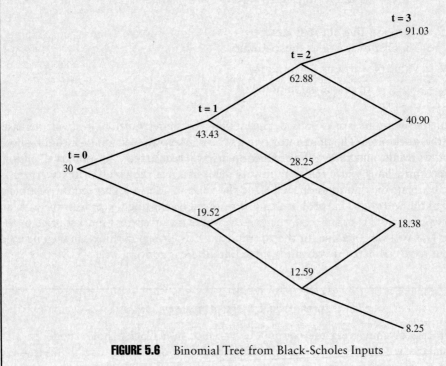

FIGURE 5.6   Binomial Tree from Black-Scholes Inputs

ILLUSTRATION 5.6:   Valuing a Warrant on Avatek Corporation

Avatek Corporation is a real estate firm with 19.637 million shares outstanding, trading at $0.38 a share. In March 2001 the company had 1.8 million options outstanding, with four years to expiration and with an exercise price of $2.25. The stock paid no dividends, and the standard deviation in ln(stock prices) was 93%. The four-year Treasury bond rate was 4.9%. (The options were trading at $0.12 apiece at the time of this analysis.)

The inputs to the warrant valuation model are as follows:

$$\text{Adjusted } S = (0.38 \times 19.637 + 0.12 \times 1.8)/(19.637 + 1.8) = \$0.3544$$

$$K = \text{Exercise price on warrant} = \$2.25$$
$$t = \text{Time to expiration} = 4 \text{ years}$$
$$r = \text{Riskless rate corresponding to life of option} = 4.9\%$$
$$\sigma^2 = \text{Variance in stock price} = 0.93$$
$$y = \text{Dividend yield on stock} = 0.0\%$$

The results of the Black-Scholes valuation of this option are:

$$d_1 = 0.0418 \qquad N(d_1) = 0.5167$$
$$d_2 = -1.8182 \qquad N(d_1) = 0.0345$$

$$\text{Value of call} = 0.3544(0.5167) - 2.25 \ \exp^{(-0.049)(4.00)} \ (0.0345) = \$0.12$$

The options were trading at $0.12 in March 2001. Since the value was equal to the price, there was no need for further iterations. If there had been a difference, we would have re-estimated the adjusted stock price and option value. If the options had been nontraded (as is the case with management options), this calculation would have required an iterative process, where the option value is used to get the adjusted value per share and the value per share to get the option value.

 warrant.xls: This spreadsheet allows you to estimate the value of an option when there is a potential dilution from exercise.

The Black-Scholes Model for Valuing Puts The value of a put can be derived from the value of a call with the same strike price and the same expiration date:

$$\text{Call} - \text{Put} = S - K \ e^{-rt}$$

where C is the value of the call and P is the value of the put. This relationship between the call and put values is called put-call parity, and any deviations from parity can be used by investors to make riskless profits. To see why put-call parity holds, consider selling a call and buying a put with exercise price K and expiration date t, and simultaneously buying the underlying asset at the current price S. The payoff from this position is riskless and always yields K at expiration (t). To see this, assume that the stock price at expiration is S^*. The payoff on each of the positions in the portfolio can be written as follows:

Position	Payoffs at t if $S^* > K$	Payoffs at t if $S^* < K$
Sell call	$-(S^* - K)$	0
Buy put	0	$K - S^*$
Buy stock	S^*	S^*
Total	K	K

Since this position yields K with certainty, the cost of creating this position must be equal to the present value of K at the riskless rate (Ke^{-rt}).

$$S + P - C = Ke^{-rt}$$
$$C - P = S - Ke^{-rt}$$

Substituting the Black-Scholes equation for the value of an equivalent call into this equation, we get:

$$\text{Value of put} = Ke^{-rt}[1 - N(d_2)] - S\ e^{-rt}[1 - N(d_1)]$$

$$d_1 = \frac{\ln\left(\frac{S}{K}\right) + \left(r - y + \frac{\sigma^2}{2}\right)t}{\sigma\sqrt{t}}$$

$$d_2 = d_1 - \sigma\sqrt{t}$$

Thus, the replicating portfolio for a put is created by selling short $[1 - N(d_1)]$ shares of stock and investing $Ke^{-rt}[1 - N(d_2)]$ in the riskless asset.

ILLUSTRATION 5.7: Valuing a Put Using Put-Call Parity: Cisco Systems and AT&T

Consider the call on Cisco Systems that we valued in Illustration 5.2. The call had a strike price of $15 on the stock, had 103 days left to expiration, and was valued at $1.87. The stock was trading at $13.62, and the riskless rate was 4.63%. The put can be valued as follows:

$$\text{Put Value} = C - S + Ke^{-rt} = 1.87 - 13.62 + 15\ e^{(-0.0463)\,(.2822)} = \$3.06$$

The put was trading at $3.38.

Also, a long-term call on AT&T was valued in Illustration 5.4. The call had a strike price of $20, 1.8333 years left to expiration, and a value of $6.63. The stock was trading at $20.50 and was expected to maintain a dividend yield of 2.51% over the period. The riskless rate was 4.85%. The put value can be estimated as follows:

$$\text{Put Value} = C - Se^{-yt} + Ke^{-rt} = 6.63 - 20.5\ e^{-(.0251)(1.8333)} + 15\ e^{(-0.0485)\,(1.8333)} = \$5.35$$

The put was trading at $3.80. Both the call and put were trading at different prices from our estimates, which may indicate that we have not correctly estimated the stock's volatility.

Jump Process Option Pricing Models

If price changes remain larger as the time periods in the binomial model are shortened, it can no longer be assumed that prices change continuously. When price changes remain large, a price process that allows for price jumps is much more realistic. Cox and Ross (1976) valued options when prices follow a pure jump process, where the jumps can only be positive. Thus, in the next interval, the stock price will either have a large positive jump with a specified probability or drift downward at a given rate.

Merton (1976) considered a distribution where there are price jumps superimposed on a continuous price process. He specified the rate at which jumps occur (λ) and the average jump size (k), measured as a percentage of the stock price. The model derived to value options with this process is called a jump diffusion model. In this model, the value of an option is determined by the five variables specified in the Black-Scholes model, and the parameters of the jump process (λ, k). Unfortunately, the estimates of the jump process parameters are so difficult to make for most firms that they overwhelm any advantages that accrue from using a more realistic model. These models, therefore, have seen limited use in practice.

EXTENSIONS OF OPTION PRICING

All the option pricing models described so far—the binomial, the Black-Scholes, and the jump process models—are designed to value options with clearly defined exercise prices and maturities on underlying assets that are traded. However, the options we encounter in investment analysis or valuation are often on real assets rather than financial assets. Categorized as real options, they can take much more complicated forms. This section considers some of these variations.

Capped and Barrier Options

With a simple call option, there is no specified upper limit on the profits that can be made by the buyer of the call. Asset prices, at least in theory, can keep going up, and the payoffs increase proportionately. In some call options, though, the buyer is entitled to profits up to a specified price but not above it. For instance, consider a call option with a strike price of K_1 on an asset. In an unrestricted call option, the payoff on this option will increase as the underlying asset's price increases above K_1. Assume, however, that if the price reaches K_2, the payoff is capped at ($K_2 - K_1$). The payoff diagram on this option is shown in Figure 5.7.

This option is called a capped call. Notice, also, that once the price reaches K_2, there is no longer any time premium associated with the option, and the option will therefore be exercised. Capped calls are part of a family of options called barrier options, where the payoff on and the life of the option are functions of whether the underlying asset price reaches a certain level during a specified period.

The value of a capped call is always lower than the value of the same call without the payoff limit. A simple approximation of this value can be obtained by valuing the call twice, once with the given exercise price and once with the cap and taking the difference in the two values. In the preceding example then, the value of the call with an exercise price of K_1 and a cap at K_2 can be written as:

$$\text{Value of capped call} = \text{Value of call } (K = K_1) - \text{Value of call } (K = K_2)$$

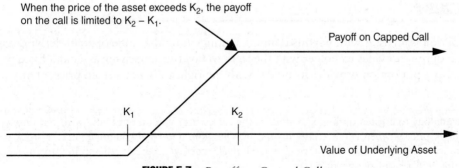

FIGURE 5.7 Payoff on Capped Call

Barrier options can take many forms. In a knockout option, an option ceases to exist if the underlying asset reaches a certain price. In the case of a call option, this knockout price is usually set below the strike price, and this option is called a down-and-out option. In the case of a put option, the knockout price will be set above the exercise price, and this option is called an up-and-out option. Like the capped call, these options are worth less than their unrestricted counterparts. Many real options have limits on potential upside, or knockout provisions, and ignoring these limits can result in the overstatement of the value of these options.

Compound Options

Some options derive their value not from an underlying asset but from other options. These options are called compound options. Compound options can take any of four forms—a call on a call, a put on a put, a call on a put, or a put on a call. Geske (1979) developed the analytical formulation for valuing compound options by replacing the standard normal distribution used in a simple option model with a bivariate normal distribution in the calculation.

In chapter 30, we will value the option to expand a project, as a real option. While we will value this option using a simple option pricing model, in reality there could be multiple stages in expansion, with each stage representing an option for the following stage. In this case, we will undervalue the option by considering it as a simple rather than a compound option.

Notwithstanding this discussion, the valuation of compound options becomes progressively more difficult as more options are added to the chain. In this case, rather than wreck the valuation on the shoals of estimation error, it may be better to accept the conservative estimate that is provided with a simple valuation model as a floor on the value.

Rainbow Options

In a simple option, the uncertainty is about the price of the underlying asset. Some options are exposed to two or more sources of uncertainty, and these options are rainbow options. Using the simple option pricing model to value such options can lead to biased estimates of value. As an example, consider an undeveloped oil reserve as an option, where the firm that owns the reserve has the right to develop the reserve. Here there are two sources of uncertainty. The first is obviously the price of oil, and the second is the quantity of oil that is in the reserve. To value this undeveloped reserve, we can make the simplifying assumption that we know the quantity of oil in the reserve with certainty. In reality, however, uncertainty about the quantity will affect the value of this option and make the decision to exercise more difficult.[4]

CONCLUSION

An option is an asset with payoffs that are contingent on the value of an underlying asset. A call option provides its holder with the right to buy the underlying asset at a fixed price, whereas a put option provides its holder with the right to sell at a fixed price, at any time

---

[4]The analogy to a listed option on a stock is the case where you do not know with certainty what the stock price is when you exercise the option. The more uncertain you are about the stock price, the more margin for error you have to give yourself when you exercise the option, to ensure that you are in fact earning a profit.

before the expiration of the option. The value of an option is determined by six variables—the current value of the underlying asset, the variance in this value, the expected dividends on the asset, the strike price and life of the option, and the riskless interest rate. This is illustrated in both the binomial and the Black-Scholes models, which value options by creating replicating portfolios composed of the underlying asset and riskless lending or borrowing. These models can be used to value assets that have option like characteristics.

QUESTIONS AND SHORT PROBLEMS

In the problems following, use an equity risk premium of 5.5 percent if none is specified.

1. The following are prices of options traded on Microsoft Corporation, which pays no dividends.

	Call		Put	
	K = 85	K = 90	K = 85	K = 90
One month	$2.75	$1.00	$4.50	$ 7.50
Three months	$4.00	$2.75	$5.75	$ 9.00
Six months	$7.75	$6.00	$8.00	$12.00

The stock is trading at $83, and the annualized riskless rate is 3.8%. The standard deviation in ln (stock prices, based on historical data) is 30%.
   a. Estimate the value of a three-month call with a strike price of $85.
   b. Using the inputs from the Black-Scholes model, specify how you would replicate this call.
   c. What is the implied standard deviation in this call?
   d. Assume now that you buy a call with a strike price of $85 and sell a call with a strike price of $90. Draw the payoff diagram on this position.
   e. Using put-call parity, estimate the value of a three-month put with a strike price of $85.
2. You are trying to value three-month call and put options on Merck with a strike price of $30. The stock is trading at $28.75, and the company expects to pay a quarterly dividend per share of $0.28 in two months. The annualized riskless interest rate is 3.6%, and the standard deviation in log stock prices is 20%.
   a. Estimate the value of the call and put options, using the Black-Scholes model.
   b. What effect does the expected dividend payment have on call values? On put values? Why?
3. There is the possibility that the options on Merck described in the preceding problem could be exercised early.
   a. Use the pseudo-American call option technique to determine whether this will affect the value of the call.
   b. Why does the possibility of early exercise exist? What types of options are most likely to be exercised early?

4. You have been provided the following information on a three-month call:

$$S = 95 \quad K = 90 \quad t = 0.25 \quad r = 0.04$$
$$N(d_1) = 0.5750 \quad N(d_2) = 0.4500$$

   a. If you wanted to replicate buying this call, how much money would you need to borrow?
   b. If you wanted to replicate buying this call, how many shares of stock would you need to buy?

5. Go Video, a manufacturer of video recorders, was trading at $4 per share in May 1994. There were 11 million shares outstanding. At the same time, it had 550,000 one-year warrants outstanding, with a strike price of $4.25. The stock has had a standard deviation of 60%. The stock does not pay a dividend. The riskless rate is 5%.
   a. Estimate the value of the warrants, ignoring dilution.
   b. Estimate the value of the warrants, allowing for dilution.
   c. Why does dilution reduce the value of the warrants?

6. You are trying to value a long-term call option on the NYSE Composite index, expiring in five years, with a strike price of 275. The index is currently at 250, and the annualized standard deviation in stock prices is 15%. The average dividend yield on the index is 3% and is expected to remain unchanged over the next five years. The five-year Treasury bond rate is 5%.
   a. Estimate the value of the long-term call option.
   b. Estimate the value of a put option with the same parameters.
   c. What are the implicit assumptions you are making when you use the Black-Scholes model to value this option? Which of these assumptions are likely to be violated? What are the consequences for your valuation?

7. A new security on AT&T will entitle the investor to all dividends on AT&T over the next three years, limiting upside potential to 20% but also providing downside protection below 10%. AT&T stock is trading at $50, and three-year call and put options are traded on the exchange at the following prices:

Strike Price	Call		Put	
	1-Year	3-Year	1-Year	3-Year
45	$8.69	$13.34	$1.99	$ 3.55
50	$5.86	$10.09	$3.92	$ 5.40
55	$3.78	$ 8.81	$6.39	$ 7.63
60	$2.35	$ 7.11	$9.92	$10.23

How much would you be willing to pay for this security?

CHAPTER 6

Market Efficiency—Definition, Tests, and Evidence

What is an efficient market? What does it imply for investment and valuation models? Clearly, market efficiency is a concept that is controversial and attracts strong views, pro and con, partly because of differences between individuals about what it really means, and partly because whether markets are efficient or not is a core belief that in large part determines how an investor approaches investing. This chapter provides a definition of market efficiency, considers the implications of an efficient market for investors, and summarizes some of the basic approaches that are used to test investment schemes, thereby proving or disproving market efficiency. It also provides a summary of the voluminous research on whether markets are efficient.

MARKET EFFICIENCY AND INVESTMENT VALUATION

The question of whether markets are efficient, and, if not, where the inefficiencies lie, is central to investment valuation. If markets are in fact efficient, the market price provides the best estimate of value, and the process of valuation becomes one of justifying the market price. If markets are not efficient, the market price may deviate from the true value, and the process of valuation is directed toward obtaining a reasonable estimate of this value. Those who do valuation well, then, will be able to make higher returns than other investors because of their capacity to spot under- and overvalued firms. To make these higher returns, though, markets have to correct their mistakes (i.e., become efficient) over time. Whether these corrections occur over six months or over five years can have a profound impact on which valuation approach an investor chooses to use and the time horizon needed for it to succeed.

There is also much that can be learned from studies of market efficiency, which highlight segments where the market seems to be inefficient. These inefficiencies can provide the basis for screening all stocks to come up with a subsample that is more likely to contain undervalued stocks. Given the size of the universe of stocks, this not only saves time for the analyst, but it increases the odds significantly of finding under- and overvalued stocks. For instance, some efficiency studies suggest that stocks that are neglected by institutional investors are more likely to be undervalued and earn excess returns. A strategy that screens firms for low institutional investment (as a percentage of the outstanding stock) may yield a subsample of neglected firms, which can then be valued to arrive at a portfolio of undervalued firms. If the research is correct, the odds of finding undervalued firms should increase in this subsample.

WHAT IS AN EFFICIENT MARKET?

An efficient market is one where the market price is an unbiased estimate of the true value of the investment. Implicit in this derivation are several key concepts:

- Contrary to popular view, market efficiency does not require that the market price be equal to true value at every point in time. All it requires is that errors in the market price be unbiased; prices can be greater than or less than true value, as long as these deviations are random.
- The fact that the deviations from true value are random implies, in a rough sense, that there is an equal chance that any stock is under- or overvalued at any point in time, and that these deviations are uncorrelated with any observable variable. For instance, in an efficient market, stocks with lower PE ratios should be no more or no less likely to be undervalued than stocks with high PE ratios.
- If the deviations of market price from true value are random, it follows that no group of investors should be able to consistently find under- or overvalued stocks using any investment strategy.

Definitions of market efficiency have to be specific not only about the market that is being considered but also the investor group being covered. It is extremely unlikely that all markets are efficient to all investors at all times, but it is entirely possible that a particular market (for instance, the New York Stock Exchange) is efficient with respect to the average investor. It is also possible that some markets are efficient while others are not, and that a market is efficient with respect to some investors and not to others. This is a direct consequence of differential tax rates and transaction costs, which confer advantages on some investors relative to others.

Definitions of market efficiency are also linked up with assumptions about what information is available to investors and reflected in the price. For instance, a strict definition of market efficiency that assumes that all information, public as well as private, is reflected in market prices would imply that even investors with precise inside information will be unable to beat the market. Fama (1970) delineated one of the earliest classifications of market efficiency, when he argued that markets could be efficient at three levels, based on what information was reflected in prices. Under *weak form efficiency*, the current price reflects the information contained in all past prices, suggesting that charts and technical analyses that use past prices alone would not be useful in finding undervalued stocks. Under *semi-strong form efficiency*, the current price reflects the information contained not only in past prices but all public information (including financial statements and news reports), and no approach that is predicated on using and massaging this information would be useful in finding undervalued stocks. Under *strong form efficiency*, the current price reflects all information, public as well as private, and no investors will be able to find undervalued stocks consistently.

Implications of Market Efficiency

An immediate and direct implication of an efficient market is that no group of investors should be able to beat the market consistently using a common investment strategy. An efficient market would also carry negative implications for many investment strategies:

■ In an efficient market, equity research and valuation would be a costly task that would provide no benefits. The odds of finding an undervalued stock would always be 50–50, reflecting the randomness of pricing errors. At best, the benefits from information collection and equity research would cover the costs of doing the research. At worst, the costs will be deadweight, and the returns to active investing will lag the market by those costs.

■ In an efficient market, a strategy of randomly diversifying across stocks or indexing to the market, carrying little or no information cost and minimal execution costs, would be superior to any other strategy that created larger information and execution costs. There would be no value added by active portfolio managers and investment strategists.

■ In an efficient market, a strategy of minimizing trading (i.e., creating a portfolio and not trading unless cash was needed) would be superior to a strategy that required frequent trading.

It is therefore no wonder that the concept of market efficiency evokes such strong reactions on the part of portfolio managers and analysts, who view it, quite rightly, as a challenge to their existence.

It is also important that there be clarity about what market efficiency does not imply. An efficient market does *not* imply that:

■ Stock prices cannot deviate from true value; in fact, there can be large deviations from true value. The only requirement is that the deviations be random.

■ No investor will beat the market in any period. To the contrary, approximately half of all investors, prior to transaction costs, should beat the market in any period.[1]

■ No group of investors, sharing commonalities, will beat the market in the long term. Given the number of investors in financial markets, the laws of probability would suggest that a fairly large number are going to beat the market consistently over long periods, not because of their investment strategies but because they are lucky. It would not, however, be consistent if a disproportionately large number of these investors used the same investment strategy.[2]

In an efficient market, the expected returns from any investment will be consistent with the risk of that investment over the long term, though there may be deviations from these expected returns in the short term.

---

[1] Since returns are positively skewed—that is, large positive returns are more likely than large negative returns (you cannot lose more than 100% on a stock)—less than half of all investors will probably beat the market.

[2] One of the enduring pieces of evidence against market efficiency lies in the performance records posted by many of the investors who learned their lessons from Benjamin Graham in the 1950s. No probability statistics could ever explain the consistency and superiority of their records.

Necessary Conditions for Market Efficiency

Markets do not become efficient automatically. It is the actions of investors, sensing bargains and putting into effect schemes to beat the market, that make markets efficient. The necessary conditions for a market inefficiency to be eliminated are:

- The market inefficiency should provide the basis for a scheme to beat the market and earn excess returns. For this to hold true:
  - The asset or assets that are the source of the inefficiency have to be traded.
  - The transaction costs of executing the scheme have to be smaller than the expected profits from the scheme.
- There should be profit-maximizing investors who:
  - Recognize the potential for excess return.
  - Can replicate the beat-the-market scheme that earns the excess return.
  - Have the resources to trade on the stock(s) until the inefficiency disappears.

The internal contradiction of claiming that there is no possibility of beating the market in an efficient market and requiring profit-maximizing investors to constantly seek out ways of beating the market, and thus making it efficient, has been explored by many. If markets were in fact efficient, investors would stop looking for inefficiencies, which would lead to markets becoming inefficient again. It makes sense to think about an efficient market as a self-correcting mechanism, where inefficiencies appear at regular intervals but disappear almost instantaneously as investors find them and trade on them. In other words, an efficient market is not a steady state but a transient one.

Propositions About Market Efficiency

A reading of the conditions under which markets become efficient leads to general propositions about where investors are most likely to find inefficiencies in financial markets.

Proposition 1: The probability of finding inefficiencies in an asset market decreases as the ease of trading on the asset increases. To the extent that investors have difficulty trading on an asset, either because open markets do not exist or because there are significant barriers to trading, inefficiencies in pricing can continue for long periods.

This proposition can be used to shed light on the differences between different asset markets. For instance, it is far easier to trade on stocks than it is on real estate, since markets are much more open, prices are in smaller units (reducing the barriers to entry for new traders), and the asset itself does not vary from transaction to transaction (e.g., one share of IBM is identical to another share, whereas one piece of real estate can be very different from another piece that is a stone's throw away). Based on these differences, there should be a greater likelihood of finding inefficiencies (both under- and overvaluation) in the real estate market.

Proposition 2: The probability of finding an inefficiency in an asset market increases as the transactions and information cost of exploiting the inefficiency increases. The cost of collecting information and trading varies widely across markets and even across investments in the same markets. As these costs increase, it pays less and less to try to exploit these inefficiencies.

Consider, for instance, the perceived wisdom that investing in "loser" stocks (i.e., stocks that have done very badly in some prior time period) should yield excess returns. This may be true in terms of raw returns, but transaction costs are likely to be much higher for these stocks since:

- They tend to be low-priced stocks, leading to higher brokerage commissions and expenses.
- The bid-ask spread, a transaction cost paid at the time of purchase, becomes a much higher fraction of the total price paid.
- Trading is often thin on these stocks, and small trades can cause prices to change, resulting in a higher buy price or a lower sell price.

Corollary 1: Investors who can establish a cost advantage (either in information collection or in transaction costs) will be more able to exploit small inefficiencies than other investors who do not possess this advantage.

There are several studies that look at the effect of block trades on prices and conclude that while block trades do affect prices, investors will not exploit these inefficiencies because of the number of times they will have to trade and their associated transaction costs. These concerns are unlikely to hold for a specialist on the floor of the exchange, who can trade quickly, often and at no or very low costs. It should be pointed out, however, that if the market for specialists is efficient, the value of a seat on the exchange should reflect the present value of potential benefits from being a specialist.

This corollary also suggests that investors who work at establishing a cost advantage, especially in relation to information, may be able to generate excess returns based on these advantages. Thus, John Templeton, who started investing in Japanese and other Asian markets well before other portfolio managers, might have been able to exploit the informational advantages he had over his peers to make excess returns on his portfolios, at least for a few years.

Proposition 3: The speed with which an inefficiency is resolved will be directly related to how easily the scheme to exploit the inefficiency can be replicated by other investors. The ease with which a scheme can be replicated is related to the time, resources, and information needed to execute it. Since very few investors single-handedly possess the resources to eliminate an inefficiency through trading, it is much more likely that an inefficiency would disappear quickly if the scheme used to exploit the inefficiency is transparent and can be copied by other investors.

To illustrate this point, assume that stocks are consistently found to earn excess returns in the month following a stock split. Since firms announce stock splits publicly and any investor can buy stocks right after these splits, it would be surprising if this inefficiency persisted over time. This can be contrasted with the excess returns made by some arbitrage funds in index arbitrage, where index futures are bought (or sold), and stocks in the index are sold short or (bought). This strategy requires that investors be able to obtain information on the index and spot prices instantaneously, have the capacity (in terms of margin requirements and resources) to trade index futures and to sell short on stocks, and to have the resources to take and hold very large positions until the arbitrage unwinds. Consequently, inefficiencies in index futures pricing are likely to persist at least for the most efficient arbitrageurs, with the lowest execution costs and the speediest execution times.

TESTING MARKET EFFICIENCY

Tests of market efficiency look at whether specific investment strategies earn excess returns. Some tests also account for transactions costs and execution feasibility. Since an excess return on an investment is the difference between the actual and expected return on that investment, there is implicit in every test of market efficiency a model for this expected return. In some cases, this expected return adjusts for risk using the capital asset pricing model (CAPM) or the arbitrage pricing model (APM), and in others the expected return is based on returns on similar or equivalent investments. In every case, a test of market efficiency is a joint test of market efficiency and the efficacy of the model used for expected returns. When there is evidence of excess returns in a test of market efficiency, it can indicate that markets are inefficient or that the model used to compute expected returns is wrong (or both). Although this may seem to present an insoluble dilemma, if the conclusions of the study are insensitive to different model specifications, it is much more likely that the results are being driven by true market inefficiencies and not just by model misspecifications.

There are several different ways of testing for market efficiency, and the approach used will depend in great part on the investment scheme being tested. A scheme based on trading on information events (stock splits, earnings announcements, or acquisition announcements) is likely to be tested using an "event study" in which returns around the event are scrutinized for evidence of excess returns. A scheme based on trading on an observable characteristic of a firm (price-earnings ratios, price–book value (BV) ratios, or dividend yields) is likely to be tested using a portfolio approach, where portfolios of stocks with these characteristics are created and tracked over time to see whether in fact they make excess returns. The following pages summarize the key steps involved in each of these approaches, and some potential pitfalls to watch out for when conducting or using these tests.

Event Study

An event study is designed to examine market reactions to and excess returns around specific information events. The information events can be market-wide, such as macroeconomic announcements, or firm-specific, such as earnings or dividend announcements. The five steps in an event study are:

1. The event to be studied is clearly identified, and the date on which the event was announced is pinpointed. The presumption in event studies is that the timing of the event is known with a fair degree of certainty. Since financial markets react to the information about an event rather than the event itself, most event studies are centered around the announcement date for the event[3].

Announcement Date

_____|_____

---

[3]In most financial transactions, the announcement date tends to precede the event date by several days and, sometimes, weeks.

2. Once the event dates are known, returns are collected around these dates for each of the firms in the sample. In doing so, two decisions must be made. First, the researcher has to decide whether to collect weekly, daily, or shorter-interval returns around the event. This will be determined in part by how precisely the event date is known (the more precise, the more likely it is that shorter return intervals can be used) and by how quickly information is reflected in prices (the faster the adjustment, the shorter the return interval to use). Second, the analyst must determine how many periods of returns before and after the announcement date will be considered as part of the event window. That decision also will be determined by the precision of the event date, since more imprecise dates will require longer windows.

$$
R_{-jn} \dots\dots\dots\dots\dots R_{j0} \dots\dots\dots\dots\dots R_{+jn}
$$
$$
\underline{\hspace{1cm}}|\underline{\hspace{3cm}}|\underline{\hspace{3cm}}|\underline{\hspace{1cm}}
$$

Return window: Period –n to +n

where R_{jt} = Returns on firm j for period $t(t = -n, \dots, 0, \dots, +n)$

3. The returns, by period, around the announcement date, are adjusted for market performance and risk to arrive at excess returns for each firm in the sample. For instance, if the capital asset pricing model is used to control for risk:

Excess return in period t = Return on period t – (Risk-free rate + Beta
$\times$ Return on market on day t)

$$
ER_{-jn} \dots\dots\dots\dots ER_{j0} \dots\dots\dots\dots ER_{+jn}
$$
$$
\underline{\hspace{1cm}}|\underline{\hspace{3cm}}|\underline{\hspace{3cm}}|\underline{\hspace{1cm}}
$$

Return window: –n to +n

where ER_{jt} = Excess returns on firm j for period $t(t = n, \dots, 0, \dots, +n) = R_{jt} - E(R_{jt})$

4. The excess returns, by period, are averaged across all observations in the sample, and a standard error is computed.

$$
\text{Average Excess Return}_t = \sum_{j=1}^{j=N} \frac{ER_{jt}}{N}
$$

$$
\text{Std error in Excess Return}_t = \sum_{j=1}^{j=N} \frac{\left(ER_{jt} - \text{Average ER}\right)}{(N-1)}
$$

where N = Number of observations (firms) in the event study

5. The question of whether the excess returns around the announcement are different from zero is answered by estimating the t statistic for each period, by dividing the average excess return by the standard error:

$$
\text{T statistics for Excess Return}_t = \frac{\text{Average Excess Return}_t}{\text{Standard error in Excess Return}_t}
$$

If the t statistics are statistically significant,[4] the event affects returns; the sign of the excess return determines whether the effect is positive or negative.

Event studies are useful in examining how markets react to news announcements or changes that have consequences for value. That said, there can be challenges, including identifying when markets become aware of the information (timing), sampling bias (both in the choice of firms to include in your sample and the events that you are testing) and statistical challenges.

ILLUSTRATION 6.1: Example of an Event Study—Effects of Option Listing on Stock Prices

Academics and practitioners have long argued about the consequences of option listing for stock price volatility. On the one hand, there are those who argue that options attract speculators, and hence increase stock price volatility. On the other hand, there are others who argue that options increase the available choices for investors and increase the flow of information to financial markets, and thus lead to lower stock price volatility and higher stock prices.

One way to test these alternative hypotheses is to do an event study, examining the effects of listing options on the underlying stocks' prices. Conrad (1989) did such a study, following these steps:

Step 1: The date of the announcement that options on a particular stock would be listed on the Chicago Board Options Exchange was collected.

Step 2: The prices of the underlying stock (j) were collected for each of the 10 days prior to the option listing announcement date, for the day of the announcement, and for each of the 10 days after.

Step 3: The returns on the stock (R_{jt}) were computed for each of these trading days.

Step 4: The beta for the stock (β_j) was estimated using the returns from a time period outside the event window (using 100 trading days from before the event and 100 trading days after the event).

Step 5: The returns on the market index (R_{mt}) were computed for each of the 21 trading days.

Step 6: The excess returns were computed for each of the 21 trading days (t) for each stock (j):

$$ER_{jt} = R_{jt} - \beta_j R_m \qquad t = -10, -9, -8, \ldots, +8, +9, +10$$

The excess returns are accumulated for each trading day.

Step 7: The average and standard error of excess returns across all stocks with option listings were computed for each of the 21 trading days. The t statistics are computed using the averages and standard errors for each trading day. Table 6.1 summarizes the average excess returns and t statistics around option listing announcement dates:

TABLE 6.1 Excess Returns around Option Listing Announcements

Trading Day	Average Excess Return	Cumulative Excess Return	T Statistic
−10	0.17%	0.17%	1.30
−9	0.48%	0.65%	1.66
−8	−0.24%	0.41%	1.43

---

[4]The standard levels of significance for t statistics are:

Level	One-Tailed	Two-Tailed
1%	2.33	2.55
5%	1.66	1.96

Trading Day	Average Excess Return	Cumulative Excess Return	T Statistic
−7	0.28%	0.69%	1.62
−6	0.04%	0.73%	1.62
−5	−0.46%	0.27%	1.24
−4	−0.26%	0.01%	1.02
−3	−0.11%	−0.10%	0.93
−2	0.26%	0.16%	1.09
−1	0.29%	0.45%	1.28
0	0.01%	0.46%	1.27
1	0.17%	0.63%	1.37
2	0.14%	0.77%	1.44
3	0.04%	0.81%	1.44
4	0.18%	0.99%	1.54
5	0.56%	1.55%	1.88
6	0.22%	1.77%	1.99
7	0.05%	1.82%	2.00
8	−0.13%	1.69%	1.89
9	0.09%	1.78%	1.92
10	0.02%	1.80%	1.91

Based on these excess returns, there is no evidence of an announcement effect on the announcement day alone, but there is mild evidence of a positive effect over the entire announcement period.[5]

Portfolio Study

In some investment strategies, firms with specific characteristics are viewed as more likely to be undervalued, and therefore to have excess returns, than firms without these characteristics. In these cases, the strategies can be tested by creating portfolios of firms possessing these characteristics at the beginning of a time period, and then examining returns over the time period. To ensure that these results are not colored by the idiosyncrasies of one time period, this analysis is repeated for a number of periods. The seven steps in doing a portfolio study are:

1. The variable on which firms will be classified is defined, using the investment strategy as a guide. This variable must be observable, and though it is easier if it is quantifiable, it can be qualitative. Quantitative examples would include market value (MV) of equity, stock prices, price-earnings ratios, and price–book value ratios. Qualitative variables could include management quality, default risk, or company reputation, though you will need measures of each to move forward.

---

[5] The t statistics are marginally significant at the 5% level.

2. The data on the variable is collected for every firm in the defined universe[6] at the *start* of the testing period, and firms are classified into portfolios based on the magnitude of the variable. Thus, if the price-earnings ratio is the screening variable, firms are classified based on PE ratios into portfolios from lowest PE to highest PE classes. The number of classes will depend on the size of the universe, since there have to be sufficient firms in each portfolio to get some measure of diversification.

3. The returns are collected for each firm in each portfolio for the testing period, and the returns for each portfolio are computed, making the decision to weight them either equally or based on value.

4. The returns should be adjusted for risk. If you are using conventional risk and return models in finance, the beta (if using a single-factor model) or betas (if using a multifactor model) of each portfolio are estimated, either by taking the average of the betas of the individual stocks in the portfolio or by regressing the portfolio's returns against market returns over a prior period (for instance, the year before the testing period). If you prefer to be model agnostic, you can compare the returns to overall market or sector returns.

5. The excess returns earned by each portfolio are computed, in conjunction with the standard error of the excess returns.

6. There are several statistical tests available to check whether the average excess returns are, in fact, different across the portfolios. Some of these tests are parametric[7] (they make certain distributional assumptions about excess returns), and some are nonparametric.[8]

7. As a final test, the extreme portfolios can be matched against each other to see whether there are statistically significant differences across these portfolios.

ILLUSTRATION 6.2:   Example of a Portfolio Study—Price-Earnings Ratios

Practitioners have claimed that low price-earnings ratio stocks are generally bargains and do much better than the market or stocks with high price-earnings ratios. This hypothesis can be tested using a portfolio approach:

Step 1: Using data on price-earnings ratios from the end of 1987, firms on the New York Stock Exchange were classified into five groups, the first group consisting of stocks with the lowest PE ratios and the fifth group consisting of stocks with the highest PE ratios. Firms with negative price-earnings ratios were ignored (which may bias the results).

Step 2: The returns on each portfolio were computed using data from 1988 to 1992. Stocks that went bankrupt or were delisted were assigned a return of −100%.

Step 3: The betas for each stock in each portfolio were computed using monthly returns from 1983 to 1987, and the average beta for each portfolio was estimated. The portfolios were assumed to be equally weighted.

---

[6] Though there are practical limits on how big the universe can be, care should be taken to make sure that no biases enter at this stage of the process. An obvious bias would be to pick only stocks that have done well over the time period for the universe.

[7] One parametric test is an F test, which tests for equality of means across groups. This test can be conducted assuming either that the groups have the same variance or that they have different variances.

[8] An example of a nonparametric test is a rank sum test, which ranks returns across the entire sample, and then sums the ranks within each group to check whether the rankings are random or systematic.

TABLE 6.2 Average Excess Returns, by PE quintile

PE Class	1988	1989	1990	1991	1992	1988–1992
Lowest	3.84%	−0.83%	2.10%	6.68%	0.64%	2.61%
2	1.75%	2.26%	0.19%	1.09%	1.13%	1.56%
3	0.20%	−3.15%	−0.20%	0.17%	0.12%	−0.59%
4	−1.25%	−0.94%	−0.65%	−1.99%	−0.48%	−1.15%
Highest	−1.74%	−0.63%	−1.44%	−4.06%	−1.25%	−1.95%

Step 4: The returns on the market index were computed from 1988 to 1992.

Step 5: The excess returns on each portfolio were computed from 1988 to 1992. Table 6.2 summarizes the excess returns each year from 1988 to 1992 for each portfolio.

Step 6: While the ranking of the returns across the portfolio classes seems to confirm our hypothesis that low-PE stocks earn a higher return, we must consider whether the differences across portfolios are statistically significant. There are several tests available, but these are a few:

- An F test can be used to accept or reject the hypothesis that the average returns are the same across all portfolios. A high F score would lead us to conclude that the differences are too large to be random.

- A chi-squared test is a nonparametric test that can be used to test the hypothesis that the means are the same across the five portfolio classes.

- We could isolate just the lowest-PE and highest-PE stocks and estimate a t statistic that the averages are different across these two portfolios.

CARDINAL SINS IN TESTING MARKET EFFICIENCY

In the process of testing investment strategies, there are a number of pitfalls that have to be avoided. Six of them are:

1. *Using anecdotal evidence to support/reject an investment strategy.* Anecdotal evidence is a double-edged sword. It can be used to support or reject the same hypothesis. Since stock prices are noisy and all investment schemes (no matter how absurd) will succeed sometimes and fail at other times, there will always be cases where the scheme works or does not work.

2. *Testing an investment strategy on the same data and period from which it was extracted.* This is the tool of choice for the unscrupulous investment strategist. An investment scheme is extracted from hundreds through an examination of the data for a particular time period. This investment scheme is then tested over the same time period, with predictable results. (The scheme does miraculously well and makes immense returns.) An investment scheme should always be tested out on a time period different from the one it is extracted from or on a universe different from the one used to derive the scheme.

3. *Choosing a biased sample.* There may be bias in the sample on which the test is run. Since there are thousands of stocks that could be considered part of this universe,

researchers often choose to use a smaller sample. When this choice is random, this does limited damage to the results of the study. If the choice is biased, it can provide results that are not true in the larger universe.

4. *Failure to control for market performance.* A failure to control for overall market performance can lead you to conclude that your investment scheme works just because it makes good returns (most schemes will make good returns if the overall market does well; the question is whether they made better returns than expected), or does not work just because it makes bad returns (most schemes will do badly if the overall market performs poorly). It is crucial therefore that investment schemes control for market performance during the period of the test.

5. *Failure to control for risk.* A failure to control for risk leads to a bias toward accepting high-risk investment schemes and rejecting low-risk investment schemes, since the former should make higher returns than the market and the latter lower, without implying any excess returns.

6. *Mistaking correlation for causation.* Consider the study on PE stocks cited in the earlier section. We concluded that low-PE stocks have higher excess returns than high-PE stocks. It would be a mistake to conclude that a low price-earnings ratio causes excess returns, since the high returns and the low PE ratio themselves might have been caused by the high risk associated with investing in the stock. In other words, high risk is the causative factor that leads to both the observed phenomena—low PE ratios on the one hand, and high returns on the other. This insight would make us more cautious about adopting a strategy of buying low-PE stocks in the first place.

SOME LESSER SINS THAT CAN BE A PROBLEM

1. *Survival bias.* Most researchers start with an existing universe of publicly traded companies and work back through time to test investment strategies. This can create a subtle bias since it automatically eliminates firms that failed during the period, with obvious negative consequences for returns. If the investment scheme is particularly susceptible to picking firms that have high bankruptcy risk, this may lead to an overstatement of returns on the scheme. For example, assume that the investment scheme recommends investing in stocks that have very negative earnings, using the argument that these stocks are the most likely to benefit from a turnaround. Some of the firms in this portfolio will go bankrupt, and a failure to consider these firms will overstate the returns from this strategy.

2. *Not allowing for transaction costs.* Some investment schemes are more expensive than others because of transaction costs—execution fees, bid-ask spreads, and price impact. A complete test will take these into account before it passes judgment on the strategy. This is easier said than done, because different investors have different transaction costs, and it is unclear which investor's trading cost schedule should be used in the test. Most researchers who ignore transaction costs argue that individual investors can decide for themselves, given their transaction costs, whether the excess returns justify the investment strategy.

3. *Not allowing for difficulties in execution.* Some strategies look good on paper but are difficult to execute in practice, either because of impediments to trading or because

trading creates a price impact. A strategy of investing in very small companies may seem to create excess returns on paper, but these excess returns may not exist in practice because the price impact that you have when trading, pushing prices up as you buy and down as you sell, is significant.

4. *Information timing.* In testing strategies, especially those built around information announcements, a key question that has to be answered is when the information would be accessible to investors, and whether you would have the time to trade on that information. For instance, later in this chapter, we will look at returns that can be made around insider buying or selling, with that information coming from filings by insiders with the Securities and Exchange Commission (SEC). However, during the period of these studies, those filings would not have been public information until weeks after the filing, altering the timing of investment.

EVIDENCE ON MARKET EFFICIENCY

This section of the chapter attempts to summarize the evidence from studies of market efficiency. Without claiming to be comprehensive, the evidence is classified into four sections—the study of price changes and their time series properties, the research on the efficiency of market reaction to information announcements, the existence of return anomalies across firms and over time, and the analysis of the performance of insiders, analysts, and money managers.

TIME SERIES PROPERTIES OF PRICE CHANGES

Investors have used price charts and price patterns as tools for predicting future price movements for as long as there have been financial markets. It is not surprising, therefore, that the first studies of market efficiency focused on the relationship between price changes over time, to see if in fact such predictions were feasible. Some of this testing was spurred by the random walk theory of price movements, which contended that price changes over time followed a random walk. As the studies of the time series properties of prices have proliferated, the evidence can be classified into two categories—studies that focus on short-term price behavior (intraday, daily, and weekly price movements) and research that examines the longer term (monthly, annual, and multi-year).

Short-Term Price Movements   The notion that today's price change conveys information about tomorrow's price change is deeply rooted in most investors' psyches. There are several ways in which this hypothesis can be tested in financial markets.

Serial Correlation   The serial correlation measures the correlation between price changes in consecutive time periods, whether hourly, daily, or weekly, and is a measure of how much the price change in any period depends on the price change over the previous period. A serial correlation of zero would therefore imply that price changes in consecutive time periods are uncorrelated with each other, and can thus be viewed as a rejection of the hypothesis that investors can learn about future price changes from past ones. A serial correlation that is positive and statistically significant could be viewed as evidence of price momentum in markets, and would suggest that returns in a period are more likely to be positive if the prior period's returns were positive, and negative if previous returns were negative. A serial correlation that is negative and statistically significant could be evidence of price reversals, and would be consistent with a market where positive returns are more likely to follow negative returns and vice versa.

From the viewpoint of investment strategy, serial correlations can be exploited to earn excess returns. A positive serial correlation would be exploited by a strategy of buying after periods with positive returns and selling after periods with negative returns. A negative serial correlation would suggest a strategy of buying after periods with negative returns and selling after periods with positive returns. Since these strategies generate transactions costs, the correlations must be large enough to allow investors to generate profits to cover these costs. It is therefore entirely possible that there is a serial correlation in returns, without any opportunity to earn excess returns for most investors.

The earliest studies of serial correlation—Alexander (1964), Cootner (1962), and Fama (1965)—all looked at large U.S. stocks and concluded that the serial correlation in stock prices was small. Fama, for instance, found that 8 of the 30 stocks listed in the Dow had negative serial correlations and that most of the serial correlations were less than 0.05. Other studies confirm these findings not only for smaller stocks in the United States, but also for other markets. For instance, Jennergren and Korsvold (1974) report low serial correlations for the Swedish equity market, and Cootner (1961) concludes that serial correlations are low in commodity markets as well. Although there may be statistical significance associated with some of these correlations, it is unlikely that there is enough correlation to generate excess returns.

The serial correlation in short period returns is affected by market liquidity and the presence of a bid-ask spread. Not all stocks in an index are liquid, and in some cases, stocks may not trade during a period. When the stock trades in a subsequent period, the resulting price changes can create a positive serial correlation. To see why, assume that the market is up strongly on day 1, but that three stocks in the index do not trade on that day. On day 2, if these stocks are traded, they are likely to go up in price to reflect the increase in the market the previous day. The net result is that you should expect to see positive serial correlation in daily or hourly returns in illiquid market indexes.

The bid-ask spread creates a bias in the opposite direction, if transaction prices are used to compute returns, since prices have an equal chance of ending up at the bid or the ask price. The bounce that this induces in prices—from bid to ask to bid again—will result in negative serial correlations in returns. Roll (1984) provides a simple measure of this relationship:

$$\text{Bid Ask Spread Effect} = \sqrt{2 \,(\text{Serial covariance in returns})}$$

where the serial covariance in returns measures the covariance between return changes in consecutive time periods. For very short return intervals, this bias induced in serial correlations might dominate and create the mistaken view that price changes in consecutive time periods are negatively correlated.

Filter Rules In a filter rule, an investor buys an investment if the price rises X percent from a previous low and holds the investment until the price drops X percent from a previous high. The magnitude of the change (X percent) that triggers the trades can vary from filter rule to filter rule, with smaller changes resulting in more transactions per period and higher transaction costs. Figure 6.1 graphs out a typical filter rule.

This strategy assumes that price changes are serially correlated and that there is price momentum (i.e., stocks that have gone up strongly in the past are more likely to keep going up than to go down). Table 6.3 summarizes results—Fama and Blume (1966) and Jensen and Bennington (1970)—from a study on returns, before and after transactions costs, on a trading strategy based on filter rules ranging from 0.5 percent to 20 percent. (A 0.5-percent rule implies that a stock is bought when it rises 0.5 percent from a previous low, and is sold when it falls 0.5 percent from a prior high.)

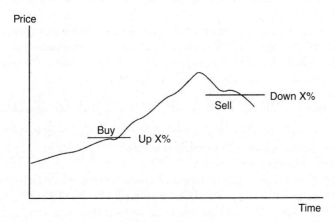

FIGURE 6.1 Filter Rule

TABLE 6.3 Returns on Filter Rule Strategies

Filter Rule Trigger	Return with Strategy	Return with Buy & Hold	Number of transactions	Return after transactions costs
0.50%	11.50%	10.40%	12,514	−103.6%
1.00%	5.50%	10.30%	8,660	−74.9%
2.00%	0.20%	10.30%	4,764	−45.2%
3.00%	−1.7%	10.10%	2,994	−30.5%
4.00%	0.10%	10.10%	2,013	−19.5%
5.00%	−1.9%	10.00%	1,484	−16.6%
6.00%	1.30%	9.70%	1,071	−9.4%
7.00%	0.80%	9.60%	828	−7.4%
8.00%	1.70%	9.60%	653	−5.0%
9.00%	1.90%	9.60%	539	−3.6%
10.00%	3.00%	9.60%	435	−1.4%
12.00%	5.30%	9.40%	289	2.30%
14.00%	3.90%	10.30%	224	1.40%
16.00%	4.20%	10.30%	172	2.30%
18.00%	3.60%	10.00%	139	2.00%
20.00%	4.30%	9.80%	110	3.00%

The only filter rule that beats the returns from the buy-and-hold strategy is the 0.5-percent rule, but it does so before transaction costs. This strategy creates 12,514 trades during the period, which generates enough transaction costs to wipe out the principal invested by the investor. While this test is dated, it also illustrates basic problems with strategies that require frequent short-term trading. Even though these strategies may earn excess returns prior to transaction costs, adjusting for these costs can wipe out the excess returns.

One popular indicator among investors that is a variant on the filter rule is the relative strength measure, which relates recent prices on stocks or other investments either to average prices over a specified period, say over six months, or to the price at the beginning of the period. Stocks that score high on the relative strength measure are considered good investments. This investment strategy is also based upon the assumption of price momentum.

Runs Tests   A runs test is a nonparametric variation on the serial correlation, and it is based on a count of the number of runs (i.e., sequences of price increases or decreases) in the price changes. Thus, the following time series of price changes, where U is an increase and D is a decrease, would result in the following runs:

UUU DD U DDD UU DD U D UU DD U DD UUU DD UU D UU D

There were 18 runs in this price series of 33 periods. The actual number of runs in the price series is compared against the number that can be expected in a series of this length, assuming that price changes are random.[9] If the actual number of runs is greater than the expected number, there is evidence of negative correlation in price changes. If it is lower, there is evidence of positive correlation. A 1966 study by Niederhoffer and Osborne of price changes in the Dow 30 stocks assuming daily, four-day, nine-day, and 16-day return intervals provided the following results:

	Differencing Interval			
	Daily	Four-day	Nine-day	Sixteen-day
Actual runs	735.1*	175.7	74.6	41.6
Expected runs	759.8	175.8	75.3	41.7

Based on these results, there is evidence of positive correlation in daily returns but no evidence of deviations from normality for longer return intervals.

Again, while the evidence is dated, it serves to illustrate the point that long strings of positive and negative changes are, by themselves, insufficient evidence that markets are not random, since such behavior is consistent with price changes following a random walk. It is the recurrence of these strings that can be viewed as evidence against randomness in price behavior.

Longer-Term Price Movements   While most of the earlier studies of price behavior focused on shorter return intervals, more attention has been paid to price movements over longer periods (one-year to five-year periods) in recent years. Here, there is an interesting dichotomy in the results. When *long term* is defined as months rather than years, there

---

[9]There are statistical tables that summarize the expected number of runs, assuming randomness, in a series of any length.

seems to be a tendency toward positive serial correlation or price momentum. However, when *long term* is defined in terms of years, there is substantial negative correlation in the returns, suggesting that markets reverse themselves over long periods.

Weekly and Monthly Price Momentum In the preceding section, we noted that the evidence of short-term price patterns is weak, and that any price dependence over very short time periods (minutes or hours) can be attributed more to market structure (liquidity, bid-ask spreads) than to inefficiency. We also argued that while chartists who track these short-term price movements abound, few seem to emerge as consistent winners. As we extend our time periods from minutes to days and from days to weeks, there is some evidence of price momentum. Put differently, stocks that have gone up in the last few weeks or months seem to tend to continue to outperform the market in the next few weeks or months, and stocks that have gone down in the recent weeks or months continue to languish in the next few weeks or months.

Jegadeesh and Titman (1993, 2001) present evidence of what they call price momentum in stock prices over time periods of up to eight months—stocks that have gone up in the last six months tend to continue to go up, whereas stocks that have gone down in the last six months tend to continue to go down. The momentum effect is just as strong in the European markets, though it seems to be weaker in emerging markets. What may cause this momentum? One potential explanation is that mutual funds are more likely to buy past winners and dump past losers, thus generating price continuity.

Annual or Multi-year Price Reversal When the long term is defined in terms of years, there is a negative correlation in returns, suggesting that markets reverse themselves over very long periods. Fama and French (1988) examined five-year returns on stocks from 1941 to 1985 and present evidence of this phenomenon. They found that serial correlation is more negative in five-year returns than in one-year returns and is much more negative for smaller stocks rather than larger stocks. Figure 6.2 summarizes one-year and five-years serial correlation by size class for stocks on the New York Stock Exchange.

Since there is evidence that prices reverse themselves in the long term, it might be worth examining whether such price reversals can be used by investors to profit. To isolate the effect of such price reversals on the extreme portfolios, DeBondt and Thaler constructed a winner portfolio of 35 stocks that had gone up the most over the prior year, and a loser portfolio of 35 stocks that had gone down the most over the prior year, each year from 1933 to 1978, and examined returns on these portfolios for the sixty months following the creation of the portfolio. Figure 6.3 summarizes the excess returns for winner and loser portfolios. This analysis suggests that loser portfolios clearly outperform winner portfolios in the 60 months following creation. This evidence is consistent with market overreaction and correction in long return intervals.

There are many academics as well as practitioners, who suggest that these findings may be interesting, but that they overstate potential returns on loser portfolios. For instance, there is evidence that loser portfolios are more likely to contain low-priced stocks (selling for less than $5), which generate higher transactions costs and are also more likely to offer heavily skewed returns; that is, the excess returns come from a few stocks making phenomenal returns rather than from consistent performance. One study of the winner and loser portfolios attributes the bulk of the excess returns of loser portfolios to low-priced stocks and finds that the results are sensitive to when the portfolios are created. Loser portfolios created every December earn significantly higher returns than portfolios created every June.

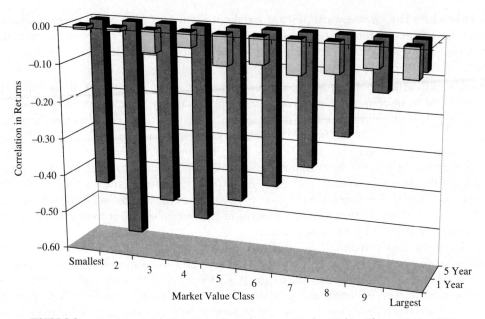

FIGURE 6.2   One-Year and Five-Year Correlations: Market Value Class, 1941–1985
Source: Adapted from Fama et. al., 1988.

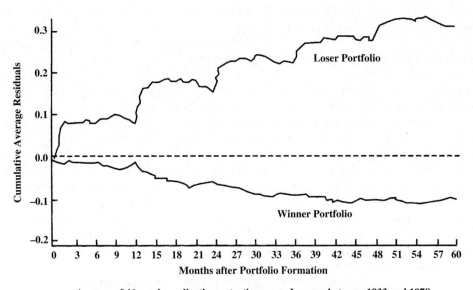

Average of 46 yearly replications, starting every January between 1933 and 1978.

FIGURE 6.3   Excess Returns for Winner and Loser Portfolios
Source: DeBondt et. al., 1985, John Wiley & Sons.

Speculative Bubbles, Crashes, and Panics   Historians who have examined the behavior of financial markets over time have challenged the assumption of rationality that underlies much of efficient market theory. They point to the frequency with which speculative bubbles have formed in financial markets as investors buy into fads or get-rich-quick schemes, and the crashes when these bubbles have ended, and suggest that there is nothing to prevent the recurrence of this phenomenon in today's financial markets. There is some evidence in the literature of irrationality on the part of market players.

Experimental Studies of Rationality   Some of the most interesting evidence on market efficiency and rationality in recent years has come from experimental studies. While most experimental studies suggest that traders are rational, there are some examples of irrational behavior in some of these studies.

One such study was done at the University of Arizona. In an experimental study, traders were told that a payout would be declared after each trading day, determined randomly from four possibilities— 0, 8, 28, or 60 cents. The average payout was 24 cents. Thus, the share's expected value on the first trading day of a 15-day experiment was $3.60 (24 cents times 15), the second day was $3.36, and so on. The traders were allowed to trade each day. The results of 60 such experiments are summarized in Figure 6.4.

There is clear evidence here of a speculative bubble forming during periods 3–5, where prices exceed expected values by a significant amount. The bubble ultimately bursts, and prices approach the expected value by the end of the period. If this mispricing is feasible in a simple market, where every investor obtains the same information, it is clearly feasible in real financial markets, where there is much more differential information and much greater uncertainty about expected value.

It should be pointed out that some of the experiments were run with students, and some with Tucson businessmen with real-world experience. The results were similar for both groups. Furthermore, when price curbs of 15 cents were introduced, the booms lasted even longer because traders knew that prices would not fall by more than 15 cents in a period. Thus, the notion that price limits can control speculative bubbles seems misguided.

Behavioral Finance   The irrationality sometimes exhibited by investors has given rise to a whole new area of finance called behavioral finance. Using evidence gathered from experimental psychology, researchers have tried both models to see how investors react to

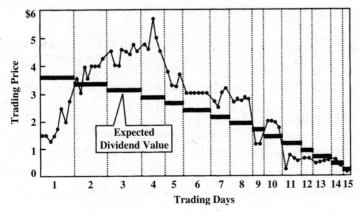

FIGURE 6.4   Trading Price by Trading Day

information and predict how prices will change as a consequence. They have been far more successful at the first endeavor than the second. For instance, the evidence seems to suggest that:

- Investors do not like to admit their mistakes. Consequently, they tend to hold on to losing stocks far too long, or in some cases double up their bets (investments) as stocks drop in value.
- More information does not always lead to better investment decisions. Investors seem to suffer both from information overload and from a tendency to react to the latest piece of information. Both result in investment decisions that lower returns in the long term.

If the evidence on how investors behave is so clear-cut, you might ask, why are the predictions that emerge from these models so noisy? The answer, perhaps, is that any model that tries to forecast human foibles and irrationalities is, by its very nature, unlikely to be a stable one. Behavioral finance may emerge ultimately as a trump card in explaining why and how stock prices deviate from true value, but its role in devising investment strategy remains questionable.

BEHAVIORAL FINANCE AND VALUATION

In 1999, Robert Shiller made waves in both academia and investment houses with his book titled *Irrational Exuberance*. His thesis is that investors are often not just irrational but irrational in predictable ways—overreacting to some information and buying and selling in herds. His work forms part of a growing body of theory and evidence of behavioral finance, which can be viewed as a congruence of psychology, statistics, and finance.

While the evidence presented for investor irrationality is strong, the implications for valuation are less so. You can consider discounted cash flow valuation to be the antithesis of behavioral finance, because it takes the point of view that the value of an asset is the present value of the expected cash flows generated by that asset. With this context, there are two ways in which you can look at the findings in behavioral finance:

1. Irrational behavior may explain why prices can deviate from value (as estimated in a discounted cash flow model). Consequently, it provides the foundation for the excess returns earned by rational investors who base decisions on estimated value. Implicit here is the assumption that markets ultimately recognize their irrationality and correct themselves.
2. It may also explain why discounted cash flow values can deviate from pricing (estimated using multiples). Since the pricing is estimated by looking at how the market prices similar assets, irrationalities that exist will be priced into the asset.

MARKET REACTION TO INFORMATION EVENTS

Some of the most powerful tests of market efficiency are event studies where market reaction to informational events (such as earnings and takeover announcements) has been scrutinized for evidence of inefficiency. While it is consistent with market efficiency for markets to react to new information, the reaction has to be instantaneous and unbiased. This point is made in Figure 6.5 by contrasting three different market reactions to information announcements containing good news.

Of the three market reactions pictured here, only the first one is consistent with an efficient market. In the second market, the information announcement is followed by a gradual increase in prices, allowing investors to make excess returns after the announcement. This is a slow learning market in which some investors will make excess returns on the price drift. In the third market, the price reacts instantaneously to the announcement but corrects itself in the days that follow, suggesting that the initial price change was an overreaction to the information. Here again, an enterprising investor could have sold short after the announcement and expected to make excess returns as a consequence of the price correction.

Earnings Announcements

When firms make earnings announcements, they convey information to financial markets about their current and future prospects. The magnitude of the information, and the size of the market reaction, should depend on how much the earnings report exceeds or falls short of investor expectations. In an efficient market, there should be an instantaneous reaction to the earnings report, if it contains surprising information, and prices should increase following positive surprises and decline following negative surprises.

Since actual earnings are compared to investor expectations, one of the key parts of an earnings event study is the measurement of these expectations. Some of the earlier studies used earnings from the same quarter in the prior year as a measure of expected earnings (i.e., firms that report increases in quarter-to-quarter earnings provide positive surprises, and those that report decreases in quarter-to-quarter earnings provide negative surprises). In more recent studies, analyst estimates of earnings have been used as a proxy for expected earnings and compared to the actual earnings.

Figure 6.6 provides a graph of price reactions to earnings surprises, classified based on magnitude into different classes from "most negative" earnings reports (group 1) to most positive earnings reports (group 10). The evidence contained in this graph is consistent with the evidence in most earnings announcement studies.

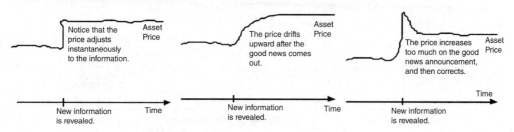

FIGURE 6.5   Information and Price Adjustment

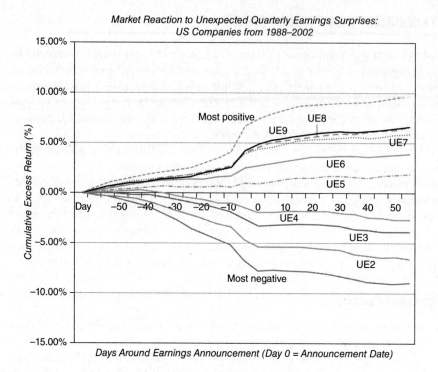

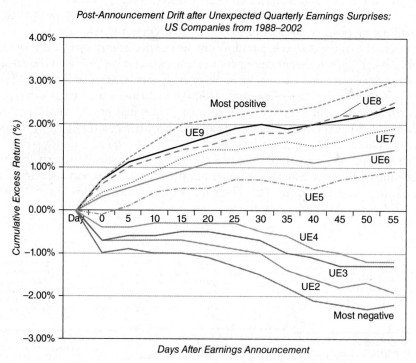

FIGURE 6.6   Pre- and Post-Announcement Drift after Unexpected Quarterly Earnings Surprises: U.S. Companies from 1988 to 2002
Source: Adapted from Nichols et. al., 2004.

■ The earnings announcement clearly conveys valuable information to financial markets; there are positive excess returns (cumulative abnormal returns) around positive announcements and negative excess returns around negative announcements.

■ There is some evidence of a market reaction in the days immediately prior to the earnings announcement that is consistent with the nature of the announcement (i.e., prices tend to go up on the day before positive announcements and down on the day before negative announcements). This can be viewed as evidence of either insider trading, information leakage, or getting the announcement date wrong.[10]

■ There is some evidence, albeit weak, of a price drift in the days following an earnings announcement. Thus, a positive report evokes a positive market reaction on the announcement date, and there are mildly positive excess returns in the days following the earnings announcement. Similar conclusions emerge for negative earnings reports.

The management of a firm has some discretion on the timing of earnings reports, and there is some evidence that the timing affects expected returns. A 1989 study of earnings reports, classified by the day of the week that the earnings are reported, reveals that earnings and dividend reports on Fridays are much more likely to contain negative information than announcements on any other day of the week. This is shown in Figure 6.7.

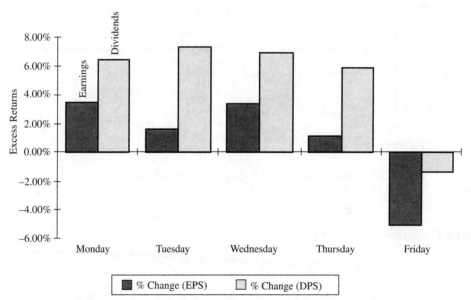

FIGURE 6.7   Earnings and Dividend Reports by Day of the Week
Source: Adapted from Damodaran (1989).

---

[10]The financial news media is often used as an information source to extract announcement dates for earnings. For some firms, news of the announcement may cross the newswire the day before the financial news announcement, leading to a misidentification of the report date and the drift in returns the day before the announcement.

There is also some evidence discussed by Chambers and Penman (1984) that earnings announcements that are delayed, relative to the expected announcement date, are much more likely to contain bad news than earnings announcements that are early or on time. This is graphed in Figure 6.8. Earnings announcements that are more than six days late relative to the expected announcement date are much more likely to contain bad news and evoke negative market reactions than earnings announcements that are on time or early.

Investment and Project Announcements

Firms frequently make announcements of their intentions of investing resources in projects and research and development. There is evidence that financial markets react to these announcements. The question of whether markets have a long-term or short-term perspective can be partially answered by looking at these market reactions. If financial markets are as short-term as some of their critics claim, they should react negatively to announcements by the firm that it plans to invest in research and development. As Table 6.4, which looks at market reactions to various investment announcements makes clear, the evidence suggests that the market reaction to investment announcements is generally positive, albeit discriminating.

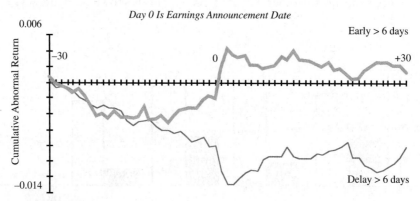

FIGURE 6.8   Cumulated Abnormal Returns and Earnings Delay
Source: Adapted from Chambers et. al., 1984.

TABLE 6.4   Market Reactions to Investment Announcements

	Abnormal Returns	
Type of Announcement	On Announcement Day	In Announcement Month
Joint venture formations	0.399%	1.412%
R&D expenditures	0.251%	1.456%
Product strategies	0.440%	−0.35%
Capital expenditures	0.290%	1.499%
All announcements	0.355%	0.984%

Source: Chan, Martin, and Kensinger (1990); McConnell and Muscarella (1985).

This table excludes the largest investments that most firms make, which are acquisitions of other firms. Here the evidence is not so favorable. In about 55 percent of all acquisitions, the stock price of the acquiring firm drops on the announcement of the acquisition, reflecting the market's beliefs that firms tend to overpay on acquisitions.

MARKET ANOMALIES

Merriam-Webster's Collegiate Dictionary defines an anomaly as a "deviation from the common rule". Studies of market efficiency have uncovered numerous examples of market behavior that are inconsistent with existing models of risk and return and often defy rational explanation. The persistence of some of these patterns of behavior suggests that the problem, in at least some of these anomalies, lies in the models being used for risk and return rather than in the behavior of financial markets. The following section summarizes some of the more widely noticed anomalies in financial markets in the United States and elsewhere.

Anomalies Based on Firm Characteristics

There are a number of anomalies that have been related to observable firm characteristics, including the market value of equity, price-earnings ratios, and price–book value ratios.

The Small Firm Effect Studies such as Banz (1981) and Keim (1983) have consistently found that smaller firms (in terms of market value of equity) earn higher returns than larger firms of equivalent risk, where risk is defined in terms of the market beta. Figure 6.9 summarizes returns for stocks in 10 market value classes, on both an equally and value-weighted basis, for the period from 1927 to 2023.

The size of the small firm premium, while it has varied across time, has been generally positive. It was highest during the 1970s and early 1980s and lowest during the 1990s before returning in the first half of the last decade. The persistence of this premium has led to several possible explanations.

1. The transaction costs of investing in small stocks are significantly higher than the transaction costs of investing in larger stocks, and the premiums are estimated prior to these costs. While this is generally true, the differential transaction costs are unlikely to explain the magnitude of the premium across time, and are likely to become even less critical for longer investment horizons.
2. The capital asset pricing model may not be the right model for risk, and betas underestimate the true risk of small stocks. Thus, the small firm premium is really a measure of the failure of beta to capture risk. The additional risk associated with small stocks may come from several sources. First, the estimation risk associated with estimates of beta for small firms is much greater than the estimation risk associated with beta estimates for larger firms. The small firm premium may be a reward for this additional estimation risk. Second, there may be additional risk in investing in small stocks because far less information is available on these stocks. In fact, studies indicate that stocks that are neglected by analysts and institutional investors earn an excess return that parallels the small firm premium.

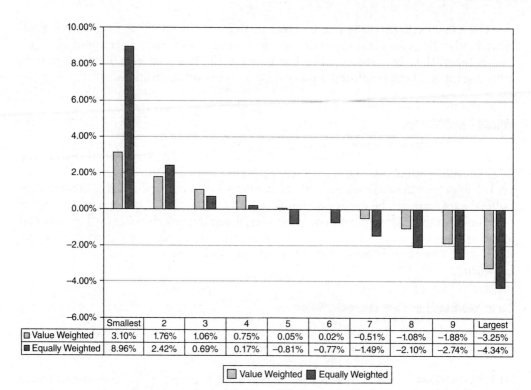

	Smallest	2	3	4	5	6	7	8	9	Largest
☐ Value Weighted	3.10%	1.76%	1.06%	0.75%	0.05%	0.02%	−0.51%	−1.08%	−1.88%	−3.25%
■ Equally Weighted	8.96%	2.42%	0.69%	0.17%	−0.81%	−0.77%	−1.49%	−2.10%	−2.74%	−4.34%

☐ Value Weighted   ■ Equally Weighted

FIGURE 6.9   Annual Returns by Size Class, 1927–2023
Source: Adapted from Ken French data.

There is evidence of a small firm premium in markets outside the United States as well. Dimson and Marsh (1986) examined stocks in the United Kingdom from 1955 to 1984 and found that the annual returns on small stocks exceeded those on large stocks by 6 percent annually over the period. Chan, Hamao, and Lakonishok (1991) report a small firm premium of about 5 percent for Japanese stocks between 1971 and 1988.

Most importantly, the small cap premium has been not only volatile but has shrunk over time. In Figure 6.10, we have graphed the differential between the annual return on the smallest cap decile and the largest cap decile, for US stocks, on a year-to-year basis from 1927 to 2023.

Since 1981, there has been no small cap premium, and stocks in the lowest decile (smallest companies) have earned, on average, returns that are 0.84% lower than the companies in the highest decile.

Price-Earnings Ratios   Investors have long argued that stocks with low price-earnings ratios are more likely to be undervalued and earn excess returns. For instance, Benjamin Graham, in his investment classic *The Intelligent Investor*,[11] used low price-earnings ratios as a screen for finding undervalued stocks. Studies (Basu 1977, 1983) that have looked at the relationship between PE ratios and excess returns confirm these priors. Figure 6.11 summarizes annual returns by PE ratio classes for stocks from 1952 to 2023. Firms in the

---

[11]Graham, B., 1949, The Intelligent Investor (New York: Harper Business, reprinted in 2005).

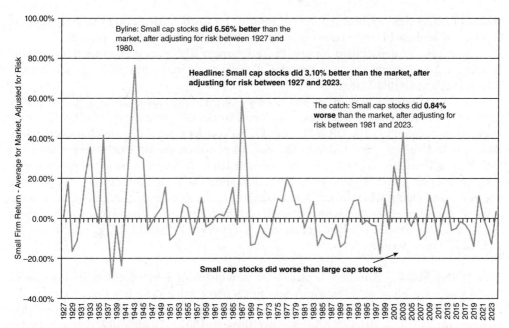

FIGURE 6.10 Small Cap Premium, by year—1927–2023
Source: Adapted from Ken French data.

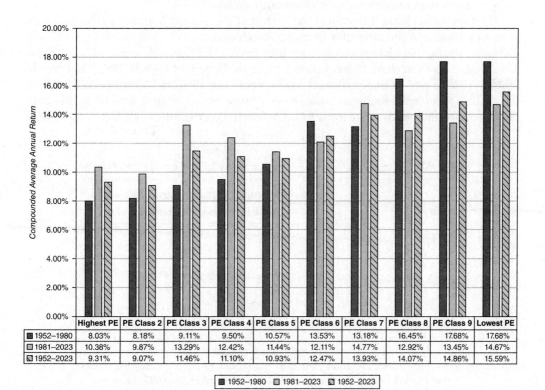

	Highest PE	PE Class 2	PE Class 3	PE Class 4	PE Class 5	PE Class 6	PE Class 7	PE Class 8	PE Class 9	Lowest PE
1952–1980	8.03%	8.18%	9.11%	9.50%	10.57%	13.53%	13.18%	16.45%	17.68%	17.68%
1981–2023	10.38%	9.87%	13.29%	12.42%	11.44%	12.11%	14.77%	12.92%	13.45%	14.67%
1952–2023	9.31%	9.07%	11.46%	11.10%	10.93%	12.47%	13.93%	14.07%	14.86%	15.59%

■ 1952–1980 ☐ 1981–2023 ▨ 1952–2023

FIGURE 6.11 PE Ratios and Stock Returns, 1952–2023

lowest PE ratio class earned an average return of 15.6 percent during the period, while firms in the highest PE ratio class earned an average return of only 9.3 percent.

The excess returns earned by low PE ratio stocks also persist in other international markets. Table 6.5 summarizes the results of studies looking at this phenomenon in markets outside the United States.

The excess returns earned by low price-earnings ratio stocks are difficult to justify using a variation of the argument used for small stocks (i.e., that the risk of low PE ratios stocks is understated in the CAPM). Low PE ratio stocks generally are characterized by low growth, large size, and stable businesses, all of which should work toward reducing their risk rather than increasing it. The only explanation that can be given for this phenomenon, which is consistent with an efficient market, is that low PE ratio stocks generate large dividend yields, which would have created a larger tax burden because dividends are taxed at higher rates. And as with the small cap premium, the premium earned by low PE stocks has also dropped, albeit not as much, between 1980 and 2023, relative to the 1952–1980 time period.

Price to Book Ratios Another statistic that is widely used by investors in investment strategy is price–book value ratios. A low price–book value ratio has been considered a reliable indicator of undervaluation in firms. In studies that parallel those done on price-earnings ratios, the relationship between returns and price–book value ratios has been examined. The consistent finding from these studies is that there is a negative relationship between returns and price–book value ratios—low price–book value ratio stocks earn higher returns than high price–book value ratio stocks.

Rosenberg, Reid, and Lanstein (1985) find that the average returns on U.S. stocks are positively related to the ratio of a firm's book value to market value. Between 1973 and 1984, the strategy of picking stocks with high book-price ratios (low price-book values) yielded an excess return of 36 basis points a month. Fama and French (1992), in examining the cross section of expected stock returns between 1963 and 1990, established that the positive relationship between book-to-price ratios and average returns persists in both the univariate and multivariate tests, and is even stronger than the size effect in explaining

TABLE 6.5 Excess Returns on Low PE Ratio Stocks by Country, 1989–1994

Country	Annual Premium Earned by Lowest-PE Stocks (Bottom Quintile)
Australia	3.03%
France	6.40%
Germany	1.06%
Hong Kong	6.60%
Italy	14.16%
Japan	7.30%
Switzerland	9.02%
United Kingdom	2.40%

Annual premium: Premium earned over an index of equally weighted stocks in that market between January 1, 1989, and December 31, 1994. These numbers were obtained from a Merrill Lynch Survey of Proprietary Indices.

returns. When they classified firms on the basis of book-to-price ratios into 12 portfolios, firms in the lowest book-to-price (highest price-book) class earned an average monthly return of 0.30 percent, while firms in the highest book-to-price (lowest price-book) class earned an average monthly return of 1.83 percent for the 1963–1990 period.

Chan, Hamao, and Lakonishok (1991) find that the book-to-market ratio has a strong role in explaining the cross section of average returns on Japanese stocks. Capaul, Rowley, and Sharpe (1993) extend the analysis of price–book value ratios across other international markets, and conclude that value stocks (i.e., stocks with low price–book value ratios) earned excess returns in every market that they analyzed between 1981 and 1992. Their annualized estimates of the return differential earned by stocks with low price–book value ratios, over the market index, are reported in Table 6.6.

A caveat is in order. Fama and French pointed out that low price–book value ratios may operate as a measure of risk, since firms with prices well below book value are more likely to be in trouble and go out of business. Investors therefore have to evaluate for themselves whether the additional returns made by such firms justify the additional risk taken on by investing in them.

Temporal Anomalies

There are several peculiarities in return differences across calendar time that not only are difficult to rationalize but are also suggestive of inefficiencies. Furthermore, some of these temporal anomalies are related to the small firm effect described in the previous section.

January Effect Studies of returns in the United States and other major financial markets (Roll, 1983; Haugen and Lakonishok, 1988) consistently reveal strong differences in return behavior across the months of the year. Figure 6.12 reports average returns by months of the year from 1926 to 2023. Returns in January are significantly higher than returns in any other month of the year. This phenomenon is called the year-end or January effect, and it can be traced to the first two weeks in January.

The relationship between the January effect and the small firm effect (Keim, 1983; Reinganum, 1983) adds to the complexity of this phenomenon. The January effect is much more accentuated for small firms than for larger firms, and roughly half of the small firm premium described in the prior section is earned in the first two weeks of January. Figure 6.13 graphs returns in January by size class for data from 1935 to 1986.

TABLE 6.6 Annual Return to Low Price to Book—Global

Country	Added Return to Low Price–Book Value Portfolio
France	3.26%
Germany	1.39%
Switzerland	1.17%
United Kingdom	1.09%
Japan	3.43%
United States	1.06%
Europe	1.30%
Global	1.88%

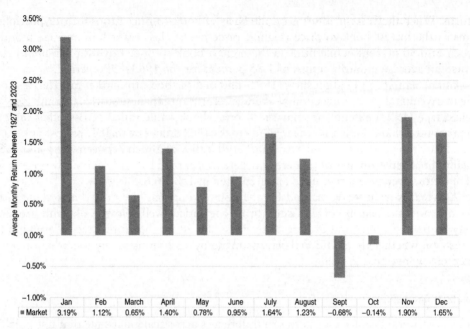

Average Monthly Return between 1927 and 2023

	Jan	Feb	March	April	May	June	July	August	Sept	Oct	Nov	Dec
■ Market	3.19%	1.12%	0.65%	1.40%	0.78%	0.95%	1.64%	1.23%	−0.68%	−0.14%	1.90%	1.65%

FIGURE 6.12   Returns by Month of the Year: U.S. Stocks from 1927 to 2023
Source: Adapted from Ken French data.

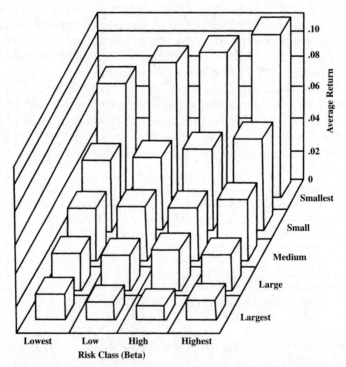

FIGURE 6.13   Returns in January by Size and Risk Class, 1935–1986
Source: Adapted from Ritter et. al., 1989.

As the small cap premium has declined since 1981, the January effect has weakened as well, although it has not completely disappeared.

A number of explanations have been advanced for the January effect, but few hold up to serious scrutiny. Reinganum suggested that there is tax loss selling by investors at the end of the year on stocks that have lost money to capture the capital gain, driving prices down, presumably below true value, in December, and a buying back of the same stocks in January,[12] resulting in the high returns. The fact that the January effect is accentuated for stocks that have done worse over the prior year is offered as evidence for this explanation. There are several pieces of evidence that contradict it, though. First, there are countries like Australia, that have a different tax year but continue to have a January effect. Second, the January effect is no greater, on average, in years following bad years for the stock market than in other years.

A second rationale is that the January effect is related to institutional trading behavior around the turn of the year. It has been noted, for instance, that the ratio of buys to sells for institutions drops significantly below average in the days before the turn of the year, and picks up to above average in the months that follow. This is illustrated in Figure 6.14. It is argued that the absence of institutional buying pushes down prices in the days before the turn of the year and pushes up prices in the days after.

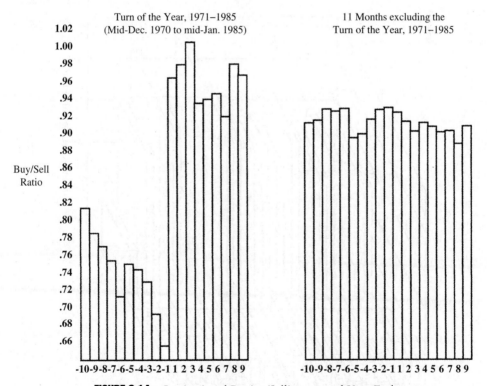

FIGURE 6.14 Institutional Buying/Selling around Year-End

---

[12]Since wash sales rules would prevent an investor from selling and buying back the same stock within 30 days, there has to be some substitution among the stocks. Thus, investor 1 sells stock A and investor 2 sells stock B, but when it comes time to buy back the stock, investor 1 buys stock B and investor 2 buys stock A.

The universality of the January effect is illustrated in Figure 6.15, which examines returns in January versus the other months of the year in several major financial markets and finds strong evidence of a January effect in every market (Haugen and Lakonishok, 1988; Gultekin and Gultekin 1983).

Weekend Effect   The weekend effect is another return phenomenon that has persisted over extraordinarily long periods and over a number of international markets. It refers to the differences in returns between Mondays and other days of the week. The significance of the return difference is brought out in Figure 6.16, which graphs returns by days of the week from 1962 to 1978 (Gibbons and Hess, 1981).

The returns on Mondays are significantly negative, whereas the returns on every other day of the trading week are not. There are a number of other findings on the Monday effect that have fleshed this out. First, the Monday effect is really a weekend effect since the bulk of the negative returns is manifested in the Friday-close-to-Monday open returns. The intraday returns on Monday are not the culprits in creating the negative returns. Second, the Monday effect is worse for small stocks than for larger stocks. Third, the Monday effect is no worse following three-day weekends than following two-day weekends.

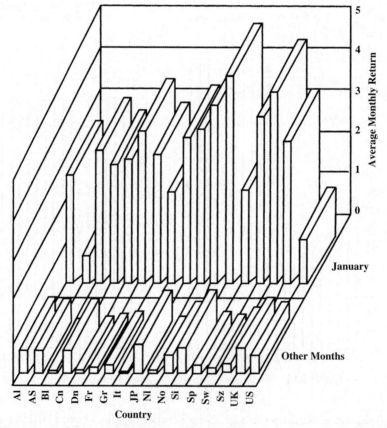

FIGURE 6.15   Returns in January versus Other Months—Major Financial Markets
Source: Adapted from Gultekin et. al., 1983.

There are some who have argued that the weekend effect is the result of bad news being revealed after the close of trading on Friday and during the weekend. They point to Figure 6.7, which reveals that more negative earnings reports are revealed after close of trading on Friday. Even if this were a widespread phenomenon, the return behavior would be inconsistent with a rational market, since rational investors would build the expectation of the bad news over the weekend into the price before the weekend, leading to an elimination of the weekend effect.

The weekend effect is fairly strong in most major international markets, as shown in Figure 6.17. The presence of a strong weekend effect in Japan, which allowed Saturday trading for a portion of the period studied here, indicates that there might be a more direct reason for negative returns on Mondays than bad information over the weekend.

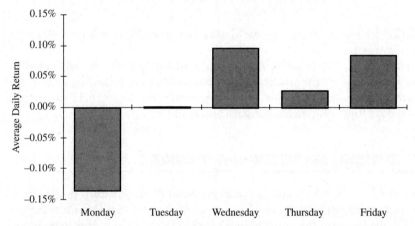

FIGURE 6.16 Average Daily Returns by Day of the Week, 1962–1978
Source: Gibbons et. al., 1981. Used with permission of University of Chicago Press.

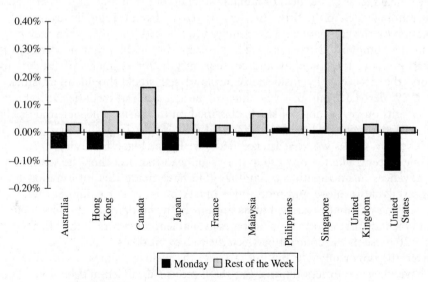

FIGURE 6.17 Weekend Effect in International Markets

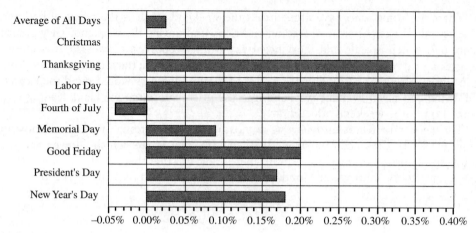

FIGURE 6.18   A Holiday Effect? Average Market Returns on Trading Days Following Holidays

As a final note, the negative returns on Mondays cannot be attributed to just the absence of trading over the weekend. The returns on days following trading holidays in general are characterized by positive, not negative, returns. Figure 6.18 summarizes returns on trading days following major holidays and confirms this pattern.

EVIDENCE ON INSIDERS AND INVESTMENT PROFESSIONALS

There is a sense that insiders, analysts, and portfolio managers must possess an advantage over the average investors in the market, and be able to convert this advantage into excess returns. The evidence on the performance of these investors is surprisingly mixed.

Insider Trading   The Securities and Exchange Commission (SEC) defines an insider to be an officer or director of the firm or a major stockholder (holding more than 5 percent of the outstanding stock in the firm). Insiders are barred from trading in advance of specific information on the company and are required to file with the SEC when they buy or sell stock in the company. If it is assumed, as seems reasonable, that insiders have better information about the company and consequently better estimates of value than other investors, the decisions by insiders to buy and sell stock should affect stock prices. Figure 6.19, derived from an early study of insider trading by Jaffe (1974), examines excess returns on two groups of stock, classified on the basis of insider trades. The "buy group" includes stocks where buys exceeded sells by the biggest margin, and the "sell group" includes stocks where sells exceeded buys by the biggest margin.

While it seems like the buy group does significantly better than the sell group in this study, advances in information technology (IT) have made this information on insider trading available to more and more investors. A more recent study (Seyhun, 1998) of insider trading examines excess returns around both the date the insiders report to the SEC and the date that information becomes available to investors in the official summary. Figure 6.20 presents the contrast between the two event dates.

Given the opportunity to buy on the date the insider reports to the SEC, investors could have marginal excess returns, but these returns diminish and become statistically insignificant if investors are forced to wait until the official summary date.

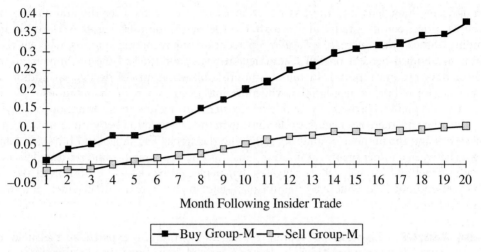

FIGURE 6.19   Cumulative Returns Following Insider Trading: Buy versus Sell Group
Source: Jaffe, 1974. Used with permission of University of Chicago Press.

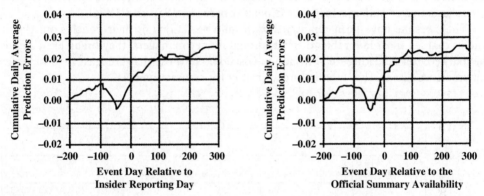

FIGURE 6.20   Abnormal Returns around Reporting Day versus Official Summary Availability Day
Source: Seyhun, 1998. Used with permission of MIT Press.

None of these studies examine the question of whether insiders themselves make excess returns. The reporting process, as set up now by the SEC, is biased toward legal and less profitable trades and away from illegal and more profitable trades. Though direct evidence cannot be offered for this proposition, insiders trading illegally on private information must make excess returns.

Analyst Recommendations   Analysts clearly hold a privileged position in the market for information, operating at the nexus of private and public information. Using both types of information, analysts issue buy and sell recommendations to their clients, who trade on this basis.

While both buy and sell recommendations affect stock prices, sell recommendations affect prices much more adversely than buy recommendations affect them positively. Interestingly, Womack (1996) documents that the price effect of buy recommendations tends to be immediate and there is no evidence of price drifts after the announcement, whereas prices continue to trend down after sell recommendations. Figure 6.21 graphs his findings. Stock prices increase by about 3 percent on buy recommendations, whereas they drop by about 4 percent on sell recommendations at the time of the recommendations (three days around reports). In the six months following, prices decline an additional 5 percent for sell recommendations, while leveling off for buy recommendations.

Though analysts provide a valuable service in collecting private information, or maybe *because* they do, there is a negative relationship in the cross section between returns earned by stocks and the number of analysts following the stock. The same kind of relationship exists between another proxy for interest—institutional ownership—and returns. This evidence (Arbel and Strebel, 1983) suggests that neglected stocks—those followed by few analysts and not held widely by institutions—earn higher returns than widely followed and held stocks.

Money Managers   Professional money managers operate as experts in the field of investments. They are supposed to be better informed, have lower transaction costs, and be better investors overall than smaller investors. The earliest study of mutual funds by Jensen (1968) suggested that this supposition might not hold in practice. His findings, summarized in Figure 6.22 as excess returns on mutual funds, were that the average portfolio manager underperformed the market between 1955 and 1964.

These results have been replicated with mild variations in their conclusions. In the studies that are most favorable for professional money managers, they break even against the market after adjusting for transaction costs, and in those that are least favorable they underperform the market even before adjusting for transaction costs.

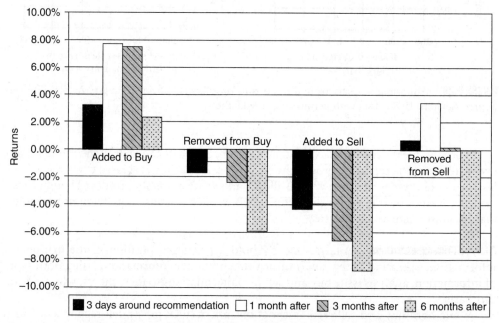

FIGURE 6.21   Market Reaction to Recommendations, 1989–1990
Source: Adapted from Womack, 1996.

The results, when categorized on a number of different bases, do not offer much solace. For instance, Figure 6.23 shows the percentage of money managers, categorized by investment style, beating the respective indices between 2013 and 2022. Money managers in every investment style underperform the market index.

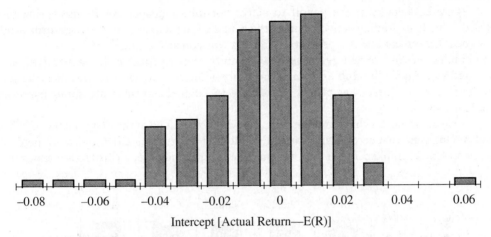

FIGURE 6.22   Mutual Fund Performance, 1955–1964—the Jensen Study
Source: Adapted from Jensen, 1968.

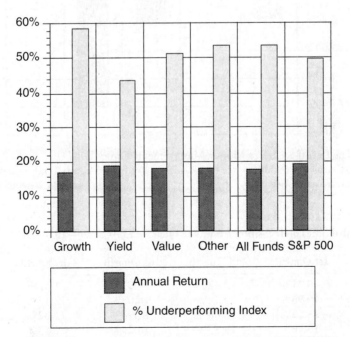

FIGURE 6.23   Performance of U.S. Equity Funds, 2013–2022
Source: SPIVA. Used with permission of S&P Dow Jones Indices.

The evidence is overwhelming, with money managers in every group underperforming the matching indices. The source of this data, SPIVA, a S&P service, now computes this measure (percentage of active money managers beating their respective indices) across the world, and while there are parts of the world where the percentage of managers losing relative to the index is lower, there is no part of the world where active money managers beat their indices.

Figure 6.24 looks at the payoff to active portfolio management by measuring the added value from trading actively during the course of the year and finds that returns drop between 0.5 percent and 1.5 percent a year as a consequence.

Finally, we find mixed evidence of continuity in performance. It classified money managers into quartiles and examined the probabilities of movement from one quartile to another in the three-year period from 2016 to 2019. The results are summarized in Table 6.7.

Table 6.7 indicates that a money manager who was ranked in the first quartile in 2016 had a 8-percent chance of being ranked in the first quartile in 2019 and a 31 percent chance of being ranked in the bottom quartile, suggesting reversal from risk exposure.

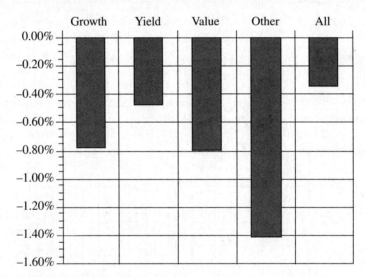

FIGURE 6.24   The Payoff to Active Money Management: Equity Funds
Note: **This chart measures the difference between actual return on equity funds and return on hypothetical portfolio frozen at beginning of period.**

TABLE 6.7   Probabilities of Transition from One Quartile to Another—2016–2019

	1st Quartile	2nd Quartile	3rd Quartile	4th Quartile	Liquidated
1st Quartile	8.21%	12.32%	24.02%	31.42%	4.52%
2nd Quartile	19.96%	19.14%	16.05%	13.17%	9.88%
3rd Quartile	18.52%	17.08%	12.96%	11.32%	13.37%
4th Quartile	13.76%	14.37%	18.28%	12.53%	18.69%

Source: Adapted from S&P Persistence Scorecard, 2023.

Among funds in the lowest quartile, a slightly higher percentage of funds transitioning to the first quartile, at 13.76 percent, than staying in the fourth quartile. In a measure of mortality in active investing, a far higher percentage of funds in the lowest quartile in 2016 have failed or been shut down by 2019.

Thus, the overall evidence is that money managers collectively add little value for investors with their active investing strategies. So, is there any good news for money managers in these studies? There are some glimmers:

- *Hot hands phenomenon:* While there is little evidence of overall continuity in mutual fund performance, there is some evidence that money managers who have performed well in the recent past are likely to outperform the market in the near future. It is unclear, however, how long this momentum lasts, before there is reversal. This evidence mirrors our earlier analysis of stock prices showing momentum over weeks and months and reversing themselves in the long term. Even this good news has to be taken with an ounce of caution, since it is possible that sheer chance and selection bias can still explain these positive runs of superior performance.
- *Skill versus luck:* There is some debate as to whether the differences in returns that money managers earn over long periods can be entirely attributed to luck. Fama and French (2010) argue that when returns are measured net of costs, there is little evidence that mutual funds beat the market. However, when they look at gross returns, there is some evidence of differences in skill; they estimate that superior managers generate about 1.25% more than the average.
- *Tax, liquidity, and time horizon arbitrage:* A money manager with a tax rate much lower than that of other money managers, lower need for liquidity or lower transactions costs than other investors, and/or a longer time horizon may be able to exploit these differences to get investments at bargain prices and earn excess returns. Although there is anecdotal evidence that such investors exist, many of them are undone by their own success; as they attract more money, they lose their focus and their competitive edge.

The bottom line: It is possible to beat the market, but it is hard work and luck plays an undeniable role. There are no magic bullets or simple formulae for investment success. The money managers who beat the market consistently over time tend to be few and far between. Although they may adopt different strategies and have different views on markets, they share some common characteristics. They have well-thought-out investment philosophies, play to their strengths, and stay disciplined.

MARKET INEFFICIENCIES AND MONEY MANAGER PERFORMANCE

The evidence on markets is contradictory. On the one hand, there seem to be numerous patterns in stock prices—stock prices reverse course in the long term and returns are higher in January—and evidence of market anomalies—small-market-cap firms with low price-to-book and price-to-earnings ratios seem to handily beat the market. On the other hand, there seems to be little evidence of money managers being able to exploit these findings to beat the market.

(continued)

(*continued*)

There are a number of possible explanations. The most benign one is that the inefficiencies show up mostly in hypothetical studies, and that the transaction cost and execution problems associated with converting these inefficiencies into portfolios overwhelm the excess returns. A second possible explanation is that the studies generally look at the long term; many are over 20–50 years. Over shorter periods, there is substantially more uncertainty about whether small stocks will outperform large stocks and whether buying losers will generate excess returns. There are no investment strategies that are sure bets for short periods. Pradhuman (2000) illustrates this phenomenon by noting that small-cap stocks have underperformed large-cap stocks in roughly one out of every four years in the past 50 years. Bernstein (1995) notes that while value investing (buying low PE and low price-to-book value stocks) may earn excess returns over long periods, growth investing has outperformed value investing over many five-year periods during the past three decades. A third explanation is that portfolio managers do not consistently follow any one strategy but jump from one strategy to another, both increasing their expenses and reducing the likelihood that the strategy can generate excess returns in the long term.

CONCLUSION

The question of whether markets are efficient will always be a provocative one, given the implications that efficient markets have for investment management and research. If an efficient market is defined as one where the market price is an unbiased estimate of the true value, it is quite clear that some markets will always be more efficient than others, and that markets will always be more efficient to some investors than to others. The capacity of a market to correct inefficiencies quickly will depend, in part, on the ease of trading, the transaction costs, and the vigilance of profit-seeking investors in that market.

While market efficiency can be tested in several different ways, the two most widely used tests to test efficiency are event studies, which examine market reactions to information events and portfolio studies, which evaluate the returns of portfolios created on the basis of observable characteristics. It does make sense to be vigilant, because bias can enter these studies, intentionally or otherwise, in a number of different ways and can lead to unwarranted conclusions and, worse still, wasteful investment strategies.

There is substantial evidence of irregularities in market behavior related to systematic factors, such as size, price-earnings ratios, and price–book value ratios, as well as to time—the January and the weekend effects. While these irregularities may be inefficiencies, there is also the sobering evidence that professional money managers, who are in a position to exploit these inefficiencies, have a very difficult time consistently beating financial markets. Read together, the persistence of the irregularities and the inability of money managers to beat the market are testimony to the gap between empirical tests on paper and real-world money management in some cases, and the failure of the models of risk and return in others.

QUESTIONS AND SHORT PROBLEMS

In the problems following, use an equity risk premium of 5.5 percent if none is specified.

1. Which of the following is an implication of market efficiency? (There may be more than one right answer.)
   a. Resources are allocated among firms efficiently (i.e., put to best use).
   b. No investor will do better than the market in any time period.
   c. No investor will do better than the market consistently.
   d. No investor will do better than the market consistently after adjusting for risk.
   e. No investor will do better than the market consistently after adjusting for risk and transaction costs.
   f. No group of investors will do better than the market consistently after adjusting for risk and transaction costs.

2. Suppose you are following a retailing stock that has a strong seasonal pattern to sales. Would you expect to see a seasonal pattern in the stock price as well?

3. Tests of market efficiency are often referred to as joint tests of two hypotheses—the hypothesis that the market is efficient and an expected returns model. Explain. Is it ever possible to test market efficiency alone (i.e., without jointly testing an asset pricing model)?

4. You are in a violent argument with a chartist. He claims that you are violating the fundamental laws of economics by trying to find intrinsic value. "Price is determined by demand and supply, not by some intrinsic value." Is finding an intrinsic value inconsistent with demand and supply?

5. You are testing the effect of merger announcements on stock prices. (This is an event study.) Your procedure goes through the following steps:
   Step 1: You choose the 20 biggest mergers of the year.
   Step 2: You isolate the date the merger became effective as the key day around which you will examine the data.
   Step 3: You look at the returns for the five days after the effective merger date.
   By looking at these returns (0.13%) you conclude that you could not have made money on merger announcements. Are there any flaws that you can detect in this test? How would you correct them? Can you devise a stronger test?

6. In an efficient market, the market price is defined to be an "unbiased estimate" of the true value. This implies that (choose one):
   a. The market price is always equal to true value.
   b. The market price has nothing to do with true value.
   c. Markets make mistakes about true value, and investors can exploit these mistakes to make money.
   d. Market prices contain errors, but the errors are random and therefore cannot be exploited by investors.
   e. No one can beat the market.

7. Evaluate whether the following actions are likely to increase stock market efficiency, decrease it, or leave it unchanged, and explain why.
   a. The government imposes a transaction tax of 1% on all stock transactions.
      Increase efficiency _____ Decrease efficiency _____ Leave unchanged _____
   b. The securities exchange regulators impose a restriction on all short sales to prevent rampant speculation.
      Increase efficiency _____ Decrease efficiency _____ Leave unchanged _____

  c. An options market, trading call and put options, is opened up, with options traded on many of the stocks listed on the exchange.

    Increase efficiency _____ Decrease efficiency _____ Leave unchanged _____

  d. The stock market removes all restrictions on foreign investors acquiring and holding stock in companies.

    Increase efficiency _____ Decrease efficiency _____ Leave unchanged _____

8. The following is a graph of cumulative abnormal returns around the announcement of asset divestitures by major corporations.

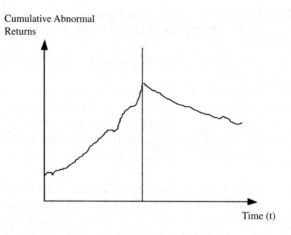

Cumulative Abnormal Returns

Time (t)

  How best would you explain the:

  a. Market behavior before the announcement?

  b. Market reaction to the announcement?

  c. Market reaction after the announcement?

9. What is the phenomenon of the size effect in stock performance? How does it relate to the turn-of-the-year effect? Can you suggest any good reasons why small stocks, after adjusting for beta, still do better than large stocks? What strategy would you follow to exploit this anomaly? What factors do you have to keep in mind?

10. A study examining market reactions to earnings surprises found that prices tend to drift after earnings surprises. What does this tell you about the market's capacity to learn from events and new information? What cross-sectional differences would you expect to find in this learning behavior? (Would you expect to see a greater price drift in some types of firms than in others? Why?) How would you try to exploit this anomaly? What possible costs would you have to keep in mind?

11. One explanation of the turn-of-the-year or January effect has to do with sales and purchases related to the tax year.

  a. Present the tax effect hypothesis.

  b. Studies have shown that the January effect occurs internationally, even in countries where the tax year does not start in January. Speculate on a good reason for this.

12. The following are the expected price appreciation and dividend yield components of returns on two portfolios—a high dividend yield portfolio and a low dividend yield portfolio.

Portfolio	Expected Price Appreciation	Expected Dividend Yield
High yield	9%	5%
Low yield	12%	1%

You are a taxable investor who faces a tax rate of 40% on dividends. What would your tax rate on capital gains need to be for you to be indifferent between these two portfolios?

13. Answer true or false to the following questions:
    a. Low price-earnings stocks, on average, earn returns in excess of expectations, while high price-earnings stocks earn less than expected. This is primarily because lower PE ratio stocks have lower risk.
       True _____ False _____
    b. The small firm effect, which refers to the positive excess returns earned, on average, by small firms, is primarily caused by a few small firms that make very high positive returns.
       True _____ False _____
    c. Investors generally cannot make money on analyst recommendations, because stock prices are not affected by these recommendations.
       True _____ False _____

14. You are examining the performance of two mutual funds. AD Value Fund has been in existence since January 1, 1988, and invests primarily in stocks with low price-earnings ratios and high dividend yields. AD Growth Fund has also been in existence since January 1, 1988, but it invests primarily in high-growth stocks, with high PE ratios and low or no dividends. The performance of these funds over the past five years is summarized as follows:

	Average from 1988–1992		
	Price Appreciation	*Dividend Yield*	*Beta*
NYSE Composite	13%	3%	1.0
AD Value	11%	5%	0.8
AD Growth	15%	1%	1.2

The average risk-free rate during the period was 6%. The current risk-free rate is 3%.
   a. How well or badly did these funds perform after adjusting for risk?
   b. Assume that the front-end load on each of these funds is 5% (i.e., if you put $1,000 in each of these funds today, you would only be investing $950 after the initial commission). Assume also that the excess returns you have calculated in part (a) will continue into the future, and that you choose to invest in the fund that outperformed the market. How many years would you have to hold this fund to break even?

CHAPTER 7

Riskless Rates and Risk Premiums

All models of risk and return in finance are built around a rate that investors can make on riskless investments and the risk premium or premiums that investors should charge for investing in the average-risk investment. In the capital asset pricing model (CAPM), where there is only one source of market risk captured in the market portfolio, this risk premium becomes the premium that investors would demand when investing in that portfolio. In multifactor models, there are multiple risk premiums, each one measuring the premium demanded by investors for exposure to a specific market risk factor. This chapter examines how best to measure a riskless rate and to estimate a risk premium or premiums for use in these models.

As noted in Chapter 4, risk is measured in terms of default risk for bonds, and this default risk is captured in a default spread that firms must pay over and above the riskless rate. This chapter closes by considering how best to estimate these default spreads and the factors that may cause these spreads to change over time.

THE RISK-FREE RATE

Most risk and return models in finance start off with an asset that is defined as risk free, and use the expected return on that asset as the risk-free rate. The expected returns on risky investments are then measured relative to the risk-free rate, with the risk creating an expected risk premium that is added to the risk-free rate. But what makes an asset risk free? And what do we do when we cannot find such an asset? These are the questions that will be dealt with in this section.

Requirements for an Asset to Be Risk Free

Chapter 4 considers some of the requirements for an asset to be risk free. In particular, an asset is risk free if we know the expected returns on it with certainty (i.e., the actual return is always equal to the expected return). Under what conditions will the actual returns on an investment be equal to the expected returns? There are two basic conditions that must be met. The first is that *there can be no default risk*. Essentially, this rules out any security issued by a private entity, since even the largest and safest ones have some measure of default risk. The only securities that have a chance of being risk free are government securities, not because governments are better run than corporations, but because they usually control the printing of currency. At least in nominal terms, they should be able to fulfill their promises. Even this assumption, straightforward though it might seem, does not always hold up, especially when governments refuse to honor claims made by previous regimes and when they borrow in currencies other than their own.

There is a second condition that riskless securities need to fulfill that is often forgotten. For an investment to have an actual return equal to its expected return, *there can be no reinvestment risk*. To illustrate this point, assume that you are trying to estimate the expected return over a five-year period and you want a risk-free rate. A six-month Treasury bill rate, even if you assume that the U.S. treasury is default free, will not be risk free, because there is the reinvestment risk of not knowing what the Treasury bill rate will be in six months. Even a five-year Treasury bond is not risk free, since the coupons on the bond will be reinvested at rates that cannot be predicted today. The risk-free rate for a five-year time horizon has to be the expected return on a default-free (government) five-year zero-coupon bond. This clearly has painful implications for anyone doing corporate finance or valuation, where expected returns often must be estimated for periods ranging from 1 to 10 years. A purist's view of risk-free rates would then require different risk-free rates for each period, and different expected returns.

As a practical compromise, however, it is worth noting that the present value effect of using year-specific risk-free rates tends to be small for most well-behaved term structures.[1] In these cases, we could use a duration-matching strategy, where the duration of the default-free security used as the risk-free asset is matched up to the duration[2] of the cash flows in the analysis. If, however, there are very large differences, in either direction, between short-term and long-term rates, it does pay to stick with year-specific risk-free rates in computing expected returns.

Practical Implications When a Default-Free Entity Exists   In some developed markets, where the government is viewed as a default-free entity, at least when it comes to borrowing in the local currency, the implications are simple. When doing investment analysis on longer-term projects or valuations, the risk-free rate should be the long-term government bond rate. The choice of a risk-free rate also has implications for how risk premiums are estimated. If, as is often the case, historical risk premiums are used, where the excess return earned by stocks over and above a government security rate over a past period is used as the risk premium, the government security chosen has to be the same one as that used for the risk-free rate. Thus, the historical risk premium used in the United States should be the excess return earned by stocks over Treasury bonds, and not Treasury bills, for purposes of long-term analysis. Implicit in this statement is the assumption that the U.S. treasury is default free, and that presumption may no longer be automatic.

Cash Flows and Risk-Free Rates: The Consistency Principle   The risk-free rate used to come up with expected returns should be measured consistently with how the cash flows are measured. Thus, if cash flows are estimated in nominal U.S. dollar terms, the risk-free rate will be the U.S. Treasury bond rate (if you are willing to also assume that there is default

---

[1] Well-behaved term structures would include a upward-sloping yield curve, where long-term rates are at most 2 to 3 percent higher than short-term rates.

[2] In investment analysis, where we look at projects, these durations are usually between 3 and 10 years. In valuation, the durations tend to be much longer, since firms are assumed to have infinite lives. The durations in these cases are often well in excess of 10 years and increase with the expected growth potential of the firm.

risk in U.S. treasuries). This also implies that it is not where a firm is domiciled which determines the choice of a risk-free rate, but the currency in which the cash flows on the firm are estimated. Thus, Nestlé can be valued using cash flows estimated in Swiss francs, discounted back at an expected return estimated using a Swiss long-term government bond rate as the risk-free rate, or it can be valued in British pounds, with both the cash flows and the risk-free rate being in British pounds. Given that the same firm can be valued in different currencies, will the results always be consistent? If we assume purchasing power parity (PPP), then differences in interest rates reflect differences in expected inflation. Both the cash flows and the discount rate are affected by expected inflation; thus, a low discount rate arising from a low risk-free rate will be exactly offset by a decline in expected nominal growth rates for cash flows, and the value will remain unchanged.

If the difference in interest rates across two currencies does not adequately reflect the difference in expected inflation in these currencies, the values obtained using the different currencies can be different. In particular, firms will be valued more highly when the currency used is the one with low interest rates relative to inflation. The risk, however, is that the interest rates will have to rise at some point to correct for this divergence, at which point the values will also converge.

Real versus Nominal Risk-Free Rates   Under conditions of high and unstable inflation, valuation can be done in real terms. Effectively, this means that cash flows are estimated using real growth rates and without allowing for the growth that comes from price inflation. To be consistent, the discount rates used in these cases have to be real discount rates. To get a real expected rate of return, we need to start with a real risk-free rate. While government bills and bonds offer returns that are risk free in nominal terms, they are not risk free in real terms, since expected inflation can be volatile. The standard approach of subtracting an expected inflation rate from the nominal interest rate to arrive at a real risk-free rate provides at best an estimate of the real risk-free rate.

Until recently, there were few traded default-free securities that could be used to estimate real risk-free rates, but the introduction of inflation-indexed Treasuries (TIPs) has filled this void. An inflation-indexed Treasury security does not offer a guaranteed nominal return to buyers, but instead provides a guaranteed real return. Thus, an inflation-indexed Treasury that offers a 3-percent real return will yield approximately 7 percent in nominal terms if inflation is 4 percent, and only 5 percent in nominal terms if inflation is only 2 percent.

The only problem is that real valuations are seldom called for or done in the United States, which has historically had stable and low expected inflation. The markets where we would most need to do real valuations, unfortunately, are markets without inflation-indexed default-free securities. The real risk-free rates in these markets can be estimated by using one of two arguments:

1. The first argument is that if capital can flow freely to those economies with the highest real returns, there can be no differences in real risk-free rates across markets. Using this argument, the real risk-free rate for the United States, estimated from the inflation-indexed Treasury, can be used as the real risk-free rate in any market.
2. The second argument applies if there are frictions and constraints in capital flowing across markets. In that case, the expected real return on an economy, in the long term, should be equal to the expected real growth rate, again in the long term, of that

economy, for equilibrium. Thus, the real risk-free rate for a mature economy like Germany should be much lower than the real risk-free rate for a economy with greater growth potential, such as India's.

Risk-Free Rates When There Is No Default-Free Entity

Our discussion, hitherto, has been predicated on the assumption that governments do not default, at least on local borrowing. There are many emerging market economies and quite a few developed markets where this assumption might not be viewed as reasonable. Governments in these markets are perceived as capable of defaulting even on local borrowing. When this is coupled with the fact that some governments do not borrow long term in the local currency, there are scenarios where obtaining a local risk-free rate, especially for the long term, becomes difficult. We consider four alternatives in the section following.

Local Currency Government Bond   If the government issues long-term bonds denominated in the local currency and these bonds are traded, you can use the interest rates on these bonds as a starting point for estimating the risk-free rate in that currency. In early 2024, for instance, the Indian government issued 10-year rupee-denominated bonds that were trading at a yield of 7.18 percent. This rate, though, is not a risk-free rate, because investors perceive default risk in the Indian government. To back out how much of the yield can be attributed to the default risk, we used the local currency sovereign rating[3] of Baa3 assigned to India by Moody's and estimated a default spread of 2.39 percent for that rating.[4]

The resulting risk-free rate in rupees is:

$$\text{Risk-free Rate in rupees} = \text{Government bond rate} - \text{Default spread}$$
$$= 7.18\% - 2.39\% = 4.79\%$$

It is true that this number assumes that the ratings agency is correct in its assessment of sovereign risk and that the default spread based on the rating is correct. An alternative approach to estimating default spreads that has become available in recent years is the credit default swap (CDS) market, where investors can buy insurance against default. The sovereign CDS spread then becomes a market-based estimate of the default spread for a country. In January 2024, the Indian 10-year sovereign CDS spread stood at 0.99%, yielding a risk-free rate of 6.19%:

$$\text{Risk-free Rate in rupees} = \text{Government bond rate} - \text{Default spread}$$
$$= 7.18\% - 0.99\% = 6.19\%$$

---

[3] Ratings agencies provide ratings for a country for borrowings in the local currency and a foreign currency. The latter rating is sometimes lower (since countries have a greater chance of defaulting when they borrow in a foreign currency), but the rating that matters for this analysis is the rating in the local currency. If the rating is Aaa (Moody's) or AAA (S&P), the government bond rate will be the risk-free rate.

[4] The default spread for a rating is computed by looking at dollar-denominated bonds issued by other governments with a Baa3 rating and comparing the rates on these bonds to the U.S. Treasury bond rate.

The CDS market does provide a more dynamic and updated measure of the default spread but it is, being a market-traded number, much more volatile. It also provides a dollar or euro-based spread, which may not apply to the local currency bonds.

Build-Up Approach   There are countries where either the government does not issue bonds denominated in the local currency, or these bonds do not trade. In this case, one alternative is to build up to a risk-free rate from fundamentals:

Build-up risk free rate = Expected inflation + Expected real growth rate

Since the risk-free rate in any currency can be written as the sum of expected inflation in that currency and the expected real rate, we can try to estimate the two components separately. To estimate expected inflation, we can start with the current inflation rate and extrapolate from that to expected inflation in the future. For the real rate, we can use the rate on the inflation-indexed U.S. Treasury bond rate, with the rationale that real rates should be the same globally. In January 2024, for instance, adding the expected inflation rate of 5 percent in India to the interest rate of 1.5 percent on the inflation-indexed U.S. Treasury would have yielded a risk-free rate of 6.5 percent in Indian rupees.

Derivatives Markets   Forward and futures contracts on exchange rates provide information about interest rates in the currencies involved, since interest rate parity governs the relationship between spot and forward rates. For instance, the forward rate between the Thai baht and the U.S. dollar can be written as follows:

$$\text{Forward Rate}^t_{\text{Thai Baht},\$} = \text{Spot Rate}_{\text{Thai Baht},\$} \times \frac{\left(1 + \text{Interest Rate}_{\text{Thai Baht}}\right)^t}{\left(1 + \text{Interest Rate}_{\text{US}\$}\right)^t}$$

For example, if the current spot rate is 35.38 Thai baht per U.S. dollar, the 10-year forward rate is 44.87 baht per dollar, and the current 10-year U.S. Treasury bond rate is 4 percent, the 10-year Thai risk-free rate (in nominal baht) can be estimated as follows:

$$44.87 = 35.38 \times \frac{\left(1 + \text{Interest Rate}_{\text{Thai Baht}}\right)^{10}}{\left(1 + .04\right)^{10}}$$

Solving for the Thai interest rate yields a 10-year risk-free rate of 6.50 percent. The biggest limitation of this approach, however, is that forward rates are difficult to come by for periods beyond a year[5] for many of the emerging markets, where we would be most interested in using them.

Risk-Free Rate Conversion   If the only reason for differences in risk-free rates in different currencies is expected inflation, you can convert the risk-free rate in a mature market

---

[5]In cases where only a one-year forward rate exists, an approximation for the long-term rate can be obtained by first backing out the one-year local currency borrowing rate, taking the spread over the one-year Treasury bill rate, and then adding this spread onto the long-term Treasury bond rate.

currency (U.S. dollars, euros) into a risk-free rate in an emerging market currency, using differences in inflation across currencies.

$$r_{\text{Local currency}} = \left(1 + r_{\text{Foreign currency}}\right)\frac{\left(1 + \text{Expected Inflation}_{\text{Local currency}}\right)}{\left(1 + \text{Expected Inflation}_{\text{Foreign currency}}\right)} - 1$$

For example, assume that the risk-free rate in U.S. dollars is 4 percent and that the expected inflation rate in Egyptian pounds is 11 percent (compared to the 2-percent inflation rate in U.S. dollars). The Egyptian pound risk-free rate can be written as follows:

$$\text{Risk-free Rate}_{\text{Egyptian pounds}} = (1.04)\frac{1.11}{1.02} - 1 = .1318 \text{ or } 13.18\%$$

To make this conversion, we still have to estimate the expected inflation in the local currency and the mature market currency.

What if none of these choices listed work? In other words, what if the government has no local currency bonds outstanding, there are no forward or futures contract on the currency, and/or expected inflation in the local currency is difficult to estimate? Faced with these problems, it is best to switch and do your valuation in a different currency. Thus, rather than value a Nigerian or Vietnamese company in the local currency, you would value it in euros or dollars. You will still have to estimate expected exchange rates in the future to convert local currency cash flows to foreign currency cash flows, but that may be a more manageable exercise.

EQUITY RISK PREMIUM

The notion that risk matters, and that riskier investments should have a higher expected return than safer investments to be considered good investments, is intuitive. Thus, the expected return on any investment can be written as the sum of the risk-free rate and an extra return to compensate for the risk. The disagreement, in both theoretical and practical terms, remains on how to measure this risk, and how to convert the risk measure into an expected return that compensates for risk. This section looks at the estimation of an appropriate equity risk premium (ERP) to use in risk and return models, in general, and in the capital asset pricing model, in particular.

Competing Models

In Chapter 4, we considered several competing models of risk, ranging from the capital asset pricing model to multifactor models. Notwithstanding their different conclusions, they all share some common views about risk. First, they all define risk in terms of variance in actual returns around an expected return; thus, an investment is riskless when actual returns are always equal to the expected return. Second, they all argue that risk has to be measured from the perspective of the marginal investor in an asset, and that this marginal investor is well diversified. Therefore, the argument goes, it is only the risk an investment adds on to a diversified portfolio that should be measured and compensated. In fact, it is this view of risk that leads models of risk to break the risk in any investment

TABLE 7.1 Comparing Risk and Return Models

Model	Assumptions	Measure of Market Risk
Capital asset pricing model (CAPM)	There are no transaction costs or private information. Therefore, the diversified portfolio includes all traded investments, held in proportion to their market value.	Beta measured against this market portfolio
Arbitrage pricing model (APM)	Investments with the same exposure to market risk have to trade at the same price (no arbitrage).	Betas measured against multiple (unspecified) market risk factors
Multifactor model	There is the same no-arbitrage assumption as with the APM.	Betas measured against multiple specified macroeconomic factors
Proxy model	Over very long periods, higher returns on investments must be compensation for higher market risk.	Proxies for market risk, for example, include market capitalization and price book value ratios.

into two components. There is a firm-specific component that measures risk that relates only to that investment or to a few investments like it; and a market component that contains risk that affects a large subset or all investments. It is the latter risk that is not diversifiable and should be rewarded.

While all risk and return models agree on this crucial distinction, they part ways when it comes to how to measure this market risk. Table 7.1 summarizes four models and the way each model attempts to measure risk.

In the first three models, the expected return on any investment can be written as:

$$E(\text{Return}) = \text{Risk-free Rate} + \sum_{j=1}^{j=k} \beta_j \left(\text{Risk Premium}_j \right)$$

where
$$\beta_j = \text{Beta of investment relative to factor j}$$
$$\text{Risk premium}_j = \text{Risk premium for factor j}$$

Note that in the special case of a single-factor model, like the CAPM, each investment's expected return will be determined by its beta relative to the market.

Assuming that the risk-free rate is known, these models all require two inputs. The first is the beta or betas of the investment being analyzed, and the second is the appropriate risk premium(s) for the factor or factors in the model. The issue of beta estimation is examined in the next chapter; this section concentrates on the measurement of the risk premium. As far as the risk premium is concerned, we would like to know for each factor what investors, on average, require as a premium over the risk-free rate for an investment with average risk. Without any loss of generality, let us consider the estimation of the beta and the equity risk premium in the capital asset pricing model. Here, the risk premium should measure what investors, on average, demand as extra return for investing in the market portfolio relative to the risk-free asset.

Determinants of Equity Risk Premiums

The equity risk premium is a barometer for the market, reflecting how the battle between fear and greed that animates markets is playing out in the price of risk. Not surprisingly, the equity risk premiums is determined by almost everything that is happening in the market from the macroeconomic (inflation, interest rates, real economy) to the political (government type and policy). In Figure 7.1, I list just a partial list of the determinants of equity risk premiums.

As you peruse the determinants, there two implications. The first is that equity risk premiums will vary across time, rising during economic crises and periods of extreme uncertainty, and falling during economic booms and stability. The second is that equity risk premiums will be different across geographies, higher in countries with more unstable governments and economic policy, and lower in countries with stable governments and legal systems that work efficiently.

Historical Risk Premiums

In practice, analysts and appraisers usually estimate the risk premium by looking at the historical premium earned by stocks over default-free securities over long time periods. The historical premium approach is simple. The actual returns earned on stocks over a

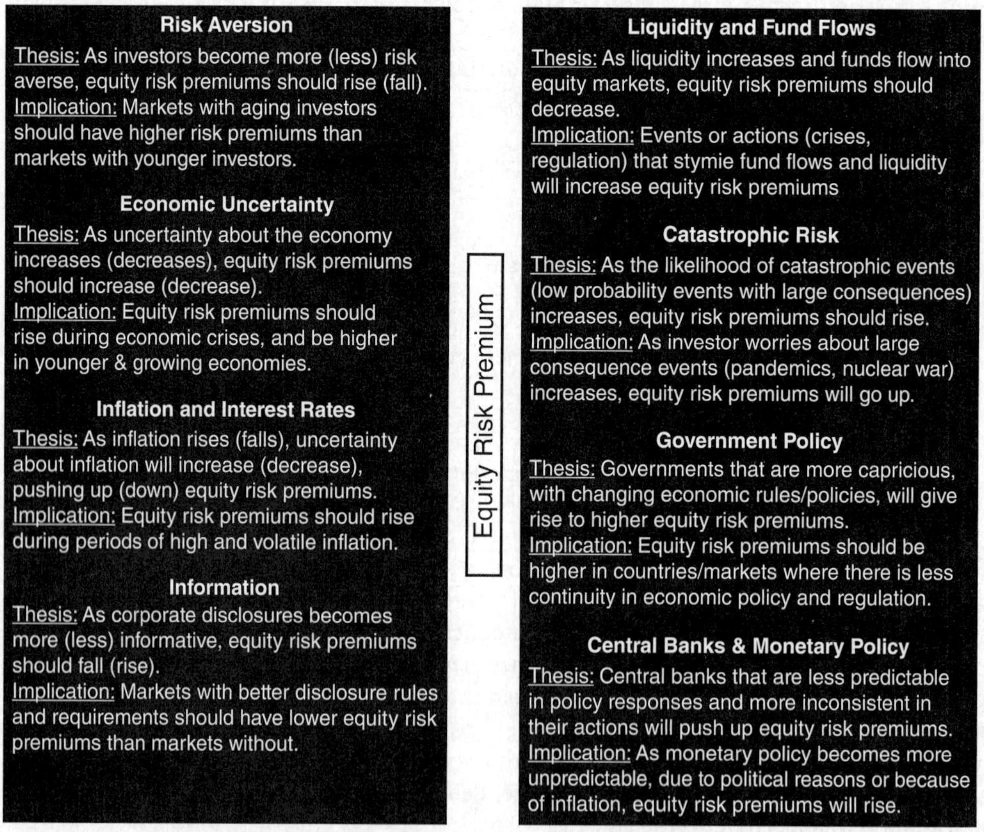

Risk Aversion
Thesis: As investors become more (less) risk averse, equity risk premiums should rise (fall).
Implication: Markets with aging investors should have higher risk premiums than markets with younger investors.

Economic Uncertainty
Thesis: As uncertainty about the economy increases (decreases), equity risk premiums should increase (decrease).
Implication: Equity risk premiums should rise during economic crises, and be higher in younger & growing economies.

Inflation and Interest Rates
Thesis: As inflation rises (falls), uncertainty about inflation will increase (decrease), pushing up (down) equity risk premiums.
Implication: Equity risk premiums should rise during periods of high and volatile inflation.

Information
Thesis: As corporate disclosures becomes more (less) informative, equity risk premiums should fall (rise).
Implication: Markets with better disclosure rules and requirements should have lower equity risk premiums than markets without.

Liquidity and Fund Flows
Thesis: As liquidity increases and funds flow into equity markets, equity risk premiums should decrease.
Implication: Events or actions (crises, regulation) that stymie fund flows and liquidity will increase equity risk premiums

Catastrophic Risk
Thesis: As the likelihood of catastrophic events (low probability events with large consequences) increases, equity risk premiums should rise.
Implication: As investor worries about large consequence events (pandemics, nuclear war) increases, equity risk premiums will go up.

Government Policy
Thesis: Governments that are more capricious, with changing economic rules/policies, will give rise to higher equity risk premiums.
Implication: Equity risk premiums should be higher in countries/markets where there is less continuity in economic policy and regulation.

Central Banks & Monetary Policy
Thesis: Central banks that are less predictable in policy responses and more inconsistent in their actions will push up equity risk premiums.
Implication: As monetary policy becomes more unpredictable, due to political reasons or because of inflation, equity risk premiums will rise.

Equity Risk Premium

FIGURE 7.1   Determinants of Equity Risk Premiums

long time period are estimated, and then compared to the actual returns earned on a default-free (usually government) security. The difference, on an annual basis, between the two returns is computed and represents the historical risk premium. This approach might yield reasonable estimates in markets like the United States, with a large and diversified stock market and a long history of returns on both stocks and government securities. However, they yield meaningless estimates for the risk premiums in other countries, where the equity markets represent a small proportion of the overall economy and the historical returns are available only for short periods.

While users of risk and return models may have developed a consensus that historical premium is, in fact, the best estimate of the risk premium looking forward, there are surprisingly large differences in the actual premiums we observe being used in practice. For instance, the risk premium estimated in the U.S. markets by different investment banks, consultants, and corporations range from 3 percent at the lower end to 12 percent at the upper end. Given that they almost all use the same database of historical returns,[6] summarizing data from 1926, these differences may seem surprising. There are, however, three reasons for the divergence in risk premiums:

1. *Time period used.* While there are many who use all the data going back to 1926 (or earlier), there are almost as many using data over shorter time periods, such as 50, 20, or even 10 years, to come up with historical risk premiums. The rationale presented by those who use shorter periods is that the risk aversion of the average investor is likely to change over time, and that using a shorter period provides a more updated estimate. This must be offset against a cost associated with using shorter time periods, which is the greater noise in the risk premium estimate. In fact, given the annual standard deviation in stock prices[7] between 1929 and 2023 of about 20 percent, the standard error[8] associated with the risk premium estimate can be estimated for different estimation periods in Table 7.2.

TABLE 7.2   Standard Errors in Risk Premium Estimates

Time Period	Standard Error in Equity Risk Premium Estimate
5 years	$20\%/\sqrt{5} = 8.94\%$
10 years	$20\%/\sqrt{10} = 6.32\%$
25 years	$20\%/\sqrt{25} = 4.00\%$
50 years	$20\%/\sqrt{50} = 2.83\%$

---

[6]See *Stocks, Bonds, Bills and Inflation*, an annual edition that reports on annual returns on stocks, Treasury bonds bills, as well as inflation rates from 1926 to the present (www.ibbotson.com).

[7]For the historical data on stock returns, bond returns, and bill returns, check under https://pages.stern.nyu.edu/~adamodar/pc/datasets/histretSP.xlsx.

[8]These estimates of the standard error are probably understated, because they are based on the assumption that annual returns are uncorrelated over time. There is substantial empirical evidence that returns are correlated over time, which would make this standard error estimate much larger.

Note that to get reasonable standard errors, we need very long time periods of historical returns. Conversely, the standard errors from 10-year and 20-year estimates are likely to be almost as large as or larger than the actual risk premium estimated. This cost of using shorter time periods seems, in our view, to overwhelm any advantages associated with getting a more updated premium.

2. *Choice of risk-free security.* With historical data, you can get returns on both Treasury bills (T-bills) and Treasury bonds (T-bonds), and the risk premium for stocks can be estimated relative to each. Given that the yield curve in the United States has been upward sloping for most of the past seven decades, the risk premium is larger when estimated relative to shorter-term government securities (such as Treasury bills). *The risk-free rate chosen in computing the premium must be consistent with the risk-free rate used to compute expected returns.* Thus, if the Treasury bill rate is used as the risk-free rate, the premium must be the premium earned by stocks over that rate. If the Treasury bond rate is used as the risk-free rate, the premium must be estimated relative to that rate. For the most part, in corporate finance and valuation, the risk-free rate will be a long-term default-free Treasury (government) bond rate and not a Treasury bill rate. Thus, the risk premium used should be the premium earned by stocks over Treasury bonds.

3. *Arithmetic and geometric averages.* The final sticking point when it comes to estimating historical premiums relates to how the average returns on stocks, Treasury bonds, and Treasury bills are computed. The arithmetic average return measures the simple mean of the series of annual returns, whereas the geometric average looks at the compounded return.[9] Conventional wisdom argues for the use of the arithmetic average. In fact, if annual returns are uncorrelated over time, and our objective were to estimate the risk premium for the next year, the arithmetic average is the best unbiased estimate of the premium. However, there are strong arguments that can be made for the use of geometric averages. First, empirical studies seem to indicate that returns on stocks are negatively correlated over time.[10] Consequently, the arithmetic average return is likely to overstate the premium. Second, while asset pricing models may be single-period models, the use of these models to get expected returns over long periods (such as 5 or 10 years) suggests that we are interested in returns over longer periods. In this context, the argument for geometric average premiums becomes even stronger.

In summary, the equity risk premium estimates vary across users because of differences in time periods used, the choice of Treasury bills or bonds as the risk-free rate, and the use of arithmetic averages as opposed to geometric averages. The effect of these choices

---

[9]The compounded return is computed by taking the value of the investment at the start of the period (Value$_0$) and the value at the end (Value$_N$), and then computing the following:

$$\text{Geometric Average} = \left(\frac{\text{Value}_N}{\text{Value}_0} \right)^{1/N} - 1$$

[10]In other words, good years are more likely to be followed by poor years, and vice versa. The evidence on negative serial correlation in stock returns over time is extensive and can be found in Fama and French (1988). While they find that the one-year correlations are low, the five-year serial correlations are strongly negative for all size classes.

TABLE 7.3 Historical Risk Premiums for the United States (with standard errors in italics)

	Arithmetic Average		Geometric Average	
	Stocks–T. Bills	Stocks–T. Bonds	Stocks–T. Bills	Stocks–T. Bonds
1928–2023	8.32%	6.80%	6.50%	5.23%
Std. Error	*(2.03%)*	*(2.14%)*		
1974–2023	8.18%	5.95%	6.79%	4.97%
Std. Error	*(2.45%)*	*(2.73%)*		
2014–2023	11.70%	11.17%	10.63%	10.44%
Std. Error	*(4.97%)*	*(3.78%)*		

is summarized in Table 7.3, which uses returns from 1928 to 2023. Note that the premiums can range from 4.97 percent to 11.70 percent, depending on the choices made. In fact, these differences are exacerbated by the fact that many risk premiums that are in use today were estimated using historical data three, four, or even 10 years ago. If forced to choose an equity risk premium on this table, we would be inclined to go with 5.23 percent, the geometric average risk premium for stocks over Treasury bonds from 1928 to 2023. No matter what premium you choose, though, there will be substantial noise (standard error) in your estimate.

 histretSP.xls: **There is a dataset on the web that summarizes historical returns on stocks, T-bonds, and T-bills in the United States going back to 1928.**

Historical Risk Premiums: Other Markets   If it is difficult to estimate a reliable historical premium for the U.S. market, it becomes doubly so when looking at markets with short and volatile histories. This is clearly true for emerging markets, but it is also true for the European equity markets. While the economies of Germany, Italy, and France may be mature, their equity markets do not share the same characteristic. Until two decades ago, they tend to be dominated by a few large companies; many businesses remain private; and trading was, except on a few stocks.

There are some practitioners who still use historical premiums for these markets. To capture some of the danger in this practice, Table 7.4 summarizes historical risk premiums[11] for major non-U.S. markets for 1970–2017.

Note that some of the countries have very low historical risk premiums, and a few others have high risk premiums. Before an attempt is made to come up with a rationale for why this might be so, it is worth noting that the standard error on every one of these estimates is high, notwithstanding the fact that the premiums are estimated over a very long time period.

If the standard errors on these estimates are high, consider how much more noise there is in estimates of historical risk premiums for emerging market equity markets,

---

[11]This data is from the Credit Suisse Global Investment Returns Sourcebook, updated by Dimson, Marsh, and Staunton at the London Business School.

TABLE 7.4 Historical Equity Risk Premiums: Markets Outside the United States

Country	Stocks minus Long-term Governments			
	Geometric Mean	Arithmetic Mean	Standard Error	Standard Deviation
Australia	5.00%	6.60%	1.70%	18.10%
Austria	2.90%	21.50%	14.10%	151.50%
Belgium	2.20%	4.30%	1.90%	20.80%
Canada	3.50%	5.10%	1.70%	18.20%
Denmark	2.20%	3.80%	1.70%	18.00%
Finland	5.20%	8.70%	2.70%	29.70%
France	3.10%	5.40%	2.10%	22.50%
Germany	5.10%	8.40%	2.60%	28.20%
Ireland	2.70%	4.70%	1.80%	19.70%
Italy	3.20%	6.50%	2.70%	29.10%
Japan	5.10%	9.10%	3.00%	32.20%
Netherlands	3.30%	5.60%	2.00%	22.10%
New Zealand	4.00%	5.60%	1.60%	17.70%
Norway	2.40%	5.40%	2.50%	27.40%
Portugal	5.30%	9.40%	2.90%	31.40%
South Africa	5.30%	7.10%	1.80%	19.40%
Spain	1.80%	3.80%	1.90%	20.50%
Sweden	3.10%	5.30%	2.00%	21.20%
Switzerland	2.20%	3.70%	1.60%	17.40%
U.K.	3.70%	5.00%	1.60%	17.00%
U.S.	4.40%	6.50%	1.90%	20.70%
Europe	3.00%	4.30%	1.40%	15.70%
World-ex U.S.	2.80%	3.80%	1.30%	14.40%
World	3.20%	4.40%	1.40%	15.30%

Source: Adapted from Credit Suisse Global Yearbook, 2018.

which often have a reliable history of 10 years or less and very large standard deviations in annual stock returns. Historical risk premiums for emerging markets may provide for interesting anecdotes, but they clearly should not be used in risk and return models.

HISTORICAL RISK PREMIUM APPROACH: SOME CAVEATS

Given how widely the historical risk premium approach is used, it is surprising how flawed it is and how little attention these flaws have attracted. Consider first the underlying assumption that investors' risk premiums have not changed over time and that the average risk investment (in the market portfolio) has remained stable over the period examined. We would be hard-pressed to find anyone who would be willing to sustain this argument with fervor.

The obvious fix for this problem, which is to use a more recent time period, runs directly into a second problem, which is the large standard error associated with risk premium estimates. Though these standard errors may be tolerable for very long time periods, they clearly are unacceptably high when shorter periods are used.

Finally, even if there is a sufficiently long time period of history available and investors' risk aversion has not changed in a systematic way over that period, there is a final problem. Markets that exhibit this characteristic, and let us assume that the U.S. market is one such example, represent so-called survivor markets. In other words, assume that one had invested in the 10 largest equity markets in the world in 1928, of which the United States was one. In the period extending from 1928 to 2023, investments in few of the other equity markets would have earned as large a premium as the U.S. equity market, and some of them (like Austria) would have resulted in investors earning little or even negative returns over the period. Thus, the survivor bias will result in historical premiums that are larger than expected premiums for markets like the United States, even assuming that investors are rational and factor risk into prices.

Modified Historical Risk Premium   While historical risk premiums for markets outside the United States cannot be used in risk models, we still need to estimate a risk premium for use in these markets. To approach this estimation question, let us start with the basic proposition that the risk premium in any equity market can be written as:

Equity risk premium$_{\text{Country}}$ = Equity risk premium$_{\text{Mature Market}}$ + Country Risk Premium

The country premium could reflect the extra risk in a specific market. This boils down our estimation to answering two questions:

1. What should the base premium for a mature equity market be?
2. Should there be a country premium, and if so, how do we estimate the premium?

To answer the first question, one can argue that the U.S. equity market is a mature market and there is sufficient historical data in the United States to make a reasonable estimate of the risk premium. In fact, reverting back to our discussion of historical premiums in the U.S. market, you could use the geometric average premium earned by stocks over Treasury bonds of 5.23 percent between 1928 and 2023, as your estimate of the mature market premium. We have chosen the long time period to reduce standard error, the Treasury bond to be consistent with our choice of a risk-free rate, and the geometric averages to reflect our desire for a risk premium that we can use for longer-term expected returns.

On the issue of country premiums, there are some who argue that country risk is diversifiable and that there should be no country risk premium. After looking at the basis for their argument, and then considering the alternative view that there should be a country risk premium, we present approaches for estimating country risk premiums—one based on country bond default spreads and one based on equity market volatility.

Should There Be a Country Risk Premium?   Is there more risk in investing in a Malaysian or Brazilian stock than there is in investing in the United States? The answer, to most, seems to be obviously affirmative. That, however, does not answer the question of whether there should be an additional risk premium charged when investing in those markets.

Note that the only risk that is relevant for purposes of estimating a cost of equity is market risk or risk that cannot be diversified away. The key question then becomes whether the risk in an emerging market is diversifiable or nondiversifiable risk. If, in fact, the additional risk of investing in Malaysia or Brazil can be diversified away, then there should be no additional risk premium charged. If it cannot, then it makes sense to think about estimating a country risk premium.

But diversified away by whom? Equity in a Brazilian or Malaysian firm can be held by hundreds or thousands of investors, some of whom may hold only domestic stocks in their portfolio, whereas others may have more global exposure. For purposes of analyzing country risk, we look at the marginal investor—the investor most likely to be trading on the equity. If that marginal investor is globally diversified, there is at least the potential for global diversification. If the marginal investor does not have a global portfolio, the likelihood of diversifying away country risk declines substantially. Stulz (1999) made a similar point using different terminology. He differentiated between segmented markets, where risk premiums can be different in each market because investors cannot or will not invest outside their domestic markets, and open markets, where investors can invest across markets. In a segmented market, the marginal investor will be diversified only across investments in that market, whereas in an open market, the marginal investor has the opportunity (even if he or she does not take it) to invest across markets.

Even if the marginal investor is globally diversified, there is a second test that must be met for country risk not to matter. All or much of country risk should be country specific. In other words, there should be low correlation across markets. Only then will the risk be diversifiable in a globally diversified portfolio. If, however, the returns across countries have significant positive correlation, country risk has a market risk component, is not diversifiable, and can command a premium. Whether returns across countries are positively correlated is an empirical question. Studies from the 1970s and 1980s suggested that the correlation was low, and this was an impetus for global diversification. Partly because of the success of that sales pitch, and partly because economies around the world have become increasingly intertwined over the past decades, more recent studies indicate that the correlation across markets has risen. This is borne out by the speed with which troubles in one market, say Russia, can spread to a market with little or no obvious relationship to it, say Brazil.

So, where do we stand? We believe that while the barriers to trading across markets have dropped, investors still have a home bias in their portfolios and that markets remain partially segmented. While globally diversified investors are playing an increasing role in the pricing of equities around the world, the resulting increase in correlation across markets has resulted in a portion of country risk being nondiversifiable or market risk. The next section considers how best to measure this country risk and build it into expected returns.

Measuring Country Risk Premiums   If country risk matters and leads to higher premiums for riskier countries, the obvious follow-up question becomes how we measure this additional premium. This section looks at three approaches. The first builds on default spreads on country bonds issued by each country, whereas the second uses equity market volatility as its basis. The third is a melded approach that uses both default spreads and equity market volatility.

Default Risk Spreads While there are several measures of country risk, one of the simplest and most easily accessible is the rating assigned to a country's debt by a ratings agency; Standard & Poor's (S&P), Moody's Investors Service, and Fitch all rate countries. These ratings measure default risk (rather than equity risk), but they are affected by many of the factors that drive equity risk—the stability of a country's currency, its budget and trade balances, and its political stability, for instance.[12] The other advantage of ratings is that they can be used to estimate default spreads over the riskless rate. The default spreads are estimated by comparing the dollar- and euro-denominated bonds issued by governments that share a sovereign rating or by using sovereign CDS spreads. For instance, a 10-year dollar-denominated bond issued by the Brazilian government, rated Ba2 by Moody's, traded at an interest rate of 6.04% in January 2024—a 2.16% spread over the U.S. Treasury bond rate of 3.88% at the time. Since there can be country-specific factors that cause these rates to vary across bonds, we average the spreads from the government bonds and the sovereign CDS market within each ratings class to arrive at the average spread for each sovereign rating. Across five countries rated Baa3 in January 2024, for example, the average default spread was 2.39%. Thus, any country with a Baa3 rating, such as India, would be assigned a spread of 2.39% in January 2024.

The perils with sovereign ratings have been documented over the past few years. Specifically, ratings agencies seem to lag markets in responding to changes in country risk. An alternative approach to estimating default spreads is the CDS market, where investors can buy insurance against default risk, by paying an annual premium. As we noted previously in the section on risk-free rates, in early 2024 there were CDS instruments traded on about 80 countries, providing an updated market measure of default risk. In January 2024, for instance, the CDS spread for Brazil was 239 basis points (2.39 percent), close to the default spread estimated from the dollar-denominated bond. If you choose to stay with sovereign ratings, Table 7.5 summarizes default spreads estimated by sovereign ratings class in January 2024, using both the sovereign rating and CDS approaches. Thus, for Brazil, with its Ba2 rating, the default spread you would estimate would be 3.28%.

TABLE 7.5   Default Spreads by Ratings Class in January 2024

	P Bond Rating	
S&P Bond Rating	**Moody's Sovereign Rating**	**Sovereign Default Spread**
AAA	Aaa	0.00%
AA+	Aa1	0.44%
AA	Aa2	0.54%
AA–	Aa3	0.65%
A+	A1	0.77%
A	A2	0.92%
A–	A3	1.31%
BBB+	Baa1	1.74%
BBB	Baa2	2.07%
BBB–	Baa3	2.39%

(continued)

[12] The process by which country ratings are obtained is explained on the S&P website at www.standardandpoors.com.

TABLE 7.5 *(continued)*

S&P Bond Rating	Moody's Sovereign Rating	Sovereign Default Spread
	P Bond Rating	
BB+	Ba1	2.73%
BB	Ba2	3.28%
BB−	Ba3	3.92%
B+	B1	4.90%
B	B2	5.99%
B−	B3	7.08%
CCC+	Caa1	8.17%
CCC	Caa2	9.81%
CCC−	Caa3	10.90%
CC+	Ca1	12.25%
CC	Ca2	14.00%
CC−	Ca3	15.00%
C+	C1	15.75%
C	C2	16.75%
C−	C3	18.00%

Analysts who use default spreads as measures of country risk typically add them on to the cost of both equity and debt of every company traded in that country. For instance, the cost of equity for a Brazilian company, estimated in U.S. dollars, will be 3.28% percent higher (based upon Brazil's sovereign rating of Ba2) than the cost of equity of an otherwise similar U.S. company. If we assume that the risk premium for the United States and other mature equity markets is 4.60 percent (and we will provide backing for that later in this chapter), the cost of equity for a Brazilian company with a beta of 1.2 can be estimated as follows (with a U.S. Treasury bond rate of 4 percent):

$$\text{Cost of equity (in U.S. dollars)} = \text{Risk-free rate}$$
$$+ \text{Beta (Equity risk premium for mature market)}$$
$$+ \text{Default spread}$$
$$= 4.0\% + 1.2(4.6\%) + 3.28\% = 12.80\%$$

To estimate the cost of equity for the same company in Brazilian reals, you would substitute in the risk-free rate in $R for the U.S. dollar risk-free rate in the calculation. If you believe that a company's exposure to country risk is similar to its exposure to other macroeconomic risk factors, analysts add the default spread to the U.S. risk premium and multiply the total risk premium by the beta.

$$\text{Cost of equity (in U.S. dollars)} = \text{Risk-free rate} + \text{Beta}$$
$$+ (\text{Mature Market Premium} + \text{Default spread})$$
$$= 4.0\% + 1.2(4.6\% + 3.28\%) = 13.46\%$$

This increases the cost of equity for high-beta companies and lowers it for low-beta firms.

While ratings provide a convenient measure of country risk, there are costs associated with using them as the only measure. First, ratings agencies often lag markets when it comes to responding to changes in the underlying default risk. Second, the ratings agency's focus on default risk may obscure other risks that could still affect equity markets. What are the alternatives? There are numerical country risk scores that have been developed by some services as much more comprehensive measures of risk. The *Economist*, for instance, has a score that runs from 0 to 100 (where 0 is no risk, and 100 is most risky) that it uses to rank emerging markets. Alternatively, country risk can be estimated from the bottom up by looking at economic fundamentals in each country. This, of course, requires significantly more information than the other approaches. Finally, default spreads measure the risk associated with bonds issued by countries and not the equity risk in these countries. Since equities in any market are likely to be more risky than bonds, you could argue that default spreads understate equity risk premiums.

Relative Standard Deviations There are some analysts who believe that investors in equity markets choose among these markets based on their assessed riskiness and that the risk premiums should reflect the differences in equity risk. A conventional measure of equity risk is the standard deviation in stock prices; higher standard deviations are generally associated with more risk. If you scale the standard deviation of one market against another, you obtain a measure of relative risk. Thus, to get the relative standard deviation for country A, relative to the United States:

$$\text{Relative Standard Deviation}_{\text{Country A}} = \frac{\text{Standard Deviation}_{\text{Country A}}}{\text{Standard Deviation}_{\text{US}}}$$

This relative standard deviation, when multiplied by the premium used for U.S. stocks, should yield a measure of the total risk premium for any market.

$$\text{Equity Risk Premium}_{\text{Country A}} = \text{ERP}_{\text{US}} \times \text{Relative Standard Deviation}_{\text{Country A}}$$

Assume, for the moment, that you are using a mature market premium for the United States of 4.60 percent and that the annual standard deviation of U.S. stocks is 12.41 percent in 2023. If the annual standard deviation of Brazilian stocks is 16.21 percent in 2023, the estimate of a total risk premium for Indonesia would be:

$$\text{Equity Risk Premium}_{\text{Indonesia}} = 4.60\% \times (16.21\%/12.41\%) = 6.01\%$$

The country risk premium can be isolated as follows:

$$\text{Country Risk Premium}_{\text{Indonesia}} = 6.01\% - 4.60\% = 1.41\%$$

While this approach has intuitive appeal, there are problems with using standard deviations computed in markets with widely different market structures and liquidity. There are very risky emerging markets that have low standard deviations for their equity markets because the markets are illiquid. This approach will understate the equity risk premiums in those markets. The second problem is related to currencies, since the standard deviations are usually measured in local currency terms; the standard deviation in the U.S. market is a dollar standard deviation, whereas the standard deviation in the Indonesian market is a rupiah standard deviation. This is a relatively simple problem to fix, though, since the standard deviations can be measured in the same currency—you could estimate the standard deviation in dollar returns for the Indonesian market.

THE DANGER OF DOUBLE COUNTING RISK

When assessing country risk, there is a substantial chance that the same risk may be counted more than once in a valuation. For instance, there are analysts who use the dollar-denominated bonds issued by a country—the Brazilian dollar bond, for instance—as the risk-free rate when estimating cost of equity for Brazilian companies. The interest rate on this bond already incorporates the default spreads discussed in the preceding section. If the risk premium is also adjusted upward to reflect country risk, there has been a double counting of the risk. This effect is made worse when betas are adjusted upward and cash flows are adjusted downward (a process called "haircutting") because of country risk.

Default Spreads + Relative Standard Deviations   The country default spreads that come with country ratings provide an important first step but still only measure the premium for default risk. Intuitively, we would expect the country equity risk premium to be larger than the country default risk spread. To address the issue of how much higher, one can look at the volatility of the equity market in a country relative to the volatility of the country bond used to estimate the spread. This yields the following estimate for the country equity risk premium:

$$\text{Country risk premium} = \text{Country Default Spread} \left[\frac{\text{Standard Deviation}_{\text{Equity}}}{\text{Standard Deviation}_{\text{Country bond}}} \right]$$

To illustrate, consider the case of Brazil. In January 2024, Brazil was rated Baa2 by Moody's, resulting in a default spread of 3.28 percent. The annualized standard deviation in the Brazilian equity index over the previous year was 16.21 percent, while the annualized standard deviation in the Brazilian dollar-denominated bond was 13.32 percent. The resulting country equity risk premium for Brazil is as follows:

$$\text{Brazil Country Risk Premium} = 3.28\% \times \frac{16.21\%}{13.32\%} = 3.99\%$$

Note that this country risk premium will increase if the country rating drops or if the relative volatility of the equity market increases. Adding this premium to the mature market (U.S.) premium of 4.60 percent would yield a total equity risk premium for Brazil of 8.59 percent.

Why should equity risk premiums have any relationship to country bond spreads? A simple explanation is that an investor who can make 3.28 percent on a dollar-denominated Brazilian government bond would not settle for a lesser premium on Brazilian equity. Playing devil's advocate, however, a critic could argue that the interest rate on a country bond, from which default spreads are extracted, is not really an expected return since it is based on the promised cash flows (coupon and principal) on the bond rather than the expected cash flows. In fact, if we wanted to estimate a risk premium for bonds, we would need to estimate the expected return based on expected cash flows, allowing for the default risk. This would result in a much lower default spread and equity risk premium.

Both this approach and the previous one use the standard deviation in equity of a market to make a judgment about country risk premium, but they measure it relative to different bases. This approach uses the country bond as a base, whereas the previous one uses the standard deviation in the U.S. market. This approach assumes that investors are more likely to choose between Brazilian bonds and Brazilian equity, whereas the previous approach assumes that the choice is across equity markets.

Choosing among the Approaches The three approaches to estimating country risk premiums will generally give you different estimates, with the bond default spread and relative equity standard deviation approaches yielding lower country risk premiums than the melded approach that uses both the country bond default spread and the equity standard deviation. We believe that the larger country risk premiums that emerge from the last approach are the most realistic for the immediate future, but that country risk premiums will change over time. Just as companies mature and become less risky over time, countries can mature and become less risky as well.

One way to adjust country risk premiums over time is to begin with the premium that emerges from the melded approach and to adjust this premium down toward either the country bond default spread or the country premium estimated from equity standard deviations. Another way of presenting this argument is to note that the differences between standard deviations in equity and bond prices narrow over longer periods, and the resulting relative volatility will generally be smaller.[13] Thus, the equity risk premium will converge on the country bond spread as we look at longer-term expected returns. For example, the country risk premium for Brazil would be 3.99 percent for the next year but decline over time to either the 3.28 percent (country default spread) or even lower.

Estimating Asset Exposure to Country Risk Premiums Once country risk premiums have been estimated, the final question that has to be addressed relates to the exposure of individual companies within that country-to-country risk. There are three alternative views of country risk:

1. *Assume that all companies in a country are equally exposed to country risk.* Thus, for Brazil with its estimated country risk premium of 3.99 percent, each company in the market will have an additional country risk premium of 3.99 percent added to its expected returns. For instance, the cost of equity for Petrobras, an integrated oil company listed in Brazil with a beta of 0.80, in U.S. dollar terms would be (assuming a U.S. Treasury bond rate of 4.00 percent and a mature market [U.S.] risk premium of 4.60 percent):

$$\text{Expected return} = 4.00\% + 0.80(4.60\%) + 3.99\% = 11.67\%$$

Note that the risk-free rate used is the U.S. Treasury bond rate and that the 4.60 percent is the equity risk premium for a mature equity market (estimated from

---

[13] Jeremy Siegel reports on the standard deviation in equity markets in his book, *Stocks for the Very Long Run: The Definitive Guide to Investment Strategies* (New York, McGraw-Hill, 2007), and notes that they tend to decrease with time horizon.

historical data in the U.S. market). The biggest limitation of this approach is that it assumes that all firms in a country, no matter what their business or size, are equally exposed to country risk. To convert this dollar cost of equity into a cost of equity in the local currency, all that we need to do is to scale the estimate by relative inflation. To illustrate, if the Brazilian inflation rate is 6 percent and the U.S. inflation rate is 2 percent, the cost of equity for Petrobras in Brazilian real (BR) terms can be written as:

$$\text{Cost of equity in } \$R = (1.1167)(1.06/1.02) - 1 = 16.05\%$$

This will ensure consistency across estimates and valuations in different currencies.

2. Assume that a company's exposure to country risk is proportional to its exposure to all other market risk, which is measured by the beta. For Petrobras, this would lead to a US $ cost of equity estimate of:

$$\text{Expected return} = 4.00\% + 0.80(4.60\% + 3.99\%) = 10.87\%$$

This approach does differentiate between firms, but it assumes that betas that measure exposure to all other market risk measure exposure to country risk as well. Thus, low-beta companies are less exposed to country risk than high-beta companies.

3. The most general approach, and most information-intensive approach, is to allow for each company to have an exposure to country risk that is different from its exposure to all other market risk. Measuring this exposure with λ, the cost of equity for any firm is estimated as follows:

$$\text{Expected return} = Rf + \text{Beta (Mature equity risk premium)}$$
$$+ \lambda(\text{Country risk premium})$$

How can we best estimate λ? This question is considered in far more detail in the next chapter, but we would argue that commodity companies that get most of their revenues in U.S. dollars[14] by selling into a global market should be less exposed than manufacturing companies that service the local market. Using this rationale, Petrobras, which derives most of its revenues in the global oil market in U.S. dollars, should be less exposed than the typical Brazilian firm to country risk.[15] Using a λ of 0.50, for instance, we get a cost of equity in U.S. dollar terms for Petrobras of:

$$\text{Expected return} = 4.00\% + 0.80(4.60\%) + 0.50(3.99\%) = 9.68\%$$

Note that the third approach essentially converts our expected return model to a two-factor model, with the second factor being country risk, with λ measuring exposure to country risk. This approach also seems to offer the most promise in analyzing companies

---

[14]While I have categorized dollar revenues, the analysis can be generalized to look at revenues in stable currencies (e.g., the dollar, euro, etc.) and revenues in risky currencies.

[15]One approach to estimating lambda is to divide the percent of revenues that a company gets from a country by how much revenue the average company in the country gets from that country.

with exposure to a single risky country in its operations. For multinationals that can have exposures to dozens of countries, we will argue that taking a weighted average of the equity risk premiums of these countries offers a more practical path.

 ctryprem.xlsx: **There is a dataset on the web that contains the updated ratings for countries and the risk premiums associated with each.**

Alternative Approach: Implied Equity Premiums

There is an alternative to estimating risk premiums that does not require historical data or corrections for country risk, but does assume that the market, overall, is correctly priced. Consider, for instance, a very simple valuation model for stocks:

$$\text{Value of equity} = \frac{\text{Expected Dividends Next Period}}{(\text{Required Return on Equity} - \text{Expected Growth Rate})}$$

This is essentially the present value of dividends growing at a constant rate. Three of the four inputs in this model can be obtained externally—the current level of the market (value), the expected dividends next period, and the expected growth rate in earnings and dividends in the long term. The only unknown is then the required return on equity; when we solve for it, we get an implied expected return on stocks. Subtracting the risk-free rate will yield an implied equity risk premium.

To illustrate, assume that the current level of the S&P 500 index is 900, the expected dividend yield on the index is 2 percent, and the expected growth rate in earnings and dividends in the long term is 7 percent. Solving for the required return on equity (r) yields the following:

$$900 = \frac{(.02 \times 900)}{(r - .07)}$$

Solving for r,

$$\text{Expected return (r)} = (18 + 63)/900 = 9\%$$

If the current risk-free rate is 6 percent, this will yield an "implied equity risk premium" of 3 percent.

This approach can be generalized to allow high growth for a period, and extended to cover cash flow–based, rather than dividend, models. Figure 7.2 contains an expanded version of the model, with dividends and buybacks replacing dividends and enabling a period of growth, before setting into a stable growth rate.

To illustrate this, consider the S&P 500 index as of January 1, 2024. The index was at 4769.83, and the cash flows from dividends and stock buybacks during 2023 were 164.25. In addition, the consensus estimate[16] of growth in earnings for companies in the index was

---

[16]We used the average of the analyst estimates for individual firms (bottom-up). Alternatively, we could have used the top-down estimate for the S&P 500 earnings (from economists).

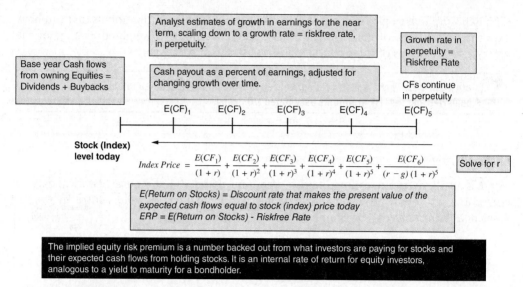

FIGURE 7.2 A Generalized Model for Implied Equity Risk Premium

approximately 8.74 percent for the next five years. Since this is not a growth rate that can be sustained forever, we employ a two-stage valuation model, where we allow growth to continue at 8.74 percent for five years, and then lower the growth rate to the Treasury bond rate of 3.88 percent after that.[17] Figure 7.3 summarizes the expected cash flows for the next five years of high growth and the first year of stable growth thereafter.

If we assume that these are reasonable estimates of the cash flows and that the index is correctly priced, then:

$$4769.83 = \frac{185.97}{(1+r)} + \frac{202.21}{(1+r)^2} + \frac{219.88}{(1+r)^3} + \frac{239.09}{(1+r)^4} + \frac{259.97}{(1+r)^5} + \frac{270.06}{(r - .0388)(1+r)^5}$$

Note that the last term in the equation is the terminal value of the index, based on the stable growth rate of 3.88 percent, discounted back to the present. Solving for r in this equation yields us the required return on equity of 8.48 percent. Netting out the Treasury bond rate of 3.88 percent yields an implied equity premium of 4.60 percent.

The advantage of this approach is that it is market-driven and current and does not require any historical data. Thus, it can be used to estimate implied equity premiums in any market. It is, however, bounded by whether the model used for the valuation is the right one, and by the availability and reliability of the inputs to that model. For instance, the equity risk premium for the Brazilian market on September 30, 2009, was estimated from the following inputs. The index (Bovespa) was at 61,172, and the aggregate cash flow yield on the index was 4.95 percent. Earnings in companies in the index are expected to grow 6 percent (in U.S. dollar terms) over the next five years, and 3.45 percent thereafter. These inputs yield a required return on equity of 9.17 percent, which when compared to the U.S.

---

[17]The Treasury bond rate is the sum of expected inflation and the expected real rate. If we assume that real growth is equal to the real rate, the long-term stable growth rate should be equal to the Treasury bond rate.

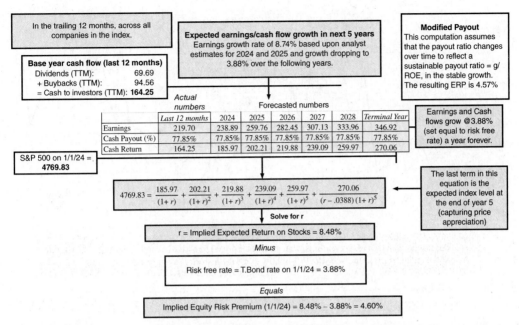

FIGURE 7.3 Implied Equity Risk Premium for S&P 500 on January 1, 2024

Treasury bond rate of 3.45 percent on that day, results in an implied equity premium of 5.72 percent. For simplicity, we have used nominal dollar expected growth rates[18] and Treasury bond rates, but this analysis could have been done entirely in the local currency.

The implied equity premiums change over time as stock prices, earnings, and interest rates change. In fact, the contrast between these premiums and the historical premiums is best illustrated by graphing out the implied premiums in the S&P 500 going back to 1960 in Figure 7.4. In terms of mechanics, smoothed historical growth rates in earnings and dividends were used as projected growth rates, and a two-stage dividend discount model was used. Looking at these numbers, the following conclusions would be drawn:

■ The arithmetic average historical risk premium, which is used by many practitioners, has been higher than the implied premium over almost the entire 50-year period (with 2009 the only exception). The geometric premium does provide a more interesting mix of results, with implied premiums exceeding historical premiums in the mid-1970s and again following 2008.

■ The implied equity premium did increase during the 1970s, as inflation increased. This does have interesting implications for risk premium estimation. Instead of assuming that the risk premium is a constant and unaffected by the level of inflation and interest rates, which is what we do with historical risk premiums, it may be more realistic to increase the risk premium if expected inflation and interest rates go up.

---

[18]The input that is most difficult to estimate for emerging markets is a long-term expected growth rate. For Brazilian stocks, I used the average consensus estimate of growth in earnings for the largest Brazilian companies that have American depositary receipts (ADRs) listed on them. This estimate may be biased as a consequence.

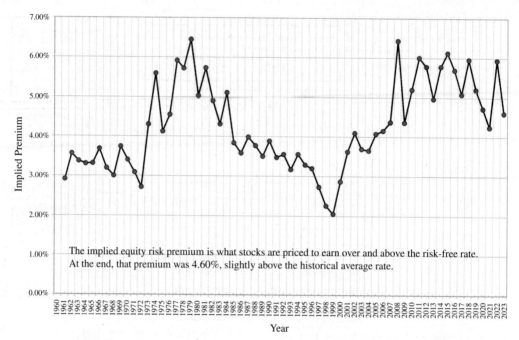

FIGURE 7.4   Implied Premiums for U.S. Equity Market (1960–2023)

▓ While historical risk premiums have generally drifted down for the last few decades, there is a strong tendency toward mean reversion in implied equity premiums. Thus, the premium, which peaked at 6.5 percent in 1978, moved down toward the average in the 1980s. By the same token, the premium of 2 percent that we observed at the end of the dot-com boom in the 1990s, quickly reverted back to the average during the market correction from 2000 to 2003.

Finally, the crisis of 2008 was unprecedented in terms of its impact on equity risk premiums. Implied equity risk premiums rose more during 2008 than in any one of the prior 50 years. Much of that change occurred in the last 15 weeks of the year when the United States and other developed markets went through gyrations more typical of emerging markets. A large portion of that increase dissipated in 2009 but returned again in 2010 and 2011. At the outset of the global pandemic, in the first quarter of 2020, equity risk premiums spiked again, before retracing its steps during the rest of the year.

As a final point, there is a strong tendency toward mean reversion in financial markets. Given this tendency, it is possible that we can end up with a far better estimate of the implied equity premium by looking not just at the current premium but also at historical data. There are two ways in which we can do this:

1. We can use the average implied equity premium over longer periods, say 10–15 years. Note that we do not need as many years of data here as we did with the historical premium estimate, because the standard errors tend to be smaller.
2. A more rigorous approach would require relating implied equity risk premiums to fundamental macroeconomic data over the period. For instance, given that implied

equity premiums tend to be higher during periods with higher inflation rates (and interest rates), we ran a regression of implied equity premiums regressed equity risk premiums against the inflation rate and GDP growth, using data from 1961 to 2023:

$$ERP = 0.0430 + 0.1061CPI - 0.155 \quad Real\ GDP\ Growth \quad R^2 = 17.34\%$$
$$(14.94^{**})\ (2.33^{**}) \qquad (2.55^{**})$$

The regression has some explanatory power, with an R-squared of 18 percent, and the t statistics (in brackets under the coefficients) indicate the statistical significance of the independent variable used. Substituting the current treasury bond rate and real GDP growth into this equation should yield an estimate of the equity risk premium. On March 8, 2024, for instance, I estimated an equity risk premium of 4.20%, from a regression where I related equity risk premiums to inflation rates, and using the 4.25% inflation rate at the time.[19]

---

 histimpl.xls: **There is a dataset on the web that summarizes our estimates of the implied equity risk premium for the S&P 500 from 1960 through today, with the inputs used.**

HISTORICAL VERSUS IMPLIED EQUITY PREMIUMS: EFFECT OF MARKET VIEWS

As you can see from the preceding discussion, historical premiums can be very different from implied equity premiums. At the end of 2000, the historical risk premium for stocks over bonds in the United States was 5.51 percent, whereas the implied equity risk premium was 2.87 percent. In contrast, at the end of 2008, the historical risk premium was 3.88%, whereas the implied premium was 6.43%. When doing discounted cash flow valuation, you have to decide which risk premium you will use in the valuation, and your choice will be determined by both your market views and your valuation mission.

Market Views: If you believe that the *market is right in the aggregate,* though it may make mistakes on individual stocks, the risk premium you should use is the current implied equity risk premium. If you believe that the market often makes mistakes in the aggregate and *risk premiums in markets tend to move back to historical norms* (mean reversion), you should go with the historical premium. A way to split the difference is to assume that *markets are right across time,* though they may make

(continued)

---

[19] On March 8, 2024, for instance, I substituted the expected inflation rate and real GDP growth rate into the regression equation to estimate an expected equity risk premium.
$$ERP = 2.97\% + 0.2903(4.25\%) = 4.20\%$$

(*continued*)

mistakes at individual points in time. If you make this assumption, you should use an average implied equity risk premium over time. The average implied equity risk premium from 1960 to 2023 is 4.25 percent. While this book uses the historical premium a few times in its valuations, it sticks with the implied premium in most of the valuations.

Valuation Mission: If your valuation requires you to be market neutral, i.e., to value a company, given where the market is today, you should use the current implied equity risk premium.

DEFAULT SPREADS ON BONDS

The interest rates on bonds are determined by the default risk that investors perceive in the issuer of the bonds. This default risk is often measured with a bond rating, and the interest rate that corresponds to the rating is estimated by adding a default spread to the riskless rate. In Chapter 4, we examined the process used by rating agencies to rate firms. This chapter considers how to estimate default spreads for a given ratings class and why these spreads may change over time.

Estimating Default Spreads

The simplest way to estimate default spreads for each ratings class is to find a sampling of bonds within that ratings class and obtain the current market interest rate on these bonds. Why do we need a sampling rather than just one bond? A bond can be mis-rated or mis-priced. Using a sample reduces or eliminates this problem. In obtaining this sample, you should try to focus on the most liquid bonds with as few special features attached to them as possible. Corporate bonds are often illiquid and the interest rates on such bonds may not reflect current market rates. The presence of special features on bonds such as convertibility can affect the pricing of these bonds and consequently the interest rates estimated on them.

Once a sample of bonds within each ratings class has been identified, you need to estimate the interest rate on these bonds. There are two measures that are widely used. The first is the yield on the bond, which is the coupon rate divided by the market price. The second is the yield to maturity on the bond, which is the interest rate that makes the present value of the coupons and face value of the bond equal to the market price. In general, it is the yield to maturity that better measures the market interest rate on the bond.

Having obtained the interest rates on the bonds in the sample, you have two decisions to make. The first relates to weighting. You could compute a simple average of the interest rates of the bonds in the sample or a weighted average, with the weights based upon the trading volume—more liquid bonds will be weighted more than less liquid bonds. The second relates to the index Treasury rate, since the average interest rate for a ratings class is compared to this rate to arrive at a default spread. In general, the maturity of the Treasury should match the average maturity of the corporate bonds chosen to estimate the average interest rate. Thus, the average interest rate for five-year BBB-rated corporate bonds should be compared to the average interest rate for five-year Treasuries to derive the spread for the BBB-rated bonds.

Data services have historically provided interest rates on at least higher-rated bonds (BBB or higher), an increasing number of online services provide the same information today for all rated bonds. Table 7.6 is extracted from one such online service in early 2024 for 10-year bonds using a 10-year T Bond rate of 3.88% as the risk-free rate.

Determinants of Default Spreads

Table 7.6 provides default spreads at a point in time, but default spreads not only vary across time, but they also can vary for bonds with the same rating but different maturities. This section considers how default spreads vary across time and for bonds with varying maturities.

Default Spreads and Bond Maturity   Empirically, the default spread for corporate bonds of a given ratings class seem to increase mildly with the maturity of the bond. Figure 7.5 presents the default spreads estimated for Aaa- and Baa -rated bonds for maturities ranging from 1 to 30 years in January 2024.

The default spreads do rise, as you increase maturities until about ten years, before leveling off and decreasing. There have been some periods in history where default spreads were an increasing function of maturity and other periods where they were a decreasing function.

TABLE 7.6   Default Spreads and Interest Rates—January 2024

Moody's/S&P Rating	Default Spread	Interest Rate
Aaa/AAA	0.59%	4.47%
Aa2/AA	0.70%	4.58%
A1/A+	0.92%	4.80%
A2/A	1.07%	4.95%
A3/A−	1.21%	5.09%
Baa2/BBB	1.47%	5.35%
Ba1/BB+	1.74%	5.62%
Ba2/BB	2.21%	6.09%
B1/B+	3.14%	7.02%
B2/B	3.61%	7.49%
B3/B−	5.24%	9.12%
Caa/CCC	8.51%	12.39%
Ca2/CC	11.78%	15.66%
C2/C	17.00%	20.88%
D2/D	20.00%	23.88%

Source: With permission of National Association of Insurance Commissioners.

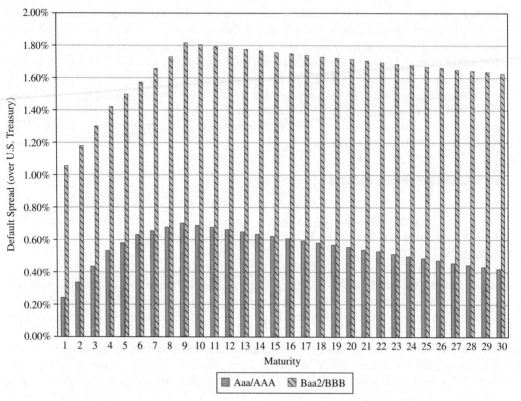

FIGURE 7.5   Default Spreads by Maturity—January 2024
Source: With permission of National Association of Insurance Commissioners.

Default Spreads over Time   The default spreads presented in Table 7.6, after a year of declining markets and a slowing economy, were significantly higher than the default spreads a year earlier. This phenomenon is not new. Historically, default spreads for every ratings class have increased during recessions and decreased during economic booms. Figure 7.6 graphs the spread between 10-year Moody's Baa-rated bonds and the 10-year Treasury bond rate each year from 1960 to 2023, and then contrasts it with the implied equity risk premium each year. The default spreads did increase during periods of low economic growth; note the increase during 1973–1974 and 1979–1981, in particular. Although default spreads and equity risk premiums in most periods have generally moved in tandem, there have been exceptional periods when they moved in different directions. In the late 1990s, for instance, the dot-com boom in stock prices resulted in declining equity risk premiums, while default spreads stayed relatively stable. In contrast, the subprime boom in 2004–2007 lowered default spreads, while equity risk premiums stayed unchanged.

 ratings.xls: **This dataset on the web summarizes default spreads by bond-rating class for the most recent period.**

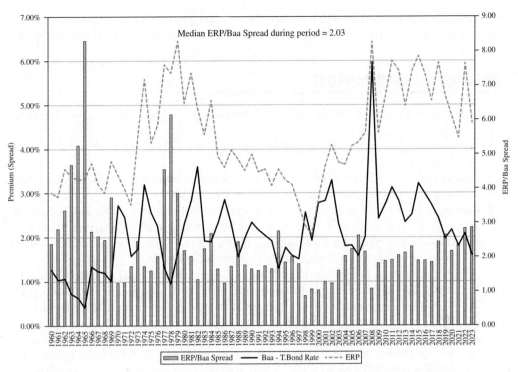

FIGURE 7.6   Baa Bond Default Spread and Implied Equity Risk Premiums: 1960–2023

CONCLUSION

The risk-free rate is the starting point for all expected return models. For an asset to be risk free, it has to be free of both default and reinvestment risk. Using these criteria, the appropriate risk-free rate to use to obtain expected returns should be a default-free (government) zero coupon rate that is matched up to when the cash flow that is being discounted occurs. In practice, however, it is usually appropriate to match up the duration of the risk-free asset to the duration of the cash flows being analyzed. In valuation, this will lead us toward long-term government bond rates as risk-free rates. It is also important that the risk-free rate be consistent with the cash flows being discounted. In particular, the currency in which the risk-free rate is denominated, and whether it is a real or nominal risk-free rate, should be determined by the currency in which the cash flows are estimated and whether the estimation is done in real or nominal terms.

The risk premium is a fundamental and critical component in portfolio management, corporate finance, and valuation. Given its importance, it is surprising that more attention has not been paid in practical terms to estimation issues. This chapter considered the conventional approach to estimating risk premiums, which is to use historical returns on equity and government securities, and evaluated some of its weaknesses. It also examined how to extend this approach to emerging markets, where historical data tends to be both limited and volatile. The alternative to historical premiums is to estimate the equity premium implied by equity prices. This approach does require that we start with a valuation model for equities, and estimate the expected growth and cash flows, collectively, on equity investments. It has the advantages of not requiring historical data and of reflecting current market perceptions.

QUESTIONS AND SHORT PROBLEMS

In the problems following, use an equity risk premium of 5.5 percent if none is specified.

1. Assume that you are valuing an Indonesian firm in U.S. dollars. What would you use as the riskless rate?
2. Explain why a six-month Treasury bill rate is not an appropriate riskless rate in discounting a five-year cash flow.
3. You have been asked to estimate a riskless rate in Indonesian rupiah. The Indonesian government has rupiah-denominated bonds outstanding, with an interest rate of 17%. S&P has a rating of BB on these bonds, and the typical spread for a BB-rated country is 5% over a riskless rate. Estimate the rupiah riskless rate.
4. You are valuing an Indian company in rupees. The current exchange rate is Rs. 45 per dollar, and you have been able to obtain a 10-year forward rate of Rs. 70 per dollar. If the U.S. Treasury bond rate is 5%, estimate the riskless rate in Indian rupees.
5. You are attempting to do a valuation of a Chilean company in real terms. While you have been unable to get a real riskless rate in Latin America, you know that inflation-indexed Treasury bonds in the United States are yielding 3%. Could you use this as a real riskless rate? Why or why not? What are the alternatives?
6. Assume you have estimated the historical risk premium, based on 50 years of data, to be 6%. If the annual standard deviation in stock prices is 30%, estimate the standard error in the risk premium estimate.
7. When you use a historical risk premium as your expected future risk premium, what are the assumptions that you are making about investors and markets? Under what conditions would a historical risk premium give you too high a number (to use as an expected premium)?
8. You are trying to estimate a country equity risk premium for Poland. You find that S&P has assigned an A rating to Poland and that Poland has issued euro-denominated bonds that yield 7.6% in the market currently. (Germany, a AAA-rated country, has euro-denominated bonds outstanding that yield 5.1%.)
   a. Estimate the country risk premium, using the default spread on the country bond as the proxy.
   b. If you were told that the standard deviation in the Polish equity market was 25% and that the standard deviation in the Polish euro bond was 15%, estimate the country risk premium.
9. The standard deviation in the Mexican Equity Index is 48%, and the standard deviation in the S&P 500 is 20%. You use an equity risk premium of 5.5% for the United States.
   a. Estimate the country equity risk premium for Mexico using relative equity standard deviations.
   b. Now assume that you are told that Mexico is rated BBB by Standard & Poor's and that it has dollar-denominated bonds outstanding that trade at a spread of about 3% above the Treasury bond rate. If the standard deviation in these bonds is 24%, estimate the country risk premium for Mexico.

10. The S&P 500 is at 1,400. The expected dividends and cash flows next year on the stocks in the index are expected to be 5% of the index. If the expected growth rate in dividends and cash flows over the long term is expected to be 6% and the riskless rate is 5.5%, estimate the implied equity risk premium.

11. The Bovespa (Brazilian equity index) is at 15,000. The dividends on the index last year were 5% of the index value, and analysts expect them to grow 15% a year in real terms for the next five years. After the fifth year, the growth is expected to drop to 5% in real terms in perpetuity. If the real riskless rate is 6%, estimate the implied equity risk premium in this market.

12. As stock prices go up, implied equity risk premiums will go down. Is this statement always true? If not, when is it not true?

CHAPTER 8

Estimating Risk Parameters and Costs of Financing

The preceding chapter laid the groundwork for estimating the costs of equity and capital for firms by looking at how best to estimate a riskless rate that operates as a base for all costs, an equity risk premium for estimating the cost of equity, and default spreads for estimating the cost of debt. It did not, however, consider how to estimate the risk parameters for individual firms. This chapter examines the process of estimating risk parameters for individual firms estimating both the cost of equity and cost of debt.

For the cost of equity, we look at the standard process of estimating the beta for a firm and consider alternative approaches. For the cost of debt, we examine bond ratings as measures of default risk and the determinants of these ratings.

The chapter closes by bringing together the risk parameter estimates for individual firms, and the economy-wide estimates of the risk-free rate and risk premiums to estimate a cost of capital for the firm. To do this, the sources of capital have to be weighted by their relative market values (MVs).

THE COST OF EQUITY AND CAPITAL

Firms raise money from both equity investors and lenders to fund investments. Both groups of investors make their investments expecting to make a return. Chapter 4 argued that the expected return for equity investors would include a premium for the equity risk in the investment. We label this expected return the cost of equity. Similarly, the expected return that lenders hope to make on their investments includes a premium for default risk, and we call that expected return the cost of debt. If we consider all the financing that the firm takes on, the composite cost of financing will be a weighted average of the costs of equity and debt, and this weighted cost is the cost of capital.

The chapter begins by estimating the equity risk in a firm and using the equity risk to estimate the cost of equity, and then follows up by measuring the default risk to estimate a cost of debt. It concludes by determining the weights we should attach to each of these costs to arrive at a cost of capital.

COST OF EQUITY

The cost of equity is the rate of return investors require on an equity investment in a firm. The risk and return models described in Chapter 4 need a riskless rate and a risk premium (in the capital asset pricing model [CAPM]) or premiums (in the arbitrage pricing model [APM] and multifactor models), which were estimated in the last chapter. They also need measures of a firm's exposure to market risk in the form of betas. These inputs are used to arrive at an expected return on an equity investment:

$$\text{Expected Return} = \text{Risk-free Rate} + \text{Beta} \times \text{Equity Risk Premium}$$

This expected return to equity investors includes compensation for the market risk in the investment and is the cost of equity. This section concentrates on the estimation of the beta of a firm. While much of the discussion is directed at the CAPM, it can be extended to apply to arbitrage pricing and multifactor model, as well.

Betas—Estimation Approaches

In the CAPM, the beta of an investment is the risk that the investment adds to a market portfolio. In the APM and multifactor model, the betas of the investment relative to each factor must be measured. There are three approaches available for estimating these parameters: One is to use historical data on market prices for individual investments; the second is to estimate the betas from the fundamental characteristics of the investment; and the third is to use accounting data. All three approaches are described in this section.

Historical Market Betas   The conventional approach for estimating the beta of an investment is a regression of returns on the investment against returns on a market index. For firms that have been publicly traded for a length of time, it is relatively straightforward to estimate returns that an investor would have made on investing in the firms' equity in intervals (such as a week or a month) over that period. In theory, these stock returns on the assets should be related to returns on a market portfolio (i.e., a portfolio that includes all traded assets) to estimate the betas of the assets. In practice, we tend to use a stock index such as the S&P 500 as a proxy for the market portfolio, and we estimate betas for stocks against the index.

Regression Estimates of Betas   The standard procedure for estimating betas is to regress stock returns (R_j) against market returns (R_m):

$$R_j = a = b\ R_m$$

where   a = Intercept from the regression

b = Slope of the regression = $\text{Covariance}\left(R_j, R_m\right)/\sigma_m^2$

The slope of the regression corresponds to the beta of the stock and measures the riskiness of the stock.

The intercept of the regression provides a simple measure of performance of the investment during the period of the regression, when returns are measured against the expected returns from the capital asset pricing model. To see why, consider the following rearrangement of the capital asset pricing model:

$$R_j = R_f + \beta(R_m - R_f)$$
$$= R_f(1 - \beta_j) + \beta_j R_m$$

Compare this formulation of the return on an investment to the return equation from the regression:

$$R_j = a + b \ R_m$$

Thus, a comparison of the intercept to $R_f(1 - \beta)$ should provide a measure of the stock's performance, at least relative to the capital asset pricing model.[1] In summary, then:

$$\text{If } \ a > R_f(1 - \beta_j): \text{Stock did better than expected.}$$

$$a = R_f(1 - \beta_j): \text{Stock did as well as expected.}$$

$$a > R_f(1 - \beta_j): \text{Stock did worse than expected.}$$

The difference between a and $R_f(1 - \beta)$ is called Jensen's alpha and provides a measure of whether the investment in question earned a return greater than or less than its required return, given both market performance and risk.[2] For instance, a firm that earned 15 percent during a period when firms with similar betas earned 12 percent will have earned an excess return of 3 percent; its intercept will also exceed $R_f(1 - \beta)$ by 3 percent. In short, the Jensen's alpha is a risk-adjusted, market-adjusted measure of performance.

The third statistic that emerges from the regression is the R-squared (R^2) of the regression. While the statistical explanation of the R-squared is that it provides a measure of the goodness of fit of the regression, the economic rationale is that it provides an estimate of the proportion of the risk of a firm that can be attributed to market risk; the balance $(1 - R^2)$ can then be attributed to firm-specific risk.

The final statistic worth noting is the standard error of the beta estimate. The slope of the regression, like any statistical estimate, may be different from the true value, and the standard error reveals just how much error there could be in the estimate. The standard error can also be used to arrive at confidence intervals for the "true" beta value from the slope estimate.

---

[1] The regression is sometimes calculated using returns in excess of the riskless rate for both the stock and the market. In that case, the intercept of the regression should be zero if the actual returns equal the expected returns from the CAPM, greater than zero if the stock does better than expected, and less than zero if it does worse than expected.

[2] The terminology is confusing since the intercept of the regression is sometimes also called the alpha, and is sometimes compared to zero as a measure of risk-adjusted performance. The intercept can be compared to zero only if the regression is run with excess returns for both the stock and the index; the riskless rate has to be subtracted from the raw return in each month for both.

ILLUSTRATION 8.1:   Estimating a Regression Beta for Microsoft in 2024

Microsoft is the largest software company in the business that over time has expanded its reach into the cloud and AI businesses. It has been traded on the NASDAQ since 1986. In assessing risk parameters for Microsoft, we compute the returns on the stock and the market index in two steps:

1. The returns to a stockholder in Microsoft are computed month by month from January 2019 to December 2023. These returns include both dividends and price appreciation, and are defined as follows:

$$\text{Stock Return}_{\text{Microsoft,j}} = \left(\text{Price}_j - \text{Price}_{j-1} + \text{Dividends}_{\text{MSFT,j}}\right)/\text{Price}_{j-1}$$

where $\text{Stock Return}_{\text{Microsoft,j}}$ = Returns on Microsoft stock in month j

Price_j = Price at the end of month j

$\text{Dividends}_{\text{MSFT,j}}$ = Dividends (if any) on Microsoft in month j

Dividends are added to the returns of the month in which stockholders are entitled to the dividend.[3]

2. The returns on the S&P 500 market index are computed for each month of the period, using the level of the index at the end of each month and the monthly dividend on stocks in the index.

$$\text{Market return}_j = \left(\text{Index}_j - \text{Index}_{j-1} + \text{Dividends}_j\right)/\text{Index}_{j-1}$$

where index_j is the level of the index at the end of month j, and dividends_j is the dividends paid on the stocks in the index in month j. Although the S&P 500 and the NYSE Composite are the most widely used indexes for U.S. stocks, they are, at best, imperfect proxies for the market portfolio in the CAPM, which is supposed to include all assets.

Figure 8.1 graphs monthly returns on Microsoft against returns on the S&P 500 index from January 2019 to December 2023. The regression statistics are as follows:

(a) *Slope of the regression = 0.88.* This is Microsoft's beta, based on monthly returns from 2019 to 2023. Using a different time period for the regression or different return intervals (weekly or daily) for the same period can result in a different beta.

(b) *Intercept of the regression = 1.30%.* This is a measure of Microsoft's performance, when it is compared with $R_f(1 - \beta)$. The monthly riskless rate (since the returns used in the regression are monthly returns) between 2019 and 2023 averaged 0.1%, resulting in the following estimate for the performance:

$$R_f\left(1 - \beta_j\right) = 0.1\%(1 - 0.88) = 0.012\%$$

$$\text{Intercept} - R_f\left(1 - \beta_j\right) = 1.30\% - 0.015\% = 1.288\%$$

This analysis suggests that Microsoft performed 1.29% better than expected, when expectations are based on the CAPM, on a monthly basis between January 2019 and December 2023. This results in an annualized excess return of approximately 16.56%.

---

[3]The stock must be bought by a day called the ex-dividend day in order for investors to be entitled to dividends. The returns in a period include dividends if the ex-dividend day is in that period.

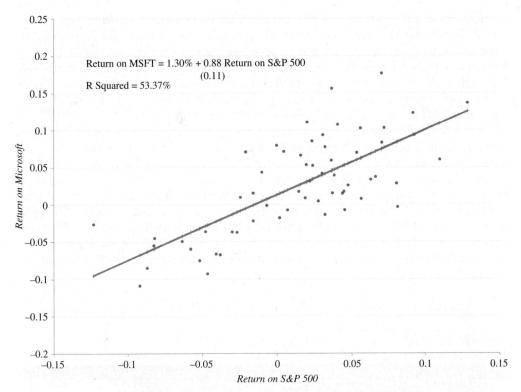

Return on MSFT = 1.30% + 0.88 Return on S&P 500
(0.11)
R Squared = 53.37%

FIGURE 8.1 Microsoft Versus S&P 500 from 2019 to 2023

$$\text{Annualized excess return} = (1 + \text{Monthly excess return})^{12} - 1$$
$$= (1 + .01288)^{12} - 1 = 16.60\%$$

Note, however, that this is entirely a post-mortem, and does not imply that Microsoft would be a good investment in the future.

The performance measure also does not provide a breakdown of how much of this excess return can be attributed to the performance of the entire sector (software) and how much is specific to the firm. To make that breakdown, we would need to compute the excess returns over the same period for other firms in the software industry and compare them with Microsoft's excess return. The difference would then be attributable to firm-specific actions. In this case, for instance, the average annualized excess return on other software firms between 2019 and 2023 was 1.15%, suggesting that the firm-specific component of performance for Microsoft is 15.45% [firm-specific Jensen's alpha = 16.60% − 1.15% = 15.45%].

(c) R-squared of the regression = 53.37%. This statistic suggests that 53.4% of the risk (variance) in Microsoft comes from market sources, and that the balance of 46.6% of the risk comes from firm-specific components. The latter risk should be diversifiable, and therefore will not be rewarded with a higher expected return. Microsoft's R-squared is higher than the median R-squared of companies listed on the New York Stock Exchange, which was approximately 25% in 2023.

(d) Standard error of beta estimate = 0.11. This statistic implies that the true beta for Microsoft could range from 0.77 to 0.99 (subtracting and adding one standard error to beta estimate of 0.56) with 67% confidence and from 0.66 to 1.10 (subtracting and adding two standard errors to beta estimate of 0.56) with 95% confidence. While these ranges may seem large, they are much larger for other (smaller, riskier) U.S. companies. This suggests that we should consider estimates of betas from regressions with caution.

Using a Service Beta   Most of us who use betas obtain them from an estimation service; Merrill Lynch, Barra, Value Line, Standard & Poor's, Morningstar, and Bloomberg are some of the well-known services. All these services begin with the regression beta just described and adjust them to reflect what they feel are better estimates of future risk. Although many of these services do not reveal their estimation procedures, Bloomberg is an exception. Figure 8.2 is the beta calculation page from Bloomberg for Microsoft, using the same period as our regression (January 2019 to December 2023).

While the period used is identical to the one used in our earlier regression, there are subtle differences between this regression and the one in Figure 8.1. First, Bloomberg uses price appreciation in the stock and the market index in estimating betas and ignores dividends.[4] The fact that dividends are ignored does not make much difference for a company like Microsoft, but it could make a difference for a company that either pays no dividends or pays significantly higher dividends than the market. This explains the mild differences in the intercept (1.33% versus 1.30%), the beta (0.876 on Bloomberg versus 0.878 in our regression) and the R-squared (54.4% on Bloomberg versus 53.4% in our regression).

Second, Bloomberg also computes what it calls an adjusted beta, which is estimated as follows:

$$\text{Adjusted beta} = \text{Raw beta}(0.67) + 1.00(0.33) = 0.876(0.67) + 0.33 = 0.917$$

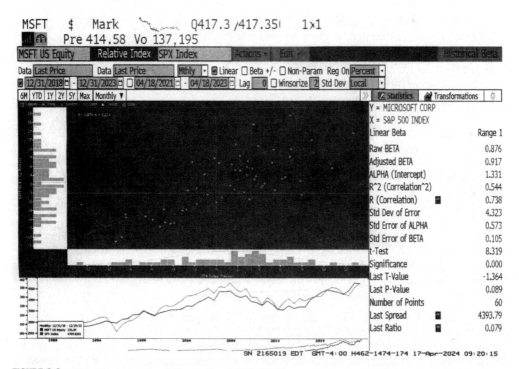

FIGURE 8.2   Beta Estimate for Microsoft—2019–2023
Source: Copyright 2001 Bloomberg LP. Reprinted with permission. All rights reserved.

---

[4]This is done purely for computational convenience. The returns in a beta regression should always include dividends, but it is far easier to run the regression with just price changes, as Bloomberg does.

These weights (0.67 and 0.33) do not vary across stocks, and this process pushes all estimated betas toward 1. Most services employ similar procedures to adjust betas toward 1. In doing so, they are drawing on empirical evidence that suggests that the betas for most companies, over time, tend to move toward the average beta, which is 1. This may be explained by the fact that firms get more diversified in their product mix and client base as they get larger. While we agree with the notion that betas move toward 1 over time, the weighting process used by most services strikes us as arbitrary and not particularly useful.

Estimation Choices for Beta Estimation   There are three decisions that must be made in setting up the regression described earlier. The first concerns the length of the estimation period. Most estimates of betas, including those by Value Line and Standard & Poor's, use five years of data, while Bloomberg uses two years of data. The trade-off is simple: A longer estimation period provides more data, but the firm itself might have changed in its risk characteristics over the time period. Microsoft, during the period of our analysis, acquired both Rockwell and McDonnell Douglas, changing its business mix and its basic risk characteristics.

The second estimation issue relates to the return interval. Returns on stocks are available on an annual, monthly, weekly, daily, and even an intraday basis. Using daily or intraday returns increases the number of observations in the regression, but it exposes the estimation process to a significant bias in beta estimates related to nontrading[5]. For instance, the betas estimated for small firms, which are more likely to suffer from nontrading, are biased downward when daily returns are used. Using weekly or monthly returns can reduce the nontrading bias significantly.[6] In this case, using weekly returns for two years yields a beta estimate for Microsoft of only 0.82, while the monthly beta estimate over the same period is 0.88.

The third estimation issue relates to the choice of a market index to be used in the regression. The standard practice used by most beta estimation services is to estimate the betas of a company relative to an index of the market in which its stock trades. Thus, the betas of German stocks are estimated relative to the Frankfurt DAX, British stocks relative to the FTSE, Japanese stocks relative to the Nikkei, and U.S. stocks relative to the NYSE Composite or the S&P 500. While this practice may yield an estimate that is a reasonable measure of risk for the domestic investor, it may not be the best approach for an international or cross-border investor, who would be better served with a beta estimated relative to an international index. For instance, Microsoft's beta between 2019 and 2023 estimated relative to the Morgan Stanley Capital International (MSCI) index that is composed of stocks from different global markets, yields a value of 0.846.

To the extent that different services use different estimation periods, use different market indexes, and adjust the regression beta differently, they will often provide different

---

[5]The nontrading bias arises because the returns in nontrading periods are zero (even though the market may have moved up or down significantly in those periods). Using these nontrading period returns in the regression will reduce the correlation between stock returns and market returns and the beta of the stock.
[6]The bias can also be reduced using statistical techniques suggested by Dimson (1979) and Scholes and Williams (1977).

beta estimates for the same firm at the same point in time. While these beta differences are troubling, note that the beta estimate delivered by each of these services comes with a standard error, and it is very likely that all the betas reported for a firm fall within the range of standard errors from the regressions.

Historical Beta Estimation for Companies in Smaller (or Emerging) Markets   The process for estimating betas in markets with fewer stocks listed on them is no different from the process described earlier, but the estimation choices on return intervals, the market index, and the return period can make a much bigger difference in the estimate.

- When liquidity is limited, as it often is in many stocks in emerging markets, the betas estimated using short return intervals tend to be biased by the absence of trading. In fact, using daily or even weekly returns in these markets will tend to yield betas that are not good measures of the true market risk of the company.
- In many emerging markets, both the companies being analyzed and the market itself change significantly over short periods of time. Using five years of returns, as we did for Microsoft, for a regression may yield a beta for a company (and market) that bears little resemblance to the company (and market) as it exists today.
- Finally, the indices that measure market returns in many smaller markets tend to be dominated by a few large companies. For instance, the Bovespa (the Brazilian index) was dominated for several years by Telebras, which represented almost half the index. Nor is this just a problem with emerging markets. The DAX, the equity index for German stocks, is dominated by Allianz, Deutsche Bank, Siemens, and Daimler. When an index is dominated by one or a few companies, the betas estimated against that index are unlikely to be true measures of market risk. In fact, the betas are likely to be close to 1 for the large companies that dominate the index and wildly variable for all other companies.

INDEX DOMINATION AND BETA ESTIMATES

There are a number of indexes that are dominated by one or a few stocks. One of the most striking cases was the Helsinki Stock Exchange (HEX) in the late 1990s. Nokia, the telecommunications giant, represented 75 percent of the Helsinki Index in terms of market value. Not surprisingly, a regression of Nokia against the HEX yielded the results shown in Figure 8.3.

The regression looks impeccable. In fact, the noise problem that we noted with Microsoft, arising from the high standard errors, disappears. The beta estimate has a standard error of 0.03, but the results are deceptive. The low standard error is the result of a regression of Nokia on itself, since it dominates the index. The beta is meaningless to a typical investor in Nokia, who is likely to be diversified, if not globally, at least across European stocks. Worse still, the betas of all other Finnish stocks against the HEX become betas estimated against Nokia. In fact, the beta of every other Finnish stock at the time of this regression was less than 1. How is this possible, you might ask, if the average beta is 1? It is the weighted average beta that is 1, and if Nokia (which comprises three-quarters of the index) has a beta greater than 1 (which it does), every other stock in the index could well end up with a beta less than 1.

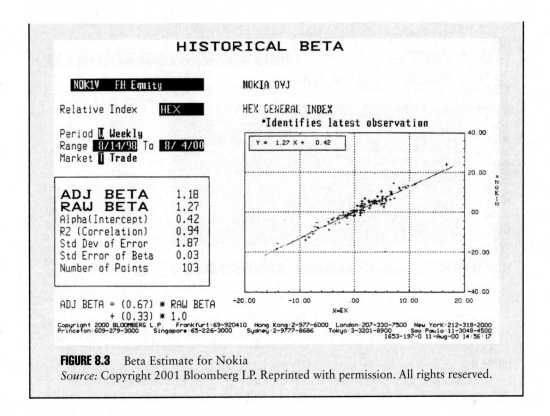

FIGURE 8.3 Beta Estimate for Nokia
Source: Copyright 2001 Bloomberg LP. Reprinted with permission. All rights reserved.

ILLUSTRATION 8.2:   Estimating a Beta for Enka Insaat (Turkey)

Enka is a construction company in Turkey. Reproduced in Figure 8.4 is the beta estimate for Enka from March 2022 to March 2024 (using weekly returns) obtained from a beta service (Bloomberg). Note that the index used is the BIST 100, an index of 100 large Turkish companies. Based on this regression, we arrive at the following equation:

$$\text{Returns}_{\text{Titan Cement}} = 0.06\% + 0.69\ \text{Returns}_{\text{BIST}} \qquad \text{R-squared} = 28\%$$
$$[0.11]$$

The beta for Enka, based upon this regression, is 0.69. The standard error of the estimate, shown in brackets below, is 0.11, but the caveats about narrow indexes apply to the BIST, which has only 100 Turkish stocks in it.

Drawing on the arguments in the previous section, if the marginal investor in Enka is, in fact, an investor diversified across European companies, the appropriate index would have been a European stock index. The Bloomberg beta calculation with the STXE European index is reported in Figure 8.5. Note the decline in beta to 0.29 and the increase in the standard error of the beta estimate to 0.30.

In fact, if the marginal investor is globally diversified, Enka's beta (as well as Microsoft's beta in Illustration 8.1) should have been estimated against a global index. Using the Morgan Stanley Capital International (MSCI) global index, we get a regression beta of 0.30 in Figure 8.6 and the standard error for the beta is 0.24.

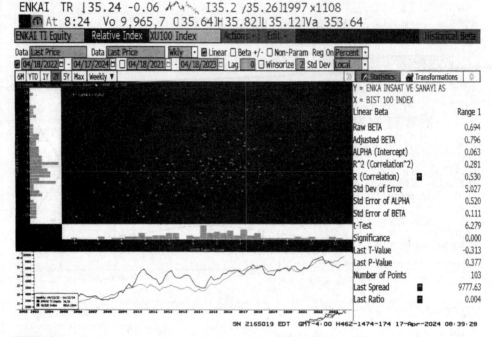

FIGURE 8.4   Beta Estimate for Enka: BIST 100 (Turkish Index)
Source: Copyright 2001 Bloomberg LP. Reprinted with permission. All rights reserved.

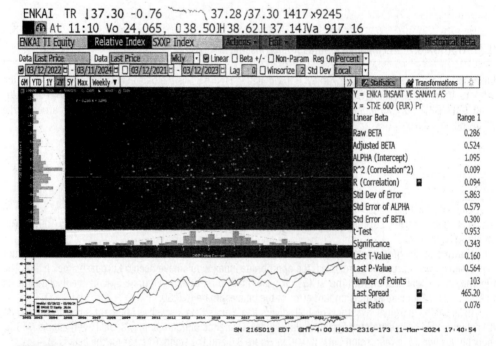

FIGURE 8.5   Beta Estimate for Enka: STXE Euro 600 Index
Source: Copyright 2001 Bloomberg LP. Reprinted with permission. All rights reserved.

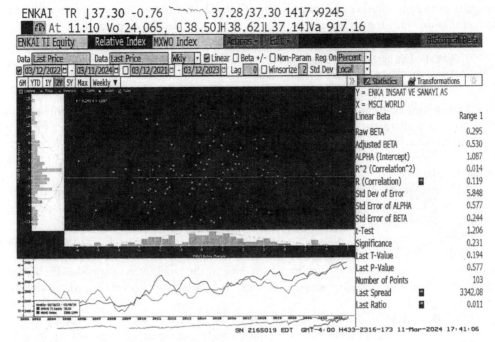

FIGURE 8.6 Beta Estimate for Enka: MSCI Global Index
Source: Copyright 2001 Bloomberg LP. Reprinted with permission. All rights reserved.

Estimating the Historical Beta for Private Firms The historical approach to estimating betas works only for assets that have been traded and have market prices. Private companies do not have a market price history. Consequently, we cannot estimate a regression beta for these companies. Nevertheless, we still need estimates of cost of equity and capital for these companies.

You might argue that this is not an issue if you do not value private companies; but you will still be confronted with this issue even when valuing publicly traded firms. Consider, for instance, the following scenarios:

- If you have to value a private firm for an initial public offering, you will need to estimate discount rates for the valuation.
- Even after a firm has gone public, there will be a period of time lasting as long as two years when there will be insufficient data for a regression.
- If you are called upon to value the division of a publicly traded firm that is up for sale, you will not have past prices to draw on to run a regression.
- Finally, if the firm has gone through significant restructuring—divestitures or recapitalization—in the recent past, regression betas become meaningless because the company itself has changed its risk characteristics.

Thus, regression betas are either unavailable or meaningless in a significant number of valuations.

Some analysts assume that discounted cash flow valuation is not feasible in these scenarios; instead, they use multiples. Others make assumptions about discount rates based on rules of thumb. Neither approach is appealing. The next section develops an approach for estimating betas that is general enough to apply to all of these companies.

 Risk.xls: This spreadsheet allows you to run a regression of stock returns against market returns and estimate risk parameters.

The Limitations of Regression Betas   Much of what has been presented in this section represents an indictment of regression betas. In the case of Microsoft, the biggest problem was that the beta had high standard error. In fact, this is not a problem unique to Microsoft. Figure 8.7 presents the distribution of standard errors on beta estimates for U.S. and global companies.

With the Nokia regression, we seem to cure the standard error problem but at a very large cost. The low standard errors reflect the domination of the index by a stock and result in betas that may be precise but bear no resemblance to true risk.

Changing the market index, the return period, and the return interval offers no respite. If the index becomes a more representative index, the standard errors on betas will increase, reflecting the fact that more of the risk in the stock is firm-specific. If the beta changes as the return period or interval changes, it creates more uncertainty about the true beta of the company.

In short, regression betas will almost always be either too noisy or skewed by estimation choices to be useful measures of the equity risk in a company. The cost of equity is far too important an input into a discounted cash flow valuation to be left to statistical chance.

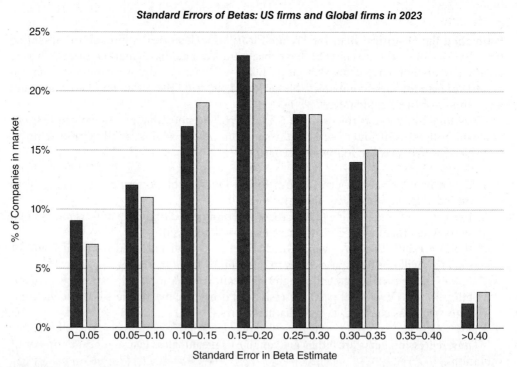

FIGURE 8.7   Distribution of Standard Errors on 2-year Beta—U.S. Firms from 2008 to 2010
Source for raw data: Bloomberg.

Fundamental Betas   A second way to estimate betas is to look at the fundamentals of the business. The beta for a firm may be estimated from a regression, but it is determined by decisions the firm has made on what business to be in and how much operating leverage to use in the business, and by the degree to which the firm uses financial leverage. This section examines an alternative way of estimating betas, where we are less reliant on historical betas and more cognizant of their fundamental determinants.

Determinants of Betas   The beta of a firm is determined by three variables: (1) the type of business or businesses the firm is in, (2) the degree of operating leverage of the firm, and (3) the firm's financial leverage. Although we will use these determinants to find betas in the capital asset pricing model, the same analysis can be used to calculate the betas for the arbitrage pricing and the multifactor model as well.

Type of Business   Since betas measure the risk of a firm relative to a market index, the more sensitive a business is to market conditions, the higher its beta. Thus, other things remaining equal, cyclical firms can be expected to have higher betas than noncyclical firms. Companies involved in housing and automobiles—two sectors of the economy that are very sensitive to economic conditions—should have higher betas than companies in food processing and tobacco, which are relatively insensitive to business cycles.

This view can be extended to a company's products. The degree to which a product's purchase is discretionary will affect the beta of the firm manufacturing the product. Firms whose products are much more discretionary to their customers—they can defer or delay buying these products—should have higher betas than firms whose products are viewed as necessary or less discretionary. Thus, the beta of Procter & Gamble, which sells diapers and daily household products, should be lower than the beta of Gucci, which manufactures luxury products.

Degree of Operating Leverage   The degree of operating leverage is a function of the cost structure of a firm and usually defined in terms of the relationship between fixed costs and total costs. A firm that has high fixed costs relative to total costs is said to have high operating leverage. A firm with high operating leverage will also have higher variability in operating income than would a firm producing a similar product with low operating leverage. Other things remaining equal, the higher variance in operating income will lead to a higher beta for the firm with high operating leverage.

Can firms change their operating leverage? While some of a firm's cost structure is determined by the business it is in (an energy utility has to build expensive power plants, and airlines have to buy or lease expensive planes), firms in the United States have become increasingly inventive in lowering the fixed cost component in their total costs. For instance, firms have made cost structures more flexible by:

- Negotiating labor contracts that emphasize flexibility and allow the firm to make its labor costs more correlated with its financial success.
- Entering into joint venture agreements, where the fixed costs are borne by someone else.
- Subcontracting manufacturing and outsourcing, which reduces the need for expensive plant and equipment.

While the arguments for such actions may be couched in terms of competitive advantage and flexibility, they do also reduce the operating leverage of the firm and its exposure to market risk.

While operating leverage affects betas, it is difficult to measure the operating leverage of a firm, at least from the outside, since fixed and variable costs are often aggregated in income statements. It is possible to get an approximate measure of the operating leverage of a firm by looking at changes in operating income as a function of changes in sales.

$$\text{Degree of operating leverage} = \frac{\%\text{ change in operating profit}}{\%\text{ change in sales}}$$

For firms with high operating leverage, operating income should see earnings change more than proportionately when sales change.

SIZE, GROWTH, AND BETAS

Generally, smaller firms with higher growth potential are viewed as riskier than larger, more stable firms. While the rationale for this argument is clear when talking about total risk, it becomes more difficult to see when looking at market risk or betas. Should a smaller software firm have a higher beta than a larger software firm? One reason to believe that it should is operating leverage. If there is a setup cost associated with investing in infrastructure or economies of scale, smaller firms will have higher fixed costs than larger firms, leading in turn to higher betas for these firms.

With growth firms, the argument for higher betas rests on the notion of discretionary versus nondiscretionary purchases. For a high-growth firm to deliver on its growth, new customers have to adopt the product, or existing customers have to buy more of the product. Whether they do so will depend, in large part, on how well-off they feel. This, in turn, will make the profits of high-growth firms much more dependent on how well the economy is doing, thus increasing their betas.

Degree of Financial Leverage   Other things remaining equal, an increase in financial leverage will increase the beta of the equity in a firm. Intuitively, we would expect that the fixed interest payments on debt result in increasing income in good times and decreasing income in bad times. Higher leverage increases the variance in net income and makes equity investment in the firm riskier. If all the firm's risk is borne by the stockholders (i.e., the beta of debt is zero),[7] and debt provides a tax benefit to the firm, then,

---

[7]This formula was originally developed by Hamada in 1972. There are two common modifications. One is to ignore the tax effects and compute the levered beta as:

$$\text{Levered Beta} = \text{Unlevered Beta} \, (1 + \text{Debt/Equity})$$

If debt has market risk (i.e., its beta is greater than zero), the original formula can be modified to take this into account. If the beta of debt is β_D, the beta of equity can be written as:

$$\text{Levered Beta} = \text{Unlevered Beta} \, (1 + (1 - t)D/E) - \text{Beta}_{\text{Debt}}((1 - t)D/E)$$

$$\beta_L = \beta_u [1 + (1 - t)(D/E)]$$

where β_L = Levered beta for equity in the firm

          β_u = Unlevered beta of the firm (i.e., the beta of the firm without any debt)

          t = Marginal tax rate

     D/E = Debt-to-equity ratio (market value)

Intuitively, we expect that as leverage increases (as measured by the debt-to-equity ratio), equity investors bear increasing amounts of market risk in the firm, leading to higher betas. The tax factor in the equation captures the tax benefits that accrue from interest payments, and since interest saves you taxes at the margin, you use the tax rate that you pay on the last dollars of income. A good estimate would be the statutory tax rate of the country in which the company is incorporated.

The unlevered beta of a firm is determined by the nature of its products and services (cyclicality, discretionary nature) and its operating leverage. It is often also referred to as the asset beta, since it is determined by the assets owned by the firm. Thus, the levered beta, which is also the beta for an equity investment in a firm, is determined both by the riskiness of the business it operates in and by the amount of financial leverage risk it has taken on.

Since financial leverage multiplies the underlying business risk, it stands to reason that firms that have high business risk should be reluctant to take on financial leverage. It also stands to reason that firms operating in stable businesses should be much more willing to take on financial leverage. Utilities, for instance, have historically had high debt ratios but have not had high betas, mostly because their underlying businesses have been stable and predictable.

ILLUSTRATION 8.3:   Effects of Leverage on Betas: Microsoft

From the regression for the period from 2019 to 2023, Microsoft had a historical beta of 0.88. Since this regression uses stock prices of Microsoft over this period, we began by estimating the average debt-to-equity ratio between 2019 and 2023, using market values for debt and equity.

Average debt-to-equity ratio between 2019 and 2023 = 6.01%

The beta over the 2019–2023 period reflects this average leverage. To estimate the unlevered beta over the period, a marginal tax rate of 25% is used:

Unlevered beta = Current beta/[1 + (1 − Tax rate) (Average Debt/Equity)]

= 0.88/[1 + (1 − 0.25)(0.0601)] = 0.842

The unlevered beta for Microsoft over the 2019–2023 period is 0.84. The levered beta at different levels of debt can then be estimated:

Levered beta = Unlevered beta × [1 + (1 − Tax rate) (Debt/Equity)]

For instance, if Microsoft were to increase its debt equity ratio to 10%, its equity beta will be:

Levered beta(@10% D/E) = 0.842 × [1 + (1 − 0.25) (0.10)] = 0.91

If the debt equity ratio were raised to 25%, the equity beta would be:

$$\text{Levered beta } (@ 25\% \text{ D/E}) = 0.84 \times [1 + (1 - 0.25)(0.25)] = 1.00$$

Table 8.1 summarizes the beta estimates for different levels of financial leverage ranging from 0% to 90% debt.

TABLE 8.1 Levered Beta and Debt to Equity Ratios

Debt to Capital	Debt to Equity	Levered Beta	Debt Effect on Beta
0%	0.00%	0.84	0.00
10%	11.11%	0.91	0.07
20%	25.00%	1.00	0.16
30%	42.86%	1.11	0.27
40%	66.67%	1.26	0.42
50%	100.00%	1.47	0.63
60%	150.00%	1.79	0.95
70%	233.33%	2.32	1.48
80%	400.00%	3.37	2.51
90%	900.00%	6.53	5.69

As Microsoft's financial leverage increases, the beta increases concurrently.

In doing these calculations, I used the total (or gross) debt for Microsoft, and the unlevered and levered betas calculated are for Microsoft the company, with the cash holdings of the company treated as an asset (which it is). Cash, though, is a riskless asset, and the unlevered beta for Microsoft's operating (or noncash) assets can be calculated by removing the cash effect:

Cash as a percent of Microsoft's value (2019–2023) = 8.41%

Unlevered beta for Microsoft's operating assets = Unlevered beta for the company

/(1 – Cash as a percent of value)

= 0.84/ (1 – .0841) = 0.92

In fact, you could arrive at close to the same value by using net debt ratios (where cash is netted out against) debt. That approach would have yielded:

Net Debt ratio between 2019 and 2023 = –2.99%

Unlevered beta (using net debt to equity) = Current Beta/[1 + (1 – Tax rate)

(Average Debt/Equity)]

= 0.88/[1 + (1 – .25) (–0299)] = .90

While we prefer the gross debt approach, with the correction for cash, the net debt ratio should work as well, as long as you stay consistent about using it all the way through the cost of capital calculation.

levbeta.xls: **This spreadsheet allows you to estimate the unlevered beta for a firm and compute the betas as a function of the leverage of the firm.**

Bottom-Up Betas Breaking down betas into their business risk and financial leverage components provides us with an alternative way of estimating betas, in which we do not need past prices on an individual firm or asset to estimate its beta.

To develop this alternative approach, we need to introduce an additional property of betas that proves invaluable. The beta of two assets put together is a weighted average of the individual asset betas, with the weights based on market value. Consequently, the beta for a firm is a weighted average of the betas of all the different businesses it is in. We can estimate the beta for a firm in five steps:

Step 1: Identify the business or businesses the firm operates in.

Step 2: Find other publicly traded firms in each business and obtain their regression betas, which we use to compute an average beta for the firms in each business.

Step 3: Estimate the average unlevered beta for the business by unlevering the average (or median) beta for the firms by their average (or median) debt-to-equity ratio (If these companies have significant cash balances, you could clean up for cash either explicitly by adjusting for cash as a percent of firm value, or implicitly, by using net debt ratios. Alternatively, we could estimate the unlevered beta for each firm, and then compute the average of the unlevered betas. The first approach is preferable because unlevering an erroneous regression beta is likely to compound the error.

$$\text{Unlevered beta}_{\text{business}} = \text{Beta}_{\text{comparable firms}} / \left[1 + \left(1 - t \right) \left(D/E_{\text{comparable firms}} \right) \right]$$

Step 4: Estimate an unlevered beta for the firm being analyzed, taking a weighted average of the unlevered betas for the businesses it operates in, using the proportion of firm value derived from each business as the weights. If values are not available, you can use operating income or revenues as weights. This weighted average is called the bottom-up unlevered beta.

$$\text{Unlevered beta}_{\text{firm}} = \sum_{j=1}^{j=k} \left(\text{Unlevered beta}_j \times \text{Value Weight}_j \right)$$

where the firm is assumed to operating in k different businesses, Unlevered beta$_j$ is the unlevered beta of each business, and Value Weight$_j$ is the percentage weight of the business.

Step 5: Finally, estimate the current market values of debt and equity at the firm, and then use this debt-to-equity ratio to estimate a levered beta.

The betas estimated using this process are called bottom-up betas.

The Case for Bottom-Up Betas At first sight, the use of bottom-up betas may seem to leave us exposed to all the problems noted with regression betas. After all, the betas for other publicly traded firms in the business are obtained from regressions.

Notwithstanding this, bottom-up betas represent a significant improvement on regression betas for the following reasons:

■ Although each regression beta is estimated with standard error, the average across a number of regression betas has much lower standard error. The intuition is simple.

A high standard error on a beta estimate indicates that it can be significantly higher or lower than the true beta. Averaging across these individual regression betas results in an average beta that is far more precise than the individual betas that went into it. In fact, if the estimation errors on individual firm betas are uncorrelated across firms, the savings in standard error can be stated as a function of the average standard error of beta estimates and the number of firms in the sample.

$$\text{Standard error}_{\text{Bottom up beta}} = \frac{\text{Average standard error in beta}_{\text{comparable firms}}}{\sqrt{n}}$$

where n is the number of firms in the sample. Thus, if the average standard error in beta estimates for software firms is 0.50 and the number of software firms is 100, the standard error of the average beta is only 0.05 ($0.50/\sqrt{100}$).

- A bottom-up beta can be adapted to reflect actual changes in a firm's business mix and expected changes in the future. Thus, if a firm divested a major portion of its operations last week, the weights on the businesses can be modified to reflect the divestiture. The same can be done with acquisitions. In fact, a firm's strategic plans to enter new businesses in the future can be brought into the beta estimates for future periods.
- Firms do change their debt ratios over time. Although regression betas reflect the average debt-to-equity ratio maintained by the firm during the regression period, bottom-up betas use the current debt-to-equity ratio. If a firm plans to change its debt-to-equity ratio in the future, the beta can be adjusted to show these changes.
- Finally, bottom-up betas wean us from our dependence on historical stock prices. While we do need these prices to get betas for comparable firms, all we need for the firm being analyzed is a breakdown of the businesses it is in. Thus, bottom-up betas can be estimated for private firms, divisions of businesses, and stocks that have just started trading in financial markets.

Computational Details   Although the idea behind bottom-up betas is fairly simple, there are several computational details that deserve attention:

- *Defining comparable firms.* First, we have to decide how narrowly we want to define a business. Consider, for instance, a firm that manufactures entertainment software. We could define the business as entertainment software and consider only companies that primarily manufacture entertainment software to be comparable firms. We could go even further and define comparable firms as firms making entertainment software with revenues similar to that of the company being analyzed. While there are benefits to narrowing the comparable firm definition, there is a cost. Each additional criterion added to the definition of *comparable* will mean that fewer firms make the list, and the savings in standard error that comprise the biggest benefit to bottom-up betas become smaller. A commonsense principle should therefore come into play. If there are hundreds of firms in a business, as there are in the software sector, you can afford to be more selective. If there are relatively few firms, not only do you have to become less selective, but you might also have to broaden the definition of comparable to bring other firms into the mix.

- *Estimating betas.* Once the comparable firms in a business have been defined, you have to estimate the betas for these firms. Although it would be best to estimate the beta for each of these firms against a common and well-diversified equity index, it is usually easier to use service betas that are available for each of these firms. These service betas may be estimated against different indexes. For instance, if you define your business to be global telecommunications and obtain betas for global telecom firms from Bloomberg, these betas will be estimated against the local indexes. This is usually not a fatal problem, especially with large samples, since errors in the estimates tend to average out.

- *Averaging method.* The average beta for the firms in the sector can be computed in one of three ways. We could use market-weighted averages, but the savings in standard error that touted in the earlier section will be muted, especially if there are one or two very large firms in the sample. We could estimate the simple average of the betas of the companies, thus weighting all betas equally. The process weights the smallest firms in the sample disproportionately (to their market value), but the savings in standard error are likely to be maximized. If the data being averaged (betas, debt to equity ratios) have large outliers, we can use the median values.

- *Controlling for differences.* In essence, when we use betas from comparable firms, we are assuming that all firms in the business are equally exposed to business risk and have similar operating leverage. Note that the process of levering and unlevering of betas allows us to control differences in financial leverage. If there are significant differences in operating leverage—cost structure—across companies, the differences in operating leverage can be controlled as well. This would require estimation of a business beta, where the effects of operating leverage are taken out from the unlevered beta:

$$\text{Business beta} = \frac{\text{Unlevered Beta}}{\left(1 + \dfrac{\text{Fixed Costs}}{\text{Variable Costs}}\right)}$$

Note the similarity to the adjustment for financial leverage; the only difference is that both fixed and variable costs are eligible for the tax deduction, and the tax rate is therefore no longer a factor. The business beta can then be relevered to reflect the differences in operating leverage across firms.

CASH AND BETAS

In the process for estimating bottom-up betas, we suggested a two-step process: getting a weighted average of the betas of the businesses that a firm is in, using the sector-average betas of other publicly traded firms in each business, and then adjusting for the debt to equity ratio of the firm in question.

In making these adjustments, though, we have to deal again with the reality that a firm may have a significant portion of its assets as cash. Since cash is usually invested in close to riskless, liquid investments, it should have a beta of zero. So, how

(continued)

(continued)

does cash enter the computation? It does so in two places. When we computed the sector-average beta, we suggested unlevering the average regression beta for the sector, using the average debt-to-equity ratio and marginal tax rate for the sector. Thus, with an average levered beta of 1.30, an average debt-to-equity ratio of 50% and an average tax rate of 40%, we estimate a sector-average unlevered beta of 1.00 for the entertainment business:

$$\text{Unlevered Beta} = \frac{1.30}{(1 + (1 - .4)(.50))} = 1.00$$

However, this is the unlevered beta for companies in this business, and these companies will generally have some of these values in cash balances. Assume, for instance, that the average cash balance of entertainment firms in the sector is 10%. The unlevered beta for the entertainment business alone can then be computed as follows:

$$\text{Unlevered beta for entertainment } (.90) + \text{Beta for cash } (.10) = 1.00$$

Plugging in a beta of zero for cash, we get a beta for just the entertainment business:

$$\text{Unlevered beta for entertainment business} = 1.00/.90 = 1.11$$

We call this the beta for the sector, corrected for cash, and use it in the computation of bottom-up betas.

The second place it shows up is when we compute the bottom-up beta for a company. To estimate the bottom-up beta for just the operating assets of a company like Microsoft, we would take a weighted average of the cash-corrected unlevered betas of the software and cloud businesses. This is the beta we would use to compute the cost of equity and cost of capital. To get a bottom-up beta for Microsoft as a company, we would then bring in the cash holdings as a separate asset and give it a beta of zero. This beta would then be a beta for all of Microsoft's assets and for Microsoft's equity in those assets. Each beta has a use in valuation.

---

 betas.xls: **This dataset on the web has updated betas and unlevered betas by business sector in the United States.**

ILLUSTRATION 8.4:   Estimating a Bottom-Up Beta for Vans Shoes—January 2001

Vans Shoes is a shoe manufacturing firm with a market capitalization of $191 million. To estimate the bottom-up beta for Vans Shoes, consider the betas of all publicly traded shoe companies in Table 8.2:

TABLE 8.2 Betas and Operating Leverage—Shoe Companies

Company Name	Beta	Market D/E	Fixed/Variable
Barry (R.G.)	1.00	40.51%	75.66%
Brown Shoe	0.80	106.64%	61.41%
Candie's Inc.	1.20	75.86%	29.78%
Converse Inc.	0.60	653.46%	39.64%
Deckers Outdoor Corp.	0.80	82.43%	62.52%
Florsheim Group Inc.	0.65	96.79%	79.03%
K-Swiss Inc.	0.65	0.69%	56.92%
Kenneth Cole 'A'	1.05	0.29%	56.97%
LaCrosse Footwear Inc.	0.55	81.15%	30.36%
Maxwell Shoe Inc.	0.75	2.24%	20.97%
Nike Inc. 'B'	0.90	9.47%	46.07%
Reebok Int'l.	1.05	171.90%	35.03%
Rocky Shoes & Boots Inc.	0.80	93.51%	26.89%
Saucony Inc.	0.15	34.93%	49.33%
Shoe Carnival	0.85	2.18%	35.03%
Stride Rite Corp.	0.80	0.00%	48.23%
Timberland Co. 'A'	1.10	15.23%	49.50%
Vulcan Int'l.	0.65	3.38%	11.92%
Wellco Enterprises Inc.	0.60	48.89%	11.52%
Weyco Group	0.30	11.91%	24.69%
Wolverine World Wide	1.35	44.37%	32.31%
Average	0.79	75.04%	42.08%
Median	0.80	40.51%	39.64%
Vans Shoes		9.41%	31.16%

In addition to the beta for each firm, Table 8.2 reports the market debt-to-equity ratio, the effective tax rate, and a measure of operating leverage obtained by dividing selling, general, and administrative (SG&A) expenses (which we consider fixed) by other operating expenses (which we consider variable). We can estimate the unlevered beta for the business using the medians for these values:

$$\text{Median Beta} = 0.80$$
$$\text{Median debt-to-equity ratio} = 40.51\%$$

Using the marginal tax rate of 40%, we can estimate the unlevered beta for the business:

$$\text{Unlevered beta} = 0.80/[1 + (1 - .40) \times .4051] = .6435$$

The beta for Vans Shoes can then be obtained using the firm's marginal tax rate of 40% and its market debt-to-equity ratio of 9.41%.

$$\text{Levered beta} = 0.6435(1 + (1 - .40) \times .0941) = 0.68$$

This levered beta is based on the implicit assumption that all shoe manufacturers have similar operating leverage. In fact, we could adjust the unlevered beta for the median fixed cost/variable cost ratio for the business, and then relever back at the operating leverage for Vans Shoes:

$$\text{Median fixed costs/variable cost} = 39.64\%$$
$$\text{Business beta} = 0.6435/(1 + (1 - .4) \times (.3964)) = 0.5199$$

We can then use Vans' fixed cost/variable cost ratio of 31.16% and Vans debt-to-equity ratio of 9.41% to estimate an adjusted unlevered and levered beta.

$$\text{Unlevered beta}_{\text{Vans}} = 0.5199 \times (1 + .3116) = 0.682$$
$$\text{Levered beta} = 0.682 \times (1 + (1 - .4) \times .0941) = 0.721$$

By having a lower debt-to-equity ratio and lower operating leverage than the median for the industry, Vans Shoes ends up with a beta much lower than that of the industry.

ILLUSTRATION 8.5: Estimating a Bottom-Up Beta for Microsoft—April 2024

Microsoft started as a software company, providing the system software for the personal computers in their nascent years. Over time, it grew to not only dominate that part of the software market but to also supplement it with Office, its suite of word processing, spreadsheet and presentation programs, ubiquitous in almost every workspace. In the last decade, Microsoft entered the crowd business with Azure, and that business has grown in size and profitability. In fact, at the time of this assessment, Microsoft seemed positioned to take advantage of a growing AI market, as a result of its partnership with OpenAI. To estimate Microsoft's beta in 2000, we broke its business into two areas:

1. *Software*, which is Microsoft's core business, composed mostly of Windows and Office revenues
2. *Intelligent Cloud*, which in their cloud business, where their revenues come from other companies that use their cloud services

Each of these areas of business has very different risk characteristics, and the unlevered beta for each business was estimated by looking at comparable firms in each business. The following table summarizes these estimates.

	Revenues in 2023	EV/Sales	Unlevered Beta	Value	Weight
		Industry Median			
Software	$ 124,008	10.72	1.27	$ 1,329,366	66.85%
Intelligent Cloud	$ 87,907	7.50	0.85	$ 659,303	33.15%
Microsoft	**$211,915**		**1.13**	**$1,988,668**	

For software, we used the 351 application and system software companies that are publicly traded in the United States, and estimated the unlevered beta and enterprise value to sales ratios; the latter is a measure of how much markets are pricing a dollar in sales in the software business. For the cloud business, a younger business with fewer players, we used about a dozen smaller companies that derived much of their revenue from the cloud business, rather than the bigger players like Google and Amazon (who derive the bulk of their value from other businesses), and computed the unlevered beta and enterprise value to sales ratios as well. The values for each of Microsoft's two businesses were estimated using the revenues from each segment[8] and a typical revenue multiple[9] for that type of business:

$$\text{Value of Microsoft's software business} = \text{Software Revenues} \times \text{EV to Sales}_{\text{Software}}$$
$$= \$124{,}008 \times 10.72 = \$1{,}329{,}366 \text{ million}$$

$$\text{Value of Microsoft's cloud business} = \text{Cloud Revenues} \times \text{EV to Sales}_{\text{Cloud}}$$
$$= \$87{,}907 \times 7.50 = \$659{,}303 \text{ million}$$

The unlevered beta for Microsoft's operating assets in 2024 can be estimated by taking a value-weighted average of the betas of each of the different business areas:

$$\text{Unlevered Beta for Microsoft Operations} = 1.27 \ (1{,}329{,}366/(1{,}329{,}366 + 659{,}303))$$
$$+ \ 0.85 \ (659{,}303/(1{,}329{,}366 + 659{,}303))$$
$$= 1.13$$

The levered beta can then be estimated using the debt-to-equity ratio for Microsoft in 2023. Combining the market value of equity of $3,023 billion and the market value of debt of $95.8 billion, and using a 25% tax rate for the firm, we arrive at the beta for Microsoft.

$$\text{Levered beta for Microsoft} = 1.13(1 + (1 - .25)(95.8/3023)) = 1.16$$

This is very different from the historical beta of 0.88 that we obtained from the regression, but it is, in our view, a much truer reflection of the risk in Microsoft in 2024. If you believe that AI will become an increasing part of Microsoft's value in the future, you can expand your assessment to bring it in as a separate business, with an estimated value, and compute a forward-looking beta for Microsoft that reflects AI.

ILLUSTRATION 8.6:   Estimating a Bottom-Up Beta for Enka—April 2024

To estimate a beta for Enka, the Turkish construction/infrastructure company in 2024, we began by defining comparable firms as other companies in the same businesses in Turkey but found only a handful. When we expanded the list to include construction and infrastructure companies across Europe, we increased our sample to about 20 firms. Since we did not see any reason to restrict our comparison to just European firms, we decided to look at the median beta for companies, in each business, globally, in Table 8.3.

---

[8]Note that Microsoft breaks its business down in its financial statements into these two segments. We could have used operating income or earnings before interest, taxes, depreciation, and amortization (EBITDA) and a typical multiple to arrive at value.

[9]To estimate these multiples, we looked at the market value of publicly traded firms relative to their revenues. This is a ratio of enterprise value to revenues.

TABLE 8.3 Bottom-up Beta for Enka

Business	Revenues	EV/Sales	Unlevered Beta	Value	Weight
Engineering/Construction	₺32,015	0.60	0.73	₺19,118	23.60%
Real Estate	₺ 5,703	3.42	0.53	₺19,481	24.05%
Transportation	₺ 4,085	0.99	0.83	₺ 4,040	4.99%
Power	₺21,494	1.79	0.44	₺38,372	47.37%
Enka Operations	₺63,297		0.55	₺81,011	100.00%

We then used Enka's market values of equity (190,358 million Turkish Lira) and debt (2,665 million lira), in conjunction with the marginal tax rate of 23% for Turkey, to estimate a levered beta for its equity:

$$\text{Debt to Equity} = 2665/190{,}358 = 1.40\%$$

$$\text{Levered beta} = 0.55[1 + (1 - .23) \times (.014)] = 0.56$$

Enka has very little debt, and its levered beta is therefore very similar to its unlevered beta.

HOW WELL DO BETAS TRAVEL?

Often when analyzing firms in small or emerging markets, we have to estimate betas by looking at firms in the same business but traded on other markets. This is what we did when estimating the beta for Enka. Is this appropriate? Should the beta for a steel company in the United States be comparable to that of a steel company in Indonesia? We see no reason why it should not be. But the company in Indonesia has much more risk, you might argue. We do not disagree, but the fact that we use similar betas does not mean that we believe that the costs of equity are identical across all steel companies. In fact, using the approach described in the preceding chapter, the risk premium used to estimate the cost of equity for the Indonesian company will incorporate a country risk premium, whereas the cost of equity for the U.S. company will not. Thus, even if the betas used for the two companies are identical, the cost of equity for the Indonesian company will be much higher.

There are a few exceptions to this proposition. Recall that one of the key determinants of betas is the degree to which a product or service is discretionary. It is entirely possible that products or services that are discretionary in one market (and command high betas) may be nondiscretionary in another market (and have low betas). For instance, phone service is viewed as a nondiscretionary product in most developed markets but is a discretionary product in emerging markets. Consequently, the average beta estimated by looking at telecom firms in developed markets will understate the true beta of a telecom firm in an emerging market. For the latter beta, the comparable firms should be restricted to include only telecom firms in emerging markets.

Calculating Betas after a Major Restructuring   The bottom-up process of estimating betas provides a solution when firms go through major restructurings that change both their business mix and their leverage. In these cases, the regression betas are misleading because they do not reflect fully the effects of these changes. Microsoft's beta estimated using the bottom-up approach is likely to provide a more precise estimate than the historical beta from a regression of Microsoft's stock prices, given Microsoft's entry into and expansion in the cloud business. At the time of this analysis, Microsoft was awaiting completion of a major acquisition of Activision Blizzard, a gaming company, for $70 billion. Illustration 8.7 estimates Microsoft's beta just before and after its acquisition of Activision.

ILLUSTRATION 8.7:   Beta of a Firm after an Acquisition: Microsoft and Activision Blizzard

In 2022, Microsoft announced that it was acquiring Activision Blizzard, to ease its entry into the gaming business and the Metaverse (virtual reality games). After delays caused by regulatory pushback, it looks like the acquisition will be completed in 2024, and the numbers for the two firms (i.e., beta and debt and equity) are provided below:

Company	Levered Beta	Unlevered Beta	Debt	Equity	Cash
Microsoft (before)	1.16	1.13	$ 95,852	$3,023,000	$80,892
Activision	0.91	0.87	$ 3,856	$ 60,444	$12,041

Note that the market values of equity used for the two firms reflect the market values after the acquisition announcement and the unlevered betas reported are the bottom-up betas for the two companies. Microsoft's unlevered beta calculation is in illustration 8.5, and we use the entertainment industry beta for Activision Blizzard.

To evaluate the effects of the acquisition on Microsoft's beta, we first examine the effects of the merger on the business risk of the combined firm. The unlevered beta for the combined firm can be calculated as the weighted average of the two unlevered betas, with the weights based on the enterprise values of the two firms.

Company	Enterprise Value	Weights	Unlevered Beta
Microsoft (before)	$ 3,037,960	98.31%	1.1300
Activision	$ 52,259	1.69%	0.8700
Microsoft (after)	**$ 3,105,725**		**1.1256**

Since the unlevered betas of the two companies reflect the market risk in their operating assets, we use the enterprise values (market value of equity plus net debt), which reflect the market's estimate of the value of operating assts, as weights to compute the weighted beta after the acquisition. Microsoft's huge capitalization, with an enterprise value exceeding $3 trillion, vastly exceeds Activision's enterprise value of $52 billion, resulting in a weighted beta very close to Microsoft's pre-acquisition beta. If Microsoft had acquired Nvidia, with an enterprise value of $2 trillion, you would have seen a greater effect on the beta, after the acquisition.

Assume that Microsoft's acquisition of Activision will be accomplished by issuing new stock in Microsoft to cover the value of Activision's equity of $60.4 billion. Since no new debt was used to finance the deal, the debt outstanding in the firm after the acquisition is just the sum of the debt outstanding at the two companies before the acquisition.

$$\text{Debt} = \text{Activision's old debt} + \text{Microsoft's old debt}$$
$$= \$3,856 + \$95,852 = \$99,708 \text{ million}$$
$$\text{Equity} = \text{Microsoft's old equity} + \text{New equity used for acquisition}$$
$$= \$3,023,000 + \$60,444 = \$3,083,444 \text{ million}$$

The debt/equity ratio can then be computed as follows:

$$\text{D/E ratio} = 99,708/3,083,444 = 3.23\%$$

This debt/equity ratio in conjunction with the new unlevered beta for the combined firm yields a new beta of 1.1571:

$$\text{Beta after acquisition} = 1.1256[1 + (1 - .25) \times (.0323)] = 1.1529$$

As you can see, the debt-to-equity ratio after an acquisition will reflect how it is funded, with more debt financing used leading to higher unlevered betas. Thus, if Microsoft finances the acquisition with a new debt issue, the post-acquisition and debt and equity values will change.

$$\text{Debt} = \text{Activision's old debt} + \text{Microsoft's old debt} + \text{New Debt}$$
$$= \$3,856 + \$95,852 + \$60,444 = \$160,152 \text{ million}$$
$$\text{Equity} = \text{Microsoft's old equity}$$
$$= \$3,023,000 \text{ million}$$

The debt/equity ratio can then be computed as follows:

$$\text{D/E ratio} = 160,152/3023000 = 5.30\%$$

This higher debt to equity ratio will result in a higher post-acquisition beta of 1.1747

$$\text{Beta after acquisition} = 1.1256[1 + (1 - .25) \times (.0530)] = 1.1703$$

Accounting Betas   A third approach is to estimate the market risk parameters from accounting earnings rather than from traded prices. Thus, changes in earnings at a division or a firm, on a quarterly or an annual basis, can be related to changes in earnings for the market, in the same periods, to arrive at an estimate of a accounting beta to use in the CAPM. While the approach has some intuitive appeal, it suffers from three potential pitfalls. First, accounting earnings tend to be smoothed out relative to the underlying value of the company, as accountants spread expenses and income over multiple periods. This results in betas that are "biased down", especially for risky firms, or "biased up" for safer firms. In other words, betas are likely to be closer to 1 for all firms using accounting data.

Second, accounting earnings can be influenced by nonoperating factors, such as changes in depreciation or inventory methods, and by allocations of corporate expenses at the divisional level. Finally, accounting earnings are measured, at most, once every quarter, and often only once every year, resulting in regressions with few observations and not much explanatory power (low R-squared, high standard errors).

ILLUSTRATION 8.8:   Estimating Accounting Betas: Defense Division of Boeing—1995

Boeing is an aerospace company with a substantial defense business. Having operated in the defense business for decades, Boeing has a record of its profitability. These profits are reported in Table 8.4, together with earnings changes for companies in the S&P 500 from 1980 to 1994.

TABLE 8.4 Boeing Defense Division Earnings vs. S&P 500 Earnings

Year	S&P 500	Boeing's Defense Business
1980	−2.10%	−12.70%
1981	−6.70%	−35.56%
1982	−45.50%	27.59%
1983	37.00%	159.36%
1984	41.80%	13.11%
1985	−11.80%	−26.81%
1986	7.00%	−16.83%
1987	41.50%	20.24%
1988	41.80%	18.81%
1989	2.60%	−29.70%
1990	−18.00%	−40.00%
1991	−47.40%	−35.00%
1992	64.50%	10.00%
1993	20.00%	−7.00%
1994	25.30%	11.00%

Regressing the changes in profits in the defense division (Δ Earnings$_{defense}$) against changes in profits for the S&P 500 (Δ Earnings$_{S\&P}$) yields the following:

$$\Delta Earnings_{defense} = -0.03 + 0.65\ \Delta Earnings_{S\&P}\quad \text{R-squared} = 19.01\%$$
$$(0.12)\ (0.37)$$

Based on this regression, the beta for the defense division is 0.65. However, that estimate comes with significant noise, with the standard error at 0.37; the range on the beta will therefore render it almost useless.

 spearn.xls: This dataset on the web has earnings changes, by year, for the S&P 500 going back to 1960.

Market, Bottom-Up, and Accounting Betas: Which One Do We Use?   For most publicly traded firms, betas can be estimated using accounting data or market data, or from the bottom-up approach. Since the betas will almost never be the same using these different approaches, the question is, which one do we use? We would almost never use accounting betas, for all the reasons specified earlier. We are almost as reluctant to use historical market betas for individual firms, because of the standard errors in beta estimates, the failures of the local indexes (as is the case with most emerging market companies), and the inability of these regressions to reflect the effects of major changes in the business mix and financial risk at the firm. Bottom-up betas, in our view, provide us with the best beta estimates for three reasons:

1. They allow us to consider changes in business and financial mix, even before they occur.
2. They use average betas across large numbers of firms, which tend to be less noisy than individual firm betas.
3. They allow us to calculate betas by area of business for a firm, which is useful both in the context of investment analysis and in valuation.

Measuring Country Risk Exposure (Lambda)

Chapter 7 introduced the concept of country risk exposure and the notion of lambda—a measure of a company's exposure to country risk. In this section, we want to consider intuitively what factors determine this exposure and how best to estimate lambda. A company's exposure to country risk is affected by almost every aspect of its operations, beginning with where its factories are located and who its customers are, and then continuing with what currency its contracts are denominated in and how well it manages its exposure to exchange rate risk. Much of this information, however, is internal information and not available to someone valuing the firm from the outside. As a practical matter, we can estimate lambda using one of the following approaches:

■ *Revenue breakdown.* The simplest way of estimating lambda is to use the proportion of a firm's revenues that are generated in a country and scale this to the proportion of the revenues generated by the average firm in that country.

$$\lambda = \frac{\text{Proportion of revenues in country}_{\text{Firm}}}{\text{Proportion of revenues in country}_{\text{Average firm in market}}}$$

Consider Embraer, a Brazilian aerospace company that in 2008 derived about 9 percent of its revenues from Brazil. If the average Brazilian company generates 60 percent of its revenues in Brazil, this will translate into a lambda of 0.15 (0.09/.060). Note, though, that if Embraer gets any of its remaining revenue in other risky emerging markets, you will have to compute lambdas against these markets as well.

■ *Regression versus country bond.* A second approach to estimating lambdas would be to run regressions of stock returns for each firm in the emerging market against the returns on the country bond. In effect, we are assuming that returns on the country bond are reflections of changes in country risk: Country bond prices increase when country risk decreases and decrease when country risk increases. When we run this regression, we are measuring how sensitive a company's stock price is to changes in country risk perceptions. To provide an illustration: Regressing the stock prices of Embraer against the dollar-denominated Brazilian government bond from 2006 to

2008 yields a slope (lambda) of 0.27. Put in intuitive terms, Embraer's returns moved 0.27 percent for every 1 percent change in returns on the bond. That would be our estimate of lambda for the company.

LAMBDAS: WORTH THE TROUBLE?

The intuition behind the use of lambdas is that a company's risk exposure should be based on where it does business and not where it is incorporated. Thus, an emerging market company that gets the bulk of its revenues in developed markets should be less exposed to the country risk in that emerging market. By the same token, a developed market company that gets large portions of its revenues in emerging markets should see its cost of equity increase because of that exposure.

Having said this, it is often difficult to obtain the information needed to estimate lambdas. The lambda for a company should depend not only on where it gets its revenues, but where it produces its goods and the degree to which it insures against country risk using derivatives or conventional insurance. For most companies, the information on these inputs is either unavailable or incomplete. Thus, any benefits from estimating lambdas may be drowned out by the estimation error in those lambdas. For firms that have revenue exposures like those of other firms in the market, it may make sense to stick with the standard approach of using beta to capture company risk. There are two factors in play that may induce you to estimate a lambda for country risk exposure:

1. *Significant exposure in one (risky) country:* For companies that have operations in many countries, which is often the standard for most multinationals, the lambda approach becomes unwieldy and unstable. It is better designed for a company that has significant exposure to one emerging market, and has the rest of its operations in developed markets (with mature market premiums). Tata Consulting Services in India and Embraer in Brazil are good examples, deriving less than 10% of their revenues in the domestic markets, while getting the rest of their revenues almost entirely in developed markets. The same can be said for developed market companies that get much of their revenues from developed markets, but either have their production or significant revenues in one emerging market.
2. *Special exposure to country risk:* For many companies, the factors that cause betas to be high or low, including whether the products or services they provide are discretionary or operating leverage also determine exposure to country risk, making betas good proxies for country risk. There are cases, though, where a company may be singled out in a country for special scrutiny or oversight, either because it used to be government owned or because it is viewed as in the national interest, and that can cause the company to be much more exposed to country risk (higher lambda).

Thus, the lambda approach is for that small subset of companies exposed to risk in a single country, and which have specific reasons for being more or less exposed to country risk than would be measured with a beta.

From Betas to Cost of Equity

Having estimated the riskless rate and the risk premium(s) in Chapter 7 and the beta(s) in this chapter, we can now estimate the expected return from investing in equity at any firm. In the CAPM, this expected return can be written as:

$$\text{Expected return} = \text{Risk-free rate} + \text{Beta} \times \text{Equity risk premium}$$

where the riskless rate would be the rate on a long-term government bond; the beta would be either the historical, fundamental, or accounting betas described earlier; and the risk premium would be either the historical premium or an implied premium.

In the arbitrage pricing and multifactor model, the expected return would be written as follows:

$$\text{Expected Return} = \text{Risk free rate} + \sum_{j=1}^{j=n} \beta_j \left(\text{Risk Premium}_j \right)$$

where the riskless rate is the long-term government bond rate; β_j is the beta relative to factor j, estimated using historical data or fundamentals; and risk premium$_j$ is the risk premium for factor j, estimated using historical data.

The expected return on an equity investment in a firm, given its risk, has implications for both equity investors in the firm and the managers of the firm. For equity investors, it is the rate they need to earn to be compensated for the risk they have taken in investing in the equity of the firm. If, after analyzing an investment, they conclude they cannot make this return, they would not buy this investment; alternatively, if they decide they can make a higher return, they would make the investment. For managers in the firm, the return investors need to make to break even on their equity investments becomes the return they have to try to deliver to keep these investors from becoming restive and rebellious. Thus, it becomes the rate they have to beat in terms of returns on their equity investments in projects. In other words, this is the cost of equity to the firm.

ILLUSTRATION 8.9:   Estimating the Cost of Equity for Microsoft—In 2024

Now that we have an estimate of beta of 1.16 (from illustration 8.5) for Microsoft, based on the bottom-up estimates, and its current debt to equity ratio, we can estimate its cost of equity. To make the estimate, we used the Treasury bond rate of 4.5% and to estimate the equity risk premium, we used Microsoft's geographic revenue breakdown to estimate an equity risk premium of 5.5%:

Geographic Regiion	Revenues in 2023	Weights	ERP in 2024
United States	$ 106,744.00	50.37%	4.25%
Other Countries	$ 105,171.00	49.63%	6.76%
Total Revenues	**$ 211,915.00**		5.50%

Note that Microsoft reports a bundled revenue for the rest of the world, rather than break that revenue down by countries or even regions. Consequently, we use an equity risk premium that reflects of weighted average of the rest of the world to these revenues. Bringing these inputs together, we estimate the cost of equity for the company to be 10.89%.

Investment
Valuation

Founded in 1807, John Wiley & Sons is the oldest independent publishing company in the United States. With offices in North America, Europe, Australia, and Asia, Wiley is globally committed to developing and marketing print and electronic products and services for our customers' professional and personal knowledge and understanding.

The Wiley Finance series contains books written specifically for finance and investment professionals as well as sophisticated individual investors and their financial advisors. Book topics range from portfolio management to e-commerce, risk management, financial engineering, valuation, and financial instrument analysis, as well as much more.

For a list of available titles, please visit our Web site at www.WileyFinance.com.

that these firms have, relative to their larger competitors. You could adjust the betas for operating leverage (as we did a few pages ago for Vans Shoes) and use the higher betas for small firms. Third, the small cap premium of 3.1 percent that we estimated from historical data comes with a significant standard error (of approximately 2 percent). Thus, the true small cap premium can be 8 percent or 0 percent. Fourth, even if your company is a small company today and deserves a small cap premium, assuming a high growth rate for your firm will make it a large cap firm eventually. It follows that you would expect the small cap premium to fade over time. Finally, as we saw in the section on the small cap premium, it has faded over time, and has disappeared in the 1981–2023 time period.

In summary, we believe that the negatives outweigh the positives, and that there remains no basis for using small cap premiums in computing costs of equity. Unfortunately, as with many other practices in valuations, once they become embedded in practice, it becomes very difficult to remove them.

FROM COST OF EQUITY TO COST OF CAPITAL

Although equity is undoubtedly an important and indispensable ingredient of the financing mix for every business, it is but one ingredient. Most businesses finance some or much of their operations using debt or some security that is a combination of equity and debt. The costs of these sources of financing are generally very different from the cost of equity, and the cost of financing for a firm should reflect their costs as well, in proportion to their use in the financing mix. Intuitively, the cost of capital is the weighted average of the costs of the different components of financing—including debt, equity, and hybrid securities—used by a firm to fund its financial requirements. This section examines the process of estimating the cost of financing other than equity, and the weights for computing the cost of capital.

Calculating the Cost of Debt

The cost of debt measures the current cost to the firm of borrowing funds to finance projects. In general terms, it is determined by the following variables:

- *The riskless rate.* As the riskless rate increases, the cost of debt for firms will also increase.
- *The default risk (and associated default spread) of the company.* As the default risk of a firm increases, the cost of borrowing money will also increase. Chapter 7 looked at how the default spread has varied across time and can vary across maturity.
- *The tax advantage associated with debt.* Since interest is tax deductible, the after-tax cost of debt is a function of the tax rate. The tax benefit that accrues from paying interest makes the after-tax cost of debt lower than the pretax cost. Furthermore, this benefit increases as the tax rate increases.

After-tax cost of debt = (Riskless Rate + Default Spread)(1 − Tax rate)

This section focuses on how best to estimate the default risk in a firm and to convert that default risk into a default spread that can be used to come up with a cost of debt.

Estimating the Default Risk and Default Spread of a Firm   The simplest scenario for estimating the cost of debt occurs when a firm has long-term bonds outstanding that are widely traded. The market price of the bond in conjunction with its coupon and maturity can serve to compute a yield that is used as the cost of debt. For instance, this approach works for a firm that has dozens of outstanding bonds that are liquid and trade frequently.

Some firms have bonds outstanding that do not trade on a regular basis. Since these firms are usually rated, we can estimate their costs of debt by using their ratings and associated default spreads. Thus, a firm with an A rating can be expected to have a cost of debt approximately 1.07 percent higher than the Treasury bond rate, since this is the spread typically paid by AA-rated firms, at least at the time of this analysis.

Many companies choose not to get rated, and smaller firms and most private businesses fall into this category. Although ratings agencies have sprung up in many emerging markets, there are still several markets where companies are not rated on the basis of default risk. When there is no rating available to estimate the cost of debt, there are two alternatives:

1. *Recent borrowing history.* Many firms that are not rated still borrow money from banks and other financial institutions. By looking at the most recent borrowings made by a firm, we can get a sense of the types of default spreads being charged the firm, and then use these spreads to come up with a cost of debt.
2. *Estimate a synthetic rating.* An alternative is to play the role of a ratings agency and assign a rating to a firm based on its financial ratios; this rating is called a synthetic rating. To make this assessment, we begin with rated firms and examine the financial characteristics shared by firms within each ratings class. To illustrate, Table 8.5 lists the range of interest coverage ratios for small (less than $5 billion in market cap) nonfinancial service firms in each S&P ratings class, with default spreads in January 2024.[11]

TABLE 8.5   Interest Coverage Ratios and Ratings: Low Market Cap Firms

Interest Coverage Ratio	Rating is	Spread is
>12.5	Aaa/AAA	0.59%
9.5–12.5	Aa2/AA	0.70%
7.5–9.5	A1/A+	0.92%
6.0–7.5	A2/A	1.07%
4.5–6.0	A3/A-	1.21%
4.0–4.5	Baa2/BBB	1.47%
3.5–4.0	Ba1/BB+	1.74%
3.0–3.5	Ba2/BB	2.21%
2.5–3.0	B1/B+	3.14%
2.0–2.5	B2/B	3.61%
1.75–2.0	B3/B-	5.24%

[11]This table was updated in early 2023 by listing out all rated firms with market capitalization lower than $5 billion and their interest coverage ratios, and then sorting firms based on their bond ratings. The ranges were adjusted to eliminate outliers and to prevent overlapping ranges.

Interest Coverage Ratio	Rating is	Spread is
1.25–1.75	Caa/CCC	8.51%
0.8–1.25	Ca2/CC	11.78%
0.5–0.8	C2/C	17.00%
<0.2	D2/D	20.00%

Source for raw data: NAIC.

Now consider a small firm that is not rated but has an interest coverage ratio of 6.15. Based on this ratio, a synthetic rating of A would be assessed for the firm, and a default spread of 1.07% would be added to the risk-free rate to arrive at the pretax cost of debt.

The interest coverage ratios tend to be lower for larger (market cap greater than $5 billion) firms for any given rating. Table 8.6 summarizes these ratios, ratings, and default spreads, as of January 2024.

TABLE 8.6   Interest Coverage Ratios, Ratings, and Default Spreads: Large Market Cap Firms

Interest Coverage Ratio	Rating is	Spread is
>8.50	Aaa/AAA	0.59%
6.5–8.5	Aa2/AA	0.70%
5.5–6.5	A1/A+	0.92%
4.25–5.5	A2/A	1.07%
3–4.35	A3/A-	1.21%
2.5–3.0	Baa2/BBB	1.47%
2.25–2.5	Ba1/BB+	1.74%
2–2.5	Ba2/BB	2.21%
1.75–2.0	B1/B+	3.14%
1.5–1.75	B2/B	3.61%
1.25–1.5	B3/B-	5.24%
0.8–1.25	Caa/CCC	8.51%
0.65–0.8	Ca2/CC	11.78%
0.2–0.65	C2/C	17.00%
<0.2	D2/D	20.00%

Source for raw data: NAIC.

This approach can be expanded to allow for multiple ratios and qualitative variables as well. Once a synthetic rating is assessed, it can be used to estimate a default spread, which when added to the risk-free rate, yields a pretax cost of debt for the firm.

EXTENDING THE SYNTHETIC RATINGS APPROACH

By basing the rating on the interest coverage ratio alone, we run the risk of missing the information that is available in the other financial ratios used by ratings agencies.

(continued)

(continued)

The approach can be extended to incorporate other ratios. The first step would be to develop a score based on multiple ratios. For instance, the Altman Z score, which is used as a proxy for default risk, is a function of five financial ratios that are weighted to generate a Z score. The ratios used and their relative weights are usually estimated by looking at past defaults. The second step is to relate the level of the score to a bond rating, much as is done in Tables 8.1 and 8.2 with interest coverage ratios.

In making this extension, though, note that complexity comes at a cost. While credit or Z scores may, in fact, yield better estimates of synthetic ratings than those based on interest coverage ratios, changes in ratings arising from these scores are much more difficult to explain than those based on interest coverage ratios. That is a reason to prefer the flawed but simpler ratings derived from interest coverage ratios.

Estimating a Tax Rate   To estimate the after-tax cost of debt, consider the fact that interest expenses are tax deductible to the firm. While the computation is fairly simple and requires that the pretax cost be multiplied by (1 − tax rate), the question of what tax rate to use can be a difficult one to answer, because there are so many choices. For instance, firms often report an effective tax rate, estimated by dividing the taxes due by the taxable income. The effective tax rate, though, is usually very different from the marginal or statutory tax rate, which is the rate at which the last dollar of income is taxed. Since interest expenses save you taxes at the margin (they are deducted from your last dollar of income), the right tax rate to use is the marginal tax rate.

The other caveat to keep in mind is that interest creates a tax benefit only if a firm has enough income to cover the interest expenses. Firms that have operating losses will not get a tax benefit from interest expenses, at least in the year of the loss. The after-tax cost of debt will be equal to the pretax cost of debt in that year. If you expect the firm to make money in future years, you would need to adjust the after-tax cost of debt for taxes in those years.

We return to this issue and examine it in more detail in Chapter 10, where we look at the same issue in the context of estimating after-tax cash flows.

ILLUSTRATION 8.11:   Estimating the Cost of Debt: Microsoft in April 2024

Microsoft was rated AAA by S&P. Using the typical default spreads for AAA-rated firms in April 2024, we could estimate the pretax cost for Microsoft by adding the default spread of 0.59% to the riskless rate of 4.5%.

$$\text{Pretax cost of debt}_{\text{actual rating}} = 4.5\% + 0.59\% = 5.09\%$$

Microsoft a marginal tax rate of 265% to estimate the after-tax cost of debt for Microsoft:

$$\text{After-tax cost of debt} = 5.09\% \times (1 - .25) = 3.82\%$$

Note that we will attach this after-tax cost of debt to all of Microsoft's debt (short term or long term). While that may seem unfair, since Microsoft could have borrowed short term at lower rates, we are assuming that the rollover cost of short-term debt will approximate to the cost of long-term debt. Furthermore, we do not want to systematically reward companies with short-term debt by giving them lower costs of capital.

One final point about ratings. The ratings agencies rate both individual bond issues and entire companies. The rating used for the pretax cost of debt should be the rating for the company and not for an individual bond. Even a risky company can structure and issue a safe bond, and estimating a cost of debt based on that bond's rating will underestimate the overall cost of debt.

Estimating the Cost of Debt for an Emerging Market Firm   In general, there are three problems that we run into when assessing the cost of debt for emerging market firms. The first is that most of these firms are not rated, leaving us with no option but to estimate the synthetic rating (and associated costs). The second is that the synthetic ratings may be skewed by differences in interest rates between the emerging market and the United States. Interest coverage ratios will usually decline as interest rates increase, and it may be far more difficult for a company in an emerging market to achieve the interest coverage ratios of companies in developed markets. Finally, the existence of country default risk hangs over the cost of debt of firms in that market.

The second problem can be fixed simply by either modifying the tables developed using U.S. firms, or restating the interest expenses (and interest coverage ratios) in dollar terms. The question of country risk is a thornier one. Conservative analysts often assume that companies in a country cannot borrow at a rate lower than the country itself can borrow at. With this reasoning, the cost of debt for an emerging market company will include the country default spread for the country:

$$\text{Cost of debt} = \text{Riskless rate} + \text{Country default spread}_{\text{sovereign rating}}$$
$$+ \text{Company default spread}_{\text{synthetic rating}}$$

The counter to this argument is that companies may be safer than the countries in which they operate, and that they bear only a portion or perhaps even none of the country default spread.

ILLUSTRATION 8.12:   Estimating the Cost of Debt: Embraer in March 2008

To estimate Embraer's cost of debt, we first estimated a synthetic rating for the firm. Based on its operating income of $527 million and interest expenses of $176 million in 2007, we arrived at an interest coverage ratio of 2.99 and a BBB rating. While the default spread for BBB-rated bonds was only 1.50% at the time, there is the added consideration that Embraer is a Brazilian firm. Since the Brazilian dollar-denominated government bond had a default spread of 2.00% at the time of the analysis, you could argue that every Brazilian company should pay this premium in addition to its own default spread. With this reasoning, the pretax cost of debt for Embraer in U.S. dollars (assuming a Treasury bond rate is 3.8%) can be calculated:

$$\text{Cost of debt} = \text{Risk-free rate} + \text{Default spread for country} + \text{Default spread for firm}$$
$$= 3.8\% + 2.00\% + 1.50\% = 7.30\%$$

Using a marginal tax rate of 34%, we can estimate an after-tax cost of debt for Embraer:

$$\text{After-tax cost of debt} = 7.30\%(1 - .34) = 4.82\%$$

With this approach, the cost of debt for a firm can never be lower than the cost of debt for the country in which it operates. Note, though, that Embraer gets a significant portion of its revenues in dollars from contracts with non-Brazilian airlines. Consequently, it could reasonably argue that it is less exposed to risk than is the

Brazilian government and should therefore command a lower cost of debt. Put differently, there are some companies (generally large companies with significant foreign operations) to which, rather than add the entire default spread for the country to the cost of debt, we may add only a portion.

 ratings.xls: This spreadsheet allows you to estimate the synthetic rating and cost of debt for any firm.

Calculating the Cost of Hybrid Securities

While debt and equity represent the fundamental financing choices available for firms, there are some types of financing that share characteristics with both debt and equity. These are called hybrid securities. This section considers how best to estimate the costs of such securities.

Preferred Stock   Preferred stock shares some of the characteristics of debt (the preferred dividend is prespecified at the time of the issue and is paid out before the common dividend) and some of the characteristics of equity (the preferred dividend is not tax deductible). If preferred stock is viewed as perpetual (as it usually is), the cost of preferred stock can be written as follows:

$$k_{ps} = \text{Preferred dividend per share/Market price per preferred share}$$

This approach assumes the dividend is constant in dollar terms forever, and that the preferred stock has no special features (convertibility, callability, etc.). If such special features exist, they will have to be valued separately to estimate the cost of preferred stock. In terms of risk, preferred stock is safer than common equity, because preferred dividends are paid before dividends on common equity. It is, however, riskier than debt since interest payments are made prior to preferred dividend payments. Consequently, on a pretax basis, it should command a higher cost than debt and a lower cost than equity.

ILLUSTRATION 8.13:   Calculating the Cost of Preferred Stock: Ford in 2011

In April 2011, Ford Motor Company had preferred stock that paid a dividend of $1.875 annually and traded at $26.475 per share. The cost of preferred stock can be estimated as follows:

$$\text{Cost of preferred stock} = \text{Preferred dividend per share/Preferred stockprice}$$
$$= \$1.875/\$26.475 = 7.08\%$$

At the same time, Ford's cost of equity, using an estimated beta of 1.40, a risk-free rate of 3.5% and an equity risk premium of 5%, was 10.5%; its pretax cost of debt, based on its S&P rating of B+, was 8.50%, and its after-tax cost of debt was 5.10%. Not surprisingly, its preferred stock was less expensive than equity but much more expensive than debt.

Other Hybrid Securities   A convertible bond is a bond that can be converted into equity at the option of the bondholder. A convertible bond can be viewed as a combination of a straight bond (debt) and a conversion option (equity). Instead of trying to calculate the cost of these hybrid securities individually, we can break down hybrid securities into their debt and equity components and treat the components separately.

ILLUSTRATION 8.14: Breaking Down a Convertible Bond into Debt and Equity Components: MGM Resorts

In 2010, MGM Resorts, the casino company, issued 5-year convertible bonds with a coupon rate of 4.25% and a 10-year maturity. Since the firm was losing money, it was rated CCC+ by S&P and would have had to pay 10% if it had issued straight bonds at the same time. A year later, the bonds were trading at a price that was 112% of par, and the total par value of the convertible bond issue was $1.15 billion. The convertible bond can be broken down into straight bond and conversion option components:

$$\text{Straight bond component} = \text{Value of a straight 4.25\% coupon bond due in}$$
$$\text{4 years with 10\% interest rate}$$
$$= \$818 (\text{assuming annual coupons})$$
$$\text{Conversion option} = \text{Market value of convertible} - \text{Straight bond component}$$
$$= \$1,120 - \$818 = \$302$$

The straight bond component of $818 is treated as debt, and has the same cost as the rest of debt. The conversion option of $302 is treated as equity, with the same cost of equity as other equity issued by the firm. For the entire bond issue of $1,150 million, with an overall market value of $1,288 million, the value of debt is $916 million, and the value of equity is $372 million.

Calculating the Weights of Debt and Equity Components

Now that we have the costs of debt, equity, and hybrid securities, we have to estimate the weights that should be attached to each. Before we discuss how best to estimate weights, we define what we include in debt. We then make the argument that weights used should be based on market value and not book value. This is so because the cost of capital measures the cost of issuing securities—stocks as well as bonds—to finance projects, and these securities are issued at market value, not at book value.

What Is Debt?   The answer to this question may seem obvious since the balance sheet for a firm shows the outstanding liabilities of the firm. There are, however, limitations with using these liabilities as debt in the cost of capital computation. The first is that some of the liabilities on a firm's balance sheet, such as accounts payable and supplier credit, are not interest-bearing. Consequently, applying an after-tax cost of debt to these items can provide a misleading view of the true cost of capital for a firm. The second is that there are items off the balance sheet that create fixed commitments for the firm, and provide the same tax deductions that interest payments on debt do. Until 2019, the most prominent of these off-balance sheet items are operating leases. Chapter 3 contrasted operating and capital leases and noted that operating leases are treated as operating expenses rather than financing expenses. Consider, though, what an operating lease involves. A retail firm leases a store space for 12 years and enters into a lease agreement with the owner of the space agreeing to pay a fixed amount each year for that period. We do not see much difference between this commitment and borrowing money from a bank, and agreeing to pay off the bank loan over 12 years in equal annual installments.

In 2019, both generally accepted accounting principles (GAAP) and international financial reporting standards (IFRS) agreed with this conclusion, and leases are now capitalized and treated as debt on balance sheets.

There are therefore two adjustments we will make when we estimate how much debt a firm has outstanding.

1. We will consider only interest-bearing debt rather than all liabilities. We would include both short-term and long-term borrowings in debt.
2. If leases are treated as debt by accountants, we will count them towards total debt. If they are not, we will capitalize leases and treat them as debt.

Capitalizing Operating Leases   Converting operating lease expenses into a debt equivalent is straightforward. The operating lease commitments in future years, which are revealed in the footnotes to the financial statements for U.S. firms, should be discounted back at a rate that reflects their status as unsecured and risky debt. As an approximation, using the firm's current pretax cost of borrowing as the discount rate yields a good estimate of the value of operating leases. There are still some countries where companies do not have to reveal their operating lease commitments to investors. When this is the case, you can get a reasonably close estimate of the debt value of operating leases by estimating the present value of an annuity equal to the current year's payment for a period that reflects a typical lease period (8–10 years).

There is one final issue relating to capitalization. Earlier in this chapter, it was stated that the interest coverage ratio could be used to estimate a synthetic rating for a firm that is not rated. For firms with little in terms of conventional debt and substantial operating leases, the interest coverage ratio used to estimate a synthetic rating has to be adapted to include operating lease expenses.

$$\text{Modified interest coverage ratio} = \frac{\text{EBIT + Current year's operating lease expense}}{\text{Interest expenses + Current year's operating lease expense}}$$

This ratio can then be used in conjunction with Tables 8.1 and 8.2 to estimate a synthetic rating.

Starting in 2019, both IFRS and GAAP have changed the rules on leases, requiring companies to capitalize all lease and show them as debt. As with all accounting rules, there are loopholes and incomplete portions, but in companies that follow the new rules, there should be a far smaller need to convert leases to debt.

ILLUSTRATION 8.15:   The Debt Value of Operating Leases: Microsoft in December 2000 versus April 2023

Microsoft has both conventional debt and operating lease commitments and in 2000, the latter were not treated as debt. This illustration estimates the "debt value" of Microsoft's operating leases by taking the present value of operating lease expenses over time. To compute the present value of operating leases in Table 8.7 (in $millions), we use the pretax cost of borrowing for the firm, estimated to be 6%:

TABLE 8.7   Capitalizing leases at Microsoft in 2000

Year	Operating Lease Expense	Present Value at 6%
1	$205	$193.40
2	$167	$146.83
3	$120	$100.75

Year	Operating Lease Expense	Present Value at 6%
4	$ 86	$ 68.12
5	$ 61	$ 45.58
6–15	$ 0	$ 0.00
Present value of operating lease expenses		$556.48

Thus, Microsoft had $556 million more in debt than is reported in the balance sheet in early 2000, since accountants ignored operating leases in 2000.

To provide a contrast on how accounting rules have changed in the treatment of debt, Microsoft's 2023 balance sheet included lease debt of $37,139 million, with $4,478 million due in the next year and the rest shown as long-term lease debt. Included in this lease debt were operating and capital leases, with accountants discounting contractual lease obligations in future years back at Microsoft's pre-tax cost of debt.

 oplease.xls: **This spreadsheet allows you to convert operating lease expenses into debt.**

Book Value (BV) versus Market Value (MV) Debt Ratios   There are three standard arguments against using market value, and none of them is convincing. First, there are some financial managers who argue that book value is more reliable than market value because it is not as volatile. While it is true that book value does not change as much as market value, this is more a reflection of book value's weakness rather than its strength, since the true value of the firm changes over time as both firm-specific and market information is revealed. We would argue that market value, with its volatility, is a much better reflection of true value than is book value.[12]

Second, the defenders of book value also suggest that using book value rather than market value is a more conservative approach to estimating debt ratios. This assumes that market value debt ratios are always lower than book value debt ratios, an assumption not based on fact. Furthermore, even if the market value debt ratios are lower than the book value ratios, the cost of capital calculated using book value ratios will be lower than those calculated using market value ratios, making it a less conservative estimate, not more. To illustrate this point, assume that the market value debt ratio is 10 percent, while the book value debt ratio is 30 percent, for a firm with a cost of equity of 15 percent and an after-tax cost of debt of 5 percent. The cost of capital can be calculated as follows:

With market value debt ratios: $15\% \times (.9) + 5\% \times (.1) = 14\%$
With book value debt ratios: $15\% \times (.7) + 5\% \times (.3) = 12\%$

---

[12]There are some who argue that stock prices are much more volatile than the underlying true value. Even if this argument is justified (and it has not conclusively been shown to be so), the difference between market value and true value is likely to be much smaller than the difference between book value and true value.

Third, it is claimed that lenders will not lend on the basis of market value, but this claim again seems to be based more on perception than on fact. Any homeowner who has taken a second mortgage on a house that has appreciated in value knows that lenders do lend on the basis of market value. It is true, however, that the greater the perceived volatility in the market value of an asset, the lower the borrowing potential on that asset.

Estimating the Market Values of Equity and Debt   The market value of equity is generally the number of shares outstanding times the current stock price. If there are other equity claims in the firm such as warrants and management options, these should also be valued and added to the value of the equity in the firm.

The market value of debt is usually more difficult to obtain directly, since very few firms have all their debt in the form of bonds outstanding trading in the market. Many firms have nontraded debt, such as bank debt, which is specified in book value terms but not market value terms. A simple way to convert book value debt into market value debt is to treat the entire debt on the books as one coupon bond, with a coupon set equal to the interest expenses on all the debt and the maturity set equal to the face-value weighted average maturity of the debt, and then to value this coupon bond at the current cost of debt for the company. Thus, the market value of $1 billion in debt, with interest expenses of $60 million (annually) and a maturity of six years, when the current cost of debt is 7.5 percent, can be estimated as follows:

$$\text{Market value of debt} = \text{PV of interest payments} + \text{PV of face value}$$

$$= 60 \left[\frac{\left(1 - \frac{1}{1.075^6} \right)}{.075} \right] + \frac{1000}{1.075^6} = \$929.59$$

This debt has a market value of approximately $930 million, with the discount coming from the fact that the book interest rate at this firm (6%) is lower than the market interest rate of 7.5%.

ILLUSTRATION 8.16:   Difference between Market Value and Book Value Debt Ratios: Microsoft in April 2024

This illustration contrasts the book values of debt and equity with the market values. The book value of debt in Microsoft in its 2023 balance sheet was $111,358 million, and much of it was untraded. Since this is the case for many firms that have debt outstanding, it is not uncommon for analysts to assume that the book value of debt is a reasonable proxy for the market value of debt:

$$\text{Total debt due at Microsoft} = \$111,358 \text{ million}$$

While that is not a bad assumption, there will be companies where the market value of debt can deviate from book value, with rapidly changing interest rates and default spreads to blame. There is a short cut that you can use to convert book value of debt to market value, at least in approximate terms, using the book value of debt, the interest expense on the debt, the average maturity of the debt, and the pretax cost of debt for each firm. For Microsoft, the book value of debt is $111,358 million, the interest expense on the debt is $2,461 million, the average maturity of the debt is about 5.69 years, and the pretax cost of debt is 5.09%. The estimated market value is:

$$\text{Market value of Microsoft's debt} = \text{PV of interest payments} + \text{PV of face value}$$

$$= 2461 \left[\frac{\left(1 - \frac{1}{1.0509^{5.69}} \right)}{.0509} \right] + \frac{111,358}{1.0509^{5.69}} = \$95,852 \text{ million}$$

The book value of equity for Microsoft was $238 billion while the market value of equity was $3,023 billion. The debt ratios in market value and book value terms are computed as follows:

	Book	Market
Equity ($ millions)	$238,268	$3,023,000
Total Debt ($ millions)	$111,358	$ 95,852
Debt to Equity	46.74%	3.17%
Debt to Capital	31.85%	3.07%

The market debt ratio is significantly lower than the book debt ratio.

GROSS DEBT VERSUS NET DEBT

Gross debt refers to all debt outstanding in a firm. Net debt is the difference between gross debt and the cash balance of the firm. For instance, a firm with $1.25 billion in interest-bearing debt outstanding and a cash balance of $1 billion has a net debt balance of $250 million. The practice of netting cash against debt is common in both Latin America and Europe, and debt ratios are usually estimated using net debt.

It is generally safer to value a firm based on gross debt outstanding, and to add the cash balance outstanding to the value of operating assets, to arrive at the firm value. The interest payment on total debt is then entitled to the tax benefits of debt, and we can assess the effect of whether the company invests its cash balances efficiently on value.

In some cases, especially when firms maintain large cash balances as a matter of routine, analysts prefer to work with net debt ratios. If you choose to use net debt ratios, you have to be consistent all the way through the valuation. To begin, the beta for the firm should be estimated using a net debt-to-equity ratio rather than a gross debt-to-equity ratio. The cost of equity that emerges from the beta estimate can be used to estimate a cost of capital, but the market value weight on debt should be based on net debt. Once you discount the cash flows of the firm at the cost of capital, you should not add back cash. Instead, you should subtract the net debt outstanding to arrive at the estimated value of equity.

Implicitly, when you net cash against debt to arrive at net debt ratios, you are assuming that cash and debt have roughly similar risk. While this assumption may not be outlandish when analyzing highly rated firms, it becomes much shakier when debt becomes riskier. For instance, the debt in a BB-rated firm is much riskier than the cash balance in the firm, and netting out one against the other can provide a misleading view of the firm's default risk. In general, using net debt ratios will overstate the value of riskier firms.

---

 wacccalc.xls: **This spreadsheet allows you to convert book values of debt into market values.**

Estimating the Cost of Capital

Since a firm can raise its money from three sources—equity, debt, and preferred stock—the cost of capital is defined as the weighted average of each of these costs. The cost of equity (k_e) reflects the riskiness of the equity investment in the firm, the after-tax cost of debt (k_d) is a function of the default risk of the firm, and the cost of preferred stock (k_{ps}) is a function of its intermediate standing in terms of risk between debt and equity. The weights on each of these components should reflect their market value proportions, since these proportions best measure how the existing firm is being financed. Thus if E, D, and PS are the market values of equity, debt, and preferred stock respectively, the cost of capital can be written as follows:

$$\text{Cost of capital} = k_e\left[E/(D + E + PS)\right] + k_d\left[D/(D + E + PS)\right] + k_{ps}\left[PS/(D + E + PS)\right]$$

ILLUSTRATION 8.17:   Estimating Cost of Capital: Microsoft in April 2024

Having estimated the costs of debt and equity in earlier illustrations, and the market value debt ratio in Illustration 8.16, we can put them together to arrive at a cost of capital for Microsoft.

Cost of equity = 10.89% (from Illustration 8.9)

Cost of debt = 3.82% (from Illustration 8.11)

Market value debt to capital ratio = 3.07% (from Illustration 8.16)

Cost of capital = 10.89% × (.9693) + 3.82% × (.0307) = 10.65%

ILLUSTRATION 8.18:   Estimating Cost of Capital: Embraer in March 2008

To estimate a cost of capital for Embraer, we again draw on the estimates of cost of equity and cost of debt we obtained in prior illustrations. The cost of capital will be estimated using gross debt ratios first in U.S. dollars:

Cost of equity = 8.31% (from Illustration 8.10)

After-tax cost of debt = 4.82% (from Illustration 8.12)

Market value of debt = 2,915 million BR (Book value = 3,128 million BR)

Market value of equity = 12,729 million BR

The cost of capital for Embraer is estimated as follows:

Cost of capital = 8.31% × [12,729/(12,729 + 2,915)] + 4.82% × [2,915/(12,729 + 2,915)] = 7.66%

To convert this into a nominal BR cost of capital, we would apply the differential inflation rates (6% in Brazil and 2% in the United States).

$$\text{Cost of equity}_{\text{nominal BR}} = \left(1 + \text{Cost of equity}_{\$}\right)\left(1 + \text{Inflation rate}_{\text{Brazil}}\right)$$
$$/\left(1 + \text{Inflation rate}_{\text{U.S.}}\right) - 1$$
$$= 1.0766(1.06/1.02) - 1 = 11.88\%$$

To estimate the cost of capital using the net debt ratio, we bring in the cash balance of 4,437 million BR that Embraer had at the time of the analysis:

Net debt = Gross debt − Cash = 2,915 million BR − 4,437 million BR = −1,422 million BR
Net Debt/Equity ratio = −1422/12,729 = −11.17%
Net Debt to Capital ratio = −1422/(12,729 − 1422) = −12.57%

Unlevered beta = 0.75
Levered beta using net debt to equity ratio = $0.75 \times [1 + (1 - .34) \times (-.1117)] = 0.695$

Intuitively, the levered beta here is lower than the unlevered beta, because we are incorporating the cash into the beta computation (with the assumption that cash is riskless):

$$\text{Cost of equity(U.S.\$)} = 3.8\% + 0.695(4\%) + 0.27(3.66\%) = 7.57\%$$

$$\text{Cost of capital(US \$)} = 7.57\% \times [12,729/(12729 - 1422)]$$
$$+ 4.82\% \times [-1422/(12729 - 1422)]$$
$$= 7.57\% \times (1.1257) + 4.82\% \times (-0.1257) = 7.91\%$$

Note that the weight on equity is greater than 100% (112.57%) and the weight on debt is negative (−12.57%) because net debt is negative. Notwithstanding these disconcerting inputs, the cost of capital is close to the cost of capital using the standard debt ratio approach, and the difference can be attributed to the fact that the net debt approach nets out the tax benefit of debt against the tax costs of earning interest income on cash.

BEST PRACTICES AT FIRMS

We have spent this chapter discussing what firms should do when it comes to estimating the cost of capital. What do they actually do? Bruner et al. (1998) surveyed 27 well-regarded corporations, and their findings are summarized in Table 8.8.

TABLE 8.8   Current Practices for Estimating Cost of Capital

Cost of Capital Item	Current Practices
Cost of equity	■ 81% of firms used the capital asset pricing model to estimate the cost of equity, 4% used a modified capital asset pricing model, and 15% were uncertain about how they estimated the cost of equity. ■ The riskless asset (R_f) is defined to be an asset for which the investor knows the expected return with certainty for the time horizon of the analysis. ■ 70% of firms used 10-year Treasuries or longer as the riskless rate, 7% used 3- to 5-year Treasuries, and 4% used the Treasury bill rate. ■ 52% used a published source for a beta estimate, while 30% estimated it themselves. ■ There was wide variation in the market risk premium used, with 37% using a premium between 5% and 6%. ■ The riskless asset (R_f) is defined to be an asset for which the investor knows the expected return with certainty for the time horizon of the analysis.

(continued)

TABLE 8.8 *(continued)*

Cost of Capital Item	Current Practices
Cost of debt	■ 52% of firms used a marginal borrowing rate and a marginal tax rate, while 37% used the current average borrowing rate and the effective tax rate.
Weights for debt and equity	■ 59% used market value weights for debt and equity in the cost of capital, 15% used book value weights, and 19% were uncertain about what weights they used.

Source: Bruner et al. (1998).

CONCLUSION

When we analyze the investments of a firm or assess its value, we need to know the cost that the firm faces in raising equity, debt, and capital. The risk and return models described in earlier chapters can be used to estimate the costs of equity and capital for a firm.

Building on the premise that the cost of equity should reflect the riskiness of equity to investors in the firm, there are three basic inputs we need to estimate the cost of equity for any firm. The riskless rate is the expected return on an investment with no default risk and no reinvestment risk. Since much of the analysis in corporate finance is long term, the riskless rate should be the interest rate on a long-term government bond. The risk premium measures what investors demand as a premium for investing in risky investments instead of riskless investments. This risk premium, which can vary across investors, can be estimated either by looking at past returns on stocks and government securities, or by looking at how the market prices stocks currently. The beta for a firm is conventionally measured using a regression of returns on the firm's stock against returns on a market index. This approach yields imprecise beta estimates, and we are better off estimating betas by examining the betas of the businesses in which the firm operates.

The cost of capital is a weighted average of the costs of the different components of financing, with the weights based on the enterprise values of each component. The cost of debt is the market rate at which the firm can borrow, adjusted for any tax advantages of borrowing. The cost of preferred stock, however, is the preferred dividend yield.

The cost of capital is useful at two levels. On a composite basis, it is what these firms have to make collectively on their investments to break even. It is also the appropriate discount rate to use to discount expected future cash flows to arrive at an estimate of firm value.

QUESTIONS AND SHORT PROBLEMS

In the problems following, use an equity risk premium of 5.5 percent if none is specified and a tax rate of 40 percent where no tax rate is provided.

1. In December 1995, Boise Cascade's stock had a beta of 0.95. The Treasury bill rate at the time was 5.8%, and the Treasury bond rate was 6.4%. The firm had debt

outstanding of $1.7 billion and a market value of equity of $1.5 billion; the corporate marginal tax rate was 36%. (The historical risk premium for stocks over Treasury bills is 8.5% and the risk premium for stocks over Treasury bonds is 5.5%.)
  a. Estimate the expected return on the stock for a short-term investor in the company.
  b. Estimate the expected return on the stock for a long-term investor in the company.
  c. Estimate the cost of equity for the company.
2. Continuing problem 1, Boise Cascade also had debt outstanding of $1.7 billion and a market value of equity of $1.5 billion; the corporate marginal tax rate was 36%.
  a. Assuming that the current beta of 0.95 for the stock is a reasonable one, estimate the unlevered beta for the company.
  b. How much of the risk in the company can be attributed to business risk and how much to financial leverage risk?
3. Biogen Inc., a biotechnology firm, had a beta of 1.70 in 1995. It had no debt outstanding at the end of that year.
  a. Estimate the cost of equity for Biogen if the Treasury bond rate is 6.4%.
  b. What effect will an increase in long-term bond rates to 7.5% have on Biogen's cost of equity?
  c. How much of Biogen's risk can be attributed to business risk?
4. Genting Berhad is a Malaysian conglomerate with holdings in plantations and tourist resorts. The beta estimated for the firm relative to the Malaysian stock exchange is 1.15, and the long-term government borrowing rate in Malaysia is 11.5%. (The Malaysian risk premium is 12% and the default spread on Malaysian local currency debt is 2%.)
  a. Estimate the expected return on the stock.
  b. If you were an international investor, what concerns, if any, would you have about using the beta estimated relative to the Malaysian Index? If you do have concerns, how would you modify the beta?
5. You have just done a regression of monthly stock returns of HeavyTech Inc., a manufacturer of heavy machinery, on monthly market returns over the past five years, and have come up with the following regression:

$$R_{HeavyTech} = 0.5\% + 1.2\ R_M$$

The variance of the stock is 50%, and the variance of the market is 20%. The current T-bill rate is 3% (it was 5% one year ago). The stock is currently selling for $50, down $4 over the past year; it has paid a dividend of $2 during the past year and expects to pay a dividend of $2.50 over the next year. The NYSE Composite has gone down 8% over the past year, with a dividend yield of 3%. HeavyTech Inc. has a tax rate of 40%.
  a. What is the expected return on HeavyTech over the next year?
  b. What would you expect HeavyTech's price to be one year from today?
  c. What would you have expected HeavyTech's stock returns to be over the past year?
  d. What were the actual returns on HeavyTech over the past year?
  e. HeavyTech has $100 million in equity and $50 million in debt. It plans to issue $50 million in new equity and retire $50 million in debt. Estimate the new beta.

6. Safecorp, which owns and operates grocery stores across the United States, currently has $50 million in debt and $100 million in equity outstanding. Its stock has a beta of 1.2. It is planning a leveraged buyout (LBO), where it will increase its debt-to-equity ratio of 8. If the tax rate is 40%, what will the beta of the equity in the firm be after the LBO?

7. Novell, which had a market value of equity of $2 billion and a beta of 1.50, announced that it was acquiring WordPerfect, which had a market value of equity of $1 billion and a beta of 1.30. Neither firm had any debt in its financial structure at the time of the acquisition, and the corporate tax rate was 40%.
   a. Estimate the beta for Novell after the acquisition, assuming that the entire acquisition was financed with equity.
   b. Assume that Novell had to borrow the $1 billion to acquire WordPerfect. Estimate the beta after the acquisition.

8. You are analyzing the beta for Hewlett Packard (HP) and have broken down the company into four broad business groups, with market values and betas for each group.

Business Group	Market Value of Equity	Beta
Mainframes	$2.0 billion	1.10
Personal computers	$2.0 billion	1.50
Software	$1.0 billion	2.00
Printers	$3.0 billion	1.00

   a. Estimate the beta for Hewlett Packard as a company. Is this beta going to be equal to the beta estimated by regressing past returns on HP stock against a market index? Why or why not?
   b. If the Treasury bond rate is 7.5%, estimate the cost of equity for Hewlett Packard. Estimate the cost of equity for each division. Which cost of equity would you use to value the printer division?
   c. Assume that HP divests itself of the mainframe business and pays the cash out as a dividend. Estimate the beta for HP after the divestiture. (HP had $1 billion in debt outstanding.)

9. The following table summarizes the percentage changes in operating income, percentage changes in revenue, and betas for four pharmaceutical firms.

Firm	% Change (Revenues)	% change (Op Income)	Beta
PharmaCorp	27%	25%	1.00
SynerCorp	25%	32%	1.25
BioMed	23%	36%	1.30
Safemed	21%	40%	1.40

   a. Calculate the degree of operating leverage for each of these firms.
   b. Use the operating leverage to explain why these firms have different betas.

10. A prominent beta estimation service reports the beta of Comcast Corporation, a major cable TV operator, to be 1.45. The service claims to use weekly returns on the stock over the prior five years and the NYSE Composite as the market index to estimate betas. You replicate the regression using weekly returns over the same period and arrive at a beta estimate of 1.60. How would you reconcile the two estimates?

11. Battle Mountain is a mining company with gold, silver, and copper in mines in South America, Africa, and Australia. The beta for the stock is estimated to be 0.30. Given the volatility in commodity prices, how would you explain the low beta?

12. You have collected returns on AnaDone Corporation (AD Corp.), a large, diversified manufacturing firm, and the NYSE index for five years:

Year	AD Corp.	NYSE
1981	10%	5%
1982	5%	15%
1983	–5%	8%
1984	20%	12%
1985	–5%	–5%

  a. Estimate the intercept (alpha) and slope (beta) of the regression.

  b. If you bought stock in AD Corp. today, how much would you expect to make as a return over the next year? (The six-month T-bill rate is 6%.)

  c. Looking back over the past five years, how would you evaluate AD Corp.'s performance relative to the market?

  d. Assume now that you are an undiversified investor and you have all of your money invested in AD Corp. What would be a good measure of the risk that you are taking on? How much of this risk would you be able to eliminate if you diversify?

  e. AD Corp. is planning to sell off one of its divisions. The division under consideration has assets that comprise half of the book value of AD Corp. and 20% of the market value. Its beta is twice the average beta for AD Corp. (before divestment). What will the beta of AD Corp. be after divesting this division?

13. You run a regression of monthly returns of Mapco Inc., an oil- and gas-producing firm, on the S&P 500 index, and come up with the following output for the period 1991–1995:

  Intercept of the regression = 0.06%
  Slope of the regression = 0.46
  Standard error of X-coefficient = 0.20
  R-squared = 5%

There are 20 million shares outstanding, and the current market price is $2 per share. The firm has $20 million in debt outstanding. (The firm has a tax rate of 36%.)

  a. What would an investor in Mapco's stock require as a return if the T-bond rate is 6%?

  b. What proportion of this firm's risk is diversifiable?

  c. Assume now that Mapco has three divisions of equal size (in market value terms). It plans to divest itself of one of the divisions for $20 million in cash and acquire another for $50 million. (It will borrow $30 million to complete this acquisition.) The division it is divesting is in a business line where the average unlevered beta is 0.20, and the division it is acquiring is in a business line where the average unlevered beta is 0.80. What will the beta of Mapco be after this acquisition?

14. You have just run a regression of monthly returns of American Airlines (AMR Corporation) against the S&P 500 over the past five years. You have misplaced some of the output and are trying to derive it from what you have.
    a. You know the R-squared of the regression is 0.36, and that your stock has a variance of 67%. The market variance is 12%. What is the beta of AMR?
    b. You also remember that AMR was not a very good investment during the period of the regression, and that it did worse than expected (after adjusting for risk) by 0.39% a month for the five years of the regression. During this period, the average risk-free rate was 4.84%. What was the intercept on the regression?
    c. You are comparing AMR to another firm, which also has an R-squared of 0.48. Will the two firms have the same beta? If not, why not?

15. You have run a regression of monthly returns on Amgen, a large biotechnology firm, against monthly returns on the S&P 500 index, and come up with the following output:

$$R_{stock} = 3.28\% + 1.65\ R_{market}\quad R^2 = 0.20$$

The current one-year Treasury bill rate is 4.8% and the current 30-year bond rate is 6.4%. The firm has 265 million shares outstanding, selling for $30 per share.
    a. What is the expected return on this stock over the next year?
    b. Would your expected return estimate change if the purpose was to get a discount rate to value the company?
    c. An analyst has estimated, correctly, that the stock did 51.1% better than expected, annually, during the period of the regression. Can you estimate the annualized risk-free rate that she used for her estimate?
    d. The firm has a debt/equity ratio of 3% and faces a tax rate of 40%. It is planning to issue $2 billion in new debt and acquire a new business for that amount, with the same risk level as the firm's existing business. What will the beta be after the acquisition?

16. You have just run a regression of monthly returns on MAD Inc., a newspaper and magazine publisher, against returns on the S&P 500, and arrived at the following result:

$$R_{MAD} = -0.05\% + 1.20\ R_{S\&P}$$

The regression has an R-squared of 22%. The current T-bill rate is 5.5%, and the current T-bond rate is 6.5%. The risk-free rate during the period of the regression was 6%. Answer the following questions relating to the regression:
    a. Based on the intercept, how well or badly did MAD do, relative to expectations, during the period of the regression?
    b. You now realize that MAD Inc. went through a major restructuring at the end of last month (which was the last month of your regression), and made the following changes:
       ■ The firm sold off its magazine division, which had an unlevered beta of 0.6, for $20 million.
       ■ It borrowed an additional $20 million, and bought back stock worth $40 million.
       After the sale of the division and the share repurchase, MAD Inc. had $40 million in debt and $120 million in equity outstanding. If the firm's tax rate is 40%, re-estimate the beta after these changes.

17. Time Warner Inc., the entertainment conglomerate, had a beta of 1.61 in 1995. Part of the reason for the high beta was the debt left over from the leveraged buyout of Time by Warner in 1989, which amounted to $10 billion in 1995. The market value of equity at Time Warner in 1995 was also $10 billion. The marginal tax rate was 40%.
    a. Estimate the unlevered beta for Time Warner.
    b. Estimate the effect of reducing the debt ratio by 10% each year for the next two years on the beta of the stock.

18. Chrysler, the automotive manufacturer, had a beta of 1.05 in 1995. It had $13 billion in debt outstanding in that year, and 355 million shares trading at $50 per share. The firm had a cash balance of $8 billion at the end of 1995. The marginal tax rate was 36%.
    a. Estimate the unlevered beta of the firm.
    b. Estimate the effect of paying out a special dividend of $5 billion on this unlevered beta.
    c. Estimate the beta for Chrysler after the special dividend.

19. You are trying to estimate the beta of a private firm that manufactures home appliances. You have managed to obtain betas for publicly traded firms that also manufacture home appliances.

Firm	Beta	Debt	MV of Equity
Black & Decker	1.40	$2,500	$3,000
Fedders Corp.	1.20	$ 5	$ 200
Maytag Corp.	1.20	$ 540	$2,250
National Presto	0.70	$ 8	$ 300
Whirlpool	1.50	$2,900	$4,000

The private firm has a debt-to-equity ratio of 25% and faces a tax rate of 40%. The publicly traded firms all have marginal tax rates of 40% as well.
    a. Estimate the beta for the private firm.
    b. What concerns, if any, would you have about using betas of comparable firms?

20. As the result of stockholder pressure, RJR Nabisco is considering spinning off its food division. You have been asked to estimate the beta for the division, and decide to do so by obtaining the beta of comparable publicly traded firms. The average beta of comparable publicly traded firms is 0.95, and the average debt-to-equity ratio of these firms is 35%. The division is expected to have a debt ratio of 25%. The marginal corporate tax rate is 36%.
    a. What is the beta for the division?
    b. Would it make any difference if you knew that RJR Nabisco had a much higher fixed cost structure than the comparable firms used here?

21. Southwestern Bell, a phone company, is considering expanding its operations into the media business. The beta for the company at the end of 1995 was 0.90, and the debt-to-equity ratio was 1. The media business is expected to be 30% of the overall firm value in 1999, and the average beta of comparable firms is 1.20; the average debt-to-equity ratio for these firms is 50%. The marginal corporate tax rate is 36%.
    a. Estimate the beta for Southwestern Bell in 1999, assuming that it maintains its current debt-to-equity ratio.
    b. Estimate the beta for Southwestern Bell in 1999, assuming that it decides to finance its media operations with a debt-to-equity ratio of 50%.

22. The chief financial officer of Adobe Systems, a growing software manufacturing firm, has approached you for some advice regarding the beta of his company. He subscribes to a service that estimates Adobe Systems' beta each year, and he has noticed that the beta estimates have gone down every year since 1991—from 2.35 in 1991 to 1.40 in 1995. He would like the answers to the following questions:
    a. Is this decline in beta unusual for a growing firm?
    b. Why would the beta decline over time?
    c. Is the beta likely to keep decreasing over time?

23. You are analyzing Tiffany & Company, an upscale retailer, and find that the regression estimate of the firm's beta is 0.75; the standard error for the beta estimate is 0.50. You also note that the average unlevered beta of comparable specialty retailing firms is 1.15.
    a. If Tiffany has a debt/equity ratio of 20%, estimate the beta for the company based on comparable firms. (The tax rate is 40%.)
    b. Estimate a range for the beta from the regression.
    c. Assume that Tiffany is rated BBB and that the default spread for BBB-rated firms is 1% over the Treasury bond rate. If the Treasury bond rate is 6.5%, estimate the cost of capital for the firm.

24. You have been asked to estimate the cost of capital for NewTel, a telecom firm. The firm has the following characteristics:
    ■ There are 100 million shares outstanding, trading at $250 per share.
    ■ The firm has a book value of debt with a maturity of six years of $10 billion, and interest expenses of $600 million on the debt. The firm is not rated, but it had operating income of $2.5 billion last year. (Firms with an interest coverage ratio of 3.5–4.5 were rated BBB, and the default spread was 1%.)
    ■ The tax rate for the firm is 35%.
    The Treasury bond rate is 6%, and the unlevered beta of other telecom firms is 0.80.
    a. Estimate the market value of debt for this firm.
    b. Based on the synthetic rating, estimate the cost of debt for this firm.
    c. Estimate the cost of capital for this firm.

CHAPTER 9

Measuring Earnings

To estimate cash flows, we usually begin with a measure of earnings. Free cash flows to the firm, for instance, are based on after-tax operating earnings. Free cash flows to equity estimates, on the other hand, commence with net income. While we obtain measures of operating and net income from accounting statements, the accounting earnings for many firms bear little or no resemblance to the true earnings of the firm.

This chapter begins by considering the philosophical difference between the accounting and financial views of firms. We then consider how the earnings of a firm, at least as measured by accountants, have to be adjusted to get a measure of earnings that is more appropriate for valuation. In particular, we examine how to treat operating lease expenses, which we argue are really financial expenses, and research and development expenses, which we consider to be capital expenses. The adjustments affect not only our measures of earnings but our estimates of book value of capital. We also look at extraordinary items (both income and expenses) and one-time charges, the use of which has expanded significantly in recent years as firms have shifted toward managing earnings more aggressively. The techniques used to smooth earnings over periods and beat analyst estimates can skew reported earnings, and, if we are not careful, the values that emerge from them.

THE LEAD-IN: FROM ACCOUNTING DATA TO FINANCIAL INFORMATION

When analyzing a firm, what are the questions to which we would like to know the answers? A firm, as defined here, includes both investments already made—assets in place—and investments yet to be made—growth assets. In addition, a firm can either borrow the funds it needs to make these investments, in which case it is using debt, or raise it from its owners in the form of equity. Figure 9.1 summarizes this description of a firm in the form of a financial balance sheet.

Note that while this summary does have some similarities with the accounting balance sheet, there are key differences. The most important one is that here we explicitly consider growth assets when we look at what a firm owns.

When doing a financial analysis of a firm, we would like to be able to answer several questions relating to each of these items. Figure 9.2 lists the questions. As we see in this chapter, accounting statements allow us to acquire some information about each of these questions, but they fall short in terms of both the timeliness with which they provide it and the way in which they measure asset value, earnings, and risk.

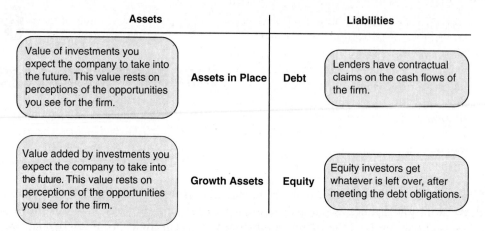

FIGURE 9.1   A Financial Balance Sheet

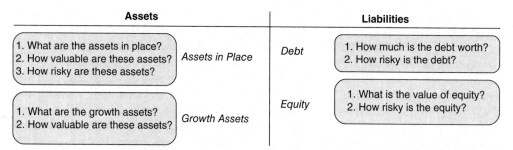

FIGURE 9.2   Financial Balance Sheet Questions

In this chapter, we will focus on a number that is the starting point for all valuations, which is accounting earnings. While we build narratives of growth and risk around these earnings, it remains unquestionably true that if your earnings are flawed, much of what flows from these earnings is also going to be flawed. We have been trained to believe that accounting earnings, as reported in income statements, represent the earnings power of the firm (i.e., the earnings generated by its assets in place). We will argue in this chapter that there are at least three considerations that come into play, when using these earnings:

1. *Updating earnings:* Unlike accounting, where updating is driven by fiscal year considerations and calendar time, valuation happens in real time. In short, if it is July 2024, there is no point to valuing a firm as of December 31, 2023, or earlier, since those valuations, even if compelling, are not actionable. In the first part of this chapter, we will look at how to update numbers, as best as we can, to reflect the reality that the accounting statements that we rely on for earnings numbers are dated.
2. *Correcting for accounting inconsistencies:* While accounting contends that, as a rule-driven discipline, it is consistent about how it categorizes expenses into capital and operating and financing groupings, the truth is that accounting, as practiced, is inconsistent in how it groups expenses are nonfinancial service firms, with capital expenditures like R&D being categorized as operating expense, and financing expenses like leases being put into the operating expense pile, at least until very recently. Without

correcting for these inconsistencies, we get skewed measures of earnings at these firms, and ripple effects on what we estimate to be their invested capital.

3. *Normalizing earnings:* It is worth remembering that the value of a business today is unaffected by its earnings in previous time periods, and that the only reason for looking at past earnings is to get a sense of earnings power at the firm that can be used not only to value assets in place but also future growth. However, earnings are volatile, sometimes for company-specific reasons and sometimes because of macroeconomic shifts, and using the most recent year's earnings as the basis for future forecasts can be dangerous. In the last section, we look at measuring earnings power better by looking at earnings over time and at cleaning up for accounting debris, including one-time or extraordinary charges that can cause earnings to gyrate.

By the end of this chapter, we will present a version of updated, consistently- measured and normalized earnings that will provide a cleaner measure of a company's current earnings power.

ADJUSTING EARNINGS

The income statement for a firm provides measures of both the operating and equity income of the firm in the form of the earnings before interest and taxes (EBIT) and net income. When valuing firms, there are two important considerations in using these measures. One is to obtain as updated an estimate as possible, given how much firms change over time. The second is that reported earnings at these firms may bear little resemblance to true earnings because of limitations in accounting rules and the firms' own actions.

Importance of Updating Earnings

Firms reveal their earnings in their financial statements and annual reports to stockholders. Annual reports are released only after the end of a firm's financial year, but you are often required to value firms all through the year. Consequently, the last annual report available for a firm being valued can contain information that is several months old. In the case of firms that are changing rapidly over time, it is dangerous to base value estimates on information that is this old. Instead, use more recent information. Since firms in the United States are required to file quarterly reports (known as 10-Qs) with the Securities and Exchange Commission (SEC) and reveal these reports to the public, a more recent estimate of key items in the financial statements can be obtained by aggregating the numbers over the most recent four quarters. The estimates of revenues and earnings that emerge from this exercise are called trailing 12-month revenues and earnings and can be very different from the values for the same variables in the most recent annual report.

There is a price paid for the updating. Unfortunately, not all items in the annual report are updated in the quarterly reports. You have to either use the numbers in the last annual report (which does lead to inconsistent inputs) or estimate their values at the end of the last quarter (which leads to estimation error). For example, many firms do not reveal details about options outstanding (issued to managers and employees) in quarterly reports, while they do reveal them in annual reports. Since you need to value these options, you can use the options outstanding as of the last annual report, or assume that the options outstanding today have changed to reflect changes in the other variables. (For instance, if revenues have doubled, you can assume that the options have doubled as well.)

For younger firms, it is critical that you stay with the most updated numbers you can find, even if these numbers are estimates. These firms are often growing exponentially, and using numbers from the last financial year will lead to misleading estimates of value. Even firms that are not growing are changing substantially from quarter to quarter, and updated information might give you a chance to capture these changes.

There are several financial markets where firms still file financial reports only once a year, thus denying us the option of using quarterly updates. When valuing firms in these markets, you may have to draw on unofficial sources to update their valuations.

ILLUSTRATION 9.1:   Updated Earnings for Apple—April 2024

Assume that you were valuing Apple in April 2024. The last 10-K was as of September 2023, and the firm had released two quarterly reports (10-Qs): one ending in December 2023 and one ending in March 2024. To illustrate how much the fundamental inputs to the valuation have changed in the six months, the information in the last 10-K is compared to the trailing 12-month information in the latest 10-Q for revenues, operating income, R&D expenses, and net income (in millions of dollars).

	Six Months Ended March 2023	Six Months Ended March 2024	Annual September 2023	Trailing 12-Month
Revenues	$211,990	$210,328	$383,285	$381,623
Operating Income	$ 64,334	$ 68,273	$114,301	$118,240
R&D	$ 15,166	$ 15,599	$ 29,915	$ 30,348
Net Income	$ 54,158	$ 57,552	$ 96,995	$100,389

The trailing 12-month revenues are down a little from the revenues reported in the latest 10-K, and the firm's operating income and net income have both increased slightly. Put simply, the trailing 12-month numbers for Apple, in April 2024, indicate a firm that is struggling with growth. Note that these are not the only inputs that will change. For younger firms, the number of shares outstanding can also change dramatically from period to period. Using the most updated numbers will give you a more realistic valuation.

Correcting Earnings Misclassification

Companies have three types of expenses, and each has a place in accounting statements, affecting reported earnings, and balance sheet values.

1. Operating expenses are expenses that generate benefits for the firm only in the current period. For instance, the fuel used by an airline during its flights is an operating expense, as is the labor cost for an automobile company associated with producing vehicles.
2. Capital expenses are expenses that generate benefits over multiple periods. For example, the expense associated with building and outfitting a new factory for an automobile manufacturer is a capital expense, since it will generate several years of revenues.
3. Financing expenses are expenses associated with nonequity capital raised by a firm. Thus, the interest paid on a bank loan would be a financial expense.

The operating income for a firm, measured correctly, should be equal to its revenues less its operating expenses. Neither financial nor capital expenses should be included in the operating expenses in the year that they occur, though capital expenses may be depreciated or amortized over the periods that the firm obtains benefits from the expenses. The net income of a firm should be its revenues less both its operating and financing expenses.

The accounting measures of earnings can be misleading because operating, capital, and financing expenses are sometimes misclassified. This section considers the two most common misclassifications and how to correct for them. The first is the inclusion of capital expenses such as research and development (R&D) in operating expenses, which skews the estimation of both operating and net income. The second adjustment is for financial expenses such as operating lease expenses that are treated as operating expenses. This affects the measurement of operating income and free cash flows to the firm.

The other factor to consider is the effect of the phenomenon of so-called managed earnings at these firms. Firms sometimes use accounting techniques to post earnings that beat analyst estimates, resulting in misleading measures of earnings.

Capital Expenses Treated as Operating Expenses   While in theory operating income in after only operating expenses, the reality is that there are several capital expenses that are treated as operating expenses. For instance, a significant shortcoming of accounting statements is the way in which they treat research and development expenses. Using the rationale that the products of research are too uncertain and difficult to quantify, accounting standards have generally required that all R&D expenses be expensed in the period in which they occur. This has several consequences, but one of the most profound is that the value of the assets created by research does not show up on the balance sheet as part of the total assets of the firm. This, in turn, creates ripple effects for the measurement of capital and profitability ratios for the firm. We consider how to capitalize R&D expenses in the first part of this section and extend the argument to other capital expenses in the second part of this section.

Capitalizing R&D Expenses   Research expenses, notwithstanding the uncertainty about future benefits, should be capitalized. To capitalize and value research assets, we make an assumption about how long it takes for research and development to be converted, on average, into commercial products. This is called the amortizable life of these assets. This life will vary across firms and reflect the time involved in converting research into products. To illustrate, research and development expenses at a pharmaceutical company should have fairly long amortizable lives, since the approval process for new drugs is long. In contrast, research and development expenses at a software firm, where products tend to emerge from research much more quickly, should be amortized over a shorter period.

Once the amortizable life of research and development expenses has been estimated, the next step is to collect data on R&D expenses over past years ranging back over the amortizable life of the research asset. Thus, if the research asset has an amortizable life of five years, the R&D expenses in each of the five years prior to the current one have to be obtained. For simplicity, it can be assumed that the amortization is uniform over time, which leads to the following estimate of the residual value of the research asset today:

$$\text{Value of research asset with n} - \text{year life} = \sum_{t=-(n-1)}^{t=0} \text{R\&D}_t \frac{(n+t)}{n}$$

Thus, in the case of the research asset with a five-year life, you cumulate one-fifth of the R&D expenses from four years ago, two-fifths of the R&D expenses from three years ago, three-fifths of the R&D expenses from two years ago, four-fifths of the R&D expenses from last year, and this year's entire R&D expense to arrive at the value of the research asset. This augments the value of the assets of the firm and, by extension, the book value of equity.

Adjusted book value of equity = Book value of equity + Value of Research Asset

Finally, the operating income is adjusted to reflect the capitalization of R&D expenses. First, the R&D expenses that were subtracted out to arrive at the operating income are added back to the operating income, reflecting their recategorization as capital expenses. Next, the amortization of the research asset is treated the same way that depreciation is and netted out to arrive at the adjusted operating income:

Adjusted operating income = Operating income + Current year R&D expense
− Amortization of research asset

This adjustment will generally increase operating income for firms which have R&D expenses that are growing over time. The net income will also be affected by this adjustment:

Adjusted net income = Net income + Current year R&D expense
− Amortization of research asset

While we would normally consider only the after-tax portion of this amount, the fact that R&D is entirely tax deductible eliminates the need for this adjustment.[1]

 R&DConv.xls: This spreadsheet allows you to convert R&D expenses from operating to capital expenses.

ILLUSTRATION 9.2:   Capitalizing R&D Expenses: Amgen in May 2024

Amgen is a biotechnology firm. Like most pharmaceutical firms, it has a substantial amount of R&D expenses, and we attempt to capitalize it in this section. The first step in this conversion is determining an amortizable life for R&D expenses. How long will it take, on an expected basis, for research to pay off at Amgen? Given the length of the approval process for new drugs by the Food and Drug Administration (FDA), we assume that this amortizable life is 10 years.

---

[1]If only amortization were tax deductible, the tax benefit from R&D expenses would be:

$$R\&D\,Amortization \times Tax\,rate$$

This extra tax benefit we get from the entire R&D being tax deductible is as follows:

$$(Current\,year's\,R\&D\,expense - R\&D\,Amortization) \times Tax\,rate$$

If we subtract out (R&D − Amortization)(1 − Tax rate) and then add the differential tax benefit that is computed above, (1 − Tax rate) drops out of the equation.

The second step in the analysis is collecting research and development expenses from prior years, with the number of years of historical data being a function of the amortizable life. The following table provides this information (in millions of dollars) for each of the years:

Calendar Year	Year (t)	R&D Expenses
Current (2023)	0	$4,784
2022	−1	$4,434
2021	−2	$4,819
2020	−3	$4,207
2019	−4	$4,116
2018	−5	$3,737
2017	−6	$3,562
2016	−7	$3,840
2015	−8	$4,006
2014	−9	$4,248
2013	−10	$4,083

The current year's information reflects the R&D in the most recent financial year (which was calendar year 2023).

The portion of the expenses in prior years that would have been amortized already and the amortization this year from each of these expenses is considered. To make estimation simpler, these expenses are amortized linearly over time; with a 10-year life, 10% is amortized each year. This allows you to estimate the value of the research asset created at each of these firms, and the amortization of R&D expenses in the current year. The procedure is illustrated in the following table:

Year	R&D Expense	Unamortized Portion		Amortization this Year
Current	$4,784.00	100.00%	4784.00	
−1	$4,434.00	90.00%	3990.60	$ 443.40
−2	$4,819.00	80.00%	3855.20	$ 481.90
−3	$4,207.00	70.00%	2944.90	$ 420.70
−4	$4,116.00	60.00%	2469.60	$ 411.60
−5	$3,737.00	50.00%	1868.50	$ 373.70
−6	$3,562.00	40.00%	1424.80	$ 356.20
−7	$3,840.00	30.00%	1152.00	$ 384.00
−8	$4,006.00	20.00%	801.20	$ 400.60
−9	$4,248.00	10.00%	424.80	$ 424.80
−10	$4,083.00	0.00%	0.00	$ 408.30
Value of Research Asset =			$23,715.60	
Amortization of Asset				$4,105.20

Note that none of the current year's expenditure has been amortized because it is assumed to occur at the end of the year (which is right now) but that 50 percent of the expense from five years ago has been amortized. The sum of the dollar values of unamortized R&D from prior years is $23,716 million. This can be viewed as the value of Amgen's research asset and would be also added to the book value of equity for computing return on equity and capital measures. The sum of the amortization in the current year for all prior year expenses is $4,105 million.

The final step in the process is the adjustment of the operating income to reflect the capitalization of research and development expenses. We make the adjustment by adding back current year's R&D expenses to the operating income (to reflect its reclassification as a capital expense) and subtracting out the amortization of the research asset, estimated in the last step. For Amgen, which reported operating income of $8,164 million in its income statement for 2023, the adjusted operating earnings would be:

$$\text{Adjusted operating income} = \text{Operating income} + \text{Current year's R\&D expense}$$
$$- \text{Amortization of research asset}$$
$$= 8{,}164 + 4{,}784 - 4{,}105 = \$8{,}843 \text{ million}$$

The stated net income of $6,717 million can be adjusted similarly.

$$\text{Adjusted net income} = \text{Net income} + \text{Current year's R\&D expense}$$
$$- \text{Amortization of research asset}$$
$$= 6{,}717 + 4{,}755 - 4{,}105 = \$7{,}367 \text{ million}$$

In the last section, we explained why there is no tax effect to consider.

Both the book value of equity and capital are augmented by the value of the research asset. Since measures of return on capital and equity are based on the prior year's values, we computed the value of the research asset at the end of 2022 using the same approach that we used in 2023.

$$\text{Value of research asset}_{2022} = \$23{,}037$$
$$\text{Adjusted book value of equity}_{2022} = \text{Book value of equity}_{2022}$$
$$+ \text{Value of research asset}_{2022}$$
$$= 6{,}232 + 23{,}037 = \$29{,}269$$
$$\text{Adjusted book value of invested capital} = \text{Book value of invested capital}_{2022}$$
$$+ \text{Value of research asset}_{2022}$$
$$= 60{,}711 + 23{,}037 = \$83{,}748$$

The returns on equity and capital are reported with both the unadjusted and adjusted numbers:

	Unadjusted	Adjusted for R&D
Return on equity	6,717/6,232 = 107.8%	7,367/29,269 = 25.17%
Pretax return on capital	8,164/60,711 = 13.45%	8.843/83,748 = 10.56%

Note that the accounting returns decline for Amgen, when the R&D adjustment is made. This is likely to happen for most firms that earn high returns on equity and capital and have substantial R&D expenses.[2]

Capitalizing Other Operating Expenses   While R&D expenses are the most prominent example of capital expenses being treated as operating expenses, there are other operating expenses that arguably should be treated as capital expenses. Consumer product companies such as Gillette and Coca-Cola could argue that a portion of advertising expenses should be treated as capital expenses, since they are designed to augment brand name value. For

---

[2] If the return on capital earned by a firm is well below the cost of capital, the adjustment could result in a higher return.

a consulting firm, the cost of recruiting and training its employees could be considered a capital expense, since the consultants who emerge are likely to be the heart of the firm's assets and provide benefits over many years. For some technology firms, including e-tailers such as Amazon.com, the biggest operating expense item is selling, general, and administrative expenses (SG&A). These firms could argue that a portion of these expenses should be treated as capital expenses, since they are designed to increase brand name awareness and bring in new customers.

While this argument has some merit, you should remain wary about using it to justify capitalizing these expenses. For an operating expense to be capitalized, there should be substantial evidence that the benefits from the expense accrue over multiple periods. Does a customer who is enticed to buy from Amazon, based on an advertisement or promotion, continue as a customer for the long term? There are some analysts who claim that this is indeed the case, and attribute significant value added to each new customer.[3] It would be logical, under those circumstances, to capitalize these expenses using a procedure similar to that used to capitalize R&D expenses.

As user and subscription-based business models proliferate, there is an argument to be made that the cost of customer acquisitions should be capitalized, with the effect depending upon how long an acquired customer stays on the platform:

- Determine the period that a customer will stay on the platform. This will depend upon subscription renewal rates or churn rates at these businesses.
- Estimate the value of the asset (similar to the process used with the research asset) created by these expenses. If the customer acquisition costs are being capitalized, there will be an asset related to these costs.
- Adjust the operating income for the expense and the amortization of the created asset.

$$\text{Adjusted operating income} = \text{Operating income} \\ + \text{Customer acquisition costs in the current year} \\ - \text{Amortization of customer acquisition asset}$$

A similar adjustment has to be made to net income:

$$\text{Adjusted net income} = \text{Net income} + \text{Customer acquisition costs in the current year} \\ - \text{Amortization of customer acquisition asset}$$

As with the research asset, the capitalization of these expenses will create an asset that augments the book value of equity (and capital).

The pushback that you will get from accountants is that you are creating an asset for expenses that may or may not create benefits, but that resistance comes from the perspective that you are rewarding a company by capitalizing expenses. In a cashflow-based valuation, capitalizing an expense does not create any cash flow benefits, moving the cash

---

[3] As an example, Jamie Kiggen, an equity research analyst at Donaldson, Lufkin, & Jenrette, valued an Amazon customer at $2,400 in an equity research report in 1999. This value was based on the assumption that the customer would continue to buy from Amazon.com and on an expected profit margin from such sales.

effect from the income to capital expenditures. In fact, the accounting returns that emerge after the capitalization will determine whether the company in question is generating returns that exceed its cost of equity and capital, and by extension, whether growth will add or destroy value at the firm.

ILLUSTRATION 9.3: Should You Capitalize Advertising Expense? Analyzing Coca Cola

Coca Cola has one of the most valuable and enduring brand names in the world, and some of its advertising expenses are directed at building up this brand name. To the extent that you can identify this portion, you can capitalize these expenses over time, using a procedure similar to the one used to capitalize R&D, starting with a determination of how long a brand name lasts and collecting brand-name related advertising over that period. The effects on earnings and invested capital will also parallel those of the R&D capitalization, with earnings and invested capital rising and accounting returns (usually) declining.

    The challenge you face in the capitalizing of advertising expenses is identifying the portion that is designed to build up brand name, as opposed to getting customers to buy the product in the current period. That judgment is difficult to make, and the most practical conclusion is recognizing that accounting returns will be overstated at brand name companies. Fair-value accounting purports to fix this problem by bringing brand name on to balance sheets, but that number is more a reflection of an estimate of the market value of brand name rather than a measure of capital invested in it.

ILLUSTRATION 9.4: Capitalizing Recruitment and Training Expenses: Cyber Health Consulting

Cyber Health Consulting (CHC) is a firm that specializes in offering management consulting services to health-care firms. CHC reported operating income (EBIT) of $51.5 million and net income of $23 million in the most recent year. However, the firm's expenses include the cost of recruiting new consultants ($5.5 million) and the cost of training ($8.5 million). A consultant who joins CHC stays with the firm, on average, four years.

    To capitalize the cost of recruiting and training, we obtained these costs from each of the prior four years. The following table reports on these human capital expenses (in $ millions) and amortizes each of these expenses over four years.

Year	Training and Recruiting Expenses	Unamortized Portion		Amoritzation this Year
		As Percent	As $ Value	
Current	$14.00	100%	$14.00	
−1	$12.00	75%	$ 9.00	$3.00
−2	$10.40	50%	$ 5.20	$2.60
−3	$ 9.10	25%	$ 2.28	$2.28
−4	$ 8.30	0%	$ 0.00	$2.08
Human capital (asset)			$30.48	
Human capital (amortization)				$9.95

The adjustments to operating and net income are as follows:

$$\text{Adjusted operating income} = \text{Operating income} + \text{Training and recruiting expenses in the current}$$
$$- \text{Amortization of training asset}$$
$$= 51.5 + 14 - 9.95 = \$55.55 \text{ million}$$

$$\text{Adjusted net income} = \text{Net income} + \text{Training and recruiting expenses in the current}$$
$$- \text{Amortization of training asset}$$
$$= 23 + 14 - 9.95 = \$27.05 \text{ million}$$

As with R&D expenses, the fact that training and recruiting expenses are fully tax deductible dispenses with the need to consider the tax effect when adjusting net income.

Capitalization and Value Capitalizing R&D, advertising, and recruiting and training expenses is not difficult to do, but it is tedious and effectively redoes the accounting statements to arrive at restated values for almost every input into valuation, as you can see in Figure 9.3.

The question is whether it has enough of an effect on value to be worth the tedium, and the answer, especially for firms where these expenses represent a significant portion of what they need to reinvest to grow, is yes.

When you capitalize these expenses, you get a clearer picture of a company's business model, especially in terms of its profitability and growth potential. Consider the Amgen example earlier in the chapter, where capitalizing R&D resulted in much lower accounting returns than you would have estimated with the unadjusted numbers. In fact, the after-tax return on capital after R&D is recapitalized, was lower than the cost of capital in 2023. It is entirely possible that Amgen had a bad year in 2023, but it does raise red flags about whether the company should be investing as much as it is in R&D, and whether growth will add value to the firm.

Put simply, capitalizing an expense may increase a company's earnings, but the effect on value will depend in large part on whether that expense generates higher earnings in future years. There is nothing inherently good or value creating about growth and R&D at

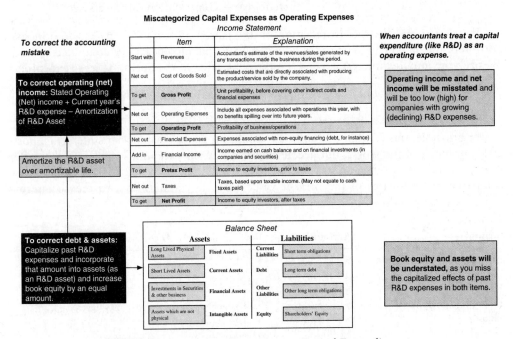

FIGURE 9.3 Converting Operating to Capital Expenditures

a business, since a business that spends vast amounts on R&D with little to show for that spending in higher earnings, will see its value decrease as it continues its R&D spending.

Adjustments for Financing Expenses The second adjustment is for financing expenses that accountants treat as operating expenses. The most significant example in much of the world, at least until 2019, was operating lease expenses, which were treated as operating expenses, in contrast to capital leases, which were presented as debt. While both international financial reporting standards (IFRS) and generally accepted accounting principles (GAAP) have now come to their senses on all lease commitments being debt, we will go through the process of converting leases to debt, not only because there are parts of the world where the accounting still lags, but also because there remain other contractual commitments that need to be meted out since they follow the same treatment as leases.

Converting Operating Leases into Debt In Chapter 8, the basic approach for converting operating leases into debt was presented. You discount future operating lease commitments back at the firm's pretax cost of debt. The present value (PV) of the operating lease commitments is then added to the conventional debt of the firm to arrive at the total debt outstanding.

$$\text{Adjusted debt} = \text{Stated debt} + \text{Present value of lease commitments}$$

Once operating leases are recategorized as debt, the operating incomes can be adjusted in two steps. First, the operating lease expense is added back to the operating income since it is a financial expense. Next, the depreciation on the leased asset is subtracted out to arrive at adjusted operating income:

$$\text{Adjusted operating income} = \text{Operating income} + \text{Operating lease expense in}$$
$$\text{current year} - \text{Depreciation on lease asset}$$

If you assume that the depreciation on the leased asset approximates the principal portion of the debt being repaid, the adjusted operating income can be computed by adding back the imputed interest expense on the debt value of the operating lease expense:

$$\text{Adjusted operating income} = \text{Operating income} + \text{Debt value}$$
$$\times \text{Interest rate on debt}$$

In principle, this is what accountants should be doing on financial statements, post-2019, in much of the world, but accounting has created exceptions for leases that offer flexibility and the income adjustment for leases is still imperfect. In 2023, for instance, we compared our estimates of the present value of lease commitments to the accounting aggregates, broken down by region:

Region	Accounting	Our Estimate	Accounting as % of Estimate
Australia, NZ, & Canada	$ 8,412	$ 13,579	61.95%
United States	$ 947,989	$1,152,870	82.23%
Europe	$ 24,337	$ 52,173	46.65%
Emerging Markets	$ 18,426	$ 109,415	16.84%
Japan	$ 1,720	$ 156,072	1.10%
Global	$1,000,885	$1,484,108	67.44%

As you can see, our estimates are consistently higher than the accounting numbers, and the differences vary across the world, from fairly close in the United States (where the accounting is 82.2% of our estimate) to gaping holes in Japan and emerging markets.

ILLUSTRATION 9.5: Adjusting Operating Income for Operating Leases: The Gap in 2011

As a specialty retailer, the Gap has hundreds of stores that are leased, with the leases being treated as operating leases. For the most recent financial year (2010), the Gap has operating lease expenses of $1,129 million. The following table presents the operating lease commitments for the firm over the next five years and the lump sum of commitments beyond that point in time:

Year	Commitment
1	$ 997
2	$ 841
3	$ 710
4	$ 602
5	$ 483
6 and beyond	$1,483

The Gap, based on its S&P bond rating of BB+, has a pretax cost of debt of 5.5%. To compute the present value of the commitments, you have to make a judgment on the lump sum commitment in year 6. Based on the average annual lease commitment over the first five years ($727 million), we arrive at an annuity of two years:[4]

Approximate life of annuity for year 6 lump sum = 1,483/727 = 2.04

The present values of the commitments at the 5.5% pretax cost of debt are estimated in the following table:

Year	Commitment	Present Value
1	$997.00	$ 945.02
2	$841.00	$ 755.60
3	$710.00	$ 604.65
4	$602.00	$ 485.94
5	$483.00	$ 369.56
6 and 7	$741.40	$1,047.50
Debt value of leases		$4,208.28

The present value of operating leases is treated as the equivalent of debt and is added onto the conventional debt of the firm. The Gap has no interest-bearing debt on its balance sheet. The cumulated debt for the firm is:

Adjusted debt = Interest − Bearing debt + Present value of lease commitments
= $0 + $4,208 = $4,208 million

---

[4] The value is rounded to the nearest integer.

To adjust the operating income for the Gap, we first use the full adjustment. To compute depreciation on the leased asset, we assume straight-line depreciation over the lease life[5] (7 years) on the value of the leased asset, which is equal to the debt value of the lease commitments:

$$\text{Depreciation on lease asset} = \text{Value of lease asset/Lease life}$$
$$= \$4,208/7 = \$601 \text{ million}$$

The Gap's stated operating income of $1,968 million is adjusted as follows:

$$\text{Adjusted operating income} = \text{Operating income} + \text{Current year's operating lease expense}$$
$$- \text{Depreciation on lease asset}$$
$$= \$1,968 + \$1,129 - \$601 = \$2,496 \text{ million}$$

The approximate adjustment is also estimated as follows, where we add the added imputed interest expense using the pretax cost of debt:

$$\text{Adjusted operating income (adjusted)} = \text{Operating income} + \text{Lease debt} \times \text{Interest rate on debt}$$
$$= \$1,968 + \$4,208 \times .055 = \$2,199 \text{ million}$$

As with the capitalization of R&D, treating leases as debt changes key numbers in the company, with mixed effects on valuation:

	Stated Value	Lease-Adjusted Value
Debt	$0	$4,208
Invested capital	$4,080	$8,288
Operating income	$1,968	$2,496
Pre-tax return on invested capital	48.24%	30.12%
Debt ratio in cost of capital	0.00%	31.74%

The Gap's return on capital remained impressive, even after converting leases to debt, but it decreased and the company's cost of capital dropped, reflecting its use of lease debt. The net effects of these two changes can therefore cause value to increase at some firms, and decrease at others, when leases are converted to debt.

 Oplease.xls: **This spreadsheet allows you to convert operating lease expenses into debt.**

WHAT ABOUT OTHER CONTRACTUAL COMMITMENTS?

The argument made about leases can be made about other long-term commitments where a firm has no escape hatches or cancellation options, or where the payment is not connected to performance/earnings. For instance, consider a professional sports

---

[5]The lease life is computed by adding the estimated annuity life of two years for the lump sum to the initial five years.

team that signs a star player to a 10-year contract, agreeing to pay $5 million a year. If the payment is not contingent on performance, this firm has created the equivalent of debt by signing this contract. In short, the Dodgers effectively borrowed money, when they committed to pay $700 million to Shohei Ohtani for ten years, as did Al Nassr, the Saudi football team, that signed Ronaldo, the soccer super star, for two and half years, paying him close to 200 million Euros a year.

The upshot of this argument is that firms that have no debt on their balance sheet may still be highly levered and subject to default risk as a consequence. For instance, Mario Lemieux, a star player for the Pittsburgh Penguins, the professional ice hockey team, was given partial ownership of the team because of its failure to meet contractual commitments it had made to him.

Value effects of converting leases to debt   Capitalizing a financial expenses also has ripple effects through the financial statements of a company, percolating through the income statement and balance sheet. To the question of whether it is worth the effort, the answer is a little more nuanced than it is for capitalizing operating expenses. If you choose to value equity directly in a company, using a dividend discount model or a free cash flow to equity model, capitalizing lease expenses and other contractual commitments will have little effect on value, because your cash flows are after those expenses. However, if you are trying to value the operating assets, capitalizing financial expenses will have effects on key fundamentals, as you can see in Figure 9.4:

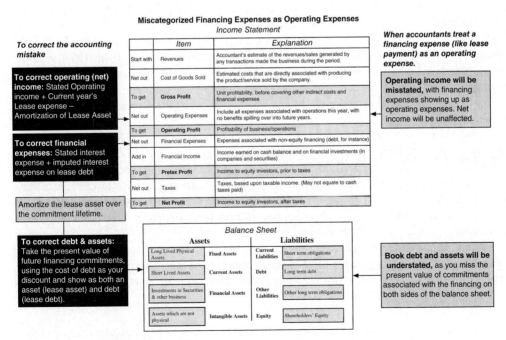

FIGURE 9.4   Effects of Capitalizing Financing Expenses

The effect on value of capitalizing leases and contractual commitments will depend on whether the company that is leasing the assets or entering into commitments is able to deliver benefits that exceed the capitalized costs. With retailers, for instance, it is only when you capitalize leases that you can start separating the retail firms which generate value from opening new stores from those that destroy value.

MEASURING EARNINGS POWER: CLEAN UP AND TIME DIFFERENCES

When you value a business, it is natural to start with the earnings in its current income statement as a starting point, but we will argue, in this section, that those numbers can be misleading for many reasons. First, firms have become particularly adept at meeting and beating analyst estimates of earnings each quarter. While beating earnings estimates can be viewed as a positive development, some firms adopt accounting techniques that are questionable to accomplish this objective. Second, there are accounting charges or income that can accrue to a firm only in a specific time period, such as the most recent one, and extrapolating them into the future can skew expected earnings. We will look at some of these charges, and how to correct for them in forecasts. Third, even if the earnings in the current period are not affected by accounting game playing, they can occur across time for many reasons, and looking at an earnings time series can often provide more information than examining the numbers in the most recent time period.

The Phenomenon of Managed Earnings

In the 1990s, firms like Microsoft and Intel set the pattern for technology firms. In fact, Microsoft beat analyst estimates of earnings in 39 of the 40 quarters during the decade, and Intel posted a record almost as impressive. As the market values of these firms skyrocketed, other technology firms followed in their footsteps in trying to deliver earnings that were higher than analyst estimates by at least a few pennies. The evidence is overwhelming that the phenomenon is spreading. For an unprecedented 18 quarters in a row from 1996 to 2000, more firms beat consensus earnings estimates than missed them.[6] In another indication of the management of earnings, the gap between the earnings reported by firms to the Internal Revenue Service and that reported to equity investors has been growing over the past decade.

Given that these analyst estimates are expectations, what does this tell you? One possibility is that analysts consistently underestimate earnings and never learn from their mistakes. While this is a possibility, it seems extremely unlikely to persist over an entire decade. The other is that technology firms particularly have far more discretion in how they measure and report earnings and are using this discretion to beat estimates. In particular, the treatment of research expenses as operating expenses gives these firms an advantage when it comes to managing earnings.

Does managing earnings really increase a firm's stock price? It might be possible to beat analysts' estimates quarter after quarter, but are markets as gullible? They are not, and the advent of so-called whispered earnings estimates is in reaction to the consistent

---

[6]The analyst consensus estimates are widely publicized, and news reports usually compare actual earnings to these estimates.

delivery of earnings that are above expectations. What are whispered earnings? Whispered earnings are implicit earnings estimates that firms have to beat to surprise the market, and these estimates are usually a few cents higher than analyst estimates. For instance, on April 10, 1997, Intel reported earnings per share of $2.10 per share, higher than analyst estimates of $2.06 per share, but saw its stock price drop 5 points because the whispered earnings estimate had been $2.15. In other words, markets had built into expectations the amount by which Intel had beaten earnings estimates historically.

Why Do Firms Manage Earnings?   Firms generally manage earnings because they believe that they will be rewarded by markets for delivering earnings that are smoother and come in consistently above analyst estimates. As evidence, they point to the success of firms like Microsoft and Intel, and the brutal punishment meted out for firms that do not meet expectations.

Many financial managers also seem to believe that investors take earnings numbers at face value, and the managers work at delivering bottom lines that reflect this belief. This may explain why any efforts by the Financial Accounting Standards Board (FASB) to change the way earnings are measured are fought with vigor, even when the changes make sense. For instance, any attempts by FASB to value the options granted by firms to their managers at a fair value, and charge them against earnings or change the way mergers are accounted, were consistently opposed by technology firms.

It may also be in the best interests of the managers of firms to manage earnings. Managers know that they are more likely to be fired when earnings drop significantly relative to prior periods. Furthermore, there are firms where managerial compensation is still built around profit targets, and meeting these targets can lead to lucrative bonuses.

Techniques for Managing Earnings   How do firms manage earnings? One aspect of good earnings management is the care and nurturing of analyst expectations, a practice that Microsoft perfected during the 1990s. Executives at the firm monitored analyst estimates of earnings and stepped in to lower expectations when they believed that the estimates were too high.[7] There are several other techniques that are used, and some of the most common are considered in this section. Not all the techniques are hurtful to the firm, and some may indeed be considered prudent management.

- *Planning ahead.* Firms can plan investments and asset sales to keep earnings rising smoothly.
- *Revenue recognition.* Firms have some leeway when it comes to measuring, earnings can preserve their credibility with analysts by letting them know when their estimates were too low. Firms that are consistently pessimistic in their analyst presentations lose their credibility and consequently their effectiveness in managing earnings. As an example, Microsoft, in 1995, adopted an extremely conservative approach to accounting for revenues from its sale of Windows 95, and chose not to show large

---

[7]Microsoft preserved its credibility with analysts by also letting them know when their estimates were too low. Firms that are consistently pessimistic in their analyst presentations lose their credibility and consequently their effectiveness in managing earnings.

chunks of revenues that it was entitled (though not obligated) to show.[8] In fact, the firm had accumulated $1.1 billion in unearned revenues by the end of 1996 that it could borrow on, to supplement earnings in a weaker quarter.

▪ *Booking revenues early.* In an opposite phenomenon, firms sometimes ship products during the final days of a weak quarter to distributors and retailers and record the revenues. Consider the case of MicroStrategy, a technology firm that went public in 1998. In the last two quarters of 1999, the firm reported revenue growth of 20 percent and 27 percent respectively, but much of that growth was attributable to large deals announced just days after each quarter ended, with some revenues attributed to the just-ended quarter.[9] In a more elaborate variant of this strategy, two firms, both of which need to boost revenues, can enter into a transaction swapping revenues, with both emerging as winners in the earnings game.

▪ *Capitalizing operating expenses.* Just as with revenue recognition, firms are given some discretion in whether they classify expenses as operating or capital expenses, especially for items like software R&D. AOL's practice of capitalizing and writing off the cost of the CDs and disks it provided with magazines, for instance, allowed it to report positive earnings through much of the late 1990s.

▪ *Write-offs.* A major restructuring charge can result in lower income in the current period, but it provides two benefits to the firm taking it. Since operating earnings are reported both before and after the restructuring charge, it allows the firm to separate the expense from operations. It also makes beating earnings easier in future quarters. To see how restructuring can boost earnings, consider the case of IBM. By writing off old plants in the year they are closed, IBM was able to drop depreciation expenses to 5 percent of revenue in 1996, from an average of 7 percent in 1990–1994. The difference, in 1996 revenue, was $1.64 billion, or 18 percent of the company's $9.02 billion in pretax profit that year. Technology firms have been particularly adept at writing off a large portion of acquisition costs as "in-process R&D" to register increases in earnings in subsequent quarters. Deng and Lev (1998) studied 389 firms that wrote off in-process R&D between 1990 and 1996;[10] these write-offs amounted, on average, to 72 percent of the purchase price on these acquisitions, and increased the acquiring firm's earnings 22 percent in the fourth quarter after the acquisition.

▪ *Use of reserves.* Firms are allowed to build up reserves for bad debts, product returns, and other potential losses. Some firms are conservative in their estimates in good years, and use the excess reserves that they have built up during these years to smooth out earnings in other years.

▪ *Income from investments.* Firms with substantial holdings of marketable securities or investments in other firms often have these investments recorded on their books

---

[8] Firms that bought Windows 95 in 1995 also bought the right to upgrades and support in 1996 and 1997. Microsoft could have shown these as revenues in 1995.

[9] *Forbes* magazine carried an article on March 6, 2000, on MicroStrategy, with this excerpt: "MicroStrategy and NCR announced what they described as a $52.5 million licensing and technology agreement. NCR agreed to pay MicroStrategy $27.5 million to license its software. MicroStrategy bought an NCR unit which had been a competitor for what was then $14 million in stock and agreed to pay $11 million in cash for a data warehousing system. MicroStrategy reported $17.5 million of the licensing money as revenue in the third quarter, which had closed four days earlier".

[10] Only three firms wrote off in-process R&D during the prior decade (1980–1989).

at values well below their market values. Thus, liquidating these investments can result in large capital gains, which can boost income in the period.

Unusual Accounting Charges and Income

In addition to managing earnings, companies often adjust earnings for items that they view as one-time or extraordinary, thus affecting earnings. In many cases, these charges are made with good intentions, and are designed to provide information to investors about occurrences at the firm; in others, they represent game playing where companies are trying to make themselves look more profitable than they truly are. This section considers a series of adjustments that we might need to make to stated earnings before using the number as a basis for projections. We begin by considering the subtle differences between one-time, recurring, and unusual items. We follow up by examining how best to deal with the debris left over by acquisition accounting. Then we consider how to deal with income from holdings in other companies and investments in marketable securities. Finally, we look at a series of tests that may help us gauge whether the reported earnings of a firm are reliable indicators of its true earnings.

Extraordinary, Recurring, and Unusual Items The rule for estimating both operating and net income is simple. The operating income, used as a base for projections, should reflect continuing operations and should not include any items that are one-time or extraordinary. Putting this statement into practice is often a challenge because there are four types of extraordinary items:

1. *One-time expense or income that is truly one-time.* A large restructuring charge that has occurred only once in the past 10 years would be a good example. These expenses can be backed out of the analysis, and the operating and net income calculated without them.
2. *Expenses and income that do not occur every year but seem to recur at regular intervals.* Consider, for instance, a firm that has taken a restructuring charge every 3 years for the past 12 years. While not conclusive, this would suggest that the extraordinary expenses are really ordinary expenses that are being bundled by the firm and taken once every three years. Ignoring such an expense would be dangerous because the expected operating income in future years would be overstated. What would make sense would be to take the expense and spread it out on an annual basis. Thus, if the restructuring expense every three years has amounted to $1.5 billion, on average, the operating income for the current year should be reduced by $0.5 billion to reflect the annual charge due to this expense.
3. *Expenses and income that recur every year but with considerable volatility.* The best way to deal with such items is to normalize them by averaging the expenses across time and reducing this year's income by this amount.
4. *Items that recur every year that change signs—positive in some years and negative in others.* Consider, for instance, the effect of foreign currency translations on income. For a firm in the United States, the effect may be negative in years in which the dollar gets stronger, and positive in years in which the dollar gets weaker. The most prudent thing to do with these expenses would be to ignore them for cash flow purposes; you may or may not adjust discount rates for the risk created by the variability.

To differentiate between these items requires that you have access to a firm's financial history. For young firms, this may not be available, making it more difficult to draw the line between expenses that should be ignored, expenses that should be normalized, and expenses that should be considered in full.

Adjusting for Acquisitions and Divestitures

Acquisition accounting can wreak havoc on reported earnings for years after an acquisition. The most common by-product of acquisitions is the amortization of goodwill. This amortization can reduce reported income in subsequent periods. Should we consider amortization to be an operating expense? We think not since it is both a noncash and often a non-tax-deductible charge. The safest route to follow with goodwill amortization is to look at earnings prior to the amortization.

Technology companies have used an unusual ploy to get the goodwill created when a premium is paid over book value off their books. Using the argument that the bulk of the market value paid for technology companies comes from the value of the research done by the firm over time, they have written off what they called in-process R&D to preserve consistency. After all, they argue, the R&D they do internally is expensed. As with amortization of goodwill, writing off in-process R&D creates a noncash and non-tax-deductible charge, and we should look at earnings prior to their write-off.

When firms divest assets, they can generate income in the form of capital gains. Infrequent divestitures can be treated as one-time items and ignored, but some firms divest assets on a regular basis. For such firms, it is best to ignore the income associated with the divestiture but to consider the cash flows associated with divestiture, net of capital gains taxes, when estimating net capital expenditures. For instance, a firm with $500 million in capital expenditures, $300 million in depreciation, and $120 million in divestitures every year would have a net capital expenditure of $80 million.

$$\text{Net capital expenditures} = \text{Capital expenditures} - \text{Depreciation} - \text{Divestiture proceeds}$$
$$= \$500 - \$300 - \$120 = \$80 \text{ million}$$

Stock-Based Compensation

There is perhaps no more abused and misused item in earnings adjustments that stock-based compensation. While we will come back and address how best to deal with stock-based compensation in the form of options and restricted stock in Chapter 16, it is worth looking at the games that companies and analysts play with stock-based compensation, in adjusting earnings before interest, taxes and depreciation.

To understand how stock-based compensation affects earnings in much of the world, it is worth remembering that until 2007, the granting of stock-based compensation, primarily in the form of options, was viewed as having no effect on earnings, at the time of the grant, because these options were usually granted at the money, i.e., the strike price was set equal to the stock price. That abominable practice finally came to an end in 2007, and companies are now required to show the value of options or restricted stock at the time that they are granted as expenses. That, of course, lowers earnings, but rightly so, at young companies that compensate their employees primarily with restricted stock and options.

Using the alluring logic that stock-based compensation is noncash, analysts and companies have started reported adjusted versions of earnings, with stock-based compensation added back, thus improving their earnings numbers. The problem with this logic is that stock-based compensation is not a noncash expense like depreciation, where adding back to get to cash flows is fully merited, but an in-kind expense where portions of equity are being given away to employees. In Chapter 16, we will look at the right way to deal with stock-based compensation, both from grants made in the past as well as expected future grants.

Income from Investments and Cross Holdings   Investments in marketable securities generate two types of income. The first takes the form of interest or dividends, and the second is the capital gains (or losses) associated with selling securities at prices that are different from their cost bases. In the 1990s, when the stock market was booming, several technology firms used the latter to augment net income and beat analyst estimates. In our view, neither type of income should be considered part of the earnings used in valuation for any firm, other than a financial service firm that defines its business as the buying and selling of securities (such as a hedge fund). The interest earned on marketable securities should be ignored when valuing the firm, since it is far easier to add the market value of these securities at the end of the process rather than mingle them with other assets. For instance, assume that you have a firm that generates $100 million in after-tax cash flows, but also assume that 20 percent of these cash flows come from holdings of marketable securities with a current market value of $500 million. The remaining 80 percent of the cash flows comes from operating assets; these cash flows are expected to grow at 5 percent a year in perpetuity, and the cost of capital (based on the risk of these assets) is 10 percent. The value of this firm can be most easily estimated as follows:

Value of operating assets of the firm = $80(1.05)/(.10 − .05)	$1,680 million	
Value of marketable securities	$ 500 million	
Value of firm	$2,180 million	

If we had chosen to discount the entire after-tax cash flow of $100 million, we would have had to adjust the cost of capital (to reflect the risk of the marketable securities). The adjustment, done right, should yield the same value as that estimated.[11] The capital gain or loss from the sale of marketable securities should be ignored for a different reason. If you incorporate this gain into your income and use it in your forecasts, not only are you counting on being able to sell your securities for higher prices each period in the future, but you risk double counting the value of these securities if you are adding them to the value of the operating assets to arrive at an estimate of value.

Firms that have a substantial number of cross holdings in other firms will often report increases or decreases to earnings reflecting income or losses from these holdings. The effect on earnings will vary, depending on how the holding is categorized. Chapter 3 differentiated among three classifications:

1. A minority passive holding, where only the dividends received from the holding are recorded in income.
2. A minority active interest, where the portion of the net income (or loss) from the subsidiary is shown in the income statement as an adjustment to net income (but not to operating income).
3. A majority active interest, where the income statements are consolidated, and the entire operating income of the subsidiary (or holding) are shown as part of the

---

[11]This will happen only if the marketable securities are fairly priced, and you are earning a fair market return on them. If they are not, you can get different values from the approaches.

operating income of the firm. In such cases, the net income is usually adjusted for the portion of the subsidiary owned by others (minority interests).

The safest route to take with the first two types of holdings is to ignore the income shown from the holding when valuing a firm, to value the holding separately and add it to the value obtained for the other assets. As a simple example, consider a firm (e.g., Holding Inc.) that generates $100 million in after-tax cash flows from its operating assets, and assume that these cash flows will grow at 5 percent a year forever. In addition, assume that the firm owns 10 percent of another firm (e.g., Subsidiary Inc.) with after-tax cash flows of $50 million growing at 4 percent a year forever. Finally, assume that the cost of capital for both firms is 10 percent. The firm value for Holding Inc. can be estimated as follows:

Value of operating assets of Holding Inc. = 100(1.05)/(.10 − .05) $2,100 million
Value of operating assets of Subsidiary Inc. = 50(1.04)/(.10 − .04) $ 867 million
Value of Holding Inc. = $2,100 + .10(867) $2,187 million

When earnings are consolidated, you can value the combined firm with the consolidated income statement, and then subtract out the value of the minority holdings. To do this, though, you must assume that the two firms are in the same business and are of equivalent risk since the same cost of capital will be applied to both firm's cash flows. Alternatively, you can strip the entire operating income of the subsidiary from the consolidated operating income and follow the process just laid out to value the holding. We will return to examine this issue is more detail in Chapter 16.

ILLUSTRATION 9.6: Adjusting Earnings for One-Time Charges

Between 1997 and 1999, Xerox's reported earnings included a significant number of one-time, extraordinary, and unusual items. The summary of the earnings is provided in the following table:

	1999	1998	1997
Sales	$10,346	$10,696	$ 9,881
Service and rentals	$ 7,856	$ 7,678	$ 7,257
Finance income	$ 1,026	$ 1,073	$ 1,006
Total revenues	$19,228	$19,447	$18,144
Costs and expenses			
Cost of sales	$ 5,744	$ 5,662	$ 5,330
Cost of service and rentals	$ 4,481	$ 4,205	$ 3,778
Inventory charges	$ 0	$ 113	$ 0
Equipment financing interest	$ 547	$ 570	$ 520
Research and development expenses	$ 979	$ 1,040	$ 1,065
SG&A expenses	$ 5,144	$ 5,321	$ 5,212
Restructuring charge and asset impairment	$ 0	$ 1,531	$ 0
Other, net	$ 297	$ 242	$ 98
Total expenses	$17,192	$18,684	$16,003
Earnings before taxes	$ 2,036	$ 763	$ 2,141
− Income taxes	$ 631	$ 207	$ 728
+ Equity in net income of unconsolidated affiliates	$ 68	$ 74	$ 127

	1999	1998	1997
– Minority interests in earnings of subsidiaries	$ 49	$ 45	$ 88
Net income from continuing operations	$ 1,424	$ 585	$ 1,452
– Discontinued operations	$ 0	$ 190	$ 0
Net income	$ 1,424	$ 395	$ 1,452

There are a few obvious adjustments to income that represent one-time charges and a host of other issues. Let us consider first the obvious adjustments:

- The inventory charge and restructuring charges seem to represent one-time charges, though there is the possibility that they represent more serious underlying problems that can create charges in future periods. The charge for discontinued operations also affects only one year's income. These expenses should be added back to arrive at adjusted operating income and net income.

- The other (net) expenses line item is a recurring but volatile item. We would average this expense when forecasting future income.

- To arrive at adjusted net income, we would also reverse the last two adjustments by subtracting out the equity in net income of subsidiaries (reflecting Xerox's minority holdings in other firms), and adding back the earnings in minority interests (reflecting minority interests in Xerox's majority holdings).

The following table adjusts the net income in each of the years for the changes suggested:

	1999	1998	1997
Net income from continuing operations	$1,424	$ 585	$1,452
– Equity in net income of unconsolidated affiliates	$ 68	$ 74	$ 127
+ Minority interests in earnings of subsidiaries	$ 49	$ 45	$ 88
+ Restructuring charge (1 – Tax rate)	$ 0	$1,116	$ 0
+ Inventory charge (1 – Tax rate)	$ 0	$ 82	$ 0
+ Other, net (1 – Tax rate)	$ 205	$ 176	$ 65
– Normalized other, net (1 – Tax rate)	$ 147	$ 155	$ 140
Adjusted net income	$1,463	$1,776	$1,338

The restructuring and inventory charges were tax deductible and the after-tax portion was added back; the tax rate was computed based on taxes paid and taxable income for that year.

Tax rate in 1998 = Taxes paid/Taxable income – 207/763 – 27.13%

We also add back the after-tax portion of the other expenses (net) and subtract out the average annual expense over the three years:

Average annual other expenses = (297 + 242 + 98)/3 = $212 million

Similar adjustments would need to be made to operating income. Xerox nets out interest expenses against interest income on its capital subsidiary to report finance income. You would need to separate interest expenses from interest income to arrive at an estimate of operating income for the firm.

What are the other issues? The plethora of one-time charges suggests that there may be ongoing operational problems at Xerox that may cause future charges. In fact, it is not surprising that Xerox had to delay its 10-K filing for 2000 because of accounting issues.

Time Variations in Earnings

If you have followed the advice meted out in this chapter and have updated your earnings to reflect the most recent reports, corrected those earnings for inconsistencies and cleaned up for unusual accounting items, you may be tempted to make those earnings the basis for assessing earnings power at a firm. There is one final and important consideration that should be considered, when assessing earnings power. The earnings of a firm can and will vary over time, for a multitude of reasons, some specific to the company and its investment and others that are macroeconomic or sector-wide. In this section, we will start by assessing the reasons for earnings volatility, and why some firms will have more volatile earnings than others, before examining how to deal with that volatility when valuing a firm.

Earnings Volatility   There are many reasons for earnings volatility, and we will list a few in this section:

1. *Stage in the corporate life cycle:* Young companies will have more volatile earnings than more mature firms, as they struggle with scaling up and shifting business models. Often, these earnings can be negative, as companies embark on building themselves up, and even after they turn positive, will still go up and down, as they settle into more established business models.
2. *Type of product or service:* A company that provides a product or service that can be classified as discretionary, i.e., their customers can delay or defer buying it, will have more volatile earnings than a firm that has a product or service that its customers need. Thus, a grocery store or power company will generally have more stable earnings than a high-end retailer or a software company.
3. *Cost structure:* Earnings represent what a company has left over after it covers its costs. If the bulk of a company's operating costs at fixed, i.e., it has high operating leverage, its operating income will be more volatile, reacting significantly to small changes in revenues. If you add on interest expense, by borrowing money, the equity earnings will become more variable over time.
4. *Macroeconomic factors:* While becoming mature businesses can bring earnings stability to some firms, there are other firms that will continue to face earnings volatility, even after they become mature, as they are subject to swings in commodity prices or the economy. Exxon Mobil is a mature oil company, but its earnings history reflects the effects of swings in oil prices over time.
5. *Country risk:* In Chapter 8, we looked at country risk, with the intent of adjusting costs of equity and capital for that risk, and noted that there can be wide variations in risk across countries, driven by economic and political considerations. A company that operates in a risky country will generally have more volatile earnings than an otherwise similar company operating in a mature market, with that higher volatility coming from both currency movements (which will track country risk) and economic variability in the country.

One way of gaining perspective on differences in earnings variability is to estimate the variance in earnings over time, and compare them across sectors and countries.

Dealing with Earnings Volatility   If earnings are volatile, using the most recent year's earnings as a measure of a company's earnings power can be misleading. Thus, if oil prices were high in the most recent period, basing the valuation of an oil company on the most recent period's earnings will skew your valuation upwards, and the reverse will occur, if oil prices are low. While we will come back and look at how best to deal with this volatility over time in later chapters, there is an obvious and low-effort fix to this problem, which is to look at earnings over time, rather than just the most recent year. With an oil or cyclical company, this will mean considering earnings over a cycle (commodity or economic) and using that time series perspective, when assessing earnings power. In practical terms, this usually involves estimating average earnings over time, with the following variants:

1. *Average absolute earnings:* The simplest fix to volatile earnings is to look at the average earnings over time, for operating income, net income, or even earnings per share. The problem with this approach is that it will understate the true earnings over the life cycle, if the company is scaling up (growing) over time, and/or there is inflation.
2. *Average scaled earnings:* The second possibility is to scale earnings to revenues or some other operating proxy, with the former yielding profit margins. Thus, the average operating margin over a cycle, earned by a firm, can be applied to revenues in the most recent period to get a "normalized" measure of earnings.
3. *Industry average earnings:* There are cases where a company either does not have a long enough history, or its history is much too volatile, for you to estimate normalized earnings. In these cases, you can look at the earnings history of companies in the sector that a firm belongs to, with the hope that your firm's numbers will converge on that average.

As you work with any of these variants, though, it is worth remembering that your aim to arrive at an estimate of earnings for your firm that you can use as a building block for forecasting its future earnings.

WARNING SIGNS IN EARNINGS REPORTS

The most troubling thing about earnings reports is that we are often blindsided not by the items that get reported (such as extraordinary charges) but by the items that are hidden in other categories. We would suggest the following checklist that should be reviewed about any earnings report to gauge the possibility of such shocks:

- Is earnings growth outstripping revenue growth by a large magnitude year after year? This may well be a sign of increased efficiency, but when the differences are large and continue year after year, you should wonder about the source of these efficiencies.
- Do one-time or nonoperating charges to earnings occur frequently? The charge itself might be categorized differently each year—an inventory charge one year, a restructuring charge the next, and so on. While this may be just bad luck, it

(continued)

(*continued*)

may also reflect a conscious effort by a company to move regular operating expenses into these nonoperating items.

- Do any of the operating expenses, as a percent of revenues, swing wildly from year to year? This may suggest that this expense item (say SG&A) includes non-operating expenses that should really be stripped out and reported separately.

- Does the company manage to beat analyst estimates quarter after quarter by a cent or two? Not every company is a Microsoft. Companies that beat estimates year after year probably are involved in earnings management and are moving earnings across time periods. As growth levels off, this practice can catch up with them.

- Does a substantial proportion of the revenues come from subsidiaries or related holdings? While the sales may be legitimate, the prices set may allow the firm to move earnings from one unit to the other and give a misleading view of true earnings at the firm.

- Are accounting rules for valuing inventory or depreciation changed frequently?

- Are acquisitions followed by miraculous increases in earnings? It is difficult to succeed with an acquisition strategy in the long term. A firm that claims instant success from such as strategy requires scrutiny.

- Is working capital ballooning out as revenues and earning surge? This can sometimes let us pinpoint those firms that generate revenues by selling on credit, often with very generous terms.

None of these factors, by themselves, suggest that we distrust earnings for these firms, but combinations of the factors can be viewed as a warning signal that the earnings statement needs to be held up to higher scrutiny.

CONCLUSION

Financial statements remain the primary source of information for most investors and analysts. There are differences, however, in how accounting and financial analysts approach answering a number of key questions about the firm.

This chapter begins our analysis of earnings by looking at the accounting categorization of expenses into operating, financing, and capital expenses. While operating and financing expenses are shown in income statements, capital expenditures are spread over several time periods and take the form of depreciation and amortization. Accounting standards used to misclassify operating leases and continue to misclassify research and development expenses as operating expenses (when the former should be categorized as financing expenses and the latter as capital expenses). We suggest ways in which earnings can be corrected to better measure the impact of these items.

In the second part of the chapter, we consider the effect of one-time, nonrecurring, and unusual items on earnings as well as the information in historic earnings. While the underlying principle is that earnings should include only normal expenses, this is put to the test by the attempts on the part of companies to move normal operating expenses into the nonrecurring column and nonoperating income into operating earnings. When earnings are volatile, looking at average earnings or profit margins over time can provide a much better basis for valuation, than just using the most recent year's numbers.

QUESTIONS AND SHORT PROBLEMS

In the problems following, use an equity risk premium of 5.5 percent if none is specified.

1. Derra Foods is a specialty food retailer. In its balance sheet, the firm reports $1 billion in book value of equity and no debt, but it has operating leases on all its stores. In the most recent year, the firm made $85 million in operating lease payments, and its commitments to make lease payments for the next five years and beyond are:

Year	Operating Lease Expense
1	$90 million
2	$90 million
3	$85 million
4	$80 million
5	$80 million
6–10	$75 million annually

If the firm's current cost of borrowing is 7%, estimate the debt value of operating leases. Estimate the book value debt-to-equity ratio.

2. Assume that Derra Foods, in the preceding problem, reported earnings before interest and taxes (with operating leases expensed) of $200 million. Estimate the adjusted operating income, assuming that operating leases are capitalized.

3. FoodMarkets Inc. is a grocery chain. It reported a book debt-to-capital ratio of 10% and a return on capital of 25% on a book value of capital invested of $1 billion. Assume that the firm has significant operating leases. If the operating lease expense in the current year is $100 million and the present value of lease commitments is $750 million, reestimate FoodMarkets' debt to capital and return on capital. (You can assume a pretax cost of debt of 8%.)

4. Zif Software is a firm with significant research and development expenses. In the most recent year, the firm had $100 million in R&D expenses. R&D expenses are amortizable over five years, and over the past five years they are:

Year	R&D Expenses
−5	$ 50 million
−4	$ 60 million
−3	$ 70 million
−2	$ 80 million
−1	$ 90 million
Current year	$100 million

Assuming a linear amortization schedule (over five years), estimate:
  a. The value of the research asset.
  b. The amount of R&D amortization this year.
  c. The adjustment to operating income.
5. Stellar Computers has a well-earned reputation for earning a high return on capital. The firm had a return on capital of 100% on capital invested of $1.5 billion last year. Assume that you have estimated the value of the research asset to be $1 billion. In addition, the R&D expense this year is $250 million, and the amortization of the research asset is $150 million. Re-estimate Stellar Computers' return on capital.

CHAPTER 10

From Earnings To Cash Flows

The value of an asset comes from its capacity to generate cash flow. When valuing a firm, these cash flows should be after taxes, prior to debt payments, and after reinvestment needs. When valuing equity, the cash flows should be after debt payments. There are three basic steps to estimating these cash flows. The first is to estimate the earnings generated by a firm on its existing assets and investments, a process we examined in the preceding chapter. The second step is to estimate the portion of this income that would go toward paying taxes. The third is to develop a measure of how much a firm is reinvesting back for future growth.

This chapter examines the last two steps. It will begin by investigating the difference between effective and marginal taxes, as well as the effects of substantial net operating losses (NOLs) carried forward. To examine how much a firm is reinvesting, we will break it down into reinvestment in tangible and long-lived assets (net capital expenditures) and short-term assets (working capital). We will use a much broader definition of reinvestment to include investments in research and development (R&D) and acquisitions as part of capital expenditures.

THE TAX EFFECT

To compute the after-tax operating income, you multiply the earnings before interest and taxes by an estimated tax rate. This simple procedure can be complicated by three issues that often arise in valuation. The first is the wide differences you observe between effective and marginal tax rates for these firms, and the choice you face between the two in valuation. The second issue arises usually with firms with large losses, leading to net operating losses that are carried forward and can save taxes in future years. The third issue arises from the capitalizing of research and development and other expenses. The fact that these expenditures can be expensed immediately leads to much higher tax benefits for the firm.

Effective versus Marginal Tax Rate

You are faced with a choice of several different tax rates. The most widely reported tax rate in financial statements is the effective tax rate, which is computed from the reported income statement as follows:

$$\text{Effective tax rate} = \text{Taxes due}/\text{Taxable income}$$

Since it is based upon numbers in the income statement, this tax rate is an accrual tax rate, rather than a cash tax rate, and indicates the estimates of tax due in the time period, as a percent of taxable income.

The second choice on tax rates is the marginal tax rate, which is the tax rate the firm faces on its last dollar of income. This rate depends on the tax code and reflects what firms must pay as taxes on their marginal income. In the United States, in 2024, the federal corporate tax rate on marginal income is 21 percent; with the addition of state and local taxes, most profitable firms face a marginal corporate tax rate of around 25 percent. The marginal tax rate therefore comes from the tax code and has little to do with what you may find about tax rates in a company's financial statements.

While the marginal tax rates for most firms in the United States should be similar, there are wide differences in effective tax rates across firms. Figure 10.1 provides a distribution of effective tax rates for moneymaking firms in the United States, as well as global firms, in January 2024.

The median effective tax rate is between 20% and 25% for both U.S. and global companies. Note that several firms report effective tax rates of less than 10 percent, as well as that a few firms have effective tax rates that exceed 50 percent. In addition, this chart does not include the firms that did not pay taxes during the most recent financial year (and most of these are money-losing companies), or that have a negative effective tax rate.[1]

Reasons for Differences between Marginal and Effective Tax Rates   Given that most of the taxable income of publicly traded firms is at the highest marginal tax bracket, why would a firm's effective tax rate be different from its marginal tax rate? There are at least four reasons:

1. Many firms, at least in the United States, follow different accounting standards for tax and for reporting purposes. For instance, firms sometimes use straight-line depreciation for reporting purposes and accelerated depreciation for tax purposes. Consequently, the reported income is significantly higher than the taxable income, on which taxes are based.[2]
2. Firms sometimes use tax credits to reduce the taxes they pay. These credits, in turn, can reduce the effective tax rate below the marginal tax rate.
3. Firms can sometimes defer taxes on income to future periods. If firms defer taxes, the taxes paid in the current period will be at a rate lower than the marginal tax rate. In a later period, however, when the firm pays the deferred taxes, the effective tax rate will be higher than the marginal tax rate.
4. Firms that generate substantial income for foreign domiciles with lower tax rates did not have to pay domestic taxes until that income is repatriated back to the domestic country, until 2017, and no additional domestic taxes, after 2017.

---

[1] A negative effective tax rate usually arises because a firm is reporting an income in its tax books (on which it pays taxes) and a loss in its reporting books.
[2] Since the effective tax rate is based on the taxes paid (which comes from the tax statement) and the reported income, the effective tax rate will be lower than the marginal tax rate for firms that change accounting methods to inflate reported earnings.

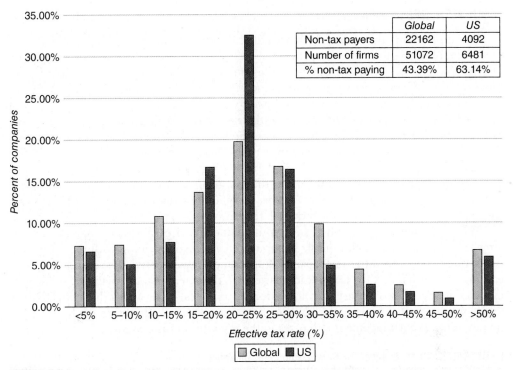

	Global	US
Non-tax payers	22162	4092
Number of firms	51072	6481
% non-tax paying	43.39%	63.14%

FIGURE 10.1 Effective Tax Rates for U.S. and Global Companies—January 2024
Source: Capital IQ. Used with permission of S&P Global Market Intelligence.

Marginal Tax Rates for Multinationals When a firm has global operations, its income is taxed at different rates in different locales. When this occurs, what is the marginal tax rate for the firm? There are three ways in which we can deal with different tax rates.

1. The first is to use a weighted average of the marginal tax rates, with the weights based on the income derived by the firm from each of these countries. The problem with this approach is that the weights will change over time if income is growing at different rates in different countries.
2. The second is to use the marginal tax rate of the country in which the company is incorporated, with the implicit assumption being that the income generated in other countries will eventually have to be repatriated to the country of origin, at which point the firm will have to pay the marginal tax rate.
3. The third approach is to keep the income from each country separate and apply a different marginal tax rate to each income stream.

Given that firms do have some flexibility in moving income across locations, it should come as no surprise that income tends to move to countries with lower taxes and away from countries with higher taxes.

Effects of Tax Rate on Value

In valuing a firm, should you use the marginal or the effective tax rates? If the same tax rate must be applied to earnings every period, the safer choice is the marginal tax rate, because three of the four reasons noted can be sustained in perpetuity. As new capital expenditures taper off, the difference between reported and tax income will narrow; tax credits are seldom perpetual, and firms eventually do have to pay their deferred taxes. For firms with income from foreign locales, with no domestic tax add-on, the global average marginal tax rate may be a better choice. There is no reason, however, why the tax rates used to compute the after-tax cash flows cannot change over time. Thus, in valuing a firm with an effective tax rate of 24 percent in the current period and a marginal tax rate of 35 percent, you can estimate the first year's cash flows using the marginal tax rate of 24 percent, and then increase the tax rate to 35 percent over time. It is good practice to assume that the tax rate used in perpetuity to compute the terminal value be the marginal tax rate.

When valuing equity, we often start with net income or earnings per share, which are after-tax earnings. Although it looks as though we can avoid dealing with the estimating of tax rates when using after-tax earnings, appearances are deceptive. The current after-tax earnings of a firm reflect the taxes paid this year. To the extent that tax planning or deferral caused this payment to be very low (low effective tax rates) or very high (high effective tax rates), we run the risk of assuming that the firm can continue to do this in the future, if we do not adjust the net income for changes in the tax rates in future years.

ILLUSTRATION 10.1: Effect of Tax Rate Assumptions on Value

Convoy Inc. is a telecommunications firm that generated $150 million in pretax operating income and reinvested $30 million in the most recent financial year. As a result of tax deferrals, the firm has an effective tax rate of 20%, while its marginal tax rate is 40%. Both the operating income and the reinvestment are expected to grow 10% a year for five years, and 5% thereafter. The firm's cost of capital is 9% and is expected to remain unchanged over time. We will estimate the value of Convoy using three different assumptions about tax rates— the effective tax rate forever, the marginal tax rate forever, and an approach that combines the two rates.

Approach 1: Effective Tax Rate Forever

We first estimate the value of Convoy if the tax rate remains at 20% forever:

Tax Rate	20%	20%	20%	20%	20%	20%	20%
	Current Year	1	2	3	4	5	Terminal Year
EBIT	$ 150.00	$165.00	$181.50	$199.65	$219.62	$ 241.58	$253.66
EBIT(1 − t)	$ 120.00	$132.00	$145.20	$159.72	$175.69	$ 193.26	$202.92
− Reinvestment	$ 30.00	$ 33.00	$ 36.30	$ 39.93	$ 43.92	$ 48.32	$ 50.73
Free cash flow to firm (FCFF)	$ 90.00	$ 99.00	$108.90	$119.79	$131.77	$ 144.95	$152.19
Terminal value						$3,804.83	
Present value		$ 90.83	$ 91.66	$ 92.50	$ 93.35	$2,567.08	
Firm value	$2,935.42						

This value is based on the implicit assumption that deferred taxes will never have to be paid by the firm.

Approach 2: Marginal Tax Rate Forever

We next estimate the value of Convoy assuming that the tax rate is the marginal tax rate of 40% forever:

Tax Rate	20%	40%	40%	40%	40%	40%	40%
	Current Year	1	2	3	4	5	Terminal Year
EBIT	$ 150.00	$165.00	$181.50	$199.65	$219.62	$ 241.58	$253.66
EBIT(1 − t)	$ 120.00	$ 99.00	$108.90	$119.79	$131.77	$ 144.95	$152.19
− Reinvestment	$ 30.00	$ 33.00	$ 36.30	$ 39.93	$ 43.92	$ 48.32	$ 50.73
FCFF	$ 90.00	$ 66.00	$ 72.60	$ 79.86	$ 87.85	$ 96.63	$101.46
Terminal value						$2,536.55	
Present value		$ 60.55	$ 61.11	$ 61.67	$ 62.23	$1,711.39	
Firm value	$1,956.94						

This firm value is based on the implicit assumption that the firm cannot defer taxes from this point on. In fact, an even more conservative reading would suggest that we should reduce this value by the amount of the cumulated deferred taxes from the past. Thus, if the firm has $200 million in deferred taxes from prior years, and expects to pay these taxes over the next four years in equal annual installments of $50 million, we would first compute the present value of these tax payments:

$$\text{Present value of deferred tax payments} = \$50 \text{ million(PV of annuity, 9\%, 4 years)}$$
$$= \$161.99 \text{ million}$$

The value of the firm would then be $1,794.95 million.

$$\text{Firm value after deferred tax} = \$1,956.94 - \$161.99 = \$1,794.95$$

Approach 3: Blended Tax Rates

In the final approach, we will assume that the effective tax will remain 20% for five years, and we will use the marginal tax rate to compute the terminal value:

Tax Rate	20%	20%	20%	20%	20%	20%	40%
	Current Year	1	2	3	4	5	Terminal Year
EBIT	$ 150.00	$165.00	$181.50	$199.65	$219.62	$ 241.58	$253.66
EBIT(1 − t)	$ 120.00	$132.00	$145.20	$159.72	$175.69	$ 193.26	$152.19
− Reinvestment	$ 30.00	$ 33.00	$ 36.30	$ 39.93	$ 43.92	$ 48.32	$ 50.73
FCFF	$ 90.00	$ 99.00	$108.90	$119.79	$131.77	$ 144.95	$101.46
Terminal value	$2,536.55						
Present value		$ 90.83	$ 91.66	$ 92.50	$ 93.35	$1,742.79	
Firm value	$2,111.12						

Note, however, that the use of the effective tax rate for the first five years will increase the deferred tax liability to the firm. Assuming that the firm ended the current year with a cumulated deferred tax liability of $200 million, we can compute the deferred tax liability by the end of the fifth year:

$$\text{Expected deferred tax liability} = \$200 + (\$165 + \$181.5 + \$199.65 + \$219.62$$
$$+ \$241.58) \times (.40 - .20) = \$401.47 \text{ million}$$

We will assume that the firm will pay this deferred tax liability after year 5, but spread the payments over 10 years, leading to a present value of $167.45 million.

$$\text{Present value of deferred tax payments} = (\$401.47/10)(\text{PV of annuity, 9\%, 10 years})/1.09^5$$
$$= \$167.45 \text{ million}$$

Note that the payments do not start until the sixth year, and hence get discounted back an additional five years. The value of the firm can then be estimated:

$$\text{Value of firm} = \$2,111.12 - \$167.45 = \$1,943.67 \text{ million}$$

---

 taxrate.xls: **This dataset on the web summarizes average effective tax rates by industry group in the United States for the most recent quarter.**

Effect of Net Operating Losses

For firms with large net operating losses carried forward or continuing operating losses, there is the potential for significant tax savings in the first few years that they generate positive earnings. There are two ways of capturing this effect.

One is to change tax rates over time. In the early years, these firms will have a tax rate of zero, as losses carried forward will offset income. Once the net operating losses are used up, the tax rates will climb toward the marginal tax rate. As the tax rates used to estimate the after-tax operating income change, the rates used to compute the after-tax cost of debt in the cost of capital computation also need to change. Thus, for a firm with net operating losses carried forward, the tax rate used for both the computation of after-tax operating income and cost of capital will be zero during the years when the losses shelter income.

The other approach is often used when valuing firms that already have positive earnings but have a large net operating loss carried forward. Analysts will value the firm ignoring the tax savings generated by net operating losses, and then add to this amount the expected tax savings from net operating losses. Often, the expected tax savings are estimated by multiplying the tax rate by the net operating loss. The limitation of doing this is that it assumes that the tax savings are both guaranteed and instantaneous. To the extent that firms must generate earnings to create these tax savings and there is uncertainty about earnings, it will overestimate the value of the tax savings.

There are two final points that need to be made about operating losses. To the extent that a potential acquirer can claim the tax savings from net operating losses sooner than the firm generating these losses, there can be potential for tax synergy that we examine in Chapter 25, when we look at acquisitions. The other is that there are countries where there are significant limitations on how far forward operating losses can be taken. If this is the case, the value of these net operating losses may be reduced.

ILLUSTRATION 10.2: The Effect of Net Operating Loss on Value: Tesla Motors in 2011

This illustration considers the effect of both net operating losses (NOLs) carried forward and expected losses in future periods on the tax rate for Tesla Motors, the electric car company, in 2011. Tesla reported an operating loss of $65.5 million in 2010, on revenues of $116.74 million, and had an accumulated net operating loss of $140.64 million by the end of that year.

While things did look bleak for the firm, we assumed that revenues will grow significantly over the next decade, and that the firm's operating margin will converge on the industry average of 10% for mature and healthy automobile firms. The following table summarizes our projections of revenues and operating income for Tesla for the next 10 years:

Year	Revenues	Operating Income	NOL at End of Year	Taxable Income	Taxes	Tax Rate
Current	$ 117	−$ 81	$141	$ 0	$ 0	0.00%
1	$ 292	−$125	$266	$ 0	$ 0	0.00%
2	$ 584	−$147	$413	$ 0	$ 0	0.00%
3	$1,051	−$142	$555	$ 0	$ 0	0.00%
4	$1,681	−$ 95	$650	$ 0	$ 0	0.00%
5	$2,354	−$ 10	$661	$ 0	$ 0	0.00%
6	$3,060	$ 93	$568	$ 0	$ 0	0.00%
7	$3,672	$197	$371	$ 0	$ 0	0.00%
8	$4,222	$292	$ 79	$ 0	$ 0	0.00%
9	$4,645	$369	$ −	$289	$116	31.40%
10	$4,877	$421	$ −	$421	$168	40.00%

Note that Tesla continues to lose money for the first five years and adds to its net operating losses. In years 6, 7, and 8, its operating income is positive, but it still pays no taxes because of its accumulated net operating losses from prior years. In year 9, it can reduce its taxable income by the remaining net operating loss ($79 million), but it begins paying taxes for the first time. We assumed a 40% tax rate and used this as our marginal tax rate after year 9. The benefits of the net operating losses are thus built into the cash flows and the value of the firm. By discounting the cash flow savings back at the cost of capital, we are incorporating both the time value of money (from having to wait) and the risk that the tax savings will not be delivered.

The Tax Benefits of R&D Expensing

The preceding chapter argued that R&D expenses should be capitalized. If we decide to do so, however, there is a tax benefit that we might be missing. Firms are allowed to deduct their entire R&D expense for tax purposes. In contrast, they are allowed to deduct only the depreciation on their capital expenses. To capture the tax benefit, therefore, you would add the tax savings on the difference between the entire R&D expense and the amortized amount of the research asset to the after-tax operating income of the firm:

$$\text{Additional tax benefit}_{\text{R\&D expensing}} = (\text{Current year's R\&D expense}$$
$$- \text{Amortization of research asset}) \times \text{Tax rate}$$

A similar adjustment would need to be made for any other operating expense that you choose to capitalize. In Chapter 9, we noted that the adjustment to pretax operating income from capitalizing R&D is:

Adjusted operating earnings = Operating earnings + Current year's R&D expense
− Amortization of research asset

To estimate the after-tax operating income, we would multiply this value by (1 − Tax rate) and add on the additional tax benefit from before:

$$
\begin{aligned}
\text{Adjusted after-tax operating earnings} = &\ (\text{Operating earnings} \\
& + \text{Current year's R\&D expense} \\
& - \text{Amortization of research asset}) \\
& \times (1 - \text{Tax rate}) \\
& + (\text{Current year's R\&D expense} \\
& - \text{Amortization of research asset}) \\
& \times \text{Tax rate} \\
= &\ \text{Operating earnings} \times (1 - \text{Tax rate}) \\
& + \text{Current year's R\&D expense} \\
& - \text{Amortization of research asset}
\end{aligned}
$$

In other words, the tax benefit from R&D expensing allows us to add the difference between R&D expense and amortization directly to the after-tax operating income (and to net income).

ILLUSTRATION 10.3:   Tax Benefit from Expensing: Amgen in 2023

In Chapter 9, we capitalize, R&D expenses for Amgen and estimated the value of the research asset to Amgen and adjusted operating income. Reviewing Illustration 9.2, we see the following adjustments:

Current year's R&D expense (2023) = $4,755 million

Amortization of research asset in 2023 = $4,105 million

To estimate the tax benefit from expensing for Amgen, first assume that the tax rate for Amgen is 25% and note that Amgen can deduct the entire $4,755 million for tax purposes:

Tax deduction from R&D expense = R&D × Tax rate = 4,755 × .25 = $1,189 million

If only the amortization had been eligible for a tax deduction in 2023, the tax benefit would have been:

Tax deduction from R&D amortization = 4,105 × .25 = $1,026 million

By expensing instead of capitalizing, Amgen was able to derive a much larger tax benefit. The differential tax benefit can be written as:

Differential tax benefit = $1,189 − $1,026 = $163 million

Thus, Amgen derives a tax benefit of $163 million because it can expense R&D expenses rather than capitalize them. Completing the analysis, we computed the adjusted after-tax operating income for Amgen. Note that in Illustration 9.2, we estimated the adjusted pretax operating income to be the following:

$$\text{Adjusted pretax operating earnings} = \text{Operating earnings} + \text{Current year's R\&D expense}$$
$$- \text{Amortization of research asset}$$
$$= 7,231 + 4,755 - 4,105 = \$7,880$$

You could convert this pretax operating income into an after-tax value and add back the tax benefit from R&D:

$$\text{After-tax operating income} = 7,880 \times (1 - .25) + 163 = \$6,073 \text{ million}$$

You can also arrive at the same answer by computing the unadjusted after-tax operating income and adjusting it for R&D:

$$\text{Adjusted after-tax operating income} = \text{After-tax operating income} + \text{Current year's R\&D expense}$$
$$- \text{Amortization of research asset}$$
$$= 7,231 \times (1 - .25) + 4,755 - 4,105 = \$6,073 \text{ million}$$

Tax Books and Reporting Books

It is no secret that many firms in the United States maintain two sets of books—one for tax purposes and one for reporting purposes—and that this practice not only is legal but is also widely accepted. While the details vary from company to company, the income reported to stockholders generally is much higher than the income reported for tax purposes. When valuing firms, we generally have access to only the former and not the latter, and this can affect our estimates in several ways:

- Dividing the taxes payable, which is computed on the taxable income, by the reported income, which is generally much higher, will yield a tax rate that may be lower than the true tax rate. If we use this tax rate as the forecasted tax rate, we could overvalue the company. This is another reason for shifting to marginal tax rates in future periods.
- If we base the projections on the reported income, we will overstate expected future income. The effect on cash flows is likely to be muted. To see why, consider one very common difference between reporting and tax income: Straight-line depreciation is used to compute the former, and accelerated depreciation is used for the latter. Since we add depreciation back to after-tax income to get to cash flows, the drop in depreciation will offset the increase in earnings. The problem, however, is that we understate the tax benefits from depreciation.
- Some companies capitalize expenses for reporting purposes (and for depreciating them in subsequent periods) but expense them for tax purposes. Here again, using the income and the capital expenditures from reporting books will result in an understatement of the tax benefits from the expensing.

Thus, the problems created by firms having different standards for tax and accounting purposes are much greater if we focus on reported earnings (as is the case when we use earnings multiples like PE or EBITDA multiples) than when we use cash flows. If we did have a choice, however, we would base our valuations on the tax books rather than the reporting books.

Deferred Tax Assets and Liabilities

As we noted earlier in the chapter, the effective tax rate estimated from the income statement of a company reflects accrual income and taxes and can result in a tax rate that is much lower or higher than the marginal tax rate. That difference can give rise to what accounts call deferred tax liabilities, if taxes are deferred to future periods, or deferred tax assets, if companies overpay taxes and expect to get savings in future periods. In an intrinsic valuation, the only effect of these deferred tax items is through the taxes that you pay in future periods and the resulting effects on cash flows:

- With deferred tax liabilities, there is the likelihood that the effective tax rate in future periods, used to estimate after-tax earnings, may be higher than the marginal tax rate until the deferred tax liability is extinguished. These higher effective tax rates will lower earnings and cash flows, and thus lower value.
- With deferred tax assets, the treatment is akin to the one for net operating losses, where the company benefits by having to pay a lower effective tax rate in future periods, and thus generates higher cash flows.

It is worth noting that in liquidation valuation, neither the deferred tax liability nor asset has much heft, since it is unlikely that the liquidation proceeds will be reduced due to deferred tax liabilities on the books, or increased as a consequence of deferred tax assets.

DEALING WITH TAX SUBSIDIES

Firms sometimes obtain tax subsidies from the government for investing in specified areas or types of businesses. These tax subsidies can take the form of either reduced tax rates or tax credits. Either way, these subsidies should increase the value of the firm. The question, of course, is how best to build in the effects into the cash flows. Perhaps the simplest approach is to first value the firm, ignoring the tax subsidies, and to then add on the value increment from the subsidies.

For instance, assume that you are valuing a pharmaceutical firm with operations in Puerto Rico, which entitles the firm to a tax break in the form of a lower tax rate on the income generated from these operations. You could value the firm using its normal marginal tax rate, and then add to that value the present value of the tax savings that will be generated by the Puerto Rican operations. There are three advantages with this approach:

1. It allows you to isolate the tax subsidy and consider it only for the period over which you are entitled to it. When the effects of these tax breaks are consolidated with other cash flows, there is a danger that they can be viewed as perpetuities.

2. The discount rate used to compute the tax breaks can be different from the discount rate used on the other cash flows of the firm. Thus, if the tax break is a guaranteed tax credit by the government, you could use a much lower discount rate to compute the present value PV of the cash flows.

3. Building on the theme that there are few free lunches, it can be argued that governments provide tax breaks for investments only because firms are exposed to higher costs or more risk in these investments. By isolating the value of the tax breaks, firms can then consider whether the trade-off operates in their favor. For example, assume that you are a sugar manufacturer that is offered a tax credit by the government for being in the business. In return, the government imposes sugar price controls. The firm can compare the value created by the tax credit with the value lost because of the price controls, and decide whether it should fight to preserve its tax credit.

REINVESTMENT NEEDS

The cash flow to the firm is computed after reinvestments. Two components go into estimating reinvestment. The first is net capital expenditures, which is the difference between capital expenditures and depreciation. The other is investments in noncash working capital.

Net Capital Expenditures

In estimating net capital expenditures, we generally deduct depreciation from capital expenditures. The rationale is that the positive cash flows from depreciation pay for at least a portion of capital expenditures, and that it is only the excess that represents a drain on the firm's cash flows. Whereas information on capital spending and depreciation are usually easily accessible in most financial statements, forecasting these expenditures can be difficult for three reasons. The first is that firms often incur capital spending in chunks— a large investment in one year can be followed by small investments in subsequent years. The second is that the accounting definition of capital spending does not incorporate those capital expenses that are treated as operating expenses such as R&D expenses. The third is that acquisitions are not classified by accountants as capital expenditures. For firms that grow primarily through acquisition, this will result in an understatement of the net capital expenditures.

Lumpy Capital Expenditures and the Need for Smoothing Firms seldom have smooth capital expenditure streams. Firms can go through periods when capital expenditures are very high (as is the case when a new product is introduced or a new plant built), followed by periods of relatively light capital expenditures. Consequently, when estimating the capital expenditures to use for forecasting future cash flows, you should normalize capital expenditures. There are at least two ways in which you can accomplish this objective.

The simplest normalization technique is to average capital expenditures over several years. For instance, you could estimate the average capital expenditures over the past four or five years for a manufacturing firm, and then use that number rather the capital expenditures from the most recent year. By doing so, you could capture the fact that the firm may invest in a new plant every four years. If instead you had used the capital expenditures from the most recent year, you would have either overestimated capital expenditures (if the firm built a new plant that year) or underestimated them (if the plant had been built in an earlier year).

There are two measurement issues that you will need to confront. One relates to the number of years of history that you should use. The answer will vary across firms and depend on how infrequently the firm makes large investments. The other is on the question of whether averaging capital expenditures over time requires us to average depreciation as well. Since depreciation is already spread out over time, the need for normalization should be much smaller. In addition, the tax benefits received by the firm reflect the actual depreciation in the most recent year, rather than an average depreciation over time. Unless depreciation is as volatile as capital expenditures, it makes more sense to leave depreciation untouched.

For firms with a limited history or firms that have changed their business mix over time, averaging over time either is not an option or will yield numbers that are not indicative of their true capital expenditure needs. For these firms, industry averages for capital expenditures are an alternative. Since the sizes of firms can vary across an industry, the averages are usually computed with capital expenditures as a percent of a base input—revenues and total assets are common choices. We prefer to look at capital expenditures as a percent of depreciation, and to average this statistic for the industry. In fact, if there are enough firms in the sample, you could look at the average for a subset of firms that are at the same stage of the life cycle as the firm being analyzed.

ILLUSTRATION 10.4: Estimating Normalized Net Capital Expenditures: BYD

BYD is China's largest electric car company, and coming into 2024, seemed poised for high growth. The firm makes substantial investments in these businesses, and the following table summarizes the capital expenditures and depreciation for the period of 2019–2023:

Year	Depreciation	Cap Ex	Net Cap Ex	Cap Ex/ Depreciation	Revenues	Net Cap Ex as % of Revenue
2019	¥ 8,321	¥ 20,627	¥12,307	247.90%	¥127,739	9.63%
2020	¥ 9,415	¥ 11,774	¥ 2,359	125.06%	¥156,598	1.51%
2021	¥11,153	¥ 37,344	¥26,191	334.83%	¥216,142	12.12%
2022	¥15,189	¥ 97,457	¥82,268	641.62%	¥424,061	19.40%
2023	¥39,108	¥122,094	¥82,985	312.19%	¥602,315	13.78%
Average			¥41,222	332.32%		11.29%

The firm's capital expenditures have been volatile, and its depreciation has been trending upward. There are two ways in which we can normalize the net capital expenditures. One is to take the average net capital expenditure over the five-year period, which would result in net capital expenditures of ¥41,222 million. Another way to normalize capital expenditures is to look at capital expenditures as a percent of depreciation over the period, and apply that to the depreciation in the most recent year (2023):

Normalized cap expenditures = ¥39,108(3.32) = ¥129,966 million

Normalized net cap expenditures = ¥129,966 − ¥39,108 = ¥90,857 million

A third approach is to scale the net capital expenditures each year to revenues and estimate it as a percentage of revenues. That yields net cap expenditures as a percent of revenues of 11.29% over the time period, and you can use that statistic to normalize net capital expenditures in 2023:

$$\text{Normalized cap expenditures} = \text{Revenues in 2023} \times \text{Net cap ex as a \% of revenues}$$
$$= ¥602,315 \, (.1129) = ¥68,984 \text{ million}$$

The advantage of the last approach, where net capital expenditures are scaled to revenues, is that it offers a basis for forecasting net capital expenditures in future periods, as a function of expected revenues.

Capital Expenses Treated as Operating Expenses   In Chapter 9, we discussed the capitalization of expenses such as R&D and personnel training, where the benefits last over multiple periods, and examined the effects on earnings. There should also clearly be an impact on our estimates of capital expenditures, depreciation, and, consequently, net capital expenditures.

■ If we decide to recategorize some operating expenses as capital expenses, we should treat the current period's value for this item as a capital expenditure. For instance, if we decide to capitalize R&D expenses, the amount spent on R&D in the current period has to be added to capital expenditures.

> Adjusted capital expenditures = Capital expenditures
> \+ R&D expenses in current period

■ Since capitalizing an operating expense creates an asset, the amortization of this asset should be added to depreciation for the current period. Thus, capitalizing R&D creates a research asset, which generates an amortization in the current period.

> Adjusted depreciation = Depreciation and amortization
> \+ Amortization of the research asset

■ If we are adding the current period's expense to the capital expenditures and the amortization of the asset to the depreciation, the net capital expenditures of the firm will increase by the difference between the two:

> Adjusted net capital expenditure = Net capital expenditures
> \+ R&D expenses in current period
> − Amortization of the research asset

Note that the adjustment that we make to net capital expenditure mirrors the adjustment we make to operating income. Since net capital expenditures are subtracted from after-tax operating income, we are, in a sense, nullifying the impact on cash flows of capitalizing R&D.

ILLUSTRATION 10.5:   Effect of Capitalizing R&D: Amgen in 2023

In Illustration 9.2, we capitalized Amgen's R&D expense and created a research asset. In Illustration 10.3, we considered the additional tax benefit generated by the fact that a company can expense the entire amount. In this illustration, we complete the analysis by looking at the impact of capitalization on net capital expenditures.

Reviewing the numbers again, Amgen had an R&D expense of $4,755 million in 2023. Capitalizing the R&D expenses, using an amortizable life of 10 years, yields a value for the research asset of $23,687 million and an amortization for the current year (2023) of $4,105 million. In addition, note that Amgen reported capital expenditures of $998 million in 2023, and depreciation and amortization amounting to $863 million. The adjustments to capital expenditures, depreciation, and amortization, and net capital expenditures are:

$$\text{Adjusted capital expenditures} = \text{Capital expenditures} + \text{R\&D expenses in current period}$$
$$= \$998\,\text{million} + \$4{,}755\,\text{million} = \$5{,}753\,\text{million}$$

$$\text{Adjusted depreciation \& amortization} = \text{Depreciation and amortization}$$
$$+ \text{Amortization of the research asset}$$
$$= \$863\,\text{million} + \$4{,}105\,\text{million} = \$4{,}968\,\text{million}$$

$$\text{Adjusted net capital expenditures} = \text{Net capital expenditures} + \text{R\&D expenses in current period}$$
$$- \text{Amortization of the research asset}$$
$$= \$5{,}753 - \$4{,}968$$
$$= \$785\,\text{million}$$

Viewed in conjunction with the adjustment to after-tax operating income in Illustration 10.3, the change in net capital expenditure (an increase of $650 million from $135 million to $785 million) is exactly equal to the change in after-tax operating income. Capitalizing R&D thus has no effect on the free cash flow to the firm. Though the bottom-line cash flow does not change, the capitalization of R&D significantly changes the estimates of earnings and reinvestment. Thus, it helps us better understand how profitable a firm is and how much it is reinvesting for future growth.

Acquisitions   In estimating capital expenditures, we should not distinguish between internal investments (which are usually categorized as capital expenditures in cash flow statements) and external investments (which are acquisitions). The capital expenditures of a firm, therefore, need to include acquisitions. Since firms seldom make acquisitions every year, and each acquisition has a different price tag, the point about normalizing capital expenditures applies even more strongly to this item. The capital expenditure projections for a firm that makes a $100 million acquisition approximately every five years should therefore include about $20 million, adjusted for inflation, every year.

Should you distinguish between acquisitions funded with cash versus those funded with stock? We do not believe so. While there may be no cash spent by a firm in the latter case, the firm is increasing the number of shares outstanding. In fact, one way to think about stock-funded acquisitions is that the firm has skipped a step in the funding process. It could have issued the stock to the public and used the cash to make the acquisitions. Another way of thinking about this issue is that a firm that uses stock to fund acquisitions year after year and is expected to continue to do so in the future will increase the number of shares outstanding. This, in turn, will dilute the value per share to existing stockholders.

ILLUSTRATION 10.6: Estimating Net Capital Expenditures: Cisco Systems in 1999

Cisco Systems increased its market value a hundredfold during the 1990s, largely based on its capacity to grow revenues and earnings at an annual rate of 60% to 70%. Much of this growth was created by acquisitions of small companies with promising technologies and Cisco's ability to convert to them into commercial successes. To estimate net capital expenditures for Cisco in 1999, we begin with the estimates of capital expenditure ($584 million) and depreciation ($486 million) in the 10-K. Based on these numbers, we would have concluded that Cisco's net capital expenditures in 1999 were $98 million.

The first adjustment we make to this number is to incorporate the effect of research and development expenses. We use a five-year amortizable life and estimate the value of the research asset and the amortization in 1999 in the following table:

Year	R&D Expense	Unamortized at Year-End		Amortization This Year
Current	$1,594.00	100.00%	$1,594.00	
−1	$1,026.00	80.00%	$ 820.80	$205.20
−2	$ 698.00	60.00%	$ 418.80	$139.60
−3	$ 399.00	40.00%	$ 159.60	$ 79.80
−4	$ 211.00	20.00%	$ 42.20	$ 42.20
−5	$ 89.00	0.00%	$ 0.00	$ 17.80
Value of the research asset			$3,035.40	
Amortization this year			$ 484.60	

The net capital expenditures for Cisco were adjusted by adding back the R&D expenses in the most recent financial year ($1,594 million) and subtracting the amortization of the research asset ($485 million).

The second adjustment is to bring in the effect of acquisitions that Cisco made during the last financial year. The following table summarizes the acquisitions made during the year and the prices paid on these acquisitions:

Acquired	Method of Acquisition	Price Paid
GeoTel	Pooling	$1,344
Fibex	Pooling	318
Sentient	Pooling	103
American Internet Corporation	Purchase	58
Summa Four	Purchase	129
Clarity Wireless	Purchase	153
Selsius Systems	Purchase	134
PipeLinks	Purchase	118
Amteva Technologies	Purchase	159
Total		$2,516

Dollars in millions

Note that both purchase and pooling transactions are included, and that the sum of these acquisitions is added to net capital expenditures in 1999. We are assuming, given Cisco's track record, that its acquisitions in 1999 are not unusual and reflect Cisco's reinvestment policy. The amortization associated with these acquisitions is already included as part of depreciation by the firm.[3] The following table summarizes the final net capital expenditures for Cisco in 1999.

Capital expenditures	$ 584.00
– Depreciation	$ 486.00
Net cap ex (from financials)	$ 98.00
+ R&D expenditures	$1,594.00
– Amortization of R&D	$ 484.60
+ Acquisitions	$2,516.00
Adjusted net cap ex	$3,723.40

IGNORING ACQUISITIONS IN VALUATION: A POSSIBILITY?

Incorporating acquisitions into net capital expenditures and value can be difficult, and especially so for firms that make large acquisitions infrequently. Predicting whether there will be acquisitions, how much they will cost, and what they will deliver in terms of higher growth can be close to impossible. You can ignore acquisitions, but only you assume that firms pay fair prices on acquisitions (i.e., a price that reflects the fair value of the target company), and you assume that the target company stockholders claim any or all synergy or control value. In these cases, acquisitions have no effect on value no matter how large they might be and how much they might seem to deliver in terms of higher growth. The reason is simple: A fair-value acquisition is an investment that earns its required return—a zero net present value investment.

If you choose not to consider acquisitions when valuing a firm, you must remain internally consistent. The portion of growth that is due to acquisitions should not be considered in the valuation. A common mistake made in valuing companies that have posted impressive historic growth numbers from an acquisition-based strategy is to extrapolate from this growth and ignore acquisitions at the same time. This will result in an overvaluation of your firm since you have counted the benefits of the acquisitions but have not paid for them.

What is the cost of ignoring acquisitions? Not all acquisitions are fairly priced, and not all synergy and control value end up with the target company stockholders. Ignoring the costs and benefits of acquisitions will result in an misvaluation of a firm that has established a reputation for growing through acquisitions. We undervalue firms that create value by making good acquisitions and overvalue firms that destroy value by overpaying on acquisitions.

---

[3] It is only the tax-deductible amortization that really matters. To the extent that amortization is not tax deductible, you would look at the EBIT before the amortization and not consider it while estimating net capital expenditures.

capex.xls: This dataset on the web summarizes capital expenditures, as a percent of revenues and firm value, by industry group in the United States for the most recent quarter.

Investment in Working Capital

The second component of reinvestment is the cash that needs to be set aside for working capital needs. Increases in working capital tie up more cash, and hence generate negative cash flows. Conversely, decreases in working capital release cash and positive cash flows.

Defining Working Capital Working capital is usually defined to be the difference between current assets and current liabilities. However, we will modify that definition when we measure working capital for valuation purposes.

▪ We will back out cash and investments in marketable securities from current assets. This is because cash, especially in large amounts, is usually invested by firms in Treasury bills, short-term government securities, or commercial paper. Although the return on these investments may be lower than what the firm may make on its real investments, they represent a fair return for riskless investments. Unlike inventory,

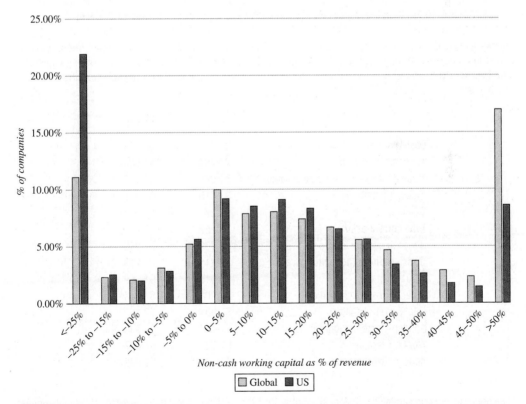

FIGURE 10.2 Noncash Working Capital as a percent of Revenues: US and Global firms in 2023
Source: Capital IQ. Used with permission of S&P Global Market Intelligence.

accounts receivable and other current assets, cash earns a fair return and should not be included in measures of working capital. Are there exceptions to this rule? When valuing a firm that has to maintain a large cash balance for day-to-day operations, or a firm that operates in a market in a poorly developed banking system, you could consider the cash needed for operations as a part of working capital but only if that cash is wasting cash, i.e., cash that is not earning a fair market return. As we shift from a cash-based economy, this operating cash requirement has become smaller and smaller.

■ We will also back out all interest-bearing debt—short-term debt and the portion of long-term debt that is due in the current period—from the current liabilities. This debt will be considered when computing the cost of capital and it would be inappropriate to count it twice.

The noncash working capital varies widely across firms in different sectors and often across firms in the same sector. Figure 10.2 shows the distribution of non-cash working capital as a percent of revenues for U.S. firms in January 2024.

In 2023, note that more than a third of all U.S. firms, and about a fifth of all global firms, had negative noncash working capital, i.e., nondebt current liabilities exceeded noncash current assets. At the other extreme, a significant percentage of firms have noncash working capital that exceeds 50% of revenues.

ILLUSTRATION 10.7: Working Capital versus Noncash Working Capital: Marks and Spencer

Marks and Spencer operated retail stores in the United Kingdom and had substantial holdings in retail firms in other parts of the world. The following table breaks down the components of working capital for the firm for 1999 and 2000 and reports both the total working capital and noncash working capital in each year:

	1999	2000
Cash and near cash	$ 282	$ 301
Marketable securities	$ 204	$ 386
Trade debtors (accounts receivable)	$1,980	$2,186
Stocks (inventory)	$ 515	$ 475
Other current assets	$ 271	$ 281
Total current assets	$3,252	$3,629
Noncash current assets	$2,766	$2,942
Trade creditors (accounts payable)	$ 215	$ 219
Short-term debt	$ 913	$1,169
Other short-term liabilities	$ 903	$ 774
Total current liabilities	$2,031	$2,162
Nondebt current liabilities	$1,118	$ 993
Working capital	$1,221	$1,467
Noncash working capital	$1,648	$1,949

The noncash working capital is substantially higher than the working capital in both years. We would suggest that the former is a much better measure of cash tied up in working capital.

Estimating Expected Changes in Noncash Working Capital   While we can estimate the noncash working capital change fairly simply for any year using financial statements, this estimate has to be used with caution. Changes in noncash working capital are unstable, with big increases in some years followed by big decreases in subsequent years. To ensure that the projections are not the result of an unusual base year, you should tie the changes in working capital to expected changes in revenues or costs of goods sold at the firm over time. The noncash working capital as a percentage of revenues can be used, in conjunction with expected revenue changes each period, to estimate projected changes in noncash working capital over time. You can obtain the noncash working capital as a percent of revenues by looking at the firm's history or at industry standards.

Should you break working capital down into more detail? In other words, is there a payoff to estimating individual items, such as accounts receivable, inventory, and accounts payable separately? The answer will depend on both the firm being analyzed and how far into the future working capital is being projected. For firms where inventory and accounts receivable behave in very different ways as revenues grow, it clearly makes sense to break working capital down into detail. The cost, of course, is that it increases the number of inputs needed to value a firm. In addition, the payoff to breaking working capital down into individual items will become smaller as we go further into the future. For most firms, estimating a composite number for noncash working capital is easier to do, and often more accurate than breaking it down into more detail.

ILLUSTRATION 10.8: Estimating Noncash Working Capital Needs: The Gap

As a specialty retailer, the Gap has substantial inventory and working capital needs. At the end of the 2000 financial year (which concluded in January 2001), the Gap reported $1,904 million in inventory and $335 million in other noncash current assets. At the same time, the accounts payable amounted to $1,067 million and other non-interest-bearing current liabilities were $702 million. The noncash working capital for the Gap in January 2001 can be estimated as follows:

Noncash working capital = $1,904 + $335 − $1,067 − $702 = $470 million

The following table reports on the noncash working capital at the end of the previous year and the total revenues in each year:

	1999	2000	Change
Inventory	$ 1,462	$ 1,904	$ 442
Other noncash current assets	$ 285	$ 335	$ 50
Accounts payable	$ 806	$ 1,067	$ 261
Other non-interest-bearing current liabilities	$ 778	$ 702	−$ 76
Noncash working capital	$ 163	$ 470	$ 307
Revenues	$11,635	$13,673	$ 2,038
Non-cash Working capital as % of revenues	1.40%	3.44%	15.06%

The noncash working capital increased by $307 million from the preceding year to this one. When forecasting the noncash working capital needs for the Gap, there are five choices:

1. One is to use the change in noncash working capital from the year ($307 million) and to grow that change at the same rate as earnings are expected to grow in the future. This is probably the least desirable option

because changes in noncash working capital from year to year are extremely volatile, and last year's change may in fact be an outlier.

2. The second is to base our changes on noncash working capital as a percentage of revenues in the most recent year and expected revenue growth in future years. In the case of the Gap, that would indicate that noncash working capital changes in future years will be 3.44% of revenue changes in that year. This is a much better option than the first one, but the noncash working capital as a percentage of revenues can also change from one year to the next.

3. The third is to base our changes on the marginal noncash working capital as a percent of revenues in the most recent year, computed by dividing the change in noncash working capital in the most recent year and the change in revenues in the most recent year, by expected revenue growth in future years. In the case of the Gap, this would lead to noncash working capital changes being 15.06% of revenues in future periods. This approach is best used for firms whose business is changing and where growth is occurring in areas different from the past. For instance, a brick-and-mortar retailer that is growing mostly online may have a very different marginal working capital requirement than the total.

4. The fourth is to base our changes on the noncash working capital as a percentage of revenues over a historical period. For instance, noncash working capital as a percent of revenues between 1997 and 2000 averaged out to 4.5% of revenues. The advantage of this approach is that it smooths out year-to-year shifts, but it may not be appropriate if there is a trend (upward or downward) in working capital.

5. The final approach is to ignore the working capital history of the firm and to base the projections on the industry average for noncash working capital as a percentage of revenues. This approach is most appropriate when a firm's history reveals a working capital that is volatile and unpredictable. It is also the best way of estimating noncash working capital for very small firms that may see economies of scale as they grow. While these conditions do not apply for the Gap, we can still estimate noncash working capital requirements using the average noncash working capital as a percent of revenues for specialty retailers, which is 7.54%.

To illustrate how much of a change each of these assumptions can have on working capital requirements, the following table forecasts expected changes in noncash working capital (WC) using each of them. In making these estimates, we have assumed a 10% growth rate in revenues and earnings for the Gap for the next five years.

	Current	1	2	3	4	5
Revenues	$13,673.00	$15,040.30	$16,544.33	$18,198.76	$20,018.64	$22,020.50
Change in revenues		$ 1,367.30	$ 1,504.03	$ 1,654.43	$ 1,819.88	$ 2,001.86
1. Change in noncash WC	$ 307.00	$ 337.70	$ 371.47	$ 408.62	$ 449.48	$ 494.43
2. Current: WC/revenues	3.44%	$ 47.00	$ 51.70	$ 56.87	$ 62.56	$ 68.81
3. Marginal: WC/revenues	15.06%	$ 205.97	$ 226.56	$ 249.22	$ 274.14	$ 301.56
4. Historical average	4.50%	$ 61.53	$ 67.68	$ 74.45	$ 81.89	$ 90.08
5. Industry average	7.54%	$ 103.09	$ 113.40	$ 124.74	$ 137.22	$ 150.94

The noncash working capital investment varies widely across the five approaches that have been described here.

Negative Working Capital (or Changes)   Can the change in noncash working capital be negative? The answer is clearly yes. Consider, though, the implications of such a change. When noncash working capital decreases, it releases tied-up cash and increases the cash flow of the firm. If a firm has bloated inventory or gives out credit too easily, managing one or both components more efficiently can reduce working capital and be a source of positive cash

Year	Current	1	2	3	4	5
Revenues	$1,000.00	$1,100.00	$1,210.00	$1,331.00	$1,464.10	$1,610.51
Noncash WC as % of revenues	10%	9%	8%	7%	6%	6%
Noncash working capital	$ 100.00	$ 99.00	$ 96.80	$ 93.17	$ 87.85	$ 96.63
Change in noncash WC		−$ 1.00	−$ 2.20	−$ 0.63	−$ 5.32	$ 8.78

flows into the immediate future—three, four, or even five years. The question, however, becomes whether it can be a source of cash flows for longer than that. At some point in time, there will be no more inefficiencies left in the system, and any further decreases in working capital can have negative consequences for revenue growth and profits. Therefore, it appears that for firms with positive working capital, decreases in working capital are feasible only for short periods. In fact, once working capital is being managed efficiently, the working capital changes from year to year should be estimated using working capital as a percentage of revenues. For example, consider a firm that has noncash working capital that represents 10 percent of revenues and that you believe that better management of working capital could reduce this to 6 percent of revenues. You could allow working capital to decline each year for the next four years from 10 percent to 6 percent, and once this adjustment is made, begin estimating the working capital requirement each year as 6 percent of additional revenues. The following table provides estimates of the change in noncash working capital on this firm, assuming that current revenues are $1 billion and that revenues are expected to grow 10 percent a year for the next 15 years.

Can working capital itself be negative? Again, the answer is yes. Firms whose non-debt current liabilities exceed noncash current assets have negative noncash working capital. This is a thornier issue than negative changes in working capital. A firm that has negative working capital is, in a sense, using supplier credit as a source of capital, especially if the negative working capital becomes larger as the firm becomes larger. Several firms, especially in the technology business, have used this strategy to grow. While this may seem like a cost-efficient strategy, there are potential downsides. The first is that supplier credit is generally not really free. To the extent that delaying paying supplier bills may lead to the loss of cash discounts and other price breaks, firms are paying for the privilege. Thus, a firm that decides to adopt this strategy will have to compare the costs of this capital to more traditional forms of borrowing.

The second downside is that a negative noncash working capital has generally been viewed by both accountants and ratings agencies as a source of default risk. To the extent that a firm's rating drops and interest rates paid by the firm increase, there may be costs created for other capital by using supplier credit as a source. As a practical question, you still have an estimation problem on your hands when forecasting working capital requirements for a firm that has negative noncash working capital. As in the previous scenario, with negative changes in noncash working capital, there is no reason why firms cannot continue to use supplier credit as a source of capital in the short term. In the long term, however, we should not assume that noncash working capital will become more and more negative over time. At some point in the future, we have to assume either that the change in noncash working capital is zero, or that pressure will build for increases in working capital.

wcdata.xls: This dataset on the web summarizes noncash working capital needs by industry group in the United States for the most recent quarter.

Reinvestment: A Consolidated Variant

As you can see, the components that go into reinvestment can take many forms, from net capital expenditures (capturing investment in long-lived and mostly fixed assets), capitalized R&D (reflecting investments made in mostly intangible assets), acquisitions (measuring investments made in acquiring entire firms) and noncash working capital. Given that each of these items is volatile and that a company may substitute one (such as acquisitions) for another (net cap expenditure), especially as it gets bigger, we believe that it makes sense, at most firms, to estimate a consolidated value for all reinvestment, rather than individual line items.

$$\text{Reinvestment} = \text{Capital Expenditures} - \text{Depreciation \& Amortization}$$
$$+ \text{Change in noncash working capital} + \text{Acquisitions}$$
$$+ (\text{Current year's R\&D expense} - \text{R\&D amortization})$$

In effect, we are replacing the long-form measure of free cash flows (to the firm or equity) with a more concise version, as can be seen in Figure 10.3.

Note that in the last version in this figure, we have divided reinvestment by revenues to estimate a *reinvestment rate*, representing the percentage of after-tax earnings that are put back into the firm. The reinvestment rate will play a starring role in the next two chapters.

At first sight, estimating a consolidated reinvestment may seem less precise that forecasting individual line items, but the precision that one gets from estimating each of the reinvestment items separately is not only false precision, but also creates a greater potential for valuation errors. In fact, there are four benefits to estimating a consolidate reinvestment, rather than individual line items:

1. *Ease of estimation:* Estimating reinvestment as a consolidated number is easier to do than forecasting individual reinvestment components, since the consolidated value will be less volatile than the component values.

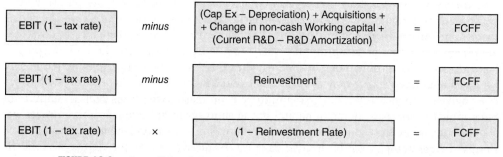

FIGURE 10.3 Consolidated Reinvestment and Free cash flow to firm (FCFF)

2. *Fewer inconsistencies:* Analysts who estimate individual line items are more likely to come up with numbers that violate basic consistency rules in valuation and sometime break accounting rules as well. Thus, estimating capital expenditure and depreciation as separate line items, basing the forecast of each on history, can result in depreciation becoming larger than depreciation not just in the near terms but in perpetuity. Ultimately, the reason we twinned capital expenditure and depreciation is because the latter comes from the former. In the same vein, as we noted when discussion working capital, negative working capital can result in noncash working can become a net plus for cash flows, and while by itself that may not be a problem, it can become one if that is your primary reinvestment line item, leading to free cash flows to the firm that run ahead of after-tax operating income in perpetuity.

3. *Easier to tie to valuation story and growth:* In the next chapter on growth, we will estimate sustainable growth rates by looking at how much firms reinvest, measured using consolidated reinvestment, and how well they reinvest. In Chapter 13, where we introduce valuation as a bridge between narrative and numbers, we will argue that it is easier to tie stories to consolidated reinvestment numbers than to reinvestment line items.

4. *Tie to invested capital:* A firm's reinvestment, in addition to representing cash set aside to deliver future growth, also has a much more prosaic effect. It becomes the change in invested capital at the firm. In fact, you can estimate the invested capital at a firm in future years, by taking the current invested capital and adding the cumulative value of all future reinvestment. That can be useful in tracking a company's return on capital (ROC) over time and linking back to its competitive advantages.

Ultimately, you may not buy into our consolidation pitch, but even if you do not, and insist on forecasting capital expenditures, acquisitions, working capital, and R&D separately, we would suggest creating a consolidate line item for all of your reinvestment that you can track over the time horizon of your valuation.

CONCLUSION

When valuing a firm, the cash flows that are discounted should be after taxes and reinvestment needs but before debt payments. This chapter considered some of the challenges in coming up with this number for firms.

The chapter began with the corrected and updated version of income described in Chapter 9. To state this income in after-tax terms, you need a tax rate. Firms generally state their effective tax rates in their financial statements, but these effective tax rates can be different from marginal tax rates. Although the effective tax rate can be used to arrive at the after-tax operating income in the early years, the tax rate used should converge on the marginal tax rate in future periods. For firms that are losing money and not paying taxes, the net operating losses that they are accumulating will protect some of their future income from taxation.

The reinvestment that firms make in their own operations is then considered in two parts. The first part is the net capital expenditure of the firm, which is the difference between capital expenditures (a cash outflow) and depreciation (effectively a cash inflow). In this net capital expenditure, we include the capitalized operating expenses (such as R&D) and acquisitions. The second part relates to investments in noncash working capital, mainly inventory and accounts receivable. Increases in noncash working capital represent cash outflows to the firm, while decreases represent cash inflows. Noncash working capital at most firms tends to be volatile and may need to be smoothed out when forecasting future cash flows. In the final part of the chapter, we argued for consolidating all of a company reinvestment into one consolidated value, and using that value as the basis for the growth and story telling that we will talk about in the next three chapters.

QUESTIONS AND SHORT PROBLEMS

In the problems following, use an equity risk premium of 5.5 percent if none is specified.

1. You are valuing GenFlex, a small manufacturing firm, which reported paying taxes of $12.5 million on taxable income of $50 million and reinvesting $15 million in the most recent year. The firm has no debt outstanding, the cost of capital is 11%, and the marginal tax rate for the firm is 35%. Assuming that the firm's earnings and reinvestment are expected to grow 10% a year for three years and 5% a year forever after that, estimate the value of this firm:
   - Using the effective tax rate to estimate after-tax operating income.
   - Using the marginal tax rate to estimate after-tax operating income.
   - Using the effective tax rate for the next three years and the marginal tax rate in year 4.

2. You are trying to estimate the free cash flow to the firm for RevTech, a technology firm. The firm reported $80 million in earnings before interest and taxes, capital expenditures of $30 million, and depreciation of $20 million in the most recent year. There are two additional complications:
   - The firm had R&D expenses of $50 million in the most recent year. You believe that a three-year amortizable life is appropriate for this firm, and the R&D expenses for the past three years have amounted to $20 million, $30 million, and $40 million, respectively.
   - The firm also made two acquisitions during the year—a cash-based acquisition for $45 million and a stock-based acquisition for $35 million.
   If the firm has no working capital requirements and a tax rate of 40%, estimate the free cash flow to the firm in the most recent year.

3. Lewis Clark, a firm in the travel business, reported earnings before interest and taxes of $60 million last year, but you have uncovered the following additional items of interest:
   - The firm had operating lease expenses of $50 million last year and has a commitment to make equivalent payments for the next eight years.
   - The firm reported capital expenditures of $30 million and depreciation of $50 million last year. However, the firm also made two acquisitions, one funded with cash for $50 million and another funded with a stock swap for $30 million. The amortization of these acquisitions is already included in the current year's depreciation.
   - The total working capital increased from $180 million at the start of the year to $200 million at the end of the year. However, the firm's cash balance was a

significant portion of this working capital and increased from $80 million at the start of the year to $120 million at the end. (The cash is invested in T-bills.)

▪ The tax rate is 40%, and the firm's pretax cost of debt is 6%.

Estimate the free cash flows to the firm last year.

4. The following is the balance sheet for Ford Motor Company as of December 31, 1994 (in millions).

Assets		Liabilities	
Cash	$ 19,927	Accounts payable	$ 11,635
Receivables	$132,904	Debt due within 1 year	$ 36,240
Inventory	$ 10,128	Other current liabilities	$ 2,721
Current assets	$ 91,524	Current liabilities	$ 50,596
Fixed assets	$ 45,586	Short-term debt	$ 36,200
		Long-term debt	$ 37,490
		Equity	$ 12,824
Total assets	$137,110	Total liabilities	$137,110

The firm had revenues of $154,951 million in 1994, and cost of goods sold of $103,817 million.

a. Estimate the net working capital.

b. Estimate the noncash working capital.

c. Estimate noncash working capital as a percentage of revenues.

5. Continuing problem 4, assume that you expect Ford's revenues to grow 10% a year for the next five years.

a. Estimate the expected changes in noncash working capital each year, assuming that noncash working capital as a percentage of revenues remains at 1994 levels.

b. Estimate the expected changes in noncash working capital each year, assuming that noncash working capital as a percent of revenues will converge on the industry average of 4.3% of revenues.

6. Newell Stores is a retail firm that reported $1 billion in revenues, $80 million in after-tax operating income, and noncash working capital of −$50 million last year.

a. Assuming that working capital as a percent of revenues remains unchanged next year and that there are no net capital expenditures, estimate the free cash flow to the firm if revenues are expected to grow 10%.

b. If you are projecting free cash flows to the firm for the next 10 years, would you make the same assumptions about working capital? Why or why not?

CHAPTER 11

Estimating Growth

The value of a firm is the present value of expected future cash flows generated by the firm. The most critical input in valuation, especially for high-growth firms, is the growth rate to use to forecast future revenues and earnings. This chapter considers how best to estimate these growth rates for firms, including those with low revenues and negative earnings.

There are four basic ways of estimating growth for any firm. One is to look at the growth in a firm's past earnings—its historical growth rate. While this can be a useful input when valuing stable firms, there are both dangers and limitations in using this growth rate for high-growth firms. The historical growth rate can often not be estimated, and even if it can, it cannot be relied on as an estimate of expected future growth.

The second is to trust the analysts who follow the firm to come up with the right estimate of growth for the firm, and to use that growth rate in valuation. Although many firms are widely followed by analysts, the quality of growth estimates, especially over longer periods, is poor. Relying on these growth estimates in a valuation can lead to erroneous and inconsistent estimates of value. An alternative source that many analysts and appraisers use for growth forecasts is the management of the firm, viewed as more informed about a company's competitive position, growth plans and market conditions than the rest of the market.

The third is to estimate the growth from a firm's fundamentals. A firm's growth ultimately is determined by how much is reinvested into new assets and the quality of these investments, with investments defined to include acquisitions, building distribution channels, or even expanding marketing capabilities. By estimating these inputs, you are, in a sense, estimating a firm's fundamental growth rate.

The fourth, and most general approach, is to estimate revenues in future years, and then, to forecast profit margins in future years, and tie up loose ends by evaluating the reinvestment needed to deliver the revenue growth.

THE IMPORTANCE OF GROWTH

A firm can be valuable because it owns assets that generate cash flows now, or because it is expected to acquire such assets in the future. The first group of assets is categorized as assets in place, and the second as growth assets. Figure 11.1 presents a financial balance sheet for a firm. Note that an accounting balance sheet can be very different from a financial balance sheet, because accounting for growth assets tends to be both conservative and inconsistent.

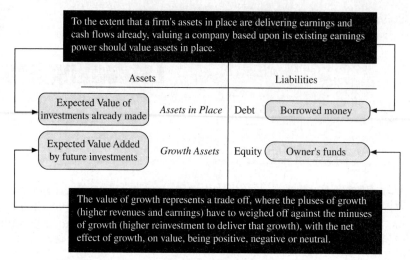

FIGURE 11.1   Growth and Value in a Financial Balance Sheet

For high-growth firms, accounting balance sheets do a poor job of summarizing the values of the assets of the firm because they mostly ignore the largest component of value, which is future growth. The problems are exacerbated for firms that invest in R&D, because the book value will not include the most important asset at these firms—the research asset.

HISTORICAL GROWTH

When estimating the expected growth for a firm, we generally begin by looking at the firm's history. How rapidly have the firm's operations, as measured by revenues or earnings, grown in the recent past? While past growth is not always a good indicator of future growth, it does convey information that can be valuable while making estimates for the future. This section begins by looking at measurement issues that arise when estimating past growth, and then considers how past growth can be used in projections.

Estimating Historical Growth

Given a firm's earnings history, estimating historical growth rates may seem like a simple exercise, but there are several measurement problems that may arise. In particular, you can get very different values for historical growth, depending on how the average is estimated and whether you allow for compounding in values over time. Estimating growth rates can also be complicated by the presence of negative earnings in the past or in the current period.

Arithmetic versus Geometric Averages   The average growth rate can vary, depending on whether it is an arithmetic average or a geometric average. The arithmetic average is the simple average of past growth rates, while the geometric mean takes into account the compounding that occurs from period to period. Thus, the arithmetic and geometric average growth rates for a firm with n years of history can be written as:

$$\text{Arithmetic average} = \frac{\displaystyle\sum_{t=-n}^{t=1} \text{Growth rate in year t}}{n}$$

$$\text{Geometric average} = \left(\frac{\text{Earnings in current year}}{\text{Earnings n years ago}}\right)^{(1/n)} - 1$$

The two estimates can be very different, especially for firms with volatile earnings. The geometric average is a much more accurate measure of true growth in past earnings, especially when year-to-year growth has been erratic.

In fact, the point about arithmetic and geometric growth rates also applies to revenues, though the difference between the two growth rates tends to be smaller for revenues than for earnings. For firms with volatile earnings and revenues, the caveats about using arithmetic growth carry even more weight.

ILLUSTRATION 11.1: Differences between Arithmetic and Geometric Averages: Amazon between 2013 and 2023

The following table reports the revenues, EBITDA, EBIT, and net income for Amazon for each year from 2018 to 2023. The arithmetic and geometric average growth rates in each series are reported at the bottom of the table.

Year	Revenues	% Change	EBITDA	% Change	EBIT	% Change	Net Income	% Change
2018	$232,887		$36,330		$14,541		$11,588	
2019	$280,522	20.45%	$48,079	32.34%	$22,899	57.48%	$21,331	84.08%
2020	$386,064	37.62%	$59,312	23.36%	$24,879	8.65%	$33,364	56.41%
2021	$469,822	21.70%	$55,269	−6.82%	$13,348	−46.35%	−$ 2,722	−108.16%
2022	$513,983	9.40%	$85,515	54.73%	$36,852	176.09%	$30,425	NA
2023	$574,785	11.83%	$96,609	12.97%	$47,385	28.58%	$37,684	23.86%
Arithmetic average		20.20%		23.32%		44.89%		14.05%
Geometric average		19.80%		21.60%		26.65%		26.60%
Standard deviation		11.10%		22.82%		82.58%		85.11%

The arithmetic average growth rate is higher than the geometric average growth rate for three of the four items, but the difference is much larger with operating income (EBIT) than it is with revenues and EBITDA. With net income, the arithmetic average is lower but only because Amazon had negative net income in 2021, making the growth rate in that number meaningless in 2022.[1] The differences between the arithmetic and

---

[1]When earnings go from a negative value to a positive one, the standard growth rate calculation yields the following:

$$\text{Growth rate in 2022} = [30{,}425 - (-2722)]/ -2722 = -1217.74\%$$

That number is nonsensical not only in terms of magnitude, but in terms of direction, yielding a negative growth rate for a year where Amazon's net income went from negative to positive.

geometric averages can be explaining by the volatility in growth rates in each of the variables, with the more volatile metrics showing a bigger disparity between the two values. Looking at the net and operating income in 2018 and 2023, it is also quite clear that the geometric averages are much better indicators of true growth.

Linear and Log-Linear Regression Models   The arithmetic mean weights percentage changes in earnings in each period equally and ignores compounding effects in earnings. The geometric mean considers compounding but focuses on the first and the last earnings observations in the series—it ignores the information in the intermediate observations and any trend in growth rates that may have developed over the period. These problems are at least partially overcome by using ordinary least squares (OLS)[2] regressions of earnings per share (EPS) against time. The linear version of this model is:

$$EPS_t = a + bt$$

where EPS_t = Earnings per share in period t

   t = Time period t

The slope coefficient on the time variable is a measure of earnings change per time period. The problem, however, with the linear model is that it specifies growth in terms of dollar EPS and is not appropriate for projecting future growth, given compounding.

The log-linear version of this model converts the coefficient into a percentage change:

$$\ln(EPS_t) = a + bt$$

where $\ln(EPS_t)$ = Natural logarithm of earnings per share in period t

   t = Time period t

The coefficient b on the time variable becomes a measure of the percentage change in earnings per unit time.

ILLUSTRATION 11.2:   Linear and Log-Linear Models of Growth: Amazon EBITDA from 2013 to 2023

The EBITDA from 2013 until 2023 are provided for Amazon (AMZN) in the following table with the percentage changes and the natural logs of the EBITDA computed each year:

Year	Time period (t)	EBITDA	% Change in EBITDA	ln(EBITDA)
2013	1	$4,365		8.3814
2014	2	$7,879	80.50%	8.9720
2015	3	$12,302	56.14%	9.4175

---

[2]An ordinary least squares (OLS) regression estimates regression coefficients by minimizing the squared differences of predicted values from actual values.

Year	Time period (t)	EBITDA	% Change in EBITDA	ln(EBITDA)
2016	4	$15,584	26.68%	9.6540
2017	5	$27,762	78.14%	10.2314
2018	6	$36,330	30.86%	10.5004
2019	7	$48,079	32.34%	10.7806
2020	8	$59,312	23.36%	10.9906
2021	9	$55,269	−6.82%	10.9200
2022	10	$85,515	54.73%	11.3564
2023	11	$96,609	12.97%	11.4784

There are several ways in which we can estimate the growth rate in EBITDA at Amazon between 2013 and 2023. One is to compute the arithmetic and geometric averages:

$$\text{Arithmetic average growth rate} = 38.89\%$$

$$\text{Geometric average growth rate} = (96{,}609/4{,}365)^{1/10} - 1 = 36.30\%$$

The second is to run a linear regression of EBITDA against a time variable (where the earliest year is given a value of 1, the next year a value of 2, and so on):

$$\text{Linear regression EBITDA} = -14{,}187 + 9{,}168\,t$$
$$(2.88^{**})\quad(12.61^{**})$$

This regression would indicate that the EBITDA increased $9,168 million a year from 2013 to 2023. We can convert it into a percent growth in earnings per share by dividing this change by the average EBITDA over the period:

$$\text{Growth rate in EBITDA} = \frac{\text{Coefficient from linear regression}}{\text{Average EBITDA}}$$

$$= \frac{9168}{44464} = 20.62\%$$

Finally, you can regress ln(EBITDA) against the time variable:

$$\text{Linear regression EBITDA} = 8.45 + 0.2978\,t$$
$$(55.72^{**})\quad(13.30^{**})$$

The coefficient on the time variable here can be viewed as a measure of compounded percent growth in EBITDA; Amazon's EBITDA grew at 29.78% a year based on this regression.

If you are wondering how you reconcile these very different estimates of growth, you cannot, and this should act as a cautionary note when you are looking historical growth rates from data services or analysts. Even though they use data from the past, these are not facts but estimates, and as such, biases will determine which variant of historical you get to see.

Negative Earnings   As you saw in the Amazon earnings example, measures of historical growth are distorted by the presence of negative earnings numbers. The percentage change in earnings on a year-by-year basis is defined as:

$$\% \text{ change in earnings in period } t = \frac{(\text{Earnings in period } t - \text{Earning in period } t - 1)}{\text{Earnings in period } t - 1}$$

If the earnings in the last period are negative, this calculation yields a meaningless number. This extends into the calculation of the geometric mean. If the earnings in the initial time period are negative or zero, the geometric average is not meaningful.

Similar problems arise in log-linear regressions since the earnings have to be greater than zero for the log transformation to exist. There are at least two ways of trying to get meaningful estimates of earnings growth for firms with negative earnings. One is to use the higher of the two numbers (EPS_t or EPS_{t-1}) in the denominator:

$$\% \text{ change in earnings in period } t = \frac{(\text{Earnings in period } t - \text{Earning in period } t - 1)}{\text{Max (Earnings in period } t, \text{ Earnings in period } t - 1)}$$

Alternatively, you could use the absolute value of EPS in the previous period. While both approaches will give you growth rates with the right sign on them, neither will give you growth rates that are useful in predicting future growth. It is correct, and, in fact, it may be appropriate to conclude that the historical growth rate is not meaningful when earnings are negative and to ignore it in predicting future growth.

ILLUSTRATION 11.3:   Negative Earnings: Tesla Motors and Aracruz Celulose

The problems with estimating earnings growth when earnings are negative can be seen even for firms that have only negative earnings. For instance, Tesla Motors reported operating earnings (EBIT) of –$52 million in 2009 and – $154 million in 2010. Clearly, the firm's earnings deteriorated, but estimating a standard earnings growth rate would lead us to the following growth rate:

Earnings growth for Tesla Motors in 2010 = [–154 – (–52)]/–52 = 1.9615 or 196.15%

Now consider Aracruz, a Brazilian paper and pulp company, susceptible like other firms in the industry to the ebbs and flows of commodity prices. The following table reports the earnings per share at the firm from 1995 to 2000.

Year	EPS in Brazilian Reals
1995	0.302
1996	0.041
1997	0.017
1998	–0.067
1999	0.065
2000	0.437

The negative net income (and earnings per share) numbers in 1998 make the estimation of a growth rate in 1999 problematic. For instance, the firm has a loss per share of 0.067 BR in 1998 and a profit per share of 0.065 BR in 1999. The growth rate in earnings per share estimated using the conventional equation would be:

Earnings growth rate in 1999 = [$0.065 − (−$0.067)]/(−$0.067) = −197%

This growth rate, a negative number, makes no sense given the improvement in earnings during the year. There are two fixes to this problem. One is to replace the actual earnings per share in the denominator with the absolute value:

Earnings growth rate in 1999$_{\text{absolute value}}$ = [$0.065 − (−$0.067)]/($0.067) = 192%

The other is to use the higher of the earnings per share from the two years, yielding:

Earnings growth rate in 1999$_{\text{higher value}}$ = [$0.065 − (−$0.067)]/($0.065) = 203%

While the growth rate is now positive, as you would expect it to be, the values for the growth rates themselves are not very useful for making estimates for the future.

Time Series Models to Predict Earnings per Share   Time series models use the same historical information as the simpler models described in the previous section. They attempt to extract better predictions from this data, however, using statistical techniques.

Box-Jenkins Models   Box and Jenkins (1976) developed a procedure for analyzing and forecasting univariate time series data using an autoregressive integrated moving average (ARIMA) model. ARIMA models model a value in a time series as a linear combination of past values and past errors (shocks). Since historical data is used, these models are appropriate if the data does not show a time trend or a dependence on outside events or variables. ARIMA models are usually denoted by the notation:

$$\text{ARIMA (p, d, q)}$$

where p = Degree of the autoregressive part
   d = Degree of differencing
   q = Degree of the moving average process

The mathematical model can then be written as follows:

$$w_t = \varphi_1 w_{t-1} + \varphi_2 w_{t-2} + \cdots + \varphi_p w_{t-p} + \theta_0 - \theta_1 a_{t-1} - \theta_2 a_{t-2} - \cdots - \theta_q a_{t-q} + \varepsilon_t$$

where w_t = Original data series or difference of degree d of the original data
$\varphi_1, \varphi_2 \cdots \varphi_p$ = Autoregressive parameters
   θ_0 = Constant term
$\theta_1, \theta_2, \cdots \theta_q$ = Moving average parameters
   ε_t = Independent disturbances, random error

ARIMA models can also adjust for seasonality in the data, in which case the model is denoted by the notation:

$$\text{SARIMA } (p, d, q) \times (p, d, q)_{s=n}$$

where   s = Seasonal parameter of length n

Time Series Models in Earnings   Most time series models used in forecasting earnings are built around quarterly earnings per share. In a survey paper, Bathke and Lorek (1984) point out that three time series models have been shown to be useful in forecasting quarterly earnings per share. All three models are seasonal autoregressive integrated moving average (SARIMA) models, since quarterly earnings per share have a strong seasonal component. The first model, developed by Foster (1977), allows for seasonality in earnings and is as follows:

$$\text{Model 1:} \text{SARIMA}(1, 0, 0) \times (0, 1, 0)_{s=4}$$

$$EPS_t = \varphi_t 1 EPS_{t-1} + EPS_{t-4} - \varphi 1 EPS_{t-5} + \theta_0 + \varepsilon_t$$

This model was extended by Griffin[3] and Watts[4] to allow for a moving average parameter:

$$\text{Model 2:} \text{SARIMA}(0, 1, 1) \times (0, 1, 1)_{s=4}$$

$$EPS_t = EPS_{t-1} + EPS_{t-4} - EPS_{t-5} - \theta_1 \varepsilon_{t-1} - \Theta \varepsilon_{t-4} - \Theta \theta_1 \varepsilon_{t-5} + \varepsilon_t$$

where θ_1 = First-order moving average [MA(1)] parameter

   Θ = First-order seasonal moving average parameter

   ε_t = Disturbance realization at the end of quarter t

The third time series model, developed by Brown and Rozeff (1979), is similar in its use of seasonal moving average parameter:

$$\text{Model 3:} \text{SARIMA}(1, 0, 0) \times (0, 1, 1)_{s=4}$$

$$EPS_t = \varphi_1 EPS_{t-1} + EPS_{t-4} - \varphi_1 EPS_{t-5} + \theta_0 - \Theta \varepsilon_{t-4}$$

How Good Are Time Series Models at Predicting Earnings?   Time series models do better than naive models (using past earnings) in predicting earnings per share in the next quarter. The forecast error (i.e., the difference between the actual earnings per share and forecasted

---

[3] Griffin, P.A., "The Time-Series Behavior of Quarterly Earnings: Preliminary Evidence," Journal of Accounting Research 15(Spring 1977): 71–83.
[4] Watts, R.L., "The Time-Series Behavior of Quarterly Earnings," Working Paper, University of Newcastle, 1975.

earnings per share) from the time series models is, on average, smaller than the forecast error from naive models (such as simple averages of past growth). The superiority of the models over naive estimates declines with longer-term forecasts, suggesting that the estimated time series parameters are not stationary.

Among the time series models themselves, there is no evidence that any one model is dominant, in terms of minimizing forecast error, for every firm in the sample. The gain from using the firm-specific best models, rather than using the same model for every firm is relatively small.

Limitations in Using Time Series Models in Valuation   There are several concerns in using time series models for forecasting earnings in valuation. First, time series models require a lot of data, which is why most of them are built around quarterly earnings per share. In most valuations, the focus is on predicting annual earnings per share and not on quarterly earnings. Second, even with quarterly earnings per share, the number of observations is limited for most firms to 10–15 years of data (40–60 quarters of data), leading to large estimation errors[5] in time series model parameters and in the forecasts. Third, the superiority of earnings forecasts from time series models declines as the forecasting period is extended. Given that earnings forecasts in valuation must be made for several years rather than a few quarters, the value of time series models may be limited. Finally, studies indicate that analyst forecasts dominate even the best time series models in forecasting earnings.

In conclusion, time series models are likely to work best for firms that have a long history of earnings and where the parameters of the models have not shifted significantly over time. For the most part, however, the cost of using these models is likely to exceed their benefits, at least in the context of valuation.

Usefulness of Historical Growth

Is the growth rate in the past a good indicator of growth in the future? Not necessarily. In this section, we consider how good historical growth is as a predictor of future growth for all firms, and why the changing size and volatile businesses of many firms can undercut growth projections.

Higgledy-Piggledy Growth   Past growth rates are useful in forecasting future growth, but they have considerable noise associated with them. In a study of the relationship between past growth rates and future growth rates, Little (1960) coined the term "higgledy-piggledy growth" because he found little evidence that firms that grew fast in one period continued to grow fast in the next period. In the process of running a series of correlations between growth rates in consecutive periods of different length, he frequently found negative correlations between growth rates in the two periods, and the average correlation across the two periods was close to zero (0.02).

If past growth is not a reliable indicator of future growth at many firms, it becomes even less so at smaller firms. The growth rates at smaller firms tend to be more volatile than growth rates at other firms in the market. We computed the correlation between

---

[5]Time series models generally can be run as long as there are at least 30 observations, but the estimation error declines as the number of observations increases.

growth rates in earnings in consecutive time periods (five-year, three-year, and one-year) for firms in the United States, across the board. In 2023, for instance, none of these correlations in net income were strong enough to pass statistical significance tests. This would suggest that you should be more cautious about using past growth, especially in earnings, for forecasting future growth at these firms.

In general, revenue growth tends to be slightly more persistent and predictable than earnings growth. This is because accounting choices have a far smaller effect on revenues than they do on earnings. In Figure 11.2, we look at the persistence of growth in four metrics—revenues, EBITDA, EBIT, and taxable income—for U.S. companies from 1997 to 2021[6]:

Note that with every metric, there is a steep drop-off in earnings growth persistence after the first year, though the drop-off is slightly less steep with revenues than with earnings numbers. The implication is that historical growth is not very useful in forecasting future growth over longer time periods, and that revenue growth is a more useful predictor that earnings growth.

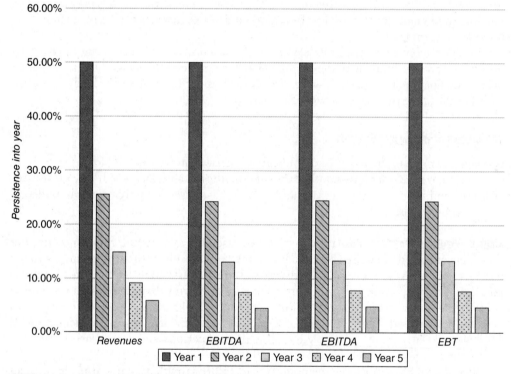

FIGURE 11.2   Growth Persistence in Operating Metrics
Source: Swedroe, L., 2022. Valuations and Earnings Growth Rates, TEBI.

---

[6] Swedroe, L., 2022, Valuations and Earnings Growth Rates, TEBI.

Effects of Firm Size   Since the growth rate is stated in percentage terms, the role of the size of the firm must be weighed in the analysis. It is easier for a firm with $10 million in earnings to generate a 50-percent growth rate than it is for a firm with $500 million in earnings. Since it becomes harder for firms to sustain high growth rates as they become larger, past growth rates for firms that have grown dramatically in size may be difficult to sustain in the future. While this is a problem for all firms, it is a particular problem when analyzing small and growing firms. While the fundamentals at these firms, in terms of management, products, and underlying markets, may not have changed, it will still be difficult to maintain historical growth rates as the firms double or triple in size.

The true test for a small firm lies in how well it handles growth. Some firms continue to deliver their products and services efficiently as they grow. In other words, they can scale up successfully. Other firms have had much more difficulty replicating their success as they become larger. In analyzing small firms, therefore, it is important that you look at plans to increase growth, but it is even more critical that you examine the systems in place to handle this growth.

ILLUSTRATION 11.4:   Cisco: Earnings Growth and Size of the Firm—The Glory Days (1990–2000) and Follow-Up (2001–2011)

Cisco's evolution from a firm with $70 million in revenues and net income of about $14 million in 1990, to revenues in excess of $18 billion and net income of about $2.7 billion in 2000, is reported in the following table:

Year	Revenues	% Change	EBIT	% Change	Net Income	% Change
1990	$70		$21		$14	
1991	$183	162.53%	$66	209.42%	$43	210.62%
1992	$340	85.40%	$129	95.48%	$84	95.39%
1993	$649	91.10%	$264	103.71%	$172	103.77%
1994	$1,334	105.60%	$500	89.77%	$323	87.83%
1995	$2,233	67.31%	$794	58.69%	$456	41.34%
1996	$4,096	83.46%	$1,401	76.49%	$913	100.08%
1997	$6,452	57.52%	$2,137	52.56%	$1,051	15.07%
1998	$8,489	31.57%	$2,664	24.66%	$1,331	26.64%
1999	$12,173	43.40%	$3,344	25.53%	$2,023	51.99%
2000	$18,928	55.49%	$4,608	37.80%	$2,668	31.88%
Arithmetic average		78.34%		77.41%		76.46%
Geometric average		75.12%		71.13%		69.16%

While this table presents the results of a phenomenally successful decade for Cisco, it does suggest that you should be cautious about assuming that the firm will continue to grow at a similar rate in the future for two reasons. First, the growth rates tapered off as the firm became larger toward the end of the 1990s. Second, if you assume that Cisco will maintain its historic growth of 1990–2000 (estimated using the geometric average) for the following five years, the revenue and earnings will be immense. If operating income continued to grow at 71.13% from 2000 to 2005, Cisco's operating income would have been almost $68 billion in 2005. Third, Cisco's growth came primarily from acquiring small firms with promising technologies and using its capabilities to commercially develop these technologies. In 1999, for instance, Cisco acquired 15 firms, and these acquisitions accounted for almost 80% of its reinvestment that year. If you assume that Cisco will continue to grow at historical rates, you are assuming that the number of acquisitions will also grow at the same rate. Thus, Cisco would have to acquire almost 80 firms five years later to maintain the growth rate it had between 1990 and 2000.

The difficulties of scaling up growth are clear when we look at Cisco between 2001 and 2011. While Cisco's game plan did not change—it continued to acquire companies and push for higher growth—the aggregate revenues and earnings were not responsive to the company's efforts.

Year	Revenues		EBIT		Net Income	
2001	$22,293		$2,270		−$1,014	
2002	$18,915	−15.15%	$3,236	42.56%	$1,893	−286.69%
2003	$18,878	−0.20%	$4,886	50.99%	$3,578	89.01%
2004	$22,045	16.78%	$6,295	28.84%	$4,401	23.00%
2005	$24,801	12.50%	$7,442	18.22%	$5,741	30.45%
2006	$28,484	14.85%	$7,156	−3.84%	$5,580	−2.80%
2007	$34,922	22.60%	$8,702	21.60%	$7,333	31.42%
2008	$39,540	13.22%	$9,478	8.92%	$8,052	9.80%
2009	$36,117	−8.66%	$7,385	−22.08%	$6,134	−23.82%
2010	$40,040	10.86%	$9,310	26.07%	$7,767	26.62%
2011	$43,218	7.94%	$8,801	−5.47%	$6,490	−16.44%
Arithmetic average		7.47%		16.58%		−11.94%
Geometric average		6.84%		14.51%		NA

The compounded annual growth rate in revenues at Cisco declined to 6.84% between 2001 and 2011, and the compounded annual growth rate in operating income at Cisco between 2001 and 2011 was 14.51%, both steep drop-offs from the growth rate in the prior decade.

 histgr.xls: **This dataset on the web summarizes historical growth rates in earnings and revenues by industry group for the United States.**

HISTORICAL GROWTH AT HIGH-GROWTH AND YOUNGER FIRMS

The presence of negative earnings, volatile growth rates over time, and the rapid changes that high-growth firms go through over time make historical growth rates unreliable indicators of future growth for these firms. Notwithstanding this, you can still find ways to incorporate information from historical growth into estimates of future growth, if you follow these general guidelines:

- Focus on revenue growth, rather than earnings growth, to get a measure of both the pace of growth and the momentum that can be carried forward into future years. Revenue growth is less volatile than earnings growth and is much less likely to be swayed by accounting adjustments and choices.

- Rather than looking at average growth over the past few years, look at growth each year. This can provide information on how the growth is changing as the firm becomes larger and can help when making projections for the future.

- Use historical growth rates as the basis for projections only in the near future (next year or two), since technologies can change rapidly and undercut future estimates.
- Consider historical growth in the overall market and in other firms that are serving it. This information can be useful in deciding what the growth rates of the firm that you are valuing will converge on over time.

OUTSOURCING GROWTH

It may surprise you to hear that many appraisers and investors, when valuing companies, do not estimate growth rates, but instead outsource that growth estimate to others, presumably more informed than they are about the company. With investors, the outsourcing is often to equity research analysts who follow the company, with the reasoning being that these analysts know far more than they do about the company and the business. With appraisers, the outsourcing is to the management of the company that has invited them in for the appraisal, with the rationale that these managers have access to information about new products, marketing plans, and reinvestment that outsiders would never possess.

While we understand the impulse, we believe that if you outsource your forecasts of growth and reinvestment to others, it is difficult to argue that you have truly valued the company. In addition, there is reason to believe that analysts and managers, while more informed than investors and appraisers, also are far more likely to be biased. In fact, the evidence that we will present in this section, especially on analysts, is that their forecasts add very little to what you could have gleaned from public data, and any added information is more relevant for the short term than the long term.

It is worth also noting that one reason for outsourcing growth is that it lets appraisers and investors off the hook on accountability, allowing them to claim that their valuation errors are the fault of others.

Analyst Estimates of Growth

Equity research analysts provide not only recommendations on the firms they follow but also estimates of earnings and earnings growth for the future. How useful are these estimates of expected growth from analysts, and how, if at all, can they be used in valuing firms? This section considers the process that analysts follow to estimate expected growth, and then follows up by examining why such growth rates may not be appropriate when valuing some firms.

Who Do Analysts Follow? The number of analysts tracking firms varies widely across firms. At one extreme are firms like Apple and Microsoft that are followed by dozens of analysts. At the other extreme, there are hundreds of firms that are not followed by any analysts.

Why are some firms more heavily followed than others? These seem to be some of the determinants:

■ *Market capitalization.* The larger the market capitalization of a firm, the more likely it is to be followed by analysts.

■ *Institutional holding.* The greater the percent of a firm's stock that is held by institutions, the more likely it is to be followed by analysts. The open question, though, is whether analysts follow institutions or whether institutions follow analysts. Given that institutional investors are the biggest clients of equity research analysts, the causality probably runs both ways.

■ *Trading volume.* Analysts are more likely to follow liquid stocks. Here again, though, it is worth noting that the presence of analysts and buy (or sell) recommendations on a stock may play a role in increasing trading volume.

Information in Analyst Forecasts   There are reasons to believe that analyst forecasts of growth should be better than using historical growth rates in earnings. Analysts, in addition to using historical data, can avail themselves of five other types of information that may be useful in predicting future growth:

1. *Firm-specific information that has been made public since the last earnings report.* Analysts can use information that has come out about the firm since the last earnings report, to make predictions about future growth. This information can sometimes lead to significant reevaluation of the firm's expected cash flows.

2. *Macroeconomic information that may impact future growth.* The expected growth rates of all firms are affected by economic news on GNP growth, interest rates, and inflation. Analysts can update their projections of future growth as new information comes out about the overall economy and about changes in fiscal and monetary policy. Information, for instance, that shows the economy growing at a faster rate than forecast will result in analysts increasing their estimates of expected growth for cyclical firms.

3. *Information revealed by competitors on future prospects.* Analysts can also condition their growth estimates for a firm on information revealed by competitors on pricing policy and future growth. For instance, a negative earnings report by one telecommunications firm can lead to a reassessment of earnings for other telecommunications firms in the same market.

4. *Private information about the firm.* Analysts sometimes have access to private information about the firms they follow that may be relevant in forecasting future growth. This avoids answering the delicate question of when private information becomes illegal inside information. There is no doubt, however, that good private information can lead to significantly better estimates of future growth. To restrict this type of information leakage, the SEC issued new regulations preventing firms from selectively revealing information to a few analysts or investors. Outside the United States, however, there are markets where firms routinely convey private information to analysts following them.

5. *Public information other than earnings.* Models for forecasting earnings that depend entirely on past earnings data may ignore other publicly available information that is useful in forecasting future earnings. It has been shown, for instance, that other financial variables, such as earnings retention, profit margins, and asset turnover, are useful in predicting future growth. Analysts can incorporate information from these variables into their forecasts.

Quality of Earnings Forecasts   If firms are followed by many analysts[7] and these analysts are indeed better informed than the rest of the market, the forecasts of growth that emerge from analysts should be better than estimates based on either historical growth or other publicly available information. But is this presumption justified? Are analyst forecasts of growth superior to other forecasts?

The consensus from studies that have looked at short-term forecasts (one quarter ahead to four quarters ahead) of earnings is that analysts provide better forecasts of earnings than models that depend purely on historical data. The mean relative absolute error, which measures the absolute difference between the actual earnings and the forecast for the next quarter, in percentage terms, is smaller for analyst forecasts than it is for forecasts based on historical data. Two other studies shed further light on the value of analysts' forecasts. Crichfield, Dyckman, and Lakonishok (1978) examined the relative accuracy of forecasts in the "Earnings Forecaster," a publication from Standard & Poor's that summarizes forecasts of earnings from more than 50 investment firms. They measured the squared forecast errors by month of the year and computed the ratio of analyst forecast error to the forecast error from time series models of earnings. They found that the time series models actually outperform analyst forecasts from April until August but underperform them from September through January. They hypothesized that this is because there is more firm-specific information available to analysts during the latter part of the year. The other study, by O'Brien (1988), compared consensus analyst forecasts from the Institutions Brokers Estimate System (I/B/E/S) with time series forecasts from one quarter ahead to four quarters ahead. The analyst forecasts that outperformed the time series model for one-quarter-ahead and two-quarters-ahead forecasts, did as well as the time series model for three-quarters-ahead forecasts, and did worse than the time series model for four-quarters-ahead forecasts. Thus, the advantage gained by analysts from firm-specific information seems to deteriorate as the time horizon for forecasting is extended.

In valuation, the focus is more on long-term growth rates in earnings than on next quarter's earnings. There is little evidence to suggest that analysts provide superior forecasts of earnings when the forecasts are over three or five years. An early study by Cragg and Malkiel (1968) that compared long-term forecasts by five investment management firms in 1962 and 1963 with actual growth over the following three years, concluded that analysts were poor long-term forecasters. This view is contested by Vander Weide and Carleton (1988), who found that the consensus prediction of five-year growth in the I/B/E/S is superior to historically oriented growth measures in predicting future growth. There is an intuitive basis for arguing that analyst predictions of growth rates must be better than time series or other historical data–based models simply because they use more information. The evidence indicates, however, that this superiority in forecasting is surprisingly small for long-term forecasts, and that past growth rates play a significant role in determining analyst forecasts.

There is one final consideration. Analysts generally forecast earnings per share, and most services report these estimates. When valuing a firm, you need forecasts of revenues or operating income, and the growth in earnings per share will usually not be equal to the

---

[7] Sell-side analysts work for brokerage houses and investment banks, and their research is offered to clients of these firms as a service. In contrast, buy-side analysts work for institutional investors, and their research is generally proprietary.

growth in operating income. In general, the growth rate in operating income should be lower than the growth rate in earnings per share. Thus, even if you decide to use analyst forecasts, you will have to adjust them if you are trying to forecast growth rates in operating income or revenues.

How Do You Use Analyst Forecasts in Estimating Future Growth? The information in the growth rates estimated by other analysts can and should be incorporated into the estimation of expected future growth. There are four factors that determine the weight assigned to analyst forecasts in predicting future growth:

1. *Amount of recent firm-specific information.* Analyst forecasts have an advantage over historical data–based models because they incorporate more recent information about the firm and its future prospects. This advantage is likely to be greater for firms where there have been significant changes in management or business conditions in the recent past, for example, a restructuring or a shift in government policy relating to the firm's underlying business.
2. *Number of analysts following the stock.* Generally, the larger the number of analysts following a stock, the more informative is their consensus forecast, and the greater should be the weight assigned to it in analysis. The informational gain from having more analysts is diminished somewhat by the well-established fact that most analysts do not act independently, resulting in a high correlation across analysts' revisions of expected earnings.
3. *Extent of disagreement between analysts.* While consensus earnings growth rates are useful in valuation, the extent of disagreement between analysts measured by the standard deviation in growth predictions is also a useful measure of the reliability of the consensus forecasts. Givoly and Lakonsihok (1984) found that the dispersion of earnings is correlated with other measures of risk such as beta and is a good predictor of expected returns.
4. *Quality of analysts following the stock.* This is the hardest of the variables to quantify. One measure of quality is the size of the forecast error made by analysts following a stock, relative to models that use only historical data—the smaller this relative error, the larger the weight that should be attached to analyst forecasts. Another measure is the effect on stock prices of analyst revisions—the more informative the forecasts, the greater the effect on stock prices. There are some who argue that the focus on consensus forecasts misses the point that some analysts are better than others in predicting earnings, and that their forecasts should be isolated from the rest and weighted more.

Analyst forecasts may be useful in coming up with a predicted growth rate for a firm, but there is a danger to blindly following consensus forecasts. Analysts often make significant errors in forecasting earnings, partly because they depend on the same data sources (which might have been erroneous or misleading), and partly because they sometimes overlook significant shifts in the fundamental characteristics of the firm. The secret to successful valuation often lies in discovering inconsistencies between analysts' forecasts of growth and a firm's fundamentals. The next section examines this relationship in more detail.

Management Forecasts

In many valuations, especially for smaller and privately owned businesses, the primary source for expected growth and cash flows is the management of the firm. There are logical reasons for this trust. First, management has access to information that neither analysts nor investors have about market conditions and the company's operations, which should give them a leg up in making forecasts for the future. Second, to the extent that growth is determined by how much investment a company will make and when, management should have be able to do better than outsiders in making these judgments.

That said, management forecasts are also likely to be biased, and especially so at poorly managed companies, where expectations of a turnaround are always overstated. There are relatively few studies of management forecasts of growth, but their findings are similar to those related to analysts. A study by Hutton, Lee, and Shu finds that analysts tend to do better than management in forecasting the effects of macroeconomic forces (interest rates, economy) on a company's earnings, but that managers are better at forecasting company-level data.[8] Both groups, though, tend to do better at short-term forecasts (next year or two), and their advantage rapidly dissipates with longer-term forecasts.

In recent years, management at publicly traded firms has also become more aggressive and active in providing guidance, at least for near-term revenues and earnings. Here again, the potential for bias remains, as management often is driven by the desire to control expectations, and it is unclear that there is much benefit in an intrinsic valuation from following that guidance.

FUNDAMENTAL DETERMINANTS OF GROWTH

With both historical and analyst estimates, growth is an exogenous variable that affects value but is divorced from the operating details of the firm. The soundest way of incorporating growth into value is to make it endogenous (i.e., tie it in more closely to the actions that a business takes to create and sustain that growth). This section begins by considering the relationship between fundamentals and growth in equity income, and then moves on to look at the determinants of growth in operating income.

Growth in Equity Earnings

When estimating cash flows to equity, we usually begin with estimates of net income, if we are valuing equity in the aggregate, or earnings per share, if we are valuing equity per share. This section begins by presenting the fundamentals that determine expected growth in earnings per share, and then moves on to consider a more expanded version of the model that looks at growth in net income.

---

[8] Hutton, A.P., L.F. Lee and S.Z. Shu, 2012, Do Managers Always Know Better? The Relative Accuracy of Management and Analyst Forecasts", Journal of Accounting Research, v50, 1217–1244.

Growth in Earnings per Share   The simplest relationship determining growth is one based on the retention ratio (percentage of earnings retained in the firm) and the return on equity on its projects. Firms that have higher retention ratios and earn higher returns on equity should have much higher growth rates in earnings per share than firms that do not share these characteristics. To establish this, note that:

$$g_t = \left(NI_t - NI_{t-1}\right)/NI_{t-1}$$

where g_t = Growth rate in net income
          NI_t = Net income in year t

Also note that the ROE in period t can be written as NI in period t divided by the Book value of equity in period t−1. Given the definition of return on equity, the net income in year t−1 can be written as:

$$NI_{t-1} = \text{Book value of equity}_{t-2} \times ROE_{t-1}$$

where ROE_{t-1} = Return on equity in year t

The net income in year t can be written as:

$$NI_t = \left(\text{Book value of equity}_{t-2} + \text{Retained earnings}_{t-1}\right) \times ROE_t$$

Assuming that the return on equity is unchanged (i.e., $ROE_t = ROE_{t-1} = ROE$):

$$g_t = \text{Retained earnings}_{t-1}/NI_{t-1} \times ROE$$
$$= \text{Retention ratio} \times ROE$$
$$= b \times ROE$$

where b is the retention ratio. Note that the firm is not being allowed to raise equity by issuing new shares. Consequently, the growth rate in net income and the growth rate in earnings per share are the same in this formulation.

ILLUSTRATION 11.5:   Growth in Earnings per Share

This illustration considers the expected growth rate in earnings based on the retention ratio and return on equity for three firms—Consolidated Edison, a regulated utility that provides power to New York City and its environs; Procter & Gamble, a leading brand-name consumer product firm; and Intel, the technology giant— in 2010. The following table summarizes the returns on equity, retention ratios, and expected growth rates in earnings for the three firms in 2010:

	Return on Equity	Retention Ratio	Expected Growth Rate
Consolidated Edison	9.79%	36.00%	3.52%
Procter & Gamble	18.22%	50.26%	9.16%
Intel	32.00%	70.00%	22.40%

Intel has the highest expected growth rate in earnings per share, assuming that it can maintain its current return on equity and retention ratio. Procter & Gamble can also be expected to post a healthy growth rate, notwithstanding the fact that it pays out more than 50% of its earnings as dividends because of its high return on equity. Con Ed, on the other hand, has a very low expected growth rate because its return on equity and retention ratio are anemic.

Growth in Net Income   If we relax the assumption that the only source of equity is retained earnings, the growth in net income can be different from the growth in earnings per share. Intuitively, note that a firm can grow net income significantly by issuing new equity to fund new projects, while earnings per share stagnates. To derive the relationship between net income growth and fundamentals, we need a measure of investment that goes beyond retained earnings. One way to obtain such a measure is to estimate how much equity the firm reinvests back into its businesses in the form of net capital expenditures and investments in working capital.

$$\text{Equity reinvested in business} = \text{Capital expenditures} - \text{Depreciation}$$
$$+ \text{Change in working capital}$$
$$- (\text{New debt issued} - \text{Debt repaid})$$

Dividing this number by the net income gives us a much broader measure of the equity reinvestment rate:

$$\text{Equity reinvestment rate} = \text{Equity reinvestment/Net income}$$

Unlike the retention ratio, this number can be well in excess of 100 percent with the excess being funded with new equity. The expected growth in net income can then be written as:

$$\text{Expected growth in net income} = \text{Equity reinvestment rate} \times \text{Return on equity}$$

Another advantage of using this more flexible version of growth in equity earnings is that you can separate net income from operating assets, from net income generated from cash and non-operating holdings, and estimate the growth just in the former. In making that distinction, you will have to adjust your definition of net income, cleansing it of non-operating income:

$$\text{Noncash net income} = \text{Net income} - \text{Interest income from cash}(1 - \text{tax rate})$$

$$\text{Noncash ROE} = \frac{\text{Noncash Net Income}}{\text{Book value of equity} - \text{Cash \& Marketable Securities}}$$

$$\text{Equity reinvestment rate} = \frac{\text{Equity reinvestment}}{\text{Noncash Net Income}}$$

In most firms, this cleaning up with reduced net income increase return on equity and equity reinvestment rates and increase the expected growth in net income from operating assets.

ILLUSTRATION 11.6:   Growth in Net Income

To estimate growth in net income based on fundamentals, we look at three firms—Coca-Cola, Nestlé, and Sony. The following table estimates the components of equity reinvestment and uses it to estimate the reinvestment rate for each of the firms. We also present the return on equity and the expected growth rate in net income at each of these firms in 2010:

	Net income	Net cap expenditure	Δ Working Capital	Net Debt Issued (Repaid)	Equity Reinvestment Rate	ROE	Expected growth rate in net income
Coca-Cola	$11,809 m	$3,006 m	$335 m	$1,848 m	12.64%	46.59%	5.89%
Nestlé	SFr 34,233 m	SFr 1,394 m	SFr 828 m	SFr 292 m	5.64%	63.83%	3.60%
Sony	JY 126.33 b	JY −33 b	JY −15 b	JY −14b	−26.91%	3.30%	−0.89%

The pluses and minuses of this approach are visible in the table. The approach much more accurately captures the true reinvestment in the firm by focusing not on what was retained but on what was reinvested. The limitation of the approach is that the ingredients that go into the reinvestment—capital expenditures, working capital change, and net debt issued—are all volatile numbers. Note that Sony had more depreciation than capital expenditures in 2010, a decrease in working capital, and paid off debt during the year. The net reinvestment rate is negative. If it continues on this path, it will have negative growth. In fact, it would probably be much more realistic to look at the average reinvestment rate over three or five years, rather than just the current year. We will return to examine this question in more depth when we look at growth in operating income.

Determinants of Return on Equity   Both earnings per share and net income growth are affected by the return on equity of a firm. The return on equity is affected by how much debt the firm chooses to use to fund its projects. In the broadest terms, increasing debt will lead to a higher return on equity if the after-tax return on capital exceeds the after-tax interest rate paid on debt. This is captured in the following formulation of return on equity:

$$ROE = ROIC + D/E[ROIC - i(1 - t)]$$

where $ROC = EBIT(1 - t)/(BV \text{ of debt} + BV \text{ of equity} - Cash)$

$D/E = BV \text{ of debt}/BV \text{ of equity (Book D/E ratio)}$

$i = \text{Interest expense on debt}/BV \text{ of debt (Book interest rate)}$

$t = \text{Tax rate on ordinary income}$

In keeping with the fact that return on equity is based on book value, all the inputs are also stated in terms of book value. The derivation is simple and is provided in a footnote.[9] Using this expanded version of ROE, the growth rate can be written as:

$$g = b(ROIC + D/E[ROC - i(1 - t)])$$

---

[9]$ROC + D/E[ROC - i(1 - t)] = [NI + Int(1 - t)]/(D + E) + D/E\{[NI + Int(1 - t)]/(D + E)$
$\qquad -Int(1 - t)/D\}$
$\qquad = \{[NI + Int(1 - t)]/(D + E)\}(1 + D/E) - Int(1 - t)/E$
$\qquad NI/E + Int(1 - t)/E - Int(1 - t)/E = NI/E = ROE$

The advantage of this formulation is that it allows users to model changes in leverage and evaluate the effects on growth. Intuitively, it allows for the fact that if the after-tax cost of borrowing is lower than what a firm can earn as a return on an investment, borrowing money will increase the return on equity.

ILLUSTRATION 11.7: Breaking Down Return on Equity

To consider the components of return on equity, the following table looks at Consolidated Edison, Procter & Gamble, and Intel, three firms whose returns on equity were shown in Illustration 11.5:

	ROIC	Book D/E	Book Interest Rate	Tax Rate	ROE
Consolidated Edison	6.66%	103.41%	5.75%	35.33%	9.70%
Procter & Gamble	12.19%	58.33%	2.56%	27.25%	18.22%
Intel	27.89%	5.32%	5.49%	28.55%	29.16%

Comparing these numbers to those reported in Illustration 11.5, you will note that the return on equity is very close to our earlier estimates for Con Ed and P&G. The return on equity computed here is lower than the earlier estimate for Intel because it posted significant nonoperating profits in its net income. We have chosen to consider only operating income in the return on capital computation. To the extent that firms routinely report nonoperating income (or losses), the return on equity computed using the standard approach (net income divided by book equity) will be different from the return on equity computed here.

While this is not a serious concern for any of the three firms examined, we should be concerned if a high ROE is caused by a high D/E ratio, a low effective tax rate, or nonoperating profits. That ROE may not be sustainable. If the firm loses its tax breaks and its sources of nonoperating income dry up, the firm could very easily find itself with a return on capital that is lower than its book interest rate. If this occurs, leverage could bring down the return on equity of the firm.

AVERAGE AND MARGINAL RETURNS

The return on equity is conventionally measured by dividing the net income in the most recent year by the book value of equity at the end of the previous year. Consequently, the return on equity measures the quality of both older projects that have been on the books for a substantial period and new projects from more recent periods. Since older investments represent a significant portion of the earnings, the average returns may not shift substantially for larger firms that are facing a decline in returns on new investments, because either of market saturation or competition. In other words, poor returns on new projects will have a lagging effect on the overall returns for the firm. In valuation, it is the returns that firms are making on their newer investments that convey the most information about a quality of a firm's projects. To measure these returns, we could compute a marginal return on equity by

(continued)

(*continued*)

dividing the change in net income in the most recent year by the change in book value of equity in the prior year:

$$\text{Marginal return on equity} = \frac{\Delta \text{ Net Income}_t}{\Delta \text{ Book value of equity}_{t-1}}$$

For example, Disney reported net income of $3.963 million on book value of equity of $35,425 million in 2010, resulting in an aggregate return on equity of 11.87 percent:

$$\text{Aggregate return on equity} = 1,963/35,425 = 11.87\%$$

The marginal return on equity is computed as follows:

$$\text{Change in net income from 2009 to 2010} = 3,963 - 3,307$$
$$= \$656 \text{ million}$$
$$\text{Change in book value of equity from 2009 to 2010} = 35,425 - 33,667$$
$$= \$1,758 \text{ million}$$
$$\text{Marginal return on equity} = 656/1,758 = 37.32\%$$

While we are not suggesting that Disney generated 37.32 percent on its new investments in 2010, it does show the momentum is upward in Disney's return on equity. Thus, a forward-looking estimate greater than 11.87 percent would be merited.

The Effects of Changing Return on Equity So far, this section has operated on the assumption that the overall return on equity remains unchanged over time. If we relax this assumption, we introduce a new component to growth—the effect of changing return on equity on existing investments over time. Consider, for instance, a firm that has a book value of equity of $100 million and a return on equity of 10 percent. If this firm improves its return on equity to 11 percent, it will post an earnings growth rate of 10 percent even if it does not reinvest any money. This additional growth can be written as a function of the change in the return on equity:

$$\text{Addition to expected growth rate} = \frac{(ROE_t - ROE_{t-1})}{ROE_{t-1}}$$

where ROE_t is the return on equity in period t. This will be in addition to the fundamental growth rate computed as the product of the return on equity and the retention ratio.

While increasing return on equity will generate a spurt in the growth rate in the period of the improvement, a decline in the return on equity will create a more than proportional drop in the growth rate in the period of the decline.

It is worth differentiating at this point between returns on equity on new investments and returns on equity on existing investments. The additional growth that we are estimating here comes not from new investments but by changing the return on existing investments. For lack of a better term, you could consider it "efficiency-generated growth."

ILLUSTRATION 11.8:   Effects of Changing Return on Equity: Con Ed

In Illustration 11.5, we looked at Con Ed's expected growth rate based on its return on equity of 9.79% and its retention ratio of 36%. Assume that the firm will be able to improve its overall return on equity (on both new and existing investments) to 11% next year and that the retention ratio remains at 36%. The expected growth rate in earnings per share next year can then be written as:

$$\text{Expected growth rate in EPS} = ROE_t \times \text{Retention ratio} + (ROE_t - ROE_{t-1})/ROE_{t-1}$$

$$= .11 \times .36 + \frac{.11 - .0979}{.0979}$$

$$= .1632 \text{ or } 16.32\%$$

After next year, the growth rate will subside to a more sustainable 3.96% (.11 × .36).

How would the answer be different if the improvement in return on equity were only on new investments but not on existing assets? The expected growth rate in earnings per share can then be written as:

$$\text{Expected growth rate in EPS} = ROE_t \times \text{Retention ratio} = .11 \times .36 = .0396$$

Thus, there is no additional growth created in this case. What if the improvement had been only on existing assets and not on new investments? Then, the expected growth rate in earnings per share next year can be written as:

$$\text{Expected growth rate in EPS} = ROE_t \times \text{Retention ratio} + (ROE_t - ROE_{t-1})/ROE_{t-1}$$

$$= .0979 \times .36 + \frac{.11 - .0979}{.0979}$$

$$= .1588 \text{ or } 15.88\%$$

Growth in Operating Income

Just as equity income growth is determined by the equity reinvested back into the business and the return made on that equity investment, you can relate growth in operating income to total reinvestment made into the firm and the return earned on capital invested.

We will consider three separate scenarios, and examine how to estimate growth in each in this section. The first is when a firm is earning a high return on capital that it expects to sustain over time. The second is when a firm is earning a positive return on capital that is expected to increase over time. The third is the most general scenario, where a firm expects operating margins to change over time, sometimes from negative values to positive levels.

Stable Return on Capital Scenario   When a firm has a stable return on capital, its expected growth in operating income is a product of the reinvestment rate (i.e., the proportion of the after-tax operating income that is invested in net capital expenditures and noncash working capital), and the quality of these reinvestments, measured as the return on the capital invested.

$$\text{Expected growth}_{\text{EBIT}} = \text{Reinvestment rate} \times \text{Return on invested capital}$$

where

$$\text{Reinvestment rate} = \frac{(\text{Cap Ex} - \text{Depreciation} + \text{Change in noncash working capital})}{\text{EBIT} (1 - t)}$$

$$\text{Return on invested capital} = \frac{\text{EBIT} (1 - t)}{(\text{Book value of equity} + \text{Book value of debt} - \text{Cash})}$$

Both measures—the reinvestment rate and return on capital—should be forward looking, and the return on invested capital should represent the expected return on capital on future investments. In the rest of this section, we consider how best to estimate the reinvestment rate and the return on capital.

Reinvestment Rate   The reinvestment rate measures how much a firm is plowing back to generate future growth. The reinvestment rate is often measured using the most recent financial statements for the firm. Although this is a good place to start, it is not necessarily the best estimate of the future reinvestment rate. A firm's reinvestment rate can ebb and flow, especially in firms that invest in relatively few large projects or acquisitions. For these firms, looking at an average reinvestment rate over time may be a better measure of the future. In addition, as firms grow and mature, their reinvestment needs (and rates) tend to decrease. For firms that have expanded significantly over the last few years, the historical reinvestment rate is likely to be higher than the expected future reinvestment rate. For these firms, industry averages for reinvestment rates may provide a better indication of the future than using numbers from the past. Finally, it is important that we continue treating R&D expenses and operating lease expenses consistently. The R&D expenses, in particular, need to be categorized as part of capital expenditures for the purpose of measuring the reinvestment rate.

Return on Capital   The return on capital is often based on the firm's return on capital on existing investments, where the book value of capital is assumed to measure the capital invested in these investments. Implicitly, we assume that the current accounting return on capital is a good measure of the true returns earned on existing investments, and that this return is a good proxy for returns that will be made on future investments. This assumption, of course, is open to question for the following reasons:

- The book value of capital might not be a good measure of the capital invested in existing investments, since it reflects the historical cost of these assets and accounting decisions on depreciation. When the book value understates the capital invested, the return on capital will be overstated; when book value overstates the capital invested, the return on capital will be understated. This problem is exacerbated if the book value of capital is not adjusted to reflect the value of the research asset or the capital value of operating leases.

■ The operating income, like the book value of capital, is an accounting measure of the earnings made by a firm during a period. All the problems in using unadjusted operating income described in Chapter 9 continue to apply.

■ Even if the operating income and book value of capital are measured correctly, the return on capital on existing investments may not be equal to the marginal return on capital that the firm expects to make on new investments, especially as you go further into the future.

Our concerns about return on invested capital are captured in Figure 11.3 below:

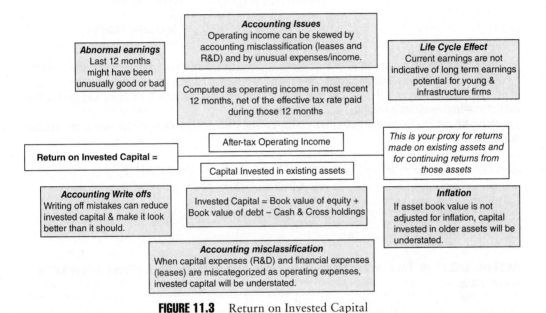

FIGURE 11.3   Return on Invested Capital

Given these concerns, we should consider not only a firm's current return on capital, but any trends in this return as well as the industry average return on capital. If the current return on capital for a firm is significantly higher than the industry average, the forecasted return on capital should be set lower than the current return to reflect the erosion that is likely to occur as competition responds.

Finally, any firm that earns a return on capital greater than its cost of capital is earning an excess return. The excess returns are the result of a firm's competitive advantages or barriers to entry into the industry. High excess returns locked in for very long periods imply that this firm has a permanent competitive advantage.

ILLUSTRATION 11.9:   Measuring the Reinvestment Rate, Return on Capital, and Expected Growth Rate: Tata Motors in 2010

In May 2010, we looked at Tata Motors, an Indian automobile company which has been aggressive in its pursuit of growth through both internal investments and acquisitions over much of the past decade. Based upon its financial statements of 2009, we estimated a reinvestment rate of 116.83% and a return on capital of 11.81%:

$$\text{Reinvestment rate}_{\text{Tata Motors}} = \frac{(\text{Cap Ex} - \text{Depreciation} + \text{Change in noncash Working Capital})}{\text{EBIT} (1 - t)}$$

$$= \frac{(₹40,291 - 25072 + 957)}{₹17,527 (1 - .21)} = 116.83\%$$

$$\text{Return on Invested Capital}_{\text{Tata Motors}} = \frac{\text{EBIT} (1 - t)}{(\text{BV of Equity} + \text{BV of Debt} - \text{Cash})}$$

$$= \frac{₹17,527 (1 - .21)}{(₹78,935 + 62,805 - 23,973)} = 11.81\%$$

Note that the effective tax rate (21%) was used to compute the after-tax operating income for both the reinvestment rate and the return on capital. The capital invested was obtained by summing up the book value of debt and equity at the end of the 2008 fiscal year (the beginning of the 2009 fiscal year), and then netting out the cash and marketable securities at that point in time.

If Tata Motors can maintain this return on capital and reinvestment rate going forward, its expected growth rate would be:

$$\text{Expected growth rate} = \text{Reinvestment rate} \times \text{Return on invested capital}$$
$$= 116.83\% \times 11.81\% = 13.80\%$$

As we will see in the next illustration, maintaining this reinvestment going forward may be very difficult to do.

ILLUSTRATION 11.10:   Current and Historical Averages: Reinvestment Rate and Return on Capital for Tata Motors

Tata Motors has had a volatile history in terms of both reinvestment and returns on capital. Although the 2009 numbers were computed in the preceding illustration, those values have been in flux over the past five years. We summarize the numbers (in millions of rupees) for 2005 to 2009, with the aggregate in the last column:

	2005	2006	2007	2008	2009	Aggregate
EBIT (1–t)	₹12,197	₹12,322	₹25,203	₹15,160	₹13,846	₹ 78,728
Capital Expenditures	₹ 8,175	₹11,235	₹24,612	₹44,113	₹40,291	₹120,251
Depreciation	₹ 5,377	₹ 6,274	₹ 6,850	₹ 7,826	₹25,072	₹ 46,022
Change in WC	₹ 4,410	₹23,191	₹ 4,520	–₹37,137	₹ 957	–₹ 8,469
Reinvestment	₹ 7,208	₹28,152	₹22,282	–₹ 850	₹16,176	₹ 65,760
Reinvestment Rate	59.10%	228.46%	88.41%	–5.61%	116.83%	83.53%

The reinvestment rate has swung between – 5.61% and 228.46% over the period, but the aggregate reinvestment rate over the period was 83.53%.

We did a similar computation with the return on capital between 2005 and 2009.

	2005	2006	2007	2008	2009	Aggregate
EBIT (1–t)	₹12,197	₹12,322	₹ 25,203	₹ 15,160	₹ 13,846	₹ 78,728
BV of debt (start)	₹33,621	₹27,142	₹ 63,293	₹ 97,479	₹ 62,805	₹284,340
BV of equity (start)	₹37,019	₹44,602	₹ 63,054	₹ 79,717	₹ 78,395	₹302,787
Cash holdings	₹ 5,546	₹20,209	₹ 4,838	₹ 6,998	₹ 23,973	₹ 61,564
Invested Capital	₹65,094	₹51,535	₹121,509	₹170,198	₹117,227	₹525,563
ROIC	18.74%	23.91%	20.74%	8.91%	11.81%	14.98%

The average return on capital between 2005 and 2009 was 14.98%.

Using these averages for the reinvestment rate and return on capital generates a growth rate of 12.51%:

$$\text{Expected growth rate} = \text{Reinvestment rate} \times \text{Return on capital}$$
$$= 83.53\% \times 14.98\% = 12.51\%$$

This does seem like a more sustainable value for the future, if the firm can maintain what it has delivered over the five-year period.

 fundgrEB.xls: **This dataset on the web summarizes reinvestment rates and return on capital by industry group in the United States for the most recent quarter.**

NEGATIVE REINVESTMENT RATES: CAUSES AND CONSEQUENCES

The reinvestment rate for a firm can be negative if its depreciation exceeds its capital expenditures, or if the working capital declines substantially during the year. For most firms, this negative reinvestment rate will be a temporary phenomenon reflecting lumpy capital expenditures or volatile working capital. For these firms, the current year's reinvestment rate (which is negative) can be replaced with an average reinvestment rate over the past few years, or an industry average reinvestment rate. For other firms, the negative reinvestment rate may reflect our failure to incorporate acquisitions into capital expenditures (if the firm grows through acquisitions) or to capitalize R&D (or like expenses). For some firms, though, the negative reinvestment rate may be deliberate, and how we deal with it will depend on why the firm is embarking on this path:

- Firms that have overinvested in capital equipment or working capital in the past may be able to live off past investment for a number of years, reinvesting little and generating higher cash flows for that period. If this is the case, we should use the negative reinvestment rate in forecasts and estimate growth based on improvements in return on capital. Once the firm has reached the point where it is efficiently using its resources, though, we should change the reinvestment rate to reflect expected growth.

(continued)

> (*continued*)
>
> - The more extreme scenario is a firm that has decided to shrink over time, by not replacing assets as they become rundown and by drawing down working capital. In this case, the expected growth should be estimated using the negative reinvestment rate. Not surprisingly, this will lead to a negative expected growth rate and declining earnings over time.

Positive and Changing Return on Capital Scenario   The analysis in the preceding section is based on the assumption that the return on capital remains stable over time. If the return on capital changes over time, the expected growth rate for the firm will have a second component, which will increase the growth rate if the return on capital increases and decrease the growth rate if the return on capital decreases.

$$\text{Expected growth rate} = \text{ROC}_t \times \text{Reinvestment rate} + (\text{ROC}_t - \text{ROC}_{t-1})/\text{ROC}_t$$

For example, a firm that sees its return on capital improve from 10 to 11 percent, while maintaining a reinvestment rate of 40 percent will have an expected growth rate of:

$$\text{Expected growth rate} = .11 \times .40 + \frac{(.11 - .10)}{.10} = 14.40\%$$

In effect, the improvement in the return on capital increases the earnings on existing assets and this improvement translates into an additional growth of 10 percent for the firm.

Marginal and Average Returns on Capital   So far, we have looked at the return on capital as the measure that determines return. In reality, however, there are two measures of returns on capital. One is the return earned by the firm collectively on all of its investments, which we define as the average return on capital. The other is the return earned by a firm on just the new investments it makes in a year, which is the marginal return on capital.

Changes in the marginal return on capital do not create a second-order effect, and the expected growth is a product of the marginal return on capital and the reinvestment rate. Changes in the average return on capital, however, will result in the additional impact on growth chronicled earlier.

Candidates for Changing Average Return on Capital   What types of firms are likely to see their return on capital change over time? One category includes firms with poor returns on capital that improve their operating efficiency and margins, and consequently their return on capital. In these firms, the expected growth rate will be much higher than the product of the reinvestment rate and the return on capital. In fact, since the return on capital on these firms is usually low before the turnaround, small changes in the return on capital translate into big changes in the growth rate. Thus, an increase in the return on capital on existing assets from 1 percent to 2 percent doubles the earnings (resulting in a growth rate of 100 percent).

Another category includes firms that have very high returns on capital on their existing investments but are likely to see these returns slip as competition enters the business, not only on new investments but also on existing investments.

ILLUSTRATION 11.11: **Estimating Expected Growth with Changing Return on Capital: Titan Cement and Motorola**

In 2000, Titan Cement, a Greek cement company, reported operating income of 55,467 million drachmas on capital invested of 135,376 million drachmas. Using its effective tax rate of 24.5%, we estimate a return on capital for the firm of 30.94%:

$$\text{Return on invested capital} = 55,467(1 - .245)/135,376 = 30.94\%$$

Assume that the firm will see its return on capital drop on both its existing assets and its new investments to 29% next year and that its reinvestment rate will stay at 35%. The expected growth rate next year can be estimated as follows:

$$\text{Expected growth rate} = .29 \times .35 + (.29 - .3094)/.3094 = 3.88\%$$

In contrast, consider Motorola in early 2000. The firm had a reinvestment rate of 52.99% and a return on capital of 12.18% in 1999. Assume that Motorola's return on capital will increase toward the industry average of 22.27% as the firm sheds the residue of its ill-fated Iridium investment and returns to its roots. Specifically, assume that Motorola's return on capital will increase from 12.18% to 17.22% over the following five years.[10] For simplicity, also assume that the change occurs linearly over the next five years. The expected growth rate in operating income each year for the next five years can then be estimated as follows:[11]

$$
\begin{aligned}
\text{Expected growth rate} &= \text{ROC}_{\text{marginal}} \times \text{Reinvestment rate}_{\text{current}} \\
&\quad + \left\{ [1 + (\text{ROC}_{\text{in 5 years}} - \text{ROC}_{\text{current}})/\text{ROC}_{\text{current}}]^{1/5} - 1 \right\} \\
&= .1722 \times .5299 + \left\{ [1 + (.1722 - .1218)/.1218]^{1/5} - 1 \right\} \\
&= .1630 \text{ or } 16.30\%
\end{aligned}
$$

The improvement in return on capital over the next five years will result in a higher growth rate in operating earnings at Motorola over that period. Note that this calculation assumes that the return on capital on new investments next year will be 17.22%. As you can see, this calculation is not only messy but makes assumptions about return improvement over time that may or may not reflect reality. For firms where returns on capital and margins are changing over time, we will develop a more general approach in the next section, for estimating future growth and cash flows.

 chgrowth.xls: This spreadsheet allows you to estimate the expected growth rate in operating income for a firm where the return on capital is expected to change over time.

---

[10] Note that 17.22% is halfway between the current return on capital and the industry average (22.27 percent).

[11] You are allowing for a compounded growth rate over time. Thus, if earnings are expected to grow 25 percent over three years, you estimate the expected growth rate each year to be: Expected growth rate each year = $(1.25)^{1/3} - 1$.

TOP-DOWN GROWTH: FROM REVENUE GROWTH TO FREE CASH FLOWS

The third and most general approach to estimating growth is for firms that are expected to see profit margins changing over time, either from negative to positive, for young firms that are scaling up and building business models, or from high margins to lower margins, for more mature firms facing increased competition. To estimate growth in these firms, we have to move up the income statement and first project growth in revenues. Next, we use the firm's expected operating margin in future years to estimate the operating income in those years. If the expected margin in future years is positive, the expected operating income will also turn positive, allowing us to apply traditional valuation approaches in valuing these firms. We also estimate how much the firm has to reinvest to generate revenue growth by linking revenues to the capital invested in the firm.

Revenue Growth

Many high-growth firms, while reporting losses, also show large increases in revenues from period to period. The first step in forecasting cash flows is forecasting revenues in future years, usually by forecasting a growth rate in revenues each period. In making these estimates, there are three points to keep in mind:

- *Scaling up:* The rate of growth in revenues will decrease as the firm's revenues increase. Thus, a tenfold increase in revenues is entirely feasible for a firm with revenues of ₹2 million but unlikely for a firm with revenues of ₹2 billion.
- *Compounding effects:* Compounded growth rates in revenues over time can seem low, but appearances are deceptive. A compounded annual growth rate in revenues of 20 percent over ten years will increase revenues about sixfold, but an increase of 40 percent over 10 years will result in an almost thirty-fold increase in revenues over the period.
- *Revenue levels:* While growth rates in revenues may be the mechanism that you use to forecast future revenues, you do have to keep track of the dollar revenues to ensure that they are reasonable, given the size of the overall market in which the firm operates. If the projected revenues for a firm 10 years out would give it a 90- or 100-percent share (or greater) of the overall market in a competitive marketplace, you clearly should reassess the revenue growth rate.

With these general propositions in mind, we will look at estimating revenues in future years by focusing on two key drivers—the total market that the company is attempting to reach with its products and services, and the share of that market it expects to gain over time.

Total Market   The expected growth in revenues for a firm is clearly a function of the size of the market that it is targeting, with larger and growing markets allowing for higher growth with other things remining equal. Thus, Indian and Chinese companies start at an advantage over companies in Peru or Slovenia, simply because their target markets are much larger. By the same token, an apparel company that goes after the mass market has the potential to grow at a higher rate and for longer, than an apparel company that caters to a niche group. That said, the higher revenue growth that comes from being in a large market may be more than offset by the lower margins that may characterize these markets.

In the last two decades, companies, especially in their nascent stages, have discovered the higher pricing that is reflected in seeking out larger markets. Venture capitalists and companies going public often tout the sizes of their total addressable markets (TAM), reflecting the total revenues in the market that these companies operate, as well as service-able addressable markets (SAM) measuring the portion of that market that can be reached with the company's existing business models. By sometimes using outlandishly large numbers for these markets, they hope to convince investors to attach higher values (or pricing) to their companies.

In a well-grounded intrinsic valuation, the total addressable market should reflect what is plausible, rather than dreams and hopes, and we will come back to examine how to test for this in Chapter 13.

Market Share Being in a big market does provide an assist when it comes to forecasting growth, but to the extent that there are competitors also drawn by the size of the market to target it, the market shares of companies operating in the market can become splintered. Thus, to estimate potential revenue growth, you often have to attempt to forecast the share of the market that a company will be able to capture, given in business model. That will require looking at the following:

a. *Industry economics:* There are some industries where there can be only a few winners, either because economies of scale give the largest players a significant advantage over smaller competitors, or because of strong network effects where the company's size and reach become factors that draw new customers to them. There are other industries that will splinter into much smaller players, often because local knowledge can translate into connections and lower costs. One of the consequences of the entry of technology in many traditional businesses has been the replacement of splintered models with winner-take-all versions; advertising was a splintered, localized business until online advertising entered, leaving Facebook and Google with dominant market shares.

b. *Competitive advantages:* In assessing market share, you must consider how your company measures up against its competitors, and what competitive advantages it does (or does not) bring to the battle. A company with strong competitive advantages, arising from lower costs, stronger brand names, or patent protection, is well positioned to gain market share at the expense of competitors who do not possess these advantages.

c. *Legal considerations:* The market shares that companies can aspire to gain are also constrained by legal restrictions. Many markets, including the United States, have anti trust laws that can be brought to bear on a company, if its market share is viewed as dominant.

Summing Up Estimating total market size and expected market share is easier in some businesses and for some companies than others. With the aircraft business, for instance, it is easy to assess the size of the market, since aircraft orders from airlines are visible, and the companies operating in the space (e.g., Airbus, Boeing, Bombardier, Embraer) are, for the most part public, disclosing revenues and order backlogs. It is also relatively simple to assess market share since the business for large aircraft is a duopoly, with Airbus and

Revenue Growth and Magnitude

Market Size and Growth	X	Market Share
1. *Current Market size*: The size of the market for the company's products & services, given geography it is targeting and product type. 2. *Expected Growth in Market*: Growth in total market, as technology and market conditions change.		1. *Company's current market share*: If company's current market share is low, potential for growth in market share at expense of competition. 2. *Industry economics*: Nature of the business (a few big winners or splintered competition). 3. *Strength of company's competitive advantages*: Stronger and more sustainable competitive advantages should allow for higher market share.

The potential for revenue growth is greater for companies with small revenues (and market share) in a big and growing market, especially if the company has strong competitive advantages in winner-take-all businesses.

FIGURE 11.4   Estimating Revenue Growth

Boeing being the large player, and the barriers to new entrants are daunting. In contrast, when valuing Uber for the first time in 2014, we faced multiple challenges, with the market, at the time, was dominated by small taxicab companies and little public disclosure, and ridesharing representing a new untested way of delivering car service with the potential to attract new users into the business. That said, the fact that you cannot estimate values precisely is not a reason to walk away from the process, since everyone valuing a ride-sharing company in 2014 would have faced similar challenges.

Figure 11.4 provides a summary of the key factors to consider when estimating a total market and market share for a company, and we will come back in the next few chapters to provide examples.

ILLUSTRATION 11.12:   Estimating Total Market and Market Share: Airbnb IPO in 2020

This illustration considers Airbnb, a company that upended the hotel business by creating a platform for home and apartment owners to list their dwellings for short-term rentals, while collecting a share of the rental revenue. After a period of intense growth, Airbnb, like other hospitality companies, was slowed down by the pandemic in 2020, but was less affected than its competitors, primarily hotels with significant fixed costs. In November 2020, the company filed for its initial public offering, and in the following table, we list the estimates for revenues in the next ten years.

We estimate the gross bookings on Airbnb's platform grew 40% in 2021, as the COVID shut down eased, and that the annual growth rate will be 25% in the next four years; that growth rate will scale down to 2% by year 10. Airbnb's revenues come from the share of these gross bookings that it claims, and we expect that percentage to increase from 12.65% in the most recent twelve months to 14% over the next decade, because of market power and economies of scale.

	Growth Rate	Gross Bookings (in $ millions)	Airbnb Share (%)	Revenues (in millions)
LTM		$ 26,492		$ 3,626
1	40.00%	$ 37,089	12.65%	$ 4,692
2	25.00%	$ 46,361	12.92%	$ 5,990
3	25.00%	$ 57,951	13.06%	$ 7,565
4	25.00%	$ 72,439	13.19%	$ 9,555
5	25.00%	$ 90,548	13.33%	$12,066
6	20.40%	$109,020	13.46%	$14,674
7	15.80%	$126,245	13.60%	$17,163
8	11.20%	$140,385	13.73%	$19,275
9	6.60%	$149,650	13.87%	$20,749
10	2.00%	$152,643	14.00%	$21,370
Terminal year	2.00%	$155,696	14.00%	$21,797

In estimating gross bookings, the driver of Airbnb's revenues we drew on two sources. The first was the collective revenues of all hotel companies globally, which amounted to $700 billion in 2019, the year prior to the pandemic. The second was the revenues of the two largest travel intermediaries in the space–Booking.com and Expedia. In our forecasts, we make Airbnb larger than both of those competitors, because of its wider reach, and estimate an overall market share of a total hospitality market of $1.2 trillion in ten years.

In assessing the Airbnb share of gross bookings, we are assuming that as the largest player in this space, it has significant networking benefits, since both renters and homeowners will want to be where most of the listings are, and that as a consequence it will be able to set the terms for listings. At the time of its IPO, Airbnb had just listed a new pricing model, where they would collect 14% of the rental price from the homeowner, and we assume that we will converge on that value over time.

Operating Margins and Taxes

Before considering how to estimate the operating margins, let us begin with an assessment of where many high-growth firms, early in their life cycle, stand when the valuation begins. They usually have low revenues and negative operating margins. If revenue growth converts low revenues into high revenues and operating margins stay negative, these firms not only will be worth nothing but are unlikely to survive. For firms to be valuable, the higher revenues eventually must deliver positive earnings. In a valuation model, this translates into positive operating margins in the future. A key input in valuing a high-growth firm then is the operating margin you would expect it to have as it matures.

Unit Economics　　Given a choice on whether you would like to earn high or low profit margins, every company would pick the former, but in most cases, your margins are constrained by what you do as a business. A manufacturing company, in general, will have lower margins than a service business, and a service business will find itself lagging software companies, and the differences tell us very little about management quality. The dominant factor determining whether a company, in a steady state, can earn high or low profit margins is unit economics, i.e., how much a company has to spend in producing that extra unit that it sells or the extra customer that it services. That is why Microsoft, which spends almost nothing on that extra unit of Windows, Office, or Office 365 that it sells can have operating margins of 40% or higher, whereas BYD and Tesla, electric car companies that have to manufacture a car before selling it, will struggle to earn operating margins that exceed 15%.

The simplest measure of unit economics is gross margins, where you net out the cost of goods sold from the revenues to get to gross profit, and scale that value to revenues:

$$\text{Gross margin} = \text{Gross profits/Revenues}$$

Just to provide a contrast, U.S. software companies had gross margins of 71.52%, in 2024, whereas auto and truck companies had gross margins of 12.45%, in the same year.

Economies of Scale As companies get larger, they will generate economies of scale, a catch-all term referring to the possibility that costs will grow at a slower rate than revenues. In general, companies with significant economies of scale will see margins improve strongly as they get bigger, whereas companies without those economies of scale will not see that improvement.

While every company uses the economies of scale mantra to explain why their margins should improve over time, the test is in the numbers. Uber, through much of its first decade of existence, from 2009 to 2019, found its costs increasing at the same rate or higher than its revenues, making their claims of economies of scale less credible. In a similar vein, Netflix has struggled through much of its existence with its biggest cost item, content costs, increasing at the same rate as subscriber count and revenues.

Business Model While gross margins will vary across businesses because of unit economics, your business model choice can also affect operating margins, with the trade-off being with growth. This contrast is most visible in the retail space, where operating margins vary widely, with discount retailers struggling to generate operating margins that exceed 5% (which is where Costco and Walmart reside) to luxury retailers who can command margins that are 15% or higher. Before you conclude that the latter have better business models than the former, it is worth remembering that discount retailers also report much higher revenues per store, and that having higher margins is of little consequences if you sell very little.

When forecasting margins for a company that has a choice to make between a higher revenues/low margin and a low revenues/high margin model, it is important that you not only identify which model better fits, but also that you stay consistent. Allowing a company to earn sky-high margins in a competitive business, while also increasing its market share, is inconsistent, for instance, and will result in an overvaluation.

Summing Up In assessing what a company can generate as an operating margin, you can start by looking at its history, and for companies like Walmart and Boeing, the historical margins can be precursors to what the company can generate in the future. If you have a younger company, one perhaps that has lost money over its lifetime, your task will become more difficult, and you will have to begin by looking at industry averages. While the margin for the business in which a firm operates provides a target value, you will still have to consider how the margin for the company that you are analyzing will improve from current levels to the target values. Generally, the improvements in margins will be greatest in the earlier years (at least in percentage terms), and then taper off as the firm moves to

Operating Margin: Target and Pathway

Target Operating Margin	Pathway to Profitability
1. Unit Economics: Profits on extra unit sold (Gross Margins), as percent of price, with higher profitability going with higher operating margin. *2. Economies of scale*: Costs growth relative to revenue growth, with greater economies of scale allowing for higher margins. *3. Competition*: Pricing behavior among competitiors, with more aggressive pricing leading to lower margins.	*1. Company's current operating margin*: The lower a company's current margin, relative to the target, the steeper the path to profitability. *2. Profitability versus Growth trade off*: Companies that put growth ahead of profitability will wait longer before getting to target margin. *3. Business model*: The more well formed a business model, the speedier the pathway to the target margin.

While all companies would like higher margins in steady state, the level of these margins will be determined by the sector in which a firm operates and its choice of business model, and the speed with which you move towards those target margins will be determined by a company's ambitions and business model choices.

FIGURE 11.5   Estimating Operating Margins

maturity. As with revenue growth, we can summarize the key determinants of operating margins in Figure 11.5.

 margins.xls: **This dataset on the web summarizes operating and net margins, by industry, for the United States.**

ILLUSTRATION 11.13:   Estimating Operating Margins for Airbnb (IPO in 2020)

To estimate the operating margins for Airbnb for its initial public offering in 2019, we looked at the operating margins for hotels, first using the aggregated values (summing up the operating income and revenues across all hotel companies), and then the median:

Aggregate operating margin for hotels = 11.24%

Median operating margin for hotels in 2019 = 14.16%

Since hotels have a very different cost structure than intermediaries, we looked at the operating margins for the two largest publicly traded travel intermediary companies in 2019:

	Expedia	*Booking.com*
Gross Bookings ($ millions)	$ 107,870.00	$ 96,400.00
Revenues ($ millions)	$ 12,067.00	$ 15,066.00
Operating Income ($ millions)	$ 961.00	$ 5,345.00
Revenues/Gross Bookings	11.19%	15.63%
Operating Margin	7.96%	35.48%

With Airbnb, we chose a target operating margin of 25%, higher than the hotel business but lower than Booking.com, reflecting our ambitious revenue growth targets. The resulting numbers are in the following table (with dollar values in millions):

	Revenues (in millions)	Operating margin	Operating income (in millions)	Tax rate	EBIT(1–t)
Base year	$ 3,626	−22.56%	−$ 818	0.00%	−$ 818
1	$ 4,692	−10.00%	−$ 469	0.00%	−$ 469
2	$ 5,990	− 3.00%	−$ 180	0.00%	−$ 180
3	$ 7,565	0.50%	$ 38	0.00%	$ 38
4	$ 9,555	4.00%	$ 382	0.00%	$ 382
5	$12,066	7.50%	$ 905	14.05%	$ 778
6	$14,674	5.98%	$ 877	25.00%	$ 658
7	$17,163	10.73%	$1,842	25.00%	$1,382
8	$19,275	15.49%	$2,985	25.00%	$2,239
9	$20,749	20.24%	$4,200	25.00%	$3,150
10	$21,370	25.00%	$5,343	25.00%	$4,007
Term year	$21,797	25.00%	$5,449	25.00%	$4,087

The margins improve over time, turning from negative to positive in year 3, and then lifting operating income as they move towards 25%. Along the way, we also track taxes dues, with no taxes due in the first two years as the company is expected to lose money, but with the net operating loss carryforward sheltering the income earned in year 3 and 4 entirely, and in year 5, partially, from taxes.[12]

MARKET SIZE, MARKET SHARE, AND REVENUE GROWTH

Estimating revenue growth rates for a young firm in a new business may seem like an exercise in futility. While it is difficult to do, there are ways in which you can make the process tractable.

One way is to work backward by first considering the share of the overall market that you expect your firm to have once it matures, and then determining the growth rate you would need to arrive at this market share. For instance, assume that you are analyzing an online toy retailer with $100 million in revenue currently. Assume also that the entire toy retail market had revenues of $70 billion last year. Assuming a 3 percent growth rate in overall toy market over the next 10 years and a market share of 5 percent for your firm in year 10, you would arrive at expected revenues of $4.703 billion for the firm in 10 years, and a compounded revenue growth rate of 46.98%.

$$\text{Expected revenues in 10 years} = \$70\,\text{billion} \times 1.03^{10} \times .05 = \$4.703\,\text{billion}$$
$$\text{Expected CAGR for next 10 years} = (4{,}703/100)^{1/10} - 1$$
$$= .4698 \text{ or } 46.98\%$$

---

[12] The net operating loss leading into the valuation was $167.6 million, with subsequent losses increasing it to $816.5 million, at the end of year 2.

Another approach is to forecast the expected growth rate in revenues over the next three to five years based on past growth rates. Once you estimate revenues in year 3 or 5, you can then forecast a growth rate based on the rate at which companies with similar revenues grow currently. For instance, assume that the online toy retailer had revenue growth of 200 percent last year (revenues went from $33 million to $100 million). You could forecast growth rates of 120 percent, 100 percent, 80 percent, and 60 percent for the next four years, leading to revenues of $1.267 billion in four years. You could then look at the average growth rate posted by retail firms with revenues between $1 billion and $1.5 billion last year, and use that as the growth rate commencing in year 5.

Reinvestment

High revenue growth is a desirable objective, especially when accompanied by positive operating margins in future years. Firms do, however, have to invest to generate both revenue growth and positive operating margins in future years. This investment can take traditional forms (plant and equipment), but it should also include acquisitions of other firms, partnerships, investments in distribution and marketing capabilities, and research and development.

The Sales-to-Capital Ratio
To link revenue growth with reinvestment needs, we look at the revenue generated by each dollar of capital that we invest.

$$\text{Sales to Capital} = \text{Sales/Invested Capital}$$

where invested capital is measured with the same inputs and caveats as when computing return on invested capital. This ratio, called the sales-to-capital ratio, allows us to estimate how much additional investment the firm must make to generate the projected revenue growth. This investment can be in internal projects as well as acquisitions, and our earlier arguments for capitalizing R&D and R&D-like investments and leases still hold.

To estimate the reinvestment needs in any year then, you divide the revenue growth that you have projected (in dollar terms) by the sales-to-capital ratio.

$$\text{Reinvestment}_t = \frac{\text{Revenues in year t} - \text{Revenues in year t} - 1}{\text{Sales-to-Invested-Capital Ratio}}$$

Thus, if you expect revenues to grow by $1 billion and you use a sales-to-capital ratio of 2.5, you will estimate a reinvestment need for this firm of $400 million ($1 billion/2.5). In making this estimate, we are assuming that reinvestment and sales growth occur contemporaneously, but as we will see in the following sections, that assumption can be easily relaxed. Put simply, the sales-to-capital ratio becomes a proxy for the efficiency with which a company is generating its revenue growth, with higher ratios indicating more efficient growth, and higher value, for any given growth rate.

To estimate the sales-to-capital ratio, you can look at both a firm's past and the business it operates in.

■ For a company's historical metrics, you can compute the current sales-to-capital ratio, by dividing the revenues in the most recent year by the invested capital at the start of the year, or you can compute the marginal sales-to-capital ratio each year, by taking the change in revenues that year and dividing by the change in invested capital

■ To the extent that a company's investment needs are determined by the business it is in, you can also look at industry averages. At the start of 2024, for instance, the businesses with the highest and lowest sales-to-capital ratios, in the aggregate, are listed in the table:

Industry	Sales to Capital	Industry	Sales to Capital
Healthcare Support Services	12.88	Green & Renewable Energy	0.20
Food Wholesalers	8.02	Utility (Water)	0.25
Retail (Grocery and Food)	4.76	Real Estate (Development)	0.27
Retail (Building Supply)	3.64	Utility (General)	0.35
Computer Services	3.59	Real Estate (General/Diversified)	0.37
Oilfield Services/Equip.	3.55	Drugs (Biotechnology)	0.41
Advertising	3.28	Power	0.41
Engineering/Construction	3.11	Telecom (Wireless)	0.47
Retail (Special Lines)	3.11	Transportation (Railroads)	0.48
Business & Consumer Services	3.11	Precious Metals	0.49

In the following sections, we will look at some of the reasons for the variation in sales-to-capital ratios across businesses.

Capital Intensity   Capital Intensity is a measure of how much a business needs as investment to be able to deliver operating results, and sales-to-capital ratios should be higher in more capital-intensive businesses. Thus, a manufacturing company that needs to build a manufacturing capacity will generate less revenues per dollar of capital invested than a service company. Looking at the industries with the highest and lowest sales-to-capital ratios, and the previous table, backs up this proposition. Utilities, real estate, and infrastructure businesses generate the least revenues per dollar of capital invested, and service business generate the most revenues per dollar of capital invested, with engineering/construction being an outlier.

When assessing the sales-to-capital ratio for an individual firm, it does make sense therefore to look at the industry that it belongs to, but within that industry a company's business model can set it apart. Thus, Tesla, while part of the capital-intensive auto business, has been able to generate much higher sales-to-capital ratios than other auto companies, through its innovative and flexible manufacturing techniques.

Leads, Lags and Excess Capacity   When companies invest for growth, there can be a time lag between the investment being made and the revenues from that investment manifesting. In the pharmaceutical business, for instance, where investing is often in R&D, the drugs that emerge from the research will often take years to get through the approval process, and may not be able to generate revenues until ten or more years after the research spending. In contrast, a company that grows through acquisitions should see revenues grow contemporaneously, augmenting its revenues with the target company revenues in the year of the acquisition. If there is a lag of n years between reinvestment and revenue generation, all it requires is a modification of the reinvestment assumption:

$$\text{Reinvestment}_t = \frac{\text{Revenues}_{t+n} - \text{Revenues in year}_{t+n-1}}{\text{Sales-to-Invested-Capital Ratio}}$$

To see how this lag effect will play out in valuation, consider valuing a company like Novo Nordisk in 2024. Coming into the year, the company was expecting healthy growth for the next few years, but much of that growth was coming from two drugs—Ozempic and Wegovy—that came out of research done a decade earlier. The company can deliver that future growth with very light reinvestment (high sales-to-capital ratio), as a consequence.

The other consideration in estimating reinvestment is a company's excess capacity, stemming from reinvestment made in the past, because that excess capacity can be used to generate revenues, at least in the near term. For instance, many of the cruise line companies, in 2024, were anticipating double-digit growth in the next few years, but given the calamitous drop in revenues during the pandemic, the future revenues, even with that growth, would have brought them back to 2019 levels. Thus, much of the expected growth can be covered with the cruise ships that these companies operated, rather than new ships, reducing reinvestment needs again for the near future.

Corporate Life Cycle   Browsing through the list of most capital-intensive industries, you will notice that green energy and biotech companies are on the list. While both industries do have capital investment needs, note that more traditional energy and drug companies are not on the list. While there are other factors at play, one key reason is where these industries fall in the corporate life cycle, with younger companies often struggling to deliver revenues on significant invested capital and more mature companies doing better, as can be seen in Figure 11.6:

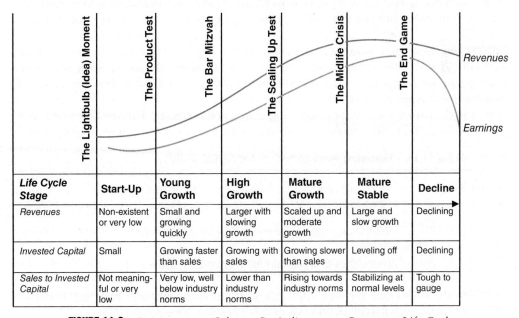

Life Cycle Stage	Start-Up	Young Growth	High Growth	Mature Growth	Mature Stable	Decline
Revenues	Non-existent or very low	Small and growing quickly	Larger with slowing growth	Scaled up and moderate growth	Large and slow growth	Declining
Invested Capital	Small	Growing faster than sales	Growing with sales	Growing slower than sales	Leveling off	Declining
Sales to Invested Capital	Not meaningful or very low	Very low, well below industry norms	Lower than industry norms	Rising towards industry norms	Stabilizing at normal levels	Tough to gauge

FIGURE 11.6   Reinvestment (Sales to Capital) across a Corporate Life Cycle

Sales to Invested Capital: Reinvestment

Current (Historical) Sales to Capital	Future Sales to Capital
The sales to invested capital ratio relates the revenues of the firm to its invested capital, with the latter defined the same way that you would in the return on invested capital calculation. Sales to Capital = Revenues/(Book Equity + Book Debt – Cash) The ratio measures the efficiency with which a firm delivers its revenue growth, with higher values indicating more efficiency. You can look at: 1. The company's historical sales to capital ratio 2. The industry average sales to capital ratio	1. Scaling Effects: As companies get bigger, the sales to invested capital ratio can rise or fall, depending on the sector being analyzed. (Looking at the peer group may give some guidance). 2. Excess Capacity: If a company has excess capacity, created by past investments, it should be able to generate revenue growth with less investment, i.e., with higher sales to capital ratios. 3. Lag between investment and growth: If reinvestment creates growth quickly (or instantaneously), the reinvestment in a year can be estimated based upon revenue change in that year. If there is a lag, the reinvestment may have to be tied to revenue change in a future year.

A company with higher expected growth in revenues will need to reinvest more, though how much will be determined by the business that it operates in, with less reinvestment needed if it has excess capacity and a lag between reinvestment and growth.

FIGURE 11.7 Estimating Reinvestment (Sales to Invested Capital)

The implications for valuation are straight forward. When valuing young or high growth companies, you should steer away from using the company's current sales-to-capital ratio as your forecasted value for the future, relying more on industry averages or subjectively estimated norms. As companies mature, the information in historical sales-to-capital ratios will increase, and you can make a stronger case for using them as forecasted values.

Summing Up In keeping with the maxim that growth requires reinvestment, it is important that you tie your reinvestment estimates to your estimates of growth for a firm, since increases in one (usually growth) should lead to increases in the other (reinvestment). It is because this linkage is broken that analysts and companies fall into the trap of believing that growth is always a positive, increasing value, as it increases. The key determinants of the sales-to-capital ratio, and the inputs that can be used to estimate it are in Figure 11.7.

ILLUSTRATION 11.14:   Estimating Reinvestment for Airbnb (IPO in 2020)

To estimate how much Airbnb would have to invest to generate its expected growth in revenues, we looked at Airbnb's history as well as the average sales-to-invested-capital ratios of the other travel intermediaries:

Airbnb's marginal sales to invested capital in 2019 = 1.86

Average sales-to-capital ratio for Booking & Expedia = 2.03

We decided to use a sales-to-invested-capital ratio of 2.00 for Airbnb, effectively making the reinvestment half of the change in annual revenues, each year (with all numbers in millions of dollars):

	Revenues	− Revenues	Sales to Capital	Reinvestment	EBIT(1−t)	FCFF
Base year	$ 3,626				−$ 818	
1	$ 4,692	$1,066	2.00	$ 533	−$ 469	−$1,002
2	$ 5,990	$1,298	2.00	$ 649	−$ 180	−$ 829
3	$ 7,565	$1,576	2.00	$ 788	$ 38	−$ 750
4	$ 9,555	$1,989	2.00	$ 995	$ 382	−$ 612
5	$12,066	$2,511	2.00	$1,255	$ 778	−$ 478
6	$14,674	$2,609	2.00	$1,304	$ 658	−$ 647
7	$17,163	$2,489	2.00	$1,244	$1,382	$ 137
8	$19,275	$2,112	2.00	$1,056	$2,239	$1,183
9	$20,749	$1,474	2.00	$ 737	$3,150	$2,413
10	$21,370	$ 621	2.00	$ 311	$4,007	$3,696

We are effectively assuming that reinvestment and growth in sales occur contemporaneously, but that assumption can be relaxed easily, enabling a lag between reinvestment and growth. Thus, with a one-year lag, the reinvestment in year 1 will be based upon the expected change in sales in year 2, and so on.

Sanity Checks

One of the dangers that you face when using a sales-to-capital ratio to generate reinvestment needs is that you might underestimate or overestimate your reinvestment needs. You can keep tabs on whether this is happening and correct it when it does by also estimating the after-tax return on capital of the firm each year through the analysis. To estimate the return on capital in a future year, you divide the estimated after-tax operating income in that year by the total capital invested in that firm in that year. The former number comes from your estimates of revenue growth and operating margins, while the latter can be estimated by aggregating the reinvestment made by the firm all the way through the future year. For instance, a firm that has $500 million in capital invested today, and is assumed to reinvest $300 million next year, and $400 million the year, after will have capital invested of $1.2 billion at the end of the second year.

For firms losing money today, the return on capital will be a negative number when the estimation begins but will improve as margins improve. If you reinvest too little, the return on capital in the later years will be too high, while if you don't reinvest enough it will be too low. Too low or high relative to what, you ask? There are two comparisons that are worth making. The first is to the average return on capital for mature firms in the business in which your firm operates—mature automobile companies in the case of Tesla Motors. The second is to the firm's own cost of capital. A projected return on capital of 40 percent for a firm, with a cost of capital of 10 percent in a sector where returns on capital hover around 15 percent, is an indicator that the firm is investing too little for the projected revenue growth and operating margins. Decreasing the sales-to-capital ratio until the return on capital converges on 15 percent would be prudent.

ILLUSTRATION 11.15:   Estimated Imputed Return on Capital for Airbnb

In illustrations 11.13 and 11.14, estimated the expected operating income and reinvestment for Airbnb. With the former, we assumed that the company would move from a money-losing enterprise to a healthy money-making firm, with pretax operating margins of 25%. With the latter, each year of reinvestment augmented the invested capital, raising from a negative value at the start of the period to a much more sustainable value by the terminal year (with all dollar values in millions):

	Revenues	EBIT(1–t)	– Reinvestment	Invested capital	ROIC
Base year	$ 3,626	($ 818)		1,370	−36.24%
1	$ 4,692	($ 469)	$ 533	$ 1,903	−24.65%
2	$ 5,990	($ 180)	$ 649	$ 2,552	−7.04%
3	$ 7,565	$ 38	$ 788	$ 3,340	1.3%
4	$ 9,555	$ 382	$ 995	$ 4,335	8.82%
5	$12,066	$ 778	$1,255	$ 5,590	13.91%
6	$14,674	$ 658	$1,304	$ 6,894	15.20%
7	$17,163	$1,382	$1,244	$ 8,139	21.18%
8	$19,275	$2,239	$1,056	$ 9,195	27.14%
9	$20,749	$3,150	$ 737	$ 9,932	33.1%
10	$21,370	$4,007	$ 311	$10,242	39.12%

The returns on capital at Airbnb rises over time, as the company becomes profitable, and reaches 39.12% in year 10.[13] While that number gave us pause, being much higher than the cost of capital, we stayed with our estimates for two reasons. The first is that technology and platform companies do generate extremely high returns on their initial platform investments, as network benefits drive up profitability. The second is that we do bring the marginal return on capital down after year 10 to 10%, to reflect the fact that Airbnb's new investments will not be as lucrative.

QUALITATIVE ASPECTS OF GROWTH

The emphasis on quantitative elements—return on capital and reinvestment rates for profitable firms, and margins, revenue growth, and sales-to-capital ratios for unprofitable firms—may strike some as skewed. After all, growth is determined by a number of subjective factors—the quality of management, the strength of a firm's marketing, its capacity to form partnerships with other firms, and the management's strategic vision, among many others. Where, you might ask, is there room in the growth equations that have been presented in this chapter for these factors?

The answer is that qualitative factors matter, but that they all ultimately have to show up in one or more of the quantitative inputs that determine growth. Consider the following:

---

[13] When invested capital is negative, the return on invested capital cannot be calculated.

■ The quality of management plays a significant role in the returns on capital that you assume firms can earn on their new investments and in how long they can sustain these returns. Thus, the fact that a firm has a well-regarded management team may be one reason why you allow a firm's return on capital to remain well above the cost of capital.

■ The marketing strengths of a firm and its choice of marketing strategy are reflected in the operating margins and turnover ratios that you assume for firms. Thus, it takes faith in a Coca-Cola's capacity to market its products effectively to assume a high turnover ratio and a high target margin. In fact, you can consider various marketing strategies, which trade off lower margins for higher turnover ratios, and consider the implications for value. The brand name of a firm's products and the strength of its distribution system also affect these estimates.

■ Defining reinvestment broadly to include acquisitions, research and development, and investments in marketing and distribution allows you to consider different ways in which firms can grow. For some firms, reinvestment and growth come from acquisitions, while for other firms it may take the form of more traditional investments in plant and equipment. The effectiveness of these reinvestment strategies is captured in the return on capital that you assume for the future, with more effective firms having higher returns on capital.

■ The strength of the competition that firms face is in the background, but it does determine how high excess returns (return on capital less cost of capital) will be, and how quickly they fade toward zero.

Thus, qualitative factors are quantified, and the growth implications are considered. If you cannot, you should remain skeptical about whether these factors truly affect value.

Why is it necessary to impose this quantitative structure on growth estimate? One of the biggest dangers in valuing firms is that storytelling can be used to justify growth rates that are neither reasonable nor sustainable. Thus, you might be told that Tesla Motors will grow 100% a year because the "green" movement is strong, or that Coca-Cola will grow 20 percent a year because it has a great brand name. While there is truth in these stories, consideration of how these qualitative views translate into the quantitative elements of growth is an essential step toward consistent valuations.

Can different investors consider the same qualitative factors and come to different conclusions about the implications for returns on capital, margins, and reinvestment rates, and consequently, about growth? Absolutely. In fact, you would expect differences in opinion about the future and different estimates of value. The payoff to knowing a firm, and the sector it operates in better than other investors, is that your estimates of growth and value will be better than theirs. Unfortunately, this does not guarantee that your investment returns will be better than theirs.

CONCLUSION

Growth is the key input in every valuation, and there are three sources for growth rates. One is the past, though both estimating and using historical growth rates can be difficult for most firms with their volatile and sometimes negative earnings. The second source is analyst estimates of growth. Though analysts may be privy to information that is not available to the rest of the market, this information does not result in growth rates that are superior to historical growth estimates. Furthermore, the analyst's emphasis on earnings per share growth can be a problem when forecasting operating income. The third and soundest way of estimating growth is to base it on a firm's fundamentals.

The relationship of growth to fundamentals will depend on what growth rate we are estimating. To estimate growth in earnings per share, we looked at return on equity and retention ratios. To estimate growth in net income, we replaced the retention ratio with the equity reinvestment rate. To evaluate growth in operating income, we used return on capital and reinvestment rate. While the details vary from approach to approach, there are some common themes that emerge from these approaches. The first is that growth and reinvestment are linked and estimates of one have to be linked with estimates of the other. Firms that want to grow at high rates over long periods have to reinvest to create that growth. The second is that the quality of growth can vary widely across firms, and the best measure of the quality of growth is the returns earned on investments. Firms that earn higher returns on equity and capital not only will generate higher growth, but that growth will add more to their value.

QUESTIONS AND SHORT PROBLEMS

In the problems following, use an equity risk premium of 5.5 percent if none is specified.

1. Walgreen Company reported the following earnings per share from 1989 to 1994.

Year	EPS
1989	$1.28
1990	$1.42
1991	$1.58
1992	$1.78
1993	$1.98
1994	$2.30

   a. Estimate the arithmetic average and geometric average growth rate in earnings per share between 1989 and 1994. Why are they different? Which is more reliable?
   b. Estimate the growth rate using a linear growth model.
   c. Estimate the growth rate using a log-linear growth model.
2. BIC Corporation reported a return on equity of 20% and paid out 37% of its earnings as dividends in the most recent year.
   a. Assuming that these fundamentals do not change, estimate the expected growth rate in earnings per share.
   b. Now assume that you expect the return on equity to increase to 25% on both new and existing investments next year. Estimate the expected growth rate in earnings per share.
3. You are trying to estimate the expected growth in net income at Metallica Corporation, a manufacturing firm that reported $150 million in net income in the just-completed financial year; the book value of equity at the beginning of the year was $1 billion. The firm had capital expenditures of $160 million, depreciation of $100 million, and an increase in working capital of $40 million during the year. The debt outstanding increased by $40 million during the year. Estimate the equity reinvestment rate and expected growth in net income.

4. You are trying to estimate a growth rate for HipHop Inc., a record producer and distributor. The firm earned $100 million in after-tax operating income on capital invested of $800 million last year. In addition, the firm reported net capital expenditures of $25 million and an increase in noncash working capital of $15 million.

   a. Assuming that the firm's return on capital and reinvestment rate remain unchanged, estimate the expected growth in operating income next year.

   b. How would your answer to (a) change if you were told that the firm's return on capital next year will increase by 2.5%? (Next year's return on capital = This year's return on capital + 2.5%.)

5. InVideo Inc. is an online retailer of videos and DVDs. The firm reported an operating loss of $10 million on revenues of $100 million in the most recent financial year. You expect revenue growth to be 100% next year, 75% in year 2, 50% in year 3, and 30% in years 4 and 5. You also expect the pretax operating margin to improve to 8% of revenues by year 5. Estimate the expected revenues and operating income (or loss) each year for the next five years.

6. SoftTech Inc. is a small manufacturer of entertainment software that reported revenues of $25 million in the most recent financial year. You expect the firm to grow significantly over time and capture 8% of the overall entertainment software market in 10 years. If the total revenues from entertainment software in the most recent year amounted to $2 billion and you expect an annual growth rate of 6% in these revenues for the next 10 years, estimate the compounded annual revenue growth rate at SoftTech for the next 10 years.

CHAPTER 12

Closure in Valuation: Estimating Terminal Value

In the previous chapter, we examined the determinants of expected growth. Firms that reinvest substantial portions of their earnings and earn high returns on these investments should be able to grow at high rates. But for how long? And what happens after that? This chapter looks at two ways of bringing closure to a valuation: a going concern approach where we assume that the firm continues to deliver cash flows in perpetuity, and a liquidation approach where we assume that the business is shut down and the assets are sold at some point in time.

Consider the going concern approach first. As a firm grows, it becomes more difficult for it to maintain high growth, and it eventually will grow at a rate less than or equal to the growth rate of the economy in which it operates. This growth rate, labeled stable growth, can be sustained either in perpetuity or for an extended finite period, allowing us to estimate the value of all cash flows beyond that point as a terminal value for a going concern. The key question that we confront is the estimation of when and how this transition to stable growth will occur for the firm that we are valuing. Will the growth rate drop abruptly at a point in time to a stable growth rate, or will it occur more gradually over time? To answer these questions, we will look at a firm's size (relative to the market that it serves), its current growth rate, and its competitive advantages.

We also consider an alternate route, which is that firms do not last forever and that they will be liquidated at some point in the future. We will consider how best to estimate liquidation value and when it makes more sense to use this approach rather than the going concern approach.

CLOSURE IN VALUATION

Since you cannot estimate cash flows forever, you generally impose closure in discounted cash flow valuation by stopping your estimation of cash flows sometime in the future, and then computing a terminal value that reflects the value of the firm at that point.

$$\text{Value of firm} = \sum_{t=1}^{t=n} \frac{E(\text{Cash Flow}_t)}{(1+r)^t} + \frac{\text{Terminal Value}}{(1+r)^n}$$

where

$$E(\text{Cash Flow}_t) = \text{Expected cash flow in period t}$$

$$r = \text{Discount rate reflecting type of and risk in cash flow}$$

You can find the terminal value in one of two ways. One is to assume a liquidation of the firm's assets in the terminal year and estimate what others would pay for the assets that the firm has accumulated at that point. The other assumes that the cash flows of the firm will grow at a constant rate forever—a stable growth rate. With stable growth, the terminal value can be estimated using a perpetual growth model. There is a third approach that is widely used by practitioners, which is to apply a multiple to earnings, revenues, or book value to estimate the value in the terminal year. In our view, that approach is incompatible with intrinsic value, closer to a forward pricing than an intrinsic valuation, and we will talk more about that in Chapter 16.

Liquidation Value

In some valuations, we can assume that the firm will cease operations at a point in time in the future and sell the assets it has accumulated to the highest bidders. The estimate that emerges is called a liquidation value. There are two ways in which the liquidation value can be estimated. One is to base it on the book value of the assets, adjusted for any inflation during the period. Thus, if the book value of assets 10 years from now is expected to be $2 billion, the average age of the assets at that point is five years and the expected inflation rate is 3 percent, then the expected liquidation value can be estimated as:

$$\text{Expected liquidation value} = \text{Book value of assets}_{\text{terminal year}}$$
$$(1 + \text{Inflation rate})^{\text{average life of assets}}$$
$$= \$2 \text{ billion } (1.03)^5 = \$2.319 \text{ billion}$$

The limitation of this approach is that it is based on accounting book value and does not reflect the earning power of the assets.

The alternative approach is to estimate the value based on the earning power of the assets. To make this estimate, we would first have to estimate the expected cash flows from the assets, and then discount these cash flows back to the present using an appropriate discount rate. In the preceding example, for instance, if we assumed that the assets in question could be expected to generate $400 million in after-tax cash flows for 15 years (after the terminal year) and the cost of capital was 10 percent, our estimate of the expected liquidation value would be:

$$\text{Expected liquidation value} = \$400 \text{ million (PV of annuity, 15 years @ 10\%)}$$
$$= \$3.042 \text{ billion}$$

When valuing equity, there is one additional step that needs to be taken. The estimated value of debt outstanding in the terminal year has to be subtracted from the liquidation value to arrive at the liquidation proceeds for equity investors.

Multiple Approach

In this approach, the value of a firm in a future year is estimated by applying a multiple to the firm's earnings or revenues in that year. For instance, a firm with expected revenues of $6 billion, ten years from now will have an estimated terminal value in that year of $12 billion, if a value-to-sales multiple of two is used. If valuing equity, we use equity multiples such as price-earnings ratios to arrive at the terminal value.

Although this approach has the virtue of simplicity, the multiple determines the final value and where it is obtained can be critical. If, as is common, the multiple is estimated by looking at how comparable firms in the business today are priced by the market, the valuation becomes a relative valuation, rather than a discounted cash flow valuation. If the multiple is estimated using fundamentals, it converges on the stable growth model (described in the next section), and there is no need for it as an alternative.

All in all, using multiples to estimate terminal value, when those multiples are estimated from comparable firms, results in a dangerous mix of pricing and discounted cash flow valuation. While there are advantages to pricing, and we consider these in a later chapter, a discounted cash flow valuation should provide you with an estimate of intrinsic value, not relative value. Consequently, the only consistent way of estimating terminal value in a discounted cash flow model is to use either a liquidation value or a stable growth model.

Stable Growth Model

In the liquidation value approach, you assume that your firm has a finite life, and that it will be liquidated at the end of that life. Firms, however, can reinvest some of their cash flows back into new assets and extend their lives. If you assume that cash flows, beyond the terminal year, will grow at a constant rate forever, the terminal value can be estimated as follows:

$$\text{Terminal valu e}_t = \frac{\text{Cash flow}_{t+1}}{(r - \text{Stable growth rate})}$$

The cash flow and the discount rate used will depend on whether you are valuing the firm or valuing equity. If you are valuing equity, the terminal value of equity can be written as:

$$\text{Terminal value of equity}_n = \frac{\text{Cash flow to equity}_{n+1}}{(\text{Cost of equity}_{n+1} - g_n)}$$

The cash flow to equity can be defined strictly as dividends (in the dividend discount model) or as free cash flow to equity. If valuing a firm, the terminal value can be written as:

$$\text{Terminal value of firm}_n = \frac{\text{Cash flow to firm}_{n+1}}{(\text{Cost of capital}_{n+1} - g_n)}$$

where the cost of capital and the growth rate in the model are sustainable forever.

In this section, we will begin by considering how high a stable growth rate can be, how to best estimate when your firm will be a stable growth firm, and what inputs need to be adjusted as a firm approaches stable growth.

Constraints on Stable Growth   Of all the inputs into a discounted cash flow valuation model, none creates as much angst as estimating the stable growth rate. Part of the reason for it is that small changes in the stable growth rate can change the terminal value significantly, and the effect gets larger as the growth rate approaches the discount rate used in the estimation.

The fact that a stable growth rate is constant forever, however, puts strong constraints on how high it can be. Since no firm can grow forever at a rate higher than the growth rate of the economy in which it operates, the constant growth rate cannot be greater than the overall growth rate of the economy. In making a judgment on what the limits on a stable growth rate are, we must consider the following three questions:

1. *Is the company constrained to operate as a domestic company, or does it operate (or have the capacity to operate) multinationally?* If a firm is a purely domestic company, either because of internal constraints (such as those imposed by management) or external constraints (such as those imposed by a government), the growth rate in the domestic economy will be the limiting value. If the company is a multinational or has aspirations to be one, the growth rate in the global economy (or at least those parts of the globe that the firm operates in) will be the limiting value.
2. *Is the valuation being done in nominal or real terms?* If the valuation is a nominal valuation, the stable growth rate should also be a nominal growth rate (i.e., include an expected inflation component). If the valuation is a real valuation, the stable growth rate will be constrained to be lower. Using a U.S. company in 2024 as an example, the stable growth rate can be as high as 4 percent if the valuation is done in nominal U.S. dollars but only 1.5 percent if the valuation is done in real terms.
3. *What currency is being used to estimate cash flows and discount rates in the valuation?* The limits on stable growth will vary depending on what currency is used in the valuation. If a high-inflation currency is used to estimate cash flows and discount rates, the stable growth rate will be much higher, since the expected inflation rate is added on to real growth. If a low-inflation currency is used to estimate cash flows, the stable growth rate will be much lower. For instance, the stable growth rate that would be used to value Cemex, the Mexican cement company, will be much higher if the valuation is done in Mexican pesos than in U.S. dollars.

Although the stable growth rate cannot exceed the growth rate of the economy in which a firm operates, it can be lower. There is nothing that prevents us from assuming that mature firms will become a smaller part of the economy, and it may, in fact, be the more reasonable assumption to make. Note that the growth rate of an economy reflects the contributions of both young higher-growth firms and mature stable-growth firms. If the former grow at a rate much higher than the growth rate of the economy, the latter have to grow at a rate that is lower.

Risk-Free Rates and Growth in Perpetuity   In valuation, the risk-free rate comes into play in the context of estimating discount rates but is generally not considered when estimating cash flows and growth rates. If there is a lesson that the low- (and negative-) interest rate world that we lived in the decade after the 2008 crisis, it is that the forces that drive interest rates up and down also affect growth rates and cash flows.

The risk-free rate, which is a nominal interest rate, in any currency can written as the sum of the expected inflation and real interest rates:

$$\text{Nominal riskless rate} = \text{Real riskless rate} + \text{Expected inflation rate}$$

In Chapter 8, we noted that risk-free rates vary across currencies, primarily because of differences in inflation, and if there are barriers to capital flowing freely, and there often are, that the real riskless rate will converge on the real growth rate of the economy. It then follows that the risk-free rate becomes a proxy for the nominal growth rate of the economy:

$$\text{Expected nominal growth rate in economy} = \text{Real growth rate in economy} \\ + \text{Expected inflation rate}$$

If this is the case, the risk-free rate becomes the cap on the growth rate in the perpetual growth model.

The pushback, of course, is that real interest rates and real growth rates do not have to be the same, especially in the short term. To test the empirical basis for the assertion, we looked at the ten-year U.S treasury bond rate (nominal dollar risk free rate) and the nominal growth rate in the U.S. economy over the last seven decades, in Figure 12.1.

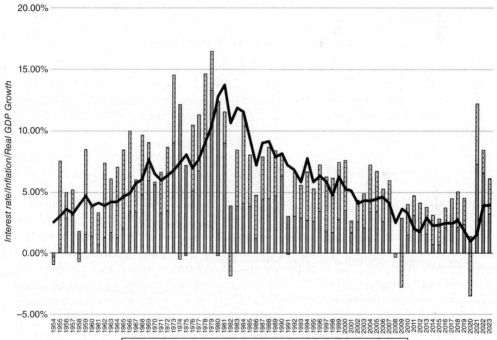

Year end	Ten-year T.Bond rate	Inflation rate	Real GDP growth	Intrinsic riskfree rate	Intrinsic - T.Bond rate
1954–2022	5.56%	3.59%	2.93%	6.52%	−0.96%
1954–1980	5.83%	4.49%	3.50%	7.98%	−2.15%
1981–2008	6.88%	3.26%	3.04%	6.30%	0.58%
2009–2020	2.36%	1.81%	1.32%	3.13%	−0.77%
2021–2023	3.09%	5.59%	3.27%	8.86%	−5.77%
1954–2023	5.54%	3.58%	2.93%	6.51%	−0.98%

FIGURE 12.1 Ten-year U.S. Treasury Bond Rate and Nominal Growth

Note that, while not in perfect sync, the ten-year treasury bond rate mirrors nominal growth rate in the U.S. economy in each decade, in high-inflation decades (like the 1970s) and low-inflation decades (like 2011–2020).

If neither of the theory and empirical arguments are convincing, there is a third rationale for capping the growth rate in perpetuity at the riskless rate, and this should resonate if you believe that central banks have the power to drive rates higher or lower than they should be, given fundamentals. In 2020 and 2021, when risk-free rates had plummeted, with the U.S. treasury bond rate dropping to historic lows and the Euro risk-free rate in negative territory, there were some investors who believed that rates were abnormally low, leading them into a conundrum. Leaving rates at current levels would result in discount rates being too low and accompanying these rates with "normal" nominal growth rates would cause value to explode. Put simply, an analyst using a treasury bond rate of 1.51% in March 2020, with a nominal growth rate of 4% as the cap for the terminal value would get too high a value. Linking the risk-free rate to the growth rate in perpetuity therefore keeps your valuation in balance, since using too low or high a value for one (discount rate) will be offset by too low or high a value for the other (expected growth in perpetuity).

CAN THE STABLE GROWTH RATE BE NEGATIVE?

The previous section noted that the stable growth rate has to be less than or equal to the growth rate of the economy. But can it be negative? There is no reason why not since the terminal value can still be estimated. For instance, a firm with $100 million in after-tax cash flows growing at −5% a year forever and a cost of capital of 10 percent has a value of:

$$\text{Value of firm} = 100(1 - .05)/(.10 - (- .05)) = \$633 \text{ million}$$

Intuitively, though, what does a negative growth rate imply? It essentially allows a firm to shrink itself each year until it just about disappears. Thus, it is an intermediate choice between complete liquidation and the going concern that gets larger each year forever.

This is the right choice to make when valuing firms in industries that are being phased out because of technological advances (such as the manufacturers of land-line phones, with the advent of the cellphones) or where an external and critical customer is scaling back purchases for the long term (as was the case with defense contractors after the end of the cold war).

Using negative growth rates may also be reflective of a changing economic order, where successful firms do not survive for a century, as was the case in the twentieth century but only for a couple of decades. For these short life cycle companies, it makes more sense when you get to your terminal year, to set them on a pathway to quickly liquidate themselves over time, by setting a stable growth rate of −5% or even −10%, a year.

Key Assumptions about Stable Growth   In every discounted cash flow valuation, there are three critical assumptions you need to make for stable growth. The first relates to when the firm that you are valuing will become a stable growth firm, if it is not one already. The second relates to what the characteristics of the firm will be in stable growth, in terms of return on investments and costs of equity and capital. The final assumption relates to how the firm that you are valuing will make the transition from high growth to stable growth.

Length of the High-Growth Period   The question of how long a firm will be able to sustain high growth is perhaps one of the more difficult questions to answer in a valuation, but two points are worth making. One is that it is not a question of whether but when firms hit the stable growth wall. All firms ultimately become stable growth firms, in the best case, because high growth makes a firm larger, and the firm's size will eventually become a barrier to further high growth. In the worst-case scenario, firms do not survive and will be liquidated. The second is that high growth in valuation, or at least high growth that creates value,[1] comes from firms earning excess returns on their marginal investments. In other words, increased value comes from firms having a return on capital that is higher than the cost of capital (or a return on equity that exceeds the cost of equity). Thus, when you assume that a firm will experience high growth for the next 5 or 10 years, you are also implicitly assuming that it will earn excess returns (over and above the required return) during that period. In a competitive market, these excess returns will eventually draw in new competitors, and the excess returns will disappear.

You should look at three factors when considering how long a firm will be able to maintain high growth.

1. *Size of the firm.* Smaller firms are much more likely to earn excess returns and maintain these excess returns than otherwise similar larger firms. This is because they have more room to grow and a larger potential market. Small firms in large markets should have the potential for high growth (at least in revenues) over long periods. When looking at the size of the firm, you should look not only at its current market share, but also at the potential growth in the total market for its products or services. A firm may have a large market share of its current market, but it may be able to grow in spite of this because the entire market is growing rapidly.
2. *Existing growth rate and excess returns.* Momentum does matter, when it comes to projecting growth. Firms that have been reporting rapidly growing revenues are more likely to see revenues grow rapidly, at least in the near future. Firms that are earning high returns on capital and high excess returns in the current period are likely to sustain these excess returns for the next few years.
3. *Magnitude and sustainability of competitive advantages.* This is perhaps the most critical determinant of the length of the high-growth period. If there are significant barriers to entry and sustainable competitive advantages, firms can maintain high growth for longer periods. If, on the other hand, there are no or minor barriers to entry, or if the firm's existing competitive advantages are fading, you should be far more conservative about allowing for long growth periods. The quality of existing

---

[1]Growth without excess returns will make a firm larger but not add value.

management also influences growth. Some top managers have the capacity to make the strategic choices that increase competitive advantages and create new ones.[2]

COMPETITIVE ADVANTAGE PERIOD (CAP)

The confluence of high-growth and excess returns that is the source of value has led to the coining of the term competitive advantage period (CAP) to capture the joint effect. This term, popularized by Michael Mauboussin at Credit Suisse First Boston, measures the period during which a firm can be expected to earn excess returns. The value of such a firm can then be written as the sum of the capital invested today and the present value of the excess returns that the firm will earn over its life. Since there are no excess returns after the competitive advantage period, there is no additional value added.

In an inventive variant, analysts sometimes try to estimate how long the competitive advantage period will have to be to sustain a current market value, assuming that the current return on capital and cost of capital remain unchanged. The resulting market-implied competitive advantage period (MICAP) can then be either compared across firms in a sector or evaluated on a qualitative basis.

ILLUSTRATION 12.1:   Length of High-Growth Period

To illustrate the process of estimating the length of the high-growth period, we will consider three companies, Consolidated Edison, Levi Strauss, and Eli Lilly in 2024, and make subjective judgments about how long each one will be able to maintain high growth.

CONSOLIDATED EDISON

Background: The firm has a near monopoly in generating and selling power in the environs of New York City. In return for the monopoly, though, the firm is restricted in both its investment and its pricing policy. A regulatory commission determines how much Con Ed can raise prices, and it makes this decision based on the returns made by Con Ed on its investments; if the firm is making high returns on its investments, it is unlikely to be allowed to increase prices. Finally, the demand for power in New York is stable, as the population levels off.

Implication: The firm is already a stable growth firm. There is little potential for either high-growth or excess returns.

LEVI STRAUSS

Background: Levi Strauss comes in with some obvious strengths. Its long history and established brand name has allowed it to earn returns on equity and invested capital that are in excess of its costs of equity and capital. The firm faces two challenges. One is that it's biggest markets, which are the United States and Europe, are saturated, making it difficult maintain high growth. The second is that the apparel market is competitive and fad-driven, posing barriers to pricing power and extended growth.

---

[2] Jack Welch (GE) and Robert Goisueta (Coca-Cola) represent traditional examples of CEOs who made a difference, though their contributions are still being debated. Steve Jobs at Apple set a new standard for the difference-making CEO, and Satya Nadella at Microsoft seems to be following.

Implication: The potential for growth in Asia, a market that Levi Strauss has a smaller presence in will enable a growth rate slightly higher than stable growth for a ten-year period. Beyond that, we will assume that the firm will be in stable growth, albeit with some residual excess returns.

ELI LILLY

Background: Eli Lilly has a stable of drugs, on which it has patent protection, that generate cash flows currently, and several drugs in its R&D pipeline. In particular, its work in developing weight-loss drugs have opened the door for higher growth in the next few years, and other blockbuster drugs, already in the works, should extend the growth to ten years, before the firm's size will push it into stable growth.

Implication: The patents that Eli Lilly has will protect it from competition, and the long lead time to drug approval will ensure that new products will take a while getting to the market. We will allow for 10 years of growth and excess returns.

There is clearly a strong subjective component to making a judgment on how long high growth will last. Much of what was said about the interrelationships between qualitative variables and growth toward the end of Chapter 11 has relevance for this discussion as well.

Characteristics of Stable Growth Firm   As firms move from high growth to stable growth, you need to give them the characteristics of stable growth firms. A firm in stable growth is different from that same firm in high growth on a number of dimensions. In general, you would expect stable growth firms to have average risk, use more debt, have lower (or no) excess returns, and reinvest less than high-growth firms. In this section, we will consider how best to adjust each of these variables.

Equity Risk   When looking at the cost of equity, high-growth firms tend to be more exposed to market risk (and have higher betas) than stable growth firms. Part of the reason for this is that they tend to be niche players supplying discretionary products, and part of the reason is high-operating leverage. Thus, young technology or social media firms will have high betas. As these firms mature, you would expect them to have less exposure to market risk and betas that are closer to 1—the average for the market. One option is to set the beta in stable growth to 1 for all firms, arguing that firms in stable growth should all be average risk. Another is to enable small differences to persist even in stable growth, with firms in more volatile businesses having higher betas than firms in stable businesses. We would recommend that, as a rule of thumb, stable period betas not exceed 1.2.[3]

But what about firms that have betas well below 1, such as commodity companies? If you assume that these firms will stay in their existing businesses, there is no harm in assuming that the beta remains at existing levels. However, if your estimates of growth in perpetuity will require them to branch out into other businesses, you should adjust the beta upward toward 1; invoking another rule of thumb, stable period betas should not be lower than 0.80.[4]

---

[3]Two-thirds of U.S. firms have betas that fall between 0.8 and 1.2. That becomes the range for stable period betas.

[4]If you are valuing a commodity company and assuming any growth rate that exceeds inflation, you are assuming that your firm will branch out into other businesses and need to adjust the beta accordingly.

betas.xls: This dataset on the web summarizes the average levered and unlevered betas, by industry group, for firms in the United States.

Project Returns   High-growth firms tend to have high returns on capital (and equity) and earn excess returns. In stable growth, it becomes much more difficult to sustain excess returns. There are some who believe that the only assumption consistent with stable growth is to assume no excess returns; the return on capital is set equal to the cost of capital. While, in principle, excess returns in perpetuity may not seem reasonable, it is difficult in practice to assume that firms will suddenly lose the capacity to earn excess returns at a point in time (say 5 years or 10 years). To provide a simple example, consider Levi Strauss, a company that we estimated a high-growth period of Ten years for in illustration 12.1. While the growth rate for Levi Strauss may drop to a stable level by year 11, the strong brand name and other competitive advantages are likely to persist for much longer (say 30–40 years). Rather than estimate cash flows for 30–40 years, we would stop estimating cash flows in year 5 but still allow the company to continue earning more than its cost of capital in perpetuity. Since entire industries often earn excess returns over long periods, assuming a firm's returns on equity and capital will move toward industry averages will yield more reasonable estimates of value.

 EVA.xls: This dataset on the web summarizes the returns on capital (equity), costs of capital (equity), and excess returns, by industry group, for firms in the United States.

Debt Ratios and Costs of Debt   High-growth firms tend to use less debt than stable growth firms. As firms mature, their debt capacity increases. When valuing firms, this will change the debt ratio that we use to compute the cost of capital. When valuing equity, changing the debt ratio will change both the cost of equity and the expected cash flows. The question of whether the debt ratio for a firm should be moved toward a more sustainable level in stable growth cannot be answered without looking at the incumbent managers' views on debt, and how much power stockholders have in these firms. If managers are willing to change their financing policy, and stockholders retain some power, it is reasonable to assume that the debt ratio will move to it optimal or target level in stable growth; if not, it is safer to leave the debt ratio at existing levels.

As earnings and cash flows increase, the perceived default risk in the firm will also change. A firm that is currently losing $10 million on revenues of $100 million may be rated B, but its rating should be much better if your forecasts of $10 billion in revenues and $1 billion in operating income come to fruition. In fact, internal consistency requires that you reestimate the rating and the cost of debt for a firm as you change its revenues and operating income. Generally, stable growth firms should have at least investment grade ratings (Baa or higher).

On the practical question of what debt ratio and cost of debt to use in stable growth, you should look at the financial leverage of larger and more mature firms in the industry. One solution is to use the industry average debt ratio and cost of debt as the debt ratio and cost of debt for the firm in stable growth.

---

 wacc.xls: **This dataset on the web summarizes the debt ratios and costs of debt, by industry group, for firms in the United States.**

Reinvestment and Retention Ratios   Stable growth firms tend to reinvest less than high-growth firms, and it is critical that we capture the effects of lower growth on reinvestment and that we ensure that the firm reinvests enough to sustain its stable growth rate in the terminal phase. The actual adjustment will vary depending on whether we are discounting dividends, free cash flows to equity, or free cash flows to the firm.

In the dividend discount model, note that the expected growth rate in earnings per share can be written as a function of the retention ratio and the return on equity.

$$\text{Expected growth rate} = \text{Retention ratio} \times \text{Return on equity}$$

Algebraic manipulation can allow us to state the retention ratio as a function of the expected growth rate and return on equity:

$$\text{Retention ratio} = \frac{\text{Expected growth rate}}{\text{Return on equity}}$$

If we assume, for instance, a stable growth rate of 3 percent (based on the growth rate of the economy) for JP Morgan Chase and a return on equity of 12 percent (based on industry averages), we would be able to compute the retention ratio of the firm in stable growth:

$$\text{Retention ratio}_{\text{JPM}} = \frac{3\%}{12\%} = 25\%$$

JP Morgan Chase will have to retain 25 percent of its earnings to generate its expected growth of 3 percent; it can pay out the remaining 75 percent.

In a free cash flow to equity model where we are focusing on net income growth, the expected growth rate is a function of the equity reinvestment rate and the return on equity:

$$\text{Expected growth rate}_{\text{Levi Strauss}} = \text{Equity reinvestment rate} \times \text{Return on equity}$$

The equity reinvestment rate can then be computed as follows:

$$\text{Equity reinvestment rate} = \frac{\text{Expected growth rate}}{\text{Return on equity}}$$

If, for instance, we assume that Levi Strauss will have a stable growth rate of 4 percent in equity income and have a return on equity in stable growth of 10 percent, we can estimate an equity reinvestment rate of 40%; the remaining 60% can be paid out as cash flows to equity investors:

$$\text{Equity reinvestment rate} = \frac{4\%}{10\%} = 40\%$$

Finally, looking at free cash flows to the firm, we estimated the expected growth in operating income as a function of the return on capital (ROC) in stable growth and the reinvestment rate:

$$\text{Expected growth rate} = \text{Reinvestment rate} \times \text{Return on invested capital}$$

Again, algebraic manipulation yields the following measure of the reinvestment rate in stable growth:

$$\text{Reinvestment rate in stable growth} = \frac{\text{Stable growth rate}}{\text{ROICn}}$$

where ROIC_n is the return on capital that the firm can sustain in stable growth. This reinvestment rate can then be used to generate the free cash flow to the firm in the first year of stable growth. With Eli Lilly, we assume a growth rate of 4% in stable growth, with a return on invested capital of 15%, reflecting the competitive advantages stemming from patent protection, resulting in a stable period reinvestment rate of 26.67%.

$$\text{Reinvestment rate}_{\text{Eli Lilly}} = \frac{4\%}{15\%} = 26.67\%$$

Linking the reinvestment rate and retention ratio to the stable growth rate also makes the valuation less sensitive to assumptions about the stable growth rate. Whereas increasing the stable growth rate, holding all else constant, can dramatically increase value, changing the reinvestment rate as the growth rate changes will create an offsetting effect. The gains from increasing the growth rate will be partially or completely offset by the loss in cash flows because of the higher reinvestment rate. Whether value increases or decreases as stable growth increases will entirely depend on what you assume about excess returns. If the return on capital is higher than the cost of capital in the stable growth period, increasing the stable growth rate will increase value. *If the return on capital is equal to cost of capital, increasing the stable growth rate will have no effect on value.* This can be proved quite easily:

$$\text{Terminal Value} = \frac{\text{EBIT}_{n+1}(1 - t)(1 - \text{Reinvestment rate})}{\left(\text{Cost of capital}_n - \text{Stable growth rate}_n\right)}$$

Substituting in the stable growth rate as a function of the reinvestment rate, from the equation, you get:

$$\text{Terminal Value} = \frac{\text{EBIT}_{n+1}(1 - t)(1 - \text{Reinvestment rate})}{\left(\text{Cost of capital}_n - \text{Reinvestment Rate} \times \text{ROIC}\right)}$$

Setting the return on capital equal to the cost of capital, you arrive at:

$$\text{Terminal Value} = \frac{\text{EBIT}_{n+1}(1 - t)(1 - \text{Reinvestment rate})}{\left(\text{Cost of capital}_n - \text{Reinvestment Rate} \times \text{Cost of capital}\right)}$$

Simplifying, the terminal value can be stated as:

$$\text{Terminal Value} = \frac{\text{EBIT}_{n+1}(1-t)}{\text{Cost of capital}_n}$$

Put simply, when there are no excess returns, your terminal value is unaffected by your assumptions about expected growth. You could establish the same proposition with equity income and cash flows and show that a return on equity equal to the cost of equity in stable growth nullifies the positive effect of growth.

 divfund.xls: **This dataset on the web summarizes retention ratios, by industry group, for firms in the United States.**

 capex.xls: **This dataset on the web summarizes the reinvestment rates, by industry group, for firms in the United States.**

ILLUSTRATION 12.2:   Stable Growth Rates and Excess Returns

Alloy Mills is a textile firm that is currently reporting after-tax operating income of $100 million. The firm has a return on capital currently of 20% and reinvests 50% of its earnings back into the firm, giving it an expected growth rate of 10% for the next five years:

$$\text{Expected growth rate} = 20\% \times 50\% = 10\%$$

After year 5 the growth rate is expected to drop to 5% and the return on capital is expected to stay at 20%. The terminal value can be estimated as follows:

$$\text{Expected operating income in year 6} = 100\,(1.10)^5(1.05) = \$169.10 \text{ million}$$
$$\text{Expected reinvestment rate from year 5} = g/\text{ROC} = 5\%/20\% = 25\%$$
$$\text{Terminal value in year 5} = \$169.10(1 - .25)/(.10 - .05) = \$2,537 \text{ million}$$

Not that the reinvestment rate in year 5 is computed based upon growth rate in year 6, as it should be, since growth should lag reinvestment. The value of the firm today would then be:

$$\text{Value of firm today} = \$55/1.10 + \$60.5/1.10^2 + \$66.55/1.10^3 + \$73.21/1.10^4$$
$$+ \$80.53/1.10^5 + \$2,537/1.10^5 = \$2,075 \text{ million}$$

If we did change the return on capital in stable growth to 10% while keeping the growth rate at 5%, the effect on value would be dramatic:

$$\text{Expected operating income in year 6} = 100\,(1.10)^5(1.05) = \$169.10 \text{ million}$$
$$\text{Expected reinvestment rate from year 5} = g/\text{ROC} = 5\%/10\% = 50\%$$
$$\text{Terminal value in year 5} = \$169.10(1 - .5)/(.10 - .05) = \$1,691 \text{ million}$$

$$\text{Value of firm today} = \$55/1.10 + \$60.5/1.10^2 + \$66.55/1.10^3 + \$73.21/1.10^4$$
$$+ \$80.53/1.10^5 + \$1,691/1.10^5 = \$1,300 \text{ million}$$

Now consider the effect of lowering the growth rate to 4% while keeping the return on capital at 10% in stable growth:

$$\text{Expected operating income in year 6} = 100\,(1.10)^5\,(1.04) = \$167.49 \text{ million}$$

$$\text{Expected reinvestment rate in year 6} = g/ROC = 4\%/10\% = 40\%$$

$$\text{Terminal value in year 5} = \$167.49(1 - .4)/(.10 - .04) = \$1{,}675 \text{ million}$$

$$\text{Value of firm today} = \$55/1.10 + \$60.5/1.10^2 + \$66.55/1.10^3 + \$73.21/1.10^4$$
$$+ \$96.53/1.10^5 + \$1{,}675/1.10^5 = \$1{,}300 \text{ million}$$

Note that the terminal value decreases by $16 million, but the cash flow in year 5 also increases by $16 million because the reinvestment rate at the end of year 5 drops to 40%. The value of the firm remains unchanged at $1,300 million. In fact, changing the stable growth rate to 0% has no effect on value:

$$\text{Expected operating income in year 6} = 100\,(1.10)^5 = \$161.05 \text{ million}$$

$$\text{Expected reinvestment rate in year 6} = g/ROC = 0\%/10\% = 0\%$$

$$\text{Terminal value in year 5} = \$161.05(1 - .0)/(.10 - .0) = \$1{,}610.5 \text{ million}$$

$$\text{Value of firm today} = \$55/1.10 + \$60.5/1.10^2 + \$66.55/1.10^3 + \$73.21/1.10^4$$
$$+ \$161.05/1.10^5 + \$1{,}610.5/1.10^5 = \$1{,}300 \text{ million}$$

Note again that the drop in the terminal value has been exactly offset by the increase in cash flows in year 5 (to equate to after-tax operating income that year, since no reinvestment is needed, with no growth expected).

ILLUSTRATION 12.3: Stable Growth Inputs

To illustrate how the inputs to valuation change as we go from high growth to stable growth, we will consider three firms—JP Morgan Chase, with the dividend discount model; Levi Strauss, with a free cash flow to equity model; and the Home Depot, with a free cash flow to firm model.

Consider JP Morgan, in May 2024, first in the context of the dividend discount model. Although we do the valuation in the next chapter, note that there are three key inputs to the dividend discount model—the payout ratio (which determines dividends), the expected return on equity (which determines the expected growth rate), and the beta (which affects the cost of equity). In Chapter 13, we will argue that JP Morgan has a ten-year high-growth period, followed by stable growth. The following table summarizes the inputs into the dividend discount model for the valuation of JP Morgan.

	High Growth	Transition	Stable growth
Time period	Years 1–5	Years 6–10	After year 10
Payout ratio	27.17%	adjusts to	75.00%
Return on equity	16.95%	adjusts to	12.00%
Expected growth rate	12.35%	adjusts to	3.00%
Beta	1.06	adjusts to	1.00
Cost of equity	9.98%	adjusts to	9.67%

Note that the payout ratio, return on equity, and beta for the high-growth period are based on the current year's values. The expected growth rate of 12.35% for the next five years is the product of the return on equity and retention ratio. In stable growth, we adjust the beta to 1, though the adjustment has little effect on value since the beta is already close to one. We assume that the stable growth rate will be 3%, just slightly below the nominal (US $) growth rate in the global economy (and the risk-free rate of 4.5% at the time). We also assume that the return on equity will drop to 12%, reflecting our assumption that returns on equity will decline for the entire industry as banking faces more competition from outsiders. The retention ratio decreases to 25%, as both growth and return on equity drop.

To analyze Levi Strauss, also in May 2024, in a free cash flow to equity model, the following table summarizes our inputs for high growth and stable growth:

	High growth	*Transition period*	*Stable growth*
Noncash ROE	32.59%	adjusts to	10.00%
Equity Reinvestment Rate	30.02%	adjusts to	40.00%
Expected Growth Rate	9.78%	adjusts to	4.00%
Beta	1.03	Unchanged	1.03
Cost of Equity	9.62%	Unchanged	9.62%

In high growth, the high return on equity allows the firm to generate an expected growth rate of 9.78% a year. In stable growth, we reduce the return on equity for Levi Strauss towards its cost of equity and estimate the expected equity reinvestment rate based on a stable growth rate of 4%, set below the risk-free rate of 4.50% at the time. The beta for the firm is left unchanged at its existing level, since it is close to one.

Finally, let us consider a valuation of Eli Lilly, in May 2024, with a firm valuation. The following table reports on the return on capital, reinvestment rate, and debt ratio for the firm in high-growth and stable growth periods.

	High-Growth Period	*Transition Period*	*Stable Growth*
Return on Invested Capital	20.43%	Adjusts to	15.00%
Reinvestment Rate	88.11%	Adjusts to	26.67%
Growth Rate in EBIT	18.00%	Adjusts to	4.00%
Cost of Capital	9.36%	Adjusts to	8.54%

Note that the reinvestment rate and return on capital for the firm reflect the decision we made to capitalize R&D. The operating income is adjusted for R&D and the book value of equity is augmented by the capitalized value of R&D (see Chapter 9). The firm has a high return on capital to begin the valuation, and we assume that this return will decrease in stable growth to 15% as the firm becomes larger and patents expire. Since the stable growth rate drops to 4%, the resulting reinvestment rate at Amgen will decrease to 26.67%. We also assume that Eli Lilly will choose to borrow more money in the future, bringing the cost of capital down to 8.54% in st.

For all of the firms, it is worth noting that we are assuming that excess returns continue in perpetuity by setting the return on capital above the cost of capital. While this is potentially troublesome, the competitive advantages that these firms have built up historically or will build up over the high-growth phase will not disappear in an instant. The excess returns will fade over time but moving them to or toward the cost of capital in stable growth seems like a reasonable compromise.

Transition to Stable Growth   Once you have decided that a firm will be in stable growth at a point in time in the future, you have to consider how the firm will change as it approaches stable growth. There are three distinct scenarios. In the first, the firm will maintain its high-growth rate for a period of time, and then become a stable growth firm abruptly; this is a two-stage model. In the second, the firm will maintain its high-growth rate for a period, and then have a transition period when its characteristics change gradually toward stable growth levels; this is a three-stage model. In the third, the firm's characteristics change each year from the initial period to the stable growth period; this can be considered an n-stage model.

Which of these three scenarios gets chosen depends on the firm being valued. Since the firm goes from high growth to stable growth in one year in the two-stage model, this model is more appropriate for firms with moderate growth rates, where the shift will not be too dramatic. For firms with very high-growth rates in operating income, a transition phase allows for a gradual adjustment not just of growth rates but also of risk characteristics, returns on capital and reinvestment rates toward stable growth levels. For very young firms or for firms with negative-operating margins, allowing for changes in each year (in an n-stage model) is prudent.

ILLUSTRATION 12.4:   Choosing a Growth Pattern

Consider the three firms analyzed in Illustration 12.3. We assumed a high-growth period of five years for all three firms (JP Morgan Chase, Levi Strauss and Eli Lilly), a transition phase between years 6 and 10 in which the inputs will change gradually from high-growth to stable growth levels. As growth rates decrease between years 6 and 10, we assume that the key inputs (accounting returns, growth rates and reinvestment rates) adjust in linear increments to stable growth levels. The following table reports on the changes in these variables over the transition periods for all three firms:

Year	JP Morgan Chase			Levi Strauss			Eli Lilly		
	Growth Rate	Payout Ratio	Cost of Equity	Growth Rate	Equity RIR	Cost of Equity	Growth Rate	Reinvestment Rate	Cost of Capital
1	12.35%	27.17%	9.98%	9.78%	30.02%	9.62%	18.00%	88.11%	9.36%
2	12.35%	27.17%	9.98%	9.78%	30.02%	9.62%	18.00%	88.11%	9.36%
3	12.35%	27.17%	9.98%	9.78%	30.02%	9.62%	18.00%	88.11%	9.36%
4	12.35%	27.17%	9.98%	9.78%	30.02%	9.62%	18.00%	88.11%	9.36%
5	12.35%	27.17%	9.98%	9.78%	30.02%	9.62%	18.00%	88.11%	9.36%
6	10.48%	36.74%	9.92%	8.63%	32.01%	9.62%	15.20%	75.82%	9.19%
7	8.61%	46.30%	9.86%	7.47%	34.01%	9.62%	12.40%	63.53%	9.03%
8	6.74%	55.87%	9.80%	6.31%	36.01%	9.62%	9.60%	51.25%	8.86%
9	4.87%	65.43%	9.73%	5.16%	38.00%	9.62%	6.80%	38.96%	8.70%
10	3.00%	75.00%	9.67%	4.00%	40.00%	9.62%	4.00%	26.67%	8.54%

With all three firms, as expected growth decreases, the reinvestment rate also decreases, from years 6 through 10. With JP Morgan, that lower reinvestment takes the form of a payout ratio that rises as growth decreases.

EXTRAORDINARY GROWTH PERIODS WITHOUT A HIGH-GROWTH RATE OR A NEGATIVE-GROWTH RATE

Can you have extraordinary growth periods for firms that have expected growth rates, which are less than or equal to the growth rate of the economy? The answer is yes, for some firms. This is because stable growth requires not just that the growth rate be less than the growth rate of the economy, but that the other inputs into the valuation are also appropriate for a stable growth firm. Consider, for instance, a firm whose operating income is growing at 2 percent a year, but whose current return on capital is 20 percent and whose beta is 1.5. You would still need a transition period in which the return on capital declined to more sustainable levels (say 12 percent) and the beta moved toward 1.

By the same token, you can have an extraordinary growth period where the growth rate is less than the stable growth rate, and then moves up to the stable growth rate. For instance, you could have a firm that is expected to see its earnings decline 5 percent a year for the next five years (which would be the extraordinary growth period) and grow 2 percent thereafter.

THE SURVIVAL ISSUE

Implicit in the use of a terminal value in discounted cash flow valuation is the assumption that the value of a firm comes from it being a going concern with a perpetual life. For many risky firms, there is the very real possibility that they might not be in existence in 5 or 10 years, with volatile earnings and shifting technology. Should the valuation reflect this chance of failure, and, if so, how can the likelihood that a firm will not survive be built into a valuation?

Life Cycle and Firm Survival

There is a link between where a firm is in the life cycle and survival. Young firms with negative earnings and cash flows can run into serious cash flow problems and end up being acquired by firms with more resources at bargain basement prices. Why are young firms more exposed to this problem? The negative cash flows from operations, when combined with significant reinvestment needs, can result in a rapid depletion of cash reserves. When financial markets are accessible and additional equity (or debt) can be raised at will, raising more funds to meet these funding needs is not a problem. However, when stock prices drop and access to markets becomes more limited, these firms can be in trouble.

A widely used measure of the potential for a cash flow problem for firms with negative earnings is the cash burn ratio, which is estimated as the cash balance of the firm divided by its earnings before interest, taxes, depreciation, and amortization (EBITDA).

$$\text{Cash burn ratio} = \frac{\text{Cash balance}}{\text{EBITDA}}$$

where EBITDA is a negative number, and the absolute value of EBITDA is used to estimate this ratio. Thus, a firm with a cash balance of $1 billion and EBITDA of –$1.5 billion will burn through its cash balance in eight months.

Likelihood of Failure and Valuation

One view of survival is that the expected cash flows, that you use in a valuation reflect cash flows under a wide range of scenarios from very good to abysmal and the probabilities of the scenarios occurring. Thus, the expected value already has built into it the likelihood that the firm will not survive. Any market risk associated with survival or failure is assumed to be incorporated into the cost of capital. Firms with a high likelihood of failure will therefore have higher discount rates and lower expected cash flows.

Another view of survival is that discounted cash flow valuations tend to have an optimistic bias, and that the likelihood that the firm will not survive is not considered adequately in value. With this view, the discounted cash flow value that emerges from the analysis in the prior section overstates the value of operating assets and must be adjusted to reflect the likelihood that the firm will not survive to deliver its terminal value or even the positive cash flows that you have forecast in future years.

Should You or Should You Not Adjust Value for Survival?

For firms that have substantial assets in place and relatively small probabilities of distress, the first view is the more appropriate one. Attaching an extra discount for nonsurvival is double counting risk.

For younger and smaller firms, it is a tougher call and depends on whether expected cash flows incorporate the probability that these firms may not make it past the first few years. If they do, the valuation already reflects the likelihood that the firms will not survive past the first few years. If they do not, you do have to discount the value for the likelihood that the firm will not survive the near future. One way to estimate this discount is to estimate a probability of failure, and adjust the operating asset value for this probability:

$$\text{Adjusted value} = \text{Discounted cash flow value} \times (1 - \text{Probability of distress})$$
$$+ \text{Distressed sale value} \times (\text{Probability of distress})$$

For a firm with a discounted cash flow value of $1 billion on its assets, a distress sale value of $500 million and a 20-percent probability of distress, the adjusted value would be $900 million:

$$\text{Adjusted value} = \$1,000 \times (.8) + \$500 \times (.2) = \$900 \text{ million}$$

There are two points worth noting here. It is not the failure to survive per se that causes the loss of value, but the fact that the distressed sale value is at a discount on the fair value. The second is that this approach requires estimating the probability of failure. This probability is difficult to estimate, because it will depend upon both the magnitude of the cash reserves of the firm (relative to its cash needs) and the state of the market. In buoyant equity markets, even firms with little or no cash can survive because they can access markets for more funds. Under more negative market conditions, even firms with significant cash balances may find themselves under threat.

Estimating The Probability of Distress

There are three ways in which we can estimate the probability that a firm will not survive.

1. *Statistical*: One is to draw on the past, look at firms that have failed, compare them to firms that did not, and look for variables that seem to set them apart. For instance, firms with high-debt ratios and negative cash flows from operations may be more likely to fail than firms without these characteristics. In fact, you can use statistical techniques such as probits to estimate the probability that a firm will fail. To run a probit, you would begin, for instance, with all listed firms in 1990 and their financial characteristics, identify the firms that failed during the 1991–1999 time period, and then estimate the probability of failure as a function of variables that were observable in 1990. The output, which resembles regression output, will then let you estimate the probability of default for any firm today.
2. *Empirical*: The Bureau of Labor Statistics maintains a database of firms that are started and tracks their survival over time. In their 2022 update, for instance, they estimated the likelihood of survival for firms that were started in 2006 for periods ranging up to 15 years, broken down by broad business grouping in Figure 12.2.

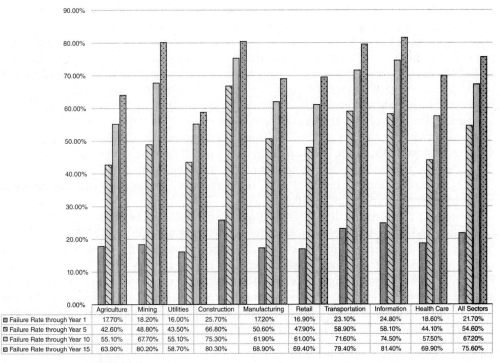

	Agriculture	Mining	Utilities	Construction	Manufacturing	Retail	Transportation	Information	Health Care	All Sectors
Failure Rate through Year 1	17.70%	18.20%	16.00%	25.70%	17.20%	16.90%	23.10%	24.80%	18.60%	21.70%
Failure Rate through Year 5	42.60%	48.80%	43.50%	66.80%	50.60%	47.90%	58.90%	58.10%	44.10%	54.60%
Failure Rate through Year 10	55.10%	67.70%	55.10%	75.30%	61.90%	61.00%	71.60%	74.50%	57.50%	67.20%
Failure Rate through Year 15	63.90%	80.20%	58.70%	80.30%	68.90%	69.40%	79.40%	81.40%	69.90%	75.60%

FIGURE 12.2 Failure (Survival) Rates by Business Grouping

3. *Bond Rating*: The third way of estimating the probability of default is to use the bond rating for the firm, if it is available. For instance, assume that the company in question has a B rating. An empirical examination of B-rated bonds over the past decade reveals that the likelihood of default with this rating is 23.74 percent, as can be seen in the table that lists default probabilities by ratings class.[5]

Default Probabilities over time (1–10 year time horizons)			
Rating	1	5	10
AAA	0.00%	0.35%	0.70%
AA	0.02%	0.31%	0.72%
A	0.05%	0.47%	1.24%
BBB	0.16%	1.58%	3.32%
BB	0.61%	6.52%	11.78%
B	3.33%	16.93%	23.74%
CCC/C	27.08%	46.19%	50.38%

While this approach is simpler, it is limiting insofar as it can be used only for rated firms, and it assumes that the standards used by ratings agencies have not changed significantly over time.

CLOSING THOUGHTS ON TERMINAL VALUE

The role played by the terminal value in discounted cash flow valuations has often been the source of much of the criticism of the discounted cash flow approach.

Critics of the approach argue that too great a proportion of the discounted cash flow value comes from the terminal value, and that it is easy to manipulate the terminal value to yield any number you want. They are wrong on both counts. It is true that a large portion of the value of any stock or equity in a business comes from the terminal value, but it would be surprising if it were not so. When you buy a stock or invest in the equity in a business, consider how you get your returns. Assuming that your investment is a good investment, the bulk of the returns come not while you hold the equity (from dividends or other cash flows) but when you sell it (from price appreciation). The terminal value is designed to capture the latter. Consequently, the greater the growth potential in a business, the higher the proportion of the value that comes from the terminal value.

The mythology around terminal value is plentiful, and Figure 12.3 summarizes these myths and tries to dispense with them:

Is it easy to manipulate the terminal value? We concede that terminal value is manipulated often and easily, but it is because analysts either use multiples to get these values, or because they violate one or both of two basic propositions in stable growth models. One is that the growth rate cannot exceed the growth rate of the economy. The other is that firms must reinvest enough in stable growth to generate the growth rate. In fact, as we showed earlier in the chapter, it is not the stable growth rate that drives value as much as what we assume about excess returns in perpetuity. When excess returns are zero, changes in the stable growth rate have no impact on value.

[5]This data is maintained and updated by the major ratings agencies, with this version of the table coming from S&P's 2023 data update.

| Myth 1: The only way to estimate terminal value is to use the perpetual growth model. | Myth 2: The perpetual growth model can give you an infinite value. | Myth 3: The growth rate is your biggest driver of terminal value. | Myth 4: Your growth rate cannot be negative in a perpetual growth model. | Myth 5: If your terminal value is a high proportion of your DCF value, it is flawed. |

$$\text{Value of an asset with life} > n \text{ years} = \frac{E(CF_1)}{(1+r)^1} + \frac{E(CF_2)}{(1+r)^2} + \ldots + \frac{E(CF_n)}{(1+r)^n} + \frac{\text{Terminal Value}_n}{(1+r)^n}$$

| Truth 1: The terminal value can be based on annuities or a liquidation value. | Truth 2: Not if growth forever is capped at the growth rate of the economy. | Truth 3: Growth is not free & increasing growth can add or destroy value. | Truth 4: Growth can be negative forever & is often more reflective of reality. | Truth 5: The terminal value should be a high percent of value today. |

FIGURE 12.3   Myth and Reality on Terminal Value

CONCLUSION

The value of a firm is the present value of its expected cash flows over its life. Since firms can have infinite lives, you apply closure to a valuation by estimating cash flows for a period, and then estimating a value for the firm at the end of the period—a terminal value. Many analysts estimate the terminal value using a multiple of earnings or revenues in the final estimation year, a non-starter if you are doing an intrinsic value. If you assume that firms have infinite lives, an approach that is more consistent with discounted cash flow valuation is to assume that the cash flows of the firm will grow at a constant rate forever beyond a point in time. When the firm that you are valuing will approach this growth rate, which you label a stable growth rate, is a key part of any discounted cash flow valuation. Small firms that are growing fast and have significant competitive advantages should be able to grow at high rates for much longer periods than larger and more mature firms, without these competitive advantages. If you do not want to assume an infinite life for a firm, you can estimate a liquidation value based on what others will pay for the assets that the firm has accumulated during the high-growth phase.

QUESTIONS AND SHORT PROBLEMS

In the problems following, use an equity risk premium of 5.5 percent if none is specified.

1. Ulysses Inc. is a shipping company with $100 million in earnings before interest and taxes that is expected to have earnings growth of 10% for the next five years. At the end of the fifth year, you estimate the terminal value using a multiple of eight times operating income (which is the average for the sector).
   a. Estimate the terminal value of the firm.
   b. If the cost of capital for Ulysses is 10%, the tax rate is 40%, and you expect the stable growth rate to be 5%, what is the return on capital that you are assuming in perpetuity if you use a multiple of 8 times operating income?
2. Genoa Pasta manufactures Italian food products and currently earns $80 million in earnings before interest and taxes. You expect the firm's earnings to grow 20 percent a

year for the next six years and 5% thereafter. The firm's current after-tax return on capital is 28%, but you expect it to be halved after the sixth year. If the cost of capital for the firm is expected to be 10% in perpetuity, estimate the terminal value for the firm. (The tax rate for the firm is 40%.)

3. Lamps Galore Inc. manufactures table lamps and earns an after-tax return on capital of 15% on its current capital invested (which is $100 million). You expect the firm to reinvest 80% of its after-tax operating income back into the business for the next four years and 30% thereafter (the stable growth period). The cost of capital for the firm is 9%.
   a. Estimate the terminal value for the firm (at the end of the fourth year).
   b. If you expect the after-tax return on capital to drop to 9% after the fourth year, what would your estimate of terminal value be?

4. Bevan Real Estate Inc. is a real estate holding company with four properties. You estimate that the income from these properties, which is currently $50 million after taxes, will grow 8% a year for the next 10 years and 3% thereafter. The current market value of the properties is $500 million, and you expect this value to appreciate at 3% a year for the next 10 years.
   a. Estimate the terminal value of the properties, based on the current market value and the expected appreciation rate in property values.
   b. Assuming that your projections of income growth are right, what is the terminal value as a multiple of after-tax operating income in the tenth year?
   c. If you assume that no reinvestment is needed after the tenth year, estimate the cost of capital that you are implicitly assuming with your estimate of the terminal value.

5. Latin Beats Corporation is a firm that specializes in Spanish music and videos. In the current year, the firm reported $20 million in after-tax operating income, $15 million in capital expenditures, and $5 million in depreciation. The firm expects all three items to grow at 10% for the next five years. Beyond the fifth year, the firm expects to be in stable growth and grow at 4% a year in perpetuity. You assume that earnings, capital expenditures, and depreciation will grow at 4% in perpetuity, and that your cost of capital is 12%. (There is no working capital.)
   a. Estimate the terminal value of the firm.
   b. What reinvestment rate and return and capital are you implicitly assuming in perpetuity when you do this?
   c. What would your terminal value have been if you had assumed that capital expenditures offset depreciation in stable growth?
   d. What return on capital are you implicitly assuming in perpetuity when you set capital expenditures equal to depreciation?

6. Crabbe Steel owns a number of steel plants in Pennsylvania. The firm reported after-tax operating income of $40 million in the most recent year on capital invested of $400 million. The firm expects operating income to grow 7% a year for the next three years, and 3% thereafter.
   a. If the firm's cost of capital is 10% and you expect the firm's current return on capital to continue in perpetuity, estimate the value at the end of the third year.
   b. If you expect operating income to stay fixed after year 3 (what you earn in year 3 is what you will earn every year thereafter), estimate the terminal value.
   c. If you expect operating income to drop 5% a year in perpetuity after year 3, estimate the terminal value.

7. How would your answers to the preceding problem change if you were told that the cost of capital for the firm is 8%?

CHAPTER 13

Narrative and Numbers –
Story to Value

After reading the last few chapters on valuation inputs, you may have concluded that both valuation and pricing are driven by numbers alone, but you would be wrong. In this chapter, we will argue that there is a story behind the numbers in the valuation and pricing of a company, and that the key to valuing companies well is being able to craft plausible business stories and connecting these stories to the numbers you use in your valuation. In this chapter, we will begin by explaining how valuations connect stories to numbers, and then describing the process of telling a business story, checking that story for reasonableness, and converting that story into valuation inputs and value.

VALUATION AS A BRIDGE

As access to data improved and the tools that we have available to use with that data became more powerful, valuation as a discipline has become increasingly not just number focused, but one built around financial modeling. In the process, we believe that valuation has lost its way, since the essence of a good valuation is that it is a bridge between stories and numbers, connecting a story about a business to inputs into a valuation, and by extension, to value. That process is encapsulated in Figure 13.1.

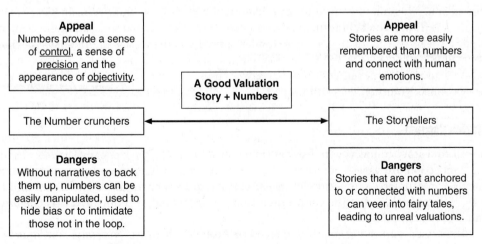

FIGURE 13.1 Valuation = Narrative Plus Numbers

Put simply, a compilation of numbers in a spreadsheet or a model will give you a financial model, not a valuation, and a story about the prospects for a business, no matter how soaring and compelling, may just be a fairy tale. For a valuation to be rooted in reality, every number in your valuation, measuring growth, risk or profitability, has to have a story that explains it, and every story that you tell about your company, from brand name to management quality, has to have a number that backs it up.

It is undeniable that each of us, when presented with numbers and stories, has a strong side, and not surprisingly, we try to play to our strengths, not our weaknesses. The peril of doing so is that focusing just on one side of the valuation bridge (stories or numbers) can lead us into danger:

- If number crunching is your strength, and you are surrounded or work with other number crunchers, the search for false precision, where estimating a discount rate to the fourth decimal point, takes precedence over far more important considerations, such as the viability of a company's business model, when valuing companies. If all you have are numbers on a spreadsheet, you have a financial model, not a valuation of a company.
- If storytelling is your forte, you have a different set of delusions. You believe that telling soaring, visionary stories entitles you to big values, even if those stories are fairy tales. Without the discipline of numbers, it is easy to use buzzwords to justify attaching high values to business.

For your valuations to make sense and become the basis for your actions, you must be either a disciplined storyteller or an imaginative number cruncher. If your strength is working with numbers, your task, if you want to value companies, should be getting more comfortable working with qualitative factors and ultimately bringing them into your numbers. If you are more drawn to storytelling, you must work on getting comfortable enough with numbers, so that you can convert your stories into valuation inputs.

THE IMPORTANCE OF STORYTELLING

If you have worked in valuation or been taught the subject, you may find the appeal to stories odd. After all, in conventional valuation, the intrinsic value of a business is driven by its cash flows, which, in turn, are determined by the growth, margins, and reinvestment needs for a firm. Why then, you may wonder, should you dilute those numbers or distract yourself by telling a story. In this section, we will start by looking at why stories connect better than numbers, even with number savvy audiences, and then look at how having a story connect your numbers will keep you from egregious errors and bias.

Stories Connect

A well-told story connects with listeners in a way that numbers never can. The reasons for the connection are varied both across stories and across listeners, and the extent of the connection can vary in intensity. In recent years, scientists have turned their attention to why and are finding that the connections may be hardwired into our brains as chemical and electrical impulses.

Let's start with the chemical explanation. Paul Zak, a neuroeconomist at Claremont Graduate University, identified a neurochemical called oxytocin, a molecule in the hypothalamus of the human brain.[1] He argues that oxytocin, whose release and synthesis is associated with trust and caring, is created and released when a person listens to a powerful story (or narrative), and that this release can lead to changes in the listener's post-narrative behavior. In addition, during stressful moments in stories, the brain releases cortisol, allowing the listener to focus. Other research also finds that happy endings to stories trigger the limbic portion of the brain, its reward center, to release dopamine, a trigger for hope and optimism.

Greg Stephens, Lauren Silbert, and Uri Hasson have a fascinating study of how electrical impulses in brains seem to respond to storytelling in what they term "neural coupling".[2] In particular, they report on an experiment, where a young woman tells a story to twelve subjects, and the brain waves of both the storyteller and the listeners are recorded. As the story gets told, they note two phenomena. The first is that the brain waves of the storyteller and listeners synchronize, with the same parts of the brain lighting up for both, with a time lag on the listeners (as they process the story). To test to see whether it is the story itself that made the difference, the story was told in Russian (which none of the listeners understood) and the brain wave activity ceased, thus illustrating that it is the story (and understanding it) that seems to make the connection. The second and more intriguing finding is that on some aspects of the story, the listeners' brain impulses precede those of the storyteller, suggesting that involved listeners start predicting the next steps in the story. Overall, as the synchronization in brain waves between the storyteller and those listening to the story increases, communication becomes more effective.

Stories are Remembered

As a teacher for more than three decades, I am lucky enough to still run into students from decades past who reminisce about classes. It is astonishing how often and how well they remember the little anecdotes and stories that have dotted our classes over time, though the details of the class have been long lost in the fog of their memories.

We are not unique in this experience, as studies indicate the staying power of stories. Stories get remembered much better and for longer periods than numbers are. In one study, subjects were read stories and expository texts and their memory was tested later.[3] Even though the content was the same, the stories were remembered about 50 percent more than the expository passages. As to why some stories get remembered more than others, researchers hypothesize that it is causal connections within the story that make them more memorable, especially if subjects have to make inferences (work) to make the connections. Thus, when subjects are given different versions of the same paragraph to read, they are less likely to remember the paragraph if the causal relationship is either too obvious or very weak. But they are more likely to remember it if the causality is understated but requires some work on the part of subjects to connect.

If there is a lesson to be learned from these studies for storytellers, it is that stories work best if they not only involve listeners but require them to think on their own and

---

[1] Zak, P., 2014, *Why your brain loves good story telling,* Harvard Business Review, October 2014.
[2] Stephens, G.J., L.J. Silbert and U. Hasson, 2010, *Speaker-listener Neuro Coupling underlies Successful Communication,* Proceedings of the National Academy of Scientists (PNAS)
[3] Graesser, A. C., Singer, M., Trabasso, T., 1994, *Constructing Inferences During Narrative Text Comprehension,* Psychological Review, 101, 371–395.

make their own connections. Those connections may very well have been the ones that you wanted them to make in the first place, but it is not only more effective but also more memorable if listeners make it, rather than have it force fed to them. As with so much else in life, when it comes to storytelling, less is more.

Stories Spur Action

Not only do stories enable emotional connections between storytellers and listeners and get remembered more vividly and for longer periods, they can elicit listeners to act. As part of his research on storytelling, Paul Zak also looked at whether the increase in oxytocin, the neurochemical that he identifies as the one released during stories, was associated with actions after the stories had been told. In one experiment where subjects were asked to watch public service announcement videos produced by the British government, the increase in oxytocin resulting from watching the video was measured, and the higher increases were associated with bigger donations to the charities mentioned in the videos.

The studies also found that some stories evoked bigger increases in neurochemicals, and thus elicited more actions than others. For instance, narratives with dramatic arcs to them resulted in more responses than flat narratives, as did stories which caused viewers to become more engaged with the story characters.

In the context of valuation, where the point, at least for investors, is to act (i.e., to buy undervalued companies and to sell overvalued ones), it is more likely that you will act on a valuation, backed by a story, than a valuation that is purely numbers.

THE DANGERS IN STORYTELLING

While we believe that it is important to establish narrative in valuation, we are also aware of the dangers of opening the door to storytelling. In the interests of balance, we will consider the downside to stories, and in the process, lay the foundations for what we will call "bounded storytelling".

Stories Can Sway Emotions

As we noted in the earlier section, stories are powerful because they connect with people's emotions, get remembered, and elicit action from listeners. It is for each of these reasons that stories can be extremely dangerous, not just for listeners, but also for storytellers. If the last section made a case for telling and listening to stories, you should consider this one a cautionary one about the dangers of letting just stories drive decisions.

The field of behavioral economics is of recent origin and represents the intersection of psychology and economics. Put succinctly, behavioral economics lays bare all of the quirks in human nature that lead people to make bad decisions, especially if they base these decisions on emotion, instinct, and gut feeling. Kahnemann, a father of this field, takes us on a romp through the fields of human irrationality in his book, *Thinking, Fast and Slow* and notes some of the biases that we bring to decision-making processes that stories can exploit easily.[4] It is not just listeners, though, who are in danger from letting emotions run away

---

[4]Kahnemann, D., 2010, Thinking, Fast and Slow, Farrar, Straus and Giroux.

from the facts. Storytellers, too, face the same problem, as they start to believe their own stories and perhaps act on them. In effect, stories feed into the biases that we already have, reinforce them, and make them worse. As Tyler Cowen pointed out in a TED talk, critiquing the wave of popular psychology books asking people to trust their instincts, *"the single, central, most important way we screw up, and that is, we tell ourselves too many stories, or we are too easily seduced by stories. And why don't these books tell us that? It's because the books themselves are all about stories. The more of these books you read, you're learning about some of your biases, but you're making some of your other biases essentially worse. So the books themselves are part of your cognitive bias."*[5]

Earlier, we noted that one of the benefits of storytelling is that as listeners get more absorbed in stories, they tend to become much more willing to suspend disbelief and let questionable assertions and assumptions go unchallenged. Much as that may be a plus for storytellers, it is exactly what enables con men and fraudsters, usually master storytellers, to spin tales of big riches and separate listeners from their money. As Oliver Stone is quoted as having said, "Master storytellers want us drunk on emotion so we will lose track of rational considerations and yield to their agenda", a benefit for a moviemaker like Stone but not a worthy testimonial for a business story.

Memories Can Be Fickle

It is true that many storytellers draw on personal memories in coming up with their stories and if they tell their stories effectively, these stories will be remembered for far longer. As researchers are discovering, human memories are fragile and easily manipulated, and it is entirely possible that both storytellers and listeners are drawing on false memories in making their judgments and decisions.

The false memory issue came to the forefront in 2014, when Brian Williams, the NBC national news anchor, admitted that stories that he had told repeatedly to audiences about his experiences during the invasion of Iraq in 2003 were made up. While it is possible that he made up these lies to advance his own case (as a heroic reporter who put his life at risk to get to a story), it is also plausible that he convinced himself over time that his version of the story was the truth. Researchers on memory were not surprised since they have been able to convince people of events in their past that had never occurred. In one study, researchers were able to convince 70 percent of their subjects that they had committed crimes as adolescents that resulted in police action, when, in fact, none of them had done so.[6] In another, researchers were able to leave their subjects with the memory (false) of having been lost in a shopping mall as children, even though they had not.[7]

This is not to suggest that stories are always made up or full of falsehoods, but to show that even well-meaning story tellers can sometimes reinvent their memories, and that those listening to those stories might not be remembering the stories the way they were actually told.

---

[5] https://www.youtube.com/watch?v=RoEEDKwzNBw
[6] Shaw, J. and S. Porter, 2015, *Constructing Rich False Memories of Committing Crime, Psychological Science* March 2015 26: 291–301.
[7] Loftus, Elizabeth F.; Pickrell, Jacqueline E., 1995, *The Formation of False Memories*, Psychiatric Annals, Vol 25(12), Dec 1995, 720–725.

Stories Can Become Fairy Tales

A key difference between telling a story for entertainment and a business story is that the latter is (or should) be bounded by reality and the real world does not reward business story tellers for just being creative. In fact, one of the perils of letting storytelling drive business decisions is that it is easy to cross the line and wander into fantasy land. In business storytelling, this can manifest itself in dysfunctional forms:

- *The Fairy Tale:* This is a business story that follows the standard script for the most part, but at some point in the story, the narrator lets his or her hopes replace expectations and the creative juices flow. Not surprisingly, these stories end well, at least in the tellng, with the narrator emerging the victor with a successful business as bounty.
- *The Runaway Story:* This is a close relative of the fairy tale, where the story sounds so good and the protagonist is so likeable that listeners overlook major gaps in the story or failures of logic, because they want the story to be true.

The bottom line is if left unchecked, that storytelling can easily lose focus and at least in the context of business stories, that can be dangerous for everyone involved. In the section that follows, we will create a process for telling business stories that are bounded by reality and common sense, cognizant of the dangers listed in this section.

FROM STORY TO NUMBERS: THE PROCESS

As we noted in the last section, each of us has a strong side and we are drawn to that side, when valuing companies. It is for this reason that it is important that we establish a process for valuing companies which requires us to bring in our weak sides. In this section, we will lay out a sequence that works for us, though you may find a variant that works for you better, with the end game being a melding of narrative with numbers.

The Sequence

As number crunchers, we find it useful to start the valuation process by forcing ourselves to tell a company's story first, but if you are a storyteller, you may find that a sequence that starts with numbers works better for you. Figure 13.2 describes the five-step process of getting from story to valuation.

Every valuation that we do starts with a valuation story for the company, and to tell that story, we need to understand what the company does well and what it does badly, as well as the business it is in. In the second step of the sequence, we stress test the story, checking to make sure that it passes what we call the 3P test—possible, plausible and probable. In the third step, we convert the story into valuation inputs, drawing on a parsimonious and generic valuation model described in Chapter 11, built around growth, profitability, reinvestment, and risk. In the fourth step, the valuation inputs are converted into story, with heed to valuation first principles. In the final step, we keep the feedback loop open, listening to those who disagree with the story, with the intent of making our stories (and valuations) better.

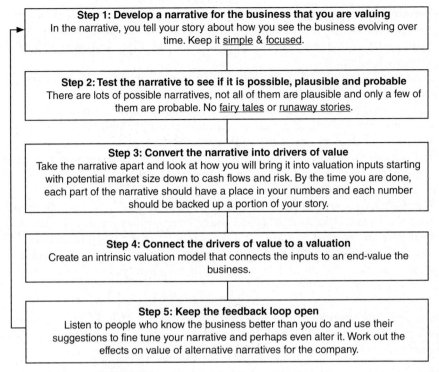

FIGURE 13.2   Story to Numbers—The Sequence

Step 1: Construct a Business Story   The first step is coming up with a valuation story that you believe best fits the company you are valuing. This, however, requires that you do your homework, understanding your company and its products, the market it competes in and the competitors it faces. In making this assessment, you can draw on the following:

- *The company's business:* One of the most crucial components in constructing a business story for a company is identifying the business it is in, and while this may seem obvious, it is more difficult than it looks. For instance, when asked what business Facebook is in, many would respond social media, but social media is a platform for delivering other businesses, not a business by itself. Facebook, at least in 2023, generated almost all of its revenues from advertising, and assuming that they will stay in advertising will frame your story for Facebook.
- *The company's financial history:* In framing your story for a company, you should look at its financial history, not because you believe that past is prologue, but because assuming that history (in terms of past growth and profitability) will repeat itself is a story that needs justification, as is assuming a break from history (from high-to-low growth, from being money-losing to money-making). As we will see in the coming chapters, one reason analysts have trouble valuing young companies and start-ups is due to an absence of history.
- *Total market history and growth:* The history of growth in the total market for the company's products and services, with assessments for growth in the future, is a key

determinant of your company story. It is easier to tell a story of high growth when you are a company in a growing market (e.g., NVIDIA in the AI chips business), than if you are one in a stagnant or declining market (e.g., Coca Cola with soft drinks and Altria with tobacco).

■ *The Competition:* While being in a growing market gives you a tailwind, if you are a company in that market, you will face competition and history is full of companies that crash and burn in growing markets. In crafting your company's story, you need to think about the competitive advantages that your company possesses (or does not possess), and how these will evolve over time. Companies that operate in businesses with few or no competitive barriers to entry will find themselves working harder to deliver growth, and their business stories will have to reflect this constraint.

■ *The macroeconomy:* To the extent that companies and industries are exposed to macroeconomic risk, your story will have to incorporate what you see occurring on that front. Thus, if you are valuing a cyclical company, your assessment of the economy may become part of your company's story, and with an oil company, what you think about the future course of oil prices may be a key part of your company story.

As you craft a business story for your company, it is worth reminding yourself that you are not a creative novelist, and that you are creating a foundation for a valuation. Consequently, you should aim to do the following:

■ *Keep it simple:* When telling business stories for companies, it is easy to get distracted by strands of these stories that may be interesting but that have little relevance for value. The most powerful business stories in valuation tend to be compact, boiling the company down to its core. In our valuations of Amazon from 1997 to 2012, our core story for Amazon was that it was a *Field of Dreams* company, built around the belief that if you build it (revenues), they (profits) will come, and in our valuations after 2013, the story shifted to that of a *Disruption Machine*, a company that would go after any business it felt had soft spots that could be exploited by a more efficient and patient player.

■ *Keep it focused:* No matter what business you are valuing, for it to be valuable, the end game is that it must make money. In short, a business story, even if it is not money-making now, must include pathways to make money in the future.

A good valuation story will benefit from brevity, steer away from buzzwords, and be relatable even to novices to valuation and the business.

BUSINESS STORIES: SPANNING THE SPECTRUM

As in literature, where it can be argued that there are only a few core story plots that get repackaged and represented as new ones, there are only a few business stories that you see play out in practice. While business stories can vary depending on the business you are in and where you stand in the corporate life cycle, which is at the risk of both overgeneralizing and not spanning the spectrum of possible stories, here are a few classic business stories:

Business Story	Type of Business	Investment Pitch
The Bully	Company with a large market share, a superior brand name, access to lots of capital, and a reputation for ruthlessness	Steamrolls competition to deliver ever-increasing revenues and profits
The Underdog	Company that is a distant second (or lower) in market share in a business, with claims to a better or cheaper product than the dominant company	Will work harder than the dominant player at pleasing customers, perhaps with a kinder, gentler corporate image
The Eureka Moment	Claims to have found an unmet need in the market, usually in a serendipitous way, and then has come up with a way of meeting that need	Will succeed as a business by filling the unmet need
The Better Mousetrap	Contends that it has a better way of delivering an existing product or service that will be more desirable and better suited to the need	Eats into the market share of the existing players in the market
The Disruptor	Changes the way a business is run, altering fundamental ways in which the product or service is delivered	Is ineffective and inefficient, believing disruption will change the business (while making money)
The Low-Cost Player	Has found a way to reduce to cost of doing business and is willing to cut prices on the expectation that it can sell a lot more	Increased sales will more than make up for lower margins
The Missionary	Presents itself as having a larger, more noble mission than just making money	Makes money while doing good (for society)

This is not a comprehensive list, but it does cover a large proportion of the businesses both in public and private capital markets. There are also two additional points worth making. The first is that it is possible for a company to have dual narratives, as was the case with Uber in September 2015, a company that is telling both a disruption story (it is changing the car service business) and a dominance story (it is presenting itself as unstoppable in the ride-sharing market). The second is that as a company moves through the life cycle, its narrative will change. Thus, when Google entered the search engine market in 1998, it was the scrappy underdog to the established players then, but in 2015 it had made the transition to being the dominant player in the market, perhaps even a bully, with a reputation to match.

ILLUSTRATION 13.1:   A Business Story for Zomato

The company we will use to illustrate this process is Zomato, an Indian restaurant-delivery company, at the time of its initial public offering in 2021. At the time of the IPO, Zomato had modest revenues and big operating losses, but it had a significant market share of the Indian restaurant delivery market, with two major competitors (Zwiggy and Amazon Foods). Building a story for Zomato requires an understanding of the Indian restaurant delivery market and its potential for growth. In Table 13.1, we look at size of the Indian restaurant food delivery market, relative to the U.S., the EU, and China.

TABLE 13.1   Indian Restaurant Delivery Market in 2021

	India	China	United States	EU
General				
GDP in 2020 (in trillions of US $)	$ 2.71	$ 14.70	$ 20.93	$ 15.17
Population (millions)	1360	1430	330	445
Per Capital GDP	$ 1,993	$ 10,280	$ 63,424	$ 34,090
Number of restaurants (in 2000s)	1000	9000	660	890
Food Delivery				
Online Access (percent)	43%	63%	88%	90%
Online Food Delivery Users (millions)	50.00	450.00	105.00	150.00
Online Food Delivery Market ($ million) in 2019	$4,200.00	$ 90,000.00	$21,000.00	$15,000.00
Online Food Delivery Market ($ million) in 2020	$2,900.00	$110,000.00	$49,000.00	$13,800.00

As you can see the Indian food delivery market lags the other three markets in size and per capita usage, but some of that difference can be attributed to differences in wealth (India's lower GDP) and internet service (because Zomato's delivery is through a phone app). Some of it can also be attributed to cultural differences, with Indians less likely to eat out at restaurants than their American and Chinese counterparts.

Our story for Zomato includes components relating to the country and trends in restaurant eating in India:

- The Indian food delivery/restaurant market will grow, as Indians become more prosperous and have increased online access, to reach $25 billion (₹1,800–₹2,000 billion) in ten years.

- The market will continue to be dominated by two or three large players, albeit with lots of localized and niche competitors who will continue to command a significant slice of the market. Zomato will be one of the winners/survivors, and will command a market share of 40% of the total restaurant-delivery market.

- Zomato's revenues represent the percentage of the gross orders placed on that platform that accrue to the company. While that number was 23.13% of gross orders in 2020 and 21.03% in 2021, we will assume that share will converge on 22% in future years.

- The biggest expenses at intermediary businesses like Zomato, which connect customers with businesses, are often on customer acquisition and marketing, and as growth scales down, these expenses should decrease, as a percent of revenues, delivering a profitability bonus. We will assume that *pre-tax operating margins will trend towards 35%*, largely because we believe that the market will be dominated by a few big players, but with the very real possibility that one rogue player that is unwilling to play the game can upend profitability.

▨ Zomato's reinvestment, to generate revenue growth, will be investments in technology and in acquisitions, and this need will continue in the near future, with a lightening up in later years, as growth declines.

▨ In terms of operating risk, the company, despite its global ambitions, is still primarily an Indian company, dependent on Indian macroeconomic growth to succeed, and our rupee cost of capital will incorporate the country risk.

▨ Zomato is a money-losing company, but it is not a start-up, facing imminent failure. On the plus side, its size and access to capital as well as its post-IPO–augmented cash balance, push down the risk of failure. On the minus side, this is a company that is still burning through cash, and will need access to capital in future years to continue to survive. Overall, we will attach a likelihood of failure of 10%, reflecting this balance.

In effect, in our story, Zomato remains primarily a restaurant delivery business, with supplemental income coming from its forays into grocery deliveries and health products.

Step 2: The 3P Test　Once you have constructed a business story for your company, you must stop and check to see if your story passes what we call the 3P test: Is it possible? Is it plausible? Is it probable? We capture the differences between the three tests in Figure 13.3.

As you go from possible to plausible to probable, you are making the tests more stringent, requiring more compelling explanations or more data from the storyteller. The "possibility" test is the weakest of the three, requiring only that you show there is some pathway that exists for your story to hold, and that it is not a fairy tale. The "plausibility" test is stronger, requiring evidence that you have succeeded, at least on a smaller scale (a market test, a geography), with your business. The "probability" test is the most difficult one, since you must show that your business story can scale up and your barriers to entry work.

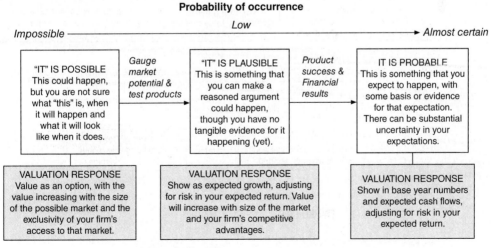

FIGURE 13.3　Valuation Stories—The 3P Test

For companies with long business histories and established track records, passing the 3P test is easy as long as you assume that they will continue in the same business. Assuming that Coca Cola will grow at the same rate as the soft-drink beverage market, or that Altria will see shrinkage in revenues as cigarette smoking continues to decline, is unlikely to get push back, but a story of Coca Cola transitioning to become an alcohol company or Altria expanding into cannabis will require more explanation and a stronger backing.

With Zomato, it was a more challenging test, since it is growing a disruptive delivery model in a market (Indian restaurant delivery), which is itself evolving and growing. Building the Zomato story around restaurant food delivery makes it easier to defend, because Zomato had succeeded in that business, at least in terms of delivering revenue growth and a significant market share. There were others telling bigger stories for Zomato in 2021, ranging from it being a grocery delivery business to a retail platform for a wider array of products, and they would have faced tougher (albeit still passable) tests.

Step 3: Connecting Stories to Inputs For a story to become part of a valuation, you must convert its parts into valuation inputs. If you have a valuation model with dozens of inputs and complex output, this will become difficult, if not impossible, to do. One reason that we believe valuations should be parsimonious, with as few inputs as possible and limited output, is because they lend themselves much more easily to story connections. In Chapter 11, we introduced the most general version of a valuation model, and we summarize those in Figure 13.4.

Breaking down the inputs, the cash flows of a firm can be written as a function of three key drivers

- *Growth:* The growth component of a business story is best captured in *revenue growth*, with that growth either coming from more units being sold or a higher price per unit. That revenue growth rate will be higher in larger markets, making the total

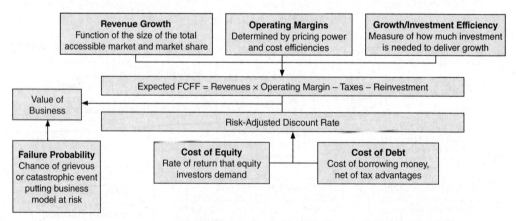

FIGURE 13.4 The Drivers of Value

market for a product or service a key driver, and lower for larger companies in that market, since scaling will work against them.

- *Profitability*: The profitability of a business story shows up in the operating margin that you estimate for the company. In making this estimate, you should start by looking at unit economics, i.e., how much it costs a company to produce an extra unit for sale, with better unit economics translating into higher operating margins. A well-run software company will generate much higher operating margins in steady state than a well-run chemical or automobile company.
- *Investment efficiency*: To grow revenues, companies must reinvest, with that reinvestment being in plant and equipment for manufacturing companies and R&D and acquisitions for technology companies. The efficiency with which growth is generated can be measured by looking at the dollars in revenues that a company can generate for every dollar invested (sales to invested capital), with more efficient companies delivering higher revenues.

There are two inputs that encapsulate the risk you see in the business:

- *Operating Risk*: In Chapter 3, we went through the process of computing the cost of capital for a company, but a big picture perspective of the cost of capital is that it measures the operating risk in a business. Suffice to say that businesses facing more operating risk should have higher costs of capita. To provide perspective on what comprises a high or low cost of capital, we report the distribution of costs of capital, by region, for global companies in January 2023 in Table 13.2.

  While these are in US dollars, converting them into other currencies is simply done by incorporating the differential inflation between the US dollar and those currencies. Thus, if expected inflation is 3% in the US and 5% in India, the median cost of capital in Indian Rupees for an Indian company would be 13.19% (adding two percent to the median cost of capital for an emerging market company).
- *Failure risk*: Discounting free cash flows to the firm back at the cost of capital yields value for the operating assets of the firm, if the firm survives as a going concern. With young firms or distressed companies, where there is a material chance of failure, you should assess the risk of this failure and assess your value if that happens, rather than try to increase your discount rate to incorporate the risk.

TABLE 13.2   Costs of Capital for U.S. and Global Companies in US $—January 2023

Decile/Quartile	US	Emerging Markets	Europe	Japan	Global
1st Decile (Lowest Risk)	6.01%	8.08%	7.26%	7.71%	7.39%
First Quartile	7.26%	9.56%	8.64%	9.07%	9.08%
Median	9.63%	11.19%	10.41%	10.72%	10.60%
Third Quartile	10.88%	12.97%	12.02%	11.50%	12.07%
9th Decile (Highest Risk)	11.63%	15.31%	14.25%	13.10%	14.04%

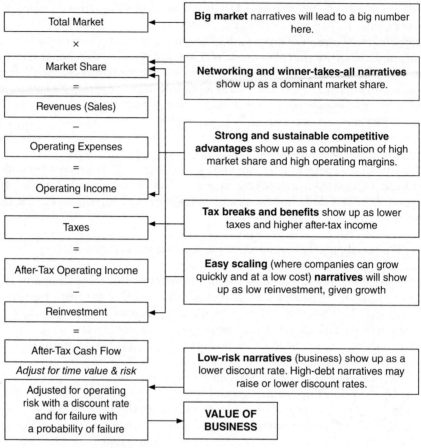

FIGURE 13.5 Stories and Valuation Inputs

Thus, to connect a business story into value, you must consider which of these inputs to change to reflect that story. Thus, if the key selling point of your business story is that it has a large potential market, it is revenue growth that will best reflect that belief, whereas if it is that your company has significant advantages (e.g., technological, brand name, patent protection) over its competition, it will show up as higher market share. Figure 13.5 summarizes the links between key components of business stories and valuation inputs.

ILLUSTRATION 13.2:   From Story to Valuation Inputs: Zomato

Applying this framework to Zomato, at the time of its IPO in 2021, we converted our story into valuation inputs with the total market being the Indian restaurant food delivery market. Figure 13.6 shows the link between the story and inputs for Zomato in June 2021.

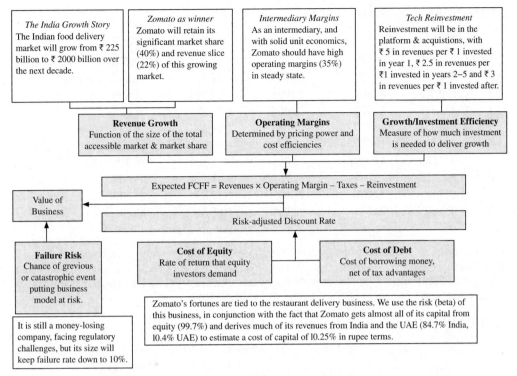

FIGURE 13.6   Stories and Valuation Inputs—Zomato in June 2021

Note that every part of the story plays out in a valuation input, and that changing your story for Zomato will alter these inputs and its value.

Step 4: From Inputs to Value   Once you have converted your story to valuation inputs, the process of converting those inputs into forecasted numbers and value is mechanical. Specifically, you use revenue growth to obtain expected revenues in future years, and then applying forecasted margins to these revenues yields operating profits. The reinvestment story converts these profits into cash flows, and the risk story allows us to discount these cash flows back in time to get a value today.

In short, if you have stayed true to the sequence, every number in your valuation should have a story behind it, and every story you tell about a company will have a number that is in your valuation. More importantly, you will lose the ability to arbitrarily change inputs to get a different value, since any significant input change requires that you retell your story, and it is very likely that you will find yourself stymied by the 3P test, when you try to do so.

ILLUSTRATION 13.3:   From Valuation Inputs to Value: Zomato

Our story for Zomato is an upbeat one, built on the presumption that the Indian economy will continue to grow strongly, pushing up demand for restaurant food and online food delivery, and that Zomato will retain a dominant market share. We start by forecasting the expected operating profits for Zomato, with the inputs that come out of that story.

EXPECTED OPERATING PROFITS AT ZOMATO

	Total Market	Market Share	Revenue Share	Revenues	Operating Margin	EBIT
1	₹ 337,500	41.72%	22.00%	₹ 30,975	−10.00%	−₹ 3,097
2	₹ 438,750	41.29%	22.00%	₹ 39,853	−1.25%	−₹ 498
3	₹ 570,375	40.86%	22.00%	₹ 51,270	6.88%	₹ 3,527
4	₹ 741,488	40.43%	22.00%	₹ 65,951	12.50%	₹ 8,244
5	₹ 963,934	40.00%	22.00%	₹ 84,826	18.13%	₹15,379
6	₹1,203,471	40.00%	22.00%	₹105,905	20.23%	₹21,425
7	₹1,440,555	40.00%	22.00%	₹126,769	27.61%	₹35,001
8	₹1,650,156	40.00%	22.00%	₹145,214	35.00%	₹50,825
9	₹1,805,271	40.00%	22.00%	₹158,864	35.00%	₹55,602
10	₹1,881,995	40.00%	22.00%	₹165,616	35.00%	₹57,965

Next, we bring in the effects of taxes and reinvestment. Note that the company pays no taxes in year 1, when it loses money, and uses carried-forward operating losses to shelter much of its profits in year 2 from settling into a 25% tax rate. The assumptions about investment efficiency about the sales to capital ratio allow you to estimate reinvestment and free cash flows, as can be seen in Table 13.3.

TABLE 13.3   Free Cash Flows to the Firm and Present Value at Zomato in 2021

Year	EBIT	Tax Rate	EBIT (1–t)	Reinvestment	FCFF	Cost of Capital	PV
1	−₹ 3,097	0.00%	−₹ 3,097	₹2,207	−₹ 5,305	10.25%	−$ 4,811
2	₹ 498	0.00%	₹ 498	₹3,551	−₹ 3,053	10.25%	−$ 2,512
3	₹ 3,527	6.63%	₹ 3,293	₹4,567	−₹ 1,273	10.25%	−$ 950
4	₹ 8,244	25.00%	₹ 6,183	₹5,872	₹ 311	10.25%	$ 210
5	₹15,379	25.02%	₹11,531	₹6,292	₹ 5,239	10.25%	$ 3,216
6	₹21,425	25.02%	₹16,065	₹7,026	₹ 9,039	10.00%	$ 5,044
7	₹35,001	24.99%	₹26,253	₹6,954	₹19,299	9.74%	$ 9,813
8	₹50,825	25.00%	₹38,119	₹6,148	₹31,970	9.48%	$14,848
9	₹55,602	25.00%	₹41,702	₹4,550	₹37,152	9.23%	$15,797
10	₹57,965	25.00%	₹43,474	₹2,251	₹41,224	8.97%	$16,085

To get to value per share, we discount the cash flows back at the costs of capital (10.25% to start, drifting down to 8.97% by year 10) that we have estimated for the company.[8] To complete the valuation, we estimate the value at the end of year 10. To do so, we assume a growth rate in perpetuity of 4.25%, in Indian rupees, and a return on capital of 12% after year 10:

$$\text{Terminal Value} = \frac{\text{After-tax Operating income in year 11} \times \left(1 - \dfrac{\text{Growth Rate}}{\text{ROC}}\right)}{(\text{Cost of Capital} - \text{Growth Rate})}$$

$$= \frac{43,474 \, (1.0425) \times \left(1 - \dfrac{.0425}{.12}\right)}{(.0897 - .0425)} = ₹620,133 \text{ million}$$

---

[8]Since the costs of capital are changing, to discount the cash flows in year 7, you have to use a cumulated cost of capital $= 19,299/(1.1025)^7(1.10)\,(1.0974) = \$9,813$ million

Discounting this value back and adding it to the present value of the cash flows yields a value for the operating assets. To get to value per share, we subtract out debt, add the cash balance (including expected proceeds from the IPO) and nonoperating assets, and net out the value of equity options. We finally divide by the number of shares that will be outstanding after the public offering.

Present value of terminal value	₹241,972
+ Present value of FCFF over next 10 years	₹ 56,739
= Value of operating assets	₹298,712
– Adjustment for failure	₹ 14,936
= Value of operating assets adjusted for failure	₹283,776
– Debt & Minority Interests	₹ 1,592
+ Cash (includes IPO proceeds)	₹105,332
+ Nonoperating assets	₹ 30,628
= Value of equity	₹418,144
– Value of equity options	₹ 73,245
Value of equity in common stock	₹344,898
Number of shares	7,946.68
Value per share	₹ 43.40

The operating asset value adjusted for failure is computed, by assuming that liquidation value will be half of fair value, if it occurs: ₹298,712 (.9) + ₹298,712 (.5) (.1) = $283,886. This process yields a value per share of about ₹43, but it is worth pausing and reminding yourself at each stage how our story is playing out in the numbers.

Step 5: Keeping the Feedback Loop Open   Let us assume that you have a story for your company, you have made sure the story passes the 3P test, you have converted the story into value inputs, and valued the company. As you celebrate, it is worth reminding yourself that this is not the value for the company, but your value, reflecting your story and inputs, and that you will be wrong. That is why it is so critical to keep the valuation process open for feedback, especially from those who disagree most strongly with you. As you read or listen to their critiques, rather than react defensively, you should consider using their arguments to strengthen and solidify your story.

ILLUSTRATION 13.4:   Keeping the Feedback Loop Open: Zomato

With the Zomato valuation, there were many who disagreed with us on our valuation, offering alternate stories for the companies, yielding much higher or lower values. Those with the higher-value stories were backed up by the market, since trading in the company opened at ₹72, and the stock continued its rise in the months after to reach ₹150. To see how alternate stories play out in valuation, we estimated the value, with these stories, and classified the valuations based upon the 3P test, in Table 13.4:

TABLE 13.4   Zomato – Alternate Stories and Value per Share

Zomato Story	Total Market (in millions)	Market Share	Revenue Slice	Target Margin	Cost of Capital	Value/ Share
Delivery Juggernaut	₹5,000,000	40%	25.00%	45.00%	9.50%	₹150.02
Delivery Star	₹5,000,000	40%	22.00%	35.00%	9.50%	₹ 93.00

(continued)

TABLE 13.4 *(continued)*

Zomato Story	Total Market (in millions)	Market Share	Revenue Slice	Target Margin	Cost of Capital	Value/ Share
Delivery Leader + Competition	₹5,000,000	40%	15.00%	25.00%	10.99%	₹ 61.55
Restaurant Delivery Juggernaut + High-Growth India	₹3,000,000	40%	25.00%	45.00%	9.50%	₹ 94.31
Restaurant Delivery Star + High-Growth India	₹3,000,000	40%	22.00%	35.00%	9.50%	₹ 59.02
Restaurant Delivery + Competition + High-Growth India	₹3,000,000	40%	20.00%	25.00%	10.99%	₹ 35.52
Our story, Positive	₹2,000,000	40%	25.00%	45.00%	10.25%	₹ 56.66
Our story	₹2,000,000	40%	22.00%	35.00%	10.25%	₹ 39.48
Our story, Negative	₹2,000,000	40%	20.00%	25.00%	10.25%	₹ 26.16
Restaurant Delivery Juggernaut + Low-Growth India	₹1,125,000	40%	25.00%	45.00%	9.50%	₹ 36.48
Restaurant Delivery Star + Low-Growth India	₹1,125,000	40%	22.00%	35.00%	9.50%	₹ 24.02
Restaurant Delivery + Competition + Low-Growth India	₹1,125,000	40%	20.00%	25.00%	10.99%	₹ 16.58

You may read this table as implying that anything goes when it comes to value, but that is not our reading of it. It is true that the value for Zomato can shift dramatically based upon the story you craft for the company, not only is that true for all young companies, but not all stories are equally plausible. Specifically when investing in a young company, you must find a story that you believe is plausible and you believe in, and accept the fact that there will other investors who will disagree with you. With more mature companies, there is less room for stories to diverge, and you will find more consensus on their valuations. Since the payoff in investing comes from being less wrong than others looking at the same company, it adds credence to the argument that the payoff to doing valuation is greater at young companies, where there is more disagreement about value than in more mature companies.

NARRATIVE AND NUMBERS ACROSS THE LIFE CYCLE

We believe that much of what we do in both corporate finance and valuation is determined by where a company is in the life cycle, and while the notion of intrinsic value as the present value of the expected cashflows from a business applies across the life cycle, there are key differences:

■ *Very different cash flow paths:* With young companies struggling with building business models, the cash flows will be negative in the early years, turn positive only as they approach high growth, and grow rapidly before settle into stability. With mature companies, you are far more likely to see positive cash flows immediately, but with far less growth in future years. With declining companies, you may see shrinkage in the cash flows over time as businesses get smaller.

■ *A changing dependence on terminal value:* Earlier in this chapter, we noted that the value of a business today will be the sum of the present value of its expected cash flows in the forecast period and the present value of the terminal value, capturing cash flows beyond the forecast period. Young companies, with negative cash flows in the early years and positive and growing cash flows later, will get a much large proportion of their values from the cash flows in the later years and the terminal value than more mature companies.

Staying with the theme that a valuation is a bridge between stories and numbers, we argue that the question of which one (story or numbers) should be given priority and dominate the valuation will also shift over the life cycle. With little historical data available on the company and big questions about business models early in the life cycle, it is the story that dominates the valuation, driving the valuation inputs and the numbers in the valuation. As a company ages, data will accumulate on the successes and failures of its business model, and the resulting numbers on revenue growth, margins, and reinvestment will move to the forefront, with the stories retreating to the background.

In Figure 13.7, we capture this shift from narrative to numbers, with key narrative drivers at each stage in the life cycle.

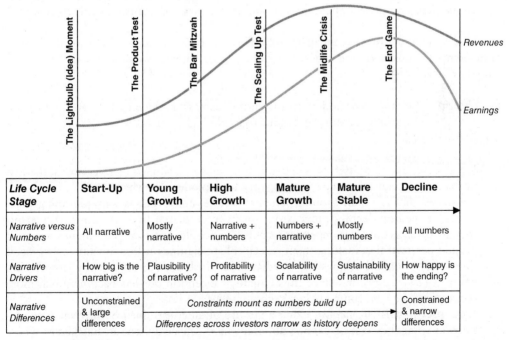

Life Cycle Stage	Start-Up	Young Growth	High Growth	Mature Growth	Mature Stable	Decline
Narrative versus Numbers	All narrative	Mostly narrative	Narrative + numbers	Numbers + narrative	Mostly numbers	All numbers
Narrative Drivers	How big is the narrative?	Plausibility of narrative?	Profitability of narrative	Scalability of narrative	Sustainability of narrative	How happy is the ending?
Narrative Differences	Unconstrained & large differences	Constraints mount as numbers build up				Constrained & narrow differences
		Differences across investors narrow as history deepens				

FIGURE 13.7 Narrative Versus Numbers Across the Corporate Life Cycle

It is worth noting also that when it is the story that drives valuation, as is often the case with young companies, we will find wide divergences in stories and value across investors, and when the numbers are dominant, those divergences will narrow, leading to more convergence on value. That is a partial explanation for why, even if markets are rational and efficient, we should expect to see far more volatility in stock prices at younger companies than at more mature ones.

STORY RESETS, CHANGES, AND BREAKS

One of the advantages of building a valuation around a story is that the process gives you perspective when examining news stories that emerge about the company or assessing the effect of earnings reports. Instead of focusing on the hype that a new CEO may bring to a company or whether a company reported earnings that beat analyst expectations by three cents or five, you can instead turn your attention to how much, if at all, the new CEO will alter the company narrative and the news in the earnings report that may lead you to change your story for a company. Broadly speaking, story changes can fall into three groups:

- In some cases, an event or action, either from within the firm or without can cause a *story to break*, with catastrophic consequences for value.
- In other cases, the core story can be proved to be either too expansive or too restrictive, and a reassessment of that story can lead you to a lower value with the former and a higher value with the latter.
- Even if the core story remains unchanged, the components of the story can change, with effects on growth, profitability, and cash flows, thus causing value to change.

In short, the notion that intrinsic value is stable or a constant is delusional, since as your company, business, and macroeconomic inputs change, so should your story and value.

Story Breaks An event that undercuts the entire business model on which your valuation story is built can cause your story and value to implode. In general, story breaks can occur for many reasons:

a. *Key person loss:* If a business is dependent on a key person for its operations, the loss of that person can cause the business story to implode. This is especially true in small businesses that are built around personal service, and explains why plumbing businesses or medical/dental practices do not have perpetual lives. As businesses grow, they tend to become less dependent upon key people, but some companies are built around personalities, making them susceptible to significant loss in value or worse, if those people falter. The question of what Elon Musk adds or takes away from Tesla's value has swirled around since the company's inception but has become much more consequential as the company has become larger.

b. *Legal and Regulatory action:* Companies are often constrained by laws and regulations in what they can or cannot do, and this is especially true in businesses where there are legal thresholds that a firm has to meet to operate. With Zomato, for instance, a decision by the government to crack down on restaurant food deliveries, could be fatal for value.

c. *Natural disasters:* While insurance has provided companies with protection against most natural disasters, in some parts of the world, there remain disasters that are almost impossible to insure against, either because they are so large that no insurance company can afford to offer protection, or because they are in parts of the world where insurance is tough to get.

d. *Fraud and malfeasance:* Acts of fraud and malfeasance can threaten a company's existence not only because they expose the firm to legal consequences, but because they break trust with customers, employees, and investors. Enron might have had a soaring story and market cap in the 1990s, but the revelations about widespread wrongdoing within the top ranks of the company doomed it. In the same vein, Theranos, a blood-testing company that soared to a $9 billion pricing, largely on promise and potential, lost all that value over the course of a few months as evidence emerged that the blood test results had been manipulated.

e. *Capital access:* With young companies, an uplifting and big story comes with capital needs, and if that capital dries up, either because of a market crisis or downturn, the story can break, even though key components remain.

f. *Other:* For many young companies, story breaks can occur for not fault of their own, with luck favoring some and working against others. With a young pharmaceutical company, this may take the form of fatal reactions to a promising drug that is in the company's product pipeline, putting an effective end to its story and value.

In general, story breaks are more likely to happen early in a company's life, but the consequences in terms of value lost are much greater when they happen, after a firm has scaled up.

Story Changes   An event that leads you to reassess your core story as either too expansive or too restrictive should lead you to change your story and value for the company. In some cases, that event can be a macroeconomic one, but often it can come from an action taken by the firm that leads you to reassess your original story.

- *Earnings reports:* When companies report earnings, many investors focus on the bottom line (i.e., whether the actual earnings per share beat or lagged what analysts expected to see reported). In our view, the more interesting and consequential news in earnings reports is in the subtext, where the company provides information that makes you reassess its story.
- *Acquisitions:* An acquisition, especially if it is of a large public target, is a calculated bet that can alter a company's story dramatically. If it fails, as was the case when Eastman Kodak bought Sterling Drugs or Time Warner bought AOL, it will take the company down with it. If it succeeds, it can alter a company's story line, perhaps moving it from a mature, steady state company to one that is a growth player.
- *Management changes:* A change at the top of a company, where a new CEO from the outside replaces a long-tenured CEO, can lead to a reassessment of the story line for the company and with it the value. That change can occur either because of a natural transition, or because of an activist investor's presence in the shareholding ranks.

With Zomato, an earnings report that contains news about a breakthrough that enables the company to expand beyond restaurant deliveries to grocery deliveries would greatly expand the story and push up value, whereas an announcement by Swiggy (a competitor) that the company plans to reduce its take (share of gross billing claimed as revenue) will spill over into the profitability part of your story for Zomato. In fact, Zomato's acquisition of Blinkit, a grocery delivery start-up, in 2022, expanded and changed its story line and value.

Story Shifts The core story may not break or change, but you may reassess the contours of that story, based upon either macroeconomic developments or stories about the company. Our story for Apple as a mature smartphone company that is a cash machine (i.e., a company capable of generating immense amounts of cash flows), remained unchanged over the last decade, but there were significant changes in our estimated intrinsic value per share as we updated the company's numbers as well as the macro inputs (risk-free rate and equity risk premium).

Month	Price per share	Value per share	% Difference
Sep-11	$ 54.47	$ 69.30	–21.39%
Sep-12	$ 95.30	$ 91.29	4.40%
Sep-13	$ 68.11	$ 86.43	–21.20%
Sep-14	$100.75	$ 97.91	2.90%
Sep-15	$110.30	$130.91	–15.74%
Sep-16	$113.05	$126.47	–10.61%
Sep-17	$154.12	$158.33	–2.66%
Sep-18	$225.74	$201.50	12.03%
Sep-19	$249.75	$243.25	2.67%
Sep-20	$462.83	$479.50	–3.48%

If the changes in intrinsic value over time trouble you, note that market prices also are affected by these changes, and investing is based upon how value measures up against price. In fact, over this decade, Apple was undervalued six times and overvalued four times, and the market price swung much more than intrinsic value did.

The growth in the Zomato story comes from the assumptions that the Indian economy will grow strongly, and that the restaurant business in the country will grow even more. Information that you receive that leads you to reassess one or both assumptions will play out as alterations in your story and value for the company.

CONCLUSION

Every valuation tells a story, and it not only makes sense to make that story explicit but check it for its weakest links. In this chapter, we started with an argument that valuations are bridges between stories and numbers, before laying out a five-step process for going from a company story to its value. We then looked at how the balance between stories and numbers can change over the life cycle, as well as why and how stories break, change, and shift. Just as warning, it is easy for investors to fall in love with their valuation narratives and resist or deny news stories that push against these stories. Maintaining a balance between having enough faith in your valuation, that you do not abandon it at the slightest hint of trouble, and not having so much conviction that you hold on to it, even when the data suggests that you should let go, is one of the toughest challenges in investing.

QUESTIONS AND SHORT PROBLEMS

In the problems following, use an equity risk premium of 5.5 percent if none is specified.

1. If every valuation is a bridge between stories and numbers, which of the following is your objective, in terms of storytelling, when valuing a company?
   a. Tell the most upbeat story that you can for the company.
   b. Tell the most realistic story that you can for the company.
   c. Tell the most pessimistic story that you can for the company.
2. In terms of getting the highest value for a young company, which of the following combinations is likely to deliver that value?
   a. High-revenue growth, high profitability, high-capital intensity.
   b. High-revenue growth, low profitability, low-capital intensity.
   c. High-revenue growth, high profitability, low-capital intensity.
   d. Low-revenue growth, high profitability, low-capital intensity.
3. You are reviewing the valuation of a small company in a large mature business, and are trying to apply the 3P test. You notice that the analyst has assumed that the company will have high-revenue growth, as it increases market share, and a target operating margin well above the industry average, and low reinvestment (a higher sales to capital ratio than the industry average). What are some of the questions that you would ask the analyst?
4. You are valuing Comet Inc., a U.S. company that has a 20% market share of the U.S. dish detergent market, which is a mature business, growing about 3% a year. The company has a new CEO who has embarked on a plan to increase market share by cutting product prices aggressively and expanding into Asia. Which of the following assumptions best captures this story? (Each one worth half a point.)
   i. Revenue Growth
      a. High
      b. Low
      c. No change
   ii. Operating Margins
      a. Increasing
      b. Decreasing
      c. No change
   iii. Cost of capital
      a. Increasing
      b. Decreasing
      c. No change
   iv. Value of the firm
      a. Increase
      b. Decrease
      c. Unclear (Depends)

CHAPTER 14

Equity Intrinsic Value Models

In the strictest sense, the only cash flow you receive when you buy shares in a publicly traded firm is a dividend. The simplest model for valuing equity is the dividend discount model (DDM)—the value of a stock is the present value of expected dividends on it. While many analysts have turned away from the dividend discount model and view it as outmoded, much of the intuition that drives discounted cash flow valuation stems from the dividend discount model. In fact, there are companies where the dividend discount model remains a useful tool for estimating value.

The biggest challenge with the dividend discount model is its dependence on dividends, which are set by managers, and may or may not reflect the capacity of a company to return cash to equity investors. In the second part of this chapter, we estimate a company's potential dividends (i.e., free cash flow to equity), and use it to estimate the equity value for a company. The equity value that you estimate will generally be different from that obtained from the dividend discount model, and we discuss the reasons for and implications of that difference.

EQUITY VALUATION

Early in this book, we drew a contrast between valuing equity in a business and valuing the entire business, with the focus on how to estimate cash flows and discount rates shifting, depending on whether you are valuing equity or the business, as can be seen in Figure 14.1.

There are three variants of cash flows to equity that can be used in equity valuation. The first and the simplest measure of cash flow to equity, at least in a publicly traded company, is the dividend that you receive from the company. The second and slightly broader measure of cash flow to equity adds cash returned in the form of buybacks to the dividends paid, to get to augmented dividends. The third and most general measure of cash flow to equity is to compute cash flows left over after reinvestment and financing needs have been met (i.e., potential dividends).

There are a few companies where the three measures of cash flows to equity may converge, because they pay out what they can afford to pay out as dividends every year. For most companies, though, there will be divergence between the three cashflow measures, which can yield different equity value estimates for the same firm, and we will talk about their differences in this chapter.

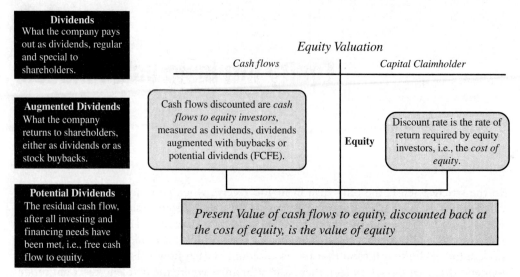

Dividends
What the company pays out as dividends, regular and special to shareholders.

Augmented Dividends
What the company returns to shareholders, either as dividends or as stock buybacks.

Potential Dividends
The residual cash flow, after all investing and financing needs have been met, i.e., free cash flow to equity.

Equity Valuation

Cash flows   *Capital Claimholder*

Cash flows discounted are *cash flows to equity investors*, measured as dividends, dividends augmented with buybacks or potential dividends (FCFE).

Equity

Discount rate is the rate of return required by equity investors, i.e., the *cost of equity*.

Present Value of cash flows to equity, discounted back at the cost of equity, is the value of equity

FIGURE 14.1   Valuing Equity in a Business

THE DIVIDEND DISCOUNT MODEL

When an investor buys stock, he or she generally expects to get two types of cash flows—dividends during the period the stock is held, and an expected price at the end of the holding period. Since this expected price is itself determined by future dividends, the value of a stock is the present value of dividends through infinity:

$$\text{Value of equity} = \sum_{t=1}^{t=\infty} \frac{E(DPS_t)}{(1 + k_e)}$$

where DPS_t = Expected dividends in period t
         k_e = Cost of equity

The rationale for the model lies in the present value rule—the value of any asset is the present value of expected future cash flows, discounted at a rate appropriate to the riskiness of the cash flows being discounted.

There are two basic inputs to the model—expected dividends and the cost on equity. To obtain the expected dividends, we make assumptions about expected future growth rates in earnings and payout ratios. The required rate of return on a stock is determined by its riskiness, measured differently in different models—the market beta in the capital asset pricing model (CAPM) and the factor betas in the arbitrage and multifactor model. The model is flexible enough to allow for time-varying discount rates, where the time variation is because of expected changes in interest rates or risk across time.

Versions of The Model

Since projections of dollar dividends cannot be made through infinity, several versions of the dividend discount model have been developed based on different assumptions about future growth. We will begin with the simplest—a model designed to value stock in a stable growth firm that pays out what it can afford to in dividends—and then look at how the model can be adapted to value companies in high growth that may be paying little or no dividends.

The Gordon Growth Model   The Gordon growth model can be used to value a firm that is in "steady state" with dividends growing at a rate that can be sustained forever.

The Model   The Gordon growth model relates the value of a stock to its expected dividends in the next time period, the cost of equity, and the expected growth rate in dividends.

$$\text{Value of stock} = \frac{\text{Expected dividends in the next period}}{(\text{Cost of equity} - \text{Growth rate in perpetuity})}$$

The Gordon model has the benefits of simplicity and parsimony, but it is dependent on the assumption of a growth rate that can be maintained in perpetuity, and dividends that are reflective of what that stable growth company can afford to pay out.

What Is a Stable Growth Rate?   While the Gordon growth model provides a simple approach to valuing equity, its use is limited to firms that are growing at a stable growth rate. There are two insights worth keeping in mind when estimating a stable growth rate. First, since the growth rate in the firm's dividends is expected to last forever, the firm's other operating metrics (including revenues and earnings) can also be expected to grow at the same rate. To see why, consider the consequences in the long term of a firm whose earnings grow 2 percent a year forever, while its dividends grow at 3 percent. Over time, the dividends will exceed earnings. If a firm's earnings grow at a faster rate than dividends in the long term, in the long term the payout ratio will converge toward zero, which is also not a steady state. Thus, though the model's requirement is for the expected growth rate in dividends, analysts should be able to substitute in the expected growth rate in earnings and get precisely the same result, if the firm is truly in steady state.

The second issue relates to what growth rate is reasonable as a stable growth rate. As noted in Chapter 12, this growth rate must be less than or equal to the growth rate of the economy in which the firm operates. No firm, no matter how well run, can be assumed to grow forever at a rate that exceeds the growth rate of the economy (or as a proxy, the risk-free rate). In addition, the caveats made in Chapter 12 about stable growth apply:

■ The return on equity (ROE) that we assume in perpetuity should reflect not what the company may have made last year nor what it is expected to make next year, but, rather, a longer-term estimate. The estimate of ROE matters because the payout ratio in stable growth must be consistent:

$$\text{Payout ratio} = 1 - \frac{\text{Stable growth rate}}{\text{Stable period ROE}}$$

■ The cost of equity must be consistent with the firm being mature; if a beta is being used, it should be close to 1.

In short, if you are valuing a firm as a mature firm with a growth rate that it can maintain in perpetuity, it should be given the characteristics (in terms of payout and risk) of a mature firm.

Limitations of the Model   As most analysts discover quickly, the Gordon growth model is extremely sensitive to assumptions about the growth rate, as long as other inputs to the model (e.g., payout ratio, cost of equity) are kept constant. Consider a stock with an expected dividend per share next period of $2.50, a cost of equity of 15 percent, and an expected growth rate of 5 percent forever. The value of this stock is:

$$\text{Value of stock} = \frac{\$2.50}{(.15 - .05)} = \$25.00$$

Note, however, the sensitivity of this value to estimates of the growth rate in Figure 14.2. As the growth rate approaches the cost of equity, the value per share approaches infinity. If the growth rate exceeds the cost of equity, the value per share becomes negative.

There are, of course, two common sense fixes to this problem. The first is to work with the constraint that a stable growth rate cannot exceed the risk-free rate; in the preceding example, this would limit the growth rate to a number well below 15 percent. The second

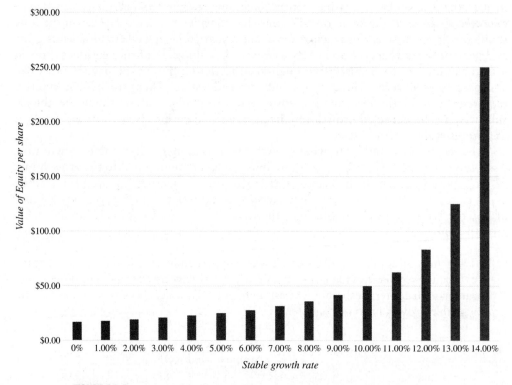

FIGURE 14.2   Value of Equity per Share and Expected Stable Growth Rate

is to recognize that growth is not free; when the growth rate is increased, the payout ratio should be decreased. This creates a trade-off on growth, with the net effect of increasing growth being positive, neutral, or even negative.

DOES A STABLE GROWTH RATE HAVE TO BE CONSTANT OVER TIME?

The assumption that the growth rate in dividends must be constant over time may seem a difficult assumption to meet, especially given the volatility of earnings. If a firm has an average growth rate that is close to a stable growth rate, the model can be used with little real effect on value. Thus a cyclical firm that can be expected to have year-to-year swings in growth rates, but has an average growth rate that is 2 percent, can be valued using the Gordon growth model, without a significant loss of generality. There are two reasons for this result. First, since dividends are smoothed even when earnings are volatile, they are less likely to be affected by year-to-year changes in earnings growth. Second, the mathematical effects on present value of using year-specific growth rates rather than a constant growth rate are small.

Model Usage   In summary, the Gordon growth model is best suited for firms growing at a rate equal to or lower than the nominal growth in the economy with well-established dividend payout policies that they intend to continue into the future. The dividend payout and cost of equity of the firm must be consistent with the assumption of stability, since stable firms generally pay substantial dividends and have betas close to 1.[1] In particular, this model will underestimate the value of the stock in firms that consistently pay out less than they can afford to and accumulate cash in the process.

Looking across the market, you can already see that the Gordon growth model can be used to value only a small subset of companies. That does not seem to stop analysts from using the model in the most inappropriate of circumstances, and blame the model for absurd results.

ILLUSTRATION 14.1:   Valuing a Regulated Monopoly: Consolidated Edison in May 2024

Consolidated Edison (Con Ed) is the electric utility that supplies power to residences and businesses in New York City. It is a quasi-monopoly whose prices and profits are regulated by the state of New York.

We will be valuing Con Ed using a stable growth dividend discount model because it fits the criteria for the model:

- The firm operates in a region where the population and power usage have leveled off over the past few decades.
- The regulatory authorities will restrict price increases to be about the inflation rate.

---

[1]The average payout ratio for large stable firms in the United States used to be in excess of 60% four decades ago, but that number has decreased to closer to 30–40%, as companies supplement dividends with stock buybacks.

- The firm has had a stable mix of debt and equity funding its operations for decades.
- Con Ed has a clientele of dividend-loving investors and attempts to pay out as much as it can in dividends. During the period 2013–2022, the firm returned about 93% of its free cash flows to equity (FCFE) as dividends.

To value the company using the stable growth dividend discount model, we start with the earnings per share of $4.07 that the firm reported for 2023, and the dividends per share of $3.26 it paid out for the year. Using the average beta of 0.60 for power utilities and an equity risk premium of 4.30% for the United States, in May 2024, allows us to estimate a cost of equity of 7.5% (the risk-free rate was 4.5%):

$$\text{Cost of equity} = 4.5\% + 0.60(4.30\%) = 7.08\%$$

We estimate the expected growth rate consistent with fundamentals for Con Ed:

$$\text{Retention ratio} = 1 - (\$3.26/\$4.07) = 19.90\%$$

$$\text{Return on equity} = 8.54\%$$

$$\text{Expected growth rate} = .199 \times .0854 = .017 \text{ or } 1.7\%$$

Setting the growth rate at the risk-free rate of 1.70%, we generated a value per share of $61.61:

$$\text{Value per share} = \frac{\text{Expected dividends per share next year}}{(\text{Cost of equity} - \text{Expected growth rate})}$$

$$= \frac{3.26\,(1.017)}{(.0708 - .017)} = \$61.61$$

The value per share, assuming that Con Ed is in stable growth, with returns on equity, retention ratios, and costs of equity that it can sustain in perpetuity is $61.61. The stock was trading at $94.34 in May 2024, making it significantly overvalued.

IMPLIED GROWTH RATE

The value for Con Ed is different from the market price, and this is likely to be the case with almost any company that you value. There are three possible explanations for this deviation. One is that you are right, and the market is wrong. While this may be the correct explanation, you should probably make sure that the other two explanations do not hold—that the market is right and you are wrong, or that the difference is too small to draw any conclusions.

To examine the magnitude of the difference between the market price and your estimate of value, you can hold the other variables constant and change the growth rate in your valuation until the value converges on the price. Figure 14.3 estimates value as a function of the expected growth rate (assuming a beta of 0.60 and current dividends per share of $3.26).

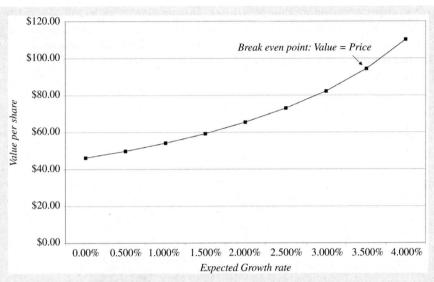

FIGURE 14.3 Con Ed: Value versus Growth Rate

Solving for the expected growth rate that provides the current price, we get:

$$\$94.34 = \frac{\$3.26\,(1 + g)}{(.0708 - g)}$$

The growth rate in earnings and dividends would have to be 3.50 percent a year to justify the stock price of $94.34. This growth rate is an implied growth rate. Since we estimate growth from fundamentals, this allows us to estimate an implied return on equity, given the retention ratio of 19.9%:

$$\text{Implied ROE} = \frac{\text{Implied growth rate}}{\text{Retention ratio}} = \frac{.035}{.199} = 17.60\%$$

That implied return on equity is much higher than what Con Ed has earned as a return on equity in the prior decade, reinforcing the conclusion that the stock looks overvalued.

 DDMst.xls: This spreadsheet allows you to value a stable growth firm, with stable firm characteristics (beta and return on equity) and dividends that roughly match cash flows.

A Two-Stage Dividend Discount Model   The two-stage growth model enables for two stages of growth—an initial phase where the growth rate is not a stable growth rate, and a subsequent steady state where the growth rate is stable and is expected to remain so for the long term. While, in most cases, the growth rate during the initial phase is higher than the stable growth rate, the model can be adapted to value companies that are expected to post low or even negative growth rates for a few years and then revert back to stable growth.

The Model   The model is based on two stages of growth, an extraordinary growth phase that lasts n years, and a stable growth phase that lasts forever after that:

$$\text{Value of equity} = \text{PV of dividends}_{\text{extraordinary growth}}$$
$$+ \text{PV of terminal value of equity}$$
$$= \sum_{t=1}^{t=n} \frac{\text{Dividends}_t}{(1 + k_{e,hg})^t} + \frac{\text{Terminal value of equity in year n}}{(1 + k_{e,hg})^n}$$

where $\text{Terminal value of equity in year n} = \dfrac{\text{Dividends in year n} + 1}{(k_{e,st} - g_n)}$

$$\text{Dividends}_t = \text{Expected dividends in year t}$$
$$K_e = \text{Cost of equity (hg: High-growth period;}$$
$$st = \text{stable growth period)}$$
$$g_n = \text{Growth rate in perpetuity after year n}$$

In the case where the high-growth period growth rate (g) and payout ratio are unchanged for the first n years, this formula can be simplified as follows:

$$\text{Value of equity today} = \frac{\text{Dividends}_0(1 + g)\left(1 - \frac{(1 + g)^n}{(1 + k_{e,hg})^n}\right)}{\left(k_{e,hg} - g\right)} + \frac{\text{Dividends}_{n+1}}{\left(k_{e,st} - g\right)\left(1 + k_{e,hg}\right)^n}$$

where the inputs are as defined previously. The first term in this equation is the present value of a growing annuity, capturing the present value of the expected dividends during the high-growth phase, and the second term is the present value of the terminal value of equity.

This model can be used either to value aggregate dividends, to estimate an aggregated value of equity today, or to value dividends per share, to get a value per share today. The two will be equivalent, if a company does not have management options or warrants outstanding, but the former is a better approach when there are options and warrants.

Calculating the Terminal Value   The same constraint that applies to the growth rate for the Gordon growth model (i.e., that the growth rate in the firm is comparable to the nominal growth rate in the economy) applies for the terminal growth rate (g_n) in this model as well.

In addition, the payout ratio must be consistent with the estimated growth rate. If the growth rate is expected to drop significantly after the initial growth phase, the payout ratio should be higher in the stable phase than in the growth phase. A stable firm can pay out more of its earnings in dividends than a growing firm. One way of estimating this new payout ratio is to use the fundamental growth model described in Chapter 12:

$$\text{Expected growth} = \text{Retention ratio} \times \text{Return on equity}$$
$$= (1 - \text{Payout ratio}) \times \text{Return on equity}$$

Algebraic manipulation yields the following stable period payout ratio:

$$\text{Stable payout ratio} = 1 - \frac{\text{Stable growth rate}}{\text{Stable ROE}}$$

Thus, a firm with a 5-percent growth rate and a return on equity of 15 percent will have a stable period payout ratio of 66.67 percent.

The other characteristics of the firm in the stable period should be consistent with the assumption of stability. For instance, it is reasonable to assume that a high-growth firm has a beta of 2.0 but unreasonable to assume that this beta will remain unchanged when the firm becomes stable. In fact, the rule of thumb that we developed in the previous chapter—that stable period betas are between 0.8 and 1.2—is worth repeating here. Similarly, the return on equity, which can be high during the initial growth phase, should come down to levels commensurate with a stable firm in the stable growth phase. What is a reasonable stable period return on equity? The industry average return on equity and the firm's own stable period cost of equity provide useful information to make this judgment.

Limitations and Uses of the Model   There are three problems with the two-stage dividend discount model; the first two would apply to any two-stage model, and the third is specific to the dividend discount model.

1. The first practical problem is in defining the length of the extraordinary growth period. Since the growth rate is expected to decline to a stable level after this period, the value of an investment will increase as this period is made longer. While we did develop criteria that might be useful in making this judgment in Chapter 12, it is difficult in practice to convert these qualitative considerations into a specific time period.
2. The second problem with this model lies in the assumption that the growth rate is high during the initial period, and is transformed overnight to a lower stable rate at the end of the period. While these sudden transformations in growth can happen, it is much more realistic to assume that the shift from high growth to stable growth happens gradually over time.
3. The focus on dividends in this model can lead to skewed estimates of value for firms that are not paying out what they can afford to in dividends. In particular, we will underestimate the value of firms that accumulate cash and pay out too little in dividends.

Model Usage   Since the two-stage dividend discount model is based on two clearly delineated growth stages—high growth and stable growth—it is best suited for firms that are in high growth and expect to maintain that growth rate for a specific time period, after which the sources of the high growth are expected to disappear. One scenario, for instance, where this may apply is when a company has patent rights to a very profitable product for the next few years, and is expected to enjoy supernormal growth during this period. Once the patent expires, it is expected to settle back into stable growth. Another scenario where it may be reasonable to make this assumption about growth is when a firm is in an industry that is enjoying supernormal growth because there are significant barriers to entry (either legal or as a consequence of infrastructure requirements), which can be expected to keep new entrants out for several years.

The assumption that the growth rate drops precipitously from its level in the initial phase to a stable rate also implies that this model is more appropriate for firms with modest growth rates in the initial phase. For instance, it is more reasonable to assume that a firm growing at 7 percent in the high-growth period will see its growth rate drop to 2 percent afterward, than it is for a firm growing at 40 percent in the high-growth period.

Finally, the model works best for firms that maintain a policy of paying out residual cash flows (i.e., cash flows left over after debt payments and reinvestment needs have been met) as dividends.

ILLUSTRATION 14.2:   Valuing a Firm with a Two-Stage Dividend Discount Model: Procter & Gamble in May 2011

Procter & Gamble (P&G) is one the leading global consumer product companies, owning some of the most valuable brands in the world, including Gillette razors, Pampers diapers, Tide detergent, Crest toothpaste, and Vicks cough medicine. P&G's long history of paying dividends makes it a good candidate for the dividend discount model, and while it is a large company, its brand names and global expansion provide it with a platform to deliver high growth at least for the next few years. Consequently, we will use the two-stage dividend discount model to value the company.

To set the stage, P&G reported $12,736 million in earnings for 2010 and paid out 49.74% of these earnings as dividends; on a per share basis, earnings were $3.82 and dividends were $1.92 in 2010. We will use a beta of 0.90, reflecting the beta of large consumer product companies in 2010, a risk-free rate of 3.50%, and a mature market equity risk premium of 5% to estimate the cost of equity:

$$\text{Cost of equity} = 3.50\% + 0.90(5\%) = 8.00\%$$

To estimate the expected growth rate, we will start with the firm's current return on equity (20.09%) and payout ratio (49.74%) and assume numbers very close to these for the next five years:

Expected ROE for next 5 years = 20%

Expected retention ratio for next 5 years = 50%

Expected growth rate for next 5 years = 20% × 50% = 10%

Applying this growth rate to earnings and dividends for the next 5 years and discounting these dividends back at the cost of equity, we arrive at a value of $10.09/share for the high-growth period in Table 14.1

TABLE 14.1   Expected dividends per share for P&G

	1	2	3	4	5	Sum
Earnings per share	$4.20	$4.62	$5.08	$5.59	$6.15	
Payout ratio	50.00%	50.00%	50.00%	50.00%	50.00%	
Dividends per share	$2.10	$2.31	$2.54	$2.80	$3.08	
Cost of equity	8.00%	8.00%	8.00%	8.00%	8.00%	
Present value	$1.95	$1.98	$2.02	$2.06	$2.09	$10.09

After year 5, we assume that P&G will be in stable growth, growing 3% a year (set just below the risk-free rate). We also assume that the return on equity for the firm will drop to a more sustainable 12% in perpetuity, resulting in an estimated payout ratio of 75% in perpetuity:

$$\text{Expected payout ratio in stable growth} = 1 - g/ROE = 1 - 3\%/12\% = 75\%$$

Assuming that the beta moves up to 1 in stable growth (resulting in a cost of equity of 8.5%), we estimate the value per share at the end of year 5:

$$\text{Value per share end of year 5} = \frac{EPS_5 \times (1 + \text{Stable growth rate}) \times (\text{Stable Payout ratio})}{(\text{Stable period cost of equity} - \text{Stable growth rate})}$$

$$= \frac{\$6.15 \times (1.03) \times (.75)}{(.085 - .03)} = \$86.41$$

Discounting this price to the present at 8% (the cost of equity for the high-growth period) and adding the present value of expected dividends during the high-growth period yields a value per share of $68.90.

$$\text{Value per share today} = \text{PV of dividends in high growth} + \text{PV of terminal value of equity}$$

$$= \$10.09 + \frac{\$86.41}{1.08^5} = \$68.90$$

The stock was trading at $68 in May 2011, making it fairly valued.

 DDM2st.xls: This spreadsheet allows you to value a growth firm, with an initial period of high growth and stable growth thereafter, using expected dividends.

The Value of Growth Investors pay a premium when they acquire companies with high-growth potential. This premium takes the form of higher price-earnings or price–book value ratios. While no one will contest the proposition that growth is valuable, it is possible to pay too much for growth. In fact, empirical studies that show low- price-earnings ratio stocks earning return premiums over high-price-earnings ratio stocks in the long term support the notion that investors overpay for growth. This section uses the two-stage dividend discount model to examine the value of growth, and it provides a benchmark that can be used to compare the actual prices paid for growth.

Estimating the Value of Growth The value of the equity in any firm can be written in terms of three components:

■ The value of assets in place, with no growth, can be calculated by assuming that the existing earnings get paid out as dividends, and discounting these dividends as a perpetuity:

$$\text{Value of equity in assets in place, with no growth} = \frac{\text{Current net income}}{\text{Cost of equity}}$$

■ The value of stable growth can be computed, by assuming a growth rate that the company sustain forever, and reinvesting enough to sustain that growth rate:

$$\text{Value of equity, with stable growth} = \frac{\text{Current net income } (1 + g)(1 - \frac{g}{ROE})}{\text{Cost of equity} - g}$$

Value of stable growth = Value of equity, with stable growth − Value of equityin assets inplace, with growth

■ The value of extraordinary growth will then be the difference in value of equity, with your assumptions about high growth over whatever period, and the value of assets in place:

Value of extraordinary growth = Value of equity − Value of equity, with stable growth[2]

In keeping with our discussion of growth having value only if you earn a return on equity that exceeds its cost of equity, the value of stable and extraordinary growth will reflect assumptions about return on equity.

ILLUSTRATION 14.3:   The Value of Growth: P&G in May 2011

In Illustration 13.3, we valued P&G using a two-stage dividend discount model at $68.90. We first value the assets in place using current earnings ($3.82) and assume that all earnings are paid out as dividends. We also use the stable growth cost of equity as the discount rate.

Value of assets in place = Current EPS/Cost of Equity = $3.82/.085 = $44.94

To estimate the value of stable growth, we assume that the expected growth rate will be 3% and that the payout ratio is the stable period payout ratio of 75%:

$$\text{Value of stable growth} = \frac{\text{Current EPS} \times \text{Stable payout ratio} \times (1 + g_n)}{(k_e - g_n)}$$
$$- \text{Value of assets in place}$$
$$= \$3.82 \times .75 \times 1.03/(.085 - .03) - \$44.94 = \$8.71$$

To get the value of extraordinary growth in the next 5 years, we subtract the value of assets in place and stable growth from the intrinsic value per share:

Value of extraordinary growth = $68.90 − $44.94 − $8.71 = $15.25

Note that $68.90 was our estimate of value per share in Illustration 13.3.

The value of both stable and extraordinary growth at P&G come from our assumption that P&G can earn a return on equity of 20% for the next five years and drives the value of extraordinary growth, and assuming that the firm will earn a 12% return on

---

[2]The payout ratio used to estimate the stable growth value should be the payout ratio that you calculate using the expected stable growth rate and the return on equity in stable growth.

equity in perpetuity determines the value of stable growth. Setting those returns on equity equal to the cost of equity will cause the value of growth to dissipate, and assuming returns on equity that are lower than the cost of equity will yield negative values for growth.

H Model for Valuing Growth   The H model is a two-stage model for growth, but unlike the classic two-stage model, the growth rate in the initial growth phase is not constant but declines linearly over time to reach the stable growth rate in steady state. This model was presented in Fuller and Hsia (1984).

The Model   The model assumes that the earnings growth rate starts at a high-initial rate (g_a) and declines linearly over the extraordinary growth period (which is assumed to last 2H periods) to a stable growth rate (g_n). It also assumes that the dividend payout and cost of equity are constant over time and are not affected by the shifting growth rates. Figure 14.4 graphs the expected growth over time in the H model.

The value of expected dividends in the H model can be written as follows:

$$\text{Value of equity} = \frac{DPS_0(1 + g_n)}{(k_e - g_n)} + \frac{DPS_0 \times H * (g_a - g_n)}{(k_e - g_n)}$$

where P_0 = Value of the firm now per share

DPS_t = DPS in year t

k_e = Cost of equity

g_a = Growth rate initially

g_n = Growth rate at end of 2H years, applies forever after that

Limitations   This model avoids the problems associated with the growth rate dropping precipitously from the high growth to the stable growth phase, but it does so at a cost. First, the decline in the growth rate is expected to follow the strict structure laid out in the model—it drops in linear increments each year based on the initial growth rate, the stable

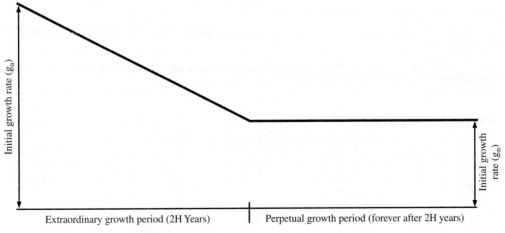

FIGURE 14.4   Expected Growth in the H Model

growth rate, and the length of the extraordinary growth period. While small deviations from this assumption do not affect the value significantly, large deviations can cause problems. Second, the assumption that the payout ratio is constant through both phases of growth exposes the model to an inconsistency—as growth rates decline, the payout ratio usually increases.

Model Usage   The allowance for a gradual decrease in growth rates over time may make this a useful model for firms that are growing rapidly right now, but where the growth is expected to decline gradually over time as the firms get larger and the differential advantage that they have over their competitors declines. The assumption that the payout ratio is constant, however, makes this an inappropriate model to use for any firm that has low or no dividends currently. Thus, by requiring a combination of high growth and high payout, the model may be quite limited[3] in its applicability. The model is also still dependent on dividends, and to the extent that companies do not pay out what they can afford to in dividends, the model can yield unrealistic estimates for the value of equity.

ILLUSTRATION 14.4:   Valuing with the H Model: Vodafone

Vodafone, a UK-based telecommunications firm, paid dividends per share of 9.8 pence on earnings per share of 16.1 pence in 2010. The firm's earnings per share had grown at 6% over the prior five years, but the growth rate is expected to decline linearly over the next five years to 3%, while the payout ratio remains unchanged. The beta for the stock is 1, the risk-free rate in British pounds is 4% and the market risk premium is 5%.

$$\text{Cost of equity} = 4\% + 1.0(5\%) = 9\%$$

The stock can be valued using the H model:

$$\text{Value of stable growth} = \frac{9.8(1.03)}{(.09 - .03)} = 168 \text{ pence}$$

$$\text{Value of high growth with H model} = \frac{9.8 \times \frac{5}{2} \times (.06 - .03)}{(.09 - .03)} = 12 \text{ pence}$$

$$\text{Value of stock} = 168 \text{ pence} + 12 \text{ pence} = 180 \text{ pence}$$

The stock was trading at 173.3 pence in May 2011, making it slightly undervalued.

 DDMH.xls: This spreadsheet allows you to value a firm, with an initial period when the high growth declines to stable growth, using expected dividends.

Generalized Dividend Discount Model   The three-stage dividend discount model combines the features of the two-stage model and the H model. It allows for an initial period of high growth, a transitional period where growth declines, and a final stable growth phase. It is the most general of the models because it does not impose any restrictions on the payout ratio.

---

[3]Proponents of the model would argue that using a stable-period payout ratio for firms that pay little or no dividends is likely to cause only small errors in valuation.

The Model   This model assumes an initial period of stable high growth, a transition period, and a third period of stable low growth that lasts forever. Figure 14.5 graphs the expected growth over the three time periods.

The value of the stock is then the present value of expected dividends during the high growth and the transitional periods, and of the terminal price at the start of the final stable growth phase.

Value of equity = PV of expected dividends during high-growth period
            + PV of expected dividends during transition period
            + PV of terminal value of equity

The key component in a three or multistage dividend discount model is to stay consistent, adjusting return on equity, cost of equity, and payout ratios as growth rates change.

Assumptions   This model removes many of the constraints imposed by other versions of the dividend discount model. In return, however, it requires a much larger number of inputs—year-specific payout ratios, growth rates, and betas. It can also be used to value firms that are expected to grow at high rates[4], before transitioning over a period (rather than instantaneously) to stable growth.

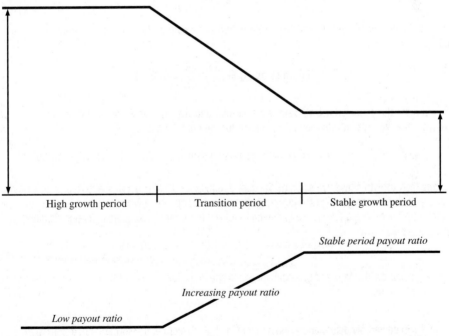

FIGURE 14.5   Expected Growth in the Three-Stage Dividend Discount Model

---

[4]The definition of a high-growth rate is subjective, but allowing for a transition period for a firm with only moderate growth (rather than high growth) will have little consequence for value. Thus, if in doubt about whether a growth rate is "high" enough, we would use a transition period to adjust inputs.

Model Usage   This model's flexibility makes it a useful model for any firm that in addition to changing growth over time is expected to change on other dimensions as well—in particular, payout policies, and risk. In fact, it can even be used to value companies that do not pay dividends currently, since the payout ratio can be zero in the high-growth period, and the value of the equity comes from expected dividends during the transition period and the terminal value of equity.

While the flexibility that the model offers is a plus, its focus remains on dividends paid, rather than what a company can afford to pay. Thus, companies that hold back cash, and pay too little in dividends, will be valued too low by this model, and companies that return more cash than they can afford to valued too high.

ILLUSTRATION 14.5:   Valuing JP Morgan Using a Three-Stage Dividend Discount Model

To value JP Morgan Chase in May 2024, we used a three-stage dividend discount model, partly because we expect the firm to maintain a growth rate higher than the economy for the next few years. More importantly, many of the ingredients for estimating cash flows (to equity or the firm) are not available for banks, leaving us with dividends because we have no choice.

In 2023, the company reported net income of $49,552 million and paid out $13,463 million in dividends, yielding a payout ratio of 27.17%:

$$\text{Payout ratio} = \frac{13,463}{49,552} = 27.17\%$$

Based upon the book value of equity of $292,332 million at the start of 2023, the firm earned a return on equity of 16.95%:

$$\text{Return on equity} = \frac{49,552}{292,332} = 16.95\%$$

To estimate the expected growth rate, we assumed that the firm would be able to generate maintain its current return on equity and retention ratio, at least for the next five years:

$$\text{Expected growth rate in net income for next 5 years} = 0.1695 \times (1 - .2717) = 12.35\%$$

During this high-growth phase, we estimate the cost of equity for JP Morgan Chase, based upon a beta of 1.06 (the average beta for money center banks), the U.S. treasury bond rate in May 2024 of 4.5% and an equity risk premium of 5.17% (with the premium augmented to reflect JP Morgan's exposure in foreign markets).

$$\text{Cost of equity} = 4.5\% + 1.06(5.17\%) = 9.98\%$$

The expected dividends over the next 5 years are shown in Table 14.2, with the present values computed using the cost of equity

TABLE 14.2   Expected dividends and Present Value in High-Growth—JP Morgan Chase

	1	2	3	4	5
Expected Growth Rate	12.35%	12.35%	12.35%	12.35%	12.35%
Return on equity	16.95%	16.95%	16.95%	16.95%	16.95%
Net Income	$49,552	$55,669	$62,542	$70,263	$78,937
Payout ratio	27.17%	27.17%	27.17%	27.17%	27.17%

	1	2	3	4	5
Dividends	$13,463	$15,125	$16,992	$19,090	$21,447
Cost of Equity	9.98%	9.98%	9.98%	9.98%	9.98%
Cumulative Cost of Equity	1.0998	1.2096	1.3303	1.4631	1.6091
Present Value	$12,241	$12,504	$12,773	$13,048	$13,328

After year 5, we allow for a transition period of 5 more years to stable growth after year 10. In the stable growth phase, we assume the following changes:

- Expected growth rate of 3% forever, set just below the risk-free rate.
- A return on equity of 12%; while this is lower than the current ROE, it is an impressive return for a mature firm and reflects our belief that JP Morgan Chase has enduring competitive advantages.
- A payout ratio of 75%, based on the return on equity and expected growth rate:

$$\text{Stable payout ratio} = 1 - \frac{g}{\text{ROE}} = 1 - \frac{.03}{.12} = 0.75 \text{ or } 75\%$$

- A cost of equity of 9.67%, based upon the assumption that the beta will increase to 1 in stable growth.

The transition period (years 6–10) allow us to change each of the inputs (payout ratio, cost of equity and growth rate) from high-growth levels to stable growth levels in linear increments. The resulting dividends and present values are summarized in Table 14.3:

TABLE 14.3 Expected Dividends and Present Value in Transition—JP Morgan Chase

	6	7	8	9	10
Expected Growth Rate	10.48%	8.61%	6.74%	4.87%	3.00%
Return on equity	15.96%	14.97%	13.98%	12.99%	12.00%
Net Income	$87,206	$94,712	$101,094	$106,016	$109,197
Payout ratio	36.74%	46.30%	55.87%	65.43%	75.00%
Dividends	$32,036	$43,853	$56,479	$69,371	$81,898
Cost of Equity	9.92%	9.86%	9.80%	9.73%	9.67%
Cumulative Cost of Equity	1.7688	1.9431	2.1334	2.3411	2.5675
Present Value	$18,112	$22,569	$26,473	$29,632	$31,898

Note that the changing cost of equity requires us to estimate a cumulated cost of equity. Thus, the cumulated cost of equity for year 7 is:

$$\text{Cumulated cost of equity in year 7} = (1.0998)^5(1.0992)(1.0986) = 1.9431$$

The value per share at the end of year 10 can now be obtained by estimating the dividends in the terminal year (11) and computing the terminal value:

$$\text{Value of equity at end of year 10} = \frac{\text{Net income in year 10} \times (1 + \text{Stable growth rate}) \times (\text{Stable Payout ratio})}{(\text{Stable period cost of equity} - \text{Stable growth rate})}$$

$$= \frac{109,197 \times 1.03 \times 0.75}{(.0967 - .03)} = \$1,265,486 \text{ million}$$

Discounting the terminal value back at the cumulated cost of equity for year 10 and adding to the present value of dividends, we get a value per share of $685,075 million.

$$\text{Value of equity} = \text{PV of dividends during high growth} + \text{PV of terminal equity value}$$

$$= \$192,578 + \frac{\$1,265,486}{2.5675} = \$685,075$$

Dividing by the number of shares outstanding (2908.3 million) in May 2024, the value per share that we obtain is $235.56:

$$\text{Value per share} = \frac{\textit{Value of equity}}{\textit{Number of shares}} = \frac{\$685,075}{2908.30} = \$235.56$$

JP Morgan was trading at $198.06 in May 2024, making it overvalued.

 DDM3st.xls: This spreadsheet enables you to value a firm with a period of high growth followed by a transition period where growth declines to a stable growth rate.

THE AUGMENTED DIVIDEND DISCOUNT MODEL

For much of the last century, cash was returned to shareholders only in the form of dividends. Starting in the mid-1980s, companies in the United States started augmenting dividends with stock buybacks, and over the last forty years, buybacks have become the dominant form of cash return to shareholders. In this section, we will expand the dividend discount model to bring in stock buybacks.

Modifying the Model to Include Stock Buybacks

The rise of buybacks to become the dominant form of cash return, for U.S. companies, is shown in Figure 14.6, which presents the cumulative amounts paid out by firms in the form of dividends and stock buybacks from 1988 to 2023. The trend toward stock buybacks was very strong, especially in the 1990s. Even the banking crisis of 2008 and the COVID shutdown created only a momentary blip in buybacks before they returned in force in the following year.

What are the implications for the dividend discount model? Focusing strictly on dividends paid as the only cash returned to stockholders exposes us to the risk that we might be missing significant cash returned to stockholders in the form of stock buybacks. The simplest way to incorporate stock buybacks into a dividend discount model is to add them onto the dividends and compute an augmented payout ratio:

$$\text{Augmented dividend payout ratio} = \frac{\text{Dividends} + \text{Buybacks}}{\text{Net Income}}$$

While this adjustment is straightforward, the resulting ratio for any one year can be skewed by the fact that stock buybacks, unlike dividends, are not smoothed out. In other words, a firm may buy back $3 billion in stock in one year, and not buy back stock for the

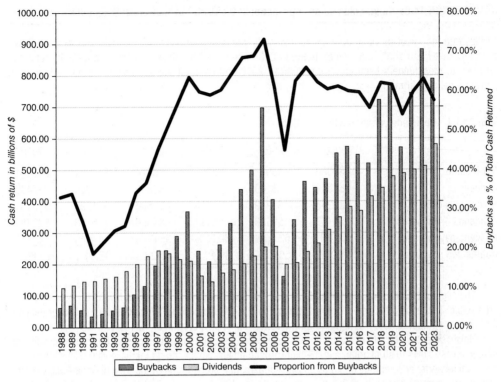

FIGURE 14.6 Stock Buybacks and Dividends: Aggregate for U.S. Firms—1988–2023

next three years. Consequently, a much better estimate of the modified payout ratio can be obtained by looking at the average value over a four- or five-year period. In addition, firms may sometimes buy back stock as a way of increasing financial leverage. We could adjust for this by netting out new debt issued from the earlier calculation:

$$\text{Debt-adjusted payout ratio} = \frac{\text{Dividends} + \text{Buybacks} - \text{Net Debt}}{\text{Net Income}}$$

Adjusting the payout ratio to include stock buybacks will have ripple effects on estimated growth and the terminal value. In particular, the modified growth rate in earnings per share can be written as:

$$\text{Augmented growth rate} = (1 - \text{Augmented payout ratio}) \times \text{Return on equity}$$

Even the return on equity can be affected by stock buybacks. Since the book value of equity is reduced by the market value of equity bought back a firm that buys back stock can reduce its book equity (and increase its return on equity) dramatically. If we use this return on equity as a measure of the marginal return on equity (on new investments), we will overstate the value of a firm. Adding back stock buybacks in recent years to the book equity and reestimating the return on equity can sometimes yield a more reasonable estimate of the return on equity on investments.

ILLUSTRATION 14.6:   Augmented versus Conventional Dividend Payout Ratios: Coca-Cola

To illustrate the effect of using augmented dividends versus actual dividends, we will look at Coca-Cola, a company that has bought back stock between 2006 and 2010. In Table 14.4, we estimate the total cash returned to stockholders each year from 2006 to 2010 and contrast the augmented payout ratio with the conventional payout ratio:

TABLE 14.4   Dividends versus Buybacks—Coca Cola

	2006	2007	2008	2009	2010	Total
Net Income	$5080	$5981	$5807	$6824	$11809	$35501
Dividends	$2911	$3149	$3521	$3800	$ 4068	$17449
Stock buybacks	$2268	$ 219	$ 493	$ 856	$ 1295	$ 5131
Dividends + buybacks	$5179	$3368	$4014	$4656	$ 5363	$22580
Dividend payout ratio	57.30%	52.65%	60.63%	55.69%	34.45%	49.15%
Augmented payout ratio	101.95%	56.31%	69.12%	68.23%	45.41%	63.60%

The augmented dividend payout is higher than the dividend payout ratio in each year, but stock buybacks are volatile. That is why we would look at the augmented dividend payout ratio in the aggregate over the entire period; that number is 63.60%, higher than the conventional payout ratio of 49.15%.

How would this play out in a valuation of Coca-Cola? Using the higher augmented payout ratio will result in higher cash flows to stockholders in the high-growth phase, which should increase value. This effect, however, will be partly or even fully offset by a lower fundamental growth rate. In the case of Coca-Cola, where we will assume a return on equity of 25%, the expected growth rate using the higher augmented payout ratio can be computed as follows:

$$\text{Expected growth rate} = ROE \times (1 - \text{Augmented payout ratio})$$
$$= 25\%(1 - .636) = 9.1\%$$

In contrast, using the conventional payout ratio would have yielded an expected growth rate of more than 12.5%.

Valuing an Entire Market Using the Augmented Dividend Discount Model

All our examples of the dividend discount model so far have involved individual companies, but there is no reason why we cannot apply the same model to value a sector or even the entire market. The market price of the stock would be replaced by the cumulative market value of all of the stocks in the sector or market. The expected dividends would be the cumulated dividends of all these stocks and could be expanded to include stock buybacks by all firms. The expected growth rate would be the growth rate in cumulated earnings of the index. There would be no need for a beta(s), since you are looking at the entire market (which should have a beta of 1), and you could add the risk premium (or premiums) to the risk-free rate to estimate a cost of equity. You could use a two-stage model, where this growth rate is greater than the growth rate of the economy, but you should be cautious about setting the growth rate too high or the growth period too long, because it will be difficult for cumulated earnings growth of all firms in an economy to run ahead of the growth rate in the economy for extended periods.

Consider a simple example. Assume that you have an index trading at 700, and that the average dividend yield of stocks in the index is 5 percent. Earnings and dividends can be expected to grow at 4 percent a year forever, and the riskless rate is 5.4 percent. If you use a market risk premium of 4 percent, the value of the index can be estimated as follows:

$$\text{Cost of equity} = \text{Riskless rate} + \text{Risk premium} = 5.4\% + 4\% = 9.4\%$$

$$\text{Expected dividends next year} = (\text{Dividend yield} \times \text{Value of the index})$$
$$(1 + \text{Expected growth rate})$$
$$= (.05 \times 700)(1.04) = 36.4$$

$$\text{Value of the index} = \frac{\textit{Expected dividends next year}}{(\textit{Cost of equity} - \textit{Growth rate})} = \frac{36.4}{(.094 - .04)} = 674$$

At its existing level of 700, the market is slightly overpriced.

ILLUSTRATION 14.7: Valuing the S&P 500 Using Augmented Dividends

---

On January 1, 2024, the S&P 500 was trading at 4,769.83, and dividends and buybacks on the index amounted to 164.25 over the previous year, on earnings of 219.70. On the same date, analysts were estimating that earnings would grow 8.74% a year for the next five years (2024–2028). Assuming that dividends grow at the same rate as earnings, we obtain the following in Table 14.5.

TABLE 14.5 Dividends and Buybacks for S&P 500

	Last 12 months	2024	2025	2026	2027	2028
Expected Earnings	219.70	238.89	259.76	282.45	307.13	333.96
Cash payout ratio	77.85%	77.85%	77.85%	77.85%	77.85%	77.85%
Dividends + Buybacks	164.25	185.97	202.21	219.88	239.09	259.97

To estimate the cost of equity, we assume a beta of 1 for the index and use the risk-free rate on January 1, 2024, of 3.88% and an equity risk premium of 5%:

$$\text{Cost of equity} = 3.88\% + 5\% = 8.88\%$$

After year 5, earnings and dividends are expected to grow at 3.88%, the same nominal rate as the economy (assumed to be equal to the risk-free rate). The value that we obtained for the index follows:

$$\text{Index value} = \frac{185.97}{(1.088)} + \frac{202.21}{(1.088)^2} + \frac{219.88}{(1.088)^3} + \frac{239.09}{(1.088)^4}$$
$$+ \frac{259.97}{(1.088)^5} + \frac{259.97\,(1.0388)}{(.0888 - .0388)(1.088)^5}$$
$$= 4381.57$$

This suggest that the index was overvalued by 8.86% on January 1, 2024.

$$\text{Index valuation} = \text{Index Price/Index Value} - 1$$
$$= (4769.83/4381.57) - 1 = .0888 \text{ or } 8.88\%$$

This valuation does assume that the cash payout ratio will not change over time, but it can be easily adapted to allow the payout ratio, at least in the terminal value calculation, to be adjusted to reflect the return on equity of the stocks in the index and the expected growth rate. At the start of 2024, for instance, using the S&P's return on equity of 17.04% yields a steady state payout ratio of 77.23% and an intrinsic value for the index of 4349.70.[5]

POTENTIAL DIVIDEND OR FCFE MODELS

Given what firms are returning to their stockholders in the form of dividends or stock buybacks, how do we decide whether they are returning too much or too little? We propose a simple measure how much cash is available to be paid out to stockholders after meeting reinvestment needs and compare this amount to the amount returned to stockholders in the form of dividends or buybacks.

Free Cash Flows to Equity

To estimate how much cash a firm can afford to return to its stockholders, we begin with the net income—the accounting measure of the stockholders' earnings during the period—and convert it to a cash flow by subtracting out a firm's reinvestment needs. First, any capital expenditures, defined broadly to include acquisitions, are subtracted from the net income since they represent cash outflows. Depreciation and amortization, on the other hand, are added back in because they are accounting but not cash expenses. The difference between capital expenditures and depreciation (net capital expenditures) is usually a function of the growth characteristics of the firm. High-growth firms tend to have high-net capital expenditures relative to earnings, whereas low-growth firms may have low, and sometimes even negative, net capital expenditures.

Second, increases in working capital drain a firm's cash flows, while decreases in working capital increase the cash flows available to equity investors. Firms that are growing fast, in industries with high-working capital requirements (retailing, for instance), typically have large increases in working capital. Since we are interested in the cash flow effects, we consider only changes in noncash working capital in this analysis.

Finally, equity investors also have to consider the effect of changes in the levels of debt on their cash flows. Repaying the principal on existing debt represents a cash outflow, but the debt repayment may be fully or partially financed by the issue of new debt, which is a cash inflow. Again, netting the repayment of old debt against the new debt issues provides a measure of the cash flow effects of changes in debt.

Allowing for the cash flow effects of net capital expenditures, changes in working capital, and net changes in debt on equity investors, we can define the cash flows left over after these changes as the free cash flow to equity (FCFE):

$$
\begin{aligned}
\text{Free cash flow to equity} = {} & \text{Net income} - (\text{Capital expenditures} - \text{Depreciation}) \\
& - (\text{Change in noncash working capital}) \\
& + (\text{New debt issued} - \text{Debt repayments})
\end{aligned}
$$

---

[5] Stable payout ratio = Stable g/ Stable ROE = 1 − 3.88%/17.04% = 77.23%.

This is the cash flow available to be paid out as dividends. Deconstructing this equation, the reinvestment by equity investors into the firm can be written as:

$$\text{Equity reinvestment} = \text{Capital expenditures} - \text{Depreciation}$$
$$+ \text{Change in noncash working capital}$$
$$- (\text{New debt issues} - \text{Debt repayments})$$
$$\text{Equity reinvestment rate} = \text{Equity reinvestment/Net income}$$

This calculation can be simplified if we assume that the net capital expenditures and working capital changes are financed using a fixed mix[6] of debt and equity. If δ is the proportion of the net capital expenditures and working capital changes that is raised from debt financing, the effect on cash flows to equity of these items can be represented as follows:

Equity cash flows associated with meeting capital expenditure needs =
$- (\text{Capital expenditures} - \text{Depreciation})(1 - \delta)$
Equity cash flows associated with meeting working capital needs =
$- (\Delta \text{Working capital})(1 - \delta)$

Accordingly, the cash flow available for equity investors after meeting capital expenditure and working capital needs is:

$$\text{Free cash flow to equity} = \text{Net income} - (\text{Capital expenditures} - \text{Depreciation})$$
$$\times (1 - \delta) - (\Delta \text{Working capital}) \times (1 - \delta)$$

Note that the net debt payment item is eliminated, because debt repayments are financed with new debt issues to keep the debt ratio fixed. It is appropriate to assume that a specified proportion of net capital expenditures and working capital needs will be financed with debt if the target or optimal debt ratio of the firm is used to forecast the free cash flow to equity that will be available in future periods. Alternatively, in examining past periods, we can use the firm's average debt ratio over the period to arrive at approximate free cash flows to equity.

WHAT ABOUT PREFERRED DIVIDENDS?

In both the long and short formulations of free cash flows to equity described in this section, we assume that there are no preferred dividends paid. Since the equity that we value is only common equity, you would need to modify the formulas slightly for the existence of preferred stock and dividends. In particular, you would subtract the preferred dividends to arrive at the free cash flow to equity:

$$\text{Free cashflow to equity} = \text{Net income} - (\text{Capital expenditures}$$
$$- \text{Depreciation}) - \text{Change in noncash working capital}$$
$$- (\text{Preferred dividends} + \text{Net preferred stock issued})$$
$$- (\text{New debt issued} - \text{Debt repaid})$$

(continued)

---

[6]The mix has to be fixed in book value terms. It can be varying in market value terms.

(*continued*)

In the short form, you would obtain the following:

Free cashflow to equity = Net income − (Capital expenditures
                                      − Depreciation) × (1 − δ)
                                      − Change in noncash working capital × (1 − δ)
                                      − Preferred dividends

The debt ratio (δ) would then have to include the expected financing from new preferred stock issues.

ILLUSTRATION 14.8: Estimating Free Cash Flows to Equity—Levi Strauss

In this illustration, we compute the free cash flows to equity generated by Levi Strauss, the apparel company, from 2019 to 2023, using the full calculation described in the last section (see Table 14.6)

TABLE 14.6 Expected Free Cashflows to Equity—Levi Strauss

	2019	2020	2021	2022	2023
Net Income	$394.61	−$127.10	$ 553.50	$569.10	$249.60
+ Depreciation & Amortization	$123.90	$141.80	$ 143.20	$158.60	$164.90
− Capital Expenditures	$175.40	$185.00	$ 557.80	$268.30	$327.60
− Change in Noncash Working Capital	$163.71	−$382.60	$ 23.80	$550.30	$108.50
+ Debt raised	$ 0.00	$806.00	$ 489.30	$404.00	$200.00
− Debt repaid	$ 23.30	$300.00	$1,023.30	$404.00	$200.00
FCFE	$156.10	$718.30	−$ 418.90	−$ 90.90	−$ 21.60

To use the shortcut, first estimate the net debt used in aggregate over the entire period as a percentage of reinvestment (net cap expenditures and change in working capital):

	2019	2020	2021	2022	2023	Total
Net Debt CF	−$ 23.30	$506.00	−$534.00	$ 0.00	$ 0.00	−$ 51.30
Reinvestment	$215.21	−$339.40	$438.40	$660.00	$271.20	$1,245.41

$$\text{Net debt ratio} = \frac{-\$51.30}{\$1,245.41} = -4.12\%$$

Note that Levi Strauss repaid more debt than they raised, making the net debt ratio a negative number. Applying this net debt ratio to reinvestment yields the shorter version of FCFE in Table 14.7.

TABLE 14.7 FCFE (Approximation) for Levi Strauss

	2019	2020	2021	2022	2023
Net Income	$394.61	−$127.10	$553.50	$569.10	$249.60
− Reinvestment (1- Debt ratio)	$224.08	−$353.38	$456.46	$687.19	$282.37
FCFE	$170.53	$226.28	$ 97.04	−$118.09	−$ 32.77

While the aggregate FCFE over the period remains the same at $343 million, the shortcut version yields smoother FCFE over the period.

Comparing Dividends to Free Cash Flows to Equity   The conventional measure of dividend policy—the dividend payout ratio—gives us the value of dividends as a proportion of earnings. The modified approach measures the total cash returned to stockholders as a proportion of the free cash flow to equity:

$$\text{Dividend payout ratio} = \frac{\text{Dividends}}{\text{Net Income}}$$

$$\text{Cash payout to FCFE ratio} = \frac{\text{Dividends} + \text{Stock buybacks}}{\text{FCFE}}$$

The ratio of cash to stockholders to FCFE shows how much of the cash available to be paid out to stockholders is returned to them in the form of dividends and stock buybacks. If this ratio, over time, is equal or close to 1, the firm is paying out all that it can to its stockholders. If it is significantly less than 1, the firm is paying out less than it can afford to, and is using the difference to increase its cash balance or to invest in marketable securities. If it is significantly over 1, the firm is paying out more than it can afford, and is either drawing on an existing cash balance or issuing new securities (stocks or bonds).

We can observe the tendency of firms to pay out less to stockholders than they have available in free cash flows to equity by examining cash returned to stockholders paid as a percentage of free cash flow to equity. In 2023, the global median of dividends as a percent of FCFE was about 75 percent, with about 60% of all companies returning less in cash than they had available in FCFE. When a firm is paying out less in dividends than it has available in free cash flows, it is generating surplus cash. For those firms, this cash surplus appears as an increase in the cash balance. Firms that pay dividends that exceed FCFE must finance these dividend payments either out of existing cash balances or by making new stock issues.

The implications for valuation are simple. If we use the dividend discount model and do not allow for the buildup of cash that occurs when firms pay out less than they can afford, we will underestimate the value of equity in firms. If we use the model to value firms that pay out more dividends than they have available, we will overvalue the firms. The rest of this chapter is designed to correct for this limitation.

 dividends.xls: **This spreadsheet allows you to estimate the free cash flow to equity and the cash returned to stockholders for a period of up to 10 years.**

divfcfe.xls: **This dataset on the web summarizes dividends, cash returned to stockholders, and free cash flows to equity, by sector, in the United States.**

Why Firms May Pay Out Less than Is Available   Many firms pay out less to stockholders, in the form of dividends and stock buybacks, than they have available in free cash flows to equity. The reasons vary from firm to firm.

Desire for Stability   Firms are generally reluctant to change dividends, and dividends are considered "sticky" because the variability in dividends is significantly lower than the variability in earnings or cash flows. The unwillingness to change dividends is accentuated when firms have to reduce dividends, and increases in dividends outnumber cuts in dividends by at least a five-to-one margin in most periods. As a consequence of this reluctance to cut dividends, firms will often refuse to increase dividends even when earnings and FCFE go up, because they are uncertain about their capacity to maintain these higher dividends. This leads to a lag between earnings increases and dividend increases. Similarly, firms frequently keep dividends unchanged in the face of declining earnings and FCFE. Figure 14.7 reports the number of dividend changes (increases, decreases, no change) between 1988 and 2023.

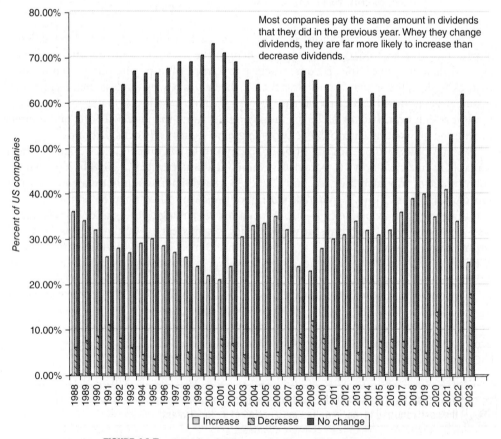

FIGURE 14.7   Dividend Changes by Year: U.S. Companies

The number of firms increasing dividends outnumbers those decreasing dividends seven to one. The number of firms, however, that do not change dividends outnumbers firms that do about four to one. Dividends are also less variable than either FCFE or earnings, but this reduced volatility is a result of keeping dividends below the FCFE.

Future Investment Needs A firm might hold back on paying its entire FCFE as dividends if it expects substantial increases in capital expenditure needs in the future. Since issuing stocks is expensive (with floatation costs and issuance fees), it may choose to keep the excess cash to finance these future needs. Thus, to the degree that a firm is unsure about its future financing needs, it will retain some cash to take on unexpected investments or meet unanticipated needs.

Tax Factors If dividends are taxed at a higher tax rate than capital gains, a firm may choose to retain the excess cash and pay out much less in dividends than it has available. This is likely to be accentuated if the stockholders in the firm are in high-tax brackets, as is the case with many family-controlled firms. If, however, investors in the firm like dividends or tax laws favor dividends, the firm may pay more out in dividends than it has available in FCFE, often borrowing or issuing new stock to do so.

Signaling Prerogatives Firms often use dividends as signals of future prospects, with increases in dividends being viewed as positive signals and decreases as negative signals. The empirical evidence is consistent with this signaling story, since stock prices generally go up on dividend increases and down on dividend decreases. The use of dividends as signals may lead to differences between dividends and FCFE.

Managerial Self-Interest The managers of a firm may gain by retaining cash rather than paying it out as a dividend. The desire for empire building may make increasing the size of the firm an objective on its own. Or management may feel the need to build up a cash cushion to tide over periods when earnings may dip; in such periods, the cash cushion may reduce or obscure the earnings drop and may allow managers to remain in control.

Free Cashflow to Equity (FCFE) Valuation Models

The free cash flow to equity model does not represent a radical departure from the traditional dividend discount model. In fact, one way to describe a free cash flow to equity model is that it represents a model where we discount potential dividends rather than actual dividends. Consequently, the three versions of the FCFE valuation model presented in this section are simple variants on the dividend discount model, with one significant change—free cash flows to equity replace dividends in the models.

Underlying Principle When we replace the dividends with FCFE to value equity, we are doing more than substituting one cash flow for another. We are implicitly assuming that the FCFE will be paid out to stockholders. There are two consequences:

1. There will be no future cash buildup in the firm since the cash that is available after debt payments and reinvestment needs is assumed to be paid out to stockholders each period.

2. The expected growth in FCFE will include growth in income from operating assets and not growth in income from increases in marketable securities. This follows directly from the last point.

How does discounting free cash flows to equity compare with the augmented dividend discount model, where stock buybacks are added back to dividends and discounted? You can consider stock buybacks to be the return of excess cash accumulated largely as a consequence of not paying out their FCFE as dividends. Thus, FCFE represents a smoothed-out measure of what companies can return to their stockholders over time in the form of dividends and stock buybacks.

Estimating Growth in FCFE   Free cash flows to equity, like dividends, are cash flows to equity investors and you could use the same approach that you used to estimate the fundamental growth rate in dividends per share:

$$\text{Expected growth rate} = \text{Retention ratio} \times \text{Return on equity}$$

The use of the retention ratio in this equation implies that whatever is not paid out as dividends is reinvested back into the firm. There is a strong argument to be made, though, that this is not consistent with the assumption that free cash flows to equity are paid out to stockholders, which underlies FCFE models. It is far more consistent to replace the retention ratio with the equity reinvestment rate, which measures the percent of net income that is invested back into the firm.

$$\text{Equity Reinvestment Rate} = \frac{\begin{array}{c}(\text{Cap Expenditures} - \text{Depreciation} + \text{Change in noncash} \\ \text{WC} - (\text{Debt raised} - \text{Debt repaid}))\end{array}}{\text{Net income}}$$

When discounting FCFE, it is safest to separate the existing cash balance from the operating assets of the firm, to value the equity in the operating assets and then add on the existing cash balance. Consequently, the return on equity can also have to be modified to reflect the fact that the conventional measure of the return includes interest income from cash and marketable securities in the numerator, and the book value of equity also includes the value of the cash and marketable securities. In the FCFE model, there is no excess cash left in the firm and the return on equity should measure the return on noncash investments. You could construct a modified version of the return on equity that measures this:

$$\text{Noncash ROE} = \frac{\text{Net Income} - \text{Income from cash holdings } (1 - \text{tax rate})}{(\text{Book value of equity} - \text{Cash and marketable securities})}$$

The product of the equity reinvestment rate and the modified ROE will yield the expected growth rate in noncash net income, and since the equity reinvestment rate is being held constant, in the FCFE:

$$\text{Expected growth in FCFE} = \text{Equity reinvestment rate} \times \text{Noncash ROE}$$

Constant Growth FCFE Model   The constant growth FCFE model is designed to value firms that are growing at a stable growth rate and are hence in steady state. It parallels the

Gordon growth model, with FCFE replacing dividends, and comes with many of the same caveats and constraints.

The Model The value of equity, under the constant growth model, is a function of the expected FCFE in the next period, the stable growth rate, and the required rate of return.

$$\text{Value of equity} = \frac{\text{Expected FCFE next year}}{(\text{Cost of equity} - \text{Stable growth rate})}$$

As in the Gordon growth model, the growth rate used in this model has to be less than or equal to the nominal growth rate in the economy in which the firm operates. The assumption that a firm is in steady state also implies that it possesses other characteristics shared by stable firms. This would mean, for instance, that capital expenditures are not disproportionately large, relative to depreciation, and the firm is of average risk. (If the capital asset pricing model is used, the beta of the equity should be close to 1.) To estimate the reinvestment for a stable growth firm, it is best to use the relationship between growth and fundamentals to estimate the required reinvestment. The expected growth in net income can be written as:

Expected growth rate in net income = Equity reinvestment rate × Return on equity

This enables us to estimate the equity reinvestment rate:

$$\text{Equity reinvestment rate} = \frac{\text{Stable Growth Rate}}{\text{ROE}}$$

To illustrate, a firm with a stable growth rate of 4 percent and a return on equity of 12 percent would need to reinvest about one third of its net income back into net capital expenditures and working capital needs. Put differently, the free cash flows to equity should be two thirds of net income.

Model Usage This model is best suited for firms growing at a rate comparable to or lower than the nominal growth in the economy. It is, however, a better model to use than the dividend discount model for stable firms that pay out dividends that are unsustainably high (because they exceed FCFE by a significant amount) or are significantly lower than the FCFE. Note, though, that if the firm is stable and pays out its FCFE as dividends the value obtained from this model, it will be the same as the one obtained from the Gordon growth model.

ILLUSTRATION 14.9: Stable Growth FCFE Model—Volkswagen

Volkswagen is a mature German automobile company. Notwithstanding the cyclical swings in net income that are characteristic of the business, the firm is assumed to be in stable growth, and the following inputs were used to value it in May 2011:

1. The net income, not including the interest income from cash, for the company in 2010 was 5,279 million euros, and we will use this as the base year income. (We did check the level to see if it was an outlier, in either direction. If it had been, we would have used a normalized value.)

2. The expected growth in net income over time is assumed to be 3% and the noncash return on equity that Volkswagen is expected to deliver is 10%. The resulting equity reinvestment rate for the stable growth model is 30%:

$$\text{Stable equity reinvestment rate} = g/ROE = 3\%/10\% = 30\%$$

The firm did report capital expenditures of 11,462 million euros, depreciation of 10,089 million euros, and an increase in noncash working capital of 423 million euros in the most recent. The reinvestment rate using those inputs was 20.41%,

$$\text{Reinvestment rate in 2010} = (11{,}462 - 10{,}089 + 423)/5{,}279 = 20.41\%$$

We could have used this reinvestment rate in the valuation, but with an expected growth rate in perpetuity of 2.04%, reflecting our ROE expectation:

$$\text{Stable growth rate with existing reinvestment rate} = 20.41\% \times 10\% = 2.04\%.$$

3. Volkswagen's cost of equity is estimated using a beta of 1.20, reflecting the average beta across European auto companies, a euro risk-free rate of 3.2%, and an equity risk premium of 5%:

$$\text{Cost of equity} = 3.2\% + 1.2(5\%) = 9.2\%$$

With the inputs, we can estimate the overall value of equity:

$$\text{Value of equity} = \frac{\text{Expected net income next year } (1 - \text{Equity reinvestment rate})}{(\text{Cost of equity} - \text{Stable growth rate})}$$
$$= \frac{5{,}279(1.03)(1 - .30)}{(.092 - .03)} = 61{,}392 \text{ million euros}$$

Note that this is the value of the equity in the noncash operating assets since we took out the income from cash from our base FCFE. Adding the cash balance of 18,670 million euros yields an overall value of equity of 80,062 million errors, significantly higher than the market capitalization of 53,560 million euros in May 2011.

 FCFEst.xls: This spreadsheet allows you to value the equity in a firm in stable growth, with all of the inputs of a stable growth firm.

LEVERAGE, FCFE, AND EQUITY VALUE

Embedded in the FCFE computation seems to be the makings of a free lunch. Increasing the debt ratio increases free cash flow to equity because more of a firm's reinvestment needs will come from borrowing and less is needed from equity investors. The released cash can be paid out as additional dividends or used for stock buybacks.

If the free cash flow to equity increases as the leverage increases, does it follow that the value of equity will also increase with leverage? Not necessarily. The discount rate used is the cost of equity, which is estimated based on a beta or betas. As leverage increases, the beta will also increase, pushing up the cost of equity. In fact, in the levered beta equation that we introduced in Chapter 8 the levered beta is:

$$\text{Levered beta} = \text{Unlevered beta}[1 + (1 - \text{Tax rate})(\text{Debt/Equity})]$$

This, in turn, will have a negative effect on equity value. The net effect on value will then depend on which effect—the increase in cash flows or the increase in betas—dominates.

Two-Stage FCFE Model   The two-stage FCFE model is designed to value a firm that is expected to grow much faster than a stable firm in the initial period and at a stable rate after that.

The Model   The value of any stock is the present value of the FCFE per year for the extraordinary growth period, plus the present value of the terminal price at the end of the period.

$$\text{Value of equity} = \sum_{t=1}^{t=n} \frac{E(FCFE)_t}{(1 + k_{e,hg})^t} + \frac{\text{Terminal value of equity in year n}}{(1 + k_{e,hg})^n}$$

Where $\qquad\qquad E(FCFE)_t$ = Expected Free cash flow to equity in period t

$$\text{Terminal value of equity in year n} = \frac{FCFE_{n+1}}{(k_{e,st} - g_n)}$$

k_e = Cost of equity in high-growth (hg) and stable period (st)

g_n = Growth rate in perpetuity after year n

As you can see, the structure of this model closely follows the two-stage dividend discount model, with free cash flows to equity replacing dividends in the model.

Calculating the Terminal Value   The same caveats that apply to the growth rate for the stable growth rate model, described in the previous section, apply here as well. In addition, the assumptions made to derive the free cash flow to equity after the terminal year have to be consistent with this assumption of stability. For instance, while capital spending may be much greater than depreciation in the initial high-growth phase, the difference should narrow as the firm enters its stable growth phase. We can use the two approaches described for the stable growth model—industry average capital expenditure requirements or the fundamental growth equation (equity reinvestment rate = g/ROE)—to make this estimate.

The beta and debt ratio may also need to be adjusted in stable growth to reflect the fact that stable growth firms tend to have average risk (betas closer to 1) and use more debt than high-growth firms.

ILLUSTRATION 14.10: Capital Expenditure, Depreciation, and Growth Rates

Assume you have a firm that is expected to have earnings growth of 20% for the next five years and 5% thereafter. The current earnings per share is $2.50. Current capital spending is $2.00, and current depreciation is $1.00. If we assume that capital spending and depreciation grow at the same rate as earnings, and there are no working capital requirements or debt:

$$\text{Earnings in year } 5 = 2.50 \times (1.20)^5 \qquad\qquad = \$6.22$$
$$\text{Capital spending in year } 5 = 2.00 \times (1.20)^5 \qquad = \$4.98$$
$$\text{Depreciation in year } 5 = 1.00 \times (1.20)^5 \qquad\quad = \$2.49$$
$$\text{Free cash flow to equity in year } 5 = \$6.22 + \$2.49 - \$4.98 = \$3.73$$

If we use the perpetual growth rate model but fail to adjust the imbalance between capital expenditures and depreciation, the free cash flow to equity in the terminal year is:

$$\text{Free cash flow to equity in year } 6 = 3.73 \times 1.05 = \$3.92$$

This free cash flow to equity can then be used to compute the value per share at the end of year 5, but it will understate the true value, since you are forcing the firm to reinvest at the same rate that it did during its high-growth phase, while lowering the growth rate.

There are two ways in which you can adjust for this:

1. Adjust capital expenditures in year 6 to reflect industry average capital expenditure needs: Assume, for instance, that capital expenditures are 150% of depreciation for the industry in which the firm operates. You could compute the capital expenditures in year 6 as follows):

$$\text{EPS in year } 6 = \$6.21 \times 1.05 = \$6.53$$
$$\text{Depreciation in year } 6 = 2.49(1.05) = \$2.61$$

$$\text{Capital expenditures in year } 6 = \text{Depreciation in year } 6 \times \text{Industry average capital}$$
$$\text{expenditures as \% of depreciation}$$
$$= \$2.61 \times 1.50 = \$3.92$$
$$\text{FCFE in year } 6 = \$6.53 + \$2.61 - \$3.92 = \$5.23$$

2. Estimate the equity reinvestment rate in year 6, based on expected growth and the firm's return on equity. For instance, if we assume that this firm's return on equity will be 15% in stable growth, the equity reinvestment rate would need to be:

$$\text{Equity reinvestment rate} = g/ROE = 5\%/15\% = 33.33\%$$
$$\text{Equity Reinvestment in year } 6 = \text{Equity reinvestment rate} \times \text{Earnings per share}$$
$$= .3333 \times \$6.53 = \$2.18$$
$$\text{FCFE in year } 6 = \$6.53 - \$2.18 = \$4.35$$

We prefer the second approach because it preserves consistency in the valuation between growth, reinvestment, and return quality assumptions.

Model Usage This model makes the same assumptions about growth as the two-stage dividend discount model (i.e., that growth will be high and constant in the initial period and drop abruptly to stable growth after that). It is different because of its emphasis on FCFE rather than dividends. Consequently, it provides much better results than the dividend discount model when valuing firms which either have dividends which are unsustainable (because they are higher than FCFE), or which pay less in dividends than they can afford to (i.e., dividends are less than FCFE).

The downside is that it requires more estimation, since rather than taking the company's dividends as its free cash flows to equity, you compute what the company could have paid out by netting out the cash flows from reinvestment and debt.

ILLUSTRATION 14.11: Two-Stage FCFE Model: Nestlé in 2024

Nestlé has operations all over the world, with most of its revenues coming from markets outside Switzerland, where it is headquartered. The firm, like many large European corporations, has a weak corporate governance system and stockholders have little power over managers.

RATIONALE FOR USING THE MODEL

- *Why two-stage?* Nestlé has a long and impressive history of growth, and while we believe that its growth will be moderate, we assume that it will be able to maintain high growth for 5 years.
- *Why FCFE?* Given its weak corporate governance structure and a history of accumulating cash, the dividends paid by Nestlé bear little resemblance to what the firm could have paid out.

BACKGROUND INFORMATION

In May 2024, Nestle's most recent financial statements reported net income of 11,209 million Swiss Francs (SFr), with 192 million SFr coming from income on cash and marketable securities during the fiscal year. During the year, the company reported the following components of reinvestment:

Capital expenditures and acquisitions = SFr 5,925 million

Depreciation and amortization = SFr 2,993 million

Change in noncash working capital = −SFr 794 million

The company did raise SFr 6,806 million in new debt, while repaying 6,126 million in debt coming due, giving it a net debt cash flow of SFr 680 million. Finally, the company's book equity, with and without cash included, is below:

	Start of 2023	End of 2023
Book Equity	SFr 41,982	SFr 35,742
Cash and marketable securities	SFr 6,744	SFr 5,851
Noncash equity	SFr 35,238	SFr 29,891

ESTIMATES

We will begin by estimating the cost of equity for Nestlé during the high-growth period in Swiss francs. We will use the 10-year Swiss government SFr bond rate of 1%, in May 2024, as the risk-free rate. To estimate the risk premium, we used the breakdown of Nestlé's revenues by region in Table 14.8.

TABLE 14.8 Nestle—Geographic Revenue Breakdown

Country	Revenues (in millions of SFr)	Weight	ERP
United States	SFr 30,034	32.33%	4.30%
Canada	SFr 2,519	2.71%	4.30%
France	SFr 3,546	3.82%	5.02%
United Kingdom	SFr 3,529	3.80%	5.18%
Germany	SFr 2,212	2.38%	4.30%
Australia	SFr 1,450	1.56%	4.30%
China	SFr 5,524	5.95%	5.33%
Brazil	SFr 4,131	4.45%	8.70%
Mexico	SFr 3,937	4.24%	7.08%
Chile	SFr 1,312	1.41%	5.54%
Rest of Latin America	SFr 3,380	3.64%	10.06%
Rest of Asia	SFr 18,330	19.73%	5.98%
Rest of Europe	SFr 13,004	14.00%	5.59%
Nestle (the firm)	SFr 92,908	100.00%	5.47%

The risk premiums for Nestle represents a revenue-weighted average of the equity risk premiums of the different parts of the world it operates in. We also estimate a bottom-up beta for Nestle of 0.67, reflecting an unlevered beta of 0.5691 for the food-processing business and its debt-to-equity ratio of 22.36% (with a global average marginal tax rate of 25%):

$$\text{Levered beta for Nestle} = 0.5691(1 + (1 - .25)(.2236)) = 0.6645$$

That yields a cost of equity of 4.64% for the firm, in Swiss francs:

$$\text{Cost of equity for Nestle} = \text{Risk-free Rate}_{\text{Swiss Francs}} + \beta(\text{ERP})$$
$$= 1.00\% + 0.6645(5.47\%) = 4.64\%$$

We will assume that this cost of equity will increase slightly in stable growth, with a beta of 0.80 being the only input that change:

$$\text{Cost of equity for Nestle}_{\text{Stable growth}} = 1.00\% + 0.80(5.47\%) = 5.38\%$$

To estimate the expected growth rate in free cash flows to equity, we first computed the free cash flow to equity in the most recent period:

$$\text{FCFE} = (\text{Net income} - \text{After-tax Interest income from cash}) - (\text{Cap expenditure} - \text{Depreciation})$$
$$- \text{Change in working capital} + \text{Debt raised} - \text{Debt repaid}$$
$$= (11,209 - 144) - (5,915 - 2,993) - (-794) + (6806 - 6126) = 9,617 \text{ SFr million}$$

The equity reinvestment rate can be estimated from this value:

$$\text{Equity reinvestment rate} = 1 - \frac{9617}{(11209 - 144)} = 13.18\%$$

The noncash return on equity in 2023 was estimated using the net income from 2023 and the book value of equity, net of cash, from the end of the previous year:

$$\text{Return on equity} = (11,209 - 144)/(41,982 - 6,744) = 31.40\%$$

The expected growth rate in FCFE is a product of the equity reinvestment rate and the return on equity:

$$\text{Expected growth in net income} = \text{ROE} \times \text{Equity reinvestment rate}$$
$$= .3140 \times .1318 = 4.14\%$$

In effect, we are assuming that Nestle will continue to earn its current return on equity and maintain its current equity reinvestment rate for the next five years. In stable growth, we assume a growth rate of 1%, set at the risk-free rate. We also assume the return on equity drops to 15%, and the equity reinvestment rate in stable growth can be estimated as follows:

$$\text{Equity reinvestment in stable growth} = g/\text{ROE} = 1\%/15\% = 6.67\%$$

VALUATION

The first component of value is the present value of the expected FCFE during the high-growth period, (see Table 14.9) net income grows at 4.14% a year, and that the equity reinvestment is 13.18% of that net income each year (in SFr), as can be seen in Table 14.9:

TABLE 14.9   FCFE and Present Value for Nestle

	1	2	3	4	5
Expected Growth Rate	4.14%	4.14%	4.14%	4.14%	4.14%
Net Income (SFr mil)	SFr11,523	SFr12,000	SFr12,496	SFr13,013	SFr13,552
Equity Reinvestment Rate	13.18%	13.18%	13.18%	13.18%	13.18%
FCFE (SFr mil)	SFr10,004	SFr10,418	SFr10,850	SFr11,298	SFr11,766
Cost of Equity	4.64%	4.64%	4.64%	4.64%	4.64%
Present Value (SFr mil)	SFr 9,561	SFr 9,516	SFr 9,471	SFr 9,426	SFr 9,381

Note that present value is computed using the high-growth period cost of equity of 4.64%.

To estimate the terminal value, we first estimate the free cash flows to equity in year 6:

$$\text{Expected net income in year 6} = \text{Net Income}_5(1 + g)$$
$$= 13,552(1.01) = \text{SFr } 13,687 \text{ m}$$

$$\text{Equity reinvestment in year 6} = \text{Net income}_6 \times \text{Stable equity reinvestment rate}$$
$$= 13,687(.0667) = \text{SFr } 912 \text{ m}$$

$$\text{Expected FCFE in year 6} = \text{Net income}_6 - \text{Equity reinvestment}_6$$
$$= 13,687 - 912 = \text{SFr } 12,775 \text{ m}$$

$$\text{Terminal value of equity per share} = \text{FCFE}_6/(\text{Cost of equity}_6 - g)$$
$$= 12,775/(.0538 - .01) = \text{SFr } 291,924 \text{ m}$$

The value per share can be estimated as the sum of the present value of FCFE during the high-growth phase and the present value of the terminal value of equity:

$$\text{Value of equity today} = \text{PV of FCFE during high-growth phase}$$
$$+ \text{Terminal equity value}/(1 + k_e)^n$$
$$= 47{,}354 + 291{,}924/1.0464^5 = \text{SFr } 280{,}102 \text{ million}$$

We discount the terminal value of equity back at the high-growth period cost of equity since that reflects the risk of the next five years. Adding in the cash and marketable securities of Sfr 5,851 million held by Nestle in its most recent balance sheet and dividing by the share count of 2621.30 million shares on May 23, 2024, we estimate a value of equity per share of 109.09 Swiss francs:

$$\text{Value of equity per share} = (\text{Value of equity} + \text{Cash \& marketable securities})$$
$$/\text{Number of shares outstanding}$$
$$= \frac{(280102 + 5851)}{2621.30} = \text{Sfr } 109.09$$

The stock was trading at 100.64 SFr per share in May 2024, at the time of this valuation, making the stock slightly undervalued.

 FCFE2st.xls: This spreadsheet allows you to value a firm with a temporary period of high growth in FCFE, followed by stable growth.

REINVESTMENT ASSUMPTIONS, TERMINAL VALUE, AND EQUITY VALUE

We have repeatedly emphasized the importance of linking growth assumptions to assumptions about reinvestment, and especially so in stable growth. A very common assumption in many discounted cash flow valuations is that capital expenditures offset depreciation in stable growth. When combined with the assumption of no working capital changes, this translates into zero reinvestment. While this may be a reasonable assumption for a year or two, it is not consistent with the assumption that operating income will grow in perpetuity. How much of a difference can one assumption make? In the Nestlé valuation, we reestimated terminal value of equity per share assuming no reinvestment:

$$\text{Terminal value of equity} = \frac{13{,}687}{(.0538 - .01)} = \text{SFr } 312{,}776 \text{ million}$$

Keeping all other assumptions intact, this results in a value of equity per share of 115.43 SFr per share—an increase in value of approximately 5 percent, with the effect being small only because the stable growth is only 1%.

A Generalized FCFE Model   In the most general version of the free cash flow to equity model, you have phases of growth, where the growth rate can either vary every year or over different periods, before settling into stable growth. In this section, we will describe consistency rules that have to be applied when allowing growth to change over time.

The Model   In the last chapter, we described a three-stage dividend discount model, with an initial period of high growth, followed by a transition period where growth declined down to stable growth:

$$\text{Value of equity today} = \sum_{t=1}^{t=n} \frac{\text{FCFE}_t}{\left(1 + k_{e,hg}\right)^t} + \frac{\text{FCFE}_{n+1}}{\left(k_{e,st} - g_n\right)\left(1 + k_{e,hg}\right)^n}$$

$$\text{FCFE}_t = \text{FCFE in year t}$$
$$k_{e,hg} = \text{Cost of equity in year t}$$
$$k_{e,st} = \text{Cost of equity in stable growth}$$
$$g_n = \text{Growth rate in stable growth period}$$

The model is adaptable, when it comes to growth, equity reinvestment rates and costs of equity in high growth, with each being changeable on a year-to-year basis.

Caveats in Using Model   Since the model assumes that the growth rate goes through three distinct phases—high growth, transitional growth, and stable growth—it is important that assumptions about other variables are consistent with these assumptions about growth.

Equity Reinvestment   It is reasonable to assume that as the firm goes from high growth to stable growth, the equity reinvestment needed to deliver that growth will change. In the high-growth phase, equity reinvestment needed to deliver that growth will be high, with that reinvestment taking the form of capital expenditures that are much higher than depreciation, significant increases in working capital, large acquisitions or large R&D investments. In the transitional phase, as growth decreases down towards stable growth, equity reinvestment rates should also decline, with the rate of decline depending upon the return on equity on new investments. (See Figure 14.8.)

Note that in stable growth, the equity reinvestment rate should level off at a level high enough to sustain the stable growth, with the sustainable growth equation providing guidance:

$$\text{Stable equity reinvestment rate} = \frac{\text{Stable growth rate}}{\text{Stable period return on equity}}$$

Risk   As the growth characteristics of a firm change, so do its risk characteristics. In the context of the CAPM, as the growth rate declines the beta of the firm can be expected to change. The tendency of betas to converge toward one in the long term has been confirmed by empirical observation of portfolios of firms with high betas. Over time, as these firms

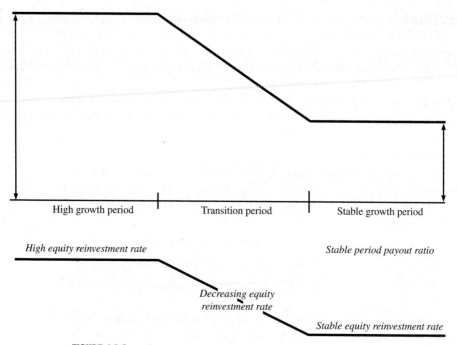

High growth period | Transition period | Stable growth period

High equity reinvestment rate | *Stable period payout ratio*

Decreasing equity reinvestment rate

Stable equity reinvestment rate

FIGURE 14.8 Three-Stage FCFE Model: Reinvestment Needs

get larger and more diversified, the average betas of these portfolios move toward 1. In sum, the costs of equity for a firm, in a generalized FCFE model, should change as growth rates change, converging on the cost of equity in a mature firm, by stable growth.

Model Usage Early in this book, we noted the equivalence of FCFE and FCFF models in delivering consistent measures of equity value for a firm. There are however estimation challenges that can make it more difficult to maintain consistency in a FCFE model, as opposed to a FCFF model. In particular, free cash flows to equity are after debt cashflows (i.e., cash inflows from raising new debt and cash outflows from repaying debt coming due). With firms where you expect debt ratios to change significantly over time, free cash flows to equity become much more difficult to estimate, since you have to forecast out the speed and extent to which you expect debt ratios to increase or decrease and convert these debt ratio changes in debt cash flows.

The companies where free cash flows to equity tend to be easiest to compute are firms that plan to maintain stable debt ratios over time, since the free cash flows to equity in future periods can then be estimated using the short cut, where equity reinvestment can be computed using that debt ratio (rather than explicitly forecasting debt repayments and issuances):

$$\text{Equity reinvestment} = (\text{Capital expenditures} - \text{Depreciation} + \text{Change in noncash} \\ \text{working capital})(1 - \text{Debt-to-capital ratio})$$

If you are unsure about whether a firm will maintain its current debt ratio into the future, you should steer away from free cash flow to equity models and use the free cash-flow to the firm models instead.

ILLUSTRATION 14.12: Generalized FCFE Model: Tsingtao Breweries (China) in 2001

Tsingtao Breweries produces and distributes beer and other alcoholic beverages in China and around the world under the Tsingtao brand name. The firm has 653.15 million shares listed on the Shanghai and Hong Kong exchanges.

RATIONALE FOR USING THE THREE-STAGE FCFE MODEL

- *Why three-stage?* Tsingtao is a small firm serving a huge and growing market—China, in particular, and the rest of Asia in general. The firm's current return on equity is low, and we anticipate that it will improve over the next five years. As it increases, earnings growth will be pushed up.

- *Why FCFE?* Corporate governance in China tends to be weak and dividends are unlikely to reflect free cash flow to equity. In addition, the firm consistently funds a portion of its reinvestment needs with new debt issues.

BACKGROUND INFORMATION

In 2000, Tsingtao Breweries earned 72.36 million CY (Chinese yuan) in net income on a book value of equity of 2,588 million CY, giving it a return on equity of 2.80%. The firm had capital expenditures of 335 million CY and depreciation of 204 million CY during the year, and noncash working capital dropped by 1.2 million CY during the year. The total reinvestment in 2000 was therefore:

$$\text{Total reinvestment} = \text{Capital expenditures} - \text{Depreciation}$$
$$+ \text{Change in noncash working capital}$$
$$= 335 - 204 - 1.2 = 129.8 \text{ million}$$

The working capital changes over the past four years have been volatile, and we normalize the change using noncash working capital as a percent of revenues in 2000:

$$\text{Normalized change in noncash working capital} = (\text{Noncash working capital}_{2000}/\text{Revenues}_{2000})$$
$$\times (\text{Revenues}_{2000} - \text{Revenues}_{1999})$$
$$= (180/2{,}253) \times (2{,}253 - 1{,}598)$$
$$= 52.3 \text{ million CY}$$

The normalized reinvestment in 2000 can then be estimated as follows:

$$\text{Normalized reinvestment} = \text{Capital expenditures} - \text{Depreciation}$$
$$+ \text{Normalized change in noncash working capital}$$
$$= 335 - 204 + 52.3 = 183.3 \text{ million CY}$$

As with working capital, debt issues have been volatile. We estimate the firm's book debt to capital ratio of 40.94% at the end of 2000 and use it to estimate the normalized equity reinvestment in 2000:

$$\text{Equity reinvestment in 2000} = \text{Reinvestment}(1 - \text{Debt ratio}) = 183.3(1 - .4094)$$
$$= 108.27 \text{ million CY}$$

As a percent of net income:

$$\text{Equity reinvestment rate in 2000} = 108.27/72.36 = 149.97\%$$

ESTIMATION

To estimate free cash flows to equity for the high-growth period, we make the assumption that the return on equity, which is 2.80% today, will drift up to 12% by the fifth year. In addition, we will assume that new investments from now on will earn a return on equity of 12%. Finally, we will assume that the equity reinvestment rate will remain at its current level (149.97%) each year for the next five years. The expected growth rate over the next five years can then be estimated as follows:

$$\text{Expected growth rate—next five years} = \text{Equity reinvestment rate} \times \text{ROE}_{new}$$
$$+ \left[(\text{ROE}_{new} - \text{ROE}_{today})/\text{ROE}_{today} \right]^{1/5} - 1$$
$$= 1.4997 \times .12 + \left\{ [(.12 - .028)/.028]^{1/5} - 1 \right\}$$
$$= 44.91\%$$

After year 5, we will assume that the expected growth rate declines linearly each year from year 6 through 10 to reach a stable growth rate of 10% in year 10. (Note that the growth rate is in nominal CY; the higher stable growth rate reflects the higher expected inflation in that currency.) As the growth rate declines, the equity reinvestment rate also drops off to a stable period equity reinvestment rate of 50%, estimated using the 10% stable growth rate and an assumed return on equity in stable growth of 20%.

$$\text{Stable period equity reinvestment rate} = g/\text{ROE} = 10\%/20\% = 50\%$$

To estimate the cost of equity, we used a risk-free rate of 10% (in nominal CY), a risk premium of 6.28% (4% for mature market risk and 2.28% as the country risk premium for China), and a beta of 0.75 (reflecting the bottom-up beta for breweries):

$$\text{Cost of equity} = 10\% + 0.75(6.28\%) = 14.71\%$$

In stable growth, we assume that the beta will drift up to 0.80 and that the country risk premium will drop to 0.95%:

$$\text{Cost of equity} = 10\% + 0.80(4.95\%) = 13.96\%$$

The cost of equity adjusts in linear increments from 14.71% in year 5 to 13.96% in year 10.

VALUATION

To value Tsingtao, we will begin by projecting the free cash flows to equity during the high-growth and transition phases, using an expected growth rate of 44.91% in net income and an equity reinvestment rate of 149.97% for the first five years. The next five years represent a transition period, where the growth drops in linear increments from 44.91% to 10% and the equity reinvestment rate drops from 149.97% to 50%. The resulting free cash flows to equity are shown in the Table 14.10:

TABLE 14.10 Expected FCFE for Tsingtao Breweries

Year	Expected	Net Income	Equity Reinv Rate	FCFE	Cost of Equity	Present Value
Current		CY 72.36	149.97%			
1	44.91%	CY 104.85	149.97%	−CY 52.40	14.71%	−CY 45.68
2	44.91%	CY 151.93	149.97%	−CY 75.92	14.71%	−CY 57.70
3	44.91%	CY 220.16	149.97%	−CY 110.02	14.71%	−CY 72.89

Year	Expected	Net Income	Equity Reinv Rate	FCFE	Cost of Equity	Present Value
4	44.91%	CY 319.03	149.97%	−CY 159.43	14.71%	−CY 92.08
5	44.91%	CY 462.29	149.97%	−CY 231.02	14.71%	−CY 116.32
6	37.93%	CY 637.61	129.98%	−CY 191.14	14.56%	−CY 84.01
7	30.94%	CY 834.92	109.98%	CY 83.35	14.41%	−CY 32.02
8	23.96%	CY 1,034.98	89.99%	CY 103.61	14.26%	CY 34.83
9	16.98%	CY 1,210.74	69.99%	CY 363.29	14.11%	CY 107.04
10	10.00%	CY 1,331.81	50.00%	CY 665.91	13.96%	CY 172.16
		Sum of present value of FCFE during high growth =				−CY 186.65

To estimate the terminal value of equity, we use the net income in the year 11, reduce it by the equity reinvestment needs in that year, and then assume a perpetual growth rate of 10%, set equal to the Chinese Yuan risk-free rate, to get to a value:

$$\text{Expected stable growth rate} = 10\%$$
$$\text{Equity reinvestment rate in stable growth} = 50\%$$
$$\text{Cost of equity in stable growth} = 13.96\%$$
$$\text{Expected FCFE in year 11} = \text{Net income}_{11} \times (1 - \text{Stable period equity reinvestment rate})$$
$$= CY1{,}331.81(1.10)(1 - .5) = CY732.50 \text{ million}$$

$$\text{Terminal value of equity in Tsingtao Breweries} = FCFE_{11}/(\text{Stable period cost of equity} - \text{Stable}$$
$$\text{growth rate}) = 732.5/(.1396 - .10)$$
$$= CY18{,}497 \text{ million}$$

To estimate the value of equity today, we sum up the present value of the FCFE over the high-growth period and add to it the present value of the terminal value of equity:

$$\text{Value of equity} = \text{PV of FCFE during the high-growth period} + \text{PV of terminal value}$$
$$= -CY186.65 + CY18{,}497/(1.1471^5 \times 1.1456$$
$$\times 1.1441 \times 1.1426 \times 1.1411 \times 1.1396) = CY4{,}596 \text{ million}$$
$$\text{Value of equity per share} = \text{Value of equity/Number of shares} = CY4{,}596/653.15$$
$$= CY7.04 \text{ per share}$$

The stock was trading at 10.10 yuan per share, which would make it overvalued based on this valuation.

NEGATIVE FCFE, EQUITY DILUTION, AND VALUE PER SHARE

Unlike dividends, free cash flows to equity can be negative. This can occur either because net income is negative or because a firm's reinvestment needs are significant; this is the case with Tsingtao in Illustration 14.5. The resulting net capital expenditure and working capital needs are much larger than the net income. In fact, this is likely to occur fairly frequently with high-growth firms.

(continued)

(*continued*)

The FCFE model is flexible enough to deal with this issue. The free cash flows to equity will be negative as the firm reinvests substantial amounts to generate high growth. As the growth declines, the reinvestment needs also drop off and free cash flows to equity turn positive.

Intuitively, though, consider what a negative free cash flow to equity implies. It indicates that the firm does not generate enough equity cash flows from current operations to meet its equity reinvestment needs. Since the free cash flow to equity is after net debt issues, the firm will have to issue new equity in years when the cash flow is negative. This expected dilution in future years will reduce the value of equity per share today. In the FCFE model, the negative free cash flows to equity in the earlier years will reduce the estimated value of equity today. Thus, the dilution effect is captured in the present value, and no additional consideration is needed of new stock issues in future years and the effect on value per share today.

 FCFE3st.xls: This spreadsheet allows you to value a firm with a temporary period of high growth in FCFE, followed by a transition period, followed by stable growth.

FCFE VALUATION VERSUS DIVIDEND DISCOUNT MODEL VALUATION

The discounted cash flow model that uses FCFE can be viewed as an alternative to the dividend discount model. Since the two approaches sometimes provide different estimates of value, it is worth examining when they provide similar estimates of value, when they provide different estimates of value, and what the difference tells us about the firm.

When They Are Similar

There are two conditions under which the value from using the FCFE in discounted cash flow valuation will be the same as the value obtained from using the dividend discount model. The first is the obvious one, where the dividends are equal to the FCFE. The second condition is more subtle, where the FCFE is greater than dividends, but the excess cash (FCFE minus dividends) is invested in projects with net present value of zero. (For instance, investing in financial assets that are fairly priced should yield a net present value of zero.)

When They Are Different

There are several cases where the two models will provide different estimates of value. First, when the FCFE is greater than the dividend, and the excess cash either earns below-market interest rates or is invested in negative net present value projects, the value from the FCFE model will be greater than the value from the dividend discount model. There is reason to believe that this is not as unusual as it would seem at first glance. There are numerous case studies of firms that, having accumulated large cash balances- by paying out low dividends relative to FCFE, have chosen to use this cash to finance unwise takeovers (where the price paid is greater than the value received from the takeover). Second, the payment of smaller dividends than can be afforded to be paid out by a firm may lead to a lower-debt ratio and a higher cost of capital, causing a loss in value.

In the cases where dividends are greater than FCFE, the firm will have to issue either new stock or new debt to pay these dividends, leading to at least three negative consequences for value. One is the issuance cost on these security issues, which can be substantial for equity issues, creates an unnecessary expenditure that decreases value. Second, if the firm borrows the money to pay the dividends, the firm may become overlevered (relative to the optimal), exposing itself to distress/default and leading to a loss in value. Finally, paying too much in dividends can lead to capital-rationing constraints where good projects are rejected, resulting in a loss of value.

There is a third possibility, and it reflects different assumptions about reinvestment and growth in the two models. If the same growth rate is used in the dividend discount and FCFE models, the FCFE model will give a higher value than the dividend discount model whenever FCFE is higher than dividends, and a lower value when dividends exceed FCFE. In reality, the growth rate in FCFE should be different from the growth rate in dividends, because the free cash flow to equity is assumed to be paid out to stockholders. This will affect the reinvestment rate of the firm. In addition, the return on equity used in the FCFE model should reflect the return on equity on noncash investments, whereas the return on equity used in the dividend discount model should be the overall return on equity. Table 14.11 summarizes the differences in assumptions between the two models.

In general, when firms pay out much less in dividends than they have available in FCFE, the expected growth rate and terminal value will be higher in the dividend discount model, but the year-to-year cash flows will be higher in the FCFE model. The net effect on value will vary from company to company.

TABLE 14.11 Differences between DDM and FCFE Models

	Dividend Discount Model	FCFE Model
Implicit assumption	Only dividends are paid. Remaining portions of earnings are invested back into the firm, some in operating assets and some in cash and marketable securities.	The FCFE is paid out to stockholders. The remaining earnings are invested only in operating assets.
Expected growth	Measures growth in income from both operating and cash assets. In terms of fundamentals, it is the product of the retention ratio and the return on equity.	Measures growth only in income from operating assets. In terms of fundamentals, it is the product of the equity reinvestment rate and the noncash return on equity.
Dealing with cash and marketable securities	The income from cash and marketable securities is built into earnings and ultimately into dividends. Therefore, cash and marketable securities do not need to be added in.	You have two choices: 1. Build income from cash and marketable securities into projections of income and estimate the value of equity. 2. Ignore income from cash and marketable securities and add their value to equity value in model.

What Does It Mean When They Are Different?

When the value using the FCFE model is different from the value using the dividend discount model, with consistent growth assumptions, there are two questions that need to be addressed: What does the difference between the two models tell us? Which of the two models is the appropriate one to use in evaluating the market price?

The less frequent scenario is that the dividend discount model yields a higher value than the FCFE model, largely because dividends exceed FCFE. In this case, it is best to go with the FCFE model because the dividends are not sustainable. The more common occurrence is for the value from the FCFE model to exceed the value from the dividend discount model. The difference between the value from the FCFE model and the value using the dividend discount model can be considered one component of the value of controlling a firm—it measures the value of controlling dividend policy. In a hostile takeover, the bidder can expect to control the firm and change the dividend policy (to reflect FCFE), thus capturing the higher FCFE value.

As for which of the two values is the more appropriate one for use in evaluating the market price, the answer lies in the openness of the market for corporate control. If there is a sizable probability that a firm can be taken over or its management changed, the market price will reflect that likelihood, and the appropriate benchmark to use is the value from the FCFE model. As changes in corporate control become more difficult because of a firm's size and/or legal or market restrictions on takeovers, the value from the dividend discount model will provide the appropriate benchmark for comparison.

CONCLUSION

When you buy stock in a publicly traded firm, the only cash flow you receive directly from this investment in expected dividends. The dividend discount model builds on this simple proposition and argues that the value of a stock then must be the present value of expected dividends over time. Dividend discount models can range from simple growing perpetuity models such as the Gordon growth model, where a stock's value is a function of its expected dividends next year, the cost of equity, and the stable growth rate, to complex three-stage models, where payout ratios and growth rates change over time. While the model is often criticized as being of limited value, it has proven to be surprisingly adaptable and useful in a wide range of circumstances. It may be a conservative model that finds fewer and fewer undervalued firms as market prices rise relative to fundamentals (e.g., earnings, dividends, etc.), but that can also be viewed as a strength.

The primary difference between the dividend discount models and the free cash flow to equity lies in the definition of cash flows; the dividend discount model uses a strict definition of cash flow to equity (i.e., the expected dividends on the stock), while the FCFE model uses an expansive definition of cash flow to equity as the residual cash flow after meeting all financial obligations and investment needs. When dividends are different from the FCFE, the values from the two models will be different. In valuing firms for takeovers or in valuing firms where there is a reasonable chance of changing corporate control, the value from the FCFE model provides the better estimate of value.

QUESTIONS AND SHORT PROBLEMS

In the problems following, use an equity risk premium of 5.5 percent if none is specified.

1. Respond true or false to the following statements relating to the dividend discount model:
   a. The dividend discount model cannot be used to value a high-growth company that pays no dividends.
      True _____ False _____
   b. The dividend discount model will undervalue stocks, because it is too conservative.
      True _____ False _____
   c. The dividend discount model will find more undervalued stocks when the overall stock market is depressed.
      True _____ False _____
   d. Stocks that are undervalued using the dividend discount model have generally made significant positive excess returns over long time periods (five years or more).
      True _____ False _____
   e. Stocks that pay high dividends and have low price-earnings ratios are more likely to come out as undervalued using the dividend discount model.
      True _____ False _____

2. Ameritech Corporation paid dividends per share of SFr3.56 in 1992, and dividends are expected to grow 5.5% a year forever. The stock has a beta of 0.90, and the Treasury bond rate is 6.25%. (Risk premium is 5.5%.)
   a. What is the value per share, using the Gordon growth model?
   b. The stock was trading for SFr80 per share. What would the growth rate in dividends have to be to justify this price?

3. Church & Dwight, a large producer of sodium bicarbonate, reported earnings per share of $1.50 in 1993 and paid dividends per share of $0.42. In 1993, the firm also reported the following:

   Net income = $30 million

   Interest expense = $0.8 million

   Book value of debt = $7.6 million

   Book value of equity = $160 million

   ▨ The firm faced a corporate tax rate of 38.5%. (The market value debt-to-equity ratio is 5%. The Treasury bond rate is 7%.)
   ▨ The firm expected to maintain these financial fundamentals from 1994 to 1998, after which it was expected to become a stable firm, with an earnings growth rate of 6%. The firm's financial characteristics were expected to approach industry averages after 1998. The industry averages were as follows:
      ▨ Return on capital = 12.5%
      ▨ Debt/equity ratio = 25%
      ▨ Interest rate on debt = 7%

Church & Dwight had a beta of 0.85 in 1993, and the unlevered beta was not expected to change over time.

    a. What is the expected growth rate in earnings, based on fundamentals, for the high-growth period (1994–1998)?

    b. What is the expected payout ratio after 1998?

    c. What is the expected beta after 1998?

    d. What is the expected price at the end of 1998?

    e. What is the value of the stock, using the two-stage dividend discount model?

    f. How much of this value can be attributed to extraordinary growth? To stable growth?

4. Oneida Inc, the world's largest producer of stainless steel and silverplated flatware, reported earnings per share of $0.80 in 1993, and paid dividends per share of $0.48 in that year. The firm was expected to report earnings growth of 25% in 1994, after which the growth rate was expected to decline linearly over the following six years to 7% in 1999. The stock was expected to have a beta of 0.85. (The Treasury bond rate is 6.25%, and the risk premium is 5.5%.)

    a. Estimate the value of stable growth, using the H model.

    b. Estimate the value of extraordinary growth, using the H model.

    c. What are the assumptions about dividend payout in the H model?

5. Medtronic Inc., the world's largest manufacturer of implantable biomedical devices, reported earnings per share in 1993 of $3.95, and paid dividends per share of $0.68. Its earnings were expected to grow 16% from 1994 to 1998, but the growth rate was expected to decline each year after that to a stable growth rate of 6% in 2003. The payout ratio was expected to remain unchanged from 1994 to 1998, after which it would increase each year to reach 60% in steady state. The stock was expected to have a beta of 1.25 from 1994 to 1998, after which the beta would decline each year to reach 1.00 by the time the firm becomes stable. (The Treasury bond rate is 6.25%, and the risk premium is 5.5%.)

    a. Assuming that the growth rate declines linearly (and the payout ratio increases linearly) from 1999 to 2003, estimate the dividends per share each year from 1994 to 2003.

    b. Estimate the expected price at the end of 2003.

    c. Estimate the value per share, using the three-stage dividend discount model.

6. Yuletide Inc. is a manufacturer of Christmas ornaments. The firm earned $100 million last year and paid out 20% of its earnings as dividends. The firm also has bought back $180 million of stock over the past four years, in varying amounts each year. The firm is in stable growth, expects to grow 5% a year in perpetuity, and has a cost of equity of 12%.

    a. Assuming that the dividend payout ratio will not change over time, estimate the value of equity.

    b. How would your answer change if your dividend payout ratio is modified to include stock buybacks?

7. Respond true or false to the following statements relating to the calculation and use of FCFE:

    a. The free cash flow to equity will generally be more volatile than dividends.
        True _____ False _____

    b. The free cash flow to equity will always be higher than dividends.
        True _____ False _____

c. The free cash flow to equity will always be higher than net income.
   True _____ False _____
d. The free cash flow to equity can never be negative.
   True _____ False _____

8. Kimberly-Clark, a household product manufacturer, reported earnings per share of $3.20 in 1993 and paid dividends per share of $1.70 in that year. The firm reported depreciation of $315 million in 1993 and capital expenditures of $475 million. (There were 160 million shares outstanding, trading at $51 per share.) This ratio of capital expenditures to depreciation is expected to be maintained in the long term. The working capital needs are negligible. Kimberly-Clark had debt outstanding of $1.6 billion, and intended to maintain its current financing mix (of debt and equity) to finance future investment needs. The firm was in steady state and earnings were expected to grow 7% a year. The stock had a beta of 1.05. (The Treasury bond rate was 6.25%, and the risk premium was 5.5%.)
   a. Estimate the value per share, using the dividend discount model.
   b. Estimate the value per share, using the FCFE model.
   c. How would you explain the difference between the two models, and which one would you use as your benchmark for comparison to the market price?

9. Ecolab Inc. sells chemicals and systems for cleaning, sanitizing, and maintenance. It reported earnings per share of $2.35 in 1993 and expected earnings growth of 15.5% a year from 1994 to 1998 and 6% a year after that.

   ▨ The capital expenditure per share was $2.25, and depreciation was $1.125 per share in 1993. Both were expected to grow at the same rate as earnings from 1994 to 1998.
   ▨ Working capital was expected to remain at 5% of revenues, and revenues, which were $1 billion in 1993, were expected to increase 6% a year from 1994 to 1998, and 4% a year after that.
   ▨ The firm had has a debt ratio [D/(D + E)] of 5%, but planned to finance future investment needs (including working capital investments) using a debt ratio of 20%. The stock was expected to have a beta of 1 for the period of the analysis, and the Treasury bond rate was 6.50%. (There were 63 million shares outstanding, and the market risk premium was 5.5%.)
   a. Assuming that capital expenditures and depreciation offset each other after 1998, estimate the value per share. Is this a realistic estimate?
   b. Assuming that capital expenditures continue to be 200% of depreciation even after 1998, estimate the value per share.
   c. What would the value per share have been, if the firm had continued to finance new investments with its old financing mix (5%)? Is it fair to use the same beta for this analysis?

10. Dionex Corporation, a leader in the development and manufacture of ion chromography systems (used to identify contaminants in electronic devices), reported earnings per share of $2.02 in 1993 and paid no dividends. These earnings were expected to grow 14% a year for five years (1994–1998) and 7% a year after that. The firm reported depreciation of $2 million in 1993 and capital spending of $4.20 million, and had 7 million shares outstanding. The working capital was expected to remain at 50% of revenues, which were $106 million in 1993, and were expected to grow 6% a year from 1994 to 1998 and 4% a year after that.

- The firm was expected to finance 10% of its capital expenditures and working capital needs with debt.
- Dionex had a beta of 1.20 in 1993, and this beta was expected to drop to 1.10 after 1998. (The Treasury bond rate was 7%, and the market risk premium was 5.5%.)
    a. Estimate the expected free cash flow to equity from 1994 to 1998, assuming that capital expenditures and depreciation grow at the same rate as earnings.
    b. Estimate the terminal price per share (at the end of 1998). Stable firms in this industry have capital expenditures that are 150% of revenues, and maintain working capital at 25% of revenues.
    c. Estimate the value per share today, based on the FCFE model.

11. Biomet Inc., which designs, manufactures, and markets reconstructive and trauma devices, reported earnings per share of $0.56 in 1993, on which it paid no dividends (it had revenues per share in 1993 of $2.91). It had capital expenditures of $0.13 per share in 1993, and depreciation in the same year of $0.08 per share.
    - The working capital was 60% of revenues in 1993 and was expected to remain at that level from 1994 to 1998, while earnings and revenues were expected to grow 17% a year.
    - The earnings growth rate was expected to decline linearly over the following five years to a rate of 5% in 2003.
    - During the high-growth and transition periods, capital spending and depreciation were expected to grow at the same rate as earnings, but capital spending would be 120% of depreciation when the firm reaches steady state.
    - Working capital was expected to drop from 60% of revenues during the 1994–1998 period to 30% of revenues after 2003. The firm had no debt currently but planned to finance 10% of its net capital investment and working capital requirements with debt.
    - The stock was expected to have a beta of 1.45 for the high-growth period (1994–1998), and the beta was expected to decline to 1.10 by the time the firm goes into steady state (in 2003). The Treasury bond rate is 7%, and the market risk premium is 5.5%.
    a. Estimate the value per share, using the FCFE model.
    b. Estimate the value per share, assuming that working capital stays at 60% of revenues forever.
    c. Estimate the value per share, assuming that the beta remains unchanged at 1.45 forever.

12. Will the following firms be likely to have a higher value from the dividend discount model, a higher value from the FCFE model, or the same value from both models?
    a. A firm that pays out less in dividends than it has available in FCFE but invests the balance in Treasury bonds.
    b. A firm that pays out more in dividends than it has available in FCFE, and then issues stock to cover the difference.
    c. A firm that pays out, on average, its FCFE as dividends.
    d. A firm that pays out less in dividends than it has available in FCFE, but uses the cash at regular intervals to acquire other firms with the intent of diversifying.
    e. A firm that pays out more in dividends than it has available in FCFE, but borrows money to cover the difference. (The firm is overlevered to begin with.)

13. You have been asked to value Oneida Steel, a midsize steel company. The firm reported $80 million in net income, $50 million in capital expenditures, and $20 million in depreciation in the just-completed financial year. The firm reported that its noncash working capital increased by $20 million during the year, and that total debt outstanding increased by $10 million during the year. The book value of equity at Oneida Steel at the beginning of the last financial year was $400 million. The cost of equity is 10%.

   a. Estimate the equity reinvestment rate, return on equity, and expected growth rate for Oneida Steel. (You can assume that the firm will continue to maintain the same debt ratio that it used last year to finance its reinvestment needs.)

   b. If this growth rate is expected to last five years and then drop to a 4% stable growth rate after that and the return on equity after year 5 is expected to be 12%, estimate the value of equity today, using the projected free cash flows to equity.

14. Luminos Corporation, a manufacturer of lightbulbs, is a firm in stable growth. The firm reported net income of $100 million on a book value of equity of $1 billion. However, the firm also had a cash balance of $200 million on which it earned after-tax interest income of $10 million last year. (This interest income is included in the net income, and the cash is part of the book value of equity.) The cost of equity for the firm is 9%.

   a. Estimate the noncash return on equity at Luminos Corporation.

   b. If you expect the cash flows from the operating assets of Luminos to increase 3% a year in perpetuity, estimate the value of equity at Luminos.

CHAPTER 15

Firm Valuation: Cost of Capital and Adjusted Present Value Approaches

The last chapter examined two approaches to valuing the equity in the firm—the dividend discount model and the free cash flow to equity (FCFE) valuation model. This chapter examines approaches to valuation in which the entire firm is valued, by either discounting the cumulated cash flows to all claim holders in the firm by the weighted average cost of capital (the cost of capital approach) or by adding the marginal impact of debt on value to the unlevered firm value—the adjusted present value (APV) approach.

In the process of looking at firm valuation, we also look at how leverage may or may not affect firm value. We note that in the presence of default risk, taxes, and agency costs, increasing leverage can sometimes increase firm value and sometimes decrease it. In fact, we argue that the optimal financing mix for a firm is the one that maximizes firm value.

FREE CASH FLOW TO THE FIRM

The free cash flow to the firm (FCFF) is the sum of the cash flows to all claim holders in the firm, including common stockholders, bondholders, and preferred stockholders. There are two ways of measuring the free cash flow to the firm.

One is to add up the cash flows to the claim holders, which would include cash flows to equity (defined either as free cash flow to equity or as dividends); cash flows to lenders (including principal payments, interest expenses, and new debt issues); and cash flows to preferred stockholders (usually preferred dividends):

$$\text{FCFF} = \text{Free cash flow to equity} + \text{Interest expense}(1 - \text{Tax rate})$$
$$+ \text{Principal repayments} - \text{New debt issues} + \text{Preferred dividends}$$

Note, however, that we are reversing the process that we used to get to free cash flow to equity, where we subtracted out payments to lenders and preferred stockholders to estimate the cash flow left for stockholders. A simpler way of getting to free cash flow to the firm is to estimate the cash flows prior to any of these claims. Thus, we could begin with the earnings before interest and taxes, net out taxes and reinvestment needs, and arrive at an estimate of the free cash flow to the firm:

$$FCFF = EBIT(1 - \text{Tax rate}) + \text{Depreciation} - \text{Capital expenditure} - \Delta\text{Working capital}$$

Since this cash flow is prior to debt payments, it is often referred to as an unlevered cash flow. Note that this free cash flow to the firm does not incorporate any of the tax benefits due to interest payments. This is by design, because the use of the after-tax cost of debt in the cost of capital already considers this benefit, and including it in the cash flows would double count it.

FCFF and Other Cash Flow Measures

The differences between FCFF and FCFE arise primarily from cash flows associated with debt—interest payments, principal repayments, and new debt issues—and other nonequity claims such as preferred dividends. For firms at their desired debt level, which finance their capital expenditures and working capital needs with this mix of debt and equity and use new debt issues to finance principal repayments, the free cash flow to the firm will exceed the free cash flow to equity.

One metric that is widely used in valuation is the earnings before interest, taxes, depreciation, and amortization (EBITDA), a rough measure of cash flows from operations. The free cash flow to the firm is a related concept, but it is more complete because it takes into account the potential tax liability from the earnings as well as capital expenditures and working capital requirements.

Some analysts also use after-tax operating income as a proxy for free cash flow to the firm, with alternative definitions of operating income. The first, earnings before interest and taxes (EBIT) or operating income, comes directly from a firm's income statements. Adjustments to EBIT yield the net operating profit or loss after taxes (NOPLAT) or the net operating income (NOI). The net operating income is defined to be the income from operations prior to taxes and nonoperating expenses.

Each of these measures is used in valuation models, and each can be related to the free cash flow to the firm. Each, however, makes some assumptions about the relationship between depreciation and capital expenditures that are made explicit in Table 15.1.

TABLE 15.1   Free Cash Flows to the Firm: Comparison to Other Measures

Cash Flow Used	Definition	Use in Valuation
FCFF	Free cash flow to firm	Discounting free cash flow to the firm at the cost of capital will yield the value of the operating assets of the firm. To do this, you would add on the value of nonoperating assets to arrive at the firm's value.
FCFE	FCFF – Interest (1–t) – Principal repaid + New debt issued – Preferred dividend	Discounting free cash flows to equity at the cost of equity will yield the value of equity in a business.

Cash Flow Used	Definition	Use in Valuation
EBITDA	FCFF + EBIT(t) + Capital expenditures + Change in working capital	If you discount EBITDA at the cost of capital to value an asset, you are assuming that there are no taxes and that the firm will actively disinvest over time. It would be inconsistent to assume a growth rate or an infinite life for this firm.
EBIT (1–t) (NOPLAT is a slightly modified version of this estimate, and it removes any nonoperating items that might affect the reported EBIT.)	FCFF + Capital expenditures– Depreciation + Change in working capital	If you discount after-tax operating income at the cost of capital to value a firm, you are assuming no reinvestment. The depreciation is reinvested back into the firm to maintain existing assets. You can assume an infinite life but no growth.

Growth in FCFE versus Growth in FCFF

Will equity cash flows and firm cash flows grow at the same rate? Consider the starting point for the two cash flows. Equity cash flows are based on net income or earnings per share—measures of equity income. Firm cash flows are based on operating income (i.e., income prior to debt payments). As a general rule, you would expect growth in operating income to be lower than growth in net income, because financial leverage can augment the latter. To see why, let us go back to the fundamental growth equations laid out in Chapter 11:

$$\text{Expected growth in net income} = \text{Equity reinvestment rate} \times \text{Return on equity}$$

$$\text{Expected growth in operating income} = \text{Reinvestment rate} \times \text{Return on invested capital}$$

We also defined the return on equity in terms of the return on invested capital (ROIC):

$$\text{Return on equity} = \text{ROIC} \times \frac{\text{Debt}}{\text{Equity}} (\text{ROIC} - \text{After-tax cost of debt})$$

When a firm borrows money and invests in projects that earn more than the after-tax cost of debt, the return on equity will be higher than the return on capital. This, in turn, will translate into a higher growth rate in equity income at least in the short term.

In stable growth, though, the growth rates in equity income and operating income must converge. To see why, assume that you have a firm whose revenues and operating income are growing at 5 percent a year forever. If you assume that the same firm's net income grows at 6 percent a year forever, the net income will catch up with operating income at some point in time in the future, and exceed revenues at a later point in time. In stable growth, therefore, even if return on equity exceeds the return on capital, the expected growth will be the same in all measures of income.[1]

---

[1]The equity reinvestment rate and firm reinvestment rate will adjust to ensure that this happens. The equity reinvestment rate will be a lower number than the firm reinvestment rate in stable growth for any levered firm.

FIRM VALUATION: THE COST OF CAPITAL APPROACH

The value of the firm is obtained by discounting the free cash flow to the firm at the weighted average cost of capital. Embedded in this value are the tax benefits of debt (in the use of the after-tax cost of debt in the cost of capital) and expected additional risk associated with debt (in the form of higher costs of equity and debt at higher debt ratios). Just as with the dividend discount model and the FCFE model, the version of the model used will depend on assumptions made about future growth.

Stable Growth Firm

As with the dividend discount and FCFE model, a firm that is growing at a rate it can sustain in perpetuity—a stable growth rate—can be valued using a stable growth model.

The Model A firm with free cash flows to the firm growing at a stable growth rate can be valued using the following equation:

$$\text{Value of enterprise} = \frac{\text{FCFF}_1}{(\text{Cost of capital} - g_n)}$$

where FCFF_1 = Expected FCFF next year

g_n = Growth rate in the FCFF forever

The Caveats There are two conditions that need to be met in using this model. First, the growth rate used in the model must be less than or equal to the growth rate in the economy—nominal growth, if the cost of capital is in nominal terms, or real growth, if the cost of capital is a real cost of capital. Second, the characteristics of the firm must be consistent with assumptions of stable growth. In particular, the reinvestment rate used to estimate free cash flows to the firm should be consistent with the stable growth rate. The best way of enforcing this consistency is to derive the reinvestment rate from the stable growth rate:

$$\text{Reinvestment rate in stable growth} = \frac{\text{Growth rate}}{\text{ROIC}}$$

If reinvestment is estimated from net capital expenditures and change in working capital, the net capital expenditures might be similar to those other firms in the industry (perhaps by setting the ratio of capital expenditures to depreciation at industry averages). A negative change in working capital creates a cash inflow, and there are businesses where this can continue as a long term component of a business model, but you should expect to see its effects on cash flows become more muted.[2] Even if industry averages are used to compute

---

[2] Early in a company's life cycle, the firm can use supplier credit and payables as a source of capital, resulting in negative working capital. While this model for funding does not usually scale up, there are some large firms where working capital continues to be negative. Even for these firms, noncash working capital as a percent of revenues should get smaller (a less negative number) over time.

the reinvestment, it is always prudent to estimate what return on capital is imputed in that reinvestment (obtained by dividing the growth rate in perpetuity by the reinvestment rate). The cost of capital should also be reflective of a stable growth firm. In particular, the beta should be close to 1—the rule of thumb presented in the earlier chapters that the beta should be between 0.8 and 1.2 still holds. While stable growth firms tend to use more debt, this is not a prerequisite for the model, since debt policy is subject to managerial discretion.

Limitations Like all stable growth models, this one is sensitive to assumptions about the expected growth rate. This is accentuated, however, by the fact that the discount rate used in valuation is the WACC, which is significantly lower than the cost of equity for most firms. So, if keeping the growth rate below the risk free rate was good practice with equity valuation models, it is even more so with firm valuation. Furthermore, the model is sensitive to assumptions made about capital expenditures relative to depreciation. As noted in Chapter 12, if the inputs for reinvestment are not a function of expected growth, the free cash flow to the firm can be inflated (or deflated) by reducing (increasing) capital expenditures relative to depreciation.

ILLUSTRATION 15.1: Valuing a Firm with the Stable Growth FCFF Model—Telesp (Brazil) in 2010

Telesp provides local telecommunication services to the Brazilian state of Sao Paulo. In 2010, the company had operating income (EBIT) of 3,544 million BR and faced an effective tax rate of 30%. In 2010, the firm reported capital expenditures of 1,659 million BR, depreciation of 1,914 million BR, and an increase in working capital of 1,119 million BR. Consequently, its reinvestment in 2010 can be computed as follows:

$$\text{Reinvestment} = \frac{\text{Capital Expenditure} - \text{Depreciation} + \text{Change in non-cash working capital}}{\text{EBIT}(1-t)}$$

$$= \frac{1,659 - 1,914 + 1,119}{3,544(1 - .30)} = 34.82\%$$

The return on capital generated by the company in 2010 was computed using the operating income for the year and the book value of capital invested at the end of the previous year (2009):

$$\text{Return on capital} = \frac{\text{EBIT}_{2010}(1-t)}{\text{BV of equity}_{2009} + \text{BV of debt}_{2009} - \text{Cash \& securities}_{2009}}$$

$$= \frac{3,544(1 - .30)}{10,057 + 8,042 - 2,277} = 15.68\%$$

The expected growth rate that emerges from these inputs is:

$$\text{Expected growth rate} = 34.82\% \times 15.68\% = 5.46\%$$

While this would be too high a growth rate for stable growth in a currency with low-expected inflation, the risk-free rate in BR in May 2011 was 7%. In conjunction with a beta of 0.8 and an equity risk premium for Brazil of 8% (composed of a mature market premium of 5% and an additional country risk premium of 3% for Brazil), this yields a cost of equity of 13.40%. Incorporating a pretax cost of debt of 9.50% and a debt ratio of

20% (based on current market values for equity and debt) results in a cost of capital of 12.05% for Telesp:

$$\text{Debt-to-capital ratio} = \frac{\text{Debt}}{\text{Debt} + \text{Market value of equity}}$$

$$= \frac{5{,}519}{5{,}519 + 21{,}982} = 20.07\%$$

$$\text{Cost of capital} = 13.40\% \,(0.7993) + 9.50\% \,(1 - .30)(2007) = 12.05\%$$

The value for the operating assets can then be estimated as follows:

$$\text{FCFF in 2010} = \text{EBIT}\,(1 - t) + \text{Depreciation} - \text{Capital expenditures} - \text{Change in noncash WC}$$

$$= 3{,}544(1 - .30) + 1{,}914 - 1{,}659 - 1{,}119 = 1{,}617 \text{ million BR}$$

$$\text{Value of operating assets} = \frac{\text{Expected FCFF next year}}{\text{Cost of capital} - \text{Expected growth rate}}$$

$$= \frac{1{,}617\,(1.0546)}{.1205 - .0546} = 25{,}901 \text{ million BR}$$

Adding the cash and marketable securities (1,557 million BR) and subtracting the debt (5,519 million BR) at the end of 2010 yields a value for the equity:

$$\text{Value of equity} = \text{Value of operating assets} + \text{Cash} - \text{Debt}$$

$$= 25{,}901 + 1{,}557 - 5{,}519 = 21{,}939 \text{ million BR}$$

The company's market capitalization in May 2011 was 21,982 million BR, making it fairly priced.

General Versions of the FCFF Model

Rather than break the free cash flow model into two-stage and three-stage models, and risk repeating what was said in the preceding chapter, we present the general version of the model in this section. We follow up by examining a firm with operating leases (Target), and a firm with substantial R&D investments (Amgen) to illustrate the differences and similarities between this approach and the FCFE approach.

The Model   The value of the firm, in the most general case, can be written as the present value of expected free cash flows to the firm:

$$\text{Value of operating assets} = \sum_{t=1}^{t=\infty} \frac{\text{FCFF}_t}{(1 + k_c)^t}$$

where FCFF_t = Expected free cash flow to firm in year t

k_c = Weighted average cost of capital

If the firm reaches steady state after n years and starts growing at a stable growth rate g_n after that, the value of the firm can be written as:

$$\text{Value of operating asset} = \sum_{t=1}^{t=n} \frac{\text{FCFF}_t}{\left(1 + k_{c,hg}\right)^t} + \frac{\text{FCFF}_{n+1}}{\left(k_c - g_n\right)\left(1 + k_{c,st}\right)^n}$$

where k_c = Cost of capital (hg = high growth; st = stable growth)

This parallels the models we used with dividends and free cash flows to equity when stable growth follows a period of high growth. Within this high-growth model, there are two variants:

a. *Stable margins:* When you expect a company's margins to remain unchanged over time, you can estimate the expected free cash flows to the firm during the high-growth period starting with operating income, and estimate the growth rate during the high-growth period, using the sustainable growth structure:

Expected growth in operating income = ROIC × Reinvestment rate

As the growth rate changes over the high-growth period, the return on capital and reinvestment rate will change to stay in sync.

b. *Changing margins:* When margins are changing, either increasing or decreasing over time, you have to start with revenues and estimate the free cashflows in three steps. First, you project revenues over time, incorporating the expected growth in revenues, based upon market size and the company's capacity to delivery market share. Second, you use your projected operating margins to estimate the expected operating income (pre- and post-tax) each year. Third, you estimate the reinvestment by tying it to the change in revenues each year, and estimating the sales-to-capital ratio. We described this process in more detail in Chapter 11.

The bottom line in both approaches is the expected free cash flow to the firm each year.

MARKET-VALUE WEIGHTS, COST OF CAPITAL, AND CIRCULAR REASONING

To value a firm, you first need to estimate a cost of capital. Every textbook is categorical that the weights in the cost-of-capital calculation be market value weights. The problem, however, is that the cost of capital is then used to estimate new values for debt and equity that might not match the values used in the original calculation. One defense that can be offered for this inconsistency is that if you bought all the debt and equity in a publicly traded firm, you would pay current market value and not your estimated value, and your cost of capital reflects this.

For those who are bothered by this inconsistency, there is a way out. You could do a conventional valuation using market value weights for debt and equity, but then use the estimated values of debt and equity from the valuation to reestimate the cost

(continued)

(*continued*)

of capital. This, of course, will change the values again, but you could feed the new values back and estimate cost of capital again. Each time you do this, the differences between the values you use for the weights and the values you estimate will narrow, and the values will converge sooner rather than later.

How much of a difference will it make in your ultimate value? The greater the difference between market value and your estimates of value, the greater the difference this iterative process will make. In the valuation of Telesp, we began with a market value of 21,982 million BR and estimated a value of 21,939 million BR. If we substituted back this estimated value and iterated to a solution, we would arrive at an estimate of value of 21,946 million BR.[3]

Model Usage   This remains the most general model for valuing firms and is adaptable enough to any firm. It can be used to value money-losing, as well as money-making companies, companies that are being restructured, and companies that are in trouble. In later chapters, we will use it to value both start-ups and distressed firms. It can also be used when valuing a firm that has changing debt ratios, whether reducing them in the aftermath of a leveraged buyout or increasing them, as a company embarks on using debt more aggressively as it matures. The calculation of FCFE is much more difficult in these cases because of the volatility induced by debt payments (or new issues), and the value of equity, which can a small slice of the total value of the firm for highly levered firms, is more sensitive to assumptions about growth and risk. It is worth noting, though, that in theory the two approaches should yield the same value for the equity. Getting them to agree in practice is an entirely different challenge, which we will return to examine later in this chapter.

Problems   There are three problems that we see with the free cash flow to the firm model. The first is that the free cash flows to equity are a much more intuitive measure of cash flows than cash flows to the firm. When asked to estimate cash flows, most of us look at cash flows after debt payments (free cash flows to equity), because we tend to think like business owners and consider interest payments and the repayment of debt as cash outflows. Furthermore, the free cash flow to equity is a real cash flow that can be traced and analyzed in a firm. The free cash flow to the firm is the answer to a hypothetical question: What would this firm's cash flow be if it had no debt (and associated payments)?

The second is that its focus on pre-debt cash flows can sometimes blind us to real problems with survival. To illustrate, assume that a firm has free cash flows to the firm of $100 million, but that its large debt load makes its free cash flows to equity equal to –$50 million. This firm will have to raise $50 million in new equity to survive, and if it cannot, all cash flows beyond this point are put in jeopardy. Using free cash flows to

---

[3] In Microsoft Excel, it is easy to set this process up. You should first go into calculation options and put a check mark in the iteration box. You can then make the cost of capital a function of your estimated values for debt and equity.

would have alerted you to this problem, but free cash flows to the firm are unlikely to reflect this.

The final problem is that the use of a debt ratio in the cost of capital to incorporate the effect of leverage requires us to make implicit assumptions that might not be feasible or reasonable. For instance, assuming that the market value debt ratio is 30 percent will require a growing firm to issue large amounts of debt in future years to reach that ratio. In the process, the book-to-debt ratio might reach stratospheric proportions and trigger covenants or other negative consequences. In fact, we count the expected tax benefits from future debt issues implicitly in the value of equity today.

ILLUSTRATION 15.2:   Valuing Target—Dealing with Operating Leases in 2010

In an earlier chapter, we noted that operating leases prior to 2019 were treated as operating, rather than financial expenses, and argued for their recategorization as debt. While the accounting treatment has changed, we will use this example to illustrate the valuation impact of the recategorization.

In 2010, Target reported $5,252 million in pretax operating income on revenues of $67,390 million. While its high-growth days were behind it, there was some potential for growth, and we will attempt to value the firm using a two-stage FCFF model.

The first step in this valuation is to recognize that the financial statement numbers for Target are skewed by the failure to consider lease commitments as debt. Using the annual report for 2010, we obtained the lease commitments for the next five years and beyond, which we discount at Target's pretax cost of debt of 4.5% (estimated based on its S&P bond rating of A) to convert the commitments to debt in Table 15.2:

TABLE 15.2   Present Value of Lease Commitments—Target

Year	Commitment	Present Value @ 4.5%
1	$190.00	$ 181.82
2	$189.00	$ 173.07
3	$187.00	$ 163.87
4	$147.00	$ 123.27
5	$141.00	$ 113.15
6–23	$172.22	$1,680.51
Debt value of leases =		$2,435.68

Note that Target reported a lump sum of $3,100 million for commitments beyond year 5, which we have converted into annual commitments of $172.22 million a year for 18 years (a judgment call based on the annual average commitment for years 1–5). We will adjust the stated debt and operating income to reflect the decision to treat lease commitments as debt:

$$\text{Adjusted operating income} = \text{Stated operating income} + \text{Current year's lease expense}$$
$$= - \text{ Depreciation on leased asset}$$
$$= \$5{,}252 \text{ million} + 200 \text{ million} - (2{,}454/23) = \$5{,}346 \text{ million}$$
$$\text{Adjusted debt} = \text{Stated debt} + \text{Debt value of leases}$$
$$= \$15{,}726 + \$2{,}436 = \$18{,}162 \text{ million}$$

To estimate the expected growth rate, we estimate the return on capital and reinvestment rate for Target in 2010, again staying true to the decision to capitalize leases:

$$\text{Reinvestment rate} = \frac{(\text{Cap Ex} - \text{Depreciation} + \text{Change in PV of Leases} + \text{Change in Noncash WC})}{\text{Adjusted EBIT} (1 - t)}$$

$$= \frac{(2,129 - 2,084 + (2,436 - 2,353) + 332)}{5,346 (1 - .35)} = 13.24\%$$

$$\text{Return on invested capital} = \frac{\text{Adjusted EBIT}_{2010} (1 - t)}{(\text{BV of debt}_{2009} + \text{PV of leases}_{2009} + \text{BV of equity}_{2009} - \text{Cash}_{2009})}$$

$$= \frac{5,346 (1 - .35)}{(16,814 + 2,353 + 15,347 - 2,200)} = 10.75\%$$

Note that we computed the present value of lease commitments at the end of 2009 by going back to the annual report for that year, extracting the lease commitments, and computing the present value of the commitments using the pretax cost of debt at the end of 2009.

Target pulled back on reinvestment in 2010, but we expect the reinvestment rate to bounce back to 40% (close to the average for the past five years) in the next five years, yielding an expected growth rate of 4.30% each year for that period:

$$\text{Expected growth rate} = \text{Return on capital} \times \text{Reinvestment rate}$$
$$= 10.75\% \times 40\% = 4.30\%$$

To compute the cost of capital over this period, we estimate a beta of 1.05 for Target (based on the average beta across general retailers) and use an equity risk premium of 5% (the risk-free rate is 3.5%):

$$\text{Cost of equity} = 3.5\% + 1.05(5\%) = 8.75\%$$
$$\text{Cost of debt} = 4.5\% (1 - .35) = 2.93\%$$
$$\text{Debt-to-capital ratio} = \frac{\$18,162}{\$18,162 + \$34,346} = 34.59\%$$
$$\text{Cost of capital} = 8.75\%(1 - .3459) + 2.93\%(.3459) = 6.74\%$$

Here again, we computed debt-to-capital ratios, with operating leases treated as part of debt, and the market capitalization for Target of $34,346 million. The resulting free cash flows to the firm for the following five years are reported in Table 15.3, with the present value computed using the cost of capital:

TABLE 15.3 Expected FCFF and Present Value—Target

	1	2	3	4	5
Expected growth rate	4.30%	4.30%	4.30%	4.30%	4.30%
Reinvestment rate	40.00%	40.00%	40.00%	40.00%	40.00%
EBIT(1− t)	$3,624	$3,780	$3,943	$4,113	$4,289
− Reinvestment	$1,449	$1,512	$1,577	$1,645	$1,715
Free cash flow to firm	$2,175	$2,268	$2,366	$2,468	$2,574
Cost of capital	6.74%	6.74%	6.74%	6.74%	6.74%
Present value	$2,037	$1,991	$1,946	$1,901	$1,858

At the end of year 5, we assume that Target will be a mature firm, with a growth rate of 3% in perpetuity and a return on capital equal to its cost of capital. The resulting reinvestment rate and terminal value are estimated in the following calculations:

$$\text{Return on capital in stable growth} = \text{Cost of capital in stable growth} = 6.74\%$$

$$\text{Reinvestment rate in stable growth} = \frac{\text{Stable growth rate}}{\text{Stable ROIC}}$$

$$= \frac{3.00\%}{6.74\%} = 44.54\%$$

$$\text{Terminal value} = \frac{\text{EBIT}_5(1 - t) \times (1 + \text{Stable growth rate}) \times (1 - \text{Reinvestment rate})}{(\text{Cost of capital} - \text{Stable growth rate})}$$

$$= \frac{4,289(1.03)(1 - .4454)}{(.0674 - .03)} = \$65,597 \text{ million}$$

Adding the present value of the terminal value to the sum of the present value of the free cash flows to the firm for the next five years, we arrive at the value of the operating assets:

$$\text{Value of operating assets} = \text{PV of FCFF} + \text{PV of terminal value}$$

$$= 9733 + \frac{\$65,597}{1.0674^5} = \$57,086 \text{ million}$$

Adding the cash balance ($1,712 million) and subtracting debt inclusive of the operating leases ($18,162 million) yields a value of equity of $40,636 million. Dividing by the number of shares (689.13 million) results in a value per share of $58.97, about 20% higher than the prevailing market price of $49 in May 2011.

As a final part of the analysis, we examine the effect that treating leases as debt has on the valuation. As Table 15.4 makes clear, staying with the current accounting treatment of operating leases as operating expenses would result in a higher return on capital, a higher cost of capital, and a slightly higher value of equity per share.

TABLE 15.4 Valuation of Target—Lease Capitalization Effect

	Operating Expense	Financial Expense
Operating income	$ 5,252.00	$ 5,346.00
Debt	$16,814.00	$19,250.00
ROIC	11.39%	10.75%
Reinvestment rate	40%	40%
Expected growth rate	4.56%	4.30%
Debt-to-capital ratio	31.41%	34.59%
Cost of capital	6.92%	6.74%
Value of firm	$56,731.00	$58,795.00
Value of equity	$41,005.00	$40,633.00
Value/share	$ 59.50	$ 58.97

While the value per share effect is small in the case of Target, it will be larger for firms with more substantial lease commitments (relative to conventional debt). A key number to track is the excess return (return on capital − cost of capital) earned by the firm. For Target, converting leases to debt lowers the excess return slightly from 4.47% (11.39% minus 6.92%) to 4.01% (10.75% minus 6.74%), which also lowers the value per share. The greater the change in the excess returns from the lease adjustment, the greater will be the impact of converting leases to debt on value per share.

ILLUSTRATION 15.3:   Valuing Amgen in May 2024: The Effects of R&D Capitalization

---

In Illustration 9.2, we used Amgen to illustrate the effects of capitalizing R&D, using a 10-year amortizable life for R&D. Using data through 2023, we estimated the capital invested in R&D and the amortization in Table 15.5:

TABLE 15.5   R&D Capitalization—Amgen

Year	R&D Expense	Unamortized portion		Amortization this year
Current	$4,784.00	100.00%	$ 4,784.00	$ 0.00
−1	$4,434.00	90.00%	$ 3,990.60	$ 443.40
−2	$4,819.00	80.00%	$ 3,855.20	$ 481.90
−3	$4,207.00	70.00%	$ 2,944.90	$ 420.70
−4	$4,116.00	60.00%	$ 2,469.60	$ 411.60
−5	$3,737.00	50.00%	$ 1,868.50	$ 373.70
−6	$3,562.00	40.00%	$ 1,424.80	$ 356.20
−7	$3,840.00	30.00%	$ 1,152.00	$ 384.00
−8	$4,006.00	20.00%	$ 801.20	$ 400.60
−9	$4,248.00	10.00%	$ 424.80	$ 424.80
−10	$4,083.00	0.00%	$ 0.00	$ 408.30
	Value of Research Asset =		$23,716.60	
	Amortization of Asset			$4,105.20

Using the financial statements from 2023, we compute the adjusted operating income and book value of invested capital at the firm:

Adjusted operating income = Operating income + Current year's R&D expense − Amortization of research asset
$$= 8,164 + 4,784 - 4,105 = \$8,843 \text{ million}$$

$$\text{Adjusted invested capital}_{2022} = \text{Book value of invested capital}_{2022}$$
$$+ \text{ Value of research asset}_{2022}$$
$$= 60,711 + 23037 = \$83,748$$

We used the adjusted operating income to compute the pretax operating margin for Amgen in 2023:

$$\text{Pretax operating margin in 2023} = \frac{\text{Adjusted operating income}}{\text{Revenues}} = \frac{8843}{28190} = 31.37\%$$

That margin was down from the 35–40% margins that the company has historically posted.

Since we expect margins to improve over time to 40%, we will use the top-down version of the model, with the following ingredients comprising its story:

a. *Revenue growth:* Amgen has had a history of strong growth, but as it has scaled up as a business, growth rates have decreased for two reasons. The first is that any new drug that the company introduces has a smaller percentage effect on overall sales. The second is that Amgen's blockbuster drugs have aged, drawing in competition for drugs produced by competitors. Given Amgen's strong pipeline in 2024, which included two obesity drugs targeting a growing market, and its acquisition of Horizon Therapeutics in 2023, we expect the company to be able to continue to grow its revenue at a 9% annual growth rate for the next five years, before growth starts to move down towards a stable growth rate of 4% in 2034 (year 10).

b. *Operating margins:* The company's R&D adjusted margin of 31.37% is healthy but is still below its ten-year average margin of 42.5%. Because some of the decline in 2023 can be attributed to special factors (including the Horizon acquisition), we will assume that margins will improve to 40%, over the next five years, before stabilizing at that level.

c. *Reinvestment:* The company will continue to invest heavily in R&D and small acquisitions for the next five years, delivering $1.50 in revenues for every $1.00 of capital invested, but will pull back on reinvestment after year 5, delivering $4.00 in revenues for every $1.00 of capital invested.

d. *Risk:* We will give Amgen a cost of capital of 9.26%, the average for U.S. biotechnology companies, to start the valuation, but we will move that cost of capital down to 8% in stable growth, closer to the median for all U.S. companies.

In sum, our story for Amgen is that it will see moderate growth, with higher operating margins and continued reinvestment in R&D, at least for the next five years. The resulting cash flows are summarized in Table 15.6:

TABLE 15.6   Expected FCFF for Amgen

	Revenue Growth	Revenues	EBIT (Operating) margin	EBIT (Operating) income	Tax rate	EBIT(1–t)	– Reinvestment	FCFF
Base year		$28,190	31.37%	$ 8,843	14.50%	$ 7,561		
1	9.00%	$30,727	31.37%	$ 9,639	14.50%	$ 8,241	$1,844	$ 6,397
2	9.00%	$33,493	34.82%	$11,662	14.50%	$ 9,971	$2,010	$ 7,962
3	9.00%	$36,507	36.55%	$13,342	14.50%	$11,408	$2,190	$ 9,217
4	9.00%	$39,792	38.27%	$15,230	14.50%	$13,022	$2,388	$10,634
5	9.00%	$43,374	40.00%	$17,350	14.50%	$14,834	$2,313	$12,521
6	8.00%	$46,844	40.00%	$18,737	16.60%	$15,627	$ 820	$14,807
7	7.00%	$50,123	40.00%	$20,049	18.70%	$16,300	$ 752	$15,548
8	6.00%	$53,130	40.00%	$21,252	20.80%	$16,832	$ 664	$16,168
9	5.00%	$55,787	40.00%	$22,315	22.90%	$17,205	$ 558	$16,647
10	4.00%	$58,018	40.00%	$23,207	25.00%	$17,405	$ 580	$16,825

At the end of year 10, we assume that Amgen is in stable growth, growing 4% a year, and generating a return on capital of 16% in perpetuity, significantly higher than its cost of capital of 8% in stable growth:

$$\text{EBIT} (1 - t) \text{ in year } 11 = 17,405 \,(1.04) = \$18,102 \text{ million}$$

$$\text{Reinvestment rate in stable growth} = \frac{\text{Stable growth rate}}{\text{Stable ROIC}} = \frac{4\%}{16\%} = 25\%$$

$$\text{Terminal value} = \frac{\text{EBIT}_{11}(1 - \text{Reinvestment rate})}{(\text{Cost of capital} - \text{Stable growth rate})}$$

$$= \frac{18,102 \,(1 - .25)}{(.08 - .04)} = \$339,406 \text{ million}$$

We used the restated numbers to estimate the value of the firm and equity per share. The valuation, where we assume 10 years of high growth, is summarized in Figure 15.1.

Amgen											May-24

Base Year and Comparison				Growth Story	Profitability Story	Growth Efficiency Story		Terminal Value			
	Company	Industry		Moderate growth driven by new drugs emerging from the pipeline, but scale will operate a growth-limiter.	The company saw margins decline in 2023, but margins will improve over time to reach historical norms (10-year average)	Continued large spending on R&D for next five years, before tapering down ahead of stable growth.		Growth Rate			4.00%
Revenue Growth	7.09%	20.21%						Cost of capital			8.00%
Revenue	$28,190							Return on capital			16.00%
Operating Margin	31.37%	−0.43%						Reinvestment Rate			25.00%
Operating Income	$8,843										
EBIT (1-t)	$7,561										

				1	2	3	4	5	6	7	8	9	10	Terminal year
PV (Terminal value)	$ 144,927													
PV (CF over next 10 years)	$ 75,170		Revenue Growth	9.00%	9.00%	9.00%	9.00%	9.00%	8.00%	7.00%	6.00%	5.00%	4.00%	4.00%
Probability of failure =	0.00%		Revenue	$ 30,727	$ 33,493	$ 36,507	$ 39,792	$ 43,374	$ 46,844	$ 50,123	$ 53,130	$ 55,787	$ 58,018	$ 60,339
Value of operating assets =	$ 220,097		Operating Margin	31.37%	34.82%	36.55%	38.27%	40.00%	40.00%	40.00%	40.00%	40.00%	40.00%	40.00%
- Debt	$65,423		Operating Income	$ 9,639	$ 11,662	$ 13,342	$ 15,230	$ 17,350	$ 18,737	$ 20,049	$ 21,252	$ 22,315	$ 23,207	$ 24,136
- Minority interests	$0		EBIT (1-t)	$ 8,241	$ 9,971	$ 11,408	$ 13,022	$ 14,834	$ 15,627	$ 16,300	$ 16,832	$ 17,205	$ 17,405	$ 18,102
+ Cash	$10,944		Reinvestment	$ 1,844	$ 2,010	$ 2,190	$ 2,388	$ 2,313	$ 820	$ 752	$ 664	$ 558	$ 580	$ 4,525
+ Non-operating assets	$4,454		FCFF	$ 6,397	$ 7,962	$ 9,217	$ 10,634	$ 12,521	$ 14,807	$ 15,548	$ 16,168	$ 16,647	$ 16,825	$ 13,576
Value of equity	$170,072												$ 339,405.96	
- Value of options	$0													
Value of equity in common stock	$170,072		Cost of Capital	9.26%	9.26%	9.26%	9.26%	9.26%	9.01%	8.76%	8.50%	8.25%	8.00%	
Number of shares	535.50		Cumulated WACC	0.9152	0.8377	0.7666	0.7017	0.6422	0.5891	0.5417	0.4992	0.4612	0.4270	
Estimated value/share	$317.60													
			Sales to Capital	1.50	1.50	1.50	1.50	1.50	4.00	4.00	4.00	4.00	4.00	
Price per share	$311.29		ROIC	9.76%	11.56%	12.92%	14.39%	15.97%	16.42%	16.98%	17.40%	17.66%	17.77%	16.00%
% Under or Over Valued	−1.99%													

Risk Story	Competitive Advantages
Cost of capital slightly higher than median company, but decreases as company matures.	Strong competitive edges, primarily from patents.

FIGURE 15.1   Valuing Amgen—May 2024

The transition period exists primarily to allow us to adjust our high-growth inputs to stable growth levels. The cost of capital for instance, which is 9.26% for the next five years, drops in linear increments to the stable growth cost of capital of 8.00%; the compounded cost of capital is therefore used to discount cash flows in those years. Our estimate of value of equity per share is $317.60 a share, a tad above the prevailing stock price of $311.29 in May 2024, but close enough for us to view the company as fairly valued.

An intriguing question is how the capitalization of R&D expenses affected value. To investigate, we valued Amgen with the standard accounting for R&D, where it is expensed, and the effect on value per share was muted; the value per share was $315.22, about $2.48 lower than our value estimated with R&D capitalized. That has not always been the case. In 2007, when we valued Amgen, capitalizing R&D increased the value per share from $42.73 per share to $74.33 a share. There are many reasons for the shift. First, Amgen is now a more mature company, with R&D expense growing slower than they used to, resulting in a much smaller effect on operating income (and margins) than the capitalization in 2007. Second, the company's pretax return on invested capital, in 2023, with R&D capitalized, is 10.56%, and with taxes incorporated, that return is about the same as the cost of capital of 9.26%. In contrast, Amgen earned an after-tax return on capital of 16.71% in 2006, significantly higher than its cost of capital (then) of 11%. That would suggest that R&D has gone from being a significant value enhancer to a more value-neutral investment at the company.

fcffginzu.xls: **This spreadsheet allows you to estimate the value of a firm using the FCFF approach.**

NET DEBT VERSUS GROSS DEBT

In valuing the companies in this chapter, we used total debt outstanding (gross debt) rather than net debt where cash was netted out against debt. What is the difference between the two approaches, and will the valuations from the two approaches agree?

A comparison of gross and net debt valuations reveals the differences in the way we approach the calculation of key inputs to the valuation, summarized as follows:

	Gross Debt	Net Debt
Levered beta	Unlevered beta is levered using gross-debt-to-market equity ratio.	Unlevered beta is levered using net-debt-to-market-equity ratio.
Cost of capital	Debt-to-capital ratio used is based on gross debt.	Debt-to-capital ratio used is based on net debt.
Treatment of cash and debt	Cash is added to value of operating assets, and gross debt is sub-tracted to get to equity value.	Cash is not added back to operating assets, and net debt is subtracted to get to equity value.

While working with net debt in valuation is not difficult to do, the more interesting question is whether the value that emerges will be the same as the value that would have been estimated using gross debt. In general, the answer is no, and the reason usually lies in the cost of debt used in the net debt valuation. Intuitively, what you are doing when you use net debt is breaking the firm into two parts—a cash business, which is funded 100 percent with riskless debt, and an operating business funded partly with risky debt. Carrying this to its logical conclusion, the cost of debt you would have for the operating business would be significantly higher than the firm's current cost of debt. This is because the current lenders to the firm will factor in the firm's cash holdings when setting the cost of debt.

To illustrate, assume that you have a firm with an overall value of $1 billion— $200 million in cash and $800 million in operating assets—with $400 million in debt and $600 million in equity. The firm's cost of debt is 7 percent, a 2-percent default spread over the risk-free rate of 5 percent; note that this cost of debt is set based on the firm's substantial cash holdings. If you net debt against cash, the firm will have $200 million in net debt and $600 million in equity. If you use the 7-percent cost of debt to value the firm now, you will overstate its value. Instead, the cost of debt you should use in the valuation is 9 percent:

$$\text{Cost of debt on net debt} = (\text{Pretax cost of debt}_{\text{gross debt}} \times \text{Gross debt}$$
$$- \text{Risk-free rate}_{\text{net debt}} \times \text{Cash})/(\text{Gross debt} - \text{Cash})$$

In general, we would recommend using gross debt rather than net debt for two other reasons. First, the net debt can be a negative number if cash exceeds the gross debt. If this occurs, you should set the net debt to zero and consider the excess cash just as you would cash in a gross debt valuation. Second, maintaining a stable net debt ratio in a growing firm will require that cash balances increase as the firm value increases.

Will Equity Value Be the Same under Firm and Equity Valuation?

This model, unlike the dividend discount model or the FCFE model, values the firm rather than equity. The value of equity, however, can be extracted from the value of the firm by subtracting the market value of outstanding debt. Since this model can be viewed as an alternative way of valuing equity, two questions arise: Why value the firm rather than equity? Will the values for equity obtained from the firm valuation approach be consistent with the values obtained from the equity valuation approaches described in the previous chapter?

The advantage of using the firm valuation approach is that cash flows relating to debt do not have to be considered explicitly since the FCFF is a pre-debt cash flow, while they have to be taken into account in estimating FCFE. In cases where the leverage is expected to change significantly over time, this is a significant time-saver, since estimating new debt issues and debt repayments when leverage is changing can become increasingly messy the further into the future you go. The firm valuation approach does, however, require information about debt ratios and interest rates to estimate the weighted average cost of capital.

The value for equity obtained from the firm valuation and equity valuation approaches will be the same if you make consistent assumptions about financial leverage. Getting them to converge in practice is much more difficult. Let us begin with the simplest case—a no-growth, perpetual firm. Assume that the firm has $166.67 million in earnings before interest and taxes, and a tax rate of 40 percent. Assume that the firm has equity with a market value of $600 million, with a cost of equity of 13.87 percent, and debt of $400 million, with a pretax cost of debt of 7 percent. The firm's cost of capital can be estimated as follows:

$$\text{Cost of capital} = 13.87\% \left(\frac{600}{1,000}\right) + 7\%(1 - .4)\left(\frac{400}{1,000}\right) = 10\%$$

$$\text{Value of the firm} = \frac{\text{Earnings before interest and taxes } (1 - t)}{\text{Cost of capital}}$$

$$= \frac{166.67(1 - .4)}{.10} = \$1,000$$

Note that the firm has no reinvestment and no growth. We can value equity in this firm by subtracting the value of debt:

Value of equity = Value of firm − Value of debt = $1,000 − $400 = $600 million

Now, let us value the equity directly by estimating the net income:

$$\text{Net income} = (\text{EBIT} - \text{Pretax cost of debt} \times \text{Debt})(1 - t)$$
$$= (166.67 - .07 \times 400)(1 - .4) = \$83.202 \text{ million}$$

The value of equity can be obtained by discounting this net income at the cost of equity:

$$\text{Value of equity} = \frac{\text{Net income}}{\text{Cost of equity}} = 83.202/.1387 = \$600 \text{ million}$$

Even this simple example works because of the following three assumptions made implicitly or explicitly during the valuation:

1. *The values for debt and equity used to compute the cost of capital were equal to the values obtained in the valuation.* Notwithstanding the circularity in reasoning—you need the cost of capital to obtain the values in the first place—it indicates that a cost

of capital based on market value weights will not yield the same value for equity as an equity valuation model, if the firm is not fairly priced in the first place.

2. *There are no extraordinary or nonoperating items that affect net income but not operating income.* Thus, to get from operating to net income, all we do is subtract interest expenses and taxes.

3. *The interest expenses are equal to the pretax cost of debt multiplied by the market value of debt.* If a firm has old debt on its books, with interest expenses that are different from this value, the two approaches will diverge.

If there is expected growth, the potential for inconsistency multiplies. You must ensure that you borrow enough money to fund new investments to keep your debt ratio at a level consistent with what you are assuming when you compute the cost of capital.

---

 fcffvsfcfe.xls: This spreadsheet allows you to compare the equity values obtained using FCFF and FCFE models.

FIRM VALUATION: THE ADJUSTED PRESENT VALUE APPROACH

The adjusted present value (APV) approach begins with the value of the firm without debt. As debt is added to the firm, the net effect on value is examined by considering both the benefits and the costs of borrowing. To do this, it is assumed that the primary benefit of borrowing is a tax benefit, and that the most significant cost of borrowing is the added risk of bankruptcy.

Mechanics of APV Valuation

We estimate the value of the firm in three steps. First, we estimate the value of the firm, with no debt; this is termed the unlevered firm value. Second, we estimate the value added by the tax benefits of borrowing; these take the form of the tax savings that you gain from deducting interest expenses. Third, you bring in the effect of borrowing on your expected bankruptcy cost, by estimating the change in the likelihood of bankruptcy from the debt and the cost of both going bankrupt (direct bankruptcy costs) and being perceived by customers, employees and suppliers are being likely to go bankrupt (indirect bankruptcy costs).

Value of Unlevered Firm   The first step in this approach is the estimation of the value of the unlevered firm. This can be accomplished by valuing the firm as if it had no debt (i.e., by discounting the expected free cash flow to the firm at the unlevered cost of equity). In the special case where cash flows grow at a constant rate in perpetuity,

$$\text{Value of unlevered firm} = E(\text{FCFF}_1)/(\rho_u - g)$$

where FCFF_1 is the expected after-tax operating cash flow to the firm, ρ_u is the unlevered cost of equity, and g is the expected growth rate. In the more general case, you can value the firm using any set of growth assumptions you believe are reasonable for the firm.

The inputs needed for this valuation are the expected cash flows, growth rates, and the unlevered cost of equity. To estimate the unlevered cost of equity, we can draw on our earlier analysis and compute the unlevered beta of the firm:

$$\beta_{unlevered} = \frac{\beta_{Current}}{[1 + (1 - t)D/E]}$$

where $\quad \beta_{unlevered}$ = Unlevered beta of the firm

$\beta_{current}$ = Current equity beta of the firm

t = Tax rate for the firm

D/E = Current debt/equity ratio

This unlevered beta can then be used to arrive at the unlevered cost of equity.

Expected Tax Benefit from Borrowing   The second step in this approach is the calculation of the expected tax benefit from a given level of debt. This tax benefit is a function of the tax rate and interest payments of the firm, and is discounted at the cost of debt to reflect the riskiness of this cash flow. If the tax savings are viewed as a perpetuity, the value can be calculated as follows:

$$\text{Value of tax benefits} = \frac{\text{Tax rate} \times \text{Cost of debt} \times \text{Debt}}{\text{Cost of debt}}$$

$$= \text{Tax rate} \times \text{Debt} = t_c D$$

The tax rate used here is the firm's marginal tax rate, and it is assumed to stay constant over time. If you anticipate the tax rate changing over time, you can still compute the present value of tax benefits over time, but you cannot use the perpetual growth equation. In addition, you would have to modify this equation if the current interest expenses do not reflect the current cost of debt.

Estimating Expected Bankruptcy Costs and Net Effect   The third step is to evaluate the effect of the given level of debt on the default risk of the firm and on expected bankruptcy costs. In theory, at least, this requires the estimation of the probability of default with the additional debt and the direct and indirect cost of bankruptcy. If π_a is the probability of default after the additional debt and BC is the present value of the bankruptcy cost, the present value (PV) of expected bankruptcy cost can be estimated:

$$\text{PV of expected bankruptcy cost} = \text{Probability of bankruptcy}$$
$$\times \text{PV of bankruptcy cost}$$
$$= \pi_a BC$$

This step of the adjusted present value approach poses the most significant estimation problems, since neither the probability of bankruptcy, nor the bankruptcy cost, can be estimated directly.

There are two basic ways in which the probability of bankruptcy can be estimated indirectly. One is to estimate a bond rating and use the empirical estimates of default probabilities for the rating. For instance, Table 15.7, extracted from Standard and Poor's,

TABLE 15.7 Ratings and Probability of Default

Rating	Default Probabilities Over Time (1-10-Year Time Horizons)		
	1	5	10
AAA	0.00%	0.35%	0.70%
AA	0.02%	0.31%	0.72%
A	0.05%	0.47%	1.24%
BBB	0.16%	1.58%	3.32%
BB	0.61%	6.52%	11.78%
B	3.33%	16.93%	23.74%
CCC/C	27.08%	46.19%	50.38%

Source: Used with permission of S&P Global, (2023).

summarizes the probability of default over 1, 5, and 10 years by bond-rating class in using the 2013–2022 time period.[4]

The other way is to use a statistical approach such as a probit to estimate the probability of default, based on the firm's observable characteristics, at each level of debt.[5]

The bankruptcy cost can be estimated, albeit with considerable error, from studies that have looked at the magnitude of this cost in actual bankruptcies. Research that has looked at the direct costs of bankruptcy concludes that they are small[6] relative to firm value. The indirect costs of bankruptcy can be substantial, but the costs vary widely across firms. Shapiro (1989) and Titman (1984) speculate that the indirect costs could be as large as 25–30 percent of firm value but provide no direct evidence of the costs.

ILLUSTRATION 15.4: Valuing a Company Using APV: The Leveraged Acquisition of J. Crew

J. Crew is a U.S. retailer that sells clothes made under its brand name through its own stores and online. In 2010, the firm was acquired in a leveraged deal by Mickey Drexler, its CEO, and two private equity firms—TPG and Leonard Green—for $2.7 billion, with about $1.85 billion coming from debt (with a rating of BB and a pretax cost of debt of 7%).

To assess the value of the deal using the APV approach, we first value the firm as an all-equity funded (unlevered) firm. To estimate the value, we first computed a cost of equity using an unlevered beta of 1.00 for specialty retailers, in conjunction with a risk-free rate of 3.5% and mature market premium of 5%:

$$\text{Unlevered cost of equity} = 3.5\% + 1.00(5\%) = 8.5\%$$

---

[4]This study estimated default rates over 10 years for only some of the ratings classes. We extrapolated the rest of the ratings.

[5]A probit is a statistical technique that can be used to estimate the probability of a discrete event (e.g., acquisition, default) using historical data on those events, and with variables that you hypothesize as determining their likelihood. Thus, you can look at companies that have defaulted in the past and contrast them with companies that did not default, using debt ratios, earnings variability, and company size as independent variabls.

[6]In Warner's 1977 study of railroad bankruptcies, the direct cost of bankruptcy seems to be about 5 percent.

J. Crew generated $230 million in operating income on revenues of $1,722 million in 2010. We assume a 35% tax rate and a growth rate of 3.5% in perpetuity, with a return on capital of 14%, resulting in the following:

$$\text{Reinvestment rate in stable growth} = g/ROC = 3.5\%/14\% = 25\%$$

$$\text{FCFF next year} = EBIT(1 - t)(1 - \text{Reinvestment rate})$$

$$= 230 \, (1.035) \, (1 - .35)(1 - .25) = \$116.05 \text{ million}$$

$$\text{Unlevered firm value} = \frac{\text{Expected FCFF next year}}{(\text{Unlevered cost of equity} - \text{Stable growth rate})}$$

$$= \frac{\$116.05}{(.085 - .035)} = \$2,321 \text{ million}$$

To estimate the tax benefits from debt, we assume that a debt schedule by which the dollar debt would be repaid in equal annual increments to a debt level of $500 million in year 10 and beyond. Using the 35% tax rate and the pretax cost of debt, we compute the interest expenses and tax benefits each year, in Table 15.8, and discount these benefits back to today using the pretax cost of debt as the discount rate.

TABLE 15.8   Present Value of Tax Benefits

Year	Debt Due at Start of Year	Interest Expense	Tax Benefit	PV @ Cost of Debt
1	$1,850.00	$129.50	$45.33	$ 42.36
2	$1,700.00	$119.00	$41.65	$ 36.38
3	$1,550.00	$108.50	$37.98	$ 31.00
4	$1,400.00	$ 98.00	$34.30	$ 26.17
5	$1,250.00	$ 87.50	$30.63	$ 21.84
6	$1,100.00	$ 77.00	$26.95	$ 17.96
7	$ 950.00	$ 66.50	$23.28	$ 14.49
8	$ 800.00	$ 56.00	$19.60	$ 11.41
9	$ 650.00	$ 45.50	$15.93	$ 8.66
10	$ 500.00	$ 35.00	$12.25	$ 6.23
In Perpetuity	$ 500.00	$ 35.00	$12.25	$ 88.96
Total				$305.45

Note that the value of tax benefits in perpetuity is computed in two steps. First, we compute the present value of $12.25 million in tax savings in perpetuity ($12.25/.07 = $175 million). Next, we discount that value back to today at the pretax cost of debt ($175/1.07^{10} = $88.96 million)

As the final piece of the analysis, we assume that bankruptcy costs (BC), direct and indirect, would amount to 30% of firm value, and that the high-debt level taken in the deal increases the probability of bankruptcy (π_{BC}) to 20%. The expected bankruptcy cost is then:

$$\text{Expected bankruptcy cost} = (\text{Unlevered firm value} + \text{PV of tax benefits}) \times BC \times \pi_{BC}$$

$$= (\$2,321 + \$305) \times .30 \times .20 = \$158 \text{ million}$$

The value for J. Crew can now be computed using all three components:

$$\text{Value of J. Crew} = \text{Unlevered firm value} + \text{PV of tax benefits from debt} - \text{Expected bankruptcy costs}$$

$$= \$2,321 + \$305 - \$158 = \$2,469 \text{ million}$$

At $2.7 billion, the private equity investors are paying too much for the firm unless they can increase operating income substantially.

apv.xls: This spreadsheet allows you to compute the value of a firm, with leverage, using the adjusted present value approach.

Benefits and Limitations of the Adjusted Present Value Approach

The advantage of the APV approach is that it separates the effects of debt into different components and allows the analyst to use different discount rates for each component. In addition, we do not assume that the debt ratio stays unchanged forever, which is an implicit assumption in the cost-of-capital approach. Instead, we have the flexibility to keep the dollar value of debt fixed, and to calculate the benefits and costs of the fixed-dollar debt.

These advantages have to be weighed against the difficulty of estimating probabilities of default and the cost of bankruptcy. In fact, many analyses that use the adjusted present value approach ignore the expected bankruptcy costs, leading them to the conclusion that firm value increases as firms borrow money. Not surprisingly, this will yield the conclusion that the optimal debt ratio for a firm is 100-percent debt.

In general, with the same assumptions, the APV and the cost-of-capital conclusions give very similar answers. However, the APV approach is more practical when firms are evaluating a dollar amount of debt, while the cost-of-capital approach is easier when firms are analyzing debt proportions.[18]

Cost of Capital versus APV Valuation

In an APV valuation, the value of a levered firm is obtained by adding the net effect of debt to the unlevered firm value.

$$\text{Value of levered firm} = \text{FCFF}_1/(\rho_u - g) + \text{tcD} - \pi_a \text{BC}$$

In the cost-of-capital approach, the effects of leverage show up in the cost of capital, with the tax benefit incorporated in the after-tax cost of debt and the bankruptcy costs in both the levered beta and the pretax cost of debt. Will the two approaches yield the same value? Not necessarily. The first reason for differences is that the models consider bankruptcy costs very differently, with the adjusted present value approach providing more flexibility in allowing you to consider indirect bankruptcy costs. To the extent that these costs do not show up, or show up inadequately in the pretax cost of debt, the APV approach will yield a more conservative estimate of value. The second reason is that the APV approach considers the tax benefit from a dollar debt value, usually based on existing debt. The cost-of-capital approach estimates the tax benefit from a debt ratio that may require the firm to borrow increasing amounts in the future. For instance, assuming a market-debt-to-capital ratio of 30 percent in perpetuity for a growing firm will require it to borrow more in the future, and the tax benefit from expected future borrowings is incorporated into value today. Generally speaking, the cost-of-capital approach is a more practical choice when valuing ongoing firms that are not going through contortions on financial leverage; it is easier to work with a debt ratio than with dollar-debt levels. The APV approach is more useful for transactions that are funded disproportionately with debt and where debt repayment schedules are negotiated or known; this is why it has acquired a footing in leveraged-buyout circles. Finally, there is a subtle distinction in how the tax benefits from debt are incorporated in value in the two approaches. While the conventional APV approach uses the pretax cost of debt as the discount rate to estimate the value of the tax savings from debt, there are variations on the APV that discount the tax savings back at the cost of capital or the unlevered cost of equity that yield values that are closer to those obtained in the cost-of-capital approach.

APV WITHOUT BANKRUPTCY COSTS

There are many who believe that adjusted present value is a more flexible way of approaching valuation than traditional discounted cash flow models. This may be true in a generic sense, but APV valuation in practice has significant flaws. The first and most important is that most practitioners who use the adjusted present value model ignore expected bankruptcy costs. Adding the tax benefits to unlevered firm value to get to levered firm value makes debt seem like an unmixed blessing. Firm value will be overstated, especially at very high-debt ratios, where the cost of bankruptcy is clearly not zero.

FIRM VALUATION: SUM OF THE PARTS

There are some practitioners who argue that there is a third way to value firms, which is as the sum of its parts. We disagree, viewing sum of the parts valuation more as a subset of firm valuation, where you apply the general principles of firm valuation to individual parts of a firm, and then aggregating these valuations.

Aggregation versus Disaggregation

One of the features of discounted cash flow valuation is that it is additive. In other words, if you have to value a company in three businesses, you can either value the combined company, by adding up its cash flows across the three businesses and discounting at a discount rate that is a value-weighted average across the business, or you can value each of the three businesses, using the cash flows and discount rate of that business in the valuation, and add up those values. In theory, at least, you should get the same value for the company doing either. We will term the first **aggregated valuation** and the second **disaggregated valuation** and explore the differences.

If your exposure in valuation has always been to aggregated valuations, there are two reasons why it is the dominant approach.

- As investors, we invest in entire companies, not in their disaggregated parts. Thus, you buy shares in General Electric (GE), the company, and not in GE Aircraft Engines or GE Capital; and in Coca Cola, the global company, and not in Coca Cola's Indian operations. That is perhaps why so much of valuation is built around aggregation, where you look at the revenues and cash flows of the company, across geographies and businesses, and discount them back at discount rates that reflect the weightings of these businesses and geographies.
- There is another reason why aggregated valuation is the rule, rather than the exception. Most information disclosure is on an aggregated business, with GE and Coca Cola's reporting full financial statements (income statements, balance sheets and statement of cash flows) for the entire companies. While there has been some attempt

to improve disclosure at the business segment and geographic region levels, that information has usually been consigned to footnotes and remains spotty, with disclosure practices varying across companies and countries.

There are occasions, though, where you may want to value a company by valuing its parts separately.

- *Fundamental Differences:* With multi-business companies and multinationals, one advantage of valuing each business or geographic segment separately is that you can then assign different risk, cash flow, and growth profiles to each one, rather than trying to create one weighted profile for the whole company.
- *Growth Differences:* If some businesses and geographic segments are growing much more quickly than others within the same company, it becomes difficult to do an aggregated valuation that reflects these different growth rates. For instance, a bottom-up beta, which represents a weighted average of the businesses that a company is in, will have to change over time, if some businesses grow more than others.
- *Transactional Reasons:* In some cases, you will need to value a portion of a company rather than an entire company, because that portion will be sold or spun off and requires a value specific to it. This need becomes acute when you are valuing a company that is on the verge of being broken up into parts.
- *Management Reasons:* Within a company, it makes sense to value each part of the business separately, both to monitor the performance of different divisional managers but also to improve that performance.

In the last decade, as social media companies like Facebook and Twitter have entered markets, there has also been an increasing focus on what the value of a user is in these companies, partly because they derive their value from having a multitude of users but also to tailor decisions to maximize that value.

Disaggregated Valuation: The Steps

To value firms that operate in multiple businesses and many regions, we will stick with the standard framework of estimating cash flows and discount rates. But we will modify how we come up with the numbers along the way.

Aggregation versus Disaggregation—The Choice   The first step in the process is perhaps the most critical, because it determines how we approach the remaining steps. We have to decide, at the start of the process, whether we intend to value the company as a whole (aggregated), or value its individual businesses separately (disaggregated). In a world with no information or time constraints, the choice would be an easy one. A disaggregated valuation should yield a better estimate of value than an aggregated valuation. In practice, though, the choice will be complicated by the following factors:

- **Availability of information:** The most critical variable determining whether we value the company or individual businesses is access to information. To value a company on an intrinsic basis, we need access to all the operating details (revenues, operating income, and taxes), the financing breakdown (book values of debt, equity and cash holdings, and market values of the same), and reinvestment numbers (capital expenditures, working capital). Very few companies provide this level of detail on individual businesses. One compromise solution would be to substitute industry averages (for each business) where information is lacking. Thus, we can use industry-average working capital ratios to determine expected investment in working capital for each business.

- **Differences across businesses/regions:** The payoff of breaking a company into component parts is greatest when big differences exist across the parts in terms of risk, growth, and profitability. Consider a multinational company that operates only in the United States and Western Europe and is in the specialty retailing and apparel businesses. Since there is very little difference in country risk across the regions that this firm operates in and only small differences in profitability and growth in its two businesses, not much would be gained by breaking it into its individual parts and valuing it.

- **Number of businesses/regions:** A pragmatic consideration also will determine whether or how much you want to disaggregate a company. If a firm operates in 30 different businesses and 60 countries, we could, in theory, value each of the company's 1,800 parts (30 businesses times 60 countries) separately, but this is clearly impractical. In such cases, we may very well value the whole company and hope that the law of averaging works in our favor.

As a final point, an intermediate solution exists, in which we break the company into the parts that are most dissimilar from the rest of the company while aggregating the rest. With Volkswagen, for instance, we may value Volkswagen Capital separately from the rest of Volkswagen, because it has fundamental differences from the rest of the company.

Currency Choice   Companies that operate in many countries have cash flows in multiple currencies. In valuing these companies, we have to decide which currency to build our valuations around:

- **Aggregated valuation:** When valuing the company as an aggregated whole, we have no choice but to pick one currency as the base currency for estimation. You cannot have one discounted cash flow valuation with different currency choices underlying different estimates. Once that currency choice has been made, all the estimates (e.g., cash flows, growth rates, and discount rates) have to be consistent with that choice. Drawing on the earlier discussion of risk-free rates in different currencies, this requires us to build the same expected inflation rate into all our estimates. While it is often easiest to work with the currency in which the parent company reports its financial statements—U.S. dollars for GE and Coca-Cola, for instance—there are two reasons why it may sometimes make sense to switch to a different currency. The first is that the company has listings in many markets, and its financial reports in a different currency may be more comprehensive or easier to work with than the domestic currency reports. Nestlé, for instance, has listings and reports financial statements in the United Kingdom and United States, where its stock is listed, in addition to its Swiss listing. It provides more information in its foreign listings than in its domestic listings. The second reason is that getting inputs in the domestic currency for the company may be difficult. Faced with the task of valuing a Russian multinational firm, we may very well find it easier to value the company in U.S. dollars than Russian rubles.

- **Disaggregated valuations:** With disaggregated valuation, you have more flexibility. You can value each of the businesses, especially if they are located in different regions of the world, in different currencies. Then you can convert the values at the last step (when you add them together), using the current exchange rates. Alternatively, you can stick with a single currency in all your valuations, estimating cash flows and discount rates in that currency. In theory, there should be no difference in the final value assessment, but given how difficult it is to work with multiple currencies in a single company valuation, we believe that the latter is less likely to be error-prone.

Ultimately, the points we made about currency choice in earlier chapters continue to apply. A firm's value should not be a function of our currency choices. If it is, it is because of inconsistencies in our forecasts.

Risk Parameters   Assessing risk in a multinational company that operates in many different businesses is more difficult than it is for a company in a single business operating in a single market. However, the measurement approaches we developed in earlier chapters will stand us in good stead:

- **Aggregated valuation:** There are two keys to preserving valuation consistency in aggregated valuations. The first is being cognizant of the differences in risk across businesses and regions when computing the cost of capital for a company that operates in many businesses and multiple countries. The second key is weighting these different risk estimates appropriately, given the firm's exposure to each one, to estimate the risk parameters for the consolidated firm. Breaking down the inputs into the cost of capital, we can generate the following implications:

  - *Betas:* In earlier chapters, we argued for the use of bottom-up betas—sector betas adjusted for financial leverage on the basis that they are more precise than regression betas. With multibusiness companies, we can add another benefit to using bottom-up betas: The beta for a multibusiness company is a weighted average of the betas of the different businesses it operates in. If we assume that estimating the sector betas, adjusted for financial leverage, follows the same process here that it did in earlier chapters, the one estimation challenge we face with companies that operate in many businesses is in coming up with the weights for the businesses. One simple solution is to base the weights on the revenues or earnings in each business, in effect assuming that a dollar in revenues in one business is worth exactly the same amount as revenues in a different business. An alternative is to estimate an approximate value for each business, perhaps based on revenues in that business and the multiple of revenues that other publicly traded companies in that business trade at.
  - *Risk premiums:* In Chapter 7, we argued that risk premiums should be higher in emerging markets than in developed markets, and we presented ways in which we could estimate the additional premium. In Chapter 16, we looked at emerging-market companies and discussed how best to estimate their country risk premiums and risk exposures. With multinational companies, which derive some of their revenues from developed markets and some from emerging markets, we face the same estimation issues that we do with emerging-market companies. We have to adjust the discount rate for the exposure that multinationals have to emerging-market risk. The simplest adjustment to make is to compute equity risk premiums

for every market that a firm operates in and to take a weighted average of these numbers, using revenues or operating income as the base. A more complex adjustment would require that we compute lambdas for the multinational against each market and then use these lambdas, in conjunction with country risk premiums, to compute a firm's cost of equity.

- *Cost of debt:* A firm's cost of debt is computed by adding the default spread to the risk-free rate and adjusting for any tax benefits generated by interest expenses:

  Cost of Debt = (Risk-Free Rate + Default Spread) (1 − Tax Rate)

  With multinational firms, we must confront three issues. The first is that the risk-free rate to use in computing the cost of debt can vary across the different currencies in which the firms may actually borrow. This is a fairly simple problem to resolve, since the risk-free rate to use will be determined by the currency you chose to do the valuation in step 2. In other words, if you decide to do your valuation in U.S. dollars, the risk-free rate will be the U.S. Treasury bond rate, no matter what currency the actual borrowing is in. The second issue is the default spread, which can vary widely across the firm's different borrowings. If the multinational firm has a rating, we can use it to compute a default spread, which can then be added to the risk-free rate to compute the costs of debt. The final issue relates to the tax rate. While it is the marginal tax rate that should use the cost of debt, the reality is that the marginal tax rates can vary across the different countries that the firm operates in. One solution is to use the marginal tax rate of the country that the multinational is incorporated in. An even better alternative is to use the highest marginal tax rate, across the countries in which the company operates, arguing that interest expenses will be directed to that country to maximize tax benefits.

- *Debt ratios:* In keeping with our objective of valuing the consolidated firm, the debt ratio we use will be based on the aggregated debt for the entire firm and the market value of all its equity.

  Using the bottom-up beta (estimated by taking a weighted average of the business betas), the consolidated equity risk premium (reflecting the country risk exposure created by operations), the cost of debt premised on the company's overall default risk, and the debt ratio for the consolidated firm, we can obtain a cost of capital. That number, though, will change over time as the firm's mix of businesses shifts.

- **Disaggregated valuations:** When we value individual businesses, we obtain more freedom in making our estimates, since the discount rates we use can vary widely across the businesses. Again, using the inputs to the discount rate as a guide, we can develop the following principles:

  - *Betas:* When valuing individual businesses, we can use bottom-up betas for those businesses in estimating the costs of equity. Since we are valuing each business individually, there is no need to compute weighted averages of the betas. For a firm with revenues from steel, mining, and technology, we would use the sector betas from each of these businesses in computing the costs of equity for each business.

  - *Risk premiums:* If we break down businesses by region and estimate each part's value separately, we should be estimating the cost of equity for each region based on the country risk premium for that region. In effect, we will be valuing Coca-Cola's

Russian operations using the country risk premium for Russia in the cost-of-equity computation and its Brazilian operations using the country risk premium for Brazil.

■ *Cost of debt:* While we will stick with the principle that the cost of debt is the sum of the risk-free rate and the default spread, the costs of debt that we estimate for the same company in different businesses/divisions can be different for two reasons. One is that we may be using different currencies to value different revenue streams; this can change the risk-free rate. The other reason is that we can estimate different default spreads for different parts of the same company, basing the spreads on the riskiness and the cash flows generated by each part.

■ *Debt ratios:* As with the other inputs into the cost of capital, the debt ratio can vary across different pieces of the same firm. In some companies, where individual divisions borrow money (rather than the consolidated firm), we may be able to estimate these debt ratios based on what firms actually do. In most companies, where debt is consolidated at the company level, we have two choices. The first is to assume that the company uses the same mix of debt and equity across all businesses, and to use the debt ratio for the company as the mix for every business. The second is to use the industry-average debt ratio for publicly traded firms in the same business, and to use this debt ratio in computing costs of capital for individual businesses.

The bottom line is that the cost of capital we use to discount cash flows in an aggregated valuation represents the cost of capital for the consolidated firm, given the mix of businesses and markets it operates in. On the other hand, the cost of capital we use to discount cash flows in a disaggregated valuation represents the cost of capital of being in a specific business in a specific country.

Expected Cashflows   Having picked a currency to do the valuation in and a discount rate that is consistent with that currency choice, we have to estimate expected cash flows to value a business. As with the previous sections, the way in which we approach this part of the process is determined in large part by whether we are valuing the consolidated firm or its individual parts:

■ **Aggregated valuation:** When we value a company on an aggregated basis, we have to estimate the cash flows for the entire firm when valuing the firm. If we stick with fundamentals for estimating growth in the cash flow, we will base the growth on the combined reinvestment rate and return on capital for the entire firm. Given that the firm operates in different businesses, with different reinvestment rates and returns on capital in each, we are using a weighted average of the business-specific values for these numbers. As with the beta computation, we have to keep an eye on how the weights shift over time and the implications for growth and cash flows.

■ **Disaggregated valuation:** When valuing the individual parts of a larger company, we acquire more flexibility. Rather than use a weighted average of the numbers across the company, we can consider each business separately, assessing the reinvestment rate and return on capital for that business as the basis of forecasting growth and expected cash flows. With large conglomerates, we may very well find that some businesses generate value from growth by earning more than their cost of capital. Other businesses within that same company destroy value, because the returns on new investments are lower than the cost of capital.

In summary, as with the other inputs into valuation, disaggregated valuation requires more of us (in terms of inputs) but also delivers more in terms of information.

Value per Share   To get from the value of operating assets to equity value per share, we have to add cash held by the firm, subtract debt outstanding, add in the value of nonoperating assets, if any, and then divide by the number of shares. While the steps in this process are identical for a multinational, multibusiness firm, there can be significant estimation questions at each stage of the process:

- **Add cash:** In general, we would argue that a dollar in cash should be valued at a dollar, and that no discounts and premiums should be attached to cash, at least in the context of an intrinsic valuation. There are two plausible scenarios in which cash may be discounted in value—in other words, in which a dollar in cash may be valued at less than a dollar by the market:

  - The first occurs when cash held by a firm is invested at a rate that is lower than the market rate, given the riskiness of the investment. While most U.S. firms can invest in government bills and bonds with ease today, the options are much more limited for small businesses and in some markets outside the United States. When this is the case, a large cash balance earning less than a fair rate of return can destroy value over time.
  - The management is not trusted with the large cash balance because of its past track record on investments. While making a large investment in low-risk or riskless marketable securities by itself is value-neutral, a burgeoning cash balance can tempt managers to accept large investments or make acquisitions even if these investments earn substandard returns. In some cases, these actions may be taken to prevent the firm from becoming a takeover target.[7] To the extent that stockholders anticipate such substandard investments, the firm's current market value reflects the cash at a discounted level. The discount is likely to be largest at firms with few investment opportunities and poor management. There may be no discount at all in firms with significant investment opportunities and good management.
- **Subtract debt:** With multinational firms, the debt we net out to derive the value of equity depends in large part on what we are valuing. If we are valuing equity in the consolidated firm, we subtract the market value of total debt outstanding to estimate the value of equity. On the other hand, if we are valuing equity in individual businesses, we should subtract the debt imputed for these individual businesses.
- **Add in values of cross holdings:** The way in which cross-holdings are valued depends on how the investment is categorized and the motive behind the investment. In general, an investment in the securities of another firm can be categorized as a minority-passive investment, a minority-active investment, or a majority-active investment. The accounting rules vary depending on the categorization. While we will cover the best ways of dealing with cross holdings in chapter 16, suffice it to say that we want to attach as close to an intrinsic value, as we can, to these cross holdings, and incorporate that value into the value of the company. In practice, though, we are hamstrung by the absence of information on subsidiaries and have to settle for market pricing (if they are publicly traded) or book value (if they are not).

---

[7]Firms with large cash balances are attractive targets, because the cash balance can be used to offset some of the cost of making the acquisition.

Post-valuation Adjustments   After we estimate the value of equity in a company with investments in multiple businesses and markets, we have to consider whether (and, if so, how) to adjust for other factors that may affect equity value. The first adjustment is for the complexity of multibusiness companies, which makes them more difficult to value, thus leading to a discount on estimated value. The second adjustment is a positive one. It reflects the likelihood that the multibusiness company will be split into individual companies, and the value increment that you expect to follow:

■ **Complexity:** Conventional valuation models have generally ignored complexity on the simple premise that, what we do not know about firms cannot hurt us in the aggregate because it can be diversified away. In other words, we trust the firm's managers to tell us the truth about what they earn, what they own, and what they owe. Why would they do this? If managers are long-term investors in the company, it is argued, they would not risk their long-term credibility and value for the sake of a short-term price gain (obtained by providing misleading information). While there might be information that is unavailable to investors about these invisible assets, the risk should be diversifiable, and thus should not have an effect on value.[8] This view of the world is not irrational, but it does create two fundamental problems. First, managers can take substantial short-term profits by manipulating the numbers (and then exercising options and selling their stock). This may well overwhelm whatever concerns they have about long-term value and credibility. Second, even managers who are concerned about long-term value may delude themselves into believing their own forecasts, optimistic though they may be. It is not surprising, therefore, that firms become sloppy during periods of sustained economic growth. Secure in the notion that there will never be another recession (at least not in the near future), they adopt aggressive accounting practices that overstate earnings. Investors, lulled by the rewards they generate by investing in stocks during these periods, accept these practices with few questions. The downside of trusting managers is obvious. If managers are not trustworthy and firms manipulate earnings, investors who buy stock in complex companies are more likely to be confronted with negative surprises than positive ones. This is because managers who deliberately hide information from investors are more likely to hide bad news than good news. While these negative surprises can occur at any time, they are more likely to occur when overall economic growth slows (a recession!) and are often precipitated by a shock. We could do a conventional valuation of a firm, using unadjusted cash flows, growth rates, and discount rates, and then apply a discount to this value to reflect the complexity of its financial statements. But how would we quantify this complexity discount? We have two options:

■ *Apply a Conglomerate Discount:* We could estimate the discount at which complex firms trade at in the marketplace, relative to simpler firms. In the last two decades, evidence has steadily mounted that markets discount the value of

---

[8]This follows from the assumption that managers are being honest. If this is the case, the information that is unavailable to investors has an equal chance of being good news and bad news. Thus, for every complex company that uncovers information reducing its value, there should be another complex company where the information that comes out increases value. In a diversified portfolio, these effects should average out to zero.

conglomerates, relative to single-business (or pure-play) firms. In a study in 1999, Villalonga compared the ratio of market value to replacement cost (Tobin's Q) for diversified firms and specialized firms, and reported that the former traded at a discount of about 8% on the latter.[9] Similar results were reported in earlier studies.[10]

■ *Measure Complexity Directly, and Estimate a Discount Based on Complexity:* A more sophisticated option is to use a complexity scoring system to measure the complexity of a firm's financial statements and to relate the complexity score to the size of the discount. Damodaran (2006) looks at different measures of complexity, ranging from the number of pages in the company's SEC filings to complexity scores that are computed from the information in financial statements, and suggests ways of adjusting value for complexity.[11]

■ **Potential restructuring:** One question that overhangs every multibusiness company is whether the company would be worth more if it were broken into independent businesses. This, in fact, is the motivation behind the sum-of-the-parts valuations that we described earlier. To the extent that a firm will be worth more as separate parts, we may have to add a premium to the value to reflect the probability that the firm will be broken up, and the value increment that will occur as a consequence.

ILLUSTRATION 15.5: Valuing GE in 2018—Sum of the parts

GE's light bulb moment might have been in Thomas Edison's lab in 1878, but at an official corporate age of 126 years in 2018, GE was an ancient company and its problems reflected its age. Other than renewable energy, all of GE's businesses were mature or declining, and by the laws of mathematics, GE itself was a mature-to-declining company, as can be seen in Table 15.9 (with dollar values in billions):

TABLE 15.9 GE Business Mix in 2018

Business	Revenues– 2017	Revenue Growth in 2017	EBIT before G&A	EBIT after G&A	EBIT Margin	Invested Capital	ROIC in 2017	ROIC: 2013– 2017	Cost of Capital
Power	$ 36.00	−1.64%	$2.80	$1.69	4.68%	$ 328.34	3.85%	9.28%	4.91%
Renewable Energy	$ 10.30	14.44%	$0.70	$0.41	4.00%	$ 49.91	6.19%	8.00%	6.88%
Oil & Gas	$ 17.20	33.33%	$0.20	−$0.31	−1.78%	$ 275.95	−0.83%	3.71%	8.82%
Aviation	$ 27.40	4.18%	$6.60	$5.80	21.19%	$ 192.73	22.59%	20.27%	8.52%
Healthcare	$ 19.10	4.37%	$3.40	$2.86	15.00%	$ 132.81	16.18%	15.07%	7.97%
Transportation	$ 4.20	−10.64%	$0.80	$0.70	16.56%	$ 20.73	25.17%	26.67%	7.49%

[9]Villalonga, B., 1999, "Does diversification cause the diversification discount?" working paper, University of California, Los Angeles.

[10]See Damodaran, A., 2006, Damodaran on Valuation (Second Edition), John Wiley and Sons.

[11]See Berger, Philip G., and Eli Ofek, 1995, "Diversification's effect on firm value," Journal of Financial Economics 37, 39–65; Lang, Larry H. P. and Rene M. Stulz, 1994, "Tobin's q, corporate diversification, and firm performance," Journal of Political Economy 102, 1248–1280; Wernerfelt, Birger and Cynthia A. Montgomery, 1988, "Tobin's q and the importance of focus in firm performance," American Economic Review, 78: 246–250.

Business	Revenues–2017	Revenue Growth in 2017	EBIT before G&A	EBIT after G&A	EBIT Margin	Invested Capital	ROIC in 2017	ROIC: 2013–2017	Cost of Capital
Lighting	$ 2.00	−58.33%	$0.10	$0.03	1.59%	$ 3.34	7.16%	9.66%	8.50%
Capital	$ 9.10	−16.51%	−$6.80	−$7.04	−77.40%	$ 723.38	−7.30%	−2.81%	3.64%
Total	$125.30	1.29%	$7.80	$4.15	3.31%	$1,727.18	1.80%	4.50%	6.23%

In 2018, GE was in three businesses (aviation, healthcare and transportation) that have low growth and high profitability (margins and returns on capital), in three energy-related businesses (power, renewable energy and oil) with higher growth but low profitability (margins & returns on capital), one business (lighting) that is fading quickly and one (capital) that is declining but dragging value down with it. Note also that the collective profits reported across businesses is before corporate expenses and eliminations of $3.83 billion (not counting a one-time restructuring charge of $4.1 billion) that effectively wipe out about half of the operating profits.

When computing return on capital, we allocated these expenses to the businesses, based upon revenues, and used a 25% effective tax rate, and while GE as a whole did not deliver a return that meets its cost of capital requirements in 2017, aviation, healthcare and transportation clear their hurdle rates by plenty. Replacing 2017 income in each business with a normalized value (computed using the average margins in each business between 2013 and 2017) improves the return on capital at the power and renewable energy businesses, but the overall conclusion remains the same. GE, as a company, did not look good, but it did have significant value creating businesses.

In broad terms, the roadmap for GE to succeed, in 2018, was a simple one, shrinking or selling off pieces of its low-margin businesses, exiting the capital business, and consolidating its presence in the aviation, healthcare and transportation businesses. To get a better sense of what the businesses would be worth, as continuing operations, we valued each of GE's business using simplistic assumptions: We used the sector cost of capital for each business, set growth in the next five years equal to revenue growth in each of GE's businesses in the last five years, and normalized operating income based upon the average operating margin that each of GE's businesses have delivered over the last five years. Table 15.10 contains the estimated values of the divisions, with other assets added in:

TABLE 15.10 Value of GE—Sum of its Parts

Business	Revenues	Normalized Operating Margin	Normalized EBIT before G&A	Normalized EBIT	Normalized EBIT(1 − t)	Cost of Capital	ROIC	Expected Growth Next 5 Years	Value of Business
Power	$ 35,990	14.34%	$ 5,162	$ 4,062	$ 3,046	4.91%	9.28%	6.10%	$ 73,138
Renewable Energy	$ 10,280	8.24%	$ 847	$ 533	$ 400	6.88%	8.00%	16.34%	$ 6,456
Oil & Gas	$ 17,231	10.97%	$ 1,891	$ 1,365	$ 1,024	8.82%	3.71%	-0.13%	$ 11,925
Aviation	$ 27,375	22.09%	$ 6.047	$ 5,209	$ 3,907	8.52%	20.27%	4.55	$ 52,849
Healthcare	$ 19,116	17.01%	$ 3,252	$ 2,668	$ 2,001	7.97%	15.07%	0.99%	$ 26,234
Transportation	$ 4,178	20.71	$ 865	$ 737	$ 553	7.49%	26.67%	-6.62%	$ 6,075
Lighting	$ 1,987	5.24%	$ 104	$ 43	$ 32	8.50%	9.66%	-24.94%	$ 280
Total (non-capital)	$116,157	15.35%	$17,830	$17,552	$13,164				$176,958
GE Capital	$ 9,070	3.00%	$ 272	-$ 6	-$ 4	6.23%	0.00%	-4.25%	$ 27,081

(*continued*)

TABLE 15.10   *(Continued)*

Business	Revenues	Normalized Operating Margin	Normalized EBIT before G&A	Normalized EBIT	Normalized EBIT(1 – t)	Cost of Capital	ROIC	Expected Growth Next 5 Years	Value of Business
Value of Businesses									$ 204,039
-Debt									$ 83,568
-GE Capital Debt									$ 51,023
-Minority Interests									$ 17.723
+Cash									$ 43,299
Value of Equity									$ 95,024
-Employee Options									$ 218.94
Value of Equity in Common Stock									$ 94,804.65
Value per Share									$ 10.92

Note that we normalized the income for each of GE's businesses, using the average operating margin over the previous five years, assessed costs of capital and expected cashflows for each business, and estimated values. We allocated GEs total G&A across the divisions, based upon revenues. At the time of this valuation, GE shares were trading at about $8 a share.

EFFECT OF LEVERAGE ON FIRM VALUE

Both the cost-of-capital approach and the APV approach make the value of a firm a function of its leverage. It follows directly, then, that there is some mix of debt and equity at which firm value is maximized. The rest of this chater considers how best to make this link.

Cost of Capital and Optimal Leverage

In order to understand the relationship between the cost of capital and optimal capital structure, we rely on the relationship between firm value and the cost of capital. The earlier section noted that the value of the entire firm can be estimated by discounting the expected cash flows to the firm at the firm's cost of capital.

The firm value can then be written as follows:

$$\text{Value of operating assets} = \sum_{t=1}^{t=\infty} \frac{\text{FCFF}_t}{(1 + k_c)^t}$$

and is a function of the firm's cash flows and its cost of capital. If we assume that the cash flows to the firm are unaffected by the choice of financing mix, and the cost of capital is reduced as a consequence of changing the financing mix, the value of the firm will increase.

If the objective in choosing the financing mix for the firm is the maximization of firm value, we can accomplish it, in this case, by minimizing the cost of capital. In the more general case where the cash flows to the firm are a function of the debt-equity mix, the optimal financing mix is the mix that maximizes firm value.[12]

ILLUSTRATION 15.6: WACC, Firm Value, and Leverage

Assume that you are given the costs of equity and debt at different debt levels for Strunks Inc., a leading manufacturer of chocolates and other candies, and that the free cash flows to this firm are currently $200 million. Strunks is in a relatively stable market, and these cash flows are expected to grow at 3% forever and to be unaffected by the debt ratio of the firm. The cost of capital schedule is provided in the Table 15.11, along with the value of the firm at each level of debt.

TABLE 15.11 Cost of Capital and Firm Value, by Debt Ratio

D/(D + E)	Cost of Equity	After-Tax Cost of Debt	Cost of Capital	Firm Value
0	10.50%	4.80%	10.50%	$2,747
10%	11.00%	5.10%	10.41%	$2,780
20%	11.60%	5.40%	10.36%	$2,799
30%	12.30%	5.52%	10.27%	$2,835
40%	13.10%	5.70%	10.14%	$2,885
50%	14.50%	6.10%	10.30%	$2,822
60%	15.00%	7.20%	10.32%	$2,814
70%	16.10%	8.10%	10.50%	$2,747
80%	17.20%	9.00%	10.64%	$2,696
90%	18.40%	10.20%	11.02%	$2,569
100%	19.70%	11.40%	11.40%	$2,452

Note that:

$$\text{Value of firm} = \frac{\text{Cash flows to firm} \times (1 + g)}{(\text{Cost of capital} - \text{Stable growth rate})}$$

$$= \frac{200\,(1.03)}{(\text{Cost of capital} - .03)}$$

The value of the firm increases as the cost of capital decreases and decreases as the cost of capital increases. This is illustrated in Figure 15.2. While this illustration makes the choice of an optimal financing mix seem easy, it obscures problems that will arise in its practice. First, we typically do not have the benefit of having the entire schedule of costs of financing prior to an analysis. In most cases, the only level of debt at which we have information on the cost of debt and equity financing is the current level. Second, the analysis assumes implicitly that the level of operating income of the firm is unaffected by the financing mix of the firm and, consequently, by the default risk (or bond rating) for the firm. While this may be reasonable in some cases, it will not be in others. Firms that borrow too much might find that there are indirect bankruptcy costs that affect revenues and operating income.

---

[12]In other words, the value of the firm might not be maximized at the point that cost of capital is minimized, if firm cash flows are much lower at that level.

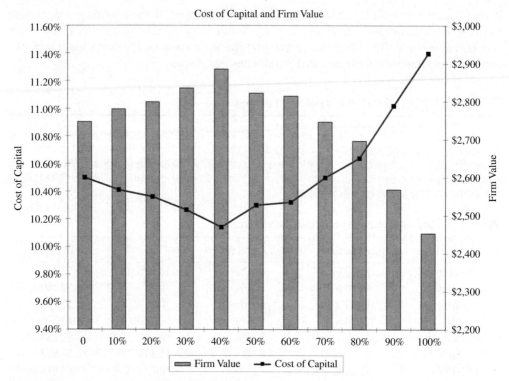

FIGURE 15.2   Cost of Capital and Firm Value
Source: Applied Corporate Finance, 2010 / John Wiley & Sons.

Steps in Cost of Capital Approach

We need three basic inputs to compute the cost of capital—the cost of equity, the after-tax cost of debt, and the weights on debt and equity. The costs of equity and debt change as the debt ratio changes, and the primary challenge of this approach is in estimating each of these inputs.

Let us begin with the cost of equity. We argued that the beta of equity will change as the debt ratio changes. In fact, we estimated the levered beta as a function of the market-debt-to-equity ratio of a firm, the unlevered beta, and the firm's marginal tax rate:

$$\beta_{levered} = \beta_{unlevered}[1 + (1 - t)\text{Debt/Equity}]$$

Thus, if we can estimate the unlevered beta for a firm, we can use it to estimate the levered beta of the firm at every debt ratio. This levered beta can then be used to compute the cost of equity at each debt ratio.

$$\text{Cost of equity} = \text{Risk-free rate} + \beta_{\text{levered}} \left(\text{Equity Risk premium}\right)$$

The cost of debt for a firm is a function of the firm's default risk. As firms borrow more, their default risk will increase and so will the cost of debt. If we use bond ratings as our measure of default risk, we can estimate the cost of debt in three steps. First, estimate a firm's dollar debt and interest expenses at each debt ratio; as firms increase their debt ratio, both dollar debt and interest expenses will rise. Second, at each debt level, compute a financial ratio(s) that measure default risk and use the ratio(s) to estimate a rating for the firm; again, as firms borrow more, this rating will decline. Third, a default spread, based on the estimated rating, is added to the risk-free rate to arrive at the pretax cost of debt. Applying the marginal tax rate to this pretax cost yields an after-tax cost of debt.

Once we estimate the costs of equity and debt at each debt level, we weight them based on the proportions used of each to estimate the cost of capital. While we have not explicitly allowed for a preferred stock component in this process, we can have preferred stock as a part of capital. However, we must keep the preferred stock portion fixed, while changing the weights on debt and equity. The debt ratio at which the cost of capital is minimized is the optimal debt ratio. Figure 15.3 summarizes the steps.

In this approach, the effect on firm value of changing the capital structure is isolated by keeping the operating income fixed and varying only the cost of capital. In practical terms, this requires us to make two assumptions. First, the debt ratio is decreased by raising new equity and retiring debt; conversely, the debt ratio is increased by borrowing money and buying back stock. This process is called recapitalization. Second, the pretax operating income is assumed to be unaffected by the firm's financing mix and, by extension, its bond rating. If the operating income changes with a firm's default risk, the basic analysis will not change, but minimizing the cost of capital may not be the optimal course of action, since the value of the firm is determined by both the cash flows and the cost of capital. The value of the firm will have to be computed at each debt level and the optimal debt ratio will be the one that maximizes firm value.

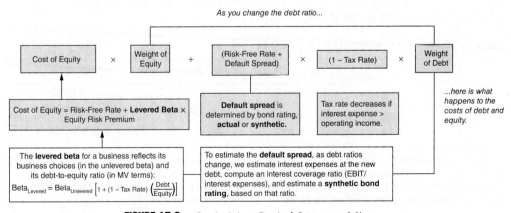

FIGURE 15.3 Optimizing Capital Structure Mix

ILLUSTRATION 15.7: Analyzing the Capital Structure for Disney: May 2024

The cost of capital approach can be used to find the optimal capital structure for a firm, as we will for Disney in May 2024. Disney had $46,431 million in interest-bearing debt on its books and adding the present value of operating lease commitments of $3,960 million to this value, we arrive at a total market value for the debt of $50,391 million.[13] The market value of equity at the same time was $183,649 million; the market price per share was $100.30, and there were 1,831 million shares outstanding. Proportionally, 21.53% of the overall financing mix was debt, and the remaining 78.46% was equity.

The unlevered beta for Disney's stock in May 2024, estimated by breaking it down into its constituent businesses and weighting the unlevered betas for each business, was 0.947. At the current market-debt-to-equity ratio, the levered beta for Disney was 1.14:

$$\text{Levered beta} = \text{Unlevered beta}\left(1 + (1 - \text{tax rate})\left(\frac{\text{Debt}}{\text{Equity}}\right)\right)$$

$$= 0.947\,(1 + (1 - .25)(50,391/183,649)) = 1.14$$

The Treasury bond rate at that time was 4.5%. Using an estimated equity risk premium of 4.78%, based upon Disney's geographical revenue exposure, we estimated the cost of equity for Disney to be 9.96%:

$$\text{Cost of equity} = 4.5\% + 1.14\,(4.78\%) = 9.96\%$$

Disney's bond rating in May 2024 was A−, and based on this rating, the estimated default spread for Disney was 1.21%, resulting in a pretax cost of debt for Disney is 5.71%. Using a marginal tax rate of 25%, we estimate the after-tax cost of debt for Disney to be 4.28%:

$$\text{After-Tax cost of debt} = 5.71\%\,(1 - .25) = 4.28\%$$

The cost of capital is calculated using these costs and the weights based on market value:

$$\text{Cost of capital} = 9.96\%\,(.7846) + 4.28\%\,(.2154) = 8.73\%$$

DISNEY'S COST OF EQUITY AND LEVERAGE

The cost of equity for Disney at different debt ratios can be computed using the unlevered beta of the firm, and the debt-equity ratio at each level of debt. We use the levered betas that emerge to estimate the cost of equity.[14] The first step in this process is to compute the levered beta at each debt ratio, using the unlevered beta and Disney's marginal tax rate of 25%, in Table 15.12.

TABLE 15.12 Cost of Equity for Disney, by Debt Ratio

D/(D + E)	D/E	Beta	Cost of Equity
0.00%	0.00%	0.95	9.02%
10.00%	11.11%	1.03	9.40%

---

[13]While Disney's accountants reported leases as debt, we chose to do the computation ourselves to ensure that the full adjustments were made to operating income and interest expenses.

[14]In computing these levered betas, we have assumed that the beta of debt is zero. As we noted in Chapter 8, there is an alternate formulation of the levered beta that enables for the beta of debt to be nonzero:

$$\text{Levered beta} = \beta_u\,(1 + (1 - t)\,D/E) - \beta_{debt}\,((1 - t)\,D/E)$$

Using this approach will reduce the levered betas, especially at high levels of debt.

D/(D + E)	D/E	Beta	Cost of Equity
20.00%	25.00%	1.12	9.87%
30.00%	42.86%	1.25	10.48%
40.00%	66.67%	1.42	11.29%
50.00%	100.00%	1.75	12.86%
60.00%	150.00%	2.20	15.02%
70.00%	233.33%	2.95	18.58%
80.00%	400.00%	4.43	25.68%
90.00%	900.00%	8.88	46.94%

We continue to use the Treasury bond rate of 4.5% and the equity risk premium of 4.78% to compute the cost of equity at each level of debt. In calculating the levered beta in this table, we assumed that all market risk is borne by the equity investors (this may be unrealistic) especially at higher levels of debt, and that the firm will be able to get the full tax benefits of interest expenses even at very high debt ratios.

Disney's Cost of Debt and Leverage

There are several financial ratios that are correlated with bond ratings, and we face two choices. One is to build a model that includes several financial ratios to estimate the synthetic ratings at each debt ratio. In addition to being more labor and data intensive, the approach will make the ratings process less transparent and more difficult to decipher. The other is to stick with the simplistic approach that we developed in Chapter 8, of linking the rating to the interest coverage ratio, with the ratio defined as:

$$\text{Interest coverage ratio} = \frac{\text{Earnings before interest and taxes}}{\text{Interest expenses}}$$

We will stick with the simpler approach for three reasons. First, we are not aiming for precision in the cost of debt, but an approximation. Given that the more complex approaches also give approximations, we will tilt in favor of transparency. Second, there is significant correlation not only between the interest coverage ratio and bond ratings but also between the interest coverage ratio and other ratios used in analysis, such as the debt coverage ratio and the funds flow ratios. In other words, we may be adding little by adding other ratios that are correlated with interest coverage ratios, including EBITDA/fixed charges, to the mix. Third, the interest coverage ratio changes as a firm changes its financing mix and decreases as the debt ratio increases, a key requirement since we need the cost of debt to change as the debt ratio changes.

To make our estimates of the synthetic rating, we will use the look-up table that we introduced in Chapter 8 for large market capitalization firms (since Disney's market capitalization is greater than $5 billion), and use the default spreads from early 2009 to estimate the pretax cost of debt. Table 15.13 reproduces those numbers:

TABLE 15.13 Ratings and Default Spreads

Interest Coverage Ratio	Rating	Typical Default Spread
>8.5	AAA	0.59%
6.5–8.5	AA	0.70%
5.5–6.5	A+	0.92%
4.25–5.5	A	1.07%
3.0–4.25	A–	1.21%
2.5–3.0	BBB	1.47%
2.25–2.5	BB+	1.74%

(continued)

TABLE 15.13   (*Continued*)

Interest Coverage Ratio	Rating	Typical Default Spread
2.0–2.25	BB	2.21%
1.75–2.0	B+	3.14%
1.5–1.75	B	3.61%
1.25–1.5	B–	5.24%
0.8–1.25	CCC	8.51%
0.65–0.8	CC	11.78%
0.2–0.65	C	17.00%
<0.2	D	20.00%

Source: Capital IQ, NAIC.

Using this table as a guideline, a firm with an interest coverage ratio of 2.75 would have a rating of BBB and a default spread of 1.47%, over the risk-free rate.

Disney's capacity to borrow is determined by its earnings power, and we will begin by looking at key numbers from the company's income statements for the most recent fiscal year (year ended September 20, 2023) and the previous year (year ended September 30, 2022) in Table 15.14.

TABLE 15.14 Base Year Operating Metrics for Disney

	Fiscal Year 2022 (10/2021–9/2022)	Fiscal Year 2023 (10/2022–9/2023)
Revenues	$82,772	$88,898
EBITDA	$11,995	$14,702
Depreciation and amortization	$ 5163	$ 5370
EBIT	$ 6832	$ 9,332
Interest expenses	$ 1,549	$ 1,973
EBITDA (adjusted for leases)	$13,102	$15,965
EBIT (adjusted for leases)	$ 7,750	$10,156
Interest expenses (adjusted for leases)	$ 1,705	$ 2,199

Note that converting leases to debt affects both the operating income and the interest expense; the imputed interest expense on the lease debt is added to both the operating income and the interest expense numbers.[15] Since the trailing 12-month figures represent more recent information, we will use those numbers in assessing Disney's optimal debt ratio. Based on the EBIT (adjusted for leases) of $10,156 million and interest expenses of $2,199 million, Disney has an interest coverage ratio of 4.62, and should command a rating of A, a notch above its actual rating of A–.

To compute Disney's ratings at different debt levels, we start by assessing the dollar debt that Disney will need to issue to get to the specified debt ratio. This can be accomplished by multiplying the total enterprise value of the firm today by the desired debt-to-capital ratio. To illustrate, Disney's dollar debt at a 10% debt ratio will be $22,242 million, computed thus:

---

[15]The present value of operating leases ($3,960 million) was multiplied by the pretax cost of debt of 5.71% to arrive at an interest expense of $226 million, which is added to interest expense. The operating income was adjusted by adding back the operating lease expense and subtracting out the depreciation on the leased asset.

$$\text{\$ Debt at 10\% Debt-to-Capital Ratio} = (\text{Market Cap} + \text{Total Debt (including leases)} - \text{Cash})*.10$$
$$= (\$183,649 + (46,491 + 3960) - 11,615)*.10$$
$$= \$22,242 \text{ million}$$

The second step in the process is to compute the interest expense that Disney will have at this debt level, by multiplying the dollar debt by the pretax cost of borrowing at that debt ratio. The interest expense is then used to compute an interest coverage ratio, which is employed to compute a synthetic rating. The resulting default spread, based on the rating, can be obtained from Table 15.13, and adding the default spread to the risk-free rate yields a pretax cost of borrowing. Table 15.15 estimates the interest expenses, interest coverage ratios, and bond ratings for Disney at 0% and 10% debt ratios, at the existing level of operating income.

TABLE 15.15   Costs of Debt for Disney, by Debt Ratio

D/(D + E)	$ Debt	EBIT	Interest Expense	Interest Coverage	Likely Rating	Pretax Cost of Debt	Adjusted Tax Rate	After-Tax Cost of Debt
0.00%	$ 0	$10,156	$ 0	∞	Aaa/AAA	5.09%	25.00%	3.82%
10.00%	$ 22,242	$10,156	$ 945	10.75	Aaa/AAA	5.09%	25.00%	3.82%
20.00%	$ 44,485	$10,156	$ 1,890	5.37	A2/A	5.57%	25.00%	4.18%
30.00%	$ 66,727	$10,156	$ 3,132	3.24	A3/A−	5.71%	25.00%	4.28%
40.00%	$ 88,970	$10,156	$ 5,223	1.94	B1/B+	7.64%	25.00%	5.73%
50.00%	$111,212	$10,156	$15,901	0.64	C2/C	21.50%	15.97%	18.07%
60.00%	$133,455	$10,156	$20,683	0.49	C2/C	21.50%	12.28%	18.86%
70.00%	$155,697	$10,156	$25,465	0.40	C2/C	21.50%	9.97%	19.36%
80.00%	$177,940	$10,156	$30,247	0.34	C2/C	21.50%	8.39%	19.70%
90.00%	$200,182	$10,156	$35,030	0.29	C2/C	21.50%	7.25%	19.94%

In reading this table, the following should be kept in mind:

▨ The EBITDA and EBIT remain fixed as the debt ratio changes. We ensure this by using the proceeds from the debt to buy back stock, thus leaving operating assets untouched and isolating the effect of changing the debt ratio.

▨ There is circular reasoning involved in estimating the interest expense. The interest rate is needed to calculate the interest coverage ratio, and the coverage ratio is necessary to compute the interest rate. To get around the problem, we use the interest rate from the previous level of debt to get started and iterate to a solution.[16]

▨ The interest expense increases more than proportionately as the debt increases since the cost of debt rises with the debt ratio. There are three points to make about these computations. First, at each debt ratio, we compute the dollar value of debt by multiplying the debt ratio by the existing enterprise value of the firm ($222,485 million). In reality, that value will change as the cost of capital changes and the dollar debt that we will need to get to a specified debt ratio, say 30%, will be different from the values that we have estimated. Second, we assume that at every debt level, all existing debt will be refinanced at the new interest rate that will prevail after the capital structure change. For instance,

---

[16] Because the interest expense rises, it is possible for the rating to drop again, when you iterate. You must continue iterating until you converge on an interest rate that does not change.

Disney's existing debt, which has an A– rating, is assumed to be refinanced at the interest rate corresponding to a B+ rating when Disney moves to a 40% debt ratio.

■ As long as interest expenses are less than $10,156 million, interest expenses remain fully tax-deductible and earn the 25% tax benefit. For instance, at the 40% debt ratio, the interest expenses are $5,223 million, and the tax benefit is therefore 25% of this amount. At a 50% debt ratio, however, the interest expenses balloon to $15,901 million, which is greater than the EBIT of $10,156 million. We consider the tax benefit on the interest expenses up to this amount, resulting in an adjusted tax rate of 15.97%:

$$\text{Adjusted Tax Rate at 50\% Debt to Capital} = \text{Marginal Tax Rate} \times \frac{\text{EBIT}}{\text{Interest Expense}}$$

$$= 25\% \times \frac{10{,}156}{15{,}901} = 15.97\%$$

This is a conservative approach because losses can be carried forward. Given that this is a permanent shift in leverage, it does make sense to be conservative. We used this tax rate to recompute the levered beta at a 50% debt ratio, to reflect the fact that tax savings from interest are depleted.

LEVERAGE AND COST OF CAPITAL

Now that we have estimated the cost of equity and the cost of debt at each debt level, we can compute Disney's cost of capital. This is done for each debt level in Table 15.16. The cost of capital, which is 9.02% when the firm is unlevered, decreases as the firm initially adds debt, reaches a minimum of 8.62% at a 30% debt ratio, and then starts to increase again.

TABLE 15.16   Cost of Capital for Disney, by Debt Ratio

Debt Ratio	Cost of Equity	Cost of Debt (After-Tax)	Cost of Capital
0%	9.02%	3.82%	9.02%
10%	9.40%	3.82%	8.84%
20%	9.87%	4.18%	8.73%
30%	10.48%	4.28%	8.62%
40%	11.29%	5.73%	9.06%
50%	12.83%	18.07%	15.45%
60%	14.98%	18.86%	17.31%
70%	18.53%	19.36%	19.11%
80%	25.61%	19.70%	20.88%
90%	46.80%	19.94%	22.63%

Note that we are moving in 10% increments and that the cost of capital flattens out between 20% and 40%. We can get a more precise reading of the optimal by looking at how the cost of capital moves between 20% and 40%, in smaller increments. It is worth noting, though, that at least the benefits of moving to the optimal debt ratio are small, at least for Disney.

 captstr.xls: **This spreadsheet allows you to compute the optimal debt ratio firm value for any firm, using the same information used for Disney. It has updated interest coverage ratios and default spreads built in.**

DEFAULT RISK, OPERATING INCOME, AND OPTIMAL LEVERAGE

The Disney analysis just completed assumed that operating income would remain constant while the debt ratios changed. While this assumption simplifies the analysis substantially, it is not realistic. The operating income, for many firms, will drop as the default risk increases; this, in fact, is the cost we label as an indirect bankruptcy cost. The drop is likely to become more pronounced as the default risk falls below an acceptable level; for instance, a bond rating below investment grade may trigger significant losses in revenues and increases in expenses.

A general model for optimal capital structure would allow both operating income and cost of capital to change as the debt ratio changes. We have already described how we can estimate cost of capital at different debt ratios, but we could also attempt to do the same with operating income. For instance, we could estimate how the operating income for Disney would change as debt ratios and default risk changes by looking at the effects of rating downgrades on the operating income of other retailers.

If both operating income and cost of capital change, the optimal debt ratio may no longer be the point at which the cost of capital is minimized. Instead, the optimal debt ratio must be defined as that debt ratio at which the value of the firm is maximized.

CONCLUSION

This chapter developed an alternative approach to discounted cash flow valuation. The cash flows to the firm are discounted at the weighted average cost of capital to obtain the value of the firm, which when reduced by the market value of outstanding debt yields the value of equity. Since the cash flow to the firm is a cash flow prior to debt payments, this approach is more straightforward to use when leverage changes over time, though the weighted average cost of capital used to discount free cash flows to the firm, must be adjusted for changes in leverage. Finally, the costs of capital can be estimated at different debt ratios and used to estimate the optimal debt ratio for a firm.

The alternative approach to firm valuation is the APV approach, where the effect on value of debt (tax benefits minus bankruptcy costs) is added to the unlevered firm value. This approach can also be used to estimate the optimal debt ratio for the firm.

QUESTIONS AND SHORT PROBLEMS

In the problems following, use an equity risk premium of 5.5 percent if none is specified.

1. Respond true or false to the following statements about the free cash flow to the firm:
   a. The free cash flow to the firm is always higher than the free cash flow to equity.
      True _____ False _____
   b. The free cash flow to the firm is the cumulated cash flow to all investors in the firm, though the form of their claims may be different.
      True _____ False _____
   c. The free cash flow to the firm is a predebt, pretax cash flow.
      True _____ False _____

  d. The free cash flow to the firm is an after-debt, after-tax cash flow.
      True _____ False _____
  e. The free cash flow to the firm cannot be estimated for a firm with debt without knowing interest and principal payments.
      True _____ False _____

2. Union Pacific Railroad reported net income of $770 million in 1993 after interest expenses of $320 million. (The corporate tax rate was 36%.) It reported depreciation of $960 million in that year, and capital spending was $1.2 billion. The firm also had $4 billion in debt outstanding on the books, rated AA (carrying a yield to maturity of 8%) and trading at par (up from $3.8 billion at the end of 1992). The beta of the stock was 1.05, and there were 200 million shares outstanding (trading at $60 per share), with a book value of $5 billion. Union Pacific's working capital requirements were negligible. (The Treasury bond rate was 7%, and the risk premium was 5.5%.)
   a. Estimate the free cash flow to the firm in 1993.
   b. Estimate the value of the firm at the end of 1993.
   c. Estimate the value of equity at the end of 1993, and the value per share, using the FCFF approach.

3. Lockheed Corporation, one of the largest defense contractors in the United States, reported EBITDA of $1,290 million in 1993, prior to interest expenses of $215 million and depreciation charges of $400 million. Capital expenditures in 1993 amounted to $450 million, and working capital was 7% of revenues (which were $13,500 million). The firm had debt outstanding of $3.068 billion (in book value terms), trading at a market value of $3.2 billion and yielding a pretax interest rate of 8%. There were 62 million shares outstanding, trading at $64 per share, and the most recent beta was 1.10. The tax rate for the firm was 40%. (The Treasury bond rate was 7%, and the risk premium was 5.5%.)

   The firm expected revenues, earnings, capital expenditures and depreciation to grow at 9.5% a year from 1994 to 1998, after which the growth rate was expected to drop to 4%. (Capital spending will be 120% of depreciation in the steady state period.) The company also planned to lower its debt/equity ratio to 50% for the steady state (which will result in the pretax interest rate dropping to 7.5%).
   a. Estimate the value of the firm.
   b. Estimate the value of the equity in the firm and the value per share.

4. In the face of disappointing earnings results and increasingly assertive institutional stockholders, Eastman Kodak was considering a major restructuring in 1993. As part of this restructuring, it was considering the sale of its health division, which earned $560 million in earnings before interest and taxes in 1993, on revenues of $5.285 billion. The expected growth in earnings was expected to moderate to 6% between 1994 and 1998 and to 4% after that. Capital expenditures in the health division amounted to $420 million in 1993, while depreciation was $350 million. Both were expected to grow 4% a year in the long term. Working capital requirements were negligible.

   The average beta of firms competing with Eastman Kodak's health division was 1.15. While Eastman Kodak had a debt ratio [D/(D + E)] of 50%, the health division could sustain a debt ratio [D/(D + E)] of only 20%, which was similar to the average debt ratio of firms competing in the health sector. At this level of debt, the health division could expect to pay 7.5% on its debt before taxes. (The tax rate was 40%, the Treasury bond rate was 7%, and the risk premium was 5.5%.)

    a. Estimate the cost of capital for the division.
    b. Estimate the value of the division.
    c. Why might an acquirer pay more than this estimated value for the division?
5. You are analyzing a valuation done on a stable firm by a well-known analyst. Based on the expected free cash flow to firm next year of $30 million and an expected growth rate of 5%, the analyst has estimated a value of $750 million. However, he has made the mistake of using the book values of debt and equity in his calculation. While you do not know the book value weights he used, you know that the firm has a cost of equity of 12% and an after-tax cost of debt of 6%. You also know that the market value of equity is three times the book value of equity, while the market value of debt is equal to the book value of debt. Estimate the correct value for the firm.
6. Santa Fe Pacific, a major rail operator with diversified operations, had earnings before interest, taxes, and depreciation of $637 million in 1993, with depreciation amounting to $235 million (offset by capital expenditure of an equivalent amount). The firm was in steady state and expected to grow 6% a year in perpetuity. Santa Fe Pacific had a beta of 1.25 in 1993, and debt outstanding of $1.34 billion. The stock price was $18.25 at the end of 1993, and there were 183.1 million shares outstanding. The expected ratings and the costs of debt at different levels of debt for Santa Fe are shown in the following table:

D/(D + E)	Rating	Cost of Debt (Pretax)
0%	AAA	6.23%
10%	AAA	6.23%
20%	A+	6.93%
30%	A−	7.43%
40%	BB	8.43%
50%	B+	8.93%
60%	B−	10.93%
70%	CCC	11.93%
80%	CCC	11.93%
90%	CC	13.43%

The earnings before interest and taxes were expected to grow 3% a year in perpetuity, with capital expenditures offset by depreciation. (The tax rate was 40%, and the Treasury bond rate was 7% and the market risk premium was 5.5%.)
    a. Estimate the cost of capital at the current debt ratio.
    b. Estimate the costs of capital at debt ratios ranging from 0% to 90%.
    c. Estimate the value of the firm at debt ratios ranging from 0% to 90%.
7. You have been asked to estimate the value of Cavanaugh Motels, a motel chain. The firm reported earnings of $200 million before interest and taxes in the most recent year and paid 40% of its taxable income in taxes. The book value of capital at the firm is $1.2 billion, and the firm expects to grow 4% a year in perpetuity. The firm has a beta of 1.2, a pretax cost of debt of 6%, equity with a market value of $1 billion, and debt with a market value of $500 million. (The risk-free rate is 5%, and the market risk premium is 5.5%.)
    a. Estimate the value of the firm, using the cost of capital approach.
    b. If you were told the probability of default at this firm at its current debt level is 10% and that the cost of bankruptcy is 25% of unlevered firm value, estimate the value of the firm using the adjusted present value approach.
    c. How would you reconcile the two estimates of value?

8. Bethlehem Steel, one of the oldest and largest steel companies in the United States, is considering the question of whether it has any excess debt capacity. The firm has $527 million in market value of debt outstanding and $1.76 billion in market value of equity. The firm has earnings before interest and taxes of $131 million, and faces a corporate tax rate of 36%. The company's bonds are rated BBB, and the cost of debt is 8%. At this rating, the firm has a probability of default of 2.3%, and the cost of bankruptcy is expected to be 30% of firm value.

   a. Estimate the unlevered value of the firm from the current market value of the firm.

   b. Estimate the levered value of the firm, using the adjusted present value approach, at a debt ratio of 50%. At that debt ratio, the firm's bond rating will be CCC, and the probability of default will increase to 46.61% of unlevered firm value.

CHAPTER 16

Estimating Equity Value per Share

Chapter 15 considered how best to estimate the value of the operating assets of the firm. To get from that value to the firm value, you have to consider the value of cash, marketable securities, and other nonoperating assets held by a firm. In particular, you have to value holdings in other firms and deal with a variety of accounting techniques used to record such holdings. To get from firm value to equity value, you have to determine the value of the nonequity claims in the firm that have to be netted out.

Once you have valued the equity in a firm, it may appear to be a relatively simple exercise to estimate the value per share. It seems that all you need to do is divide the value of the equity by the number of shares outstanding. But in the case of some firms, even this simple exercise can become complicated by the presence of management and employee options. This chapter discusses the magnitude of this option overhang on valuation, and then considers ways of incorporating the effect into the value per share.

VALUE OF NONOPERATING ASSETS

Firms have several assets on their books that can be categorized as nonoperating assets. The first and most obvious one is cash and near-cash investments—investments in riskless or very low-risk investments that most companies with large cash balances make. The second is investments in equities and bonds of other firms, sometimes for investment reasons and sometimes for strategic ones. The third is holdings in other firms, private and public, which are categorized in a variety of ways by accountants. Finally, there are assets that firms own that do not generate cash flows but nevertheless could have value—say, undeveloped land in New York City or Tokyo.

Cash and Near-Cash Investments

Investments in short-term government securities or commercial paper, which can be converted into cash quickly and with very low cost, are considered near-cash investments. This section considers how best to deal with these investments in valuation.

Operating Cash Requirements If a firm needs cash for its operations—an operating cash balance—and this cash does not earn a fair market return, you should consider such cash part of working capital requirements rather than as a source of additional value. Any cash and near-cash investments that exceed the operating cash requirements can be then viewed as nonoperating assets and added to the value of operating assets. How much cash does a firm need for its operations? The answer depends on both the firm and the economy in which the firm operates. A small retail firm in an emerging market, where cash transactions are more common than credit card transactions, may require an operating cash balance that is substantial. In contrast, a manufacturing firm in a developed market may not need any operating cash. If the cash held by a firm is interest-bearing and the interest earned on the cash reflects a fair rate of return,[1] you would not consider that cash to be part of working capital. Instead, you consider it to be part of nonoperating assets and kept separate from the operating asset valuation.

Dealing with Nonoperating Cash Holdings   There are two ways in which we can deal with cash and marketable securities in valuation. One is to lump them in with the operating assets and value the firm (or equity) as a whole. The other is to value the operating assets and the cash and marketable securities separately.

Consolidated Valuation   Is it possible to consider cash as part of the total assets of the firm, and to value it on a consolidated basis? The answer is yes, and it is, in a sense, what we do when we forecast the total net income for a firm and estimate dividends and free cash flows to equity from those forecasts. The net income will then include income from investments in government securities, corporate bonds, and equity investments. While this approach has the advantage of simplicity and can be used when financial investments comprise a small percent of the total assets, it becomes much more difficult to use when financial investments represent a larger proportion of total assets for two reasons.

First, the cost of equity or capital used to discount the cash flows has to be adjusted on an ongoing basis for the cash. In specific terms, you would need to use an unlevered beta that represents a weighted average of the unlevered beta for the operating assets of the firm and the unlevered beta for the cash and marketable securities. For instance, the unlevered beta for a steel company where cash represents 10 percent of the value would be a weighted average of the unlevered beta for steel companies and the beta of cash (which is usually zero). If 10 percent were invested in riskier securities, you would need to adjust the beta accordingly. While this can be done if you use bottom-up betas, you can see that it would be much more difficult to do if you obtain a beta from a regression.[2]

Second, as the firm grows, the proportion of income that is derived from operating assets is likely to change. When this occurs, you have to adjust the inputs to the valuation model—cash flows, growth rates, and discount rates—to maintain consistency.

What will happen if you do not make these adjustments? You will tend to misvalue the financial assets. To see why, assume that you were valuing the aforementioned steel company with 10 percent of its value coming from cash. This cash is invested in government securities and earns an appropriate rate—say 3 percent. If this income is added onto the other income of the firm and discounted back at a cost of equity appropriate for a steel company—say 11 percent—the value of the cash will be discounted. A billion dollars in cash will be valued at $800 million, for instance, because the discount rate used is incorrect.

Separate Valuation   It is safer to separate cash and marketable securities from operating assets and to value them individually. We do this almost always when we use the firm

---

[1]Note that if the cash is invested in riskless assets such as Treasury bills, the riskless rate is a fair rate of return.

[2]The unlevered beta that you can back out of a regression beta reflects the average cash balance (as a percent of firm value) over the period of the regression. Thus, if a firm maintains this ratio at a constant level, you might be able to arrive at the correct unlevered beta.

valuation approaches described in the preceding chapter. This is because we use operating income to estimate free cash flows to the firm, and operating income generally does not include income from financial assets. If, however, this is not the case and some of the investment income has found its way into the operating income, you would need to back it out before you did the valuation. Once you value the operating assets, you can add the value of the cash and marketable securities to it to arrive at firm value.

We also followed this practice with the FCFE models in Chapter 14. While net income includes income from financial assets, we can still separate cash and marketable securities from operating assets if we wanted to. To do this, we would first back out the portion of the net income that represents the income from financial investments (interest on bonds, dividends on stock), and use this adjusted net income to estimate free cash flows to equity. These free cash flows to equity would be discounted back using a cost of equity that would be estimated using a beta that reflected only the operating assets. Once the equity in the operating assets has been valued, you could add the value of cash and marketable securities to it to estimate the total value of equity.

ILLUSTRATION 16.1: Consolidated versus Separate Valuation

To examine the effects of a cash balance on firm value, consider a firm with investments of $1,200 million in noncash assets and $200 million in cash. For simplicity, let us assume the following:

- The noncash assets have a beta of 1 are expected to earn $120 million in net income each year in perpetuity, and there are no reinvestment needs.
- The cash is invested at the riskless rate, which we assume to be 4.5%.
- The market risk premium is assumed to be 5.5%.

Under these conditions, we can value the equity using both the consolidated and separate approaches.

Let us first consider the consolidated approach. Here, we will estimate a cost of equity for all the assets (including cash) by computing a weighted average beta of the noncash and cash assets:

$$\text{Beta of the firm} = \text{Beta}_{\text{operating assets}} \times \text{Weight}_{\text{operating assets}}$$
$$+ \text{Beta}_{\text{cash assets}} \times \text{Weight}_{\text{cash assets}}$$
$$= 1.00 \times (1200/1,400) + 0.00 \times (200/1,400) = 0.8571$$
$$\text{Cost of equity} = 4.5\% + 0.8571(5.5\%) = 9.21\%$$
$$\text{Expected earnings for the firm} = \text{Net income from operating assets} + \text{Interest income from cash}$$
$$= (120 + .045 \times 200) = \$129 \text{ million (which is also the FCFE since}$$
$$\text{there are no reinvestment needs)}$$

$$\text{Value of the equity} = \text{FCFE/Cost of equity} = 129/.0921 = \$1,400 \text{ million}$$

The equity is worth $1,400 million.

Now, let us try to value them separately, beginning with the noncash investments:

$$\text{Cost of equity for noncash investments} = \text{Riskless rate} + \text{Beta} \times \text{Risk premium}$$
$$= 4.5\% + 1.00 \times 5.5\% = 10\%$$
$$\text{Expected earnings from operating assets} = \$120 \text{ million (which is the FCFE from these assets)}$$
$$\text{Value of noncash assets} = \text{Expected earnings/Cost of equity for noncash assets}$$
$$= 120/.10 = \$1,200 \text{ million}$$

To this we can add the value of the cash, which is $200 million, to get a value for the equity of $1,400 million.

To see the potential for problems with the consolidated approach, note that if you had discounted the total FCFE of $129 million at the cost of equity of 10% (which reflects only the operating assets) you would valued the firm at $1,290 million. The loss in value of $110 million can be traced to the mishandling of cash:

$$\text{Interest income from cash} = 4.5\% \times 200 = \$9 \text{ million}$$

If you discount the cash at 10%, you will value the cash at $90 million instead of the correct value of $200 million—hence the loss in value of $110 million.

Should You Ever Discount Cash?   In Illustration 16.1, cash was reduced in value for the wrong reason—a riskless cash flow was discounted at a discount rate that reflects risky investments. However, there are two conditions under which you might legitimately apply a discount to a cash balance:

1. The cash held by a firm is invested at a rate that is lower than the market rate, given the riskiness of the investment.
2. The management is not trusted with the large cash balance because of its past track record on investments.

Cash Invested at Below-Market Rates   The first and most obvious condition occurs when much or all the cash balance does not earn a market interest rate. If this is the case, holding too much cash will clearly reduce the firm's value. While most firms in the United States can invest in government bills and bonds with ease today, the options are much more limited for firms in many emerging markets. When this is the case, a large cash balance earning less than a fair return can destroy value over time.

ILLUSTRATION 16.2: Cash Invested at Below-Market Rates

Illustration 16.1 assumed that cash was invested at the riskless rate. Assume, instead, that the firm was able to earn only 3% on its cash balance, while the riskless rate is 4.5%. The estimated value of the cash kept in the firm would then be:

$$\text{Estimated value of cash invested at } 3\% = (.03 \times 200)/.045 = 133.33$$

The firm would have been worth only $1,333 million instead of $1,400 million. The cash returned to stockholders would have a value of $200 million. In this scenario, returning the cash to stockholders would yield them a surplus value of $66.67 million. In fact, liquidating any asset that has a return less than the required return would yield the same result, as long as the entire investment can be recovered on liquidation.[3]

---

[3] While this assumption is straightforward with cash, it is less so with real assets, where the liquidation value may reflect the poor earning power of the asset. Thus, the potential surplus from liquidation may not be as easily claimed.

Distrust of Management While making a large investment in low-risk or no-risk marketable securities by itself is value neutral, the burgeoning cash balance can tempt managers to accept large investments or make acquisitions even if these investments earn substandard returns. In some cases, managers may take these actions to prevent the firm from becoming a takeover target.[4] To the extent that stockholders anticipate such substandard investments, the current value of the firm will reflect the cash at a discounted level. The discount is likely to be largest at firms with few investment opportunities and poor management, and there will be no discount in firms with significant investment opportunities and good management.

ILLUSTRATION 16.3: Discount for Poor Investments in the Future

Return now to the firm described in Illustration 16.1, where the cash is invested at the riskless rate of 4.5%. Normally, we would expect this firm to trade at a total value of $1,400 million. Assume, however, that the managers of this firm have a history of poor acquisitions, and that the presence of a large cash balance increases the probability from 0% to 30% that they will try to acquire another firm. Further, assume that the market anticipates that they will overpay by $50 million on this acquisition. The cash will then be valued at $185 million, with the discount estimated as follows:

$$\text{Estimated discount on cash balance} = \Delta \text{Probability}_{\text{acquisition}} \times \text{Expected overpayment}_{\text{acquisition}}$$
$$= 0.30 \times \$50 \text{ million} = \$15 \text{ million}$$
$$\text{Value of cash} = \text{Cash balance} - \text{Estimated discount}$$
$$= \$200 \text{ million} - \$15 \text{ million} = \$185 \text{ million}$$

The firm will therefore be valued at $1,385 million instead of $1,400 million. The two factors that determine this discount—the incremental likelihood of a poor investment and the expected net present value of the investment—are likely to be based on investors' assessments of management quality.

Cash Held in Foreign Markets As U.S. companies globalized, they also generate a significant portion of their income in foreign markets, many with much lower corporate tax rates. Until 2017, this income was taxed in the foreign market, and taxed again, when repatriated to the United States, at which point companies have to pay the differential tax rate (between the U.S. corporate and the foreign corporate rates). Not surprisingly, many companies chose to let cash accumulate in foreign markets and subsidiaries, trying to delay and, in some cases, avoid the tax impact. This cash was referenced to as trapped cash and amounted to close to $200 billion at Apple in 2016. The conservative approach to valuing this trapped cash was to assume that you would have to pay the differential tax rate on repatriation and compute the value net of this tax. Thus, if a company has

---

[4]Firms with large cash balances are attractive targets, since the cash balance reduces the cost of making the acquisition.

$200 billion in trapped cash, where you estimate that repatriation will require the payment of 20% in differential taxes, the value of the cash is only $160 billion.

We face two practical problems in making this adjustment. The first is that companies are not transparent about how much of the cash balance that they show in their financial statements is tied up in foreign subsidiaries or markets. The second is that the tax effect of repatriating this cash may be clear in the very short term, but not so clear in the long term because (1) U.S. tax rates may change over time and (2) there is a chance that Congress may allow for a tax holiday, companies are given a one-time reprieve and allowed to bring the cash back without paying taxes or paying a much lower rate.

Since 2017, the United States has joined much of the rest of the globe in not taxing foreign income earned by U.S. companies at the U.S. tax rate. Thus, if a U.S. multinational earns $6 billion in the United States, with a corporate tax rate of 25%, and $4 billion in another country, with a tax rate of only 10%, its total taxes due will be:

$$\text{Tax due} = \$6 \times 0.25 + \$4 \times 0.10 = \$1.6$$

Thus, the company will pay an effective tax rate of 16% on is overall income of $10 billion, and will have no deferred taxes or taxes due.

Investments in Risky Securities

So far, this chapter has looked at how to value cash and near-cash investments. In some cases, firms invest in risky securities, which can range from investment-grade bonds to high-yield bonds to publicly traded equity in other firms. This section examines the motivation, consequences, and accounting for such investments.

Reasons for Holding Risky Securities

Why do firms invest in risky securities issued by other firms? Some do so for the allure of the higher returns they can expect to make investing in stocks and corporate bonds, relative to Treasury bills and commercial paper. In recent years, there has also been a trend for firms (especially technology) to take equity positions in other firms to further their strategic interests. Still other firms take equity positions in firms they view as undervalued by the market; and finally, investing in risky securities is part of doing business for banks, insurance companies, and other financial service companies.

To Make a Higher Return   Near-cash investments such as Treasury bills and commercial paper are liquid and have little or no risk, but they also earn low returns. When firms have substantial amounts invested in marketable securities, they can expect to earn considerably higher returns by investing in riskier securities. For instance, investing in corporate bonds will yield a higher interest rate than investing in Treasury bonds, and the rate will increase with the riskiness of the investment. Investing in stocks will provide an even higher expected return, though not necessarily a higher actual return, than investing in corporate bonds. Figure 16.1 summarizes returns on risky investments—Baa corporate bonds and equities—and compares them to the returns on treasuries (bills and bonds) in three decades: 1991–2000, 2001–2010, and 2011–2020. In the first decade, stocks vastly outpaced corporate bonds and treasuries; in the second, they did much worse and in the third, they returned to dominance.

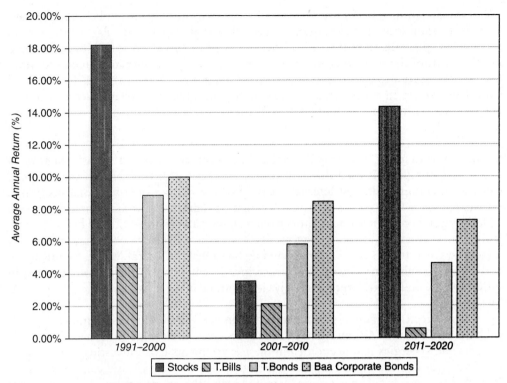

FIGURE 16.1 Returns on Investment Classes: 1991–2020

While investing in riskier investments may earn a higher return for the firm, it does not make the firm more valuable. In fact, using the same reasoning that we used to analyze near-cash investments, we can conclude that investing in riskier investments and earning a fair market return (which would reward the risk taken) will be value neutral.

To Invest in Undervalued Securities A good investment is one that earns a return greater than its required return. That principle, developed in the context of investments in projects and assets, applies just as strongly to financial investments. A firm that invests in undervalued stocks is accepting positive net present value investments, since the return it will make on these equity investments will exceed the cost of equity on these investments. Similarly, a firm that invests in underpriced corporate bonds will also earn an excess return and a positive net present value.

How likely is it that a firm will find undervalued stocks and bonds to invest in? It depends on how efficient markets are and how good the managers of the firm are at finding undervalued securities. In unique cases, a firm may be more adept at finding good investments in financial markets than it is at competing in product markets. Consider the case of Berkshire Hathaway, a firm that has been a vehicle for Warren Buffett's investing acumen over the past few decades. At the end of 2010, Berkshire Hathaway had billions invested in securities of other firms. Among its holdings were investments in Coca-Cola, American Express, and the *Washington Post*. While Berkshire Hathaway also has real business interests, including ownership of a well-regarded insurance company (GEICO), investors in the firm get a significant portion of their value from the firm's passive equity investments.

Notwithstanding Berkshire Hathaway's success, most firms in the United States steer away from looking for bargains among financial investments. Part of the reason for this is their realization that it is difficult to find undervalued securities in financial markets. Part of the reluctance on the part of firms to make equity investments in other firms can be traced to a recognition that investors in firms like Procter & Gamble and Coca-Cola invest in these firms because of their competitive advantages in product markets (e.g., brand name, marketing skills, etc.) and not for their perceived skill at picking stocks.

Strategic Investments   During the 1990s, Microsoft accumulated a cash balance in excess of $40 billion. It used this cash to make a series of investments in the equity of software, entertainment, and Internet-related firms. It did so for several reasons.[5] First, investing in these firms gave Microsoft a say in the products and services these firms were developing and preempted competitors from forming partnerships with the firms. Second, it allowed Microsoft to work on joint products with these firms. In 1998 alone, Microsoft announced investments in 14 firms, including ShareWave, General Magic, RoadRunner, and Qwest Communications. In an earlier investment in 1995, Microsoft invested in NBC to create the MSNBC network to give it a foothold in the television and entertainment business.

Can strategic investments be value enhancing? As with all investments, it depends on how much is invested and what the firm receives as benefits in return. If the side benefits and synergies that are touted in these investments exist, investing in the equity of other firms can earn much higher returns than the hurdle rate and can create value. It is clearly a much cheaper option than acquiring the entire equity of the firm. It is worth noting, though, that Microsoft's investments in other companies have gained it little in terms of added value. In 2011, Microsoft doubled down on this strategy and announced that it would be buying Skype, the Internet phone service company, for $8.5 billion, with questionable payoffs.

Business Investments   Some firms hold marketable securities not as discretionary investments but because it is the nature of their business. For instance, insurance companies and banks often invest in marketable securities in the course of their business, the former to cover expected liabilities on insurance claims and the latter in the course of trading. While these financial service firms have financial assets of substantial value on their balance sheets, these holdings are not comparable to those of the firms described so far. In fact, they are more akin to the raw material used by manufacturing firms than to discretionary financial investments.

Dealing with Marketable Securities in Valuation   Marketable securities can include corporate bonds, with default risk embedded in them, and traded equities, which have even more risk associated with them. As the marketable securities held by a firm become riskier, the choices on how to deal with them become more complex. You have three ways of accounting for marketable securities:

---

[5]One of Microsoft's oddest investments was in one of its primary competitors, Apple Computer, early in 1998. The investment may have been intended to fight the antitrust suit brought against Microsoft by the Justice Department.

1. The simplest and most direct approach is to estimate the current market value of these marketable securities and add the value to the value of operating assets. For firms valued on a going-concern basis, with multiple holdings of marketable securities, this may be the only practical option.
2. The second approach is to estimate the current market value of the marketable securities and net out the effect of capital gains taxes that may be due if those securities were sold today. This capital gains tax bite depends on how much was paid for these assets at the time of the purchase and the value today. This is the best way of estimating value when valuing a firm on a liquidation basis, or when the firm has provided a clear indication that it plans to sell its holdings.
3. The third and most difficult way of incorporating the value of marketable securities into firm value is to value the firms (using a discounted cash flow approach) that issued these securities and estimate the value of these securities. This approach tends to work best for firms that have relatively few but large holdings in other publicly traded firms.

ILLUSTRATION 16.4: Microsoft's Cash and Marketable Securities—2001

During the 1990s, Microsoft accumulated a huge cash balance, largely as a consequence of holding back on free cash flows to equity that could have been paid to stockholders. In 1999 and 2000, for instance, the firm reported the following holdings of near-cash investments (in $millions), as can be seen in Table 16.1:

TABLE 16.1 Microsoft Cash Holdings—1999 and 2000

	1999	2000
Cash and equivalents:		
Cash	$ 635	$ 849
Commercial paper	$ 3,805	$ 1,986
Certificates of deposit	$ 522	$ 1,017
U.S. government and agency securities	$ 0	$ 729
Corporate notes and bonds	$ 0	$ 265
Money market preferreds	$ 13	$ 0
Total cash and equivalents	$ 4,975	$ 4,846
Short-term investments:		
Commercial paper	$ 1,026	$ 612
U.S. government and agency securities	$ 3,592	$ 7,104
Corporate notes and bonds	$ 6,996	$ 9,473
Municipal securities	$ 247	$ 1,113
Certificates of deposit	$ 400	$ 650
Total short-term investments	$12,261	$18,952
Cash and short-term investments	*$17,236*	*$23,798*

When valuing Microsoft in 2000, we should clearly consider the $23.798 billion investment as part of the firm's value. The interesting question is whether there should be a discount reflecting investors' fears about poor investments in the future. Through 2000, Microsoft had not been punished for holding on to cash, largely because of its impeccable track record in delivering ever-increasing profits on the one hand and high stock returns on the other. While 1999 and 2000 were not good years for the firm, investors were probably giving the firm the benefit of the doubt at least for the near future. We would have added the cash balance at face value to the value of Microsoft's operating assets.

The more interesting component is the $17.7 billion that Microsoft showed as investments in riskier securities in 2000. Microsoft reported the following information about these investments (in $millions) in Table 16.2:

TABLE 16.2   Microsoft investments in Riskier Securitiess

	Cost Basis	Unrealized Gains	Unrealized Losses	Recorded Basis
Debt securities at market				
Within 1 year	$ 498	$ 27	$ 0	$ 525
Between 2 and 10 years	$ 388	$ 11	−$ 3	$ 396
Between 10 and 15 years	$ 774	$ 14	−$ 93	$ 695
Beyond 15 years	$ 4,745		−$ 933	$ 3,812
Total debt securities at market	$ 6,406	$ 52	−$1,029	$ 5,429
Equities:				
Common stock and warrants	$ 5,815	$5,655	−$1,697	$ 9,773
Preferred stock	$ 2,319			$ 2,319
Other investments	$ 205		$ 205	
Equities & other investments	$14,745	$5,707	−$2,726	$17,726

Microsoft had generated a paper profit of almost $3 billion on its original cost of $14.745 billion and reported a current value of $17.726 billion. Most of these investments are traded in the market and recorded at market value. The easiest way to deal with these investments is to add the market value to the value of the operating assets of Microsoft to arrive at firm value. The most volatile item is the investment in common stock of other firms. The value of these holdings had almost doubled, as reflected in the recorded basis of $9,773 million. Should we reflect this at current market value when we value Microsoft? The answer is generally yes. However, if these investments are overvalued, you risk building in this overvaluation into your valuation. The alternative is to value each of the equities that the firm has invested in, but this will become increasingly cumbersome as the number of equity holdings increases.

In summary, then, you would add the values of both the near-cash investments of $23.798 billion and the equity investments of $17.726 billion to the value of the operating assets of Microsoft in 2000.

More than a decade later, in 2011, Microsoft still had a large cash balance, invested in a mix of near-cash investments and marketable securities. However, Microsoft's stock price and operating performance lagged the market and the sector between 2000 and 2010. When valuing Microsoft in 2011, you may attach a discount to the cash holdings.

Premiums or Discounts on Marketable Securities?   Generally, you should not attach a premium or discount for marketable securities, unless you are willing to do intrinsic valuations of the underlying companies. There is an exception to this rule, though, and it relates to firms that make it their business to buy and sell financial assets. These are the closed-end mutual funds, of which there are several hundred listed on the U.S. stock exchanges, and investment companies, such as Fidelity and T. Rowe Price. Closed-end mutual funds sell shares to investors and use the funds to invest in financial assets. The number of shares in a closed-end fund remains fixed, and the share price changes. Since the investments of a closed-end fund are in publicly traded securities, this sometimes creates a phenomenon in which the market value of the shares in a closed-end fund is greater than or less than the market value of the securities owned by the fund. For these firms, it may be appropriate to attach a discount or premium to the marketable securities to reflect their capacity to generate excess returns on these investments.

A closed-end mutual fund that consistently finds undervalued assets and delivers much higher returns than expected (given the risk) should be valued at a premium on the value of its marketable securities. The amount of the premium will depend on how large the excess return is, and how long you would expect the firm to continue to make these excess returns. Conversely, a closed-end fund that delivers returns that are much lower than expected should trade at a discount on the value of the marketable securities held by the fund. The stockholders in this fund would clearly be better off if it were liquidated, but that may not be a viable option.

ILLUSTRATION 16.5: Valuing a Closed-End Fund

The Rising Asia fund is a closed-end fund with investments in traded Asian stocks, valued at $4 billion at today's market prices. The fund has earned a return of 13% over the past 10 years, but based on the riskiness of its investments and the performance of the Asian market over the period, it should have earned 15%. Looking forward, your expected return for the Asian market for the future is 12%, but you anticipate that the Rising Asia fund will continue to underperform the market by 2%.

To estimate the discount, you would expect to see on the fund, let us begin by assuming that the fund will continue in perpetuity earning 2% less than the return on the market index. The discount would then be:

$$\text{Estimated discount} = \text{Excess return} \times \text{Fund value/Expected return on the market}$$
$$= (.10 - .12)(4,000)/.12 = \$667 \text{ million}$$

On a percentage basis, the discount represents 16.67% of the market value of the investments.

If you assume that the fund will either be liquidated or begin earning the expected return at a point in time in the future—say 10 years from now—the expected discount will become smaller.

Holdings in Other Firms

In this category, we consider a broader category of nonoperating assets, where we look at holdings in other companies, public as well as private. We begin by looking at the differences in accounting treatment of different holdings and how this treatment can affect the way they are reported in financial statements.

Accounting Treatment   The way in which these assets are valued depends on the way the investment is categorized and the motive behind the investment. In general, an investment in the securities of another firm can be categorized as a minority passive investment. A minority active investment, or a majority active investment, and the accounting rules vary depending on the categorization.

Minority Passive Investments   If the securities or assets owned in another firm represent less than 20 percent of the overall ownership of that firm, an investment is treated as a minority passive investment. These investments have an acquisition value, which represents what the firm originally paid for the securities, and often a market value. Accounting principles require that these assets be subcategorized into one of three groups—investments that will be held to maturity, investments that are available for sale, and trading investments. The valuation principles vary for each.

- For investments that will be held to maturity, the valuation is at historical cost or book value, and interest or dividends from this investment are shown in the income statement.
- For investments that are available for sale, the valuation is at market value, but the unrealized gains or losses are shown as part of the equity in the balance sheet and not in the income statement. Thus, unrealized losses reduce the book value of the equity in the firm, and unrealized gains increase the book value of equity.
- For trading investments, the valuation is at market value, and the unrealized gains and losses are shown in the income statement.

Firms are allowed an element of discretion in the way they classify investments and through this choice in the way they value these assets. This classification ensures that firms such as investment banks, whose assets are primarily securities held in other firms for purposes of trading, revalue the bulk of these assets at market levels each period. This is called marking to market and provides one of the few instances in which market value trumps book value in accounting statements.

Minority Active Investments   If the securities or assets owned in another firm represent between 20 percent and 50 percent of the overall ownership of that firm, an investment is treated as a minority active investment. While these investments have an initial acquisition value, a proportional share (based on ownership proportion) of the net income and losses made by the firm in which the investment was made is used to adjust the acquisition cost. In addition, the dividends received from the investment reduce the acquisition cost. This approach to valuing investments is called the equity approach.

The market value of these investments is not considered until the investment is liquidated, at which point the gain or loss from the sale relative to the adjusted acquisition cost is shown as part of the earnings in that period.

Majority-Active Investments   If the securities or assets owned in another firm represent more than 50 percent of the overall ownership of that firm, an investment is treated as a majority-active investment.[6] In this case, the investment is no longer shown as a financial investment but is instead replaced by the assets and liabilities of the firm in which the investment was made. This approach leads to a consolidation of the balance sheets of the two firms, where the assets and liabilities of the two firms are merged and presented as one balance sheet. The share of the firm that is owned by other investors is shown as a minority interest on the liability side of the balance sheet. A similar consolidation occurs in the other financial statements of the firm as well, with the statement of cash flows reflecting the cumulated cash inflows and outflows of the combined firm. This contrasts with the

---

[6] Firms have evaded the requirements of consolidation by keeping their share of ownership in other firms below 50 percent.

equity approach, used for minority active investments, in which only the dividends received on the investment are shown as a cash inflow in the cash flow statement.

Here again, the market value of this investment is not considered until the ownership stake is liquidated. At that point, the difference between the market price and the net value of the equity stake in the firm is treated as a gain or loss for the period.

Valuing Cross Holdings in Other Firms   Given that the holdings in other firms can be accounted for in three different ways, how do you deal with each in valuation? The best way to deal with each of them is the same. You would value the equity in each holding separately and estimate the value of the proportional holding. This value would then be added to the value of the equity of the parent company. Thus, to value a firm with minority holdings in three other firms, you would value the equity in each of these firms, take the percent share of the equity in each, and add it to the value of equity in the parent company.

When income statements are consolidated, you first need to strip the income, assets, and debt of the subsidiary from the parent company's financials before you do any of the aforementioned steps. If you do not do so, you will double-count the value of the subsidiary.

Why, you might ask, do we not value the consolidated firm? You could, and in some cases because of the absence of information, you might have to. The reason we would suggest separate valuations is because the parent and its subsidiaries may have very different characteristics—costs of capital, growth rates, and reinvestment rates. Valuing the combined firm under these circumstances will yield misleading results. There is another reason: Once you have valued the consolidated firm, you will have to subtract the portion of the equity in the subsidiary that the parent company does not own. If you have not valued the subsidiary separately, it is not clear how you would do this. Note that the conventional practice of netting out the minority interest does not accomplish this, because minority interest reflects book rather than market value.

As a firm's holdings become more numerous, estimating the values of the holdings will become more onerous. If the holdings are publicly traded, substituting the market values of the holdings for estimated value is an alternative worth exploring. While you risk building into your valuation any mistakes the market might be making in valuing these holdings, this approach is more time efficient.

ESTIMATING THE VALUE OF HOLDINGS IN PRIVATE COMPANIES

When a publicly traded firm has a cross holding in a private company, it is often difficult to obtain information on the private company and to value it. Consequently, you might have to make your best estimate of how much this holding is worth based on the limited information that you have available. One way to do this is to estimate the multiple of book value at which firms in the same business (as the private business in which you have holdings) typically trade at, and then apply this multiple to the book value of the holding in the private business. Assume, for instance, that you are trying to estimate the value of the holdings of a pharmaceutical firm in five privately held biotechnology firms, and that these holdings collectively have a book value of $50 million. If biotechnology firms typically trade at 10 times book value, the estimated market value of these holdings would be $500 million.

(continued)

(continued)

In fact, this approach can be generalized to estimate the value of complex holdings, when you lack the information to estimate the value for each holding, or there are too many such holdings. For example, you could be valuing a Japanese firm with dozens of cross holdings. You could estimate the value for the cross holdings by applying a multiple of book value to their cumulative book value.

ILLUSTRATION 16.6:   Valuing Holdings in Other Companies

Segovia Entertainment operates in a wide range of entertainment businesses. The firm reported $300 million in operating income (EBIT) on capital invested of $1,500 million in the current year; the total debt outstanding is $500 million. A portion of the operating income ($100 million), capital invested ($400 million), and debt outstanding ($150 million) represent Segovia's holdings in Seville Television, a television station owner. Segovia owns only 51% of Seville, but Seville's financials are fully consolidated with those of Segovia.[7] In addition, Segovia owns 15% of LatinWorks, a record and CD company. These holdings have been categorized as minority passive investments, and the dividends from the investments are shown as part of Segovia's net income but not as part of its operating income. LatinWorks reported operating income of $80 million on capital invested of $250 million in the current year; the firm has $100 million in debt outstanding. We will assume the following:

- The cost of capital for Segovia Entertainment, without considering its holdings in either Seville or LatinWorks, is 10%. The firm is in stable growth, with operating income (again not counting the holdings) growing 5% a year in perpetuity.

- Seville Television has a cost of capital of 9% and is in stable growth, with operating income growing 5% a year in perpetuity.

- LatinWorks has a cost of capital of 12% and is in stable growth, with operating income growing 4.5% a year in perpetuity.

- None of the firms has a significant balance of cash and marketable securities.

- The tax rate for all of these firms is 40%.

We can value Segovia Entertainment in three steps:

STEP 1: **Value the equity in the operating assets of Segovia without counting any of the holdings. To do this, we first have to cleanse the operating income of the consolidation:**

Operating income from Segovia's operating assets = Consolidated income − Income from Seville = $300 − $100 = $200 million

Capital invested in Segovia's operating assets = Consolidated capital − Capital from Seville = $1,500 − $400 = $1,100 million

Debt in Segovia's operating assets = Consolidated debt − Debt from Seville = $500 − $150 = $350 million

Return on capital invested in Segovia's operating assets = 200(1 − .4)/1,100 = 10.91%

Reinvestment rate = g/ROC = 5%/10.91% = 45.83%

---

[7]Consolidation in the United States requires that you consider 100 percent of the subsidiary, even if you own less. There are other markets in the world where consolidation requires only that you consider the portion of the firm that you own.

$$\text{Value of Segovia's operating assets} = \frac{\text{EBIT } (1 - t)(1 + g)(1 - \text{Reinvestment Rate})}{(\text{Cost of capital} - \text{Expected growth rate})}$$

$$= \frac{200(1 - .4)(1.05)(1 - .4583)}{(.10 - .05)} = \$1{,}365 \text{ million}$$

Value of equity in Segovia's operating assets = Value of operating assets − Value of Segovia's debt = 1,365 − 350 = $1,015 million

STEP 2: Value the 51% of equity in Seville Enterprises:

Operating income from Seville's operating assets = $100 million

Capital invested in Seville's operating assets = $400 million

Debt owed in Seville = $150 million

Return on capital invested in Seville's operating assets = 100(1 − .4)/400 = 15%

Reinvestment rate = g/ROC = 5%/15% = 33.33%

$$\text{Value of Seville's operating assets} = \frac{\text{EBIT } (1 - t)(1 + g)(1 - \text{Reinvestment Rate})}{(\text{Cost of capital} - \text{Expected growth rate})}$$

$$= \frac{100(1 - .4)(1.05)(1 - .3333)}{(.09 - .05)} = \$1{,}050 \text{ million}$$

Value of equity in Seville's operating assets = Value of operating assets − Value of Seville's debt = 1,050 − 150 = $900 million

Value of Segovia's stake in Seville = .51(900) = $459 million

STEP 3: Value the 15% stake in LatinWorks:

Operating income from LatinWorks' operating assets = $75 million

Capital invested in LatinWorks' operating assets = $250 million

Return on capital invested in LatinWorks' operating assets = 75(1 − .4)/250 = 18%

Reinvestment rate = g/ROC = 4.5%/18% = 25%

$$\text{Value of LatinWorks operating assets} = \frac{\text{EBIT } (1 - t)(1 + g)(1 - \text{Reinvestment Rate})}{(\text{Cost of capital} - \text{Expected growth rate})}$$

$$= \frac{75(1 - .4)(1.045)(1 - .25)}{(.12 - .045)} = \$470.25 \text{ million}$$

Value of LatinWorks equity = Value of LatinWorks operating assets − Value of LatinWorks Debt = $470.25 million − $100 million = $370.25 million

Value of Segovia's stake in LatinWorks = .15(370.25) = $55 million

The value of Segovia as a firm can now be computed (assuming that it has no cash balance):

Value of equity in Segovia = Value of equity in Segovia + 51% of equity in Seville
+15% of equity in LatinWorks
= $1,015 + $459 + $55 = $1,529 million

In our view, this is the best estimate of Segovia's equity value, at least in intrinsic value terms.

To provide a contrast, consider what would have happened if we had used the consolidated income statement and Segovia's cost of capital to do this valuation, and used the book values of the minority interest and minority holdings to adjust value. We would have valued Segovia and Seville together as follows:

Operating income from Segovia's consolidated assets = $300 million

Capital invested in Segovia's consolidated assets = $1,500 million

Consolidated debt = $500 million

Return on capital invested in Segovia's operating assets = 300(1 − .4)/1,500 = 12%

Reinvestment rate = g/ROC = 5%/12% = 41.67%

$$\text{Value of Segovia's consolidated operating assets} = \frac{\text{EBIT}(1 - t)(1 + g)(1 - \text{Reinvestment Rate})}{(\text{Cost of capital} - \text{Expected growth rate})}$$

$$= \frac{300(1 - .4)(1.05)(1 - .4167)}{(.10 - .05)} = \$2,205 \text{ million.}$$

Value of equity in Segovia = Value of consolidated operating assets − Consolidated debt − Minority interests in Seville + Minority holdings in LatinWorks = 2,205 − 500 − 122.5 + 22.5 = $1,605 million

Note that the minority interests in Seville are computed as 49% of the book value of equity at Seville.

$$\text{Book value of equity in Seville} = \text{Capital invested in Seville} - \text{Seville's debt}$$
$$= 400 - 150 = 250 \text{ million}$$

$$\text{Minority interest value} = (1 - \text{Parent company holding}) \times \text{Book value of equity}$$
$$= (1 - .51) \times 250 = \$122.5 \text{ million}$$

The minority holdings in LatinWorks are computed as 15% of the book value of equity in LatinWorks, which is $250 million (capital invested minus debt outstanding). It would be pure chance if this value were equal to the true value of equity, as first estimated, of $1,529 million.

There is an intermediate approach, where you can start with the consolidated firm value ($2,205 million), and incorporate the market value (instead of the book value) of the equity in minority interests and holdings derived earlier, to arrive at Segovia's equity value:

Value of equity in Segovia (using market value)

= Value of consolidated operating assets − Consolidated debt

− Market value of Minority interests in Seville

+ Market value of Minority holdings in LatinWorks

= 2,205 − 500 − .49(900) + .15(370.25) = $1,320 million

The difference between this value and the one estimated earlier, using stand-alone valuations of the three companies, comes from the divergence in costs of capital and expected growth across these firms.

You can see from the discussion that you need a substantial amount of information to value holdings correctly. This information may be difficult to come by when the holdings are in private companies.

ILLUSTRATION 16.7: Valuing Cross Holdings—Real-World Concerns

In Illustration 16.6, we were able to value each of the cross holdings separately because we were able to access the information on each of the subsidiaries. That may not always be possible or feasible in the real world. To illustrate, we will use two examples: Hyundai Heavy, a Korean shipbuilder, in May 2008, and Tata Motors in May 2010.

Hyundai Heavy, a part of a Hyundai Group in Korea, has cross holdings in seven other Hyundai Group companies, four of which are publicly traded and three of which are privately held. The company reported the book values of its holdings in these subsidiaries in the financial statements for 2007 in Table 16.3:

TABLE 16.3 Hyundai Heavy Cross Holdings

Cross Holding	Book Value (in billions of won)
Hyundai Merchant Marine	380.00
Hyundai Motors	355.00
Hyundai Elevator	9.20
Hyundai Corp	2.00
Hyundai Oil Bank	329.80
Hyundai Samho	1,068.50
Hyundai Finance	88.20
Value of Cross Holdings	2,232.70

To estimate the market value of these holdings, we use two approaches. For the four publicly traded firms, we use the market values of the firms in May 2008 to estimate the values of the holdings. For the three private businesses, we used the price-to-book ratio at which publicly traded Korean companies in the underlying businesses traded to estimate market value in Table 16.4:

TABLE 16.4 Valuing Hyundai Heavy's Crossholdings

Publicly Traded Cross Holdings			
Cross Holding	% of Shares Held	Total Market Cap	Value of Holding
Hyundai Merchant Marine	17.60%	4,806.00	845.86
Hyundai Motors	3.46%	17,540.00	606.88
Hyundai Elevator	2.16%	688.00	14.86
Hyundai Corp.	0.36%	602.00	2.17
Private Cross Holdings			
	Book Value	Price BV for Sector	
Hyundai Oil Bank	329.80	1.10	362.78
Hyundai Samho	1,068.50	1.80	1,923.30
Hyundai Finance	88.20	1.10	97.02
Value of cross holdings			3,852.87

Thus, the value of the cross holdings that we add on to the discounted cash flow value for operating assets is 3,853 billion Korean won, not the book value of 2,233 billion won.

For Tata Motors, the cross holdings were more widespread (20-plus companies) and more opaque. Two of the holdings were in publicly traded companies, and we use the market values for those: Rs 13,527 million in Tata Steel, and Rs 24.3 million in Tata Chemicals; the total market value of Rs 13,596 million replace the book value of Rs 2,701 million in these holdings. In addition, though, Tata Motors reported book value of Rs 137,875 million in other cross holdings, where we were unable to estimate a market value. The cumulated value that we estimate for the cross holdings is therefore Rs 151,471 million:

$$\text{Value of Tata Motors' cross holdings} = 13,596 + 137,875 = \text{Rs } 151,471 \text{ million}$$

While we are not comfortable with this value, we see little choice, given the information that we have available on the cross holdings. Adding to our disquiet is the fact that these cross holdings amount to almost 42% of our estimated value for Tata Motors as a company; the value that we obtained for the operating assets is Rs 210,832 million. In effect, buying stock in Tata Motors is an investment in the company (58%) and the Tata Group (42%).

Other Nonoperating Assets

Firms can have other nonoperating assets, but they are likely to be of less importance than those listed in the previous section. In particular, firms can have unutilized assets that do not generate cash flows and have book values that bear little resemblance to market values. An example would be prime real estate holdings that have appreciated significantly in value since the firm acquired them but produce little if any cash flows. An open question also remains about overfunded pension plans. Do the excess funds belong to stockholders, and, if so, how do you incorporate the effect into value?

VALUE OF TRANSPARENCY

The difficulty we often face in identifying and valuing holdings in other companies highlights a cost faced by firms that have complicated cross-holding structures and that make little or no effort to explain what they own to investors. In fact, many companies seem to adopt a strategy of making it difficult for their own stockholders to see what they own lest they be questioned about the wisdom of their choices. Not surprisingly, the market values of these firms often understate the value of these hidden holdings.

Many firms outside the United States use, as an excuse, the argument that the disclosure laws are not as strict in their countries as they are in the United States, but disclosure laws provide a floor for information that has to be revealed to markets and not a ceiling. For instance, InfoSys, an Indian software company, has one of the most informative financial reports of any company anywhere in the world. In fact, the firm has reaped substantial financial rewards because of its openness, as investors are better able to gauge how the firm is doing and tend to be much more willing to listen to management views.

So, what can undervalued firms with cross holdings do to improve their value? First, they can break down complicated holdings structures that impede understanding and valuation. Second, they can adopt a strategy of revealing as much as they can to investors about their holdings—private as well as public. Third, they need to stick with this strategy when they have bad news to report. A firm that is generous with positive information and stingy with negative information will rapidly lose credibility as an information source. Finally, if all else fails, they can consider divesting or spinning off their holdings.

Unutilized Assets   The strength of discounted cash flow models is that they estimate the value of assets based on expected cash flows that these assets generate. In some cases, however, this can lead to assets of substantial value being ignored in the final valuation.

For instance, assume that a firm owns a plot of land that has not been developed, and that the book value of the land reflects its original acquisition price. The land obviously has significant market value but does not generate any cash flow for the firm yet. If a conscious effort is not made to bring the expected cash flows from developing the land into the valuation, the value of the land will be left out of the final estimate.

How do you reflect the value of such assets in firm value? An inventory of all such assets (or at least the most valuable ones) is a first step, followed up by estimates of market value for each of the assets. These estimates can be obtained by looking at what the assets would fetch in the market today, or by projecting the cash flows that could be generated if the assets were developed and discounting the cash flows at the appropriate discount rate.

The problem with incorporating unutilized assets into firm value is an informational one. Firms do not reveal their unutilized assets as part of their financial statements. While it may sometimes be possible for investors and analysts to find out about such assets, it is far more likely that they will be uncovered only when you have access to information about what the firm owns and uses.

Pension Fund Assets   Firms with defined pension liabilities sometimes accumulate pension fund assets in excess of these liabilities. While the excess does belong to stockholders, they usually face a tax liability if they claim it. The conservative rule in dealing with overfunded pension plans would be to assume that the social and tax costs of reclaiming the excess funds are so large that few firms would ever even attempt to do it. The more realistic approach would be to add the after-tax portion of the excess funds into the valuation.

As an illustration, consider a firm that reports pension fund assets that exceed its liabilities by $1 billion. Since a firm that withdraws excess assets from a pension fund is taxed at 50% on these withdrawals (in the United States), you would add $500 million to the estimated value of the operating assets of the firm. This would reflect the 50% of the excess assets that the firm will be left with after paying the taxes.

No Double Counting   There is one simple rule to follow when incorporating non-operating assets into value, and that is you cannot double count an asset, i.e., value the cash flows that come from the asset and add the asset value to it. That is why, when valuing a hotel, you cannot add the real estate value of the hotel to the present value of the expected cash flows from running the hotel. That does give rise to a challenging scenario, especially in real-estate based businesses, where the value of the real estate may exceed the value that you obtain for the business, by discounting expected cash flows back at a risk-adjusted discount rate. As an investor, with little or no power to control how the asset gets used, you may choose to go with the latter, but in an acquisition, you may go with the higher of teh two values, as long as you follow through by shutting the business down, and selling the real estate, after you take it over.

The consequences of following a no double counting rule are that most accounting assets are operating assets. Thus, adding items like goodwill or accounting estimates of brand name value to an intrinsic valuation is accounting malpractice, since these assets are what allow the company to generate its expected cash flows.

---

 cash.xls: **This dataset on the web summarizes the value of cash and marketable securities by industry group in the United States for the most recent quarter.**

FIRM VALUE AND EQUITY VALUE

Once you have estimates of the values of the operating assets, cash and marketable securities, and the other nonoperating assets owned by a firm, you can estimate the value of the firm as the sum of the three components. To get to the value of the equity from the firm value, you subtract out the nonequity claims on the firm. Nonequity claims would include debt and preferred stock, though the latter are often treated as equity in financial statements.

What Nonequity Claims Should Be Subtracted?

The general rule that you should use is that the debt you subtract from the value of the firm should be at least equal to the debt that you use to compute the cost of capital. Thus, if you decide to capitalize operating leases as debt, to compute the cost of capital, you should subtract the debt value of operating leases from the value of operating assets to estimate the value of equity. If the firm you are valuing has preferred stock, you would use the market value of the stock (if it is traded) or estimate a market value (if it is not)[8], and deduct it from firm value to get to the value of common equity:

There may be other claims on the firm that do not show up in debt that you should subtract from firm value:

- *Expected liabilities on lawsuits.* You could be analyzing a firm that is the defendant in a lawsuit, where it potentially could have to pay tens of millions of dollars in damages. You should estimate the probability that this will occur and use this probability to estimate the expected liability. Thus, if there is a 10-percent chance that you could lose a case that you are defending, and the expected damage award is $1 billion, you would reduce the value of the firm by $100 million (probability × expected damages). If the expected liability is not anticipated until several years from now, you would compute the present value of the payment.
- *Unfunded pension and health care obligations.* If a firm has significantly underfunded a pension or a health plan, it will need to set aside cash in future years to meet these obligations. While it would not be considered debt for cost of capital purposes, it should be subtracted from firm value to arrive at equity value.
- *Deferred tax liability.* The deferred tax liability that shows up on the financial statements of many firms reflects the fact that firms often use tax-deferral strategies that reduce their taxes in the current year while increasing their taxes in future years. Of the three items listed here, this one is the least clearly defined, because it is not clear when or even whether the obligation will come due. Ignoring it may be foolhardy, though, since the firm could find itself making these tax payments in the future. The most sensible way of dealing with this item is to consider it an obligation, but one that will come due only when the firm's growth rate moderates. Thus, if you expect your firm to be in stable growth in 10 years, you will discount the deferred tax liability back 10 years and deduct this amount from firm value to get to equity value.

---

[8]Estimating market value for preferred stock is relatively simple. Preferred stock generally is perpetual, and the estimated market value of the preferred stock is therefore:

Value of preferred stock = Preferred dividend/Cost of preferred stock

The cost of preferred stock should be higher than the pretax cost of debt, because debt has a prior claim on the cash flows and assets of the firm.

What about Future Claims?

As you forecast earnings growth for your firm, you generally also assume that the firm will increase its debt as it grows. A question that arises then is whether you should be subtracting the value of these future debt issues when estimating equity value today. The answer is no, since the value of the equity is a current value, and these future claims do not exist today. To illustrate, assume that you have a firm with no debt today, and that you assume that it will have a 30-percent debt ratio in stable growth. Assume further that your estimate of the terminal value for this firm is $10 billion in five years. You are implicitly assuming that your firm will borrow $3 billion in five years to raise its debt ratio to 30 percent. This higher debt ratio may affect your firm value today, but the value of equity today is the firm value less the current debt (which is zero).

STOCK-BASED COMPENSATION

Companies sometimes pay employees by giving them equity in the firms at which they work. Until 2007, much of this compensation took the form of options, partly because companies were not required to record options as expenses, at least at the time of the grant. In the years since, many companies have moved away from options to restricted stock, where employees are given shares in the firm, with restrictions on trading those shares for a period after receipt. With both options and restricted stock, employees must work for a specified tenure, called a vesting period, before laying claim on them. In this section, we will begin by looking at how to deal with options and restricted stock grants in the past, before examining how to incorporate continued grants into the future.

Employee Options

Firms use options to reward managers as well as other employees. There are two effects that these options have on value per share. One is created by options that have already been granted. These options, some of which have exercise prices well below the stock price, reduce the value of equity per share, since a portion of the existing equity in the firm has to be set aside to meet these eventual option exercises. The other is the likelihood that these firms will use options on a continuing basis to reward employees or to compensate them. These expected option grants reduce the portion of the expected future cash flows that accrue to existing stockholders.

The use of options in management compensation packages is not new to firms. Many firms in the 1970s and 1980s initiated option-based compensation packages to induce top managers to think like stockholders in their decision-making. In most cases, though, the drain on value created by these options was small enough that it could be ignored without affecting the value per share substantially. In the 1990s, however, the surge in both the number and the value of technology firms has highlighted the importance of dealing with these options in valuation.

What is different about technology firms? One is that management contracts at these firms are much more heavily weighted toward options than are those at other firms. The second is that the paucity of cash at these firms has meant that options are granted not just to top managers but to employees all through the organization, making the total option grants much larger. The third is that some of the smaller firms have used options to meet operating expenses and pay for supplies.

Characteristics of Option Grants   Firms that use employee options usually restrict when and whether these options can be exercised. It is standard, for instance, that the options granted to an employee cannot be exercised until they are vested. For this to occur, the employee usually has to remain for a period that is specified in the contract. While firms do this to keep employee turnover low, it also has implications for the value of these options. Firms that issue options generally do not face any tax consequences in the year in which they make the issue. When the options are exercised, however, they are allowed to treat the difference between the stock price and the exercise price as an employee expense and claim it as a tax deduction.

The accounting for stock options has evolved over time. Until 2006, options were generally expensed at the time of exercise, paralleling the tax treatment. With the passage of FAS 123R in 2006, the rules have changed, and options now must be expensed at the time of the grant, with the value based upon option-pricing models. As we will note later in this section, this has made the task of incorporating expected future options grants easier for those valuing companies.

Existing Options   Why do existing options affect value per share? Note that not all options do. In fact, options issued and listed by the options exchanges have no effect on the value per share of the firms on which they are issued. The options issued by firms themselves do have an effect on value per share, since there is a chance that they will be exercised in the near or far future. Given that these options offer the right to individuals to buy stock at a fixed price, they will be exercised only if the stock price rises above that exercise price. When they are exercised, the firm has two choices, both of which have negative consequences for existing stockholders. It can issue additional shares to cover the option exercise. But this increases the number of shares outstanding and reduces the value per share to existing stockholders.[9] Alternatively, it can use cash flows from operations to buy back shares in the open market, and then use these shares to meet the option exercise. This reduces the cash flows available to current equity investors in future periods and makes their equity less valuable today.

There are four approaches that are used to incorporate that effect of options that are already outstanding into the value per share. However, the first three approaches can lead to misleading estimates of value.

Use Fully Diluted Number of Shares to Estimate Per-Share Value   The simplest way to incorporate the effect of outstanding options on value per share is to divide the value of equity by the number of shares that will be outstanding if all options are exercised today—the fully diluted number of shares. While this approach has the virtue of simplicity, it will lead to too low an estimate of value per share for two reasons:

1. It considers all options outstanding, not just ones that are in-the-money and vested. To be fair, there are variants of this approach where the shares outstanding are adjusted to reflect only in-the-money and vested options.
2. It does not incorporate the expected proceeds from exercise, which will comprise a cash inflow to the firm.

---

[9]This would be dilution in the true sense of the word, rather than the term that is used to describe any increase in the number of shares outstanding. The reason there is dilution is because the additional shares are issued only to the option holders at a price below the current price. In contrast, the dilution that occurs in a rights issue where every stockholder gets the right to buy additional shares at a lower price is value neutral. The shares will trade at a lower price, but everyone will have more shares outstanding.

Finally, this approach does not build in the time premium on the options into the valuation.

Estimate Expected Option Exercises in the Future and Build in Expected Dilution In this approach, you forecast when options will be exercised and build in the expected cash outflows associated with the exercise, by assuming that the firm will buy back stock to cover the exercise. The biggest limitation of this approach is that it requires estimates of what the stock price will be in the future and when options will be exercised on the stock. Given that your objective is to examine whether the price today is correct, forecasting future prices to estimate the current value per share seems circular. In general, this approach is neither practical nor particularly useful in coming up with reasonable estimates of value.

Use Treasury Stock Approach This approach is a variant of the fully diluted approach. Here the number of shares is adjusted to reflect options that are outstanding, but the expected proceeds from the exercise (exercise price times number of options) are added to the value of equity. The limitations of this approach are that, like the fully diluted approach, it does not consider the time premium on the options, and there is no effective way of dealing with vesting. Generally, this approach, by underestimating the value of options granted, will overestimate the value of equity per share.

The biggest advantage of this approach is that it does not require a value per share (or stock price) to incorporate the option value into per-share value. As you will see with the final (and recommended) approach, there is a circularity that is created when the stock price is an input when estimating value per share.

ILLUSTRATION 16.8: The Option Overhang at Cisco—Fully Diluted versus Treasury Stock Approaches

---

Cisco Systems has used management options liberally over its lifetime to supplement compensation packages. After a troubled decade of failed acquisitions and stagnant stock prices, the company's stock was trading at $16.26 a share in May 2011. At that point in time, the company had 5,528 million shares outstanding, but it also reported 732 million options that were outstanding, with the following breakdown on exercise prices and maturity (see Table 16.5):

TABLE 16.5 Cisco—Options outstanding

Exercise Price	Number (in millions)	Weighted Average Life	Weighted Average Exercise Price
$0.01–$15.00	71	2.50	$10.62
$15.01–$18.00	137	3.18	$17.38
$18.01–$20.00	177	2.90	$19.29
$20.01–$25.00	188	4.26	$22.48
$25.01–$35.00	158	6.02	$30.63
>$35	1	0.61	$54.22
Total	732	3.94	$21.39

To evaluate Cisco, we first value the company using a discounted cash flow model and estimate an aggregate value for the equity of $113,331 million. Note that it this value that has to be allocated across two claimholders - the owners of the common stock and the option holders.

To estimate the value using the fully diluted approach, we divide the total value of equity by the fully diluted number of shares:

$$\text{Value of equity} = \frac{\text{Value of equity}}{\text{\# primary share} + \text{\# of options}} = \frac{113{,}331}{(5{,}528 + 732)} = \$18.10/\text{share}$$

Note that this is an extremely conservative estimate since not only are we ignoring the exercise proceeds from the options but also because many of these options are out-of-the money currently.

With the treasury stock approach, rather than add the exercise proceeds from all options outstanding, we incorporate only the 208 million options that are in-the-money and add the exercise proceeds of $3,135 million from these options being exercised (with an average exercise price of $15.07).

$$\text{Value of equity} = \frac{\text{Value of equity} + \text{Exercise proceeds}}{\text{\# primary share} + \text{\# of options}}$$

$$= \frac{113{,}331 + \$3{,}135}{(5{,}528 + 732)} = \$20.30/\text{share}$$

Note that the treasury stock approach ignores the time premium on options in-the-money. It is therefore likely to give you too high an estimate of value of equity per share. (In fact, incorporating the out-of-the-money options into a treasury stock approach will push up the value per share.)

Value Options Using the Option Pricing Model   The correct approach to dealing with options is to estimate the value of the options today, given today's value per share and the time premium on the option. Once this value has been estimated, it is subtracted from the equity value, and then divided by the number of shares outstanding to arrive at value per share.

$$\text{Value of equity per share} = \frac{\text{Aggregate Value of Equity} - \text{Value of Employee Options}}{\text{Number of shares outstanding}}$$

In valuing these options, however, there are four measurement issues that you must confront. One relates to the fact that not all of the options outstanding are vested, and some of the nonvested options might never be vested. The second relates to the stock price to use in valuing these options. As the description in the preceding paragraph clarifies, the value per share is an input to the process as well as the output. The third issue is taxation. Since firms are allowed to deduct a portion of the expense associated with option exercises, there may be a potential tax saving when the options are exercised. The final issue relates to private firms(s) on the verge of a public offering. Key inputs to the option pricing model, including the stock price and the variance, cannot be obtained for these firms, but the options have to be valued, nevertheless.

Dealing with Vesting   As noted earlier in the chapter, firms granting employee options usually require that the employee receiving the options stay with the firm for a specified period for the option to be vested. Consequently, when you examine the options outstanding at a firm, you are looking at a mix of vested and nonvested options. The nonvested options should be worth less than the vested options, but the probability of vesting will depend on how in-the-money the options are and the period left for an employee to vest. While there have been attempts to develop option pricing models that allow for the possibility that employees may leave a firm before vesting and forfeit the value of their options,[10] the likelihood of such an occurrence when a manager's holdings are substantial should be small. Carpenter (1998) developed a simple extension of the standard option pricing model to allow for early exercise and forfeiture and used it to value executive options.

Which Stock Price? The answer to this question may seem obvious. Since the stock is traded and you can find a stock price, it would seem that you should be using the current stock price to value options. However, you are valuing these options to arrive at a value per share that you will then compare to the market price to decide whether a stock is under- or overvalued. Thus, using the current market price to arrive at the value of the options, and then using this option value to estimate an entirely different value per share seems inconsistent.

There is a solution. You can value the options using the estimated value per share. However, this creates circular reasoning in your valuation. In other words, you need the option value to estimate value per share, and value per share to estimate the option value. We would recommend that the value per share be initially estimated using the treasury stock approach, and that you then converge on the proper value per share by iterating.[11]

There is another related issue. When options are exercised, they increase the number of shares outstanding, and by doing so, there can be an effect on the stock price. In conventional option pricing models, the exercise of the option does not affect the stock price. These models have to be adapted to allow for the dilutive effect of option exercise. This can be done simply by adjusting the current stock price for the expected effects of dilution (as we did with warrants in Chapter 5).

WHAT ABOUT OTHER OPTIONS?

While we have considered the effects of management options specifically in this section, everything that has been said here about management and employee options applies to other equity options issued by the firm as well. In particular, warrants issued to raise equity capital and conversion options in convertible securities (bonds and preferred stock) also dilute the value of the common stock in a firm. Consequently, you would need to reduce the value of equity by the value of these options as well. Generally speaking, though, warrants and conversions tend to be easier to value than management options because they are traded. The market values of the warrants and the conversion options can be used as measures of their estimated values.

ILLUSTRATION 16.9: Valuing Management Options as Options: Cisco Systems

---

In Illustration 16.8, we estimated the value of equity per share at Cisco Systems using both the fully diluted approach, which we argued would give us too low a value per share, and the treasury stock approach, which yields too high a value. To get it right, we valued the 732 million options outstanding as options, using the actual stock price ($16.26), the average exercise price of $21.39, the weighted-average maturity of 3.94 years,

---

[10] Cuny and Jorion (1995) examine the valuation of options when there is the possibility of forfeiture.
[11] The value per share, obtained using the treasury stock approach, will become the stock price in the option pricing model. The option value, which results from using this price, is used to compute a new value per share, which is fed back into the option pricing model, and so on.

and an estimated standard deviation in stock prices of 40%. With these inputs and using the Black-Scholes model adjusted for dilution, we arrived at an estimate of value of $2.96 per option and an aggregate value of $2,165 million for the 732 million options. (Cisco had a dividend yield of 1.48% that we incorporated into the model; see Chapter 5 for details).

The value of equity per share can now be computed, using the estimated value of equity of $113,331 million that we arrived at, using discounted cash flows:

Value of equity	$113,331
Value of options	$ 2,165
Value of equity in common stock	$111,166
Primary number of shares	5528
Value per share	$ 20.10

Thus, after incorporating the option value, we arrive at a value per share higher than that estimated using the fully diluted approach, and lower than that estimated from the treasury stock approach. This value ($20.10) is still much higher than the price of $16.26 that the stock was trading at in May 2011.

In valuing Cisco's options, we used the current stock price rather than the estimated value per share. If we did use the estimated value per share, it would create an iterative process—the value of the options affects the value per share, and the value per share affects the value of the options. Employing this iterative process would have increased the after-tax value of the options to $2,637 million, and reduced the value per share to $20.00.

Future Option Grants   Just as options outstanding currently represent potential dilution or cash outflows to existing equity investors, expected option grants in the future will affect value per share by increasing the number of shares outstanding in future periods. The simplest way of thinking about this expected dilution is to consider the terminal value in the discounted cash flow model. As constructed in the previous chapter, the terminal value is discounted to the present and divided by the shares outstanding today to arrive at the value per share. However, expected option issues in the future will increase the number of shares outstanding in the terminal year, and therefore reduce the portion of the terminal value that belongs to existing equity investors.

Future Option Grants and Value   Until 2006, when the accounting rules on options changed, incorporating the effect of future option issuances required a restatement of current earnings to reflect the option grants as expenses. Since it is now standard accounting practice to treat option grants as expenses, that is no longer required.

However, you still must forecast how option expenses will evolve over time in forecasting future earnings. In general, when firms are young with small revenues, stock-based compensation will be a disproportionately high percentage of revenues. As they scale up and develop working business models, these companies will often shift from stock-based compensation to cash compensation, and compensation expenses in total will become a smaller percentage of revenues. You can draw on industry averages for compensation expenses to make these judgments, and the effects will play out in your target operating margins.

Since 2007, U.S. and international accounting standards have converged on the accounting for option grants. Both require that options be expensed when granted, rather than when exercised (which used to be the practice until 2007). As a result, the current operating expenses for a firm include the value of options granted in the current year. If we then keep current operating margins, we are implicitly assuming that the firm will continue to grant options at the same pace (as a percent of revenues). If we converge on industry margins, we are assuming that the firm's option grants will converge on industry averages (as a percent of revenue). In the Cisco valuation, we assumed that current margins would remain unchanged for the future, thus locking in option grants at their current percent of revenues into the future.

warrants.xls: **This spreadsheet allows you to value the options outstanding in a firm, enabling the dilution effect.**

Restricted Stock

The change in the accounting rules on option grants in 2006 also had effects on the composition of stock-based compensation. While companies, especially young and growing, continue to use compensate employees with equity, they have shifted away from options to restricted stocks (i.e., shares in the company with restrictions on trading). From a valuation perspective that has been a blessing, since dealing with restricted stock in valuation is far simpler than dealing with employee options. As with options, we will break the discussion down into restricted stock granted in the past and expected future restricted stock issuances.

Past Restricted Stock Issuance   Companies that have made it a practice to issue restricted shares to employees will build up a count of these restricted shares, with a mix of vesting. There are three strategies that you can adopt when valuing a company to deal with these restricted shares:

1. *Only vested restricted shares*: Once you have valued the aggregate value of equity for the firm, you can divide that value by a share count that includes only vested restricted shares:

$$\text{Value per share} = \frac{\text{Value of equity in common stock}}{(\text{Primary shares} + \text{Vested restricted shares})}$$

   To the extent that you are missing the restricted shares that may get vested in the future, you will overvalue shares in the company.
2. *All restricted stock*: Once you have valued the aggregate value of equity for the firm, you can divide that value by a share count that includes all restricted shares:

$$\text{Value per share} = \frac{\text{Value of equity in common stock}}{(\text{Primary shares} + \text{All restricted shares})}$$

   To the extent that you are counting restricted shares that may not get vested in the future, you will undervalue shares in the company.

3. *Restricted stock, with expected vesting*: Once you have valued the aggregate value of equity for the firm, you can divide that value by a share count, which includes all vested restricted shares and an expected value for existing restricted shares that will get vested in the future:

$$\text{Value per share} = \frac{\text{Value of equity in common stock}}{(\text{Primary shares} + \text{Expected vested restricted shares})}$$

While this is the most logical and complete way to deal with restricted shares when a significant portion are nonvested, it requires making judgments about whether employees will remain employed long enough to become vested.

In most valuations, we go with the second approach and count all restricted shares, on the assumption that employees with significant nonvested restricted stock holdings will stay on to vest.

There are some analysts who argue that there should an illiquidity discount attached to restricted shares, but with publicly traded companies where employees can find ways to monetize their holdings, once vested, without trading shares, we would argue that this discount should be negligible.

Expected Future Restricted Stock Issuance   If you expect a company to continue to grant restricted shares as compensation for employees in future periods, you should adopt a variant of the approach used to deal with future option grants. Put simply, recognize that with accounting rules, as they stand now, the earnings in the most recent time period already incorporate the effect of restricted stock grants in that period.

In forecasting the effects of future restricted stock grants on future earnings, we would suggest again that you look at where firms fall in the life cycle. For young firms, restricted stock grants as a percentage of revenues will decrease as revenues scale up, helping improve operating margins. For more mature firms, assuming that the overall compensation expenses will remain at prevailing levels, as a percentage of revenues, is a reasonable assumption, and changes in how the compensation is paid (from stock to cash) will have no effect on value.

ILLUSTRATION 16.10:   Valuation with Stock-based compensation—Tesla in January 2024

- In January 2024, we valued Tesla's equity, in the aggregate, to be worth $635.32 billion, based upon an expansive story of growth not just in automobiles but also in software and energy.
- The company had 3,174 million common shares outstanding at the time of the valuation, but also had restricted stock awards that added 19.1 million to the share count.
- In addition, the company had 344 million options outstanding, with an average exercise price of $35.11 and a remaining maturity of 4.31 years. Using a standard deviation of 40%, in stock prices and the prevailing market price of $182.58, we valued the options outstanding at $51.76 billion.

To estimate the value of equity per share, we adjusted for both the options outstanding as well as the restricted stock:

Value of equity (aggregate)	= $635.32 billion
−Value of options outstanding	= $51.76 billion
Value of equity in common stock	= $583.56 billion
/ Shares outstanding	= 3193.1 million
Value per share	= $182.76

This value does not include the residual options which may come due to Elon Musk from a huge option grant that he received in 2017, and that is conditional on the market capitalization of the company hitting targets. While those options have value, a judgment from the Delaware courts had nullified that grant at the time of this valuation.

Gaming Stock-based Compensation

Even as accountants have made the right decisions on stock-based compensation, requiring that it be expensed at the time it is granted, at option value rather than exercise value, analysts and companies have worked at neutralizing this positive by reversing accountants.

- Companies routinely add back the stock-based compensation earnings to arrive at adjusted earnings and EBITDA. The rationale is that stock-based compensation is not a cash expense, and that you should therefore be treating it like you do depreciation and adding it back to get to free cash flows. That logic does not hold up, because stock-based compensation, unlike depreciation, is an in-kind expense rather than a non-cash expense. Giving away pieces of your equity as compensation is giving away something of value, which needs to be netted out from earnings. Just as a thought experiment, if a company had taken the options and restricted stock that they were planning to give to employees and issued them to markets, using the cash proceeds to pay employees, it would have been a cash expense.
- With options, managers and analysts often argue that it is uncertain whether options will be exercised, and that counting them in as a reduction in equity value is jumping the gun. That argument very quickly falls apart because assuming that these options are worth nothing is a much more dangerous assumption than using an option-pricing model to estimate their value. In fact, option-pricing models reflect a probability-adjusted present value of the dilution that equity investors face in the future.
- The third argument in ignoring options, in particular, is that you can adjust the share count in future years for option exercise, but the problem with doing that, in intrinsic valuation, is that it puts your into endless do loop, where you have to estimate the intrinsic value of your equity in future years, to estimate the intrinsic value today.

Put simply, augmenting earnings by adding back stock-based compensation will generally lead you to overvalue companies, and that skew will only grow, as you value young companies. Loosely paraphrasing Warren Buffett, if management options are not employee compensation, what are they? And if employee compensation is not an operating expense, what is it?

VALUE PER SHARE WHEN VOTING RIGHTS VARY

When you divide the value of the equity by the number of shares outstanding, you assume that the shares all have the same voting rights. If different classes of shares have different voting rights, the value of equity per share must reflect those differences, with the shares with more voting rights having a higher value. Note, though, that the total value of equity is still unchanged. To illustrate, assume that the value of equity in a firm is $500 million and that there are 50 million shares outstanding; 25 million of these shares have voting rights while 25 million do not. Furthermore, assume that the voting shares will have a value 10-percent higher than the nonvoting shares. To estimate the value per share:

$$\text{Value per nonvoting share} = \frac{\$500 \text{ million}}{(25 \text{ million} \times 1.10 + 25 \text{ million})}$$

$$= \frac{\$500 \text{ million}}{52.5} = \$9.52$$

$$\text{Value per voting share} = \$9.52(1.10) = \$10.48$$

The key issue that you face in valuation then is in coming up with the discount to apply for nonvoting shares or, alternatively, the premium to attach to voting shares.

Voting Shares Versus Nonvoting Shares

What premium should be assigned to the voting shares? You have two choices. One is to look at studies that empirically examine the size of the premium for voting rights and to assign this premium to all voting shares. Lease, McConnell, and Mikkelson (1983) examined 26 firms that had two classes of common stock outstanding, and they concluded that the voting shares traded at a premium relative to nonvoting shares.[12] The premium, on average, amounted to 5.44 percent, and the voting shares sold at a higher price in 88 percent of the months for which data were available. In four firms that also had voting preferred stock, however, the voting common stock traded at a discount of about 1.17 percent relative to nonvoting shares.

The other option is to be more discriminating and vary the premium depending on the firm being valued. Voting rights have value because they give shareholders a say in the management of the firm. To the extent that voting shares can make a difference—by removing incumbent management, forcing management to change policy, or selling to a hostile bidder in a takeover—their price will reflect the possibility of a change in the way the firm is run.[13] Nonvoting shareholders do not participate in these decisions.

To estimate the value of the voting versus nonvoting shares, we go through the following four-step sequence:

1. Value the firm under existing management (status quo value); this will lock in current investment, financing and dividend policies, even if these policies are suboptimal.

---

[12] The two classes of stock received the same dividend.

[13] In some cases, the rights of nonvoting stockholders are protected in the specific instance of a takeover by forcing the bidder to buy the nonvoting shares as well.

2. Divide the status quo value by the total number of shares (voting and nonvoting) to get the value per nonvoting share.

$$\text{Value per nonvoting share} = \frac{\text{Status quo value}}{\text{\# voting shares} + \text{\# nonvoting shares}}$$

3. Value the firm under new and presumably better management (optimal value); this will require reassessing how much and how well the firm invests, how much debt it uses in its capital structure, and how much cash it returns to stockholders.

4. Estimate a probability that the firm's management will change (π_{change}) and divide the expected value of changing management by the number of voting shares:

$$\text{Control premium per voting share} = \frac{\pi_{change}(\text{Optimal value} - \text{Status quo value})}{\text{\# of voting shares}}$$

The value per voting share will be the sum of the values of the nonvoting shares and the control premium. Thus, the value per voting share will be determined by how badly the firm is managed (the worse run a firm, the greater the premium) and the likelihood of management change (the higher the likelihood, the greater the premium).

ILLUSTRATION 16.11: Estimating the Value of Voting and Nonvoting Shares

Adris Grupa is a Croatia-based tobacco company, with holdings in other businesses. In June 2010, we estimated the status quo and optimal values for the firm:

- The status quo value for equity was 5,484 million HRK. In deriving this value, we assumed that the firm would continue to finance itself almost entirely with equity (its debt ratio in 2010 was 2.6% and its cost of capital was 10.55%), and that it would continue its aggressive investment strategy (it generated a return on capital of 9.69% and reinvested 70.83% of its operating income back in 2009, resulting in a growth rate of 6.86%).

- The optimal value for equity was 5,726 million HRK. To arrive at this value, we assumed a higher debt ratio (10%), resulting in a slightly lower cost of capital (10.45%). We also assumed that the firm would maintain its reinvestment rate of 70.83%, while earning a return on capital equal to its cost of capital (10.45%).

The firm has 9.616 million voting shares and 6.748 million nonvoting shares. The value for the nonvoting shares is computed by dividing the status quo value by the total number of shares:

Value per nonvoting share = 5,484/(9.616 + 6.748) = 335.13 HRK/share

To estimate the value per voting share, we estimate the premium, with a 30% probability attached to a change in management. (We assess a low likelihood of management changing because the company is family controlled.):

Premium per voting share = (5,726 − 5,484) × .30/9.616 = 7.55 HRK/share

Value per voting share = 335.13 + 7.55 = 342.68 HRK/share

CONCLUSION

Incorporating the value of nonoperating assets into firm value can be very simple to do in some cases—cash and near-cash investments—and very complicated in other cases— holdings in other companies. The principle, though, should remain the same. You want to estimate a fair value for these nonoperating assets and bring them into value. As noted, it is often better to value nonoperating assets separately from operating assets, but the absence of information may impede this process.

The existence of options and the possibility of future option grants makes getting from equity value to value per share a complicated exercise. To deal with options outstanding at the time of the valuation, there are four approaches. The simplest is to estimate the value per share by dividing the value of equity by the fully diluted number of shares outstanding. This approach ignores both the expected proceeds from exercising the options and the time value of the options. The second approach of forecasting expected option exercises in the future and estimating the effect on value per share is not only tedious but unlikely to work. In the treasury stock approach, you add the expected proceeds from option exercise to the value of equity and then divide by the fully diluted number of shares outstanding. While this approach does consider the expected proceeds from exercise, it still ignores the option time premium.

In the final and preferred approach, the options are valued using an option-pricing model, and the value is subtracted from the value of equity. The resulting estimate is divided by the primary shares outstanding to arrive at the value of equity per share. While the current price of the stock is usually used in option-pricing models, the value per share estimated from the discounted cash flow valuation can be substituted to arrive at a more consistent estimate.

To deal with expected option grants in the future, you have to estimate the options as an expense item, specified as a percentage of revenues. A firm expected to grant more options in the future will have lower earnings and cash flows, and thus, a lower value.

Once the value per share of equity has been estimated, that value may need to be adjusted for differences in voting rights. Shares with disproportionately high-voting rights will sell at a premium relative to shares with low- or no voting rights. The difference will be larger for firms that are badly managed and smaller for well-managed firms.

QUESTIONS AND SHORT PROBLEMS

In the problems following, use an equity risk premium of 5.5 percent if none is specified.

1. ABV Inc. has earnings before interest and taxes of $250 million, is expected to grow 5% a year forever, and the tax rate is 40%. Its cost of capital is 10%, its reinvestment rate is 33.33%, and it has 200 million shares outstanding. If the firm has $500 million in cash and marketable securities and $750 million in debt outstanding, estimate the value of equity per share.
2. How would your answer to the previous problem change if you were told that ABV had options outstanding for 50 million shares, and that each option had a value of $5?
3. If you were told that the average exercise price of the 50 million options in the previous problem was $6, estimate the value per share for ABV using the treasury stock approach.

4. LSI Logic has 1 billion shares outstanding, trading at $25 per share. The firm also has $5 billion in debt outstanding. The cost of equity is 12.5% and the cost of debt, after taxes, is 5%. If the firm has $3 billion in cash outstanding and is fairly valued, estimate how much the firm earned in operating income in the current year. (The return on capital is 15%, the tax rate is 30%, and earnings are growing 6% a year in perpetuity.)

5. Lava Lamps Inc. had $800 million in earnings before interest and taxes last year. It has just acquired a 50% stake in General Lamps Inc., which had $400 million in earnings before interest and taxes last year. Because Lava Lamps has a majority active stake, it has been asked to consolidate last year's income statements for the two firms.

   a. What earnings, before interest and taxes, would you see in the consolidated statement?

   b. If both firms have a 5% stable growth rate, a 10% cost of capital, a 40% tax rate, and a return on capital of 11%, estimate the value of equity in Lava Lamps.

   c. How would your answer change if you were told that General Lamps has a 9% cost of capital and a 15% return on capital?

6. Genome Sciences is a biotechnology firm that had after-tax operating income of $300 million last year; these earnings are expected to grow 6% a year forever, the reinvestment rate is 40%, and the firm has a cost of capital of 12%. Genome also owns 10% of the stock of Gene Therapies Inc., another publicly traded firm. Gene Therapies has 100 million shares outstanding, trading at $50 per share. If Genome has $800 million in debt outstanding, estimate the value of equity per share in Genome Sciences. (Genome has 50 million shares outstanding.)

7. Fedders Asia Closed End fund is a closed-end equity fund that holds Asian securities with a market value of $1 billion. Over the past 10 years, the fund has earned a return of 9% a year, 3% less than the return earned by index funds investing in Asia. You expect annual returns in the future to be similar to those earned in the past, both for your fund and for index funds in general.

   a. Assuming no growth in the fund and investment in perpetuity, estimate the discount at which you would expect the fund to trade.

   b. How would your answer change if you expect the fund to be liquidated in 10 years?

8. You have been asked to review another analyst's valuation of System Logic Inc., a technology firm. The analyst estimated a value per share of $11, while the stock was trading at $12.50 per share. In making this estimate, however, the analyst divided the value of equity by the fully diluted 1.4 million shares outstanding. Reviewing this number, you discover that the firm has only 1 million shares outstanding, and that the remaining 400,000 shares represent options with an average maturity of three years and an average exercise price of $5.

   a. Estimate the correct value per share, using the treasury stock approach.

   b. If the standard deviation in the stock price is 80%, estimate the value of the options using an option-pricing model (and the current stock price) and the correct value per share.

   c. Will your value per share increase or decrease if you reestimate the value of the options using your estimated value per share?

CHAPTER 17

Fundamental Principles of Relative Valuation

In discounted cash flow valuation, the objective is to find the value of assets, given their cash flow, growth, and risk characteristics. In relative valuation, the objective is to value assets based on how similar assets are currently priced in the market. While multiples are easy to use and intuitive, they are also easy to misuse. Consequently, a series of tests are developed in this chapter that can be used to check that multiples are correctly used.

There are two components to relative valuation. The first is that, to value assets on a relative basis, prices have to be standardized, usually by converting prices into multiples of earnings, book values, or sales. The second is to find similar firms, which is difficult to do since no two firms are identical and firms in the same business can still differ on risk, growth potential, and cash flows. The question of how to control these differences, when comparing pricing across several firms, becomes a key one.

USE OF RELATIVE VALUATION

The use of relative valuation is widespread. Most equity research reports and many acquisition valuations are based on a comparison of a company to comparable firms, using a multiple such as PE as the basis. In fact, firms in the same business as the firm being valued are called comparable, though, as you will see later in this chapter, that is not always true. In this section, the reasons for the popularity of relative valuation are considered first, followed by some potential pitfalls.

Reasons for Popularity

There are several reasons why relative valuation or pricing is so widely used. First, a pricing based on multiple and comparable firms can be completed with far fewer explicit assumptions and far more quickly than a discounted cash flow valuation. Second, a relative valuation is simpler to understand and easier to present to clients and customers than a discounted cash flow valuation. Put differently, it is far easier to frame an asset as cheap or expensive using a multiple rather than a discounted cash flow valuation. Finally, a relative valuation is much more likely to reflect the current mood of the market, since it is an attempt to measure relative and not intrinsic value. Thus, in a market where all social media stocks see their prices bid up, relative valuation is likely to yield higher pricing for these stocks than discounted cash flow valuations. In fact, relative valuations will generally yield values that are closer to the market price than discounted cash flow valuations for all companies. This is particularly important for those whose job it is to make judgments on relative value, and who are themselves judged on a relative basis. Consider, for instance, managers of growth mutual funds. These managers will be judged based on how their funds do relative to other growth funds. Consequently, they will be rewarded if they pick growth stocks that are underpriced relative to other growth stocks, even if all growth stocks are overvalued.

Potential Pitfalls

The strengths of relative valuation are also its weaknesses. First, the ease with which a relative valuation can be put together, pulling together a multiple and a group of comparable firms, can also result in inconsistent estimates of value where key variables such as risk, growth, or cash flow potential are ignored. Second, the fact that multiples reflect the market mood also implies that using relative valuation to estimate the value of an asset can result in values that are too high when the market is overvaluing comparable firms, or too low when it is undervaluing these firms. Third, while there is scope for bias in any type of valuation, the lack of transparency regarding the underlying assumptions in relative valuations makes them particularly vulnerable to manipulation. A biased analyst who is allowed to choose the multiple on which the valuation is based and to pick the comparable firms can essentially ensure that almost any value can be justified.

STANDARDIZED VALUES AND MULTIPLES

The price of a stock is a function of both the value of the equity in a company and the number of shares outstanding in the firm. Thus, a 2-for-1 stock split that doubles the number of units will approximately halve the stock price. Since stock prices are determined by the number of units of equity in a firm, stock prices cannot be compared across different firms. To compare the pricing of similar firms in the market, you need to standardize the prices in some way. Values for businesses can be standardized relative to the earnings generated, to the book value or replacement value of the assets employed, to the revenues generated, or to measures that are specific to firms in a sector.

Earnings Multiples

One of the more intuitive ways to think of the value of any asset is as a multiple of the earnings that asset generates. When buying a stock, it is common to look at the price paid as a multiple of the earnings per share generated by the company. The earnings per share themselves can be estimated before or after extraordinary items and can reflect what the company earned in prior periods or a future period.

When buying a business, as opposed to just the equity in the business, it is common to examine the value of the operating assets of the firm (also called enterprise value) as a multiple of the operating income or the earnings before interest, taxes, depreciation, and amortization (EBITDA). While, for a buyer of the equity or the operating assets, a lower multiple is better than a higher one, these multiples will be affected by the growth potential and risk of the business being acquired.

Book Value or Replacement Value Multiples

While markets provide one estimate of the value of a business, accountants often provide a very different estimate of the same business. The accounting estimate of book value is determined by accounting rules, and is heavily influenced by the original price paid for assets and any accounting adjustments (such as depreciation) made since. Investors often look at the relationship between the price they pay for a stock and the book value of equity (or net worth) as a measure of how over- or undervalued a stock is; the price–book value (PBV) ratio that emerges can vary widely across industries, depending again on the growth potential and the quality of the investments in each. When pricing businesses, you estimate this ratio using the enterprise value relative to the the book value of all invested capital (rather than just the equity). For those who believe that book value is not a good measure of the true value of the assets, an alternative is to use the replacement cost of the assets; the ratio of the value of the firm to replacement cost is called Tobin's Q, which is discussed in Chapter 19.

Revenue Multiples

Both earnings and book value are accounting measures and are determined by accounting rules and principles. An alternative measure, which is far less affected by accounting choices, is revenue, and you can scale either equity or enterprise value to it. For equity investors, this ratio is the price-sales (PS) ratio, where the market value of equity is divided by the revenues. For enterprise value, this ratio can be modified as the value-sales (VS) ratio, where the numerator becomes the enterprise value of the firm. This ratio, again, varies widely across sectors, largely as a function of the profit margins in each. The advantage of using revenue multiples, however, is that it becomes far easier to compare firms in different markets, with different accounting systems at work, than it is to compare earnings or book value multiples. It is also useful in sectors composed of young companies, where most or all are losing money.

Sector-Specific Multiples

While earnings, book value, and revenue multiples are multiples that can be computed for firms in any sector and across the entire market, there are some multiples that are specific to a sector. For instance, when dot-com firms first appeared on the market in the later 1990s, they had negative earnings and negligible revenues and book value. Analysts looking for a multiple to value these firms divided the market value of each of these firms by the number of hits generated by that firm's website. Firms with a low market value per customer hit were viewed as more undervalued. More recently, social media companies such as Linkedin and Facebook have been judged by the market value of equity per subscriber or user.

While there are conditions under which sector-specific multiples can be justified, and a few are discussed in Chapter 20, they are dangerous for two reasons. First, since they cannot be computed for other sectors or for the entire market, sector-specific multiples can result in persistent over- or undervaluations of sectors relative to the rest of the market. Thus, investors who would never consider paying amounts 80 times the revenues for a firm might not have the same qualms about paying $2,000 for every page hit (on the website), largely because they have no sense of what high, low, or average is on this measure. Second, it is far more difficult to relate sector-specific multiples to fundamentals, which is an essential ingredient to using multiples well. For instance, does a visitor to a company's website translate into higher revenues and profits? And how much value is created by an additional user on a social media site? The answer will not only vary from company to company but will also be difficult to estimate looking forward.

FOUR BASIC STEPS TO USING MULTIPLES

Multiples are easy to use and easy to misuse. There are four basic steps to using multiples wisely and for detecting misuse in the hands of others. The first step is to ensure that the multiple is defined consistently and measured uniformly across the firms being compared. The second step is to be aware of the cross-sectional distribution of the multiple, not only across firms in the sector being analyzed but also across the entire market. The third step is to analyze the multiple and understand not only what fundamentals determine the multiple but also how changes in these fundamentals translate into changes in the multiple. The final step is finding the right firms to use for comparison, and controlling for differences that may persist across these firms.

Definitional Tests

Even the simplest multiples can be defined differently by different analysts. Consider, for instance, the price-earnings (PE) ratio. Most analysts define it to be the market price divided by the earnings per share, but that is where the consensus ends. There are a number of variants on the PE ratio. While the current price is conventionally used in the numerator, there are some analysts who use the average price over the prior six months or year. The earnings per share in the denominator can be the earnings per share from the most recent financial year (yielding the current PE), the last four quarters of earnings (yielding the trailing PE), or expected earnings per share in the next financial year (resulting in a forward PE). In addition, earnings per share can be computed based on primary shares outstanding or fully diluted shares, and can include or exclude extraordinary items. Figure 17.1 provides the PE ratios for Nvidia in May 2024, using each of these measures.

Not only can these variants on earnings yield vastly different values for the price-earnings ratio, but the one that gets used by analysts depends on their biases. For instance, in periods of rising earnings, the forward PE yields consistently lower values than the trailing PE, which, in turn, is lower than the current PE. A bullish analyst will tend to use the forward PE to make the case that the stock is trading at a low multiple of earnings, while a bearish analyst will focus on the current PE to make the case that the multiple is too high. The first step when discussing a valuation based on a multiple is to ensure that everyone in the discussion is using the same definition for that multiple.

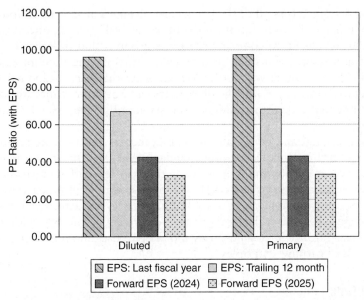

FIGURE 17.1   PE Ratios—Nvidia in May 2024

Consistency   Every multiple has a numerator and a denominator. The numerator can be either an equity value (such as market price or value of equity) or a firm value (such as enterprise value, which is the sum of the values of debt and equity, net of cash). The denominator can be an equity measure (such as earnings per share, net income, or book value of equity) or a firm measure (such as operating income, EBITDA, or book value of capital).

One of the key tests to run on a multiple is to examine whether the numerator and denominator are defined consistently. *If the numerator for a multiple is an equity value, then the denominator should be an equity value as well. If the numerator is a firm value, then the denominator should be a firm value as well.* To illustrate, the price-earnings ratio is a consistently defined multiple, since the numerator is the price per share (which is an equity value) and the denominator is earnings per share (which is a measure of equity earnings). So is the enterprise value to EBITDA multiple, since the numerator and denominator are both operating asset measures.

Are there any multiples in use that are inconsistently defined? Consider the Price-to-EBITDA multiple, a multiple that acquired a few adherents in the past few years. The numerator in this multiple is an equity value, and the denominator is a measure of earnings to the firm. The analysts who use this multiple will probably argue that the inconsistency does not matter since the multiple is computed the same way for all of the comparable firms; but they would be wrong. If some firms on the list have no debt and others carry significant amounts of debt, the latter will look cheap on a Price-to-EBITDA basis, when in fact they might be overpriced or correctly priced.

Uniformity   In relative valuation, the multiple is computed for all of the firms in a group, and then compared across these firms to make judgments on which firms are overpriced and which are underpriced. For this comparison to have any merit, the multiple has to be defined uniformly across all of the firms in the group. Thus, if the trailing PE is used for one firm, it has to be used for all of the others as well. In fact, one of the problems with using the current PE to compare firms in a group is that different firms can have different fiscal year-ends. This can lead to some firms having their prices divided by earnings from July to June, with other firms having their prices divided by earnings from January to December. While the differences can be minor in mature sectors where earnings do not make quantum jumps over six months, they can be large in high-growth sectors.

With both earnings and book value measures, there is another component to be concerned about, and that is the accounting standards used to estimate earnings and book values. Differences in accounting standards can result in very different earnings and book value numbers for similar firms. This makes comparisons of multiples across firms in different markets, with different accounting standards, very difficult. Even with the same accounting standards, the fact that some firms use different accounting rules (on depreciation and expensing) for reporting purposes and tax purposes and others do not can throw off comparisons of earnings multiples.[1]

Descriptional Tests

When using a multiple, it is always useful to have a sense of what a high value, a low value, or a typical value for that multiple is in the market. In other words, knowing the distributional characteristics of a multiple is a key part of using that multiple to identify under- or overvalued firms. In addition, you need to understand the effects of outliers on averages and unearth any biases in these values introduced in the process of estimating multiples.

Distributional Characteristics   Many analysts who use multiples have a sector focus and a sense of how different firms in their sector rank on specific multiples. What is often lacking, however, is a sense of how the multiple is distributed across the entire market. Why, you might ask, should a software analyst care about price-earnings ratios of utility stocks? Because both software and utility stocks are competing for the same investment dollar, they have to, in a sense, play by the same rules. Furthermore, an awareness of how multiples vary across sectors can be very useful in detecting when the sector you are analyzing is over- or undervalued.

What are the distributional characteristics that matter? The standard statistics—the average and standard deviation—are where you should start, but they represent the beginning of the exploration. The fact that multiples such as the price-earnings ratio can never be less than zero and are unconstrained in terms of a maximum result in distributions for these multiples that are skewed toward the positive values. Consequently, the average values for these multiples will be higher than median values,[2] and the latter are much more representative of the typical firm in the group. While the maximum and

---

[1] Firms that adopt different rules for reporting and tax purposes generally report higher earnings to their stockholders than they do to the tax authorities. When they are compared on a price-earnings basis to firms that do not maintain different reporting and tax books, they will look cheaper (lower PE).

[2] With the median, half of all firms in the group fall below this value and half will lie above.

minimum values are usually of limited use, the percentile values (10th percentile, 25th percentile, 75th percentile, 90th percentile, and so on) can be useful in judging what is a high or low value for the multiple in the group.

Outliers and Averages   As noted earlier, multiples are unconstrained on the upper end, and firms can have price-earnings ratios of 500, 2,000, or even 10,000. This can occur not only because of high stock prices but also because earnings at firms can sometimes drop to a fraction of a cent. These outliers will result in averages that are not representative of the sample. In most cases, services that compute and report average values for multiples either throw out these outliers when computing the averages, or constrain the multiples to be less than or equal to a fixed number. For instance, any firm that has a price-earnings ratio greater than 500 may be given a price-earnings ratio of 500.

When using averages obtained from a service, it is important that you know how the service dealt with outliers in computing the averages. In fact, the sensitivity of the estimated average to outliers is another reason for looking at the median values for multiples.

Biases in Estimating Multiples   With every multiple, there are firms for which the multiple cannot be computed. Consider again the price-earnings ratio. When the earnings per share are negative, the price-earnings ratio for a firm is not meaningful and is usually not reported. When looking at the average price-earnings ratio across a group of firms, the firms with negative earnings will all drop out of the sample because the price-earnings ratio cannot be computed. Why should this matter when the sample is large? The fact that the firms, which are taken out of the sample, are the firms losing money creates a bias in the selection process and skews the statistics.

There are three solutions to this problem. The first is to be aware of the bias and build it into the analysis. In practical terms, this will mean adjusting the average PE to reflect the elimination of the money-losing firms. The second is to aggregate the market value of equity and net income (or loss) for all of the firms in the group, including the money-losing ones, and compute the price-earnings ratio using the aggregated values. Figure 17.2 summarizes the average PE ratio, the median PE ratio, and the PE ratio, based on aggregated earnings for four industry groups for U.S. companies: software, basic chemicals, banks, and tobacco companies in 2024. While the values are very different for software companies, they are very similar for banks, mostly because the software sector has more companies with negative earnings and extreme (high) PE ratios. In the same vein, basic chemical companies show more converge on the three PE ratio metrics than do tobacco companies, again indicating the presence of outliers and negative earnings companies in the latter. Note that the median PE ratio is lower than the average PE ratio in three of the industry groups but is higher with banks. The third choice is to use a multiple that can be computed for all the firms in the group. The inverse of the price-earnings ratio, which is called the earnings yield, can be computed for all firms, including those losing money.

Analytical Tests

In discussing why analysts were so fond of using multiples, it was argued that relative valuations require fewer assumptions than discounted cash flow valuations. While this is technically true, it is so only on the surface. In reality, you make just as many assumptions

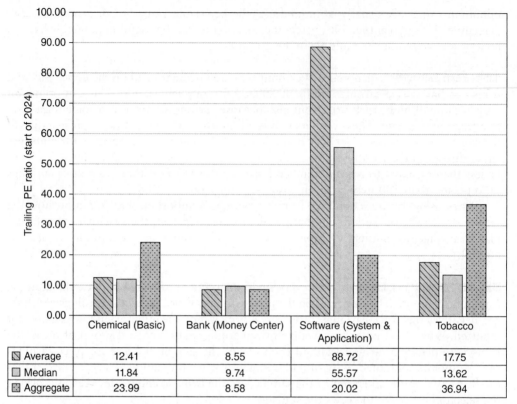

	Chemical (Basic)	Bank (Money Center)	Software (System & Application)	Tobacco
Average	12.41	8.55	88.72	17.75
Median	11.84	9.74	55.57	13.62
Aggregate	23.99	8.58	20.02	36.94

FIGURE 17.2   PE Ratio in 2024: Average, Median, and Aggregate in May 2024

when you do a relative valuation as you make in a discounted cash flow valuation. The difference is that the assumptions in a relative valuation are implicit and unstated, whereas those in discounted cash flow valuation are explicit. The two primary questions that you need to answer before using a multiple are: What are the fundamentals that determine at what multiple a firm should trade? How do changes in the fundamentals affect the multiple?

Determinants   In the chapters on discounted cash flow valuation, we observed that the value of a firm is a function of three variables—its capacity to generate cash flows, its expected growth in these cash flows, and the uncertainty associated with these cash flows. Every multiple, whether it is of earnings, revenues, or book value, is a function of the same three variables—risk, growth, and cash flow generating potential. Intuitively, then, firms with higher growth rates, less risk, and greater cash flow generating potential should trade at higher multiples than firms with lower growth, higher risk, and less cash flow potential.

The specific measures of growth, risk, and cash flow generating potential that are used will vary from multiple to multiple. To look under the hood, so to speak, of equity and firm value multiples, you can go back to simple discounted cash flow models for equity and enterprise value (EV) and use them to derive the multiples. Figure 17.3 summarizes

	Step 1	Step 2	Step 3
	Start with a basic intrinsic value model	*Divide both sides of the equation by the denominator of the multiple that you are trying to deconstruct.*	*You should end up with an intrinsic version of your multiple, which should relate it to fundamentals.*
If Equity Multiple	*Start with a dividend or FCFE model, preferably simple.*	*Divide your dividend or FCFE model by denominator of equity multiple.*	*Intrinsic version of equity multiple, with drivers of value*
	$Price = EPS * Payout/(r-g)$	$Price/Book = ROE * Payout/(r-g)$	$Price/Book = f(ROE, r, g, Payout)$
If EV Multiple	*Start with a operating asset value model, preferably simple*	*Divide your operating asset model by denominator of EV multiple.*	*Intrinsic version of EV multiple, with drivers of value*
	$EV = EBIT (1-t)(1-RIR)/(WACC-g)$	$EV/Sales = After\text{-}tax\ Operating\ Margin\ (1-RIR)/(WACC-g)$	$EV/Sales = f(After\text{-}tax\ Operating\ Margin, RIR, WACC, g)$

FIGURE 17.3 Analyzing Multiples—Equity and Enterprise Value (using Price-to-Book ratio and EV to Sales as illustrative examples)

the process for both equity and enterprise value multiples, using price-to-book ratios (for equity multiples) and enterprise value to sales (for enterprise value multiples) to illustrate the process.

For example, to estimate the determinants of the PE ratio, start with the simplest discounted cash flow model for equity, which is a stable growth dividend discount model, the value of equity is:

$$\text{Value of equity per share} = \frac{\text{Expected Dividends per share next year}}{(\text{Cost of equity} - \text{Expected growth rate})}$$

Dividing both sides by the expected earnings per share next year (forward earnings), you obtain the discounted cash flow equation specifying the forward PE ratio for a stable growth firm:

$$\frac{\text{Value per share}}{\text{Earnings per share}} = \text{PE} = \frac{\dfrac{\text{Dividends per share}}{\text{Earnings per share}}}{(\text{Cost of equity} - \text{Expected growth rate})}$$
$$= \frac{\text{Payout ratio}}{(\text{Cost of equity} - \text{Expected growth rate})}$$

The equation can be easily modified to yield the trailing PE ratio:

$$\text{Trailing PE} = \frac{\text{Payout ratio} (1 + g)}{(\text{Cost of equity} - \text{Expected growth rate})}$$

Dividing both sides by the book value (BV) of equity, you can estimate the price-book value ratio for a stable growth firm:

$$\frac{\text{Value per share}}{\text{BV of equity per share}} = \text{PBV} = \frac{\dfrac{\text{Dividends per share}}{\text{Earnings per share}} \times \dfrac{\text{Earnings per share}}{\text{BV of equity per share}}}{(\text{Cost of equity} - \text{Expected growth rate})}$$

$$= \frac{\text{Payout ratio} \times \text{Return on equity}}{(\text{Cost of equity} - \text{Expected growth rate})}$$

You can do a similar analysis to derive enterprise value multiples. The value of the operating assets of a firm in stable growth can be written as:

$$\text{Value of operating assets (enterprise value)} = \frac{\text{Expected FCFF next year}}{(\text{Cost of capital} - \text{Expected growth rate})}$$

Dividing both sides by the expected free cash flow to the firm yields the EV-to-FCFF multiple for a stable growth firm:

$$\frac{\text{EV}}{\text{FCFF}} = \text{EV to FCFF} = \frac{1}{(\text{Cost of capital} - \text{Expected growth rate})}$$

Since the free cash flow the firm is the after-tax operating income netted against the net capital expenditures and working capital needs of the firm, the multiples of EBIT, after-tax EBIT, and EBITDA can also be estimated similarly. The model can be expanded to allow for high growth and inputs that vary over time, with no loss of generality.

The point of this analysis is not to suggest that you go back to using discounted cash flow valuation but to understand the variables that may cause these multiples to vary across firms in the same sector. If you ignore these variables, you might conclude that a stock with a PE of 8 is cheaper than one with a PE of 12, when the true reason may be that the latter has higher expected growth; or you might decide that a stock with a PBV ratio of 0.7 is cheaper than one with a PBV ratio of 1.5, when the true reason may be that the latter has a much higher return on equity.

Relationship   Knowing the fundamentals that determine a multiple is a useful first step but understanding how the multiple changes as the fundamentals change is just as critical to using the multiple. To illustrate, knowing that higher-growth firms have higher PE ratios is not a sufficient insight, if you are called on to analyze whether a firm with a growth rate, which is twice as high as the average growth rate for the sector, should have a PE ratio that is 1.5 times, 1.8 times, 2 times the average price-earnings ratio for the sector. To make this judgment, you need to know how the PE ratio changes as the growth rate changes.

A surprisingly large number of analyses assume that there is a linear relationship between multiples and fundamentals. For instance, the price-earnings/growth (PEG) ratio, which is the ratio of the PE to the expected growth rate of a firm and widely used to analyze high-growth firms, implicitly assumes that PE ratios and expected growth rates are linearly related.

One of the advantages of deriving the multiples from a discounted cash flow model, as was done in the last section, is that you can analyze the relationship between each fundamental variable and the multiple by keeping everything else constant and changing the value of that variable.

Companion Variable   While the variables that determine a multiple can be extracted from a discounted cash flow model, and the relationship between each variable and the multiple can be developed by holding all else constant and asking what-if questions, there is one variable that dominates when it comes to explaining each multiple. This variable, which is called the companion variable, can usually be identified by looking at how multiples vary across firms in a sector or across the entire market. In the next three chapters, the companion variables for the most widely used multiples from the price-earnings ratio to the value-to-sales multiples are identified and then used in analysis.

Application Tests

When multiples are used, they tend to be used in conjunction with comparable firms to determine the value of a firm or its equity. But what is a comparable firm? While the conventional practice is to look at firms within the same industry or business as comparable firms, this is not necessarily always the correct or the best way of identifying these firms. In addition, no matter how carefully you choose comparable firms, differences will remain between the firm you are valuing and the comparable firms. Figuring out how to control these differences is a significant part of relative valuation.

What Is a Comparable Firm?   A comparable firm is one with cash flows, growth potential, and risk similar to the firm being valued. It would be ideal if you could value a firm by looking at how an exactly identical firm—in terms of risk, growth, and cash flows—is priced. Nowhere in this definition is there a component that relates to the industry or sector to which a firm belongs. Thus, a telecommunications firm can be compared to a software firm if the two are identical in terms of cash flows, growth, and risk. In most analyses, however, analysts define comparable firms to be other firms in the firm's business or businesses. If there are enough firms in the industry to allow for it, this list is pruned further using other criteria; for instance, only firms of similar size may be considered. The implicit assumption being made here is that firms in the same sector have similar risk, growth, and cash flow profiles, and therefore can be compared with much more legitimacy.

The key question that you face in coming up with the list of comparable firms then becomes how narrowly you define a comparable firm. If you define it as a firm that looks just like the firm you are valuing on every dimension (e.g., risk, growth, and cash flows), you may find only a handful of comparable firms. If you define it more broadly and are willing to accept differences on one or all the dimensions, your comparable firm list will be longer. If you can find ways of controlling for differences across companies (and the next section presents a few choices), you will get more reliable estimates of relative value using a larger sample of less comparable firms than a very small sample of more comparable ones.

With globalization, you are faced with a new challenge, where companies in a sector are incorporated and trade in different markets. Thus, in the automobile sector, you can have U.S., European, and Asian firms all competing for market share globally. Can you compare companies that are listed on different markets? Sure, as long as you recognize that these companies can have different risk, growth, and cash flow characteristics. Thus, Asian automobile companies may have higher growth potential and risk exposure than European firms. In addition, differences in accounting standards and currencies can skew both market and accounting numbers and must be controlled.

Sampling Choices   In creating peer groups for pricing, we are torn between two impulses, in terms of getting a better pricing:

- One is to find companies that are like the one we are pricing on every dimension. Thus, you may decide to price a U.S. entertainment software company against other entertainment software companies located in the United States and of similar size, and perhaps even with similar growth potential.
- The other is to get a large enough sample of comparable firms so that the law of large numbers works in your favor, where mistakes average out.

The two impulses work at cross purposes, since adding more criteria to control for, in coming up with peer companies, will cause smaller samples. In a large market, like the United States, and in a industry like software where there hundreds of firms listed, you may be able to have your cake and eat it too. In smaller markets like Turkey or Indonesia or in industry grouping, adding more criteria can very quickly reduce your peer group to a handful of companies. Figure 17.4 illustrates the trade off on peer group choices.

If you are choosing between a small group of companies that are similar to your company and a larger group that may include companies that vary in terms of fundamentals (cash flows, growth, and risk), your choice will depend on whether you plan to just compare your company's pricing metrics to the median (or average) for the peer group, or whether you have mechanisms for controlling for differences. In the next section, we will develop tools that allow us to control for differences, and with these tools, the choice of a larger peer group, albeit one with differences, will trump a smaller, more homogenous grouping.

Controlling for Differences Across Firms   No matter how carefully you construct your list of comparable firms, you will end up with firms that are different from the firm you are valuing. The differences may be small on some variables and large on others, and you will have to control these differences in a relative valuation. There are three ways of controlling these differences: subjective adjustments, modified multiples, and sector or market regressions.

FIGURE 17.4   Peer Group Choice

Subjective Adjustments   Relative valuation begins with two choices—the multiple used in the analysis, and the group of firms that comprises the comparable firms. The multiple is calculated for each of the comparable firms, and the average is computed. To evaluate an individual firm, you then compare the multiple it trades at to the average computed; if it is significantly different, you make a subjective judgment about whether the firm's individual characteristics (growth, risk, or cash flows) may explain the difference. Thus, a firm may have a PE ratio of 22 in a sector where the average PE is only 15, but you may conclude that this difference can be justified because the firm has higher growth potential than the average firm in the industry. If, in your judgment, the difference on the multiple cannot be explained by the fundamentals, the firm will be viewed as overvalued (if its multiple is higher than the average) or undervalued (if its multiple is lower than the average).

This may seem like an extension of the storytelling that we described in Chapter 13, as a necessary precursor to a good intrinsic valuation, but there is an important difference. When stories alone are used to justify pricing, whether it be at a premium or a discount, they are unconstrained, enabling investors and analysts to confirm their biases. In May 2024, for instance, Nvidia was trading at a trailing PE ratio of more than 100, more than three times the median PE for a semiconductor company at the time. An investor intent on buying Nvidia could have justified paying the higher PE, because the company had higher earnings growth, without having to consider whether the higher growth justified a pricing premium that large.

Modified Multiples   In this approach, you modify the multiple to take into account the most important variable determining it—the companion variable. Thus, the PE ratio is divided by the expected growth rate in EPS for a company to determine a growth-adjusted PE ratio or the PEG ratio. These modified ratios are then compared across companies in a sector. The implicit assumption you make is that these firms are comparable on all the measures of value, other that the one being controlled for. In addition, you are assuming that the relationship between the multiples and fundamentals is linear.

ILLUSTRATION 17.1:   Comparing PE Ratios and Growth Rates across Firms: Beverage Companies in 2001

The PE ratios in 2001 and expected growth rates in EPS over the next five years (2002–2006), based on consensus estimates from analysts, for the firms that are categorized as beverage firms are summarized in the following table:

Company Name	Trailing PE	Expected Growth	Standard Deviation	PEG
Coca-Cola Bottling	29.18	9.50%	20.58%	3.07
Molson Inc. Ltd. "A"	43.65	15.50%	21.88%	2.82
Anheuser-Busch	24.31	11.00%	22.92%	2.21
Corby Distilleries Ltd.	16.24	7.50%	23.66%	2.16
Chalone Wine Group Ltd.	21.76	14.00%	24.08%	1.55
Andres Wines Ltd. "A"	8.96	3.50%	24.70%	2.56
Todhunter Int'l.	8.94	3.00%	25.74%	2.98
Brown-Forman "B"	10.07	11.50%	29.43%	0.88
Coors (Adolph) "B"	23.02	10.00%	29.52%	2.30

(*continued*)

(continued)

Company Name	Trailing PE	Expected Growth	Standard Deviation	PEG
PepsiCo, Inc.	33.00	10.50%	31.35%	3.14
Coca-Cola	44.33	19.00%	35.51%	2.33
Boston Beer "A"	10.59	17.13%	39.58%	0.62
Whitman Corp.	25.19	11.50%	44.26%	2.19
Mondavi (Robert) "A"	16.47	14.00%	45.84%	1.18
Coca-Cola Enterprises	37.14	27.00%	51.34%	1.38
Hansen Natural Corp.	9.70	17.00%	62.45%	0.57
Average	*22.66*	*12.60%*	*33.30%*	*2.00*

Andres Wines undervalued on a relative basis. A simple view of multiples would lead you to conclude this because its PE ratio of 8.96 was significantly lower than the average for the industry.

In making this comparison, we are assuming that Andres Wines had growth and risk characteristics similar to the average for the sector. One way of bringing growth into the comparison is to compute the PEG ratio, which is reported in the last column. Based on the average PEG ratio of 2.00 for the sector and the estimated growth rate for Andres Wines, you obtain the following value for the PE ratio for Andres:

$$\text{PE ratio} = 2.00 \times 3.50\% = 7.00$$

Based on this adjusted PE, Andres Wines looks overvalued even though it had a low PE ratio. While this may seem like an easy adjustment to resolve the problem of differences across firms, the conclusion holds only if these firms are of equivalent risk. Implicitly, this approach also assumes a linear relationship between growth rates and PE.

Regressions   When firms differ on more than one variable, it becomes difficult to modify the multiple to account for the differences across firms. You can run a regression of the multiple, as dependent variable, against the variables that you believe determine that multiple, and then use this regression to find the predicted value for each firm. This approach works reasonably well when the number of comparable firms is large, and the relationship between the multiple and the variables is stable. When these conditions do not hold, a few outliers can cause the coefficients to change dramatically and make the predictions much less reliable.

In running these regressions, you have to hew to statistical first principles, and consider the following:

- Your sample size must be large enough to accommodate the terms of your regression. With a simple regression, for instance, where you have only one independent variable, you can get away with sample sizes as small as ten. With multiple regressions, you need larger samples, with a simple rule of thumb of ten additional firms for each additional independent variable in the regression. Thus, you need a sample of at least twenty firms, with two variables, and thirty, with three, and so on.
- Every regression makes an assumption about the nature of the relationship between your dependent and independent variables. The standard ordinary least squares regression assumes that the relationship between your dependent and independent variables is linear, and if that is not the case, there are statistical variants that you can that will incorporate nonlinear relationships.

■ While there are statistics (t statistics, p values) that you can use to measure the statistical significance of the relationship between your dependent and independent variables, and a higher R-squared indicates that you can explain more of the variation in the dependent variable with the independent variables, you can still use a regression with a low R-squared. The predictions that you get from this regression will come with a wider range, making it more difficult to reject the hypothesis that a stock with a PE ratio different from the predicted value is under or overpriced.

■ Finally, regressions are tools in an analyst's arsenal that can be used to test hypotheses about the relationships between a multiple and fundamentals as well as debunking or proving rules of thumb.

ILLUSTRATION 17.2: Revisiting the Beverage Sector in 2001: Sector Regression

The price-earnings ratio is a function of the expected growth rate, risk, and the payout ratio. While there is not a wide variation in payout ratios across beverage companies, they differ in terms of risk and growth. In Illustration 17.1, we looked at beverage companies in 2001, estimating the PE ratios for these companies, in conjunction with expected growth in earnings per share (in the next five years) and a measure of risk (standard deviation in stock prices).

Since these firms differ on both risk and expected growth, a regression of PE ratios on both variables is run:

$$PE = 20.87 - 63.98 \text{ Standard deviation} + 183.24 \text{ Expected growth} \quad R^2 = 51\%$$
$$\quad (3.01) \quad (2.63) \quad\quad\quad\quad\quad\quad (3.66)$$

The numbers in brackets are t-statistics and suggest that the relationships between PE ratios and both variables in the regression are statistically significant. The R-squared indicates the percentage of the differences in PE ratios that is explained by the independent variables. Finally, the regression itself can be used to get predicted PE ratios for the companies in the list.[3] Thus, the predicted PE ratio for Coca-Cola, based on its standard deviation of 35.51% and the expected growth rate of 19%, would be:

$$\text{Predicted PE}_{\text{Coca-Cola}} = 20.87 - 63.98(.3551) + 183.24(.19) = 32.97$$

Since the actual PE ratio for Coca-Cola was 44.33, this would suggest that the stock was overvalued, given how the rest of the sector was priced.

If you are uncomfortable with the assumption that the relationship between PE and growth is linear, which is what we have assumed in the preceding regression, you could either run nonlinear regressions or modify the variables in the regression to make the relationship more linear. For instance, using the ln (growth rate) instead of the growth rate in the regression yields much better-behaved residuals.

Market Regressions Searching for comparable firms within the sector in which a firm operates is fairly restrictive, especially when there are relatively few firms in the sector or when a firm operates in more than one sector. Since the definition of a comparable firm is not one that is in the same business, but one that has the same growth, risk, and cash flow characteristics as the firm being analyzed, you need not restrict your choice of comparable

---

[3] Both approaches described assume that the relationship between a multiple and the variables driving value are linear. Since this is not always true, you might have to run nonlinear versions of these regressions.

firms to those in the same industry. The regression introduced in the previous section controls for differences on those variables that you believe cause multiples to vary across firms. Based on the variables that determine each multiple, you should be able to regress any multiple (PE, EV/EBITDA, PBV) against the variables, using all of the firms in the market in your sample. You can then use the market regression to get predicted values for individual companies. A company that trades at a PE ratio lower (higher) than the predicted PE from the market regression is undervalued (overvalued) relative to the market.

The first advantage of this approach over the subjective comparison across firms in the same sector is that it does quantify, based on actual market data, the degree to which higher growth or risk should affect the multiples. It is true that these estimates can have error associated with them, but this error reflects the reality that many analysts choose not to face when they make subjective judgments. Second, by looking at all firms in the market, this approach allows you to make more meaningful comparisons of firms that operate in industries with relatively few firms. Third, it allows you to examine whether all firms in an industry are under- or overvalued by estimating their values relative to other firms in the market.

RECONCILING RELATIVE AND DISCOUNTED CASH FLOW VALUATIONS

The two approaches to valuation—discounted cash flow valuation and relative valuation—will generally yield different estimates of value for the same firm. Furthermore, even within relative valuation, you can arrive at different estimates of value, depending on which multiple you use and on what firms you based the relative valuation.

The differences in value between discounted cash flow valuation and relative valuation come from different views of market efficiency, or, put more precisely, market inefficiency. In discounted cash flow valuation, you assume that markets make mistakes, that they correct these mistakes over time, and that these mistakes can often occur across entire sectors or even the entire market. In relative valuation, you assume that while markets make mistakes on individual stocks, they are correct on average. In other words, when you value Adobe Systems relative to other software companies, you are assuming that the market has priced these companies correctly on average even though it might have made mistakes in the pricing of each of them individually. Thus, a stock may be overvalued on a discounted cash flow basis but undervalued on a relative basis, if the firms used in the relative valuation are all overpriced by the market. The reverse would occur, if an entire sector or market were underpriced.

CONCLUSION

In relative valuation, you estimate the value of an asset by looking at how similar assets are priced. To make this comparison, you begin by converting prices into multiples—standardizing prices—and then comparing these multiples across firms that you define as comparable. Prices can be standardized based on earnings, book value, revenue, or sector-specific variables.

While the allure of multiples remains their simplicity, there are four steps in using them soundly. First, you have to define the multiple consistently and measure it uniformly across the firms being compared. Second, you need to have a sense of how the multiple varies across firms in the market. In other words, you need to know what a high value, a low value, and a typical value are for the multiple in question. Third, you need to identify the fundamental variables that determine each multiple and how changes in these fundamentals affect the value of the multiple. Finally, you need to find truly comparable firms and adjust for differences between the firms on fundamental characteristics.

QUESTIONS AND SHORT PROBLEMS

In the problems following, use an equity risk premium of 5.5 percent if none is specified.

1. You can compute the PE ratio using current earnings, trailing earnings, and forward earnings.
   a. What is the difference between the ratios?
   b. Which one is likely to yield the highest value and why?
2. An analyst has computed a ratio of firm value (which he has defined as the market value of equity plus long-term debt minus cash) to earnings after all interest expenses and taxes.
   a. Explain why this ratio is not consistently estimated.
   b. Explain why this might be a problem when comparing firms using this multiple.
3. The chapter noted that multiples have skewed distributions.
   a. What is meant by skewed distributions?
   b. Why do multiples generally have skewed distributions?
   c. What are the implications for analysts who might use industry averages to compare firms?
4. Generally, we cannot compute PE ratios for firms that have negative earnings. What are the implications for statistics such as industry-average PE ratios?

CHAPTER 18

Earnings Multiples

Earnings multiples remain the most used measure of relative value. Even market novices have heard of price earnings ratios, and many market strategists make judgments on whether the market is under- or overpriced by looking at the PE ratio for the market, relative to history. Analysts, when pricing individual stocks, often use price earnings ratios to make their case that a stock is under- or overpriced, relative to the market.

This chapter begins with a detailed examination of the price-earnings ratio, and then moves on to consider variants of the multiple—the PEG ratio and relative PE. It also looks at cash flow multiples, and, in particular, the Enterprise Value to EBITDA multiple in the last part of the chapter. The four-step process described in Chapter 17 is used to look at each of these multiples.

PRICE-EARNINGS RATIO

The price-earnings (PE) multiple is the most widely used and misused of all multiples. Its simplicity makes it an attractive choice in applications ranging from pricing initial public offerings to making judgments on relative value, but its relationship to a firm's financial fundamentals is often ignored, leading to significant errors in applications. This chapter provides some insight into the determinants of price-earnings ratios and how best to use them in valuation.

Definitions of PE Ratio

The price-earnings ratio is the ratio of the market price per share to the earnings per share:

$$PE = \frac{\text{Market price per share}}{\text{Earnings per share}} \text{ or } \frac{\text{Market value of equity}}{\text{Net income}}$$

The two variants should yield the same value, as long as the share count used to compute per share numbers and the market capitalization are the same. The PE ratio is consistently defined, with the numerator being the value of equity per share and the denominator measuring earnings per share, which is a measure of equity earnings. The biggest problem with PE ratios is the variations on earnings per share used in computing the multiple. In

Chapter 17, we saw that PE ratios could be computed using current earnings per share, trailing earnings per share, forward earnings per share, fully diluted earnings per share, and primary earnings per share.

Especially with high-growth (and high-risk) firms, the PE ratio can be very different depending on which measure of earnings per share is used. This can be explained by two factors:

1. *The volatility in earnings per share at these firms.* Forward earnings per share can be substantially higher (or lower) than trailing earnings per share, which, in turn, can be significantly different from current earnings per share.
2. *Management options and restricted shares.* Since high-growth firms tend to have far more employee options and restricted stock outstanding, relative to the number of shares, the differences between diluted and primary earnings per share tend to be large.

When the PE ratios of firms are compared, it is difficult to ensure that the earnings per share are uniformly estimated across the firms for the following reasons:

- Firms often grow by acquiring other firms, and they do not account for acquisitions the same way. While all companies now must use purchase accounting and record goodwill as an asset, there is enough discretion in the process to make a material difference in reported earnings. These differences lead to different measures of earnings per share and different PE ratios.
- Using diluted earnings per share in estimating PE ratios might bring the shares that are covered by management options into the multiple, but they treat options that are deep in-the-money or only slightly in-the-money as equivalent.
- Firm often have discretion in whether they expense or capitalize items, at least for reporting purposes. The expensing of a capital expense gives firms a way of shifting earnings from period to period and penalizes those firms that are reinvesting more.

Cross-Sectional Distribution of PE Ratios

A critical step in using PE ratios is to understand how the cross-sectional multiple is distributed across firms in the sector and the market. In this section, the distribution of PE ratios across the entire market is examined.

Market Distribution   Figure 18.1 presents the distribution of PE ratios for U.S. stocks in January 2024. The current PE, trailing PE, and forward PE ratios are all presented in this figure.

Table 18.1 presents summary statistics on all three measures of the price-earnings ratio, starting with the mean and the median, and the 25th and 75th percentile values.

Looking at all three measures of the PE ratio, the average is consistently higher than the median, reflecting the fact that PE ratios can be very high numbers but cannot be less than zero. In fact, with current PE ratios, there is one firm with a PE ratio of 103,000, skewing the average upwards. The current PE ratios are also higher than the trailing PE

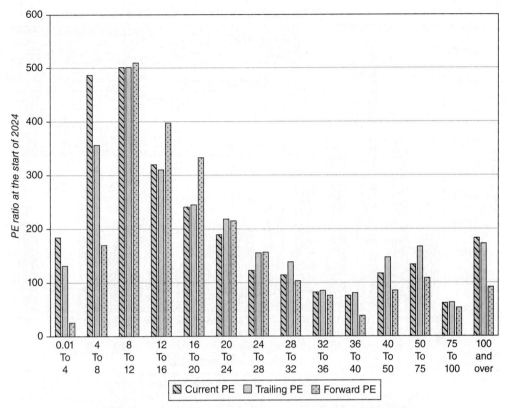

FIGURE 18.1 PE Ratios for U.S. Companies—January 2024

TABLE 18.1 Distribution for PE ratios—U.S. Companies in January 2024

	Current PE	Trailing PE	Forward PE
Average	121.65	52.28	31.98
First Quartile	8.19	9.34	11.19
Median	14.95	17.08	16.85
Third Quartile	29.89	32.71	27.20
Maximum	103000.00	6471.43	2183.33
Number with PE	2817	2779	2363
Number missing	3601	3639	4055

ratios, which, in turn, are usually higher than the forward PE ratios, reflecting the fact that forward earnings are expected to be higher than trailing earnings. Finally, note the number of firms where PE ratios cannot be calculated. With all three measures of PE ratios, companies with negative earnings per share have PE ratios that are not meaningful. The additional drop off in companies, with forward PE ratios, comes from the fact that companies that are not tracked by analysts will have no forward earnings estimates.

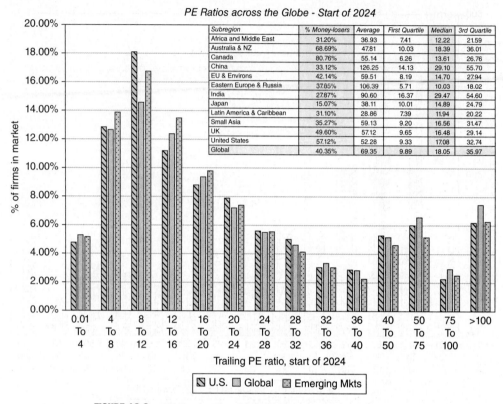

Subregion	% Money-losers	Average	First Quartile	Median	3rd Quartile
Africa and Middle East	31.20%	36.93	7.41	12.22	21.59
Australia & NZ	68.69%	47.81	10.03	18.39	36.01
Canada	80.76%	55.14	6.26	13.61	26.76
China	33.12%	126.25	14.13	29.10	55.70
EU & Environs	42.14%	59.51	8.19	14.70	27.94
Eastern Europe & Russia	37.85%	106.39	5.71	10.03	18.02
India	27.87%	90.60	16.37	29.47	54.60
Japan	15.07%	38.11	10.01	14.89	24.79
Latin America & Caribbean	31.10%	28.86	7.39	11.94	20.22
Small Asia	35.27%	59.13	9.20	16.56	31.47
UK	49.60%	57.12	9.65	16.48	29.14
United States	57.12%	52.28	9.33	17.08	32.74
Global	40.35%	69.35	9.89	18.05	35.97

FIGURE 18.2   PE Ratios for Global Companies—January 2024

While the numbers in Figure 18.1 and the table were based on just U.S. companies at the start of 2024, expanding the analysis to look at global stocks does not change the distributional characteristics. In Figure 18.2, we look at the distribution of PE ratios for global stocks, compared to U.S. and emerging market stocks, and report on the statistics for geographical regions:

All three distribution (U.S., global, emerging markets) share the same skewness—with the peak to the left of the distribution and long positive tails on the distribution. The median values vary across geographies, with Eastern Europe and Latin American stocks trading at the lowest multiples of earnings, and China and India trading at the highest multiples, the former perhaps because they are perceived as risky and the latter because of the potential for high growth.

 pedata.xls: This dataset on the web summarizes price-earnings ratios and fundamentals by industry group in the United States for the most recent year.

Determinants of the PE Ratio

In Chapter 17, the fundamentals that determine multiples were extracted using a discounted cash flow model—an equity model like the dividend discount model for equity multiples and a firm value model for firm multiples. The price-earnings ratio, being an equity multiple, can be analyzed using a equity valuation model. In this section, the fundamentals that determine the price-earnings ratio for a high-growth firm are analyzed.

Discounted Cash Flow Model Perspective on PE Ratios   In Chapter 17, we derived the PE ratio for a stable growth firm from the stable growth dividend discount model:

$$\text{Trailing PE} = \frac{\text{Payout ratio } (1 + g)}{(\text{Cost of equity} - \text{Stable growth rate})}$$

If the PE ratio is stated in terms of expected earnings in the next time period, this can be simplified to:

$$\text{Forward PE} = \frac{\text{Payout ratio}}{(\text{Cost of equity} - \text{Stable growth rate})}$$

The PE ratio is an increasing function of the payout ratio and the growth rate, and a decreasing function of the riskiness of the firm. In fact, we can state the payout ratio as a function of the expected growth rate (g_n) and return on equity (ROE_n):

$$\text{Payout ratio} = 1 - \frac{\text{Stable growth rate}}{\text{Return on equity}} = 1 - \frac{g_n}{ROE_n}$$

Substituting back into the equation,

$$\text{Forward PE} = \frac{1 - \dfrac{g_n}{ROE_n}}{(\text{Cost of equity} - \text{Stable growth rate})}$$

The price-earnings ratio for a high-growth firm can also be related to fundamentals. Using the two-stage dividend discount model, this relationship can be made explicit simply. When a firm is expected to be in high growth for the next n years and stable growth thereafter, the dividend discount model can be written as follows:

$$\text{Value per share}_0 = \frac{EPS_1 \times \text{Payout ratio} \times \left(1 - \dfrac{(1 + g)^n}{\left(1 + k_{e,hg}\right)^n}\right)}{\left(k_{e,hg} - g\right)}$$
$$+ \frac{EPS_{n+1} \times \text{Payout ratio}_{st}}{\left(k_{e,st} - g_{st}\right)\left(1 + k_{e,hg}\right)^n}$$

where

EPS_0 = Earnings per share in current year (year 0)

g = Growth rate in EPS in the first n years

$k_{e,hg}$ = Cost of equity in high-growth period

$k_{e,st}$ = Cost of equity in stable growth

Payout = Payout ratio in the first n years

g_{st} = Stable growth rate

$Payout_{st}$ = Payout ratio in stable growth

Bringing EPS_0 to the left-hand side of the equation, we can derive the intrinsic value equations for both trailing and forward PE ratios:

$$\text{Trailing PE} = \frac{\text{Payout ratio}\,(1+g)\left(1 - \dfrac{(1+g)^n}{\left(1+k_{e,hg}\right)^n}\right)}{\left(k_{e,hg} - g\right)} + \frac{(1+g)^n\left(1+g_{st}\right)\text{Payout ratio}_{st}}{\left(k_{e,st} - g_{st}\right)\left(1+k_{e,hg}\right)^n}$$

$$\text{Forward PE} = \frac{\text{Payout ratio}\left(1 - \dfrac{(1+g)^n}{\left(1+k_{e,hg}\right)^n}\right)}{\left(k_{e,hg} - g\right)} + \frac{(1+g)^{n-1}\left(1+g_{st}\right)\text{Payout ratio}_{st}}{\left(k_{e,st} - g_{st}\right)\left(1+k_{e,hg}\right)^n}$$

Here again, we can substitute in the fundamental equation relating ROE for payout ratios:

$$\text{Forward PE} = \frac{\left(1 - \dfrac{g}{ROE_{hg}}\right)\left(1 - \dfrac{(1+g)^n}{(1+k_{e,hg})^n}\right)}{\left(k_{e,hg} - g\right)} + \frac{(1+g)^{n-1}\left(1+g_{st}\right)\left(1 - \dfrac{g_{st}}{ROE_{st}}\right)}{\left(k_{e,st} - g_{st}\right)\left(1+k_{e,hg}\right)^n}$$

where ROE_{hg} is the return on equity in the high-growth period, and ROE_{st} is the return on equity in stable growth.

The left-hand side of the equation is the price-earnings ratio. It is determined by:

- *Payout ratio (and return on equity) during the high-growth period and in the stable period.* The PE ratio increases as the payout ratio increases, for any given growth rate. An alternative way of stating the same proposition is that the PE ratio increases as the return on equity increases, for any given growth rate, and decreases as the return on equity decreases.
- *Riskiness (through the discount rate).* The PE ratio becomes lower as riskiness increases. Put differently, the PE ratio will be higher for a firm where is growth is more predictable and stable than for an otherwise similar firm with unstable growth.
- *Expected growth rate in earnings in both the high-growth and stable phases.* The PE increases as the growth rate increases, assuming that the ROE > cost of equity.

This formula is general enough to be applied to any firm, even one that is not paying dividends right now. In fact, the ratio of FCFE to earnings can be substituted for the payout ratio for firms that pay significantly less in dividends than they can afford to.

ILLUSTRATION 18.1:   Estimating the PE Ratio for a High-Growth Firm in the Two-Stage Model

Assume that you have been asked to estimate the PE ratio for a firm that has the following characteristics in Table 18.2:

TABLE 18.2   High growth firm—Fundamentals

Length of high growth = five years

Growth rate in first five years = 20%	Payout ratio in first five years = 20%
Growth rate after five years = 4%	Payout ratio after five years = 60%
Beta = 1.0	Risk-free rate = T-bond rate = 4.5%
Cost of equity[1] = 4.5% + 1(5%) = 9.5%	Risk premium = 5%

Plugging in the values for growth, payout ratio, and the cost of equity into the intrinsic PE equation for a high-growth firm:

$$\text{Trailing PE} = \frac{(0.20)\,(1.20)\left(1 - \dfrac{(1.20)^5}{(1.095)^5}\right)}{(.095 - .20)} + \frac{(1.20)^5\,(1.04)\,(0.60)}{(.095 - .04)\,(1.095)^5} = 19.26$$

The estimated trailing PE ratio for this firm is 19.26. Note that the return on equity implicit in these inputs can also be computed as follows:

$$\text{Return on equity in the first five years} = \frac{\text{High-growth rate}}{(1 - \text{Payout ratio during high growth})} = \frac{.20}{(1 - .20)} = .25$$

$$\text{Return on equity in the stable growth} = \frac{\text{Stable growth rate}}{(1 - \text{Payout ratio during stable growth})} = \frac{.04}{(1 - .60)} = .10$$

ILLUSTRATION 18.2:   Estimating an Intrinsic PE Ratio—P&G in May 2011

In Chapter 13, we valued P&G using a two-stage dividend discount model. We reproduce the inputs that we used in the valuation in the Table 18.3:

TABLE 18.3   Intrinsic PE ratio inputs for P&G

	High Growth	Stable Growth
Return on equity	20%	12%
Length of growth	5 years	After year 5
Expected growth rate	10.00%	3.00%
Payout ratio	50.00%	75.00%
Cost of equity	8.00%	8.50%

Note that we derived the payout ratio in stable growth from the stable growth rate and the stable period ROE:

$$\text{Stable payout ratio} = 1 - \frac{\text{Stable growth rate}}{\text{Stable period ROE}} = 1 - \frac{3\%}{12\%} = 75\%$$

---

[1]For purposes of simplicity, the beta and cost of equity are estimated to be the same in both the high-growth and stable growth periods. They could have been different.

We plug these values into the two-stage PE ratio equation:

$$\text{Trailing PE} = \frac{(0.50)(1.10)\left(1 - \frac{(1.10)^5}{(1.08)^5}\right)}{(.08 - .10)} + \frac{(1.10)^5\,(1.03)\,(0.75)}{(.08 - .03)\,(1.08)^5} = 18.04$$

Based on its fundamentals, we would expect P&G to trade at 18.04 times earnings. Not surprisingly, multiplying this intrinsic PE ratio by the trailing EPS of $3.82 yields $68.90, the same value that we estimated using the two-stage dividend discount model in Chapter 13.

PE Ratios and Expected Extraordinary Growth   The PE ratio of a high-growth firm is a function of the expected extraordinary growth rate—the higher the expected growth, the higher the PE ratio for a firm. In Illustration 18.1, for instance, the PE ratio that was estimated to be 19.26, with a growth rate of 20 percent, will change as that expected growth rate changes. Figure 18.3 graphs the PE ratio as a function of the expected growth rate during the high-growth period. As the firm's expected growth rate in the first five years declines from 25 percent to 5 percent, the PE ratio for the firm also decreases from 19.26 to just above 11.

The effect of changes in the expected growth rate varies depending on the level of interest rates. In Figure 18.4, the PE ratios are estimated for different expected growth rates at four levels of riskless rates—2 percent, 4 percent, 6 percent, and 8 percent.

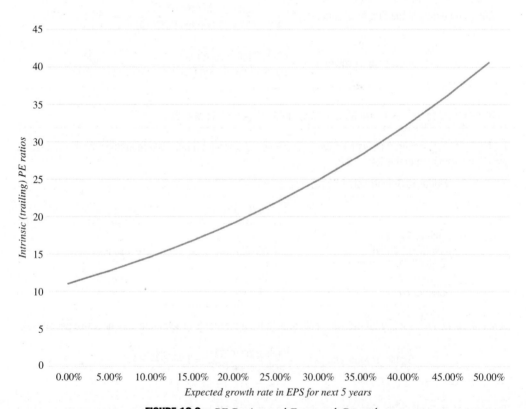

FIGURE 18.3   PE Ratios and Expected Growth

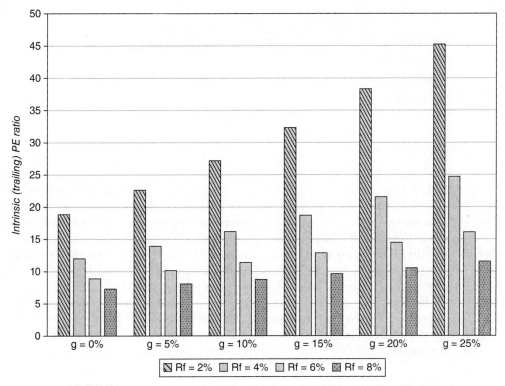

FIGURE 18.4 PE Ratios and Expected Growth: Interest Rate Scenarios

The PE ratio is much more sensitive to changes in expected growth rates when interest rates are low than when they are high. The reason is simple. Growth produces cash flows in the future, and the present value of these cash flows is much smaller at high-interest rates. Consequently, the effect of changes in the growth rate on the present value tends to be smaller.

There is a possible link between this finding and how markets react to earnings surprises from high-growth firms. When firm reports earnings that are significantly higher than expected (a positive surprise) or lower than expected (a negative surprise), investors' perceptions of the expected growth rate for this firm can change concurrently, leading to a value effect. You would expect to see much greater price reactions for a given earnings surprise, positive or negative, in a low-interest-rate environment than you would in a high-interest-rate environment.

PE Ratios and Risk   The PE ratio is a function of the perceived risk of a firm, and the effect shows up in the cost of equity. A firm with a higher cost of equity will trade at a lower multiple of earnings than a similar firm with a lower cost of equity.

Again, the effect of higher risk on PE ratios can be seen using the firm in Illustration 18.1. Recall that the firm, which has an expected growth rate of 20 percent for the next five years and 4 percent thereafter, has an estimated PE ratio of 19.26, if its beta is assumed to be 1.

$$\text{Trailing PE} = \frac{(0.20)(1.20)\left(1 - \frac{(1.20)^5}{(1.095)^5}\right)}{(.095 - .20)} \frac{(1.20)^5 (1.04) (0.60)}{(.095 - .04) (1.095)^5} = 19.26$$

If you assume that the beta is 1.5, the cost of equity increases to 12 percent, leading to a PE ratio of 12.25:

$$\text{Trailing PE} = \frac{(0.20)(1.20)\left(1 - \frac{(1.20)^5}{(1.12)^5}\right)}{(.12 - .20)} \frac{(1.20)^5 (1.04) (0.60)}{(.12 - .04) (1.12)^5} = 12.25$$

The higher cost of equity reduces the value created by expected growth. In Figure 18.5, you can see the impact of changing the beta on the price earnings ratio for three high-growth scenarios—0 percent, 10 percent, and 20 percent—for the next five years.

As the beta increases, the PE ratio decreases in all four scenarios. However, the difference between the PE ratios across the four growth classes is less when the beta is very high and increases as the beta decreases. This would suggest that at very high risk levels, a firm's PE ratio is likely to increase more as the risk decreases than as growth increases. For many high-growth firms that are viewed as both very risky and having good growth potential, reducing risk may increase value much more than increasing expected growth.

The effect of higher interest rates and higher beta is an increase in the cost of equity, but the effect on value per share and PE ratios comes from what a company can generate

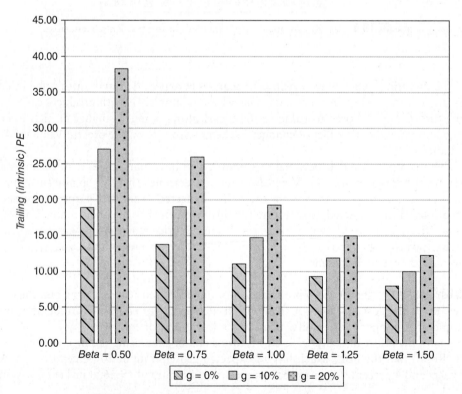

FIGURE 18.5 PE Ratios and Beta: Growth Rate Scenarios

as excess returns (i.e., the difference between its return on equity, relative to its cost of equity). At the limit, if you set earn a return on equity equal to its cost of equity, its intrinsic PE will remain unchanged as the growth rate changes, since the benefits of growth will exactly be offset by its costs. In our hypothetical example, the return on equity during high growth was 25%, well above the cost of equity, resulting in the positive relationship between the PE ratios and expected growth rates. If we has set the return on equity to 5% instead, which is below the cost of equity, the PE ratio will decrease as growth increases.

---

 eqmult.xls: This spreadsheet allows you to estimate the price-earnings ratio for a stable growth or high-growth firm, given its fundamentals.

Using the PE Ratio for Comparisons

Now that we have defined the PE ratio, looked at the cross-sectional distribution, and examined the fundamentals that determine the multiple, we can use PE ratios to make pricing judgments. This section begins by looking at how best to compare the PE ratio for a market over time, and follows up by a comparison of PE ratios across different markets. Finally, it uses PE ratios to analyze firms within a sector, and then expands the analysis to the entire market. In doing so, note that PE ratios should vary across time, markets, industries, and firms because of differences in fundamentals—higher growth, lower risk, and higher payout generally result in higher PE ratios. When comparisons are made, you must control for these differences in risk, growth rates, and payout ratios.

Comparing a Market's PE Ratio across Time   Analysts and market strategists often compare the PE ratio of a market to its historical average to make judgments about whether the market is under- or overvalued. Thus, a market that is trading at a PE ratio is much higher than its historical norms is often considered to be overvalued, whereas one that is trading at a ratio lower than its historical norms is considered undervalued.

While reversion to historic norms remains a very strong force in financial markets, you should be cautious about drawing too strong a conclusion from such comparisons. As the fundamentals (interest rates, risk premiums, expected growth, and payout) change over time, the PE ratio for a market will also change. Other things remaining equal, for instance, you would expect the following:

- An increase in interest rates should result in a higher cost of equity for the market and a lower PE ratio.
- A greater willingness to take risk on the part of investors will result in a lower risk premium for equity and a higher PE ratio across all stocks.
- An increase in expected growth in earnings across firms will result in a higher PE ratio for the market.
- An increase in the return on equity at firms will result in a higher payout ratio for any given growth rate [g = (1 − Payout ratio) ROE] and a higher PE ratio for all firms.

In other words, it is difficult to draw conclusions about PE ratios without looking at these fundamentals. A more appropriate comparison is therefore not between PE ratios across time, but between the actual PE ratio and the predicted PE ratio based on fundamentals existing at that time.

ILLUSTRATION 18.3:   PE Ratios Across Time

Table 18.4 the summary economic statistics at two points in time for the same stock market. The interest rates in the first period were significantly higher than the interest rates in the second period.

TABLE 18.4   PE Ratios and Macroeconomic Factors

	Period 1	Period 2
T-bond rate	11.00%	6.00%
Market premium	5.50%	5.50%
Expected inflation	5.00%	4.00%
Expected growth in real GNP	3.00%	2.50%
Average payout ratio	50%	50%
Expected PE ratio	$(0.5 \times 1.08)/(.165 - .08) = 6.35$	$(0.5 \times 1.065)/(.115 - .065) = 10.65$

The PE ratio in the second time period is significantly higher than the PE ratio in the first period, largely because of the drop in real interest rates (nominal interest rate – expected inflation).

ILLUSTRATION 18.4:   PE Ratios across Time for the S&P 500

Figure 18.5 summarizes the earnings-price (EP) ratios for S&P 500 and Treasury bond rates at the end of each year from 1960 to 2023. There is a strong positive relationship between EP ratios and T-bond rates, as evidenced by the correlation of 0.689 between the two variables. In addition, there is evidence that the term structure also affects (or as we will see, affected) the PE ratio as can be seen in the correlation matrix below.

	Earnings Yield	T.Bond Rate	T.Bond – T.Bill
Earnings yield	1.0000		
T.Bond rate	0.6876	1.0000	
T.Bond – T.Bill	−0.0766	−0.0256	1.0000

In Figure 18.6, we look at the movements in earnings yields (earnings to price ratios), ten-year treasury bond rates, and the difference between the treasury bond and bill rates between 1960 and 2023:

As you can see, when long-term rates are low, the earnings to price ratio tends to be low (PE ratios are high), perhaps explaining the high multiples of earnings that stocks traded at through much of the last decade (2010–2020). In the following regression, we regress EP ratios against the level of T-bond (10-year) rates and the yield spread (10-year T-bond minus 3-month T-bill rate), using data from 1960 to 2023.

$$EP = 0.0350 + 0.5576 \text{ T-bond rate} - 0.1161(\text{T-bond rate} - \text{T-bill rate}) \qquad R^2 = 0.478$$
$$(6.57) \quad (7.40) \qquad\qquad (-0.04)$$

Other things remaining equal, this regression suggests that:

- Every 1% increase in the T-bond rate increases the EP ratio by 0.5576%. This is not surprising, but it quantifies the impact that higher interest rates have on the PE ratio.
- Every 1% increase in the difference between T-bond and T-bill rates reduces the EP ratio by 0.1161%. Flatter or negatively sloping term yield curves seem to correspond to lower PE ratios, and upwardly sloping yield curves to higher PE ratios. While, at first sight, this may seem surprising, the slope of the yield curve, at least in the United States, has been a leading indicator of economic growth, with

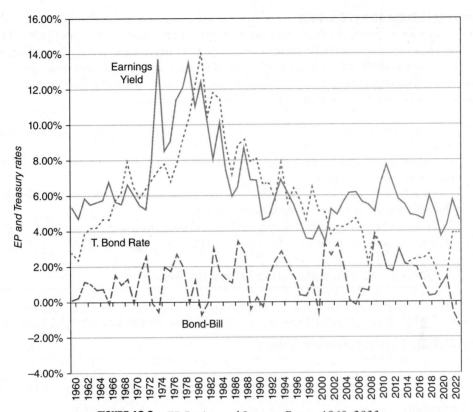

FIGURE 18.6 EP Ratios and Interest Rates: 1960–2023

more upwardly sloped curves going with higher growth. That said, there seems to be no statistical significance to this relationship, and that is a break from the past. For instance, when we ran the same regression in 2008, we arrived at the following:

$$\text{EP} = 0.0256 + 0.7044 \text{ T-bond rate} - 0.3289 \text{ (T-bond rate - T-bill rate)} \qquad R^2 = 0.507$$
$$(4.71) \quad (7.10) \qquad\qquad (1.46)$$

Put simply, it looks like the yield curve effect has weakened over the last few decades, perhaps because long-term interest rates hit historic lows during that period.

Based on this regression, the predicted EP ratio at the beginning of 2024, with the T-bill rate at 4.61% and the T-bond rate at 3.88%, would have been:

$$\text{Predicted EP} = 0.0350 + 0.5576(.0388) - 0.1161(.0388 - .0461) = 0.0575 \text{ or } 5.75\%$$
$$\text{Predicted PE} = 1/.0575 = 17.40$$

Since the S&P 500 was trading at a multiple of 21.71 times earnings in early 2024, this would have indicated an overvalued market. This regression can be enriched by adding other variables that should be correlated to the price-earnings ratio, such as expected growth in gross national product (GNP) and payout ratios as independent variables. In fact, an argument can be made that the influx of technology stocks into the S&P 500 over the past two decades, the increase in return on equity at U.S. companies over the same period, and a decline in risk premiums could all explain the increase in PE ratios over the period.

Comparing PE Ratios Across Countries Comparisons are often made between price-earnings ratios in different countries with the intention of finding undervalued and overvalued markets. Markets with lower PE ratios are viewed as undervalued, and those with higher PE ratios are considered overvalued. Given the wide differences that exist between countries on fundamentals, it is misleading to draw these conclusions. For instance, you would expect to see the following, other things remaining equal:

- Countries with higher real interest rates should have lower PE ratios than countries with lower real interest rates.
- Countries with higher expected real growth should have higher PE ratios than countries with lower real growth.
- Countries that are viewed as riskier (and thus command higher risk premiums) should have lower PE ratios than safer countries.
- Countries where companies are more efficient in their investments (and earn a higher return on equity on these investments) should trade at higher PE ratios.

ILLUSTRATION 18.5: PE Ratios in Markets with Different Fundamentals

Table 18.5 summary economic statistics for stock markets in two different countries—country 1 and country 2. The key difference between the two countries is that real interest rates are much higher in country 1.

TABLE 18.5 Summary Macroeconomic Statistics

	Country 1	Country 2
T-bond rate	10.00%	5.00%
Market premium	4.00%	5.50%
Expected inflation	4.00%	4.00%
Expected growth in real GNP	2.00%	3.00%
Average payout ratio	50%	50%
Expected PE ratio	$(0.5 \times 1.06)/(.14 - .06) = 6.625$	$(0.5 \times 1.07)/(.105 - .07) = 15.29$

In this case, the expected PE ratio in country 2 is significantly higher than the PE ratio in country 1, but it can be justified on the basis of differences in financial fundamentals. (Note that nominal growth = real growth rate + expected inflation.)

ILLUSTRATION 18.6: Comparing PE Ratios across Markets—July 2000

This principle can be extended to broader comparisons of PE ratios across countries. Table 18.6 summarizes PE ratios across different developed markets in July 2000, together with dividend yields and interest rates (short-term and long-term) at that time:

TABLE 18.6 Market Characteristics—Country comparison

Country	PE	Dividend Yield	2-Year Rate	10-Year Rate	10-Year – 2-Year
United Kingdom	22.02	2.59%	5.93%	5.85%	−0.08%
Germany	26.33	1.88%	5.06%	5.32%	0.26%
France	29.04	1.34%	5.11%	5.48%	0.37%

Country	PE	Dividend Yield	2-Year Rate	10-Year Rate	10-Year – 2-Year
Switzerland	19.60	1.42%	3.62%	3.83%	0.21%
Belgium	14.74	2.66%	5.15%	5.70%	0.55%
Italy	28.23	1.76%	5.27%	5.70%	0.43%
Sweden	32.39	1.11%	4.67%	5.26%	0.59%
Netherlands	21.10	2.07%	5.10%	5.47%	0.37%
Australia	21.69	3.12%	6.29%	6.25%	−0.04%
Japan	52.25	0.71%	0.58%	1.85%	1.27%
United States	25.14	1.10%	6.05%	5.85%	−0.20%
Canada	26.14	0.99%	5.70%	5.77%	0.07%

A naive comparison of PE ratios suggests that Japanese stocks, with a PE ratio of 52.25, were overvalued, while Belgian stocks, with a PE ratio of 14.74, are undervalued. There were, however, a strong negative correlation between PE ratios and 10-year interest rates (−.73) and a positive correlation between the PE ratio and the spread between long- and short-term rates (.70). A cross-sectional regression of PE ratio on interest rates and expected growth yields the following:

PE ratio = 42.62 − 360.9 10-year rate + 846.61(10-year rate − 2-year rate) $R^2 = 59\%$

      [2.78]   [1.41]   [1.08]

The coefficients are of marginal significance, partly because of the small size of the sample. Based on this noisy regression, the predicted PE ratios for the countries are shown in the Table 18.7:

TABLE 18.7   Actual versus Predicted PE ratios

Country	Actual PE	Predicted PE	Under- or Overvalued
United Kingdom	22.02	20.83	5.71%
Germany	26.33	25.62	2.76%
France	29.04	25.98	11.80%
Switzerland	19.60	30.58	−35.90%
Belgium	14.74	26.71	−44.81%
Italy	28.23	25.69	9.89%
Sweden	32.39	28.63	13.12%
Netherlands	21.10	26.01	−18.88%
Australia	21.69	19.73	9.96%
Japan	52.25	46.70	11.89%
United States	25.14	19.81	26.88%
Canada	26.14	22.39	16.75%

From this comparison, Belgian and Swiss stocks would be the most undervalued, while U.S. stocks would have been the most overvalued. It is worth remembering that the low R-squared on the regression will result in wide ranges on the predicted values.

ILLUSTRATION 18.7:   An Example with Emerging Markets—End of 2000

This example is extended to examine PE ratio differences across emerging markets at the end of 2000. In Table 18.8, the country risk factor is that estimated by the *Economist* for these emerging markets, scaled from 0 (safest) to 100 (riskiest).

TABLE 18.8   Summary Macroeconomic Statistics—Emerging Markets

Country	PE Ratio	Interest Rate	GDP Real Growth	Country Risk
Argentina	14	18.00%	2.50%	45
Brazil	21	14.00%	4.80%	35
Chile	25	9.50%	5.50%	15
Hong Kong	20	8.00%	6.00%	15
India	17	11.48%	4.20%	25
Indonesia	15	21.00%	4.00%	50
Malaysia	14	5.67%	3.00%	40
Mexico	19	11.50%	5.50%	30
Pakistan	14	19.00%	3.00%	45
Peru	15	18.00%	4.90%	50
Philippines	15	17.00%	3.80%	45
Singapore	24	6.50%	5.20%	5
South Korea	21	10.00%	4.80%	25
Thailand	21	12.75%	5.50%	25
Turkey	12	25.00%	2.00%	35
Venezuela	20	15.00%	3.50%	45

The regression of PE ratios on these variables provides the following:

PE = 16.16 − 7.94 Interest rates + 154.40 Real growth − 0.112 Country risk $R^2 = 74\%$
    [3.61]   [0.52]   [2.38]   [1.78]

Countries with higher real growth and lower country risk have higher PE ratios, but the level of interest rates seems to have only a marginal impact. The regression can be used to estimate the price- earnings ratio for Turkey:

Predicted PE for Turkey = 16.16 − 7.94(.25) + 154.40(.02) − 0.112(35) = 13.354

At a PE ratio of 12, the market would have been viewed as slightly undervalued.

Comparing PE Ratios across Firms in a Sector   The most common approach to estimating the PE ratio for a firm is to choose a group of comparable firms, to calculate the average PE ratio for this group, and to subjectively adjust this average for differences between the firm being valued and the comparable firms. There are several problems with this approach. First, the definition of a comparable firm is essentially a subjective one. The use of other firms in the industry as the control group is often not the solution because firms within the same industry can have very different business mixes and risk and growth profiles. There is also plenty of potential for bias. One clear example of this is in takeovers, where a high PE ratio for the target firm is justified using the price earnings ratios of a control group of other firms that have been taken over. This group is designed to give an upwardly biased estimate of the PE ratio and other multiples. Second, even when a legitimate group of comparable firms can be constructed, differences will continue to persist in fundamentals between the firm being valued and this group. It is very difficult to subjectively adjust for differences across firms. Thus, knowing that a firm has much higher growth potential than other firms in the comparable firm list would lead you to expect to see a higher PE ratio for that firm, but how much higher is an open question.

The alternative to subjective adjustments is to control explicitly for the one or two variables that you believe account for the bulk of the differences in PE ratios across companies in the sector in a regression. The regression equation can then be used to estimate predicted PE ratios for each firm in the sector, and these predicted values can be compared to the actual PE ratios to make judgments on whether stocks are under- or overpriced.

ILLUSTRATION 18.8:   Comparing PE Ratios for Global Telecom Firms—September 2000

Table 18.9 summarizes the trailing PE ratios for global telecom firms with American depositary receipts (ADRs) listed in the United States in September 2000. The earnings per share used are those estimated using generally accepted accounting principles in the United States, and thus should be much more directly comparable than the earnings reported by these firms in their local markets.

TABLE 18.9   Global Telecom Company Pricing in 2000

Company Name	Trailing PE	Expected Growth in EPS	Emerging Market Dummy Variable
APT Satellite Holdings ADR	31.00	33.00%	1
Asia Satellite Telecom Holdings ADR	19.60	16.00%	1
British Telecommunications PLC ADR	25.70	7.00%	0
Cable & Wireless PLC ADR	29.80	14.00%	0
Deutsche Telekom AG ADR	24.60	11.00%	0
France Telecom SA ADR	45.20	19.00%	0
Gilat Communications	22.70	31.00%	1
Hellenic Telecommunication ADR	12.80	12.00%	1
Korea Telecom ADR	71.30	44.00%	1
Matav RT ADR	21.50	22.00%	1
Nippon Telegraph & Telephone ADR	44.30	20.00%	0
Portugal Telecom SA ADR	20.80	13.00%	0
PT Indosat ADR	7.80	6.00%	1
Royal KPN NV ADR	35.70	13.00%	0
Swisscom AG ADR	18.30	11.00%	0
Tele Danmark AS ADR	27.00	9.00%	0
Telebras ADR	8.90	7.50%	1
Telecom Argentina ADR B	12.50	8.00%	1
Telecom Corp of New Zealand ADR	11.20	11.00%	0
Telecom Italia SPA ADR	42.20	14.00%	0
Telecomunicaciones de Chile ADR	16.60	8.00%	1
Telefonica SA ADR	32.50	18.00%	0
Telefonos de Mexico ADR L	21.10	14.00%	1
Telekomunikasi Indonesia ADR	28.40	32.00%	1
Telstra ADR	21.70	12.00%	0

The earnings per share represent trailing earnings, and the price-earnings ratios for the firms are reported in the second column. The analyst estimates of expected growth in earnings per share over the next five years are shown in the next column. In the last column, we introduce a dummy variable indicating whether the firm is from an emerging market or a developed one, since emerging market telecom firms are likely to be exposed to far more risk. Not surprisingly, the firms with the lowest PE ratios, such as Telebras and PT Indosat, are from emerging markets.

Regressing the PE ratio for the sector against the expected growth rate and the emerging market dummy yields the following results:

$$\text{PE ratio} = 13.12 + 121.22 \text{ Expected growth} - 13.85 \text{ Emerging market dummy} \qquad R^2 = 66\%$$
$$[3.78] \quad [6.29] \qquad\qquad\qquad\qquad [3.84]$$

Firms with higher growth have significantly higher PE ratios than firms with lower expected growth. In addition, this regression indicates that an emerging market telecom firm should trade at a much lower PE ratio than one in a developed market. Using this regression to get predicted values in Table 18.10:

TABLE 18.10   Actual versus Predicted PE ratios

Company Name	Actual PE	Predicted PE	Under- or Overvalued
APT Satellite Holdings ADR	31.00	39.27	−21.05%
Asia Satellite Telecom Holdings ADR	19.60	18.66	5.05%
British Telecommunications PLC ADR	25.70	21.60	18.98%
Cable & Wireless PLC ADR	29.80	30.09	−0.95%
Deutsche Telekom AG ADR	24.60	26.45	−6.99%
France Telecom SA ADR	45.20	36.15	25.04%
Gilat Communications	22.70	36.84	−38.38%
Hellenic Telecommunication SA ADR	12.80	13.81	−7.31%
Korea Telecom ADR	71.30	52.60	35.55%
Matav RT ADR	21.50	25.93	−17.09%
Nippon Telegraph & Telephone ADR	44.30	37.36	18.58%
Portugal Telecom SA ADR	20.80	28.87	−27.96%
PT Indosat ADR	7.80	6.54	19.35%
Royal KPN NV ADR	35.70	28.87	23.64%
Swisscom AG ADR	18.30	26.45	−30.81%
Tele Danmark AS ADR	27.00	24.03	12.38%
Telebras ADR	8.90	8.35	6.54%
Telecom Argentina ADR B	12.50	8.96	39.51%
Telecom Corp of New Zealand ADR	11.20	26.45	−57.66%
Telecom Italia SPA ADR	42.20	30.09	40.26%
Telecomunicaciones de Chile ADR	16.60	8.96	85.27%
Telefonica SA ADR	32.50	34.94	−6.97%
Telefonos de Mexico ADR L	21.10	16.23	29.98%
Telekomunikasi Indonesia ADR	28.40	38.05	−25.37%
Telstra ADR	21.70	27.66	−21.55%

Based on the predicted PE ratios, Telecom Corporation of New Zealand is the most undervalued firm in this group, and Telecomunicaciones de Chile is the most overvalued firm. A Chilean analyst might point out that this is because Chile, at least in 2000, was much safer than other emerging markets, with justification, but that is the peril with using a dummy variable for this risk. Using country risk scores or ratings for countries may allow us to differentiate better between countries.

Comparing PE Ratios across Firms in the Market In the preceding section, comparable firms were narrowly defined to be other firms in the same business. This section considers ways in which we can expand the number of comparable firms by looking at an entire sector or even the market. There are two advantages in doing this. The first is that the estimates may become more precise as the number of comparable firms increase. The second is that it enables you to pinpoint when firms in a small subgroup are being under- or overvalued relative to the rest of the sector or the market. Since the differences across firms will increase when you loosen the definition of comparable firms, you have to adjust for these differences. The simplest way of doing this is with a multiple regression, with the PE ratio as the dependent variable, and proxies for risk, growth, and payout forming the independent variables.

Past Studies One of the earliest regressions of PE ratios against fundamentals across the entire market was done by Kisor and Whitbeck in (1963). Using data from the Bank of New York as of June 1962 for 135 stocks, they arrived at the following regression:

$$PE = 8.2 + 1.5 \text{ (Growth rate in earnings)} + 6.7 \text{ (Payout ratio)}$$
$$- .2 \text{ (Standard deviation in EPS changes)}$$

Cragg and Malkiel followed up by estimating the coefficients for a regression of the price-earnings ratio on the growth rate, the payout ratio, and the beta for stocks for the time period from 1961 to 1965, in Table 18.11:

TABLE 18.11 Market Regressions from 1961 to 1965

Year	Equation	R-Squared
1961	$PE = 4.73 + 3.28 \, g + 2.05 \, \pi - 0.85 \, \beta$	0.70
1962	$PE = 11.06 + 1.75 \, g + 0.78 \, \pi - 1.61 \, \beta$	0.70
1963	$PE = 2.94 + 2.55 \, g + 7.62 \, \pi - 0.27 \, \beta$	0.75
1964	$PE = 6.71 + 2.05 \, g + 5.23 \, \pi - 0.89 \, \beta$	0.75
1965	$PE = 0.96 + 2.74 \, g + 5.01 \, \pi - 0.35 \, \beta$	0.85

where
PE = Price-earnings ratio at the start of the year
g = Growth rate in earnings
π = Earnings payout ratio at the start of the year
β = Beta of the stock

They concluded that while such models were useful in explaining PE ratios, they were of little use in predicting performance. In both these studies, the three variables used—payout, risk, and growth—represent the three variables that were identified as the determinants of PE ratios in an earlier section.

The regressions were updated from 1987 to 1991 in the first edition of this book using a much broader sample of stocks.[2] The results are summarized in Table 18.12:

---

[2]These regressions look at all stocks listed on the Compustat database. The growth rate over the previous five years was used as the expected growth rate, and the betas were estimated from the CRSP tape.

TABLE 18.12   Market Regressions from 1987 to 1991

Year	Regression	R-Squared
1987	PE = 7.1839 + 13.05 Payout − 0.6259 Beta + 6.5659 EGR	0.9287
1988	PE = 2.5848 + 29.91 Payout − 4.5157 Beta + 19.9143 EGR	0.9465
1989	PE = 4.6122 + 59.74 Payout − 0.7546 Beta + 9.0072 EGR	0.5613
1990	PE = 3.5955 + 10.88 Payout − 0.2801 Beta + 5.4573 EGR	0.3497
1991	PE = 2.7711 + 22.89 Payout − 0.1326 Beta + 13.8653 EGR	0.3217

where EGR is a historical growth rate in EPS. Note the volatility in the R-squared over time and the changes in the coefficients on the independent variables. For instance, the R-squared in the regressions reported declines from 0.93 in 1987 to 0.32 in 1991, and the coefficients change dramatically over time. Part of the reason for these shifts is that earnings are volatile, and price-earnings ratios reflect this volatility. The low R-squared for the 1991 regression can be ascribed to the recession's effects on earnings in that year. These regressions are clearly not stable, and the predicted values are likely to be noisy.

Updated Market Regressions   The data needed to run market regressions is much more easily available today than it was for these earlier studies. In this section, the results of two regressions are presented. In the first regression, run in January 2024, the PE ratio was regressed against payout ratios, betas, and expected growth for all firms in the market:[3]

$$PE = -2.11 + 69.57 \text{ (Expected growth rate)} + 20.76 \text{ (Beta)} + 11.38 \text{ (Payout ratio)}$$
$$[1.89] \quad [13.57] \qquad\qquad\qquad [13.83] \qquad\qquad [7.87]$$
$$\text{R-squared} = 33.4\% \qquad\qquad \text{Number of observations} = 1755$$

With the sample size of 1,755 firms, this regression represents the broadest measure of relative value. This regression has a low R-squared, but it is more a reflection of the noise in PE ratios than it is on the regression methodology. As you will see, the market regressions for price-to-book value tend to be better behaved and have a higher R-squared than PE ratio regressions. The other disquieting finding is that the coefficients on the variables do not always have the signs you would expect them to have. For instance, higher-risk stocks (higher betas) have higher PE ratios, when fundamentals would lead you to expect the opposite.

The coefficient on the expected growth rate in the regressions offers some useful insight into how the market is pricing growth differences across stocks. In Table 18.13, we report this number at the end of each year from 2000 to 2024, in conjunction with the implied equity risk premiums that we computed in Chapter 7 (as a price of risk).

In January 2000, at the peak of the dot-com boom, the market was paying a very high price for growth, while charging very little for risk; not surprisingly, high-growth,

---

[3] The t statistics are reported in brackets below the coefficients.

high-risk firms traded at sky-high PE ratios. By January 2002, the mood had shifted, with the price for growth dropping by more than 50 percent and the price of risk increasing almost 80 percent. In January 2009, right after the banking crisis, the market price for risk was 6.43 percent (the highest level in 30 years), and the price paid for growth was low; the median PE ratio for U.S. firms was in single digits, as a consequence. As you can see, this table reflects the battle in markets between greed (in the desire for growth) and fear (in the price of risk), with one winning out in some periods, and the other in other periods.

Global Regressions As access to data has improved, we have started running these regressions across global markets. In table 18.14, we summarize the regression results at the start of 2024 for geographical groupings—Europe, Emerging markets, Australia, New Zealand & Canada, Japan and the United States, as well as for a global universe of companies. The results are in Table 18.14.

There are clearly differences across markets both in terms of explanatory power (R squared) and the relationship with variables (coefficients), but notice also what they share in common. In every geographical segment, growth remains the dominant variable explaining differences in PE ratios fo companies operating in that segment.

TABLE 18.13 ERP and Growth Coefficients—2000–2024

Start of Year	g Coefficient	ERP	Start of Year	g Coefficient	ERP
2000	2.11	2.05%	2013	5.78%	0.58
2001	1.46	2.75%	2014	1.49	4.96%
2002	1.00	3.62%	2015	0.99	5.78%
2003	2.62	4.10%	2016	0.75	6.12%
2004	0.81	3.69%	2017	1.71	5.69%
2005	0.91	3.65%	2018	1.14	5.08%
2006	1.13	4.07%	2019	1.40	5.96%
2007	1.18	4.16%	2020	1.37	5.20%
2008	1.43	4.37%	2021	2.28	4.72%
2009	0.78	6.43%	2022	0.49	4.24%
2010	0.55	4.36%	2023	0.46	5.94%
2011	0.84	5.20%	2024	0.70	4.60%
2012	0.41	6.04%			

TABLE 18.14 PE Market Regressions—Start of 2024

Region	Regression	R-squared
United States	PE = − 2.11 + 20.76 Beta + 69.57 g_{EPS} + 11.38 Payout	33.6%
Europe	PE = 11.89 + 1.47 Beta + 32.44 g_{EPS} + 13.18 Payout	15.5%
Japan	PE = 4.65 + 6.94 Beta + 25.75 g_{EPS} + 17.17 Payout	23.2%
Australia, NZ & Canada	PE = 15.02 + 0.06 Beta + 41.70 g_{EPS} + 3.71 Payout	24.8%
Emerging markets	PE = 14.41 − 1.24 Beta + 92.94 g_{EPS} + 7.49 Payout	24.8%
Global	PE = 16.90 + 3.20 Beta + 51.53 g_{EPS} + 2.68 Payout	17.2%

Problems with the Regression Methodology The regression methodology offers a convenient way of compressing large amounts of data into one equation capturing the relationship between PE ratios and financial fundamentals. But it does have its limitations. First, the independent variables are correlated with each other.[4] For example, high-growth firms tend to have high-risk and low-payout ratios, as is clear from Table 18.15, which summarizes the correlations between beta, growth, and payout ratios for all U.S. firms. Note the negative correlation between payout ratios and growth, and the positive correlation between beta and growth. This multicollinearity makes the coefficients of the regressions unreliable (increased standard error), and may explain the wrong signs on the coefficients (such as beta having a positive coefficient) and the large changes in these coefficients from period to period. Second, the regression is based on a linear relationship between PE ratios and the fundamentals, and that might not be appropriate. An analysis of the residuals from a regression may suggest transformations of the independent variables (squared or natural logs) that work better in explaining PE ratios. Third, the basic relationship between PE ratios and financial variables itself is not stable, and if it shifts from year to year, the predictions from the regression equation may not be reliable for extended periods. For all these reasons, the regression approach is useful, but it has to be viewed as one more tool in the search for true value.

TABLE 18.15 Pearson Correlations between Independent Variables

		Correlation[a]			
		Trailing PE	Beta	Payout ratio	Expetced growth rate in EPS—Next 5 years
Trailing PE	Correlation	1	.116**	.167**	.091**
	Sig. (2-tailed)		<.001	<.001	.002
	N	2607	2481	2586	1114
Beta	Correlation	.116**	1	−.005	.140**
	Sig. (2-tailed)	<.001		.797	<.001
	N	2481	5634	2589	1444
Payout ratio	Correlation	.167**	−.005	1	−.154**
	Sig. (2-tailed)	<.001	.797		<.001
	N	2586	2589	2728	1157
Expetced growth rate in EPS- Next 5 years	Correlation	.091**	.140**	−.154**	1
	Sig. (2-tailed)	.002	<.001	<.001	
	N	1114	1444	1157	1462

** Correlation is significant at the 0.01 level (2–tailed).
[a] Broad Group = United States

---

[4]In a multiple regression, the independent variables should be independent of each other.

ILLUSTRATION 18.9: Valuing Procter & Gamble (PG) Using the Market Regression in 2024

In an earlier illustration, we estimated the intrinsic PE ratio for Procter and Gamble in 2011, using a 2-stage dividend discount model. In this illustration, we will price P&G in 2024 using the PE market regression for U.S. stocks in January 2024. To price P&G using the broader regression, you would first have to estimate the values, for P&G, of the independent variables in the regression:

P&G's beta = 0.65

P&G's payout ratio = 61.48%

P&G's expected growth rate = 11.45%

Note that these variables have been defined consistently with the variables in the regression. Thus, the growth rate over the next five years, the beta over the past five years, and the payout ratio over the most recent four quarters are used to make the prediction. Based on the price-earnings ratio regression for all stocks in the market, you would get a predicted PE ratio of:

$$PE = -2.11 + 20.76(0.65) + 69.57(.1145) + 11.38(.6148) = 26.35$$

Based on the market regression, you would expect P&G to be trading at 26.35 times earnings. At its actual PE ratio of 26.50, the stock looks close to fairly priced, relative to the market.

 MReg.htm: This dataset on the web reports the results of the latest regression of PE ratios against fundamentals, using all firms in the market.

NORMALIZING EARNINGS FOR PE RATIOS

The dependence of PE ratios on current earnings makes them particularly vulnerable to the year-to-year swings that often characterize reported earnings. In making comparisons, therefore, it may make much more sense to use normalized earnings. The process used to normalize earnings varies widely, but the most common approach is a simple averaging of earnings across time. For a cyclical firm, for instance, you would average the earnings per share across a cycle. In doing so, you should adjust for inflation. If you do decide to normalize earnings for the firm you are valuing, consistency demands that you normalize them for the comparable firms in the sample as well.

THE PEG RATIO

Portfolio managers and analysts sometimes compare PE ratios to the expected growth rate to identify undervalued and overvalued stocks. In the simplest form of this approach, firms with PE ratios less than their expected growth rate are viewed as undervalued. In its more general form, the ratio of PE ratio to growth (PEG) is used as a measure of relative value, with a lower value believed to indicate that a firm is undervalued. For many analysts, especially those tracking firms in high-growth sectors, these approaches offer the promise of a way of controlling for differences in growth across firms, while preserving the inherent simplicity of a multiple.

Definition of PEG Ratio

The PEG ratio is defined to be the price-earnings ratio divided by the expected growth rate in earnings per share:

$$\text{PEG ratio} = \frac{\text{PE ratio}}{\text{Expected growth in earnings per share (in absolute terms)}}$$

For instance, a firm with a PE ratio of 20 and a growth rate of 10 percent is estimated to have a PEG ratio of 2. Consistency requires that the growth rate used in this estimate be the growth rate in earnings per share rather than operating income, because PEG ratio is an equity multiple.

Given the many definitions of the PE ratio, which one should you use to estimate the PEG ratio? The answer depends on the base on which the expected growth rate is computed. If the expected growth rate in earnings per share is based on earnings in the most recent year (current earnings), the PE ratio that should be used is the current PE ratio. If it is based on trailing earnings, the PE ratio used should be the trailing PE ratio. The forward PE ratio should never be used in this computation, since it may result in a double-counting of growth. To see why, assume that you have a firm with a current price of $30 and current earnings per share of $1.50. The firm is expected to double its earnings per share over the next year (forward earnings per share will be $3.00), and then have earnings growth of 5 percent a year for the following four years. An analyst estimating growth in earnings per share for this firm, with the current earnings per share as a base, will estimate a growth rate of 19.44%:

$$\text{Expected earnings growth} = \left[\left(1 + \text{Growth rate}_{\text{year 1}}\right)\right.$$
$$\left.\left(1 + \text{Growth rate}_{\text{years 2–5}}\right)^4\right]^{1/5} - 1$$
$$= [(1 + 1)(1.05)4]^{1/5} - 1 = .1944$$

If you used the forward PE ratio and this estimate of earnings growth to estimate the PEG ratio, you would get:

$$\text{PEG ratio based on forward PE} = \text{Forward PE/Expected growth}_{\text{next 5 years}}$$
$$= (\text{Price/Forward EPS})/\text{Expected growth}_{\text{next 5 years}}$$
$$= (\$30/\$3)/19.44 = 0.51$$

On a PEG ratio basis, this firm seems to be cheap. Note, however, that the growth in the first year has been counted twice—the forward earnings are high because of the doubling of earnings, leading to a low forward PE ratio, and the growth rate is high for the same reason. A consistent estimate of the PEG ratio would require using a current PE and the expected growth rate over the next five years:

$$\text{PEG ratio based on current PE} = (\text{Price/Current EPS})/\text{Expected growth rate}_{\text{next 5 years}}$$
$$= (\$30/\$1.50)/19.44 = 1.03$$

Alternatively, you could compute the PEG ratio based on forward earnings per share and the growth rate from years 2 through 5:

$$\text{PEG ratio based on forward PE} = (\text{Price/Forward EPS})/\text{Expected growth}_{\text{years 2--5}}$$
$$= (\$30/\$3)/5 = 2.0$$

If this approach is used, the PEG ratio would have to be estimated uniformly for all of the other comparable firms as well, using the forward PE and the expected growth rate from years 2 through 5.

Building on the theme of uniformity, the PEG ratio should be estimated using the same growth estimates for all firms in the sample. You should not, for instance, use five-year growth rates for some firms and one-year growth rates for others. One way of ensuring uniformity is to use the same source for earnings growth estimates for all the firms in the group. For instance, many data services provide consensus estimates from analysts of earnings per share growth over the next five years for most U.S. firms. Alternatively, you could estimate expected growth rates for each company in the group.

Cross-Sectional Distribution of PEG Ratios

Now that the PEG ratio has been defined, the cross-sectional distribution of PEG ratios across U.S. and global firms, at the start of 2024, is examined in Figure 18.7. In estimating these PEG ratios, the estimates of growth in earnings per share over the next five years are

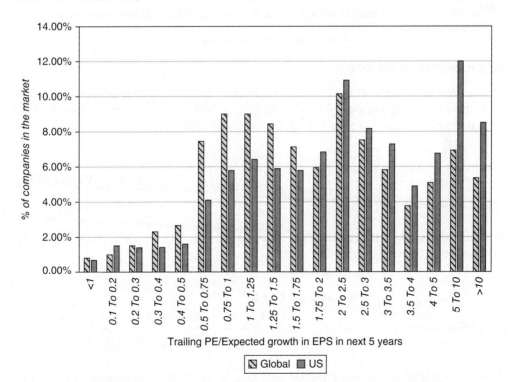

FIGURE 18.7 PEG Ratios for U.S and Global Firms—January 2024

TABLE 18.16 PEG ratio comparison—Software versus Market

Industry Name	PE	Expected growth—next 5 years	PEG Ratio
Software (Entertainment)	27.58	31.53%	0.87
Software (Internet)	33.60	37.52%	0.90
Software (System & Application)	42.07	24.30%	1.73
Total Market	21.45	13.02%	1.65

used in conjunction with the current PEs. The distribution of PEG ratios is less skewed than the distribution of PE ratios, with one important caveat. The PEG ratio can be computed only for those firms where there is an expected growth rate in earnings. Since this growth rate is usually provided by analysts, any firm that is not tracked by analysts will not have a PEG ratio (at least in our sample). Since smaller, younger firms tend not to be followed by analysts, this can create a subtle selection bias in the sample.

PEG ratios are most widely used in analyzing technology firms, but they need to be used with caution, because as we will see in the next section, risk is a wild card. In Table 18.16, we list out the PEG ratios for software companies in the United States at the start of 2024, and contrast them with the PEG ratio for the market:

At first sight, it looks like entertainment and internet software companies are a bargain, trading at PEG ratios that are much lower than the market, but that may be misleading because of the risk differences.

 pedata.xls: This dataset on the web summarizes the PEG ratios by industry for firms in the United States.

Determinants of the PEG Ratio

The determinants of the PEG ratio can be extracted using the same approach used to estimate the determinants of the PE ratio. In fact, we will start with the intrinsic (trailing) PE ratio that we derived for a high-growth firm earlier in this chapter:

$$\text{Trailing PE} = \frac{\text{Payout ratio} (1 + g) \left(1 - \dfrac{(1 + g)^n}{(1 + k_{e,hg})^n} \right)}{\left(k_{e,hg} - g \right)} + \frac{(1 + g)^n (1 + g_{st}) \text{Payout ratio}_{st}}{\left(k_{e,st} - g_{st} \right) \left(1 + k_{e,hg} \right)^n}$$

Dividing both sides of the equation the expected growth rate over the high-growth period (g) next, you can estimate the PEG ratio:

$$\text{PEG} = \frac{\text{Payout ratio} (1 + g) \left(1 - \dfrac{(1 + g)^n}{\left(1 + k_{e,hg} \right)^n} \right)}{\left(k_{e,hg} - g \right) \times g} + \frac{(1 + g)^n (1 + g_{st}) \text{Payout ratio}_{st}}{g \times \left(k_{e,st} - g_{st} \right) \left(1 + k_{e,hg} \right)^n}$$

Even a cursory glance at this equation suggests that analysts who believe that using the PEG ratio neutralizes the growth effect are mistaken. Instead of disappearing, the growth rate becomes even more deeply enmeshed in the multiple. In fact, as the growth rate increases, the effects on the PEG ratio can be both positive and negative and the net effect can vary depending on the level of the growth rate.

ILLUSTRATION 18.10:   Estimating the PEG Ratio for a Firm

Assume that you have been asked to estimate the PEG ratio for a firm that has the same characteristics as the firm described in Illustration 18.1:

Growth rate in first five years = 20%	Payout ratio in first five years = 20%
Growth rate after five years = 4%	Payout ratio after five years = 60%
Beta = 1.0	Risk-free rate = T-bond rate = 4.5%
Required rate of return = 4.5% + 1(5%) = 9.5%	Equity risk premium = 5%

The PEG ratio can be estimated as follows:

$$PEG = \frac{0.20\,(1.20)\,\left(1 - \dfrac{(1.20)^5}{(1.095)^5}\right)}{(.095 - .20) \times (.20)} + \frac{(1.20)^5\,(1.04)\,(0.60)}{.20\,(.095 - .04)\,(1.095)^5} = 0.96$$

The PEG ratio for this firm, based on fundamentals, is 0.96.

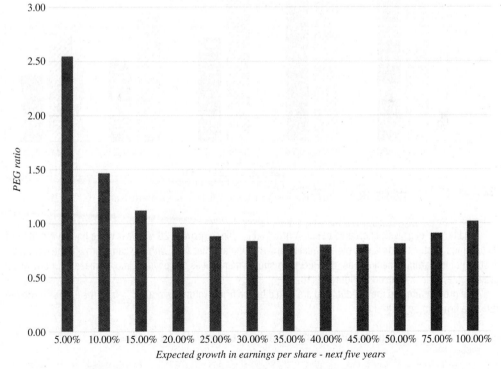

Expected growth in earnings per share - next five years

FIGURE 18.8   PEG Ratios, Expected Growth, and Interest Rates

Exploring the Relationship with Fundamentals

Consider first the effect of changing the growth rate during the high-growth period (next five years) from 20%. Figure 18.8 presents the PEG ratio as a function of the expected growth rate. As the growth rate increases, the PEG ratio initially decreases, flattens out at higher-growth rates, and then starts increasing again. This complicated relationship between PEG ratios and growth suggests that comparing PEG ratios across firms with widely different growth rates can be complicated.

Next, consider the effect of changing the riskiness (beta) of this firm on the PEG ratio. Figure 18.9 presents the PEG ratio as a function of the beta. Here, the relationship is clear. As the risk increases, the PEG ratio of a firm decreases. When comparing the PEG ratios of firms with different risk levels, even within the same sector, this would suggest that riskier firms should have lower PEG ratios than safer firms.

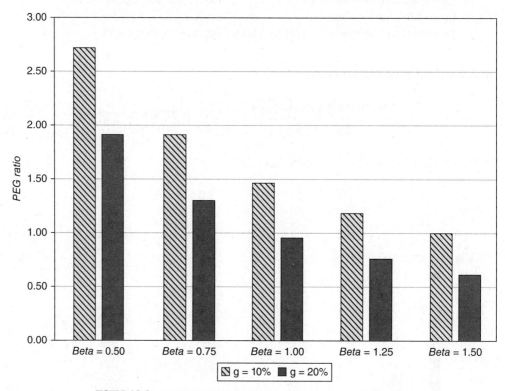

FIGURE 18.9   PEG Ratios and Beta: Different Growth Rates

Finally, not all growth is created equal. A firm that is able to grow at 20% a year while paying out 50% of its earnings to stockholders has higher-quality growth than another firm with the same growth rate that reinvests all of its earnings back. Thus, the PEG ratio should increase as the payout ratio increases, for any given growth rate, as is evidenced in Figure 18.10.

The growth rate and the payout ratio are linked by the firm's return on equity. In fact, the expected growth rate of a firm can be written as:

$$\text{Expected growth rate} = \text{Return on equity} \times (1 - \text{Payout ratio})$$

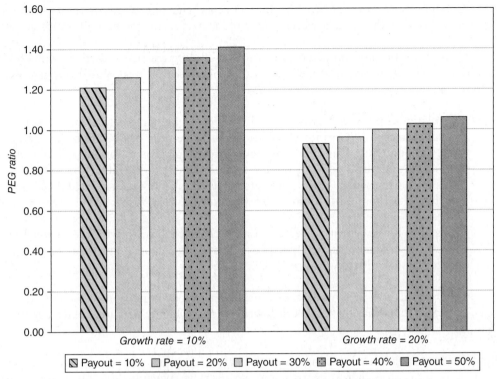

FIGURE 18.10   PEG Ratios and Payout Ratios

The PEG ratio should therefore be higher for firms with higher returns on equity for a given growth rate. In summary, even if fairly priced, you should expect see riskier firms and firms that earn lower returns on equity trade at lower PEG ratios than safer firms that generate higher returns on equity.

eqmult.xls: This spreadsheet allows you to estimate the PEG ratio for a stable-growth or high-growth firm, given its fundamentals.

Using the PEG Ratio for Comparisons

As with the PE ratio, the PEG ratio is used to compare the valuations of firms that are in the same business. As noted in the preceding section, the PEG ratio is a function of the risk, growth potential, and payout ratio of a firm. This section looks at ways of using the PEG ratio and examines some of the problems in comparing PEG ratios across firms.

Direct Comparisons   Most analysts who use PEG ratios compute them for firms within a sector (or comparable firm group) and compare these ratios. Firms with lower PEG ratios are usually viewed as undervalued, even if growth rates are different across the firms being compared. This approach is based on the incorrect perception that PEG ratios control for differences in growth. In fact, direct comparisons of PEG ratios work only if firms are similar in terms of growth potential, risk, and payout ratios (or returns on equity). If this were the case, however, you could just as easily compare PE ratios across firms.

When PEG ratios are compared across firms with different risk, growth, payout characteristics, and judgments are made about valuations based on this comparison, you will tend to find that:

- The relationship between growth and PEG ratios is a unpredictable one. Initially, as growth increases, PEG ratios decrease, but at some point the relationship reverses itself. Put differently, firms with very low or very high growth rates will have higher PEG ratios than firms whose growth rates fall in the middle. (See Figure 18.8.)
- Higher-risk firms will have lower PEG ratios and look more undervalued than lower-risk firms, because PEG ratios tend to decrease as a firm's risk increases (see Figure 18.9).
- Firms with lower returns on equity (or lower payout ratios) will have lower PEG ratios and look more undervalued than firms with higher returns on equity and higher payout ratios (see Figure 18.10).

In short, firms that look undervalued based on direct comparison of the PEG ratios may, in fact, be firms with higher risk or lower returns on equity that are, in fact, correctly valued.

Controlled Comparisons   When comparing PEG ratios across firms, it is important that you control for differences in risk, growth, and payout ratios when making the comparison. While you can attempt to do this subjectively, the complicated relationship between PEG ratios and these fundamentals can pose a challenge. A far more promising route is to use the regression approach suggested for PE ratios, and to relate the PEG ratios of the firms being compared to measures of risk, growth potential, and the payout ratio.

As with the PE ratio, the comparable firms in this analysis can be defined narrowly (as other firms that look just like the firm you are valuing), more expansively as firms in the same sector, or as all firms in the market. In running these regressions, all the caveats that were presented for the PE regression continue to apply. The independent variables continue to be correlated with each other, and the relationship is both unstable and likely to be nonlinear. In fact, Figure 18.11, which provides a scatter plot of PEG ratios against growth rates for all U.S. stocks in January 2024, indicates the degree of nonlinearity.

In running the regression, especially when the sample contains firms with very different levels of growth, you could transform the growth rate to make the relationship more linear. A scatter plot of PEG ratios against the natural log of the expected growth rate, for instance, yields a much more linear relationship, as evidenced in Figure 18.12.

The results of the regression of PEG ratios against ln(expected growth), beta, and payout ratio are reported here for markets, broken down by geography, in January 2024, are reported in Table 18.17.

The low R-squared is indicative of the problems with this multiple and the difficulties you will run into in using it in comparisons across firms. In fact, the requirement for a long-term expected growth rate in earnings not only reduces the sample size substantially, but also creates bias, because smaller companies that are not tracked by analysts and companies in emerging markets that are lightly analyzed are lost in the sample.

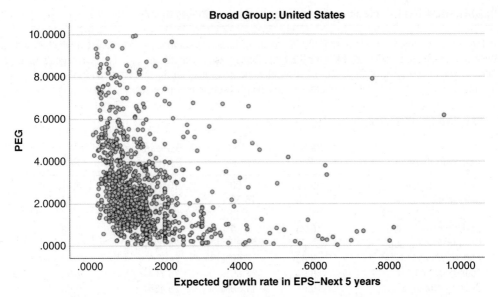

FIGURE 18.11 PEG Ratios versus Expected Growth Rates—January 2024

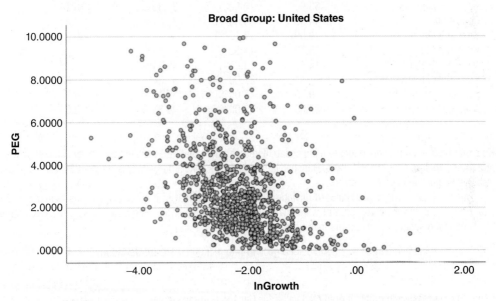

FIGURE 18.12 PEG Ratios versus ln(Expected Growth)—January 2024

TABLE 18.17 PEG Market Regressions—Start of 2024

Region	Regression	R-squared
United States	PEG = 0.24 + 0.87 Payout − 0.58 ln(g$_{EPS}$) − 1.28 Beta	8.6%
Europe	PEG = 0.42 + 0.96 Payout − 0.92 ln(g$_{EPS}$) − 0.12 Beta	19.5%
Japan	PEG = −0.31 Payout − 1.06 ln(g$_{EPS}$) + 0.16 Beta	23.2%
Australia, NZ, & Canada	PEG = 0.05 + 0.32 Payout − 1.64 ln(g$_{EPS}$) − 0.54 Beta	46.2%
Emerging markets	PEG = 1.06 + 0.20 Payout − 0.43 ln(g$_{EPS}$) − 0.12 Beta	9.0%
Global	PEG = 1.21 + 0.17 Payout − 0.70 ln(g$_{EPS}$) + 0.001 Beta	8.0%

ILLUSTRATION 18.11:   Revisiting the Beverage Sector in 2001—PEG Ratio

In the preceding chapter, we looked at the PE ratios for beverage companies and evaluated whether Andres Wine was cheap because it traded at a low PE ratio. Since there are significant differences in expected growth rates across the sector, in Table 18.18, we computed the PEG ratios for the firms and report these along with the annualized standard deviations of stock prices over the previous two years:

TABLE 18.18   PEG ratios for Beverage companies

Company Name	Trailing PE	Expected Growth	Standard Deviation	PEG
Coca-Cola Bottling	29.18	9.50%	20.58%	3.07
Molson Inc. Ltd. "A"	43.65	15.50%	21.88%	2.82
Anheuser-Busch 24.	31	11.00%	22.92%	2.21
Corby Distilleries Ltd.	16.24	7.50%	23.66%	2.16
Chalone Wine Group	21.76	14.00%	24.08%	1.55
Andres Wines Ltd. "A"	8.96	3.50%	24.70%	2.56
Todhunter Int'l	8.94	3.00%	25.74%	2.98
Brown-Forman "B"	10.07	11.50%	29.43%	0.88
Coors (Adolph) "B"	23.02	10.00%	29.52%	2.30
PepsiCo, Inc.	33.00	10.50%	31.35%	3.14
Coco-Cola	44.33	19.00%	35.51%	2.33
Boston Beer "A"	10.59	17.13%	39.58%	0.62
Whitman Corp.	25.19	11.50%	44.26%	2.19
Mondavi (Robert) "A"	16.47	14.00%	45.84%	1.18
Coca-Cola Enterprises	37.14	27.00%	51.34%	1.38
Hansen Natural Corp.	9.70	17.00%	62.45%	0.57
Average	22.66	13.00%	0.33%	2.00

Note that Andres Wine is no longer looking cheap, if you compare that PEG ratio to the average; its low-growth rate translates into a higher PEG ratio. Hansen Natural still looks like a bargain, trading at a PEG ratio of 0.57, well below the average for the sector.

Hansen is still riskier (its standard deviation is almost twice that of the sector) and has higher growth than other firms in the sector, both of which can contribute to a lower PEG ratio. Regressing the PEG ratios for firms in the sector, we obtain the following:

$$PEG = 3.61 - 2.86 \text{ Expected growth rate} - 3.38 \text{ (Standard deviation)}$$
$$[6.86] \quad [0.75] \qquad\qquad\qquad [2.04]$$

Using this regression to obtain a predicted value for Hansen Natural, we get:

$$PEG_{Hansen} = 3.61 - 2.86(.1700) - 3.38(.6245) = 1.01$$

At a PEG ratio of 0.57, the firm remains significantly undervalued.

 MReg.xls: This dataset on the web summarizes the results of the most recent regression of PEG ratios against fundamentals for U.S. stocks.

WHOSE GROWTH RATE?

In computing PEG ratios, we are often faced with the question of whose growth rate we will use in estimating the PEG ratios. If the number of firms in the sample is small, you could estimate expected growth for each firm yourself. If the number of firms increases, you will have no choice but to use analyst estimates of expected growth for the firms. Will this expose your analyses to all of the biases in these estimates? Not necessarily. If the bias is uniform—for instance, analysts overestimate growth for all of the firms in the sector—you will still be able to make comparisons of PEG ratios across firms and draw reasonable conclusions.

OTHER VARIANTS ON THE PE RATIO

While the PE ratio and the PEG ratio may be the most widely used earnings multiples, there are other equity earnings multiples that are also used by analysts. In this section, three variants are considered. The first is the relative PE ratio, the second is a multiple of price to earnings in a future year (say 5 or 10 years from now), and the third is a multiple of price to earnings prior to R&D expenses (used primarily for technology firms).

Relative PE Ratios

Relative price earnings ratios measure a firm's PE ratio relative to the market average. It is obtained by dividing a firm's current PE ratio by the average for the market:

$$\text{Relative PE ratio} = \frac{\text{Current PE ratio}_{\text{firm}}}{\text{Current PE ratio}_{\text{market}}}$$

Not surprisingly, the distribution of relative PE ratios mimics the distribution of the actual PE ratios, with one difference—the average relative PE ratio is 1. This measure can be generalized and relative PE ratios can be computed relative to the PE ratio for the industry that the company belongs or even to its own historical PE ratios.

Note that the relative PE ratio is a function of all of the variables that determine the PE ratio—the expected growth rate, the risk of the firm, and the payout ratio—but stated in terms relative to the market. Thus, a firm's relative PE ratio is a function of its relative growth rate in earnings per share (growth rate$_{\text{firm}}$/growth rate$_{\text{market}}$), its relative cost of equity (cost of equity$_{\text{firm}}$/cost of equity$_{\text{market}}$), and its relative return on equity (ROE$_{\text{firm}}$/ROE$_{\text{market}}$). Firms with higher relative growth, lower relative costs of equity, and higher relative returns on equity should trade at higher relative PE ratios.

There are two ways in which relative PEs are used in valuation. One is to compare a firm's relative PE ratio to its historical norms; Ford, for instance, may be viewed as undervalued because its relative PE ratio today is lower than the relative PE at which it has historically traded. The other is to compare relative PE ratios of firms in different markets; this allows comparisons when PE ratios in different markets vary significantly. For instance, we could have divided the PE ratios for each telecom firm in Illustration 18.8 by the PE ratio for the market in which this firm trades locally to estimate relative PE ratios and could have compared those ratios.

ILLUSTRATION 18.12:   Relative PE Ratios—Automobile Stocks in May 2011

In Table 18.19, we list all automobile companies with a market cap greater than $10 billion in May 2011. Because these firms are listed on different markets, we divide the PE ratio for each company by the aggregate PE ratio for the primary market in which each one trades.

TABLE 18.19   Relative PE ratios for auto companies in 2011

Company	Trailing PE	Primary Market	PE for Market	Relative PE
SAIC Motor Corporation	9.69	China	20.66	0.47
Dongfeng Motor Group Co.	9.01	China	20.66	0.44
Renault SA	3.25	France	15.86	0.21
Volkswagen AG	6.71	Germany	16.82	0.40
Daimler AG	10.37	Germany	16.82	0.62
BMW Group	9.29	Germany	16.82	0.55
Porsche Automobile Holding SE	2.81	Germany	16.82	0.17
Audi AG	10.32	Germany	16.82	0.61
Astra International tbk PT	15.63	Indonesia	21.82	0.72
Fiat S.p.A	14.64	Italy	15.02	0.97
Honda Motor Co., Ltd.	10.55	Japan	17.50	0.60
Toyota Motor Corp.	26.10	Japan	17.50	1.49
Nissan Motor Co. Ltd.	10.63	Japan	17.50	0.61
Suzuki Motor Corp.	22.42	Japan	17.50	1.28
Hyundai Motor Co.	8.50	S. Korea	16.98	0.50
Kia Motors Corp.	11.64	S. Korea	16.98	0.69
General Motors Co.	5.65	U.S.	19.16	0.30
Ford Motor Co.	7.87	U.S.	19.16	0.41

Porsche and Renault remain the cheapest firms on both a PE ratio and a relative PE basis, and Toyota and Suzuki are the most expensive firms, on both a PE and relative PE basis. In fact, the differences in PE ratios across markets are small enough that the rankings on a relative PE basis are very close to those on a PE basis. That would not have been true a decade ago, when Japanese stocks traded at much higher PE ratios than firms in other markets.

The average relative PE for Ford (to the U.S. market) has been 0.50 over the past four decades. At its current relative PE of 0.41, Ford looks cheap. GM also looks cheap, making the same type of comparison, but GM in 2011, after its near-death experience in 2009, is a very different company from the one that existed in previous decades.

Price-to-Future (Forward) Earnings

The price-earnings ratio cannot be estimated for firms with negative earnings per share. While there are other multiples such as the price-to-sales ratio that can still be estimated for these firms, there are analysts who prefer the familiar ground of PE ratios. One way in which the price-earnings ratio can be modified for use in these firms is to use expected earnings per share in a future year in computing the PE ratio. For instance, assume that a firm has negative earnings per share currently of −$2.00 but is expected to report earnings per share in five years of $1.50 per share. You could divide the price today by the expected earnings per share in five years to obtain a PE ratio.

How would such a PE ratio be used? The PE ratio for all of the comparable firms would also have to be estimated using expected earnings per share in five years, and the resulting values can be compared across firms. Assuming that all of the firms in the sample share the same risk, growth, and payout characteristics after year 5, firms with low price-to-future-earnings ratios will be considered undervalued. An alternative approach is to estimate a target price for the negative-earnings firm in five years, dividing that price by earnings in that year and then comparing this PE ratio to the PE ratio of comparable firms today.

While this modified version of the PE ratio increases the reach of PE ratios to cover many firms that have negative earnings today, it is difficult to control for differences between the firm being valued and the comparable firms, because you are comparing firms at different points in time.

RELATIVE PE RATIOS AND MARKET GROWTH

As the expected growth rate on the market increases, the divergence in PE ratios increases, resulting in a bigger range for relative PE ratios. This can be illustrated very simply, if you consider the relative PE for a company that grows at half the rate of the market. When the market growth rate is 4 percent, this firm will trade at a PE that is roughly 80 percent of the market PE. When the market growth rate increases to 10 percent, the firm will trade at a PE that is 60 percent of the market PE.

This has consequences for analysts who use relative PE ratios. Stocks of firms whose earnings grow at a rate much lower than the market growth rate will often look cheap on a relative PE basis when the market growth rate is high and expensive when the market growth rate is low.

Price to Earnings before R&D Expenses

In the discussion of cash flows and capital expenditures in Chapter 4, it was argued that research and development expenses should be capitalized, since they represent investments for the future. Since accounting standards require that R&D be expensed rather than capitalized, the earnings of high-growth firms with substantial research expenses are likely to be understated, and the PE ratio is, therefore, likely to be overstated. This will especially be true if you are comparing technology firms, which have substantial research expenditures, to nontechnology firms, which usually do not. Even when comparing only across technology stocks, firms that are growing faster with larger R&D expenses will end up with lower earnings and higher PE ratios than more stable firms in the sector with lower R&D expenses. There are some analysts who argue that the PE ratio should be estimated using earnings prior to R&D expenses:

$$PE_{pre-R\&D} = \frac{\text{Market value of equity}}{(\text{Net Income} + \text{R\&D expense})}$$

The PE ratios that emerge from this calculation are likely to be much lower than the PE ratios using conventional definitions of earnings per share.

While the underlying logic behind this approach is sound, adding back R&D to earnings represents only a partial adjustment. To complete the adjustment, you would need to capitalize R&D expenses and compute the amortization of R&D expenses, as was done in Chapter 9. The adjusted PE would then be:

$$PE_{pre-R\&D} \frac{\text{Market value of equity}}{(\text{Net Income} + \text{R\&D expense} - \text{Amortization of research asset})}$$

These adjusted PE ratios can then be computed across firms in the sample.

This adjustment to the PE ratio, while taking care of one problem—the expensing of R&D—will still leave you exposed to all of the other problems associated with PE ratios. Earnings will continue to be volatile and affected by accounting choices, and differences in growth, risk, and cash flow characteristics will still cause price-earnings ratios to be different across firms. In addition, you will also have to estimate expected growth in earnings (pre-R&D) on your own, since consensus estimates from analysts will not be available for growth in this variable.

ILLUSTRATION 18.13: Forward PE Ratios—Amylin Pharmaceuticals in May 2011

In May 2011, there were dozens of biotechnology firms that were traded on the U.S. exchanges, but many of these firms were reporting losses, either because they had no commercial products yet or because the earnings were being outstripped by significant R&D expenses. We consider one such company: Amylin Pharmaceuticals, which was trading at $13.28 in May 2011. In the trailing 12 months leading into the valuation, the company reported a loss of −$1.05 and analysts were projecting losses of roughly 90 cents a share for both 2011 and 2012.

While conventional PE ratios cannot be estimated with negative earnings, there are two ways in which we can still employ PE ratios to analyze Amylin:

1. *Forward PE:* Analysts expect the firm's products to start generating significant profits in 2013, and the firm to generate earnings per share of $1.25 in 2016. Dividing the price today by the expected earnings per share in 2016 yields a value of 10.62:

   Forward PE = Price today/EPS in 2016 = $13.28/$1.25 = 10.62

   Note that this PE ratio cannot be compared to the current PE ratios of other traded companies today. For instance, arguing that Amylin is cheap because the forward PE of 10.62 is less than Amgen's current PE of 12.42 does not stand up to scrutiny, because Amgen's earnings are in 2010 and not in 2016. Consequently, to use the forward PE, you would have to obtain forecasted EPS in 2016 for each firm in the sector and compute the forward PE for each one. (Amgen's PE based on forecasted EPS in 2016 is 7.45, for instance.)

2. *P/E before R&D:* A significant reason for Amylin's losses is the substantial R&D expense incurred by the firm. If you add back the R&D to the reported net loss and compute the per share value, you get earnings per share before R&D of about $0.15. The price-earnings ratio can be computed using this estimated earnings per share:

   Price/EPS before R&D = $13.28/$0.15 = 88.53

Here again, you have to be consistent and compute PE ratios based on earnings per share before R&D expenses for all of the firms in the sector.

ENTERPRISE VALUE TO EBITDA MULTIPLE

Unlike the earnings multiples discussed so far in this chapter, the enterprise value to EBITDA multiple is a firm value multiple. In the past two decades, this multiple has acquired a number of adherents among analysts for several reasons. First, there are far fewer firms with negative EBITDA than there are firms with negative earnings per share, and thus fewer firms are lost from the analysis. Second, differences in depreciation methods across different companies—some might use straight-line while others use accelerated depreciation—can cause differences in operating income or net income but will not affect EBITDA. Third, this multiple can be compared far more easily than other earnings multiples across firms with different financial leverage (the numerator is firm value and the denominator is a pre-debt earnings). For all of these reasons, this multiple is particularly useful for firms in sectors that require large investments in infrastructure with long gestation periods. Telecom companies or companies involved in airport or toll road construction would be good examples.

Definition

The enterprise value to EBITDA multiple relates the total market value of the firm, net of cash, to the earnings before interest, taxes, depreciation, and amortization of the firm:

$$\text{EV/EBITDA} = \frac{\text{(Market value of equity} + \text{Market value of Debt} - \text{Cash)}}{\text{EBITDA}}$$

In practice, analysts and investors use the book value of debt as a proxy for market value of debt, since the two numbers tend to be similar (at least for healthy firms). Why is cash netted out of firm value for this calculation? Since the interest income from the cash is not counted as part of the EBITDA, not netting out the cash will result in an overstatement of the EV-to-EBITDA multiple.

The enterprise value to EBITDA multiple can be difficult to estimate for firms with cross holdings. To see why, note that cross holdings can be categorized as either majority-active, minority-active, or minority-passive holdings. When a holding is categorized as minority holding, the operating income of a firm does not reflect the income from the holding. The numerator, on the other hand, includes the market value of equity, which should incorporate the value of the minority holdings. Consequently, the EV to EBITDA multiple will be too high for these firms, leading a casual observer to conclude that they were overvalued. When a holding is categorized as a majority holding, a different problem arises. The EBITDA includes 100 percent of the EBITDA of the holding, but the numerator reflects only the portion of the holding that belongs to the firm. Thus the EV to EBITDA multiple will be too low, leading it to be categorized as an undervalued stock.

The correction for cross holdings is tedious and difficult to do when the holdings are in private firms. With minority holdings, you can either subtract the estimated value of the holdings from the numerator or add the portion of the EBITDA of the subsidiary to the denominator. With consolidated holdings, you can subtract the proportional share of the value of the holding from the numerator and the entire EBITDA of the holding from the denominator.

$$\text{EV/EBITDA}_{\text{Consolidated}} = \frac{\begin{pmatrix}\text{Market value of equity} + \text{Debt}_{\text{Consolidated}} \\ + \text{Minority interest} - \text{Minority holdings} \\ -\text{Cash}_{\text{Consolidated}}\end{pmatrix}}{\text{EBITDA}_{\text{Consolidated}}}$$

While analysts who make these adjustments often use the book values of minority holdings and interests, a correct adjustment would require that we net out the market values of both.

You could also entirely remove all cross holdings, whether minority or majority, and compute an EV / EBITDA for just the parent company

$$\text{EV/EBITDA}_{\text{Parent}} = \frac{\begin{pmatrix}\text{Market value of equity} + \text{Debt}_{\text{Parent}} - \\ \text{Market value of cross holdings} - \text{Cash}_{\text{Parent}}\end{pmatrix}}{\text{EBITDA}_{\text{Parent}}}$$

As you can see, cross holdings are a source of headaches in intrinsic valuation remain troublesome when pricing companies.

ILLUSTRATION 18.14:   Estimating Value to EBITDA with Cross Holdings

In Illustration 16.6, we estimated a discounted cash flow value for Segovia, a firm with two holdings—a 51% stake in Seville Televison and a 15% stake of LatinWorks, a record and CD company. The first holding was categorized as a majority-active holding (resulting in consolidation) and the second as a minority-passive holding. Here, we will try to estimate an enterprise value to EBITDA multiple for Seville, using the following information:

- The market value of equity at Segovia is $1,529 million, and the consolidated debt outstanding at the firm is $500 million. The firm reported $500 million in EBITDA on its consolidated income statement. A portion of the EBITDA ($180 million) and debt outstanding ($150 million) represent Segovia's holdings in Seville Televison.
- Seville Television is a publicly traded firm with a market value of equity of $459 million.
- LatinWorks is a private firm with an EBITDA of $120 million on the capital invested of $250 million in the current year; the firm has $100 million in debt outstanding.
- None of the firms have significant cash balances.

If we estimate an enterprise value to EBITDA multiple for Segovia using its consolidated financial statements, we would obtain the following:

$$\text{EV/EBITDA} = (\text{Market value of equity} + \text{Value of debt} - \text{Cash})/\text{EBITDA}$$
$$= (1{,}529 + 500 - 0)/500 = 4.06$$

This multiple is contaminated by the cross holdings. There are three ways you can correct for these holdings. One is to net out from the market value of equity of Segovia the value of the equity in the holdings and the debt of the consolidated holding from Segovia's debt, and then divide by the EBITDA of just the parent company.

To do this, you would first need to estimate the market value of equity in LatinWorks, which is a private company. We will use the estimate of equity value that we obtained in Illustration 16.6:

$$\text{Value of equity in LatinWorks} = \$370.25 \text{ million}$$

$$\text{EV/EBITDA}_{\text{parent}} = \frac{(1{,}529 - .51 \times 459 - .15 \times 370.25) + (500 - 150)}{(500 - 180)} = 5.70$$

This will yield a EV/EBITDA for just the parent company. The alternative is to adjust just the denominator to make it consistent with the numerator. In other words, the EBITDA should include only 51% of the majority active holding's EBITDA and should add in the 15% of the EBITDA in the minority holdings. Since you are now counting only your portion of the consolidated holding, you should net out the portion of the consolidated company's debt that is not yours:

$$\text{EV/EBITDA}_{\text{Adjusted EBITDA}} = \frac{1{,}529 + (500 - 150 \times .49)}{(500 - .49 \times 180 + .15 \times 120)} = 4.55$$

In the last approach, you estimate the EV-to-EBITDA multiple for the consolidated firm, correcting for just the minority holding. To accomplish this, you need to add the estimated value of the equity in the subsidiary that you have consolidated (since the market value of equity of the parent company reflects only the 51% of the subsidiary that you own) to the numerator, and subtract the estimated value of equity in the minority holding in Latin Works from that value. The denominator can be left untouched since it already includes 100% of the EBITDA from the consolidated subsidiary; the same argument applies to the cash and debt items in Segovia:

$$\text{EV/EBITDA}_{\text{Consolidated}} = \frac{(1{,}529 + .49 \times 459 - .15 \times 370.25) + (500 - 150)}{500} = 3.40$$

Note that 49% of the market value of equity in Seville is added back to the numerator, to stay consistent with equity value being measured in market terms. In practice, though, many analysts would have used the minority interests on Segovia's balance sheet, which is the book value measure of the 49% of Seville, to get to enterprise value. While this may be convenient, it does introduce an inconsistency into the estimate.

Since the approaches yield very different values, you may wonder which one is correct. Since the only reason we compute the multiple is to compare it to values computed for similar companies, the answer depends on that comparison. If each of the three companies is in a different sector, it is best to use the first approach and get EV/EBITDA multiples for each company separately and compare that company to other companies in its sector. If you can find consolidated companies that look just like Segovia, in terms of both minority and majority holdings, you can use the second approach. If Segovia and Seville are both in the same sector, you can use the third approach, because you can compare the consolidated value to the values that other companies in the sector trade at.

Description

Figure 18.13 summarizes the enterprise value to EBITDA multiples for U.S. and global firms in January 2024. As with the price-earnings ratio, you have a heavily skewed distribution. The median EV/EBITDA multiple across U.S. firms in January 2024 was 14.05, and the European, emerging market, and Japanese firms all have skewed distributions, with positive outliers pushing the average well above the median.

This distribution illustrates why rules of thumb based upon absolute values will be misleading in many markets and in many time periods. For instance, the rule of thumb

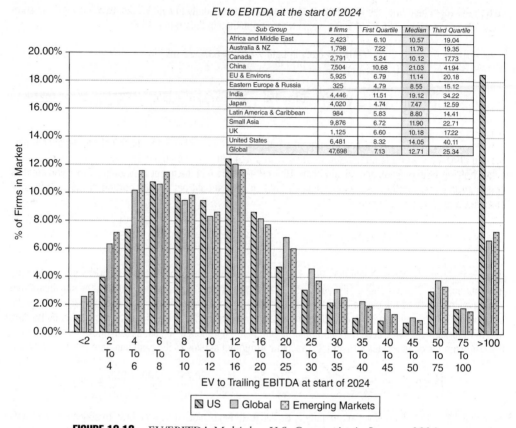

FIGURE 18.13 EV/EBITDA Multiples: U.S. Companies in January 2024

that many private equity investors used in the 1980s is that any company that traded at less than six times EBITDA is cheap may hold up in the U.S. in 2024, but would not have in 2010 when the median value was 6.25. In 2024, it would lead you to conclude that almost half of all Japanese stocks were cheap, since the median value is 7.47.

Analysis

To analyze the determinants of enterprise value to EBITDA multiples, we will revert back to a free cash flow to the firm valuation model that we developed in Chapter 15. Specifically, we estimated the value of the operating assets (or enterprise value) of a firm to be:

$$\text{Value of operating assets} = EV = \frac{FCFF_1}{(\text{Cost of capital} - \text{Expected growth rate})}$$

We can write the free cash flow to the firm in terms of the EBITDA:

$$FCFF = EBIT(1-t) - (Cap\ ex - DA; + \Delta Working\ capital)$$
$$= (EBITDA - DA)(1-t) - (Cap\ ex - DA + \Delta Working\ capital)$$
$$= EBITDA(1-t) - DA(1-t) - Reinvestment$$

Substituting back into the equation, we get:

$$EV = \frac{EBITDA_1(1-t) - DA(1-t) - \text{Reinvestment}}{(\text{Cost of capital} - \text{Expected growth rate})}$$

Dividing both sides by the EBITDA and removing the subscripts yields the following:

$$\frac{EV}{EBITDA} = \frac{(1-t) - \dfrac{DA}{EBITDA}(1-t) - \dfrac{\text{Reinvestment}}{EBITDA}}{(\text{Cost of capital} - \text{Expected growth rate})}$$

The five determinants of the enterprise value to EBITDA multiple are visible in this equation:

1. *Tax rate.* Other things remaining equal, firms with lower tax rates should command higher enterprise value to EBITDA multiples than otherwise similar firms with higher tax rates.
2. *Depreciation and amortization.* Other things remaining equal, firms that derive a greater portion of their EBITDA from depreciation and amortization should trade at lower multiples of EBITDA than otherwise similar firms.
3. *Reinvestment requirements.* Other things remaining equal, the greater the portion of the EBITDA that needs to be reinvested to generate expected growth, the lower the value to EBITDA will be for firms.
4. *Cost of capital.* Other things remaining equal, firms with lower costs of capital should trade at much higher multiples of EBITDA.
5. *Expected growth.* Other things remaining equal, firms with higher expected growth should trade at much higher multiples of EBITDA.

This can be generalized to consider firms in high growth. The variables will remain unchanged but will need to be estimated for each phase of growth.

ILLUSTRATION 18.15: Analyzing Value to EBITDA Multiples

Castillo Cable is a cable and wireless firm with the following characteristics:

- ▩ The firm has a cost of capital of 10% and faces a tax rate of 36% on its operating income.
- ▩ The firm has capital expenditures that amount to 45% of EBITDA and depreciation that amounts to 20% of EBITDA. There are no working capital requirements.
- ▩ The firm is in stable growth and its operating income is expected to grow 5% a year in perpetuity.

To estimate the enterprise value to EBITDA, we first estimate the reinvestment needs as a percent of EBITDA:

Reinvestment/EBITDA = Cap ex/EBITDA − Depreciation/EBITDA + Δ Working capital/EBITDA
= .45 − .20 − 0 = .25

$$\frac{EV}{EBITDA} = \frac{(1-.36) - (0.20)(1-.36) - 0.25}{(.10-.05)} = 5.24$$

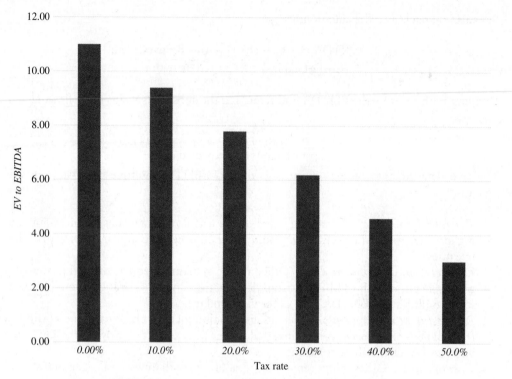

FIGURE 18.14 EV/EBITDA Multiples and Tax Rates

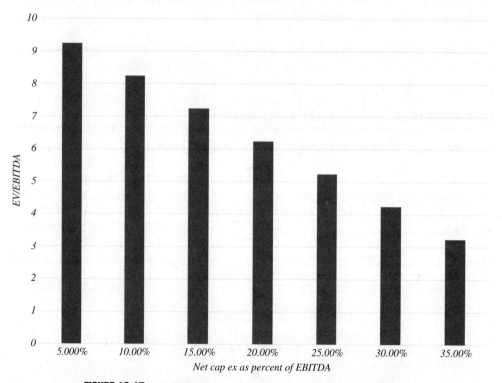

FIGURE 18.15 EV/EBITDA and Net Capital Expenditure Ratios

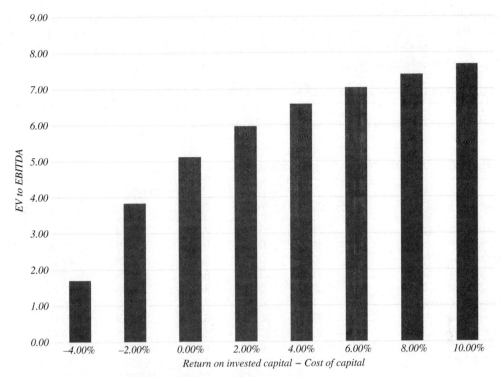

FIGURE 18.16   EV/EBITDA and Excess Returns

This multiple is sensitive to the tax rate, as evidenced in Figure 18.14. It is also sensitive to the reinvestment rate (stated as a percent of EBITDA), as shown in Figure 18.15.

However, changing the reinvestment rate while keeping the growth rate fixed is the equivalent of changing the return on capital. In fact, at the existing reinvestment rate and growth rate, we are assuming a return on capital of 10.24%, slightly higher than the cost of capital of 10.00%. Figure 18.16 looks at the enterprise value to EBITDA multiple as a function of the excess return, i.e., the difference between the return on capital and the cost of capital.

In short, firms with low returns on capital and high reinvestment rates should trade at low multiples of EBITDA.

 firmmult.xls: **This spreadsheet enables you to estimate firm value multiples for a stable-growth or high-growth firm, given its fundamentals.**

Application

Having established the fundamentals that determine the enterprise value to EBITDA multiple, we can now examine how best to apply the multiple. The multiple is most widely used in capital-intensive firms with heavy infrastructure investments. The rationale that is given for using the multiple—that EBITDA is the operating cash flow of the firm—does not really hold up, because many of these firms also tend to have capital expenditure needs that drain cash flows. There are, however, good reasons for using this multiple when depreciation methods vary widely across firms and the bulk of the investment in infrastructure has already been made.

ILLUSTRATION 18.16: Comparing the EV-to-EBITDA Multiples: Steel Companies in 2001

Table 18.20 summarizes the enterprise value to EBITDA multiples for steel companies in the United States in March 2001:

TABLE 18.20 EV/EBITDA Multiples for Steel Companies in 2001

Company Name	EV/EBITDA	Tax Rate	ROIC	Net Cap ex % of EBITDA	Depreciation % of EBITDA
Ampco-Pittsburgh	2.74	26.21%	12.15%	15.72%	20.05%
Bayou Steel	5.21	0.00%	5.95%	12.90%	41.01%
Birmingham Steel	5.60	0.00%	6.89%	−28.64%	51.92%
Carpenter Technology	5.05	33.29%	9.16%	15.51%	28.87%
Castle (A.M.) & Co.	9.26	0.00%	8.92%	9.44%	27.22%
Cleveland-Cliffs	5.14	0.00%	7.65%	51.84%	26.33%
Commercial Metals	2.40	36.86%	16.60%	1.19%	26.44%
Harris Steel	4.26	37.18%	15.00%	3.23%	4.92%
Huntco Inc.	5.40	0.00%	4.82%	−48.84%	53.02%
IPSCO Inc.	5.06	23.87%	9.22%	50.57%	16.88%
Kentucky Elec. Steel Inc.	1.72	37.26%	6.75%	−25.51%	38.78%
National Steel	2.30	0.00%	8.46%	68.49%	53.84%
NN Inc.	6.00	34.35%	15.73%	−15.04%	24.80%
Northwest Pipe Co.	5.14	39.47%	9.05%	8.73%	17.22%
Nucor Corp.	3.88	35.00%	18.48%	15.66%	26.04%
Olympic Steel Inc.	4.46	37.93%	5.80%	−3.75%	26.62%
Oregon Steel Mills	5.32	0.00%	7.23%	−31.77%	49.57%
Quanex Corp.	2.90	34.39%	16.38%	−3.45%	29.50%
Ryerson Tull	7.73	0.00%	5.10%	3.50%	38.36%
Samuel Manu-Tech Inc.	3.13	31.88%	14.90%	−2.91%	21.27%
Schnitzer Steel Inds. "A"	4.60	8.70%	7.78%	−16.21%	38.74%
Slater STL Inc.	4.48	26.00%	11.25%	0.80%	27.96%
Steel Dynamics	5.83	36.33%	10.09%	33.13%	23.14%
Steel Technologies	3.75	36.87%	9.22%	11.95%	27.69%
Steel-General	4.14	38.37%	9.80%	21.69%	28.75%
Unvl. Stainless & Alloy Prods.	4.28	37.52%	14.51%	12.73%	15.15%
Worthington Inds.	4.80	37.50%	12.54%	0.16%	22.79%

The enterprise value to EBITDA multiples vary widely across these firms, and many of these firms have negative net capital expenditures (depreciation > Cap Ex), partly reflecting the industry's maturity and partly the lumpy nature of reinvestments. Many of them also pay no taxes because they lose money. We regressed the EV/EBITDA multiple against the tax rate and depreciation as a percent of EBITDA:[5]

---

[5]Depreciation as a percent of EBITDA operates as a proxy for reinvestment needs, and seems to work better as a better proxy than cap ex or net cap ex as a percent of EBITDA; the latter two were statistically insignificant.

$$EV/EBITDA = 8.64 - 8.07 \text{ Tax rate } - 7.19\left(\frac{DA}{EBITDA}\right) \quad R^2 = 35.1\%$$
$$(6.36) \quad (3.44) \qquad\qquad (2.35)$$

We did not use expected growth or cost of capital as independent variables because they are very similar across these firms. Using this regression, the predicted value to EBITDA multiple for Birmingham Steel would be:

$$\text{Predicted EV/EBITDA}_{\text{Birmingham Steel}} = 8.64 - 8.07(0.00) - 7.19(.5192) = 4.91$$

At 5.60 times EBITDA, the firm is overvalued by about 14.26%.

---

 vebitda.xls: **This dataset on the web summarizes value-to-earnings multiples and fundamentals by industry group in the United States for the most recent year.**

VALUE MULTIPLES: VARIANTS

While enterprise value to EBITDA may be the most widely used value multiple, there are close variants that are sometimes used by analysts—EV/EBIT, EV/after-tax EBIT, and EV/FCFF. Each of these multiples is determined by many of the same variables that determine the EV/EBITDA multiple, but the actual relationship is slightly different. In particular, note that for a stable growth firm these multiples can be written as follows:

$$EV/FCFF = 1/(\text{Cost of capital } - \text{ Expected growth rate})$$
$$EV/EBIT(1 - t) = (1 - RIR)/(\text{Cost of capital } - \text{ Expected growth rate})$$
$$EV/EBIT = (1 - t)(1 - RIR)/(\text{Cost of capital } - \text{ Expected growth rate})$$

where RIR is the reinvestment rate and t is the tax rate.

In other words, higher costs of capital and lower expected growth decrease all of these multiples. A higher reinvestment rate lowers the last two multiples but does not affect the multiple of FCFF (since FCFF is already after reinvestment). A higher tax rate will affect just the last multiple, since the first two look at earnings after taxes.

CONCLUSION

The price-earnings ratio and other earnings multiples, which are widely used in valuation, have the potential to be misused. These multiples are ultimately determined by the same fundamentals that determine the value of a firm in a discounted cash flow model—expected growth, risk, and cash flow potential. Firms with higher growth, lower risk, and higher payout ratios, other things remaining equal, should trade at much higher multiples of earnings than other firms. To the extent that there are differences in fundamentals across countries, across time, and across companies, the multiples will also be different. A failure to control for these differences in fundamentals can lead to erroneous conclusions based purely on a direct comparison of multiples.

There are several ways in which earnings multiples can be used in valuation. One way is to compare earnings multiples across a narrowly defined group of comparable firms and to control for differences in growth, risk, and cash flows subjectively. Another is to expand the definition of a comparable firm to the entire sector (such as technology) or the market, and to control for differences in fundamentals using statistical techniques.

In the last part of the chapter, we turned our attention from equity multiples to multiples of operating earnings and cash flows. As with the PE ratio, these multiples are a function of growth (in operating income), reinvestment, and risk.

QUESTIONS AND SHORT PROBLEMS

In the problems following, use an equity risk premium of 5.5 percent if none is specified.

1. National City Corporation, a bank-holding company, reported earnings per share of $2.40 in 1993, and paid dividends per share of $1.06. The earnings had grown 7.5% a year over the prior five years, and were expected to grow 6% a year in the long term (starting in 1994). The stock had a beta of 1.05 and traded for 10 times earnings. The Treasury bond rate was 7%, and the risk premium is 5.5%.
   a. Estimate the PE ratio for National City Corporation.
   b. What long-term growth rate is implied in the firm's current PE ratio?
2. On March 11, 1994, the New York Stock Exchange Composite was trading at 16.9 times earnings, and the average dividend yield across stocks on the exchange was 2.5%. The Treasury bond rate on that date was 6.95%. The economy was expected to grow 2.5% a year, in real terms, in the long term, and the consensus estimate for inflation, in the long term, was 3.5%. (Market risk premium is 5.5%.)
   a. Based on these inputs, estimate the appropriate PE ratio for the exchange.
   b. What growth rate in dividends/earnings would justify the PE ratio on March 11, 1994?
   c. Would it matter whether this higher growth comes from higher inflation or higher real growth? Why?
3. International Flavors and Fragrances, a leading creator and manufacturer of flavors and fragrances, paid out dividends of $0.91 per share on earnings per share of $1.64 in 1992. The firm was expected to have a return on equity of 20% between 1993 and 1997, after which the firm was expected to have stable growth of 6% a year. (The return on equity was expected to drop to 15% in the stable growth phase.) The dividend payout ratio was expected to remain at the current level from 1993 to 1997. The stock had a beta of 1.10, which was not expected to change. The Treasury bond rate was 7%, and the risk premium is 5.5%.
   a. Estimate the PE ratio for International Flavors based on fundamentals.
   b. Estimate how much of this PE ratio can be ascribed to the extraordinary growth in earnings that the firm expects to have between 1993 and 1997.
4. Cracker Barrel, which operates restaurants and gift shops, reported dramatic growth in earnings and revenues between 1983 and 1992. During this period, earnings grew from $0.08 per share in 1983 to $0.78 per share in 1993. The dividends paid in 1993

amounted to only $0.02 per share. The earnings growth rate was expected to ease to 15% a year from 1994 to 1998, and to 6% a year after that. The payout ratio was expected to increase to 10% from 1994 to 1998, and to 50% after that. The beta of the stock was 1.55, but it was expected to decline to 1.25 for the 1994–1998 time period and to 1.10 after that. (The Treasury bond rate was 7%, and the risk premium is 5.5%.)

a. Estimate the PE ratio for Cracker Barrel.

b. Estimate how much higher the PE ratio would have been if it had been able to maintain the growth rate in earnings that it had posted between 1983 and 1993. (Assume that the dividend payout ratios are unaffected.)

c. Now assume that disappointing earnings reports in the near future lower the expected growth rate between 1994 and 1998 to 10%. Estimate the PE ratio. (Again, assume that the dividend payout ratio is unaffected.)

5. The S&P 500 was trading at 21.2 times earnings on December 31, 1993. On the same day, the dividend yield on the index was 2.74%, and the Treasury bond rate was 6%. The expected growth rate in real GNP was 2.5%.

a. Assuming that the S&P 500 is correctly priced, what is the inflation rate implied in the PE ratio? (Assume stable growth and a 5.5% risk premium.)

b. By February 1994, Treasury bond rates had increased to 7%. If payout ratios and expected growth remain unchanged, what would the effect on the PE ratio be?

c. Does an increase in interest rates always imply lower prices (and PE ratios)?

6. The following were the PE ratios of firms in the aerospace/defense industry at the end of December 1993, with additional data on expected growth and risk.

Company	PE Ratio	Growth	Beta	Payout
Boeing	17.3	3.5%	1.10	28%
General Dynamics	15.5	11.5%	1.25	40%
General Motors—Hughes	16.5	13.0%	0.85	41%
Grumman	11.4	10.5%	0.80	37%
Lockheed Corporation	10.2	9.5%	0.85	37%
Logicon	12.4	14.0%	0.85	11%
Loral Corporation	13.3	16.5%	0.75	23%
Martin Marietta	11.0	8.0%	0.85	22%
McDonnell Douglas	22.6	13.0%	1.15	37%
Northrop	9.5	9.0%	1.05	47%
Raytheon	12.1	9.5%	0.75	28%
Rockwell	13.9	11.5%	1.00	38%
Thiokol	8.7	5.5%	0.95	15%
United Industrial	10.4	4.5%	0.70	50%

a. Estimate the average and median PE ratios. What, if anything, would these averages tell you?

b. An analyst concludes that Thiokol is undervalued, because its PE ratio is lower than the industry average. Under what conditions is this statement true? Would you agree with it here?

c. Using a regression, control for differences across firms on risk, growth, and payout. Specify how you would use this regression to spot under- and overvalued stocks. What are the limitations of this approach?

7. The following was the result of a regression of PE ratios on growth rates, betas, and payout ratios for stocks listed on the Value Line Database in April 1993.

$$PE = 18.69 + 0.0695 \, \text{Growth} - 0.5082 \, \text{Beta} - 0.4262 \, \text{Payout} \quad R^2 = 0.35$$

Thus a stock with an earnings growth rate of 20%, a beta of 1.15, and a payout ratio of 40% would have had an expected PE ratio of:

$$PE = 18.69 + 0.0695 \times 20 - 0.5082(1.15) - 0.4262 \times 0.40 = 19.33$$

You are attempting to value a private firm with the following characteristics:

- The firm had net profits of $10 million. It did not pay dividends, but had depreciation allowances of $5 million and capital expenditures of $12 million in the most recent year. Working capital requirements were negligible.
- The earnings had grown 25% over the previous five years, and are expected to grow at the same rate over the next five years.
- The average beta of publicly traded firms, in the same line of business, is 1.15, and the average debt-equity ratio of these firms is 25%. (The tax rate is 40%.) The private firm is an all-equity-financed firm, with no debt.

a. Estimate the appropriate PE ratio for this private firm using the regression.
b. What would some of your concerns be in using this regression in valuation?

CHAPTER 19

Book Value Multiples

The relationship between price and book value has always attracted the attention of investors. Stocks selling for well below the book value of equity have generally been considered undervalued, while those selling for more than book value have been targeted as overvalued. This chapter begins by examining the price–book value (PBV) ratio in more detail, the determinants of this ratio, and how best to evaluate or estimate the ratio.

In the next part of the chapter, we turn our attention to variants of the price-to-book ratio. In particular, we focus on the value-to-book ratio and Tobin's Q—a ratio of market value of assets to their replacement cost.

PRICE-TO-BOOK EQUITY

The market value of the equity in a firm reflects the market's expectation of the firm's earning power and cash flows. The book value of equity is the difference between the book value of assets and the book value of liabilities, a number that is largely determined by accounting conventions. In the United States, the book value of assets is the original price paid for the assets reduced by any allowable depreciation on the assets. Consequently, the book value of an asset generally decreases as it ages. The book value of liabilities similarly reflects the at-issue values of the liabilities. Since the book value of an asset reflects its original cost, it might deviate significantly from market value if the earning power of the asset has increased or declined significantly since its acquisition.

Why Analysts Use Book Value and the Downside

There are several reasons why investors find the price–book value ratio useful in investment analysis. The first is that the book value provides a relatively stable, intuitive measure of value that can be compared to the market price. For investors who instinctively mistrust discounted cash flow estimates of value, the book value is a much simpler benchmark for comparison. The second is that, given reasonably consistent accounting standards across firms, price–book value ratios can be compared across similar firms for signs of under- or overvaluation. Finally, even firms with negative earnings, which cannot be valued using price-earnings ratios, can be evaluated using price–book value ratios; there are far fewer firms with negative book value for equity than there are firms with negative earnings.

There are several disadvantages associated with measuring and using price–book value ratios. First, book values, like earnings, are affected by accounting decisions on depreciation and other variables. When accounting standards vary widely across firms, the price–book value ratios may not be comparable. A similar statement can be made about comparing price–book value ratios across countries with different accounting standards. Second, book value may not carry much meaning for service and technology firms that do not have significant tangible assets. Third, the book value of equity can become negative if a firm has a sustained string of negative earnings reports, leading to a negative price–book value ratio.

Definition

The price-to-book ratio is computed by dividing the market price per share by the current book value of equity per share.

$$\text{Price to book} = \frac{\text{Price per share}}{\text{Book value of equity per share}}$$

While the multiple is fundamentally consistent—the numerator and denominator are both equity values—there is a potential for inconsistency if you are not careful about how you compute book value of equity per share. In particular,

- If there are multiple classes of shares outstanding, the price per share can be different for different classes of shares, and it is not clear how the book equity should be apportioned among shares.
- You should not include the portion of the equity that is attributable to preferred stock in computing the book value of equity, since the market value of equity refers only to common equity.

Some of the problems can be alleviated by computing the price-to-book ratio using the total market value of equity and book value of equity, rather than per-share values.

$$\text{Price to book} = \frac{\text{Market capitalization}}{\text{Book value of equity}}$$

The safest way to measure this ratio when there are multiple classes of equity is to use the composite market value of all classes of common stock in the numerator and the composite book value of equity in the denominator—you would still ignore preferred stock for this computation.

There are two other measurement issues that you must confront in computing this multiple. The first relates to the book value of equity, which as an accounting measure gets updated infrequently—once every quarter for Most companies, and once every year for some companies. While most analysts use the most current book value of equity, there are some who use the average over the previous year or the book value of equity at the end of the latest financial year. Consistency demands that you use the same measure of book equity for all firms in your sample. The second and more difficult problem concerns the value of options outstanding. Technically, you would need to compute the estimated market value of management options and conversion options (in bonds and preferred stock) and add them to the market value of equity before computing the price to book value ratio.[1] If you have a small sample of comparable firms and options represent a large and variable portion of equity value, you should do this. With larger samples and less significant option issues, you can stay with the conventional measure of market value of equity.

Accounting standards can affect book values of equity and price-to-book ratios and skew comparisons made across firms. For instance, assume that you are comparing the price-to-book ratios of technology firms in two markets, and that one of them enables research expenses to be capitalized and the other does not. You should expect to see lower price-to-book value ratios in the former, since the book value of equity will be augmented by the value of the research asset.

ADJUSTING BOOK EQUITY FOR BUYBACKS AND ACQUISITIONS

In recent years, U.S. firms have increasingly turned to buying back stock as a way of returning cash to stockholders. When a firm buys back stock, the book equity of the firm declines by the amount of the buyback. Although this is precisely what happens when firms pay a cash dividend as well, buybacks tend to be much larger than regular dividends, and thus have a bigger impact on book equity. To illustrate, assume that you have a firm that has an market value of equity of $100 million and a book value of equity of $50 million; its price-to-book ratio is 2.00. If the firm borrows $25 million and buys back stock, both its book and market equity drop by $25 million. The resulting price-to-book ratio is 3.

With acquisitions, the effect on price-to-book ratios can vary dramatically depending on how the acquisition is accounted for. While all firms are now required to show goodwill as an asset, when they do acquisition, there is some discretion in how the purchase price on an acquisition is allocated across the target firm's assets. Furthermore, the goodwill line item has to be revisited in subsequent years and impaired if the value of the target company has declined since the acquisition. Both actions can affect the book value of equity and the price-to-book ratio.

To compare price-to-book ratios across firms, when some firms in the sample buy back stocks and some do not, or when there are wide differences in both the magnitude and the accounting for acquisitions, that can be problematic. One way to adjust for the differences is to take out the goodwill from acquisitions and to add back the market value of buybacks to the book equity to come up with an adjusted book value of equity. The price-to-book ratios can then be computed based on this adjusted book value of equity.

---

[1] If you do not do this and compare price-to-book ratios across firms with widely different amounts of options outstanding, you could misidentify firms with more options outstanding as undervalued—the market value of traded common stock at these firms will be lower because of the option overhang.

Description

To get a sense of what comprises a high, low, or average price to book value ratio, we computed the ratio for every firm listed in the United States, and Figure 19.1 summarizes the distribution of price-to-book ratios for U.S. and global companies in January 2024. Note that this distribution is heavily skewed, as is evidenced by the fact that the average price-to-book ratio for U.S. (global) firms is 9.94 (6.15) while the median price-to-book ratio is much lower at 1.62 (1.49).

Another point worth making about price-to-book ratios is that there are firms with negative book values of equity—the result of continuously losing money—for which price-to-book ratios cannot be computed. In this sample of 6,481 firms, in the United States, there were almost 2,000 firms where this occurred. Those negative book equities can sometimes reflect companies that are in trouble, but more often they are the result of accounting adjustments to the book value of equity for stock buybacks and write-offs.

 pbvdata.xls: This dataset on the web summarizes price-to-book ratios and fundamentals by industry group in the United States for the most recent year.

Analysis

The price–book value ratio can be related to the same fundamentals that determine value in discounted cash flow models. Since this is an equity multiple, we will use an equity discounted cash flow model—the dividend discount model—to explore the

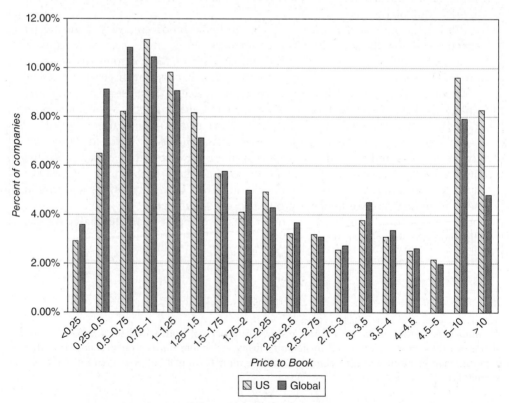

FIGURE 19.1   Price-to-Book Value—U.S. Companies in January 2024.

determinants. The value of equity in a stable growth dividend discount model can be written as:

$$\text{Value of equity today} = \frac{\text{Expected Dividends next year}}{(\text{Cost of equity} - \text{Expected growth rate})}$$

The expected dividends next year can be written as the product of the net income next year and the payout ratio.

$$\text{Dividends next year} = \text{Net Income next year} \times \text{Payout ratio}$$

The value of the equity can be written as:
Defining the return on equity (ROE) = Net Income$_1$/Book value of equity$_0$, the value of equity can be written as:

$$\text{Value of equity today} = \frac{\text{BV of equity}_0 \times \text{ROE} \times \text{Payout ratio}}{(\text{Cost of equity} - \text{Expected growth rate})}$$

Rewriting in terms of the PBV ratio,

$$\frac{\text{Value of equity today}}{\text{Book value of equity today}} = \text{PBV} = \frac{\text{ROE} \times \text{Payout ratio}}{(\text{Cost of equity} - \text{Expected growth rate})}$$

The PBV ratio is an increasing function of the return on equity, the payout ratio, and the growth rate, and a decreasing function of the riskiness of the firm.

This formulation can be simplified even further by relating growth to the return on equity:

$$g = (1 - \text{Payout ratio}) \times \text{ROE}$$

Substituting back into the PBV equation,

$$\text{PBV} = \frac{\text{ROE} - \text{Expected growth rate}}{\text{Cost of equity} - \text{Expected growth rate}}$$

The price–book value ratio of a stable firm is determined by the differential between the return on equity and its cost of equity. If the return on equity exceeds the cost of equity, the price will exceed the book value of equity; if the return on equity is lower than the cost of equity, the price will be lower than the book value of equity.

ILLUSTRATION 19.1: Estimating the Intrinsic Price-to-Book Ratio—Stable Growth, Dividend-Paying Firm

In Chapter 13, we valued Vodafone with the H model, where we assumed a slightly higher growth rate initially that scaled down in linear increments to a stable growth rate. In this illustration, we will assume that Vodafone is already in stable growth and estimate the price-to-book ratio for the firm. Vodafone paid out 4,468 million BP in dividends on net income of 7,968 million BP in 2010, giving it a payout ratio of 55.82%:

$$\text{Payout ratio} = \text{Dividends/Net income} = 4,468/7,968 = 55.82\%$$

Based on its book value of equity of 90,810 million BP at the end of 2009, the return on equity generated by the firm in 2010 was 8.77%:

$$\text{Return on equity} = \frac{\text{Net income}_{2010}}{\text{Book value of equity}_{2009}} = \frac{7,968}{90,810} = 8.77\%$$

The expected growth rate, based on maintaining this payout ratio and return on equity, is 3.88%, which we will assume is the growth rate forever. To estimate the cost of equity, we will use the risk-free rate in British pounds (4%), an equity risk premium of 5%, assume a beta of 1 for the company:

$$\text{Cost of equity} = 4\% + 1.00\,(5\%) = 9.00\%$$

There are two ways in which we can estimate the price-to-book ratio for the firm, and they yield the same result:

$$\text{PBV} = \frac{\text{ROE} \times \text{Payout ratio}}{\text{Cost of equity} - \text{Expected growth rate}} = \frac{.0877 \times .5582}{.09 - .0388} = 0.96$$

$$\text{PBV} = \frac{\text{ROE} - \text{Expected growth rate}}{\text{Cost of equity} - \text{Expected growth rate}} = \frac{.0877 - .0388}{.09 - .0388} = 0.96$$

The stock is expected to trade at slightly below book value, because its return on equity is less than its cost of equity.

ILLUSTRATION 19.2: Estimating the Price–Book Value Ratio for a Privatization Candidate: Jenapharm in 1991

One of the by-products of German reunification was the Treuhandanstalt, the German privatization agency set up to sell hundreds of East German firms to other German companies, individual investors, and the public. One of the handful of firms that seemed to be a viable candidate for privatization was Jenapharm, the most respected pharmaceutical manufacturer in East Germany. Jenapharm, which was expected to have revenues of 230 million DM in 1991, also was expected to report net income of 9 million DM in that year. The firm had a book value of assets of 110 million DM and a book value of equity of 58 million DM at the end of 1990.

The firm was expected to maintain sales in its niche product, a contraceptive pill, and grow at 5% a year in the long term, primarily by expanding into the generic drug market. The average beta of pharmaceutical firms traded on the Frankfurt Stock Exchange was 1.05, though many of these firms had much more diversified product portfolios and less volatile cash flows. Allowing for the higher leverage and risk in Jenapharm, a beta of 1.25 was used for Jenapharm. The 10-year bond rate in Deutsche Marks at the time of this valuation in early 1991 was 7%, and the equity risk premium was assumed to be 3.5%.

Expected net income = 9 million DM

$$\text{Return on equity} = \frac{\textit{Expected net income}}{\textit{Book value of equity}} = \frac{9}{58} = 15.52\%$$

$$\text{Cost of equity} = 7\% + 1.25(3.5\%) = 11.375\%$$

$$\text{Estimated price-to-book ratio} = \frac{(\text{ROE} - g)}{(\textit{Cost of equity} - g)} = \frac{(.1552 - .05)}{(.11375 - .05)} = 1.65$$

Estimated market value of equity = Estimated price to book × Book equity

$$= 58 \times 1.65 = 95.70 \text{ million DM}$$

PBV Ratio for a High-Growth Firm   The price–book value ratio for a high-growth firm can also be related to fundamentals. In the special case of the two-stage dividend discount model, this relationship can be made explicit fairly simply. The value of equity of a high-growth firm in the two-stage dividend discount model can be written as:

Value of equity = Present value of expected dividends
+ Present value of terminal value of equity

When the growth rate is assumed to be constant after the initial high-growth phase, the dividend discount model can be written as follows:

$$\text{Value per share}_0 = \frac{EPS_1 \times \text{Payout ratio} \times \left[1 - \dfrac{(1+g)^n}{\left(1+k_{e,hg}\right)^n} \right]}{\left(k_{e,hg} - g\right)} + \frac{EPS_{n+1} \times \text{Payout ratio}_{st}}{\left(k_{e,st} - g_{st}\right)(1 + k_{e,hg})^n}$$

where g = Growth rate in the first n years

Payout = Payout ratio in the first n years

g_{st} = Growth rate after n years forever (stable growth rate)

Payout_{st} = Payout ratio after n years for the stable firm

k_e = Cost of equity (hg: high-growth period; st: stable-growth period)

Defining ROE_{hg} as the return on equity for the high-growth period, and rewriting EPS_1 in terms of the return on equity, we get:

$$EPS_1 = BV \, of \, equity_0 \times ROE_{hg}$$

Bringing BV_0 to the left-hand side of the equation, we get:

$$\frac{\text{Price}}{\text{Book}} = ROE_{hg} \times \left[\frac{\text{Payout ratio} \times \left(1 - \dfrac{(1+g)^n}{\left(1+k_{e,hg}\right)^n} \right)}{\left(k_{e,hg} - g\right)} + \frac{(1+g)^{n-1}\left(1+g_{st}\right)\text{Payout ratio}_{st}}{\left(k_{e,st} - g_{st}\right)(1+k_{e,hg})^n} \right]$$

where ROE_{hg} is the return on equity in the high-growth period and k_e is the cost of equity. The left-hand side of the equation is the price–book value ratio. It is determined by:

▮ *Return on equity.* The price–book value ratio is an increasing function of the return on equity.

▮ *Payout ratio during the high-growth period and in the stable period.* The PBV ratio increases as the payout ratio increases, for any given growth rate.

■ *Riskiness (through the discount rate r).* The PBV ratio becomes lower as riskiness increases; the increased risk increases the cost of equity.
■ *Growth rate in earnings, in both the high-growth and stable phases.* The PBV increases as the growth rate increases, in either period, holding the payout ratio constant.

This formula is general enough to be applied to any firm, even one that is not paying dividends right now. Note, in addition, that the fundamentals that determine the price-to-book ratio are the same as they were for a stable growth firm—the payout ratio, the return on equity, the expected growth rate, and the cost of equity.

Chapter 14 noted that firms may not always pay out what they can afford to and recommended that the free cash flows to equity be substituted in for the dividends in those cases. You can, in fact, modify the equation to state the price-to-book ratio in terms of free cash flows to equity. The only substitution that we must make in the equation is the replacement of the payout ratio by the FCFE as a percent of earnings.

ILLUSTRATION 19.3:   **Estimating the PBV Ratio for a High-Growth Firm in the Two-Stage Model**

Assume that you have been asked to estimate the PBV ratio for a firm that is expected to be in high growth for the next five years. Table 19.1 lists the characteristics of the firm:

TABLE 19.1   Firm characteristics—High Growth and Stable Growth

EPS growth rate in first five years = 20%	Payout ratio in first five years = 20%
EPS growth rate after five years = 4%	Payout ratio after five years = 60%
Beta = 1.0	Risk-free rate = T-bond rate = 4.5%
Return on equity$_{high growth}$ = 25%	Equity risk premium = 5%
Return on equity$_{stable}$ = 10%	
Cost of equity = 4.5% + 1(5%) = 9.5% (in perpetuity)	

$$\frac{Price}{Book} = 0.25 \times \left[\frac{0.20 \times \left(1 - \frac{(1.20)^5}{(1.095)^5} \right)}{(.095 - .20)} + \frac{(1.20)^4 (1.04)(0.60)}{(.095 - .04)(1.095)^5} \right] = 4.01$$

The estimated PBV ratio for this firm is 4.01.[2]

ILLUSTRATION 19.4:   **Estimating the Intrinsic Price-to-Book Ratio (with High Growth)**

To extend the reach of the intrinsic valuation model, we will use a two-stage model to estimate the price-to-book ratio for Nestle, a company we valued with a two-stage FCFE model in Chapter 14. Rather than use the actual dividends paid (and payout ratio), we will use the FCFE as potential dividends and measure a payout ratio accordingly.

Expected growth rate = ROE × Equity reinvestment rate

---

[2]You may be puzzled by the fact that the return on equity in stable growth does not explicitly affect the price-to-book ratio, but it affects it implicitly by determining the payout ratio in stable growth. If, for instance, the return on equity had stayed at 25% in perpetuity, the stable payout ratio would become 68%, and the intrinsic PBV ratio would have been higher at 4.99.

Using the illustration in Chapter 14, we summarize the inputs for Nestle in Table 19.2:

TABLE 19.2 Firm characteristics—Nestle

	High Growth	*Stable Growth*
Length of growth	5 years	Forever
ROE	21.35%	10%
Equity reinvestment rate	37.17%	25.00%
FCFE/Net income	62.83%	75.00%
Expected growth rate	7.94%	2.50%
Cost of equity	6.90%	6.90%

Plugging back into the two-stage model, we get:

$$\frac{Price}{Book} = 0.2135 \times \left[\frac{0.6283 \times \left(1 - \frac{(1.0794)^5}{(1.069)^5}\right)}{(.069 - .0794)} + \frac{(1.0794)^4 \, (1.025) \, (0.75)}{(.069 - .025)(1.069)^5} \right] = 4.27$$

In this illustration, we assumed that Nestle's expected ROE for the next five years will be equal to its current ROE of 21.35%. Note that the stable period return on equity of 10% gets used only to compute the payout ratio in stable growth and that the high-growth period ROE is used everywhere else. Lowering this high-growth period return on equity will reduce the price-to-book ratio for the firm.

PBV Ratios and Return on Equity   The ratio of price to book value is strongly influenced by the return on equity. A lower return on equity affects the price–book value ratio directly through the formulation specified in the prior section and indirectly by lowering the expected growth or payout.

Expected growth rate = Retention ratio × Return on equity

The effects of lower return on equity on the price–book value ratio can be seen by going back to Illustration 19.3 and changing the return on equity for the firm valued in that example.

ILLUSTRATION 19.5:   Return on Equity and Price–Book Value

In Illustration 19.3, we estimated a price-to-book ratio for the firm of 4.01, based on a return on equity of 25% for the next five years of high growth, which, in turn, allowed the firm to generate growth rates of 20% in high growth. The expected return on equity of 10%, after year 5, sustained the stable growth rate of 4% in perpetuity:

Growth rate in first five years = Retention ratio × ROE = 0.8 × 25% = 20%

Growth rate after year 5 = Retention ratio × ROE = 0.40 × 10% = 4%

If the firm's return on equity, during the next five years, drops to 12%, the price–book value ratio will reflect the drop. The lower return on equity will also lower expected growth in the initial high-growth period:

Growth rate in first five years = Retention ratio × ROE = 0.8 × 12% = 9.6%

Assuming that the return on equity after year 5 remains 10%, the new price–book value ratio can then be calculated as follows:

$$\frac{\text{Price}}{\text{Book}} = 0.12 \times \left[\frac{0.20 \times \left(1 - \frac{(1.096)^5}{(1.095)^5}\right)}{(.095 - .096)} + \frac{(1.096)^4 (1.04)(0.60)}{(.095 - .04)(1.095)^5} \right] = 1.36$$

The drop in the ROE has a two-layered impact. First, it lowers the growth rate in earnings and/or the expected payout ratio, thus having an indirect effect on the PBV ratio. Second, it reduces the PBV ratio directly.

The price–book value ratio is also influenced by the cost of equity, with higher costs of equity leading to lower price–book value ratios. The influence of the return on equity and the cost of equity can be consolidated in one measure by taking the difference between the two—a measure of excess equity return. The larger the return on equity relative to the cost of equity, the greater the price–book value ratio. In Illustrations 19.3 and 19.5, for instance, the firm, which had a cost of equity of 9.5 percent, went from having a return on equity that was 15.5 percent greater than the required rate of return to a return on equity that was only 2.5 percent greater than the required rate of return. Consequently, its price–book value ratio declined from 7.89 to 1.25. Figure 19.2 shows the price–book value ratio as a function of the difference between the return on equity and the cost of equity. Note that when the return on equity is equal to the cost of equity, the price is equal to the book value.

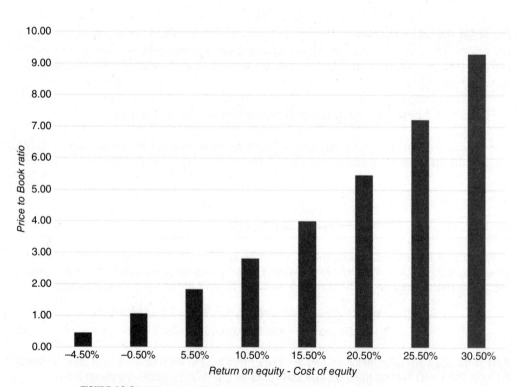

FIGURE 19.2   Price–Book Value as a Function of Return Differential

Determinants of Return on Equity   The difference between return on equity and the cost of equity is a measure of a firm's capacity to earn excess returns in the business in which it operates. Corporate strategists have examined the determinants of the size and expected duration of these excess profits (and high ROE) using a variety of frameworks. One of the better known is the "forces of competition" framework developed by Porter (1980). In his approach, competition arises not only from established producers producing the same product but also from suppliers of substitutes and from potential new entrants into the market. Figure 19.3 summarizes the five forces of competition.

In Porter's framework, a firm can maintain a high return on equity because there are significant barriers to entry by new firms, or because the firm has significant advantages over its competition. The analysis of the return on equity of a firm can be made richer and much more informative by examining the competitive environment in which it operates. There may also be clues in this analysis to the future direction of the return on equity. Value investors have their own variant on this theme that they call the "moat". A firm with strong and sustainable competitive advantages is considered to have a strong moat, which in turn makes it more valuable. In the framework developed in this chapter, the strength of the moat is measured by the level of the ROE and how long it can be maintained.

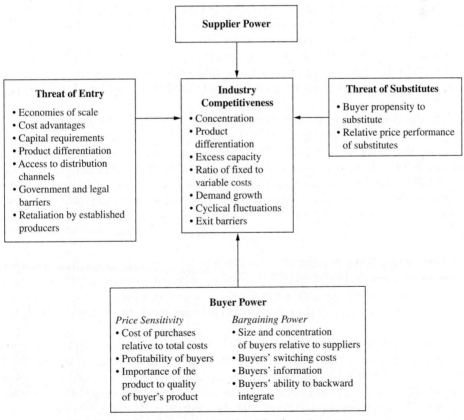

FIGURE 19.3   Five Forces of Competition and Return on Equity
Source: Adapted from Porter, 1980.

eqmult.xls: This spreadsheet enables you to estimate the price-earnings ratio for a stable-growth or high-growth firm, given its fundamentals.

Applications of Price–Book Value Ratios

There are several potential applications for the principles developed in the preceding section, and we will consider three in this section. We will first look at what causes price-to-book ratios for entire markets to change over time, and when a low- or high-price-to-book ratio for a market can be viewed as a sign of undervaluation (or overvaluation). We will next compare the price-to-book ratios of firms within a sector and extend this to look at firms across the market and what you need to control in making these comparisons. Finally, we will look at the factors that cause the price-to-book ratio of an individual firm to change over time and how this can be used as a tool for analyzing restructurings.

PBV Ratios for a Market   The price-to-book value ratio for an entire market is determined by the same variables that determine the price-to-book value ratio for an individual firm. Other things remaining equal; you would expect the price-to-book ratio for a market to go up as the equity return spread (ROE minus cost of equity) earned by firms in the market increases. Conversely, you would expect the price-to-book ratio for the market to decrease as the equity return spread earned by firms decreases.

Chapter 18 noted the increase in the price-earnings ratio for the S&P 500 from 1960 to 2023. Over that period, the price-to-book value ratio for the market also increased. Figure 19.4 reports on the price-to-book ratio for the S&P 500 and the return on equity for S&P 500 firms.

Note the rise in price to book ratios between 1980 and 2000, as the returns on equity rose for the index during that period, partly because of the influx of technology stocks into the index. In the 2001–2010 time period, returns on equity and price-to-book ratios both trended downwards, before reversing themselves between 2011 and 2021. While it may be a stretch to attribute the rise in price-to-book ratios to any one fact, it is undeniable that lower interest rates contributed to raising the price-to-book in the last decade, since building off a 2% treasury bond rate yields a much lower cost of equity.

Comparisons Across Firms in a Sector   Price–book value ratios vary across firms for a number of reasons—different expected growth, different payout ratios, different risk levels, and most importantly, different returns on equity. Comparisons of price–book value ratios across firms that do not take into account these differences are likely to be flawed.

The most common approach to estimating PBV ratios for a firm is to choose a group of comparable firms, to calculate the average PBV ratio for this group, and to base the PBV ratio estimate for a firm on this average. The adjustments made to reflect differences in fundamentals between the firm being valued and the comparable group are usually made subjectively. There are several problems with this approach. First, the definition of a comparable firm is essentially a subjective one. The use of other firms in the industry as the

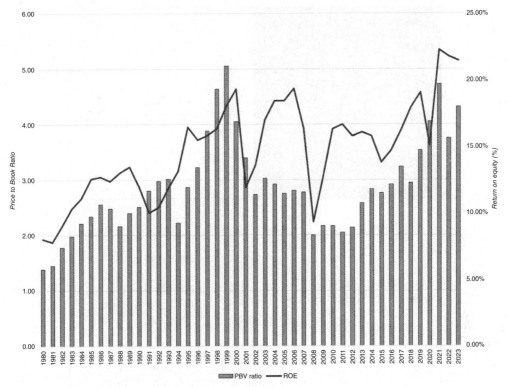

FIGURE 19.4 Price-to-Book Ratios and ROE—S&P 500

control group is often not a complete solution, because firms within the same industry can have very different business mixes and risk and growth profiles. There is also plenty of potential for bias. Second, even when a legitimate group of comparable firms can be constructed, differences will continue to persist in fundamentals between the firm being valued and this group. Adjusting for differences subjectively does not provide a satisfactory solution to this problem, since these judgments are only as good as the analysts making them.

Given the relationship between price–book value ratios and returns on equity, it should not be surprising to see firms that have high returns on equity sell for well above book value and firms that have low returns on equity sell at or below book value. The firms that should draw attention from investors are those that provide mismatches of price–book value ratios and returns on equity—low PBV ratios and high ROE, or high PBV ratios and low ROE. There are two ways in which we can bring home these mismatches—a matrix approach and a sector regression.

Matrix Approach   If the essence of misvaluation is finding firms that have price-to-book ratios that do not go with their equity return spreads, the mismatch can be brought home by plotting the price-to-book value ratios of firms against their excess returns (i.e., the difference between return and cost of equity). Figure 19.5 presents such a plot.

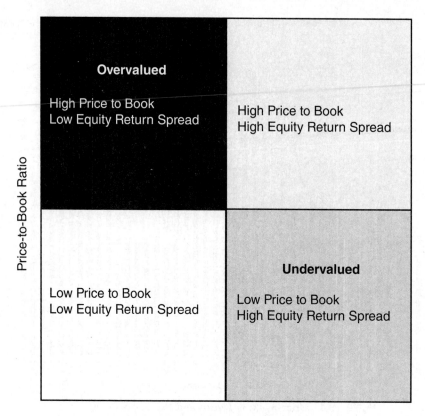

FIGURE 19.5   Price-to-Book Ratios and Return on Equity

If we assume that firms within a sector have similar costs of equity, we could replace the equity return spread with the raw return on equity. Though we often use current returns on equity in practice, the matrix is based on expected returns on equity in the future.

Regression Approach   If the price-to-book ratio is largely a function of the return on equity, we could regress the former against the latter:

$$\text{Price to Book} = a + b \text{ Return on equity}$$

If the relationship is strong and linear, we could use this regression to obtain predicted price-to-book ratios for all the firms in the sector, separating out those firms that are undervalued from those that are overvalued.

This regression can be enriched in two ways. The first is to allow for nonlinear relationships between price-to-book and return on equity; this can be done either by transforming the variables (e.g., natural logs, exponentials, etc.) or by running nonlinear regressions. The second is to expand the regression to include other independent variables such as risk and growth.

ILLUSTRATION 19.6:   **Comparing Price-to-Book Value Ratios: European Apparel Companies in May 2024**

Table 19.3 reports on the price-to-book ratios for European apparel companies with market capitalizations exceeding $1 billion in May 2024:

TABLE 19.3   PBV and ROE of European Apparel firms

Company Name	PBV	ROE	Company Name	PBV	ROE	Company Name	PBV	ROE
LVMH	5.88	24.87%	Pandora A/S	23.11	121.57%	Capri Holdings Limited	2.52	−14.32%
Hermès International	14.71	28.36%	The Swatch Group	0.76	7.12%	Hugo Boss AG	2.54	19.61%
Christian Dior	5.77	29.28%	Birkenstock Holding	3.93	3.13%	Ermenegildo Zegna N.V.	3.32	14.46%
Compagnie Financière Richemont	4.25	11.51%	LPP SA	6.91	34.10%	CCC S.A.	11.07	−6.69%
adidas AG	8.53	2.75%	Amer Sports, Inc	1.93	−5.53%	Coats Group plc	3.11	10.12%
Kering SA	2.51	19.61%	PUMA SE	2.59	9.94%	Salvatore Ferragamo S.p.A.	2.10	3.61%
Prada S.p.A.	4.95	17.41%	Brunello Cucinelli S.p.A	13.94	25.95%	TOD'S S.p.A.	1.28	4.59%
Moncler S.p.A.	5.05	19.04%	Burberry Group plc	3.24	23.54%	New Wave Group AB (publ)	2.32	14.91%
On Holding AG	10.34	10.70%	Samsonite International S.A.	2.99	27.51%	Dr. Martens plc	2.30	18.80%

The average (median) price-to-book ratio for the sector is 5.63 (3.28), but the range in price-to-book ratios is large, with the Swatch Group trading at 0.76 times book value and Pandora AS trading at 23.11 times book value.

We will begin by plotting price-to-book ratios against returns on equity for these firms in Figure 19.6. Pandora, with a return on equity of 121.57% and a price-to-book ratio of 23.11 is the outlier in the distribution.

While the scatter plot indicates a positive relationship between PBV and return on equity, we extend the analysis by regressing the price-to-book ratio against return on equity, and we obtain the following:

$$PBV = 3.05 + 14.64 \text{ Return on equity} \quad R^2 = 47.0\%$$
$$(3.34) \ (4.71)$$

If we extend this regression to include expected growth in earnings per share (EPS: g_{EPS}) as a measure of risk, we get:

$$PBV = 1.66 + 14.44 \text{ Return on equity} + 11.73 \ g_{EPS} \quad R^2 = 58.9\%$$
$$(1.70) \ (5.17) \qquad\qquad\qquad (2.64)$$

The latter regression can be used to estimate predicted price-to-book ratios for these companies in Table 19.4:

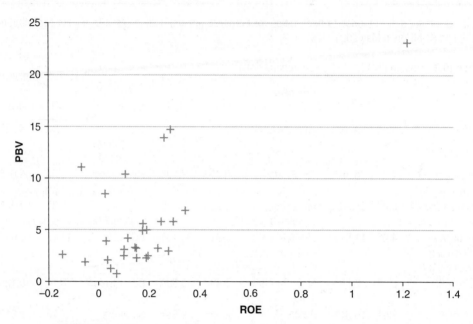

FIGURE 19.6   Price to Book versus Return on Equity: European Apparel

TABLE 19.4   Predicted PBV of European Apparel Firms

Company Name	PBV	ROE	Expected growth in EPS	Predicted PBV	Under- or Over-valued
LVMH	5.88	24.87%	10.70%	6.51	−9.62%
Hermès International	14.71	28.36%	10.80%	7.02	109.47%
Christian Dior	5.77	29.28%	0.00%	5.89	−1.98%
Compagnie Financière Richemont	4.25	11.51%	10.10%	4.51	−5.67%
adidas AG	8.53	2.75%	59.50%	9.04	−5.61%
Kering SA	2.51	19.61%	−0.81%	4.40	−42.96%
Prada S.p.A.	4.95	17.41%	14.80%	5.91	−16.17%
Moncler S.p.A.	5.05	19.04%	10.20%	5.61	−9.86%
On Holding AG	10.34	10.70%	54.20%	9.56	8.15%
Pandora A/S	23.11	121.57%	16.80%	21.19	9.10%
The Swatch Group	0.76	7.12%	4.18%	3.18	−76.20%
Birkenstock Holding	3.93	3.13%	21.80%	4.67	−15.74%
LPP SA	6.91	34.10%	19.70%	8.89	−22.29%
Amer Sports, Inc	1.93	−5.53%	0.00%	0.86	124.37%
PUMA SE	2.59	9.94%	19.50%	5.38	−51.88%
Brunello Cucinelli S.p.A	13.94	25.95%	22.00%	7.99	74.56%
Burberry Group plc	3.24	23.54%	−3.05%	4.70	−31.11%
Samsonite International S.A.	2.99	27.51%	0.00%	5.63	−46.88%
Capri Holdings Limited	2.52	−14.32%	7.43%	0.46	443.76%
Hugo Boss AG	2.54	19.61%	17.00%	6.49	−60.91%

Company Name	PBV	ROE	Expected growth in EPS	Predicted PBV	Under- or Over-valued
Ermenegildo Zegna	3.32	14.46%	9.86%	4.90	−32.30%
CCC S.A.	NA	−6.69%	NA	0.69	NA
Coats Group plc	3.11	10.12%	10.50%	4.35	−28.57%
Salvatore Ferragamo S.p.A.	2.10	3.61%	0.00%	2.18	−3.59%
TOD'S S.p.A.	1.28	4.59%	0.00%	2.32	−44.98%
New Wave Group AB	2.32	14.91%	11.70%	5.19	−55.29%
Dr. Martens	2.30	18.80%	1.00%	4.49	−48.78%

The most undervalued firm, in percentage terms, in the group is the Swatch, with an actual price-to-book ratio of 0.76 and a predicted price-to-book ratio of 3.18, and the most overvalued, again in percentage terms, is Capri Holdings, with an actual price-to-book ratio of 2.52 and a predicted price-to-book ratio of 0.46.

Comparing Firms Across the Market   In contrast to the comparable firm approach, you could look at how firms are priced across the entire market to predict PBV ratios for individual firms. The simplest way of summarizing this information is with a multiple regression, with the PBV ratio as the dependent variable, and proxies for risk, growth, return on equity, and payout forming the independent variables.

Past Studies   The relationship between price–book value ratios and the return on equity has been highlighted in other studies. Wilcox (1984) posited a strong relationship between the price-to-book value ratio (plotted on a logarithmic scale) and return on equity. Using data from 1981 for 949 Value Line stocks, he arrived at the following equation:

$$\text{Log (Price-to-Book value)} = -1.00 + 7.51(\text{Return on equity})$$

He also found that this regression has much smaller mean squared error than competing models using price-earnings ratios and/or growth rates.

These PBV ratio regressions were updated in the first edition of this book using data from 1987 to 1991. The Compustat database was used to extract information on price–book value ratios, return on equity, payout ratios, and earnings growth rates (for the preceding five years) for all NYSE and AMEX firms with data available in each year. The betas were obtained from the CRSP tape for each year. All firms with negative book values were eliminated from the sample, and the regression of PBV on the independent variables yielded the following for each year (in Table 19.5):

TABLE 19.5   PBV Market Regressions—1987 to 1991

Year	Regression	R-Squared
1987	PBV = 0.1841 + 2.00 Payout − 0.3940 Beta + 133.89 EGR + 9.35 ROE	0.8617
1988	PBV = 0.7113 + 0.007 Payout − 0.5082 Beta + 46.05 EGR + 6.9374 ROE	0.8405
1989	PBV = 0.4119 + 0.63 Payout − 0.6406 Beta + 100.38 EGR + 9.55 ROE	0.8851
1990	PBV = 0.8124 + 0.99 Payout − 0.1857 Beta + 111.30 EGR + 6.61 ROE	0.8846
1991	PBV = 1.1065 + 35.05 Payout − 0.6471 Beta + 100.87 EGR + 10.51 ROE	0.8601

where   PBV = Price–book value ratio at the end of the year
    Payout = Dividend payout ratio at the end of the year
      Beta = Beta of the stock
      EGR = Growth rate in earnings over prior five years
      ROE = Return on equity = Net income/Book value of equity

Updated Regressions   In January 2024, we regressed the price-to-book ratios against the fundamentals identified in the preceding section—the return on equity, the payout ratio, the beta, and the expected growth rate over the next five years (from analyst forecasts) for stocks broken down by geography. Table 19.6 contains the results:

TABLE 19.6   PBV Market Regressions—Start of 2024

Region	Regression	R-squared
United States	$PBV = 2.10 + 6.07\, g_{EPS} + 0.69\, Beta + 5.09\, ROE - 0.33\, Payout$	21.9%
Europe	$PBV = 1.20 + 3.25\, g_{EPS} + 0.06\, Beta + 5.78\, ROE + 1.36\, Payout$	17.1%
Japan	$PBV = 0.05 + 0.48\, g_{EPS} + 0.78\, Beta + 10.30\, ROE + 0.10\, Payout$	34.9%
Australia, NZ, & Canada	$PBV = 3.07 + 1.60\, g_{EPS} - 1.49\, Beta + 9.50\, ROE + 1.80\, Payout$	32.9%
Emerging markets	$PBV = 0.99 + 1.80\, g_{EPS} - 0.13\, Beta + 5.52\, ROE - 0.09\, Payout$	36.9%
Global	$PBV = 2.29 + 3.12\, g_{EPS} - 0.16\, Beta + 6.61\, ROE - 0.29\, Payout$	19.8%

The strong positive relationship between price-to-book ratios and returns on equity is not unique to the United States. In fact, as you can see in the table, return on equity remains the most significant explanatory variable for price-to-book ratios across the world, albeit with different coefficients.

ILLUSTRATION 19.7:   Valuing Nike Using the Cross-Sectional Regressions

Assume that you had been asked to value Nike early in January 2024, and that you had obtained the following data on the company:

    Book value of equity = \$14, 004 million
    Payout = 41.76 %
    Earnings growth rate = 12.37 %
    Return on equity = 36.38%
    Beta = 1.06

Plugging into the U.S. market regression, we get:

Predicted price-book value ratio = $2.10 + 6.07\,(.1237) + 0.69\,(1.06) + 5.09\,(.3638) - 0.33\,(.4176) = 5.30$

With the global regression, we get:

Predicted price-book value ratio = 2.29 + 3.12(.1237) − 0.16(1.06) + 6.61(.3638) − 0.29(.4176) = 4.79

The stock was trading at a price to book value ratio of 11.10, suggesting that it is overvalued, given its fundamentals, in both the U.S. and global markets.

 MReg.xls: **This dataset on the web reports the results of the latest regression of PBV ratios against fundamentals, using all firms in the market.**

CURRENT VERSUS EXPECTED RETURNS ON EQUITY

In all the comparisons that we have made in this section, we have used a firm's current return on equity to make judgments about valuation. While it is convenient to focus on this current number, the market value of equity is determined by expectations of future returns on equity.

To the extent that there is a strong positive correlation between current ROE and future ROE, using the current return on equity to identify under- or overvalued companies is appropriate. Focusing on the current ROE can be dangerous, however, when the competitive environment is changing, it can lead to significant errors in valuation. In such cases, you should use a forecast return on equity that can be very different from the current return on equity. There are two ways to obtain this forecast:

1. Compute a historical average (over the past three or five years) of the return on equity earned by the firm and substitute this value for the current return on equity when the latter is volatile.
2. Push the firm's current return on equity toward the industry average to reflect competitive pressures. For instance, assume that you are analyzing a computer software firm with a current return on equity of 35 percent and that the industry average return on equity is 20 percent. The forecast return on equity for this firm would be a weighted average of 20 percent and 35 percent, with the weight on the industry average increasing with the speed with which you expect the firm's return to converge on industry norms.

Comparing a Firm's Price-to-Book Ratio across Time   As a firm's return on equity changes over time, you would expect its price-to-book ratio to also change. Specifically, firms that increase their returns on equity should increase their price-to-book ratios, and firms that see their returns on equity deteriorate should see a fall in their price-to-book ratios as well. Another way of thinking about this is in terms of the matrix presented in Figure 19.5, where we argued that firms with low (or high) returns on equity should have low (or high) price-to-book ratios. Thus, one way to measure the effect of the restructuring of a poorly

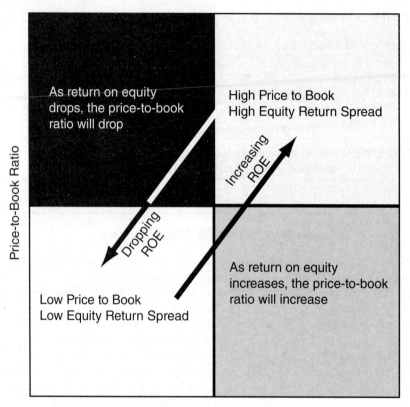

Price-to-Book Ratio

As return on equity drops, the price-to-book ratio will drop

High Price to Book
High Equity Return Spread

Increasing ROE

Dropping ROE

Low Price to Book
Low Equity Return Spread

As return on equity increases, the price-to-book ratio will increase

Return on Equity—Cost of Equity

FIGURE 19.7   Changes in ROE and Changes in PBV Ratio

performing firm (with low return on equity and low price-to-book ratio) is to see where it moves on the matrix. If it succeeds in its endeavor, it should move from the low PBV/low ROE quadrant toward the high PBV/high ROE quadrant. (See Figure 19.7.)

ILLUSTRATION 19.8:   ROE and PBV Ratios: The Case of IBM

IBM provides a classic example of the effects of returns on equity on price–book value ratios. In 1983, IBM was trading at three times its book value, one of the highest price to book value multiples among the Dow 30 stocks at that time. By 1992, the stock was trading at roughly book value, significantly lower than the average ratio for Dow 30 stocks. This decline in the price–book value ratio was triggered by the decline in return on equity at IBM, from 25% in 1983 to negative values in 1992 and 1993. In the years following Lou Gerstner becoming CEO, the firm recovered dramatically and was trading at nine times book value in 1999. Even after the dot-com crash, IBM was able to sustain a strong record of high ROE and high price-to-book ratios from 2001 to 2010. Figure 19.8 illustrates both PBV and ROE between 1983 and 2010 for IBM.

    An investor buying IBM at its low point would have obtained a stock with a low price-to-book and a low return on equity, but the bet would have paid off. As the return on equity improved, IBM migrated from the bottom-left quadrant to the top-right quadrant in the matrix. As its price-to-book ratio improved, the investor would have seen substantial price appreciation and profits.

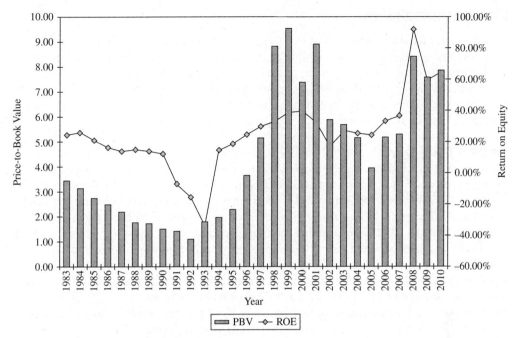

FIGURE 19.8   IBM: The Fall and Rise Again

Tangible and Non-Cash Price-to-Book Ratios   In some value investing circles, it is not the book value of equity that is the metric that market value of equity should be compared, but just the tangible book value of equity. There is a basis for this caution, and it is rooted in the presence of goodwill as an asset on balance sheets—an item that we argued earlier in the book is more plug-in value (reflecting the difference between the price paid to acquire a company and its book value of equity). Thus, the simplest version of price-to-tangible book equity just removes goodwill from the invested capital:

$$\text{Price to tangible book} = \frac{\text{Market capitalization}}{(\text{Book value of equity} - \text{Goodwill})}$$

That adjustment changes very little in terms of our assessment of price-to-book equity, and everything that we said in the context of price-to-book ratios also applies to tangible price to book, with the caveat that the return on equity, a key driver of price-to-book ratios be recomputed on just tangible book equity:

$$\text{Return on tangible equity} = \frac{\text{Net Income}}{(\text{Book value of equity} - \text{Goodwill})}$$

For companies that grow primarily through acquisitions, adjusting book value of equity for goodwill increases return on equity and raises price-to-book ratios, but it is an imperfect adjustment. After all, goodwill reflects many acquisition motives including control and synergy, but it is also a receptacle for overpayment. If you are trying to estimate what a company earns on its equity, as a return on equity, you should incorporate the overpayment in the book equity, and bring down the return on equity, since consistently overpaying on acquisitions will make your equity less valuable over time.

Use in Investment Strategies

Investors have used the relationship between price and book value in a number of investment strategies ranging from the simple to the sophisticated. Some have used low price–book value ratios as a screen to pick undervalued stocks. Others combine price-to-book value ratios with other fundamentals to make the same judgment. Finally, the sheer persistence of higher returns earned by low price-to-book stocks is viewed by some as an indication that the price-to-book value ratio is a proxy for equity risk.

The Link to Excess Returns   Several studies have established a relationship between price–book value ratios and excess returns. Rosenberg, Reid, and Lanstein (1985) found that the average returns on U.S. stocks are positively related to the ratio of a firm's book value to market value. Between 1973 and 1984, the strategy of picking stocks with high book–price ratios (low price–book values) yielded an excess return of 36 basis points a month. Fama and French (1992), in examining the cross section of expected stock returns between 1963 and 1990, established that the positive relationship between book-to-price ratios and average returns persists in both the univariate and multivariate tests, and is even stronger than the small-firm effect in explaining returns. When they classified firms on the basis of book-to-price ratios into 12 portfolios, firms in the lowest book-to-price (highest PBV) class earned an average monthly return of 0.30 percent, while firms in the highest book-to-price (lowest PBV) class earned an average monthly return of 1.83 percent for the 1963–1990 period.

Chan, Hamao, and Lakonishok (1991) found that the book-to-market ratio has a strong role in explaining the cross section of average returns on Japanese stocks. Capaul, Rowley, and Sharpe (1993) extended the analysis of price–book value ratios across other international markets between 1981 and 1992, and concluded that value stocks (stocks with low price–book value ratios) earned excess returns in every market that they analyzed. Their annualized estimates of the return differential earned by stocks with low price–book value ratios, over the market index, are summarized in Table 19.7:

Although this study is dated, the conclusion that lower price-to-book stocks earn higher returns than higher price-to-book stocks look robust.

Using Price–Book Value Ratios as Investment Screens   The excess returns earned by firms with low price–book value ratios have been exploited by investment strategies that use price–book value ratios as a screen. Benjamin Graham, for instance, in his classic book on

TABLE 19.7   PBV Excess Return by Country

Country	Added Return to Low PBV Portfolio
France	3.26%
Germany	1.39%
Switzerland	1.17%
United Kingdom	1.09%
Japan	3.43%
United States	1.06%
Europe	1.30%
Global	1.88%

security analysis, listed price being less than two-thirds of book value as one of the criteria to be used to pick stocks.

The discussion in the preceding section emphasized the importance of return on equity in determining the price–book value ratio and noted that only firms with high return on equity and a low price–book value ratio could be considered undervalued.

Price to Book as a Proxy for Risk   The persistence of excess returns earned by firms with lower price-to-book ratios indicates either that the market is inefficient, or that the price-to-book ratio is a proxy for equity risk. In other words, if lower price-to-book ratio stocks are viewed by the market as riskier than firms with higher price-to-book ratios, the higher returns earned by these stocks would be a fair return for this risk. In fact, this is the conclusion that Fama and French (1992) reached after examining the returns earned by lower price-to-book stocks.

While you cannot reject this hypothesis out of hand, you would need to put it to the test. What is the additional risk that low price-to-book stocks are exposed to? It is true that some low price-to-book ratio companies are highly levered and may not stay in business. For the most part, though, a portfolio composed of low price-to-book ratio stocks does not seem any more risky than a portfolio of high price-to-book stocks—their leverage and earnings variability are similar.

VALUE-TO-BOOK RATIOS

Instead of relating the market value of equity to the book value of equity, the value-to-book ratio relates the firm value to the book value of capital of the firm. Consequently, it can be viewed as the firm value analogue to the price-to-book ratio.

Definition

The value-to-book ratio is obtained by dividing the market value of both debt and equity by the book value of capital invested in a firm:

$$\text{Firm Value to book} = \frac{(\text{Market value of equity} + \text{Market value of debt})}{(\text{Book value of equity} + \text{Book value of debt})}$$

If the market value of debt is unavailable, the book value of debt can be used in the numerator as well. Needless to say, debt has to be consistently defined for both the numerator and denominator. For instance, if you choose to convert operating leases to debt for computing market value of debt, you have to add the present value of operating leases to the book value of debt as well.

There are two common variants of this multiple that do not pass the consistency test. One uses the book value of assets, which will generally exceed the book value of capital by the magnitude of current liabilities, in the denominator. This will result in value-to-book ratios that are biased down for firms with substantial current liabilities. The other uses the enterprise value in the numerator, with cash netted from the market values of debt and equity. Since the book value of equity incorporates the cash holdings of the firm, this will also bias the multiple down. If you decide to use enterprise value in the numerator, you should net cash out of the denominator as well. Netting out cash from book capital creates a measure called invested capital:

$$\text{Invested capital} = \text{Market value of equity} + \text{Market value of debt} - \text{Cash}$$

In practice, in the absence of easily accessible market values for debt, analysts often use book value as a proxy and cash includes marketable securities.

$$\text{EV to IC} = \frac{(\text{Market value of equity} + \text{Market value of debt} - \text{Cash})}{(\text{Book value of equity} + \text{Book value of debt} - \text{Cash})}$$

In addition, the multiple may need to be adjusted for a firm's cross holdings just as EV/EBITDA multiples were. The adjustment was described in detail for the enterprise value to EBITDA multiple in Chapter 18, and will require that you net out the portion of the market value and book value of equity that is attributable to subsidiaries.

Description

The distribution of the EV-to-book ratio resembles that of the price-to-book ratio. Figure 19.9 presents the distributions for EV/invested capital for U.S. and global companies in January 2024. As with the other multiples, it is a heavily skewed and the average values

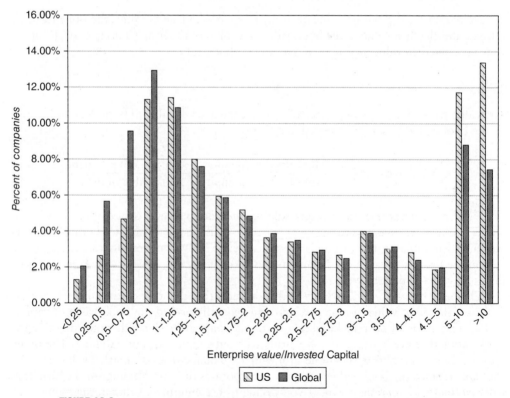

FIGURE 19.9   EV/Invested Capital: U.S. and Global Firms in January 2024

are much higher than the medians: The median EV/Invested capital for U.S. (global) firms in January 2024 was 1.97 (1.54), and there are firms where enterprise value is negative (because cash exceeds the combined market values of debt and equity).

One of the interesting by-products of switching from price-to-book ratios to value-to-book ratios is that we lose very few firms in the sample with the latter. It is rarer for firms to have negative invested capital than it is for them to have negative book value of equity.

---

 pbvdata.xls: **This dataset on the web summarizes value-to-book multiples and fundamentals by industry group in the United States for the most recent year.**

Analysis

The value-to-book ratio is a firm value multiple. To analyze it, we go back to a free cash flow to the firm valuation model, and use it to value a stable growth firm:

$$\text{Enterprise value} = \frac{\text{FCFF}_1}{(\text{Cost of capital} - \text{Expected growth rate})}$$

Substituting in FCFF = EBIT $(1 - t)$ (1-Reinvestment rate) into the equation, we get:

$$\text{Enterprise value} = \frac{\text{EBIT}_1(1 - t)(\text{Reinvestment rate})}{(\text{Cost of capital} - \text{Expected growth rate})}$$

Dividing both sides by the invested capital, we arrive at the intrinsic value equation for EV to invested capital for a stable growth firm:[3]

$$\frac{\text{Enterprise value}}{\text{Invested capital}} = \frac{\text{ROIC} \times \text{Reinvestment rate}}{(\text{Cost of capital} - \text{Expected growth rate})}$$

The EV-to-invested capital ratio is fundamentally determined by its return on capital—firms with high returns on capital tend to have high EV-to-invested capital ratios. In fact, the determinants of value-to-book mirror the determinants of price-to-book equity, but we replace equity measures with firm value measures—the ROE with the ROC, the cost of equity with the cost of capital, and the payout ratio with (1 − Reinvestment rate). In fact, if we substitute in the fundamental equation for the reinvestment rate:

$$\text{Reinvestment rate} = \text{Expected growth rate}/\text{ROIC}$$

$$\frac{\text{Enterprise value}}{\text{Invested capital}} = \frac{\text{ROIC} - \text{Expected growth rate}}{\text{Cost of capital} - \text{Expected growth rate}}$$

---

[3] As with the return on equity, if return on capital is defined in terms of contemporaneous earnings (ROIC = EBIT_0/Book capital), there will be an extra $(1 + g)$ in the numerator.

The analysis can be extended to cover high-growth firms, with the value-to-book capital ratio determined by the return on capital, cost of capital, growth rate, and reinvestment—in the high growth and stable growth periods:

$$\frac{EV}{IC} = ROIC_{hg} \times \left[\frac{\left(1 - RIR_{hg}\right) \times \left(1 - \dfrac{(1+g)^n}{\left(1 + k_{c,hg}\right)^n}\right)}{\left(k_{c,hg} - g\right)} + \frac{(1+g)^{n-1}\left(1 + g_{st}\right)\left(1 - RIR_{st}\right)}{\left(k_{c,st} - g_{st}\right)(1 + k_{c,hg})^n} \right]$$

where ROC = Return on capital (hg: high-growth period; st: stable-growth period)

RIR = Reinvestment rate (hg: high-growth period; st: stable-growth period)

k_c = Cost of capital (hg: high-growth period; st: stable-growth period)

 firmmult.xls: This spreadsheet enables you to estimate firm value multiples for a stable-growth or high-growth firm, given its fundamentals.

ROC, ROIC, ROA, AND ROE

We have emphasized the importance of measuring the returns generated by a firm on its investments through both the DCF and relative valuation sections, but we have used different measures of accounting returns: return on equity, return on capital, and return on invested capital. In fact, there are many who also compute return on assets as a measure. So, how do they relate to each other, and which one should you use?

Let's start with what they have in common. They all relate current earnings in the numerator to the book value in the denominator, but they measure earnings and book value differently.

- With return on equity, we divide earnings to equity investors (net income) by the book value of equity to get a measure of how much return is being earned by equity investors. This is the measure we use when our comparison metric is the cost of equity and to get growth rates in equity earnings (for the dividend discount and FCFE models).

- We use return on capital (ROC) and return on invested capital (ROIC) interchangeably and obtain them by dividing operating income by the book value of invested capital; this is the sum of the book value of debt and equity with cash netted out. We compare this return to the cost of capital and to derive growth rates in operating income (for FCFF calculations).

- The return on assets is a mixed measure that really does not fit in well. Since it is obtained by dividing net income or operating income by total assets, it is not directly comparable to either cost of equity or capital. We would suggest that it not be used in valuation.

Finally, we prefer to compute all of these returns by taking the income in a given year and dividing it by the book value at the end of the prior year. There are others who prefer to use the average over the year, and if that is the practice, it should be followed consistently.

Application

The value-to-book ratios can be compared across firms just as the price-to-book value of equity ratio was in the preceding section. The key variable to control in making this comparison is the return on capital. The value matrix developed for price-to-book ratios can be adapted for the value-to-book ratio in Figure 19.10. Firms with high return on capital will tend to have high value-to-book value ratios, whereas firms with low return on capital will generally have lower value-to-book ratios.

This matrix also yields an interesting link to a widely used value enhancement measure—economic value added (EVA). One of the biggest sales pitches for EVA, which is computed as the product of the return spread (ROC minus cost of capital) and capital invested, is its high correlation with market value added (MVA), which is defined as the

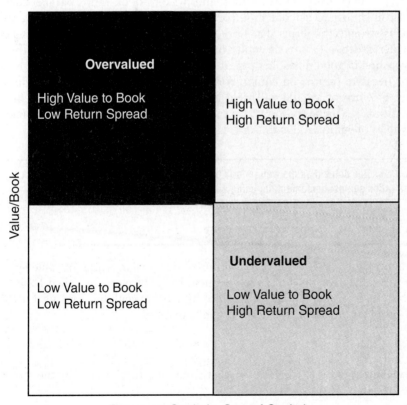

FIGURE 19.10 Valuation Matrix: Value to Book and Excess Returns

TABLE 19.8   EV-to-IC Market Regressions—Start of 2024

Region	Regression	R-squared
United States	EV/IC= 5.78 + 0.66 $g_{Revenue}$ + 0.57 ROIC − 6.20 DFR	44.2%
Europe	EV/IC= 3.56 + 2.82 $g_{Revenue}$ + 4.10 ROIC − 3.54 DFR	51.7%
Japan	EV/IC= 3.55 + 1.22 $g_{Revenue}$ + 0.64 ROIC − 4.30 DFR	41.1%
Australia, NZ, & Canada	EV/IC= 2.38 + 0.71 $g_{Revenue}$ + 4.62 ROIC − 2.06 DFR	44.4%
Emerging markets	EV/IC= 3.29 + 1.25 $g_{Revenue}$ + 0.96 ROIC − 3.76 DFR	50.1%
Global	EV/IC= 4.70 + 0.70 $g_{Revenue}$ + 0.86 ROIC − 5.00 DFR	44.3%

difference between market value and book value of capital. This is not surprising, since MVA is a variant on the value-to-book ratio and EVA is a variant on the return spread.

Is the link between value-to-book and return on capital stronger or weaker than the link between price-to-book and return on equity? To examine this question, we regressed the EV/invested capital (IC) against return on capital using data on all firms in January 2024, broken down by geography in Table 19.8, where DFR = Debt-to-capital ratio (market value). The regression yields results similar to those obtained for price-to-book ratios, with return on invested capital being the prime driver of differences in enterprise value to invested capital ratios.

If the results from using value-to-book and price-to-book ratios parallel each other, why would you choose to use one multiple over the other? The case for using value-to-book ratios is stronger for firms that have high and/or shifting leverage. Firms can use leverage to increase their returns on equity, but in the process they also increase the volatility in the measure: in good times they report very high returns on equity, and in bad times, very low or negative returns on equity. For such firms, the value-to-book ratio and the accompanying return on capital will yield more stable and reliable estimates of relative value. In addition, the value-to-book ratio can be computed even for firms that have negative book values of equity, and is thus less likely to be biased.

 MReg.xls: **This dataset on the web reports the results of the latest regression of book value ratios against fundamentals, using all firms in the market.**

TOBIN'S Q: MARKET VALUE/REPLACEMENT COST

James Tobin presented an alternative to traditional financial measures of value by comparing the market value of an asset to its replacement cost. His measure, called Tobin's Q, has several adherents in academia but still has not broken through into practical use, largely because of problems in getting the necessary information.

Definition

Tobin's Q is estimated by dividing the market value of a firm's assets by the replacement cost of these assets.

$$\text{Tobin's Q} = \frac{\text{Market value of assets in place}}{\text{Replacement cost of assets in place}}$$

In cases where inflation has pushed up the replacement cost of the assets or where technology has reduced the cost of the assets, this measure may provide a more updated measure of the value of the assets than accounting book value. The rationale for the measure is simple. Firms that earn negative excess returns and do not utilize their assets efficiently will have a Tobin's Q that is less than 1. Firms that utilize their assets more efficiently will trade at a Tobin's Q that exceeds 1.

While this measure has some advantages in theory, it does have some practical problems. The first is that the replacement value of some assets may be difficult to estimate, especially if assets are not traded on a market. The second is that even where replacement values are available, substantially more information is needed to construct this measure than the traditional price–book value ratio. In practice, analysts often use shortcuts to arrive at Tobin's Q, using book value of assets as a proxy for replacement value and market value of debt and equity as a proxy for the market value of assets. In these cases, Tobin's Q resembles the value-to-book value ratio described in the preceding section.

Description

If we use the strict definition of Tobin's Q, we cannot get a cross-sectional distribution of the multiple because the information to estimate it is neither easily accessible nor even available. This is a serious impediment to using the multiple, in pricing, because we have no sense of what a high, low, or average number for the multiple would be. For instance, assume that you find a firm trading at 1.2 times the replacement cost of the assets. You would have no way of knowing whether you were paying too much or too little for this firm without knowing the summary statistics for the market.

Analysis

The value obtained from Tobin's Q is determined by two variables—the market value of the firm and the replacement cost of assets in place. In inflationary times, when the cost of replacing assets increases over time, Tobin's Q will generally be lower than the unadjusted price–book value ratio, and the difference will increase for firms with older assets. Conversely, if the cost of replacing assets declines much faster than the book value (because of technological changes), Tobin's Q will generally be higher than the unadjusted price–book value ratio.

Tobin's Q is also determined by how efficiently a firm manages its assets and extracts value from them relative to the next best bidder. To see why, note that the market value of an asset will be equal to its replacement cost when assets earn their required return. (If the return earned on capital is equal to the cost of capital, investments have a zero-net present value, and the present value of the cash flows from the investment will be equal to the replacement cost.) Carrying this logic forward, Tobin's Q will be less than 1 if a firm earns less than its required return on investments, and more than 1 if it earns positive excess returns.

Applications

Tobin's Q is a practical measure of value for a mature firm with most or all its assets in place, where replacement cost can be estimated for the assets. Consider, for example, a steel company with little or no growth potential. The market value of this firm can be used as a proxy for the market value of its assets, and you could adjust the book value of the assets owned by the firm for inflation. In contrast, estimating the market value of assets owned would be difficult for a high-growth firm, since the market value of equity for this firm will include a premium for future growth.

Tobin's Q is more a measure of the perceived quality of a firm's management than it is of misvaluation, with poorly managed firms trading at market values that are lower than the replacement cost of the assets that they own. In fact, several studies have examined whether such firms are more likely to be taken over. Lang, Stulz, and Walkling (1991) concluded that firms with low Tobin's Q are more likely to be taken over for purposes of restructuring and increasing value. They also find that shareholders of high Tobin's Q bidders gain significantly more from successful tender offers than shareholders of low Tobin's Q bidders.

CONCLUSION

The relationship between price and book value is much more complex than most investors realize. The price–book value ratio of a firm is determined by its expected payout ratio, its expected growth rate in earnings, and its riskiness. The most important determinant, however, is the return on equity earned by the firm—higher returns lead to higher price–book value ratios, and lower returns lead to lower PBV ratios. The mismatch that should draw investor attention is the one between return on equity and price–book value ratios—high price–book value ratios with low returns on equity (overvalued) and low price–book value ratios with high returns on equity (undervalued).

The value-to-book ratio is the firm value analogue to the price-to-book ratio, and it is a function of the return on capital earned by the firm, its cost of capital, and the reinvestment rate. Again, though, firms with low value-to-book ratios and high expected returns on capital can be viewed as undervalued.

QUESTIONS AND SHORT PROBLEMS

In the problems following, use an equity risk premium of 5.5 percent if none is specified.

1. Answer true or false to the following statements, with a short explanation.
   a. A stock that sells for less than book value is undervalued.
      True ___ False ___
   b. If a company's return on equity drops, its price–book value ratio will generally drop more than proportionately (e.g., if the return on equity drops by half, the price–book value ratio will drop by more than half).
      True ___ False ___
   c. A combination of a low price–book value ratio and a high expected return on equity suggests that a stock is undervalued.
      True ___ False ___
   d. Other things remaining equal, a higher-growth stock will have a higher price–book value ratio than a lower-growth stock.
      True ___ False ___
   e. In the Gordon growth model, firms with higher dividend payout ratios will have higher price–book value ratios.
      True ___ False ___

2. NCH Corporation, which markets cleaning chemicals, insecticides, and other products, paid dividends of $2 per share in 1993 on earnings of $4 per share. The book value of equity per share was $40, and earnings were expected to grow 6% a year in the long term. The stock had a beta of 0.85 and was selling for $60 per share. (The Treasury bond rate was 7%, and the market risk premium was 5.5%.)
   a. Based on these inputs, estimate the price–book value ratio for NCH.
   b. How much would the return on equity have to increase to justify the price–book value ratio at which NCH was selling for in 1993?

3. You are analyzing the price–book value ratios for firms in the trucking industry, relative to returns on equity and required rates of return. The data on the companies is as follows:

Company	PBV	ROE	Beta
Builders Transport	2.00	11.5%	1.00
Carolina Freight	0.60	5.5%	1.20
Consolidated Freight	2.60	12.0%	1.15
J.B. Hunt	2.50	14.5%	1.00
M.S. Carriers	2.50	12.5%	1.15
Roadway Services	3.00	14.0%	1.15
Ryder System	2.25	13.0%	1.05
Xtra Corporation	2.80	16.5%	1.10

The Treasury bond rate is 7%, and the market risk premium is 5.5%.
   a. Compute the average PBV ratio, return on equity, and beta for the industry.
   b. Based on these averages, are stocks in the industry under- or overvalued relative to book values?

4. United Healthcare, a health maintenance organization, is expected to have earnings growth of 30% for the next five years and 6% after that. The dividend payout ratio will be only 10% during the high-growth phase but will increase to 60% in steady state. The stock has a beta of 1.65 currently, but the beta is expected to drop to 1.10 in steady state. (The Treasury bond rate is 7.25%.)
   a. Estimate the price–book value ratio for United Healthcare, given the inputs as given.
   b. How sensitive is the price–book value ratio to estimates of growth during the high-growth period?
   c. United Healthcare trades at a price–book value ratio of 7.00. How long would extraordinary growth have to last (at a 30% annual rate) to justify this PBV ratio?

5. Johnson & Johnson, a leading manufacturer of health care products, had a return on equity of 31.5% in 1993, and paid out 37% of its earnings as dividends. The stock had a beta of 1.25. (The Treasury bond rate was 6%, and the risk premium was 5.5%.) The extraordinary growth was expected to last for 10 years, after which the growth rate was expected to drop to 6% and the return on equity to 15% (the beta would move to 1.)
   a. Assuming the return on equity and dividend payout ratio continue at current levels for the high-growth period, estimate the PBV ratio for Johnson & Johnson.
   b. If health care reform passes, it is believed that Johnson & Johnson's return on equity will drop to 20% for the high growth phase. If the company chooses to maintain its existing dividend payout ratio, estimate the new PBV ratio for Johnson & Johnson. (You can assume that the inputs for the steady state period are unaffected.)

6. Assume that you have done a regression of PBV ratios for all firms on the New York Stock Exchange, and arrived at the following result:

$$PBV = 0.88 + 0.82\,\text{Payout} + 7.79\,\text{Growth} - 0.41\,\text{Beta} + 13.81\,\text{ROE} \quad R^2 = 0.65$$

where   Payout = Dividend payout ratio during most recent period

         Growth = Projected growth rate in earnings over next five years

           Beta = Beta of the stock in most current period

To illustrate, a firm with a payout ratio of 40%, a beta of 1.25, a ROE of 25%, and expected growth rate of 15% would have had a price–book value ratio of:

$$PBV = 0.88 + 0.82(0.4) + 7.79(.15) - 0.41(1.25) + 13.81(.25) = 5.3165$$

     a. What use, if any, would you put the R-squared of the regression to?

     b. Assume that you have also run a sector regression on a company and estimated a price-to-book ratio based on that regression. Why might your result from the market regression yield a different result from the sector regression?

7. SoftSoap Corporation is a large consumer product firm that reported after-tax operating income of $600 million in the recent financial year. At the beginning of the year, the firm reported book value of equity of $4 billion and book value of debt of $1 billion. The market value of equity was $8 billion, the market value of debt was $1 billion, and the firm had a cost of equity of 11% and an after-tax cost of debt of 4%. If the firm is in stable growth, expecting to grow 4% a year in perpetuity, estimate the correct value-to-book value ratio for the firm.

8. Lyondell Inc. is a conglomerate with a value-to-book capital ratio of 2.0. If the firm is in stable growth, expecting to grow 4% a year in perpetuity, and has a cost of capital of 10%, what return on capital is the market assuming in perpetuity for Lyondell?

9. Estimate the value-to-book capital ratio for Zapata Enterprises, a trading firm in high growth, with the following characteristics:

	High Growth	Stable Growth
After-tax return on capital	15%	12%
Expected growth rate	12%	4%
Cost of capital	10%	9%

If high growth is expected to last 10 years, estimate the correct value-to-book ratio for Zapata.

10. If Tobin's Q is computed by dividing the market value of traded equity and debt by the book value of assets, you will overestimate the value for high-growth firms. Explain why.

CHAPTER 20

Revenue Multiples and Sector-Specific Multiples

While earnings and book value multiples are intuitively appealing and widely used, analysts in recent years have increasingly turned to alternative multiples to value companies. For young firms that have negative earnings, multiples of revenues have replaced multiples of earnings. In addition, these firms are being valued on multiples of sector-specific measures, such as the number of customers, subscribers, or other revenue drivers. In this chapter, the reasons for the increased use of revenue multiples are examined first, followed by an analysis of the determinants of these multiples and how best to use them in valuation. This is followed by a short discussion of the sector-specific multiples, the dangers associated with their use and the adjustments that might be needed to make them work.

REVENUE MULTIPLES

A revenue multiple measures the value of the equity or a business relative to the revenues that it generates. As with other multiples, other things remaining equal, firms that trade at low multiples of revenues are viewed as cheap relative to firms that trade at high multiples of revenues.

Revenue multiples have proved attractive to analysts for a number of reasons. First, unlike earnings and book value ratios, which can become negative for many firms and thus not meaningful, revenue multiples are available even for the most troubled firms and for very young firms. Thus, the potential for bias created by eliminating firms in the sample is far lower. Second, unlike earnings and book value, which are heavily influenced by accounting decisions on depreciation, inventory, research and development (R&D), acquisition accounting, and extraordinary charges, revenue is relatively difficult to manipulate. Third, revenue multiples are not as volatile as earnings multiples, and hence are less likely to be affected by year-to-year swings in a firm's fortunes. For instance, the price-earnings ratio of a cyclical firm changes much more than its price-sales ratios, because earnings are much more sensitive to economic changes than revenues are.

The biggest disadvantage of focusing on revenues is that it can lull you into assigning high values to firms that are generating high-revenue growth while losing significant amounts of money. Ultimately, a firm has to generate earnings and cash flows for it to have value. While it is tempting to use revenue multiples to value firms with negative earnings and book value, the failure to control differences across firms in costs and profit margins can lead to misleading valuations.

Definition of Revenue Multiple

There are two basic revenue multiples in use. The first, and more popular, one is the multiple of the market value of equity to the revenues of a firm; this is termed the price-to-sales ratio. The second, and more robust, ratio is the multiple of the value of the operating assets to revenues; this is the EV-to-sales ratio.

$$\text{Price-to-sales ratio} = \frac{\text{Market value of equity}}{\text{Revenues}}$$

$$\text{EV-to-sales ratio} = \frac{(\text{Market value of equity} + \text{Market value of debt} - \text{Cash})}{\text{Revenues}}$$

As with the EV-to-EBITDA multiple, we net cash out of firm value, because the income from cash is not part of revenue. The enterprise value-to-sales ratio is a more robust multiple than the price-to-sales ratio because it is internally consistent. It divides the total value of the operating assets by the revenues generated by those assets. The price-to-sales ratio divides an equity value by revenues that are generated for the firm. Consequently, it will yield lower values for more highly levered firms and may lead to misleading conclusions when price-to-sales ratios are compared across firms in a sector with different degrees of leverage.

Accounting standards across different sectors and markets are fairly similar when it comes to how revenues are recorded. There have been firms in recent years, though, that have used questionable accounting practices in recording installment sales and intracompany transactions to make their revenues higher. Notwithstanding these problems, revenue multiples suffer far less than other multiples from differences in accounting treatment across firms.

Cross-Sectional Distribution

As with the earnings and book value multiples, the place to begin the examination of revenue multiples is with the cross-sectional distribution of price-to-sales and enterprise value to-sales ratios across firms in the United States. Figure 20.1 summarizes this distribution in January 2024.

There are two things worth noting in this distribution. The first is that revenue multiples are not as skewed as earnings or book value multiples and are much disparate across companies; there is not central or median value around which they congregate. The second is that the price-to-sales ratio is generally lower than the EV-to-sales ratio, which should not be surprising since the former includes only equity while the latter considers enterprise value. For firms that carry debt of much magnitude, the enterprise value will generally be higher than the market value of just equity.

Table 20.1 provides summary statistics on both the price-to-sales and the value-to-sales ratios. The average values for both multiples are much higher than the median values, largely as the result of outliers—there are firms that trade at multiples that exceed 1,000 or more.

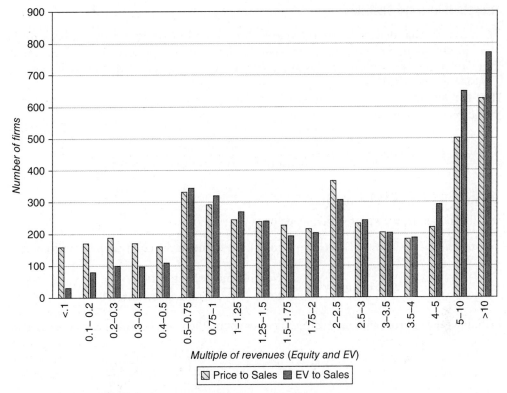

FIGURE 20.1 Revenue Multiples—U.S. firms in January 2024

TABLE 20.1 Price-to-sales and EV/Sales Multiples: Distributional Statistics for U.S. firms in January 2024

	PS Ratio	EV/Sales Ratio
Number of firms	4761	4637
Average	217.88	230.53
Median	1.95	2.56
25th percentile	0.73	1.05
75th percentile	4.59	6.32

Since there are 6,481 firms in the sample, you may be wondering why you lose firms when computing revenue multiples. First, in most financial service firms, such as banks, insurance companies, and investment banks, revenues are not easily defined, and are thus left as not meaningful. Second, there remain 124 firms that have negative-enterprise values, because cash exceeds the sum of the market values of equity and debt.

 psdata.xls: **This dataset on the web summarizes price-to-sales and value-to-sales ratios and fundamentals by industry group in the United States for the most recent year.**

Analysis of Revenue Multiples

The variables that determine the revenue multiples can be extracted by going back to the appropriate discounted cash flow models—dividend discount model (or an FCFE valuation model) for price-to-sales ratios and a firm valuation model for value-to-sales ratios.

Price-to-Sales Ratios   The price-to-sales ratio for a stable firm can be extracted from a stable growth dividend discount model:

$$\text{Value of equity} = \frac{\text{Dividends}_1}{(\text{Cost of equity} - \text{Stable growth rate})}$$

where P_0 = Value of equity

Dividends$_1$ = Expected dividends next year

Substituting in for $\text{DPS}_1 = \text{EPS}_1(\text{Payout ratio})$, the value of the equity can be written as:

$$\text{Value of equity} = \frac{\text{Net Income}_1 \times \text{Payout ratio}}{(\text{Cost of equity} - \text{Stable growth rate})}$$

Defining the net profit margin = $\text{EPS}_0/\text{Sales per share}$, the value of equity can be written as:

$$\text{Value of equity} = \frac{\text{Sales}_1 \times \text{Net margin} \times \text{Payout ratio}}{(\text{Cost of equity} - \text{Stable growth rate})}$$

Rewriting in terms of the price-forward sales ratio,

$$\frac{\text{Value of equity}}{\text{Sales}_1} = \frac{\text{Net margin} \times \text{Payout ratio}}{(\text{Cost of equity} - \text{Stable growth rate})}$$

If the revenue multiple is relative to current revenues,

$$\frac{\text{Value of equity}}{\text{Sales}_0} = \frac{\text{Net margin} \times \text{Payout ratio} \times (1 + \text{Stable growth rate})}{(\text{Cost of equity} - \text{Stable growth rate})}$$

The PS ratio is an increasing function of the profit margin, the payout ratio, and the growth rate, and a decreasing function of the riskiness of the firm. As with the price earnings and price-to-book ratios, the price-to-forward-sales ratio can be estimated for a high-growth firm:

$$\frac{\text{Price}}{\text{Forward Sales}} = \text{Net margin}_{hg} \times \left[\frac{\text{Payout ratio}_{hg} \times \left(1 - \frac{(1+g)^n}{\left(1 + k_{e,hg}\right)^n}\right)}{\left(k_{e,hg} - g\right)} + \frac{(1+g)^{n-1}\left(1 + g_{st}\right) \text{Payout ratio}_{st}}{\left(k_{e,st} - g_{st}\right)\left(1 + k_{e,hg}\right)^n} \right]$$

The left-hand side of the equation is the price-sales ratio. Holding all else constant, it is determined by:

- *Net profit margin: net income/revenues.* The price-sales (PS) ratio is an increasing function of the net profit margin. Firms with higher net margins, other things remaining equal, should trade at higher price-to-sales ratios.[1]
- *Payout ratio.* The PS ratio increases as the payout ratio increases, for any given growth rate; paying more out as dividends, for any given growth rate, implies that you generate growth more efficiently and should thus be priced higher.
- *Riskiness (through the discount rate).* The PS ratio becomes lower as riskiness increases since higher risk translates into a higher cost of equity.
- *Expected growth rate in earnings, in both the high-growth and stable phases.* The PS increases as the growth rate increases, in both the high-growth and stable-growth periods.

As with the price-to-book ratio, you can substitute in the free cash flows to equity for the dividends in making this estimate. Doing so will yield a more reasonable estimate of the price-to-sales ratio for firms that pay out dividends that are far lower than they can afford to pay out. As with the price-to-book ratio, the firm can have a different net margin during the stable-growth phase. That margin, though, will affect only the payout ratio during the stable phase.

ILLUSTRATION 20.1: Estimating the Price-to-Sales Ratio for a High-Growth Firm in the Two-Stage Model

Assume that you have been asked to estimate the PS ratio for a firm that is expected to be in high growth for the next five years. Table 20.2 is a summary of the inputs for the valuation:

TABLE 20.2 Characteristics of a High Growth firm

Growth rate in first five years = 20%	Cost of equity = 4.5% + 1(5%) = 9.5%
Growth rate after five years = 4%	Payout ratio in first five years = 20%
Beta = 1.0	Payout ratio after five years = 60%
Net profit margin = 10%	Risk-free rate = T-bond rate = 4.5%
	Equity risk premium = 5%

This firm's price-to-forward-sales ratio can be estimated as follows:

$$\frac{\text{Price}}{\text{Forward Sales}} = 0.10 \times \left[\frac{0.20 \times \left(1 - \frac{(1.20)^5}{(1.095)^5}\right)}{(.095 - .20)} + \frac{(1.20)^4(1.04)(0.60)}{(.095 - .04)(1.095)^5} \right] = 1.61$$

---

[1]If the net margin changes, but only in the stable-growth period, the equation has a glitch, since it assumes that earnings in the terminal year is equal to the earnings in the last year of high growth scaled up one year at the stable-growth rate. If the margin changes in the terminal year, there has to be either a one-time change in earnings in that year to accommodate that change, or a one-time drop in revenues. If you assume the latter, the equation holds. If you assume the former, the terminal value has to be adjusted upwards.

The price-to-training-sales ratio can be computed simply:

$$\frac{Price}{Trailing\ Sales} = Forward\ Price\ to\ sales(1 + Expected\ growth\ rate) = 1.61 \times 1.20 = 1.93$$

Based on this firm's fundamentals, you would expect its equity to trade at 1.61 (3.21) times trailing (forward) revenues.

ILLUSTRATION 20.2:   Estimating the Intrinsic Price-to-Sales Ratio for a High-Growth Firm: Whole Foods Markets in May 2011

Whole Foods Markets was founded as a grocery chain designed to provide alternatives for health-conscious shoppers willing to pay a premium for organic food. The retailer grew significantly between 2005 and 2010 and had more than 300 stores open by May 2011. The firm reported net income of $246 million in 2010 on revenues of $9,006 million, giving it a net profit margin of 2.73%:

$$Net\ profit\ margin = Net\ income/Sales = \$246/\$9,006\ million = 2.73\%$$

Based on its book value of equity of $1,628 million at the end of 2009, the firm generated a return on equity of 15.11%:

$$Return\ on\ equity = \frac{Net\ income_{2010}}{Book\ value\ of\ equity_{2009}} = \frac{246}{1628} = 15.11\%$$

We will assume that the firm will be able to maintain a growth rate in net income of 10% a year for the next 10 years, while preserving its current net margin and return on equity. After the tenth year, we will assume that the firm will be in stable growth, growing 3% a year in perpetuity, with a net margin of 2.5% and a return on equity of 10%. To estimate the cost of equity, we will assume that the firm has a beta of 1.00 for the high growth period and 0.90 in stable growth; the risk-free rate is 3.5% and the equity risk premium is 5%. The inputs used in the estimation are summarized in Table 20.3:

TABLE 20.3   Valuation Inputs—High Growth Firm

	High Growth	Stable Growth
Length of growth	10 years	Forever
Net margin	2.73%	2.50%
Sales/BV of equity	5.53	4.00
ROE	15.11%	10.00%
Payout ratio	$1 - 10\%/15.11\% = 33.82\%$	$1 - 3\%/10\% = 70\%$
Expected growth rate	10.00%	3.00%
Cost of equity	$3.5\% + 1(5\%) = 8.50\%$	$3.5\% + .9(5\%) = 8.00\%$

Note that we are backing out a payout ratio from the expected growth rate and ROE, rather than use actual dividends paid. Consequently, we are effectively using FCFE instead of actual dividends. The price-to-sales ratio, based on these inputs, is estimated here.

$$\frac{\text{Price}}{\text{Forward Sales}} = 0.0273 \times \left[\frac{0.3382 \times \left(1 - \frac{(1.10)^{10}}{(1.085)^{10}} \right)}{(.085 - .10)} + \frac{(1.10)^9 \, (1.03)(0.70)}{(.08 - .03)(1.085)^{10}} \right]$$

$$= 0.50$$

$$\frac{\text{Price}}{\text{Trailing Sales}} = 0.50(1.10) = 0.55$$

Whole Foods was trading at a price-to-sales ratio of 1.11 in May 2011, making it significantly overvalued.

Enterprise Value-to-Sales Ratios   To analyze the relationship between value and sales, consider the value of a stable-growth firm:

$$\text{Enterprise value} = \frac{\text{EBIT} \, (1 - t)(1 - \text{Reinvestment rate})}{(\text{Cost of capital} - \text{Expected growth rate})}$$

Dividing both sides by the revenue, you get:

$$\frac{\text{Enterprise value}}{\text{Sales}} = \frac{\frac{\text{EBIT} \, (1 - t)}{\text{Sales}} \times (1 - \text{Reinvestment rate})}{(\text{Cost of capital} - \text{Expected growth rate})}$$

$$\frac{\text{Enterprise value}}{\text{Sales}} = \frac{\text{After-tax operating margin} \times (1 - \text{Reinvestment rate})}{(\text{Cost of capital} - \text{Expected growth rate})}$$

Just as the price-to-sales ratio is determined by net profit margins, payout ratios, and costs of equity, the value-to-sales ratio is determined by after-tax operating margins, reinvestment rates, and the cost of capital. Firms with higher after-tax operating margins (ATOM), lower reinvestment rates (for any given growth rate), and lower costs of capital will trade at higher value-to-sales multiples.

This equation can be expanded to cover a firm in high growth by using a two-stage firm valuation model:

$$\frac{\text{EV}}{\text{Forward Sales}} = \text{ATOM}_{\text{hg}} \times \left[\frac{(1 - \text{RIR}_{\text{hg}}) \times \left(1 - \frac{(1 + g)^n}{(1 + k_{\text{c,hg}})^n} \right)}{(k_{\text{c,hg}} - g)} + \frac{(1 + g)^{n-1}(1 + g_{\text{st}})(1 - \text{RIR}_{\text{st}})}{(k_{\text{c,st}} - g_{\text{st}})(1 + k_{\text{c,hg}})^n} \right]$$

where ATOM = After-tax operating margin = $\text{EBIT}(1 - t)/\text{Sales}$

   RIR = Reinvestment rate(RIR_n is for stable growth period)

   k_c = Cost of capital(hg:high growth and st: stable growth periods)

   g = Growth rate in operating income in high growth

   g_{st} = Growth rate in operating income in stable growth

Note that the determinants of the EV-to-sales ratio remain the same as they were in the stable-growth model—the growth rate, the reinvestment rate, the operating margin, and the cost of capital—but the number of estimates increases to reflect the existence of a high-growth period.

ILLUSTRATION 20.3: Estimating the Intrinsic EV-to-Sales Ratio for a High-Growth Firm: Coca-Cola in May 2011

Coca-Cola has been successful in delivering high growth with impressive margins for decades. In 2010, Coca-Cola reported pretax operating income of $8,449 million on revenues of $35,119 million; the tax rate for the company was approximately 40%. At the end of 2009, the firm had total capital invested of $31,679 million, leading to the following inputs:

$$\text{Invested capital} = \text{BV of equity} + \text{BV of debt} - \text{Cash} = 24,799 + 11,859 - 4,979 = \$31,679 \text{ million}$$

$$\text{After-tax operating margin} = \frac{\text{Operating income}(1-t)}{\text{Revenues}} = \frac{8,449(1-.40)}{35,119} = 14.43\%$$

$$\frac{\text{Sales}}{\text{capital}} = \frac{\$35,119}{\$31,169} = 1.11$$

$$\text{Return on invested capital} = \text{After-tax operating margin} \times \frac{\text{Sales}}{\text{Capital}} = 14.43\% \times 1.11 = 16\%$$

We will assume that the firm will be able to maintain its current margin and return on capital for the next 10 years, while reinvesting 60% of its after-tax operating income back into the business (the average over the past five years). During this period, we also assume that Coca-Cola will have a beta of 0.90 and a pretax cost of debt of 4.50%, and that it will remain at its existing debt-to-capital ratio of 7.23%, resulting in a cost of capital of 8.03% (the equity risk premium of 5.5% reflects Coca-Cola's exposure to emerging markets):

$$\text{Cost of equity} = \text{Risk-free rate} + \text{Beta}(\text{Equity risk premium}) = 3.5\% + .9(5.5\%) = 8.45\%$$

$$\text{Cost of capital} = 8.45\%(1 - .0723) + 4.5\%(1 - .40)(.0723) = 8.03\%$$

After year 10, we assume that Coca-Cola will be in stable growth, growing 3.5% a year, and that its operating margin and sales-to-capital ratio will drop back toward (but not all the way to) industry averages (after-tax operating margin will be 12% and the sales-to-capital ratio will converge on 1). In stable growth, we also assume that the beta for the company will be 1 and that the debt ratio will rise to 20%.

$$\text{Cost of equity} = 3.5\% + 1(5.5\%) = 9\%$$

$$\text{Cost of capital} = 9\%(.80) + 4.5\%(1 - .4)(.20) = 7.74\%$$

The inputs that we will use to estimate the EV/Sales ratio for Coca-Cola are listed in Table 20.4:

TABLE 20.4 Valuation Inputs—Coca Cola

	High Growth	Stable Growth
Length of period	10	After year 5
After-tax operating margin	14.43%	12.00%
Sales/capital	1.11	1.00
Return on capital	16.00%	12.00%

	High Growth	Stable Growth
Reinvestment rate	60%	3.5%/12% = 29.17%
Expected growth rate	9.60%	3.50%
Cost of capital	8.03%	7.74%

Plugging these numbers into the two-stage EV/Sales equation, we get:

$$\frac{\text{Enterprise value}}{\text{Forward Sales}} = 0.1443 \times \left[\frac{(1 - .60) \times \left(1 - \frac{(1.096)^{10}}{(1.0803)^{10}} \right)}{(.0803 - .096)} + \frac{(1.096)^9 \, (1.035)(1 - .2917)}{(.0774 - .035)(1.0803)^{10}} \right]$$

$$= 3.20$$

$$\frac{\text{Enterprise value}}{\text{Trailing Sales}} = \frac{\text{Enterprise value}}{\text{Forward Sales}} \times (1.096) = 3.51$$

Based on our inputs, the enterprise value for Coca-Cola should be 3.51 times trailing revenues:

$$\text{Expected enterprise value} = \$35,119 \times 3.51 = \$123,197 \text{ million}$$

In May 2011, Coca-Cola's market capitalization was \$152,200 million. Incorporating the debt outstanding (\$11,859 million) and the cash balance (\$4,979 million) yields an enterprise value of:

$$\text{Actual enterprise value} = \$152,200 + \$11,859 - \$4,979 = \$159,080 \text{ million}$$

The company looks overvalued, based on our assumptions, by about 23%.

---

 firmmult.xls: **This spreadsheet enables you to estimate the value-to-sales ratio for a stable-growth or high-growth firm, given its fundamentals.**

Revenue Multiples and Profit Margins The key determinant of revenue multiples is the profit margin—the net margin for price-to-sales ratios and operating margin for value-to-sales ratios. Firms involved in businesses that have high margins can expect to sell for high multiples of sales. However, a decline in profit margins has a twofold effect. First, the reduction in profit margins reduces the revenue multiple directly. Second, the lower profit margin can lead to lower growth, and hence lead to even lower revenue multiples.

The profit margin can be linked to expected growth fairly easily if an additional term is defined—the ratio of sales-to book value (BV), which is also called a turnover ratio. This turnover ratio can be defined in terms of book equity (Equity turnover = Sales/Book value of equity) or book capital (Capital turnover = Sales/Book value of capital). Using a relationship developed between growth rates and fundamentals, the expected growth rates in equity earnings can be written as a function of net profit margins and turnover ratios:

$$\text{Expected growth}_{\text{Net income}} = \text{Retention ratio} \times \text{Return on equity}$$

$$= \text{Retention ratio} \times \left(\frac{\text{Net profit}}{\text{Sales}}\right) \times \left(\frac{\text{Sales}}{\text{BV of equity}}\right)$$

$$= \text{Retention ratio} \times \text{Net margin} \times \text{Sales/BV of equity}$$

For example, in the valuation of Whole Foods in Illustration 20.2, the expected return on equity is 15.11%. This return on equity can be derived from Whole Foods' net margin (2.73%) and sales-to-book value of equity ratio (5.53):

$$\text{Net margin} = 2.73\%$$
$$\text{Sales/BV of equity} = \$9,006/\$1,628 = 5.53$$
$$\text{Return on equity} = 2.73\% \times 5.53 = 15.11\%$$

For growth in operating income, the equation has to be restated in terms of reinvestment rates (instead of retention ratios) and returns on capital (instead of returns on equity):

$$\text{Expected growth}_{\text{Operating income}} = \text{Reinvestment rate} \times \text{Return on capital}$$

$$= \text{Reinvestment rate} \times \frac{EBIT\ (1-t)}{Sales}$$

$$\times \frac{Sales}{Invested\ capital}$$

$$= \text{Reinvestment rate} \times \text{After-tax operating margin}$$
$$\times \text{Sales to Capital}$$

In the valuation of Coca-Cola in Illustration 20.3, the return on capital is 16%. This return on capital can be derived from Coca-Cola's after-tax operating margin (14.43%) and sales/capital ratio (1.11):

$$\text{After-tax operating margin} = 14.43\%$$
$$\text{Sales/invested capital} = \$35,119/\$31,679 = 1.11$$
$$\text{Return on capital} = 14.43\% \times 1.11 = 16\%$$

As the profit margin is reduced, the expected returns on equity and capital will decrease, if the sales do not increase proportionately.

ILLUSTRATION 20.4:   Estimating the Effect of Lower Margins on Price-Sales Ratios

Consider again the firm analyzed in Illustration 20.1. If the firm's net profit margin declines, and total revenue remains unchanged, the price-sales ratio for the firm will decline with it. For instance, if the firm's profit margin declines from 10% to 5% and the sales/BV ratio remains unchanged:

$$\text{New growth rate in first five years} = \text{Retention ratio} \times \text{Profit margin} \times \frac{\text{Sales}}{\text{BV}}$$

$$= .8 \times .05 \times 2.50 = 10\%$$

$$\text{New return on equity} = \text{Net Profit margin} \times \text{Sales/BV of equity}$$
$$= .05 \times 2.5 = 12.5\%$$

The new price-sales ratio can then be calculated as follows:

$$\frac{\text{Price}}{\text{Forward Sales}} = 0.05 \times \left[\frac{0.20 \times \left(1 - \frac{(1.10)^5}{(1.095)^5}\right)}{(.095 - .10)} + \frac{(1.10)^4 \ (1.04)(0.60)}{(.095 - .04)(1.095)^5} \right] = 0.57$$

The relationship between profit margins and the price-sales ratio is illustrated more comprehensively in Figure 20.2. The price-sales ratio is estimated as a function of the profit margin, keeping the sales/book value of equity ratio fixed. This linkage of price-sales ratios and profit margins can be utilized to analyze the value effects of changes in corporate strategy as well as the value of a brand name.

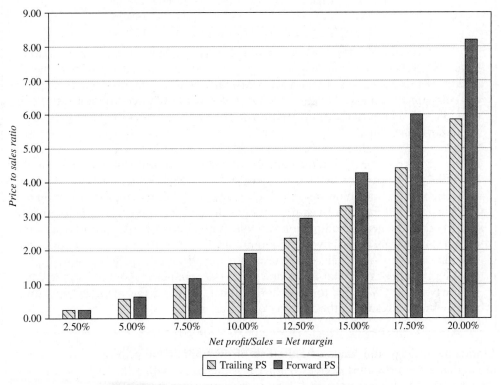

FIGURE 20.2 Price-to-Sales Ratios and Profit Margins

Note that the price-to-sales ratio decreases (and increases) more than proportionately as the net margin decreases (increases).

MULTIPLES AND COMPANION VARIABLES

By this point in the relative valuation discussion, the process of deconstructing multiples should no longer be a mystery. In fact, with each multiple, while we have highlighted multiple variables that affect its value, there is one variable that operates as a

(continued)

(*continued*)

key driver. We call this variable the companion variable, and Table 20.5 lists it out for each multiple:

TABLE 20.5   Pricing Multiples and Companion Variables

Multiple	Companion Variable
PE ratio	Expected growth rate in EPS
PBV	Return on equity
PS	Net margin
EV/EBITDA	Reinvestment rate
EV/Invested capital	Return on invested capital
EV/sales	After-tax operating margin

These variables matter for two reasons. The first is that changes in the variables have big effects on the multiples to which they relate to. The second is that when a stock looks cheap, because it has a low value on a multiple, the first item to check is the companion variable. Thus, if a stock trades at a low price-to-book ratio, you should check its return on equity; most low price-to-book stocks have low or negative returns on equity.

How do you find the companion variable for a multiple? One way is to run the market regression for the multiple against all the independent variables that should determine it. The variable that has the most statistical significance (highest t statistic) is invariably the companion variable. The other, more intuitive, approach is to do the following: If working with an equity multiple, divide net income by the denominator of the multiple to get the companion variable. With price-to-book value of equity, for instance, using this approach would require dividing net income by the book value of equity, which would yield the return on equity. With enterprise value multiples, dividing the after-tax operating income by the denominator should yield the companion variable. With EV-to-sales, for instance, dividing the after-tax operating income by sales results in the after-tax operating margin.

Marketing Strategy and Value   At the risk of oversimplifying pricing strategy, you can argue that every firm must decide whether it wants to go with a low-price, high-volume strategy (volume leader) or with a high-price, lower-volume strategy (price leader). In terms of the variables that link growth to value, this choice will determine the profit margin and turnover ratio to use in valuation.

You could analyze the alternative pricing strategies, which are available to a firm, by examining the impact that each strategy will have on margins and turnover, and valuing the firm under each strategy. The strategy that yields the highest value for the firm is, in a sense, the optimal strategy.

Note that the effect of price changes on turnover ratios will depend, in large part, on how elastic or inelastic the demand for the firm's products are. Increases in the price of a product will have a minimal effect on turnover ratios if demand is inelastic. In this case, the value of the firm will generally be higher with a price leader strategy. On the other hand, the turnover ratio could drop more than proportionately if the product price is increased, and demand is elastic. In this case, firm value will increase with a volume leader strategy.

ILLUSTRATION 20.5: Choosing between a High-Margin and a Low-Margin Strategy

Assume that a firm must choose between the two pricing strategies. In the first strategy, the firm will charge higher prices (resulting in higher operating margins) and sell less (resulting in lower turnover ratios). In the second strategy, the firm will charge lower prices and sell more. Assume that the firm has done market testing and arrived at the following inputs:

	High Margin, Low Volume	Low Margin, High Volume
Operating margin	10%	5%
Sales/book value of invested capital	2.5	5.0

Assume, in addition, that the firm is expected to reinvest 80% of its after-tax operating earnings over the next five years, and 40% of earnings after that, and that these numbers will be unaffected by the margin strategy adopted. The growth rate after year 5 is expected to be 4%. The book value of equity per share is $10. The cost of capital for the firm is 8%.

HIGH-MARGIN STRATEGY

$$\text{Expected growth rate in first 5 years} = \text{After-tax operating margin} \times \frac{\text{Sales}}{\text{BV of capital}}$$
$$\times \text{Reinvestment rate}$$
$$= .10 \times 2.5 \times .80 = 20\%$$

$$\frac{\text{Enterprise value}}{\text{Forward Sales}} = 0.10 \times \left[\frac{(1 - .80) \times \left(1 - \frac{(1.20)^5}{(1.08)^5}\right)}{(.08 - .20)} + \frac{(1.20)^4(1.04)(1 - .40)}{(.08 - .04)(1.08)^5} \right] = 2.32$$

LOW-MARGIN STRATEGY

$$\text{Expected growth rate in first 5 years} = \text{After-tax operating margin} \times \frac{\text{Sales}}{\text{BV of capital}}$$
$$\times \text{Reinvestment rate}$$
$$= .05 \times 4.0 \times .80 = 16\%$$

$$\frac{\text{Enterprise value}}{\text{Forward Sales}} = 0.05 \times \left[\frac{(1 - .80) \times \left(1 - \frac{(1.16)^5}{(1.08)^5}\right)}{(.08 - .16)} + \frac{(1.16)^4(1.04)(1 - .40)}{(.08 - .04)(1.08)^5} \right] = 1.01$$

Holding invested capital constant, and allowing for the fact that the low margin strategy allows revenues to be 60% higher, we still get higher enterprise value from the high-margin strategy:

$$\text{Enterprise value}_{\text{High margin}} = \frac{\text{EV}}{\text{Sales}} \times \text{Sales} = 2.32 \times 2.5 = 5.80$$
$$\text{Enterprise value}_{\text{Low margin}} = 1.01 \times 4 = 4.04$$

The high-margin strategy is the better one to follow here, if the objective is value maximization.

ILLUSTRATION 20.6:   Effects of Changing Pricing Strategy: Whole Foods in May 2011

In Illustration 20.2, we estimated an intrinsic forward price-to-sales ratio of 0.50 for Whole Foods. In making the estimate of 0.50, we assumed that Whole Foods would be able to sustain a net profit margin of 2.73% and a sales-to-book equity of 5.53.

Assume now that concerned about sales erosion if the company continues with its premium-pricing strategy, Whole Foods is considering reducing prices to get back market share. If it does cut prices by 10%, its net profit margin will drop to 2.5% but assume that same store sales will surge by 7.5% raising expected revenues next year from $10 billion to $10.75 billion and increasing the sales-to-book ratio to 6.36 (5.53 × 1.075). Assuming that the stable growth inputs remain unchanged (growth rate = 3%; ROE = 10%), the effect of the strategy change on the price-to-sales ratio, and more importantly on equity value can be summarized in Table 20.6:

TABLE 20.6   Valuation Inputs for Pricing Strategies

	Premium Price Strategy (current)	Lower Price Strategy
Expected revenues ($ millions)	$10,000	$10.750
Expected net margin	2.73%	2.50%
Expected sales/capital	5.53	6.36
Expected ROE	15.11%	15.90%
Expected growth rate	10.00%	10.00%
Payout ratio	33.82%	37.10%
Price to Forward sales	0.50	0.47
Value of equity ($ millions)	$5,000	$5,053

The new price-to-sales ratio is computed using the same two-stage model we used in Illustration 20.2:

$$\frac{Price}{Forward\ Sales} = 0.025 \times \left[\frac{0.3710 \times \left(1 - \frac{(1.10)^{10}}{(1.085)^{10}}\right)}{(.085 - .10)} + \frac{(1.10)^{9}(1.03)(0.70)}{(.08 - .03)(1.085)^{10}} \right] = 0.47$$

Note that the expected revenues increase by 7.5% from the current level of $10,000 million to $10,750 million. While the net effect on the price-to-sales ratio is very small (decreases from 0.50 to 0.47), the value of equity increases mildly from $5 billion to $5.05 billion.

Value of a Brand Name   One of the critiques of traditional valuation is that it fails to consider the value of brand names and other intangibles. Hiroyumi Itami, in his 1987 book *Mobilizing Invisible Assets*, provides a summary of this criticism. He says:

> *Analysts have tended to define assets too narrowly, identifying only those that can be measured, such as plant and equipment. Yet the intangible assets, such as a particular technology, accumulated consumer information, brand name, reputation, and corporate culture, are invaluable to the firm's competitive power. In fact, these invisible assets are the only real source of competitive edge that can be sustained over time.*

While this criticism is clearly overstated, the approaches used by analysts to value brand names are often ad hoc and may significantly overstate or understate their value. Firms with well-known brand names often sell for higher multiples than lesser-known firms. The standard practice of adding on a "brand name premium", often set arbitrarily, to discounted cash flow value can lead to erroneous estimates. Instead, the value of a brand name can be estimated using the approach that relates profit margins to price-sales ratios.

One of the benefits of having a well-known and respected brand name is that its owner can charge higher prices for the same products, leading to higher profit margins, and hence to higher price-sales ratios and firm value. The larger the price premium that a firm can charge, the greater is the value of the brand name. In general, the value of a brand name can be written as:

$$\text{Value of brand name} = \left(\text{EV/Sales}_{\text{brand}} - \text{EV/Sales}_{\text{generic}}\right) \times \text{Sales}$$

where $\text{EV/Sales}_{\text{brand}}$ = EV-sales ratio of the firm with brand name

$\text{EV/Sales}_{\text{generic}}$ = EV-sales ratio of the same firm with the generic product

---

PRICING STRATEGY, MARKET SHARE, AND COMPETITIVE DYNAMICS

All too often, firms analyze the effects of changing prices in a static setting, where only the firm is acting, and the competition stays still. The problem, though, is that every action (especially when it comes to pricing) generates reactions from competition, and the net effects can be unpredictable.

Consider, for instance, a firm that cuts prices, hoping to increase market share and sales. If the competition does nothing, the firm may be able to accomplish its objectives. If, on the other hand, the competition reacts by also cutting prices, the firm may find itself with lower margins and the same turnover ratios that it had before the price cut—a recipe for lower firm value. In competitive industries, you have to assume that the latter will happen and plan accordingly.

There are some firms that have focused on maximizing market share as their primary objective function. The linkage between increased market share and market value is a tenuous one, and can be examined using the profit-margin/revenue multiple framework developed in the preceding section. If increasing market share leads to higher margins, either because of economies of scale driving down costs, or because of increased market power driving out competitors, it will lead to higher value. If the increase in the market share is accompanied by lower prices and profit margins, the net effect on value can be negative.

ILLUSTRATION 20.7:   Valuing a Brand Name Using the Enterprise Value to Sales Ratio

Consider two firms that produce similar products that compete in the same marketplace: Famous Inc. has a well-known brand name and has an after-tax operating profit margin of 10%, while NoFrills Inc. makes a generic version and has an after-tax operating margin of 5%. Both firms have the same sales-book capital ratio (2.50) and the cost of capital of 9%. In addition, both firms are expected to reinvest 80% of their operating income in the next five years and 40% of earnings after that. The growth rate after year 5, for both firms, is 4%. Both firms are expected to have total sales of $2.5 billion next year.

Valuing Famous

$$\text{Expected return on invested capital} = \text{After-tax operating margin} \times \text{Reinvestment rate}$$
$$= 10\% \times 2.5 = 25\%$$
$$\text{Expected growth rate} = \text{Return on invested capital} \times \text{Reinvestment rate}$$
$$= 25\% \times .80 = 20\%$$

Using these inputs, you can estimate the enterprise value to-sales ratio:

$$\frac{\text{Enterprise value}}{\text{Forward Sales}} = 0.10 \times \left[\frac{(1 - .80) \times \left(1 - \frac{(1.20)^5}{(1.09)^5}\right)}{(.09 - .20)} + \frac{(1.20)^4(1.04)(1 - .40)}{(.09 - .04)(1.09)^5} \right] = 1.79$$

Valuing No Frills

$$\text{Expected return on invested capital} = \text{After-tax operating margin} \times \text{Reinvestment rate}$$
$$= 5\% \times 2.5 = 12.5\%$$
$$\text{Expected growth rate} = \text{Return on invested capital} \times \text{Reinvestment rate}$$
$$= 12.5\% \times .80 = 10\%$$

With these inputs, the enterprise value to sales ratios can be computed:

$$\frac{\text{Enterprise value}}{\text{Forward Sales}} = 0.10 \times \left[\frac{(1 - .80) \times \left(1 - \frac{(1.10)^5}{(1.09)^5}\right)}{(.09 - .10)} + \frac{(1.10)^4 \, (1.04)(1 - .40)}{(.09 - .04)(1.09)^5} \right] = 0.64$$

$$\text{Value of brand name} = \left(\text{EV to Sales}_{\text{Brand Name}} - \text{EV to Sales}_{\text{Generic}} \right)$$
$$\times \text{Expected revenue next year}$$

$$= (1.79 - 0.64) \times 2,000 = \$2.3 \text{ billion}$$

ILLUSTRATION 20.8: Valuing a Brand Name: Coca-Cola in May 2011

We estimated an enterprise value-to-sales ratio of 3.20 (3.51) times forward (trailing) revenues 3.51 for Coca-Cola in May 2011 in Illustration 20.3, based on its strong operating margin and return on capital. It is undeniable that Coca-Cola has one of the most recognizable and valuable brand names in the world, but there are two key questions that need to be answered:

1. Should we be adding a premium to the estimated EV/sales ratio for the strength of the brand name?
2. How much is the brand name adding to Coca-Cola's overall value?

The answer to the first question is no. After all, it is the strength of the brand name that has enabled Coca-Cola to generate an after-tax operating margin of 14.43% and a return on capital of 16%. Adding a premium to estimated value would amount to double-counting. The answer to the second question is nuanced. A segment of the estimated enterprise value can be attributed to the strong brand name, and it becomes a matter of isolating its impact.

The first step in estimating the value added by the brand name is finding out how much differential advantage Coca-Cola generates as a result of its brand name. In this pursuit, we were lucky to find a manufacturer of generics, Cott Corporation, that is publicly traded. In table 20.7, we summarize the values for Coca-Cola and Cott in 2010 (in millions for dollar values):

TABLE 20.7   Valuation Inputs—Coca Cola and Cott

	Coca-Cola	Cott
Market value of equity	$152,200	$ 809
Debt	$ 11,859	$ 345
Cash	$ 4,979	$ 27
Enterprise value	$159,080	$1,127
Sales	$ 35,119	$1,803
Pretax operating income	$ 8,449	$ 99
EBITDA	$ 9,892	$ 173
Capital Invested	$ 31,679	$ 626
Tax rate	40%	40%
Beta—High growth	0.9	1.25
Pretax cost of debt	4.50%	6%
Computed Values		
After-tax operating margin	14.43%	3.29%
Sales to invested capital	1.11	2.88
Return on capital	16.00%	9.49%
Cost of capital	8.03%	8.35%
Excess return	7.97%	1.14%

Note that Cott is much smaller than Coca-Cola and has weaker margins, a lower return on capital, and a higher cost of capital. While the scale differences make the companies difficult to compare directly, we will use the information gleaned from Cott in valuing Coca-Cola's brand name.

OPTION 1: BRAND NAME AFFECTS ONLY PRICING POWER

In the first and simplest version of valuing brand name, we assume that brand name affects only pricing power and through it, the operating margin. In effect, we value Coca-Cola with all its other characteristics intact but giving it Cott's after-tax operating margin. During stable growth, we assume that Coca-Cola will earn its cost of capital if it loses its brand name advantage. Table 20.8 summarizes the effects.

TABLE 20.8   Coca Cola Brand Name Value—Pricing Power

	Coca-Cola	Coca-Cola with Cott's Margin
Current tax rate	40.00%	40.00%
Current revenues	$35,119	$35,119

(continued)

TABLE 20.8 (*Continued*)

	Coca-Cola	Coca-Cola with Cott's Margin
High Growth Period		
Length of high growth period (n)	10	10
Reinvestment rate	60%	60%
After-tax operating margin	14.43%	3.29%
Sales/Invested capital	1.11	1.11
Return on capital	16.00%	3.65%
Growth rate during period (g)	9.60%	2.19%
Cost of capital during period	8.03%	8.03%
Stable Growth Period		
Growth rate in steady state	3.50%	3.50%
Return on capital in steady state	12.00%	7.74%
Reinvestment rate in stable growth	29.17%	45.22%
Cost of capital in steady state	7.74%	7.74%
EV/Trailing Sales	3.51	0.35
Enterprise value	$123,199	$12,291

Note that lowering the margin, while keeping the sales-to-capital-ratio reduces the return on capital to 3.65%. The EV/Sales ratio for Coca-Cola drops to 0.35 if it earns Cott's margins, while preserving all its own characteristics for the other variables. The estimated enterprise value drops to $12.3 billion, and the brand name value accounts for almost 90% of Coca-Cola's estimated value:

$$\text{Value of brand name} = \$123,199 - \$12,291 = \$110,908 \text{ million}$$

Option 2: Brand Name Affects Pricing Power And Sales Turnover

Generic companies that purse high-volume strategies may be able to generate more revenue per dollar of capital invested. To capture this effect, we assume that Coca-Cola, if it loses its brand name, will have Cott's margin and sales-to-capital ratio. In effect, this will give Coca-Cola the return on capital generated by Cott (see Table 20.9):

TABLE 20.9 Coca Cola Brand Name Value—Pricing Power & Turnover

	Coca-Cola	Coca-Cola with Cott's ROIC
Current tax rate	40.00%	40.00%
Current revenues	$ 35,119	$35,119
Capital invested (Book values of debt and equity)	$ 31,679	$31,679
High Growth Period		
Length of high-growth period (n)	10	10
Reinvestment rate	60.00%	60%
After-tax operating margin	14.43%	3.29%
Sales/Invested capital	1.11	2.88

	Coca-Cola	Coca-Cola with Cott's ROIC
Return on capital	16.00%	9.49%
Growth rate during period (g)	9.60%	5.69%
Cost of capital during period	8.03%	8.03%
Stable Growth Period		
Growth rate in steady state	3.50%	3.50%
Return on capital in steady state	12.00%	7.74%
Reinvestment rate in stable growth	29.17%	45.22%
Cost of capital in steady state	7.74%	7.74%
After-tax cost of debt	2.70%	2.70%
Debt ratio D/(D + E)	20.00%	20.00%
EV/sales	3.51	0.47
Enterprise value	$123,199	$16,506

There is a drop in value, but it is less precipitous than under option 1, since the return on capital, even under the no-brand name scenario, is 9.49%, higher than the cost of capital during high growth. With the enterprise value to sales ratio of 0.47, the value of the brand name is still a substantial $106.69 billion:

Value of brand name = $123,199 − $16,506 = $106,693 million

Option 3: All Excess Returns Earned Are Due To Brand Name

The first two options presuppose the existence of a generic competitor with accessible financial statements. In many cases, there is no truly generic alternative, or even if one exists, it is not public. If that is the case, valuing a brand name becomes more difficult. One alternative is to assume that the brand name is the only competitive advantage and that all excess returns (returns over and above the cost of capital) can be attributed to brand name. Using that approach in Table 20.10 for Coca-Cola, we get:

TABLE 20.10   Coca Cola Brand Name Value—All Excess Returns

	Coca-Cola	Coca-Cola—No Excess Returns
Current tax rate	40.00%	40.00%
Current revenues	$35,119.00	$35,119.00
Capital invested	$31,679.00	$31,679.00
High Growth Period		
Length of high-growth period (n)	10	10
Reinvestment rate	60%	60%
Return on capital	16.00%	8.03%
Growth rate during period (g)	9.60%	4.82%
Cost of capital during period	8.03%	8.03%
Stable Growth Period		
Growth rate in steady state	3.50%	3.50%
Return on capital in steady state	12.00%	7.74%

(continued)

TABLE 20.10   (*Continued*)

	Coca-Cola	Coca-Cola—No Excess Returns
Reinvestment Rate	29.17%	45.22%
Cost of capital in steady state	7.74%	7.74%
EV/Trailing sales	3.51	0.44
Value of firm	$123,199	$15,452

If we remove the excess returns generated by Coca-Cola, leaving all else unchanged, the enterprise value to sales ratio drops to 0.96, and the value of the brand name becomes $117.74 billion.

$$\text{Value of brand name} = \$123,199 - \$15,452 = \$ 107,747 \text{ million}$$

The three approaches yield a range for brand name value from $106.7 billion to $110.9 billion. In short, no matter which approach you use, the bulk of Coca Cola's value comes from its brand name.

AN ASIDE ON BRAND NAME VALUE

It is common to see brand name premiums attached to discounted cash flow valuations. As you can see from the preceding example, this is a mistake. Done right, the value of a brand name is already built into the valuation in a number of places—higher operating margins, higher turnover ratios, and consequently higher returns on capital. These, in turn, have ripple effects, increasing expected growth rates and value. Adding a brand name premium to this value would be double-counting.

What about firms that do not exploit a valuable brand name? You might add a premium to the values of these firms, but the premium is not for the brand name but rather for control. In fact, you could estimate similar premiums for any underutilized or mismanaged assets, but you would pay the premiums only if you could acquire control of the firm.

Using Revenue Multiples in Investment Analysis

The key determinants of the revenue multiples of a firm are its expected margins (net and operating), risk, cash flow, and growth characteristics. To use revenue multiples in analysis and to make comparisons across firms, you would need to control differences on these characteristics. This section examines different ways of comparing revenue multiples across firms.

Looking for Mismatches   While growth, risk, and cash flow characteristics affect revenue multiples, the key determinants of revenue multiples are profit margins—net profit margin for equity multiples and operating margins for firm value multiples. Thus, it is not

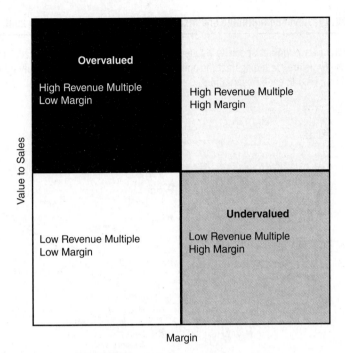

FIGURE 20.3 Value/Sales and Margins

surprising to find firms with lowprofit margins and lowrevenue multiples, and firms with high profit margins and high revenue multiples. However, firms with high revenue ratios and low profit margins as well as firms with low revenue multiples and high profit margins should attract investors' attention as potentially overvalued and undervalued securities respectively. In Figure 20.3, this is presented in a matrix. You can identify under- or overvalued firms in a sector or industry by plotting them on this matrix and looking for potential mismatches between margins and revenue multiples.

While intuitively appealing, there are at least three practical problems associated with this approach. The first is that data is more easily available on historical (current) profit margins than on expected profit margins. If a firm's current margins are highly correlated with future margins (a firm that has earned high margins historically will continue to do so, and one that have earned low margins historically will also continue to do so), using current margins and current revenue multiples to identify under- or overvalued securities is reasonable. If the current margins of firms are not highly correlated with expected future margins, it is no longer appropriate to argue that firms are overvalued just because they have low current margins and trade at high price-to-sales ratios. The second problem with this approach is that it assumes that revenue multiples are linearly related to margins. In other words, as margins double, you would expect revenue multiples to double as well. The third problem is that it ignores differences in other fundamentals, especially risk. Thus, a firm that looks undervalued because it has a high current margin and is trading at a low multiple of revenues may in fact be a fairly valued firm with very high risk.

ILLUSTRATION 20.9: Revenue Multiples and Margins: Specialty Retailers in July 2000

In the first comparison, we look at specialty retailers in the United States. In Figure 20.4 the EV-to-trailing-sales ratios of these firms are plotted against the operating margins of these firms in July 2000 (with the stock symbols for each firm next to each observation).

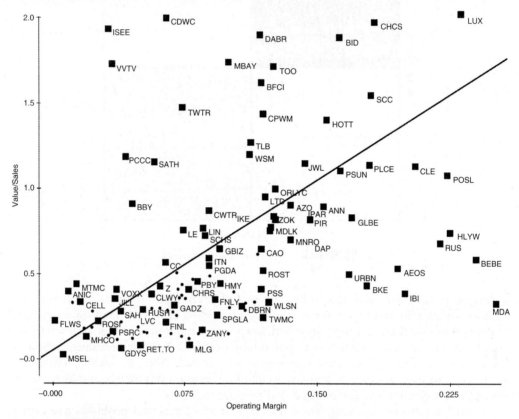

FIGURE 20.4 Enterprise Value-to-Sales Ratios and Operating Margins

Firms with higher operating margins tend to have higher EV-to-sales ratios, while firms with lower margin have lower EV-to-sales ratios. Note, though, that there is a considerable amount of noise even in this subset of firms in the relationship between value-to-sales ratios and operating margins

ILLUSTRATION 20.10: Revenue Multiples and Margins: Internet Retailers in July 2000

In the second comparison, the enterprise value-to-trailing sales ratios in July 2000 of Internet retailers are plotted against the net margins earned by these firms in the most recent year in Figure 20.5.

Here, there seems to be almost no relationship between enterprise value-to-sales ratios and operating margins. This should not be surprising. Most Internet firms have negative operating income and operating margins. The market values of these firms are based not on what they earn now but what they are expected to earn in the future, and there is little correlation between current and expected future margins

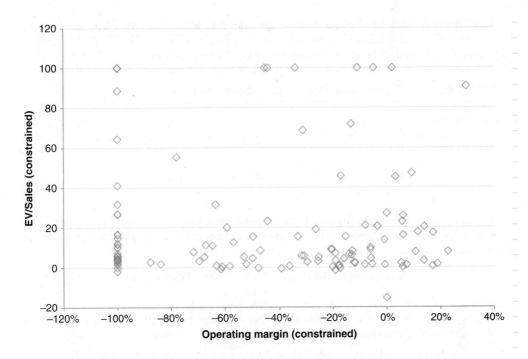

FIGURE 20.5   EV-to-Sales Ratios versus Operating Margins: Internet Stocks

Statistical Approaches   When analyzing price-earnings and price-to-book value ratios, we used regressions to control differences in risk, growth, and payout ratios across firms. We could also use regressions to control differences across firms to analyze revenue multiples. In this section, we begin by applying this approach to comparables defined narrowly as firms in the same business, and then expanded to cover the entire sector and the market.

Comparable Firms in the Same Business   In the last section, we examined firms in the same business looking for mismatches—firms with high margins and low revenue multiples were viewed as undervalued. In a simple extension of this approach, we could regress revenue multiples against profit margins across firms in a sector:

$$\text{Price-to-sales ratio} = a + b \text{ (Net profit margin)}$$
$$\text{EV-to-sales ratio} = a + b \text{ (After-tax operating margin)}$$

These regressions can be used to estimate predicted values for firms in the sample, helping to identify undervalued and overvalued firms.

If the number of firms in the sample is large enough to allow for it, this regression can be extended to add other independent variables. For instance, the standard deviation in stock prices or the beta can be used as an independent variable to capture differences in risk, and analyst estimates of expected growth can control for differences in growth. The regression can also be modified to account for nonlinear relationships between revenue multiples and any or all of these variables.

Can this approach be used for sectors such as the Internet where there seems to be little or no relationship between revenue multiples and fundamentals? It can, but only if you adapt it to consider the determinants of value in these sectors.

ILLUSTRATION 20.11:   Regression Approach—Specialty Retailers in July 2000

Consider again the scatter plot of value-to-sales ratios and operating margins for retailers in Illustration 20.9. There is clearly a positive relationship and a regression of enterprise value to sales ratios against operating margins for specialty retailers yields the following:

$$\text{EV to sales} = 0.0563 + 6.6287 \text{ After-tax operating margin}\quad R^2 = 39.9\%$$
$$(0.72)\quad (10.39)$$

This regression has 162 observations, and the t statistics are reported in brackets. To estimate the predicted value-to-sales ratio for Talbots, one of the specialty retailers in the group, which has an 11.22% as after-tax operating margin:

$$\text{Predicted EV-to-sales ratio} = 0.0563 + 6.6287(.1122) = 0.80$$

With an actual EV-to-sales ratio of 1.27, Talbots be consider overvalued.

This regression can be modified in two ways. One is to regress the EV-to-sales ratio against the ln(Operating margins) to enable the nonlinear relationship between the two variables:

$$\text{EV to sales} = 1.8313 + 0.4339 \text{ ln(After-tax operating margin)}\quad R^2 = 22.40\%$$
$$(10.76)\quad (6.89)$$

The other is to expand the regression to include a proxy for growth:

$$\text{EV to sales} = -0.1488 + 0.2494 \text{ Operating Margin} + 1.545 \text{ Growth}\quad R^2 = 45.4\%$$
$$(1.62)\quad (10.09)$$

where   Operating Margin = After-tax operating margin in most recent year
           Growth = Expected growth rate in earnings over next five years

This regression has fewer observations (124) than the previous two but a higher R-squared of 45.4%. The predicted enterprise value-to-sales ratio for Talbots using this regression is:

$$\text{Predicted EV-to-sales ratio} = -0.1488 + 0.2494(0.1122) + 1.545(0.225) = 0.90$$

Talbots remained overvalued even after adjusting for differences in growth.

ILLUSTRATION 20.12:   Regression Approach—Internet Retailers in July 2000

In the case of the Internet stocks graphed in Illustration 20.10, the regression of enterprise value-to-sales ratios against operating margins yields the following:

$$\text{Price-to-sales ratio} = 18.4015 - 8.5823(\text{Operating margin})\quad R^2 = 1.27\%$$
$$(4.27)\quad (1.21)$$

Not only is the R-squared close to zero, but the relationship between current operating margins and EV-to-sales ratios is negative. Thus, there is little relationship between the pricing of these stocks and their current profitability.

What variables might do a better job of explaining the differences in price-to-sales ratios across Internet stocks? Consider the following propositions:

■ Since this sample contains some firms with very little in revenues and other firms with much higher revenues, you would expect the firms with less in revenues to trade at a much higher multiple of revenues than firms with higher revenues. Thus, Amazon, with revenues of almost $2 billion can be expected to trade at a lower multiple of this value than iVillage with revenues of less than $60 million.

■ There is a high probability that some or many of these Internet firms will not survive because they will run out of cash. A widely used measure of this potential for cash problems is the cash burn ratio, which is the ratio of the cash balance to the absolute value of EBITDA (which is usually a negative number). Firms with a low cash burn ratio are at higher risk of running into a cash crunch and should trade at lower multiples of revenues.

■ Revenue growth is a key determinant of value at these firms. Firms that have faster growing revenues are likely to reach profitability sooner, other things remaining equal.

The following regression relates price-to-sales ratios to the level of revenues [ln(Revenues)], the cash burn ratio (absolute value of Cash/EBITDA) and revenue growth over the past year for Internet firms:

$$\text{EV to sales} = 29.23 - 2.46 \ \ln(\text{Revenues}) + 0.48(\text{Cash/EBITDA}) + 9.34 \ \text{Growth}_{\text{revenue}}$$
$$(1.45) \quad (0.54) \quad\quad\quad (2.70) \quad\quad\quad\quad (1.18)$$

The regression has 116 observations and an R-squared of 8.23%. The coefficients all have the right signs but are of marginal statistical significance. You could obtain a predicted EV-to-sales ratio for Amazon.com in July 2000 using this regression:

$$\text{EV to Sales}_{\text{Amazon.com}} = 29.23 - 2.46 \ \ln(1,920) + 0.48(2.12) + 9.34(1.4810) = 25.48$$

At its actual EV-to-sales ratio of 6.69, Amazon looks significantly undervalued relative to other Internet firms.

In any case, the regressions are much too noisy to attach much weight to the predictions. In fact, the low explanatory power with fundamentals and the huge differences in measures of relative value should sound a note of caution on the use of multiples in sectors such as this one, where firms are in transition and changing dramatically from period to period.

ILLUSTRATION 20.13:   Revenue Multiples and Margins: Whole Foods and the Grocery Sector over Time

If the essence of finding cheap stocks in relative valuation is spotting mismatches, making money from these stocks is possible only if the mismatches get corrected over time. Put differently, you can buy a stock with high margins that trades at a low multiple of revenues, but you need the revenue multiple to increase to match the high margins to make money on the stock.

To provide an illustration of the process, we will track Whole Foods from January 2007 through May 2011. We will begin by plotting Whole Foods in January 2007 in Figure 20.6, relative to the rest of the companies in the grocery sector; the regression line for price-to-sales ratio is also shown on the graph.[2] As the scatter plot of price to sales against net margins for the sector reveals, Whole Foods stood out with the highest price-to-sales ratio (1.40) and the second highest operating margin (3.41%) in the sector.

To see if the higher margin earned by Whole Foods should justify a price to sales ratio of 1.41, we regressed the price-to-sales ratio against net margins for the sector:

$$PS = -0.16 + 33.26(\text{Net profit margin})$$

---

[2] At the time of this analysis, grocery stores had similar debt ratios, with the debt taking the form of leases on stores. If were redoing the analysis in 2024, where differences in leverage across grocery firms has become more significant, we would use enterprise value to sales ratios, twinned with operating margins.

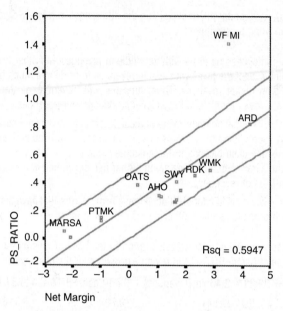

FIGURE 20.6   Price-to-Sales Ratios and Net Margins: Grocery Sector in January 2007

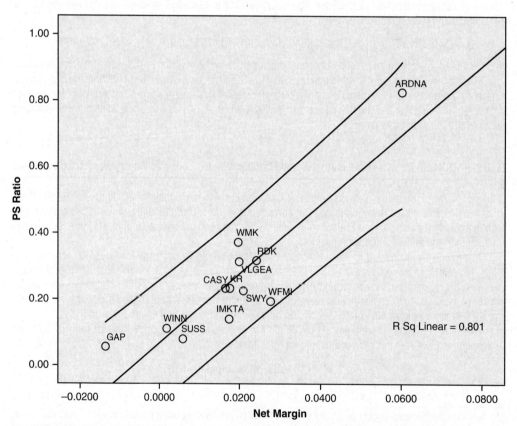

FIGURE 20.7   Price-to-Sales Ratios and Net Margins: Grocery Sector in January 2009

Plugging Whole Food's net margin into the regression, we get:

$$PS_{WFM} = -0.16 + 33.26(.0341) = .97$$

Even after controlling for the higher margin, Whole Foods looks significantly overvalued at 1.41 times sales.

In January 2009, we revisited the grocery sector and plotted price-to-sales ratios against net margins (see Figure 20.7). In the intervening two years, Whole Foods seems to have fallen out of favor with investors. As its net profit margin dropped to 2.77% its price-to-sales ratio took a more significant drop to 0.31.

To assess whether the market over reacted to the decline in margin, we regressed the price-to sales ratio against the net margin and arrived at the following:

$$PS = 0.07 + 10.49 \text{ Net profit margin}$$

Plugging in Whole Food's net margin into the regression, we get:

$$PS_{WFM} = 0.07 + 10.49(.0277) = 0.36$$

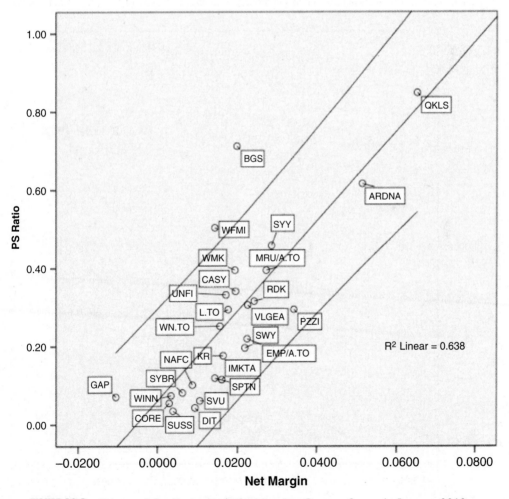

FIGURE 20.8   Price-to-Sales Ratios and Net Margins: Grocery Sector in January 2010

Whole Foods now looks undervalued at 0.31 times revenues, though it falls just above the lower bound for statistical significance.

Moving forward a year to January 2010, we plotted price-to-sales ratio against the net margins for grocery stores again. While the net margin for Whole Foods dropped to 1.44% over the year, its price-to-sales ratio increased to 0.50, putting it right in the middle of the pack (see Figure 20.8).

Again, we regressed price-to-sales ratios against net margins for the sector:

$$PS = 0.06 + 11.43 \text{ Net profit margin}$$

Plugging Whole Foods' net margin into the regression, we get:

$$PS_{WFM} = 0.06 + 11.43(.0144) = 0.22$$

Whole Foods reverted to being overvalued in 2010, and it falls just above the upper bound for statistical significance.

Finally, we revisited the sector in May 2011 and plotted price-to-sales ratios against net margins for firms in the sector. As noted in the earlier illustrations, Whole Foods has reclaimed its premium status in terms of pricing, trading at 1.11 times revenues, and its net profit margin has increased to 2.73%. (See Figure 20.9.)

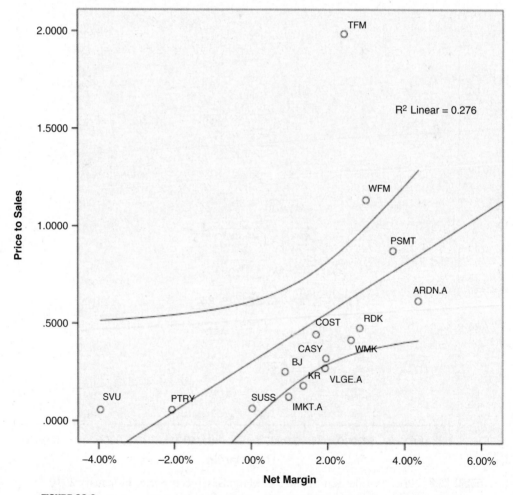

FIGURE 20.9   Price-to-Sales Ratios and Net Margins: Grocery Sector in May 2011

Regressing price-to-sales ratio against net margins, we get:

$$PS = 0.304 + 0.126 \text{ Net profit margin}$$

Plugging Whole Foods' net margin into the regression, we get:

$$PS_{WFM} = 0.304 + 12.60(.0273) = 0.65$$

Whole Foods looks significantly overvalued in May 2011.

In hindsight, these regressions would have suggested selling short on Whole Foods in January 2007, buying the stock again in January 2009, and reverting to selling short in January 2010. The first two actions would have generated significant profits, but the last one would have been a money loser since the stock became even more overvalued between 2010 and 2011.

Market Regressions   If you can control differences across firms using a regression, you can extend this approach to look at much broader cross sections of firms. Here, the cross-sectional data is used to estimate the price-to-sales ratio as a function of fundamental variables—profit margin, dividend payout, beta, and growth rate in earnings.

This approach can be extended to cover the entire market. In the first edition of this book, regressions of price-sales ratios on fundamentals—dividend payout ratio, growth rate in earnings, profit margin, and beta—were run for each year from 1987 to 1991 in Table 20.11:

TABLE 20.11   Market Regressions for Price to Sales—1987–1991

Year	Regression	R-Squared
1987	PS = 0.7894 + .0008 Payout – 0.2734 Beta + 0.5022 EGR + 6.46 Margin	0.4434
1988	PS = 0.1660 + .0006 Payout – 0.0692 Beta + 0.5504 EGR + 10.31 Margin	0.7856
1989	PS = 0.4911 + .0393 Payout – 0.0282 Beta + 0.2836 EGR + 10.25 Margin	0.4601
1990	PS = 0.0826 + .0105 Payout – 0.1073 Beta + 0.5449 EGR + 10.36 Margin	0.8885
1991	PS = 0.5189 + 0.2749 Payout – 0.2485 Beta + 0.4948 EGR + 8.17 Margin	0.4853

where   PS = Price-sales ratio at the end of the year

Payout = Payout ratio = Dividends/earnings at the end of the year

Beta = Beta of the stock

Margin = Profit margin for the year = Net income/sales for the year(in %)

EGR = Earnings growth rate over the previous five years

These regressions were updated in Table 20.12 in January 2024 for EV/Sales ratios for publicly traded companies, broken down by geography:

TABLE 20.12   Market Regressions for EV to Sales—Start of 2024

Region	Regression	R-Squared
United States	EV/S = 0.81 + 9.86 g + 8.19 OM – 1.60 DFR– 5.88 Tax rate	36.0%
Europe	EV/S = 1.52 + 5.96 g + 6.13 OM – 2.04 DFR– 0.15 Tax rate	14.3%
Japan	EV/S = 1.13 + 3.82 g + 8.97 OM + 0.33 DFR– 1.59 Tax rate	29.1%
Australia, NZ & Canada	EV/S = 1.39 + 3.02 g + 4.31 OM + 1.21 DFR+ 3.18 Tax rate	14.7%

(*continued*)

TABLE 20.12 (*continued*)

Region	Regression	R-Squared
Emerging markets	EV/S = 3.07 + 1.48 g + 4.29 OM − 0.24 DFR- 2.22 Tax rate	8.9%
Global	EV/S= 3.35 + 3.36 g + 6.45 OM - 0.52 DFR− 3.82 Tax rate	18.0%

where   g = Expected growth rate in earnings per share(next 5 years)

         OM = Trailing operating income/Revenues

         DFR = Debt/(Debt + Equity) in market value

   Tax rate = Effective tax rate in most recent year

Differences in the revenue multiples are explained best by variation in operating margins, though the explanatory power varies widely around the world.

ILLUSTRATION 20.14: Pricing Costco and Tesco

We will try to estimate EV-to-sales multiples for Costco (a U.S. big-box retailer, with a subscription model) and Tesco (a UK-based retailer) in May 2024, based upon the previous market regressions.

First, we plug the numbers for Costco into the U.S. EV-to-sales regression, with the following inputs:

Costco's operating margin = 3.76%

Costco's expected revenue growth rate = 7.20%

Costco's deb-to-capital ratio = 3.00%

Costco's tax rate = 22.15%

The resulting pricing, using the U.S. market regression is:

US Regression: EV/S = 1.81 + 9.86(g) + 8.19(OM) − 1.60(DFR) − 5.88(Tax rate)

Costco's EV/Sales = 1.81 + 9.86(.072) + 8.19(.0376) − 1.60(.03) − 5.88(.2215) = 1.48

This is higher than the actual price-to-sales ratio for Costco, of 1.31, in May 2024; the stock looks undervalued, given how the rest of the market is being priced.

Next, we estimate the EV-to-sales ratio for Tesco, using the European EV-to-sales regression. The following inputs:

Tesco's operating margin (OM) = 4.11%

Tesco's expected revenue growth rate (g) = 1.5%

Tesco's debt-to-capital ratio (DFR) = 40.35%

Tesco's tax rate = 18.5%

The resulting pricing, using the U.S. market regression is:

Europe Regression: EV/Sales = 1.52 + 5.96 g + 6.13 OM − 2.04 DFR − 0.15 Tax rate

Tesco's: EV/Sales = 1.52 + 5.96(.015) +6.13(.0411) −2.04(.4035)

−0.15(.185)

= 1.01

Tesco was trading at 0.47 times trailing revenues in May 2024, making it significantly underpriced.

Multiples of Revenues in Future Years   Chapter 18 examined the use of market value of equity as a multiple of earnings in a future year. Revenue multiples can also be measured in terms of future revenues. Thus, you could estimate the value as a multiple of revenues five years from now. There are some advantages to doing this:

- For firms that have little in revenues currently but are expected to grow rapidly over time, the revenues in the future—say five years from now—are likely to better reflect the firm's true potential than revenues today.
- It is easier to estimate multiples of revenues when growth rates have leveled off, and the firm's risk profile is stable. This is more likely to be the case five years from now than it is today for young, growth firms.

Assuming that revenues five years from now are to be used to estimate value, what multiple should be used on these revenues? You have three choices. One is to use the average multiples of value (today) to revenues today of comparable firms to estimate a value five years from now, and then discount that value back to the present. Consider, for example, Tesla in 2010, where current revenues are only $117 million, but which we expected to grow to $4,877 billion in 10 years. If the average EV-to-sales ratio of more mature automobile firms is 0.82, the estimated value of Tesla can be estimated as follows:

$$\text{Revenues at Tesla Motors in 10 years} = \$4,877 \text{ million}$$

$$\text{Estimated EV for Tesla Motors in 10 years} = \$4,877 \times 0.82 = \$3,999 \text{ million}$$

If Tesla's cost of capital for the next ten years is expected to be 12%, you could estimate the enterprise value today:

$$\text{Value of firm today} = \text{Estimated EV in ten years}/(1 + \text{Cost of capital})^{10}$$
$$= \$3,999/(1.12)^{10} = \$1288 \text{ million}$$

We are ignoring the cash flows over the next 10 years in this computation. Adding the current cash balance ($196 million), subtracting out debt outstanding ($106 million), netting out the value of management options ($152 million), and dividing by the number of shares (94.908 million) yields a value per share of $12.91:

$$\text{Value per share} = \frac{1,288 + 196 - 106 - 152}{94.908} = \$12.91$$

The second approach is to forecast the expected revenue in ten years for each of the comparable firms, and to divide each firm's current value by these revenues. This multiple of current value to future revenues can be used to estimate the value today. To illustrate, if current value is 0.4 times revenues in 10 years for other automobile firms, the value of Tesla Motors can be estimated as follows:

$$\text{Revenues at Tesla in 10 years} = \$4,877 \text{ million}$$

$$\text{Enterprise value today} = \text{Revenues in 10 years} \times (\text{EV today}/\text{Revenues}_{\text{year 10}})$$
$$= \$4,877(0.4) = \$1,951 \text{ million}$$

In the third approach, you can adjust the multiple of future revenues for differences in operating margin, growth, and risk for differences between the firm and comparable firms. For instance, Tesla Motors, 10 years from now will have an expected operating margin of 10%, and an expected growth rate of 3.5% in subsequent years.

You could run a regression of EV/sales ratios against expected growth rates and operating margins at automobile companies today, and then plug in the values for Tesla Motors into the regression to get the predicted EV-to-sales ratio for the firm in 10 years. That predicted EV would be used instead of the industry average to estimate the future value.

SECTOR-SPECIFIC MULTIPLES

The value of a firm can be standardized using a number of sector-specific multiples. The value of steel companies can be compared based on market value per ton of steel produced, and the value of electricity generators can be computed on the basis of kilowatt hour (kwh) of power produced. In the past few years, analysts following new technology firms have become particularly inventive with multiples that range from value per subscriber for online service providers to value per website visitor for Internet portals to value per member for social media companies.

Why Analysts Use Sector-Specific Multiples

The increase in the use of sector-specific multiples in the last few years has opened up a debate about whether they yield good estimates of relative value. There are several reasons why analysts use sector-specific multiples:

- They link firm value to operating details and output. For analysts who begin with these forecasts—predicted number of subscribers or number of social media site members, for instance—they provide a much more intuitive way of estimating value.
- Sector-specific multiples can often be computed with no reference to accounting statements or measures. Consequently, they can be estimated for firms where accounting statements are nonexistent, unreliable, or just not comparable. Thus, you could compute the value per kwh sold for Latin American power companies and not have to worry about accounting differences across these countries.
- Though this is usually not admitted to, sector-specific multiples are sometimes employed in desperation because none of the other multiples can be estimated or used. For instance, an impetus for the use of sector-specific multiples for dot-com companies in the late 1990s was that they often had negative earnings and little in terms of book value or revenues.

Limitations

Though it is understandable that analysts sometimes turn to sector-specific multiples, there are two significant problems associated with their use:

- They feed into the tunnel vision that plagues analysts who are sector focused, and thus they enable entire sectors to become overpriced. A service company trading at

$50 a subscriber might look cheap next to another one trading at $125 a subscriber, but it is entirely possible that they are both overpriced or underpriced.

- As will be shown later in this section, the relationship of sector-specific multiples to fundamentals is complicated, and consequently it is very difficult to control differences across firms when comparing them on these multiples.

Definitions of Sector-Specific Multiples

The essence of sector-specific multiples is that the way they are measured vary from sector to sector. In general, though, they share some general characteristics:

- The numerator is usually enterprise value—the market values of both debt and equity netted out against cash and marketable securities.
- The denominator is defined in terms of the operating units that generate revenues and profits for the firm.

For commodity companies such as oil refineries and gold-mining companies, where revenue is generated by selling units of the commodity, the market value can be standardized by dividing by the value of the reserves that these companies have of the commodity:

$$\text{Value per commodity unit in reserve} = \frac{\text{Enterprise value}}{\text{Number of units of commodity in reserves}}$$

Oil companies can be compared on enterprise value per barrel of oil in reserves and gold-mining companies on the basis of enterprise value per ounce of gold in reserves.

For manufacturing firms that produce a homogeneous product (in terms of quality and units), the market value can be standardized by dividing by the number of units of the product that the firm produces or has the capacity to produce:

$$\text{Value per commodity unit produced} = \frac{\text{Enterprise value}}{\text{Number of units of produced}}$$

For instance, steel companies can be compared based on their enterprise value per ton of steel produced or in capacity, and auto companies based upon their enterprise value per automobile sold.

For subscription-based firms such as cable companies, online service providers, and information providers, revenues come from the number of subscribers to the base service provided. Here, the value of a firm can be stated in terms of the number of subscribers:

$$\text{Enterprise Value per subscriber} = \frac{\text{Enterprise value}}{\text{Number of subscribers}}$$

In each of the cases we have discussed, you could make an argument for the use of a sector-specific multiple because the units (whether they be barrels of oil, kwh of electricity, or subscribers) generate similar revenues. Sector multiples become much more problematic when the units used to scale value are not homogeneous. Let us consider two examples.

For retailers that generate revenue from customers who shop at their stores or websites, the value of the firm can be stated in terms of the number of regular customers:

$$\text{Enterprise Value per customers} = \frac{\text{Enterprise value}}{\text{Number of paying customers}}$$

The problem, here, is that the amount spent can vary widely across customers, so it is not clear that a firm that looks cheap on this basis is undervalued.

For online or social media portals that generate revenue from advertising revenues that are based on traffic to the sites, the revenues can be stated in terms of the number of users of the site:

$$\text{Enterprise Value per user} = \frac{\text{Enterprise value}}{\text{Number of user of social media site}}$$

Here, again, the link between visitors and advertising revenues is neither clearly established nor obvious. In 2024, for instance, there are social media sites like Meta that derive immense advertising revenues from those who visit its sites (Facebook, Instagram) and there are other sites (SnapChat and Twitter), where it has been much more difficult to monetize users.

Determinants of User/Subscriber Value   What are the determinants of value for these sector-specific multiples? Not surprisingly, they are the same as the determinants of value for other multiples—cash flows, growth, and risk—though the relationship can be complex. If you are a user- or subscriber-based company with an existing user (or subscriber), that user/subscriber has value to you because you expect to generate cash flows from his or her interactions with you. There are, broadly speaking, three ways (or revenue models) in which you can generate these cash flows:

- **Subscription fees:** The user or subscriber pays a fee, usually fixed, each period for using your service. That fee can be the same for every subscriber or tiered, with different fees for different levels of service, and generally will continue until the subscriber cancels the service. Netflix, Microsoft's Office 365 and Adobe's Creative Cloud are all subscription fee-based models.
- **Advertising:** With this model, users pay nothing for being on your service, but other businesses are attracted by your user base (its size and focus) to try to sell them products and services. Facebook, Twitter, Snap, and Google are all user-based companies that generate their revenues from selling access to their user bases to other companies in the form of advertising.
- **Transactions:** With a transaction-based model, the user or subscriber transacts with or through you, and you generate profits from the transaction. Uber, for instance, enables the download of its app for free, but it generates revenues only when you use the app to call for a car service or delivery, sharing in the revenue from that transaction.

As you can see, there are hybrid versions that draw on more than one of these models. LinkedIn has both a subscription-based premium model, for users who want to use its network more extensively, as well as a free model, where it generates revenues from online advertising. Amazon Prime has an annual subscription fee that it charges members, but also generates revenues (and associated costs) when Prime members buy products on the Amazon portal.

Whatever revenue model you use, the value of a user or a subscriber is the present value of the expected after-tax cash flows that you will generate from that user/subscriber over the period that you expect them to stay on your platform. To derive this value, you will need the following information:

1. **User life:** Whether your users are individuals or businesses, the lifetime of that user to you will be finite, due to mortality. In most cases, though, you will use a lifetime much shorter than the remaining life of a user, because your technology may have a more limited life, and/or users' preferences for a brand may change over time. Generally speaking, the more tied your product or service is to a specific technology, the shorter the user life will be.
2. **User renewal rate:** If your users renew 100% of the time, every user will stay on for his or her full lifetime, and you can count on the cash flows each year for that period. If the renewal rate is less than 100%, the expected cash flows in future years must reflect the survival likelihood for that customer. For instance, if you have an annual renewal rate of 90%, the probability that a customer will be around in year 8 of a fifteen-year life-time is only 43% (survival rate until year $10 = .9^8 = 0.43$). In fact, if you have data that is rich enough, you could estimate year-specific renewal rates for the collective customer base, since it is not just possible but also likely that renewal rates will change as you go through time, usually from lower values in the early years to higher ones in the later years. It is also worth noting that renewal rates, even when reported by companies, can be difficult to generalize, since some subscribers can cancel their subscriptions and renew them multiple times during a period. Finally, the importance of renewal rates in value is far greater for subscription-based companies, where nonrenewal leads to a loss of income, than it is for transaction-based companies, where you get value from a user only if a transaction occurs. If users and members stop transacting or trans-act with lower frequency, it should show up a lower user revenues and cash flow. Thus, the renewal rate assumption will have far more consequence in our valuation of Netflix than in the valuation of Uber, with Amazon Prime falling somewhere in the middle.
3. **User cash flow (current):** Your current cash flow per user is not just the revenue that you expect to generate from that user—you must net out against the cost of servicing that user. Thus, if Netflix generates $120/subscriber per year and spends $30 providing direct services to that subscriber, the base year cash flow for Netflix will be $90 per subscriber on a pre-tax basis, and perhaps only $72 per subscriber, if it faces an effective tax rate of 20%. With an advertising-based company, this is a more diffuse number to estimate, but dividing your total advertising revenue in the most recent period by the number of users you had during the period may be a reasonable starting point for revenues, but you will still need to net out costs.
4. **Growth in per-user cash flow:** Once you have acquired a user, you may be able to sell that user other products and services in the future, leading to growth in the per-user revenues, and if some of your service costs are fixed, your operating profits per user will grow even more quickly. That growth, though, will depend on your business model. For Netflix, with its monthly subscription-based model, there are limits to how much it can raise that subscription price over time. For Amazon Prime, there is a much larger poten-tial for growth, since a Prime member can be targeted with new products and services.

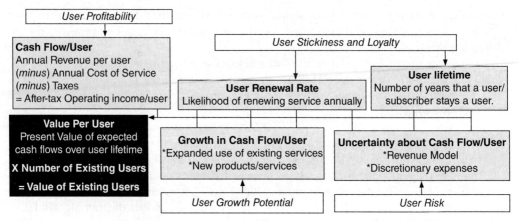

FIGURE 20.10   Value of an Existing User/Subscriber

One outgrowth from Amazon's acquisition of Whole Foods in 2017, for instance, is that the company can offer prepared meals to its Prime members as an added product.
5. **Risk in Cash Flow:** Since the risk of losing a user is already built into the expected cash flow, the primary risk here comes from both variations in renewal rates over time and from how much cash flow you can generate from each user. Again, your revenue model matters, with subscription-based models delivering more predictable revenues than transaction-based models, and the discount rates you use to value the cash flows have to reflect the risk differences.

Figure 20.10 brings together all these variables into a picture, tying user value to key user inputs.

As you look at the information that you will need to derive this value, you probably also recognize that the information disclosures that we have from user-based companies are seriously lacking. While we will try to patch our way to valuing a user in the example at the end of this section, we believe that the path forward must include more complete user-related information from companies.

ILLUSTRATION 20.15:   Estimating Subscriber value: Netflix in April 2018

Since going public in 2002, Netflix has disrupted two businesses. First, it displaced the brick-and-mortal video rental business, dominated by Blockbuster, with its subscription-based, mailed-video model. Second, starting in 2012, it has broken into the entertainment business, on both the content side by spending immense amounts on original content, and on the customer side by changing the way we watch television. In the process, it has built a business with more than a hundred million subscribers globally, who not only pay more on average than a hundred dollars, to watch Netflix content, but also provide data on their watching habits to the company, which it uses to create new content.

To describe Netflix as a streaming company misses its complexity, since it has long since left that label behind. It does make its revenues from subscribers who pay a monthly or an annual fee to watch its offerings, but its content now is just as likely to be homemade as it is to be leased from a studio. Figure 20.11 breaks down the Netflix business model, at least as of April 2018.

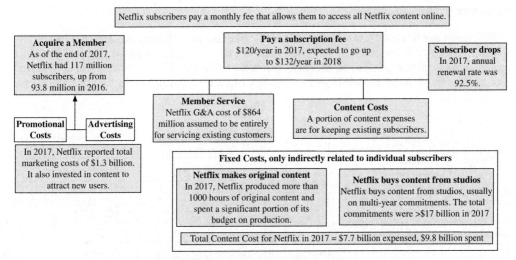

FIGURE 20.11 Netflix Business Model

Note that while Netflix's biggest expense, creating and licensing content, is clearly directed at keeping and acquiring subscribers. At the same time, it is not directly related to user count, and this will have important consequences for value.

To value Netflix, we start by breaking Netflix expenses into three parts: those associated with (a) servicing existing subscribers, (2) acquiring new subscribers, and (3) corporate costs, not directly related to user numbers. We then value the company by valuing each of these three segments separately.

DECONSTRUCTING THE FINANCIALS

Netflix reported $838 million in operating profit in 2017, on revenues of $11.693 billion, while also reporting a surge in the number of users from 93.8 million to $117.6 million. Using the information in the financial statement, we began by breaking down the total operating expenses at the company, shown in figure 20.12 into costs associated with servicing existing subscribers (G&A cost and 20% of expensed content costs), getting new subscribers (capitalized content cost and marketing costs) and corporate costs (technology and development and 80% of expensed content costs). Figure 20.12 summarizes the deconstruction of the financials.

The allocation of content costs between existing subscribers, new subscribers, and into corporate costs reflects our subjective input, but in the absence of clear information from Netflix, we had no other option. Based upon our estimates, the cost of acquiring a new subscriber is $111.01, lower than the $143.87 in the most recent year, and the cost of servicing an existing subscriber is $21.39.

Subscriber Statistics					Cost of acquiring new subscribers	
	2017	2016	Change			
Number of Subscribers	117.60	93.80	23.80		Total User Acquisition Costs	$3,424.00
Revenue/Subscriber	$113.16	$103.32			Change in Subscribers in 2017	23.80
Content Cost Breakdown					Cost per new Subscriber	$ 143.87
Content Costs (Cash expense)	$9,806.00					
Content Costs Expensed	$ 7,660.00				*Cost of Servicing Existing Subscribers*	
Content Costs Capitalized	$2,146.00				Revenue/Subscriber in 2017	$113.16
Netflix: Operating Income in 2017					G&A Cost as % of Revenue	7.39%
Revenues	$11,693.00	As % of Sales			Subscriber-related Content Costs	$1,532.00
Marketing Costs	$ 1,278.00	10.93%				
G&A Costs	$ 864.00	7.39%			*Corporate Costs (unrelated to Subscribers)*	
Technology & Development	$ 1,053.00	9.01%			Technology & Development	$1,053.00
Content Costs Expensed	$ 7,660.00	65.51%			Corporate Content Costs	$6,128.00
Operating Profit	$ 838.00	7.17%				

FIGURE 20.12 Netflix Finances Deconstructed

VALUING EXISTING SUBSCRIBERS

In 2017, Netflix reported that it generated $113.16 per subscriber per year, reflecting its geographical mix of subscribers. Netting out $21.39, the cost of servicing a subscriber each year, yields an operating profit of $91.77 per subscriber before taxes, and $68.83 per subscriber after taxes. In Figure 20.13, we estimate the value of existing subscribers at Netflix, further considering Netflix's cost of capital and the average lifetime of Netflix subscribers.

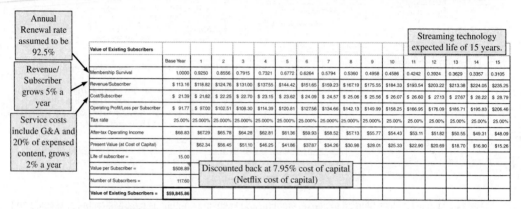

Value of Existing Subscribers	Base Year	1	2	3	4	5	6	7	8	9	10	11	12	13	14	15
Membership Survival	1.0000	0.9250	0.8556	0.7915	0.7321	0.6772	0.6264	0.5794	0.5360	0.4958	0.4586	0.4242	0.3924	0.3629	0.3357	0.3105
Revenue/Subscriber	$ 113.16	$118.82	$124.76	$ 131.00	$137.55	$144.42	$151.65	$159.23	$ 167.19	$175.55	$184.33	$193.54	$203.22	$213.38	$224.05	$235.25
Cost/Subscriber	$ 21.39	$ 21.82	$ 22.25	$ 22.70	$ 23.15	$ 23.62	$ 24.09	$ 24.57	$ 25.06	$ 25.56	$ 26.07	$ 26.60	$ 27.13	$ 27.67	$ 28.22	$ 28.79
Operating Profit/Loss per Subscriber	$ 91.77	$ 97.00	$102.51	$108.30	$114.39	$120.81	$127.56	$134.66	$142.13	$149.99	$158.25	$166.95	$176.09	$185.71	$195.83	$206.46
Tax rate	25.00%	25.000%	25.000%	25.000%	25.000%	25.000%	25.000%	25.000%	25.000%	25.000%	25.00%	25.00%	25.00%	25.00%	25.00%	25.00%
After-tax Operating Income	$68.83	$67.29	$65.78	$64.28	$62.81	$61.36	$59.93	$58.52	$57.13	$55.77	$54.43	$53.11	$51.82	$50.55	$49.31	$48.09
Present Value (at Cost of Capital)		$62.34	$56.45	$51.10	$46.25	$41.86	$37.87	$34.26	$30.98	$28.01	$25.33	$22.90	$20.69	$18.70	$16.90	$15.26
Life of subscriber =	15.00															
Value per Subscriber =	$508.89															
Number of Subscribers =	117.60															
Value of Existing Subscribers =	**$59,845.86**															

FIGURE 20.13   Value of Netflix's Existing Subscribers

Assuming that Netflix has pricing power and can increase subscriber fees by 5% a year, while keeping content costs growing at only 2% a year, results in higher operating income over time. Finally, incorporating another of Netflix's strengths, it high renewal rate of 92.5%,[3] and discounting back at Netflix's cost of capital of 7.95%, reflecting its business mix and debt ratio, we arrive at a value of $508.89 per user and a total value of $59.8 billion for all 117 million subscribers.

VALUING NEW SUBSCRIBERS

To value new subscribers, we start with the value of an existing subscriber of $508.89, derived in the last section, and net out the cost of $111.01, for acquiring a new subscriber, to arrive at a value per new subscriber of $397.88 in today's dollars. In Figure 20.14, we value new subscribers at Netflix.

To complete the process, we assumed that the net subscriber base would grow 15% a year for the next five years and 10% a year from years six through ten, before subsiding to a 1% growth rate thereafter.[4] Also enabling the value of a new subscriber to grow at the inflation rate of 2%, and discounting back at the Netflix cost of capital of 7.95%, yields a value of $137.3 billion for new users.

THE CORPORATE COST DRAG

The final component of the analysis is the weightiest, at least for Netflix, since it includes $1,053 million in technology and development costs, and $6,128 million in content costs. If those costs grow with subscriber

---

[3]The renewal rate is a key number here, and we tried to use the more sophisticated approach that McCarthy and Fader suggest for a more refined value but quickly ran into data constraints.

[4]Note that to get net subscribers to grow at 15% a year, Netflix has to add more than number in new subscribers, because its renewal rate is 92.5%. To illustrate, we start the first year with 117.6 million members but will lose 7.5% of those members due to nonrenewal. To be able to grow the net subscriber base by 15%, you will have to add enough members to also cover the nonrenewals, giving you a total add on of 26.46 million members in year 1.

$$\text{New Subscribers in year 1} = 117.6\,(.15) + 117.6\,(1 - .925) = 26.46 \text{ million}$$

We repeat this process each year.

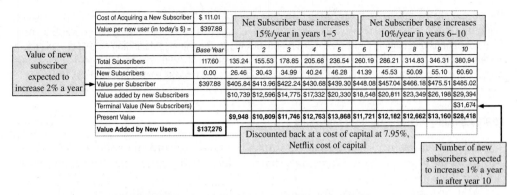

FIGURE 20.14   Valuing New Subscribers at Netflix

count and revenues, Netflix will drown in these costs. In Figure 20.15, we assume that once Netflix gets through its immediate growth phase, it will find a way to get these costs under control.

Even with content costs growing 3% a year, the value of the corporate cost drag reduces the value of Netflix by $111.3 billion.

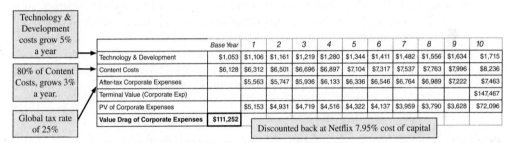

FIGURE 20.15   The Corporate Drag at Netflix

VALUING NETFLIX

With the value of existing and new subscribers in hand as well as the corporate cost drag, we can estimate the value of Netflix, as a company, in table 20.13.

TABLE 20.13   Value of Netflix on April 16, 2018

Valuing Netflix	
Value of Existing Subscribers	$ 59,845.86
+ Value of New Subscribers	$137,276.49
− PV of Corporate Drag	$111,251.70
= Value of Operating Assets	$ 85,870.65
+ Cash & Cross Holdings	$ 2,823.00
− Debt	$ 6,500.00
Value of Equity	**$ 82,193.65**
− Value of Equity Options	$ 4,978.00
Value of Equity in common stock	**$ 77,215.65**
Number of Shares	446.81
Value per Share	**$ 172.82**

The value of the operating assets of $85.9 billion is augmented with Netflix's cash holdings of $2.8 billion and reduced by Netflix debt of $6.5 billion, yielding a value of equity of $82.2 billion. Netting out the value of management options outstanding at the end of 2017, and dividing by the shares outstanding on that date yielded a value per share of $172.82 on April 16, 2018. The stock was trading at $280 per share, suggesting either that we have been too pessimistic about Netflix's prospects, or that the market is over valuing the company.

Analysis Using Sector-Specific Multiples

To analyze firms using sector-specific multiples, you have to control the differences across firms on any or all of the fundamentals that you identified as affecting these multiples in the last part.

With value per subscriber, for instance, you have to control differences in the value generated by each subscriber. In particular:

■ Firms that are more efficient in delivering a service for a given subscription price (resulting in lower costs) should trade at a higher value per subscriber than comparable firms. This would also apply if a firm has significant economies of scale. In Illustration 20.13, the value per subscriber would be higher if each existing subscriber generated $120 in net cash flows for the firm each year, instead of $100.

■ Firms that can add new subscribers at a lower cost (through advertising and promotion) should trade at a higher value per subscriber than comparable firms.

■ Firms with higher expected growth in the subscriber base (in percentage terms) should trade at a higher value per subscriber than comparable firms.

You could make similar statements about value per customer.

ILLUSTRATION 20.16: Cascading Values: Value per Member and Social Media Companies

In May 2011, Linkedin became the first of the major social media companies to go public to a rapturous response: The stock price doubled on the offering day and the company was valued at about $10 billion, even though it had revenues of only $243 million. At about the same time, Microsoft acquired Skype for $8.5 billion, though Skype reported an operating loss of $7 million in the prior year. Facebook and Twitter, while not public, also commanded lofty valuations in private markets for shares in the companies.

One justification for the high valuations was the number of members/users of the resources offered by these companies. Table 20.14 lists these four social media companies, the market (or estimated) values of these companies, the value per user/member, and a more conventional EV/sales multiple:

TABLE 20.14 User Data for Social Media Companies

Company	Users (millions)	EV (millions)	EV/user (user)	Revenues (millions)	EV/Sales
Facebook	500	$50,000*	$100.00	$710.00	70.42
Twitter	175	$ 6,000*	$ 34.29	$ 1.30	4615.38
Skype	170	$ 8,500	$ 50.00	$860.00	9.88
Linkedin	75	$10,000	$133.33	$243.00	41.15

Note that the values for Skype and LinkedIn represent public transactions, whereas the estimated values for Facebook and Twitter are based on private transactions. All four of the companies look hopelessly overvalued on the EV/sales multiple, with Twitter trading at 4,615 times revenues in 2010. On the value/member dimension, though, Twitter looks cheap, and Microsoft seems to have bought Skype at a bargain.

In making these comparisons, though, note that we are assuming that the revenue models for all four firms are similar and will generate roughly the same value per member (user). It is possible that LinkedIn, as a professional, business-oriented site, can generate higher value per member and that it will be tougher for Twitter to commercialize its site, but at this stage in the process, it is entirely speculative.

CONCLUSION

The price-to-sales multiple and value-to-sales ratio are widely used to value technology firms and to compare value across these firms. An analysis of the fundamentals highlights the importance of profit margins in determining these multiples, in addition to the standard variables—the dividend payout ratio, the cost of equity, and the expected growth rates in net income for price to sales, and the reinvestment rate, cost of capital, and growth in property income for value to sales. Comparisons of revenue multiples across firms have to take into account differences in profit margins. One approach is to look for mismatches—low margins and high revenue multiples suggesting overvalued firms and high margins and low revenue multiples suggesting undervalued firms. Another approach that controls differences in fundamentals is the cross-sectional regression approach, where revenue multiples are regressed against fundamentals across firms in a business, an entire sector, or the market.

Sector-specific multiples relate value to sector-specific variables, but they have to be used with caution. It is often difficult to compare these multiples across firms without making stringent assumptions about their operations and growth potential.

QUESTIONS AND SHORT PROBLEMS

In the problems following, use an equity risk premium of 5.5 percent if none is specified.

1. Longs Drug Stores, a large U.S. drugstore chain operating primarily in Northern California, had sales per share of $122 in 1993, on which it reported earnings per share of $2.45 and paid a dividend per share of $1.12. The company is expected to grow 6% in the long term and has a beta of 0.90. The current T-bond rate is 7%, and the market risk premium is 5.5%.
   a. Estimate the appropriate price-sales multiple for Longs Drug.
   b. The stock is currently trading for $34 per share. Assuming the growth rate is estimated correctly, what would the profit margin need to be to justify this price per share?
2. You are examining the wide differences in price-sales ratios that you can observe among firms in the retail store industry, and are trying to come up with a rationale to explain these differences:

Company	Price	Sales	Earnings	Growth	Beta	Payout
Bombay Co.	$38	$ 9.70	$0.68	29.00%	1.45	0%
Bradlees	$15	$168.60	$1.75	12.00%	1.15	34%
Caldor	$32	$147.45	$2.70	12.50%	1.55	0%

(continued)

(continued)

Company	Price	Sales	Earnings	Growth	Beta	Payout
Consolidated	$21	$ 23.00	$0.95	26.50%	1.35	0%
Dayton Hudson	$73	$272.90	$4.65	12.50%	1.30	38%
Federated	$22	$ 58.90	$1.40	10.00%	1.45	0%
Kmart	$23	$101.45	$1.75	11.50%	1.30	59%
Nordstrom	$36	$ 43.85	$1.60	11.50%	1.45	20%
Penney	$54	$ 81.05	$3.50	10.50%	1.10	41%
Sears	$57	$150.00	$4.55	11.00%	1.35	36%
Tiffany	$32	$ 35.65	$1.50	10.50%	1.50	19%
Wal-Mart	$30	$ 29.35	$1.05	18.50%	1.30	11%
Woolworth	$23	$ 74.15	$1.35	13.00%	1.25	65%

    a.   There are two companies that sell for more than revenues, the Bombay Company and Wal-Mart. Why?

    b.   What is the variable that is most highly correlated with price-sales ratios?

    c.   Which of these companies is most likely to be over or undervalued? How did you arrive at this judgment?

3. Walgreen, a large retail drugstore chain in the United States, reported net income of $221 million in 1993 on revenues of $8,298 million. It paid out 31% of its earnings as dividends, a payout ratio it was expected to maintain between 1994 and 1998, during which period earnings growth was expected to be 13.5%. After 1998, earnings growth was expected to decline to 6%, and the dividend payout ratio was expected to increase to 60%. The beta was 1.15 and was expected to remain unchanged. The Treasury bond rate was 7%, and the risk premium was 5.5%.

    a.   Estimate the price/sales ratio for Walgreens, assuming its profit margin remains unchanged at 1993 levels.

    b.   How much of this price/sales ratio can be attributed to extraordinary growth?

4. Tambrands, a leading producer of tampons, reported net income of $122 million on revenues of $684 million in 1992. Earnings growth was anticipated to be 11% over the next five years, after which it was expected to be 6%. The firm paid out 45% of its earnings as dividends in 1992, and this payout ratio was expected to increase to 60% during the stable period. The beta of the stock was 1.00. During the course of 1993, erosion of brand loyalty and increasing competition for generic brands lead to a drop in net income to $100 million on revenues of $700 million. The sales/book value ratio was comparable to 1992 levels. (The Treasury bond rate in 1992 and 1993 was 7%, and the risk premium was 5.5%.)

    a.   Estimate the price-sales ratio, based on 1992 profit margins and expected growth.

    b.   Estimate the price-sales ratio, based on 1993 profit margins and expected growth. (Assume that the extraordinary growth period remains five years, but that the growth rate will be impacted by the lower margins.)

5. Gillette Inc. was faced with a significant corporate strategy decision early in 1994 on whether it would continue its high-margin strategy, or shift to a lower margin to increase sales revenues in the face of intense generic competition. The two strategies being considered are as follows:

Status Quo High-Margin Strategy
- Maintain profit margins at 1993 levels from 1994 to 2003. (In 1993, net income was $575 million on revenues of $5,750 million.)
- The sales/book value ratio, which was 3 in 1993, can then be expected to decline to 2.5 between 1994 and 2003.

Low-Margin Higher-Sales Strategy
- Reduce net profit margin to 8% from 1994 to 2003.
- The sales/book value ratio will then stay at 1993 levels from 1994 to 2003.
  The book value per share at the end of 1993 was $9.75. The dividend payout ratio, which was 33% in 1993, was expected to remain unchanged from 1994 to 2003 under either strategy, as is the beta, which was 1.30 in 1993. (The T-bond rate was 7%, and the risk premium was 5.5%.) After 2003, the earnings growth rate was expected to drop to 6%, and the dividend payout ratio was expected to be 60% under either strategy. The beta would decline to 1.0.
  a. Estimate the price-sales ratio under the status quo strategy.
  b. Estimate the price-sales ratio under the low-margin strategy.
  c. Which strategy would you recommend and why?
  d. How much would sales have to drop under the status quo strategy for the two strategies to be equivalent?
6. You have regressed price-sales ratios against fundamentals for NYSE stocks in 1994 and come up with the following regression:

$$PS = 0.42 + 0.33 \text{ Payout} + 0.73 \text{ Growth} - 0.43 \text{ Beta} + 7.91 \text{ Margin}$$

For instance, a firm with a 35% payout, a 15% growth rate, a beta of 1.25, and a profit margin of 10% would have had a price-sales ratio of:

$$PS = 0.42 + 0.33 \times 0.35 + 0.73 \times 0.15 - 0.43 \times 1.25 + 7.91 \times 0.10$$
$$= 0.8985$$

  a. What do the coefficients on this regression tell you about the independent variable's relationship with the dependent variable? What statistical concerns might you have with this regression?
  b. Estimate the price-sales ratios for all the retail chains described in question 2. Why might this answer be different from the one obtained from the regression of only the retail firms? Which one would you consider more reliable and why?
7. Ulysses Inc. is a retail firm that reported $1.5 billion in after-tax operating income on $15 billion in revenues in the just-ended financial year; the firm also had a capital turnover ratio of 1.5. The firm's cost of capital is 10%.
  a. If you expect operating income to grow 5% a year in perpetuity, estimate the value-to-sales ratio for the firm.
  b. How would your answer change if you were told that the operating income will grow 10% a year for the next five years, and then grow 5% in perpetuity?
8. You have run a regression of enterprise value/sales ratios against operating margins for cosmetics firms:

$$\text{Enterprise Value/Sales} = 0.45 + 8.5(\text{After-tax operating margin})$$

You are trying to estimate the brand name value of Estée Lauder. The firm earned $80 million after interest and after taxes on revenues of $500 million. In contrast, GenCosmetics, a manufacturer of generic cosmetics, had an after-tax operating margin of 5%. Estimate the brand name value for Estée Lauder.

9. You are trying to estimate the brand name value for Steinway, one of the world's best-known piano manufacturers. The firm reported operating income of $30 million on revenues of $100 million in the most recent year; the tax rate is 40%. The book value of capital at the firm is $90 million, and the cost of capital is 10%. The firm is in stable growth and expects to grow 5% a year in perpetuity.

   a. Estimate the value/sales ratio for this firm.

   b. Assume now that the operating profit margin (EBIT/sales) for generic piano manufacturers is half of the operating profit margin for Steinway. Assuming generic piano manufacturers have the same stable growth rate, capital turnover ratio, and cost of capital as Steinway, what is the value of the Steinway brand name?

CHAPTER 21

Valuing Financial Service Firms

Banks, insurance companies, and other financial service firms pose unique challenges for an analyst attempting to value them for two reasons. The first is that the nature of their businesses makes it difficult to define both debt and reinvestment, making the estimation of cash flows much messier. The other is that they tend to be heavily regulated, and the effects of regulatory requirements on value have to be considered.

This chapter begins by considering what makes financial service firms unique and ways of dealing with the differences. It then looks at how best we can adapt discounted cash flow models to value financial service firms and looks at three alternatives—a traditional dividend discount model, a cash flow to equity discount model, and an excess return model. With each, we look at a variety of examples from the financial services arena. We move on to look at how relative valuation works with financial service firms, and what multiples may work best with these firms.

The last part of the chapter examines a series of issues that, if not specific to financial service firms, are accentuated in those firms, ranging from the effect of changes in regulatory requirements on risk and value to how best to consider the quality of loan portfolios at banks.

CATEGORIES OF FINANCIAL SERVICE FIRMS

Any firm that provides financial products and services to individuals or other firms can be categorized as a financial service firm. We would break down financial service businesses into four groups from the perspective of how they make their money. A bank makes money on the spread between the interest it pays to those from whom it raises funds, and the interest it charges those who borrow from it, and from other services it offers its depositors and its lenders. Insurance companies make their income in two ways. One is through the premiums they receive from those who buy claims from them, and the other is income from the investment portfolios that they maintain to service these claims. An investment bank provides advice and supporting products for nonfinancial service firms who are desirous of raising capital or to consummate deals such as acquisitions or divestitures. Investment firms provide investment advice or manage portfolios for clients. Their income comes from advisory fees for the advice, and management and sales fees for investment portfolios.

With the consolidation in the financial services sector, an increasing number of firms operate in more than one of these businesses. For example, most large money-center banks in the United States operate in at least three of these businesses. At the same time, however, there remain a large number of small banks, boutique investment banks, and specialized insurance firms that still derive the bulk of their income from one source.

In emerging markets, financial service firms tend to have an even higher profile and account for a larger proportion of overall market value than they do in the United States. If we bring these firms into the mix, it is quite clear that no one template will value all financial service firms, and that we have to be able to be flexible in model design to allow for all types of financial service firms.

WHAT IS UNIQUE ABOUT FINANCIAL SERVICE FIRMS?

Financial service firms have much in common with nonfinancial service firms. They must negotiate the trade-off between profits and risk, to worry about competition, and want to grow rapidly over time. If they are publicly traded, they are judged by the total return they make for their stockholders, just as other firms are. This section, though, focuses on those aspects of financial service firms that make them different from other firms and considers the implications for valuation.

Debt: Raw Material or Source of Capital

When we talk about capital for nonfinancial service firms, we tend to talk about both debt and equity. A firm raises funds from both equity investors and bondholders (and banks) and uses these funds to make its investments. When we value the firm, we value the assets owned by the firm, rather than just the value of its equity.

With a financial service firm, debt takes on a different connotation. Rather than view debt as a source of capital, most financial service firms view it as a raw material. In other words, debt to a bank is akin to steel for an automobile company—something to be molded into other financial products that can then be sold at a higher price and yield a profit. Consequently, capital at financial service firms is more narrowly defined as including only equity capital. This definition of capital is reinforced by the regulatory authorities who count only equity or equity-like financing in regulatory capital.

The definition of what comprises debt also is murkier with a financial service firm than it is with a nonfinancial service firm. For instance, should deposits made by customers into their checking accounts at a bank be treated as debt by that bank? Especially on interest-bearing deposits, there is little distinction between a deposit and debt issued by the bank. If we do categorize this as debt, the operating income for a bank should be measured prior to interest paid to depositors, which would be problematic since interest expenses are usually the biggest single expense item for a bank.

The Regulatory Overlay

Financial service firms are heavily regulated all over the world, though the extent of the regulation varies from country to country. In general, these regulations take three forms. First, banks and insurance companies are required to maintain capital ratios to ensure that they do not expand beyond their means and put their claimholders or depositors at risk.

Second, financial service firms are often constrained in terms of where they can invest their funds. For instance, the Glass-Steagall Act in the United States restricted commercial banks from investment banking activities and from taking active equity positions in manufacturing firms for decades after the Great Depression. Third, the entry of new firms into the business is often restricted by the regulatory authorities, as are mergers between existing firms.

Why does this matter? From a valuation perspective, assumptions about growth are linked to assumptions about reinvestment. With financial service firms, these assumptions have to be scrutinized to ensure that they pass regulatory constraints. There might also be implications for how we measure risk at financial service firms. If regulatory restrictions are changing or are expected to change, it adds a layer of uncertainty to the future, which can influence value.

Reinvestment at Financial Service Firms

The preceding section noted that financial service firms are often constrained in both where they invest their funds and how much they invest. If we define reinvestment, as we have so far in this book, as necessary for future growth, there are other problems associated with measuring reinvestment with financial service firms. Note that Chapter 10 considers two items in reinvestment—net capital expenditures and working capital. Unfortunately, measuring either of these items at a financial service firm can be problematic.

Consider net capital expenditures first. Unlike manufacturing firms that invest in plant, equipment, and other fixed assets, financial service firms invest in intangible assets such as their brand name and human capital. Consequently, their investments for future growth often are categorized as operating expenses in accounting statements. Not surprisingly, the statement of cash flows to a bank shows little or no capital expenditures and correspondingly low depreciation. With working capital, we run into a different problem. If we define working capital as the different between current assets and current liabilities, a large proportion of a bank's balance sheet would fall into one or the other of these categories. Changes in this number can be both large and volatile, and may have no relationship to reinvestment for future growth.

As a result of this difficulty in measuring reinvestment, we run into two practical problems in valuing these firms. The first is that we cannot estimate cash flows without estimating reinvestment. In other words, if we cannot identify net capital expenditures and changes in working capital, we cannot estimate cash flows, either. The second is that estimating expected future growth becomes more difficult if the reinvestment rate cannot be measured.

GENERAL FRAMEWORK FOR VALUATION

Given the unique role of debt at financial service firms, the regulatory restrictions that they operate under, and the difficulty of identifying reinvestment at these firms, how can we value these firms? In this section, we suggest some broad rules that can enable us to deal with these issues. First, it makes far more sense to value equity directly at financial service firms, rather than the entire firm. Second, we either need a measure of cash flow that does not require us to estimate reinvestment needs, or need to redefine reinvestment to make it more meaningful for a financial service firm.

Equity versus Firm

Early in this book, we noted the distinction between valuing a firm and valuing the equity in the firm. We value firms by discounting expected cash flows prior to debt payments at the weighted average cost of capital. We value equity by discounting cash flows to equity investors at the cost of equity.

Estimating cash flows prior to debt payments or a weighted average cost of capital is problematic when debt and debt payments cannot be easily identified, which, as we argued earlier, is the case with financial service firms. Equity can be valued directly, however, by discounting cash flows to equity at the cost of equity. Consequently, we would argue for the latter approach for financial service firms. We would extend this argument to multiples as well. Equity multiples, such as price-to-earnings or price-to-book ratios, are a much better fit for financial service firms than value multiples such as EV to EBITDA.

Estimating Cash Flows

To value the equity in a firm, we normally estimate the free cash flow to equity. In Chapter 10, we defined the free cash flow to equity thus:

$$\text{Free cash flow to equity} = \text{Net income} - \text{Net capital expenditures}$$
$$- \text{Change in noncash working capital}$$
$$- (\text{Debt repaid} - \text{New debt issued})$$

If we cannot estimate the net capital expenditures or noncash working capital, we clearly cannot estimate the free cash flow to equity. Since this is the case with financial service firms, we have two choices. The first is to use dividends as cash flows to equity and assume that firms over time pay out their free cash flows to equity as dividends. Since dividends are observable, we do not have to confront the question of how much firms reinvest. The second is to adapt the free cash flow to equity measure to enable for the types of reinvestment that financial service firms. For instance, given that banks operate under a regulatory capital ratio constraint, it can be argued that these firms have to reinvest in regulatory capital to be able to grow in the future.

DISCOUNTED CASH FLOW VALUATION

In a discounted cash flow model, we consider the value of an asset to be the present value of the expected cash flows generated by that asset. In this section, we will first consider the use of dividend discount models to value banks and other financial service firms, then move on to analyze cash flow to equity models, and conclude with an examination of excess return models.

Dividend Discount Models

Chapter 13 considered how to value the equity in a firm based on dividend discount models. Using the argument that the only cash flows that a stockholder in a publicly traded firm receives are dividends, we valued equity as the present value of the expected dividends.

We looked at the range of dividend discount models, from stable to high growth, and considered how best to estimate the inputs. While much of what was said in that chapter applies here as well, we will consider some of the unique aspects of financial service firms in this section.

Basic Models   In the basic dividend discount model, the value of a stock is the present value of the expected dividends on that stock. Assuming that equity in a publicly traded firm has an infinite life, we arrive at:

$$\text{Value of equity} = \sum_{t=1}^{t=\infty} \frac{\text{Dividends}_t}{(1 + k_e)^t}$$

where DPS_t = Expected dividend per share in period t

   k_e = Cost of equity

As we saw in Chapter 14, in the special case where the expected growth rate in dividends can be sustained forever, this model collapses into the Gordon growth model:

$$\text{Value of equity} = \frac{\text{Expected dividends next period}}{(\text{Cost of equity} - \text{Stable growth rate})}$$

In the more general case, where dividends are growing at a rate that is not expected to be sustainable or constant forever for a period (called the extraordinary growth period), we can still assume that the growth rate will be constant forever at some point in time in the future. This enables us to then estimate the value of a stock, in the dividend discount model, as the sum of the present values of the dividends over the extraordinary growth period and the present value of the terminal price, which itself is estimated using the Gordon growth model.

$$\text{Value of equity} = \sum_{t=1}^{t=n} \frac{\text{Dividends}_t}{(1 + k_{e,hg})^t} + \frac{\text{Dividends}_{n+1}}{(k_{e,st} - g_n)(1 + k_{e,hg})^n}$$

The extraordinary growth is expected to last n years, g_n is the expected growth rate after n years, and k_e is the cost of equity (hg: high growth period and st: stable growth period).

Inputs to Model   This section will focus purely on the estimation issues relating to financial service firms, when it comes to the inputs to these models. In general, to value a stock using the dividend discount model, we need estimates of the cost of equity, the expected payout ratios, and the expected growth rate in earnings per share over time.

Cost of Equity   In keeping with how we have estimated the cost of equity for firms so far in this book, the cost of equity for a financial service firm has to reflect the portion of the risk in the equity that cannot be diversified away by the marginal investor in the stock. This risk is estimated using a beta (in the capital asset pricing model) or betas (in a multifactor or arbitrage pricing model).

In our earlier discussions of betas, we argued against the use of regression betas because of the noise in the estimates (standard errors) and the possibility that the firm has changed over the period of the regression. How relevant are these arguments with financial service firms? If regulatory restrictions have remained unchanged over the period and are not expected to change in the future, this may be one of the few sectors where regression betas can continue to be used with some confidence. In periods when the rules are changing and regulatory environments are shifting, the caveat about not using regression betas continues to hold.

There is a second area of difference. When estimating betas for nonfinancial service firms, we emphasized the importance of unlevering betas (whether they be historical or sector averages) and then relevering them, using a firm's current debt to equity ratio. With financial service firms, we would skip this step for two reasons. First, financial service firms tend to be much more homogeneous in terms of capital structure—they tend to all be highly levered. Second, and this is a point made earlier, debt is difficult to measure for financial service firms. In practical terms, this means that we will use the average-levered beta for comparable firms as the bottom-up beta for the firm being analyzed.

Payout Ratios   The expected dividend per share in a future period can be written as the product of the expected earnings per share in that period and the expected payout ratio. There are two advantages of deriving dividends from expected earnings. The first is that it enables us to focus on expected growth in earnings, which is tied to the fundamentals of the firm more closely than dividends. The second is that the payout ratio can be changed over time, to reflect changes in growth and investment opportunities.

The payout ratio for a bank, as it is for any other firm, is the dividend divided by the earnings. This said, financial service firms have conventionally paid out more in dividends than most other firms in the market. The dividend payout ratios and dividend yields for banks, insurance companies, investment banks, and investment firms are much higher than similar statistics for the rest of the market.

Why do financial service firms pay out more in dividends than other firms? An obvious response would be that they operate in much more mature businesses than firms in sectors such as technology, but this is only part of the story. Even if we control differences in expected growth rates, financial service firms pay out far more in dividends than other firms for two reasons. One is that banks and insurance companies have less in reinvestment needs than other firms. This, in turn, means that far more of the net income of these firms can be paid out as dividends than for a manufacturing firm. A second factor is history. Banks and insurance companies have developed a reputation as reliable payers of high dividends. Over time, they have attracted investors who like dividends, making it difficult for them to change dividend policy.

In recent years, in keeping with a trend that is visible in other sectors as well, financial service firms have increased stock buybacks as a way of returning cash to stockholders. In this context, focusing purely on dividends paid can provide a misleading picture of the cash returned to stockholders. An obvious solution is to add the stock buybacks each year to the dividends paid and to compute the composite payout ratio. If we do so, however, we should look at the number over several years, since stock buybacks vary widely across time—a buyback of billions in one year may be followed by three years of relatively meager or no buybacks, for instance.

Expected Growth   If dividends are based on earnings, the expected growth rate that will determine value is the expected growth rate in earnings. For financial service firms, as with other firms, earnings growth can be estimated in one of three ways:

1. *Historical growth in earnings.* Many banks and insurance companies have very long histories, and estimating historical growth is usually feasible. Furthermore, the correlation between past earnings growth and expected future growth used to be much higher for financial service firms than for other firms.

   This would suggest that historical growth in earnings is a much better predictor of future earnings at these firms. If the regulatory environment is changing, however, you have to be cautious about projecting past growth into the future.

2. *Analyst estimates in growth in earnings.* Analysts estimate expected growth rates in earnings for many publicly traded firms, though the extent of coverage varies widely. Many large banks and insurance companies are widely followed, enabling you to get these estimates of future growth. As noted in Chapter 11, it is an open question as to whether the long-term forecasts from analysts are any better than historical growth for estimating future growth.

3. *Fundamental growth.* In Chapter 11, we suggested that the expected growth in earnings per share be written as a function of the retention ratio and the return on equity (ROE):

$$\text{Expected growth}_{\text{EPS}} = (1 - \text{Payout ratio}) \times \text{ROE} = \text{Retention ratio} \times \text{ROE}$$

This equation enables you to estimate the expected growth rate for firms with stable returns on equity. If you consider stock buybacks in addition to dividends when looking at payout, the retention ratio should be defined consistently as well.

If the return on equity is expected to change over time, the expected growth rate in earnings per share can be written as:

$$\text{Expected growth}_{\text{EPS}} = \text{Retention ratio} \times \text{ROE}_{t+1} + (\text{ROE}_{t+1} - \text{ROE}_t)/\text{ROE}_t$$

In both formulations, the expected growth rate is a function of the retention ratio, which measures the quantity of reinvestment, and the return on equity, which measures their quality. How well do fundamental growth models work for financial service firms? Surprisingly well. The retention ratio in a bank measures the equity reinvested back into the firms, which in turn, given the regulatory focus on capital ratios, determines in large part how much these firms can expand in the future. The return on equity is also a more meaningful measure of investment quality because financial assets are more likely to be marked up to market.

Stable Growth   To get closure with dividend discount models, you have to assume that the financial service firms that you are valuing will be in stable growth at some point in time in the future, where stable growth is defined to be growth that is less than or equal to the growth rate of the economy (or the risk-free rate). In some cases, especially with larger firms in more mature businesses, the expected growth rate today may already be a stable growth rate.

In making the judgment of when a financial service firm will become a stable growth firm, you must consider three factors.

- *The first is the size of the firm, relative to the market that it serves.* Larger financial service firms will find it more difficult to sustain high growth for long periods, especially in mature markets.
- *The second is the nature of the competition.* If competition is intense, stable growth will arrive sooner rather than later. If competition is restricted, high growth and excess returns can last much longer.
- *Finally, the way in which financial service firms are regulated can affect the convergence to stable growth, since regulation can operate both as a help and as a hindrance.* By restricting new entrants, regulations may help financial service firms maintain high growth for long periods. At the same time, though, regulatory restrictions may prevent firms from entering new and potentially lucrative businesses, and thus reduce the length of the high growth period.

As noted in prior chapters, it is not only the growth rate that changes in stable growth. The payout ratio must adjust to reflect the stable growth rate (g), and can be estimated from the payout ratio:

$$\text{Payout ratio in stable growth} = 1 - \frac{\text{Stable growth rate}}{\text{Stable return on equity}}$$

The risk of the firm should also adjust to reflect the stable growth assumption. In particular, if betas are used to estimate the cost of equity, they should converge toward 1 in stable growth.

ILLUSTRATION 21.1:   Valuing HSBC Stable Growth Dividend Discount Model

Founded in Hong Kong and headquartered now in London, HSBC is one of the largest commercial banks in the world. In 2010, the company reported earnings per share of 74.8 pence/share and paid out dividends of 36 pence/share, resulting into a dividend payout ratio of 48.13%:

$$\text{Payout ratio} = \frac{\text{Dividends per share}}{\text{Earnings per share}} = \frac{36}{74.8} = 48.13\%$$

The firm is assumed to have a beta of 1.00, and the cost of equity is computed in British pounds, with a risk-free rate of 4% and an equity risk premium of 5.5% (composed of a mature market premium of 5% and an additional country risk premium of 0.5% to reflect HSBC's substantial exposure in Asia). The cost of equity is computed to be 9.5%:

$$\text{Cost of equity} = \text{Riskless rate} + \text{Beta(Equity risk premium)} = 4\% + 1(5.5\%) = 9.5\%$$

We will assume that the firm is in stable growth, with a growth rate of 3.5% in perpetuity, leading to a value per share of 621 pence/share:

$$\text{Value per share} = \frac{\text{Expected dividends next year}}{(\text{Cost of equity} - \text{Stable growth rate})} = \frac{36(1.035)}{(.095 - .035)}$$
$$= 621 \text{ pence per share}$$

The stock was trading at 635 pence/share, making it close to fairly valued. That said, this is a conservative estimate of value per share for HSBC, since we are assuming a growth rate of 3.5% and a payout ratio of 48.13%, implicitly leading to a return on equity of 6.75% (3.5%/(1-.4813)), lower than the cost of equity of 9.5%. If HSBC is able to maintain a ROE equal to its cost of equity of 9.5%, it should be able to pay out significantly more dividends and still deliver the same expected growth rate:

$$\text{Payout ratio assuming ROE is 9.5\%} = 1 - \frac{(.035)}{(.095)} = 63.16\%$$

Applying this payout ratio to earnings in 2010 would have resulted in higher dividends (47.24 pence instead of 36 pence) and a value per share of 815 pence/share:

$$\text{Value per share} = \frac{\text{Expected earnings next year} \times \text{Sustainable payout ratio}}{(\text{Cost of equity} - \text{Stable growth rate})}$$

$$= \frac{74.8 \times 1.035 \times .6316}{(.095 - .035)}$$

$$= 815 \text{ pence per share}$$

ILLUSTRATION 21.2:   A High-Growth Dividend Discount Model: State Bank of India in 2001

State Bank of India is one of India's largest banks, created in the aftermath of a nationalization of all banks in India in 1971. For the two decades that followed, it operated as a monopoly and was entirely government owned. In the 1990s, the Indian governments privatized portions of the bank while retaining control of its management and operations.

In 1999, State Bank of India earned 205 million Indian rupees on a book value of equity of 1,042 million rupees (at the beginning of 1999), resulting in a return on equity of 19.72%. The bank also paid out dividends of Rs 2.50 per share from earnings per share of Rs 38.98; this yielded a payout ratio of 6.41%. The high retention ratio suggests that the firm investing substantial amounts in the expectation of high growth in the future. We will analyze its value over three phases—an initial period of sustained high growth, a transition period in which growth drops toward stable growth, and a stable growth phase.

High Growth Phase

If State Bank of India can maintain the current return on equity of 19.72% and payout ratio of 6.41%, the expected growth rate in earnings per share will be 18.46%:

$$\text{Expected growth rate} = \text{ROE} \times \text{Retention ratio} = 19.72\% \times (1 - .0641) = 18.46\%$$

The key question is how long the bank can sustain this growth. Given the large potential size of the Indian market, we assume that this growth will continue for four years. During this period, we also allow for the fact that there will be substantial risk associated with the Indian economy by allowing for a country risk premium in estimating the cost of equity. Using the approach developed earlier in the book, we estimate a risk premium for India based on its rating of BB+ in 2001 and the relative equity market volatility of the Indian market.

$$\text{Country risk premium for India} = \text{Country default spread} \times \text{Relative equity market volatility}$$
$$= 3.00\% \times 2.1433 = 6.43\%$$

To estimate the cost of equity during the high-growth period—the next four years—we estimate the average beta for Asian commercial banks as 0.80, and assume that State Bank of India will have a similar beta. In conjunction with the risk-free rate in Indian rupees of 12.00%, we estimate a cost of equity as 20.34%.

Cost of equity = Risk-free rate + Beta × (Mature market premium + Country risk premium)

= 12.00% + 0.80 × (4.00% + 6.43%) = 20.34%

With these estimates of expected growth, payout ratio, and the cost of equity, we can estimate the present value of expected dividends per share over the next four years in Table 21.1:

TABLE 21.1   Expected Dividends in Years 1 Through 4

	1	2	3	4
Expected growth rate	18.46%	18.46%	18.46%	18.46%
Earnings per share	₹46.17	₹54.70	₹64.79	₹76.75
Payout ratio	6.41%	6.41%	6.41%	6.41%
Dividends per share	₹2.96	₹3.51	₹4.16	₹4.92
Cost of equity	20.34%	20.34%	20.34%	20.34%
Present value	₹2.46	₹2.42	₹2.38	₹2.35

TRANSITION PHASE

We expect State Bank to continue growing beyond year 4 but at a declining rate. Each year, we reduce the expected growth rate linearly from 18.46% to a stable growth rate of 10.00%—these growth rates are all in nominal rupees. As the growth rate declines, we allow the return on equity to decline (as competition increases) to 18% and the payout ratio to rise to reflect the lesser need for reinvestment.[1] To illustrate, the payout ratio in year 8, when the expected growth rate is 10%, can be computed to be:

$$\text{Payout ratio in year 8} = 1 - \frac{\text{Expected growth}}{\text{Return on equity}} = 1 - \frac{.10}{.18} = 0.4444 \text{ or } 44.44\%$$

We also adjust the country risk premium down from 6.43% to 3.00% to reflect our expectation that there will be less risk in investing in India as the country's economy matures. Table 21.2 summarizes expected dividends during the transition phase:

TABLE 21.2   Expected Dividends in Years 1 Through 4

	5	6	7	8
Expected growth rate	16.34%	14.23%	12.11%	10.00%
Earnings per share	₹89.29	₹102.00	₹114.35	₹125.79
Payout ratio	15.92%	25.43%	34.94%	44.44%
Dividends per share	₹14.22	₹25.94	₹39.95	₹55.91
Cost of equity	19.66%	18.97%	18.29%	17.60%
Cumulative cost of equity	2.5098	2.9860	3.5320	4.1536
Present value	₹5.66	₹8.69	₹11.31	Rs13.46

[1] The adjustment in the payout ratio is linear. The current payout ratio is 6.41% and the stable period payout ratio is 44.44%. Dividing the difference of 38.03% over four years yields an increase in the payout ratio of 9.51% each year.

Note that the cost of equity in year 8 reflects the lower country risk premium:

$$\text{Cost of equity in year 8} = 12.00\% + 0.80 \times (4.00\% + 3.00\%) = 17.60\%$$

The beta and the mature market risk premium of 4% have been left unchanged. To compute the present values of the expected dividends over the transition period, we compound the cost of equity and discount the cash flows.[2]

STABLE GROWTH

In stable growth, we assume that State Bank's earnings and dividends will grow in perpetuity at 10% a year, and discount them at the stable period cost of equity of 17.60%. The present value of these dividends in perpetuity, which yield the terminal price per share, can be computed to be:

$$
\begin{aligned}
\text{Terminal price per share} &= \frac{\text{Expected EPS}_9 \times \text{Payout ratio}_9}{(\text{Cost of equity} - \text{Stable growth rate})} \\
&= \frac{125.79\,(1.10)(.4444)}{(.176 - .10)} \\
&= ₹809.18
\end{aligned}
$$

FINAL VALUATION

The final value per share for State Bank can be computed by adding the present values of the dividends during the high-growth phase, the dividends during the transition period, and the terminal price at the end of the transition period, discounted back eight years using the compounded cost of equity.

$$
\begin{aligned}
\text{Value per share} &= \text{PV of dividends: high growth} + \text{PV of dividends: transition phase} + \text{PV of terminal price} \\
&= 2.46 + 2.42 + 2.38 + 2.35 + 5.66 + 8.69 + 11.31 + 13.46 + \frac{809.18}{4.1536} \\
&= ₹243.55
\end{aligned}
$$

Note that the terminal price is discounted back at the compounded cost of equity for the eighth year. In January 2001, at the time of this valuation, State Bank was trading at ₹235 per share.

Valuing a Non-dividend-Paying Financial Service Firm While many financial service firms do pay dividends, a large number of young high-growth financial service firms, in recent years, have chosen not to pay dividends and to reinvest all of their earnings back into their operations. In fact, some of these firms lose money. While it may seem inappropriate to use the dividend discount model to value such firms, we will argue that the model is flexible enough to deal with them. How, if dividends are zero, will we ever be able to get a positive value for a share? The answer is simple, at least for firms that have positive earnings currently. While dividends are zero currently and are expected to be zero for the foreseeable future when the firm is growing, the growth will ultimately subside. As the growth drops, the firm's capacity to pay

---

[2] As in earlier chapters, when the cost of equity or capital changes, you must compute a cumulated cost of equity. The cumulated cost of equity calculation for year 7 is shown here:

$$\text{Cumulated cost of equity discount factor} = (1.2034)^4(1.1966)(1.1897)(1.1829) = 3.5320$$

out dividends will increase. In fact, using the fundamental equation for growth from the preceding section, we can estimate the expected payout ratio in future periods to be:

$$\text{Expected payout ratio} = 1 - g/ROE$$

The equity will derive its value from expected future dividends.

If earnings are negative currently, the mechanics become a little more involved. We first have to estimate earnings in future periods. Presumably, we would expect earnings to become positive during some period in the future. (If we did not, the value of equity would be zero, and the valuation exercise would be unnecessary.) Once earnings become positive, the rest of the analysis resembles what we did before.

Cash Flow to Equity Models

At the beginning of this discussion, we noted the difficulty in estimating cash flows when net capital expenditures and noncash working capital cannot be easily identified. It is possible, however, to estimate cash flows to equity even for financial service firms if we define reinvestment differently.

Defining Cash Flow to Equity   The cash flow to equity is the cash flow left over for equity investors after debt payments have been made and reinvestment needs met. With financial service firms, the reinvestment generally does not take the form of plant, equipment, or other fixed assets. Instead, the investment is in human capital and regulatory capital; the latter is the capital as defined by the regulatory authorities, which, in turn, determines the limits on future growth. There are ways in which we could incorporate both of these items into the reinvestment.

Capitalize Training and Employee Development Expenses   If human capital is a large factor in determining the success or failure of a financial service firm, we could capitalize the expenses associated with developing this capital. The process for doing so closely mirrors the process for capitalizing research and development expenses for technology firms and involves the following five steps:

1. *Identify the amortizable life for the asset.* To determine the period over which these expenses will be written off, we have to begin with how long a typical employee that the firm has invested its resources in stays with the firm.
2. *Collect information on employee expenses in prior years.* The amount spent by the firm on employee training and development in prior years is collected, with the number of years matching the amortizable life specified in the first step.
3. *Compute the current year's amortization expense.* The expenses in each of the prior years is amortized. With a linear amortization schedule, the expense will be spread equally over the amortizable life. The sum total of the amortization of all of the expenses in previous years will become the current year's amortization expense.
4. *Adjust the net income for the firm.* The net income for the firm is adjusted for the capitalization of employee expenses:

   Adjusted net income = Reported net income

   + Employee development expense in the current year

   − Amortization of the employee expenses (from step 3)

5. *Compute the value of the human capital.* The value of human capital in the firm can be computed by adding up the unamortized portion of the employee development expenses in each of the prior years.

Employee development expenses are more difficult to capitalize than research and development expenses for two reasons. The first is that, while research expenses are usually consolidated and reported as one item on a financial statement, employee development expenses tend to be widely spread across the firm and may be included in several different items in an income statement. Disentangling these expenses from employee salary and benefits may be difficult to do. The second is that the patents and licenses that emerge from R&D belong to the firm, and often give it exclusive rights in commercial use. A firm's employees, on the other hand, are mobile and may, and often do, move to competitors who offer them better terms.

Assuming that we can get over these practical difficulties in valuing human capital, let us consider the factors that determine the value that human capital adds to a firm. The first is the employee turnover ratio; as this ratio rises, the amortizable life for employee expenses will fall, and with it, the value of human capital. The second relates to the resources spent by the firm in employee development and training; the greater the resources, the greater the value assigned to human capital.

There is a third, and often ignored, factor. If we consider human capital as an asset, it is the excess returns that we make on the asset that create value. To create excess returns, a firm will have to pay an employee less than what he or she generates in value to the firm. To illustrate, an investment bank will generate value from a bond trader that works for it only if it pays that trader less than what he or she generates in profits for the firm. Why might the trader settle for less? One reason might be that the investment bank has some unique capability that enables the trader to earn these profits; this unique capability might come from proprietary information, client lists, or market position. Another reason might be noneconomic; the trader may have enough goodwill toward the investment bank that he or she might be willing to give up higher compensation elsewhere. Firms that treat their employees well and are loyal to them in bad times are more likely to earn this goodwill and have higher value as a consequence.

Investments in Regulatory Capital For a financial service firm that is regulated based on capital ratios, equity earnings that are not paid out increase the equity capital of the firm and enable it to expand its activities. For instance, a bank that has a 5-percent equity capital ratio can make $100 in loans for every $5 in equity capital. When this bank reports net income of $15 million and pays out only $5 million, it increases its equity capital by $10 million. This, in turn, will enable it to make $200 million in additional loans and presumably increase its growth rate in future periods.

Using this argument, the portion of net income that does not get paid out, either in dividends or buybacks, can be viewed as reinvestment. It works, however, only if the firm takes advantage of its larger capital base and grows. If it does not, the equity retained is more akin to cash accumulating in the firm rather than reinvestment. A firm that reports an equity capital ratio that rises over time, well above the regulatory constraint, is not using its equity capital to grow.

The portion of net income that does not get paid out to shareholders is also retained earnings, and it accumulates in the book value of equity of the firm as well. Thus, the regulatory capital, at least as defined in this model, and the book value of equity will move in sync, in this model. It is for this reason that we would recommend using the narrowest measures of regulatory capital; tier 1 capital, which is mostly composed of equity, is better suited for this reason than tier 2 or tier 3 capital.[3]

ILLUSTRATION 21.3: Valuing Deutsche Bank in Early 2009 with an FCFE Model

For much of the last century, Deutsche Bank has been a profitable commercial bank. During 2008, the landscape for financial service firms changed as banks entered crisis mode and financial markets collapsed. After taking billions of dollars of write-offs, Deutsche Bank reported a loss of 3,835 million euros for 2008 and cut dividends to 285 million euros. While neither of these numbers represents a stable starting point, we made the following four assumptions to value Deutsche Bank:

1. *Net income bounce-back.* We will assume that net income will bounce back to 3.147 billion euros in 2009, and base this assumption on the improved earnings for the first quarter of 2009 reported by Deutsche Bank (1.12 billion euros in quarterly profits) and the average net income between 2003 and 2007 (approximately 3.95 billion euros).
2. *Asset base and target ROE.* We will assume that the current asset base for the firm (312,882 million euros) will grow 4% a year for the next five years, and that the return on equity will improve to 10% over this period.
3. *Potential dividends.* Rather than focus on current dividends, which have been cut drastically, we estimate the potential dividends, based upon the assumption that the firm will move towards a target regulatory capital ratio of 10%, a small decline from its current regulatory capital ratio of 10.20%.
4. *Cost of equity.* To arrive at the cost of equity, we use a bottom-up beta of 1.162 that reflects Deutsche Bank's exposure in the investment banking and commercial banking businesses, in conjunction with the euro risk-free rate of 3.6% at the start of 2009, and an equity risk premium of 6% for mature markets.

$$\text{Cost of equity} = \text{Risk-free rate} + \text{Beta} \times (\text{Equity risk premium})$$
$$= 3.6\% + 1.162 \times (6\%) = 10.572\%$$

Table 21.3 summarizes the estimates of net income, potential dividends, and the present value of these dividends over the next five years:

TABLE 21.3 Expected Potential Dividends (in millions of euros) over Next Five Years—Deutsche Bank in 2009

	Current	1	2	3	4	5
Asset base	312,882	325,398	338,414	351,950	366,028	380,669
Capital ratio	10.20%	10.16%	10.12%	10.08%	10.04%	10.00%
Regulatory capital	31,914	33,060	34,247	35,477	36,749	38,067
Change in reg capital		1,146	1,187	1,229	1,273	1,318
ROE	9.40%	9.52%	9.64%	9.76%	9.88%	10.00%
Net Income	3,000	3,147	3,302	3,463	3,631	3,807
−Investment in reg capital		1,146	1,187	1,229	1,273	1,318
FCFE (potential dividend)		2,001	2,114	2,233	2,358	2,489
Present value@ 10.572%		1,810	1,729	1,652	1,578	1,506

[3]Tier 1 capital, at least as defined by the Basel accords, is built around equity capital. That said, the banking definition of equity does not always correspond to common equity as defined by accountants.

The sum of the present value of potential dividends over the five-year period is 8,275 million euros. At the end of year 5, we assume that the firm will be in stable growth, growing 3% a year in perpetuity. In addition, we will also assume that the beta will decrease to 1, resulting in a drop in cost of equity to 9.60%.

$$\text{Cost of equity} = \text{Risk-free rate} + \text{Beta} \times \text{Equity risk premium}$$
$$= 3.6\% + 1 \times (6\%) = 9.60\%$$

The return on equity after year 5 will be equal to the stable period cost of equity of 9.60%.

Given the expected growth rate of 3% after year five and the stable ROE of 9.60%, the potential cash payout ratio in stable growth is 68.75%.

$$\text{Stable payout ratio} = 1 - \frac{\text{Stable growth rate}}{\text{Stable ROE}} = 1 - \frac{.03}{.096} = 68.75\%$$

The value of equity at the end of year 5 can be estimated as follows:

$$\text{Terminal value of equity} = \frac{\text{Expected earnings}_6 \times \text{Stable payout ratio}}{(\text{Cost of equity} - \text{Stable growth rate})}$$
$$= \frac{3,807 \times 1.03 \times .6875}{(.096 - .03)} = 39,728 \text{ million euros}$$

Discounting the terminal value back at the cost of equity for the high-growth period:

$$\text{PV of terminal value} = \frac{\text{Terminal value in year n}}{(1 + \text{Cost of equity}_{\text{high growth}})^n} = \frac{39,728}{(1.10572)^5} = 24,036 \text{ million euros}$$

Adding the present value of dividends to this number yields the value of equity for Deutsche Bank in early 2009:

$$\text{Value of equity} = €8,275 \text{ million} + €24,036 \text{ million} = €32,311 \text{ million}$$

Dividing by the number of shares outstanding at the start of 2009 (581.85 million), we can obtain the value of equity per share:

$$\text{Value of equity per share} = \frac{\text{Value of equity}}{\text{Number of shares}} = \frac{32,311}{581.85} = 55.53 \text{ euros/share}$$

In June 2009, Deutsche Bank was trading at 48.06 euros per share and looked slightly undervalued.

WHY EARNINGS ARE NOT CASH FLOWS

There are some analysts who value banks by discounting their earnings back to the present. They make the argument that banks have little or no net capital expenditure needs, and that working capital needs (e.g., inventory, accounts receivable, etc.) are nonexistent. The problem, though, is that they couple the discounting of earnings with an expected growth rate in these earnings. This is clearly not consistent.

(continued)

(continued)

To see why, consider a bank that does pay out 100 percent of its earnings as dividends. If this firm issues no new equity, its book equity will stay frozen at current levels forever. If this bank continues to grow its loan portfolio, it will end up with capital ratios that are lower than the regulatory minimum sooner rather than later.

That is why reinvestment has to include investments in regulatory capital, acquisitions, and other such investments that banks need to make to continue to grow. That is also why even mature banks with low growth rates cannot afford to pay out 100 percent of their earnings as dividends.

Excess Return Models

The third approach to valuing financial service firms is to use an excess return model. In such a model, the value of a firm can be written as the sum of capital invested currently in the firm and the present value of dollar excess returns that the firm expects to make in the future. This section considers how this model can be applied to valuing equity in a bank.

Basic Model   Given the difficulty associated with defining total capital in a financial service firm, it makes far more sense to focus on just equity when using an excess return model to value a financial service firm. The value of equity in a firm can be written as the sum of the equity invested in a firm's current investments and the expected excess returns to equity investors from these and future investments.

Value of equity = Current equity capital
+ Present value of expected excess returns to equity investors

The most interesting aspect of this model is its focus on excess returns. A firm that invests its equity and earns just the fair-market rate of return on these investments should see the market value of its equity converge on the equity capital currently invested in it. A firm that earns a below-market return on its equity investments will see its equity market value dip below the equity capital currently invested.

The other point that must be emphasized is that this model considers expected future investments as well. Thus, it is up to the analyst using the model to forecast not only where the financial service firm will direct its future investments, but also the returns it will make on those investments.

Inputs to Model   There are two inputs needed to value equity in the excess return model. The first is a measure of equity capital currently invested in the firm. The second and more difficult input is the expected excess returns to equity investors in future periods.

The equity capital invested currently in a firm is usually measured as the book value of equity in the firm. While the book value of equity is an accounting measure and is affected by accounting decisions, it should be a much more reliable measure of equity invested in a financial service firm than in a manufacturing firm for two reasons. The first is that the assets of a financial service firm are often financial assets that are marked up to market; the assets of manufacturing firms are real assets, and deviations between book and market value are usually much larger. The second is that depreciation, which can be a big factor in determining book value for manufacturing firms, is often negligible at financial service firms. Notwithstanding this, the book value of equity can be affected by stock buybacks and extraordinary or one-time charges. The book value of equity for financial service firms that buy back stock or take extraordinary charges may understate the equity capital invested in the firm.

The excess returns, defined in equity terms, can be stated in terms of the return on equity and the cost of equity:

Excess equity return = (Return on equity − Cost of equity) × (Equity capital invested)

Here again, we are assuming that the return on equity is a good measure of the economic return earned on equity investments. When analyzing a financial service firm, we can obtain the return on equity from the current period and past periods, but the return on equity that is required is the expected future return. This requires an analysis of the firm's strengths and weaknesses, as well as the competition faced by the firm and changes in regulatory capital requirements.

In making estimates of expected equity return spreads, we have to allow for the fact that the presence of large excess returns is likely to attract competition. These excess returns will fade over time, and this should be reflected in the forecasts.

ILLUSTRATION 21.4: Valuing Goldman Sachs with an Excess Return Model—May 2011

In May 2011, Goldman Sachs, regarded at the time as perhaps the best investment bank in the world, was trading at a market capitalization for equity of $75.4 billion, just a tad below its book value of equity of $78.228 billion (from the end of 2010).

To value Goldman Sachs, we begin with the current cost of equity. Using the average beta of 1.20, reported by investment banks in 2010, in conjunction with a Treasury bond rate of 3.5% and an equity risk premium of 5%, yields a cost of equity of 9.5% for the firm:

$$\text{Cost of equity} = 3.5\% + 1.2 \times 5\% = 9.5\%$$

In 2010, Goldman earned net income of $8,354 million, which in conjunction with the book value of equity of $71,674 million at the end of 2009 resulted in a return on equity of 11.66%:

$$\text{Return on equity} = \frac{\text{Net income}_{2010}}{\text{Book value of equity}_{2009}} = \frac{\$8,354}{\$71,674} = 11.66\%$$

Note that this is a steep drop-off from the returns on equity that Goldman posted in the years prior to the banking crisis of 2008. During 2010, Goldman Sachs also paid out dividends per share of $1.40 on earnings per share of $13.99, resulting in a payout ratio of 10%. Assuming that Goldman can maintain its return on equity, payout ratio, and cost of equity at current levels for the next five years, the excess returns and the present value are summarized in Table 21.4:

TABLE 21.4 Expected Excess Returns—Goldman Sachs

	1	2	3	4	5
Net Income	$ 9,118	$10,074	$11,131	$ 12,299	$ 13,589
− Equity cost (see below)	$ 7,432	$ 8,211	$ 9,073	$ 10,024	$ 11,076
Excess equity return	**$ 1,686**	**$ 1,863**	**$ 2,059**	**$ 2,275**	**$ 2,513**
Present value	**$ 1,540**	**$ 1,554**	**$ 1,568**	**$ 1,582**	**$ 1,596**

(continued)

(*continued*)

	1	2	3	4	5
Beginning BV of equity	$78,228	$86,434	$95,501	$105,519	$116,588
Cost of equity	9.50%	9.50%	9.50%	9.50%	9.50%
Equity cost	$7,432	$8,211	$9,073	$10,024	$11,076
Return on equity	11.66%	11.66%	11.66%	11.66%	11.66%
Net income	$9,118	$10,074	$11,131	$12,299	$13,589
Dividend payout ratio	10.00%	10.00%	10.00%	10.00%	10.00%
Dividends paid	$912	$1,007	$1,113	$1,230	$1,359
Retained earnings	$8,206	$9,067	$10,018	$11,069	$12,230

The net income each year is computed by multiplying the return on equity in that year by the beginning book value of equity. The book value of equity each year is augmented by the portion of earnings that is not paid out as dividends.

To put closure to this valuation, we must make assumptions about excess returns after year 5. We assume that the net income would grow 3% a year beyond year 5, and that the beta for the stock would remain unchanged at 1.20. For Goldman Sachs, we will assume that the return on equity after year 5 will be 9.50%, set equal to the cost of equity. Since the firm earns its cost of equity after year 5, there is no value gained or lost after that year. The value of equity can then be computed as the sum of the three components—the book value of equity invested today, the present value of excess equity returns over the next five years, and the present value of the terminal value of equity.

Book value of equity invested currently	$78,228
PV of equity excess return—next five years	$ 7,880
PV of terminal value of excess returns	$ 0
Value of equity	$86,068
Number of shares	517.735
Value per share	$166.24

At the time of this valuation in May 2011, Goldman Sachs was trading at $140.63 a share, making it undervalued by about 18%.

Asset-Based Valuation

In asset-based valuation, we value the existing assets of a financial service firm, net out debt and other outstanding claims, and report the difference as the value of equity. For example, with a bank, this would require valuing the loan portfolio of the bank (which would comprise its assets) and subtracting outstanding debt to estimate the value of equity. For an insurance company, you would value the policies that the company has in force and subtract out the expected claims resulting from these policies and other debt outstanding to estimate the value of the equity in the firm.

How would you value the loan portfolio of a bank or the policies of an insurance company? One approach would be to estimate the price at which the loan portfolio can be sold to another financial service firm, but the better approach is to value it based on the expected cash flow. Consider, for instance, a bank with a $1 billion loan portfolio with a weighted average maturity of eight years, on which it earns interest income of $70 million. Furthermore, assume that the default risk on the loans is such that the fair market interest rate on the loans would be 6.50 percent; this fair market rate can be estimated by either getting the loan portfolio rated by a ratings agency, or by measuring the potential for default risk in the portfolio. The value of the loans can be estimated as follows:

$$\text{Value of loans} = \$70 \text{ million(PV of annuity, 8 years, 6.5\%)} + \$1,000 \text{ million}/1.065^8$$
$$= \$1,030 \text{ million}$$

This loan portfolio has a fair market value that exceeds its book value because the bank is charging an interest rate that exceeds the market rate. The reverse would be true if the bank charged an interest rate that is lower than the market rate. To value the equity in this book, you would subtract out the deposits, debt, and other claims on the bank.

This approach has merit if you are valuing a mature bank or insurance company with little or no growth potential, but it has two significant limitations. First, it does not assign any value to expected future growth and the excess returns that flow from that growth. A bank, for instance, that consistently is able to lend at rates higher than justified by default risk should be able to harvest value from future loans as well. Second, it is difficult to apply when a financial service firm enters multiple businesses. A firm like Citigroup that operates in multiple businesses would prove to be difficult to value because the assets in each business— insurance, commercial banking, investment banking, portfolio management—would need to be valued separately, with different income streams and different discount rates.

RELATIVE VALUATION

The chapters on relative valuation examined a series of multiples that are used to value firms, ranging from earnings multiples to book value multiples to revenue multiples. This section considers how relative valuation can be used for financial service firms.

Choices in Multiples

Firm value multiples, such as EV-to-EBITDA or EV-to-EBIT, cannot be easily adapted to value financial service firms, because neither enterprise value nor operating income can be easily estimated for banks or insurance companies. In keeping with our emphasis on equity valuation for financial service firms, the multiples that we will work with to analyze financial service firms are equity multiples. The three most widely used equity multiples are price-earnings ratios, price-to-book value ratios, and price-to-sales ratios. Since sales or revenues are not really measurable for financial service firms, price-to-sales ratios cannot be estimated or used for these firms. This section looks at the use of price-earnings and price-to-book value ratios for valuing financial service firms.

Price-Earnings Ratios The price-earnings ratio for a bank or an insurance company is measured in much the same way as it is for any other firm.

$$\text{PE ratio} = \frac{\text{Market capitalization}}{\text{Net income}}$$

Chapter 18 noted that the price-earnings ratio is a function of three variables—the expected growth rate in earnings, the payout ratio, and the cost of equity. As with other firms, the price-earnings ratio should be higher for financial service firms with higher expected growth rates in earnings, higher payout ratios, and lower costs of equity.

An issue that is specific to financial service firms is the use of provisions for expected expenses. For instance, banks routinely set aside provisions for bad loans. These provisions reduce the reported income and affect the reported price-earnings ratio. Consequently, banks that are more conservative about categorizing bad loans will report lower earnings and have higher price-earnings ratios, whereas banks that are less conservative will report higher earnings and lower price-earnings ratios.

Another consideration in the use of earnings multiples is the diversification of financial service firms into multiple businesses. The multiple that an investor is willing to pay for a dollar in earnings from commercial lending should be very different from the multiple that the same investor is willing to pay for a dollar in earnings from proprietary trading. When a firm is in multiple businesses with different risk, growth, and return characteristics, it is very difficult to find truly comparable firms and to compare the multiples of earnings paid across firms. In such a case, it makes far more sense to break the firm's earnings down by business and assess the value of each business separately.

ILLUSTRATION 21.5:   Comparing PE Ratios—U.S. Insurance Companies in May 2011

Table 21.5 summarizes the price-earnings ratios and relevant fundamentals (analysts' estimates of expected growth in EPS over the next five years, payout, return on equity, and beta) for U.S. insurance companies with a market capitalization exceeding $1 billion.

TABLE 21.5   PE Ratios and Fundamentals—U.S. Insurance Companies

Company	PE	Payout	ROE	Growth	Beta
CNO Financial Group, Inc. (NYSE:CNO)	6.31	0.00%	7.04%	13.00%	2.91
Hartford Financial Services Group Inc. (NYSE:HIG)	6.31	4.49%	9.48%	7.95%	2.78
Reinsurance Group of America Inc. (NYSE:RGA)	7.53	5.74%	12.16%	12.20%	1.33
Travelers Companies, Inc. (NYSE:TRV)	7.56	0.00%	13.41%	8.60%	0.65
Protective Life Corp. (NYSE:PL)	8.01	18.60%	7.75%	10.30%	2.28
American Financial Group Inc. (NYSE:AFG)	8.03	14.04%	10.20%	9.00%	1.00
Delphi Financial Group, Inc. (NYSE:DFG)	8.44	12.79%	11.72%	10.30%	1.68
Chubb Corporation (NYSE:CB)	8.56	21.00%	14.29%	9.33%	0.80
American International Group, Inc. (NYSE:AIG)	8.73	0.00%	17.26%	12.00%	2.48
Lincoln National Corp. (NYSE:LNC)	8.74	0.00%	8.09%	12.00%	2.48
ProAssurance Corporation (NYSE:PRA)	8.82	0.00%	13.00%	10.30%	0.83
AmTrust Financial Services, Inc. (NasdaqGS:AFSI)	8.90	11.95%	20.78%	13.00%	0.98
Fidelity National Financial, Inc. (NYSE:FNF)	8.91	37.57%	11.56%	11.50%	0.81
Unum Group (NYSE:UNM)	9.11	13.27%	9.86%	12.30%	1.50
Unitrin Inc. (NYSE:UTR)	9.48	29.19%	9.01%	7.00%	1.72

Company	PE	Payout	ROE	Growth	Beta
RLI Corp. (NYSE:RLI)	9.71	23.36%	16.39%	11.00%	0.76
Prudential Financial, Inc. (NYSE:PRU)	9.92	18.74%	9.58%	12.90%	2.22
Torchmark Corp. (NYSE:TMK)	10.01	10.00%	12.47%	10.10%	1.62
W.R. Berkley Corporation (NYSE:WRB)	10.39	9.06%	12.08%	11.00%	0.58
AFLAC Inc. (NYSE:AFL)	10.68	25.63%	19.02%	11.90%	1.87
StanCorp Financial Group Inc. (NYSE:SFG)	11.19	22.89%	9.05%	11.00%	1.42
HCC Insurance Holdings Inc. (NYSE:HCC)	11.62	20.11%	9.73%	10.00%	0.76
CNA Financial Corporation (NYSE:CNA)	12.10	4.04%	6.10%	7.50%	1.69
Allstate Corporation (NYSE:ALL)	12.29	32.40%	6.98%	9.00%	0.98
Progressive Corp. (NYSE:PGR)	12.42	22.53%	18.77%	8.20%	0.79
Hanover Insurance Group Inc. (NYSE:THG)	13.15	33.31%	5.78%	9.00%	0.76
Cincinnati Financial Corp. (NasdaqGS:CINF)	13.22	68.19%	7.37%	7.50%	0.97
Assurant Inc. (NYSE:AIZ)	13.57	25.86%	5.52%	9.00%	1.07
Principal Financial Group Inc. (NYSE:PFG)	14.12	25.00%	7.25%	11.40%	2.44
Transatlantic Holdings Inc. (NYSE:TRH)	14.76	26.71%	4.58%	8.00%	0.78
Mercury General Corporation (NYSE:MCY)	15.17	87.40%	8.31%	7.30%	0.67
MetLife, Inc. (NYSE:MET)	15.62	26.48%	6.09%	12.70%	1.80
Markel Corp. (NYSE:MKL)	17.26	0.00%	7.33%	10.50%	0.74
Marsh & McLennan Companies, Inc. (NYSE:MMC)	18.08	49.36%	14.64%	9.25%	0.85
Arthur J. Gallagher & Co. (NYSE:AJG)	19.75	84.57%	14.47%	9.00%	0.70
Aon Corporation (NYSE:AON)	21.94	23.90%	9.38%	7.50%	0.61
Brown & Brown Inc. (NYSE:BRO)	22.74	27.39%	10.88%	11.60%	0.60
Erie Indemnity Co. (NasdaqGS:ERIE)	24.74	62.26%	17.43%	7.00%	0.58
Genworth Financial Inc. (NYSE:GNW)	118.27	0.00%	0.33%	17.00%	3.31

Looking at the PE ratio, CNO Financial and Hartford look cheap, but they are also extremely risky and have very low payout ratios. We regressed PE ratios against expected growth, payout ratios and betas but removed expected growth from the list, since it was not statistically significant. The regression of PE ratios against expected growth and payout ratios yielded the following:

$$PE = 12.311 - 1.953 \text{ Beta} + 9.70 \text{ Payout ratio} \qquad R^2 = 37.6\%$$
$$[7.04] \qquad [2.08] \qquad [3.21]$$

Plugging the values for CNO Financial into this regression, we get a predicted PE ratio of 6.63:

$$PE = 12.311 - 1.953(2.91) + 9.70(0) = 6.63$$

At 6.31 times earnings, CNO Financial looks close to fairly valued. In contrast, the predicted PE ratio for Aon Corporation is:

$$PE = 12.311 - 1.953(0.61) + 9.70(.239) = 13.44$$

At 21.94 times earnings, Aon looks overvalued.

ILLUSTRATION 21.6:   Pricing a Company Based on Business Units: JP Morgan Chase in May 2011

JP Morgan Chase is in multiple businesses and breaks down its net profit by business. Table 21.6 lists the net profit reported in 2010 by business, and applies a PE ratio based on other firms that operate primarily or only in that segment:

TABLE 21.6   Pricing JP Morgan Chase, by Segment

Business	Net Income	PE for sector	Estimated Equity Value
Investment Banking	$ 6,639	12.15	$ 80,664
Retail Financial Services	$ 2,526	14.8	$ 37,385
Credit Card Services	$ 2,074	14.8	$ 30,695
Commercial Bank	$ 2,084	10.8	$ 22,507
Treasury & Security Services	$ 1,079	10.8	$ 11,653
Asset Management	$ 1,710	15.67	$ 26,796
Private equity	$ 1,258	8.08	$ 10,165
J.P. Morgan	$17,370		$219,864.59

Note that for some segments, such as Treasury and security services, where there are no stand-alone competitors, we have used the average PE of firms that offer that product or service. Cumulating the equity values across the businesses, we obtain a value of $219.865 billion for the equity in JP Morgan Chase. In May 2011, the company had a market capitalization of $168.29 billion, making it undervalued by about 30%.

Price-to-Book Value Ratios   The price-to-book value ratio for a financial service firm is the ratio of the market capitalization (or price per share) to the book value of equity (or book value of equity per share).

$$\text{Price to book} = \frac{\text{Market capitalization}}{\text{Book value of equity}}$$

This definition is identical to the one presented in Chapter 19, and it is determined by the variables specified in that chapter—the expected growth rate in earnings per share, the dividend payout ratio, the cost of equity, and the return on equity. Other things remaining equal, higher growth rates in earnings, higher payout ratios, lower costs of equity, and higher returns on equity should all result in higher price-to-book ratios. Of these four variables, the return on equity has the biggest impact on the price-to-book ratio, leading us to identify it as the companion variable for the ratio.

If anything, the strength of the relationship between price-to-book ratios and returns on equity should be stronger for financial service firms than for other firms, because the book value of equity is much more likely to track the market value of equity invested in existing assets. Similarly, the return on equity is less likely to be affected by accounting decisions. The strength of the relationship between price-to-book ratios and returns on equity can be seen when we plot the two on a scatter plot for commercial banks, in May 2024, in the United States, in Figure 21.1.

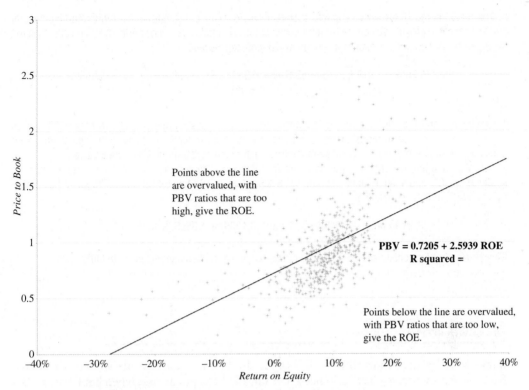

FIGURE 21.1 PBV Ratios and ROE—U.S. Banks in May 2024

As you can see, banks with higher returns on equity tend to trade at higher price-to-book ratios, but there is plenty of noise in the relationship, reflecting differences in other fundamentals. For instance, banks vary in terms of risk, and we would expect for any given return on equity, riskier banks should have lower price-to-book value ratios. Similarly, banks with much greater potential for growth should have much higher price-to-book ratios, for any given level of the other fundamentals.

ILLUSTRATION 21.7: PBV and ROE for European Banks in May 2024

In May 2024, there were seventy publicly traded European banks, with information available on regulatory capital ratios. Table 21.7 summarizes the price-to-book ratios, returns on equity and tier 1 capital ratios (as a percent of regulatory capital) of the banks:

TABLE 21.7 Price to Book and Fundamentals—European Banks

	Average	First Quartile	Median	Third Quartile
Price to book	0.89	0.55	0.77	1.09
Return on equity	15.22%	11.04%	13.99%	17.69%
Tier 1 capital ratio	17.78%	15.38%	16.97%	19.51%

While 50 of the 70 banks trade at less than book value, many of these firms have low returns on equity and low expected growth. To control for differences in fundamentals, we regress price-to-book ratios against return on equity and tier 1 capital as a percent of risk-adjusted assets:

$$\text{Price to book} = -0.4063 + 3.4563\ \text{ROE} + 4.3595\ \text{Tier 1 Capital Ratio}\quad R^2 = 37.45\%$$
$$\phantom{\text{Price to book} = }(1.48)\quad\ (4.65)\qquad\quad (2.72)$$

A significant portion of the differences in returns on equity across European banks in May 2024 can be explained by differences in return on equity and tier 1 capital ratios, with companies with higher returns on equity and healthier (higher) tier 1 capital ratios trading at much higher multiples of book value.

To illustrate the use of this regression, consider Banco Santander, the Spanish bank, with a return on equity of 12.86% and a tier 1 capital ratio of 13.75%, trading at 0.63 times book value. Plugging the company's numbers into the regression:

$$\text{Price to book} = -0.4063 + 3.4563\ (0.1286) + 4.3595\ (0.1375) = 0.64$$

Given how other European banks were priced in May 2024, Banco Santander is close to fairly priced.

THE CRISIS EFFECT

Banks have been an integral part of business for centuries, and while we have benefited from their presence, we have also been periodically been put at risk, when banks overreach or get into trouble, with their capacity to create costs that the rest of us have to bear. After every banking crisis, new rules are put into place to reduce or minimize these risks to the economic system, but in spite of these rules or sometimes because of them, there are new crises. To understand the roots of bank troubles, it is important that we understand how the banking business works, with the intent of creating criteria that we can use to separate good banks from average or bad ones.

The Banking Business Model

The banking business, when stripped down to basics, is a simple one. A bank collects deposits from customers, offering the quid quo pro of convenience, safety, and sometimes interest income (on those deposits that are interest-beating), and lends this money out to borrowers (individuals and businesses), charging an interest rate that is high enough to cover defaults and leave a surplus profit for the bank. In addition, banks can also invest some of the cash in securities, usually fixed-income, and with varying maturities and degrees of default risk, again earning income from these holdings. The profitability of a bank rests on the spread between its interest income (from loans and financial investments) and its interest expenses (on deposits and debt), with leakages from that spread to cover defaulted loans and losses on investment securities. Figure 21.2 captures these effects. To ensure that a bank survives, its owners must hold enough equity capital to buffer against unanticipated defaults or losses.

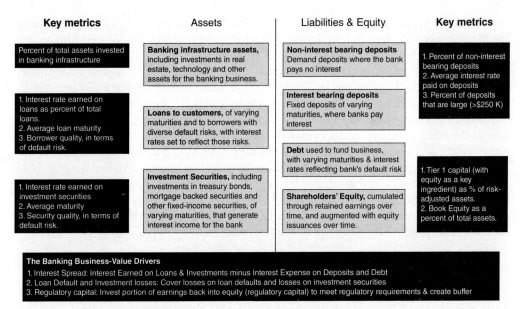

Key metrics	Assets	Liabilities & Equity	Key metrics
Percent of total assets invested in banking infrastructure	**Banking infrastructure assets,** including investments in real estate, technology and other assets for the banking business.	**Non-interest bearing deposits** Demand deposits where the bank pays no interest	1. Percent of non-interest bearing deposits 2. Average interest rate paid on deposits 3. Percent of deposits that are large (>$250 K)
1. Interest rate earned on loans as percent of total loans. 2. Average loan maturity 3. Borrower quality, in terms of default risk.	**Loans to customers,** of varying maturities and to borrowers with diverse default risks, with interest rates set to reflect those risks.	**Interest bearing deposits** Fixed deposits of varying maturities, where banks pay interest	
		Debt used to fund business, with varying maturities & interest rates reflecting bank's default risk	1. Tier 1 capital (with equity as a key ingredient) as % of risk-adjusted assets. 2. Book Equity as a percent of total assets.
1. Interest rate earned on investment securities 2. Average maturity 3. Security quality, in terms of default risk.	**Investment Securities,** including investments in treasury bonds, mortgage backed securities and other fixed-income securities, of varying maturities, that generate interest income for the bank	**Shareholders' Equity,** cumulated through retained earnings over time, and augmented with equity issuances over time.	

The Banking Business-Value Drivers
1. Interest Spread: Interest Earned on Loans & Investments minus Interest Expense on Deposits and Debt
2. Loan Default and Investment losses: Cover losses on loan defaults and losses on investment securities
3. Regulatory capital: Invest portion of earnings back into equity (regulatory capital) to meet regulatory requirements & create buffer

FIGURE 21.2 The Banking Business Model

The Banking Regulators

If you are wondering where bank regulators enter the business model, it is worth remembering that banks predate regulators, and for centuries were self-regulated (i.e., were responsible for ensuring that they had enough equity capital to cover unexpected losses). Predictably, bank runs were frequent, and the banks that survived and prospered set themselves apart from the others by being better capitalized and better assessors of default risk than their competition. In the United States, it was during the civil war that the National Banking Act was passed, laying the groundwork for chartering banks and requiring them to maintain safety reserves. After a 1907 banking panic where it fell upon J.P. Morgan and other wealthy bankers to step in and save the system, the Federal Reserve Bank was created in 1913. The Great Depression gave rise to the Glass-Steagall Act in 1933, which restricted banks to commercial banking, with the intent of preventing them from investing their deposit money in riskier businesses. The notion of regulatory capital has always been part of bank regulation, with the FDIC defining "capital adequacy" as having enough equity capital to cover one-tenth of assets. In subsequent decades, these capital adequacy ratios were refined to allow for risk variations across banks, with the logic that riskier assets needed more capital backing than safer ones. These regulatory capital needs were formalized and globalized after the G-10 countries created the Basel Committee on Banking Supervision and explicitly created the notions of "risk-weighted assets" and "Tier 1 capital" composed of equity and equity-like instruments, as well as specified minimum capital ratios that banks had to meet to continue to operate. Regulators were given punitive powers, ranging from restrictions of executive pay and acquisitions at banks that fall below the highest capitalization ranks, to putting banks that were undercapitalized into receivership.

The Basel Accord and the new rules on regulatory capital have largely shaped banking for the last few decades, and while they have provided a safety net for depositors, they have also given rise to a dangerous game where some banks arrived at the distorted conclusion that their endgame was exploiting loopholes in regulatory capital rules, rather than build solid banking businesses. In short, these banks found ways of investing in risky assets that the regulators did not recognize as risky, either because they were new or came in complex packages and using nonequity capital (debt and deposits), while getting that capital classified as equity or equity-like for regulatory purposes. The 2008 crisis exposed the ubiquity and consequences of this regulatory capital game but at great cost to the economy and taxpayers, with the troubled assets relief program (TARP) investing $426 billion in bank stocks and mortgage-backed securities to prop up mostly large money-center banks, rather than small or regional banks, that had overreached. The phrase "too big to fail" has been overused, but it was the rationale behind TARP, and may influence how we value bigger banks relative to smaller ones.

Good and Bad Banks

If the banking business is a simple one, what separates good from bad banks? If you look back at the Figure 21.2, you can see that I have highlighted key metrics at banks that can help gauge not just current risk but their exposure to future risk.

1. *Deposits:* Every bank is built around a deposit-base, and there are deposit-base characteristics that clearly determine risk exposure. First, to the extent that some deposits are not interest-bearing (as is the case with most checking accounts), banks that have higher percentages of non-interest-bearing deposits start off at an advantage, lowering the average interest rate paid on deposits. Second, because a big deposit base can very quickly become a small deposit base, if depositors flee, having a stickier deposit base gives a bank a benefit. As to the determinants of this stickiness, there are numerous factors that come into play, including deposit size (bigger and wealthier depositors tend to be more sensitive to risk whispers and to interest rate differences than smaller ones), depositor homogeneity (more diverse depositor bases tend to be less likely to indulge in groupthink), and deposit age (depositors who have been with a bank longer are stickier). In addition to these bank-specific characteristics, there are two other forces that are shaping deposit stickiness in 2023. One is that the actions taken to protect the largest banks after 2008 have also tilted the scales of stickiness towards them, since the perception, fair or unfair, among depositors, that your deposits are safer at a Chase or Citi than they are at a regional bank. The other is the rise of social media and online news made deposits less sticky across the board, as rumors (based on truth or otherwise) can spread much faster now than a few decades ago.
2. *Equity and Regulatory Capital:* Banks that have more book equity and Tier 1 capital have built bigger buffers against shocks than banks without those buffers. Within banks that have accumulated high amounts of regulatory capital, we would argue that banks that get all or the bulk of their capital from equity are safer than those that have created equity-like instruments that get counted as equity.
3. *Loans:* While your first instinct on bank loans is to look for banks that have lent to safer borrowers (less default risk), it is not necessarily the right call when it comes to measuring bank quality. A bank that lends to safe borrowers but charges them too low a rate, even given their safer status, is undercutting its value, whereas a bank that lends to riskier borrowers but charges them a rate that incorporates that risk and more, is

creating value. In short, to assess the quality of a bank's loan portfolio, you need to consider the interest rate earned on loans in conjunction with the expected loan losses on that loan portfolio, with a combination of high (low) interest rates on loans and low (high) loan losses characterizing good (bad) banks. In addition, banks that lend to a more diverse set of clients (small and large, across different business) are less exposed to risk than banks that lend to homogeneous clients (with similar profiles or operate in the same business), since default troubles often show up in clusters.

4. *Investment Securities:* In the aftermath of the 2008 crisis where banks were burned by their holdings in riskier mortgage-backed securities, regulators pushed for more safety in investment securities held by banks, with safety defined around default and liquidity risk. While that push was merited and banks with safer and more liquid holdings are safer than banks with riskier illiquid holdings, there are two other components that also determine risk exposure. The first is the duration of these securities, relative to the duration of the deposit base, with a greater mismatch associated with more risk. A bank that is funded primarily with demand deposits, which invests in 10-year bonds, is exposed to more risk than if it invests in commercial paper or treasury bills. The second is whether these securities, as reported on the balance sheet, are marked to market or not, a choice determined (at least currently) by how banks classify these holdings, with assets held to maturity being left at original cost and assets held for trading being marked to market. As an investor, you have more transparency about the value of what a company holds and, by extension, its equity and Tier 1 capital, when securities are marked to market, as opposed to when they are not.

At the risk of oversimplifying the discussion, Figure 21.3 below draws a contrast between good and bad banks, based upon the previous discussion:

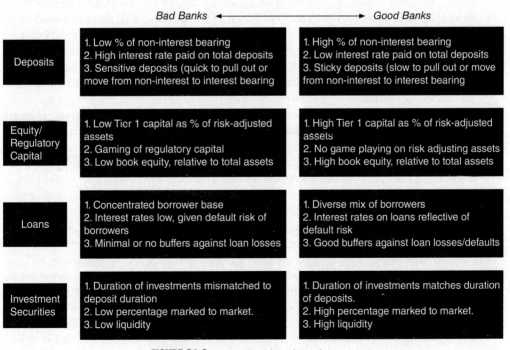

FIGURE 21.3 Good and Bad Banks

Banks with sticky deposits, on which they pay low interest rates (because a high percentage are noninterest bearing) and big buffers on equity and Tier 1 capital, which also earn "fair interest rates" given the default risk on the loans and investments they make, add more value and are usually safer than banks with depositor bases that are sensitive to risk perceptions and interest rates paid, while earning less than they should on loans and investments, given their default risk.

Macro Stressors

While we can differentiate between good and bad banks, and some of these differences are driven by the choices banks make on how they build their deposit bases and the loans and investments that they make with that deposit money, these differences are often either ignored or overlooked in the good times by investors and regulators. It often requires a crisis for both groups to wake up and respond, and these crises are usually macro-driven:

1. *Recessions:* Through banking history, it is the economy that has been the biggest stressor of the banking system, since recessions increase default across the board, but more so at the most default-prone borrowers and investment securities. Since regulatory capital requirements were created in response to one of the most severe recessions in history (the Great Depression), it is not surprising that regulatory capital rules are perhaps most effective in dealing with this stress test.
2. *Overvalued Asset Classes:* While banks should lend money using a borrower's earnings capacity as collateral, it is a reality that many bankers lend against the value of assets, rather than their earning power. The defense that bankers offer is that these assets can be sold, if borrowers default, and the proceeds used to cover the outstanding dues. That logic breaks down when asset classes get overvalued, since the loans made against the assets can no longer be covered by selling these assets if prices correct. This boom-and-bust cycle has long characterized lending in real estate, but became the basis for the 2008 crisis, as housing prices plunged around the country, taking down not just lenders but also holders of real-estate–based securities. In short, when these corrections happen, no matter what the asset class involved, banks that are overexposed to that asset class will take bigger losses and perhaps risk failure.
3. *Inflation and Interest Rates:* Rising inflation and interest rates are a mixed blessing for banks. On the one hand, as rates rise, longer life loans and longer-term securities will become less valuable, causing losses. After all, the market price of even a default-free bond will change when interest rates change, and bonds that were acquired when interest rates were lower will become less valuable as interest rates rise.

ILLUSTRATION 21.8:   U.S. Banks in Crisis—The Silicon Valley Bank Meltdown in March 2023

When interest rates change, those changes will affect the value of fixed income securities, with the effect increasing for longer maturiities. In most years, those changes in rates, at least in developed markets like the United States, are small enough that they create little damage. However, 2022 was an uncommon year, as the treasury bond rate rose from 1.51% to 3.88%, causing the price of a ten-year treasury bond to drop by more than 19%. Put simply, every bank holding ten-year treasury bonds in 2022 would have seen a markdown of 19% in the value of these holdings during the year, but as investors you would have seen the decline in value only at those few banks that classified those holdings as held for sale. That pain was worse with bonds with default-risk, with Baa (investment grade) corporate bonds losing 27% of their value. On the other hand, banks that had higher percentages of noninterest-bearing deposits would have gained value from accessing these interest-free deposits in a high interest world. The net effect would have determined how rising rates play out in bank value, and may explain why the damage from the crisis has varied across U.S. banks in 2023. It is worth noting that all the pain that would have come from writing down investment security holdings at banks, from the surge in interest rates, was clearly visible at the start of 2023, but there was no talk of a banking crisis. The implicit belief was that banks would be able to gradually realize or at least recognize these losses on the books, and then use the time to fix the resulting drop in their equity and regulatory capital.

The presumption that time was an ally was challenged by the implosion of Silicon Valley Bank in March 2023, where over the course of a week a large bank effectively was wiped out of existence. To see why Silicon Valley Bank (SVB) was particularly exposed, let us go back and look at it through the lens of good/bad banks from the last section:

1. *An Extraordinary Sensitive Deposit Base:* SVB was a bank designed for Silicon Valley (founders, VCs, employees) and it succeeded in that mission, with deposits almost doubling in 2021. That success created a deposit base that was anything but sticky, sensitive to rumors of trouble, with virally connected depositors drawn from a common pool, and big depositors who were well-positioned to move money quickly to other institutions.
2. *Equity and Tier 1 capital that was overstated:* While SVB's equity and Tier 1 capital looked robust at the start of 2023, that look was deceptive because it did not reflect the write-down in investment securities that was looming. While it shared this problem with other banks, SVB's exposure was greater than most (see later for why), and explains its attempt to raise fresh equity to cover the impending shortfall.
3. *Loans:* A large chunk of SVB's loan portfolio was composed of venture debt (i.e., lending to prerevenue and money-losing firms), and backed up by expectations of cash inflows from future rounds of VC capital. Since the expected VC rounds were conditional on these young companies being repriced at higher and higher prices over time, venture debt is extraordinarily sensitive to the pricing of young companies. In 2022, risk capital pulled back from markets, and as venture capital investments dried up and down rounds proliferated, venture debt suffered.
4. *Investment Securities:* All banks put some of their money in investment securities, but SVB was an outlier in terms of how much of its assets (55–60%) were invested in treasury bonds and mortgage-backed securities. Part of the reason was the surge in deposits in 2021, as venture capitalists pulled back from investing and parked their money in SVB, and with little demand for venture debt, SVB had no choice but to invest in securities. That said, the choice to invest in long-term securities was one that was made consciously by SVB and driven by the interest rate environment in 2021 and early 2022, where short-term rates were close to zero and long-term rates were low (1.5–2%) but still higher than what SVB was paying its depositors. If there is an original sin in this story, it is in this duration mismatch, which caused SVB's fall.

In short, if you were building a bank that would be susceptible to a blow-up from rising rates, SVB would fit the bill, but its failure opened the door for investors and depositors to reassess risk at banks at precisely the time when most banks did not want that reassessment done.

In the aftermath of SVB's failure, Signature Bank was shut down in the weeks after and First Republic has followed, and the question of what these banks shared is one that must be answered, not just for intellectual curiosity, because that answer will tell us whether other banks will follow. It should be noted that neither of these banks were as exposed as SVB to the macro-shocks of 2022, but the nature of banking crises is that as banks fall, each subsequent failure will be at a stronger bank than the one that failed before.

▨ With Signature Bank, the trigger for failure was a run on deposits, since more than 90% of deposits at the bank were uninsured, making those depositors far more sensitive to rumors about risk. The FDIC, in shuttering the bank, also pointed to "poor management" and failure to heed regulatory concerns, which clearly indicate that the bank had been on the FDIC's watchlist for troubled banks.

▧ With First Republic bank, a bank that had a large and lucrative wealth management arm, it was a dependence on those wealthy clients who increased their exposure. Wealthy depositors not only were more likely to have deposits that exceed $250,000, technically the cap on deposit insurance, but also had access to information on alternatives and the tools to move money quickly. Thus, in the first quarter of 2023, the bank reported a 41% drop in deposits, triggering forced sale of investment securities and the realization of losses on those sales.

In short, it was the stickiness of deposits that seemed to be the biggest indicator of banks getting into trouble, rather than the composition of their loan portfolios or even the nature of their investment securities, though having a higher percentage invested in long-term securities leaves you more exposed, given the interest rate environment.

In addition, U.S. banks collectively came under selling pressure after the Silicon Valley Bank crisis, and we looked at the pricing of the twenty-five largest U.S. banks, with the intent of finding under, and overpriced banks. Keeping in mind the discussion of risk and profitability leading in, here is what you would want to see in your underpriced bank, in Table 21.8:

TABLE 21.8 Bank Cheapness Indicators

Metric	What it measures	Under valued indicator
Price-to-Book ratio	**Cheapness of the stock,** measured by scaling market cap to accounting book value.	Low
Return on Equity	**Return Profitability**, measured by scaling profitability to shareholders equity	High
Interest spread	**Profitability of banking model**, measured as spread between interest earned on loans and investments and interest paid on deposits	High
Deposit growth	**Growth in bank deposit base**, proxying for stickiness, with higher growth -> more stickiness	Low
Tier 1 Capital Ratio	**Risk from Capitalization**, with higher Tier 1 capital ratios indicating more buffer and safety	High
% of Securities held to maturity	**Risk from undisclosed write-downs** from higher interest rates, since securities held to maturity are not marked to market	Low
Dividend Yield	**Cash yield on the stock**, with dividends divided by market capitalization	High

Applying this approach to the 25 largest banks, for instance, we computed the median values for each of these variables for the 25 largest U.S. banks, in terms of market cap, and used it as the dividing line for good and bad on each of the variables. Thus, a return on equity higher than the median of 12% is considered a good (and in green) and less than 12% is considered bad (and in red). Table 21.9 presents the statistics for the twenty-five biggest U.S. banks.

Put simply, you are looking for a preponderance of bold numbers for your underpriced banks, and while there no all-bold banks, there are banks that stand out, in both directions.

▧ Citi comes closest to meeting the tests, scoring well on risk (with a higher than median Tier 1 capital ratio, and a lower percent of securities held to maturity among the five biggest banks), deposit stickiness (with low deposit growth), and trades at half of book value (the lowest price-to-book ratio). Its weakest link is a return on equity of 8.11% (in 2022) and 9.50% (average from 2018–2022), lower than the median for U.S. banks, and while that would suggest a lower than median price-to-book

TABLE 21.9 Cheapness Screens for Large U.S. Banks

Company Name	Exchange: Ticker	Cheapness — Price to Book	Profitability — Return on Equity (ROE) (2022)	Profitability — Average ROE (2018–22)	Interest Spread (2022)	Stickiness — Deposit Growth: Last 5 years	Riskiness — Tier 1 Capital Ratio	Riskiness — % of Securities Held to Maturity	Cash Yield — Dividend Yield
Citigroup Inc. (NYSE:C)	NYSE:C	0.50	8.11%	9.50%	9.39%	3.74%	14.80%	51.85%	4.40%
Citizens Financial Group, Inc.	NYSE:CFG	0.69	9.68%	8.72%	3.57%	9.20%	11.12%	29.06%	3.47%
Valley National Bancorp	NasdaqGS:VLY	0.77	11.67%	10.61%	3.38%	21.21%	9.46%	75.21%	3.11%
Truist Financial Corporation	NYSE:TFC	0.81	10.00%	9.84%	3.84%	21.23%	10.54%	44.56%	4.25%
Webster Financial Corporation	NYSE:WBS	0.84	19.56%	13.68%	3.69%	20.62%	11.23%	45.41%	1.76%
Prosperity Bancshares, Inc.	NYSE:PB	0.85	8.16%	8.43%	4.24%	9.39%	15.88%	96.85%	2.62%
M&T Bank Corporation	NYSE:MTB	0.90	12.33%	12.10%	3.86%	11.94%	11.79%	55.73%	2.27%
New York Community Bancorp, Inc.	NYSE:NYCB	0.93	9.94%	8.16%	2.00%	13.56%	9.78%	0.00%	5.39%
Wells Fargo & Company	NYSE:WFC	0.93	7.84%	9.36%	3.88%	1.60%	12.11%	72.34%	3.08%
Bank of America Corporation	NYSE:BAC	0.95	11.22%	10.87%	5.98%	8.75%	12.99%	100.00%	3.18%
KeyCorp	NYSE:KEY	0.96	12.35%	12.64%	3.44%	7.45%	10.60%	18.21%	4.45%
SouthState Corporation	NasdaqGS:SSB	1.03	10.33%	8.83%	3.85%	26.19%	10.96%	33.50%	1.70%
Huntington Bancshares Incorporated	NasdaqGS:HBAN	1.04	13.06%	12.30%	3.86%	13.97%	10.90%	42.13%	3.02%
Fifth Third Bancorp	NasdaqGS:FITB	1.17	12.17%	12.57%	3.87%	9.75%	10.53%	0.01%	5.30%
Comerica Incorporated	NYSE:CMA	1.19	15.34%	13.84%	3.93%	4.34%	10.50%	0.00%	4.28%
Regions Financial Corporation	NYSE:RF	1.19	13.47%	11.83%	4.17%	6.88%	10.91%	2.79%	2.95%
U.S. Bancorp	NYSE:USB	1.20	12.00%	14.23%	3.26%	9.82%	9.83%	54.90%	3.82%
BOK Financial Corporation	NasdaqGS:BOKF	1.20	9.70%	10.76%	4.04%	10.66%	11.71%	0.00%	2.07%
East West Bancorp, Inc.	NasdaqGS:EWBC	1.22	19.33%	16.18%	3.85%	15.57%	12.68%	33.22%	1.70%
The PNC Financial Services Group, Inc.	NYSE:PNC	1.30	11.92%	12.79%	3.38%	11.20%	10.43%	68.31%	3.11%
First Horizon Corporation	NYSE:FHN	1.30	11.72%	13.09%	3.77%	15.36%	11.92%	13.43%	1.69%
JPMorgan Chase & Co.	NYSE:JPM	1.53	14.53%	15.30%	6.80%	9.69%	14.85%	67.38%	2.93%
First Citizens BancShares, Inc	NasdaqGS:FCNC	1.65	24.97%	16.02%	3.84%	24.77%	11.06%	53.33%	0.15%
Cullen/Frost Bankers, Inc.	NYSE:CFR	2.37	13.49%	12.12%	4.24%	10.73%	13.35%	12.64%	2.10%
Commerce Bancshares, Inc.	NasdaqGS:CBSH	2.83	14.21%	14.67%	3.89%	5.80%	14.13%	0.00%	1.42%
Median		1.04	12.00%	12.12%	3.86%	10.66%	11.12%	42.13%	3.02%

ratio, the discount at Citi exceeds that expectation. Citi's banking business, though slow growing, remains lucrative with the higher interest rate spread in this sample.

- At the other end of the expectation scales, JP Morgan Chase scores well on operating metrics, with a high ROE, low deposit growth, and a high Tier 1 capital ratio, but it trades at a much higher price-to-book ratio than the other banks and with a lower dividend yield.

As a value investor, we would be uncomfortable making an investment in Citi purely based upon this pricing analysis, and it is for that reason that we would do an intrinsic valuation of the bank before making a buy decision. That reinforces a more general point that even investors who are true believers in valuation can benefit from understanding and using pricing, just as traders, who play the pricing game, can benefit from an understanding of the core principles of intrinsic valuation.

DEPOSIT INSURANCE AND BANK VALUE

In most countries, the state provides insurance to bank depositors by guaranteeing the deposits up to a specified limit. What effect will such deposit insurance have on value? If banks are charged a fair price for the insurance, it should have no effect on value. In practice, though, deposit insurance can skew value in two ways:

1. In many countries, including the United States, the deposit insurance rate does not vary across banks. Thus, banks with safe loan portfolios are charged the same rate as banks with risky loan portfolios. If the rate set is based on average default, this will result in the former being overcharged and the latter being undercharged. It will also create an incentive system for banks to take on more and more risk. In fact, you can consider deposit insurance to be a put option provided to the bank—the bank can put its deposit liabilities to the insurance agency if the value of its loan portfolio drops below the value of the liabilities. If the put price does not vary with the volatility in the value of the loan portfolio, banks with riskier portfolios will become more valuable (the value of the put will exceed the price paid), and banks with safer portfolios will become less valuable.
2. Even if deposit insurance rates vary across banks, the price of the insurance may not fully reflect the risk of the bank's assets for two reasons. The first is that the risk can change from period to period and the pricing may not keep up. The second is that the insurance may be subsidized by taxpayers, in which case all banks will become more valuable as a result of the insurance.

NONBANK FINANCIAL SERVICE FIRMS

In much of this chapter, we have focused our attention on banks, because they are a dominant segment of the financial services business. That said, there are other financial service segments that do not contain some of the complexities that bedevil bank valuation but still need to be valued and priced.

Asset Management Companies

Asset management firms derive their value from managing client money invested in equities, fixed income, and other assets. They include mutual funds, which often invest client money, as well as advisory firms that direct the investment, but often don't directly invest.

(a) *Drivers of earnings power:* There are three key drivers of earnings power at asset management firms. The first, and perhaps most critical one, is assets under management (AUM), reflecting the total value of the assets that clients are investing through you. The second is the fee rate, where the asset management firm is remunerated, and while that fee is usually a percent of assets under management, there are variations, from fixed fees per client to a fee structures, where the asset management firm gets a share of the upside (hedge funds that take 2% of assets under management and 20% of the upside).[4] The third is the expenses incurred by the asset management firm in managing the AUM, which will vary depending on the service provided. For an active money manager, these expenses will include the cost of paying analysts and portfolio managers, and for wealth management, it is the pay and commissions of the wealth managers that handle their client networks.

(b) *Reinvestment:* The lesson that growth requires reinvestment applies just as much to asset managers as it does to any other company, but the nature of reinvestment can make it difficult to identify and isolate the expenditure. For instance, in a wealth management firm, a portion of every wealth manager's job may be seeking out and signing up new clients, but that cost is often not broken out. In general, though, asset management is not a capital-intensive business, and successful asset managers should be able to earn high returns on equity.

(c) *Risk:* There are two groups of risks that asset managers are exposed to, and they require different treatments. First, the asset class that you manage (stocks, bonds, real estate) may perform badly during a period, dragging down the value of assets under management, and fees. Second, to the extent that money chases success, an asset manager who underperforms their peer group may find their assets under management shrink in the aftermath. Using the language of stickiness that we introduced with banks, asset managers with stickier clients will be more valuable than asset managers with more fickle clients, and that stickiness can come from multiple factors.

While we can debate the pluses and minuses of active money management, it is undeniable that the business has become a more difficult one to create value in for many reasons. First, clients cannot only more easily find out more about how their asset managers have performed but can do so in a far timelier fashion. Second, the growth of passive investment vehicles (exchange traded funds and index funds) has put pressure on the fee structures of asset managers, in general, and the rise of robot advisors and fin-tech investing platforms has added to that pressure. Third, technology has given clients access to information and trading platforms that only professional traders and investments could have accessed a few decades ago, making do-it-yourself investing a more viable choice for many.

---

[4]If you find asset managers who seem to be providing their services for nothing, there is usually other mechanics that they use to derive profits, some of which are questionable.

In short, the investment world has become flatter, and the values of asset management firms reflect that development.

Transaction and Payment Processors

Transaction and payment processing firms generate their value from taking a slice of transactions that happen on their platforms. While the rise of fintech payment processors such as Paypal and Venmo have brought these businesses attention, they have been a factor in markets for decades. In fact, Mastercard, Visa, and American Express have derived significant portions of their value from credit card transactions that they facilitate.

(a) *Drivers of earnings power:* There are three key drivers of earnings power at payment processing firms. The first is the gross transaction value, reflecting the gross value of all transactions that occur on a transaction platform. The second is the take rate (i.e., the percentage of transaction value that accrues to the payment processor). The third is the expenses incurred by the firm in maintaining the platform, including customer and merchant processing services and technology.

(b) *Reinvestment:* The growth in gross transaction value over time is driven by two forces, with the first being the number of customers on the platform and the second being the transaction value per customer. Using the language introduced in Chapter 20 for user- and subscriber-based companies, the amount spent by payment processing companies in signing up new merchants and acquiring new customers will be their prime reinvestment, with the caveat that acquiring another payment processing company can deliver both quickly.

(c) *Risk:* The macro risk in a payment processing firm comes from the economy since people spend more in a strong economy than during a recession. The company-specific risks that can affect the earnings and cash flows of the company include the risk of fraud on the platform, which the company must cover, as well as the potential for bad debts if customers do not fulfil their financial obligations.

After decades of dominance, where the large credit card companies used network benefits to grow and acquire market share, the advent of digital payments has opened the door to newcomers, not only from newcomers like Venmo and Paytm but also from technology companies like Apple and Google flexing their platform reach.

Brokerage Firms

As long as markets have existed, there are businesses that have derived their value as intermediaries, taking a piece of transactions that occur in these markets. From real estate brokers, to stock market intermediaries, to even antique dealers, value comes from transactions in these asset classes and their transaction fees.

(a) *Drivers of earnings power:* There are three key drivers of earnings power at asset management firms. The first is in transaction value, reflecting the gross value of all transactions that are brokered. The second is the dealer and broker commission (the percentage of transaction value that accrues to the broker). The third is the expenses incurred by the brokerage firm in providing brokerage services, which can include information, legal, and monitoring costs.

(b) *Reinvestment:* The growth in brokerage revenues comes from having more transactions, often requiring hiring more brokers, or from investing in a more powerful or expansive platform that enables for more transactions.

(c) *Risk:* The macro-risk in a brokerage firm comes from the business that they broker, with real estate broker revenues seesawing with real estate transaction and stock market brokers ebbing and flowing with equity markets. Extending into the crypto space, Coinbase, the prime intermediary when it comes to crypto trades, has seen its operating results move with the price of Bitcoin. The company-specific risks that can affect the earnings and cash flows of the company include regulatory and legal risks.

The rise of technology has put a debt on intermediation revenues, and it can be seen especially in equity markets where bid-ask spreads and brokerage commissions have plummeted. The decline in brokerage revenues has been slower in other markets, and especially so in real estate where real estate commissions have barely budged, even as technology competitors like Zillow and Redfin have emerged.

CONCLUSION

The basic principles of valuation apply just as much for financial service firms as they do for other firms. There are, however, a few aspects relating to financial service firms that can affect how they are valued. The first is that debt for a financial service firm is difficult to define and measure, making it difficult to estimate firm value or costs of capital. Consequently, it is far easier to value the equity directly in a financial service firm by discounting cash flows to equity at the cost of equity. The second is that capital expenditures and working capital, which are required inputs to estimating cash flows, are often not easily estimated at financial service firms. In fact, much of the reinvestment that occurs at these firms is categorized under operating expenses. To estimate cash flows to equity, therefore, we have to either use dividends (and assume that what is not paid out as dividend is the reinvestment) or modify our definition of reinvestment to consider investments in regulatory capital.

Even if we choose to use multiples, we run into many of the same issues. The difficulties associated with defining debt make equity multiples such as price-earnings or price-to-book value ratios better suited for comparing financial service firms than value multiples. In making these comparisons, we have to control for differences in fundamentals—risk, growth, cash flows, loan quality—that affect value.

Finally, regulatory considerations and constraints overlay financial firm valuations. In some cases, regulatory restrictions on competition enable financial service firms to earn excess returns and increase value. In other cases, the same regulatory authorities may restrict the potential excess returns that a firm may be able to make by preventing the firm from entering a business.

QUESTIONS AND SHORT PROBLEMS

In the problems following, use an equity risk premium of 5.5 percent if none is specified.

1. You have been asked to assess the value per share of Secure Savings, a mature savings and loan company. The company had earnings per share in the just-completed financial year of $4 per share and paid dividends of $2.40 per share. The book value of equity at the beginning of the year was $40 per share. The beta for the stock is 0.90, the risk-free rate is 6%, and the market risk premium is 4%.
   a. Assuming that the firm will continue to earn its current return on equity in perpetuity and maintain its current dividend payout ratio, estimate the value per share.
   b. If the stock is trading at $40 a share, estimate the implied growth rate.
2. You are now valuing the Southwest Bank, a small bank that is growing rapidly. The bank reported earnings per share of $2 in the just-completed financial year and paid out dividends per share of $0.20. The book value of equity at the beginning of the year was $14. The beta for the stock is 1.10, the risk-free rate is 6% and the risk premium is 4%.
   a. Assuming that it will maintain its current return on equity and payout ratio for the next five years, estimate the expected growth rate in earnings per share.
   b. Assuming that the firm will start growing at a constant rate of 5% a year beyond that point in time, estimate the value per share today. (You can assume that the return on equity will drop to 12% in stable growth, and that the beta will become 1.)
3. You have been asked to analyze LongLife Insurance company, a firm in stable growth, with earnings expected to grow 4% in the long term. The firm is trading at a multiple of 1.4 times book value and has a cost of equity of 11%.
   a. If the market is pricing the stock correctly, estimate the return on equity that LongLife is expected to earn in perpetuity.
   b. If the regulatory authorities constrain LongLife to earn a return on equity equal to its cost of equity, what would you expect the price-to-book ratio to be?
4. Now assume that you are comparing the price-to-book ratios of the 13 largest banks in the United States in 2000. The following table summarizes the price-to-book ratios and the returns on equity earned by these firms:

Company Name	PBV	ROE
Wachovia Corp.	2.05	18.47%
PNC Financial Serv.	2.54	21.56%
SunTrust Banks	1.91	15.35%
State Street Corp.	6.63	19.52%
Mellon Financial Corp.	4.59	23.95%
Morgan (J.P.) & Co.	1.74	19.39%
First Union Corp.	1.52	19.66%
FleetBoston Fin'l.	2.25	20.15%
Bank of New York	7.01	25.36%
Chase Manhattan Corp.	2.60	24.60%
Wells Fargo	3.07	17.72%
Bank of America	1.69	19.31%
Bank of Montreal	1.23	18.08%

a. If you were valuing SunTrust Banks relative to these firms, would you expect it to have a higher or lower price-to-book ratio than the average for the group? Explain why.

b. If you regress price-to-book ratios against returns on equity, what would your predicted price-to-book ratios be for each of these companies?

5. Signet Bank has asked you to estimate the value of its loan portfolio. The bank has $1 billion in loans outstanding, with an average maturity of six years, and expected interest income of $75 million a year. You have been able to get a synthetic rating of A for the entire loan portfolio, and the current market interest rate on A-rated bonds is 6.5%.

a. Estimate the value of the loan portfolio.

b. If Signet Bank has $800 million in debt outstanding, estimate the value of the equity in the bank based on the loans it has in place.

6. Loomis Capital is a boutique investment bank that reported a return on equity of 20% on its book equity of $100 million in the just-completed financial year. The beta for the bank is 1.20, the risk-free rate is 5.2%, and the risk premium is 4%. You assume that the current return on equity and cost of equity will continue unchanged for the next 10 years, and that there will be no excess returns after year 10. The payout ratio for the firm is 30%.

a. Estimate the dollar excess equity returns every year for the next 10 years.

b. Estimate the value of equity today, using the excess return approach.

c. How would your answer to (b) change if you were told that the return on equity will drop to 15% after year 10 and remain at that level forever?

CHAPTER 22

Valuing Money-Losing Firms

In most of the valuations thus far in this book, we have looked at firms that have positive earnings. In this chapter, we consider the subset of firms with negative earnings or abnormally low earnings and examine how best to value them. We begin by looking at why firms have negative earnings in the first place, and then look at the ways that valuation has to be adapted to reflect these underlying reasons.

For firms with temporary problems—a strike or a product recall, for instance—we argue that the adjustment process is a simple one, where we back out of current earnings the portion of the expenses associated with the temporary problems. For a firm with a single, long-gestation period infrastructure investment (e.g., toll road, a dam), we look at how best to deal with the resulting cash flow patterns. For cyclical firms, where the negative earnings are due to a deterioration of the overall economy, and for commodity firms, where cyclical movements in commodity prices can affect earnings, we argue for the use of normalized earnings in valuation. For firms with long-term strategic or operating problems (e.g., outdated plants, a poorly trained workforce, or poor investments in the past), the process of valuation becomes more complicated because we must make assumptions about whether the firm will be able to outlive its problems and restructure itself. Finally, we look at firms that have negative earnings because they have borrowed too much, and consider how best to deal with the potential for default.

There is a final group of firms (i.e., start-ups and young firms, some of which can have immense potential), where earnings are negative because they have not found a working business model (or in some cases, a product or a service that they can market) yet, or because they are still in the process of scaling up. We will look at those firms in Chapter 23.

NEGATIVE EARNINGS: CONSEQUENCES AND CAUSES

A firm with negative earnings or abnormally low earnings is more difficult to value than a firm with positive earnings. This section looks at why such firms create problems for analysts in the first place, and then follows up by examining the reasons for negative earnings.

Consequences of Negative or Abnormally Low Earnings

Firms that are losing money currently create several problems for the analysts who are attempting to value them. While none of these problems are conceptual, they are significant from a measurement standpoint:

1. *Earnings growth rates cannot be estimated or used in valuation.* The first and most obvious problem is that we can no longer estimate an expected growth rate of earnings and apply it to current earnings to estimate future earnings. When current earnings are negative, applying a growth rate will just make it more negative. In fact, even estimating an earnings growth rate becomes problematic, whether one uses historical growth, analyst projections, or fundamentals.

   ▪ Estimating historical growth when current earnings are negative is difficult, and the numbers, even if estimated, often are meaningless. To see why, assume that a firm's operating earnings have gone from –\$200 million last year to –\$100 million in the current year. The traditional historical growth equation yields the following:

   $$\text{Earnings growth rate} = \frac{-100}{-200} - 1 = -50\%$$

   This clearly does not make sense since this firm has improved its earnings over the period. In fact, we looked at this problem in Chapter 11.

   ▪ An alternative approach to estimating earnings growth is to use analyst estimates of projected growth in earnings, especially over the next five years. The consensus estimates of this growth rate across all analysts following a stock is generally available as public information for many U.S. companies, and is often used as the expected growth rate in valuation. For firms with negative earnings in the current period, this estimate of a growth rate will not be available or meaningful.

   ▪ A third approach to estimating earnings growth is to use fundamentals. This approach is also difficult to apply for firms that have negative earnings, since the two fundamental inputs—the return made on investments (return on equity or capital) and the reinvestment rate (or retention ratio)—are usually computed using current earnings. When current earnings are negative, both these inputs become meaningless from the perspective of estimating expected growth.

2. *Tax computation becomes more complicated.* The standard approach to estimating taxes is to apply the marginal tax rate on the pretax operating income to arrive at the after-tax operating income:

   $$\text{After-tax operating income} = \text{Pretax operating income}(1 - \text{Tax rate})$$

   This computation assumes that earnings create tax liabilities in the current period. While this is generally true, firms that are losing money can carry these losses forward in time and apply them to earnings in future periods. Thus, analysts valuing firms with negative earnings must keep track of the net operating losses of these firms, and remember to use them to shield income in future periods from taxes.

3. *The going concern assumption may not apply.* The final problem associated with valuing companies that have negative earnings is the very real possibility that these firms

will go bankrupt if earnings stay negative, and that the assumption of infinite lives that underlies the estimation of terminal value may not apply in these cases.

The problems are less visible but exist nevertheless for firms that have abnormally low earnings; that is, the current earnings of the firm are much lower than what the firm has earned historically. Though you can compute historical growth and fundamental growth for these firms, they are likely to be meaningless because current earnings are depressed. The historical growth rate in earnings will be negative, and the fundamentals will yield very low estimates for expected growth.

Causes of Negative Earnings

There are several reasons why firms have negative or abnormally low earnings, some of which can be viewed as temporary, some of which are long-term, and some of which relate to where a firm stands in the life cycle.

Temporary Problems   For some firms, negative earnings are the result of temporary problems, sometimes affecting the firm alone, sometimes affecting an entire industry, and sometimes the result of a downturn in the economy:

- Firm-specific reasons for negative earnings can include a strike by the firm's employees, an expensive product recall, or a large judgment against the firm in a lawsuit. While these will undoubtedly lower earnings, the effect is likely to be one-time and not affect future earnings.
- Sector-wide reasons for negative earnings can include a downturn in the price of a commodity for a firm that produces that commodity. It is common, for instance, for paper and pulp firms to go through cycles of high paper prices (and profits), followed by low paper prices (and losses). In some cases, the negative earnings may arise from the interruption of a common source of supply for a necessary raw material or a spike in its price. For instance, an increase in oil prices will negatively affect the profits of all airlines.
- For cyclical firms, a recession will affect revenues and earnings. It is not surprising, therefore, that automobile companies report low or negative earnings during bad economic times.

The common thread for all these firms is that we expect earnings to recover sooner rather than later as the problem dissipates. Thus, we would expect a cyclical firm's earnings to bounce back once the economy revives, and an airline's profits to improve once oil prices level off.

Infrastructure Firms   The nature of infrastructure investments is that they not only require large amounts of investment up front, but also that you have wait for a few or many years before the investment starts delivering operating results. With a mature infrastructure company, this is generally not a problem since it owns a portfolio of infrastructure projects at different stages in the cycle, and the earnings and cash flows will reflect that diverse portfolio.

There are cases, however, where a company is created for a single infrastructure investment, such as building an airport or a toll road, with only investment costs occurring in the near term, as the infrastructure is created, and the potential for monetizing this investment with fees and revenues in later years. Figure 22.1 summarizes the challenge.

By itself, there is nothing exceptional about this cash flow stream, but there are valuation questions that need to be answered, especially when you value it ahead of or early in the construction period including, and we will look at answers to these questions later in this chapter.

If the business that a firm is in requires large infrastructure investments early in the life cycle and the firm must wait for a long period before it can generate earnings, it is entirely possible that the firm will report large losses in the initial periods when the investments are made. In fact, as an added complication, many of these firms must borrow large amounts to fund their infrastructure investments, creating a fairly toxic combination—negative earnings and high leverage.

Given this combination of extended losses and high debt loads, how can an infrastructure firm—a telecom firm or cable company—ever be valuable? Consider one possible path to success. A firm borrows money and makes large investments in infrastructure. Having made these investments, though, it has a secure market where entry for competitors is prohibitively expensive. In some cases, the firm may have a legally sanctioned monopoly to provide the service. No further large investments are needed in infrastructure, but depreciation on the existing investments continues to generate large tax benefits. The net effect is that the firm will be sitting on a cash machine that allows it to not only pay off its debt but ready itself for the next generation of investments. In a sense, phone companies and power companies, as well as some cable and cellular firms, followed this path to success in the last century.

In the 1990s, we saw an explosion both in the number of telecom firms and the capital raised by these firms in a variety of ventures. While they followed the timeworn path of high debt and large up-front infrastructure investments laid by their predecessors, we believe that there were two critical ingredients that were missing with this generation of firms. The first was that technology had become a wild card, and large investments in infrastructure did not guarantee future profitability or even that a market would exist. The second is that the protection from competition that allowed the old-time infrastructure firms to generate large and predictable profits was unlikely to be there for this new generation of firms. As a consequence, many of these firms exposed themselves to default and bankruptcy.

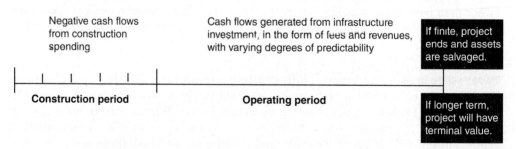

FIGURE 22.1   Infrastructure Investment—Cash Flow Profile

Long-Term Problems   Negative earnings are sometimes reflections of deeper and much more long-term problems in a firm. Some of these are the results of poor strategic choices made in the past, some reflect operational inefficiencies, and some are purely financial, the result of a firm borrowing much more than it can support with its existing cash flows.

- A firm's earnings may be negative because its strategic choices in terms of product mix or marketing policy might have backfired. For such a firm, financial health is generally not around the corner and will require a substantial makeover and, often, new management.
- A firm can have negative earnings because of inefficient operations. For instance, the firm's plant and equipment may be obsolete or its workforce may be poorly trained. The negative earnings may also reflect poor decisions made in the past by management and the continuing costs associated with such decisions. For instance, firms that have gone on acquisition binges and overpaid on a series of acquisitions may face several years of poor earnings as a consequence.
- In some cases, a firm that is in generally good health operationally can end up with negative equity earnings because it has chosen to use too much debt to fund its operations.

MAKING THE CALL: SHORT-TERM VERSUS LONG-TERM PROBLEMS

In practice, it is often difficult to disentangle temporary or short-term problems from long-term ones. There is no simple rule of thumb that works, and accounting statements are not always forthcoming about the nature of the problems. Most firms, when reporting negative earnings, will claim that their problems are transitory, and that recovery is around the corner. Analysts must make their own judgments on whether this is the case, and they should consider the following:

- *The credibility of the management making the claim.* The managers of some firms are much more forthcoming than others in revealing problems and admitting their mistakes, and their claims should be given much more credence.

- *The amount and timeliness of information provided with the claim.* A firm that provides detailed information backing up its claim that the problem is temporary is more credible than a firm that does not provide such information. In addition, a firm that reveals its problems promptly is more believable than one that delays reporting problems until its hand is forced.

- *Confirming reports from other companies in industry.* A cyclical company that claims that its earnings are down because of an economic slowdown will be more believable if other companies in the sector also report similar slowdowns.

- *The persistence of the problem.* If poor earnings persist over multiple periods, it is much more likely that the firm is facing a long-term problem. Thus, a series of restructuring charges should be viewed with suspicion.

VALUING MONEY-LOSING FIRMS

The way we deal with negative earnings will depend on why the firm has negative earnings in the first place. This section explores the alternatives that are available for working with negative earnings firms.

Firms with Temporary Problems

When earnings are negative because of temporary or short-term problems, the expectation is that earnings will recover in the near term. Thus, the solutions we devise will be fairly simple ones, which for the most part will replace the current earnings (which are negative) with normalized earnings (which will be positive). How we normalize earnings will vary depending on the nature of the problem.

Firm-Specific Problems   A firm can have a bad year in terms of earnings, but the problems may be isolated to that firm and be short-term in nature. If the loss can be attributed to a specific event—a strike or a lawsuit judgment, for instance—and the accounting statements report the cost associated with the event, the solution is simple. You should estimate the earnings prior to these costs, and use these earnings not only for estimating cash flows but also for computing fundamentals such as return on capital. In making these estimates, though, note that you should remove not just the expense, but also all of the tax benefits created by the expense as well, assuming that it is tax deductible.

If the cause of the loss is more diffuse or if the cost of the event causing the loss is not separated from other expenses, you face a tougher task. First, you must ensure that the loss is in fact temporary and not the symptom of long-term problems at the firm. Next, you have to estimate the normal earnings of the firm. The simplest and most direct way of doing this is to compare each expense item for the firm, for the current year with the same item in previous years, scaled to revenues. Any item that looks abnormally high, relative to prior years, should be normalized (by using an average from previous years). Alternatively, you could apply the operating margin that the firm earned in prior years to the current year's revenues and estimate an operating income to use in the valuation.

In general, you will have to consider adjusting the earnings of firms after years in which they have made major acquisitions, since the accounting statements in these years will be skewed by large items that are generally nonrecurring and related to the acquisition.

ILLUSTRATION 22.1:   Normalizing Earnings for a Firm after a Poor Year: Daimler-Benz in 1995

In 1995, Daimler-Benz reported an operating loss of DM 2,016 million and a net loss of DM 5,674 million. Much of the loss could be attributed to firm-specific problems, including a large write-off of a failed investment in Fokker Aerospace, an aircraft manufacturer. To estimate normalized earnings at Daimler-Benz, we eliminated all charges related to these items and estimated a pretax operating income of DM 5,693 million. To complete the valuation, we made the following additional assumptions:

- Revenues at Daimler had been growing 3% to 5% a year prior to 1995, and we anticipated that the long-term growth rate would be 5% in both revenues and operating income.
- The firm had a book value of capital invested of DM 43,558 million at the beginning of 1995, and was expected to maintain its return on capital (based on the adjusted operating income of DM 5,693 million).
- The firm's tax rate is 44%.

To value Daimler, we first estimated the return on invested capital at the firm, using the adjusted operating income:

$$\text{Return on invested capital} = \frac{\text{EBIT } (1-t)}{\text{Invested capital}} = \frac{5,693 (1-.44)}{43,558} = 7.32\%$$

Based on the expected growth rate of 5%, this would require a reinvestment rate of 68.31%:

$$\text{Reinvestment rate} = g/\text{ROC} = 5\%/7.32\% = 68.31\%$$

With these assumptions, we were able to compute Daimler's expected free cash flows in 1996:

EBIT $(1 - t) = 5,693(1.05)(1 - .44) =$	DM 3,347.48 million
$-$ Reinvestment $= 5,693(1.05)(1-.44)(.6831) =$	DM 2,286.66 million
Free cash flow to firm	DM 1,060.82 million

To compute the cost of capital, we used a bottom-up beta of 0.95, estimated using automobile firms listed globally. The long-term bond rate (on a German government bond denominated in DM) was 6%, and Daimler-Benz could borrow long-term at 6.1%. We assumed a market risk premium of 4%. The market value of equity was DM 50,000 million, and there was DM 26,281 million in debt outstanding at the end of 1995.

$$\text{Cost of equity} = 6\% + 0.95(4\%) = 9.8\%$$
$$\text{Cost of debt} = 6.1\% (1-.44) = 3.42\%$$
$$\text{Debt ratio} = 26,281/(50,000 + 26,281) = 34.45\%$$
$$\text{Cost of capital} = 9.8\%(.6555) + 3.42\%(.3445) = 7.60\%$$

Note that all the costs are computed in DM terms, to be consistent with our cash flows. Note also that we are assuming that Daimler will generate a return on capital (7.32%) that is lower than its cost of capital in perpetuity. While value destruction in the long term may not seem rational, the corporate governance system structure in Daimler leaves us with few options. The firm value can now be computed, if we assume that earnings and cash flows will grow at 5% a year in perpetuity:

$$\text{Value of operating assets at end of 1995} = \frac{\text{Expected FCFF in 1996}}{(\text{Cost of capital} - \text{Expected growth rate})}$$
$$= \frac{1,060.82}{(.076 - .05)} = \text{DM 40,787 million}$$

Adding to this is the value of the cash and marketable securities (DM 13,500 million) held by Daimler at the time of this valuation, and netting out the market value of debt ($26,281) yields an estimated value of DM 28,006 million for equity, significantly lower than the market value of DM 50,000 million.

$$\text{Value of equity} = \text{Value of operating assets} + \text{Cash and marketable securities} - \text{Debt}$$
$$= 40,787 + 13,500 - 26,281 = \text{DM 28,006 million}$$

As in all firm valuations, there is an element of circular reasoning involved in this valuation.[1]

---

[1] The circular reasoning comes in because we use the current market value of equity and debt to compute the cost of capital. We then use the cost of capital to estimate the value of equity and debt. If this is unacceptable, the process can be iterated, with the cost of capital being recomputed using the estimated values of debt and equity, and continued until there is convergence.

Sector-Wide or Market-Driven Problems   The earnings of cyclical firms are, by definition, volatile and depend on the state of the economy. In economic booms, the earnings of these firms are likely to increase, while in recessions the earnings will be depressed. The same can be said of commodity firms that go through price cycles, where periods of high prices for the commodity are often followed by low prices. In both cases, you can get misleading estimates of value if you use the current year's earnings as your base year earnings.

Valuing Cyclical Firms   Cyclical firm valuations can be significantly affected by the level of base year earnings. There are two potential solutions: One is to adjust the expected growth rate in the near periods to reflect cyclical changes, and the other is to value the firm based on normalized rather than current earnings.

Adjust Expected Growth   Cyclical firms often report low earnings at the bottom of an economic cycle, but the earnings recover quickly when the economy recovers. One solution, if earnings are not negative, is to adjust the expected growth rate in earnings, especially in the near term, to reflect expected changes in the economic cycle. This would imply using a higher growth rate in the next year or two, if both the firm's earnings and the economy are depressed currently but are expected to recover quickly. The strategy would be reversed if the current earnings are inflated (because of an economic boom), and if the economy is expected to slow down. The disadvantage of this approach is that it ties the accuracy of the estimate of value for a cyclical firm to the precision of the macroeconomic predictions of the analyst doing the valuation. The criticism, though, may not be avoidable because it is difficult to value a cyclical firm without making assumptions about future economic growth. The actual growth rate in earnings in turning-point years (years when the economy goes into or comes out of a recession) can be estimated by looking at the experience of this firm (or similar firms) in prior recessions.

ILLUSTRATION 22.2:   Valuing a Cyclical Company Using a Higher Growth Rate—Dana Corporation in May 2011

Dana manufactures automotive components and systems and was badly hurt by the global recession in 2008 and 2009; the company reported operating losses of $123 million in 2008 and $141 million in 2009. Although the company reported an operating profit of $196 million in 2010, the operating margin for the year amounted to only 3.21%. While the company is mature, it is anticipated that as the economy continues to improve, operating profits will grow 15% a year for the 2011–2015 time period as margins improve. After 2015, the firm is expected to revert to stable growth, with revenues and operating income growing at 3% a year forever, and with the firm earning a return on capital equal to its cost of capital in perpetuity.

   The firm is expected to have a beta of 1.20 in perpetuity and maintain its existing debt-to-capital ratio of 26.32%. However, while the pretax cost of debt for the 2011–2015 time period will remain at the existing level of 6.85% (based on its bond rating), we assume that it will drop to 5% after 2015. Using a marginal tax rate of 40%, a risk-free rate of 3.5%, and an equity risk premium of 5%, we estimate the cost of capital for Dana in both high and stable growth:

$$\text{Cost of capital}_{\text{high growth}} = \text{Cost of equity } [E/(D+E)] + \text{Cost of debt}(1-t) \, [(D/(D+E)]$$

$$= [3.5\% + 1.2(5\%)](1 - .2632) + 6.85\%(1 - .4)(.2632) = 8.08\%$$

$$\text{Cost of capital}_{\text{stable growth}} = [3.5\% + 1.2(5\%)](1 - .2632) + 5\%(1 - .4)(.2632) = 7.79\%$$

In Table 22.1, we estimate the free cash flows to the firm for the 2011–2015 time period and discount them back at the cost of capital of 8.08%:

TABLE 22.1 Expected Earnings and Cash Flows—Dana Corp

	Current	1	2	3	4	5
Expected growth rate		15.00%	15.00%	15.00%	15.00%	15.00%
EBIT × (1 − Tax rate)	$117.60	$135.24	$155.53	$178.85	$205.68	$236.54
− (Capex–Depreciation)	$ 11.00	$ 12.72	$ 14.63	$ 16.83	$ 19.35	$ 22.25
− Change in WC	$ 16.00	$ 18.33	$ 21.08	$ 24.24	$ 27.87	$ 32.05
Free cash flow to firm	$ 90.60	$104.19	$119.82	$137.79	$158.46	$182.23
Cost of capital		8.08%	8.08%	8.08%	8.08%	8.08%
Present value @8.08%		$ 96.40	$102.57	$109.14	$116.12	$123.55

The sum of the present value amounts to $547.78 million. Note that we have assumed that the net cap ex and change in working capital will grow at the same rate as operating income.

To estimate the value at the end of the high growth period, we estimate the reinvestment rate based on the stable growth rate and return on capital:

Stable growth rate = 3%

Stable return on capital = 7.79% (equal to cost of capital in stable growth)

Stable reinvestment rate = g/ROC = 3%/7.79% = 38.51%

$$\text{Terminal value} = \frac{\text{EBIT}_5(1 + g_{stable})(1 - \text{Reinvestment rate})}{(\text{Cost of capital} - g_{stable})}$$

$$= \frac{236.54(1.03)(1 - .3851)}{(.0779 - 0.03)} = \$3,127.69$$

Discounting the terminal value back at 8.08% for five years and adding to the present value of the cash flows over the five years yields a value for the operating assets of $2668 million:

Value of operating assets = $547.78 + $3127.69/1.0808^5 = $2,668 million

Adding the cash balance of $1,134 million, subtracting out debt outstanding of $947 million and dividing by the number of shares outstanding (146.26 million) yields a value per share of $19.52.

$$\text{Value of equity per share} = \frac{2668 + 1134 - 947}{146.26} = \$19.52/\text{share}$$

This was about 8% higher than the stock price of $18.13 at the end of May 2011.

Normalize Earnings   For cyclical firms, the easiest solution to the problem of volatile earnings over time and negative earnings in the base period, is to normalize earnings. When normalizing earnings for a firm with negative earnings, we are simply trying to answer the question: "What would this firm earn in a normal year?" Implicit in this statement is the assumption that the current year is not a normal year, and earnings will recover quickly to normal levels. This approach, therefore, is most appropriate for cyclical firms in mature businesses. There are several ways in which earnings can be normalized:

■ *Average the firm's dollar earnings over prior periods.* The simplest way to normalize earnings is to use the average earnings over prior periods. How many periods should you go back in time? For cyclical firms, you should go back long enough to cover an entire economic cycle—between 5 and 10 years. While this approach is simple, it is best suited for firms that have not changed in scale (or size) over the period. If it is applied to a firm that has become larger or smaller (in terms of the number of units it sells or total revenues) over time, it will result in a normalized estimate that is incorrect.

■ *Average the firm's return on investment or profit margins over prior periods.* This approach is similar to the first one, but the averaging is done on scaled earnings (operating margins or return on capital) instead of dollar earnings. The advantage of the approach is that it allows the normalized earnings estimate to reflect the current size of the firm. Thus a firm with an average return on capital of 12 percent over prior periods and a current capital invested of $1,000 million would have normalized operating income of $120 million. Using average return on equity and book value of equity yields normalized net income. A close variant of this approach is to estimate the average operating or net margin in prior periods and apply this margin to current revenues to arrive at normalized operating or net income. The advantage of working with revenues is that they are less susceptible to accounting manipulation.

There is one final question that we have to deal with when normalizing earnings, and it relates to when earnings will be normalized. Replacing current earnings with normalized earnings essentially is equivalent to assuming that normalization will occur quickly (i.e., in the very first time period of the valuation). If earnings will not return to normalized levels for several periods, the value obtained by normalizing current earnings will be too high. A simple correction that can be applied is to discount the value back by the number of periods it will take to normalize earnings.

ILLUSTRATION 22.3: Valuing a Cyclical Company Using Normalized Earnings: Toyota Motor Corporation in March 2009

In the years leading up to 2008, Toyota Motor Corporation acquired a reputation for efficiency and innovation. The banking crisis of 2008 and the slowing down of the global economy, however, led to Toyota reporting a loss in the last quarter of 2008, a precursor to much lower earnings in its 2008–2009 fiscal year (stretching from April 2008 to March 2009). To normalize Toyota's operating income, we looked at its operating performance from 1998 to 2008 in Table 22.2:

TABLE 22.2 Expected Earnings and Cash Flows—Toyota

Year	Revenues (millions)	Operating Income (millions)	EBITDA	Operating Margin	EBITDA Margin
1998	¥11,678,400	¥ 779,800	¥1,382,950	6.68%	11.84%
1999	¥12,749,010	¥ 774,947	¥1,415,997	6.08%	11.11%
2000	¥12,879,560	¥ 775,982	¥1,430,982	6.02%	11.11%
2001	¥13,424,420	¥ 870,131	¥1,542,631	6.48%	11.49%
2002	¥15,106,300	¥1,123,475	¥1,822,975	7.44%	12.07%
2003	¥16,054,290	¥1,363,680	¥2,101,780	8.49%	13.09%

Year	Revenues (millions)	Operating Income (millions)	EBITDA	Operating Margin	EBITDA Margin
2004	¥17,294,760	¥1,666,894	¥2,454,994	9.64%	14.20%
2005	¥18,551,530	¥1,672,187	¥2,447,987	9.01%	13.20%
2006	¥21,036,910	¥1,878,342	¥2,769,742	8.93%	13.17%
2007	¥23,948,090	¥2,238,683	¥3,185,683	9.35%	13.30%
2008	¥26,289,240	¥2,270,375	¥3,312,775	8.64%	12.60%
2009 (est)	¥22,661,325	¥ 267,904	¥1,310,304	1.18%	5.78%
Average		¥1,306,867		7.33%	

We considered three different normalization techniques:

- *Average income:* Averaging operating income from 1998 to 2008 yields a value of 1,306.9 billion yen. Since the revenues over the period more than doubled, this will understate the normalized operating income for the firm.

- *Industry average margin:* The average pretax operating margin of automobile firms (global) over the same time period (1998–2008) is about 6%. In 2009, however, many of these firms were in far worse shape than Toyota, and many are likely to report large losses. While we could apply the industry average margin to Toyota's 2009 revenues to estimate a normalized operating income (6% of 22,661 billion yen = 1,360 billion yen), this would understate the normalized operating income, since it will not reflect the fact that Toyota has been among the most profitable firms in the sector.

- *Historical margin:* Averaging the pretax operating margin from 1998 to 2008 yields an average operating margin of 7.33%. Applying this margin to the revenues in 2009 yields a normalized operating income of 1,660.7 billion yen (7.33% of 22,661 billion yen), an estimate that captures both the larger scale of the firm today and its success in this business. We will use this value as our normalized operating income.

To value the firm, we made the following assumptions.

- To estimate Toyota's cost of equity, we used a bottom-up beta (estimated from the automobile sector) of 1.10. Using the 10-year Japanese yen government bond rate of 1.50% as the risk-free rate and an equity risk premium of 6.5% (reflecting a mature market premium of 6% in early 2009 and an additional 0.50% for Toyota's exposure to emerging market risk), we computed a cost of equity of 8.65%.

$$\text{Cost of equity} = \text{Risk-free rate} + \text{Beta} \times \text{Equity risk premium}$$
$$= 1.50\% + 1.10 \times (6.5\%) = 8.65\%$$

- In early 2009, Toyota had 11,862 billion yen in debt outstanding, and the market value of equity for the firm was 10,551 billion (3.448 billion shares outstanding at 3,060 yen/share). Using a rating of AA and an associated default spread of 1.75% over the risk-free rate, we estimated a pretax cost of debt of 3.25%. Assuming that the current debt ratio is a sustainable one, we estimated a cost of capital of 5.09%; the marginal tax rate for Japan in 2009 was 40.7%.

$$\text{Debt ratio} = 11,862/(11,862 + 10,551) = 52.9\%$$
$$\text{Cost of capital} = 8.65\%(.471) + 3.25\%(1 - .407)(.529) = 5.09\%$$

- We estimated the cost of capital for Toyota over time, and since neither the debt ratio nor the cost of capital has moved substantially over time, we will use this as the normalized cost of capital.

■ Since Toyota was already the largest automobile firm in the world in terms of market share, we assumed that the firm was in stable growth, growing at 1.50% (capped at the risk-free rate) in perpetuity. We also assumed that the firm will be able to generate a return on capital equal to its cost of capital on its investments. The reinvestment rate that emerges from these two assumptions is 29.46%:

$$\text{Stable period reinvestment rate} = \frac{g}{ROIC} = \frac{.015}{.0509} = .2946$$

Bringing together the normalized operating income (1,660.7 billion yen), the marginal tax rate for Japan (40.7%), the reinvestment rate (29.46%), the stable growth rate of 1.5%, and the cost of capital of 5.09%, we estimated the value of the operating assets at Toyota:

$$\text{Value}_{\text{operating assets}} = \frac{\text{Operating income } (1 + g)(1 - \text{tax rate})(1 - \text{Reinvestment rate})}{(\text{Cost of capital} - g)}$$

$$= \frac{1{,}660.7 \,(1.015)(1 - 0.407)(1 - .2946)}{(0.0509 - 0.015)} = 19{,}640 \text{ billion yen}$$

Adding in cash (2,288 billion yen) and nonoperating assets (6,845 billion yen), subtracting out debt (11,862 billion yen) and minority interests in consolidated subsidiaries (583 billion yen), and dividing by the number of shares (3.448 billion) yielded a value per share of 4,735 yen/share.

$$\text{Value per share} = \frac{\text{Operating assets} + \text{Cash} + \text{Nonoperating assets} - \text{Debt} - \text{Minority interests}}{\text{Number of shares}}$$

$$= \frac{19640 + 2288 + 6845 - 11862 - 583}{3.448} = 4735 \text{ yen/share}$$

Based on the normalized income, Toyota looked significantly undervalued at its stock price of 3,060 yen per share in early 2009.

 normearn.xls: **This spreadsheet allows you to normalize the earnings for a firm, using a variety of approaches.**

Valuing Commodity and Natural Resource Firms   Commodity prices are not only volatile but go through cycles—periods of high prices followed by periods with lower prices. Some natural resource companies smooth out their earnings using futures and options contracts, but many let the price changes flow through into their bottom lines. As a consequence, the earnings of commodity companies tend to move up and down with commodity prices. To value natural resource companies—and that group would include not just oil and mining firms but also forest product firms (such as timber) and agricultural businesses—you have three choices:

1. One is to try to forecast future commodity prices—the commodity price cycle—and build these forecasts into expected revenues in future years. This is not only difficult to do since the cycles are unpredictable but dangerous, since the value that you obtain will then be the joint result of your assessment of the company and your views on commodity prices. Put simply, if you value Royal Dutch on the assumption that oil prices will double over the next five years, you will almost certainly find it to be undervalued, but mostly because of your oil price views.

2. You could value the firms using a normalized commodity price, estimated by looking at the average price of the commodity over a cycle. Thus, the average price of coffee over the past decade can be used to estimate the value of a coffee plantation. The danger, of course, is that the price of coffee may stay well above or below this average price for an extended period, throwing off estimates of value.

3. You could value the firm's current production using the observable market prices for the commodity, in the spot and forward markets, even if these prices are at historic lows or highs, and then use simulations to incorporate the effect of commodity price swings.

In choosing between these approaches, recognize that you are making assumptions about future commodity prices implicitly in the first two approaches, and that can be dangerous. If your response is that your strength is in taking a commodity price view, you can take advantage of that strength by buying or selling commodity futures/options, rather than through commodity companies.

MACROECONOMIC VIEWS AND VALUATION

The earnings of cyclical firms tend to be volatile, with volatility linked to how well or badly the economy is performing. One way to incorporate these effects into value is to build in expectations of when future recessions and recoveries will occur into the cash flows. This exercise is fraught with danger, since the error in such predictions is likely to be very large. Economists seldom agree on when a recovery is imminent, and most categorizations of recessions occur after the fact. Furthermore, a valuation that is based on specific macroeconomic forecasts makes it difficult for users to separate how much of the final recommendation (i.e., that the firm is under- or overvalued) comes from the firm being mispriced and how much reflects the analyst's optimism or the pessimism about the overall economy.

The other way to incorporate earnings variability into the valuation is through the discount rate—cyclical firms tend to be more risky and require higher discount rates. This is what we do when we use higher unlevered betas and/or costs of debt for cyclical firms.

ILLUSTRATION 22.4:   A Commodity-Price-Neutral Valuation of a Commodity Company: Exxon Mobil in 2009

Exxon Mobil may be the largest of the oil companies, with diversified operations in multiple locations, but it is as dependent on oil prices as the rest of the companies in its sector. Figure 22.2 shows Exxon's operating income as a function of the average oil price each year from 1985 to 2008.

The operating income clearly increases (or decreases) as the oil price increases (or decreases). We regress the operating income against the oil price per barrel over the period and obtain the following:

$$\text{Operating Income} = -6,395 + 911.32 \, (\text{Average Oil Price}) \quad R^2 = 90.2\%$$
$$(2.95) \quad (14.59)$$

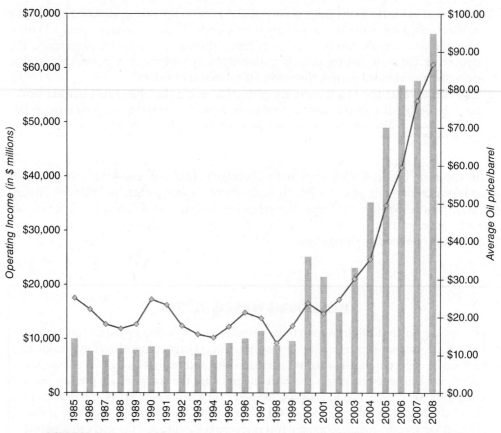

FIGURE 22.2   Exxon Mobil – Operating income versus Oil prices—1985 to 2008

Put another way, Exxon Mobil's operating income increases about $9.11 billion for every $10 increase in the price per barrel of oil, and 90% of the variation in Exxon's earnings over time comes from movements in oil prices.[2]

To get from operating income to equity value at Exxon, we make the following assumptions:

▨   We estimate a bottom-up beta of 0.90 for Exxon Mobil. Then we use the Treasury bond rate of 2.5% and an equity risk premium of 6.5% to estimate a cost of equity:

$$\text{Cost of Equity} = 2.5\% + 0.90\ (6.5\%) = 8.35\%$$

Exxon has $9.4 billion of debt outstanding and a market capitalization of $320.4 billion (4,941.63 million shares, trading at $64.83 per share), resulting in a debt ratio of 2.85%. As an AAA-rated company, its cost of debt is expected to be 3.75%, reflecting a default spread of 1.25% over the

---

[2] The relationship is very strong at Exxon because it has been a large and stable firm for decades. It is likely that the relationship between earnings and oil prices will be weaker at smaller, evolving oil companies.

risk-free rate. Using a marginal tax rate of 38% (rather than the effective tax rate), we estimate a cost of capital of 8.18% for the firm:

$$\text{Cost of Capital} = 8.35\% \, (.9715) + 3.75\% \, (1 - .38) \, (.0285) = 8.18\%$$

▓ Exxon Mobil is in stable growth, with the operating income growing at 2% a year in perpetuity. New investments are expected to generate a return on capital that reflects the normalized operating income and current capital invested. This return on capital is used to compute a reinvestment rate.

Exxon reported pre-tax operating income in excess of $60 billion in 2008, but that reflects the fact that the average oil price during the year was $86.55. By March 2009, the price per barrel of oil had dropped to $45, and the operating income for the coming year will be much lower. Using the regression results, the expected operating income at this oil price is $34,614 billion:

$$\text{Operating Income (given current oil price)} = -6,395 + 911.32 \, (\$45) = \$34,614$$

This operating income translates into a return on capital of approximately 21% and a reinvestment rate of 9.52%, based on a 2% growth rate[3]:

$$\text{Return on invested capital} = \frac{34,614 \, (1 - .38)}{101,629} = 21.11\%$$

$$\text{Reinvestment Rate} = \frac{\text{Stable growth rate}}{\text{ROIC}} = \frac{2.00\%}{21.11\%} = 9.52\%$$

$$\text{Value of Operating Assets} = \frac{\text{Operating income } (1 - \text{tax rate})(1 + \text{Stable growth rate})}{(1 - \text{Reinvestment Rate})} \bigg/ (\text{Cost of capital} - \text{Stable growth rate})$$

$$= \frac{34,614 \times (1 - .38) \times (1.02)(1 - .0952)}{(.0818 - .02)}$$

$$= \$320,472 \text{ million(with rounding)}$$

Adding the current cash balance ($32,007 million), subtracting debt ($9,400 million), and dividing by the number of shares (4,941.63 million) yields the value per share:

$$\text{Value per share} = \frac{\text{Operating assets} + \text{Cash} - \text{Debt}}{\text{Number of shares}}$$

$$= \frac{320472 + 32007 - 9400}{4941.63} = \$69.43$$

At its stock price of $64.83 in 2009, the stock looked slightly undervalued, at the prevailing oil price of $45/barrel. Figure 22.3 shows the value of Exxon Mobil as a function of the oil price.

---

[3] To compute the return on capital, we aggregate the book value of equity ($126,044 million), the book value of debt ($9,566 million), and netted-out cash ($33,981 million) from the end of 2007 to arrive at an invested capital value of $101,629 million. Exxon's effective tax rate of 38% is used in the calculation.

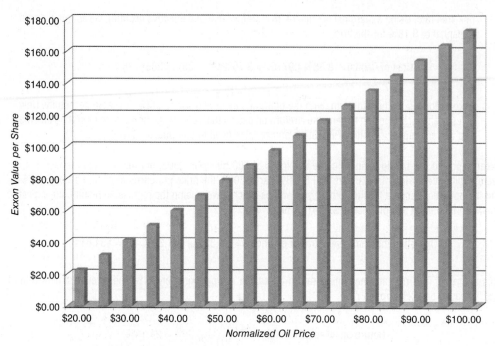

FIGURE 22.3   Oil Price and Value per Share for Exxon Mobil

As the oil price changes, the operating income and the return on capital change. We keep the capital-invested number fixed and reestimate the return on capital with the estimated operating income. If the oil price is $42.52, the value per share is $64.83, equal to the current stock price. Put another way, any investor who believes that the oil price will stabilize above this level will find Exxon Mobil to be undervalued. Since the value per share is so dependent on the oil price, it would make more sense to allow the oil price to vary and value the company as a function of this price. In Chapter 33, we will return to look at this valuation, using simulation to look at the effect of uncertain oil prices on estimated value.

Infrastructure Investments (Firms)   As we noted at the start of this chapter, a mature infrastructure company that holds a portfolio of infrastructure investments, at different stages in the investment cycle, can be valued using conventional approaches, since the cash flow patterns across time (an initial extended period of negative cashflows followed by a long period of positive cash flows) will get averaged out across the portfolio. In this section, we will focus on the more difficult scenario of a firm with a single infrastructure investment, with the valuation occurring at the start of the investment period.

Investment Cash (out)Flows   The feature that sets apart infrastructure investments is that they often require large investments up front, and that you must wait for long periods before these investments are functional (i.e., you are able to generate revenues and earnings). Building a new airport can take a decade or more, partly because of the complexities of construction and partly because of legal and regulatory barriers to overcome. The Dubai International Airport, which was completed in ten years, was regarded as a model for timeliness. The construction of a toll road can take years, again with legal challenges to overcome. The very first toll road in the world, the Lancaster turnpike, connecting Philadelphia to Lancaster, was initiated in 1795, funded by an equity issuance, and was operational in 1797. The Mumbai Trans Harbor Link, a 23-mile toll road connecting Mumbai with Navi Mumbai, was proposed in 2012, initiated in 2016, and operational in 2024.

During the period of construction, the cashflows are not only negative but are often structured around contractual agreements, where there are cash payments due to a variety of contractors. That insight is key to assessing how these cash flows should be treated in valuation, since the core rule in discounting is that the discount rate should reflect the risk in the cash flow. In short, since the initial investment cash flows are not operating cash flows but contractual claims, they should be discounted back at a "lower" rate. In practical terms, and assuming that you are contracted to spend these cash flows, the right discount rate should be the cost of debt for investing company.

As a stand-alone investment, the fact that there are no revenues and only expenses in the investment period implies that there are no tax savings to these expenses at the time they are incurred, though you will still have to keep track of the net operating losses to carry forward into the operating period.

Operating Cashflows   Once an infrastructure investment becomes operational, you can start generating revenues and perhaps even profits, though the volatility in these cash flows will depend in large part on how the infrastructure investment is monetized.

- *Fixed fees:* If the cash flows that will be generated from the infrastructure investment are fixed and contractually set, they are generally lower-risk, and the right discount rate to apply on these cash flows will be one that reflects the default risk of the guarantor. Thus, if an airport owner is set to receive contractually set payments from the government, the discount rate will be the government bond rate, whereas if the payments are from the airlines that will be using the airport, the discount rate will be the pretax cost of debt of the airlines.
- *Usage revenues:* If the revenues from the infrastructure investments is tied to the usage of the infrastructure, with users paying, the discount rate should reflect the resulting uncertainty. Thus, a toll road operator's cash flow will reflect the volatility in toll road revenues over time, and can perhaps be estimated by looking at the costs of capital of publicly traded companies that derive their revenues from road transportation.
- *Other:* There are other revenue models that can be tied to infrastructure investments, including advertising revenues and subscription revenues, and the discount rates used should reflect the uncertainty in each stream.

Cost of Capital   The cost of capital for a infrastructure project/company is, as is the case with all other firms, a weighted average of its cost of equity and an after-tax cost of debt, with the weights reflecting the estimated or market values of each, with a few key divergences:

- *Shifting Debt ratio and cost of debt:* While is not a requirement, many infrastructure companies choose to borrow significant amounts to fund their investment needs in the early years of the project, and often pay that debt down over the lifetime of the project. As a result, the mix of debt and equity will change over the project's lifetime, from high debt in the early years to little or no debt in the later years. In tandem, the cost of debt may also start high, before a project becomes operational, and decrease as it starts generating cash flow.

▪ *Tax benefits:* Since infrastructure investments are money-losing in the early years, there will be no taxes due or tax benefits from debt. Since these tax benefits will accrue once the investment starts making money, the effect on value of assuming a tax benefit on debt, even in the money-losing years, will be small.

▪ *Cost of equity:* In Chapter 8, we introduced the notion of a levered beta, a function of the operating risk in an investment and the debt used in funding it:

$$\text{Levered beta} = \text{Unlevered beta} \, (1 + (1 - \text{tax rate}) \, (\text{Debt/Equity}))$$

If the debt ratio changes over time for an infrastructure investment, it follows that the cost of equity will also change over time, decreasing as the debt ratio decreases.

In the face of a shifting capital structure, there are two choices that you face, when valuing infrastructure investments:

1. *Year-specific costs of capital:* In the first approach, the cost of capital is computed each year, with the estimated debt ratio and costs of debt and equity in that year, with the tax advantage being applied to debt, only if the project's earnings are taxable.
2. *Average cost of capital across project life:* In the second approach, the cost of capital is computed using an average debt ratio and cost of debt over the project life, with a beta reflecting that average debt ratio.

As you have probably noted in earlier chapters, we are not averse to using time-varying costs of capital when valuing company, but in the case of a stand-alone infrastructure investment, we believe that using an average cost of capital as the discount rate, at least for the operating cash flows, is the better approach.

Terminal Value   As we noted in the introduction to this chapter, closure when valuing infrastructure projects will depend upon what you assume about the project's life:

▪ If individual projects have finite lives, the terminal value will reflect what you can get as salvage value at the end of those lives. That will however require estimating cash flows for the entire investment life; a 30-year life will require estimating expected cash flows for the next 30 years, before the salvage or liquidation value calculation. Thus, the value of an infrastructure investment with a n-year life can be written as:

$$\text{Value of investment} = \sum_{t=1}^{t=n} \frac{E(\text{Cashflow}_t)}{(1 + r)^t} + \frac{\text{Salvage value in year n}}{(1 + r)^n}$$

▪ If the investment life is long enough, say 80 or 100 years, you will be better served estimating cashflows for a finite period much lower than the investment life, and then estimating a terminal value that reflects the expected value of cash flows for the remaining life. Thus, with a 80-year project, you can estimate expected cash flows for the next ten years, and then estimate the terminal value as the present value of expected cash flows for the next 70 years. For an investment with a life of n years, and assuming that you stop estimating cash flows over a shorter time period of n1, and assuming a growth rate:

$$\text{Value of investment} = \sum_{t=1}^{t=n1} \frac{E(\text{Cashflow}_t)}{(1 + r)^t}$$
$$+ \frac{\text{PV of expected cashflows from years n1 to n}}{(1 + r)^{n1}}$$

■ If, with sufficient reinvestment, you can keep an infrastructure investment alive for an indefinite period, you can borrow the perpetual growth equation used for most publicly traded companies, with the caveat that the growth rate in stable growth (g_n) has to be set to the inflation rate or below, and not include real growth.

$$\text{Value of investment} = \sum_{t=1}^{t=n} \frac{E(\text{Cashflow}_t)}{(1 + r)^t} + \frac{E(\text{Cashflow}_{n+1})}{(r - g_n)(1 + r)^n}$$

ILLUSTRATION 22.5:   Valuing a Toll Road

Roadways Inc. is a company that has been created to construct and manage a single toll road, and the following information relates to the investment:

■ *Investment costs/timeline:* The toll road will take five years to construct, with an expected investment cost of $50 million next year, growing 2% a year for the following four years. This investment will be depreciated straight line over fifty years, starting in year 6.

■ *Revenues details:* The toll road will be ready for operation in year 6, and Roadways expects to generate $75.92 million in revenues that year. These revenues are expected to grow 4% a year for the following nine years; after year 15, the expected growth rate will converge on the inflation rate of 2%, and continue through year 75, at which point ownership of the roads will revert to the government, with no compensation to Roadways.

■ *Operating expenses:* The direct cost of operating the toll road will amount to 20% of revenues, but there are fixed costs of $10 million starting in year 6, expected to grow at the inflation rate after that.

■ *Taxes:* The company faces a marginal tax rate of 25%, and net operating losses can be carried forward until utilized.

■ *Capital maintenance:* Once operational, the company plans to utilize 40% of its depreciation each year in capital maintenance.

■ *Cost of capital:* While the company plans to borrow much of the initial investment, it plans to pay that debt down over the project life. The average debt to capital ratio across the project life if 40%, and the cost of equity at that debt ratio is estimated to be 12% and the pre-tax cost of borrowing, on average, will be 5%.

We begin by estimating the present value of the cost of building the toll roads over the next five years in Table 22.3:

TABLE 22.3 Construction costs and present value

	1	2	3	4	5
Toll road costs (in millions)	−$50.00	−$51.00	−$52.02	−$53.06	−$54.12
Discount rate used	5.00%	5.00%	5.00%	5.00%	5.00%
Present value (in millions)	−$47.62	−$46.26	−$44.94	−$43.65	−$42.41

Note that the costs of construction are mostly contractually set, and the pretax cost of debt is used as the discount rate, yielding a total investment cost of −$224.87 million.

The expected operating income in the first ten years of operation are in Table 22.4:

TABLE 22.4 Expected Earnings on Investment

Year	Revenues	Operating expenses	Depreciation	EBIT	Taxes	EBIT (1−t)
6	$ 75.92	$25.18	$5.20	$45.53	$ 0.00	$45.53
7	$ 78.96	$25.99	$5.20	$47.76	$ 0.00	$47.76
8	$ 82.11	$26.83	$5.20	$50.08	$ 0.00	$50.08
9	$ 85.40	$27.69	$5.20	$52.50	$ 0.00	$52.50
10	$ 88.81	$28.59	$5.20	$55.02	$ 0.00	$55.02
11	$ 92.37	$29.51	$5.20	$57.65	$12.09	$45.56
12	$ 96.06	$30.47	$5.20	$60.38	$15.10	$45.29
13	$ 99.90	$31.47	$5.20	$63.23	$15.81	$47.42
14	$103.90	$32.50	$5.20	$66.20	$16.55	$49.65
15	$108.06	$33.56	$5.20	$69.29	$17.32	$51.97

Note that the company has enough accumulated losses to fully shelter income from taxes from years 6 through 10 and partially in year 11. Adding back depreciation and subtracting capital maintenance yields free cashflows to the firm, and discounting back at a cumulated cost of capital results in the present value of the free cashflows to the firm (in Table 22.5):

TABLE 22.5 Cash Flows and present value

Year	EBIT (1−t)	+ Depreciation	− Capital Maintenance	FCFF	WACC[4]	Cumulated WACC[5]	PV
6	$45.53	$5.20	$2.08	$48.65	9.20%	1.3937	$34.91
7	$47.76	$5.20	$2.08	$50.88	9.20%	1.5219	$33.43
8	$50.08	$5.20	$2.08	$53.21	9.20%	1.6619	$32.01
9	$52.50	$5.20	$2.08	$55.63	9.20%	1.8148	$30.65

---

[4]We use the cost of equity of 12%, the pretax cost of debt of 5% and the debt ratio of 40% all through the project life, but the cost of capital changes over time because the tax rate is zero from years 6–10, is 20.97% in year 11 and reaches 25% only in year 12.

[5]Cumulated WACC in year 6 = $(1.05)^5 \times (1.092)$; Cumulated WACC in year 7 = $(1.05)^5 \times (1.092)^2$

Year	EBIT (1−t)	+ Depreciation	− Capital Maintenance	FCFF	WACC[4]	Cumulated WACC[5]	PV
10	$55.02	$5.20	$2.08	$58.15	9.20%	1.9818	$29.34
11	$45.56	$5.20	$2.08	$48.68	8.78%	2.1558	$22.58
12	$45.29	$5.20	$2.08	$48.41	8.70%	2.3434	$20.66
13	$47.42	$5.20	$2.08	$50.55	8.70%	2.5472	$19.84
14	$49.65	$5.20	$2.08	$52.77	8.70%	2.7689	$19.06
15	$51.97	$5.20	$2.08	$55.09	8.70%	3.0097	$18.30

The sum of the present value of the expected cash flows over year 6 through 15 is $260.80 million. At the end of year 15, when the cash flow growth drops to the inflation rate, we estimate a terminal value of the cash flows from years 16–75, using a growing annuity formula:[6]

$$\text{Terminal value} = \frac{FCFF_{15}(1 + g_n)\left(1 - \dfrac{(1 + g)^n}{(1 + r)^n}\right)}{(Cost\ of\ capital - g)}$$

$$= \frac{55.09(1.02)\left(1 - \dfrac{(1.02)^{60}}{(1.087)^{60}}\right)}{(0.087 - 0.02)} = \$820.24\ \text{million}$$

To compute the present value of the terminal value, we use the cumulated cost of capital for year 15:

$$\text{PV of terminal value} = \frac{\$820.24}{3.0097} = \$272.53$$

We can now estimate the value of the toll road, in total, by adding the present value of the expected cash flows and the terminal value:

$$\text{Value of toll road} = \text{PV of investment costs} + \text{PV of cash flows during years 6–15} +$$
$$\text{PV of terminal value}$$
$$= -\$224.87 + \$260.80 + \$272.53 = \$308.45\ \text{million}$$

To estimate the value of equity, you would net out the debt due, which will vary over time. At the start of the project, when the debt due is $123.38 million, the value of equity in the project is as follows:

$$\text{Value of equity} = \text{Value of toll road} - \text{Debt}$$
$$= \$308.45 - \$123.38 = \$185.07\ \text{million}$$

Firms with Long-Term Problems

In all the valuations presented in the last section, earnings were adjusted either instantaneously to reflect normal levels or very quickly, reflecting our belief that the negative earnings will soon pass. In some cases, though, the negative earnings are a manifestation of

---

[6]Assuming that cash flows last forever would have increased the terminal value but only marginally to $838.69 million, explaining why the growing perpetuity assumption works well for very long term investments.

more long-term problems at the firm. In such cases, we will be forced to make judgments on whether the problem will be overcome, and if so, when this will occur. This section presents a range of solutions for companies in this position.

MULTIPLES AND NORMALIZED EARNINGS

Would you have to make these adjustments to earnings if you were doing relative valuation rather than discounted cash flow valuation? The answer is generally yes, and when adjustments are not made, you are implicitly assuming normalization of earnings.

To see why, assume that you are comparing steel companies using price-earnings ratios and that one of the firms in your group has just reported very low earnings because of a strike during the past year. If you do not normalize the earnings, this firm will look overvalued relative to the sector, because the market price will be based on the expectation that the labor troubles, though costly, are in the past. If you use a multiple such as price-to-sales to make your relative valuation judgments and you compare this firm's price-to-sales ratio to the industry average, you are assuming that the firm's margins will converge on industry averages sooner rather than later.

What if an entire sector's earnings are affected by an event? Would you still need to normalize? We believe so. Though the earnings of all automobile stocks may be affected by a recession, the degree to which they are affected can vary widely depending on differences in operating and financial leverage. Furthermore, you will find yourself unable to compute multiples such as price-earnings ratios for many of the firms in the group that lose money during recessions. Using normalized earnings will yield multiples that are more reliable measures of true value.

Strategic Problems   Firms can sometimes make mistakes in terms of the product mixes they offer, the marketing strategies they adopt, or even the markets that they choose to target. They often end up paying a substantial cost in terms of negative or lower earnings and perhaps a permanent loss of market share. Consider the following examples:

- IBM found its dominant position in the mainframe computer business and the extraordinary profitability of that business was challenged by the explosion of the personal computer market in the 1980s. While IBM could have developed the operating system for personal computers early in the process, it ceded that business to an upstart called Microsoft. By 1989, IBM had lost more than half its market value and its return on equity had dropped into the single digits.[7]
- For decades, Xerox dominated the copier business to the extent that its name became synonymous with the product. In the 1970s and 1980s, it was challenged for the market by Asian firms with lower cost structures like Ricoh and Canon. After initial losses, Xerox was able to recoup some of its market share. However, the last part of

---

[7]It is worth noting that IBM made a fulsome recovery in the following decades by going back to basics, cutting costs, and refocusing its efforts on business services.

the 1990s saw a steady decline in Xerox's fortunes as technology (in the form of e-mails, faxes, and low-cost printers) took its toll. By the end of 2000, there were questions about whether Xerox had a future.

▪ Under the leadership of Michael Armstrong, AT&T tried to shed its image as a stodgy phone company and become a technology firm. After some initial successes, a series of miscues and poor acquisitions saw the firm enter the new millennium with a vastly reduced market capitalization and no clear vision on where to go next.

When firms have low or negative earnings that can be traced to strategic missteps, you must determine whether the shift is a permanent one. If it is, you will have to value the firm on the assumption that it will never recover lost ground and scale down your expectations of revenue growth and expected margins. If, on the other hand, you are more optimistic about the firm's recovery or its entry into new markets, you can assume that the firm will be able to revert to its traditional margins and high growth.

Operating Problems Firms that are less efficient in the delivery of goods and services than their competitors will also be less profitable and less valuable. But how and why do firms become less efficient? In some cases, the reasons can be traced to a failure to keep up with the times and replenish assets and keep up with the latest technology. A steel company whose factories are decades old and whose equipment is outdated will generally bear higher costs for every ton of steel that it produces than its newer competitors. In other cases, the problem may be labor costs. A steel company with plants in the United States faces much higher labor costs than a similar company in Asia.

The variable that best measures operating efficiency is the operating margin, with firms that have operating problems tending to have much lower margins than their competitors. One way to build in the effect of operating improvements over time is to increase the margin toward the industry average, but the speed with which the margins will converge will depend on several factors:

▪ *Size of the firm.* Generally, the larger the firm, the longer it will take to eliminate inefficiencies. Not only is inertia a much stronger force in large firms, but the absolute magnitude of the changes that have to be made are much larger. A firm with $10 billion in revenues will have to cut costs by $300 million to achieve a 3-percent improvement in pretax operating margin, whereas a firm with $100 million in revenues will have to cut costs by $3 million to accomplish the same objective.

▪ *Nature of the inefficiency.* Some inefficiencies can be fixed far more quickly than others. For instance, a firm can replace outdated equipment or a poor inventory system quickly, but retraining a labor force will take much more time.

▪ *External constraints.* Firms are often restricted in terms of how much and how quickly they can move to fix inefficiencies by contractual obligations and social pressure. For instance, laying off a large portion of the workforce may seem an obvious solution for a firm that is overstaffed, but union contracts and the potential for negative publicity may make firms reluctant to do so.

▪ *Management quality.* A management that is committed to change is a critical component of a successful turnaround. In some cases, a replacement of top management may be necessary for a firm to be able to resolve its operating problems.

The Special Case of Privatizations   In many privatizations, we are called on to value firms with long financial histories but not very profitable ones. The lack of profitability is not surprising, since many of these firms have been run with objectives other than maximizing value or profitability. In some cases, employment in these firms has been viewed as a source of political patronage. Consequently, they end up overstaffed and inefficient.

Will this all change as soon as they are privatized? Not necessarily, and certainly not immediately. The power of unions to preserve existing jobs, the power that governments continue to have on how they are run, and the sheer size of these firms makes change both daunting and slow. While it is reasonable to assume that these firms will, in fact, become more efficient once they are privatized, the speed of the improvement will vary from firm to firm. In general, you would expect the adjustment to be much quicker if the government relinquishes its power to control the management of the firm and if there are strong competitive pressures to become more efficient. It will be slower if the firm is a monopoly, and the government continues to handpick the top management of the firm.

GOLDEN SHARES AND THE VALUE OF PRIVATIZED FIRMS

Whereas governments are always eager to receive the cash proceeds from privatizing the firms that they own, they are generally not as eager to give up control of these firms. One way they attempt to preserve power is by maintaining what is called a golden share in the firm that gives them veto power and control over some or many aspects of the firm's management.

For instance, the Brazilian government maintains a golden share in Vale, allowing it the final decision on whether mines can be closed and other major financial decisions. While governments often view these golden shares as a costless way to privatize and preserve control at the same time, there is a cost that they will bear. Investors valuing firms with golden shares will generally be much less willing to assume radical changes in management and improvements in efficiency. Consequently, the values attached to these firms by the market will be much lower. The more inefficient the firm being privatized and the more restrictive the golden share, the greater will be the loss in value to the government.

ILLUSTRATION 22.6:   Valuing a Privatization: Compahnia Vale Dio Roce (CVRD) in 1995

In 1995, the Brazilian government privatized Compahnia Vale Dio Roce (CVRD), Latin America's biggest mining company. In the year the firm was privatized, it reported after-tax operating income of 717 million BR on revenues of 4,714 million BR. Based on the capital invested in the firm at the beginning of the year of 14,722 million BR, the after-tax return on capital earned by the firm was 5.33%.

If we assumed a stable real growth rate of 3% and a real cost of capital of 10%, and valued CVRD based on these inputs, we would have estimated the following value for the firm:

$$\text{Reinvestment rate} = g/ROC = 3\%/5.33\% = 56.29\%$$

$$\text{Value of the firm} = \frac{\text{EBIT}(1-t)(1+g)(1-\text{Reinvestment rate})}{(\text{Cost of capital} - \text{Growth rate})}$$

$$= \frac{717\,(1.03)(1-0.5629)}{(.10-.03)}$$

$$= \$R\,4,611 \text{ million}$$

Note, though, that this assumes that CVRD's return on capital will remain at existing levels in perpetuity. If privatization leads to operating efficiencies at the firm, its margins and return on capital can be expected to improve. For instance, if we valued CVRD using the real return on capital of 7% earned by mining companies in the United States, we would have estimated the following:

$$\text{Reinvestment rate} = g/ROC = 3\%/7\% = 42.86\%$$

$$\text{Value of the firm} = \frac{\text{EBIT } (1 - t)(1 + g)(1 - \text{Reinvestment rate})}{(\text{Cost of capital} - \text{Growth rate})}$$

$$= \frac{717 \, (1.03)(1 - 0.4286)}{(.10 - .03)}$$

$$= \$R \, 6,029 \text{ million}$$

Is it reasonable to assume this improvement in margins? It depends on which side of the transaction you are on. If you were an investor interested in buying the stock, you might argue that the firm is too entrenched in its ways to make the changes needed for higher profitability, and you would then use the value estimated with current margins. If you are the government and want to obtain the highest value you can, you would argue for the latter.

Financial Leverage   In some cases, firms get into trouble because they borrow too much and not because of operating or strategic problems. In these cases, it will be the equity earnings that will be negative, while operating earnings will be positive. The solution to the problem depends, in large part, on how distressed the firm really is. If the distress is not expected to push the firm into bankruptcy, there are a variety of potential solutions. If, however, the distress could be terminal, finding a solution is much more difficult.

Overlevered with No Immediate Threat of Bankruptcy   Firms that borrow too much are not always on the verge of bankruptcy. In fact, firms with valuable operating assets and substantial operating cash flows can service much more debt than is optimal for them, even though they might not do so comfortably. So, what are the costs of being over levered? First, the firm might end up with a large enough exposure to default risk that it affects its operations—customers might not buy its products, suppliers might demand speedier payment, and it might have trouble retaining valued employees. Second, the higher beta and cost of debt that go with the higher leverage will increase the firm's cost of capital and reduce its value. It is, therefore, in the best interests of the firm to reduce its debt ratio, if not immediately, at least over time.

There are two choices when it comes to valuing levered firms as going concerns:

1. You can estimate free cash flows to the firm and value the firm. If the firm is operationally healthy (the operating margins are both positive and similar to those of comparable firms), the only modification you have to make is to reduce the debt ratio over time—in practical terms, a disproportionate share of the reinvestment each year has to come from equity—and compute costs of capital that change with the debt ratio. If the firm's operating margins have suffered because it borrowed too much, you might need to adjust the operating margins over time toward industry averages as well.

2. You can use the adjusted present value approach and value the firm as an unlevered firm and add to this unlevered firm value the costs (expected bankruptcy costs) and benefits (tax benefits) of debt. As noted in Chapter 15, though, estimating the expected bankruptcy cost can be difficult to do.

ILLUSTRATION 22.7:   Adjust Debt Ratio over Time: Hyundai

Hyundai Corporation is a Korean company that is part of the Hyundai Group and handles the trading operations for the firm. Like many other Korean companies, Hyundai borrowed large amounts to fund expansion until the late 1990s. By the end of 2000, Hyundai had debt outstanding of 848 billion Korean won (krw) and had a market value of equity of 163 billion krw, resulting in a debt-to-capital ratio of 83.85%. The high leverage has three consequences:

1. The bottom-up beta for the firm is 2.60, reflecting the firm's high debt-to-equity ratio. With a risk-free rate of 9% in Korean won and the risk premium of 7% (4% as the mature market premium and 3% for Korean country risk), we estimate a cost of equity in Korean won for the firm of 27.20%.

$$\text{Cost of equity} = 9\% + 2.6(7\%) = 27.20\%$$

2. The firm has a high default risk, leading to a pretax cost of borrowing in Korean won terms of 12.5%; the tax rate for the firm is 30%.
3. The firm reported pretax operating income of 89.42 billion krw, but the interest expenses of the firm amounted to 99 billion krw, resulting in a loss for the firm. Note, though, that the firm is still obtaining the tax benefits of almost all its interest payments.[8]

We assume that the operating income will grow 10% a year for the next six years and 8% a year beyond that point in time. Over that period, we assume that the firm's capital expenditures (which are currently 12 billion krw), depreciation (which is currently 4 billion krw), and noncash working capital (which is currently 341 billion krw) will grow at the same rate as operating income, yielding the following estimates for the cash flows (in Table 22.6):

TABLE 22.6   Expected free cash flows for years 1 through 6

	1	2	3	4	5	6
EBIT(1 − t)	$68.86	$75.74	$83.32	$91.65	$100.81	$110.89
+ Depreciation	$ 4.40	$ 4.84	$ 5.32	$ 5.86	$ 6.44	$ 7.09
− Capital spending	$13.20	$14.52	$15.97	$17.57	$ 19.33	$ 21.26
− Change in working capital	$34.11	$37.52	$41.27	$45.40	$ 49.94	$ 54.93
Free cash flow to firm	$25.95	$28.54	$31.40	$34.54	$ 37.99	$ 41.79

Over the next six years, we assume that the firm will reduce its debt ratio from 83.85% to 50%, which will result in the beta decreasing from 2.60 to 1.00 and the pretax cost of debt dropping from 12.5% to 10.5% (we assume that the changes occur linearly over the period.) The costs of capital for Hyundai are estimated each year for the next six years (in Table 22.7):

TABLE 22.7   Debt Ratios and Costs of Capital

	1	2	3	4	5	6
Beta	2.60	2.28	1.96	1.64	1.32	1.00
Cost of equity	27.20%	24.96%	22.72%	20.48%	18.24%	16.00%
Cost of debt (after-tax)	8.75%	8.47%	8.19%	7.91%	7.63%	7.35%
Debt ratio	83.85%	77.08%	70.31%	63.54%	56.77%	50.00%
Cost of capital	11.73%	12.25%	12.50%	12.49%	12.22%	11.68%

---

[8]Without interest expenses, Hyundai would have paid taxes on its operating income of 89 billion krw. Because of its interest payments, Hyundai was able to not pay taxes. Of the 99 billion krw in interest payments, Hyundai is receiving tax benefits on 89 billion krw.

To estimate the terminal value, we assume a growth rate of 8% in perpetuity after year 6, and a return on capital of 16%. This allows us to estimate a reinvestment rate and terminal value for the firm at the end of year 6:

$$\text{Reinvestment rate} = \frac{\textit{Stable growth rate}}{\textit{Stable period ROIC}} = \frac{.08}{.16} = .50$$

$$\text{Terminal value} = \frac{\text{After-tax operating income}_6 \,(1 + \text{Stable growth rate})}{\text{(Cost of capital} - \text{Stable growth rate)}} \times (1 - \text{Reinvestment rate})$$

$$= \frac{110.89\,(1.08)(1 - .50)}{(.1168 - .08)} = 1{,}629 \text{ billion krw}$$

Discounting the cash flows over the next six years and the terminal value using the cumulated cost of capital yields the following:

Present value of FCFF in high-growth phase	132.34 billion krw
Present value of terminal value	819.19 billion krw
Value of the operating assets	951.52 billion krw
+ Cash and marketable securities	80.46 billion krw
− Market value of debt	847.73 billion krw
Market value of equity	184.25 billion krw

Note that while the valuation is based upon the assumption that the firm will be able to reduce its debt burden, you still have to subtract the debt due today to get to equity value. Dividing by the number of shares results in an estimated value of equity for the firm of 2,504 krw per share:

$$\text{Value per share} = \frac{\textit{Value of equity}}{\textit{Number of shares in billions}} = \frac{184.25}{0.07357} = 2{,}50 \text{ krw per share}$$

This was a little higher than the actual trading price of 2,220 krw per share.

CAN EQUITY VALUE BE NEGATIVE?

We generally subtract the value of outstanding debt from firm value to get to the value of equity. But can the value of the outstanding debt exceed the value of the firm? If you are using market values for both the firm (obtained by adding the market values of debt and equity) and debt, this should not occur. This is because the market value of equity can never be less than zero. However, if you are using your estimated value for the firm, obtained by discounting cash flows to the firm at the cost of capital, the estimated firm value can be less than the market value of the outstanding debt. When this occurs, there are three possible interpretations:

1. The first and most obvious reading is that you have made a mistake in estimating firm value and that your estimate is too low. In this case, the obvious solution is to redo the firm valuation.
2. The second possibility is that the market value of debt is overstated. This can happen if you are using the book value of debt as a proxy for market value for

(continued)

(continued)

troubled firms, or if the bond market is making a mistake pricing the debt. Estimating the correct market value of debt will eliminate the problem.[9]

3. The third and most intriguing possibility is that your estimate of firm value and the market value of debt are both correct, in which case the equity value is, in fact, negative. Since the market price of equity cannot be less than zero, the implication is that the equity in this firm is worth nothing. However, as you will see later, equity may still continue to command value, even under these circumstances, if it is viewed as a call option on the firm's assets.

Overlevered with High Probability of Bankruptcy   Discounted cash flow valuation is conditioned on a firm being a going concern, with cash flows continuing into the future. When a firm's financial problems are severe enough to suggest a strong likelihood of bankruptcy, two other approaches may need to be used to value a firm and the equity claim in it. One is to estimate a liquidation value for the assets today, and the other is to value the company on the assumption that it stays a going concern, and then adjust that value for the likelihood and consequences of distress.

Liquidation Value   The liquidation value of a firm is the aggregate of the value that the assets of the firm would command on the market, net of transactions and legal costs. The value of equity can be obtained by subtracting the value of the outstanding debt from the asset value.

$$\text{Value of equity} = \text{Liquidation value of assets} - \text{Outstanding debt}$$

Estimating liquidation value is complicated when the assets of the firm are not easily separated, and thus, cannot be valued individually. Furthermore, the likelihood that assets will fetch their fair market value will decrease as the urgency of the liquidation increases. A firm in a hurry to liquidate its assets may have to accept a discount on fair market value as a price for speedy execution.

As a note of caution, it is almost never appropriate to treat the book value of the assets as the liquidation value. Most distressed firms earn subpar returns on their assets, and the liquidation value will reflect the earning capacity of the assets rather than the original capital invested in the assets (which is what the book value measures, net of depreciation).

Distress-Adjusted DCF   Discounted cash flow valuation will yield too high a value for a firm where there is a significant likelihood of distress or default, because we assume that the firm will survive as a going concern. One way of counteracting this bias is to first value

---

[9]You could discount the expected cash flows on the debt at a pretax cost of debt that reflects the firm's current standing.

the firm using a DCF approach, assuming that it makes it back to financial health and profitability. We then follow this up by estimating two inputs:

1. *The probability that the firm will not make it as a going concern* (i.e., the probability of default). This can be estimated in one of three ways:
   a. If the company has traded bonds outstanding, it can be backed out of the price of the bonds.

$$\text{Bond price} = \sum_{t=1}^{t=n} \frac{\text{Coupon}\left(1 - \pi_{\text{Distress}}\right)}{(1 + \text{Riskfree rate})^t} + \frac{\text{Face value of bond}\left(1 - \pi_{\text{Distress}}\right)}{(1 + \text{Risk-free rate})^n}$$

   We are solving for an annualized probability of default over the life of the bond and ignoring the possibility that the annualized probability of default will be higher in the earlier years and decline in the later years.
   b. If the company has a bond rating, we can use historical data to evaluate the likelihood of default. Table 22.8 reproduces a table from Chapter 12, where we report on default rates over 3-, 5- and 10-year periods for bonds in different ratings classes. Based on this table, a CCC-rated company has a 61.67% probability of default over 10 years.
   c. If neither bonds nor ratings exist, we can use statistical techniques (such as probits) to estimate the probability of bankruptcy.
2. *The value that the firm will be able to get for its assets in the event of default.* In effect, we are using the techniques for estimating liquidation value that we described in the last section. Netting out the debt outstanding should yield a value for equity in default. (In most cases, the equity investors will get nothing.)

   Once these numbers have been estimated, the value for the equity in the firm today can be written as a probability weighted average of the going concern value and the distress value:

Value of equity today = Value of equity in going concern (1 − Probability of default)
+ Value of equity in default (Probability of default)

TABLE 22.8 Probability of Default by Bond Ratings Class

Rating	Default Probabilities over Time (1–10-year Time Horizons)		
	1	5	10
AAA	0.00%	0.35%	0.70%
AA	0.02%	0.31%	0.72%
A	0.05%	0.47%	1.24%
BBB	0.16%	1.58%	3.32%
BB	0.61%	6.52%	11.78%
B	3.33%	16.93%	23.74%
CCC/C	27.08%	46.19%	50.38%

ILLUSTRATION 22.8:   Valuing a Company with Depressed Operating Income and Substantial Debt—MGM Resorts in May 2011

MGM Resorts is one of the leading gaming companies in the world, with casinos in the United States and Macau. Like other companies in the sector, the firm borrowed large amounts to fund its expansion between 2002 and 2008. As the economy slowed, the operating income for the firm dropped from $1,425 million in 2007 to $371 million in 2010, and net income decreased even more precipitously from $1,584 million in 2007 to –$1,437 million in 2010. In May 2011, the company was rated CCC, and the potential for default loomed.

For MGM to survive as a going concern, it needs to fix two problems. First, it has to mend its operating margins and return to positive revenue growth; its revenues declined from $7,962 million in 2007 to $6,019 million in 2010. Second, it has to reduce its debt burden; its market debt-to-capital ratio of 59.70% in May 2011 was significantly higher than the industry average of 46.21%. To value MGM as a going concern, we made the following assumptions:

- *Revenue growth.* We see revenue growth returning in 2011, with a 6% growth rate, followed by 15% growth for the following four years and then declining growth to a stable growth rate of 3% beyond year 10.

- *Operating margin.* The current pretax operating margin of 6.23% is expected to increase to the industry average of 19.84% over the next 10 years, with more substantial improvements in the earlier years.

- *Debt ratio and cost of capital.* While we leave the debt ratio at 59.7% for the next five years, we assume that the debt ratio will decrease in linear increments after year 5 to the industry average of 46.21% by year 10. As the debt ratio decreases, we expect the beta (currently 2.63, because of the high debt ratio) to decrease to 1.20 in stable growth. The pretax cost of debt (set at 11.5% to reflect the current CCC rating) remains unchanged for the first five years, and then decreases in linear increments to a pretax cost of debt of 6% in perpetuity.

- *Reinvestment.* Since the bulk of the growth will come from utilizing existing assets more efficiently, MGM will be able to deliver the growth with relatively little reinvestment in the first five years, but the reinvestment rate will climb over the following five years to reach a stable growth level of 30%. That level is estimated using the stable growth rate of 3% and assuming a return on capital in perpetuity of 10%.

Pulling all these assumptions together, we estimated revenues, operating income, and free cash flow to the firm in Table 22.9:

TABLE 22.9 Expected Free Cash Flows

Year	Revenues	Revenue Growth	Operating Margin	EBIT	EBIT (1–t)	Reinvestment Rate (%)	Reinvestment $ Value	FCFF
Base	$ 6,019		6.23%	$ 375	$ 233	19.78%	$ 46	$ 187
1	$ 6,380	6.00%	10.77%	$ 687	$ 426	–5.91%	–$ 25	$ 451
2	$ 7,656	20.00%	13.79%	$1,056	$ 655	0.95%	$ 6	$ 649
3	$ 8,805	15.00%	15.81%	$1,392	$ 863	3.74%	$ 32	$ 831
4	$10,125	15.00%	17.15%	$1,737	$1,077	7.80%	$ 84	$ 993
5	$11,644	15.00%	18.05%	$2,102	$1,303	12.95%	$169	$1,134
6	$13,041	12.00%	18.65%	$2,432	$1,508	16.97%	$256	$1,252
7	$14,345	10.00%	19.04%	$2,732	$1,694	20.80%	$352	$1,342
8	$15,493	8.00%	19.31%	$2,992	$1,855	23.82%	$442	$1,413
9	$16,423	6.00%	19.49%	$3,200	$1,984	25.52%	$506	$1,478
10	$17,080	4.00%	19.60%	$3,348	$2,076	25.99%	$540	$1,536
Terminal	$17,592	3.00%	19.84%	$3,490	$2,164	30.00%	$649	$1,515

Note that these cash flows get discounted back at costs of capital that will also change over time, as debt ratios and risk parameters change (see Table 22.10):

TABLE 22.10 Costs of Capital and Discount Factors

Year	Debt ratio	Beta	Cost of Equity	Cost of Debt		Cost of capital	Cumulated WACC
				Pre-tax	After-tax		
Current	59.70%	2.63	16.63%	11.50%	7.13%	10.96%	
1	59.70%	2.63	16.63%	11.50%	7.13%	10.96%	1.1096
2	59.70%	2.63	16.63%	11.50%	7.13%	10.96%	1.2311
3	59.70%	2.63	16.63%	11.50%	7.13%	10.96%	1.3660
4	59.70%	2.63	16.63%	11.50%	7.13%	10.96%	1.5157
5	59.70%	2.63	16.63%	11.50%	7.13%	10.96%	1.6818
6	57.00%	2.34	15.20%	10.40%	6.45%	10.21%	1.8535
7	56.33%	2.06	13.78%	10.13%	6.28%	9.55%	2.0306
8	55.20%	1.77	12.35%	9.67%	5.99%	8.84%	2.2101
9	52.96%	1.49	10.93%	8.75%	5.43%	8.01%	2.3872
10	46.21%	1.20	9.50%	6.00%	3.72%	6.83%	2.5502

The terminal value for MGM's operating assets can be estimated using the FCFF in the terminal year, the cost of capital, and the stable growth rate:

$$\text{Reinvestment rate} = \frac{\text{Stable growth rate}}{\text{Stable ROIC}} = \frac{.03}{.10} = 0.30 \text{ or } 30\%$$

$$\text{Terminal value} = \frac{EBIT_{10}\,(1 + \text{stable growth rate})(1 - \text{Tax rate})(1 - \text{Reinvestment rate})}{(\text{Cost of capital} - \text{Stable growth rate})}$$

$$= \frac{17{,}080\,(1.03)(1 - .38)(1 - .30)}{(.0683 - .03)} = \$39{,}560 \text{ million}$$

The value of the operating assets can be obtained by discounting the cash flows back at the cumulated cost of capital in Table 22.11.

TABLE 22.11 FCFF and Present value

Year	FCFF	Terminal Value	Cumulated WACC	Value
1	$ 451		1.1096	$406.60
2	$ 649		1.2311	$526.76
3	$ 831		1.3660	$608.13
4	$ 993		1.5157	$655.02
5	$1,134		1.6818	$674.42
6	$1,252		1.8535	$675.36
7	$1,342		2.0306	$660.67
8	$1,413		2.2101	$639.33
9	$1,478		2.3872	$619.07
10	$1,536	$39,560	2.5502	$16,115

(continued)

TABLE 22.11 (*continued*)

Year	FCFF	Terminal Value	Cumulated WACC	Value
Value of operating assets				$21,580
+ Cash				$ 499
− Debt				$10,952
Value of equity				$11,127
/ Number of shares				488.59
Value per share				$ 22.77

If MGM can improve its operating performance and reduce its debt load over time, its value per share in May 2011 is $22.77.

This going-concern value was much higher than the stock price of $15.13 that MGM was trading at in May 2011, but MGM's high-debt burden and low-bond rating (CCC) both raise red flags about potential default. To bring in the potential for default, we estimated the probability of and proceeds from default.

Probability of default: Using Table 22.1, we can assess a probability of default based on the CCC bond rating to be 61.67%. There is an alternative. Since MGM has publicly traded bonds, we chose one of the most liquid—a bond with seven years to maturity and a 7.625% coupon rate that was trading at 97.4% of par and estimated the probability of distress ($\pi_{distress}$) from the bond price:

$$\text{Bond price} = 917 = \sum_{t=1}^{t=7} \frac{76.25\,(1 - \pi_{Distress})}{(1.035)^t} + \frac{1000\,(1 - \pi_{Distress})}{1.035^7}$$

Solving for the probability of distress, we get an annual probability of 4.28% and a cumulative probability of 35.42% over 10 years:

$$\text{Probability of default over 10 years} = 1 - (1 - .0428)^{10} = .3542.$$

Default proceeds: In the event of default, we assumed that MGM could sell its assets (primarily real estate) for 80% of book value and that liquidation costs would be 5% of the proceeds.

$$\text{Distress proceeds} = \text{Book value of assets (Distress proceeds as \% of book value)}$$
$$(1 - \text{Liquidation cost \%})$$
$$= \$14,548(.80)(1 - .05) = \$11,531 \text{ million}$$

Since the book value of debt is $12,048 million, the equity will be worth nothing in the event of default.

The distress-adjusted value of equity can then be written as a function of the DCF value and the distress-adjusted value:

	Going Concern	Distress/Default
Probability	64.58%	35.42%
Value of firm	$22,079	$11,531
Debt outstanding	$10,952	$12,048
Value of equity	$11,127	$0
Value per share	$22.77	$0.00

$$\text{Value of equity} = \$22.77(.6458) + \$0.00(.3542) = \$14.71$$

Since the stock price was $15.13 in May 2011, the stock looks fairly valued.

dbtfund.xls: **This dataset on the web summarizes book and market value debt ratios by industry group in the United States for the most recent year.**

Life Cycle Earnings   As noted earlier in the chapter, it is normal for firms to lose money at certain stages in their life cycles. When valuing such firms, you cannot normalize earnings, as we do with cyclical firms or firms with temporary problems. Instead, you have to estimate the cash flows of the firm over its life cycle and let them turn positive at the right stage of the cycle. Earlier in this chapter we looked at infrastructure firms, as one example, where cash flows will be negative, early in the period. We will add two more groups of firms to the mix: young biotechnology companies that derive their value primarily from a patent or patents and start-up companies.

Firms with Patents   The value of a firm generally comes from two sources—assets in place and expected future growth opportunities. The value of the former is generally captured in current cash flows, while the value of the latter is reflected in the expected growth rate. In the special case of a firm that derives a large portion of its value from a product patent or patents, expected growth will be from developing the patents. Ignoring them in a discounted cash flow valuation will understate the value of the firm.

There are three possible solutions to the problems associated with valuing firms with product options:

1. Price the product options on the open market and add them to the value from discounted cash flow DCF valuation. If there is an active market trading in product options, this offers a viable and simple way of valuing these options. In the absence of such a market, or when the product options are not separable and tradable, this approach becomes difficult to apply.
2. Use a higher growth rate than the one justified by existing projects and assets to capture the additional value from product options. While this keeps the analysis within the traditional discounted cash flow valuation framework, the increase in the growth rate is essentially subjective, and it converts contingent cash flows (where the product option will be exercised if and only if it makes economic sense) to expected cash flows.
3. Use an option pricing model to value product options and add the value to that obtained from DCF valuation of assets in place. The advantage of this approach is that it mirrors the cash flow profile of a product option much more precisely.

The primary problem in valuing firms with product options is not that these options are ignored, but that they are often double-counted. Analysts all too frequently use a higher growth rate to reflect the product options that a firm owns, but then add on a premium to the DCF value for the same product options. We will return to examine the valuation of these firms in Chapter 28.

Young Start-Up Firms   Many firms begin as ideas in the minds of entrepreneurs and develop into commercial ventures over time. During this transition from idea companies to commercial ventures, it is not unusual for these firms to lose money. This does not make them worthless. In fact, the boom in the market value of new economy companies in the late 1990s brought home the fact that good ideas can have substantial value, though the correction in 2000 also illustrated how volatile these values can be.

Valuing young start-up firms is perhaps the most difficult exercise in valuation and one that was, until very recently, the domain of venture capitalists and private equity investors, who often compensated for uncertainty by demanding very high returns on these investments. The challenge becomes much more daunting if a young start-up firm is publicly traded. The next chapter will examine the estimation issues that we face in valuing such a firm.

CONCLUSION

There are many cases where traditional discounted cash flow valuation has to be modified or adapted to provide reasonable estimates of value. Some of these cases are presented in this chapter. Cyclical firms can be difficult to value because their earnings track the economy. The same can be said about commodity firms in relation to the commodity price cycle. A failure to adjust the earnings for these cyclical ups and downs can lead to significant undervaluation of these firms at the depth of a recession and a significant overvaluation at the peak of a boom.

When a firm's earnings are negative because of long-term strategic, operating, or financial problems, the process of valuing these firms becomes more complicated. You have to make a judgment of whether the firm's problems will be solved and, if so, when. For those firms where there is a significant chance of bankruptcy, you might have to consider the liquidation value of the assets or adjust going concern valuations for the likelihood and consequences of distress. Valuing firms early in their life cycles poses similar problems, but they are accentuated when earnings, cash flow, and book value are all negative. In most of these cases, discounted cash flow valuation is flexible enough to be used to estimate value.

QUESTIONS AND SHORT PROBLEMS

In the problems following, use an equity risk premium of 5.5 percent if none is specified.

1. Intermet Corporation, the largest independent iron foundry organization in the country, reported a deficit per share of $0.15 in 1993. The earnings per share from 1984 to 1992 were as follows:

Year	EPS
1984	$0.69
1985	$0.71
1986	$0.90
1987	$1.00
1988	$0.76
1989	$0.68
1990	$0.09
1991	$0.16
1992	−$0.07

The firm had capital expenditures of $1.60 per share and depreciation per share of $1.20 in 1993. Working capital was expected to increase $0.10 per share in 1994. The stock has a beta of 1.2, which is expected to remain unchanged; the company finances its capital expenditure and working capital requirements with 40% debt [D/(D + E)]. The firm was expected, in the long term, to grow at the same rate as the economy (6%).

   a. Estimate the normalized earnings per share in 1994, using the average earnings approach.

   b. Estimate the normalized free cash flow to equity per share in 1994, using the average earnings approach.

2. General Motors Corporation reported a deficit per share in 1993 of $4.85, following losses in the two earlier years. (The average earnings per share is negative.) The company had assets with a book value of $25 billion, and spent almost $7 billion on capital expenditures in 1993, which was partially offset by a depreciation charge of $6 billion. The firm had $19 billion in debt outstanding, on which it paid interest expenses of $1.4 billion. It intended to maintain a debt ratio [D/(D + E)] of 50%. The working capital requirements of the firm were negligible, and the stock has a beta of 1.10. In the last normal period of operations for the firm between 1986 and 1989, the firm earned an average return on capital of 12%. The Treasury bond rate was 7%, and the market risk premium is 5.5%. Once earnings are normalized, GM expected them to grow 5% a year forever, and capital expenditures and depreciation to grow at the same rate.

   a. Estimate the value per share for GM, assuming earnings are normalized instantaneously.

   b. How would your valuation be affected if GM is not going to reach its normalized earnings until 1995 (in two years)?

3. Toro Corporation, which manufactures lawnmowers and tractors, had revenues of $635 million in 1992, on which it reported a loss of $7 million (largely as a consequence of the recession). It had interest expenses of $17 million in 1992, and its bonds were rated BBB; a typical BBB-rated company had an interest coverage ratio (EBIT/interest expenses) of 3.10. The company faced a 40% tax rate. The stock had a beta of 1.10. (The Treasury bond rate was 7%, and the risk premium is 5.5%.)

   Toro spent $25 million on capital expenditures in 1992, and had depreciation of $20 million. Working capital amounted to 25% of sales. The company expected to maintain a debt ratio of 25%. In the long term, growth in revenues and profits was expected to be 4%, once earnings return to normal levels.

   a. Assuming that the bond rating reflects normalized earnings, estimate the normalized earnings for Toro Corporation.

   b. Allowing for the long-term growth rate on normalized earnings, estimate the value of equity for Toro Corporation.

4. Kollmorgen Corporation, a diversified technology company, reported sales of $194.9 million in 1992, and had a net loss of $1.9 million in that year. Its net income had traced a fairly volatile course over the previous five years:

Year	Net Income
1987	$ 0.3 million
1988	−$11.5 million
1989	−$ 2.4 million
1990	$ 7.2 million
1991	−$ 4.6 million

The stock had a beta of 1.20, and the normalized net income was expected to increase 6% a year until 1996, after which the growth rate was expected to stabilize at 5% a year. (The beta will drop to 1.00.) The depreciation amounted to $8 million in 1992, and capital spending amounted to $10 million in that year. Both items were expected to grow 5% a year in the long term. The firm expected to maintain a debt ratio of 35%. (The Treasury bond rate was 7%, and the risk premium is 5.5%.)

   a. Assuming that the average earnings from 1987 to 1992 represents the normalized earnings, estimate the normalized earnings and free cash flow to equity.

   b. Estimate the value per share.

5. OHM Corporation, an environmental service provider, had revenues of $209 million in 1992 and reported losses of $3.1 million. It had earnings before interest and taxes of $12.5 million in 1992, and had debt outstanding of $104 million (in market value terms). There were 15.9 million shares outstanding, trading at $11 per share. The pretax interest rate on debt owed by the firm was 8.5%, and the stock had a beta of 1.15. The firm's EBIT was expected to increase 10% a year from 1993 to 1996, after which the growth rate is expected to drop to 4% in the long term. The return on capital in stable growth is 10%. (The corporate tax rate was 40%, the Treasury bond rate was 7%, and the market risk premium is 5.5%.)

   a. Estimate the cost of capital for OHM.

   b. Estimate the value of the firm.

   c. Estimate the value of equity (both total and on a per share basis).

6. You have been provided the following information on CEL Inc., a manufacturer of high-end stereo systems.

   ■ In the most recent year, which was a bad one, the company made only $40 million in net income. It expects next year to be more normal. The book value of equity at the company is $1 billion, and the average return on equity over the previous 10 years (assumed to be a normal period) was 10%.

   ■ The company expects to make $80 million in new capital expenditures next year. It expects depreciation, which was $60 million this year, to grow 5% next year.

   ■ The company had revenues of $1.5 billion this year, and it maintained a noncash working capital investment of 10% of revenues. It expects revenues to increase 5% next year and working capital to decline to 9.5% of revenues.

   ■ The firm expects to maintain its existing debt policy (in market value terms). The market value of equity is $1.5 billion, and the book value of equity is $500 million. The debt outstanding (in both book and market terms) is $500 million.

   ■ The cost of equity for the firm is 9%.

   a. Estimate the FCFE next year.

   b. Estimate the value of the equity assuming that the firm can grow 5% a year in perpetuity.

7. Tenet Telecommunications is in serious financial trouble and has just reported an operating loss of $500 million on revenues of $5 billion. The firm also had capital expenditures of $1.8 billion and depreciation of $800 million in the most recent financial year, and no significant noncash working capital requirements. You assume that:

   ■ Revenues will continue to grow 10% a year for the next five years and 5% in perpetuity after that.

   ■ EBITDA as a percentage of sales will increase in linear increments from existing levels to 20% of revenues in year 5.

■ Capital expenditures can be cut to $600 million each year for the next five years, while depreciation will remain at $800 million each year.

■ The net operating loss carried forward is $700 million.

■ Return on capital in perpetuity after year 5 will be 10%.

■ Cost of capital for the firm is 9% in perpetuity.

  a. Estimate the EBITDA, EBIT, and after-tax EBIT for the firm each year for the next five years, assuming a corporate tax rate of 40%.

  b. Estimate the FCFF each year for the next five years.

  c. Estimate the terminal value of the firm.

  d. Estimate the value of the firm today.

  e. How would your valuation change if you were told that there is a 20% chance that the firm will go bankrupt and that assets will have a distress sale value amounting to 60% of the current book value of $1.25 billion?

CHAPTER 23

Valuing Young or Start-Up Firms

Many of the firms that we have valued in this book are publicly traded firms with established operations. But what about young firms that have just come into being? There are many analysts who argue that these firms cannot be valued because they have no history, and in some cases, no products or services to sell. This chapter presents a dissenting point of view. While conceding that valuing young firms is more difficult to do than valuing established firms, we argue that the fundamentals of valuation do not change. The value of a young start-up firm is the present value of the expected cash flows from its operations, though estimates of these expected cash flows may require us to go outside our normal sources of information.

INFORMATION CONSTRAINTS

When valuing a firm, you draw on information from three sources. The first is the current financial statements for the firm. You use these to determine how profitable a firm's investments are or have been, how much it reinvests back to generate future growth and for all of the inputs that are required in any valuation. The second is the past history of the firm, in terms of both earnings and market prices. A firm's earnings and revenue history over time let you make judgments on how cyclical a firm's business has been and how much growth it has shown, while a firm's price history can help you measure its risk. Finally, you can look at the firm's competitors or peer group to get a measure of how much better or worse a firm is than its competition, and also to estimate key inputs on risk, growth, and cash flows from more mature companies in the peer group.

While you would optimally like to have substantial information from all three sources, you may often have to substitute more of one type of information for less of the other if you have no choice. Thus, the fact that there exists 75 years or more of history on each of the large automakers in the United States compensates for the fact that there are only a few of them. In contrast, there may be only a few years of information on the current version of a young software firm, but the firm is in a sector (software) where there are more than 600 comparable firms. The ease with which you can obtain industry averages, and the precision of these averages compensate for the lack of history at the firm.

There are some firms, especially in new sectors of the economy, where you might run into information problems. First, these firms usually have not been in existence for more than a year or two, leading to a very limited history. Second, their current financial statements reveal very little about the component of their assets—expected growth—that contributes the most to their value. Third, these firms often represent the first of their kind of business. In many cases, there are no competitors or a peer group against which they can be measured. When valuing these firms, therefore, you may find yourself constrained on all three counts when it comes to information. How have investors responded to this absence of information? Some have decided that these stocks cannot be valued and should not, therefore, be held in a portfolio. Others have argued that while these stocks cannot be valued with traditional models, the fault lies in the models. They have come up with new and inventive ways, based on the limited information available, of justifying the prices paid for them. We will argue in this chapter that discounted cash flow models can be used to value these firms.

New Paradigms or Old Principles: A Life Cycle Perspective

The value of a firm is based on its capacity to generate cash flows, and the uncertainty associated with these cash flows. Generally speaking, more profitable firms have been valued more highly than less profitable ones. However, young start-up firms often lose money but still sometimes have high values attached to them. This seems to contradict the proposition about value and profitability going hand in hand. There seems to be, at least from the outside, one more key difference between young start-up firms and other firms in the market. A young firm does not have significant investments in land, buildings, or other fixed assets, and seems to derive the bulk of its value from growth assets.

The negative earnings and the dependence on future growth for value are used by analysts as a rationale for abandoning traditional valuation models and developing new ways that can be used to justify investing in young firms. For instance, as noted in Chapter 20, Internet companies in their infancy were compared based on their pricing per site visitor, computed by dividing the market value of a firm by the number of visitors to the website. Implicit in these comparisons were the assumptions that more visitors to your site translated into higher revenues, which, in turn, would lead to greater profits in the future. All too often, though, these assumptions were neither made explicit nor tested, leading to unrealistic valuations. In fact, the cycle seemed to repeat itself with social media companies in 2011 and AI companies in 2023 and 2024.

This search for new paradigms is misguided. The problem with young firms is not that they lose money, have no history, or do not have substantial tangible assets. It is that they are far earlier in their life cycles than established firms, and often must be valued before they have an established market for their products. In fact, in some cases, the firms being valued have an interesting idea that could be a commercial success but has not been tested yet. The problem, however, is not a conceptual problem but one of estimation. The value of a firm is still the present value of the expected cash flows from its assets, but those cash flows are likely to be much more difficult to estimate.

Figure 23.1 offers a view of the life cycle of the firm and how the availability of information and the source of value changes over that life cycle:

▪ *Start-up*. This represents the initial stage after a business has been formed. The product is generally still untested and does not have an established market. The firm has little in terms of current operations, no operating history, and no comparable firms, and with little in revenues and big operating losses; you will learn little by poring over

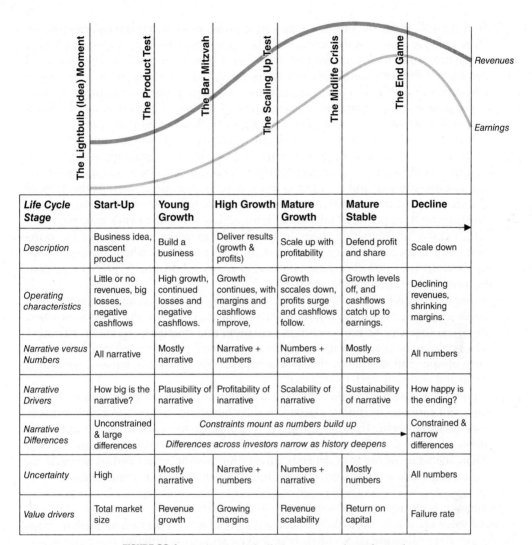

FIGURE 23.1 Valuation Challenges across the Life Cycle

financial statements. Not only does all of the value comes from your assessment of the value of future growth, and these based on assessments of the competence of existing managers and their capacity to convert a promising idea into commercial success. Using the language of Chapter 13, these valuations are almost entirely driven by the story you tell about the company, and there will be wide differences across investor stories.

- *Young growth.* Once a firm succeeds in attracting customers and establishing a presence in the market, its revenues increase rapidly, though it still might be reporting losses. The current operations of the firm start to provide clues on pricing, margins, and expected growth, but there is not much data with which to work. Your valuation narratives will have a little more basis to them, allowing you to at least assess whether they pass the 3P test, but your judgments can change from day to day, as new information comes out about the firm.

■ *High growth*. While the firm's revenues are growing rapidly at this stage, earnings are likely to lag revenues. At this stage, both the current operations and operating history of the firm contain information that can be used in valuing the firm. The number of comparable firms is generally highest at this stage, and these firms are more diverse in where they are in the life cycle, ranging from small, high-growth competitors to larger, lower-growth competitors. The existing assets of this firm have value, but the larger proportion of value still comes from future growth. There is more information available at this stage, and the estimation of inputs becomes more straightforward.

■ *Mature growth*. As revenue growth starts decreasing, firms generally find two phenomena occurring. The earnings and cash flows continue to increase rapidly, reflecting past investments, and the need to invest in new projects declines. At this stage in the process, the firm has current operations that are reflective of the future, an operating history that provides substantial information about the firm's markets, and a large number of comparable firms at the same stage in the life cycle. The key question you will face in building a narrative for this company is whether you can scale up its success (i.e., whether it can continue to grow and deliver the profits that it has historically) as it becomes larger.

■ *Mature stable:* As revenue growth levels off, firms are mature, and as reinvestment needs go down, cash flows catch up with earnings. These are the companies where historical data can be most useful in valuation, and numbers can trump narrative. The key tests in your narrative will be on how well the company can hold off its competition, and if and whether it will behave like a mature company, borrowing more and returning cash to shareholders.

■ *Decline*. The last stage in this life cycle is decline. Firms in this stage find both revenues and earnings starting to decline, as their businesses mature, and new competitors overtake them. Existing investments are likely to continue to produce cash flows, albeit at a declining pace, and the firm has little need for new investments. Thus, the value of the firm depends entirely on existing assets and on whether the firm will gamble with its shareholders' money in an attempt at reincarnation.

Valuation is clearly more of a challenge in the earlier stages in a life cycle, and estimates of value are much more likely to contain errors for start-up or high-growth firms. But the payoff to valuation is also likely to be highest with these firms for two reasons. The first is that the absence of information scares many analysts away, and analysts who persist and end up with a valuation, no matter how imprecise, are likely to be rewarded. The second is that these are the firms that are most likely to be coming to the market in the form of initial public offerings and new issues and need estimates of value.

Venture Capital Valuation

Until very recently, young start-up firms raised additional equity primarily from venture capitalists. It is useful to begin by looking at how venture capitalists assess the value of these firms. While venture capitalists sometimes use discounted cash flow models to value firms, they are much more likely to price private businesses using what is called the venture capital method. Here, the earnings of the private firm are forecast in a future year when the company can be expected to go public. These earnings, in conjunction with an earnings multiple that is estimated by looking at publicly traded firms in the same business, are used to assess the value of the firm at the time of the initial public offering; this is called the exit or terminal value.

For instance, assume that you are pricing InfoSoft, a small software firm, that is expected to have an initial public offering in three years, and that the net income in the third year for the firm is expected to be \$4 million. If the price-earnings ratio of publicly traded software firms is 25, this would yield an estimated exit value of \$100 million. This pricing is discounted back to the present at what venture capitalists call a target rate of return, which measures what venture capitalists believe is a justifiable return, albeit one untethered from stamdard measures of risk. This target rate of return is usually set at a much higher level than the conventional cost of equity for the firm.[1]

$$\text{Pricing today} = \frac{\text{Estimated Pricing at exit in year n}}{(1 + \text{Target return})^n}$$

Using the InfoSoft example again, if the venture capitalist requires a target return of 30 percent on his or her investment, the discounted terminal value for InfoSoft would be:

$$\text{Pricing today} = \frac{(\text{Net income}_4 \times \text{PE ratio in year 4})}{(1 + \text{Target return})^4} = \frac{4 \times 25}{(1.30)^4} = \$35.01 \text{ million}$$

So, how do venture capitalists come up with target rates of return and why are they so high? It is possible that there are some venture capitalists who have developed sophisticated risk-return models that yield target returns, but for the most part, the target returns represent a mix of judgment, historical experience, and guesswork. As for why they are so high, it is a combination of three factors:

1. Young and start-up firms are more exposed to macroeconomic risk than the rest of the market. In CAPM terms, they should command high betas.
2. Venture capitalists are often sector-focused and not diversified. Consequently, they demand a premium for firm-specific risk that can be diversified away.
3. Many young, start-up companies don't make it, and the target rate of return incorporates the risk of failure.

In practice, target rates of return become more instruments of negotiation than conventional discount rates. Put differently, the interests of a venture capitalist are served by using a high target rate of return and demanding a much larger stake in the start-up company. The interests of the owners of the company are advanced with a lower target rate of return. The final number used will depend upon the relative bargaining power of the two sides.

The venture capital approach is also exposed to another problem. To the extent that exit multiples are based on how comparable firms are priced today, they can result in serious misevaluations if the market is wrong. For instance, venture capitalists who valued Internet firms in 2000 on the assumption that they would be able to sell these firms at 80 times revenues (which was what the market was pricing small publicly traded Internet firms at that time) would have overestimated the value of these firms.

---

[1] In 2024, for instance, the target rate of return for venture capitalists ranged from 30% to 60%, depending upon whether the company in question was in the earlier or later stages of the start-up cycle. In contrast, using a conventional risk and return model, you would be hard pressed to get costs of equity that exceed 15%.

VENTURE CAPITAL, PRIVATE EQUITY, AND DIVERSIFICATION

Venture capitalists historically have been sector focused—they tend to concentrate their investments in one or two industries. Part of the reason for this is that the demand for venture capital tends to be concentrated in a few sectors at any point in time—social media companies in 2011, new technology stocks in the late 1990s, biotechnology stocks in the late 1980s—and part of the reason is that venture capitalists draw on their knowledge of the industry both to value firms that ask for equity capital and to help in the management of these firms.

There is a cost to not being diversified, however, and it affects how these companies get valued in the first place. The cost of equity in a firm to a diversified investor will be lower than the cost of equity in the same firm to an undiversified investor, and as we will see in the next chapter, this will result in a lower value being assigned to the firm by the latter.

In recent years, public market investors have emerged as competition for traditional venture capitalists. Since these investors tend to be more diversified, they can settle for lower costs of equity, and thus will attach a much higher value for the same private firm. In the long term, will public equity funds drive out venture capitalists? As long as localized knowledge about an industry matters in valuing firms in that industry, we do not believe so.

GENERAL FRAMEWORK FOR ANALYSIS

To value firms with negative earnings, little or no historical data, and few comparables, the steps involved are essentially the same as in any valuation. This section will look at some of the issues that are likely to come up at each step when valuing young companies.

Step 1: Assess the Firm's Current Standing: The Importance of Updated Information

It is conventional, when valuing firms, to use data from the most recent financial year to obtain the current year's inputs. For firms with negative earnings and high growth in revenues, the numbers tend to change dramatically from period to period. Consequently, it makes more sense to look at the most recent information that one can obtain, at least on revenues and earnings. Using the revenues and earnings from the trailing 12 months, for instance, will provide a much better estimate of value than using earnings from the last financial year. It is true that some items, such as operating leases and options outstanding, may not be updated as frequently. Even so, we would argue for using estimates for these inputs[2] and valuing firms with more recent data.

---

[2] One simple approach is to scale all of the inputs to reflect the growth in revenues that has occurred between the last financial year and the trailing 12 months.

Step 2: Estimate Revenue Growth

Young firms tend to have fairly small amounts of revenues, but the expectation is that these revenues will grow at a substantial rate in the future. Not surprisingly, this is a key input in these valuations, and we would suggest drawing on several sources:

- *Past growth rate in revenues at the firm itself.* Since the firm increases in scale as it grows, it will become more and more difficult to maintain very high growth rates. Thus, a firm that grew 300 percent two years ago and 200 percent last year is likely to grow at a lower rate this year.
- *Growth rate in the overall market that the firm serves.* It is far easier for firms to maintain high growth rates in markets that are themselves growing at high rates than it is for them to do so in stable markets.
- *Barriers to entry and competitive advantage possessed by the firm.* For a firm to be able to sustain high growth rates, it has to have some sustainable competitive advantage. This may come from legal protection (as is the case with a patent), a superior product or service, or a brand name, or from being the first mover into a market. If the competitive advantage looks sustainable, high growth is much more likely to last for a long period. If it is not, it will taper off much faster.

We looked at the process of estimating revenue growth in more detail in Chapter 11.

ILLUSTRATION 23.1:   Revenue Growth Rates— Airbnb in 2020

We will value Airbnb (ABNB), a company that upended the hospitality and hotel business, at the time of its IPO in November 2020. While we introduced the company in chapter 11 in the context of estimating cash flows, we will value the company fully in this chapter, albeit with slightly modified assumptions about growth, profitability and reinvestment. The firm had been in existence just over a decade, but had shown high growth potential, with revenues increasing almost five-fold, from $919 million in 2015 and to $4.8 billion in 2019. However, the company's business model was still in flux, as it reported operating losses of $501 million in 2019. Adding to the uncertainty in this valuation was the COVID shut down of the global economy, with the hospitality business among the most affected. As a result, in the trailing 12 months, leading into this valuation, Airbnb's revenues dropped to $3.6 billion, and its losses ballooned to $818 million.

There are three key numbers in forecasting future cash flows. The first is revenue growth, which can be obtained by either extrapolating from the recent past or by estimating the total market for a product or service and an expected market share. The potential market for a company will be smaller, if the product or service offered by the firm is defined narrowly and will expand if we use a broader definition. Defining Airbnb as a apartment-rental company will result in a smaller market than categorizing it as being in the hospitality business. The next step is to estimate the share of that market that will be captured by the firm being analyzed, both in the long term and in the time periods leading up to it. It is at this stage that you will consider both the quality of the products and management of the young company and the resources that the company can draw on to accomplish its objectives.

Airbnb's management has shown competence and creativity and the networking benefits of being the largest network for rentals will allow it not only to continue winning market share from hotels, but give it an advantage over other companies that try to imitate it. We estimate the gross bookings on Airbnb's platform will grow 40% in 2021, as the COVID shut down eases, and that the annual growth rate will be 25% in the next four years; that growth rate will scale down to 2% by year 10. Airbnb's revenues come from the share of these gross bookings that it claims, and we expect that percentage to increase from 12.65% in the most recent twelve months to 14% over the next decade, because of market power and economies of scale. Table 23.1 summarizes the gross bookings and revenue projections for Airbnb:

TABLE 23.1 Expected Revenues for Airbnb (in $ millions)

	Growth Rate	Gross Bookings	Airbnb Share (%)	Revenues
LTM		$ 26,492		$ 3,626
1	40.00%	$ 37,089	12.65%	$ 4,692
2	25.00%	$ 46,361	12.92%	$ 5,990
3	25.00%	$ 57,951	13.06%	$ 7,565
4	25.00%	$ 72,439	13.19%	$ 9,555
5	25.00%	$ 90,548	13.33%	$12,066
6	20.40%	$109,020	13.46%	$14,674
7	15.80%	$126,245	13.60%	$17,163
8	11.20%	$140,385	13.73%	$19,275
9	6.60%	$149,650	13.87%	$20,749
10	2.00%	$152,643	14.00%	$21,370
Terminal year	2.00%	$155,696	14.00%	$21,797

Note that with the high growth rate, the projected gross bookings of $156 billion in year 11 will make Airbnb almost as big as Booking.com in term of revenues and give it about 10% of the overall hospitality market (including hotels and private bookings). Since Airbnb is an intermediary that keeps a slice (14%) of these gross bookings, its revenues will be $21.8 billion in the terminal year, making it larger (in revenue terms) than the largest hotel companies in the world in 2019.

Step 3: Estimate a Sustainable Operating Margin in Stable Growth

For a firm losing money, high revenue growth alone will accomplish little more than make the losses become larger over time. A key component for a young firm to be valuable is the expectation that the operating margin, while negative now, will become positive in the future. In many ways the true test in valuation is being able to evaluate what a young, high-growth firm will have as an operating margin when growth stabilizes. In the absence of comparables, the difficulty of this task is magnified. Again, a few guidelines help:

- Looking at the underlying business that this firm is in, consider its true competitors. A company with strong competitors will find its margins under pressure, and that has to be reflected in a lower operating margin. In making this assessment, though, we may need to look at potential competitors that may be drawn into the business.
- Look at the company's business model: When choose business models, companies are also picking a combination of revenue growth and operating margins, with the two often working at cross purposes. A firm that is intent on scaling up may accept a lower target margin than a firm that chooses to stay in a niche portion of the market, with higher profit margins.
- Deconstruct the firm's current income statement to get a truer measure of its operating margin.

Many young start-up firms that report losses do so, not because their operating expenses from generating current revenues are large, but because a significant portion of operating expenses are in pursuit of future growth and should really be capital expenses. Since many of these expenses are treated as selling, general, and administrative (SG&A)

expenses in income statements, estimating margins and profitability prior to these expenses is a useful exercise in figuring out how profitable a company's products truly are.

ILLUSTRATION 23.2: Estimating Sustainable Margin and Path to Margin: Airbnb in 2000

We assume that Airbnb's pretax operating margin, currently an abysmal −22.56 percent, will improve to 25 percent, a little lower than the margins delivered by Booking.com, the only competitor of similar scale and business model. In the second part, we can then look at how the margin will evolve over time; this "pathway to profitability" can be rockier for some firms than others, with fixed costs and competition playing significant roles in the estimation. The product of the forecasted revenues and expected operating margins yields the expected operating income (in millions of dollars) in Table 23.2:

TABLE 23.2 Expected Operating Income for Airbnb (in $ millions)

	Revenues	Operating margin	Operating income	Tax rate	EBIT(1−t)
Base year	$ 3,626	−22.56%	−$ 818		−$ 817.96
1	$ 4,692	−10.00%	−$ 469	0.00%	−$ 469
2	$ 5,990	−3.00%	−$ 180	0.00%	−$ 180
3	$ 7,565	0.50%	$ 38	0.00%	$ 38
4	$ 9,555	4.00%	$ 382	0.00%	$ 382
5	$12,066	7.50%	$ 905	14.05%	$ 778
6	$14,674	5.98%	$ 878	25.00%	$ 658
7	$17,163	10.73%	$1,842	25.00%	$1,381
8	$19,275	15.49%	$2,986	25.00%	$2,239
9	$20,749	20.24%	$4,200	25.00%	$3,150
10	$21,370	25.00%	$5,343	25.00%	$4,007
Terminal year	$21,797	25.00%	$5,449	25.00%	$4,087

To estimate taxes due on this income, consider the possibility of carrying forward operating losses from earlier years to offset income in later years. The net operating loss of $167.6 million that Airbnb has accumulated in the past and the losses it is expected to generate over the next two years shelter its income from taxes until the sixth year.

Step 4: Estimate Reinvestment to Generate Growth

To grow, firms must reinvest, and this principle cannot be set aside when you are looking at a young firm. Unlike a mature firm, though, there is likely to be little in the firm's history that will help in determining how much the firm will need to reinvest. As the firm grows, the nature of its reinvestment and the amount reinvested will probably change, and the challenge is to estimate this amount.

Chapter 11 related growth in operating income to how much a firm reinvests and how well it reinvests (measured by the return on capital).

$$\text{Expected growth} = \text{Reinvestment rate} \times \text{Return on capital}$$

In fact, this equation has been used to estimate growth in most of the valuations done so far in this book. However, note that this equation becomes inoperable when operating earnings are negative, which is the position we are in when valuing young firms. In those cases, the growth in revenues must be estimated first, and the reinvestment must be based on the revenue growth. To make this link, we used a sales-to-capital ratio, that is, a ratio that specifies how many additional dollars of revenue will be generated by each additional dollar of capital:

$$\text{Expected reinvestment} = \frac{\text{Expected change in revenues}}{\text{Sales to invested capital}}$$

For instance, to grow revenues by $1 billion, with a sales-to-capital ratio of 4, would require a reinvestment of $250 million. The key input required for this formulation is the sales-to-capital ratio, and it can be estimated by looking at the firm's history, limited though it might be, and at industry averages, with the industry defined broadly to reflect the business the firm is in.

In steady state, however, the reinvestment needs can be computed using the expected growth rate and the expected return on invested capital:

$$\text{Expected reinvestment rate} = \frac{\text{Expected stable growth rate}}{\text{ROIC in stable growth}}$$

An alternative approach is to use the industry-average reinvestment rates (broken up into capital expenditures and working capital needs) to estimate cash flows.

ILLUSTRATION 23.3:   Estimating Reinvestment Needs—Aribnb

Airbnb is an intermediary, and while that may suggest that the company is not capital intensive, its growth has come with significant reinvestments not just in platform technology but also in acquisitions that the company has made to generate growth quickly and to add more users. Based on Airbnb's reinvestment history and the reinvestment at competitors (Expedia and Booking), we estimate that every $2.00 in additional revenue will require a dollar in capital invested. To get to free cash flows, we estimate reinvestment each year, and net that reinvestment out from the after-tax operating income (with all dollar values in millions) in Table 23.3:

TABLE 23.3   Expected FCFF for Airbnb (in $ millions)

	Revenues	Change in revenues	EBIT(1−t)	Sales to capital	Reinvestment	FCFF
Base year	$ 3,626		($ 818)			
1	$ 4,692	$1,066	($ 469)	2.00	$ 533	($1,002)
2	$ 5,990	$1,298	($ 180)	2.00	$ 649	($ 829)
3	$ 7,565	$1,576	$ 38	2.00	$ 788	($ 750)
4	$ 9,555	$1,989	$ 382	2.00	$ 995	($ 612)
5	$12,066	$2,511	$ 778	2.00	$1,255	($ 478)
6	$14,674	$2,609	$ 658	2.00	$1,304	($ 647)
7	$17,163	$2,489	$1,382	2.00	$1,244	$ 137
8	$19,275	$2,112	$2,239	2.00	$1,056	$1,183
9	$20,749	$1,474	$3,150	2.00	$ 737	$2,413
10	$21,370	$ 621	$4,007	2.00	$ 311	$3,696

We make no attempt to break reinvestment down into its constituent parts—capital expenditures, R&D, acquisitions, and working capital—because we know too little about how the firm will evolve over time. We also assume that the reinvestment, since it takes the form of acquisitions, creates revenue growth contemporaneously. To the extent that there is a lag between reinvestment and growth, it can be built into your forecasts.[3]

One of the dangers of estimating reinvestment independently from operating income (which is what we have done) is that our estimates may become internally inconsistent over time. To make sure that the expected return on capital as the firm matures is a number that we can live with, we estimated the imputed return on capital each year (with the dollar values in millions) in Table 23.4:[4]

TABLE 23.4   Reinvestment and Imputed ROIC for Airbnb (in $ millions)

	EBIT(1−t)	Reinvestment	Invested capital (end of year)	ROIC
Base year	($ 818)		($ 448)	104.82%
1	($ 469)	$ 533	$ 85	−210.48%
2	($ 180)	$ 649	$ 734	5.15%
3	$ 38	$ 788	$1,522	25.11%
4	$ 382	$ 995	$2,517	30.90%
5	$ 778	$1,255	$3,772	17.44%
6	$ 658	$1,304	$5,077	27.21%
7	$1,382	$1,244	$6,321	35.42%
8	$2,239	$1,056	$7,377	42.71%
9	$3,150	$ 737	$8,114	49.38%
10	$4,007	$ 311	$8,425	104.82%

The capital invested at the start of year 1 is the capital invested in the most recent balance sheet, computed as follows:

$$\text{Invested capital} = \text{Book value of equity} + \text{Book value of debt} - \text{Cash}$$
$$= 1{,}855.22 + 2{,}192.38 - 4{,}495.21 = -\$447.61 \text{ million}$$

The capital invested in subsequent years is estimated by adding the reinvestment for the year to the capital invested at the start:

$$\text{Invested capital}_t = \text{Invested capital}_{t-1} + \text{Reinvestment}_t$$

The expected return on capital improves over time as margins improve. In fact, the return on capital reaches 104.38% in year 10, a number that is very high, but reflects the low capital intensity of the business.

---

[3]With a two-year lag, for instance, you can estimate reinvestment in year 1 based upon revenue growth between years 2 and 3:

$$\text{Reinvestment in year 1} = \frac{(7{,}565.48 - 5{,}989.79)}{2.0} = \$787.34$$

[4]The return on capital is estimated using the invested capital at the start of the year. Thus, the return on capital in year 3 is computed by dividing the after-tax operating income in year 3 by the invested capital at the end of year 2. In year 1, it cannot be computed since the invested capital is negative.

The free cash flows to the firm are negative for the next six years, partly because of operating losses (through year 2) and partly because of reinvestment needs. Based on our estimates, Airbnb will need to raise about $4.3 billion in new capital (from debt and equity) over the next seven years; that amount comes from summing up the negative free cash flows over the next six years.

REINVESTMENT AND GROWTH: LAGGED EFFECTS

In our valuation of Aribnb, we have assumed that reinvestment and growth occur contemporaneously. In other words, the increase in revenues and the reinvestment that creates that increase occur simultaneously. This may seem like a radical assumption, but it is realistic for service businesses or when growth occurs through acquisitions.

If, in fact, there is a lag between reinvestment and growth, it is relatively simple to build this lag into the analysis. In the Airbnb valuation, assuming a one-year lag, you could estimate the reinvestment in year 1 from expected revenue growth in year 2. The length of the lag will depend on both the firm being valued—it will be longer for firms that have to make capital-intensive and infrastructure investments—and the form of the reinvestment—whether it is internal or external (acquisitions).

Step 5: Estimate Risk Parameters and Discount Rates

In the standard approaches for estimating beta, we regress stock returns against market returns. Young start-up firms, even when publicly traded, have little historical data, and we cannot use the conventional approach to estimate risk parameters.[5] In Chapter 7, though, we suggested alternative approaches for estimating betas that are useful to bridge this gap. One is the bottom-up approach. If there are comparable firms that have been listed for two or more years, the current risk parameters for the firm can be estimated by looking at the averages for these firms. If such firms do not exist, risk parameters can be estimated using the financial characteristics of the firm—the volatility in earnings, their size, cash flow characteristics, and financial leverage.[6]

If a young firm has debt, we run into a different problem when estimating the cost of debt. The firm will generally not be rated, thus denying us a chance to estimate the cost of debt based on the rating. We could try estimating a synthetic rating, but the negative operating income will yield a negative interest coverage ratio and a default rating for the firm. One solution is to estimate an expected interest coverage ratio for the firm based on expected operating income in future periods (note that these forecasts were already made in steps 2 and 3) and to use this expected interest coverage ratio to estimate a synthetic rating.

Whatever approach we use to estimate costs of equity and debt, they should not be left unchanged over the estimation period. As the firm matures and moves toward its

---

[5] The conventional approach is to regress returns on a stock against returns on a market index over a past period, say two to five years.
[6] For a description of this approach, refer back to Chapter 7.

sustainable margin and stable growth, the risk parameters should also approach those of an average firm—the betas should move toward 1, and the cost of debt should adjust toward a mature firm's cost of debt.

In addition to estimating the cost of equity for these firms, we have to estimate how leverage will change over time. Again, targeting an industry average or an optimal debt ratio for this firm (as it will look in steady state) should yield reasonable estimates for the cost of capital over time.

OPERATING LEVERAGE AND RISK

One argument that is made for why young firms should have much higher betas than larger, more mature firms in their business is that they have much higher operating leverage. The costs for young firms are for the most part fixed and do not vary with revenues. If you are estimating a bottom-up beta for a young firm by looking at comparable firms, you have two choices:

1. You can use only small, publicly traded firms as your comparable firms. This will work only if there are significant numbers of publicly traded firms in the business.
2. The other and more promising approach is to adjust the bottom-up beta for differences in operating leverage. Chapter 7 noted how betas can be adjusted for differences in fixed cost structures:

Unlevered beta = Business beta [1 + (Fixed costs/Variable costs)]

ILLUSTRATION 23.4: Estimating Risk Parameters and Cost of Capital—Airbnb

Since this was a valuation of Airbnb, at the time of its IPO, the traditional market measures of risk are not available. Since the stock is not traded, there are no regression betas available for the firm or measure of stock price volatility. The company had no bond rating available.

We made an initial assessment of the company's cost of capital, by looking at the hotel/gaming business, and the debt ratio for the company, while using the 10-year treasury bond rate of 0.90% as the risk free rate:

Unlevered beta for the hotel/gaming business = 0.91

Debt to equity ratio for Airbnb = 6.75%

Levered beta = 0.91(1 + (1 − .25)(.0675)) = 0.96
Cost of equity = 0.90% + 0.96(6.09%) = 6.75%

Cost of debt (pre-tax) = 3.85%

$$\text{Cost of capital} = \textit{Cost of equity} \times \frac{\textit{Equity}}{\textit{Debt} + \textit{Equity}} + \textit{Cost of debt} \times (1 - \textit{tax rate})$$

$$\times \frac{\textit{Debt}}{\textit{Debt} + \textit{Equity}}$$

$$= 6.75\%(.9367) + 3.85\%(1 - .25)(.0633) = 6.50\%$$

That cost of capital is low, but it reflects the timing of the IPO, in late 2020, when the 10-year treasury bond rate had dropped to 0.90%. As the firm matures, we expect the cost of capital will rise slightly to 7.12 percent as Airbnb's risk moves towards that of the average company in the market and treasury bond rates return to 2% (which, in 2020, seemed like a reasonable norm).

Step 6: Estimate the Value of the Firm

With the inputs on earnings, reinvestment rates, and risk parameters over time, this valuation starts resembling a conventional valuation. In many cases, the cash flow in the early years will be negative, driven by negative earnings and large reinvestment needs, but turn positive in later years as margins improve and reinvestment drops off. The bulk of the value will generally be in the terminal value. Note, though, that the magnitude of the terminal value is determined by your growth and target margin assumptions during the high growth phase.

Having valued the operating assets of the firm, you need to consider two other factors—the possibility that the firm will not survive to become a going concern and the value of nonoperating assets—to value the firm.

Survival When we value firms using discounted cash flow valuation, we tend to assume that the firm will be a going concern and continue to generate cash flows in perpetuity. This assumption might be suspect when valuing young companies, since many of them will not survive the tests that they will be put to over the next few years. If we ignore this possibility and consider only the best-case scenario of expansion and perpetual profitability, we will overestimate the value of these firms. We have two choices when it comes to dealing with this possibility.

1. The first is to build into the expected growth rates and earnings the likelihood of unfavorable outcomes. Thus, the growth rate used in revenues will be the expected growth rate over all scenarios, both optimistic and pessimistic, and incorporate the likelihood that the firm will not make it. For young firms, this will become progressively more difficult to do as you get further and further into the future.
2. The second is to estimate a discounted cash flow value across only the scenarios where the firm is a going concern, and then apply a probability that the firm will be a going concern to this value. Once we have estimated the probability of surviving as a going concern, the value of a firm can then be estimated as follows:

> Value of firm = Probability of surviving as a going concern
> $\times$ DCF value of firm
> + (1 − Probability of surviving as a going concern)
> $\times$ Distress or liquidation sale value

One approach to estimating the probability of survival is to look at the empirical data. Knaup (2005) and Knaup and Piazza (2008) used data from the U.S. Bureau of Labor Statistics Quarterly Census of Employment and Wages (QCEW) to compute survival statistics across firms. This census contains information on more than 8.9 million U.S. businesses in both the public and private sector. Using a seven-year database from 1998 to

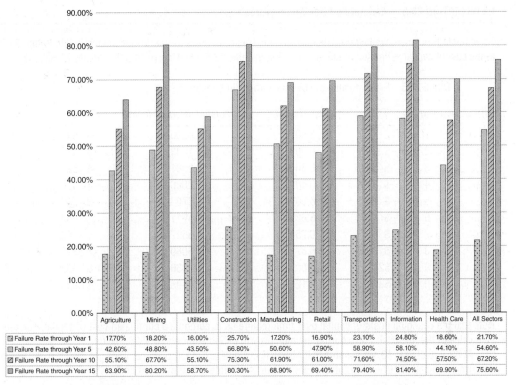

	Agriculture	Mining	Utilities	Construction	Manufacturing	Retail	Transportation	Information	Health Care	All Sectors
Failure Rate through Year 1	17.70%	18.20%	16.00%	25.70%	17.20%	16.90%	23.10%	24.80%	18.60%	21.70%
Failure Rate through Year 5	42.60%	48.80%	43.50%	66.80%	50.60%	47.90%	58.90%	58.10%	44.10%	54.60%
Failure Rate through Year 10	55.10%	67.70%	55.10%	75.30%	61.90%	61.00%	71.60%	74.50%	57.50%	67.20%
Failure Rate through Year 15	63.90%	80.20%	58.70%	80.30%	68.90%	69.40%	79.40%	81.40%	69.90%	75.60%

FIGURE 23.2   Survival of New Establishments Founded in 2007

2005, the authors concluded that only 44 percent of all businesses that were founded in 1998 survived at least four years, and only 31 percent made it through all seven years. In addition, they categorized firms into 10 sectors and estimated survival rates for each. Figure 23.2 provides the updated version of this table, showing survival rates across sectors. Note that survival rates vary across sectors, with only 25 percent of firms in the information sector (which includes technology) surviving ten years, whereas almost 42.5 percent of health services businesses made it through that period.

Value of Nonoperating Assets   As with the valuation of any firm, you have to consider cash, marketable securities, and holdings in other companies when you value a firm. The only note of caution that we would add is that young firms can burn through significant cash balances in short periods because their operations drain cash rather than generate it. Thus, the cash balance from the last financial statements, especially if those statements are more than a few months old, can be very different from the current cash balances.

To the extent that young firms often have holdings in other young firms, there is also the danger that investments in other firms may be shown on the books at values that are not reflective of their true value. If there are only one or two large holdings, you should value those holdings using cash flow-based approaches as well.

ILLUSTRATION 23.5:   Estimating Firm Value—Airbnb

To estimate firm value, we begin by discounting the free cash flows to the firm estimated in Illustration 23.3 at the cost of capital estimated in Illustration 23.4, in Table 23.5 following (with dollar values in millions):

TABLE 23.5   Present value of FCFF for Airbnb (in $ millions)

Year	FCFF	Cost of capital	Cumulated discount factor	PV(FCFF)
1	−$1,002	6.50%	1.0650	−$ 941
2	−$ 829	6.50%	1.1343	−$ 731
3	−$ 750	6.50%	1.2081	−$ 621
4	−$ 612	6.50%	1.2866	−$ 476
5	−$ 478	6.50%	1.3703	−$ 349
6	−$ 647	6.63%	1.4611	−$ 442
7	$ 137	6.75%	1.5597	$ 88
8	$1,183	6.87%	1.6669	$ 710
9	$2,413	7.00%	1.7836	$1,353
10	$3,696	7.12%	1.9105	$1,935

Note that the changing costs of capital over time require us to compute a cumulated cost of capital. The present value of the free cash flows during the high growth period amounts to $526 million.

At the end of year 10, we assume that Airbnb is in stable growth, growing at 2% a year, while maintaining a return on capital of 10%. The stable period reinvestment rate is computed to be 20%:

$$\text{Stable reinvestment rate} = \frac{\text{Stable growth rate}}{\text{Stable ROIC}} = \frac{2\%}{10\%} = 20\%$$

The terminal value (at the end of year 10) can then be computed using the operating income in year 11 (see Illustration 23.2):

$$\text{Terminal value} = \frac{\text{EBIT}_{10}(1-t)(1+\text{stable growth rate})(1-\text{Reinvestment rate})}{(\text{Cost of capital} - \text{Stable growth rate})}$$

$$= \frac{4,007(1.02)(1-0.20)}{(.0712 - .02)} = \$63,860 \text{ million}$$

Discounting the terminal value back at the cumulated cost of capital in year 10 and adding to the present value of FCFF over the next 10 years, we get (in thousands of dollars)

$$\text{Value of operating assets} = \text{PV of cashflows in years } 1-10 + \text{PV of terminal value}$$

$$= \$526 + \frac{\$63,860}{1.9105} = \$33,951 \text{ million}$$

While Airbnb has potential, it is a money-losing enterprise, with years of cash burn ahead of it. The IPO will add to its cash balance, but we assess a 10% chance of failure, and assume that if it occurs, the company will have to be sold for half its fair value. The expected value of the operating assets, with failure risk built into it:

$$\text{Value of operating assets(adjusted for failure)} = \text{Value of operating assets }(1 - \text{Probability of failure})$$
$$+ \text{Value of distress sale (Probability of failure)}$$
$$= \$33,951(.90) + \$33,951(0.50)(.10)$$
$$= \$32,253 \text{ million}$$

Adding the current cash balance of $4,495 million to this estimate and netting out debt of $2,192 million we get the value of the equity:

$$\text{Value of equity} = \text{Value of operating assets} + \text{Cash} - \text{Debt}$$
$$= \$32{,}253 + \$4{,}495 - \$2{,}192 = \$34{,}556 \text{ million}$$

Finally, Airbnb expects to raise $3 billion from its initial public offering, and since that cash will be held by the firm, the augmented value of equity after the IPO can be computed:

$$\text{Value of equity (post-IPO)} = \text{Value of equity} + \text{IPO proceeds}$$
$$= \$34{,}556 \text{ million} + \$3{,}000 = \$37{,}556 \text{ million}$$

Step 7: Estimate the Value of Equity and Per-Share Value

To get from firm value to equity value, we generally subtract out all nonequity claims on the firm. For mature firms, the nonequity claims take the form of bank debt and bonds outstanding. For young firms, there can also be preferred equity claims that have to be valued and subtracted to get to the value of the common equity.

To get from equity value to value per share, you have to consider equity options outstanding on the firm. In Chapter 16, we argued that this is something that needs to be done for all firms, but it becomes particularly important with young start-up firms, because the value of the options outstanding can be a much larger share of the overall equity value. Given the importance of these claims, we would suggest that the options— vested as well as nonvested—be valued using an option pricing model, and that the value of the options be subtracted from the value of the equity to arrive at the value of equity in common stock. This value should then be divided by the actual number of shares outstanding to arrive at the equity value per share. Since Airbnb will have to issue more shares in the next few years to cover its reinvestment needs, you may wonder why we do not incorporate these additional shares when computing value per share. The reduction in value of $1,306 million in Illustration 23.5, from bringing in the expected cash flows over the next 10 years, can be considered the dilution discount to current value, and incorporating the additional shares in the denominator would be double-counting.

ILLUSTRATION 23.6: Valuing Equity per Share—Airbnb

In Illustration 23.5, we estimated the value of Airbnb's equity to be worth $37,556 million. There are 671.06 million shares outstanding, including restricted stock, but Airbnb (reflecting its technology roots) also has 44.84 million options outstanding, with an average exercise price of $11.43 and 5 years left to expiration. Drawing on Chapter 16, there are three ways we can adjust for these options:

1. *Fully diluted approach:* We divide the value of equity by the fully diluted number of shares:

$$\text{Value per share} = 37556/(671.06 + 44.84) = \$52.46/\text{share}$$

2. *Treasury stock approach:* We add the exercise proceeds from the options to the equity value before dividing by the fully diluted number of shares:

$$\text{Value per share} = (37556 + 44.84 \times \$11.43)/(671.06 + 44.84) = \$53.18$$

3. *Option valuation approach:* Using a standard deviation of 40%, reflecting the expected high volatility in a freshly public company, in the dilution-adjusted Black-Scholes model, and setting the price equal to the estimated intrinsic value per share of $53.18, yields a value of $1,877 million for the options and a value per share of $53.17.

$$\text{Value per share} = \frac{\text{Equity value} - \text{Value of options}}{\text{Number of shares outstanding}} = \frac{37,556 - 1,877}{671.06} = \$53.17/\text{share}$$

The initial offering price set for Airbnb was $68, but the stock soared on the offering to hit a high of $146/share.

VALUE DRIVERS

What are the key inputs that determine the value of a young high-growth firm with negative earnings? In general, the inputs that have the greatest impact on value are the estimates of sustainable margins and revenue growth. To a lesser extent, assumptions about how long it will take the firm to reach a sustainable margin and reinvestment needs in stable growth also have an impact on value.

In practical terms, the bulk of the value of these firms is derived from the terminal value. While this will be troublesome, it mirrors how an investor makes returns in these firms. The payoff to these investors takes the form of price appreciation rather than dividends or stock buybacks. Another way of explaining the dependence on terminal value and the importance of the sustainable growth assumption is in terms of assets in place and future growth. The value of any firm can be written as the sum of the two:

$$\text{Value of firm} = \text{Value of assets in place} + \text{Value of growth potential}$$

For start-up firms with negative earnings, almost all the value can be attributed to the second component. Not surprisingly, the firm value is determined by assumptions about the latter.

SHOULD THERE BE A DISCOUNT FOR LOW FLOAT?

Some publicly traded stocks are lightly traded, and the number of shares available for trade (often referred to as the float) is small relative to the total number of shares outstanding.[7] Investors who want to sell their stock quickly in these companies often have a price impact when they sell, and the impact will increase with the size of the holding.

---

[7]The float is estimated by subtracting from the shares outstanding the shares that are owned by insiders and 5 percent owners and the rule 144 shares. (Rule 144 refers to restricted stock that cannot be traded.)

Investors with longer time horizons and a lesser need to convert their holdings into cash quickly have a smaller problem associated with illiquidity than investors with shorter time horizons and a greater need for cash. Investors should consider the possibility that they will need to convert their holdings quickly into cash, when they look at lightly traded stocks as potential investments and require much larger discounts on value before they take large positions. Assume, for instance, that an investor is looking at a young firm that she has valued at $19.05 per share. The stock would be underpriced if it were trading at $17, but it might not be underpriced enough for a short-term investor to take a large position in it. In contrast, a long-term investor may find the stock an attractive buy at that price.

ILLUSTRATION 23.7: Airbnb—Dealing with uncertainty

While there are literally dozens of assumptions, which underlie the value per share of $53.17 that we obtained for Airbnb, there are two key ones that drive the value per share. One is the growth rate in revenues over the next 10 years: We assumed a growth rate of 25% in gross bookings for years 2 through 5, before growth rates declined to stable growth. The other is the target pretax operating margin; we assumed that it would be 25%, higher than the automobile sector average but lower than the average for technology firms.

In Table 23.6, we estimate the value per share as a function of the revenue growth rate over the next five years and the target operating margin:

TABLE 23.6 Value per Share, Growth and Margins—Airbnb

		Target operating margin (in year 10)				
		15%	20%	25%	30%	35%
Revenue Growth rate in next 5 years	10%	$ 16.63	$ 21.00	$ 25.35	$ 29.68	$ 34.00
	20%	$ 23.02	$ 30.90	$ 38.74	$ 46.57	$ 54.39
	30%	$ 33.89	$ 47.57	$ 61.22	$ 74.86	$ 88.49
	40%	$ 51.63	$ 74.65	$ 97.64	$120.62	$143.60
	50%	$ 79.73	$117.33	$154.90	$192.47	$230.03
	60%	$122.99	$182.79	$242.57	$302.33	$362.10

To justify the offering price of $68, you would not need to change your assumptions by much, since a slightly higher growth rate would get you there, but it is a far bigger stretch to get to the $146 that the stock was trading at shortly after its offering.

ESTIMATION NOISE

The framework for valuation provided in this section should not be considered a recipe for precision. The valuation of a firm with negative earnings, high growth, and limited information will always have estimation error. One way to present this error is in terms of a valuation range, and the range on the value for these firms will be large. This is often used as an excuse by analysts who do not want to go through the process of valuing such firms. It also provides critics with a simplistic argument against trusting the numbers that emerge from these models.

We have a different view. The error in the valuation is not always a reflection of the quality of the valuation model, or the analyst using it, but of the underlying real uncertainty about the future prospects of the firm. This uncertainty is a fact of life when it comes to investing in these firms. In a valuation, we attempt to grapple with this uncertainty and make our best estimates about the future. Note that those who disdain valuation models for their potential errors end up using far cruder approaches, such as comparing price-sales ratios across firms. The difference, as we see it, is that they choose to sweep the uncertainties under the rug and act as if they do not exist.

There are two other points to make about the precision in these valuations. First, even if a valuation is imprecise, it provides a powerful tool to answer the question of what has to occur for the current market price of a firm to be justified. Investors can then decide whether they are comfortable with these assumptions and make their decisions on buying and selling stock. Second, even if individual valuations are noisy, portfolios constructed based on these valuations will be more precisely valued. Thus, an investor who buys 40 stocks that he or she has found to be undervalued using traditional valuation models, albeit with significant error, should find that error averaging out across the portfolio. The ultimate performance of the portfolio then should reflect the valuation skills, or the absence of them, of the analyst.

Implications for Investors

From a valuation perspective, there are a number of useful lessons that emerge for investors in young firms with negative earnings and limited information.

- *Focus on sustainable margins and survival*, rather than quarter-to-quarter or even year-to-year swings in profitability. Understanding what a firm's operating margins will look like when it reaches financial health might be the single most important determinant of whether one is successful investing, in the long term, in such firms. Separating those firms that have a greater chance of surviving and reaching financial health from those that will not survive is a closely connected second determinant. After all, most start-up firms never survive to enjoy their vaunted growth prospects.
- *Earnings reports can be misleading*, especially when reinvestment costs are expensed (as is the case with research, development, and long-term marketing expenses). Thus, when a firm with high-growth potential and poor earnings reports a significant improvement in earnings, investors should examine the report for the reasons. If the earnings are improving because the costs of generating current revenues are coming down (due to economies of scale or pricing power), this is clearly good news. If, however, the earnings are increasing because the firm has reduced or eliminated discretionary reinvestment expenditures (such as development costs), the net effect on value can be very negative, since future growth is being put at risk.
- *Diversify.* This age-old rule of investing becomes even more critical when investing in stocks that derive the bulk of their value from uncertain future growth. The

antidote to estimation error is often a more diversified portfolio both across firms and across sectors.[8]

■ *Keep track of barriers of entry* and competitive advantages; they will, in large part, determine whether the firm will continue to maintain high growth.

■ *Be ready to be wrong.* The noise in these valuations is such that no matter how much information is brought into the process and how carefully a valuation is done, the value obtained is an estimate. Thus, investors in these stocks will be spectacularly wrong sometimes, and it is unfair to judge them on individual valuations. They will also be spectacularly right in other cases, and all that we can hope for is that with time as an ally, the successes outweigh the failures.

Implications for Managers

If the future growth potential for a firm is uncertain, what are the implications for managers? The first is that the uncertainty about future growth will almost certainly translate into more uncertainty in traditional investment analysis. It is far more difficult to estimate cash flows and discount rates for individual projects in young start-up firms than in more stable sectors. While the reaction of some managers at these firms is to give up and fall back on more intuitive approaches, the managers who persevere and attempt to estimate cash flows will have a much better sense of what they need to do to make new investments pay off. The second is that the company's value comes as much from the narrative that you give the company as it does from the proverbial bottom line. Put simply, managers of young companies have to not only provide vision, but convert that vision into a consistent and deliverable business story.

THE EXPECTATIONS GAME

As the proportion of value determined by future growth increases, expectations become a more critical determinant of how markets react to new information. In fact, the expectations game largely explains why stock prices change in ways that do not seem consistent with the news being announced (good earnings news leading to stock price drops; bad earnings news resulting in stock price increases) and the volatility in stock prices of young start-up firms in general.

Expectations, Information, and Value

The value of a firm is the present value of the expected cash flows on the firm, and implicit in these expected cash flows and the discount rates used to discount the cash flows are investors' views about the firm, its management, and the potential for excess returns. While this is true for all firms, the larger proportion of value that comes from future growth potential at young start-up firms makes them particularly vulnerable to shifts in expectations about the future.

---

[8]The simple rules of diversification that suggest 20 stocks are enough may not apply here. Since these investments tend to come from the same sector and have higher correlations with each other, and since there is so much noise in estimation, more stocks will be needed to accomplish the same degree of diversification that one would have got by buying 20 large-capitalization, mature companies.

How are these expectations formed? While the past history of these firms and industry averages are sometimes used as the basis for estimates, the firms and the industries themselves both evolve and change over time. The fact that information is both noisy and limited suggests that expectations can change relatively quickly and in response to small shifts in information. An earnings announcement, for instance, that suggests that a firm's strategy is not working as well as anticipated may lead to a reassessment of expectations and a sharp drop in value.

Lessons for Investors

The power of expectations in determining the value of a stock has to be considered when investors choose stocks for their portfolios and when they assess new information about the firm. There are several important implications:

- *Risk is always relative to expectations.* The risk in a firm does not come from whether it performs well or badly but from how it does relative to expectations. Thus, a firm that reports earnings growth of 35 percent a year when it was expected to grow 50 percent a year is delivering bad news and will probably see its stock price drop. In contrast, a firm that reports a 20-percent drop in earnings when it was expected to report a 40-percent drop will generally see its stock price increase.
- *Good companies do not always make good investments.* It is not how well or badly a company is managed that determines stock returns; it is how well or badly managed it is relative to expectations. A company that meets every financial criterion for excellence may be a poor investment if markets are expecting too much of it. Conversely, a firm that is universally viewed as a poorly managed, poorly run company may be a good investment if expectations have been set too low.[9]
- *Small news can lead to big price jumps.* As noted in the preceding section, you should expect to see what seem like disproportionate stock price responses to relatively small pieces of information. A report from a high-growth firm that earnings in the most recent quarter were a few cents less than expected may lead to a significant drop in the stock price.
- *Focus on information about value drivers.* On a positive note, investors can assess what it is that drives value the most at a firm, and get a sense of what they should focus on when looking at new information. Looking past the aggregate earnings numbers for information on these value drivers may provide clues of both upcoming trouble and potential promise.

Lessons for Managers

If the expectation game affects investors, it is even more critical to managers at young firms. One of the ironies that emerges from this game is that it is far easier to manage a firm that is perceived to be a poor performer than it is to manage one that is perceived to be a star.[10]

---

[9] The empirical evidence backs up this proposition. Studies of investments seem to indicate that companies that are viewed as well-managed underperform companies that are less well regarded as investments.
[10] Steve Jobs's job at Apple Computer was far easier when he took over in 1998 (when the stock price had hit a 10-year low) than it was two years later, when he had succeeded in changing investor perceptions of the company (and pushed the stock price up tenfold in the process).

■ *Find out what is expected of you.* If you are going to be judged against expectations, it is critical that you gauge what these expectations are. While this translates, for many firms, into keeping track of what analysts are estimating earnings per share or revenue growth to be in the next quarter, there is more to it than this. Understanding why investors value your firm the way they do, and what they think are your competitive advantages are, is much more important in the long term.

■ *Learn to manage expectations.* When firms are first listed on public markets, managers and insiders sell the idea that their firm has great potential and should be valued highly. While this is perfectly understandable, managers have to learn to manage expectations. Specifically, they have to talk down expectations when they feel that their firm is being set up to do things that it cannot accomplish. Again, though, some firms damage their credibility when they talk down expectations incessantly, even when they know the expectations are reasonable.[11]

■ *Do not delay the inevitable.* No matter how well a firm manages expectations, there are times when managers realize that they cannot meet expectations anymore because of changes in the sector or the overall economy. While managers try to delay revealing this realization to financial markets, often by shifting earnings from future periods into the current one or using accounting ploys, it is far better to deal with the consequences immediately. This may mean reporting lower earnings than expected and a lower stock price, but firms that delay their day of reckoning tend to be punished much more.

CONCLUSION

Valuation, fundamentally, remains the same no matter what type of firm one is analyzing. There are three groups of firms where the exercise of valuation becomes more difficult and estimates of value noisier. The first group includes firms that have negative earnings. Given the dependence of most models on earnings growth to make projections for the future, analysts have to consider approaches that allow earnings to become positive, at least over time. They can do so by normalizing earnings in the current period, by adjusting margins from current levels to sustainable levels over time, or by reducing leverage. The approach used will depend on why the firm has negative earnings in the first place. The second group of firms where estimates are difficult to make are young firms with little or no financial history. Here, information on comparable firms can substitute for historical data and allow analysts to estimate the inputs needed for valuation. The third group of firms where valuation can be difficult includes unique firms with few or no comparable companies.

If all three problems come together for the same firm—negative earnings, limited history, and few comparables—the difficulty is compounded. This chapter has laid out a broad framework that can be used to value such firms. It should be noted again that the question is not whether these firms can be valued—they certainly can—but whether we are willing to live with noisy estimates of value. To those who argue that these valuations are too noisy to be useful, our counter would be that much of this noise stems from real uncertainty about the future. As we see it, investors who attempt to measure and confront this uncertainty are better prepared for the volatility that comes with investing in these stocks.

---

[11] In the 1990s, Microsoft developed a reputation for talking down expectations, and then beating them on a consistent basis.

QUESTIONS AND SHORT PROBLEMS

In the problems following, use an equity risk premium of 5.5 percent if none is specified.

1. Intellitech is a technology firm that has been in operating for two years. In the most recent year, the firm reported revenues of $500 million, five times revenues in the previous year. The firm also reported an operating loss of $400 million. You expect revenues to grow 100% next year, 80% the year after, and 40% a year for the following three years, and the pretax operating margin to improve—in linear increments—to 10% by the fifth year. Estimate the revenues and operating income each year for the next five years.
2. You are trying to estimate the trailing 12-month earnings for Fiber Networks. The firm has just reported an operating loss for the first quarter of 2001 of $180 million on revenues of $600 million, a jump from the operating loss of $30 million on revenues of $120 million in the first quarter of 2000. In its annual report for 2000, Fiber Networks reported an operating loss of $330 million on revenues of $1.1 billion. Estimate the operating loss and revenues for the past four quarters.
3. Verispace Software sells inventory management software and reported revenues of $25 million in the most recent financial year. You estimate that the total market for inventory management software to be $25 billion, growing at 5% a year for the foreseeable future. If you expect Verispace to have 10% market share of this market in 10 years, estimate the compounded revenue growth rate over that period.
4. Lumin Telecomm produces specialized telecommunication equipment and has made losses each year over the three years it has been in existence—it has an accumulated net operating loss of $180 million. In the most recent year, the firm reported an operating loss of $90 million on revenues of $1 billion. If you expect the growth rate in revenues to be 20% a year for the next five years, and the pretax operating margin to be –6% next year, –3% two years from now, 0% the year after, 6% in four years, and 10% in five years (tax rate = 40%), estimate:
   a. The revenues and pretax operating income each year for the next five years.
   b. The taxes you would have to pay and your after-tax operating income each year for the next five years.
5. In problem 4, assume that Lumin Telecomm has a beta of 2.0 currently and that you expect it to drop in linear increments to 1.2 by year 5. If the current cost of borrowing is 9% and you expect this to remain unchanged over the next five years, estimate the cost of capital for the firm each year for the next five years. (The risk-free rate is 5.6%, and the risk premium is 4%.) The debt ratio is expected to decline from 70% in the current year to 50% in year 5 in linear increments.
6. You have estimated the value of Vitale Systems, an Internet software firm, to be $700 million as a going concern, seven times its book value. However, you are concerned that Vitale might not survive the next five years and estimate the probability of failure at 40%. If the firm fails, you expect its assets to sell for 1.5 times book value. If there are 30 million shares outstanding, estimate the value per share. (The firm has no debt or options outstanding.)

CHAPTER 24

Valuing Private Firms

So far, this book has concentrated on the valuation of publicly traded firms. In this chapter, we turn our attention to the thousands of firms that are private businesses. These businesses range in size from small family businesses to some that rival large publicly traded firms in revenues and profitability. The principles of valuation remain the same, but there are estimation problems that are unique to private businesses. The information available for valuation tends to be much more limited in terms of both history and depth, since private firms are often not governed by the standardized accounting and reporting standards of publicly traded firms. In addition, the standard techniques for estimating risk parameters such as beta and standard deviation require market prices for equity, an input that is lacking for private firms.

When valuing private firms, the motive for the valuation matters and can affect the value. In particular, the value that is attached to a publicly traded firm may be different when it is being valued for sale to an individual, for sale to a publicly traded firm, or for an initial public offering. In particular, whether there should be a discount on value for illiquidity and nondiversifiable risk or a premium for control will depend on the potential buyer. Each of these components will be considered over the course of this chapter.

WHAT MAKES PRIVATE FIRMS DIFFERENT?

There are a number of common characteristics shared by private firms with publicly traded firms, but there are four significant differences that can affect how we estimate inputs for valuation.

1. Publicly traded firms are governed by a set of accounting standards that allow us not only to identify what each item in a financial statement includes but also to compare earnings across firms. Private firms, especially if they are not incorporated, operate under far looser standards, and there can be wide differences between firms on how items are accounted.

2. There is far less information about private firms in terms of both the number of years of data that is typically available and, more importantly, the amount of information available each year. For instance, publicly traded firms have to break down operations by business segments in their filings with the SEC and provide information on revenues and

earnings by segment. Private firms do not have to provide this information, and usually do not.

3. A constantly updated price for equity and historical data on this price are very useful pieces of information that we can obtain easily for publicly traded firms but not for private firms. In addition, the absence of a ready market for private firm equity also means that liquidating an equity position in a private business can be far more difficult (and expensive) than liquidating a position in a publicly traded firm.

4. In publicly traded firms, the stockholders tend to hire managers to run the firms, and most stockholders hold equity in several firms in their portfolios. The owner of a private firm tends to be very involved with management, and often has all his or her wealth invested in the firm. The absence of separation between the owner and management can result in an intermingling of personal expenses with business expenses, and a failure to differentiate between management salary and dividends (or their equivalent). The absence of diversification can affect our measurement of risk.

Each of the differences cited can change value by affecting discount rates, cash flows, and expected growth rates.

To examine the issues that arise in the context of valuing private firms, we will consider two firms. The first firm is Chez Pierre, an upscale French restaurant in New York City, and the second is a private software firm called InfoSoft. We will value Chez Pierre for sale in a private transaction, whereas we will value InfoSoft for sale in an initial public offering (IPO).

ESTIMATING VALUATION INPUTS AT PRIVATE FIRMS

The value of a private firm is the present value of expected cash flows, discounted back at an appropriate discount rate. Since this construct is not different from the one we used to value publicly traded firms, the differences between private firms and publicly traded firms have to show up in how we estimate these inputs to the discounted cash flow model.

Discount Rates

If we choose to value equity, we discount cash flows to equity at the cost of equity, whereas if we choose to value the firm, we discount cash flows at the cost of capital. While the fundamental definitions of these costs have not changed, the process of estimating them may have to be changed given the special circumstances surrounding private firms.

Cost of Equity In assessing the cost of equity for publicly traded firms, we looked at the risk of investments through the eyes of the marginal investors in these firms. With the added assumption that these investors were well diversified, we were able to define risk in terms of risk added on to a diversified portfolio or market risk. The beta in the capital asset pricing model (CAPM) and betas (in the multifactor models) that measure this risk are usually estimated using historical stock prices. The absence of historical price information for private firm equity and the failure on the part of many private firm owners to diversify can create serious problems with estimating and using betas for these firms.

Approaches to Estimating Market Betas   The standard process of estimating the beta in the capital asset pricing model involves running a regression of stock returns against market returns. Multifactor models use other statistical techniques, but they also require historical price information. In the absence of such information, as is the case with private firms, there are three ways in which we can estimate betas: accounting betas, fundamental betas, and bottom-up betas.

Accounting Betas   While price information is not available for private firms, accounting earnings information is. We could regress changes in a private firm's accounting earnings against changes in earnings for an equity index (such as the S&P 500) to estimate an accounting beta:

$$\Delta \text{Earnings}_{\text{private firm}} = a + b\,\Delta \text{Earnings}_{\text{S\&P 500}}$$

The slope of the regression (b) is the accounting beta for the firm. Using operating earnings would yield an unlevered beta, whereas using net income would yield a levered or equity beta.

There are two significant limitations with this approach. The first is that private firms usually measure earnings only once a year, leading to regressions with few observations and limited statistical power. The second is that earnings are often smoothed out and subject to accounting judgments, leading to mismeasurement of accounting betas.

ILLUSTRATION 24.1:   Estimating an Accounting Beta—InfoSoft

InfoSoft, even though it is a private business, has been in existence since 1992 and has accounting earnings going back to that year. Table 24.1 summarizes the annual accounting earnings changes at InfoSoft and for the S&P 500 for each year between 1992 and 2010.

TABLE 24.1   Accounting Earnings—Infosoft versus S&P 500

Year	S&P 500 Earnings	Δ Earnings (%)	Infosoft Earnings ('000s)	Δ Earnings (%)
1992	20.87		$ 25	
1993	26.90	28.89%	$ 45	80.00%
1994	31.75	18.03%	$ 80	7.78%
1995	37.70	18.74%	$125	56.25%
1996	40.63	7.77%	$135	8.00%
1997	44.09	8.52%	$160	18.52%
1998	44.27	0.41%	$165	3.13%
1999	51.68	16.74%	$200	21.21%
2000	56.13	8.61%	$220	10.00%
2001	38.85	−30.79%	$150	−31.82%
2002	46.04	18.51%	$280	86.67%
2003	54.69	18.79%	$420	50.00%

(*continued*)

TABLE 24.1   *(continued)*

Year	S&P 500		Infosoft	
	Earnings	Δ Earnings (%)	Earnings ('000s)	Δ Earnings (%)
2004	67.68	23.75%	$600	42.86%
2005	76.45	12.96%	$750	25.00%
2006	87.72	14.75%	$900	20.00%
2007	82.54	−5.91%	$800	−11.11%
2008	65.39	−20.78%	$600	−25.00%
2009	60.8	−7.02%	$550	−8.33%
2010	83.66	37.60%	$900	63.64%

Regressing the changes in earnings at InfoSoft against changes in earnings for the S&P 500 yields the following.

$$\text{InfoSoft Earnings change} = 0.10 + 1.84(\text{S \& P 500 Earnings change})$$
$$(1.93)\ (6.91)$$

Based on this regression, the beta for InfoSoft is 1.84. In calculating this beta, we used net income to arrive at an equity beta. Using operating earnings for both the firm and the S&P 500 should yield the equivalent of an unlevered beta.

Fundamental Betas   There have been attempts made by researchers to relate the betas of publicly traded firms to observable variables, such as earnings growth, debt ratios, and variance in earnings. Beaver, Kettler, and Scholes (1970) examined the relationship between betas and seven variables: dividend payout, asset growth, leverage, liquidity, asset size, earnings variability, and the accounting beta. Rosenberg and Guy (1976) also attempted a similar analysis.

Updating this regression using data for 1,710 U.S. companies from January 2024, we obtained the following:

$$\text{Beta} = 0.74 - 0.01(\text{Cash/Capital}) + 0.2898\ \text{DFR} + 0.0467\ \text{Earnings Growth}$$
$$(34.58)(2.05) \qquad\qquad (6.39) \qquad\qquad (2.43)$$

Where   Cash/Capital = Cash/(BV of debt + BV of equity)
          DFR = BV of debt/(BV of debt + BV of equity)
   Earnings growth = CAGR in Earnings − last 3 years

Thus, firms that have higher debt-to-capital ratios and expected growth have higher betas, whereas firms that have more cash, as a percent of book value of capital, have lower betas. Since all the independent variables can be obtained for a private business, you could estimate a fundamental beta for the business. A caveat on using this regression is that the R-squared of the regression is only 2.8 percent, suggesting that the predictions will come with large standard errors.

ILLUSTRATION 24.2: Estimating a Fundamental Beta: InfoSoft

To use the cross-sectional regression that we reported earlier to estimate a beta for InfoSoft, we have to estimate the value for each of the independent variables for the firm.

Variable	Value
Cash/(BV of debt + BV of equity)	25%
BV of debt/(BV of debt + BV of equity)	0%
CAGR in net income – last 3 years	50%

Inputting these values into the regression, we obtain a predicted value for the beta:

$$\text{Beta} = 0.74 - 0.01(.25) + 0.2898(0) + 0.0467(0.50) = 0.76$$

This would yield an estimate of 0.76 for InfoSoft's beta. The standard error on this estimate is 0.07, resulting in a range of 0.62–0.90 for the beta, with 95% probability.

Bottom-Up Betas When valuing publicly traded firms, we used the unlevered betas of the businesses that the firms operated in to estimate bottom-up betas—the costs of equity were based on these betas. We did so because of the low standard errors on these estimates (due to the averaging across large numbers of firms) and the forward-looking nature of the estimates (because the business mix used to weight betas can be changed). We can estimate bottom-up betas for private firms, and these betas have the same advantages that they do for publicly traded firms. Thus, the beta for a private steel firm can be estimated by looking at the average betas for publicly traded steel companies. Any differences in financial or even operating leverage can be adjusted for in the final estimate.

In making the adjustment of unlevered betas for financial leverage, we do run into a problem with private firms, since the debt-to-equity ratio that should be used is a market value ratio. While many analysts use the book value debt-to-equity ratio to substitute for the market ratio for private firms, we would suggest one of the following alternatives:

■ Assume that the private firm's market debt-to-equity ratio will resemble the average for the industry. If this is the case, the levered beta for the private firm can be written as:

$$\beta_{\text{private firm}} = \beta_{\text{unlevered}}[1 + (1 - \text{Tax rate})(\text{Industry average Debt/Equity})]$$

■ Use the private firm's target debt-to-equity ratio (if management is willing to specify such a target) or its optimal debt ratio (if one can be estimated) to estimate the beta:

$$\beta_{\text{private firm}} = \beta_{\text{unlevered}}[1 + (1 - \text{Tax rate})(\text{Optimal Debt/Equity})]$$

The adjustment for operating leverage is simpler and is based on the proportion of the private firm's costs that are fixed. If this proportion is greater than is typical in the industry, the beta used for the private firm should be higher than the average for the industry.

 spearn.xls: **This dataset on the web has earnings changes, by year, for the S&P 500 going back to 1960.**

ILLUSTRATION 24.3:   Estimating Bottom-Up Betas—Chez Pierre and InfoSoft

---

To estimate a bottom-up beta for Chez Pierre, we looked at publicly traded restaurants in the United States. In January 2011, these firms had an average unlevered beta of 1.21 and an average market debt-to-equity ratio of 22.08%. We will assume that Chez Pierre will have the same unlevered beta and maintain a debt-to-equity ratio similar to that of publicly traded firms. Using a 40% tax rate, we get a levered beta for Chez Pierre of 1.37.

$$\text{Levered beta for Chez Pierre} = 1.21 \times [1 + (1 - .40) \times (.2208)] = 1.37$$

To estimate a beta for InfoSoft, we obtained the betas and market debt-equity ratios for publicly traded software firms. Since there are 333 software firms in the sample, with wide variations in market capitalization and growth prospects, we also look at subclasses of these firms that might be more comparable to InfoSoft.

Grouping	# of Firms	D/E Ratio	Unlevered Beta
All software firms	333	5.61%	1.08
Small-cap software firms (Market cap <$1 billion)	108	6.35%	1.60
Entertainment software firms	26	4.55%	1.45

Note that the debt-equity ratios are market value debt-equity ratios, and that that the difference in the size of the firms should not affect the betas directly, but it might have an indirect effect, since smaller firms tend to have higher operating leverage. We will use an unlevered beta of 1.60 for InfoSoft, based on the average beta of small cap software firms. To estimate a levered beta, we recognize that Infosoft has no debt outstanding and no plans to borrow money. Its levered beta is, therefore, equal to its unlevered beta of 1.60.

Adjusting for Nondiversification   Betas measure the risk added by an investment to a diversified portfolio. Consequently, they are best suited for firms where the marginal investor is diversified. With private firms, the owner is often the only investor, and thus, can be viewed as the marginal investor. Furthermore, in most private firms, the owner tends to have much of his or her wealth invested in the private business and does not have an opportunity to diversify. Consequently, it can be argued that betas will understate the exposure to market risk in these firms.

At the limit, if the owner has all his or her wealth invested in the private business and is completely undiversified, he or she is exposed to all risk in the firm and not just the market risk (which is what the beta measures). There is a fairly simple adjustment that can allow us to bring in this nondiversifiable risk into the beta computation. To arrive at this adjustment, assume that the standard deviation in the private firm's equity value (which measures total risk) is σ_j, and that the standard deviation in the market index is σ_m. If the correlation between the stock and the index is defined to be ρ_{jm}, the market beta can be written as:

$$\text{Market beta} = \rho_{jm}\sigma_j/\sigma_m$$

Note that the numerator is the portion of the risk in the firm. To measure exposure to total risk (σ_j), we could divide the market beta by ρ_{jm}. This would yield the following:

$$\text{Market beta}/\rho_{jm} = \sigma_j/\sigma_m$$

This is a relative standard deviation measure, where the total standard deviation of the private firm's equity value is scaled against the market index's standard deviation to yield what we will call a total beta:

$$\text{Total beta} = \text{Market beta}/\rho_{jm}$$

The total beta will be higher than the market beta and will depend on the correlation between the firm and the market—the lower the correlation, the higher the total beta. Intuitively, it scales the beta to reflect all risk in the firm and not just the portion of the risk that is market risk.

You might wonder how a total beta can be estimated for a private firm, where the absence of market prices seems to rule out the calculation of either a market beta or a correlation coefficient. Note, though, that we were able to estimate the market beta of the sector by looking at publicly traded firms in the business. We can obtain the correlation coefficient by looking at the same sample and use it to estimate a total beta for a private firm.

The question of whether the total beta adjustment should be made cannot be answered without examining why the valuation of the private firm is being done in the first place. If the private firm is being valued for sale, whether and how much the market beta should be adjusted will depend on the potential buyer or buyers. If the valuation is for an initial public offering, there should be no adjustment for nondiversification, since the potential buyers are stock market investors. If the valuation is for sale to another individual or private business, the extent of the adjustment will depend on the degree to which the buyer's portfolio is diversified; the more diversified the buyer, the higher the correlation with the market and the smaller the total beta adjustment.

ILLUSTRATION 24.4: Estimating a Bottom-Up Beta—Chez Pierre

Consider the estimate of market beta that we obtained for Chez Pierre in the previous illustration. Using publicly traded restaurants as our comparable firms, we obtained an unlevered beta of 1.21 for Chez Pierre. The average correlation coefficient for these publicly traded firms with the markets is 48.41%. The total unlevered beta for Chez Pierre can be estimated as follows:

$$\text{Total unlevered beta} = \frac{\text{Market unlevered beta}}{\text{Correlation with market}} = \frac{1.21}{0.4841} = 2.50$$

Using Chez Pierre's tax rate of 40% and a debt-to-equity ratio of 22.08% (the restaurant sector's average) yields a total levered beta of 2.07.

$$\text{Total levered beta} = 2.50 \times [1 + (1 - .40) \times (.2208)] = 2.83$$

This total beta estimate, in a sense, takes the limiting view that the potential buyer will own only Chez Pierre. To the extent that the buyer has some diversification, the correlation coefficient will be adjusted upward; if the buyer has a diversified portfolio, the correlation coefficient will approach 1 and the total beta will converge on the market beta.

ALTERNATIVE ADJUSTMENTS FOR PRIVATE FIRM RISK

If you are leery about using the total beta approach to estimate the cost of equity for a private firm, there are three alternatives:

1. *Venture capital returns:* Look at the actual returns earned by investors who invest in private companies over long periods of history, relative to the risk-free rate and returns on publicly traded firms. Thus, if venture capital investors have earned 5 percent more than the S&P 500 after adjusting for risk, you could view this as a premium for investing in private businesses and add the number to your cost of equity, computed using a conventional risk and return model:

Adjusted cost of equity = Risk-free rate + Market beta
× Equity risk premium + Venture capital premium

The counter argument is that venture capitalists cannot really be compared to private business owners, since they are not only more diversified but may also have other exit strategies in mind (such as going public eventually).

2. *Build up approach:* In this approach, you again start with the expected return from a conventional risk and return model, and then add premiums to reflect the special risks associated with investing in small, private businesses. Two commonly used premiums are the small cap premium, reflecting the actual premium earned by very small, publicly traded companies over and above the market return (about 4 to 5 percent between 1928 and 2010) and the illiquidity premium, reflecting the higher returns earned by less liquid, public investments (with liquidity measured in trading volume and bid-ask spreads).

Adjusted cost of equity = Risk-free rate + Market beta
× Equity risk premium + Small cap premium
+ Illiquidity premium + Company-specific
risk premium

Notwithstanding its popularity, there are multiple problems with this approach. The first is that even if the premiums used as back-up with data, these premiums come from studies that measure them in isolation. Thus, it is true that there is a historical small cap premium of about 4%, if you go back to 1927, though as we noted in Chapter 8, that small cap premium has largely disappeared since 1981. It is also true that illiquid stocks earn higher returns (of about 2%) than liquid stocks, if you classify stocks based upon liquidity, and look at returns over the last few decades. It is however dangerous to add the two premiums together, since some of the small cap premium may come from their lower liquidity, creating a double counting. The second is that once appraisers are given the license to adjust discount rates, especially with premiums that have no basis in the data, like the company-specific risk premium, the integrity of intrinsic valuation breaks down.

3. *Implied private costs of equity:* As data on private transactions gets richer, it is possible that we could use transactions prices to back out internal rates of return, given the expected cash flows. These internal rates of return will be the implied costs of equity to buyers. While there have been attempts to do this in the last few decades, they have been stymied by the fact that the prices observed in private company transactions are not always arm's length, and the cash flows used in the valuation are not always accessible or reliable.

From Cost of Equity to Cost of Capital   To get from the cost of equity to the cost of capital, we need two additional inputs—the cost of debt, which measures the rate at which firms can borrow, and the debt ratio, which determines the weights in the cost of capital computation. This section considers how best to estimate each of these inputs for a private firm.

Cost of Debt   The cost of debt represents the rate at which a firm can borrow money. To estimate it for publicly traded firms, we generally use either the yields on bonds issued by these firms or the ratings for these bonds to get default spreads. Private firms generally are not rated and do not have bonds outstanding. Consequently, we have to use one of the following alternative approaches:

- If the private firm has borrowed money recently (in the past few weeks or months), we can use the interest rate on the borrowing as a cost of debt. Since the cost of debt has to be current, the book interest rate[1] on debt issued in the past is generally not a good measure of the cost of debt.
- If the private firm is being valued for an initial public offering, we can assume that the cost of debt for the private firm will move toward the average cost of debt for the industry to which the firm belongs. We are essentially assuming that the private firm, once public, will structure its debt policy to resemble those of comparable firms.
- When estimating the cost of debt for publicly traded firms in Chapter 8, we used the interest coverage ratios of these firms to estimate synthetic ratings, and then used the default spreads on these ratings to arrive at the costs of debt. To allow for the fact that private firms tend to be smaller and riskier than most publicly traded firms, we would use the relationship between interest coverage ratios and ratings for a subset of smaller, publicly traded firms, summarized in Table 24.2.

TABLE 24.2   Interest Coverage Ratios and Bond Ratings

Interest Coverage Ratio	Rating
>12.50	AAA
9.50–12.50	AA
7.50–9.50	A+
6.00–7.50	A
4.50–6.00	A–

(continued)

---

[1]Book interest rate = Interest expenses/Book value of debt.

TABLE 24.2 (*continued*)

Interest Coverage Ratio	Rating
3.50–4.50	BBB
3.00–3.50	BB
2.50–3.00	B+
2.00–2.50	B
1.50–2.00	B–
1.25–1.50	CCC
0.80–1.25	CC
0.50–0.80	C
<0.50	D

To estimate the cost of debt for a private firm with an interest coverage ratio of 5.1, for instance, we would use a synthetic rating of A– and the default spread associated with that rating. Thus, if firms that are rated A– typically pay 1.25 percent above the riskless rate to borrow, we would add that default spread to the riskless rate to estimate the cost of debt for the private firm.

This approach may underestimate the cost of debt if banks charge higher interest rates for private firms than for otherwise similar publicly traded firms. In that case, you would add an additional spread to reflect this difference, if you were valuing the firm for sale in a private transaction, but not if you were valuing it for sale to a publicly traded firm or an initial public offering.

Debt Ratios The debt ratio represents the proportion of the market value of a firm that comes from debt financing. For publicly traded firms, we use the market prices of publicly traded stocks and bonds to arrive at this ratio. Since neither input will be available for private firms, we have to consider one of the following options:

- In estimating levered betas, we suggested that the industry-average or target debt ratios could be used in the computation. Consistency demands that we use the same debt ratio for computing the cost of capital. Thus, if the industry-average debt-to-equity ratio is used to estimate the levered beta, the industry-average debt-to-capital ratio should be used to estimate the cost of capital. If the target debt-to-equity ratio is used for the levered beta computation, the target debt-to-capital ratio should be used in the cost of capital calculation.
- While market values of equity and debt are not available for private firms, we can use our estimated values of equity and debt from the valuation, though this creates circular reasoning in the analysis. You need the cost of capital (and the debt ratio) to estimate firm and equity value, and you need the equity value to estimate the cost of capital. You could overcome this problem by iterating toward a value—you could start with the book-debt ratio and cost of capital, estimate a firm and equity value, use these values to arrive at a new debt ratio and cost of capital, and reestimate firm and equity value. You would continue until the debt and equity values in the cost of capital computation converge on the estimated values.[2]

---

[2] The values will always converge.

ILLUSTRATION 24.5: Estimating Cost of Debt

InfoSoft has no debt, and we did not estimate a cost of debt for the firm. For Chez Pierre, we estimated an interest coverage ratio based on the operating income of $400,000 and its annual lease expenses of $120,000:

$$\text{Interest coverage ratio} = \$400,000/\$120,000 = 3.33$$

That interest-coverage ratio yielded a synthetic rating of BB based on Table 24.1.

Adding the default spread of 4%, for a BB-rated bond, to the risk-free rate of 3.5% provides a pretax cost of debt of 7.5% for the firm.

$$\text{Pretax cost of debt} = \text{Risk-free rate} + \text{Default spread} = 3.5\% + 4\% = 7.5\%$$

$$\text{After tax cost of debt} = 7.5\% \times (1 - .40) = 4.5\%$$

ILLUSTRATION 24.6: Estimating Cost of Capital

To estimate the cost of capital for Chez Pierre and InfoSoft, we will stay consistent with the assumptions we have made about leverage so far in this chapter. Chez Pierre, we assumed, would stay close to industry average debt-to-equity ratio of 22.08%, which translates into a market debt-to-capital ratio of 18.09%. For InfoSoft, we stayed with the assumption that the firm has a debt ratio of 0%.

For Chez Pierre, given that we are valuing the firm for sale to an undiversified individual, we estimated a total beta of 2.83. Using the Treasury bond rate of 3.5% prevalent at the time of this valuation and a market risk premium of 5%, we estimate a cost of equity of 17.65%.

$$\text{Cost of equity} = 3.5\% + 2.83 \times (5\%) = 17.65\%$$

Using the after-tax cost of debt of 4.5% estimated in Illustration 24.5, we can estimate the cost of capital.

$$\text{Cost of capital} = 17.65\% \times (0.8191) + 4.5\% \times (0.1809) = 15.27\%$$

For InfoSoft, where we are pricing an initial public offering, we use the market beta estimate of 1.60. Using the Treasury bond rate of 3.5% and a risk premium of 5% yields a cost of equity of 11.50%.

$$\text{Cost of equity} = 3.5\% + 1.60 \times (5\%) = 11.50\%$$

Since the firm has no debt, the cost of capital is also 11.50%.

Cash Flows

The definitions of the cash flow to equity and cash flow to the firm are identical for both private and publicly traded firms. The cash flow to equity is the cash flow after taxes, debt payments and issues, and reinvestment needs. The cash flow to the firm is the cash flow after taxes and reinvestment needs but before debt payments. There are three issues that do affect estimation of cash flows with private firms. The first is that many private firms do not adequately consider the salaries for owner-managers, since many owners do not distinguish between income that they receive as dividends and income obtained as salaries. The second is the intermingling of personal and business expenses that often occurs at small private businesses can cause income to be mismeasured. The third is the effect of taxes on value, since individual tax status and tax rates vary much more widely than corporate tax rates.

Owner Salaries and Equity Cash Flows

In valuing firms, we draw a simple distinction between salaries and dividends. Salaries are compensation for professional services rendered to the firm and should be treated as operating expenses. Dividends or other equity cash withdrawals from the firm are returns on equity capital invested and determine the value of equity. The separation between managers and stockholders in publicly traded firms results in a distinction between salaries (which are paid to managers) and dividends (which are paid to stockholders) that is clear. In a private business, the owner is often the firm's manager and its only equity investor. If the private firm is not incorporated, the income earned by the owner is taxed at the same rate, whether it is categorized as a salary or as a dividend. Consequently, an owner will be indifferent between receiving a salary of $10,000 and a dividend of $90,000 and a salary of $90,000 and a dividend of $10,000. As a consequence, owners do not pay themselves a salary in many small private firms, or even if they do, the salary does not reflect the services they render to the firm.

When valuing a private firm, we generally make forecasts based on the operating income reported by the firm. If that operating income does not reflect a salary adjustment for the owner, it will be overstated and result in a value that is too high. To get a more precise estimate of operating income, we have to estimate the appropriate compensation for the owner-managers, based on the role they play in the firm and the cost of hiring replacements for them. Thus, the owner of a private business might play several roles—cashier, accountant, stockperson, and salesperson, and the management salary would have to include the cost of hiring a person or outside entity to provide the same services.

Intermixing Business and Personal Expenses

The intermingling of business and personal expenses is a particular problem in small private businesses, since owners often have absolute power over many aspects of these businesses. Many private business owners maintain offices in their residences, have vehicles that they use for personal and business use, and share other services between work and home. In some cases, family members are hired to fill phantom positions to distribute income or to reduce taxes.

If personal expenses are consolidated with business expenses or are otherwise a part of business expenses, the operating income for a private firm has to be estimated prior to these expenses. The problem with making these adjustments, however, is that private firm owners are usually not forthcoming about the extent of these expenses, and there may be tax consequences.

Tax Effects

When valuing publicly traded firms, the tax rate that we use in valuation is centered on the marginal corporate tax rate. While different firms may face different marginal tax rates, the differences in tax rates across potential buyers of a private firm will be much larger. In fact, the tax rate can vary from the corporate tax rate (if the potential buyer is a corporation), to the highest marginal tax rate for individuals (if the potential buyer is a wealthy individual), to zero if the potential buyer has lower income like a nonprofit. The tax rate will affect both the cash flows (through the after-tax operating income) and the cost of capital (through the cost of debt). As a consequence, the value of a private firm can vary across different buyers.

TO PRETAX OR AFTER-TAX

Private businesses can be organized in many different ways, with very different tax consequences. In its simplest form, a private business can be a sole proprietorship, where the line between business and the individual is blurred and the income from the business is reported on the owner's tax returns. Here, the solution is simple. Compute the cash flows, after taking into account the owner's tax liability, and discount those cash flows back at a rate of return that the owner would need on an after-tax basis, to compensate for the risk taken. It is possible, however, that this business could be worth a different amount to a potential buyer who faces a different tax rate.

Things become more interesting when you have a partnership, where income is split among the partners based on the proportion of the partnership that they own and is shown as income (and taxed) on their individual tax returns. To the extent that they face similar tax rates, you can use a consensus tax rate that reflects the partners' standing and compute after-tax cash flows and discount back at a risk-adjusted after-tax rate of return.

Finally, consider a subchapter S corporation. The entity is not taxed on its income, but the stockholders in the corporation are taxed on their share of the income, even if it is not paid out as dividends. (A stockholder in a publicly traded company is taxed only on the dividend paid and can defer paying capital gains taxes until he or she sells the stock.) You can value this firm, using one of two approaches:

1. You can use the same logic that we used for partnerships and find a tax rate that reflects what the stockholders pay. You can then estimate after-tax cash flows and discount back at a rate of return that is risk-adjusted and after taxes.
2. You can hone in on pretax cash flows and discount them back at a risk-adjusted pretax rate of return.

The key to all of these valuations is to use the appropriate discount rate, given the cash flows.

When you use the CAPM or its variants to estimate discount rates for publicly traded companies, you are estimating a *post-corporate tax* and *pre-personal tax required rate of return*. If you draw on the same risk and return models to estimate discount rates for private businesses, you have to recognize that if the cash flows are after personal taxes, you will have to adjust the discount rates accordingly. In June 2011, for instance, the cost of equity for a public company was about 8 percent. The tax rate on dividends and capital gains was 15 percent. If we assume that the marginal investor pays this tax rate on the entire return, the post-personal tax cost of equity is 6.8 percent.

ILLUSTRATION 24.7: Operating and Net Income

To estimate the cashflows for Chez Pierre, we started with the stated income from the owner's financial statements. Those statements (with all the numbers reported in thousands) indicated that the restaurant generated $400,000 in operating income and $240,000 in net income on revenues of $1.2 million in the most recent year (see Table 24.3):

TABLE 24.3 Income Statements—Chez Pierre

	Stated	Adjusted
Revenues	$1,200.00	$1,200.00
– Operating lease expense	$ 120.00	
– Imputed depreciation on leased asset		$ 50.38
– Wages	$ 200.00	$ 350.00
– Material	$ 300.00	$ 300.00
– Other operating expenses	$ 180.00	$ 180.00
Operating income	$ 400.00	$ 319.62
– Imputed interest expenses	$ 0.00	$ 69.62
Taxable income	$ 400.00	$ 250.00
– Taxes	$ 160.00	$ 100.00
Net income	$ 240.00	$ 150.00

We made two key adjustments. First, we noticed that the owner (and chef) was not paying himself a salary. We added $150,000 to wages to reflect the expected expense associated with a new chef. Second, we converted operating lease expenses into financial expenses, by capitalizing the lease commitments ($120,000/ year for the next 12 years), using the pretax cost of debt of 7.5% that we estimated in Illustration 24.5:

$$\text{PV of lease commitments} = \$120,000(\text{PV of annuity, 7.5\%, 12 years}) = \$928,230$$

This conversion then results in two new items on the income statement:

$$\text{Imputed interest expenses} = \$828,233 \times .075 = \$69,620$$

$$\text{Imputed depreciation} = \text{Current year's lease expense} - \text{Imputed interest expense}$$
$$= \$120,000 - \$69,620 = \$50,380$$

These two adjustments reduce the operating income to $319,620 and the net income to $180,230.

InfoSoft, though a private firm, has essentially been run like a public firm, probably as a lead-in to the initial public offering. This table reflects the operating income for InfoSoft.

Income Statement—InfoSoft (in '000s)

Sales and other operating revenues	$10,000
– Operating costs and expenses	$ 8,300
– Depreciation	$ 200
Operating income	$ 1,500
– Interest expenses	$ 0

Income Statement—InfoSoft (in '000s)

Taxable income	$ 1,500
– Taxes	$ 600
Net income	$ 900

Growth

The growth rate for a private firm can be estimated by looking at the past (historical growth) or from fundamentals (the reinvestment rate and return on invested capital). This section will consider some of the issues in estimating private firm growth.

Estimating Growth   In estimating growth for publicly traded firms, we noted that we could draw on three sources—historical growth, analyst estimates, and fundamentals. With private firms, we will not find analyst estimates of growth, and historical growth numbers have to be used with caution. The shifting accounting standards that characterize many private firms will mean that reported earnings changes over time may not reflect actual earnings changes. Furthermore, the fact that earnings are measured annually rather than quarterly, and the reality that private firms tend to be younger than publicly traded firms will mean far less data in the historical growth estimate.

As a consequence of these gaps in past growth and analyst estimates, there should be an even greater reliance on fundamentals in private firms. The expected growth rate in operating income is the product of the reinvestment rate and the return on capital, though changes in return on capital in existing assets can create an additional impact.

$$\text{Expected growth rate} = \text{Reinvestment rate} \times \text{Return on invested capital}$$

In making the estimates of reinvestment rates and returns on capital for private firms, we can look at both the histories of these firms and the industry averages for publicly traded companies in the same businesses.

ILLUSTRATION 24.8:   Estimating Growth

The process of estimating growth is different for the two firms under consideration in this chapter. With Chez Pierre, we are looking at a well-run restaurant operating at close to capacity and that is unlikely to grow at rate higher than the inflation rate. Consequently, we will assume a growth rate of 2% in nominal terms for the next 12 years, which is the remaining lease term. At the end of year 12, we assume that the business will be liquidated. Since we are assuming a finite life and no real growth, we also assume a reinvestment rate of zero for the firm.

To estimate the growth rate at InfoSoft, we follow a more conventional route. We first estimate the return that the firm earns on its capital invested currently, by dividing the after-tax operating income from the most recent year by the book value capital invested[3] at the beginning of the year. We use the operating income from Illustration 24.7 and a marginal tax rate of 40%.

---

[3] As with publicly traded firms with R&D expenses, we capitalized the expenses, and the capital invested reflects the value of the research asset.

$$\text{Return on invested capital} = \frac{\text{Operating income } (1 - \text{tax rate})}{\text{BV of debt}_{\text{Last year}} + \text{BV of equity}_{\text{Last year}} - \text{Cash}_{\text{Last year}}}$$

$$= \frac{1500 \, (1 - .40)}{0 + 5000 - 500} = 20.00\%$$

We then estimate InfoSoft's reinvestment rate by dividing its reinvestment (in capital expenditures and working capital) in the most recent year by the after-tax operating income. Given that the firm reported capital expenditures of \$960,000, depreciation of \$200,000, and an increase in noncash working capital from \$100,000 to \$150,000, we estimated a reinvestment rate of:

$$\text{Reinvestment rate} = \frac{\text{Cap ex} - \text{Depreciation} + \text{Change in WC}}{\text{EBIT } (1 - t)}$$

$$= \frac{960 - 200 + 50}{1500 \, (1 - .4)} = 90\%$$

The expected growth rate in operating income for InfoSoft for the immediate future assumes that the return on capital and reinvestment rate will remain unchanged over the next five years.

$$\text{Expected growth rate} = 20\% \times .90 = 18\%$$

If we had expected the return on capital or the reinvestment rate to change over time, we would have reflected those changes in this growth rate.

Persistence of Growth   In valuing publicly traded firms, we generally assumed infinite lives, even though we did allow for the risk that the firms would not survive. With private firms, the perpetual life assumption has to be made with far more caution. Unlike publicly traded firms, where the transition from one CEO to another is common, the transition is much more complicated in a private firm where the owner-manager often looks to the next generation in his or her family for the successor, a process that is not always successful.

What are the implications for valuation? One is that the terminal value for a private firm will be lower than the terminal value for a publicly traded firm. If we assume, in fact, that the firm will cease operations at some point in time in the future—say when the current owner retires—we would use a liquidation value for the assets as the terminal value. In general, liquidation values are lower than the value of continuing operations. The other is that private firms where owners plan for the transition to the next generation will be worth more than private firms that do not make these arrangements.

Some private firms, especially as they get larger, resemble publicly traded firms in terms of having professional managers. With these firms, the assumption of infinite growth that we used with publicly traded firms can be sustained.

ILLUSTRATION 24.9: Closure in Valuation and Terminal Values

As we noted earlier, we assume a 12-year life for Chez Pierre. When the lease ends, we assume that the restaurant will be closed and that the assets will be liquidated at a book value of \$500,000.

With InfoSoft, we are assuming a growing and healthy publicly traded firm, based on our projections over the next 10 years. The firm should be worth more based on continuing operations than from liquidation. Consequently, we assume an expected growth rate of 3% beyond year 10 for the firm. As the firm becomes larger, it will become more and more difficult for it to sustain its current return on capital of 20%. We assume that the return on capital will drop to 12% after year 10. These two assumptions yield a reinvestment rate of 25% after year 10.

$$\text{Reinvestment rate} = \frac{\text{Stable growth rate}}{\text{Stable ROIC}} = \frac{3\%}{12\%} = 25\%$$

We also assume that the beta for InfoSoft will drop to 1.20 after year 10, and that the firm will use some of its debt capacity (its debt ratio will rise from 0% to 10% and the cost of debt will be 5%). The resulting cost of equity and capital are estimated here:

$$\text{Cost of equity} = 3.5\% + 1.2 \times (5\%) = 9.5\%$$
$$\text{After-tax cost of debt} = 5\% \times (1 - .40) = 3\%$$
$$\text{Cost of capital} = 9.5\% \times (.9) + 3\% \times (.1) = 8.85\%$$

"Key Person" Effect on Value

Young companies, especially in service businesses, are often dependent upon the owner or a few key people for their success. While we generally think of key people as those at the top of entities (i.e., top managers and founders), their role can vary in different businesses, as shown in Figure 24.1.

Consequently, the value we estimate for these businesses can change significantly if one or more of these key people will no longer be associated with the firm. To assess a key person discount in valuations, we suggest that the firm be first valued with the status quo

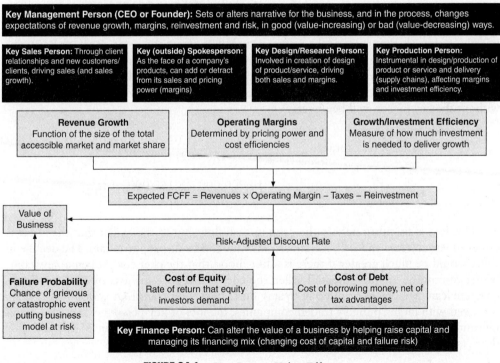

FIGURE 24.1   Key Person Value Effect

(with key people involved in the business), and then be valued again with the loss of these individuals built into revenues, earnings, and expected cash flows. To the extent that earnings and cash flows suffer when key people leave, the value of the business will be lower with the loss of these individuals, and the effect can show up in each of the value drivers, and Figure 24.1 illustrates these effects. To value a key person or persons, you should value the firm twice, once with the status quo (with the key persons continuing to work for the firm) and once without, leading to the key person effect:

$$\text{Key person value effect(\$)} = \text{Value of firm}_{\text{status quo}} - \text{Value of firm}_{\text{no key person}}$$

In percentage terms, the key person effect can be stated as a percent of the status quo value:

$$\text{Key person value effect(\%)} = \frac{\text{Value of firm}_{\text{status quo}} - \text{Value of firm}_{\text{no key person(s)}}}{\text{Value of firm}_{\text{status quo}}}$$

To illustrate, assume that you are valuing a restaurant that is being offered for sale by its well-known chef/owner. Assume that the restaurant generated $1 million in after-tax cash flow last year, has an expected growth rate of 2 percent and a cost of capital of 12 percent. The value of the restaurant should be $10 million, based on these inputs:

$$\begin{aligned} \text{Value of restaurant}_{\text{status quo}} &= \frac{\text{Expected FCFF next year}}{(\text{Cost of capital} - \text{Growth rate})} \\ &= \frac{1{,}000{,}000\,(1.02)}{(.12 - .02)} = \$10{,}200{,}000 \end{aligned}$$

It is likely, though, that some of the revenues/cash flows from this restaurant can be attributed to the chef and that his departure will cause a drop-off in cash flows. Assume that as the potential buyer, you survey customers in the restaurant and realize that there will be a 20-percent drop-off in cash flow if the current chef leaves. The value of the restaurant without the key person will be lower:

$$\text{Value of restaurant}_{\text{no key person(s)}} = \frac{800{,}000\,(1.02)}{(.12 - .02)} = \$8{,}160{,}000$$

$$\text{Key person value effect(\%)} = \frac{10{,}200{,}000 - 8{,}160{,}000}{10{,}200{,}000} = 20\%$$

This loss is proportionate to the drop in cash flow, but to the extent that the effect is on revenues, margins and risk, the effects on value can be disproportionate. The decline in value would be much greater if there is a likelihood that the chef could open a new competing restaurant. As the potential seller, the chef can reduce his loss by signing a noncompete legal agreement or offering to stay on as chef for a transition period.

Even with larger, publicly traded companies, the loss of key personnel can have a significant impact on value. In fact, the question of how much an Elon Musk adds (or detracts) from Tesla's value in 2024 was widely discussed.

Illiquidity Discounts

When you take an equity position in an entity, you generally would like to have the option to liquidate that position if needed. The need for liquidity arises not only because of cash flow considerations but also because you might want to change your portfolio holdings. With publicly traded firms, liquidation is simple and generally has a low cost—the transaction costs for liquid stocks are a small percent of the value. With equity in a private business, liquidation costs as a percent of firm value can be substantial. Consequently, the value of equity in a private business may need to be discounted for this potential illiquidity. This section will consider the determinants of this discount and how best to estimate it.

Determinants of Illiquidity Discount   The illiquidity discount is likely to vary across both firms and buyers, which renders rules of thumb useless. Let us consider four factors that may cause the discount to vary across firms:

1. *Liquidity of assets owned by the firm.* The fact that a private firm is difficult to sell may be rendered moot if its assets are liquid and can be sold with no significant loss in value. A private firm with significant holdings of cash and marketable securities should have a lower illiquidity discount than one with factories or other assets for which there are relatively few buyers.
2. *Financial health and cash flows of the firm.* A private firm that is financially healthy should be easier to sell than one that is not healthy. In particular, a firm with solid profits and positive cash flows should be subject to a smaller illiquidity discount than one with negative income and cash flows.
3. *Possibility of going public in the future.* The greater the likelihood that a private firm can go public in the future, the lower should be the illiquidity discount attached to its value. In effect, the probability of going public is built into the valuation of the private firm. To illustrate, the owner of a private e-commerce firm in 1998 or 1999 would not have had to apply much of an illiquidity discount to his or her firm's value, if any, because of the ease with which these firms could be taken public in those years.
4. *Size of the firm.* If we state the illiquidity discount as a percent of the value of the firm, it should become smaller as the size of the firm increases. In other words, the illiquidity discount should be smaller as a percent of firm value for private firms like Cargill and Koch Industries, which are worth billions of dollars, than it should be for a small firm worth $15 million a million.

The illiquidity discount is also likely to vary across potential buyers because the desire for liquidity varies with individuals. It is likely that those long-term buyers who have deep pockets and see little or no need to cash out their equity positions will attach much lower illiquidity discounts to value for similar firms than short-term buyers that have less of a safety margin.

Empirical Evidence and Typical Practice   How large is the illiquidity discount attached to private firm valuations? This is a very difficult question to answer empirically because the discount itself cannot be observed. Even if we were able to obtain the terms of all private firm transactions, note that what is reported is the price at which private firms are bought and sold. The value of these firms is not reported, and the illiquidity discount is the difference between the value and the price.

In fact, much of the evidence on illiquidity discounts comes from examining restricted stock at publicly traded firms. Restricted securities are securities issued by a publicly traded company but not registered with the SEC, that can be sold through private placements to investors but cannot be resold in the open market for a one-year holding period, and only limited amounts can be sold after that. When this stock is issued, the issue price is set much lower than the prevailing market price, and the difference is viewed as a discount for illiquidity. The results of three studies that have looked at the magnitude of this discount are listed here:

1. Maher (1976) examined restricted stock purchases made by four mutual funds in the period 1969–1973 and concluded that they traded at an average discount of 35.43 percent on publicly traded stock in the same companies.
2. Moroney (1973) reported a mean discount of 35 percent for acquisitions of 146 restricted stock issues by 10 investment companies, using data from 1970.
3. Silber (1991) examined restricted stock issues from 1984 to 1989 and found that the median discount for restricted stock was 33.75 percent.

In summary, there seems to be a substantial discount attached, at least on average, when an investment is not liquid. Much of the practice of estimating illiquidity discounts seems to build on these averages. For instance, rules of thumb often set the illiquidity discount at 20–30 percent of estimated value, and there seems to be little or no variation across firms.

Silber (1991) also examined factors that explained differences in discounts across different restricted stocks by relating the size of the discount to observable firm characteristics, including revenues and the size of the restricted stock offering. He reported the following regression:

$$\ln(\text{RPRS}) = 4.33 + 0.036 \ \ln(\text{REV}) - 0.142 \ \ln(\text{RBRT})$$
$$+ 0.174 \ \text{DERN} + 0.332 \ \text{DCUST}$$

where RPRS = Restricted stock price/Unrestricted stock price
         = 1 – Illiquidity discount
     REV = Revenues of the private firm (in millions of dollars)
    RBRT = Restricted block relative to total common stock in %
    DERN = 1 if earnings are positive; 0 if earnings are negative
   DCUST = 1 if there is a customer relationship with the investor; 0 otherwise

The illiquidity discount tends to be smaller for firms with higher revenues, decreases as the block offering decreases, and is lower when earnings are positive and when the investor has a customer relationship with the firm.

These findings are consistent with some of the determinants that we identified in the previous section for the illiquidity premium. In particular, the discounts tend to be smaller for large firms (at least as measured by revenues) and for healthy firms (with positive earnings being the measure of financial health). This would suggest that the conventional practice of using constant discounts across private firms is wrong and that we should be adjusting for differences across firms.

Estimating the Illiquidity Discount   If we do decide to adjust the illiquidity discount to reflect the differences across private firms, we are faced with an estimation question. How are we going to measure these differences and build them into an estimate? There are two ways of doing this. The first is to extend the analysis done for restricted securities into the illiquidity discount; in other words, we could adjust the discount factor for the magnitude of a firm's revenues and whether it has positive earnings. The second is to extend some of the empirical work that has been done examining the magnitude of the bid-ask spread for publicly traded firms to estimating illiquidity discounts.

Restricted Stocks and Initial Public Offerings   Consider again the regression that Silber presents on restricted stock. Not only does it yield a result specific to restricted stock, but it also provides a measure of how much lower the discount should be as a function of revenues. A firm with revenue of $20 million should have an illiquidity discount that is 1.19 percent lower than a firm with revenues of $10 million. Thus, we could establish a benchmark discount for a profitable firm with specified revenues (say $10 million) and adjust this benchmark discount for individual firms that have revenues much higher or lower than this number. The regression can also be used to differentiate between profitable and unprofitable firms. Figure 24.2 presents the difference in illiquidity discounts across both profitable and unprofitable firms with different revenues, using a benchmark discount of 25 percent for a firm with positive earnings and $10 million in revenues.

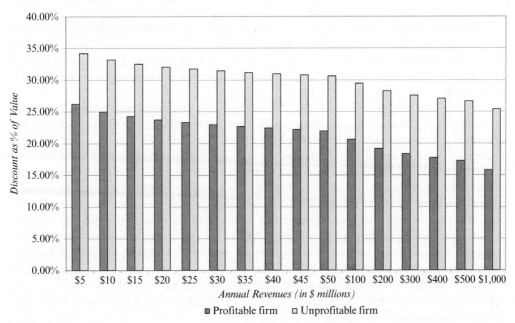

FIGURE 24.2   Illiquidity Discounts: Base Discount of 25 Percent for Profitable Firm with $10 Million in Revenues

There are clearly dangers associated with extending a regression run on a small amount of restricted stock to estimating discounts for private firms, but it does provide at least a road map for adjusting discount factors.

In follow-up studies, there have been attempts to quantify the illiquidity discount by looking at transactions that occur just before an IPO, where founders or venture capitalists sell stakes in the firm to each other. The illiquidity discount can then be measured as the difference between the IPO price (which is observable) and the transaction price, with the latter being lower because it occurs prior to the IPO, when equity is still illiquid. The discounts that show up in these studies are so large (>40%) that they are not credible, and are more likely to reflect sampling bias than a true illiquidity discount

Bid-Ask Spread Approach   The biggest limitations of using studies based on restricted stock or IPOs is that the samples are small and biased. The bias, in particular, comes from the fact that healthy publicly traded firms are unlikely to issue restricted shares, at large discounts on market value, and that there are many firms that plan IPOs that never go through with public offerings (but are ignored in the IPO studies).

We would be able to make better estimates if we could obtain a large sample of firms with illiquidity discounts. We would argue that such a sample exists, if we consider the fact that an asset that is publicly traded is not completely liquid. In fact, liquidity varies widely across publicly traded stock. A small company listed over-the-counter is much less liquid than a company listed on the New York Stock Exchange, which in turn is much less liquid than a large-capitalization company that is widely held. In fact, the difference between the bid price and the ask price that we observe on publicly traded assets can be viewed as a measure of the cost of instant liquidity. An investor who buys an asset, changes his or her mind, and decides to sell the asset immediately will pay the bid-ask spread.

While the bid-ask spread might only be a quarter or half a dollar, it looms as a much larger cost when it is stated as a percent of the price per unit. For a stock that is trading at $2, with a bid-ask spread of 25 cents, this cost is 12.5 percent. For higher-price and very liquid stocks, the illiquidity discount may be less than 0.5 percent of the price, but it is not zero.

What relevance does this have for illiquidity discounts on private companies? Think of equity in a private company as a stock that never trades. On the continuum just described, you would expect the bid-ask spread to be high for such a stock, and this would essentially measure the illiquidity discount.

To make estimates of the illiquidity discounts using the bid-ask spread, scaled to the price of the stock, as the measure, you would need to relate the bid-ask spread of publicly traded stocks to variables that can be measured for a private business. For instance, you could regress the bid-ask spread against the revenues of the firm and a dummy variable reflecting whether the firm is profitable, and extend the regression done on restricted stocks to a much larger sample. You could even consider the trading volume for publicly traded stocks as an independent variable and set it to zero for a private firm. Using data from the end of 2000, for instance, we regressed the bid-ask spread for Nasdaq stocks against revenues, a dummy variable for positive earnings, cash as a percent of firm value, and trading volume.

$$\text{Spread} = 0.145 - 0.0022\ \ln(\text{Annual revenues}) - 0.015(\text{DERN})$$
$$- 0.016(\text{Cash/Firm value}) - 0.11(\$\ \text{Monthly trading volume/Firm value})$$

where

DERN = Dummy variable, set to one (zero) if earnings are positive (negative)

Cash/Firm value = Cash/(Total Debt + Market capitalization)

Plugging in the corresponding values—with a trading volume of zero—for a private firm should yield an estimate of the bid-ask spread for the firm.

Illiquidity as an Option   What is the value of liquidity? Put differently, when does an investor feel the loss of liquidity most strongly when holding an asset? There are some who would argue that the value of liquidity lies in being able to sell an asset, when it is most overpriced; the cost of illiquidity is not being able to do this. In the special case, where the owner of an asset has the information to know when this overpricing occurs, the value of illiquidity can be considered an option.

Longstaff (1995) presents an upper bound for the option by considering an investor with perfect market timing abilities who owns an asset on which they is not allowed to trade for a period (t). In the absence of trading restrictions, this investor would sell at the maximum price that an asset reaches during the time- period, and the value of the look-back option estimated using this maximum price should be the outer bound for the value of illiquidity.[4] Using this approach, Longstaff estimates how much marketability would be worth as a percent of the value of an asset for different illiquidity periods and asset volatilities.

It is worth emphasizing that these are upper bounds on the value of illiquidity since it is based upon the assumption of a perfect market timer. To the extent that investors are unsure about when an asset has reached its maximum price, the value of illiquidity will be lower than these estimates. The more general lessons will still apply. The cost of illiquidity, stated as a percent of firm value, will be greater for more volatile assets, and will increase with the length of the period for which trading is restricted. There have been attempts to extend option pricing models to valuing illiquidity, with mixed results. In one widely used variation, liquidity is modeled as a put option for the period when an investor is restricted from trading. Thus, the illiquidity discount on value for an asset where the owner is restricted from trading for two years will be modeled as a two-year at-the-money put option.[5] There are several flaws, both intuitive and conceptual, with this approach. The first is that liquidity does not give you the right to sell a stock at today's market price anytime over the next two years. What it does give you is the right to sell at the prevailing market price anytime over the next two years.[6] The second (and smaller) problem is that option pricing models are based upon continuous price movements and arbitrage, and it is difficult to see how these assumptions will hold up for an illiquid asset.

---

[4]It is the outer bound because it assumes that you know how the price will move and sell when it optimal for you to do so.

[5]In a 1993 study, David Chaffe used this approach to estimate illiquidity discounts rangings from 28–49% for an asset, using the Black Scholes option pricing model and volatilities ranging from 60 to 90% for the underlying asset.

[6]There is a simple way to illustrate that this put option has nothing to do with liquidity. Assume that you own stock in a liquid, publicly traded company and that the current stock price is $50. A 2-year put option on this stock with a strike price of $50 will have substantial value, even though the underlying stock is completely liquid. The value has nothing to do with liquidity, but is a price you are willing to pay for insurance.

The value of liquidity ultimately must derive from the investor being able to sell at some predetermined price during the nontrading period, rather than being forced to hold until the end of the period. The look-back option approach that assumes a perfect market timer, as explained earlier, assumes that the sale would have occurred at the high price and allows us to estimate an upper bound on the value. Can we use option pricing models to value illiquidity without assuming perfect market timing? Consider one alternative. Assume that you have a disciplined investor who always sells investments, when the price rises 25% above the original buying price. Not being able to trade on this investment for a period (say, two years) undercuts this discipline, and it can be argued that the value of illiquidity is the produce of the value of the put option (estimated using a strike price set 25% above the purchase price and a two-year life), and the probability that the stock price will rise 25% or more over the next two years.

If you decide to apply option pricing models to value illiquidity in private businesses, the value of the underlying asset (which is the private business) and the standard deviation in that value will be required inputs. While estimating them for a private business is more difficult to do than for a publicly traded firm, we can always use industry averages.

ILLUSTRATION 24.10:   Estimating the Illiquidity Discount for Chez Pierre

Since Chez Pierre is being valued for a private transaction, it is appropriate to consider an illiquidity discount. We can use both approaches described earlier to estimate the magnitude of that discount

1. *Restricted stock approach:* To estimate the illiquidity discount for Chez Pierre, we assume that the base discount for a firm with $10 million in revenues would be 25%. Chez Pierre's revenues of $1.2 million, being smaller than the typical firm, should result in a higher discount on their value. We estimate the difference in the illiquidity discount between a firm with $10 million in revenue and $1.2 million in revenue to be 3.75%. To do this, we first estimated the illiquidity discount in the Silber equation for a firm with $10 million in revenues.

$$\text{Illiquidity discount}_{\text{Base}} = \frac{100 - \exp(4.33 + 0.36 \times \ln(10) - 0.142 \times \ln(100) + 0.174 \times (1)}{100}$$

$$= 48.94\%$$

We then reestimated the illiquidity discount with revenues of $1.2 million:

$$\text{Illiquidity discount}_{\text{Revenue}=\$12\text{mil}} = \frac{100 - \exp(4.33 + 0.36 \times \ln(1.2) - 0.142 \times \ln(100) + 0.174 \times (1)}{100}$$

$$= 52.69\%$$

Increase in discount, based on revenues = 52.69% − 48.94% = 3.75%

The estimated illiquidity discount for Chez Pierre would, therefore, be 28.75%, which is the base discount of 25% adjusted for the additional discount to reflect smaller revenues that the firm possesses.

2. *Bid-ask spread approach:* We could substitute in the revenues of Chez Pierre the fact that it has positive earnings and the cash as a percent of revenues held by the firm (1%):

Spread $= 0.145 - 0.0022 \ \ln(\text{Annual revenues}) - 0.015(\text{DERN})$

$\qquad - 0.016(\text{Cash/firm value}) - 0.11(\$\text{ Monthly trading volume/Firm value})$

$\qquad = 0.145 - 0.0022 \times \ln(1.2) - 0.015 \times (1) - 0.016 \times (.03) - 0.11 \times (0) = .1294 \text{ or } 12.94\%$

Based on this approach, we would estimate an illiquidity discount of 12.94%.

---

 liqdisc.xls: **This spreadsheet allows you to estimate the illiquidity discount for private firms using both the restricted stock approach and the bid-ask spread approach.**

VALUATION MOTIVES AND VALUE ESTIMATES

In the preceding section, we considered how best to estimate the inputs to use in valuing a private firm. As we considered each input, though, we noted that the process of estimation might be different depending on the potential buyer of the firm. With betas, for instance, we argued that the market beta should be used if the potential buyer is a publicly traded firm or a stock market investor (in an initial public offering), and that a total beta should be used if the potential buyer is a private party. We made similar arguments about the cost of debt and cash flows. Table 24.4 summarizes the differences in the way we estimate the inputs to valuation for different valuation motives.

TABLE 24.4　Estimation of Inputs for Valuation: Valuation Motives

	Valuation for Sale to a Private Entity	Valuation for Sale to a Publicly Traded Firm or for an Initial Public Offering
Cost of equity	Based on total beta, with correlation reflecting diversification of potential buyer	Based on market beta, since marginal investor is diversified
Cost of debt	May reflect additional spread associated with being a private business	Based on synthetic rating, estimated by looking at publicly traded firms
Operating cash flows	Private business tax rate used in valuation	Corporate marginal tax rates used in valuation
Firm life	Finite life terminal value or liquidation value	Perpetual life when estimating terminal value
Illiquidity discount	Value discounted for illiquidity	No illiquidity discount

The results of using different approaches to estimating discount rates and cash flows, depending on the potential buyer, can have significant effects on value. In general, a private business that is up for sale will be valued much more highly by a publicly traded firm than by a private entity. This can be traced to the fact that the discount rates are higher when we assume that the buyer is not diversified. Thus, the owners of private businesses who are interested in selling their businesses will be well served looking for potential buyers who are publicly traded firms. While they might not be able to extract the entire value, they can try to obtain at least a share of the additional value created because the marginal investors are diversified.

The same implications arise when looking at the alternative of going public. The value that a firm can obtain from a public offering will exceed the value that it will receive from a private entity. The values obtained from an initial public offering and sale to a publicly traded firm will be based on similar discount rates but may vary because of cost and revenue synergies. If the potential for these synergies is large, selling to a publicly traded firm may result in a higher value than going public.

ILLUSTRATION 24.11: Valuing Chez Pierre for a Private Sale

To value Chez Pierre for a private sale, we draw on the inputs that we have estimated in prior illustrations:

After-tax operating income in most recent year = $319,620(1 − .40) = $191,770
(from illustration 24.7)

Cost of capital = 15.27% (from illustration 24.6)

Expected Growth rate = 2% a year for the next 12 years (from illustration 24.8)

Reinvestment rate = 0% (from illustration 24.8)

Pretax operating income in most recent year = $319,620 (from illustration 24.7)

FCFF in most recent year = $319,620(1 − .40) (1 − 0) = $191,770

At the end of year 12, we assume that the restaurant will be closed, and that the liquidation proceeds will be $500,000 (from illustration 24.9).

The present value of the operating cash flows over the next 12 years is estimated first:

$$\text{PV of FCFF for next 12 years} = \frac{191,770 \times \left(1 - \frac{1.02^{12}}{1.1527^{12}}\right)}{(0.1527 - .02)} = \$1,134,121$$

Adding the present value of the liquidation proceeds (discounted back 12 years at 15.27%) and subtracting out the present value of lease commitments yields the value of equity:

PV of operating cash flows for next 12 years	= $1,134,121
+ PV of liquidation value = $500,000/1.152710	= $ 90,821
− PV of operating lease commitments	= $ 928,333
Value of equity	= $ 296,709

Based on our estimates for growth and cost of capital, the value of the equity in Chez Pierre is $296,709.

ILLUSTRATION 24.12: Valuing InfoSoft for an Initial Public Offering

To value InfoSoft for an initial public offering, we gather the inputs that we have already estimated for the company:

1. *Cost of capital:* In illustration 24.6, we use a bottom-up market beta for InfoSoft and estimated a cost of equity and capital of 11.50%:

   Cost of equity = 3.5% + 1.60 (5%) = 11.50%
   Cost of capital = Cost of equity = 11.50%

In the terminal value computation (in illustration 24.9), we argued for a decrease in beta of 1.20 and an increase in the debt ratio to 10%, leading to a cost of capital of 8.85% in stable growth.

2. *Cash flows and growth rates:* In illustration 24.7, we presented the current income statement for InfoSoft, with pretax operating income of $1.5 million and a tax rate of 40%. In illustration 24.8, we estimated a return on capital of 20% and a reinvestment rate of 90% for InfoSoft, which we assumed would be maintained for the next five years, allowing for expected growth of 18% in earnings.

3. *Terminal value:* In illustration 24.9, we assumed that the firm would be in stable growth after year 10, growing 3% a year, while maintaining a return on capital of 12%. The five years between the high growth period (lasting five years) and the stable growth (after year 10) represent a transition phase, where growth rates, reinvestment rates, and costs of capital all change from high growth levels to stable growth levels. Table 24.5 summarizes the cash flows and the present value (in '000s).

TABLE 24.5   Expected Earnings, Cash Flows, and Present Value

Year	EBIT $(1-t)$	Expected growth	Reinvestment Rate	FCFF	Cost of capital	Cumulated WACC	PV
Current	$ 900						
1	$1,062	18.00%	90.00%	$ 106	11.50%	1.1150	$ 95
2	$1,253	18.00%	90.00%	$ 125	11.50%	1.2432	$ 101
3	$1,479	18.00%	90.00%	$ 148	11.50%	1.3862	$ 107
4	$1,745	18.00%	90.00%	$ 174	11.50%	1.5456	$ 113
5	$2,059	18.00%	90.00%	$ 206	11.50%	1.7234	$ 119
6	$2,368	15.00%	77.00%	$ 545	10.97%	1.9124	$ 285
7	$2,652	12.00%	64.00%	$ 955	10.44%	2.1121	$ 452
8	$2,891	9.00%	51.00%	$1,416	9.91%	2.3214	$ 610
9	$3,064	6.00%	38.00%	$1,900	9.38%	2.5391	$ 748
10	$3,156	3.00%	25.00%	$2,367	8.85%	2.7638	$ 856
Sum							$3,487

At the end of year 10, the firm is in stable growth and the terminal value is estimated as follows:

$$\text{Terminal value} = \frac{\text{EBIT}_{10}(1 - \text{tax rate})(1 + \text{Stable growth rate})(1 - \text{Reinvestment rate})}{(\text{Cost of capital} - \text{Stable growth rate})}$$

$$= \frac{3,156\ (1.03)(1 - .25)}{(0.0885 - 0.03)} = \$41.675 \text{ million}$$

Discounting the terminal value back, adding it to the present value of cash flows during the high-growth period and subtracting out debt (zero) yields a value of $18.566 million for the value of the operating assets.

$$\text{Value of operating assets} = \text{PV of cash flows from years } 1 - 10 + \frac{\text{Terminal value}}{\text{Cumulated WACC}_{10}}$$

$$= \$3.487 + \frac{41.675}{2.7638} = \$18.566 \text{ million}$$

Adding the cash balance ($500,000) and netting out debt ($), yields a value for the equity:

$$\text{Value of equity} = \text{Value of operating assets} + \text{Cash} - \text{Debt}$$

$$= \$18.566 + 0.5 - 0 = \$19.066 \text{ million}$$

Getting to value of equity per share: To get to value of equity per share, we value the 100,000 equity options that are held by managers and venture capitalists in the company, subtract the value from the value of equity, before dividing by the 1 million shares outstanding.

$$\text{Value of management options (in millions)} = \$1.161$$

$$\text{Value of equity in common stock} = \$19.066 - \$1.161 = \$17.904 \text{ million}$$

$$\text{Value of equity per share} = \$17.904/1.00 = \$17.90$$

MANAGEMENT FORECASTS AND THE GAMING OF PRIVATE COMPANY VALUATION

When valuing public companies, we talked about using analyst forecasts of growth and management guidance in estimating cash flows and growth for companies, and cautioned that while analysts and managers have an information advantage over outsiders, biases can very quickly dilute that advantage. In private company valuation, it is not just common for appraisers to rely on managers of private companies for future cash flow estimates, but often required by appraisal rules. The defense that appraisers offer for the dependence is that with many small private businesses, the information that managers have about market conditions and investment plans is indispensable in forecasting cash flows. That may true, but the bias in management forecasts is also likely to much greater, since there is no market price check.

It is no surprise, therefore, that appraisers, especially as they acquire more experience, accept that management forecasts of cashflows are biased upwards and try to offset that by using higher discount rates. In an earlier part of this chapter, we talked about a company-specific risk premium added to private company discount rates, with nebulous basis and no real data to back it up. For appraisers, the company-specific risk premium becomes a device used to increase discount rates by enough to compensate for cash flows that are too high and hopefully deliver a reasonable value.

This process, in our view, opens the door to meaningless intrinsic values, where made-up cash flows get discounted at made-up discount rates to arrive at predetermined values. To appraisers who argue that they have no choice, we need to debate why management forecasts are taken as a starting point and change that practice.

Control Issues

When valuing a firm, you need to consider the competence and strengths of the management of the firm. With private firms where the owner is also the manager, this consideration carries special weight, since the owner has absolute control. In a publicly traded firm, in contrast, incompetent management can often be replaced, if enough stockholders can be convinced that it is in their best interests to do so.

There are implications for valuation if a portion of a private firm is offered for sale. If that portion provides a controlling interest (i.e., the right to pick the firm's management), it should have a substantially higher value than if it does not provide this power. Normally, this would mean that 51 percent of a private firm's equity should trade at a substantial premium over 49 percent. This applies whether a firm is being sold to a private entity or a publicly traded firm, and may arise in an initial public offering. If, for instance, only non-voting shares or shares with diluted voting rights are offered to investors in the public offering, they should trade at a discount on shares with full voting rights.

While the intuition about the value of control is simple, estimating how much it is worth is a little more difficult. We will defer a full discussion of the topic until the next chapter on acquisitions, but we will value it as the difference between two values—the value of the firm run optimally and the value of the firm with the incumbent management. For instance, if the value of a private firm run by incumbent management is $100 million and the value of the firm run optimally is $150 million, the difference in values between the 51-percent and 49-percent shares can be computed as follows:

Value of controlling interest = 51% of optimal value = .51 × 150 = $76.5 million

Value of noncontrolling interest = 49% of status quo value = .49 × 100 = $49 million

The additional 2-percent interest (from 49 to 51 percent) has a disproportionate effect on value because of control. This value of control will be greatest for private firms that are poorly run and will be close to zero for well-run firms.

As we noted in Chapter 16, the same approach can be used to compute the discount that nonvoting shares will trade at relative to voting shares in initial public offerings. The values of the two classes can be estimated as follows:

$$\text{Value per nonvoting share} = \frac{\text{Status quo value}}{(\text{Number of voting share} + \text{Number of nonvoting shares})}$$

$$\text{Value per voting share} = \frac{\text{Status quo value}}{(\text{Number of voting share} + \text{Number of nonvoting shares})} + \frac{(\text{Optimal value} - \text{Status quo value}) \times \text{Probability of change}}{\text{Number of voting shares}}$$

By assuming that voting shares get the entire expected value of control, we are perhaps overstating the premium, since nonvoting shares may be able to claim some or perhaps an equal claim, depending on the change is made.[7]

---

[7]If change comes from an acquisition, and the acquirer has to buy only the voting shares to complete the acquisition, the voting shares will get the bulk or all of the premium. If change comes from within, where managers are replaced, nonvoting shareholders will also benefit from the change.

ILLUSTRATION 24.13:   Valuing Voting and Nonvoting Shares: InfoSoft

In the last illustration, we valued the equity in InfoSoft at $17.904 million. Based upon the 1 million shares outstanding, we estimated a value per share of $17.90. Assume that the firm decides to create .9 million nonvoting shares and .1 million voting shares. In the initial offering, only the nonvoting shares will be sold to the public, and the current owners will retain all of the voting shares.

To value the voting and nonvoting shares, we need to value InfoSoft under optimal management. Assume that the firm would be worth $20 million under optimal management.[8] The value of the voting and nonvoting shares can then be computed.

$$\text{Value per nonvoting share} = \frac{\text{Status quo value}}{(\text{Number of voting share} + \text{Number of nonvoting shares})}$$

$$= \frac{17.904}{(.1 + .9)}$$

$$= \$17.90$$

Assuming that incumbent managers will retain the voting shares reduces the probability of management change to 25%.

$$\text{Value per voting share} = \frac{\text{Status quo value}}{(\text{Number of voting share} + \text{Number of nonvoting shares})}$$

$$+ \frac{(\text{Optimal value} - \text{Status quo value}) \times \text{Probability of change}}{\text{Number of voting shares}}$$

$$= \frac{17.904}{(.1 + .9)} + \frac{(20 - 17.904) \times 0.25}{0.1} = \$23.14$$

VALUING VENTURE CAPITAL AND PRIVATE EQUITY STAKES

In the previous illustrations we looked at two extremes in the private company valuation spectrum: a private-to-private transaction, where the buyer and the seller were completely undiversified (and thus exposed to total risk), and a private-to-public transaction, an IPO, or sale of a private to a public company, where more conventional valuation approaches work.

There is an intermediate case, where venture capitalists and private equity investors take stakes in private businesses, with the intent of cashing out when the company goes public or is sold to a public entity. Venture capitalists and private equity investors are more diversified than private owners, but they are not as diversified as investors in public markets are for two reasons. The first is that they specialize in a few businesses: Many venture capitalists invest only in biotechnology companies or software businesses. The second is that the size of their positions (which tend to be large) and the need for oversight restrict them from having more than a handful of open positions at any time.

---

[8] InfoSoft was revalued at its optimal debt ratio. We assumed that the existing investment policy was optimal.

In a sense, if you think of total beta as the appropriate measure for the completely undiversified end of the spectrum and market beta as the right risk measure for the completely diversified buyer, venture capitalists and private equity investors fall in the middle of the spectrum. In fact, we can modify the total beta equation to reflect these differences:

$$\text{VC or private equity beta} = \frac{\text{Market beta}}{\text{Correlation of VC or PE portfolio with market}}$$

Thus, we are replacing the correlation of the private firm with the market with the correlation of the investor's portfolio. At the limit, a private equity may have so many holdings spread over so many different businesses that the correlation of their portfolios with the market will approach 1, and the beta that they should use is a market beta. In fact, as some of the biggest private equity firms like Blackstone have gone public, you can argue that they should be assessing the valuations of all private firms, as if they were fully diversified.

To see how this will play out, assume that you are valuing a private business operating in a sector where publicly traded companies have an average beta of 1 and the average correlation of firms with the market is 0.25. Assume that this company will be fully owned by its current owner for two years, will raise capital from a technology venture capitalist at the start of year 3, and is expected to either go public or be sold to a publicly traded firm at the end of year 5. We estimate the cost of equity at three stages (risk-free rate = 4%; equity risk premium = 5%):

Stage 1: The nascent business, with a private owner who is fully invested in that business:
 Perceived beta = 1/0.25 = 4
 Cost of equity = 4% + 4(5%) = 24%
Stage 2: Angel financing provided by specialized venture capitalist who holds multiple investments in high-technology companies. (Correlation of portfolio with market is 0.5.):
 Perceived beta = 1/0.5 = 2
 Cost of equity = 4% + 2(5%) = 14%
Stage 3: Public offering where investors are retail and institutional investors with diversified portfolios:
 Perceived beta = 1
 Cost of equity = 4% + 1(5%) = 9%

Now assume that you have projected cash flows for this company for the next five years and expect it to be a stable growth firm after it goes public in year 5, growing 2% a year in perpetuity. The value of the business can be estimated in Table 24.6:

TABLE 24.6 Expected Cash Flows and Present Value

	1	2	3	4	5	Terminal Year
Expected Cash Flows	$100	$125	$150	$165	$170	$175
Market beta	1.00	1.00	1.00	1.00	1.00	1.00
Correlation	0.25	0.25	0.50	0.50	0.50	1.00

(continued)

TABLE 24.6 *(continued)*

	1	2	3	4	5	Terminal Year
Beta used	4.00	4.00	2.00	2.00	2.00	1.00
Cost of equity	24.00%	24.00%	14.00%	14.00%	14.00%	9.00%
Terminal value					$2,500	
Cumulated COE	1.2400	1.5376	1.7529	1.9983	2.2780	2.4830
PV	$80.65	$81.30	$85.57	$82.57	$1,172.07	
Value of firm	$1,502					

The terminal value of equity is computed using the cost of equity of 9% in perpetuity, but is discounted back to today using the much higher costs of equity for the next five years. Note that using the private owner's cost of equity (24%) forever would have yielded too low a value ($1,221) and using the market beta cost of equity (9%) forever would resulted in too high a value ($2,165).

PRECASH AND POSTCASH VALUATIONS

When valuing private companies, many analysts draw a distinction between precash and postcash valuations. In general, this is done when an infusion of cash is anticipated either from venture capitalists or from an initial public offering. The precash valuation values the firm before the cash influx, and the postcash valuation values it after.

There are two reasons why the valuations may yield different values. The first is that the firm may face capital rationing constraints without the infusion of the cash, resulting in a scaling down of how much it can reinvest, and consequently how quickly it can grow. If the firm's return on capital is greater than the cost of capital, this will cause the value to be lower before the cash influx. The second is that the value of cash and marketable securities is added to the value of the operating assets to arrive at firm value. After a large cash influx, firms may have excess cash to invest in marketable securities, which when added to the value of operating assets will increase value. If the cash is taken out of the firm, though, by the existing owners, you should not add the cash to the value.

Which of these two values should be used to estimate the value per share in a public offering? Since stockholders in the firm will hold stock in the postcash firm, the postcash value should be used. In the case of a venture capitalist, though, the answer may be different. If the venture capitalist has bargaining power—he or she is the only person who is interested in providing venture capital—he or she can ask for a share of the firm value based on the precash valuation, arguing that the increase in value is feasible only with the additional venture capital. If two or more venture capitalists are interested in the firm, odds are that the postcash valuations will be the basis for deciding how much of the firm will be yielded to the venture capitalist.

ILLUSTRATION 24.14: Valuing a Private Equity Stake

Assume that you work for a publicly traded firm and have been asked to value a potential stake in a small, privately held firm that wants you to invest $10 million in its equity, which it plans to use to expand operations.

First, you would value the private firm assuming that you do not invest the $10 million. Based on the projected cash flows, assume that you value the equity in the firm at $30 million:

$$\text{Precash valuation} = \$30 \text{ million}$$

Now assume that your investment of $10 million will enable the firm to grow faster, and that the present value of the expected cash flows is $50 million for the equity. (This present value does not include the cash inflow of $10 million from the private equity investment.)

$$\text{Postcash valuation} = \$50 \text{ million} + \$10 \text{ million} = \$60 \text{ million}$$

The key question, assuming that you decide to make this investment, is the percentage of the private firm you should demand in return for the $10 million investment. At the minimum, you would demand a share of the postcash valuation:

$$\text{Share of ownership}_{minimum} = \frac{\text{Capital infusion}}{\text{Postcash valuation}} = \frac{10}{60} = 16.66\%$$

However, you would bargain for a larger share. At the limit, you could argue for a share of the precash valuation, with your capital infusion counted in:

$$\text{Share of ownership}_{maximum} = \frac{\text{Capital infusion}}{\text{Precash valuation} + \text{Capital infusion}} = \frac{10}{30 + 10} = 25\%$$

PRICING PRIVATE BUSINESSES

The essence of relative valuation is that you value a firm based on how much the market is paying for similar firms. This premise is clearly more challenging for private businesses. Notwithstanding these problems, analysts have tried to extend the relative valuation practices that have been developed for public companies into the private business space. In general, there are two approaches used by analysts for coming up with comparable firms in private company valuation. Some analysts focus on transaction prices paid for other private businesses, arguing that these businesses are likely to have more in common with the young business being valued. Other analysts, distrustful of private transaction prices, draw on the market prices of publicly traded companies in the same business, and try to adjust for differences in fundamentals.

Private Transaction Multiples

Since you are valuing a young, private business, it seems logical that you should look at what others have paid for similar businesses in the recent past. That is effectively the foundation on which private transaction multiples are based. In theory, at least, you pull together a dataset of other young private businesses, similar to the one that we are valuing (same business, similar size, and at the same stage in the life cycle), that have been bought/ sold and the transaction values. You then scale these values to a common variable (revenues, earnings, or something even sector-specific) and compute a typical multiple that acquirers have been willing to pay. Applying this multiple to the same variable for the company being valued should yield an estimated value for the company.

Potential Problems   The biggest problem used to be the absence of organized databases of private business transactions, but that is no longer the case. Many private services offer databases (for a price) that contain this data, but other problems remain:

- *Arms-length transactions.* One of the perils of using prices from private transactions is that some of them are not arms'-length transactions, where the price reflects just the value of business being sold. In effect, the price includes other services and side factors that may be specific to the transaction. Thus, a doctor selling a medical practice may get a higher price because he agrees to stay on for a period of time after the transaction to ease the transition.
- *Timing differences.* Private business transactions are infrequent and reflect the fact that the same private business will not be bought and sold dozens of times during a particular period. Unlike public firms, where the current price can be used to compute the multiples for all firms at the same point in time, private transactions are often staggered across time. A database of private transactions can, therefore, include transactions from June 2008 and December 2008, a period when the public markets lost almost 45 percent of their value.
- *Scaling variable.* To compare firms of different scale, we generally divide the market price by a standardizing variable. With publicly traded firms, this can take the form of revenues (price/sales, EV/sales), earnings (PE, EV/EBITDA), or book value. While we could technically do the same with private transactions, there is a potential roadblock. There are broad differences in accounting standards across private businesses, and these differences can result in bottom lines that are not quite equivalent.
- *Nonstandardized equity.* Equity claims in private businesses can vary widely in terms of cash flow, control claims, and illiquidity. The transaction price for equity in a private business will reflect the claims that are embedded in the equity in that business and may not easily generalize to equity in another firm with different characteristics.
- *Non-U.S. firms.* Most of the transaction databases that are available and accessible today are databases of transactions of private businesses in the United States. As we are called upon increasingly to value businesses in other markets, some of which are riskier emerging markets, it is not clear how or even whether this data can be used in that context.

Usefulness and Best Practices   So, when is it appropriate to use private transaction data to value a private business? As a general rule, this approach works best for small businesses that plan to stay small and private, rather than expand their reach and perhaps go public. It also helps if the firm being valued is in a business where there are not only a large number of other private businesses but also where transactions are common. For instance, this approach should work well for valuing a medical/dental practice or a small retail business. It will get more difficult to apply for firms that are in unique or unusual businesses.

If you decide to employ private company transactions to value a business, there are five general practices that can help to deliver more dependable valuations:

- *Scale to variables that are less affected by discretionary accounting choices:* As a counter to the problem of wide differences in accounting and operating standards across private companies, you can focus on variables where discretionary choice matters less. For instance, multiples of revenues (which are more difficult to fudge or manipulate) should be preferred to multiples of earnings. You could even scale value to units specific to the business being valued—number of patients for a general medical practice or the number of customers for a plumbing business.
- *Value businesses, not equity.* In Chapter 16, we classified multiples into equity multiples (where equity value is scaled to equity earnings or book value) and enterprise value multiples (where the value of the business is scaled to operating earnings, cash flows, or the book value of capital). Given the wide differences in equity claims and the use of debt across private businesses, it is better to focus on enterprise value multiples rather than equity multiples. In other words, it is better to value the entire business, and then work out the value of equity than it is to value equity directly.
- *Start with a large dataset:* Since transactions with private businesses are infrequent, it is best to start with a large dataset of companies and collect all transaction data. This will then enable you to screen the data for transactions that look suspicious (and are thus, likely to fail the arm's-length test).
- *Adjust for timing differences.* Even with large datasets of private transactions, there will timing differences across transactions. While this is not an issue in a period where markets are stable, you should make adjustments to the value (even if they are crude) to account for the timing differences. For instance, using June 2008 and December 2008 as the transaction dates, you would reduce the transaction prices from June 2008 by the drop in the public market (a small cap index like the Russell 5000 dropped by about 40 percent over that period) to make the prices comparable.
- *Focus on differences in fundamentals.* The notion that the value of a business depends on its fundamentals—growth, cash flows, and risk—cannot be abandoned just because you are doing relative valuation. The estimated value is likely to be more reliable if you can collect other measures of the transacted private businesses that reflect these fundamentals. For instance, it would be useful to obtain not only the transaction prices of private businesses but also the growth in revenues recorded in these businesses in the period prior to the transactions and the age of the business (to reflect maturity and risk). You can explore the data to see if there is a relationship between transaction value and these variables, and if there is one, to build it into the valuation.

Public Multiples

It is far easier to obtain timely data on pricing and multiples for publicly traded firms. In fact, for those analysts who do not have access to private transaction data, this is the only option when it comes to relative valuation. The peril, though, is that you are extending the pricing lessons that you learn from looking at more mature, publicly traded firms to a private business.

Problems   The issues we face in applying public market multiples to private businesses, especially early in the life cycle, are fairly obvious:

- *Life cycle affects fundamentals.* If you accept the premise that only those young firms that make it through the early phase of the life cycle and succeed are likely to go public, you also have to accept the reality that public firms will have different fundamentals from private firms. Generally, public firms will be larger, have less potential for growth, and have more established markets than private businesses, and these differences will manifest themselves in the multiples investors pay for public companies.
- *Diversified versus undiversified investors.* When we discussed estimating risk and discount rates for young private businesses, we noted the different perspectives on risk that diversified investors in public companies have, relative to equity investors in private businesses, and how that difference can manifest itself as higher costs of equity for the latter. When you use multiples of earnings or revenues, obtained from a sample of publicly traded firms with diversified investors, to value a private business with undiversified investors, you will overvalue the latter.
- *Liquidity.* Since equity in publicly traded companies is more liquid than equity in private businesses, the value obtained by using public multiples will be too high if used for a private business. Just as we had to adjust for illiquidity in intrinsic valuation, we have to adjust for illiquidity with relative valuation.

Usefulness and Best Practices   What types of private businesses are best valued using public company multiples? Generally, companies that aspire to reach a larger market and either go public or be acquired by a public company are much better candidates for this practice. In effect, you are valuing the company for what it wants to be, rather than what it is today.

There are three simple practices that cannot only prevent egregious valuation errors but also lead to better valuations:

1. *Adjust for survival.* To the extent that private businesses have limited access to capital, they are also more exposed to failure. When valuing private businesses using public company multiples, you have to adjust for this additional risk of failure.
2. *Adjust for nondiversification.* Earlier in the chapter, we developed the total beta measure for undiversified investors and argued that the higher cost of equity that results from using it will lower intrinsic value. The same rationale should be applied when doing relative valuation. If the average PE ratio for publicly traded restaurants is twelve, you would expect Chez Pierre to trade at a lower PE ratio, even if it has the same characteristics.
3. *Adjust for illiquidity.* In the last section on intrinsic valuation, we presented different ways of estimating illiquidity discounts for equity in private businesses. We could adopt the same techniques to adjust the public multiple value for illiquidity.

All of these adjustments will result in lowering the pricing multiple, thus causing the EV-to-EBITDA multiple of ten for public companies to become six or seven with private businesses.

CONCLUSION

The value of a private firm is the present value of the cash flows it is expected to generate, discounted back at a rate that reflects both the risk in the private firm and the mix of debt and equity it uses. While this statement is identical to the one used to describe the value of a publicly traded firm, there are differences in the way we estimate these inputs for private firms, and even among private firms, depending on the motive for the valuation.

When valuing a private firm for sale to an individual or private entity, we have to consider three specific issues. The first is that the cost of equity, which we have hitherto assumed to be determined purely by the risk that cannot be diversified, might have to be adjusted for the fact that the potential buyer is not well diversified. The second is that equity holdings in private businesses are illiquid, leading to a discount on the estimated value. The discounts on restricted stock issues made by publicly traded firms or the bid-ask spreads of these firms may provide us with useful information on how large this discount should be. The third is that a controlling interest in equity of a private firm can trade at a significant premium over a minority interest.

The valuation of a private firm for sale to a publicly traded firm or initial public offering follows a much more conventional route. We can continue to assume that the cost of equity should be based only on nondiversifiable risk, and there is no need for an illiquidity discount. There can still be a control value if less than a controlling interest is sold to the publicly traded firm or if nonvoting shares are issued in the initial public offering.

QUESTIONS AND SHORT PROBLEMS

In the problems following, use an equity risk premium of 5.5 percent if none is specified.

1. You have been asked to value Barrista Espresso, a chain of espresso coffee shops that have opened on the East Coast of the United States.
   - The company had earnings before interest and taxes of $10.50 million in the most recent year on revenues of $50 million. However, the founders of the company had never charged themselves a salary, which would have amounted to $1 million if based on comparable companies.
   - The tax rate is 36% for all firms, and working capital is 10% of revenues.
   - The capital expenditures in the most recent year amounted to $4.5 million, while depreciation was only $1 million.
   - Earnings, revenues, and net capital expenditures are expected to grow 30% a year for five years, and 6% after that forever.
   - The comparable firms have an average beta of 1.3567 and an average D/E ratio of 13.65%. The average correlation with the market is 0.50. Barrista Espresso is expected to maintain a debt ratio of 12% and face a cost of debt of 8.75%. The risk-free rate is 6%, and the market risk premium is 5.5%.
   a. Estimate the value of Barrista Espresso as a firm.
   b. Estimate the value of equity in Barrista Espresso.
   c. Would your valuation be different if you were valuing the firm for an IPO?

2. You have valued a business, using discounted cash flow models, at $250 million for a private sale. The business, which does make money, had revenues of $200 million in the most recent year. (The average firm has revenues of $10 million.) How much of a liquidity discount would you apply to this firm:
   a. Based on the Silber regression?
   b. Based on correcting the average discount (25%) for the size of the firm?
3. You are valuing a bed-and-breakfast in Vermont with the following information:
   ▪ The business had pretax operating income of $100,000 in the most recent year. This income has grown 5% a year for the past three years and is expected to continue growing at that rate for the foreseeable future.
   ▪ About 40% of this operating income can be attributed to the fact that the owner is a master chef. He does not plan to stay on if the business is sold.
   ▪ The business is financed equally with debt and equity. The pretax cost of borrowing is 8%. The beta for publicly traded firms in the hospitality business is 1.10. The Treasury bond rate is 7%, the market risk premium is 5.5%, and the tax rate is 40%.
   ▪ The capital maintenance expenditure, net of depreciation, was $10,000 in the most recent year, and it is expected to grow at the same rate as operating income.
   ▪ The business is expected to have an operating life of 10 years, after which the building will be sold for $500,000, net of capital gains taxes.
   a. Value the business for sale.
   b. How much would the value change if the owner offered to stay on for the next three years?
4. You have been asked by the owner of Tectonics Software, a small firm that produces and sells computer software, to come up with an estimate of value for the firm for an initial public offering. The firm had revenues of $20 million in the most recent year, on which it made earnings before interest and taxes of $2 million. The firm had debt outstanding of $10 million, on which pretax interest expenses amounted to $1 million. The book value of equity is $10 million. The average unlevered beta of publicly traded software firms is 1.20, and the average market value of equity of these firms is, on average, three times the book value of equity. All firms face a 40% tax rate. Capital expenditures amounted to $1 million in the most recent year and were twice the depreciation charge in that year. Both items are expected to grow at the same rate as revenues for the next five years. The return on capital after year 5 is expected to be 15%. The revenues of this firm are expected to grow 20% a year for the next five years and 5% after that, and the operating margins will remain at existing levels. The Treasury bond rate is 6%.
   a. Estimate the cost of capital for the firm.
   b. Estimate the value of the equity in the firm.
   c. If the firm plans to issue 1 million shares, estimate the value per share.
5. How would your answer to the previous question change if you were valuing Tectonics Software for sale to a private individual? The individual in question has a portfolio that is not diversified and has a correlation of 0.60 with the market index. In addition, use the following bid-ask spread equation to estimate the illiquidity discount:

$$\text{Bid} - \text{Ask spread} = 0.14 - 0.015 \ln(\text{Revenues})$$

Estimate the value of equity in the private transaction.

CHAPTER 25

Acquisitions and Takeovers

Firms are acquired for several reasons. In the 1960s and 1970s, firms such as Gulf & Western and ITT built themselves into conglomerates by acquiring firms in other lines of business. In the 1980s, corporate giants like Time Inc., Beatrice Foods, and RJR Nabisco were acquired by other firms, their own management, or wealthy raiders, who saw potential value in restructuring or breaking up these firms. The 1990s saw a wave of consolidation in the media business as telecommunications firms acquired entertainment firms, and entertainment firms acquired cable businesses. In the 2010s, the locus of acquisitions shifted again to technology firms, many with large cash buffers buying other technology firms to expand the reach of their platforms and to augment user bases. Through time, firms have also acquired or merged with other firms to gain the benefits of synergy, in the form of either higher growth or lower costs.

Acquisitions seem to offer firms a shortcut to their strategic objectives, but the process has its costs. This chapter examines the four basic steps in an acquisition, starting with establishing an acquisition motive, continuing with the identification and valuation of a target firm, and following up with structuring and paying for the deal. The final, and often the most difficult, step is making the acquisition work after the deal is consummated.

BACKGROUND ON ACQUISITIONS

When we talk about acquisitions or takeovers, we are talking about several different types of transactions. These transactions can range from one firm merging with another firm to create a new firm, to managers of a firm acquiring the firm from their own stockholders and creating a private firm. This section begins by looking at the different forms taken by acquisitions, continues by providing an overview on the acquisition process, and concludes by examining the history of the acquisitions in the United States.

Classifying Acquisitions

There are several ways in which an acquisition can be structured. In a merger, the boards of directors of two firms agree to combine and seek stockholder approval for the combination. In most cases, at least 50 percent of the shareholders of the target and the bidding firm have to agree to the merger. The target firm ceases to exist and becomes part of the acquiring firm; Digital Equipment Corporation was absorbed by Compaq after it was acquired in 1997. In a consolidation, a new firm is created after the merger, and both the

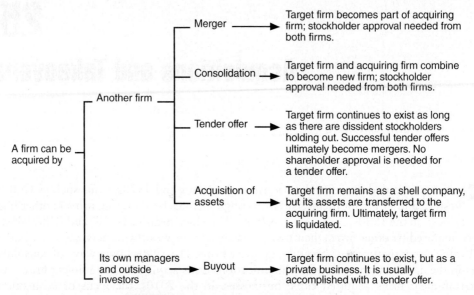

FIGURE 25.1 Classification of Acquisitions

acquiring firm and target firm stockholders receive stock in this firm; Citigroup, for instance, was the firm created after the consolidation of Citicorp and Travelers Group.

In a tender offer, one firm offers to buy the outstanding stock of the other firm at a specific price, and then communicates this offer in advertisements and mailings to stockholders. By doing so, it bypasses the incumbent management and board of directors of the target firm. Consequently, tender offers are often used to carry out hostile takeovers. The acquired firm will continue to exist as long as there are minority stockholders who refuse the tender. From a practical standpoint, however, most tender offers eventually become mergers if the acquiring firm is successful in gaining control of the target firm.

In a purchase of assets, one firm acquires the assets of another, though a formal vote by the shareholders of the firm being acquired is still needed.

There is a one final category of acquisitions that does not fit into any of the four described so far. Here, a firm is acquired by its own management or by a group of investors, usually with a tender offer. After this transaction, the acquired firm can cease to exist as a publicly traded firm and become a private business. These acquisitions are called management buyouts, if managers are involved, and leveraged buyouts, if the funds for the tender offer come predominantly from debt.

Figure 25.1 summarizes the various transactions and the consequences for the target firm.

Process of an Acquisition

Acquisitions can be friendly or hostile events. In a friendly acquisition, the managers of the target firm welcome the acquisition and, in some cases, seek it out. In a hostile acquisition, the target firm's management does not want to be acquired. The acquiring firm offers a price higher than the target firm's market price prior to the acquisition, and then invites stockholders in the target firm to tender their shares for the price.

In both friendly and hostile acquisitions, the difference between the acquisition price and the market price prior to the acquisition is called the acquisition premium.

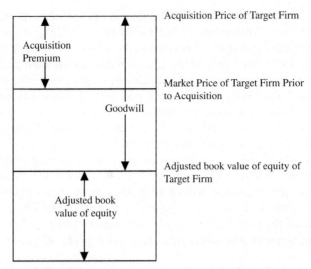

FIGURE 25.2 Breaking Down the Acquisition Price

The acquisition price, in the context of mergers and consolidations, is the price that will be paid by the acquiring firm for each of the target firm's shares. In a friendly merger, this price is usually based on negotiations between the acquiring firm and the target firm's managers. In a tender offer, it is the price at which the acquiring firm receives enough shares to gain control of the target firm. This price may be higher than the initial price offered by the acquirer, especially if there are other firms bidding for the same target firm or if an insufficient number of stockholders tender at that initial price. For instance, in 1991, AT&T initially offered to buy NCR for $80 per share, a premium of $25 over the stock price at the time of the offer. AT&T ultimately paid $110 per share to complete the acquisition.

There is one final comparison that can be made, and that is between the price paid on the acquisition and the accounting book value of the equity in the firm being acquired. After the acquisition is complete, the target firm's assets can be reappraised, following accounting rules, to fair value to estimate the adjusted book value of equity. Depending on how the acquisition is accounted for, the difference between the acquisition price and the adjusted book value of equity will be recorded as goodwill on the acquiring firm's books, or may not be recorded at all. Figure 25.2 presents the breakdown of the acquisition price into these component parts.

Empirical Evidence on the Value and Pricing Effects of Takeovers

Many researchers have studied the effects of takeovers on the value of both the target firm and the bidder firm. The evidence indicates that the stockholders of target firms are the clear winners in takeovers; they earn significant excess returns[1] not only around the announcement of the acquisitions but also in the weeks leading up to it. Jensen and Ruback (1983) reviewed 13 studies that looked at returns around takeover announcements and reported an average excess return of 30 percent to target stockholders in successful tender

---

[1]Excess returns represent returns over and above the returns you would have expected an investment to make, after adjusting for risk and market performance.

offers and close to 20 percent to target stockholders in successful mergers. Jarrell, Brickley, and Netter (1988) reviewed the results of 663 tender offers made between 1962 and 1985, and noted that premiums averaged 19 percent in the 1960s, 35 percent in the 1970s, and 30 percent between 1980 and 1985. Many studies report an increase in the stock price of the target firm prior to the takeover announcement, suggesting either a very perceptive financial market or leaked information about prospective deals. The effect of takeover announcements on bidder firm stock prices is not as clear-cut. Jensen and Ruback report excess returns of 4 percent for bidding firm stockholders around tender offers, and no excess returns around mergers. Jarrell, Brickley, and Netter, in their examination of tender offers from 1962 to 1985, note a decline in excess returns to bidding firm stockholders from 4.4 percent in the 1960s, to 2 percent in the 1970s, to –1 percent in the 1980s. Other studies indicate that approximately half of all bidding firms earn negative excess returns around the announcement of takeovers, suggesting that shareholders are skeptical about the perceived value of the takeover in a significant number of cases. Figure 25.3 provides the findings on the acquirer and target firm stock price performance around acquisition announcements.

Some attempts at takeovers fail, either because the bidding firm withdraws the offer, or because the target firm fights it off. Bradley, Desai, and Kim (1983) analyzed the effects of takeover failures on target firm stockholders and found that, while the initial reaction to the announcement of the failure is negative, albeit statistically insignificant, a substantial number of target firms are taken over within 60 days of the first takeover failing, eventually earning significant excess returns (50 percent to 66 percent).

When there are multiple bidders and a bidder fails, what are the consequences? While the initial reaction of markets is often negative, reflecting the costs of a failed bid, the long-term results are more revealing. As we will see later in this chapter, failed bidders outperform successful bidders both in terms of operating profitability and stock price performance

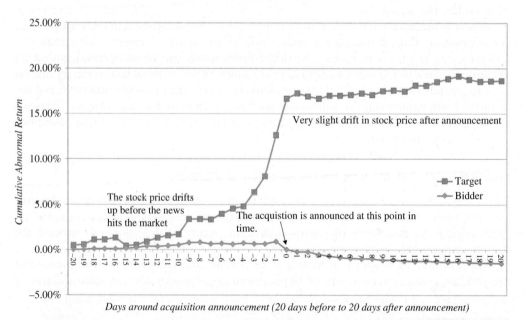

Days around acquisition announcement (20 days before to 20 days after announcement)

FIGURE 25.3 Acquirer and Target Firm Stock Returns around Acquisition Events

in the five years after the bidding war. At least with acquisitions, it seems to be much better for stockholders in acquiring firms to lose a bidding war than win one.

STEPS IN AN ACQUISITION

There are four basic and not necessarily sequential steps in acquiring a target firm. The first is the development of a rationale and a strategy for doing acquisitions, and what this strategy requires in terms of resources. The second is the choice of a target for the acquisition and the valuation of the target firm, with premiums given the motive. The third is the determination of how much to pay on the acquisition, how best to raise funds to do it, and whether to use stock or cash to pay for the target. The final step in the acquisition, and perhaps the most challenging one, is to make the acquisition work after the deal is complete.

Developing an Acquisition Strategy

Not all firms that make acquisitions have acquisition strategies, and not all firms that have acquisition strategies stick with them. This section considers a number of different motives for acquisitions and suggests that a coherent acquisition strategy has to be based on one or another of these motives.

Acquire Undervalued Firms Firms that are undervalued by financial markets can be targeted for acquisition by those who recognize this mispricing. The acquirer can then gain the difference between the value and the purchase price as surplus. For this strategy to work, however, three basic components need to come together:

1. *A capacity to find firms that trade at less than their true value.* This capacity would require either access to better information than is available to other investors in the market, or a better analytical tool than those used by other market participants.
2. *Access to the funds that will be needed to complete the acquisition.* Knowing a firm is undervalued does not necessarily imply having capital easily available to carry out the acquisition. Access to capital depends on the size of the acquirer—large firms will have more access to capital markets and internal funds than smaller firms or individuals—and upon the acquirer's track record—a history of success at identifying and acquiring undervalued firms will make subsequent acquisitions easier.
3. *Skill in execution.* If the acquirer, in the process of the acquisition, drives the stock price up to and beyond the estimated value, there will be no value gained from the acquisition. To illustrate, assume that the estimated value for a firm is $100 million and that the current market price is $75 million. In acquiring this firm, the acquirer will have to pay a premium. If that premium exceeds 33 percent of the market price, the price exceeds the estimated value, and the acquisition will not create any value for the acquirer.

While the strategy of buying undervalued firms has a great deal of intuitive appeal, it is daunting, especially when acquiring publicly traded firms in reasonably efficient markets, where the premiums paid on market prices can very quickly eliminate the valuation surplus. The odds are better in less efficient markets or when acquiring private businesses.

Diversify to Reduce Risk An argument was made in Chapter 4 that diversification reduces an investor's exposure to firm-specific risk. In fact, the risk and return models used in this book have been built on the presumption that the firm-specific risk will be diversified away, and hence, will not be rewarded. By buying firms in other businesses and diversifying, acquiring firms' managers believe they can reduce earnings volatility and risk and increase potential value.

Although diversification has benefits, it is an open question whether it can be accomplished more efficiently by investors diversifying across traded stocks, or by firms diversifying by acquiring other firms. If we compare the transaction costs associated with investor diversification with the costs and the premiums paid by firms doing the same, investors in most publicly traded firms can diversify far more cheaply than firms can.

There are two exceptions to this view. The first is in the case of a private firm, where the owner may have all or most of his or her wealth invested in the firm. Here, the argument for diversification becomes stronger, since the owner alone is exposed to all risk. This risk exposure may explain why many family-owned businesses in Asia, for instance, diversified into multiple businesses and became conglomerates. The second, albeit weaker, case is the closely held firm, whose incumbent managers may have the bulk of their wealth invested in the firm. By diversifying through acquisitions, they reduce their exposure to total risk, though other investors (who presumably are more diversified) may not share their enthusiasm.

Create Operating or Financial Synergy The third reason to explain the significant premiums paid in most acquisitions is synergy. Synergy is the potential additional value from combining two firms. It is probably the most widely used and misused rationale for mergers and acquisitions.

Sources of Operating Synergy Operating synergies are those synergies that enable firms to increase their operating income, increase growth, or do both. Operating synergies can be categorized into five types:

1. *Economies of scale* that may arise from the merger, allowing the combined firm to become more cost-efficient and profitable.
2. *Greater pricing power* from reduced competition and higher market share, which should result in higher margins and operating income.
3. *Combination of different functional strengths*, as would be the case when a firm with strong marketing skills acquires a firm with a good product line.
4. *Higher growth in new or existing markets*, arising from the combination of the two firms. This would be case when a U.S. consumer products firm acquires an emerging market firm, with an established distribution network and brand name recognition, and uses these strengths to increase sales of its products.
5. *Defensive synergy*, emanating from preempting competitors in acquisitions, and thus preventing market share or margin slippage that would have occurred otherwise.

Operating synergies can affect margins and growth, and through these the value of the firms involved in the merger or acquisition.

Sources of Financial Synergy With financial synergies, the payoff can take the form of either higher cash flows or a lower cost of capital (discount rate). Included are the following:

- A combination of a firm with excess cash or *cash slack* (and limited project opportunities), and a firm with high-return projects (and constraints on raising capital), can yield a payoff in terms of higher value for the combined firm. The increase in value comes from the projects, that were taken with the excess cash that otherwise would not have been taken. This synergy is likely to show up most often when large firms acquire smaller firms, or when publicly traded firms acquire private businesses.
- *Debt capacity* can increase, because when two firms combine, their earnings and cash flows may become more stable and predictable. This, in turn, allow them to borrow more than they could have as individual entities, which creates a tax benefit for the combined firm. This tax benefit can either be shown as higher cash flows (when estimating cash flows to equity), or take the form of a lower cost of capital for the combined firm.
- *Tax benefits* can arise from the combined firm paying less in taxes than the individual firms would have paid. Thus, a profitable firm that acquires a money-losing firm may be able to use the net operating losses of the latter to reduce its tax burden. Alternatively, a firm that is able to increase its depreciation charges after an acquisition will save in taxes and increase its value. In most cases, goodwill amortization is not tax deductible, and hence, does not provide tax benefits.

Clearly, there is potential for synergy in many mergers. The more important issues are whether that synergy can be valued and, if so, how to value it.

Empirical Evidence on Synergy Synergy is a stated motive in many mergers and acquisitions. Bhide (1993) examined the motives behind 77 acquisitions in 1985 and 1986 and reported that operating synergy was the primary motive in one-third of these takeovers. A number of studies examine whether synergy exists and, if it does, how much it is worth. If synergy is perceived to exist in a takeover, the value of the combined firm should be greater than the sum of the values of the bidding and target firms, operating independently.

$$V(AB) > V(A) + V(B)$$

where V(AB) = Value of a firm created by combining A and B (synergy)

  V(A) = Value of firm A, operating independently

  V(B) = Value of firm B, operating independently

Studies of stock returns around merger announcements generally conclude that the value of the combined firm does increase in most takeovers, and that the increase is significant. Bradley, Desai, and Kim (1988) examined a sample of 236 interfirm tender offers between 1963 and 1984 and reported that the combined value of the target and bidder firms increased 7.48 percent ($117 million in 1984 dollars), on average, on the announcement of the merger. This result has to be interpreted with caution, however, since the increase in the value of the combined firm after a merger is also consistent with a number of other hypotheses explaining acquisitions, including undervaluation and a change in corporate control. It is, thus, a weak test of the synergy hypothesis.

The existence of synergy generally implies that the combined firm will become more profitable or grow at a faster rate after the merger than will the firms operating separately. A stronger test of synergy is to evaluate whether merged firms improve their performance (profitability and growth) *relative to their competitors*, after takeovers. On this test, as shown later in this chapter, many mergers fail.

Take Over Poorly Managed Firms and Change Management　　Some firms are not managed optimally, and other individuals often believe they can run them better than the current managers. Acquiring poorly managed firms and removing incumbent management, or at least changing existing management policy or practices, should make these firms more valuable, allowing the acquirer to claim the increase in value. This value increase is often termed the value of control.

Prerequisites for Success　　While this corporate control story can be used to justify large premiums over the market price, the potential for its success rests on the following:

- The poor performance of the firm being acquired should be attributable to bad management, rather than to market or industry factors that are not under management control.
- The acquisition has to be followed by a change in management practices, and the change has to increase value. Using the framework for intrinsic value developed in this book, actions that enhance value increase cash flows from existing assets, increase expected growth rates, increase the length of the growth period, or reduce the cost of capital.
- The market price of the acquisition should reflect the status quo—the current management of the firm and their poor business practices. If the market price already has the control premium built into it, there is little potential for the acquirer to earn the premium.

In general, control is more likely to be a motive for hostile takeovers than friendly ones, because of its premise that existing managers are not up to the task.

Empirical Evidence on the Value of Control　　The strongest support for the existence of a market for corporate control lies in the types of firms that are typically acquired in hostile takeovers. Research indicates that the typical target firm in a hostile takeover has the following characteristics:

- It has underperformed other stocks in its industry and the overall market, in terms of returns to its stockholders in the years preceding the takeover.
- It has been less profitable than firms in its industry in the years preceding the takeover.
- It has a much lower stock holding by insiders than do firms in its peer groups.

In a comparison of target firms in hostile and friendly takeovers, Bhide illustrates their differences. His findings are summarized in Figure 25.4. As you can see, target firms in

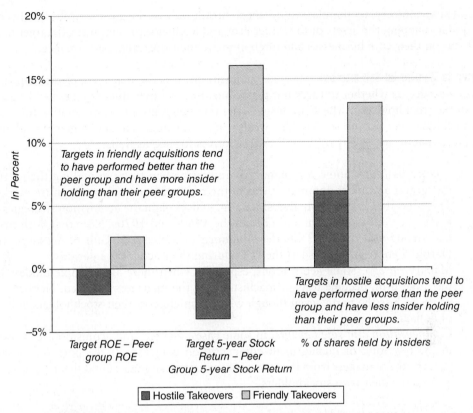

FIGURE 25.4 Target Characteristics—Hostile versus Friendly Takeovers
Source: Bhide.

hostile takeovers have earned a 2.2 percent lower return on equity, on average, than other firms in their industry; they have earned returns for their stockholders that are 4 percent lower than the market; and only 6.5% of their stock is held by insiders.

There is also evidence that firms make significant changes in the way they operate after hostile takeovers. In his study, Bhide examined the aftermaths of hostile takeovers and noted the following four changes:

1. Many of the hostile takeovers were followed by an increase in debt, which resulted in a downgrading of the debt. The debt was quickly reduced with proceeds from the sale of assets, however.
2. There was no significant change in the amount of capital investment in these firms.
3. Almost 60 percent of the takeovers were followed by significant divestitures, in which half or more of the firm was divested. The overwhelming majority of the divestitures were units in business areas unrelated to the company's core business (i.e., they constituted reversal of corporate diversification done in earlier time periods).
4. There were significant management changes in 17 of the 19 hostile takeovers, with the replacement of the entire corporate management team in seven of the takeovers.

Thus, contrary to popular view,[2] most hostile takeovers are not followed by the acquirer stripping the assets of the target firm and leading it to ruin. Instead, target firms refocus on their core businesses and often improve their operating performance.

Cater to Managerial Self-Interest In most acquisitions, it is the managers of the acquiring firm who decide whether to carry out the acquisition and how much to pay for it, rather than the stockholders of the same firm. Given these circumstances, the motive for some acquisitions may not be stockholder wealth maximization, but rather managerial self-interest, manifested in any of the following motives for acquisitions:

- *Empire building.* Some top managers' interests seem to lie in making their firms the largest and most dominant firms in their industry or even in the entire market. This objective, rather than diversification, may explain the acquisition strategies of firms like Gulf & Western and ITT[3] in the 1960s and 1970s. Note that both firms had strong-willed CEOs; Charles Bludhorn in the case of Gulf & Western, and Harold Geneen in the case of the ITT) during their acquisitive periods.
- *Managerial ego.* Some acquisitions, especially when there are multiple bidders for the same firm, become tests of machismo[4] for the managers involved. Neither side wants to lose the battle, even though winning might cost their stockholders billions of dollars.
- *Compensation and side benefits.* In some cases, mergers and acquisitions can result in the rewriting of management compensation contracts. If the potential private gains to the managers from the transaction are large, it might blind them to the costs created for their own stockholders.

In a 1986 paper titled "The Hubris Hypothesis of Corporate Takeovers", Roll suggested that we might be underestimating how much of the acquisition process, and the prices paid can be explained by managerial pride and ego. There is also significant evidence that has accumulated in behavioral finance that overconfident CEOs are more likely to push for acquisitions, often overestimating the benefits and underestimating the costs of these deals.

SHOULD THERE BE AN EGO DISCOUNT?

If managerial self-interest and egos can cause firms to pay too much on acquisitions, should the values of firms run by strong-willed CEOs be discounted? In a sense, this discount is probably already applied if the firm's current return on capital and reinvestment rate reflect the failed acquisitions of the past, and we assume that the firm will continue to generate the same return on capital in the future.

---

[2] Even if it is not the popular view, it is the populist view that has found credence in Hollywood, in movies like *Wall Street* and *Other People's Money*, and in books like *Barbarians at the Gate*.

[3] In a delicious irony, ITT itself became the target of a hostile acquisition bid by Hilton Hotels and responded by shedding what it termed its noncore businesses (i.e., all the businesses it had acquired during its conglomerate period).

[4] An interesting question that is whether these bidding wars will become less likely as more women rise to become CEOs of firms. They might bring in a different perspective on what winning and losing in a merger means.

By the same token, though, this is a good reason to revisit a firm valuation when there is a change at the top. If the new CEO does not seem to have the same desire to empire-build or overpay on acquisitions as the old one, the firm's future return on capital can be expected to be much higher than its past return on capital, and its value will rise.

Choosing a Target Firm and Valuing Control/Synergy

Once a firm has an acquisition motive, there are two key questions that need to be answered. The first relates to how to best identify a potential target firm for an acquisition, given the motives described in the previous section. The second is the more concrete question of how to value a target firm, again given the different motives that we have outlined in the last section.

Choosing a Target Firm   Once a firm has identified the reason for its acquisition program, it has to find the appropriate target firm.

- If the motive for acquisitions is undervaluation, the target firm must be undervalued. How such a firm will be identified depends on the valuation approach and model used. With pricing, an undervalued stock is one that trades at a multiple (of earnings, book value, or sales) well below that of the rest of the industry, after controlling for significant differences on fundamentals. Thus, a bank with a price-to-book value ratio of 1.2 would be an undervalued bank if other banks have similar fundamentals (return on equity, growth, and risk) but trade at much higher price-to-book value ratios. In discounted cash flow valuation approaches, an undervalued stock is one that trades at a price well below the estimated discounted cash flow value.
- If the motive for acquisitions is diversification, the most likely target firms will be in businesses that are unrelated to and uncorrelated with the business of the acquiring firm. Thus, a cyclical firm should try to acquire countercyclical or at least noncyclical firms to get the fullest benefit from diversification.
- If the motive for acquisitions is operating synergy, the typical target firm will vary depending on the source of the synergy. For economies of scale, the target firm should be in the same business as the acquiring firm. Thus, the acquisition of Continental Airlines by United Airlines was motivated by potential cost savings from economies of scale. For functional synergy, the target firm should be strongest in those functional areas where the acquiring firm is weak. For financial synergy, the target firm will be chosen to reflect the likely source of the synergy—a risky firm with limited or no standalone capacity for borrowing, if the motive is increased debt capacity, or a firm with significant net operating losses carried forward, if the motive is tax benefits.
- If the motive for the merger is control, the target firm will be a poorly managed firm in an industry where there is potential for excess returns. In addition, its stock holdings will be widely dispersed (making it easier to carry out the hostile acquisition), and the current market price will be based on the presumption that incumbent management will continue to run the firm.
- If the motive is managerial self-interest, the choice of a target firm will reflect managerial interests rather than economic reasons.

TABLE 25.1   Target Firm Characteristics Given Acquisition Motive

If Motive Is...	Then the Target Firm...
Undervaluation	Trades at a price below the estimated value.
Diversification	Is in a business different from the acquiring firm's business.
Operating synergy	Has the characteristics that create the operating synergy: *Cost savings:* Creates in the same business economies of scale. *Higher growth:* Has potential to open up new markets or expand existing ones.
Financial synergy	Has the characteristics that create financial synergy: 1. *Tax savings:* Provides a tax benefit to acquirer. 2. *Debt capacity:* Is unable to borrow money or pay high interest rates. 3. *Cash slack:* Has great projects/capital constraints.
Control	Is a badly managed firm whose stock has underperformed the market.
Manager's interests	Has characteristics that best meet CEO's ego and power needs.

Table 25.1 summarizes the typical target firm, given the motive for the takeover.

There are two final points worth making here before moving on to valuation. The first is that firms often choose a target firm and a motive for the acquisition simultaneously, rather than sequentially. That does not change any of the analysis in these sections. The other point is that firms often have more than one motive in an acquisition—say, control and synergy. If this is the case, the search for a target firm should be guided by the dominant motive.

Valuing the Target Firm   The valuation of an acquisition is not fundamentally different from the valuation of any firm, although the existence of control and synergy premiums introduces some complexity into the valuation process. Given the interrelationship between synergy and control, the safest way to value a target firm is in steps, starting with a status quo valuation of the firm, and following up with a value for control and a value for synergy.

Status Quo Valuation   The valuation of the target firm starts by estimating the firm value with existing investing, financing, and dividend policies, assuming existing management stays in place. This valuation, termed the status quo valuation, provides a base from which control and synergy premiums can be estimated. All the basic principles presented in the earlier chapters on valuation continue to apply here. In particular, the value of the firm is a function of its cash flows from existing assets, the expected growth in these cash flows during a high-growth period, the length of the high-growth period, and the firm's cost of capital.

ILLUSTRATION 25.1:   A Status Quo Valuation of SAB Miller

In September 2015, Inbev, the largest beer company in the world, announced that it would be acquiring SAB Miller, the second largest brewer in the world, in a friendly merger. The merger was motivated by synergies, both from growth, with the two firms having different geographic strongholds and cost savings from consolidation. In addition, Inbev, controlled by Brazil-based 3G Capital, was considered one of the most efficient brewers in the world, and it was expected that they would be able to bring some of these efficiencies into SAB Miller's operations. Figure 25.5 captures the details of the deal, including the market values at the time that the acquisition was announced and when the deal was consummated:

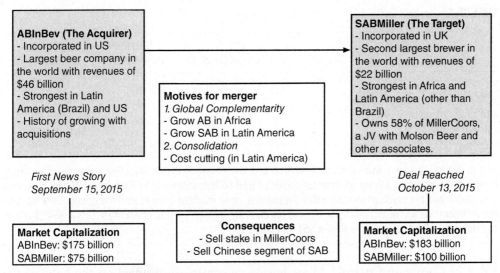

FIGURE 25.5 The Inbev-SAB Miller Acquisition Deal

To analyze the acquisition, we begin with a status quo valuation of SAB Miller, including its joint venture ownership of Coors as well as its minority holdings in associates, in Table 25.2:

TABLE 25.2 Status Quo Valuation of SAB Miller (in $ millions)

	SAB Miller	+ 58% of Coors JV	+ Share of Associates	SAB Miller Consolidated
Revenues	$22,130.00	$ 5,201.00	$6,099.00	
Operating Margin	19.97%	15.38%	10.72%	
Operating Income (EBIT)	$ 4,420.00	$ 800.00	$ 654.00	
Invested Capital	$31,526.00	$ 5,428.00	$4,459.00	
Beta	0.7977	0.6872	0.6872	
Equity risk premium	8.90%	6.00%	7.90%	
Cost of Equity	9.10%	6.12%	7.43%	
After-tax cost of debt	2.24%	2.08%	2.24%	
Debt-to-Capital Ratio	14.67%	0.00%	0.00%	
Cost of capital	8.09%	6.12%	7.43%	
After-tax return on capital =	10.33%	11.05%	11.00%	
Reinvestment Rate =	16.02%	40.00%	40.00%	
Expected growth rate =	1.65%	4.42%	4.40%	
Number of years of growth	5	5	5	
Value of firm				
PV of FCFF in high growth =	$11,411.72	$ 1,715.25	$1,351.68	
Terminal value =	$47,711.04	$ 15,094.36	$9,354.28	
Value of operating assets today =	**$43,747.24**	**$12,929.46**	**$7,889.56**	**$64,566.26**

(continued)

TABLE 25.2　*(continued)*

	SAB Miller	+ 58% of Coors JV	+ Share of Associates	SAB Miller Consolidated
+ Cash				$ 1,027.00
− Debt				$ 12,918.00
− Minority Interests				$ 1,183.00
Value of equity				**$51,492.26**

As you can see, we have used the simple version of a firm valuation model, with five years of extraordinary growth and stable margins for all three segments of SAB Miller's value – operating assets, the joint venture with Coor's and the holdings in associates. This allows us to estimate growth as the product of the existing reinvestment rate and return on capital and the resulting aggregated value of operating assets is $64.57 billion and the value of the equity in the firm is $51.49 billion.

Value of Corporate Control　Many hostile takeovers are justified on the basis of the existence of a market for corporate control. Investors and firms are willing to pay large premiums over the market price to control the management of firms, especially those that they perceive to be poorly run. This section explores the determinants of the value of corporate control and attempts to value it in the context of an acquisition.

Determinants of the Value of Corporate Control　The value of wresting control of a firm from incumbent management is inversely proportional to the perceived quality of that management and its capacity to maximize firm value. In general, the value of control will be much greater for a poorly managed firm that operates at below optimum capacity than for a well-managed firm.

The value of controlling a firm comes from changes made to existing management policy that can increase the firm value. Assets can be acquired or liquidated, the financing mix can be changed, and the dividend policy reevaluated, and the firm can be restructured to maximize value. If we can identify the changes that we would make to the target firm, we can value control. The value of control can then be written as:

$$\text{Value of control} = \text{Value of firm optimally managed}$$
$$- \text{Value of firm with current management}$$

The value of control is negligible for firms that are operating at or close to their optimal value since a restructuring will yield little additional value. It can be substantial for firms operating at well below optimal, since a restructuring can lead to a significant increase in value.

ILLUSTRATION 25.2:　The Value of Control at SAB Miller

We said earlier that one of the reasons SAB Miller might have been targeted by Inbev is because of the potential for higher value from running the former's operations more efficiently. There is basis for this belief, since Inbev had managed to pull of a similar feat at Modela, the Mexican brewer, in a prior acquisiton. To assess the potential for value change at SAB Miller, we will use the industry averages as our rough proxy for optimal, and assume that SAB Miller run more efficiently will raise its debt ratio from 14.67% (status quo) to 18.82% (industry average), and that it will also be able to raise its operating margins and returns on invested capital to industry averages. The value of control can then be calculated in Table 25.3:

TABLE 25.3   Value of Control at SAB Miller

	Status Quo Value	Restructured	Changes made
Cost of Equity =	9.10%	9.37%	Increases with debt ratio
After-tax cost of debt =	2.24%	2.24%	Left unchanged
Debt-to Capital Ratio	14.67%	18.82%	Set to industry average
Cost of capital =	8.09%	8.03%	Due to debt ratio change
Pretax return on capital	14.02%	17.16%	Set to industry average
After-tax return on capital =	10.33%	12.64%	Result of pretax ROIC change
Reinvestment Rate =	16.02%	33.29%	Set to industry average
Expected growth rate =	1.65%	4.21%	Result of reinvestment/ROIC
Value of firm			
PV of FCFF in high growth	$11,411.72	$ 9,757.08	
Terminal value	$47,711.04	$56,935.06	***Value of Control***
Value of operating assets	**$43,747.24**	**$48,449.42**	**$4,702.17**
+ Cash	$ 1,027.00	$ 1,027.00	
+ Minority Holdings	$20,819.02	$20,819.02	
− Debt	$12,918.00	$12,918.00	
− Minority Interests	$ 1,183.00	$ 1,183.00	
Value of equity	**$51,492.26**	**$56,194.44**	

The lower cost of capital and higher growth rate increases the value of the operating assets from $43.7 billion to $48.5 billion to $48.5 billion. We can then estimate the value of control:

Value of operating assets (optimally managed) =	$48,449 million
Value of operating assets (status quo) =	$43,747 million
Value of control =	$ 4,702 million

Note that we have assume that there will be no changes at the Coor's joint venture or the associates, and bringing in those holdings, as well as the cash and debt at the time of the merger into the analysis, causes the value of equity to increase from its status quo value of $51.5 billion to $56.2 billion, mirroring the change in operating asset value.

Valuing Operating Synergy   There is a potential for operating synergy, in one form or the other, in many takeovers. Some disagreement exists, however, over whether synergy can be valued and, if so, what that value should be. One school of thought argues that synergy is too nebulous to be valued and that any systematic attempt to do so requires so many assumptions that it is pointless. If this is true, a firm should not be willing to pay large premiums for synergy to which it cannot attach a value.

While valuing synergy requires us to make assumptions about future cash flows and growth, the lack of precision in the process does not mean we cannot obtain an unbiased estimate of value. Thus, we maintain that synergy can be valued by answering two fundamental questions:

1. *What form is the synergy expected to take?* Will it reduce costs as a percentage of sales and increase profit margins (e.g., when there are economies of scale)? Will it increase future growth (e.g., when there is increased market power) or the length of the growth period? Synergy, to have an effect on value, has to influence one of the four inputs into the valuation process—cash flows from existing assets, higher expected growth rates (market power, higher growth potential), a longer growth period (from increased competitive advantages), or a lower cost of capital (higher debt capacity).
2. *When will the synergy start affecting cash flows?* Synergies can sometimes show up instantaneously, but they are more likely to show up over time. Since the value of synergy is the present value of the cash flows created by it, the longer it takes for it to show up, the smaller its value.

Once we answer these questions, we can estimate the value of synergy using discounted cash flow techniques. First, we value the firms involved in the merger independently, by discounting expected cash flows to each firm at the weighted average cost of capital for that firm. Second, we estimate the value of the combined firm, with no synergy, by adding the values obtained for each firm in the first step. Third, we build in the effects of synergy into expected growth rates and cash flows, and we value the combined firm with synergy. The difference between the value of the combined firm with synergy and the value of the combined firm without synergy provides a value for synergy.

Table 25.4 summarizes the effects of synergy and control in valuing a target firm for an acquisition. Notice the difference between Figure 25.2, which is based on the market price of the target firm before and after the acquisition, and Table 25.4, where we are looking at the value of the target firm with and without the premiums for control and synergy. A fair-value acquisition, which would leave the acquiring firm neither better nor worse off, would require that the total price (in Figure 25.4) be equal to the consolidated value (in Table 25.2) with the synergy and control benefits built in.

TABLE 25.4   Valuing an Acquisition

Component	Valuation Guidelines	Should You Pay?
Synergy	Value the combined firm with synergy built in. This value may include: • A higher growth rate in revenues: *growth synergy.* • Higher margins because of *economies of scale.* • Lower taxes because of tax benefits: *tax synergy.* • Lower cost of debt: *financing synergy.* • Higher debt ratio because of lower risk: *debt capacity.* Subtract the value of the target firm (with control premium) + value of the bidding firm (preacquisition). This is the value of synergy.	*Which firm is indispensable for synergy?* If it is the target, you should be willing to pay up to the value of synergy. If it is the bidder, you should not.

Component	Valuation Guidelines	Should You Pay?
Control premium	Value the company as if optimally managed. This will usually mean altering investment, financing, and dividend policy: *Investment policy*: Earn higher returns on projects and divest unproductive projects. *Financing policy*: Move to a better financing. structure(e.g., optimal capital structure). *Dividend policy*: Return cash for which the firm has no need. Practically, • Look at industry averages as optimal. • Do a full-fledged corporate financial analysis to compute optimal debt ratio.	If motive is control or in a stand-alone valuation, this is the maximum you should pay.
Status quo valuation	Value the company as is, with existing inputs for investment, financing, and dividend policy.	If motive is undervaluation, the status quo value is the maximum you should pay.

ILLUSTRATION 25.3:   Valuing Synergy: Inbev and SAB Miller

Returning to the Inbev/SAB Miller merger, note that synergy was one of the stated reasons for the acquisition. To value this synergy, we need to first value Inbev as a standalone firm, since synergy requires valuations of both the acquiring and the target firms, and in Table 25.5, we summarize the valuations of the two firms— Inbev and SAB Miller with control incorporated into the numbers, and the consolidated firm, with no synergy benefits built in:

TABLE 25.5   Inbev and SAB Miller Consolidated—No synergy

	Inbev	*SAB Miller*	*Combined firm (no synergy)*
Cost of Equity =	8.93%	9.37%	9.12%
After-tax cost of debt =	2.10%	2.24%	2.10%
Cost of capital =	7.33%	8.03%	7.51%
Revenues	$ 45,762.00	$22,130.00	$ 67,892.00
Operating Margin	32.28%	19.97%	28.27%
Operating Income (EBIT)	$ 14,771.97	$ 4,419.36	$ 19,191.33
After-tax return on capital	12.10%	12.64%	11.68%
Reinvestment Rate =	50.99%	33.29%	43.58%
Length of growth period =	5	5	5
After-tax return on capital =	12.10%	12.64%	11.68%
Reinvestment Rate =	50.99%	33.29%	43.58%
Expected growth rate =	6.17%	4.21%	5.09%
Value of firm			
PV of FCFF in high growth =	$ 28,732.57	$ 9,806.49	$ 38,539.06
Terminal value =	$260,981.86	$58,735.57	$319,717.43
Value of operating assets =	$211,952.80	$50,065.35	$262,018.16

Note that all the dollar values (for inputs like revenues and operating income, and output like FCFF and operating asset value) for the consolidated firm are just the sums of the individual firm values. The cost of capital for the consolidated firm is obtained by estimating the unlevered beta for the combined firm as a weighted average of the unlevered betas for the individual firms, and then using the consolidated firm's debt-to-equity ratio. With no synergy, the value of the consolidated firm should be $262 billion.

To bring in the effects of synergy, we assume that synergy will come from two sources. The first is from the cost cuts from consolidation, playing out as an increase in the operating margin for the consolidated firm from 28.27 to 29.00%, a small percentage increase but one that will require almost $500 million in cost cuts. The second is an increase in the return on capital from 11.68 to 12.00%, as the company uses its higher market share to improve its competitive position. Table 25.6 estimates the value effects of these changes:

TABLE 25.6   Value of Synergy

	Combined firm (status quo)	Combined firm (synergy)
Cost of Equity =	9.12%	9.12%
After-tax cost of debt =	2.10%	2.10%
Cost of capital =	7.51%	7.51%
Debt-to-Equity Ratio	29.71%	29.71%
Revenues	$ 67,892.00	$ 67,892.00
Operating Margin	28.27%	29.00%
Operating Income (EBIT)	$ 19,191.33	$ 19,688.68
After-tax return on capital	11.68%	12.00%
Reinvestment Rate	43.58%	50.00%
Length of growth period	5	5
Reinvestment Rate	43.58%	50.00%
Expected growth rate	5.09%	6.00%
Value of firm		
PV of FCFF in high growth =	$ 38,539.06	$ 39,150.61
Terminal value =	$319,717.43	$340,174.63
Value of operating assets =	$262,018.16	$276,609.92

The value of the combined firm, with synergy, is $276.6 billion. This can be compared to the value of the combined firm without synergy of $262 billion, and the difference is the value of the synergy in the merger.

Value of combined firm (with synergy)	$276,610 million
Value of combined firm (with no synergy)	$262,018 million
Value of synergy	$ 14,592 million

This valuation is based on the presumption that synergy will be created instantaneously. In reality, it can take years before the firms are able to see the benefits of synergy. A simple way to account for the delay is to consider the present value of synergy. Thus, if it will take Inbev and SAB Miller three years to create the synergy, the present value of synergy can be estimated, using the combined firm's cost of capital as the discount rate:

$$\text{Present value of synergy} = \$14,592 \text{ million}/1.0751^3 = \$11,746 \text{ million}$$

synergy.xls: **This spreadsheet enables you to estimate the approximate value of synergy in a merger or acquisition.**

Valuing Financial Synergy Synergy can also be created from purely financial factors. We will consider three legitimate sources of financial synergy: better use for excess cash or cash slack; a greater tax benefit from accumulated losses or tax deductions; and an increase in debt capacity, and therefore, firm value. The discussion begins, however, with diversification, which though a widely used rationale for mergers is not a source of increased value by itself, at least at publicly traded companies.

Diversification A takeover motivated only by diversification considerations has no effect on the combined value of the two firms involved in the takeover, when the two firms are both publicly traded, and when the investors in the firms can diversify on their own. Consider the following example. Dalton Motors, which is an automobile parts manufacturing firm in a cyclical business, plans to acquire Lube & Auto, which is an automobile service firm whose business is noncyclical and high-growth, solely for the diversification benefit. The characteristics of the two firms are summarizes in Table 25.7.

TABLE 25.7 Company Characteristics (Dalton and Lube & Auto)

	Lube & Auto	Dalton Motors
Current free cash flow to the firm	$100 million	$200 million
Expected growth rate—next five years	20%	10%
Expected growth rate—after year 5	6%	6%
Debt/(Debt + Equity)	30%	30%
After-tax cost of debt	6%	5.40%
Levered Beta for equity—next five years	1.20	1.00
Levered Beta for equity—after year 5	1.00	1.00

The Treasury bond rate is 7 percent, and the market premium is 5.5 percent. The calculations for the weighted average cost of capital and the value of the firms are shown in Table 25.8.

TABLE 25.8 Value of Lube & Auto, Dalton Motors, and Combined Firm

	Lube & Auto	Dalton Motors	Combined Firm
Debt (%)	30%	30%	30%
Cost of debt	6.00%	5.40%	5.65%
Equity (%)	70%	70%	70%
Cost of equity	13.60%	12.50%	12.95%
Cost of capital—year 1	11.32%	10.37%	10.76%
Cost of capital—year 2	11.32%	10.37%	10.76%
Cost of capital—year 3	11.32%	10.37%	10.77%

(continued)

TABLE 25.8   *(continued)*

	Lube & Auto	Dalton Motors	Combined Firm
Cost of capital—year 4	11.32%	10.37%	10.77%
Cost of capital—year 5	11.32%	10.37%	10.77%
Cost of capital after	10.55%	10.37%	10.45%
FCFF in year 1	$ 120.00	$ 220.00	$ 340.00
FCFF in year 2	$ 144.00	$ 242.00	$ 386.00
FCFF in year 3	$ 172.80	$ 266.20	$ 439.00
FCFF in year 4	$ 207.36	$ 292.82	$ 500.18
FCFF in year 5	$ 248.83	$ 322.10	$ 570.93
Terminal value	$5,796.97	$7,813.00	$13,609.97
Value today	$4,020.91	$5,760.47	$ 9,781.38

The cost of equity and debt for the combined firm is obtained by taking the weighted average of the individual firm's costs of equity (debt); the weights are based on the relative market values of equity (debt) of the two firms. Since these relative market values change over time, the costs of equity and debt for the combined firm also change over time. The value of the combined firm is the same as the sum of the values of the independent firms, indicating that there is no value gain from diversification.

This equality does not imply, however, that the shareholders in the bidding and target firms are indifferent about such takeovers, since the bidding firm pays a significant premium over the market price. To the extent that these firms were correctly valued before the merger (market value of Lube & Auto = $4,020.91; market value of Dalton Motors = $5,760.47), the payment of a premium over the market price will transfer wealth from the bidding firm to the target firm.

The absence of added value from this merger may seem puzzling, given the fact that the two firms are in unrelated businesses, and thus, should gain some diversification benefit. In fact, if the earnings of the two firms are not highly correlated, the variance in earnings of the combined firm should be significantly lower than the variance in earnings of the individual firms operating independently. This reduction in earnings variance does not affect value, however, because it is firm-specific risk, which is assumed to have no effect on the cost of equity. (The betas, which are measures of market risk, are always value-weighted averages of the betas of the two merging firms.) But what about the impact of reduced variance on debt capacity? Firms with lower variability in earnings can increase debt capacity, and thus, value. This can be a real benefit of conglomerate mergers and will be considered separately later in this section.

Cash Slack   Managers may reject profitable investment opportunities if they have to raise new capital to finance them. Myers and Majluf (1984) suggest that since managers have more information than investors about prospective projects, new stock may have to be issued at less than true value to finance these projects, leading to the rejection of good projects and capital rationing for some firms. It may, therefore, make sense for a company with excess cash and no investment opportunities to take over a cash-poor firm with good investment opportunities, or vice versa. The additional value of combining these two firms is the present value of the projects that would not have been taken if they had stayed apart but can now be taken because of the availability of cash.

Cash slack can be a potent rationale for publicly traded firms that have ready access to capital or huge cash balances to acquire small or private firms that have capital constraints. It may also explain why acquisition strategies concentrating on buying smaller, private firms have worked fairly well in practice. Blockbuster Inc. (video rental), Browning and Ferris (waste disposal), and Service Merchandise (funeral homes) were all built by rolling up smaller private businesses into one publicly traded corporate entity.

Tax Benefits Several possible tax benefits accrue from takeovers. If one of the firms has tax deductions that it cannot use because it is losing money, whereas the other firm has income on which it pays significant taxes, combining the two firms can result in tax benefits that can be shared by the two firms. The value of this synergy is the present value of the tax savings that result from this merger. In addition, the assets of the firm being taken over can be written up to reflect new market values in some forms of mergers, leading to higher tax savings from depreciation in future years.

ILLUSTRATION 25.4:   Tax Benefits of Writing Up Asset Values after Takeover: Congoleum Inc.

One of the earliest leveraged buyouts (LBOs) occurred in 1979 and involved Congoleum Inc., a diversified firm in shipbuilding, flooring, and automotive accessories. Congoleum's own management bought out the firm. The favorable treatment that would be accorded the firm's assets by tax authorities was a major reason behind the takeover. After the takeover—estimated to cost approximately $400 million—the firm was enabled to write up its assets to reflect the new market values and claim depreciation on these new values. The estimated change in depreciation and the present value effect of this depreciation tax benefit, based on a tax rate of 48%, discounted at the firm's cost of capital of 14.5%[5], are shown in Table 25.9:

TABLE 25.9 Tax Benefits from Depreciation—Congoleum

Year	Depreciation			Tax Savings	Present Value
	Before	After	Change		
1980	$ 8.00	$ 35.51	$ 27.51	$13.20	$11.53
1981	$ 8.80	$ 36.26	$ 27.46	$13.18	$10.05
1982	$ 9.68	$ 37.07	$ 27.39	$13.15	$ 8.76
1983	$ 10.65	$ 37.95	$ 27.30	$13.10	$ 7.62
1984	$ 11.71	$ 21.23	$ 9.52	$ 4.57	$ 2.32
1985	$ 12.65	$ 17.50	$ 4.85	$ 2.33	$ 1.03
1986	$ 13.66	$ 16.00	$ 2.34	$ 1.12	$ 0.43
1987	$ 14.75	$ 14.75	$ 0.00	$ 0.00	$ 0.00
1988	$ 15.94	$ 15.94	$ 0.00	$ 0.00	$ 0.00
1989	$ 17.21	$ 17.21	$ 0.00	$ 0.00	$ 0.00
1980–1989	$123.05	$249.42	$126.37	$60.66	$41.76

Note that the increase in depreciation occurs in the first seven years, primarily as a consequence of higher book values and accelerated depreciation. After 1986, however, the old and new depreciation schedules

---

[5]The risk in the tax benefit cash flows arises primarily from the risk that you will not generate enough in earnings to take advantage of the tax benefits. While we have used the cost of capital as the discount rate here, reasonable arguments can be made for the use of the cost of equity (if you are uncertain about taxable income) or even the cost of debt (if you feel that you will get the tax benefits almost certainly, unless you go bankrupt).

converge. The present value of the additional tax benefits from the higher depreciation, based amounted to $41.76 million, about 10% of the overall price paid on the transaction.

In recent years, the tax code covering asset revaluations has been significantly tightened. While acquiring firms can still reassess the value of the acquired firm's assets, they can do so only up to fair value.

Debt Capacity　If the cash flows of the acquiring and target firms are less than perfectly correlated, the cash flows of the combined firm will be less variable than the cash flows of the individual firms. This decrease in variability can result in an increase in debt capacity and in the value of the firm. The increase in value, however, has to be weighed against the immediate transfer of wealth to existing bondholders in both firms from the stockholders of both the acquiring and target firms. The bondholders in the premerger firms find themselves lending to a safer firm after the takeover. The interest rates they are receiving are based on the riskier premerger firms, however. If the interest rates are not renegotiated, the bonds will increase in price, increasing the bondholders' wealth at the expense of the stockholders.

There are several models available for analyzing the benefits of higher debt ratios as a consequence of takeovers. Lewellen (1971) analyzes the benefits in terms of reduced default risk, since the combined firm has less variable cash flows than do the individual firms. He provides a rationale for an increase in the value of debt after the merger but at the expense of equity investors. It is not clear, therefore, that the value of the firm will increase after the merger. Stapleton (1985) evaluates the benefits of higher debt capacity after mergers using option pricing. He shows that the effect of a merger on debt capacity is always positive, even when the earnings of the two firms are perfectly correlated. The debt capacity benefits increase as the earnings of the two firms become less correlated and as investors become more risk averse.

Consider again the merger of Lube & Auto and Dalton Motors. The value of the combined firm was the same as the sum of the values of the independent firms. The fact that the two firms were in different business lines reduced the variance in earnings, but value was not affected, because the capital structure of the firm remained unchanged after the merger and the costs of equity and debt were the weighted averages of the individual firms' costs.

The reduction in variance in earnings can increase debt capacity, which can increase value. If, after the merger of these two firms, the debt capacity for the combined firm were increased to 40 percent from 30 percent (leading to an increase in the beta to 1.21 and no change in the cost of debt), the value of the combined firm after the takeover can be estimated as shown in Table 25.10. As a consequence of the added debt, the value of the firm will increase from $9,781.38 million to $11,429.35 million.

TABLE 25.10　Value of Debt Capacity—Lube & Auto and Dalton Motors

	Lube & Auto	Dalton Motors	Combined firm	
			No new debt	Added debt
Debt (%)	30%	30%	30%	40%
Cost of debt	6.00%	5.40%	5.65%	5.65%
Equity (%)	70%	70%	70%	60%
Cost of equity	13.60%	12.50%	12.95%	13.65%

	Lube & Auto	Dalton Motors	Combined firm	
			No new debt	Added debt
Cost of capital—year 1	11.32%	10.37%	10.76%	10.45%
Cost of capital—year 2	11.32%	10.37%	10.76%	10.45%
Cost of capital—year 3	11.32%	10.37%	10.77%	10.45%
Cost of capital—year 4	11.32%	10.37%	10.77%	10.45%
Cost of capital—year 5	11.32%	10.37%	10.77%	10.45%
Cost of capital after	10.55%	10.37%	10.45%	9.76%
FCFF in year 1	$ 120.00	$ 220.00	$ 340.00	$ 340.00
FCFF in year 2	$ 144.00	$ 242.00	$ 386.00	$ 386.00
FCFF in year 3	$ 172.80	$ 266.20	$ 439.00	$ 439.00
FCFF in year 4	$ 207.36	$ 292.82	$ 500.18	$ 500.18
FCFF in year 5	$ 248.83	$ 322.10	$ 570.93	$ 570.93
Terminal value	$5,796.97	$7,813.00	$13,609.97	$16,101.22
Present value	$4,020.91	$5,760.47	$ 9,781.38	$11,429.35

Increase Growth and Price-Earnings Multiples   Some acquisitions are motivated by the desire to increase growth and pricing multiples. Though the benefits of higher growth are undeniable, the price paid for that growth will determine whether such acquisitions make sense. If the price paid for the growth exceeds the fair market value, the stock price of the acquiring firm will decline even though the expected future growth in its cash flows may increase as a consequence of the takeover.

This can be seen in the previous example. Dalton Motors, with projected growth in cash flows of 10 percent, acquires Lube & Auto, which is expected to grow 20 percent. The fair market value for Lube & Auto is $4,020.91. If Dalton Motors pays more than this amount to acquire Lube & Auto, its stock price will decline, even though the combined firm will grow at a faster rate than Dalton Motors alone. Similarly, Dalton Motors, which sells at a lower multiple of earnings than Lube & Auto, will increase its PE ratio after the acquisition, but the effect on the stockholders in the firm will still be determined by whether the price paid on the acquisition exceeds the fair value. Interestingly, there is an alternate rationale that is provided for acquisitions, which is almost the inverse of this higher growth/PE strategy, and that is the accretive acquisition strategy. In this strategy, an acquisition is considered to be accretive (good) if it increases the earnings per share of the acquiring company and dilutive (bad) if it decreases earnings per share. That strategy makes no sense either, since Lube & Auto (as the higher PE ratio company) will see its earnings per share go up when it buys Dalton. But that higher earnings per share will be accompanied by a lower PE ratio and a price that can be higher or lower, depending on the price paid for Dalton.

HOW OFTEN DOES SYNERGY ACTUALLY SHOW UP?

McKinsey & Co. examined 58 acquisition programs between 1972 and 1983 for evidence on two questions: (1) Did the return on the amount invested in the acquisitions exceed the cost of capital? (2) Did the acquisitions help the parent companies

(continued)

(*continued*)

outperform the competition? McKinsey concluded that 28 of the 58 programs failed both tests, and 6 failed at least one test. In a follow-up study of 115 mergers in the United Kingdom and the United States in the 1990s, McKinsey concluded that 60 percent of the transactions earned returns on capital less than the cost of capital and that only 23 percent earned excess returns.[6] In 1999, KPMG examined 700 of the most expensive deals between 1996 and 1998 and concluded that only 17 percent created value for the combined firm, 30 percent were value-neutral, and 53 percent destroyed value.[7]

A study looked at the eight largest bank mergers in 1995 and concluded that only two (Chase/Chemical, First Chicago/NBD) subsequently outperformed the bank-stock index.[8] The largest, Wells Fargo's acquisition of First Interstate, was a significant failure. Sirower (1996) takes a detailed look at the promises and failures of synergy and draws the gloomy conclusion that synergy is often promised but seldom delivered.

The most damaging piece of evidence on the outcome of acquisitions is the large number of acquisitions that are reversed within fairly short time periods. Mitchell and Lehn (1990) note that 20.2 percent of the acquisitions made between 1982 and 1986 were divested by 1988. Studies that have tracked acquisitions for longer time periods (10 years or more) have found the divestiture rate of acquisitions rises to almost 50 percent, suggesting that few firms enjoy the promised benefits from acquisitions. In another study, Kaplan and Weisbach (1992) found that 44 percent of the mergers they studied were reversed, either because the acquirer paid too much or because the operations of the two firms did not mesh.

TAKEOVER VALUATION: BIASES AND COMMON ERRORS

The process of takeover valuation has potential pitfalls and biases that arise from the desire of the management of both the bidder and target firms to justify their points of view to their stockholders. The bidder firm aims to convince its stockholders that it is getting a bargain (i.e., that it is paying less than what the target firm is truly worth). In friendly takeovers, the target firm attempts to show its stockholders that the price it is receiving is a fair price (i.e., it is receiving at least what it is worth). In hostile takeovers, there is a role reversal, with bidding firms trying to convince target firm stockholders that they are not being cheated out of their fair share, and target firms arguing otherwise. Along the way, there are a number of common errors and biases in takeover valuation.

---

[6]This study was referenced in an article titled "Merger Mayhem" that appeared in *Barron's* on April 20, 1998.

[7]KPMG measured the success at creating value by comparing the postdeal stock price performance of the combined firm to the performance of the relevant industry segment for a year after the deal was completed.

[8]This study was done by Keefe, Bruyette, and Woods, an investment bank. It was referenced in an article titled "Merger Mayhem" in *Barron's*, April 20, 1998.

Use of Comparable Firms and Multiples

The prices paid in most takeovers are justified using the following sequence of actions: The acquirer assembles a group of firms comparable to the one being valued, selects a multiple to value the target firm, computes an average multiple for the comparable firms, and then makes subjective adjustments to this average. Each of these steps provides an opening for bias to enter into the process. Since no two firms are identical, the choice of comparable firms is a subjective one and can be tailored to justify the conclusion we want to reach. Similarly, in selecting a multiple, there are a number of possible choices—price-earnings ratios, price-cash flow ratios, price-book value ratios, and price-sales ratios, among others—and the multiple chosen will be the one that best suits our biases. Finally, once the average multiple has been obtained, subjective adjustments can be made to complete the story. In short, there is plenty of room for bias to be used to justify any price, using reasonable valuation models.

In some acquisition valuations, only firms that have been target firms in acquisitions are used as comparable firms, with the prices paid on the acquisitions being used to estimate multiples. The average multiple paid, which is called a transaction multiple, is then used to justify the price paid in an acquisition. This clearly creates a biased sample, and the values estimated using transactions multiples will generally be too high.

Mismatching Cash Flows and Discount Rates

One of the fundamental principles of valuation is that cash flows should be discounted using a consistent discount rate. Cash flows to equity should be discounted at the cost of equity and cash flows to the firm at the cost of capital; nominal cash flows should be discounted at the nominal discount rate and real cash flows at the real rate; after-tax cash flows should be discounted at the after-tax discount rate and pretax cash flows at the pretax rate. The failure to match cash flows with discount rates can lead to significant under- or overvaluation. Two of the more common mismatches include:

1. *Using the bidding firm's cost of equity or capital to discount the target firm's cash flows.* If the bidding firm raises the funds for the takeover, it is argued that its cost of equity should be used. This argument fails to take into account the fundamental investment principle that, it is not who raises the money that determines the cost of equity, as much as where the money is invested. The same firm will face a higher cost of equity for funds raised to finance riskier projects and a lower cost of equity to finance safer projects. Thus, the cost of equity in valuing the target should reflect that firm's riskiness (i.e., it is the target firm's cost of equity). Note also that since the cost of equity, as we have defined it, includes only nondiversifiable risk, arguments that the risk will decrease after the merger cannot be used to reduce the cost of equity, since the risk being decreased is firm-specific risk.

2. *Using the cost of capital to discount the cash flows to equity.* If the bidding firm uses a mix of debt and equity to finance the acquisition of the equity in a target firm, the argument goes that the cost of capital should be used in discounting the target firm's cash flows to equity (cash flows left over after interest and principal payments). The bottom line is that discounting the cash flows to equity at the cost of capital to obtain the value of equity is always wrong and will result in a significant overvaluation of the equity in the target firm.

Subsidizing the Target Firm

In a rational setting, the price paid for the target firm should not include any portion of the value that should be attributed to the acquiring firm. For instance, assume that a firm with excess debt capacity or a high debt rating uses a significant amount of low-cost debt to finance an acquisition. If we estimated a low cost of capital for the target firm with a high debt ratio and a low after-tax cost of debt, we would overestimate the value of the firm. If the acquiring firm paid this price on the acquisition, it would represent a transfer of wealth from the acquiring firm's stockholders to the target firm's stockholders. Thus, it is not appropriate to use the acquiring firm's cost of debt or debt capacity to estimate the cost of capital for the target firm. Instead, you should use the target company's debt ratio (actual or target) and cost of debt to compute the cost of capital for use in valuing the target company.

STRUCTURING THE ACQUISITION

Once the target firm has been identified and valued, the acquisition moves forward into the structuring phase. There are three interrelated steps in this phase. The first is the decision on how much to pay for the target firm, given that we have valued it with synergy and control built into the valuation. The second is the determination of how to pay for the deal (i.e., whether to use stock, cash, or some combination of the two) and whether to borrow any of the funds needed. The final step is the choice of the accounting treatment of the deal, because it can affect both taxes paid by stockholders in the target firm and how the purchase is accounted for in the acquiring firm's income statement and balance sheets.

Deciding on an Acquisition Price

The preceding section explained how to value a target firm with control and synergy considerations built into the value. This value represents a ceiling on the price that the acquirer can pay on the acquisition rather than a floor. If the acquirer pays the full value, there is no surplus value to claim for the acquirer's stockholders, and the target firm's stockholders get the entire value of the synergy and control premiums. This division of value is unfair if the acquiring firm plays an indispensable role in creating the synergy and control premiums.

Consequently, the acquiring firm should try to keep as much of the premium as it can for its stockholders. Several factors, however, will act as constraints. They include:

- *The market price of the target firm, if it is publicly traded, prior to the acquisition.* Since acquisitions have to be based on the current market price, the greater the current market value of equity, the lower the potential for gain to the acquiring firm's stockholders. For instance, if the market price of a poorly managed firm already reflects a high probability that the management of the firm will be changed, there is likely to be little or no value gained from control.
- *The relative scarcity of the specialized resources that the target and the acquiring firm bring to the merger.* Since the bidding firm and the target firm are both contributors to the creation of synergy, the sharing of the benefits of synergy among the two parties will depend in large part on whether the bidding firm's contribution to the creation of the synergy is unique or easily replaced. If it can be easily replaced, the bulk of the synergy benefits will accrue to the target firm. If it is unique, the

benefits will be shared much more equitably. Thus, when a firm with cash slack acquires a firm with many high-return projects, value is created. If there are a large number of firms with cash slack and relatively few firms with high-return projects, the bulk of the value of the synergy will accrue to the latter.

▨ *The presence of other bidders for the target firm.* When there is more than one bidder for a firm, the odds are likely to favor the target firm's stockholders. Bradley, Desai, and Kim (1988) examined an extensive sample of 236 tender offers made between 1963 and 1984 and concluded that the benefits of synergy accrue primarily or entirely to the target firms when multiple bidders are involved in the takeover. They estimated the market-adjusted stock returns around the announcement of the takeover for the successful bidder to be 2 percent in single-bidder takeovers and –1.33% in contested takeovers.

Payment for the Target Firm

Once a firm has decided to pay a given price for a target firm, it has to follow up by deciding how it is going to pay for this acquisition. In particular, decisions have to be made about the following aspects of the deal: debt versus equity and cash versus stock.

Debt versus Equity   A firm can raise the funds for an acquisition from either debt or equity. The mix will generally depend on the excess debt capacities of both the acquiring and the target firms. Thus, the acquisition of a target firm that is significantly under levered may be carried out with a larger proportion of debt than the acquisition of one that is already at its optimal debt ratio. This, of course, is reflected in the value of the firm through the cost of capital. It is also possible that the acquiring firm has excess debt capacity, and that it uses its ability to borrow money to carry out the acquisition. Although the mechanics of raising the money may look the same in this case, it is important that the value of the target firm not reflect this additional debt. As noted in the last section, the cost of capital used in valuing the acquisition should not reflect what it would have cost the target company to raise the funds, and not what the acquiring company may actually end up paying. The additional debt has nothing to do with the target firm, and building it into the value will only result in the acquiring firm paying a premium for a value enhancement that rightfully belongs to its own stockholders.

Cash versus Stock   There are three ways in which a firm can use equity in a transaction. The first is to use cash balances that have been built up over time to finance the acquisition. The second is to issue stock to the public, raise cash, and use the cash to pay for the acquisition. The third is to offer stock as payment for the target firm, where the payment is structured in terms of a stock swap—shares in the acquiring firm in exchange for shares in the target firm. The question of which of these approaches is best utilized by a firm cannot be answered without looking at the following factors:

▨ *The availability of cash on hand.* Clearly, the option of using cash on hand is available only to those firms that have accumulated substantial amounts of cash.

▨ *The perceived value of the stock.* When stock is issued to the public to raise new funds or when it is offered as payment on acquisitions, the acquiring firm's managers are making a judgment about what the perceived value of the stock is. In other words, managers who believe that their stock is trading at a price significantly below value should not use stock as currency on acquisitions, since what they gain on the acquisitions can be more than lost in the stock issue. However, firms that believe their stocks are overvalued are much more likely to use stock as currency in transactions. The stockholders in the target firm are also aware of this and may demand a larger premium when the payment is made entirely in the form of the acquiring firm's stock.

▪ *Tax factors.* When an acquisition is a stock swap, the stockholders in the target firm may be able to defer capital gains taxes on the exchanged shares. Since this benefit can be significant in an acquisition, the potential tax gains from a stock swap may be large enough to offset any perceived disadvantages.

The final aspect of a stock swap is the setting of the terms of the stock swap (i.e., the number of shares of the acquired firm that will be offered per share of the acquiring firm). While this amount is generally based on the market price at the time of the acquisition, the ratio that results may be skewed by the relative mispricing of the two firms' securities, with the more overpriced firm gaining at the expense of the more underpriced (or at least less overpriced) firm. A fairer ratio would be based on the intrinsic values of the two firms' shares. This can be seen quite clearly in the following illustration.

ILLUSTRATION 25.5:   **Setting the Exchange Ratio**

The Inbev SAB Miller acquisition was funded with debt, but in this illustration, we will look at how, if it had been structured as an exchange offering, the exchange ratio would have been computed. We will begin by reviewing our valuation for SAB Miller and synergy in Table 25.11. The value of SAB Miller with the synergy and control components is $70,786 million. This is obtained by adding the value of control ($4,702 million) and the value of synergy ($14,592 million) to the status quo value of $51,492 million. SAB Miller also has net debt outstanding of $13,074 million, other investments (JV and crossholdings) of $20,819 million, and 1,607.4 million shares outstanding. The maximum value per share for SAB Miller can then be estimated as follows (assuming no cash):

$$\text{Maximum Value per share (SAB Miller)} = \frac{(51492 + 14592 + 4702) - 13074 + 20819}{1607.4}$$

$$= \$48.86$$

TABLE 25.11   Valuing SAB Miller for Inbev

Component	Valuation Guidelines	Value
Synergy	Value the combined firm with synergy built in. In the case of Inbev, the synergy comes from cost savings and a slightly higher growth rate. (See Illustration 25.3.)	$14,592 million
Control premium	Value SAB Miller as a stand-alone firm, with changed management: (See Illustration 25.2.) ● Debt ratio to match industry average ● Higher margins and return on capital to match industry average.	$4,702 million
Status quo valuation	Value SAB Miller as is, with existing inputs for investment, financing, and dividend policy. (See Illustration 25.1.)	$51,492 million

The estimated value per share for Inbev is $104.57, based on the total value of the operating assets of $211,953 million, and incorporating the net debt outstanding of $44,720 million, and accounting for 1,599.2 million shares, we get:

$$\text{Value per share (Inbev)} = \frac{211953 - 44720}{1599.2} = \$104.57$$

The appropriate exchange ratio, based on value per share, can be estimated:

$$\text{Exchange ratio}_{\text{inbev,SAB}} = \frac{\text{Value per share}_{\text{SAB}}}{\text{Value per share}_{\text{Inbev}}} = 48.86/104.57 = 0.4672$$

If Inbev exchanges 0.4672 shares of its stock in SAB Miller, SAB Miller shareholders will get 100% of the benefits of control and synergy, and Inbev shareholders will just break even. If the exchange ratio is set below this number, Inbev shareholders will receive some of the benefits of synergy and control, and at a low enough value, it is conceivable that they can claim all or more than the full benefits from both sources.

As we noted earlier, Inbev paid almost $100 billion to acquire SAB Miller, paying $67.59 per share, and funding the acquisition primarily with debt. At that price, and based upon our estimates of the value of control and synergy, SAB Miller shareholders clearly were the winners from this deal, with the wealth transfer computed here:

Price paid by Inbev for SAB Miller shares = $108,644 million
Value of SAB Miller, with control and synergy = $ 78,531 million
Excess payment = $ 30,113 million

Since Inbev did not assume any of SAB Miller's debt in the acquisition, the net debt of $13,074 million can be netted out of this excess payment value to arrive at an overpayment of $17,039 million.

---

 exchratio.xls: This spreadsheet enables you to estimate the exchange ratio on an acquisition, given the value of control and synergy.

Accounting Considerations

While much of the discussion in this chapter has been about value and price, the accounting for acquisitions seems to play a key role not only in whether a deal is made but the price paid for that deal. To the extent that the accounting treatment of acquisitions can affect cash flows, the attention paid to them is appropriate. All too often, though, accounting choices affect only reported earnings (and not cash flows) and should have little or no impact on deal making.

Asset Revaluation The rules on asset revaluation after mergers vary widely across countries, with some countries allowing much more leeway to companies on how much of the purchase price they allocate to acquired company assets and depreciation schedules based upon the appraised values. This increases the tax benefits from acquisitions and may enable higher premiums to be paid.

The good news is that generally accepted accounting principles (GAAP) and international financial reporting standards (IFRS) are converging on how to account for acquisition, with a move towards fair value accounting. After an acquisition, the acquiring firm is required to reappraise the value of the target company's assets. For some assets that have a traded market price, this is simple to do, but for others it does require an appraisal of what a buyer would pay for that asset in the marketplace. This is also one of the few occasions where intangible assets, such as customer lists and trademarks, can be valued and put on the books. When assets are revalued or valued for the first time (as is the case with many intangible assets in acquisitions), there can be tax consequences that affect cash flows, and through them the value.

Goodwill   Goodwill is the debris of acquisition accounting. It reflects the accountant's attempt to reconcile two irreconcilable items: the adjusted book value (with the assets being revalued as specified earlier) and market value. To see why, assume that firm A is considering acquiring firm B for $ 2.5 billion, and that the adjusted book value of assets at firm B currently is $ 1.5 billion. When firm A acquires firm B, the difference between the price paid and the book value ($2.5 billion minus $1.5 billion) will be termed goodwill and be shown as an asset, with a value of $ 1 billion, on the balance sheet.

Once goodwill is valued as an asset, its value has to be estimated in each subsequent year. Until about two decades ago, goodwill was amortized in equal annual increments over 40 years, and accountants were given little or no discretion on the schedule. Now, accountants are required to revalue the acquired company (or its assets) each year after the acquisition. If the value has gone up, the goodwill is left intact. If the value has declined, the goodwill is considered to be "impaired", and the firm has to take an impairment charge. For the most part, impairment of goodwill that is generated as a result of acquisitions of companies is not tax deductible. Hence, whether it is impaired or not has no effect on cash flows, though it can have dramatic effects on earnings. It is only in the exceptional circumstance where the assets of a firm are acquired (rather than the firm itself) that acquirers can qualify for tax deductions for goodwill impairment.

The bottom line for acquirers is that goodwill measurement, for the most part, should not make a good deal into a bad deal or vice versa. It should also have little or no impact on the value that you attach to a target companies, unless it qualifies for tax deductions. In the special cases, where goodwill amortization/impairment is tax deductible, it will affect cash flows and values.

Restructuring Charges   Common by-products of acquisitions are restructuring and acquisition-related charges associated with consolidating the merged companies. These charges can be categorized into three groups:

- Cash expenses that clearly reduce the expected cash flows in the first few years of the merger and will offset or at least reduce any potential gains from synergy.
- Noncash expenses that are tax deductible. These reduce earnings but can increase cash flows by reducing taxes paid.
- Noncash expenses that are not tax deductible, which are similar to amortization of goodwill, insofar as they reduce earnings but have no effect on cash flows.

IMPROVING THE ODDS

If the message that you have received in this chapter is that creating value from acquisitions and its by-products (control and synergy) is difficult to pull off, that was intentional. If history is a guide, the history of acquisitions is that much is promised at the time of the merger, but less is delivered, and even when there is success, the fruits of that success go mostly or entirely to the shareholders in the target company. In this section, we will look at the types of acquisitions where the odds are better for acquirers, and actions that can be taken to improve those odds.

Sole Bidder versus Bidding War

It is not uncommon for acquirers to get caught up in bidding wars, especially when the target has qualities that are much sought after by the market. The lesson from acquisitions for value creation, on this front, are clear. If you are in a bidding war, drop out, since winning a bidding war often requires paying a higher premium. In a paper that isolates mergers with bidding wars, Malmendier, Moretti, and Peters (2018) look at the returns earned in bidding wars, by both the winning and losing bidders. Figure 25.6 summarizes their findings on how the stock returns of winning and losing bidders do, relative to their industry peer groups.

In short, this study concludes that while the returns for winning and losing bidders are similar in the thirty-six months leading into the bidding war, losing bidders outperform winning bidders by about 24% in the three years after the bidding war concludes.

Small versus Large Targets

In acquisitions, acquiring firms often face a choice when it comes to target firms. Should you acquire small targets, with the caveat that you will have to do a lot more acquisitions to make a dent in your own operating metrics, or should acquire much larger targets, where you can fewer acquisitions, with more due diligence? The empirical evidence on this front is in favor of small acquisitions, with a multitude of factors (including cultural fits between

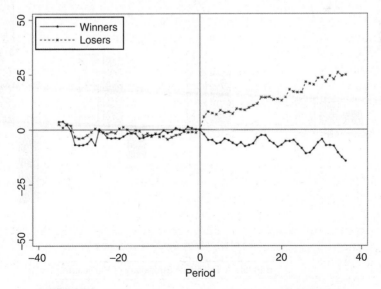

FIGURE 25.6   Winning versus Losing Bidders in Acquisitions

the merged companies) working against success with large acquisitions. Robert Bruner's look at "deals from hell" highlights twelve bad merger and acquisitions (M&A) deals, and one the characteristics that they share in common is that they are all mergers of large publicly traded enterprises.

In related findings, studies also find that the returns to acquisitions are greater at smaller acquirers than at larger acquirers. Moeller, Schlingemann, and Stulz (2004) looked at U.S-based acquisitions and found that while they collectively earned a slightly positive excess return on acquisitions, smaller acquirers earned significantly higher returns than larger acquirers, perhaps suggesting that acquisition-based strategies do not scale up well.

Public versus Private Targets

When looking for target firms, you can look at public markets for companies that may be good fits, or at privately owned businesses. With the former, you have the benefit of accounting standards that are close to your own, and market assessments of the firm's business that you can use in making your own judgments. With the latter, your biggest advantage is that there is no market price acting as a floor on your bid, creating room for a more reasoned assessment of value. However, private businesses may come with more strings attached, including key people that determine its value and opaque accounting practices. Studies that have looked at these targets concluded, fairly categorically, that there is a much greater chance for acquirers to generate value from buying privately owned businesses, as opposed to their publicly traded counterparts, as can be seen in Figure 25.7.

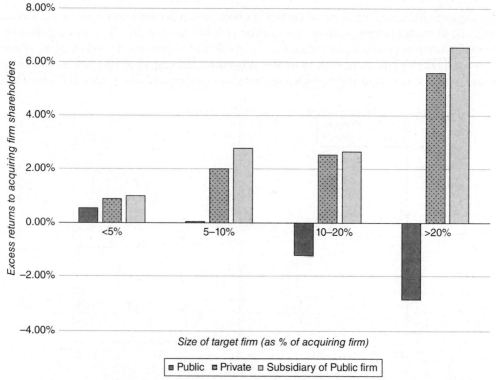

FIGURE 25.7   Private versus Public Targets in Acquisitions

Note that for acquisitions of every size, acquiring companies do much better with private target acquisitions than with public company acquisitions. However, there is a third category which seems to deliver even better results, at least for larger acquisitions, which is acquiring divisions of public companies. It seems fair to conclude, therefore, that it is not the private/public divide that is at the core of why public acquisitions often fail, it is the fact that you have to pay market price plus a premium.

Cost versus Growth Synergies

In the section on synergies, we noted that operating synergies can take the form of either growth synergies (higher revenue and earnings in future periods) or cost synergies. In theory, both synergies contribute to higher cash flows, and should lead to higher value. In practice, though, there is a much greater likelihood that cost synergies, that are promised at the time of an acquisition, come to fruition than growth synergies, as can be seen in Figure 25.8, where we summarize the results of a study by McKinsey of the breakdown of firms that deliver their promised synergies.

The percentage of firms that deliver on promised cost synergies is significantly higher than the percentage of firms that deliver growth synergies, and you are far more likely to see dramatic shortfalls in growth synergy deliveries.

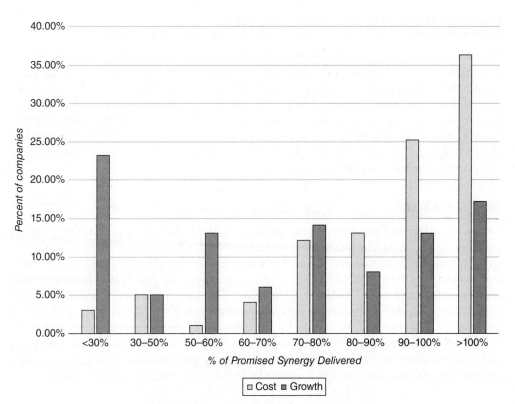

FIGURE 25.8 Cost versus Growth Synergies

Other Factors

While the ecosystem that makes money on acquisitions is wide and influential, including consultants and quite a few strategists, blaming bankers or consultants for overpayment on acquisitions cannot pass muster. When a company overpays on an acquisition, there has to be accountability, where those who most actively pushed for that acquisition should be held responsible for delivering its promise (in synergy and control) and pay a price when it does not. Unfortunately, that accountability is absent in the real world, since bad deals become orphans where everyone involved in the deal finds way to distance themselves from the deal.

Even if you do find an acquisition strategy that works at delivering value, you must recognize when to stop, since even the most successful deal-focused strategies will run out of steam, partly because your success makes you bigger. Cisco was an M&A success story in the 1990s, where it adopted a disciplined strategy of buying small private companies, often with technology that it could incorporate into its products, to grow from a market capitalization of $4 billion in 1990 to more than $400 billion briefly in 1999. By 1999, the company had become big enough that it often had to acquire two dozen or more firms every year to be able to deliver the growth that investors were expecting of it. As the dot-com bubble burst and investors started looking for results, Cisco's strategy of acquisitions turned against it between 2000 and 2009 as the company's capitalization stagnated, even as it spent tens of billions on acquisitions.

ANALYZING MANAGEMENT AND LEVERAGED BUYOUTS

The first section, when describing the different types of acquisitions, pointed out two important differences between mergers and buyouts. The first is that, unlike a merger, a buyout does not involve two firms coming together and creating a consolidated entity. Instead, the target firm is acquired by a group of investors that may include the management of the firm. The second is that the target firm in a buyout usually becomes a private business. Some buyouts in the 1980s also used large proportions of debt, leading to their categorization as leveraged buyouts. Each of these differences does have an effect on how we approach the valuation of buyouts.

Valuation of a Buyout

The fact that buyouts involve only the target firm, and that there is no acquiring firm to consider, makes valuation much more straightforward. Clearly, there is no potential for synergy, and therefore, no need to value it. However, the fact that the managers of a firm are also the acquirers of the firm does create two issues. The first is that managers have access to information that investors do not have. This information may enable managers to conclude, with far more certainty than would an external acquirer, that their firm is undervalued. This may be one reason for the buyout. The second is that the management of the firm remains the same after the buyout, but the way in which investment, financing, and dividend decisions are made may change. This happens because managers, once they become owners, may become much more concerned about maximizing firm value.

The fact that firms that are involved in buyouts become private businesses can also have an effect on value. Chapter 24 noted that investments in private businesses are much more difficult to liquidate than investments in publicly traded firms. This can create a significant discount on value. One reason this discount may be smaller in the case of buyouts is that many of them are done with the clear intention, once the affairs of the firm have been put in order, of going public again.

If going private is expected to increase managers' responsiveness to value maximization in the long term—since they are part owners of the firm—the way to incorporate this in value is to include it in the cash flows. The increased efficiency can be expected to increase cash flows if it increases operating margins. The emphasis on long-term value should be visible in investment choices, and should lead to a higher return on capital and higher growth. This advantage has to be weighed against the capital rationing the firm might face because of limited access to financial markets, which might reduce future growth and profits. The net effect will determine the change in value. The empirical evidence on going-private transactions, however, is clear-cut. DeAngelo, DeAngelo, and Rice (1984) reported, for example, an average abnormal return of 30 percent for 81 firms in their sample that went private. Thus, financial markets, at least, seem to believe that there is value to be gained for some public firms in going private.

Valuing a Leveraged Buyout

We have seen that leveraged buyouts are financed disproportionately with debt. This high leverage is justified in several ways. First, if the target firm initially has too little debt relative to its optimal debt ratio, the increase in debt can be explained partially by the increase in value moving to the optimal ratio provides. The debt level in most leveraged buyouts exceeds the optimal debt ratio, however, which means that some of the debt will have to be paid off quickly in order for the firm to reduce its cost of capital and its default risk. A second explanation is provided by Michael Jensen, who proposes that managers cannot be trusted to invest free cash flows wisely for their stockholders; they need the discipline of debt payments to maximize cash flows on projects and firm value. A third rationale is that the high debt ratio is temporary and will disappear once the firm liquidates assets and pays off a significant portion of the debt.

The extremely high leverage associated with leveraged buyouts creates two problems in valuation, however. First, it significantly increases the riskiness of the cash flows to equity investors in the firm, by increasing the fixed payments to debt holders in the firm and exposure to failure risk. Thus, the cost of equity and failure risk to be adjusted to reflect the higher financial risk the firm will face after the leveraged buyout. Second, the expected decrease in this debt over time, as the firm liquidates assets and pays off debt, implies that the cost of equity will also decrease over time. Since the cost of debt and debt ratio will change over time as well, the cost of capital will also change in each period.

In valuing a leveraged buyout, we begin with the estimates of free cash flow to the firm, just as we did in traditional valuation. However, instead of discounting these cash flows back at a fixed cost of capital, we discount them back at a cost of capital that will vary from year to year. Once we value the firm, we then can compare the value to the total amount paid for the firm.

ILLUSTRATION 25.6:   Valuing a Leveraged Buyout: Congoleum Inc.

The managers of Congoleum Inc. targeted the firm for a leveraged buyout in 1979.[9] They planned to buy back the stock at $38 per share (it was trading at $24 prior to the takeover), and to finance the acquisition primarily with debt. The breakdown of the cost and financing of the deal is:

Cost of Takeover	
Buy-back stock: $38 × 12.2 million shares	$463.60 million
Expenses of takeover	$7.00 million
Total cost	$470.60 million
Financing Mix for Takeover	
Equity	$117.30 million
Debt	$327.10 million
Preferred stock (@13.5%)	$26.20 million
Total proceeds	$470.60 million

There were three sources of debt:

1. Bank debt of $125 million, at a 14% interest rate, to be repaid in annual installments of $16.666 million starting in 1980.
2. Senior notes of $115 million, at 11.25% interest rate, to be repaid in equal annual installments of $7.636 million each year from 1981.
3. Subordinated notes of $92 million, at 12.25% interest, to be repaid in equal annual installments of $7.636 million each year from 1989.

The firm also assumed $12.2 million of existing debt, at the advantageous rate of 7.50%; this debt would be repaid in 1982.[10]

The firm projected operating income (EBIT), capital spending, depreciation, and change in working capital from 1980 to 1984 as shown in the Table 25.12 (in millions of dollars):

The earnings before interest and taxes were expected to grow 8% after 1984, and the capital spending was expected to be offset by depreciation.[11]

TABLE 25.12   Forecasted Earnings and Reinvestment

Year	EBIT	Capital Spending	Depreciation	Δ Working Capital
Current	$ 89.80	$ 6.8	$ 7.5	$ 4.0
1980	$ 71.69	$15.0	$35.51	$ 2.0
1981	$ 90.84	$16.2	$36.26	$14.0
1982	$115.73	$17.5	$37.07	$23.3
1983	$133.15	$18.9	$37.95	$11.2
1984	$137.27	$20.4	$21.93	$12.8

[9] The numbers in this illustration were taken from the Harvard Business School case titled "Congoleum". The case is reprinted in Fruhan, Kester, Mason, Piper, and Ruback (1992).

[10] The debt value exceeds the transaction amount, reflecting transaction costs and investment banking fees.

[11] We have used the assumptions provided by the investment banker in this case. It is troubling, however, that the firm has an expected growth rate of 8% a year forever without reinvesting any money back. In fact, this violation of valuation first principles may drown out any benefits from finessing the capital structure and calculating the cost of capital correctly.

Congoleum had a beta of 1.25 in 1979 prior to the leveraged buyout. The Treasury bond rate at the time of the leveraged buyout was 9.5%, and the tax rate was 48%.

We begin the analysis by estimating the expected cash flows to the firm from 1980 to 1985. To obtain these estimates, we subtract the net capital expenditures and changes in working capital (which were provided) from the after-tax operating income in Table 25.13:

TABLE 25.13 Expected Free Cashflows to the Firm

	1980	1981	1982	1983	1984	1985
EBIT	$71.69	$90.84	$115.73	$133.15	$137.27	$148.25
− EBIT(t)	$34.41	$43.60	$ 55.55	$ 63.91	$ 65.89	$ 71.16
= EBIT(1 − t)	$37.28	$47.24	$ 60.18	$ 69.24	$ 71.38	$ 77.09
+ Depreciation	$35.51	$36.26	$ 37.07	$ 37.95	$ 21.93	$ 21.62
− Capital expenditures	$15.00	$16.20	$ 17.50	$ 18.90	$ 20.40	$ 21.62
− Δ WC	$ 2.00	$14.00	$ 23.30	$ 11.20	$ 12.80	$ 5.00
= FCFF	$55.79	$53.30	$ 56.45	$ 77.09	$ 60.11	$ 72.09

We follow up by estimating the cost of capital for the firm each year, based on our estimates of debt and equity each year. The value of debt for future years is estimated based on the repayment schedule, which decreases over time. The value of equity in each of the future years is estimated by discounting the expected cash flows in equity beyond that year at the cost of equity. (This explains why the equity in 1980 is greater than the book value of equity.)

	1980	1981	1982	1983	1984	1985
Debt	$327.10	$309.96	$285.17	$260.62	$236.04	$211.45
Equity	$275.39	$319.40	$378.81	$441.91	$504.29	$578.48
Preferred stock	$26.20	$26.20	$26.20	$26.20	$26.20	$26.20
Debt/capital	52.03%	47.28%	41.32%	35.76%	30.79%	25.91%
Equity/capital	43.80%	48.72%	54.89%	60.64%	65.79%	70.88%
Preferred stock/capital	4.17%	4.00%	3.80%	3.60%	3.42%	3.21%
Beta	2.02547	1.87988	1.73426	1.62501	1.54349	1.4745
Cost of equity	20.64%	19.84%	19.04%	18.44%	17.99%	17.61%
After-tax cost of debt	6.53%	6.53%	6.53%	6.53%	6.53%	5.00%
Cost of preferred stock	13.51%	13.51%	13.51%	13.51%	13.51%	13.51%
Cost of capital	13.00%	13.29%	13.66%	14.00%	14.31%	14.21%

An alternative approach to estimating equity that does not require iterations or circular reasoning is to use the book value of equity, rather than the estimated market value in calculating debt-equity ratios.[12]

The cash flows to the firm and the cost of capital in the terminal year (1985), in conjunction with the expected growth rate of 8% are used to estimate the terminal value of the business (at the end of 1984):

$$\text{Terminal value of the firm}_{1984} = \frac{\text{FCFF}_{1985}}{(\text{Cost of capital in 1985} - \text{Expected growth rate})}$$

$$= \frac{\$72.09}{(0.1421 - 0.08)} = \$1{,}161 \text{ million}$$

---

[12]The book value of equity can be obtained as follows:

Book value of equity$_t$ = Book value of equity$_{t-1}$ + Net income$_t$ − Dividends$_t$

It is assumed that there will be no dividends paid to equity investors in the initial years of a leveraged buyout.

The expected cash flows to the firm and the terminal value were discounted back to the present at the cost of capital to yield a present value of $820.21 million.[13] Since the acquisition of Congoleum cost only $470.6 million, this acquisition creates value for the acquiring investors.

---

 merglbo.xls: **This spreadsheet enables you to evaluate the cash flows and the value of a leveraged buyout.**

CONCLUSION

Acquisitions take several forms and occur for different reasons. Acquisitions can be categorized based on what happens to the target firm after the acquisition. A target firm can be consolidated into the acquiring entity (merger), create a new entity in combination with the acquiring firm, or remain independent (buyout).

There are four steps in analyzing acquisitions. First, we specify the reasons for acquisitions and list five: the undervaluation of the target firm, benefit from diversification, the potential for synergy, the value created by changing the way the target firm is run, and management self-interest. Second, we choose a target firm whose characteristics make it the best candidate, given the motive chosen in the first step. Third, we value the target firm, assuming it would continue to be run by its current managers, and then revalue it assuming better management. We define the difference between these two values as the value of control. We also value each of the different sources of operating and financial synergy, and consider the combined value as the value of total synergy. Fourth, we look at the mechanics of the acquisition. We examine how much the acquiring firm should consider paying, given the value estimated in the prior step for the target firm, including control and synergy benefits. We also look at whether the acquisition should be financed with cash or stock, and how the choice of the accounting treatment of the acquisition affects this choice.

Buyouts share some characteristics with acquisitions, but they also vary on a couple of important ones. The absence of an acquiring firm, the fact that the managers of the firm are its acquirers, and the conversion of the acquired firm into a private business all have implications for value. If the buyout is financed predominantly with debt, making it a leveraged buyout, the debt ratio will change in future years, leading to changes in the costs of equity, debt, and capital in those years.

---

[13]When the cost of capital changes on a year-to-year basis, the discounting has to be based on a cumulative cost. For instance, the cash flow in year 3 will be discounted back as follows:

PV of cash flow in year 3 = 56.45/(1.13)(1.1329)(1.1366)

QUESTIONS AND SHORT PROBLEMS

In the problems following, use an equity risk premium of 5.5 percent if none is specified.

1. The following are the details of two potential merger candidates, Northrop and Grumman, in 1993:

	Northrop	Grumman
Revenues	$4,400.00	$3,125.00
Cost of goods sold (without depreciation)	87.50%	89.00%
Depreciation	$200.00	$74.00
Tax rate	35.00%	35.00%
Working capital	10% of revenue	10% of revenue
Market value of equity	$2,000.00	$1,300.00
Outstanding debt	$160.00	$250.00

Both firms are expected to grow 5% a year in perpetuity. Capital spending is expected to be 20% of depreciation. The beta for both firms is 1, and both firms are rated BBB, with an interest rate on their debt of 8.5% (The Treasury bond rate is 7%, and the risk premium is 5.5%.)

As a result of the merger, the combined firm is expected to have a cost of goods sold of only 86% of total revenues. The combined firm does not plan to borrow additional debt.
   a. Estimate the value of Grumman, operating independently.
   b. Estimate the value of Northrop, operating independently.
   c. Estimate the value of the combined firm, with no synergy.
   d. Estimate the value of the combined firm, with synergy.
   e. How much is the operating synergy worth?
2. In the Grumman-Northrop example described in the previous question, the combined firm did not take on additional debt after the acquisition. Assume that as a result of the merger the firm's optimal debt ratio increases to 20% of total capital from current levels. (At that level of debt, the combined firm will have an A rating, with an interest rate on its debt of 8%.) If it does not increase debt, the combined firm's rating will be A+ (with an interest rate of 7.75%).
   a. Estimate the value of the combined firm if it stays at its existing debt ratio.
   b. Estimate the value of the combined firm if it moves to its optimal debt ratio.
   c. Who gains this additional value if the firm moves to the optimal debt ratio?
3. In April 1994, Novell, Inc. announced its plan to acquire WordPerfect Corporation for $1.4 billion. At the time of the acquisition, the relevant information about the two companies was as follows:

	Novell	WordPerfect
Revenues	$1,200.00	$600.00
Cost of goods sold (without depreciation)	57.00%	75.00%
Depreciation	$ 42.00	$ 25.00
Tax rate	35.00%	35.00%

	Novell	WordPerfect
Capital spending	$ 75.00	$ 40.00
Working capital (as % of revenue)	40.00%	30.00%
Beta	1.45	1.25
Expected growth rate in revenues/EBIT	25.00%	15.00%
Expected period of high growth	10 years	10 years
Growth rate after high growth period	6.00%	6.00%
Beta after high growth period	1.10	1.10

Capital spending will be 115% of depreciation after the high-growth period. Neither firm has any debt outstanding. The Treasury bond rate is 7%.

a. Estimate the value of Novell, operating independently.

b. Estimate the value of WordPerfect, operating independently.

c. Estimate the value of the combined firm, with no synergy.

d. As a result of the merger, the combined firm is expected to grow 24% a year for the high growth period. Estimate the value of the combined firm with the higher growth.

e. What is the synergy worth? What is the maximum price Novell can pay for WordPerfect?

4. Assume, in the Novell-WordPerfect merger described in the preceding question, that it will take five years for the firms to work through their differences and start realizing their synergy benefits. What is the synergy worth under these circumstances?

5. In 1996, Aetna, a leading player in health insurance, announced its intentions to acquire U.S. Healthcare, the nation's largest health maintenance organization, and provided synergy as a rationale. On the announcement of the merger, Aetna's stock price, which was $57, dropped to $52.50, while U.S. Healthcare's stock price surged from $31 to $37.50. Aetna had 400 million shares, and U.S. Healthcare had 50 million shares outstanding at the time of the announcement.

a. Estimate the value, if any, that financial markets are attaching to synergy in this merger.

b. How would you reconcile the market reaction to the rationale presented by management for the acquisition?

6. IH Corporation, a farm equipment manufacturer, has accumulated almost $2 billion in losses over the past seven years of operations and is in danger of not being able to carry forward these losses. EG Corporation, an extremely profitable financial service firm, which had $3 billion in taxable income in its most recent year, is considering acquiring IH Corporation. The tax authorities will allow EG Corporation to offset its taxable income with the carried-forward losses. The tax rate for EG Corporation is 40%, and the cost of capital is 12%.

a. Estimate the value of the tax savings that will occur as a consequence of the merger.

b. What is the value of the tax savings if the tax authorities allow EG Corporation to spread the carried-forward losses over four years (i.e., allow $200 million of the carried-forward losses to offset income each year for the next four years)?

7. You are considering a takeover of PMT Corporation, a firm that has significantly underperformed its peer group over the past five years, and you wish to estimate the value of control. The data on PMT Corporation, the peer group, and the best-managed firm in the group are:

	PMT Corp	*Peer Group*	*Best-managed firm*
Return on assets (after-tax)	8.00%	12.00%	18.00%
Dividend payout ratio	50.00%	30.00%	20.00%
Debt-equity ratio	10.00%	50.00%	50.00%
Interest rate on debt	7.50%	8.00%	8.00%
Beta	Not available	1.30	1.30

PMT Corporation reported earnings per share of $2.50 in the most recent time period and is expected to reach stable growth in five years, after which the growth rate is expected to be 6% for all firms in this group. The beta during the stable-growth period is expected to be 1 for all firms. There are 100 million shares outstanding, and the Treasury bond rate is 7% (the tax rate is 40% for all firms).

a. Value the equity in PMT Corporation assuming that the current management continues in place.

b. Value the equity in PMT Corporation assuming that it improves its performance to peer group levels.

c. Value the equity in PMT Corporation assuming that it improves its performance to the level of the best managed firm in the group.

8. You are attempting to do a leveraged buyout of Boston Turkey but have run into some roadblocks. You have some partially completed projected cash flow statements and need help to complete them.

	Year 1	*Year 2*	*Year 3*	*Year 4*	*Year 5*	*Terminal Year*
Revenues	$1,100,000	$1,210,000	$1,331,000	$1,464,100	$1,610,510	$1,707,141
– Expenses	$ 440,000	$ 484,000	$ 532,400	$ 585,640	$ 644,204	$ 682,856
– Depreciation	$ 100,000	$ 110,000	$ 121,000	$ 133,100	$ 146,410	$ 155,195
= EBIT	$ 560,000	$ 616,000	$ 677,600	$ 745,360	$ 819,896	$ 869,090
– Interest	$ 360,000	$ 324,000	$ 288,000	$ 252,000	$ 216,000	$ 180,000
Taxable income	$ 200,000	$ 292,000	$ 389,600	$ 493,360	$ 603,896	$ 689,090
– Tax	$ 80,000	$ 116,800	$ 155,840	$ 197,344	$ 241,558	$ 275,636
= Net income	$ 120,000	$ 175,200	$ 233,760	$ 296,016	$ 362,338	$ 413,454

The capital expenditures are expected to be $120,000 next year and to grow at the same rate as revenues for the rest of the period. Working capital will be kept at 20% of revenues (revenues this year were $1 million).

The leveraged buyout will be financed with a mix of $1 million of equity and $3 million of debt (at an interest rate of 12%). Part of the debt will be repaid by the end of year 5, and the debt remaining at the end of year 5 will remain on the books permanently.

a. Estimate the cash flows to equity and the firm for the next five years.

b. The cost of equity in year 1 has been computed. Compute the cost of equity each year for the rest of the period. (Use book value of equity for the calculation).

Item	*Year 1*
Equity	$1,000,000
Debt	$3,000,000
Debt-equity ratio	3
Beta	2.58
Cost of equity	24.90%

    c. Compute the terminal value of the firm.

    d. Evaluate whether the leveraged buyout will create value.

9. J & L Chemical is a profitable chemical manufacturing firm. The business, however, is highly cyclical, and the profits of the firm have been volatile. The management of the firm is considering acquiring a food-processing firm to reduce the earnings volatility and exposure to economic cycles.

    a. Would such an action be in the best interests of stockholders? Explain.

    b. Would your analysis be any different if J & L was a private firm? Explain.

    c. Is there any condition under which you would argue for such an acquisition for a publicly traded firm?

CHAPTER 26

Valuing Real Estate

The valuation models developed for financial assets are applicable for real assets as well. Real estate investments comprise the most significant component of real asset investments. For many years, analysts in real estate have used their own variants on valuation models to value real estate. Real estate is too different an asset class, they argue, to be valued with models developed to value publicly traded stocks.

This chapter presents a different point of view: that while real estate and stocks may be different asset classes, the principles of valuation should not differ across the classes. The intrinsic and relative valuation techniques that we used to value stocks should work for real estate as well. That said, there are serious estimation issues to confront that are unique to real estate and will be dealt with in this chapter.

REAL VERSUS FINANCIAL ASSETS

Real estate and financial assets share several common characteristics: Their value should be determined by the cash flows they generate, the uncertainty associated with these cash flows, and the expected growth in the cash flows. Other things remaining equal, the higher the level and growth in the cash flows, and the lower the risk associated with the cash flows, the greater is the value of the asset.

There are also significant differences between the two classes of assets. There are many who argue that the risk and return models used to evaluate financial assets cannot be used to analyze real estate because of the differences in liquidity across the two markets and in the types of investors in each market. The alternatives to traditional risk and return models will be examined in this chapter. There are also differences in the nature of the cash flows generated by financial and real estate investments. In particular, real estate investments often have finite lives, and have to be valued accordingly. Many financial assets, such as stocks, have infinite lives. These differences in asset lives manifest themselves in the value assigned to these assets at the end of the estimation period. The terminal value of a stock, 5 or 10 years hence, is generally much higher than the current value because of the expected growth in the cash flows, and because these cash flows are expected to continue forever. The terminal value of a building may be lower than the current value because the usage of the building might depreciate its value. However, the land component will have an infinite life and, in some cases, may be the overwhelming component of the terminal value.

THE EFFECT OF INFLATION: REAL VERSUS FINANCIAL ASSETS

For the most part, real and financial assets seem to move together in response to macroeconomic variables. A downturn in the economy seems to affect both adversely, as does a surge in real interest rates. There is one variable, though, that seems to have dramatically different consequences for real and financial assets, and that is inflation. Historically, higher than anticipated inflation has had negative consequences for financial assets, with both bonds and stocks being adversely impacted by unexpected inflation. Fama and Schwert, for instance, in a study on asset returns report that a 1-percent increase in the inflation rate causes bond prices to drop by 1.54 percent and stock prices by 4.23 percent. In contrast, unanticipated inflation seems to have a positive impact on real assets. In fact, the only asset class that Fama and Schwert tracked that was positively affected by unanticipated inflation was residential real estate.

Why is real estate a potential hedge against inflation? There are a variety of reasons, ranging from more favorable tax treatment when it comes to depreciation, to the possibility that investors lose faith in financial assets when inflation runs out of control and prefer to hold real assets. It is also possible that the income from real estate can be adjusted more quickly to changing inflation; property owners can raise rents more in high inflation periods. More importantly, the divergence between real estate and financial assets, in response to inflation, indicates that the risk of real estate will be very different if viewed as part of a portfolio that includes financial assets than if viewed as a standalone investment.

REAL ESTATE: THE UNDERFOLLOWED INVESTMENT CLASS

Most investors own real estate as part of their portfolios, but many of them don't consider it as part of their portfolios for two reasons. The first is that it often takes the form of residential property, which seems to get a carve out, at least psychologically, from investments in other asset classes (like stocks and bonds). The other is that much of real estate remains untraded, and consequently, the owners, at least until recently, did not have observable market prices for their holdings. With the growth of services like Redfin and Zillow, that is starting to change.

Value Relative to Other Asset Classes

How big is real estate as an asset class? If you focus just on traded real estate and look at the market value of market-traded real estate companies and securities, it is a small slice of a very large market pie. In 2023, for instance, the aggregated market value of real estate companies and real estate investment trust comprised 4.15% of U.S. companies and 2.69% of global companies, as can be seen in Table 26.1.

These statistics however miss a key component of real estate, which is that unlike most other asset classes, the bulk of real estate is not traded. If you bring in that untraded portion of real estate into the picture, the global asset pie changes dramatically. In 2023, for instance, it is estimated that the total value of real estate globally is $614 trillion, with $115 trillion in residential and $499 trillion in commercial real estate. In short, the collective value of real estate is far greater than the collective value of financial assets, with stocks in 2023 having a collective value of $109 trillion.

TABLE 26.1   Real Estate Companies and REITs in the Market in 2023

	US	Global
REITs	$ 1,120,897	$ 1,515,764
Real Estate (Development)	$ 6,734	$ 512,953
Real Estate (General/Diversified)	$ 4,950	$ 349,936
Real Estate (Operations & Services)	$ 107,958	$ 605,711
Rest of the market	$28,628,250	$107,882,319
Real estate as % of market	4.15%	2.69%

Given how much of our wealth is tied in real estate and viewing it as an alternative to investing in financial or other assets, it seems critical that we adopt approaches to analyzing real estate investments that are consistent with the way we value stocks or bonds, and that is what we will try to do in this chapter.

Historical Returns

In addition to chronicling how much of our wealth is invested in real estate and determining how much should be invested in the future, it is important that we chronicle real estate's history in delivering returns, especially relative to financial asset classes. To make this judgment, we need indices that capture the performance of real estate as a class, and there have been attempts to estimate market indices and risk parameters for classes of real estate investments.

The obvious and imperfect solution to the nontrading problem in real estate is to construct indices of real estate investment trusts (REITs), which are traded and have market prices. The reason this might not be satisfactory is because the properties owned by real estate investment trusts may not be representative of the real estate property market, and the securitization of real estate may result in differences between real estate and REIT returns. An alternative index more closely tied to real estate property values is the National Council of Real Estate Investment Fiduciaries (NCREIF), which estimates annual returns for commercial property as well as for farmland. Since transactions on individual properties are infrequent, NCREIF uses appraised values for properties to measure returns. Finally, Case and Shiller constructed an index using actual transaction prices, rather than appraised values, to estimate the value of residential real estate. Table 26.2 summarizes the returns on real estate indexes, the S&P 500, and an index of bonds.

There are several interesting results that emerge from this table. First, not all real estate series behave the same way. Returns on REITs seem to have more in common with returns on the stock market than returns on other real estate indexes. Second, there is high-positive serial correlation in many of the real estate return series, especially those based on appraised data. This can be attributed to the smoothing of appraisals that are used in these series. Thirds, the standard deviation in securitized real estate (REITs) is significantly higher than the standard deviation in the non-market-traded real estate series.

Looking at historical returns on real estate, there are two patterns in history that emerge.

TABLE 26.2 Returns by Asset Class

Asset class	Data Source	Time Period	Return Measure	Arithmetic Average	Standard Deviation	Geometric Average
Stocks	S&P 500	1928–2023	Dividend + Price appreciation	11.66%	19.55%	9.80%
Treasury Bonds (10-yr)	FRED	1928–2023	Total return on 10-year	4.86%	7.95%	4.57%
Treasury bills (3-mth)	FRD	1928–2023	3-month T-bill	3.34%	3.01%	3.30%
Corporate bills (3-mth)	FRED	1928–2023	Total return on Baa (Moody's)	6.95%	7.71%	6.68%
Equity REITs	FTSE	1972–2023	Dividend + Price appreciation	12.74%	18.41%	10.89%
Mortgage REITs	FTSE	1972–2023	Dividend + Price appreciation	8.40%	27.64%	4.68%
All REITS	FTSE	1971–2023	Dividend + Price appreciation	11.27%	20.42%	9.00%
Commercial real estate	NCREIF	1978–2023	Total return, appraised values	9.20%	7.40%	NA
Residential real estate	Case & Shiller	1928–2023	Transaction prices	4.42%	6.24%	4.23%

■ The first is that the price appreciation in real estate over time, has been modest, with residential real estate delivering a compounded average return of 4.23% a year from 1928 to 2003, lower than the 4.57% that investors could have earned on a ten-year treasury bond. The returns are better on a total return basis, with income cash flows supplementing the price appreciation, with the NCREIF index of commercial real estate indicating annual returns of 9.20% between 1978 to 2023, with less than half of those returns coming from price appreciation.

■ The standard deviation in the appraised real estate indices (NCREIF and Case-Shiller) is low, but that is because these indices are based on either appraised values or infrequent transactions. Investors who use this as an indication that real estate is less risky than other asset classes will be making a serious mistake.

Co-movement with Other Asset Classes

At the core of the advice given to investors that adding real estate to a portfolio would produce a better risk/return trade-off is the belief that real estate was a unique asset class, that delivered returns that were different from other asset classes. There is evidence that, real estate investments and financial assets have not historically moved together in reaction to larger economic events. In Table 26.3, we reproduce a correlation table that measured the correlation between different asset classes from 1947 to 1982, and found that real estate was lightly or negatively correlated with financial assets.

As noted earlier in this chapter, the differences between real asset and financial asset returns widen when inflation rates change. In fact, three of the five real estate indices are negatively correlated with stocks, and the other two have low correlations. The role of real estate in a portfolio can be seen best if you break down returns by assets classes for U.S. stocks, can be seen in Table 26.4:

TABLE 26.3 Correlations Across Asset Classes: 1947–1982

	I&S	CREF	Home	C&S	Farm	S&P	T-bonds	T-bills	Inflation
I&S	1.00								
CREF	0.79	1.00							
Home	0.52	0.12	1.00						
C&S	0.26	0.16	0.62	1.00					
Farm	0.06	−0.06	0.51	0.49	1.00				
S&P	0.16	0.25	−0.13	−0.20	−0.10	1.00			
T-bonds	−0.04	0.01	−0.22	−0.54	−0.44	0.11	1.00		
T-bills	0.53	0.42	0.13	−0.56	−0.32	−0.07	0.48	1.00	
Inflation	0.70	0.35	0.77	0.56	0.49	−0.02	−0.17	0.25	1.00

I&S: Ibbotson & Siegal; CREF: CREF index; Home: Index of home prices; C&S: Case & Shiller; Farm: Index of farmland prices.
Source: Ibbotson and Brinson (1996).

TABLE 26.4 Returns, by Decade, by Asset Class

			Nominal Return					
Decade	Actual Inflation	Unexpected Inflation	Stocks	T.Bills	T.Bonds	Baa Corporate Bonds	Gold	Real Estate
1930–39	−1.92%	0.07%	4.27%	0.99%	4.01%	7.77%	NA	−1.05%
1940–49	5.51%	3.08%	9.64%	0.48%	2.52%	5.18%	NA	8.56%
1950–59	2.24%	−1.89%	20.93%	2.00%	0.83%	2.32%	NA	3.09%
1960–69	2.53%	0.84%	8.60%	3.98%	2.51%	3.23%	NA	2.18%
1970–79	7.41%	2.80%	7.52%	6.29%	5.58%	7.29%	37.46%	8.80%
1980–89	5.14%	−2.33%	17.95%	8.82%	12.59%	14.46%	−0.96%	5.90%
1990–99	2.94%	−0.90%	18.82%	4.85%	7.83%	9.69%	−2.72%	2.70%
2000–09	2.53%	−0.02%	1.16%	2.69%	6.62%	8.61%	14.95%	4.30%
2010–19	1.76%	−0.38%	14.02%	0.52%	4.35%	7.23%	4.43%	3.86%
2020	1.36%	−0.39%	18.01%	0.09%	11.33%	10.41%	24.17%	10.35%

While real estate returns lag stock returns in most decades, they outperform financial asset classes in the 1970s, a period with unexpectedly high inflation.

The advice to diversify by adding real estate to your portfolio may need to be revised considering the changes to the real estate market in the past three decades. As real estate has been increasingly securitized, there is evidence that real estate as an asset class has started behaving more and more like other financial asset classes (stocks and bonds). Perhaps the best way to bring this home is to use a measure for equities that we presented in Chapter 7—the implied equity risk premium. In Figure 26.1, we bring together the equity risk premium, the default spread on a Baa-rated bond (the risk premium for bonds), and a real estate risk premium, computed by subtracting the risk-free rate from the capitalization rate (a required return measure used by real estate investors). Note that while stock and bond premiums have always moved together for the most part over the entire time period, the behavior of real estate has changed dramatically over the past three decades. In the early 1980s, real estate risk premiums followed a course completely unrelated to the paths followed by stocks and bonds, which is consistent with the low or negative correlations reported in Table 26.3. Starting in the mid-1990s and accelerating through the last decade, real estate risk premiums have converged both in magnitude and direction with equity and bond risk premiums. In practical terms, this suggests that not only is the correlation between real estate and financial assets much higher today, but that the former adage of diversifying your portfolio by adding real estate to it may no longer be good advice.

While few economists would argue with the value of incorporating real estate investments into the market portfolio, most are stymied by the measurement problems. These problems, while insurmountable until recently, are becoming more solvable as real estate investments get securitized and traded. The downside is that as real estate has become more easily tradeable, it is losing some of its uniqueness and behaving more like traded financial assets.

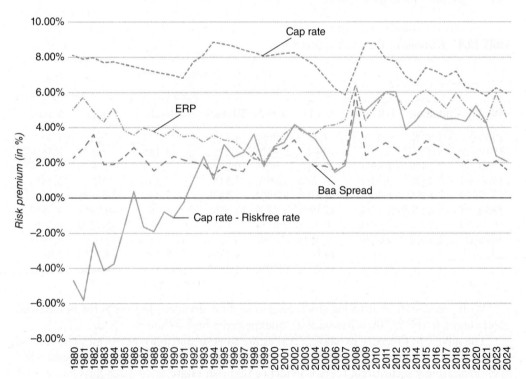

FIGURE 26.1 Equity Risk Premium, Cap Rates, and Bond Spreads

INTRINSIC VALUATION OF REAL ESTATE

The value of any cash-flow-producing asset is the present value of the expected cash flows on it. Just as discounted cash flow valuation models, such as the dividend discount model, can be used to value financial assets, they can also be used to value cash-flow-producing real estate investments.

To use discounted cash flow valuation to value real estate investments it is necessary to first measure the riskiness of real estate investments and estimate a discount rate, based on the riskiness, and then follow up by estimating the expected cash flows on these investments.

The following section examines these issues.

Estimating Discount Rates

Chapters 7 and 8 presented the basic models that are used to estimate the costs of equity, debt, and capital for an investment. Do those models apply to real estate as well? If so, do they need to be modified? If not, what do we use instead?

This section examines the applicability of risk and return models to real estate investments. In the process, we consider whether the assumption that the marginal investor is well diversified is a justifiable one for real estate investments, and if so, how best to measure the parameters of the model—risk-free rate, beta, and risk premium—to estimate the cost of equity. We also consider other sources of risk in real estate investments that are not adequately considered by traditional risk and return models, and how to incorporate these into valuation.

Cost of Equity   In the basic models used to estimate the cost of equity for financial assets, the risk of any asset, real or financial, is defined to be that portion of that asset's variance that cannot be diversified away. This nondiversifiable risk is measured by the market beta in the capital asset pricing model (CAPM), and by multiple factor betas in the arbitrage pricing and multifactor models. The primary assumptions that these models make to arrive at these conclusions are that the marginal investor in the asset is well diversified, and that the risk is measured in terms of the variability of returns. If one assumes that these models apply for real assets as well, the risk of a real asset should be measured by its beta relative to the market portfolio in the CAPM, and by its factor betas in multifactor models. If we do so, however, we are assuming, as we did with publicly traded stocks, that the marginal investor in real assets is well diversified.

A strong argument can be made that many investors in real estate are concentrated in that asset class, and as a consequence, it is inappropriate to use conventional risk models to measure risk. If that is the case, we need alternate models to measure risk in and the cost of equity, and in this section, we will present two choice—a variant on the total beta approach that we used with private businesses, and a survey approach where real estate investors are asked what they would accept as required returns.

ARE THE MARGINAL INVESTORS IN REAL ESTATE DIVERSIFIED?

Many analysts argue that real estate requires investments so large that investors in it may not be able to diversify sufficiently. In addition, they note that real estate investments require localized knowledge, and that those who develop this knowledge choose to invest primarily or only in real estate. Consequently, they note that the use of the capital asset pricing model or multifactor models, which assume that only nondiversifiable risk is rewarded, is inappropriate as a way of estimating cost of equity.

There is a kernel of truth to this argument, but it can be countered easily by noting that:

- Many investors who concentrate their holdings in real estate do so by choice. They see it as a way of leveraging their specialized knowledge of real estate. Thus, we would view them the same way we view investors who choose to hold only technology stocks in their portfolios.
- Even large real estate investments can be broken up into smaller pieces, allowing investors the option of holding real estate investments in conjunction with financial assets. This is especially true now with the securitization of real estate.
- Just as the marginal investor in stocks is often an institutional investor with the resources to diversify and keep transactions costs low, the marginal investor in many real estate markets today has sufficient resources to diversify.

If real estate developers and private investors insist on higher expected returns because they are not diversified, real estate investments will increasingly be held by real estate investment trusts, private equity investors, and corporations, which attract more diversified investors with lower required returns. This trend is well in place in the United States and may spread over time to other countries as well.

Conventional Asset Pricing Models   Even if it is accepted that the risk of real estate is its market beta in the CAPM and its factor betas in multifactor models, there are several issues related to the measurement and use of these risk parameters that need to be examined. To provide some insight into the measurement problems associated with real assets, consider the standard approach to estimating betas in the capital asset pricing model for a publicly traded stock. First, the prices of the stock are collected from historical data, and returns are computed on a periodic basis (daily, weekly, or monthly). Second, these stock returns are regressed against returns on a stock index over the same period to obtain the beta. For real estate, these steps are not as straightforward.

Individual Assets: Prices and Risk Parameters   The betas of individual stocks can be estimated simply because stock prices are available for extended time periods. The same cannot be said for individual real estate investments. A piece of property does not get bought and sold very frequently, though similar properties might. Consequently, price indexes are available for classes of assets (e.g., downtown Manhattan office buildings), and risk parameters can be estimated for these classes.

Even when price indices are available for classes of real estate investments, questions remain about the comparability of assets within a class (e.g., Is one downtown building the same as any other? How does one control for differences in age and quality of construction? What about location?), and about the categorization itself (office buildings versus residential buildings; single-family versus multifamily residences).

The Market Portfolio   In estimating the betas of stocks, we generally use a stock index as a proxy for the market portfolio. In theory, however, the market portfolio should include all assets in the economy in proportion to their market values. This is of particular significance when the market portfolio is used to estimate the risk parameters of real estate investments. The use of a stock index as the market portfolio will result in the marginalization[1] of real estate investments and the underestimation of risk for these assets. The differences between a stock and an all-asset portfolio can be large, because the market value of real estate and other nonstock investments not included in the stock index is significant.

A Pragmatic Solution   If one accepts the proposition that the risk of a real estate investment should be measured using traditional risk and return models, there are some practical approaches that can be used to estimate risk parameters:

- The risk of a class of real estate investments can be obtained by regressing returns on the class (using the NCREIF series, for instance, on commercial and residential property) against returns on a consolidated market portfolio. The primary problems with this approach are (1) these returns series are based on smoothed appraisals and may understate the true volatility in the market, and (2) the returns are available only for longer return intervals (annual or quarterly).
- The risk parameters of traded real estate securities (REITs and master limited partnerships [MLPs]) can be used as a proxy for the risk in real estate investment. The limitations of this approach are that securitized real estate investments may behave differently from direct investments in real estate, and that it is much more difficult to estimate risk parameters for different classes of real estate investment (unless one can find REITs that restrict themselves to one class of investments such as commercial property).
- The demand for real estate is in some cases a derived demand. For instance, the value of a shopping mall is derived from the value of retail space, which should be a function of how well retailing is doing as a business. It can be argued, in such a case, that the risk parameters of a mall should be related to the risk parameters of publicly traded retail stores. Corrections should obviously be made for differences in operating and financial leverage.

Augmented Risk Models   In this approach, you start with the conventional risk and return models such as the CAPM, and then adjust your required return for the additional risks that you believe are unique to real estate investments. In particular, you can incorporate the additional risk that real estate investors may face in their investments,

---

[1] When the beta of an asset is estimated relative to a stock index, the underlying assumption is that the marginal investor has the bulk of his or her portfolio in stocks and measures risk relative to this portfolio.

because they are not fully diversified, the liquidity risk associated with the fact that real estate holdings are not as easily bought and sold as publicly traded stock, the increased exposure to legal and regulatory risk that is part of some real estate investments, and the need for localized information to value individual real estate investments.

Limited Diversification   Using risk and return models that assume that the marginal investor is well diversified may be reasonable, even though many investors in real estate choose not to be diversified. Part of the justification for this statement is the presence of firms with diversified investors, such as real estate investment trusts and master limited partnerships, in the real estate market. But what if no such investors exist and the marginal investor in real estate is not well diversified? How would we modify our estimates of cost of equity?

Chapter 24 examined how to adjust the cost of equity for a private business for the fact that its owner was not diversified. In particular, we recommended the use of a total beta that reflected not just the market risk but also the extent of nondiversification on the part of the potential investor:

$$\text{Total beta} = \frac{\text{Market beta}}{\text{Correlation between investor's portfolio and the market}}$$

This measure could be adapted to estimate a total beta for real estate. For instance, assume that the marginal investor in commercial real estate has a portfolio that has a correlation of 0.50 with the market, and that commercial real estate as a property class has a market beta of 0.40. The beta you would use to estimate the cost of equity for an investment would be 0.80:

$$\text{Total beta} = \frac{0.40}{0.50} = 0.80$$

Using this higher beta would result in a higher cost of equity and a lower value for the real estate investment. Using this approach to estimating cost of equity will also create differential costs of equity across investors in real estate, with investors with more diversified portfolios accepting lower costs of equity and being willing to pay higher prices for the same properties. This may explain why broadly diversified investors like Blackrock are acquiring larger stakes in real estate, outbidding local real estate developers and purely real estate investors for properties.

Lack of Liquidity   Another critique of traditional risk measures is that they assume that all assets are liquid (or, at least that there are no differences in liquidity across assets). Real estate investments are often less liquid than financial assets; transactions occur less frequently, transactions costs are higher, and there are fewer buyers and sellers. The less liquid an asset, it is argued, the riskier it is.

Again, as we noted in Chapter 24, the link between illiquidity and risk is difficult to quantify for several reasons. One is that it depends on the time horizon of the investor. An investor who intends to hold an investment long term will care less about liquidity than one who is uncertain about his or her time horizon or wants to trade short term. Another is that it is affected by the external economic conditions. For instance, real estate is much more liquid during economic booms when prices are rising, than during recessions when prices are depressed.

The alternative to trying to view the absence of liquidity as an additional risk factor and building into discount rates is to value the illiquid asset as if it were liquid, and then applying a illiquidity discount to it. This is often the practice in valuing closely held and illiquid businesses and enables the illiquidity discount to be a function of the investor and external economic conditions at the time of the valuation. The process of estimating the discount was examined in more detail in Chapter 24.

Exposure to Legal Changes   The values of all investments are affected by changes in the tax law—changes in depreciation methods and changes in tax rates on ordinary income and capital gains. Real estate investments are particularly exposed to changes in the tax law, because they derive a significant portion of their value from tax treatment and tend to be highly levered.

Unlike manufacturing or service businesses, which can move operations from one locale to another to take advantage of locational differences in tax rates and other legal restrictions, real estate is not mobile and is, therefore, much more exposed to changes in local laws (such as zoning requirements, property taxes, and rent control).

The question becomes whether this additional sensitivity to changes in tax and local laws is an additional source of risk, and, if so, how this risk should be priced. Again, the answer will depend on whether the marginal investor is diversified, not only across asset classes, but also across real estate investments in different locations. For instance, a real estate investor who holds real estate in New York, Miami, Los Angeles, and Houston is less exposed to legal risk than one who holds real estate in only one of those locales. The trade-off, however, is that the localized knowledge that allows a real estate investor to do well in one market may not carry well into other markets.

Information Costs and Risk   Real estate investments often require specific information about local conditions that is difficult (and costly) to obtain. That information is also likely to contain more error. There are some who argue that this higher cost of acquiring information, and the greater error in this information, should be built into the risk and discount rates used to value real estate. This argument is not restricted to real estate. It has been used as an explanation for the small stock premium—that is small stocks make higher returns than larger stocks, after adjusting for risk (using the CAPM). Small stocks, it is argued, generally have less information available on them than larger stocks, and the information tends to be noisier.

An Alternative Approach to Estimating Discount Rates: The Survey Approach   The problems with the assumptions of traditional risk and return models, and the difficulties associated with the measurement of risk for nontraded real assets in those models, have led to alternative approaches to estimating discount rates for those real estate investments. In the context of real estate, for instance, discount rates are often obtained by surveying potential investors in real estate on what rates of return they would demand for investing in different types of property investments. In many cases, those surveys are done in terms of capitalization rates, which—as we noted earlier—are just required rates of return in another guise. Figure 26.2 summarizes the cap rates for different classes of real estate investments in 2019 and 2024.[2]

---

[2]CBRE is a service that estimates real-estate transaction related data, including cap rates for U.S. real estate investments.

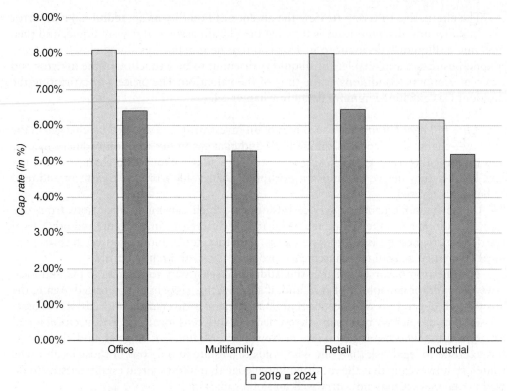

FIGURE 26.2   Cap Rates by Real Estate Investment Grouping
Source: *CBRE*.

This approach is justified on the following grounds:

▨ These surveys are not based on some abstract models of risk and return (which may ignore risk characteristics unique to the real estate market), but on what actual investors in real estate want to make as a return.
▨ These surveys enable the estimation of discount rates for specific categories of properties (e.g., hotels, apartments, etc.) by region, without requiring a dependence on past prices like risk and return models.
▨ There are relatively few large investors who invest directly in real estate (rather than in securitized real estate). It is, therefore, feasible to do such a survey.

There are, however, grounds for contesting this approach as well:

▨ Surveys, by their very nature, yield different "desired rates of return" for different investors for the same property class. Assuming that a range of desired returns can be obtained for a class of investments, it is not clear where one goes next. Presumably, those investors who demand returns at the high end of the scale will find themselves priced out of the market, and those whose desired returns are at the low end of the scale will find plenty of undervalued properties. The question of who the marginal investor in an investment should be is not answered in these surveys.

- The survey approach bypasses the issue of risk, but it does not really eliminate it. Clearly, investors demand the returns that they do on different property classes, because they perceive them to have different levels of risk.
- The survey approach works reasonably well when there are relatively few and fairly homogeneous investors in the market. While this might have been true a decade ago in the real estate business, it is becoming less so as new institutional investors enter the market, and the number of investors increases and becomes more heterogeneous.
- The survey approach also becomes suspect when the investors who are surveyed act as pass-throughs—they invest in real estate, securitize their investments, and sell them to others and then move on. If they do so, it is the desired returns of the ultimate investor (the buyer of the securitized real estate) that should determine value, not the desired return of the intermediate investor.

There are several advantages to using a model that measures risk and estimates a discount rate based on the risk measure, rather than using a survey:

- A risk and return model, properly constructed, sets reasonable bounds for the expected returns. For instance, the expected return on a risky asset in both the CAPM and the APM will exceed the expected return on a riskless asset. There is no such constraint on survey responses.
- A risk and return model, by relating expected return to risk and risk to prespecified factors, allows an analyst to be proactive in estimating discount rates rather than reactive. For instance, in the context of the CAPM, the expected return on an investment is determined by its beta, which in turn is determined by the cyclicality of the business (in which the investment is made) and the financial leverage taken on. Thus, an analyst who knows how the financial leverage in an investment is expected to change over time can adjust the beta of that investment accordingly and use it in valuation. There is no such mechanism available when the survey approach is used.
- When the ultimate investor is not known at the time of the analysis, as is the case in real estate investments that are securitized, a risk and return model provides the framework for estimating the discount rate for a hypothetical marginal investor.

As real estate markets become more accessible to institutional investors and more investments are made with the objective of eventual securitization, the need for a good risk and return model becomes more acute. These same trends will also make real estate investments more like financial investments (by making them more liquid). Sooner rather than later, the same models used to estimate risk and discount rates for financial assets will also be used to estimate risk and discount rates for real estate investments.

DIVERSIFICATION IN REAL ESTATE: TRENDS AND IMPLICATIONS

As we look at the additional risk factors—estimation errors, legal and tax changes, volatility in specific real estate markets—that are often built into discount rates and valuations, the rationale for diversification becomes stronger. A real estate firm that is diversified across holdings in multiple locations will be able to diversify away some

(continued)

(*continued*)

of this risk. If the firm attracts investors who are diversified into other asset classes, you diversify away even more risk, thus reducing its exposure to risk and its cost of equity.

Inexorably then, you would expect to see diversified real estate investors—real estate corporations, REITs, and MLPs—drive local real estate investors who are not diversified (across either locations or asset classes) out of the market by bidding higher prices for the same properties. If this is true, you might ask, why has it not happened already? There are two reasons. The first is that knowledge of local real estate market conditions is still a critical component driving real estate values, and real estate investors with this knowledge may be able to compensate for their failure to diversify. The second is that a significant component of real estate success still comes from personal connections—to other developers, to zoning boards, and to politicians. Real estate investors with the right connections may be able to get much better deals on their investments than corporations bidding for the same business.

As real estate corporations and REITs multiply, you should expect to see much higher correlation in real estate prices across different regions and a drop-off in the importance of local conditions. Furthermore, you should also expect to see these firms become much savvier at dealing with the regulatory authorities in different regions.

From Cost of Equity to Cost of Capital

Once you have estimated a cost of equity, there are two other inputs needed to estimate the cost of capital. The first is the cost of debt, and estimating it is much more straightforward than estimating the cost of equity. You have two choices:

1. If you are raising capital for a new real estate investment, you could use the stated interest rate on bank loans used to fund the investment. In making this estimate, though, you have to be aware of the terms of the bank loan and whether there will be other costs not captured in the interest rate. For instance, a requirement that a compensating balance be maintained over the life of the loan will increase the effective cost of debt.
2. You could look at the capacity that the real estate investment has to cover bank payments (this is the equivalent of an interest coverage ratio), estimate a synthetic rating, and use this rating to estimate a pretax cost of debt. In fact, you could modify the numerator to include depreciation, since the investment is a finite life investment and should not require significant reinvestment.

To estimate an after-tax cost of debt, you would use the marginal tax rate of the individual or entity investing in the property. The debt ratio in most real estate investments is usually estimated by looking at the proportion of the funds raised from debt and equity. Thus, if a property costs $4 million to build and the investor borrows $3 million to fund it, the debt ratio used is 75 percent. While we will stick with this convention, it is worth bearing in mind that the ratios should be based on the value of the property rather than the funding needs. Thus, if the value of the property is expected to be $5 million after it is built, the debt ratio used should be 60 percent ($3 million/$5 million). This, of course, creates circular reasoning since the cost of capital is necessary to estimate the value of the property in the first place.

The distinction between cost of equity and the cost of capital, drawn in Chapter 7, is significant. If the cash flows being discounted are predebt cash flows (i.e., cash flows to the firm), the appropriate discount rate is the cost of capital. If you use this approach, you will value the property, and if you are the equity investor, you would then subtract out the value of the outstanding debt to arrive at the value of the equity in the real estate investment. If the cash flows being discounted on a real estate deal are cash flows after interest and principal payments or cash flows to equity, the appropriate discount rate is the cost of equity. You would then value the equity in the real estate investment directly.

Estimating Cash Flows

Not all real estate investments generate cash flows but for those that do, cash flows can be estimated in much the same way that they can be estimated for financial investments. The ultimate objective is to estimate cash flows after taxes. Just as with financial assets, these cash flows can be estimated to equity investors. This is the cash flow left over after meeting all operating expenses, debt obligations (interest expenses and principal payments), and capital expenditures. The cash flows can also be estimated for all investors (debt as well as equity) in the real estate investment. This is the equivalent of cash flows to the firm, which is the cash flow prior to meeting debt obligations.

Cash Inflows   The cash flows from a commercial real estate investment to the owner generally take the form of rents and lease income. In estimating rents for future years, you must consider past trends in rents, demand and supply conditions for space provided by the property, and general economic conditions.

In office/multiple residential buildings all space may not be rented at a particular time. Thus, the vacancy rate (i.e., the percentage of the space that will not be rented out at any point in time) has to be projected in conjunction with market rents. Even in tight markets, there will be periods of time where space cannot be rented out, leading to a vacancy rate. Thus, no building, no matter how sought after, can be expected to have a 100-percent occupancy rate in perpetuity. With new buildings, the projections also have to factor in how long it will take initially to get occupants to rent/lease space. Clearly, the longer it takes, the smaller is the discounted cash flow value of the building.

In the case of leased property, the terms of the lease can affect the projected lease revenues. If income properties are subject to existing leases, the terms of the lease such as the length of the lease, the contracted lease income future increases, additional reimbursable expenses, and provisions on lease renewal will determine cash flow estimates. The leases may also be net leases, where the tenant is responsible for paying taxes, insurance, and maintenance.

Cash Outflows   Expenses on real estate investments include property taxes, insurance, repairs and maintenance, and advertising—which are unrelated to occupancy and are fixed—as well as items such as utility expenses, which are a function of occupancy and are variable. In addition, the following factors will affect projected expenses:

- *Reimbursability.* Some expenses incurred by the owner in connection with a property may be reimbursed by the tenant as part of a contractual agreement.
- *Expense stops.* Many office leases include provisions to protect the owner from increases in operating expenses beyond an agreed-on level. Any increases beyond that level have to be paid by the tenant.

Finally real estate taxes represent a large item of expenditures, and they can be volatile, not only because the tax laws change, but because they are based often on assessed values.

Expected Growth

To estimate future cash flows, we need estimates of the expected growth rate in both rents/leases and expenses. A key factor in estimating the growth rate is the expected inflation rate. In a stable real estate market, the expected growth in cash flows should be close to the expected inflation rate. In tight markets with low vacancy rates, the expected growth rate in rents may be higher than the expected inflation rate at least until the market shortages disappear. The reverse is likely to be true in markets with high vacancy rates.

The surveys used to estimate discount rates mentioned earlier in the chapter, also collect information on investors' expectations of expected growth. It is interesting that while there are significant differences between investors on discount rates, the expected growth rates in cash inflows and outflows fall within a tight band. In 2000, for instance, the Cushman and Wakefield survey of investors in a wide range of markets found that they all estimated expected growth in cash flows to be between 4 and 6 percent.

How will rent control affect these estimates? By putting a cap on how high the increases can be without limiting the downside, it will generally lower both the expected cash flows and the expected growth rate in cash flows over time and lower value. Uncertainty about rent control laws, in terms of both how much the cap will be and whether the laws will be revised, will add to the estimation error in the valuation.

Terminal Value

In all discounted cash flow valuation models, a key input is the estimate of terminal value, that is, the value of the asset being valued at the end of the investment time horizon. There are two basic approaches that can be used to estimate the terminal value:

1. One approach is to assume that the cash flows in the terminal year (the last year of the investment horizon) will continue to grow at a constant rate forever. If this assumption is made, the terminal value of the asset is:

$$\text{Terminal value of equity or asset}_n = \frac{\text{Expected CF}_{n+1}}{(r - g)}$$

where r is the discount rate (cost of equity if it is the terminal value of equity, and cost of capital if it is the terminal value of the asset) and CF_t is the cash flow (cash flow to equity if terminal value is for equity, and to firm if terminal value is total terminal value).

Thus, if a property is expected to produce a net cash flow, prior to debt payments, of $1.2 million in year 10, this cash flow is expected to grow 3 percent a year forever and the cost of capital was 13 percent, the terminal value of the property can be written as:

$$\text{Terminal value of asset}_{10} = \frac{\text{Expected CF}_{11}}{(\text{Cost of capital} - g)}$$

$$= \frac{1.20\,(1.03)}{(.13 - .03)} = \$12.36 \text{ million}$$

The assumption of perpetual cash flows may make some analysts uncomfortable, but one way to compensate is to require that more cash be set aside each year to ensure that the property life can be extended. If you use this approach, for instance, you could assume that the cash flow from depreciation be reinvested back into the building in the form of maintenance capital expenditures.

2. A close variation on the infinite growth model is the capitalization rate (cap rate) used by many real estate appraisers to value properties. In its most general form, the cap rate is the rate by which operating income is divided to get the value of the property.

$$\text{Property value} = \frac{\text{Operating income after taxes}}{\text{Capitalization rate}}$$

The capitalization rate is, in fact, the inverse of the value-to-EBIT multiple used to value publicly traded companies in Chapter 18.

There are three ways in which capitalization rates are estimated. One is to use the average capitalization rate of similar properties that have sold recently. This is the equivalent of using the industry-average earnings multiple to estimate terminal value in a publicly traded company, and thus converts your intrinsic value into a forward pricing. The second is to use the surveys mentioned earlier to obtain an average cap rate used by other real estate investors. The third is to estimate the cap rate from a discounted cash flow model. To see the linkage with the infinite growth model, assume that the net operating income (prior to debt payments) is also the free cash flow to the firm (note that this essentially is the equivalent of assuming that capital maintenance expenditures equal depreciation). Then the capitalization rate can be written as a function of the discount rate and the expected growth rate:

$$\text{Capitalization rate} = \frac{r - g}{(1 + g)}$$

where r is the discount rate (the cost of equity if net income is being capitalized and the cost of capital if operating income is being capitalized) and g is the expected growth rate forever. In this example, the capitalization rate would have been:

$$\text{Capitalization rate} = \frac{.13 - .03}{(1.03)} = 9.70\%$$

If the capitalization rate is being applied to next year's operating income rather than this year's value, you can ignore the denominator and use a cap rate of 10 percent.

A SPECULATIVE INVESTMENT IN UNDEVELOPED LAND

Developers sometimes buy undeveloped land not with the intention of developing it, but to hold onto in the hope that the value of the land will appreciate significantly over the holding period. An investment in undeveloped land does not generate positive cash flows during the holding period. The only positive cash flow, in fact, is the estimated value of the land at the end of the holding period. If you have to pay

(continued)

(*continued*)

property taxes and other expenses during the holding period, you will have negative cash flows during the holding period.

There are two ways you can approach the analysis of this investment. The first with the traditional discounted cash flow approach. You could discount the expected property taxes and other expenses during the holding period, and the estimated value of the land at the end of the period back to the present at the cost of capital, and see if it exceeds the cost of the land today. In fact, the expected appreciation in the price of the land will have to be greater than the cost of capital and the expected annual property tax rate for this investment to have a positive net present value. To illustrate, if your cost of capital is 10 percent and the annual property tax rate is 2 percent of land value, you would need a price appreciation rate of 12 percent a year for the present value of the inflow to exceed the present value of the outflows.[3]

The other is to view the land as an option and developing the property as exercising the option. You would then consider the cost of the land as the price of the option. The interesting implication is that you might choose to buy the land even if the expected price appreciation rate is lower than your cost of capital, if there is substantial volatility in land prices. This application is considered in more detail in Chapter 28.

DCF Valuation Models

Once a discount rate has been chosen and cash flows estimated, the value of an income-producing real asset can be estimated either in whole (by discounting cash flows to the firm at the weighted average cost of capital) or to its equity investors (by discounting cash flows to equity at the cost of equity). The following illustrations provide examples of DCF valuation in real estate.

ILLUSTRATION 26.1: Valuing an Office Building in 2000

In this illustration, we will be valuing an office building located at 711 Third Avenue in New York City. The operating details of the building are as follows:

- The building has a capacity of 528,357 square feet of rentable space. While 95% of this space is rented out for the next year, the occupancy rate is expected to climb 0.5% a year for the following four years to reach 97% of capacity in year 5. This is expected to be the occupancy rate in steady state.

- The average rent per square foot[4] was $28.07 in the most recent year, and is expected to grow 3% a year in perpetuity. Historically, there has been a credit loss, associated with tenants failing to make payments, of 2.5% of rental revenues.

- The building has a garage that generated $800,000 in income for the most recent year. This income is also expected to grow 3% a year in perpetuity.

---

[3]We are assuming that the property taxes are based on the estimated value of the land each year and not the original cost. If it is the latter, the price appreciation rate can be lower.
[4]The rents vary depending on location in the building, with lower rents in the basement and lower floors and higher rents on the top floors.

▨ Real estate taxes were $5.24 a square foot in the most recent year, and are expected to grow 4% a year for the next five years and 3% a year thereafter.

▨ The land under the building is rented under a long-term lease, and the ground rent in the most recent year was $1.5 million. This rent is expected to remain unchanged for the next five years and grow 3% a year thereafter.

▨ Other expenses, including insurance, maintenance, and utilities, amounted to $6.50 a square foot in the most recent year, and are expected grow 3% a year in perpetuity. Approximately 10% of these expenses will be reimbursed by tenants each year (and thus will become a part of the revenues).

▨ The management fee for the most recent year was $300,000, and is expected to grow 3% a year in perpetuity.

▨ The depreciation in the building is expected to be $2 million a year for the next five years. The capital maintenance and upgrade expenditures (including leasehold improvements for new tenants) last year amounted to $1.5 million, and are expected to grow 3% a year for the next five years. Beyond year 5, depreciation is expected to increase 3% a year in perpetuity, and capital maintenance expenditures will offset depreciation.

The potential buyer of the building is a corporation that faces a marginal tax rate of 38% and expects to finance the building with a mix of 60% debt and 40% equity. Then debt will take the form of a long-term balloon payment loan with an interest rate of 6.5%

STEP 1: ESTIMATING A COST OF CAPITAL

We begin by trying to estimate a cost of equity. While we had access to a survey that provided typical hurdle rates used by real estate investors for office buildings in New York, we chose to estimate the cost of equity from the capital asset pricing model because the potential buyer is a corporation (whose investors are diversified).[5] To make this estimate, we began with the unlevered beta of 0.62 of equity REITs with office properties. We estimated a levered beta using the debt-equity mix proposed for the building:

$$\text{Levered beta} = \text{Unlevered beta} \left[1 + (1 - \text{Tax rate}) \left(\frac{\text{Debt}}{\text{Equity}} \right) \right]$$
$$= 0.62[1 + (1 - .38) (.6/.4)] = 1.20$$

To estimate the cost of equity, we used a risk-free rate of 5.4% and a risk premium of 4%:

$$\text{Cost of equity} = \text{Risk-free rate} + \text{Beta} \times \text{Equity Risk premium}$$
$$= 5.4\% + 1.20 \times (4\%) = 10.20\%$$

Using the interest rate of 6.5% on the bank borrowing as the pretax cost of debt, we estimated a cost of capital:

$$\text{Cost of capital} = 10.20\% \times (.40) + 6.5\% \times (1 - .38) \times (.60) = 6.49\%$$

We assumed that this would be the cost of capital in perpetuity.[6]

STEP 2: ESTIMATING CASH FLOWS ON THE BUILDING

We used the operating information specified earlier to estimate the cash flows prior to debt payments on the building for the next five years in the Table 26.5.

---

[5]Note that it is the investors in the corporation who need to be diversified and not the corporation itself.
[6]This implies that the existing loan will be refinanced with a new loan set at 60% of the value of the property when it comes due.

TABLE 26.5 Cash Flows to the Firm (Predebt) on Building

	Base year	1	2	3	4	5	Terminal year
Building space(sq ft)		528357	528357	528357	528357	528357	528357
Occupancy		95%	95.50%	96.00%	96.50%	97%	97%
Rent/square foot	$28.07	$28.91	$29.78	$30.67	$31.59	$32.54	
Rental income		$14,512,115	$15,026,149	$15,557,965	$16,108,166	$16,677,377	$17,177,698
Garage income	$800,000	$ 824,000	$ 848,720	$ 874,182	$ 900,407	$ 927,419	$ 955,242
Reimbursement revenue	10.00%	$ 353,735	$ 364,347	$ 375,277	$ 386,536	$ 398,132	$ 410,076
Credit loss	2.50%	$ 362,803	$ 375,654	$ 388,949	$ 402,704	$ 416,934	$ 429,442
Total revenues		$15,327,047	$15,863,563	$16,418,475	$16,992,404	$17,585,993	$18,113,573
Expenses							
Real estate taxes	$5.24	$ 2,879,334	$ 2,994,508	$ 3,114,288	$ 3,238,860	$ 3,368,414	$ 3,469,466
Ground rent	$1,500,000	$ 1,500,000	$ 1,500,000	$ 1,500,000	$ 1,500,000	$ 1,500,000	$ 1,545,000
Other expenses	$6.50	$ 3,537,350	$ 3,643,471	$ 3,752,775	$ 3,865,358	$ 3,981,319	$ 4,100,758
Management fee	$300,000	$ 309,000	$ 318,270	$ 327,818	$ 337,653	$ 347,782	$ 358,216
Total expenses		$ 8,225,684	$ 8,456,248	$ 8,694,881	$ 8,941,870	$ 9,197,515	$ 9,473,440
EBITDA		$ 7,101,363	$ 7,407,314	$ 7,723,594	$ 8,050,534	$ 8,388,478	$ 8,640,133
Depreciation	$2,000,000	$ 2,000,000	$ 2,000,000	$ 2,000,000	$ 2,000,000	$ 2,000,000	$ 2,060,000
Operating income		$ 5,101,363	$ 5,407,314	$ 5,723,594	$ 6,050,534	$ 6,388,478	$ 6,580,133
Taxes	38%	$ 1,938,518	$ 2,054,779	$ 2,174,966	$ 2,299,203	$ 2,427,622	$ 2,500,450
EBIT (1−t)		$ 3,162,845	$ 3,352,535	$ 3,548,628	$ 3,751,331	$ 3,960,857	$ 4,079,682
+ Depreciation		$ 2,000,000	$ 2,000,000	$ 2,000,000	$ 2,000,000	$ 2,000,000	$ 2,060,000
− Capital maintenance	$1,500,000	$ 1,545,000	$ 1,591,350	$ 1,639,091	$ 1,688,263	$ 1,738,911	$ 2,060,000
Cash flow to firm		$ 3,617,845	$ 3,761,185	$ 3,909,538	$ 4,063,068	$ 4,221,946	$ 4,079,682

Since all the items grow at 3% beyond year 5, we estimated a cash flow for year 6 as the terminal year. The terminal value of the building was calculated based on this cash flow, a perpetual growth rate of 3%, and a cost of capital of 6.49%:

$$\text{Terminal value} = \frac{\text{FCFF}_6}{(\text{Cost of capital} - \text{Stable growth rate})}$$

$$= \frac{\$4,079,682}{(0.0649 - 0.03)} = \$116,810,659$$

The present value of the expected cash flows for the next five years and the terminal value, summarized in the following table, yields the value of the building:

	1	2	3	4	5
Cash flow to firm	$3,617,845	$3,761,185	$3,909,538	$4,063,068	$ 4,221,946
Terminal value					$116,810,659
Present value @ 6.49%	$3,397,275	$3,316,547	$3,237,186	$3,159,199	$ 90,928,871

The sum of the present value of the cash flows is $101.48 million. This is the estimated value of the building.

ILLUSTRATION 26.2: Valuing the Equity Stake in a Building

The preceding analysis can be done for just the equity stake in 711 Third Avenue. To do so, we will first estimate the dollar debt that will be borrowed to buy this building. Assuming that the building has a value of $101.48 million (from the previous illustration) and using a debt ratio of 60%, we estimate debt to be $60.89 million.

$$\text{Debt} = \text{Value of building} \times \text{Debt ratio} = 101.48 \times .6 = \$60.89 \text{ million}$$

Since this is a balloon payment loan, the interest payments on the debt will remain the same each year, based on the 6.5% interest rate:

$$\text{Annual interest expenses} = \text{Dollar debt} \times \text{Interest rate}$$

$$= \$60.89 \times .065 = \$3.96 \text{ million}$$

The appropriate discount rate to use while valuing the equity stake in the building is the cost of equity, estimated to be 10.20% in this analysis.

ESTIMATING CASH FLOWS TO EQUITY

The estimated cash flows to equity are estimated each year by netting out interest expenses from income and adjusting the taxes accordingly. Table 26.6 summarizes cash flows to equity each year for the next five years.

In year 5, we also estimate the terminal value of equity by subtracting the debt due from the terminal value of the building estimated in the previous illustration:

$$\text{Terminal value of equity} = \text{Terminal value of building} - \text{Debt}$$

$$= \$116.81 \text{ million} - \$60.89 \text{ million} = \$55.92 \text{ million}$$

TABLE 26.6   Cash Flows to the Equity (Post-debt) on Building

	1	2	3	4	5
Building space (square feet)	5,28,357	5,28,357	5,28,357	5,28,357	5,28,357
Occupancy	95.00%	95.50%	96.00%	96.50%	97.00%
Rent/square foot	$28.91	$29.78	$30.67	$31.59	$32.54
Rental income	$14,512,115	$15,026,149	$15,557,965	$16,108,166	$16,677,377
Garage income	$ 824,000	$ 848,720	$ 874,182	$ 900,407	$ 927,419
Reimbursement revenue	$ 353,735	$ 364,347	$ 375,277	$ 386,536	$ 398,132
Credit loss	$ 362,803	$ 375,654	$ 388,949	$ 402,704	$ 416,934
Total revenues	$15,327,047	$15,863,563	$16,418,475	$16,992,404	$17,585,993
Expenses					
Real estate taxes	$ 2,879,334	$ 2,994,508	$ 3,114,288	$ 3,238,860	$ 3,368,414
Ground rent	$ 1,500,000	$ 1,500,000	$ 1,500,000	$ 1,500,000	$ 1,500,000
Other expenses	$ 3,537,350	$ 3,643,471	$ 3,752,775	$ 3,865,358	$ 3,981,319
Management fee	$ 309,000	$ 318,270	$ 327,818	$ 337,653	$ 347,782
Interest expenses	$ 3,957,737	$ 3,957,737	$ 3,957,737	$ 3,957,737	$ 3,957,737
Total expenses	$12,183,422	$12,413,986	$12,652,618	$12,899,608	$13,155,252
Net income before depreciation and taxes	$ 3,143,625	$ 3,449,577	$ 3,765,856	$ 4,092,797	$ 4,430,741
Depreciation	$ 2,000,000	$ 2,000,000	$ 2,000,000	$ 2,000,000	$ 2,000,000
Operating income	$ 1,143,625	$ 1,449,577	$ 1,765,856	$ 2,092,797	$ 2,430,741
Taxes	$ 434,578	$ 550,839	$ 671,025	$ 795,263	$ 923,682
Net income	$ 709,048	$ 898,738	$ 1,094,831	$ 1,297,534	$ 1,507,059
+ Depreciation −	$ 2,000,000	$ 2,000,000	$ 2,000,000	$ 2,000,000	$ 2,000,000
Capital maintenance	$ 1,545,000	$ 1,591,350	$ 1,639,091	$ 1,688,263	$ 1,738,911
Cash flow to equity	$ 1,164,048	$ 1,307,388	$ 1,455,741	$ 1,609,271	$ 1,768,148

ESTIMATING THE VALUE OF EQUITY

The present value of the cash flows to equity for the next five years and the terminal value are computed in the following table:

	1	2	3	4	5
Cash flow to equity	$1,164,048	$1,307,388	$1,455,741	$1,609,271	$ 1,768,148
Terminal value					$55,922,390
Present value @ 10.20%	$1,056,435	$1,076,833	$1,088,178	$1,091,735	$35,519,318

The value of the equity stake in the building is $39.83 million. Adding this value to the value of the debt raised of $60.89 million gives us an estimate for the value of the building:

Estimated value of building = $60.89 million + $39.83 million = $100.72 million

Why is there a difference between this estimate of the property value and the one we arrived at in the previous illustration? The reason is simple. The debt ratio of 60% that we assumed and kept constant when estimating cost of capital will require us to borrow an additional amount each year for the next five years, since the building's value will appreciate by about 3% a year. The tax benefits from this additional debt were implicitly built into the valuation of the building in the previous illustration but were ignored while valuing equity in this one. If we consider those tax benefits, we will arrive at the same value.

REAL ESTATE VALUATION IN PRACTICE: A COMPARISON

The building at 711 Third Avenue was valued for sale by an appraiser using discounted cash flow valuation. While many of the base assumptions in our valuation were borrowed from that appraisal, the estimate of value in the appraisal was $70 million, about a third below our estimate. The main differences between our valuation and the appraiser's valuation are as follows:

- The appraisal was done entirely in terms of pretax cash flows. Depreciation was therefore, not considered, and the tax benefits from it were ignored.
- The discount rate used was 11.5 percent, based on a proprietary survey of real estate investors done by the appraiser. While nothing was mentioned in the appraisal, this discount rate presumably was in pretax terms (to ensure consistency with how the cash flows were estimated) and stated as a return on the overall investment (and not just the equity investment). This is higher than the cost of capital we used.
- The terminal value was estimated based on a capitalization rate of 9.0 percent, which was also based on the survey. (The operating income in year 5 was divided by 9.0 percent to arrive at terminal value.)

We believe that using pretax cash flows and pretax discount rates will miss the segment of value that comes from depreciation and interest expenses being tax deductible and understate the value of the building. Assuming that the discount rate is defined correctly as a pretax cost of capital, the use of surveys to estimate both this number and the terminal multiple makes us uncomfortable, especially given the fact that the buyer of this building is a corporation with diversified investors.

Limitations of Discounted Cash Flow Valuation

There are many reasons given for why discounted cash flow valuation is not appropriate for real estate. First, it is argued the discount rates are difficult, if not impossible, to estimate for most real estate investments. Our counter is that this is not necessarily true. Second, it is posited that estimating cash flows for the time horizon is tedious and difficult to do, as is the estimation of the terminal value. However, it would seem that it is much easier to estimate cash flows for real estate than for some financial investments (for instance, a high-growth stock). Third, it is argued that discounted cash flow valuation does not reflect market conditions—that the market is strong or weak at the time of the valuation. This argument could be rejected at two levels. On one level, the cash flows should reflect the market conditions, since they will be higher (higher rents and lower vacancy rates) and grow faster in strong market conditions. On the other level, a market-based valuation that is not in sync with the cash flows of the property being valued is a misvaluation, and the focus in intrinsic or DCF valuation is to steer away from that practice.

COMPARABLE/RELATIVE VALUATION

Just as price-earnings and price–book value ratios are used to value financial assets, real estate investments can be priced using standardized value measures and comparable assets. There are several reasons for doing so:

- It provides a mechanism for pricing no-cash-flow-producing assets. For instance, the value of a single-family residential building bought as a primary residence can be estimated by looking at similar properties in the same area.
- It takes into account market trends that might not be reflected in the cash flows yet for a number of reasons. Existing leases might have frozen outdated lease payments in place, while market values have risen, and rent control laws might have prevented rents from rising with market values. To the extent that the market sees the possibility that both leases and rents will revert to market levels, the market prices may be higher than the intrinsic valuations.
- It is also argued that pricing based on comparables is much simpler to do than discounted cash flow valuation since it does not require, at least explicitly, the estimation of discount rates and cash flows.

What Is a Comparable Asset?

The key limitation of all comparable-based approaches is in the definition of comparable. In the case of stocks, differences in growth, risk, and payout ratios between stocks have to be adjusted before price-earnings ratios are compared. Many analysts choose to restrict their comparisons of stocks to those within the same industry group, to keep it relatively homogeneous. In the case of real estate, differences in income production, size, scale, location, age, and quality of construction must be accounted for, before comparisons are made. Some of these adjustments are simple (such as differences in size), while others are subjective (such as differences in quality of construction).

Use of Standardized Pricing Estimates

When pricing assets based on comparable assets, the pricing has to be standardized for the comparison. In stocks, this standardization is often done by dividing the price per share by the earnings per share (PE) or the book value per share (PBV). In the case of real estate, this adjustment is made by:

- *Size.* The simplest standardized measure is the price per square foot, which standardizes value using the size of the building. In office rentals, where square footage is a key factor determining rental revenues, this may by a useful adjustment. It does not, however, factor in differences on any of the other dimensions.
- *Income.* The value of an asset can be standardized using its income. For instance, the gross income multiplier (price of property/gross annual income) is an income-standardized value measure. The advantage of this approach is that the income incorporates differences in scale, construction quality, and location.[7] The gross

---

[7] Buildings of better quality in better locations should command higher rents/leases and higher expected income than other buildings.

income should be prior to debt payments, since differences in leverage can cause large differences in the income available to equity investors.

Why Comparables Often Work Better for Real Estate Than Stocks

One of the difficulties in using comparables to value stocks is that risk and growth characteristics can vary widely across stocks, even in the same industry class. In the case of real estate properties in the same locale, the argument can be made that the growth and risk characteristics are very similar across these properties.

ILLUSTRATION 26.3: Pricing a Property Based on Comparables in 2000

Consider the property at 711 Third Avenue that was valued using discounted cash flow valuation. The appraisal also noted eight other properties in that part of Manhattan with roughly the same characteristics as the building being appraised that had sold recently. Table 26.7 summarizes the details of these properties and the prices that they were sold for, as well as the net operating income (NOI) of each property:

TABLE 26.7 Property Pricing—Peer Group

Property	Size (Sq. Feet)	Occupancy Rate	Price for Sale	Price/ Sq foot	NOI/ Sq foot	Price/ NOI
900 Third Avenue	5,60,000	99%	$182,000,000	$325.00	26.98	12.05
767 Third Avenue	4,56,007	95%	$ 95,000,000	$208.33	NA	
350 Madison Avenue	3,10,000	97%	$ 70,060,000	$226.00	17.6	12.84
888 Seventh Avenue	8,38,680	96%	$154,500,000	$184.22	NA	
622 Third Avenue	8,74,434	97%	$172,000,000	$196.70	NA	
150 East 58th Street	5,07,178	95%	$118,000,000	$232.66	16.52	14.08
1065 Avenue of the Americas	5,80,000	95%	$ 59,000,000	$101.72	NA	
810 Seventh Avenue	6,46,000	95%	$141,000,000	$218.27	15.17	14.39
Average		96.13%		$211.61		13.34

The property at 711 Third Avenue has 528,357 square feet of rental space, had an occupancy rate of 95%, and generated net operating income of $6.107 million in the most recent year. Based on the average price per square foot, the value of the property is:

Pricing of 711 Third Avenue = Square footage × Price per square foot
= 528,357 sq. ft. × $211.61 per square foot = $111.807 million

If we adjust for the fact that the occupancy rate is slightly lower at 711 Third Avenue than at the average building, we would estimate the following:

Pricing of 711 Third Avenue = Square footage × (Occupancy rate 711 Third/Average occupancy rate)
× Price per square foot
= 528,357 sq. ft. × (95%/96.13%) × $211.61 per square foot
= $110.498 million

Finally, if we apply to this property the multiple of operating income based on the four properties for which it is available:

$$\text{Pricing of 711 Third Avenue} = \text{Net operating income} \times \text{Average price/NOI}$$
$$= \$6.107 \times 13.34 = \$81.470 \text{ million}$$

Which of these values gets used will depend on whether you view the lower operating income per square foot at 711 Third Avenue to be the consequence of poor management or the building's characteristics—location and condition. If it is the former, you might be willing to pay the higher values ($111 million). If it is the latter, you would pay only $81.4 million.

Regression Approach

One way to extend the reach of relative valuation for stocks is the regression approach, where price-earnings or price–book value multiples are regressed against independent variables that cause differences in these multiples—risk, growth, and payout. Since the variables causing differences in real estate values in a locale are fairly obvious—vacancy rates, size, and capacity to generate income, among others—it should be relatively simple to use this approach to analyze properties. In fact, it is the approach that Zillow uses to provide z-estimates for residential properties on its site.

ILLUSTRATION 26.4:   Regression Approach

You could regress the price per square foot for the eight properties in Illustration 26.3 against occupancy rates and obtain the following:

$$\text{Price per square foot} = -2,535.50 + 2,857.86 \text{ Occupancy rate} \quad R^2 = 46\%$$
$$\qquad\qquad\qquad\qquad\quad [2.07] \qquad\quad [2.25]$$

Using this regression, we would obtain an estimated price per square foot for 711 Third Avenue, with its 95% occupancy rate:

$$\text{Price per square foot} = -2,535.70 + 2,857.86(.95) = \$179.46$$
$$\text{Pricing of 711 Third Avenue} = 528,357 \times \$179.46 = \$94.820 \text{ million}$$

This regression is clearly limited in its power because there are only eight observations, and the occupancy rates are very similar. If we can obtain information on more properties and include variables on which there are bigger differences—a variable measuring the age of the building, for instance—we would be able to get much stronger predictions.

VALUING REAL ESTATE BUSINESSES

Much of this chapter has focused on valuing real estate properties. This section considers extending this analysis to value a real estate business. To value such a business, you have to consider its sources of income, and then look at its organization structure.

Sources of Income

Real estate businesses vary widely in terms of how they generate income, and how you approach valuation will vary as well. In particular, we could categorize real estate firms into four businesses.

1. *Service income.* Some firms generate income from providing just management services or support services to the owners of real estate—for instance, selling, security, or maintenance. Valuing these firms is relatively straightforward and requires assumptions about how fees will be assessed (many management service contracts, for instance, are stated as a percent of the gross income on a property), and how much the fee income will increase over time. More efficient firms or firms with better reputations (brand names) may be able to charge higher fees and be worth more.
2. *Real estate construction.* These businesses make their income from real estate construction—building residential or commercial properties. They usually agree to deliver the units at a contractually fixed price and generate profits from being able to construct them at a lower cost. Firms that are more cost-efficient will generally earn higher profits and be worth more. Here again, though, reputation can make a difference, and firms that are associated with quality construction may be able to charge premium prices.
3. *Real estate development.* These businesses usually buy vacant or underutilized land, put up new construction, and sell the units to real estate investors. They generally do not hold on to the properties for purposes of generating ongoing income. The values of these businesses will be determined by their capacity to gauge market demand and complete construction both quickly and at low cost.
4. *Real estate investment.* These are businesses that buy real estate property as income-generating investments. The simplest way of valuing these businesses is to value each of the properties that they own and to aggregate them. However, a premium may be attached to this value if a business has shown the capacity to repeatedly buy undervalued properties.

Thus, the factors we should think about when valuing real estate businesses are the same factors we think about in any valuation—the capacity to generate not just cash flows but also excess returns, and the uncertainty associated with these cash flows.

Organizational Structure

There are four basic organizational forms available to real estate business—the real estate investment trust (REIT), a master limited partnership (MLP), a business trust, and a real estate corporation. They differ in two major areas:

Structure of Taxation   Single taxation is a characteristic of REITs and MLPs, since both are taxed at the investor level, but not at the firm level. This tax benefit is given to REITs to compensate for certain investment and dividend policy restrictions to which REITs must adhere. MLPs receive single-taxation status only if they invest in certain activities, such as real estate or oil and gas. Otherwise, for tax purposes, MLPs are treated as corporations.

This tax advantage does not exist for business trusts and corporations that are taxed at both the entity level on income and at the investor level on dividends.

What are the implications for valuation? When valuing real estate investment trusts and master limited partnerships, the entity level tax rate used to estimate cash flows and discount rates is zero. That does not mean that there are no tax benefits from depreciation or interest expenses, since these benefits still flow through to the ultimate investors. When valuing real estate corporations, the corporate tax rate should be used for estimating cash flows and discount rates.

Restrictions on Investment and Dividend Policy   The tax code requires REITs to distribute 95 percent of their taxable income to shareholders, which effectively limits REITs' use of internal financing (or retained earnings). Consequently, REITs must return to the capital markets on a regular basis, which in turn limits their growth potential. The code further requires that a minimum of 75 percent of a REIT's gross income must come from real estate. A REIT must also be a passive investment conduit; that is, less than 30 percent of a REIT's income must come from the operation of real estate held less than four years, and income from the sale of securities held less than one year. REITs cannot engage in active real estate operations. They cannot operate a business, develop or trade properties for sale, or sell more than five properties per year. A REIT is prohibited from entering into tax-free exchanges to acquire properties. Although no dividend payout restrictions exist for MLPs, a high payout ratio is likely, since partners are taxed regardless of whether they actually receive the income or the MLP retains it, and the evidence suggests that MLPs pay out a high proportion of their earnings as dividends. Although MLPs are restricted to engaging in real estate activities, there are no restrictions on the nature or management of these activities. Consequently, MLPs can actively and directly engage in the real estate trade or business. There are no MLP restrictions on the number of properties that can be sold in any given year. Business trusts and corporations have no restrictions on dividend payout and can engage in any real estate or non–real estate activity except those prohibited in the declaration of trust or corporate charter, respectively.

The implications for valuation are significant. When valuing REITs and MLPs, you have to assume much of the earnings will be paid out in dividends. If you do not assume external financing, your estimates of expected growth in per share earnings will be low, no matter how well managed the entities are. If you do allow for external financing, you can have high-expected growth in net income, but the number of shares in the firm will have to increase proportionately, thus limiting the potential price appreciation on a per-share basis. The restrictions on investment policy will constrain how much returns on capital can be changed over time.

CONCLUSION

There is much that is said in this chapter that repeats what was said in earlier chapters on stock valuation. This is because a real estate investment can (and should) be valued with the same approaches used to value financial assets. While the structure and caveats of discounted cash flow models remain unchanged for real estate investments, there are some practical problems that have to be faced and overcome. In particular, real estate investments do not trade regularly, and risk parameters (and discount rates) are difficult to estimate. A real estate investment can also be priced using comparable investments, but the difficulties in identifying comparable assets and controlling for differences across them remain significant problems.

QUESTIONS AND SHORT PROBLEMS

In the problems following, use an equity risk premium of 5.5 percent if none is specified.

1. An analyst who looks at real estate decides to apply the capital asset pricing model to estimate the risk (beta) for real estate. He regresses returns on a real estate index (based on appraised values) against returns on a stock index and estimates a beta of 0.20 for real estate. Would you agree with this estimate? If you do not, what might be the sources of your disagreement?

2. An alternative way of estimating risk for real estate is to use prices on traded REITs to compute returns, and to regress these returns against a stock index to arrive at a beta estimate. Would this beta be a more reliable estimate of risk? Why or why not?

3. The risk for real estate can be viewed as a derived demand. If this is the case, the risk of real estate can be estimated from the underlying business it supports. Under this view, what would be the appropriate proxy to use for risk in the following types of real estate investments:

    a. Commercial real estate in New York City.
    b. Commercial real estate in Houston, Texas.
    c. Commercial real estate in San Jose, California (Silicon Valley).
    d. Hotel complex in Orlando, Florida.

4. Would your valuation of real estate by affected by who the potential investors in the property are? (For instance, would your analysis be any different if the primary investors were individuals involved primarily in real estate or if they were institutional investors?)

5. How would you factor in the absence of liquidity into your valuation?

6. You have been asked to value an office building in Orlando, Florida, with the following characteristics:

    ▨ The building was built in 1988 and has 300,000 square feet of rentable area.
    ▨ There would be an initial construction and renovation cost of $3.0 million.
    ▨ It will take two years to fill the building. The expected vacancy rates in the first two years are:

Year	Vacancy Rate
1	30%
2	20%
After year 2	10%

    ▨ The market rents in the building were expected to average $15.00 per square foot in the current year, based on average rents in the surrounding buildings.
    ▨ The market rents were assumed to grow 5% a year for five years and at 3% a year after that forever.
    ▨ The variable operating expenses were assumed to be $3.00 per square foot, and are expected to grow at the same rate as rents. The fixed operating expense in 1994 amounted to $300,000, and was expected to grow at 3% forever.
    ▨ The real estate taxes are expected to amount to $300,000 in the first year, and grow 3% a year after that. It is assumed that all tenants will pay their prorate share of increases in real estate taxes that exceed 3% a year.

■ The tax rate on income was assumed to be 42%.

■ The cost of borrowing was assumed to be 8.25%, pretax. It was also assumed that the building would be financed with 30% equity and 70% debt.

■ A survey suggests that equity investors in real estate require a return of 12.5% of their investments.

a. Estimate the value of the building, based on expected cash flows.

b. Estimate the value of just the equity stake in this building.

7. You are trying to value the same building based on comparable properties sold in recent years. There have been six property sales of buildings of comparable size in the surrounding area.

Property	Sale Price	Size (Sq. Ft.)	Gross Rent
A	$20,000,000	400,000	$5,000,000
B	$18,000,000	425,000	$4,750,000
C	$22,000,000	450,000	$5,100,000
D	$25,000,000	400,000	$5,500,000
E	$15,000,000	350,000	$4,000,000
F	$12,000,000	300,000	$3,000,000

a. Estimate the value of the building based on price per square foot.

b. Estimate the value of the building based on price/gross rent.

c. What are some of the assumptions you make when you value a building based on comparable buildings?

CHAPTER 27

Valuing Other Assets

One of the fundamental precepts of this book is that all assets, financial as well as real, can be valued systematically using traditional valuation models. The bulk of this book examines the valuation of stocks, but the preceding chapter extended the reach of valuation models to cover real estate. This chapter considers other assets that are usually considered unique and different and attempts to value them using the principles developed in the earlier chapters.

While the assets covered in this chapter have very different characteristics and attract different investors, they can be broadly classified into three categories:

1. Assets that are expected to generate cash flows over time and can be valued with discounted cash flow models.
2. Assets that do not generate cash flows but attain value because they are scarce and are perceived to be valuable (e.g., collectibles, coins) and/or generate utility to their owners (e.g., antiques, paintings). These assets can be valued using relative valuation.
3. Assets that do not generate cash flows but could be valuable in the event of a contingency—they have option characteristics. These assets can be valued using option pricing models.

Within each category, there are a surprising number of commonalties both across different assets and with the financial assets described in the earlier chapter.

INVESTMENT CLASSIFICATION

For much of this book, we have focused on assets that generate cash flows, either in contractual form (bonds) or in residual form (equities, ownership in private businesses and real estate). In this chapter, we will look at varied investments, some of which (franchises) generate cash flows and some that do not (bitcoin, collectives), and argue that not everything can be valued but almost everything can be priced.

To understand the distinction between value and price, let us start by positing that every investment that we look at must fall into one of the following four groupings:

1. *Cash Generating Asset:* An asset generates or is expected to generate cash flows in the future. A business that you own is definitely an asset, as is a claim on the cash flows of that business. Those claims can be either contractually set (bonds or debt), residual (equity or stock), or even contingent (options). What assets have in common is that these cash flows can be valued, and assets with high cash flows and less risk should be valued more than assets with lower cash flows and more risk. At the same time, assets

can also be priced, relative to each other, by scaling the price that you pay to a common metric. With stocks, this takes the form of comparing pricing multiples (PE ratio, enterprise value (EV)/ earnings before interest, taxes, depreciation, and amortization (EBITDA), Price-to-Book or EV/Sales) across similar companies to form pricing judgments of which stocks are cheap and which ones are expensive.

2. *Commodity:* A commodity derives its value from its use as raw material to meet a fundamental need, whether it be energy, food, or shelter. While that value can be estimated by looking at the demand for and supply of the commodity, there are long lag and lead times in both that make that valuation process much more difficult than for an asset. Consequently, commodities tend to be priced, often relative to their own history, with normalized oil, coal, wheat, or iron ore prices being computed by averaging prices across long cycles.

3. *Currency:* A currency is a medium of exchange that you use to denominate cash flows, and is a store of purchasing power, if you choose not to invest. Standing alone, currencies have no cash flows and cannot be valued, but they can be priced against other currencies, taking the form of exchange rates. In the long term, currencies that are accepted more widely as a medium of exchange, and that hold their purchasing power better over time should see their prices rise, relative to currencies that don't have those characteristics. In the short term, though, other forces, including governments trying to manipulate exchange rates, can dominate.

4. *Collectible:* A collectible has no cash flows and is not a medium of exchange, but it can sometimes have aesthetic value (e.g., a master painting or a sculpture) or an emotional attachment (e.g., a baseball card or team jersey). A collectible cannot be valued since it too generates no cash flows, but it can be priced based upon how other people perceive its desirability and the scarcity of the collectible.

Table 27.1 summarizes the contrast between these different investment groupings, with indications the value/pricing divide:

As we go through this chapter, we will follow this rubric, valuing and pricing those investments that generate cash flows and pricing those investments that do not. As you navigate this divide, we will also talk about investments that fit into more than one category—trophy assets, which have cash flows like conventional assets but are priced as collectibles, precious metals like gold which are both commodities and collectibles and bitcoin, which can viewed as a currency or a collectible.

TABLE 27.1 Investment Classes—Value versus Price

Investment	To value	To price
Assets	Can be valued based upon expected cash flows, with higher cash flows & lower risk = higher value.	Can be priced against similar assets, after controlling for cash flows and risk
Commodity	Can be value based upon utilitarian demand and supply, but with long lags in both.	Can be priced against its own history (normalized price over time)
Currency	Cannot be valued	Can be priced against other currencies, with greater acceptance and more stable purchasing power = higher price
Collectible	Cannot be valued	Can be priced based upon scarcity and desirability.

CASH-FLOW–PRODUCING ASSETS

Several assets derive their value from their capacity to generate cash flows to their owners. The value of such assets is a function of the expected cash flows in the future and the uncertainty associated with these cash flows. The basic principles of discounted cash flow valuation, described in earlier chapters, apply for any of these assets and require the following steps:

- Estimate cash flows on the asset for the estimation period. These cash flows can either be predebt (cash flows to the firm) or after-debt cash flows (cash flows to equity).
- Estimate the value of the asset, if any, at the end of the estimation period. This value will decline over time if the asset loses value with use or has a limited life, and may, in some cases, be zero.
- Estimate a discount rate that reflects the riskiness of the cash flows. This discount rate will be the cost of equity, if the cash flows discounted are cash flows to equity, and the cost of capital, if the cash flows are cash flows to the firm.
- Calculate the present value of the cash flows to arrive at the value of the asset or the value of the equity in the assets.

There are several practical problems associated with applying these steps to assets when cash flows are difficult to estimate and risk cannot be easily quantified (and converted into a discount rate). In most cases, these problems are not insurmountable and can be overcome. Since the problems and the solutions vary from case to case, we consider a series of examples, ranging from the valuation of a simple franchise to more complex businesses.

Valuing a Franchise

A franchise gives you the right to market or sell a product or service of a brand-name company. Examples of franchises would include the thousands of McDonald's restaurants around the world, dealerships for the automobile companies, and, loosely defined, even a New York City cab medallion. In each case, the franchisee (the person who buys the franchise) pays the franchisor (e.g., McDonald's or Ford) either an up-front price or an annual fee for running the franchise. In return, he or she gets the power of the brand name, corporate support, and advertising backing.

Franchise Value and Excess Returns   The acquisition of a franchise provides the franchisee with the opportunity to earn excess returns for the life of the franchise. While the sources of these above-market returns vary from case to case, they can arise from several factors:

- *Brand name value.* The franchise might have a brand name value that enables the franchisee to charge higher prices and attract more customers than an otherwise similar business. Thus, an investor may be willing to pay a significant up-front fee to acquire a McDonald's franchise, in order to take advantage of the brand-name value associated with the company.
- *Exclusivity.* In some cases, a franchise has value because it enables a franchisee to produce a product, the rights to which are owned by the franchisor. For instance, an investor may pay a fee to Disney for the right to manufacture Mickey Mouse watches or toys, and hope to recoup the fee by selling more of the product or charging a higher price for it.

■ *Legal monopolies.* Sometimes, a franchise may have value because the franchisee is given the exclusive right to provide a service. For instance, a company may pay a large fee for the right to operate concession stands in a baseball stadium, knowing that it will face no competition within the stadium. In a milder variant of this, multiple franchises are sometimes sold, but the number of franchises is limited to ensure that the franchisees earn excess returns. New York City, for example, sells cab medallions that are a prerequisite for operating a yellow cab in the city, and has tight restrictions on nonmedallion owners offering the same service. Consequently, a market where cab medallions are bought and sold exists.

In essence, the value of a franchise is directly tied to the capacity to generate excess returns. Any action or event that affects these excess returns will affect the value of the franchise.

Special Issues in Valuing Franchises   Buying a franchise is often a mixed blessing. While the franchisee gets the backing of a well-known firm with significant resources to back up his or her efforts, there are some costs that may affect the value of the franchise. Among these costs are the following:

■ The problems of the franchisor can spill over onto the franchisee. For instance, when Daewoo, the Korean automaker, borrowed too much and got into financial trouble, its dealers around the world felt the repercussions. Similarly, McDonald's franchisees around the world have been targeted by anti-globalization activists. Thus, an efficient and well-run franchise's value can be affected by actions that it has little or no control over.
■ Since franchisors tend to be large corporations and franchisees tend to be small businesspeople, the former often have much more bargaining power and sometimes take advantage of it to change the terms of franchise agreements in their favor. Franchisees can increase their power by banding together and bargaining as a collective unit.
■ The value of a franchise derives from the exclusive rights it grants the franchisee to sell the products of a firm. This value can be diluted if a franchise is granted to a competitor. For instance, the value of a Days Inn franchise may be diluted if another Days Inn is allowed to open five miles down the highway.

ILLUSTRATION 27.1:   Valuing a New York City Cab Medallion—June 2014

BACKGROUND

■ Starting in 1937, New York City has required cab operators to own cab medallions, endowing its owners the right to operate a yellow taxi in perpetuity.
■ While the cab medallions were initially issued by the city, the number of medallions has increased only marginally over the last few decades. Consequently, the primary way to acquire a medallion is in the secondary market.
■ In 2014, New York City had 13,437 cab medallions outstanding. The owner of a cab medallion has the right to operate a yellow cab in the five boroughs of New York City—Manhattan, Brooklyn, the Bronx, Queens, and Staten Island. New York City restricts nonmedallion owners from picking up customers on the street, though they can still be summoned in other ways.

- There are two classes of medallions, one for driver-owners, who buy medallions for the cabs that they operate, and one for taxi operators, who buy the medallions and then lease the cabs to drivers who pay them a lease rate each day.

- All yellow cabs in the city are regulated by the Taxi and Limousine Commission, which sets fares and reserves the right to fine owners who do not follow its numerous requirements.

Cash Flows on a Leased Cab Medallion to a Taxi Operator

- To value a medallion to a taxi operator, we will start with the economics of cab leasing. The taxi operator can lease out a cab for two ten-hour lease shifts each day, and in 2014, the Taxi and Limousine Commission capped that lease rate at about $130/shift for the next year.

- A cab can be expected to be on the road 330 days of the year, with an expected down time (for maintenance) of 35 days. While the driver is responsible for gas and operating expenses, the taxi operator must pay for maintenance and repairs, amounting to $2,000 a year, for next year.

- The typical New York City cab used to be a Chevrolet Caprice or Ford Victoria, but the fleet now includes more hybrid cars. In 2014, the cost of a cab was approximately $25,000, and it has an expected life of 5 years.[1] The cab can be depreciated over the life down to a salvage value of zero, but an amount equivalent to depreciation is set aside to cover the cost of a new car in the future.

- All taxi cabs that operate in New York city must carry $100,000 in liability insurance and $300,000 to cover injuries to individuals involved in the accident. The cost of automobile insurance, covering the cost of collision, theft, and bodily harm, is expected to be $1,500 per year.

- The annual fee to be paid to the Taxi and Limousine Commission is $500. Other licensing costs are expected to amount to $500 a year. The taxi operator is expected to pay a tax rate of 30% on taxable income.

The expected cash flows, next year, to the taxi operator, based on these assumptions is shown in Table 27.2:

TABLE 27.2 Expected Earnings to Taxi Operator

Item	Calculation	Amount
Lease revenues	$2 \times 130 \times 330$	$85,800.00
− Maintenance & Repairs		$ 2,000.00
− Insurance		$ 1,500.00
− Fees and license costs		$ 1000.00
− Depreciation	Straight line over 5 years	$ 5,000.00
EBIT		$76,300.00
− Taxes	Tax rate = 30%	$22,890.00
EBIT (1 − tax rate)		$53,410.00
+ Depreciation	Straight line − 5 years	$ 5,000.00
− Capital Expenditures	Set aside for new car	$ 5,000.00
Free cash flow to firm		$53,410.00

Cash Flows on a Cab Medallion to a Driver owner

Looking at the cash flows through the eyes of a driver/owner alters the cash-flow mechanics. While some of the expenses (maintenance and repairs, depreciation, fees, and insurance) will apply to the driver owner, the

---

[1] A New York city cab typically is driven 70,000 miles a year or more, putting wear and tear on the vehicle and shortening vehicle life.

driver owner is entitled to the cash flows left over after all these expenses have been factored in as well as gas and the driver's time. Assuming that the driver values his time at $60,000 for driving a ten-hour day all year, spends $10,000 on gas each year, and that the annual fare revenues are expected to be $150,000, the expected cash flows to a driver owner can be calculated in Table 27.3:

TABLE 27.3 Expected Earnings to Cab Driver/Owner

Item	Calculation	Amount
Cab fare	Annual fare	$150,000.00
− Gas		$ 10,000.00
− Driver salary		$ 60,000.00
− Maintenance & Repairs		$ 2,000.00
− Insurance		$ 1,500.00
− Fees and license costs		$ 1000.00
− Depreciation	Straight line over 5 years	$ 5,000.00
EBIT		$ 70,500.00
− Taxes	Tax rate = 30%	$ 21,150.00
EBIT (1 − tax rate)		$ 49,350.00
+ Depreciation		$ 5,000.00
− Capital Expenditures	Set aside for new car	$ 5,000.00
Free cash flow to firm		$ 49,350.00

A driver/owner can clear more in cash flows, before factoring in the cost of driver time, than a taxi operator, but less, after driver time is factored into the cash flows.

ESTIMATING RISK AND DISCOUNT RATES

In assessing risk and discount rates to a taxi operator, it is worth recognizing that the lease revenues are contractually set, and that the only risk these operators face is from drivers defaulting. Consequently, the discount rate that we will use to discount the cash flows back will be the cost of debt to a driver. In 2014, cab drivers who were buying their own medallions were facing a cost of debt of 5%. Note that this discount rate is just a reflection of the risk in the cash flows and does not presuppose that the taxi operators will borrow the money to buy the medallions.

In assessing risk to a driver/owner, we must consider the additional risk in the discount rate. The capacity of a cab to pull in the expected revenues is a function of several variables:

- *State of the city's economy.* The more buoyant the economy of the city, the greater are the potential revenues from owning and operating a cab in it. Since the condition of New York City's economy is, in large part, driven by the state of the financial services sector, there is likely a positive correlation between cab revenues and financial service sector health.

- *Scarcity of cabs.* The value of a cab medallion is derived directly from the fact that there are a limited number of medallions sold. To the extent that the city can either issue more medallions or allow gypsy cabs (unlicensed taxis) to operate within the environs of the city, it can affect the expected revenues.

- *Fare structure.* Since the fare structure is regulated, the expected revenues from owning a cab in the future will be dependent on the generosity of raises that the Taxi and Limousine Commission allows.

- *Other risks.* There are a number of other potential sources of risk, including collision and theft, that have already been built into the cost structure. To the extent that these are estimates, they could also create swings in the cash flows.

Assuming that the expected revenues already factors in the number of medallions outstanding and the expected changes in the fare structure, the primary source of risk in owning a cab medallion is expected to be from shifts in the city's economy. If the health of the city's economy is a function of the financial service sector, the risk of owning a cab medallion should be similar to the risk of investing in a financial service firm. The average beta of financial service firms headquartered in New York City is 1.15. In June 2014, with Treasury bond rates at 2.5% and using the then-prevailing equity risk premium of 5.0%, the cost of equity would have been:

$$\text{Cost of equity} = 2.5\% + 1.15 \times (5.0\%) = 8.25\%$$

This will be used as the cost of equity in valuing a cab medallion. Assume that the medallion will be financed 40% with equity and 60% with debt, and that the debt will carry an annual interest rate of 5%. Allowing for a marginal tax rate (federal, state, and city) of 25%, the cost of capital for valuing the medallion is:

$$\text{Cost of capital} = 8.25\% \times (0.4) + 5\% \times (1 - 0.25) \times (0.6) = 5.55\%$$

ESTIMATING FUTURE GROWTH AND VALUE

It is assumed that the expected operating income (to both taxi operators and driver/owners) from owning a cab will keep up with expected inflation, which is assumed to be 2%. Given that technology was already disrupting cab service in New York city, we assume an operating life for the medallion. The value of the cab medallion can then be calculated to taxi operators and driver owners:[2]

$$\text{Value to taxi operator} = \text{Expected FCFF next year} \times \frac{\left(1 - \frac{(1+g)^n}{(1+r)^n}\right)}{(r-g)}$$

$$= \$53,410 \times \frac{\left(1 - \frac{(1.02)^{50}}{(1.05)^{50}}\right)}{(.05 - .02)} = \$1,362,460$$

$$\text{Value to driver owner} = \text{Expected FCFF next year} \times \frac{\left(1 - \frac{(1+g)^n}{(1+r)^n}\right)}{(r-g)}$$

$$= \$49,350 \times \frac{\left(1 - \frac{(1.02)^{50}}{(1.0825)^{50}}\right)}{(.0825 - .02)} = \$1,138,862$$

Note that the high value for the medallions are premised on two assumptions. The first is that they will continue to endow their owners with the franchise power to operate a cab in New York city for the next 50 years, with little or no competition. The other is that the Taxi and Limousine Commission will allow fares and lease caps to rise with inflation over time.

A PRICING UPDATE

For much of the last century, a taxicab medallion in New York city provided its owner with a business opportunity, with little competition from outside. While car and limousine services coexisted with taxicabs, they served a different population and different needs. As tourism increased through the late nineties and into this century, the price of a taxicab medallion marched steadily upwards, reaching more than a million dollars in 2014, increasing more than fivefold between 2004 and 2014, as indicated in Figure 27.1.

As a cautionary note on how even the most protected franchises can be undercut by unanticipated developments, the rise of ride-sharing companies has devastated the economic payoff to owning a medallion and its pricing has reflected that devastation, as can be seen in Figure 27.2:

---

[2]We are assuming that the expected cash flows computed in the last section are for next year, and thus there is no need to grow them out in the present value calculation.

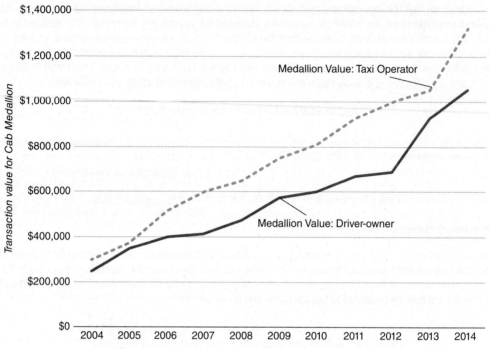

FIGURE 27.1   Cab Medallion Values from 2004 to 2014

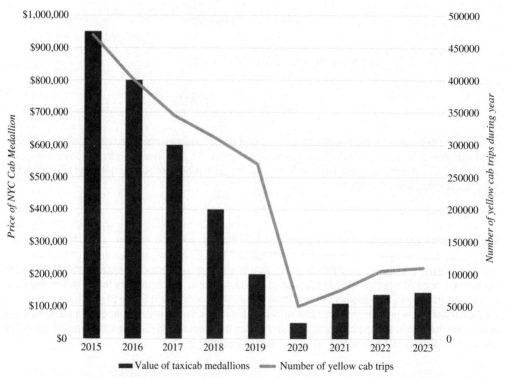

FIGURE 27.2   The Decline and Fall of NYC Cabs

Since cab medallion purchases have historically been funded with borrowed the money, the drop in medallion prices has been catastrophic for owners, with even the largest taxi operators declaring bankruptcy. In fact, while there are 13,587 medallions in circulation, it is estimated that almost half of them are not in use in 2022.[3]

ILLUSRATION 27.2: Valuing a Movie Franchise—Star Wars in 2015

The Star Wars story began in 1977 when George Lucas produced the first *Star Wars* movie, the fourth episode in what he saw as a six-episode series. That movie made history and remains one of the highest grossing movies of all time. It was followed in 1980 by the fifth episode, *The Empire Strikes Back*, and in 1983 with the sixth in the series, *The Return of the Jedi*. Those first three movies created an entire generation of *Star Wars* fans, who then had to wait 16 years for the first movie in the series, *The Phantom Menace,* which was followed by *Attack of the Clones* in 2002, and *Revenge of the Sith* in 2005. The six movies represent one of the most valuable movie franchises of all time, generating billions of dollars in box office receipts, with the appeal spreading globally.

THE DISNEY ACQUISITION

In 2012, Disney acquired the *Star Wars* franchise for $4 billion, from George Lucas, with plans to produce three more *Star Wars* movies. At the time of the acquisition, we argued that it was a fair price, given Disney's history with developing, maintaining, and merchandising franchises but had to draw on the potential for synergy to justify the number. With the release of *Star Wars: The Force Awakens* in 2015, Disney seemed to be more than delivering on its promise, as the movie has broken box office records and is on its way to delivering a global box office of $2 billion or more. This valuation of the *Star Wars* franchise was done at the time of that movie release, and reflects our expectations for the future, as seen then.

In 2015, the next two movies were scheduled for 2017 and 2019, and there were expected to be three spin offs in the intermediate years, with less ambitious budgets. After 2020, Disney's plans were not specific, but if the appetite remains, there will be undoubtedly more movies in the pipeline. More importantly, the movies were not only expected to create a new base of younger fans but to also augment the sales of merchandise, toys, and games in the coming decade. The revenues that would have come from DVDs and video rentals would be replaced with streaming revenues, and there will undoubtedly be games and apps directed at smartphones, devices, and gaming systems.

VALUING THE STAR WARS FRANCHISE

To value the franchise in 2015, we started with our estimates of worldwide box office receipts for *Star Wars: The Force Awakens* and the subsequent movies in the series. Though, the first two weekends have blown away expectations (with the movie making $1 billion), we estimate $2 billion in revenues, for each of the three main movies, and half those proceeds for the spin-offs, with an inflation adjustment of 2% a year. As with the prior movies, the bulk of the revenues from the franchise will come from add-ons, and in assessing the potential, here are some of our assumptions:

1. *Streaming:* As viewers increasingly turn to watching streamed movies from Netflix, we assumed, based on what we knew in 2015, that the bulk of the revenues for the Star Wars franchise woudl come from movie theaters office receipts for movies, and by 2017, the total revenues from streaming were expected to exceed box office revenues. We assumed that each dollar in box office revenues from the new *Star*

---

[3] In 2022, it was estimated that 6,400 out of the 13,587 medallions were inactive. That may explain the partial recovery in both taxi cab trips and medallion prices in 2023.

Wars movies would generate $1.20 in additional revenue in streaming, slightly higher than historical numbers (1.14).

2. *Toys/Merchandise:* The *Star Wars* movies have historically generated $1.80 in revenues from toys/merchandise for every dollar in box office revenues. Given Disney's prowess at merchandising, we would not be surprised to see this number go up, and we assume that each dollar at the box office will translate into two dollars in merchandising revenues, a little higher than the historical value of $1.80 per box office dollar. Keep in mind that this franchise is a merchandisers' dream, with an almost endless potential for new opportunities in the Expanded Universe.

3. *Books and eBooks:* This is the stream that is perhaps most at risk, and we assume that, while a way will be found to adapt the publishing stream to changing tastes in reading, the revenues from these books/e-books will drop to $0.20 per box office dollar (from $0.27, the historical number).

4. *Gaming:* In keeping with the history of *Star War* games, we were convinced that those games would be adapted not only to gaming platforms (Xbox, Playstation, and Nintendo) but also to smartphones and tablets. We leave the gaming revenues at $0.50 per dollar in box office receipts.

5. *TV Shows/Other:* This is the one add-on where we assume a significant improvement over historical numbers, as Disney, Netflix, and others find ways to adapt the franchise to television viewers. We will assume that the revenues from TV shows will increase to $0.50 per dollar in box office receipts.

Figure 27.3 summarizes the valuation of the *Star Wars* movie and merchandising franchises:

	Add-On $ per Box Office $
Streaming/Video	$1.20
Toys & Merchandise	$2.00
Books/eBooks	$0.20
Gaming	$0.50
Other	$0.50

Main Movies
World Box office of $1.5 billion, adjusted for 2% inflation.

Spin Off Movies
World Box office of 50% of main movies.

Add-On $ per box office $		Main Star Wars Movies			Star Wars Spin-Offs		
		Star Wars VII	Star Wars VIII	Star Wars IX	Rogue One	Hans Solo?	Boba Fett?
	Years from now	0.0	2.0	4.0	1.0	3.0	5.0
	Movies - Revenues	$2,000	$2,081	$2,165	$1,020	$1,061	$1,104
	Streaming/Video - Revenues	$2,400	$2,497	$2,598	$1,224	$1,273	$1,325
	Toys & Merchandise - Revenues	$4,000	$4,162	$4,330	$2,040	$2,122	$2,208
	Books/eBooks - Revenues	$400	$416	$433	$204	$212	$221
	Gaming - Revenues	$1,000	$1,040	$1,082	$510	$531	$552
	Other Revenues	$1,000	$1,040	$1,082	$510	$531	$552
Operating Margin 20.14% for movies 15% for non-movies 30% tax rate	Total - Revenues	$10,800	$11,236	$11,690	$5,508	$5,731	$5,962
	After-Tax Operating Income (movies)	$ 282	$ 293	$ 305	$ 144	$ 150	$ 156
	After-Tax Operating Income (non-movies)	$ 924	$ 961	$ 1,000	$ 471	$ 490	$ 510
	Present Value (PV)	$ 1,206	$ 1,083	$ 973	$ 572	$ 514	$ 461
Discounted back @ 7.61% cost of capital of entertainment companies	Value of New Star Wars movies =	$4,809					
	Value of Continuing Income =	$5,163					
	Value of Star Wars =	$9,972					

Assumes that revenues from add ons continue after 2020, growing at 2% a year, with 15% operating margin

FIGURE 27.3 Valuing the Star Wars Franchise in December 2015

To estimate the franchise value, we used the operating margins of the movie (20.14%) and toy/merchandise businesses (15%), and netted out taxes (at a 30% tax rate), before discounting back at a 7.61% cost of capital, the entertainment sector average. (We assumed that Disney would license most of the merchandise, passing of the risk to others but settling for a share of the operating income.) At least based on our projections, the value of the *Star Wars* franchise, if it can maintain my estimated numbers (for add-ons) and deliver at the box office, is almost $10 billion. The value is obviously a function of movie revenues, and the add-on dollar values, as can be seen in Table 27.4:

TABLE 27.4 *Star Wars* Franchise Value and Add-Ons

		Add-On $ as Multiple of Box Office $		
		$ 3.00	$ 4.50	$ 6.00
Box Office Revenue	$1,500.00	$ 7,308	$ 8,250	$ 9,193
(in $ millions)	$2,000.00	$ 8,800	$10,056	$11,312
	$2,500.00	$10,291	$11,862	$13,432

Not only does that make Disney's $4 billion investment in 2012 a very good one, but any synergies that Disney can gain in its other businesses (like this one) will create more upside.

A 2024 Postscript, with a Streaming Add-on

In 2024, Disney has run through its *Star Wars* movie gamut, at least for the moment. Looking back, it seems clear that we overshot our estimates on movie revenues on the movies released by Disney. In fact, while *Force One* delivered $2.5 billion in global ticket receipts, *The Last Jedi* and *The Rise of Skywalker,* the most recent movies, made closer to $1.5 billion than the $2 billion that we estimated. Along the way, Disney did make a major investment in its own streaming platform in November 2019, and used *The Mandalorian,* a *Star Wars* spin-off, as a driver for new subscriptions. In the years since, Disney has added more *Star Wars* shows to its streaming mix, which has the potential to increase the value of the franchise. One danger of the proliferation of *Star Wars*-streaming shows is that it may be undercutting the box office potential for new movies, because of viewer exhaustion.

While we are in a holding pattern, waiting for Disney's plans with the franchise, we believe that the value of the franchise has only increased since 2015, partly because of the additional revenue streams on streaming and at the parks.

Valuing Businesses with a Personal Component

In Chapter 24, we introduced the notion of a *key person* in a business and the effect on value of losing that key person. We suggested that the key person effect on value be estimated, by looking at the impact of the loss of that key person on cash flows. There are several examples we can offer for businesses with personal components. Consider the following:

- In Chapter 24, we used the example of a restaurant with a star chef with drawing power. Thus, when a chef is incapacitated or moves to a competitor, the number of customers may drop off dramatically.
- Many service businesses, ranging from plumbing, to dentistry, to tax accounting, have a personal component. Hence, when the person providing the service moves on, a large portion of the value of the business could be lost. A dentist who pays a large amount for a thriving dental practice of another dentist may see a drop-off in business after the purchase. This effect will be accentuated if the seller can start a competing business.
- A mutual fund company may derive its value from its most recognized fund managers. If they move to a competitor or start their own funds, they could take a large portion of the money they manage with them.

So, how should we value these businesses and the component of value that is attributable to the key person? The answer depends on why you are doing the valuation in the first place. If the objective is to value the business for the existing owner, you may separate out the portion of value due to the owner's personal connections and skill, but there are no immediate consequences. If the objective is to value the business for a potential buyer, the simplest way to avoid overpaying is to do two valuations—one with the business as is, with the existing owner, and one without the owner, making reasonable assumptions about the degree to which business will drop off. The latter will be much lower than the former, and will represent the price you would be willing to pay.

FRANCHISE VALUE: CAN THE FRANCHISEE MAKE A DIFFERENCE?

We do not intend to leave you with the impression that the value of a franchise is entirely attributable to the franchisor, and that the franchisee cannot affect the value. Clearly, franchisees can make a difference, which explains why the value of a McDonald's can increase when it passes from one franchisee to another. There are several factors that explain these differences:

- *Efficiency.* Some franchisees do a much better job in controlling costs and generating higher margins than others. To illustrate, a large proportion of low-cost hotels and inns in the United States is owned by a group of immigrants from Asia. Since the owner's entire family often works at the hotel at low or no pay, employee costs tend to be lower, allowing the owner to turn a larger profit than a passive owner would have.

- *Personal component.* There remains a personal component in many franchises that can make a significant difference to value. For instance, while there are thousands of automobile dealers around the country, a few of them account for a significant portion of the total revenues.

- *Economies of scale.* There are economies of scale associated with owning several franchises from the same firm. For instance, you often see individuals who own more than one franchise of the same company. By pooling several franchises, you might be able to reduce your administrative costs and increase the profitability of each.

ILLUSTRATION 27.3:   Valuing a Dental Practice in 2011

Assume that you are a young dentist specializing in pediatric dentistry, and that you are interested in buying a dental practice located in Chatham, New Jersey. The dentist who owns the practice has built it up over the past two decades, and the practice generated $500,000 in revenues last year. The expenditures associated with running this practice last year include the following:

- Employee expenses (including dental hygienists and secretarial help) amounted to $150,000 last year, and are expected to grow 3% a year for the next 10 years.
- The annual rent for the facilities last year was $50,000, and is expected to grow 3% a year for the next 10 years.
- Rentals of medical equipment cost $40,000 last year, and this expense is expected to grow 3% for the next 10 years.

- The cost of medical insurance last year was $60,000 and is expected to grow 3% a year for the next 10 years.
- The tax rate on the income, including state and local taxes, is 40%.
- The cost of capital is 10%. We estimate this number by looking at the costs of capital of publicly traded health care clinics and using the median value.

To value the practice, assume that revenues would have grown 3% a year for the next 10 years if the current dentist continued to run the practice, but that there will be a drop-off of 20% in the first year's revenues if a new dentist comes into the practice. The growth rate of 3% will still occur in the following years but on the lower base revenues.

First, value the practice with the current dentist. To make this estimate, begin by estimating the cash flows in the first year to the practice:

$$\text{Cash flow in year 1} = (\text{Revenues}_1 - \text{Operating expenses}_1) \times (1 - \text{tax rate})$$
$$= [500,000(1.03) - (150,000 + 50,000 + 40,000 + 60,000) \times (1.03)] \times (1 - .40)$$
$$= \$123,600$$

Using the cost of capital as the discount rate and the growing annuity equation for a 10-year period, you can estimate the value of the practice:

$$\text{Value of practice} = CF_1 \times \frac{1 - \frac{(1 + g)^n}{(1 + r)^n}}{(r - g)} = 123,600 \times \frac{1 - \frac{(1.03)^{10}}{(1.10)^{10}}}{(.10 - .03)} = \$850,831$$

We assume that the value of the practice fades after 10 years, and therefore, attach no terminal value.

Follow up by valuing the practice with a new dentist in place. The cash flow in year 1 will be lower because the revenues will be lower:

$$\text{Cash flow in year 1} = (\text{Revenues}_1 - \text{Operating expenses}_1) \times (1 - \text{Tax rate})$$
$$= [400,000(1.03) - (150,000 + 50,000 + 40,000 + 60,000)(1.03)] \times (1 - .40)$$
$$= \$61,800$$

$$\text{Value of practice} = CF_1 \times \frac{1 - \frac{(1 + g)^n}{(1 + r)^n}}{(r - g)} = 61,800 \times \frac{1 - \frac{(1.03)^{10}}{(1.10)^{10}}}{(.10 - .03)} = \$425,415$$

Notice that the value is halved, and the difference can be viewed as the value of the key person.

As a potential buyer, the new dentist should offer the latter value for the practice. However, if the buyer can arrange for a transition period where the current dentist stays with the practice after the transaction, he or she may be willing to pay a higher price.

ILLUSTRATION 27.4: Valuing a Five-Star Restaurant: Lutèce in 1994

Lutèce is a renowned restaurant located at 249 East 50th Street in Manhattan. In 1994, Lutèce was sold by its owner/chef Andre Soltner to Ark Restaurants, a publicly traded restaurant chain, for an undisclosed amount. The *New York Times*, blanching as a result of the sale, ran the headline, "Lutèce, a Dining Landmark, Is Sold to a Chain Operator", which was then followed by an article detailing the surprise marriage of the classic French restaurant to Ark, a company largely known for operating theme restaurants. Bryan Miller, the *Times'* former restaurant reviewer and writer of the piece, likened the addition of Lutèce to Ark's portfolio to "hanging a Van Gogh in a community art exhibit".

BACKGROUND

Lutèce was founded in 1961 by Andre Soltner, and quickly acquired a reputation for serving food of exceptional quality. It had received a five-star rating from Mobil for 24 consecutive years, and was one of five New York City restaurants that got a four-star rating (the highest) from the *New York Times*. In a sign of slippage, however, its ranking in the *Zagat Survey of New York City Restaurants* dropped to eighth from being perennially at or near the top for much of the 1970s and 1980s.

ESTIMATING CASH FLOWS

The following are some of the background facts on Lutèce:

- The restaurant can seat 92 diners. It has one seating for lunch and two seatings for dinner. It fills in 70% of its seats at lunchtime and 80% of its seats at dinner.
- The restaurant is open 340 days every year and closed for the remaining 25 days.
- The average price of lunch is $30, and the average price of a dinner is $66. Approximately one-third of this is for liquor.
- There are 42 employees on the staff of the restaurant. The cost of food is approximately 30% of the price of the meal, and the payroll amounts to $1.25 million a year.
- The annual rent for the space used by Lutèce is $600,000.

Table 27.5 is an estimation of the after-tax operating cash flows in 1994 for Lutèce:

TABLE 27.5   Earnings in most recent year—Lutèce

Revenues	Assumption	Base year
Lunch	70% occupancy; $30 per person	$ 656,880
Dinner	80% occupancy; $66 per person	$3,303,168
Total Expenses		$3,960,048
Food	30% of revenues	$1,188,014
Staff $	1,250,000 for staff expenses	$1,250,000
Rent	Annual rent for premises	$ 600,000
Total		$3,038,014
EBIT		$ 922,034
Taxes	Tax rate of 40%	$ 368,813
EBIT(1 − t)		$ 553,220

These cash flows are expected to grow 6% a year for three years and 3% a year after that. Table 27.6 summarizes the expected after-tax earnings over the next three years.

ESTIMATING DISCOUNT RATES

The acquirer in this case, Ark Restaurants, has a relatively low beta (0.7) and gets only about 10% of its financing needs from debt. Assuming that the underlying risk in investing in Lutèce is similar, the cost of equity can be estimated as follows:

$$\text{Cost of equity} = 8\% + 0.7(5.5\%) = 11.85\%$$

(This assumes that the long-term Treasury bond rate is 8% and an equity risk premium of 5.5%.)

TABLE 27.6 Expected After-tax Earnings—Lutèce

=	Base Year	1	2	3
Revenues	$3,960,048	$4,197,651	$4,449,510	$4,716,481
Expenses	$3,038,014	$3,220,295	$3,413,513	$3,618,324
EBIT	$ 922,034	$ 977,356	$1,035,997	$1,098,157
Taxes	$ 368,813	$ 390,942	$ 414,399	$ 439,263
EBIT(1 − t)	$ 553,220	$ 586,413	$ 621,598	$ 658,894

If Ark Restaurants can borrow money at 9% and faces a 40% tax rate, the cost of capital can be calculated as follows:

$$\text{Cost of capital} = 11.85\% \times (.90) + 9\%(1 - 0.4) \times (.10) = 11.21\%$$

ESTIMATING VALUE

The value of Lutèce can be estimated by discounting the cash flows at the weighted average cost of capital. Allowing for a growth rate of 6% over the next three years and 3% after that, the value of the restaurant can be estimated as follows:

$$\text{Value at end of high-growth period} = \frac{\text{EBIT}_3(1 - t)/(1 + g_n)}{\text{WACC} - g_n}$$

$$= \frac{\$658,894(1.03)}{(.1121 - .03)} = \$8,271,309$$

$$\text{Value of Lutèce} = \frac{586,413}{1.1121} + \frac{\$621,598}{1.1121^2} + \frac{\$658,894 + \$8,271,309}{1.1121^3}$$

$$= \$7,524,559$$

VALUING THE KEY PERSON

There would probably be no argument that some of Lutèce's value derives from Andre Soltner's presence as chef. It would be worth examining how much this value would change if he were to be replaced by somebody else. The simplest way to evaluate this effect is to:

- Estimate the effect on occupancy of replacing Mr. Soltner with another chef and on cash flows. To the extent that occupancy and cash flows decline, the value of the restaurant will decline.
- Calculate the value of the restaurant based on the discounted cash flows.

In extreme cases, where the entire value of an enterprise depends on one person, the value can drop to essentially zero if the key person were to leave or die. In less extreme cases, the value of the key person can be estimated to be the difference in value of the enterprise with and without that person in place.

Valuing Trademarks, Copyrights, and Licenses

Trademarks, copyrights, and licenses all give the owner the exclusive right to produce a product or provide a service. Fundamentally, their value is derived from the cash flows that can be generated from the exclusive right. To the extent that there is a cost associated with production, the value comes from the excess returns that come from having the exclusive right.

As with other assets, you can value trademarks or copyrights in one of two ways. You can estimate the expected cash flows from owning the asset, attach a discount rate to these cash flows that reflects their uncertainty, and take the present value, which will yield a discounted cash flow valuation of the asset. Alternatively, you can attempt a relative valuation, where you apply a multiple to the revenues or income that you believe you can generate from the trademark or copyright. The multiple is usually estimated by looking at what similar products have sold for in the past.

In making these estimates, you are likely to run into estimation issues unique to these assets. First, you have to consider the fact that a copyright or trademark provides you with exclusive rights for a finite period. Consequently, the cash flows you will estimate will be for only this period, and there will generally be no terminal value. Second, you have to factor in the expected costs of violations of the copyright and trademark. These costs can include at least two items. The first is the legal and monitoring cost associated with enforcing exclusivity. The second is the fact that no matter how careful you are with the monitoring, you cannot ensure that there will be no violations, and the lost revenues (profits) that arise as a consequence will lower the value of the right.

ILLUSTRATION 27.5:   Valuing the Copyright on Investment Valuation in 2024

Assume that John Wiley & Sons has been approached by another publisher that is interested in buying the copyright to this book (*Investment Valuation*). To estimate the value of the copyright, we will make the following assumptions[4]:

■ The book is expected to generate $150,000 in after-tax cash flows (hopeful thinking, I know) each year for the next three years to Wiley, and $100,000 a year for the subsequent two years. These are the cash flows after author royalties, promotional expenses, and production costs.

■ About 40% of these cash flows are from large organizations that make bulk orders and are considered predictable and stable. The cost of capital applied to these cash flows is 7%.

■ The remaining 60% of the cash flows are to the general public, and this segment of the cash flows is considered much more volatile. The cost of capital applied to these cash flows is 10%.

The value of the copyright can be estimated in Table 27.7 using these cash flows and the cost of capital that has been supplied:

TABLE 27.7   Expected Cash flows from Trademark

Year	Cash Flows (Stable)	PV@ 7%	Cash Flows (Volatile)	PV@ 10%
1	$60,000	$ 56,075	$90,000	$ 81,818
2	$60,000	$ 52,406	$90,000	$ 74,380
3	$60,000	$ 48,978	$90,000	$ 67,618
4	$40,000	$ 30,516	$60,000	$ 40,981
5	$40,000	$ 28,519	$60,000	$ 37,255
Total		$216,494		$302,053

The value of the copyright, with these assumptions, is $518,547 (the sum of $216,494 and $302,053).

---

[4]We are intentionally making these assumptions as optimistic as I can. We hope you, as the reader, can make the actual cash flows resemble our estimates.

COLLECTIBLES

Assets that do not produce cash flows cannot be valued using discounted cash flow models. They derive their value from a combination of factors—a scarcity of supply relative to demand, consumption utility, and individual perceptions. While they can be valued relative to comparables, their values are also much more volatile since they are based entirely on perceptions. There are a wide range of investments that fall under this category, from limited edition Barbie dolls, to rare coins, to wine.

Pricing a Investment with No cash Flows

The biggest difference between these investment and cash-flow–generating assets is that there is no intrinsic value backing up the price. Consequently, the only way to value these assets is by using relative valuation (i.e., by looking at how similar assets are priced in the market).

The process of using comparables in valuing an asset is straightforward, at least in the abstract. The first step in the process is to collect the pricing statistics of comparable assets. The second is to estimate a measure of standardized pricing for this group. The third is to control for differences between assets in this group, and the asset being valued to arrive at a measure of reasonable value for the asset. The problems in applying this approach are:

- Finding comparable assets may be difficult to do for some noncash-flow–producing assets. While there are indices compiled on various unconventional assets, there are substantial differences between the assets within each index.
- The markets for many of these assets are neither liquid nor public. Many transactions are private, and the reported prices are therefore, unreliable.
- It is not clear how one controls for differences across assets that are comparable when these differences are not quantitative but relate to perception.
- The prices of many of these assets are directly related to how scarce the supply of the asset is. For instance, the reason that the Honus Wagner T-206 baseball card is the most highly valued card on the market is because there are only 58 known cards in existence, and only one in mint condition.[5] The flip side of this is that any event that alters this balance will affect the price. Thus, a surprise find of another mint-condition Honus Wagner card in someone's attic can cause the price to change dramatically.

Artwork

There are many investors who view investments in art and collectibles as part of their overall portfolios. In that context, it is worth asking the following questions.

The first relates to the returns that these investments generate for investors over long periods. There are a number of studies that have looked at this question. In one of the more comprehensive analyses of art as an investment, Mei and Moses (2001) constructed an index based on repeated sales of artwork. Extending their index to 2010, their results are summarized in Table 27.8.

---

[5] This is the card that sold for $640,000 in 1996 to Michael Gidwitz, an investor from Chicago. The card had been earlier owned by Wayne Gretzky, the hockey great, who bought it for $451,000 in 1991.

TABLE 27.8 Returns on Fine Art versus Financial Investments 1961–2010

	Art		Stocks	
	Average	Std deviation	Average	Std deviation
1875–2010	4.63%	44.30%	8.02%	17.79%
1910–2010	5.67%	28.40%	7.79%	19.09%
1960–2010	9.49%	17.10%	11.10%	17.06%

TABLE 27.9 Correlation between Investments: 1961–2010

	Art	S&P 500	T-bonds
Art	1.00		
S&P 500	−0.02	1.00	
T-bonds	−0.13	0.06	1.00

As a stand-alone investment, art has earned low returns historically. In the past 50 years, the returns on art have become less volatile, but that may reflect the fact that there have been more transactions in this period than in earlier ones. Does the low return make art a bad investment? Not necessarily. Table 27.9 examines the correlation between the returns on art, stocks, and Treasury bonds. The low correlation between art and stocks may give it a place in a well-diversified portfolio of financial assets but only at the margin.

The second relates to how best to price investments in art and collectibles. In practice, they are almost always priced on a relative basis. Thus, a Picasso is usually priced by looking at what other Picassos have sold for recently. There are at least three problems that we run into in the context of valuation:

▓ The first is that this is not a very liquid market, and there are relatively few transactions. Thus, the most recent sale of a Picasso might have occurred three years ago, and a great deal might have changed in the art market since then.

▓ The second is that no two Picassos are alike, and there are substantial differences (both in style and pricing) across different paintings.

▓ The third problem is that there is the very real possibility of forgery and fraud, and much of it can be detected only by an expert eye. Consequently, the relative pricing of art and collectibles remains the province of expert appraisers, who try to overcome these problems (though not always successfully) and estimate a fair price. Like all analysts, however, they are susceptible to market moods, and bubbles and busts are just as common in this market as they are in others.

So, what are the lessons for individual investors? The first is that while art and collectibles, as a class, may balance a portfolio, you must spend substantially more time acquiring specialized knowledge to be successful with these investments than you would with financial investments. The second is that you should expect to have much higher transaction costs with investments in art and collectibles, especially at the high end of the market. The third is that you should collect baseball cards or old master paintings because you enjoy them and not just as investments. The psychological returns that you receive will then compensate for the substandard financial returns that you may well earn.

Gold

Paraphrasing Winston Churchill, gold is a "riddle, wrapped up in a mystery inside an enigma", at least as far as we are concerned. That does not mean, however, that we are not fascinated by the price of gold and immune from its movements. In Figure 27.4, we look at gold prices over time, in nominal and real terms:

The nominal and inflation-adjusted prices of gold soared between 2000 and 2012, dropped back between 2012 and 2015, before soaring again in the last few years. In June 2024, the nominal price was at an all-time high of 2320, and the inflation-adjusted price was close to its previous high set at the end of the 1970s.

Does Gold Have an Intrinsic Value?   The intrinsic value of an asset is a function of its expected cash flows, growth, and risk. Since gold is not a cash-flow generating asset, you cannot estimate an intrinsic value for gold. If one of the central tenets of value investing is that you should never invest in an asset without estimating its value, that would seem to rule out gold as an investment for a classic value investor. In fact, Warren Buffett has repeatedly argued against investing in gold because it's value cannot be estimated.

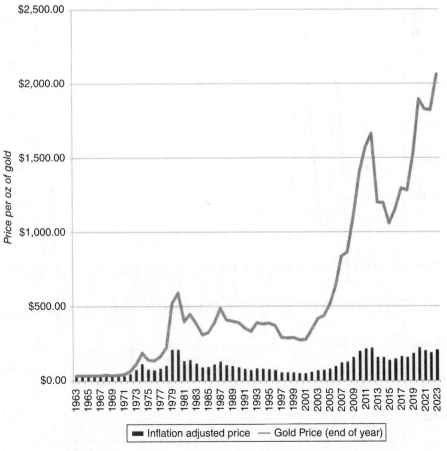

FIGURE 27.4   Gold Prices—Historical Data from 1964 to 2023

There is an alternate route that can be used to estimate the "fundamental" value of a commodity by gauging the demand for the commodity (based on its uses) and the supply. While that may work, at least in principle, for industrial commodities, it is tough to put into practice with precious metals in general and gold, because the demand is not driven primarily by practical uses.

The Drivers of Gold Prices   If gold does not have an intrinsic value, what is it that drives its price? There are at least three factors historically that have influenced the price of gold:

1. *Inflation:* If as is commonly argued that gold is an alternative to paper currency, you can then argue that the price of gold will be determined by how much trust individuals have in paper currency. Thus, it is widely believed that if the value of paper currency is debased by inflation, gold will gain in value. To see if the widely held view of gold as a hedge against inflation has a basis, we looked at changes in gold prices and the inflation rate each year from 1963–2023 in Figure 27.5:
    The co-movement of gold and inflation is particularly strong in the 1970s, a decade where the U.S. economy was plagued by high inflation and the correlation between

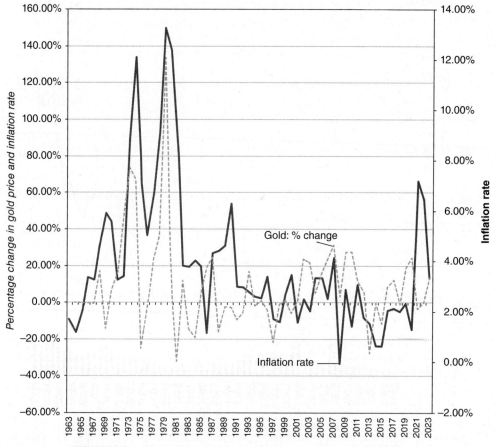

FIGURE 27.5   Returns on Gold versus Inflation Rate: 1963—2023

gold prices and the inflation rate is brought home, when you regress returns on gold against the inflation rate for the entire period:

$$\text{Annual \% Change in Gold price} = -0.06 + 3.97(\text{Inflation rate}) \quad R^2 = 19.4\%$$
$$(1.27) \quad (3.86)$$

While this regression does back the conventional view of gold as an inflation hedge, there are two potential weak spots. The first is that the R-squared is only 20%, suggesting that factors other than inflation have a significant effect on gold prices. The second is that removing the 1970s essentially removes much of the significance from this regression. In fact, while the large move in gold prices in the 1970s can be explained by unexpectedly high inflation during the decade, the rise of oil prices between 2001 and 2012 cannot be attributed to inflation. In fact, taking a closer look at the data, gold is more a hedge against extreme (and unexpected) movements in inflation, and does not really provide much protection against smaller inflation changes.

2. *Fear of crisis:* Through the centuries, gold has been the "asset" of last resort for investors fleeing a crisis. Thus, as investor fears ebb and flow, gold prices should go up and down. To test this effect, we used two forward-looking measures of investor fears—the default spread on a Baa-rated bond and the implied equity risk premium (which is a forward-looking premium, computed based upon stock prices and expected cash flows). As investor fears increase, you should expect to see these premiums in both the equity and the bond market increase, and gold rise in concurrence. Figure 27.6 summarizes the risk premiums in financial markets (bond default spreads and equity risk premiums) and gold returns each year.

While the relationship is harder to decipher than the one with inflation, higher equity risk premiums correlate with higher gold prices. Again, regressing annual returns on gold against these two measures separately, we get:

$$\text{Annual \% Change in Gold price} = -0.13 + 5.20(\text{ERP}) \quad R \text{ squared} = 5.0\%$$
$$(0.98) \quad (1.76)$$

$$\text{Annual \% Change in Gold price} = 0.12 - 1,01(\text{Baa Rate} - \text{T.Bond Rate})$$
$$(0.15) \quad (0.23)$$
$$R \text{ squared} = 0\%$$

These regressions suggest little or no relationship between bond default spreads and gold prices, but a modest positive relationship, albeit one with substantial noise, between gold prices and equity risk premiums. Thus, gold prices seem to move more with fear in the equity markets than with concerns in the bond market. Every 1% increase in the equity risk premium translates into an increase of 5.20% in gold prices.

3. *Real interest rates:* One of the costs of holding gold is that while you hold it, it earns nothing in the form of cash flows. The magnitude of this opportunity cost is captured by the real interest rate, with higher real interest rates translating into much higher opportunity costs, and thus, lower prices for gold. The real interest rate can be measured directly using the inflation-indexed treasury bond (TIPs) rate, or indirectly by netting out the expected inflation from a nominal risk-free (or close to risk free) rate. Figure 27.7 summarizes real interest rates and gold price changes on a year-by-year basis from 1963 to 2023.

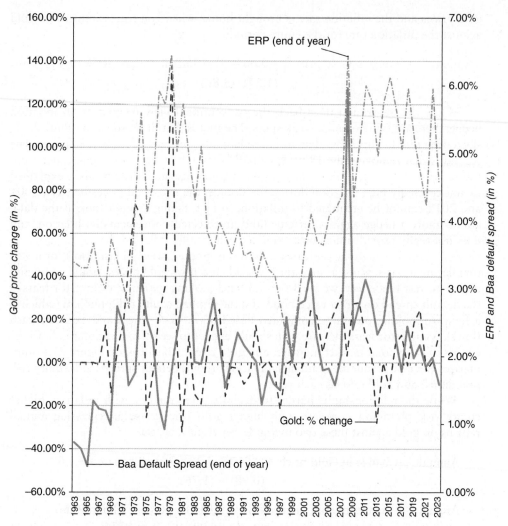

FIGURE 27.6 Market Risk Premia and Returns on Gold

Note that the TIPs rate is available only for the two decades, and that the real interest rate is computed as the difference between the ten-year U.S. treasury bond rate in that year and the realized inflation rate (rather than the expected inflation rate). Regressing changes in gold prices against the real interest rate yields the following:

$$\text{Annual \% Change in Gold price} = 0.18 - 4.68(\text{T.Bond Rate} - \text{Inflation Rate})$$
$$(0.55) \quad (2.93)$$
$$\text{R squared} = 22.0\%$$

High real interest rates are negative for gold prices, and low real interest rates, or negative real interest rates, push gold prices higher.

FIGURE 27.7 Market Risk Premia and Returns on Gold

Pricing Gold Knowing that gold prices move with inflation, equity risk premiums, and real interest rates is useful, but it still does not help us answer the fundamental question of whether gold prices today are too high or low. Can you price gold against other investments or itself?

A. Against Inflation In companion papers, Erb and Harvey (2015) examine the relationship between gold prices and inflation. In these papers, the price of gold is related to the CPI index and a ratio of gold prices to the CPI index is computed. We try to replicate their findings, and we use the U.S. Department of Labor CPI index for all items (and all urban consumers) set to a base of 100 in 1982–1984 but with data going back to 1947. The level of the index in December 2023 was 308.742. Dividing the gold price of $2,063/oz on December 31, 2023, by the CPI index level, yields a value of 6.68. To get a measure of whether that number is high or low, we computed it every year going back to 1963 in Figure 27.8.

The median value is 2.93 for the 1963–2023 time period, and 3.77 for the 1971–2023 period. Thus, based purely on the comparison of the current measure of the Gold/CPI ratio to the historical medians does miss the fact that lower interest rates and inflation in the last decade may be skewing the statistics. Consequently, we regressed the Gold/CPI index

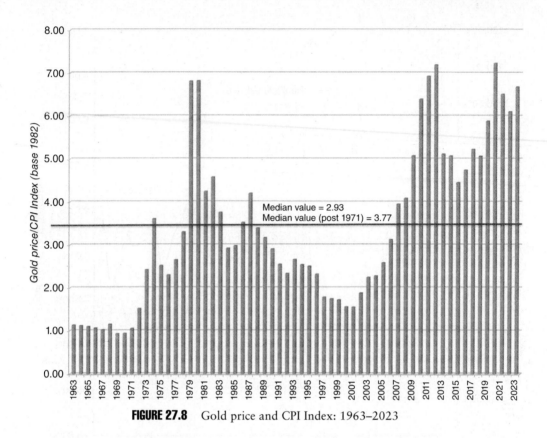

FIGURE 27.8   Gold price and CPI Index: 1963–2023

against equity risk premiums and real interest rates using the 1960–2023 time period, and while real interest rates seem to have little effect on the Gold/CPI ratio, there is strong evidence that it moves with the ERP, increasing (decreasing) as the ERP increases (decreases):

$$\text{Gold/CPI} = -1.86 + 123.24 \text{ Equity Risk Premium} \quad R^2 = 52.7\%$$
$$(2.76) \quad (8.11)$$

The implied equity risk premium for the S&P 500 at the start of June 2024 was 4.27 equity risk premium, and plugging that value into the gold/CPI regression yields the following:

$$\text{Gold/CPI (given ERP of 4.27\% in 6/24)} = -1.86 + 123.24(.0427) = 3.41$$

Put simply, gold looks overpriced in June 2024, even after correcting for changing equity risk premiums.

B. Against Other Precious Metals   There is another way that you can frame the relative value of gold, which is against other precious metals. For instance, you can price gold, relative to silver, and make a judgment on whether it is cheap or expensive (on a relative basis). At the end of December 2023, the gold price was $2062.92/oz, and the silver price was $29.47/oz, yielding a ratio of 70.00 for gold to silver prices (2602.92/29.47). To get a measure of where this number stands in a historical context, we looked at the ratio of gold prices to silver prices from 1963 to 2023 in Figure 27.9.

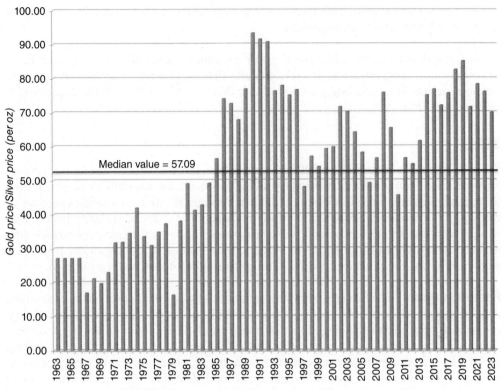

FIGURE 27.9   Gold and Silver Prices: 1963–2023

The median value of 57.09 over the 1963–2012 period would suggest that gold is overpriced, relative to silver. Given that gold and silver move together more often than they move in opposite directions, we are not sure that this relationship can be mined to address the question of whether gold is fairly priced today, but it can still be the basis for trading across precious metals.

C. Gold as Insurance   It can be argued that pricing gold relative to silver or against the inflation index misses the primary rationale for investors holding gold (i.e., as insurance against uncommon but potentially catastrophic risks to their assets, from hyperinflation to war and terrorism). Viewed from that perspective, gold operates as insurance for an investor whose assets are primarily financial, and thus, exposed to these catastrophic risks. Put in less abstract terms, if you add gold to your portfolio, it is not to make money, per se, but to buy protection against "black swan" events that could swamp your other investments. If you view gold as a hedge/insurance against event risk, there are two implications:

1. You should not expect gold to generate high annual returns over long periods. In fact, notwithstanding boom periods (the 1970s and the last decade) gold has, for the most part, generated low returns over long periods, relative to other risky investments.
2. It also follows that the price of gold should reflect the cost of buying the insurance, which in turn, will be driven by the uncertainty you feel about the future and the likelihood of catastrophic events. Thus, the multiple crises over the last decade (banking,

war, terrorism) explain both the surge in gold prices over the last decade and the cor-relation with equity risk premiums.

It is worth noting that gold is not the only insurance against black swan events. There are other ways, using other real assets (e.g., collectibles, real estate, other commodities) or financial derivatives (including puts on indices) that can deliver the same hedging results, perhaps at a lower cost.

Bitcoin

Since its inception in November 2008, there has been more written about and discussion about Bitcoin than would be merited by its collective market capitalization, which even at its peak price amounted to less than the market capitalization of a single company at the top of the market cap tables. That said, it has had advocates who clearly believe that it represents the future, unchained to governments and central banks, and critics who argue that it is worth nothing. In the section, we will look at the argument from both sides, and assess the evidence, at least in the period that Bitcoin has been around.

Pathways for Bitcoin   The first step towards a serious debate on bitcoin then has to be deciding whether it is an asset, currency, commodity, or collectible. Bitcoin is not an asset, since it does not generate cash flows standing alone for those who hold it (until you sell it). It is not a commodity, because it is not raw material that can be used in the production of something useful. The only exception that we can think of is that, if it becomes a necessary component of smart contracts, it could take on the role of a commodity; that may be Ethereum's saving grace, since it has been marketed less as a currency and more as a smart contracting lubricant. The choice then becomes whether it is a currency or a collectible, with some of its supporters tilting towards the former and others the latter. Broadly, there are three possible paths that we see for Bitcoin, looking at it even through the eyes of its advocates and critics.

1. *A Global Digital Currency:* In the best-case scenario, Bitcoin gains wide acceptance in transactions across the world, becoming a widely used global digital currency. For this to happen, it must become more stable (relative to other currencies), central banks and governments around the world have to accept its use (or at least not actively try to impede it), and the aura of mystery around it has to fade. If that happens, it could compete with fiat currencies, and given the algorithm set limits on its creation, its high price could be justified.
2. *Gold for Millennials:* In this scenario, Bitcoin becomes a haven for those who do not trust central banks, governments, and fiat currencies. In short, it takes on the role that gold has, historically, for those who have lost trust in or fear centralized authority. It is interesting that the language of Bitcoin is filled with mining terminology, since it suggests that intentionally or otherwise, the creators of Bitcoin shared this vision. In fact, the hard cap on Bitcoin of 21 million is more compatible with this scenario than the first one. If this scenario unfolds, and Bitcoin shows the same staying power as gold, it will behave like gold does, rising during crises and dropping in more sanguine time periods.
3. *The 21ˢᵗ Century Tulip Bulb:* In this, the worst case scenario, Bitcoin is like a shooting star, attracting more money as it soars, from those who see it as a source of easy prof-its, but just as quickly flares out as these traders move on to something new and dif-ferent (which could be a different and better designed digital currency), leaving Bitcoin

holders with memories of what might have been. If this happens, Bitcoin could very well become the equivalent of tulip bulbs, a speculative object that saw its prices soar in the sixteen hundreds in Holland, before collapsing in the aftermath.

As to which of these pathways will unfold, if you are trading in Bitcoin, you may very well not care, since your time horizon may be in minutes and hours, not weeks, months, or years. If you have a longer-term interest in Bitcoin, though, your focus should be less on the noise of day-to-day price movements, and more on advancements on its use as a currency. Note also that you could be a pessimist on Bitcoin and other crypto currencies, but be an optimist about the underlying technology, especially block chain, and its potential for disruption.

Bitcoin as Digital Currency   In the aftermath of the 2008 crisis, when investors had lost trust in institutions, advocates for Bitcoin argued that it was well positioned to replace fiat currencies as a global digital currency. In the world that they foresaw, more and more businesses would accept Bitcoin as payment for goods and services, and consumers would be making use of their Bitcoin wallets for purchases, small and large.

More than a decade later, that promise has largely not been delivered on. Even as Bitcoin has risen in price and minted millionaires among those who were able to time their entry and exit from the Bitcoin trading market, the use of Bitcoin in transactions has lagged, as can be seen in Figure 27.10, where we look at the use of Bitcoin in transactions on a year-to-year basis.

As you can see, the number of transactions in Bitcoin stayed stagnant between 2018 and 2022, and while it did increase in 2023, the fact that it is still lightly used is backed up by other statistics. A Federal Reserve survey of U.S. households in May 2023, for instance, found that while 8% of households remained open to trading Bitcoin as investments, only 2% had used it buy something or make a payment.[6]

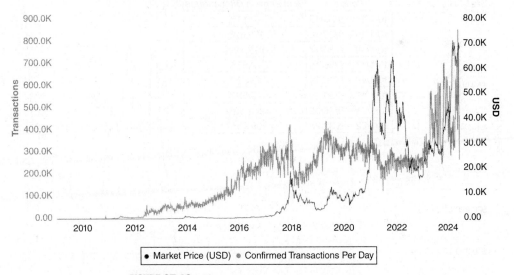

FIGURE 27.10   Business Transactions in Bitcoin

----

[6] Report on the economic well-being of U.S. households in 2022—May 2023, U.S. Federal Reserve Bank.

There are good reasons why Bitcoin has not found a foothold as a currency in wide use in business. Many of them lie in its design, with features that are not compatible with a good currency.

■ The absolute limit of 21 million bitcoin in circulation implies that, as economies adopt bitcoin as currency experience real growth, they will have to deal with deflation.
■ The dependence on blockchain to check whether buyers have blockchain in their wallets and to transfer that bitcoin to sellers removes dependence on centralized institutions, but it comes at a cost. Bitcoin is an inefficient currency, with more time and higher costs associated with every transaction.

The fact that Bitcoin has become a speculative trade adds to the problem, since there are wild swings in its price, as can be seen in Figure 27.11.

Businesses that attempt to price their goods and services in bitcoin will have to constantly reset their pricing as its price swings, and worry about the post-transaction volatility. Good currencies tend to be stable, and bitcoin is anything but.

Bitcoin advocates have been quick to celebrate small successes that the currency has enjoyed over time. In September 2021, El Salvador announced that Bitcoin would be legal tender in that country, requiring businesses to accept it, if buyers chose to pay with it. While that is an advance, it comes with two caveats. The first is that even in El Salvador, 89% of Salvadorans did not use the currency in 2023, and the government has seen instability in its

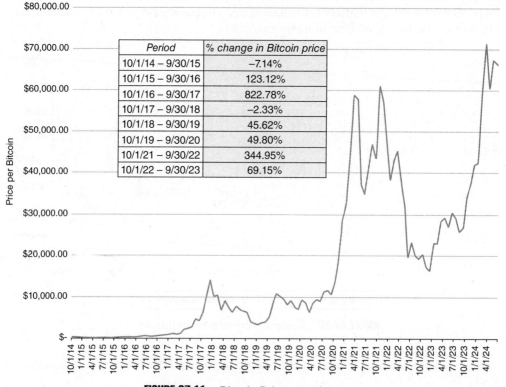

Period	% change in Bitcoin price
10/1/14 – 9/30/15	–7.14%
10/1/15 – 9/30/16	123.12%
10/1/16 – 9/30/17	822.78%
10/1/17 – 9/30/18	–2.33%
10/1/18 – 9/30/19	45.62%
10/1/19 – 9/30/20	49.80%
10/1/21 – 9/30/22	344.95%
10/1/22 – 9/30/23	69.15%

FIGURE 27.11 Bitcoin Price over time

fortunes, driven by Bitcoin price volatility. The second is, that if your argument is that Bitcoin would be good replacement for countries with failed currencies (currencies that have been ravaged by inflation and misbehaving central banks), it is a niche market and a small one.

Bitcoin as a Collectible   There is a second argument for Bitcoin, and this one is rooted in the arguments that we posited for gold in the last section. In fact, the bitcoin as millennial gold is not a bad analogy, but it needs to be stress tested. For an investment to be a good collectible, it must meet two characteristics. The first is scarcity, since any investment where the number of units can be increased significantly will lose value. The second is enduring appeal, since the investment has to be attractive to investors not just now but well into the future. Gold, the most enduring collectible in history, meets both requirements. The quantity is limited, though mining for more gold can increase the quantity but only gradually over time. The appeal is enduring, since it seems to have found a place even in ancient civilizations. With Bitcoin, the scarcity test is met, since there can be only 21 million in circulation, but the challenge will be if other digital currencies become near substitutes. The enduring appeal test is tough to run, since Bitcoin has been around for less than two decades. But advocates can point to the fact that Bitcoin, left for dead multiple times, has bounced back from repeated sell-offs during the period.

There is another test for a collectible, which is to map its behavior during crisis, since the essence of a good collectible is that it holds its value when financial assets melt down or during a crisis. While it is still early in Bitcoin's life to make a final judgment, the early returns on Bitcoin as a collectible have not been favorable. In every market crisis between 2010 and 2023, Bitcoin has behaved less like gold and more like stocks, and the riskiest stocks at that. To provide an illustration, consider the COVID market crisis in 2020, and Bitcoin's price behavior during the crisis, shown in Figure 27.12:

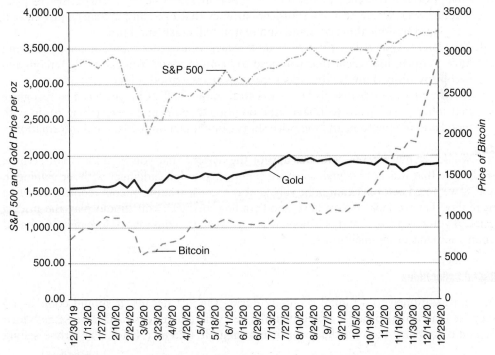

FIGURE 27.12   Bitcoin, Gold, and Stocks—The COVID Market Crisis in 2020

As stocks collapsed in the first quarter of 2020, with the S&P 500 losing a third of its value between February 14, 2020, and March 31, 2020, gold held its value, but bitcoin plummeted more than 50%, and as stocks recovered by the end of the year, bitcoin soared in price. If you are tempted to dismiss this as specific to COVID, it is worth remembering that the correlation of Bitcoin with the NASDAQ between 2014 and 2024 is 0.45, indicating that they move together much of the time and not a statistic that you would expect to see in a good collectible.

Bitcoin Reality Checks   Combining the section where we classified investments into assets, commodities, currencies, and collectibles with the one where we argued that Bitcoin is a "young" currency allows us to draw the following conclusions:

1. *Bitcoin is not an asset class:* To those who are carving out a portion of their portfolios for Bitcoin, be clear about why you are doing it. It is not because you want to have a diversified portfolio and hold all asset classes, it is because you want to use your trading skills on Bitcoin to supercharge your portfolio returns. Lest you view this as a swipe at cryptocurrencies, we would hasten to add that fiat currencies (like the U.S. dollar, Euro, or Yen) are not asset classes either.
2. *You cannot value Bitcoin, you can only price it:* This follows from the acceptance that Bitcoin is a currency, not an asset or a commodity. Anyone who claims to value Bitcoin either has a very different definition of value than we do, or is just making up stuff as they go along.
3. *It will be judged as a currency:* In the long term, the price that you attach to Bitcoin will depend on how well it will perform as a currency. If it is accepted widely as a medium of exchange and is stable enough to be a store of value, it should command a high price. If it becomes a fringe currency that investors flee to during crises, its price will be lower. Worse, if it is a transient currency that loses all purchasing power, as it is replaced by something new and different, it will crash and burn.
4. *You don't invest in Bitcoin, you trade it:* Since you cannot value Bitcoin, you don't have a critical ingredient that you need to be an investor. You can trade Bitcoin and become wealthy doing so, but it is because you are a good trader.
5. *Good trader ingredients:* To be a successful trader in Bitcoin, you need to recognize that moves in its price will have little do with fundamentals, everything to do with mood and momentum, and big price shifts can happen on incremental information.

Would we buy Bitcoin? No, but not for the reasons that you think. It is not because we believe that it is overvalued, since we cannot make that judgment without valuing it, and as we noted before, it cannot be valued. It is because trading bitcoin requires a trading mentality that we lack. If you have good trading instincts, you should play the pricing game, if you recognize that it is a game where you can win millions or lose millions, based upon your calls on momentum.

Digital Collectibles

As we transitioned to a digital economy during the last decade, it should come as no surprise that you also saw a rise in digital asset, where investors paid for original video or audio content, many in the form of nonfungible tokens (NFTs). The prime selling

TABLE 27.10 Most Highly Priced NFTs (as of 2023)

NFT	Price paid (in $ millions)
Everydays: The First 5000 Days by Beeple	$ 69.30
Clock by Pak	$ 52.70
Human One by Beeple	$ 28.90
CryptoPunk 5822	$237.00
CryptoPunk 7523	$ 11.75
Tpunk 3442	$ 10.50
CryptoPunk 4156	$ 10.26
CryptoPunk 5577	$ 7.70
CryptoPunk 3100	$ 7.58
CryptoPunk 7804	$ 7.57

point was that each NFT is unique, and therefore, would see prices rise over time. We accept the scarcity argument, but we are skeptical about the enduring appeal of these digital assets.

Just to provide a measure of how much investors (or traders) have paid for NFTs in recent years, Table 27.10 lists the most highly priced NFTs of the last few years:

A decade from now, will any of these still be on the list? We cannot rule it out, but until we feel more secure in NFTs holding their appeal, they are, at best, short-term trades, and at worst, complete speculation.

TROPHY ASSETS

Earlier in this chapter, we drew a divide between assets, which generate cash flows, and collectibles, which do not. There is a subgrouping of assets, though, that is worth carving out and considering differently, and we will call these *trophy assets*. A trophy asset has expected cash flows and can be valued like any other asset, but the people who buy it often do so, less for its asset status and more as a collectible. Powered by emotional factors, the prices of trophy assets can rise above values and stay higher, since, unlike other assets, there is no catalyst that will cause the gap between price and value to close. So, what is it that makes it a "trophy asset"?

1. *Emotional appeal overwhelms financial characteristics:* The key to a trophy asset is that the core of its attraction, to potential buyers or investors, lies less in business models and cash flows, and more in the emotional appeal it has to buyers. That appeal may be only to a subset of individuals, but these buyers want to own the asset more for the emotional dividends, not the cashflows.
2. *It is unique:* Trophy assets pack a punch because they are unique, insofar as they cannot be replicated by someone, even if that someone has substantial financial resources.
3. *It is scarce:* For trophy assets to command a pricing that is significantly higher than value, they have to be scarce.
4. *It is bought and held for nonfinancial reasons:* If trophy assets are opened for bidding, the winning bidder will almost always be an individual or entity that is buying the asset more for its history or provenance, not its financial characteristics.

Examples of trophy assets can range the spectrum from legendary real estate properties, such as the Ritz Carlton in London, to publications like the *Economist* or the *Financial Times* and as we'll argue in this chapter, many of the most prominent sports franchises in the world.

Consequences   Once an asset crosses the threshold to trophy status, you can expect the following to occur. First, it will look overpriced, relative to financial fundamentals (earnings, revenues, cash flows), and relative to peer group assets that do not enjoy the same trophy status. Second, and this is critical, even as price increases relative to value, the mechanism that causes the gap to close, often stemming from a recognition that that you have paid too much for something, given its capacity to generate earnings and cash flows, will stop working. After all, if buyers price trophy assets based upon their emotional connections, they are entering into the transaction knowing that they have paid too much and do not care. Third, and this follows from the first point, the forces that cause the prices of trophy assets to change from period to period will have a *weak or no relationship to the fundamentals* that would normally drive value.

There is an interesting question of whether a publicly traded company can acquire trophy status, and while our answer, ten or twenty years ago, would have been a quick no, we must pause before we answer it now. As many of you know, we have tried to value Tesla many times, and while some of the pushback has come from those who disagree with the contours of our story and our expectations, some of it has come from people who have not only invested a large proportion of their wealth in the company, but have done so because they want to be part of what they see as a historical disruptor—one that will upend the way we not only drive but live. The implication then is that Tesla will trade at prices that are difficult to justify, given the company's financials, that it will attract a subset of investors who receive emotional dividends from owning the stock and that short-selling the stock, on the expectation that the gap will close, will be a perilous exercise.

Sports Franchises as Trophy Assets   When the Rooney family bought the Pittsburg Steelers, now a storied franchise in the most highly priced sports league (NFL) in 1932 for $2,500, it was very likely that they were buying it as a business, hoping to generate enough in ticket sales to cover their costs and earn a profit. After all, football (at least the American version) was a nascent sport not widely followed, with just a few teams, and no organized structure. In fact, you can still view the Steelers as a business and value them as such, but as we will argue in this section, that number will bear little resemblance to the $4 billion pricing that Forbes attached to the team in 2022. In fact, sports franchises across the world have already become, or are increasingly on the pathway to becoming, trophy assets.

Prices Disconnect from Fundamentals   To value a sports franchise as a business, it is worth examining how the revenues for franchises have evolved over time. Until the last 50 years, almost all the revenues for sports franchises came from gate receipts collected from fans coming in to watch games, and the food and merchandise that these fans bought, usually at the games they attended. With television entering the picture and streaming augmenting it, the portion of revenues that sports franchises get from media has become a larger and larger slice of the pie, as can be seen in Figure 27.13, where we look at gate receipts, media revenue, and other (merchandizing and sponsorship) revenues for all U.S. sports franchises between 2006 and 2022:

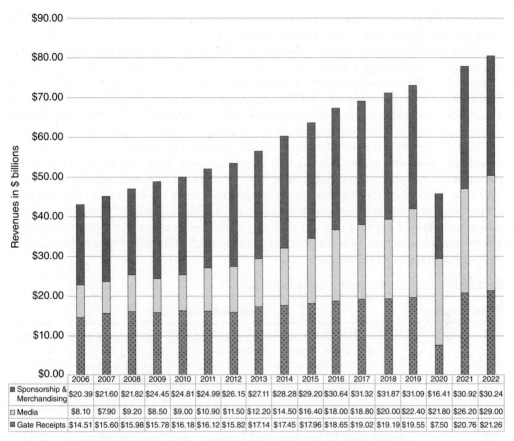

	2006	2007	2008	2009	2010	2011	2012	2013	2014	2015	2016	2017	2018	2019	2020	2021	2022
■ Sponsorship & Merchandising	$20.39	$21.60	$21.82	$24.45	$24.81	$24.99	$26.15	$27.11	$28.28	$29.20	$30.64	$31.32	$31.87	$31.09	$16.41	$30.92	$30.24
▢ Media	$8.10	$7.90	$9.20	$8.50	$9.00	$10.90	$11.50	$12.20	$14.50	$16.40	$18.00	$18.80	$20.00	$22.40	$21.80	$26.20	$29.00
▨ Gate Receipts	$14.51	$15.60	$15.98	$15.78	$16.18	$16.12	$15.82	$17.14	$17.45	$17.96	$18.65	$19.02	$19.19	$19.55	$7.50	$20.76	$21.26

FIGURE 27.13   Revenues at U.S. Sports Franchises—2006–2022

As you can see, the overall revenues for sports franchises has grown between 2006 and 2022, with 2020 being the COVID outlier, but much of that growth has come from the media slice of revenues, as gate receipts have flatlined. This is clearly not just a U.S. phenomenon, and you are seeing the same process play out in Europe (with soccer the big beneficiary) and in India (with cricket the winner).

To value a sports franchise, you not only have to consider how much of a draw the team is at the stadium, but how much revenue the team gets from its media contracts as well as merchandising and sponsorship revenues. While the gate receipts and merchandising revenues are significant, they are relatively easy to forecast, given the history and ticket sales. Media revenues, though, are tricky, since they are determined partly by the size of the media market in which the team operates, and partly by how the sports franchise that the team belongs to shares its media revenues. In the United States, for example, baseball teams get a significant portion of their broadcasting revenues from local TV rights, and as a consequence, teams in the biggest media markets (e.g., Yankees and Mets in New York, Dodgers in Los Angeles) have higher revenues than teams in smaller media market (e.g., Mariners in Seattle). In contrast, the media revenues for football (NFL) are mostly national, and those revenues are equally divided across the teams, resulting in more equitable media revenues across NFL teams. That difference explains why the divergence between the highest- and lowest-priced teams is greater in baseball than the NFL. Table 27.11 provides a comparison of how media revenues are shared across teams by franchise.

While all the franchises pay lip service to the need for balance, with large media-market teams subsidizing small media-market teams, there is wide variation across franchises in how they follow through on fixing that imbalance. Only the NFL has a strong enough system in place to create full balance, and that is partly because of the fact that almost all of its broadcasting revenues are national (rather than local), and partly because it is a league with a strong commissioner and weaker owners.

While revenues have risen, aided by richer broadcasting contracts, sports franchises have been faced with rising player costs; in almost every major sports franchise in the United States, player expenses account to 50% of revenues or more, and they have risen over time. Once the other expenses associated with a team are netted out, the operating profits at sports franchises are, for the most part, moderate. Looking across sports franchises, in Table 27.12, you can see that the cumulated revenue and operating income numbers, in conjunction with the collective pricing (in $ millions) of teams (as estimated by Forbes), in the most recent year.

TABLE 27.11   Revenue Sharing, by Sports Franchise

Sports Franchise	Media Revenue sharing
NFL	Almost all media revenues are from national TV contract, and every team gets an equal share of those revenues
MLB	National revenues from media rights are equally shared, but teams keep 52% of revenues from local broadcasting, giving big-market teams more revenues
MBA	National TV is equally shared, but local TV accounts for a large portion of media revenues. Revenue sharing across teams does enable some of these revenues to be transferred from richer to poorer teams
NHL	Mostly local TV revenues, with revenue sharing; richer teams provide subsidies to poorer teams
MLS	Teams do not have owners, with the investor–operators who run these teams invested in the MLS, which collects all television revenues
Premier League	Every Premier League team splits base payments of the broadcasting rights each season. Additional revenue is then added to each club, based on how often their matches are selected for live TV.
IPL	Share of media revenue, based upon ranking of team at the end of the season, with higher-ranked teams getting a higher percent.

TABLE 27.12   Operating Metrics, by Sports Franchise

Sports Franchise	Collective Pricing	Revenues	Operating Income	Operating Margin	EV/ Revenues	EV/Operating Profit
NFL	$132,500	$16,101	$4,671	29.01%	8.23	28.37
MLB	$ 69,550	$10,320	$ 874	8.46%	6.74	79.62
NBA	$ 85,910	$10,023	$2,948	29.41%	8.57	29.15
NHL	$ 32,350	$ 5,931	$1,573	26.53%	5.45	20.56
MLS	$ 16,200	$ 1,549	$ 34	2.19%	10.46	476.47
Premier League	$ 30,255	$ 6,442	$ 520	8.07%	4.70	58.23
IPL	$ 10,430	$ 1,087	$ 150	13.80%	9.60	69.53

While team financials tend to be opaque, Forbes estimated that the NFL, the richest sports franchise in the world, generated about $4.7 billion in operating profit on revenues of approximately $16 billion in 2022. The NBA is the next-most profitable franchise, whereas baseball collectively struggles to make money. More to the point, if you use the Forbes pricing estimates for teams, note that four of the seven franchises (NFL, NBA, MLS and IPL) trade at eight to ten times revenues and at high multiples of operating income. It is true that there are tech companies in the market that trade at similar multiples, but those companies have extraordinary growth potential ahead of them and new markets to conquer. Even if you believe that media rights will continue to be the goose that lays the golden eggs for sports franchises, it is difficult to see how you justify these pricing multiples. To show that the disconnect between what buyers are paying for franchises and what they are getting back in return has been growing over time, we look at the pricing of NFL teams over time, relative to revenues at these teams (which include the richer media contracts) from 2012 to 2022 in Figure 27.14.

Over the last decade, you can see that the pricing of NFL teams has risen from just over four times revenues in 2012 to more than seven times revenues in 2022. In short, NFL franchise prices are rising at rates that cannot be explained by revenue growth, richer media contracts notwithstanding, or higher profitability.

A New Breed of Owners   At the start of this section, we noted that the Rooneys bought the Pittsburg Steelers in 1932 for $2,500, and that they continue to own the Steelers. While it is conceivable that they think of the Steelers as a business they own that has to continue to deliver earnings for them, much of the rest of the NFL has seen a changing of

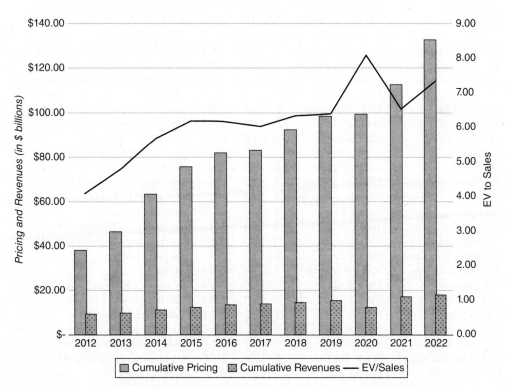

FIGURE 27.14   Pricing of NFL Franchises Over—Time

the guard, with new owners replacing the older holdouts. Many of these new owners are already wealthy, with their wealth accumulated in a different setting (real estate, private equity, venture capital), when they buy professional sports teams, and from the outset, it seems clear that they are less interested in turning a profit, and more in playing the role of team owner. To illustrate, we focus on the NBA, where there has been much turnover in the ownership ranks, with close to two-thirds of the teams acquiring new owners in the last two decades, in Table 27.13.

As you browse this list, you will note that while many of the owners are billionaires, not counting their NBA team ownership, there are a few owners towards the bottom of the list whose wealth is primarily in their team ownership. Looking for trends, the more

TABLE 27.13   NBA Team Owners in 2023

Team	Owner	Wealth (billions)	Year Bought	Business Background
Indiana Pacers	Herb Simon	$ 2.80	1983	Real estate
Chicago Bulls	Jerry Reinsdorf	$ 1.50	1985	Real estate
Portland Trailblazers	Paul Allen (family)	$20.30	1988	Microsoft co-founder
Orlando Magic	Richard DeVos	$ 5.40	1991	Amway co-founder
San Antoni Spurs	Peter Holt	$ 0.20	1993	Tractor dealership
Minnesota Timberwolves	Glen Taylor	$ 2.50	1994	Taylor Corporation owner
New York Knicks	James Dolan	$ 2.00	1994	Cablevision (Founder's son)
Miami Heat	Mickey Arison	$ 5.90	1995	Carnival Corp (Founder's son)
LA Lakers	Phillip Anschutz	$10.10	1998	Oil, Railroad,Telecom, Entertainment
Toronto Raptors	Larry Tanenbaum	$ 1.50	1998	Construction and Broadcasting
Denver Nuggets	Stanley Kroenke	$ 8.30	2000	Real Estate
Dallas Mavericks	Mark Cuban	$ 4.20	2000	Company founder and Venture Capital
Boston Celtics	Wyc Grousbeck	$ 0.40	2002	Venture capital
Cleveland Cavaliers	Dan Gilbert	$44.80	2005	Quicken founder
Oklahoma City Thunder	Clay Bennett	$ 0.40	2006	Media (inheritance)
Utah Jazz	Gail Miller	$ 1.90	2009	Car dealerships
Charlotte Hornets	Michael Jordan	$ 1.60	2010	Basketball player (and legend)
Washington Wizards	Theodore Leonsis	$ 1.40	2010	Media and Entertainment
Golden State Warriors	Joe Lacob	$ 1.20	2010	Venture Capital
Detroit Pistons	Tom Gores	$ 5.70	2011	Private Equity (Platinum Equity)
Philadelphia 76ers	Joshua Harris	$ 4.60	2011	Private Equity (Apollo Global)
Memphis Grizzliers	Robert Pera	$14.10	2012	Ubiquiti founder
Sacramento Kings	Vivek Ranadive	$ 0.70	2013	Software
LA Clippers	Steve Ballmer	$75.60	2014	Microsoft CEO (and employee #30)
Milwaukee Bucks	Marc Lasry	$ 1.80	2014	Private equity
Phoenix Suns	Robert Sarver	$ 0.40	2014	Banking and Real Estate
Atlanta Hawks	Tony Ressler	$ 3.90	2015	Private Equity and Venture Capital
Houston Rockets	Tilman Fertitta	$ 4.10	2017	Restaurant & hotel owner
New Orleans Pelicans	Gayle Benson	$ 3.30	2018	Car dealerships and banks
Brooklyn Nets	Joseph Tsai	$14.20	2019	Alibaba co-founder

recent a sports franchise transaction, the more likely it is that the buyer is not just wealthy, but immensely so, and this pattern is playing out across the world.

So, why would these wealthy, and presumably financially savvy, individuals put their money into sports teams? In 2014, at the end of a post on the Clippers, and after attempting in every conceivable way to find a financial justification why Ballmer would pay $2 billion for an NBA team that was a distant second to the other NBA team that played in the same city, we threw up our hands and concluded that Ballmer was buying a toy. By our estimates, it was an expensive toy that we estimated to cost about a billion (the estimate of the difference between the price he paid and our estimated value), but one that he could well afford, given his wealth.

In many ways, sports franchises are the ultimate trophy assets, since they are scarce and owning them not only allows you to live out your childhood dreams, but also gives you a chance to indulge your friends and family with front-row seats and player introductions. In fact, it also explains the entry of sovereign wealth funds, especially from the Middle East, into the ownership ranks, especially in the Premier League. If you couple this reality with the fact that winner-take-all economies of the twenty-first century deliver more billionaires in our midst, you can see why there is no imminent correction on the horizon for sports franchise pricing. As long as the number of billionaires exceeds the number of sports franchises on the face of the Earth, you should expect to see fewer and fewer owners like the Rooneys, and more and more like the Steves (Cohen and Ballmer).

ILLUSTRATION 27.6:   Valuing a Sports Franchise—The Clippers in 2014

Steve Ballmer offered $2 billion for the Los Angeles Clippers in 2014. At the time, we estimated the intrinsic value of the franchise, looking at four scenarios, ranging from an extrapolation of the Clipper's 2012 financials to a best-case scenario, where we modeled out a much larger media revenue stream, in Table 27.14.

As you can see, none of the measures of intrinsic value are close to the $2 billion pricing.

TABLE 27.14   Clippers—Intrinsic Value

	Clipper: 2012 numbers	*Median values*	*Laker-like (2012)*	*Best/best scenario*
Revenues	$128.00	$139.00	$295.00	$ 295.00
EBITDA margin	11.72%	11.29%	22.51%	49.31%
EBITDA	$ 15.00	$ 15.70	$ 66.40	$ 145.45
DA	$ 0.00	$ 0.00	$ 0.00	$ 0.00
EBIT	$ 15.00	$ 15.70	$ 66.40	$ 145.45
Taxes	$ 6.00	$ 6.28	$ 26.56	$ 58.18
EBIT (1 − t)	$ 9.00	$ 9.42	$ 39.84	$ 87.27
Reinvestment	$ 1.80	$ 1.88	$ 3.98	$ 8.73
FCFF	$ 7.20	$ 7.54	$ 35.86	$ 78.55
ROIC	12.50%	12.50%	25.00%	25.00%
Risk-free rate	2.50%	2.50%	2.50%	2.50%
Cost of capital	7.50%	7.50%	7.50%	7.50%
Expected growth rate	2.50%	2.50%	2.50%	2.50%
Value of team	$147.60	$154.48	$735.05	$1,610.18

With information on how investors/buyers have priced sports franchises in hand, we tried to price the Clippers using a rudimentary combination of variables: the annual revenues of the franchise and a multiple of revenues gleaned from the historical transactions, in Table 27.15:

TABLE 27.15 Clippers—The Pricing

	Clipper revenues + Median EV/Sales for NBA	Laker-like revenues + Median EV/Sales for NBA	Laker-like revenues + Maximum EV/Sales for NBA	Your estimates
Revenues	$128.00	$295.00	$ 295.00	$ 300.00
EV/Sales	3.30	3.30	5.14	5.25
Estimated Enterprise value	$422.56	$973.87	$1,516.36	$1,575.00

As with the intrinsic valuations, it is difficult to justify a $2 billion price tag on the Clippers, even with assumptions that stretch credibility. There may be more fanciful multiples that deliver a price closer to $2 billion. For instance, you could divide the transaction prices by the population of the metro area served by the team, and then scale this up to reflect the larger LA media market. Thus, taking the $550 million that was paid recently for Milwaukee, which has a media market one-tenth the size of the LA media market, and assuming a 50:50 split of the LA market with the Lakers, you would arrive at a value of $2.75 billion for the Clippers.

The most likely explanation for Ballmer's $2 billion offer does not lie either in intrinsic valuation or in pricing, but in his desire for an expensive toy—one that gives him a great deal of pleasure as he cheers it on from the sidelines.

CONCLUSION

This chapter provides an insight into the breadth of use that valuation models can be put to, ranging from valuing a New York City cab medallion to a five-star restaurant. The basic models remain unchanged, but the inputs may be more difficult to get and have more noise associated with them. That should, however, not be viewed as a barrier to their use.

We also looked at how best to price investments that do not generate cash flows, ranging the spectrum from artwork to gold to bitcoin, and ended the chapter with a discussion of trophy assets, where the pricing dominates intrinsic value.

QUESTIONS AND SHORT PROBLEMS

In the problems following, use an equity risk premium of 5.5 percent if none is specified.

1. Cool Café is a well-regarded restaurant in the Denver area, owned and run by Joanne Arapacio, a star chef specializing in Southwestern cuisine. You are interested in buying the restaurant and have been provided the income statement for the firm for the most recent year is reported here (in '000s):

Revenues	$5,000
– Operating expenses	$3,500
EBIT	$1,500
– Interest expenses	$ 300
– Taxes	$ 480
Net income	$ 720

The owner did not pay herself a salary last year, but you believe that you will have to pay $200,000 a year for a new chef. The restaurant is in stable growth and is expected to grow 5% a year for the next decade. You estimate the unlevered beta of publicly traded restaurants to be 0.80. The average debt-to-capital ratio for these firms is 30%, and you believe that Cool Café will have to operate at close to this average. The risk-free rate is 6%, the market risk premium is 4% and the cost of debt is 7%.

   a. Estimate the value of Cool Café.
   b. Now assume that you will see a drop-off in revenues of 15% if Joanne Arapacio leaves the restaurant. Assuming that 70% of the current operating expenses are variable and that the remaining 30% of fixed, estimate the value Ms. Arapacio to the restaurant.

2. Sick and tired of the investment banking grind, you decide to quit and buy a franchise for a fast-growing bagel chain in your town. You have been able to get information on what another franchise for the same chain is generating in revenues in the neighboring town:

   ■ The franchise has revenues of $1 million and earnings before interest and taxes of $150,000 last year, but the owner did not assess a salary for himself. He does the accounting and oversees the bagel shop, and you believe that hiring someone else to do what he does will cost you $50,000 annually.
   ■ The revenues and operating income are expected to grow 3% a year in perpetuity.
   ■ You expect to pay 35% of your income in taxes and use all of your investment savings to buy the shop. The unlevered beta for franchise food chains is 0.80, and the average correlation with the market is 0.40.
   ■ The owner has a bank loan outstanding of $300,000 and the book value of equity in the business is $200,000. However, the average market-debt-to-capital ratio of publicly traded restaurants is 20% and the average pretax cost of debt for restaurants is 8%.
   ■ The riskless rate is 5% and the market risk premium is 4%.
   Estimate the value of the bagel shop to you.

3. You work for a publishing company and are considering bidding for the copyright to *Cook Light, Cook Right*, a cookbook of low-fat recipes. While the book was out of print last year, you believe that you can generate $120,000 in after-tax cash flows next year, $100,000 the year after, and $80,000 in the following three years. If your cost of capital is 12%, estimate the value of the copyright.

4. You have been asked to value the practice of Dr. Vong, a pediatrician in your town, and are provided with the following facts:

   ■ The practice generated $800,000 in revenues last year, and these revenues are expected to grow 4% a year for the next 10 years.
   ■ Employee expenses (including nurses and secretarial help) amounted to $200,000 last year and are expected to grow 4% a year for the next 10 years.

■ The annual rent for the facilities last year was $100,000 and is expected to grow 4% a year for the next 10 years.

■ Rentals of medical equipment cost $75,000 last year, and this expense is expected to grow 5% for the next 10 years.

■ The cost of medical insurance last year was $75,000 and is expected to grow 7% a year for the next 10 years.

■ The tax rate on the income, including state and local taxes, is 40%.

■ The cost of capital is 11%.

Assuming that there will be no drop-off in revenues if a new pediatrician takes over the practice, estimate the value of the practice.

5. You are trying to decide how much you should bid on a Ken Griffey Jr. rookie baseball card in good condition on eBay. You notice that there have been eight transactions involving Ken Griffey Jr. cards in the last month on eBay:

Transaction #	Condition of Card	Price Paid for Card
1	Excellent	$800
2	Poor	$200
3	Good	$550
4	Good	$500
5	Excellent	$850
6	Good	$400
7	Poor	$350
8	Excellent	$650

a. Estimate how much you would be willing to pay for the card.

b. Now assume that the seller of the card has been rated poorly by other buyers because he has misrepresented other items he has sold to them. What effect would this information have on how much you would be willing to bid for the card?

6. Assume that you are a wealthy investor with your entire portfolio invested in stocks. Your financial adviser has suggested that you buy some fine art to balance the portfolio and based this suggestion on the low correlation between returns on stocks and returns on fine art (.10).

a. If the standard deviation of stock returns is 20% and the standard deviation in fine art returns is 15%, estimate what the standard deviation of your portfolio would be if you invested 10% of your portfolio in fine art.

b. If the expected return on stocks is 12.5% and the expected return on fine art is only 5%, would you add fine art to your portfolio? Explain why or why not. (The risk-free rate is 6%.)

CHAPTER 28

The Option to Delay and Valuation Implications

In traditional investment analysis, a project or new investment should be accepted only if the returns on the project exceed the hurdle rate; in the context of cash flows and discount rates, this translates into investing in projects with positive net present values (NPVs). The limitation of this view of the world, which analyzes projects based on expected cash flows and discount rates, is that it fails to consider fully the options that are usually associated with many investments.

This chapter considers an option that is embedded in many projects, namely the option to wait and take the project in a later period. Why might a firm want to do this? If the present value of the cash flows on the project are volatile and can change over time, a project or technology that does not pass muster now may become valuable in the future. Furthermore, a firm may gain by waiting on a project even after a project has a positive net present value, because the project may have a higher value taken at a future date. This option is most valuable in projects where a firm has the exclusive right to invest in a project and becomes less valuable as the barriers to entry decline.

There are at least three cases where the option to delay can make a difference when valuing a firm. The first is undeveloped land in the hands of a real estate investor or company. The choice of when to develop rests in the hands of the owner, and presumably development will occur when real estate values increase enough to justify it. The second is a firm that owns a patent or patents. Since a patent provides a firm with the exclusive rights to produce the patented product or service, it can and should be valued as an option. The third is a natural resource company that has undeveloped reserves it can choose to develop at a time of its choosing—presumably when the price of the resource is high.

REAL OPTIONS: PROMISE AND PITFALLS

In Chapter 5, we introduced the basics of option pricing, drawing on their unique payoff diagrams, with limited losses and potentially unlimited profits, to talk about why risk (uncertainty) becomes an ally, increasing option value. We also introduced option pricing models, including the Black-Scholes and Binomial models, to value both short-term and long-term options. In this and the next two chapters, we will use these option mechanics to value what we loosely classify as real options, where projects, assets, and companies that have option-like characteristics, also have option value.

The Allure of Real Options

To understand the allure of real options, we will start with a very simple decision tree, with the payoff in millions, in Figure 28.1.

The expected value of this tree is −$10 million, and it would not make sense to take this investment. Now consider a variant of this tree, in Figure 28.2, with the same total upside (positive cash flows of $100 million and negative cash flows of $120 million), but with an initial branch, with smaller amounts at play.

The expected value of this tree is positive:

$$\text{Expected value} = 0.25 \times (-20) + 0.75 \times \left[20 + \frac{2}{3} \times (80) + \frac{1}{3} \times (-100)\right]$$

$$= \$25 \text{ million}$$

If you are wondering why the expected value increases from −$10 million to $25 million, it comes from having the initial branch of the tree, where you observe the outcome and adapt your behavior. In other words, a negative outcome in the first branch leads you to cut your losses at $20 million and abandon the investment. In short, you learn by observing market outcomes, and you adapt your behavior accordingly.

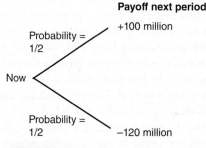

FIGURE 28.1   A Simple Decision Tree

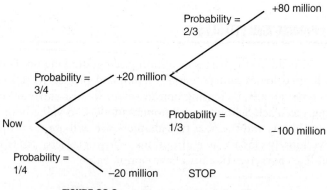

FIGURE 28.2   A Two-Step Decision Tree

Real options derive their value from those same forces. We will value undeveloped oil reserves as options later in this chapter, and the optionality comes from the owners of oil reserves observing the actual oil price and adjusting their oil development/production accordingly, developing and producing more oil when oil prices are high and less when oil prices drop. In valuation terms, an asset with a real option embedded in it will have an option value that is on top of its intrinsic.

Detecting Optionality

How do you know if there is an optionality embedded in a company or an asset? The answer lies in revisiting what makes an option an option. First, it derives its value from an underlying asset, with its value changing as the asset value changes. Second, there is a contingency that determines whether you will get cash flows from the asset. With an oil reserve, the underlying asset is the oil under the ground, and the contingency is that the value of the oil has to exceed the cost of extracting it, for it to be an in-the-money or viable option.

The follow-up test is to draw a payoff diagram for the asset, graphing cash flows on the asset against the price of the underlying asset. If that payoff diagram resembles the payoff diagram in Figure 28.3 on an option, call, or put, you have optionality that must be valued.

Does the Optionality Have Value?

Most assets have some aspect of optionality, but most of these options have little or no value. For an option to have value, you need some degree of exclusivity. Many real option advocates often use the optionality argument to justify paying premiums for entering big markets, either geographically (e.g., China at the start of this century) or technologically (e.g., AI in 2024). However, opportunities are not options, and the opportunity to enter a big market may be valuable for other reasons, but there is no optionality, unless you can offer an additional argument that the company in question has some degree of exclusivity in that big market. That exclusivity can range the spectrum from absolute (e.g., when a

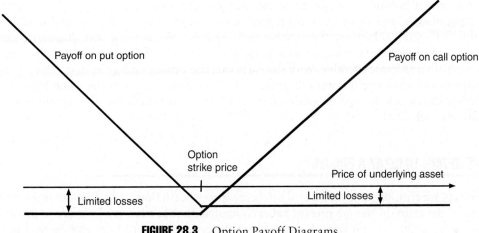

FIGURE 28.3 Option Payoff Diagrams

government or patent protects you from competition) to relative (e.g., a first mover may have an advantage over later entrants).

As we look at examples of real options in the next three chapters, we will try to identify the exclusivity that drives the option value. In this chapter, for instance, we will value patents and oil reserves as options, with the exclusivity in the form coming from legal protection and with the latter from natural scarcity.

Can an Option Pricing Model be Used?

In Chapter 5, we introduced option pricing models by noting that they were built on two planks—replication, where you create a position with the underlying stock and borrowing/lending that has the same cash flows as the option; and arbitrage, where if they trade at different prices, trading will remove the difference. Those plans work best when the underlying asset and the option are traded, and when you can lend and borrow money at the risk-free rate. Setting the second requirement apart for the moment and focusing just on the first one, real options can be problematic when it comes to pricing. First, often, neither the underlying asset nor the option is traded, making replication and arbitrage an abstraction. Second, many of the inputs you need for option pricing, and in particular, the variance comes from traded prices, and those will not be accessible for many real options.

Focusing on patents and undeveloped oil reserves, the two real options that we value in this chapter, you can see these problems come into play. With patents, where the underlying asset is the product that you have patented and the patent is the option, neither is traded and you are stretching the limits of option pricing. With undeveloped oil reserves, where it is oil under the ground that is the underlying asset, the underlying asset is traded (oil is a traded commodity), and oil companies do buy and sell reserves from each other, albeit infrequently. Since you can also use observed volatility in oil prices in your option pricing models, you are on more solid ground using option pricing models to value oil reserves.

There is a final component to real options that may affect how you price them. Unlike many listed and traded options, where early exercise is rare, and most owners hold the option until exercise, most real options generate their value by being exercised early. If, for instance, you view a patent as an option, viewing the years left of patent protection as the option life, you do not want to wait until the last moment of patent life to develop the patent into a product. The prevalence of early exercise can affect your choice of option pricing models, and there are practitioners who choose to use only binomial models to value real options, because they enable early exercise. We are not that dogmatic, since using a Black-Scholes model, notwithstanding its European option roots, will give you a conservative estimate of value, with the early exercise option adding to that value. In this chapter, with each option, we will provide the contrasting estimates of value from both models (Black-Scholes and Binominal), so that you can see the difference (or more truthfully, the lack of it).

THE OPTION TO DELAY A PROJECT

Projects are typically analyzed based on their expected cash flows and discount rates at the time of the analysis; the net present value computed on that basis is a measure of its value and acceptability at that time. Expected cash flows and discount rates change over time, however, and so does the net present value. Thus, a project that has a negative net present value now may have a positive net present value in the future. In a competitive environment, in which individual firms have no special advantages over their competitors on these projects, the fact that net present values can be positive in the future may not be significant (since they will be positive for the competitors as well). In an environment in which a project can be taken by only one firm because of legal restrictions or other entry barriers to competitors, however, the changes in the project's value over time give it the characteristics of a call option.

Payoff on the Option to Delay

Assume that a project requires an initial up-front investment of X, and that the present value of expected cash inflows from investing in the project, computed today, is V. The net present value of this project is the difference between the two:

$$NPV = V - X$$

Now assume that the firm has exclusive rights to this project for the next n years, and that the present value of the cash inflows may change over that time (but that the cost of the project stays fixed at X), because of changes in either the cash flows or the discount rate. Thus, the project may have a negative net present value right now, but it may still be a good project if the firm waits. Defining V again as the present value of the cash flows, the firm's decision rule on this project can be summarized as follows:

If V > X Invest in the project: Project has positive NPV

V < X Do not invest in the project: Project has negative NPV

If the firm does not invest in the project over its life, it incurs no additional cash flows, though it will lose what it invested to get exclusive rights to the project. This relationship can be presented in a payoff diagram of cash flows on this project, as shown in Figure 28.4, assuming that the firm holds out until the end of the period for which it has exclusive rights to the project.

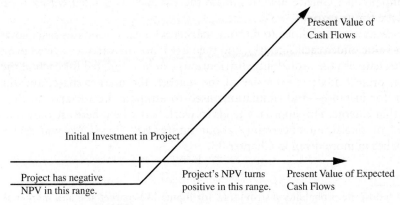

FIGURE 28.4   The Option to Delay a Project

Note that this payoff diagram is that of a call option—the underlying asset is the project, the strike price of the option is the investment needed to take the project, and the life of the option is the period for which the firm has rights to the project. The present value of the cash flows on this project and the expected variance in this present value represent the value and variance of the underlying asset.

Inputs for Valuing the Option to Delay

The inputs needed to apply option pricing theory to valuing the option to delay are the same as those needed for any option. We need the value of the underlying asset, the variance in that value, the time to expiration on the option, the strike price, the riskless rate, and the equivalent of the dividend yield.

Value of the Underlying Asset   In the case of product options, the underlying asset is the project to which the firm has exclusive rights. The current value of this asset is the present value of expected cash flows from initiating the project now, not including the up-front investment. This present value can be obtained from a standard investment analysis, discounting expected cash flows at a risk-adjusted discount rate. There is likely to be a substantial amount of error in the cash flow estimates and the present value, especially if the project is in a new business or involves an untested technology. Rather than being viewed as a problem, this uncertainty should be viewed as the reason the project delay option has value. If the expected cash flows on the project were known with certainty and were not expected to change, there would be no need to adopt an option pricing framework, since there would be no value to the option.

Variance in the Value of the Asset   As noted in the prior section, there is likely to be considerable uncertainty associated with the cash flow estimates and the present value that measures the value of the project now. This is partly because the potential market for the product may be unknown, and partly because technological shifts can change the cost structure and profitability of the product. The variance in the present value of cash flows from the project can be estimated in one of three ways:

1. If we have invested in similar projects in the past, the variance in the cash flows from those projects can be used as an estimate. This may be the way that a consumer product company like Gillette might estimate the variance associated with introducing a new blade for its razors.
2. We can assign probabilities to various market scenarios, estimate cash flows and a present value under each scenario, and then calculate the variance across present values. Alternatively, the probability distributions can be estimated for each of the inputs into the project analysis—the size of the market, the market share, and the profit margin, for instance—and simulations used to estimate the variance in the present values that emerge. This approach tends to work best when there are only one or two sources[1] of significant uncertainty about future cash flows. We will review these approaches in more detail in Chapter 33.

---

[1] In practical terms, the probability distributions for inputs like market size and market share can often be obtained from market testing.

3. We can use the variance in the value of firms involved in the same business (as the project being considered) as an estimate of the variance in present value for the project. Thus, the average variance in the value of firms involved in the software business can be used as the variance in present value of a software project.

The value of the option is largely derived from the variance in cash flows; the higher the variance, the higher the value of the project delay option. Thus, the value of an option to invest in a project in a stable business will be less than the value of one in an environment where technology, competition, and markets are all changing rapidly.

Exercise Price on Option   The option to delay a project is exercised when the firm owning the rights to the project decides to invest in it. The cost of making this initial investment is the exercise price of the option. The underlying assumption is that this cost remains constant (in present value dollars) and that any uncertainty associated with the investment is reflected in the present value of cash flows on the product. That is more an assumption of convenience than necessity, since it makes valuing the option a little easier.

Expiration of the Option and the Riskless Rate   The project delay option expires when the rights to the project lapse. Investments made after the project rights expire are assumed to deliver a net present value of zero as competition drives returns down to the required rate. The riskless rate to use in pricing the option should be the rate that corresponds to the expiration of the option. While expiration dates can be estimated easily when firms have the explicit right to a project (through a license or a patent, for instance), they become far more difficult to obtain when the right is less clearly defined. If, for instance, a firm has a competitive advantage on a product or project, the option life can be defined as the expected period over which the advantage can be sustained.

Cost of Delay   Chapter 5 noted that an American option generally will not be exercised prior to expiration. When you have the exclusive rights to a project, though, and the net present value turns positive, you would not expect the owner of the rights to wait until the rights expire to exercise the option (invest in the project). Note that there is a cost to delaying investing in a project, once the net present value turns positive. If you wait an additional period, you may gain if the variance pushes value higher, but you also lose one period of protection against competition. You have to consider this cost when analyzing the option, and there are two ways of estimating it:

1. Since the project rights expire after a fixed period, and excess profits (which are the source of positive present value) are assumed to disappear after that time as new competitors emerge, each year of delay translates into one less year of value-creating cash flows.[2] If the cash flows are evenly distributed over time, and the life of the patent is n years, the cost of delay can be written as:

$$\text{Annual cost of delay} = \frac{1}{n}$$

---

[2] A value-creating cash flow is one that adds to the net present value because it is in excess of the required return for investments of equivalent risk.

Thus, if the project rights are for 20 years, the annual cost of delay works out to 1/20, or 5% in the first year. Note, though, that this cost of delay rises each year, to 1/19 in year 2, 1/18 in year 3, and so on, making the cost of delaying exercise larger over time.

2. If the cash flows are uneven, the cost of delay can be more generally defined in terms of the cash flow that can be expected to occur over the next period as a percent of the present value today:

$$\text{Cost of delay} = \frac{\text{Expected cash flow next period}}{\text{Present value now}}$$

3. In either case, the likelihood that a firm will delay investing in a project is higher early in the exclusive rights period rather than later and will increase as the loss in cash flows from waiting a period increases.

---

 optvar.xls: **This dataset on the web summarizes standard deviations in firm value and equity value by industry group in the United States.**

ILLUSTRATION 28.1:   Valuing the Option to Delay a Project

Assume that you are interested in acquiring the exclusive rights to market a new product that will make it easier for people to access files from their work computers on the road. If you do acquire the rights to the product, you estimate that it will cost you $50 million up front to set up the infrastructure needed to provide the service. Based on your current projections, you believe that the service will generate only $10 million in after-tax cash flow each year. In addition, you expect to operate without serious competition for the next five years.

From a static standpoint, the net present value of this project can be computed by taking the present value of the expected cash flows over the next five years. Assuming a discount rate of 15% (based on the riskiness of this project), we obtain the following net present value for the project:

$$\text{NPV of project} = -\$50 \text{ million} + \$10 \text{ million(PV of annuity, 15\%, 5 years)}$$
$$= -\$50 \text{ million} + \$33.5 \text{ million} = -\$16.5 \text{ million}$$

This project has a negative net present value.

The biggest source of uncertainty about this project is the number of people who will be interested in the product. While current market tests indicate that you will capture a relatively small number of business travelers as your customers, they also indicate the possibility that the potential market could be much larger. In fact, a simulation of the project's cash flow yields a standard deviation of 42% in the present value of the cash flow, with an expected value of $33.5 million.

To value the exclusive rights to this project, we first define the inputs to the option pricing model:

Value of underlying asset(S) = PV of cash flows from product if introduced now = $33.5 million
Strike price(K) = Initial investment needed to introduce the product = $50 million
Variance in underlying asset's value = $0.42^2 = 0.1764$
Time to expiration = Period of exclusive rights to product = 5 years
Dividend yield (Cost of delay) = 1/Life of the patent = 1/5 = 0.20

Assume that the five-year riskless rate is 5%. The value of the option can be estimated as follows:

$$\text{Call value} = 33.5\ \exp^{(-0.2)(5)}(0.2250) - 50\ \exp^{(-0.05)(5)}(0.0451) = \$1.019\ \text{million}$$

The rights to this product, which has a negative net present value if introduced today, is \$1.019 million. Note, though, as measured by $N(d_2)$, the likelihood is low that this project will become viable before expiration.

---

 delay.xls: **This spreadsheet enables you to estimate the value of an option to delay an investment.**

ARBITRAGE POSSIBILITIES AND OPTION PRICING MODELS

The discussion of option pricing models in Chapter 5 noted that they are based on two powerful constructs—the idea of replicating portfolios and arbitrage. Models such as the Black-Scholes and binomial models assume that you can create a replicating portfolio, using the underlying asset and riskless borrowing or lending that has cash flows identical to those on an option. Furthermore, these models assume that since investors can then create riskless positions by buying the option and selling the replicating portfolio, they have to sell for the same price. If they do not, investors should be able to create riskless positions and walk away with guaranteed profits— the essence of arbitrage. This is why the interest rate used in option pricing models is the riskless rate.

With listed options on traded stocks or assets, arbitrage is clearly feasible, at least for some investors. With options on nontraded assets, it is almost impossible to trade the replicating portfolio, although you can create it on paper. In Illustration 28.1, for instance, you would need to buy 0.225 units (the option delta) of the underlying project (a nontraded asset) to create a portfolio that replicates the call option.

There are some who argue that the impossibility of arbitrage makes it inappropriate to use option pricing models to value real options, whereas others try to adjust for this limitation by using an interest rate higher than the riskless rate in the option pricing model. We do not think that either of these responses is appropriate. Note that while you cannot trade on the replicating portfolios in many real options, you still can create them on paper (as we did in Illustration 28.1) and value the options. The difficulties in creating arbitrage positions may result in prices that deviate by a large amount from this value. Increasing the riskless rate to reflect the higher risk associated with real options may seem like an obvious fix, but doing this will only make call options (such as the one valued in Illustration 28.1) more valuable, not less.

If you want to be more conservative in your estimate of value for real options to reflect the difficulty of arbitrage, you have two choices. One is to use a higher discount rate in computing the present value of the cash flows that you would expect

(continued)

(*continued*)

to make from investing in the project today, thus lowering the value of the underlying asset (S) in the model. In Illustration 28.1, using a 20-percent discount rate rather than a 15-percent rate would result in a present value of $29.1 million, which would replace the $33.5 million as S in the model. The other choice is to value the option, and then apply an illiquidity discount to it (similar to the one we used in valuing private companies), because you cannot trade it easily.

Problems in Valuing the Option to Delay

While it is quite clear that the option to delay is embedded in many projects, several problems are associated with the use of option pricing models to value these options. First, the underlying asset in this option, which is the project, is not traded, making it difficult to estimate its value and variance. The value can be estimated from the expected cash flows and the discount rate for the project, albeit with error. The variance is even more difficult to estimate, however, since we are attempting to estimate a variance in project value over time.

Second, the behavior of prices over time may not conform to the price path assumed by the option pricing models. In particular, the assumption that value follows a diffusion process, and that the variance in value remains unchanged over time, may be difficult to justify in the context of a project. For instance, a sudden technological change may dramatically change the value of a project, either positively or negatively.

Third, there may be no specific period for which the firm has rights to the project. Unlike the case of a patent, in which the firm has exclusive rights to produce the patented product for a specified period, the firm's rights to a specific project often are less clearly defined in terms of both exclusivity and time. For instance, a firm may have significant advantages over its competitors, which may, in turn, provide it with the virtually exclusive rights to a project for a period of time. An example would be a company with strong brand-name recognition in retailing or consumer products. The rights are not legal restrictions, however, and will erode over time. In such cases, the expected life of the project itself is uncertain and only an estimate. In the previous section the valuation of the rights to the product with a life of five years for the option was used, but competitors could, in fact, enter sooner than anticipated. Alternatively, the barriers to entry may turn out to be greater than expected, and enable the firm to earn excess returns for longer than five years. Ironically, uncertainty about the expected life of the option can increase the variance in present value, and through it, the expected value of the rights to the project.

Implications and Extensions of Delay Options

Several interesting implications emerge from the analysis of the option to delay a project as an option. First, a project may have a negative net present value currently based on expected cash flows, but the rights to it may still be valuable because of the option characteristics. By the same token, the exclusive rights to nonviable technology in a risky business can be worth a great deal.

Second, a project may have a positive net present value but still not be accepted right away. This can happen because the firm may gain by waiting and accepting the project in a future period, for the same reasons that investors do not always exercise an option that is in the money. A firm is more likely to wait if it has the rights to the project for a long time, as protection against competition and the variance in project inflows is high. To illustrate, assume a firm has the patent rights to produce a new type of storage for computer systems, and building a new plant will yield a positive net present value today. If the technology for manufacturing the storage is in flux, however, the firm may delay investing in the project, in the hopes that the improved technology will increase the expected cash flows, and consequently the value of the project. It has to weigh this benefit against the cost of delaying the project, which will be the cash flows that will be forsaken by not investing in it.

Third, factors that can make a project less attractive in a static analysis can actually make the rights to the project more valuable. As an example, consider the effect of uncertainty about the size of the potential market and the magnitude of excess returns. In a static analysis, increasing this uncertainty increases the riskiness of the project and may make it less attractive. When the project is viewed as an option, an increase in the uncertainty may actually make the option more valuable, not less. This chapter will consider two cases, product patents and natural resource reserves, where the project delay option allows value to be estimated more precisely.

Option Pricing Models

Once you have identified the option to delay a project as a call option and identified the inputs needed to value the option, it may seem like a trivial task to actually value the option. There are, however, some serious estimation issues that we have to deal with in valuing these options. Chapter 5 noted that while the more general model for valuing options is the binomial model, many practitioners use the Black-Scholes model, which makes far more restrictive assumptions about price processes and early exercise to value options. With listed options on traded assets, you can do this at fairly low cost. With real options, there can be a substantial cost to this practice for the following reasons:

- Unlike listed options, real options tend to be exercised early, if they are in the money. While there are ways in which the Black-Scholes model can be adjusted to allow for this early exercise, the binomial model allows for much more flexibility.
- The binomial option pricing model allows for a much wider range of price processes for the underlying asset than the Black-Scholes model, which assumes that prices are not only continuous but non-normally distributed. With real options, where the present value of the cash flows is often equivalent to the price, the assumptions of non-normality and continuous distributions may be difficult to sustain.

The biggest problem with the binomial model is that the prices at each node of the binomial tree must be estimated. As the number of periods expands, this will become more and more difficult to do. You can, however, use the variance estimate in the Black-Scholes to come up with measures of the magnitude of the upward and downward movements, which can be used to obtain the binomial tree.

Having made a case for the binomial model, you may find it surprising that we use the Black-Scholes model to value any real options. We do so not only because the model is more compact and elegant to present, but because we believe that it will provide a lower bound on the value in most cases. To provide a frame of reference, we will present the values that we would have obtained using a binomial model in each case.

From Black-Scholes to Binomial   It is a fairly simple exercise to convert the inputs to the Black-Scholes model into a binomial model. To make the adjustment, you have to assume a multiplicative binomial process, where the magnitude of the jumps, in percent terms, remains unchanged from period to period. If you assume symmetric probabilities, the upward (u) and downward (d) movements can be estimated as a function of the annualized variance in the price process and how many periods you decide to break each year into (t).

$$u = \exp^{\sigma\sqrt{dt}+\left(r-y-\frac{\sigma^2}{2}\right)dt}$$

$$d = \exp^{-\sigma\sqrt{dt}+\left(r-y-\frac{\sigma^2}{2}\right)dt}$$

where dt = 1/Number of periods each year.

To illustrate, consider the project delay option valued in Illustration 28.1. The standard deviation in the value was assumed to be 42 percent, the risk-free rate was 5%, and the dividend yield was 20 percent. To convert the inputs into a binomial model, assume that each year is a time period, and estimate the upward and downward movements as follows:

$$u = \exp^{.42\sqrt{1}+\left(.05-.20-\frac{.42^2}{2}\right)\sqrt{t}} = 1.1994$$

$$d = \exp^{-.42\sqrt{1}+\left(.05-.20-\frac{.42^2}{2}\right)1t} = 0.5178$$

The value today is $33.5 million. To estimate the end values for the first branch:

> Value with upward movement = $33.5(1.1994) = $40.179 million
> Value with downward movement = $33.5(0.5178) = $17.345 million

You could use these values then to get the three potential values at the second branch. Note that the value of $17.345 million growing at 19.94 percent is exactly equal to the value of $40.179 million dropping by 48.22 percent. The binomial tree for the five periods is shown in Figure 28.5.

You could estimate the value of the option from this binomial tree to be $1.02 million, slightly higher than the estimate obtained from the Black-Scholes model of $1.019 million. The differences will narrow as the option becomes more in-the-money, and you shorten the time periods you use in the binomial model.

VALUING A PATENT

A number of firms, especially in the technology and pharmaceutical sectors, can patent products or services. A product patent provides a firm with the exclusive right to develop and market a product, and thus can be viewed as an option.

Patents as Call Options

The firm will develop a patent only if the present value of the expected cash flow from the product sales exceeds the cost of development, as shown in Figure 28.6. If this does not occur, the firm can shelve the patent and not incur any further costs. If I is the present of

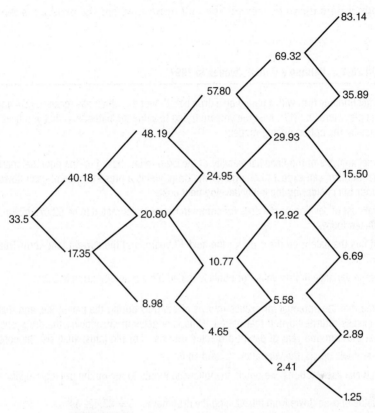

FIGURE 28.5 Binomial Tree for Delay Option

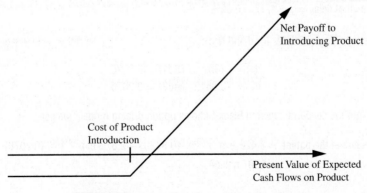

FIGURE 28.6 Payoff to Introducing Product

the costs of commercially developing the patent, and V is the present value of the expected cash flows from development, then:

$$\text{Payoff from owning a product patent} = V - I \quad \text{if } V > I$$
$$= 0 \qquad \text{if } V \leq I$$

Thus, a product patent can be viewed as a call option, where the product is the underlying asset.

ILLUSTRATION 28.2:   Valuing a Patent: Avonex in 1997

Biogen is a biotechnology firm with a patent on a drug called Avonex, which has received FDA approval for use in treating multiple sclerosis (MS). Assume you are trying to value the patent and that you have the following estimates for use in the option pricing model:

▪ An internal analysis of the financial viability of the drug today, based on the potential market and the price that the firm can expect to charge for the drug, yields a present value of cash flows of $3.422 billion prior to considering the initial development cost.

▪ The initial cost of developing the drug for commercial use is estimated to be $2.875 billion, if the drug is introduced today.

▪ The firm has the patent on the drug for the next 17 years, and the current long-term Treasury bond rate is 6.7%.

▪ The average variance in firm value for publicly traded biotechnology firms is 0.224.

We assume that the potential for excess returns exists only during the patent life, and that competition will eliminate excess returns beyond that period. Thus, any delay in introducing the drug, once it becomes viable, will cost the firm one year of patent-protected returns. (For the initial analysis, the cost of delay will be $\frac{1}{17}$, next year it will be $\frac{1}{16}$, the year after $\frac{1}{15}$, and so on.)

Based on these assumptions, we obtain the following inputs to the option pricing model:

Present value of cash flows from introducing the drug now = S = $3.422 billion
Initial cost of developing drug for commercial use (today) = K = $2.875 billion
Patent life = t = 17 years
Riskless rate = r = 6.7% (17 − year Treasury bond rate)
Variance in expected present values = σ^2 = 0.224
Expected cost of delay = y = 1/17 = 5.89%

These yield the following estimates for d and N(d):

$$d1 = 1.1362 \quad N(d1) - 0.8720$$
$$d2 = -0.8512 \quad N(d2) = 0.2076$$

Plugging back into the dividend-adjusted Black-Scholes option pricing model,[3] we get:

$$\text{Value of the patent} = 3{,}422 \ \exp^{(-0.0589)(17)}(0.8720) - 2{,}875 \ \exp^{(-0.067)(17)}(0.2076)$$
$$= \$907 \text{ million}$$

---

[3]With a binomial model, we estimate a value of $915 million for the same option.

To provide a contrast, the net present value of this project is only $547 million:

$$NPV = \$3,422 \text{ million} - \$2,875 \text{ million} = \$547 \text{ million}$$

The time premium of $360 million on this option ($907–$547) suggests that the firm will be better off waiting rather than developing the drug immediately, the cost of delay notwithstanding. However, the cost of delay will increase over time, and make exercise (development) more likely in future years. In addition, to the extent that there are competitors working on similar drugs to treat MS, Biogen may find that the cost of waiting becomes prohibitive and develop the drug immediately.

To illustrate, we will value the call option, assuming that all of the inputs, other than the patent life, remain unchanged and changing the patent life. For instance, assume that there are 16 years left on the patent. Holding all else constant, the cost of delay increases as a result of the shorter patent life:

$$\text{Cost of delay} = 1/16$$

The decline in the present value of cash flows (which is S) and increase in the cost of delay (y) reduce the expected value of the patent. Figure 28.7 graphs the option value and the net present value of the project each year.

Based on this analysis, if nothing changes, you expect Avonex to be worth more as a commercial product than as a patent if there were less than twelve years left on the patent, which would also then be the optimal time to commercially develop the product.[4]

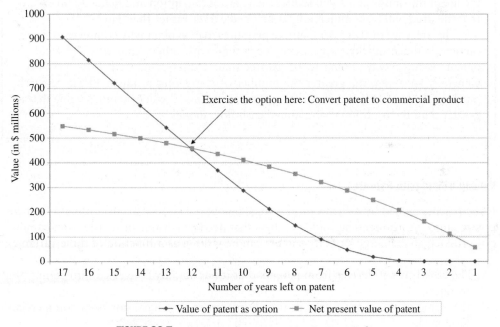

FIGURE 28.7   Patent Value versus Net Present Value

---

[4]The net present values each year were computed on the assumption that the NPV at the start of $547 million is converted into an annuity over seventeen years of $64.02 million (using a 9% cost of capital). In year 2, when there are sixteen years left on the project, the net present value decreases to $532 million, the present value of $64.02 million for 16 years at a 9% cost of capital.

product.xls: This spreadsheet allows you to estimate the value of a patent, if you input the values for the expected cash flows (today) from developing the patent, and the cost of converting the patent into a commercial product.

COMPETITIVE PRESSURES AND OPTION VALUES

The preceding section has taken the view that a firm is protected from competition for the life of the patent. This is generally true only for the patented product or process, but the firm may still face competition from other firms that come up with their own products to serve the same market. More specifically, Biogen can patent Avonex, but Merck or Pfizer can come up with their own drugs to treat multiple sclerosis and compete with Biogen.

What are the implications for the value of the patent as an option? First, the life of the option will no longer be the life of the patent but the lead time that the firm believes it has until a competing product is developed. For instance, if Biogen knows that another pharmaceutical firm is working on a drug to treat MS and where this drug is in the research pipeline (early research or stage in the FDA approval process), it can use its estimate of how long it will take before the drug is approved for use as the life of the option. This will reduce the value of the option and make it more likely that the drug will be commercially developed earlier rather than later.

The presence of these competitive pressures may explain why commercial development is much quicker with some drugs than with others, and why the value of patents is not always going to be greater than a discounted cash flow valuation. Generally speaking, the greater the number of competing products in the research pipeline, the less likely it is that the option pricing model will generate a value that is greater than the traditional discounted cash flow model.

Valuing a Firm with Patents

If the patents owned by a firm can be valued as options, how can this estimate be incorporated into firm value? The value of a firm that derives its value primarily from commercial products that emerge from its patents can be written as a function of three variables:

1. The cash flows it derives from patents that it has already converted into commercial products.
2. The value of the patents that it already possesses that have not been commercially developed.
3. The expected value of any patents that the firm can be expected to generate in future periods from new patents it might obtain as a result of its research.

> Value of firm = Value of commercial products + Value of existing patents
> + (Value of new patents that will be obtained in the future
> − Cost of obtaining these patents)

The expected cash flows from existing products can be estimated for their commercial lives and discounted back to the present at the appropriate cost of capital to arrive at the value of these products. The value of the second component can be obtained using the option pricing model described earlier to value each patent. The value of the third component will be based on perceptions of a firm's research capabilities. In the special case where the expected cost of research and development in future periods is equal to the value of the patents that will be generated by this research, its value will become zero. In the more general case, firms that have a history of generating value from research will derive positive value from this component as well. There is also the possibility that some companies destroy value with ongoing research, where the cost of the research exceeds the value created.

How would the overall estimate of value obtained using this approach contrast with the estimate obtained in a traditional discounted cash flow model? In traditional discounted cash flow valuation, the second and the third components of value are captured in the expected growth rate in cash flows. Firms are allowed to grow at much higher rates for longer periods because of the patents they possess and their research prowess. In contrast, the approach described in this section looks at each patent separately and allows for the option component of value explicitly.

The biggest limitation of the option-based approach is the information needed to put it in practice. To value each patent separately, you need access to proprietary information that is usually available only to managers of the firm. In fact, some of the information, such as the expected variance to use in option pricing, may not even be available to insiders and will have to be estimated for each patent separately.

Given these limitations, the real option approach should be used to value small firms with one or two patents and little in terms of established assets. A good example would be Biogen in 1997, which is valued in Illustration 28.3. For more established firms that have significant assets in place and dozens of patents, discounted cash flow valuation is a more pragmatic choice.

ILLUSTRATION 28.3: Valuing Biogen as a Firm in 1997

In illustration 28.2, the patent that Biogen owns on Avonex was valued as a call option, and the estimated value was $907 million. To value Biogen as a firm, two other components of value would have to be considered:

1. Biogen had two commercial products (a drug to treat hepatitis B and a cancer drug called Intron) at the time of this valuation that it had licensed to other pharmaceutical firms. The license fees (pretax) on these products were expected to generate $50 million in after-tax cash flows each year for the next twelve years. To value these cash flows, which were guaranteed contractually, the pretax cost of debt of the licensing firms (7%) was used as the discount rate, since the primary risk is that of default by these firms:

$$\text{Present value of license fees} = \$50 \times \frac{(1 - 1.07^{-12})}{.07} = \$397.13 \text{ million}$$

2. Biogen continued to fund research into new products, spending about $100 million on R&D in the most recent year. These R&D expenses were expected to grow 20% a year for the next 10 years and 5% thereafter. While it was difficult to forecast the specific patents that would emerge from this research, it was assumed

that every dollar invested in research would create $1.25 in value in patents[5] (valued using the option pricing model described earlier) for the next 10 years, and break even after that (i.e., generate $1 in patent value for every $1 invested in R&D). There was a significant amount of risk associated with this component, and the cost of capital was estimated to be 15%.[6] The value of this component was then estimated as follows:

$$\text{Value of future research} = \sum_{t=1}^{t=n} \frac{(\text{Value of patents}_t - \text{R\&D}_t)}{(1 + r)^t}$$

Table 28.1 summarizes the value of patents generated each period, and the R&D costs in that period. Note that there is no surplus value created after the tenth year:

TABLE 28.1   Valuing Continuing R&D at Biogen

Year	Value of Patents	R&D Cost	Excess Value	PV at 15%
1	$150.00	$120.00	$ 30.00	$ 26.09
2	$180.00	$144.00	$ 36.00	$ 27.22
3	$216.00	$172.80	$ 43.20	$ 28.40
4	$259.20	$207.36	$ 51.84	$ 29.64
5	$311.04	$248.83	$ 62.21	$ 30.93
6	$373.25	$298.60	$ 74.65	$ 32.27
7	$447.90	$358.32	$ 89.58	$ 33.68
8	$537.48	$429.98	$107.50	$ 35.14
9	$644.97	$515.98	$128.99	$ 36.67
10	$773.97	$619.17	$154.79	$ 38.26
Value of R&D				$318.30

The total value created by new research is $318.3 million.

The value of Biogen as a firm is the sum of all three components—the present value of cash flows from existing products, the value of Avonex (as an option), and the value created by new research:

Value = Commercial products + Value : undeveloped patents + Value : future R&D

= $397.13 million + $907 million + $318.30 million = $1,622.43 million

Since Biogen had no debt outstanding or a significant cash balance, this value was divided by the number of shares outstanding (35.5 million) to arrive at a value per share:

Value per share = $1,622.43 million/35.5 = $45.70

---

[5]This is not an estimate based on any significant facts other than Biogen's history of success in coming up with new products. You can obtain an estimate of this number from the return and cost of capital. For instance, if you assume a return on invested capital of 15% and cost of capital of 10% in perpetuity, $1 invested would yield the following:

$$\text{Value created by a \$ investment} = 1 + \frac{\text{ROIC} - \text{Cost of capital}}{\text{Cost of capital}}$$

$$= 1 + \frac{(.15 - .10)}{.10} = \$1.50$$

[6]This discount rate was estimated by looking at the costs of equity of young publicly traded biotechnology firms with little or no revenue from commercial products.

IS THERE LIFE AFTER THE PATENT EXPIRES?

In these valuations, it has been assumed that the excess returns are restricted to the patent life, and that they disappear the instant the patent expires. In the pharmaceutical sector, the expiration of a patent does not necessarily mean the loss of excess returns. In fact, many firms continue to be able to charge a premium price for their products and earn excess returns even after the patent expires, largely as a consequence of the brand-name image that they built up over the project life. A simple way of adjusting for this reality is to increase the present value of the cash flows on the project (S), and decrease the cost of delay (y) to reflect this reality. The net effect is a greater likelihood that firms will delay commercial development, while they wait to collect more information and assess market demand.

The other thing that might increase the value of the patent is the capacity that drug companies have shown to lobby legislators or use the legal system to extend the patent lives of profitable drugs. If we consider this as a possibility when we value a patent, it will increase the expected life of the patent and its value as an option.

NATURAL RESOURCE OPTIONS

Natural resource companies, such as oil and mining companies, generate cash flows from their existing reserves but also have undeveloped reserves that they can develop if they choose to do so. They will be much more likely to develop these reserves if the price of the resource (e.g., oil, gold, copper, etc.) increases and these undeveloped reserves can be viewed as call options. This section begins by looking at the value of an undeveloped reserve, and then considers how this can be extended to look at natural resource companies that have both developed and undeveloped reserves.

Undeveloped Reserves as Options

In a natural resource investment, the underlying asset is the natural resource, and the value of the asset is based on the estimated quantity and the price of the resource. Thus, in a gold mine, the underlying asset is the value of the estimated gold reserves in the mine, based on the price of gold. In most such investments, there is an initial cost associated with developing the resource; the difference between the value of the estimated reserves and the cost of the development is the profit to the owner of the resource (see Figure 28.8). Defining the cost of development as X, and the estimated value of the resource as V, makes the potential payoffs on a natural resource option the following:

$$\text{Pay off on natural resource investment} = V - X \quad \text{if } V > X$$
$$= 0 \qquad \text{if } V \le X$$

Thus, the investment in a natural resource option has a payoff function that resembles a call option.

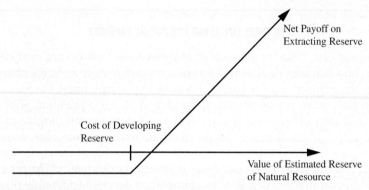

FIGURE 28.8   Payoff from Developing Natural Resource Reserves

Inputs for Valuing a Natural Resource Option   To value a natural resource investment as an option, we need to make assumptions about a number of variables:

- *Available reserves of the resource and estimated value if extracted today.* Since the quantity of the reserve is not known with certainty at the outset, it has to be estimated. In an oil tract, for instance, geologists can provide reasonably accurate estimates of the quantity of oil available in the tract. The value of the reserves is then the product of the estimated reserves and the contribution (current price of the resource minus variable cost of extraction) per unit of reserve.

- *Estimated cost of developing the resource.* The estimated cost of developing the resource reserve is the exercise price of the option. In an oil reserve, this would be the fixed cost of installing the rigs to extract oil from the reserve. With a mine, it would be the cost associated with making the mine operational. Since oil and mining companies have done this before in a variety of settings, they can use their experience to come up with a reasonable measure of development cost.

- *Time to expiration of the option.* The life of a natural resource option can be defined in one of two ways. First, if the ownership of the investment has to be relinquished at the end of a fixed period of time, that period will be the life of the option. In many offshore oil leases, for instance, the oil tracts are leased to the oil company for a fixed period. The second approach is based on the inventory of the resource and the capacity output rate, as well as estimates of the number of years it would take to exhaust the inventory. Thus, a gold mine with a mine inventory of 3 million ounces and a capacity output rate of 150,000 ounces a year will be exhausted in 20 years, which is defined as the life of the natural resource option.

- *Variance in value of the underlying asset.* The variance in the value of the underlying asset is determined by the variability in the price of the resource and the variability in the estimate of available reserves. In the special case where the quantity of the reserve is known with certainty, the variance in the underlying asset's value will depend entirely on the variance in the price of the natural resource.

- *Cost of delay.* The net production revenue is the annual cash flow that will be generated, once a resource reserve has been developed, as a percentage of the value of the reserve. This is the equivalent of the dividend yield and is treated the same way in calculating option values. An alternative way of thinking about this cost is in terms of the cost of delay. Once a natural resource option is in-the-money (value of the reserves is greater than the cost of developing these reserves), by not developing the reserve, the firm is costing itself the net production revenue it could have generated by doing so.

An important issue in using option pricing models to value natural resource options is the effect of development lags on the value of these options. Since oil, gold, or any other natural resource reserve cannot be developed instantaneously, a time lag has to be allowed between the decision to extract the resources and the actual extraction. A simple adjustment for this lag is to reduce the value of the developed reserve for the loss of cash flows during the development period. Thus, if there is a one-year lag in development, you can estimate the cash flow you would make over the year as a percent of your reserve value, and then discount the current value of the developed reserve at that rate. This is the equivalent of removing the first year's cash flow from your investment analysis and lowering the present value of your cash flows.

ILLUSTRATION 28.4: Valuing an Oil Reserve[7]

Consider an offshore oil property with an estimated oil reserve of 50 million barrels of oil; the cost of developing the reserve is expected to be $600 million, and the development lag is two years. Exxon has the rights to exploit this reserve for the next 20 years, and the marginal value (price per barrel minus marginal cost per barrel) per barrel of oil is currently $12.[8] Once developed, the net production revenue each year will be 5% of the value of the reserves. The riskless rate is 8%, and the variance in oil prices is 0.03.

Given this information, the inputs to the Black-Scholes model can be estimated as follows:

Current value of the asset = Value of developed reserve discount back the length of the development lag
$$= (\$12 \times 50)/1.05^2 = \$544.22 \text{ million}$$

Exercise price = Cost of developing reserve = $600 million
Time to expiration on the option = 20 years
Variance in the value of the underlying asset = 0.03
Riskless rate = 8%
Dividend yield = Net production revenue/Value of reserve = 5%

Based on these inputs, the Black-Scholes model provides the following call value:

$$d1 = 1.0359 \quad N(d1) = 0.8498$$
$$d2 = 0.2613 \quad N(d2) = 0.6030$$

Call value = $544.22 \exp^{(-0.05)(20)}(0.8498) - 600 \exp^{(-0.08)(20)}(0.6030) = \$97.08$ million

This oil reserve, though not viable at current prices, is still valuable because of its potential to create value if oil prices go up.[9]

---

[7]The following is a simplified version of the illustration provided by Siegel, Smith, and Paddock (1993) to value an offshore oil property.
[8]For simplicity, we will assume that, while this marginal value per barrel of oil will grow over time, the present value of the marginal value will remain unchanged at $12 per barrel. If we do not make this assumption, we will have to estimate the present value of the oil that will be extracted over the extraction period.
[9]With a binomial model, we arrive at an estimate of value of $99.15 million.

natres.xls: **This spreadsheet allows you to estimate the value of an undeveloped natural resource reserve.**

MULTIPLE SOURCES OF UNCERTAINTY

In the preceding example, we assumed that there was no uncertainty about the quantity of the reserve. Realistically, the oil company has an estimate of the reserve of 50 million barrels but does not know it with certainty. If we introduce uncertainty about the quantity of the reserve into the analysis, there will be two sources of variance, and both can affect value. There are two ways we can address this problem:

- *Combine the uncertainties into one value.* If we consider the value of the reserves to be the product of the price of oil and the oil reserves, the variance in the value should reflect the combined effect of the variances in each input.[10] This would be the variance we would use in the option pricing model to estimate a new value for the reserve.

- *Keep the variances separate and value the option as a rainbow option.* A rainbow option enables explicitly for more than one source of variance and enables us to keep the variances separate and still value the option. While option pricing becomes more complicated, you may need to do this if you expect the two sources of uncertainty to evolve differently over time—the variance from one source (say, oil prices) may increase over time whereas the variance from the other source (say, oil reserves) may decrease over time.

Valuing a Firm with Undeveloped Reserves

The examples provided earlier illustrate the use of option pricing theory in valuing individual mines and oil tracts. Since the assets owned by a natural resource firm can be viewed primarily as options, the firm itself can be valued using option pricing models.

Individual Reserves versus Aggregate Reserves   The preferred approach would be to consider each reserve separately, value it, and cumulate the values of the reserves to get the value of the firm. Since this information is likely to be difficult to obtain for large natural resource firms such as oil companies, which own hundreds of such reserves, a variant of this approach is to value the entire firm's undeveloped reserves as one option. A purist would probably disagree, arguing that valuing an option on a portfolio of assets (as in this approach) will provide a lower value than valuing a portfolio of options (which is what the natural resource firm really owns). Nevertheless, the assumption that the only source of variance is the price of the natural resource effectively makes the values of the reserves perfectly correlated and enables us to use the short cut with limited or no cost.

---

[10]This is the variance of a product of two variables.

Inputs to Option Valuation   If you decide to apply the option pricing approach to estimate the value of aggregate undeveloped reserves, you have to estimate the inputs to the model. In general terms, while the process resembles the one used to value an individual reserve, there are a few differences.

- *Value of underlying asset.* You should cumulate all of the undeveloped reserves owned by a company and estimate the value of these reserves, based on the price of the resource today and the average variable cost of extracting these reserves today. The variable costs are likely to be higher for some reserves and lower for others, and weighting the variable costs at each reserve by the quantity of the resource of that reserve should give you a reasonable approximation of this value. At least hypothetically, we are assuming that the company can decide to extract all its undeveloped reserves at one time and not affect the price of the resource.
- *Exercise price.* For this input, you should consider what it would cost the company today to develop all of its undeveloped reserves instantly. Again, the costs might be higher for some reserves than for others, and you can use a weighted average cost.
- *Life of the option.* A firm will probably have different lives for each of its reserves. As a consequence, you will have to use a weighted average of the lives of the different reserves.[11]
- *Variance in the value of the asset.* Here, there is a strong argument for looking at only the oil price as the source of variance, since a firm should have a much more precise estimate of its total reserves than it does of any one of its reserves.
- *Dividend yield (cost of delay).* As with an individual reserve, a firm with viable reserves will be giving up the cash flows it could receive in the next period from developing these reserves if it delays exercise. This cash flow, stated as a percent of the value of the reserves, becomes the equivalent of the dividend yield. The development lag reduces the value of this option just as it reduces the value of an individual reserve. The logical implication is that undeveloped reserves will be worth more at oil companies that can develop their reserves quicker than at less efficient companies.

ILLUSTRATION 28.5:   Valuing an Oil Company: Gulf Oil in 1984

Gulf Oil was the target of a takeover in early 1984 at $70 per share. (It had 165.30 million shares outstanding and total debt of $9.9 billion.) It had estimated reserves of 3,038 million barrels of oil, and the total cost of developing these reserves at that time was estimated to be $30.38 billion. (The development lag is approximately two years.) The average relinquishment life of the reserves is 12 years. The price of oil was $22.38 per barrel, and the production costs, taxes, and royalties were estimated at $7 per barrel. The bond rate at the time of the analysis was 9.00%. If Gulf were to choose to develop these reserves, it was expected to have cash flows next year of approximately 5% of the value of the developed reserves. The variance in oil prices is 0.03.

Value of underlying asset = Value of estimated reserves, adjusted for development lag

$$= 3{,}038 \times (\$22.38 - \$7)/1.05^2 = \$42{,}380.44$$

---

[11]If you own some reserves in perpetuity, you should cap the life of the reserve at a large value—say, 30 years—in making this estimate.

Note that the development lag creates a two-year waiting period for the cash flow, effectively reducing their value by the absence of cash flows (5%) in years one and two. While this assumes, unrealistically, that you can extract the oil instantaneously without affecting prices, you could have set a production capacity and used forecasted oil prices to estimate cash flows over the production period and the value of the underlying asset to be the present value of all these cash flows.[12] We have used a shortcut of assuming that the current contribution margin of $15.38 a barrel will remain unchanged in present value terms over the production period.

Exercise price = Estimated cost of developing reserves today = $30,380 million
Time to expiration = Average length of relinquishment option = 12 years
Variance in value of asset = Variance in oil prices = 0.03
Riskless interest rate = 9%
Dividend yield = Net production revenue/Value of developed reserves = 5%

Based on these inputs, the Black-Scholes model provides the following value for the call[13]:

$$d1 = 1.6548 \quad N(d1) = 0.9510$$
$$d2 = 1.0548 \quad N(d2) = 0.8542$$

Call value = 42,380.44 $\exp^{(-0.05)(12)}$(0.9510) − 30,380 $\exp^{(-0.09)(12)}$(0.8542) = $13,306 million

This stands in contrast to the discounted cash flow value of $12 billion that you obtain by taking the difference between the present value of the cash flows of developing the reserve today ($42.38 billion) and the cost of development ($30.38 billion). The difference can be attributed to the option possessed by Gulf to choose when to develop its reserves.

The option value ($13.3 billion) represents the value of the undeveloped reserves of oil owned by Gulf Oil. In addition, Gulf Oil had free cash flows to the firm from its oil and gas production of $915 million from already developed reserves, and we assume that these cash flows are likely to be constant and continue for 10 years (the remaining lifetime of developed reserves). The present value of these developed reserves, discounted at the weighted average cost of capital of 12.5%, yields:

Value of already developed reserves = 915(1 − 1.125^{-10})/125 = $5,065.83

Adding the value of the developed and undeveloped reserves of Gulf Oil provides the value of the firm.

Value of undeveloped reserves	$13,306 million
Value of production in place	$5,066 million
Total value of firm	$18,372 million
Less outstanding debt	$9,900 million
Value of equity	$8,472 million
Value per share	$8,472/165.3 = $51.25

This analysis would suggest that Gulf Oil was overvalued at $70 per share.

---

[12] If you assume that the company can extract 250 million barrels a year for twelve years, assuming that oil prices increase at 10% a year, from current prices, the present value of the cashflows would be the following (using a 10% inflation rate and a 12.5% cost of capital):

$$\text{Value of reserves} = 250 \times (\$22.38 - \$7) \left[\frac{\left(1 - \frac{1.10^{12}}{1.125^{12}}\right)}{(.125 - .10)} \right]$$

$$= \$36,814 \text{ million}$$

[13] With a binomial model, we estimate the value of the reserves to be $13.73 billion.

PRICE VOLATILITY AND NATURAL RESOURCE COMPANY VALUATION

An interesting implication of this analysis is that the value of a natural resource company depends not just on the price of the natural resource but also on the expected volatility in that price. Thus, if the price of oil goes from $25 a barrel to $40 a barrel, you would expect all oil companies to become more valuable. If the price drops back to $25, the values of oil companies may not decline to their old levels, since the perceived volatility in oil prices may have changed. If investors believe that the volatility in oil prices has increased, you can expect an increase in values, but the increase will be greatest for companies that derive a higher proportion of their value from undeveloped reserves.

If you regard undeveloped reserves as options, discounted cash flow valuation will generally underestimate the value of natural resource companies, because the expected price of the commodity is used to estimate revenues and operating profits. As a consequence, you miss the option component of value. Again, the difference will be greatest for firms with significant undeveloped reserves and with commodities whose price volatility is highest.

OTHER APPLICATIONS

While patents and undeveloped reserves of natural resource companies lend themselves best to applying option pricing, there are other assets referenced in earlier chapters that can also be valued as options:

- Chapter 26, in the context of real estate valuation, noted that vacant land could be viewed as an option on commercial development.
- Chapter 27 presented an argument that copyrights and licenses could be viewed as options, even if they are not commercially viable today.

Table 28.2 presents the inputs you would use to value each of these options in an option pricing model. Much of what we have said about the other option applications apply here as well. The value is derived from the exclusivity that you have to commercially develop the asset. That exclusivity is obtained by legal sanction in the case of licenses and copyrights, and from the scarcity of land in the case of undeveloped land.

TABLE 28.2   Inputs to Value Other Options to Delay

	Undeveloped Land	License/Copyright
Value of the underlying asset	Present value of the cash flows that would be obtained from commercial development of land today	Present value of the cash flows that would be obtained from commercially utilizing the license or copyright today
Variance in value of underlying asset	Variance in the values of commercial property in the area where the real estate is located	Variance in the present values from commercial utilization of copyright or license (from a simulation)

(continued)

TABLE 28.2   *(continued)*

	Undeveloped Land	License/Copyright
Exercise price	Cost of commercially developing land today	Up-front cost of commercially utilizing copyright or license today
Life of the option	If land is under long-term lease, you could use the lease period. If not, you should set the option life equal to the period when the loan that you used to buy the land comes due	Period for which you have rights to copyright or license
Cost of delay	Property taxes and other costs associated with holding land	Cash flow you could generate in next year as a percent of present value of the cash flows today

CONCLUSION

In traditional investment analysis, we compute the net present value of a project's cash flows and conclude that firms should not invest in a project with a negative net present value. This is generally good advice, but it does not imply that the rights to this project are not valuable. Projects that have negative net present values today may have positive net present values in the future, and the likelihood of this occurring is directly a function of the volatility in the present value of the cash flows from the project.

This chapter valued the option to delay an investment and considered the implications of this option for three valuation scenarios—the value of a firm that derives all or a significant portion of value from patents that have not yet been commercially exploited, the value of a natural resource company with undeveloped reserves of the resource, and the value of a real estate firm with undeveloped land. In each case, using discounted cash flow valuation would result in an understatement of the values of these firms.

QUESTIONS AND SHORT PROBLEMS

In the problems following, use an equity risk premium of 5.5 percent if none is specified.

1. A company is considering delaying a project with after-tax cash flows of $25 million but that costs $300 million to take on (the life of the project is 20 years, and the cost of capital is 16%). A simulation of the cash flows leads you to conclude that the standard deviation in the present value of cash inflows is 20%. If you can acquire the rights to the project for the next 10 years, what is the value of the rights? (The six-month T-bill rate is 8%, the 10-year bond rate is 12%, and the 20-year bond rate is 14%.)

2. You are examining the financial viability of investing in some abandoned copper mines in Chile, which still have significant copper deposits in them. A geologist survey suggests that there might be 10 million pounds of copper in the mines still, and that the cost of opening up the mines will be $3 million (in present value dollars). The capacity

output rate is 400,000 pounds a year, and the price of copper is expected to increase 4% a year. The Chilean government is willing to grant a 25-year lease on the mine. The average production cost is expected to be 40 cents a pound, and the current price per pound of copper is 85 cents. (The production cost is expected to grow 3% a year, once initiated.) The annualized standard deviation in copper prices is 25%, and the 25-year bond rate is 7%.

a. Estimate the value of the mine using traditional capital budgeting techniques.

b. Estimate the value of the mine based on an option pricing model.

c. How would you explain the difference between the two values?

3. You have been asked to analyze the value of an oil company with substantial oil reserves. The estimated reserves amount to 10 million barrels, and the estimated cost of developing these reserves today is $120 million. The current price of oil is $20 per barrel, and the average production cost is estimated to be $6 per barrel. The company has the rights to these reserves for the next 20 years, and the 20-year bond rate is 7%. The company also proposes to extract 4% of its reserves each year to meet cash flow needs. The annualized standard deviation in the price of the oil is 20%. What is the value of this oil company?

4. You are analyzing a capital-budgeting project. The project is expected to have a PV of cash inflows of $250 million and will cost $200 million today to take on. You have done a simulation of the project cash flows, and the simulation yields a variance in present value of cash inflows of 0.04. You have the rights to this project for the next 20 years. The 20-year Treasury bond rate is 8%.

a. What is the value of the project based on traditional NPV?

b. What is the value of the project as an option?

c. Why are the two values different? What factor or factors determine the magnitude of this difference?

5. Cyclops Inc., a high-technology company specializing in state-of-the-art visual technology, is considering going public. While the company has no revenues or profits yet on its products, it has a 10-year patent to a product that will enable contact lens users to get no-maintenance lenses that will last for years. While the product is technically viable, it is exorbitantly expensive to manufacture, and the potential market for it will be relatively small currently. (A cash flow analysis of the project suggests that the present value of the cash inflows on the project, if adopted now, would be $250 million, while the cost of the project will be $500 million.) The technology is rapidly evolving, and a simulation of alternative scenarios yields a wide range of present values, with an annualized standard deviation of 60%. The 10-year bond rate is 6%.

a. Estimate the value of this company.

b. How sensitive is this value estimate to the variance in project cash flows? What broader lessons would you draw from this analysis?

The Options to Expand and to Abandon: Valuation Implications

The preceding chapter noted that traditional discounted cash flow valuation does not consider the value of the option that many firms have to delay making an investment, and consequently understates the value of these investments. This chapter considers two other options that are often embedded in investments (and consequently in the values of the firms that possess them). The first of these is the option to expand an investment, not only in new markets but to new products, to take advantage of favorable conditions. We argue that this option may sometimes make young start-up firms significantly more valuable than the present value of their expected cash flows. The second option is the option to abandon or scale down investments, which can reduce the risk and downside from large investments, and therefore, make them more valuable.

THE OPTION TO EXPAND

Firms sometimes invest in projects because the investments enable them either to make further investments, or to enter other markets in the future. In such cases, we can view the initial projects as yielding options, and these options have value. Put another way, a firm may accept a negative net present value on the initial project, because of the possibility of high positive net present values on future projects.

Payoff on the Option to Expand

The option to expand can be evaluated at the time the initial project is analyzed. Assume that this initial project will give the firm the right to expand and invest in a new project in the future. Assessed today, the expected present value of the cash flows from investing in the future project is V, and the total investment needed for this project is X. The firm has a fixed time horizon, at the end of which it has to make the final decision on whether to make the future investment. Finally, the firm cannot move forward on this future investment if it does not take the initial project. This scenario implies the option payoffs shown in Figure 29.1.

As you can see, at the expiration of the fixed time horizon, the firm will expand into the new project if the present value of the expected cash flows at that point in time exceeds

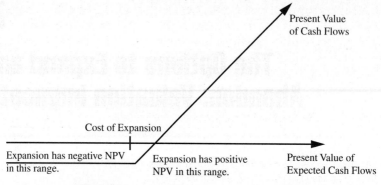

FIGURE 29.1   The Option to Expand a Project

the cost of expansion. Note again that the initial project is a conventional investment, and it is the expansion option that tilts the scales.

Inputs to Value the Option to Expand

To understand how to estimate the value of the option to expand, let us begin by recognizing that there are two linked projects. The first project generally has a negative net present value and is recognized as a poor investment, even by the firm investing in it. The second project is the potential to expand that comes with the first project. It is the second project that represents the underlying asset for the option. The inputs have to be defined accordingly:

- The present value of the cash flows that you would generate if you were to invest in the second project today (the expansion option) is the value of the underlying asset— S in the option pricing model.
- If there is substantial uncertainty about the expansion potential, the present value is likely to be volatile and change over time as circumstances change. It is the variance in this present value that you would want to use to value the expansion option. Since projects are not traded, you must either estimate this variance from simulations, or use the variance in values of publicly traded firms in the business.
- The cost that you would incur up front, if you were to invest in the expansion today, is the equivalent of the strike price.
- The life of the option is difficult to define, since there is usually no externally imposed exercise period. (This is in contrast to the patents valued in the preceding chapter, which have a legal life that can be used as the option life.) When valuing the option to expand, the life of the option will be an internal constraint imposed by the firm on itself. For instance, a firm that invests on a small scale in China might impose a constraint that it will either expand within five years or pull out of the market. Why might it do so? There may be considerable costs associated with maintaining the small presence, or the firm may have scarce resources that have to be committed elsewhere.

■ As with other real options, there may be a cost to waiting once the expansion option becomes viable. That cost may take the form of cash flows that will be lost on the expansion project if it is not taken, or a cost imposed on the firm until it makes its final decision. For instance, the firm may have to pay a fee every year until it makes its final decision.

ILLUSTRATION 29.1: Valuing an Option to Expand: Ambev and Guarana

Guarana is a very popular caffeine-based soft drink in Brazil, and Ambev is the Brazilian beverage manufacturer that is the largest producer of Guarana in the world. Assume that Ambev is considering introducing the drink into the United States and that it has decided to do so in two steps:

1. Ambev will initially introduce Guarana in just the large U.S. metropolitan areas to gauge potential demand. The expected cost of this limited introduction is $500 million, and the estimated present value of the expected cash flows is only $400 million. In other words, Ambev expects to have a negative net present value of $100 million on this first investment.
2. If the limited introduction turns out to be a success, Ambev expects to introduce Guarana to the rest of the U.S. market. At the moment, though, the firm is not optimistic about this expansion potential and believes that while the cost of the full-scale introduction will be $1 billion, the expected present value of the cash flows is only $750 million (making this a negative net present value investment as well).

At first sight, investing in a poor project to get a chance to invest in an even poorer project may seem like a bad deal, but the second investment does have a redeeming feature. It is an option, and Ambev will not make the second investment (of $1 billion) if the expected present value of the cash flow stays below that number. Furthermore, there is considerable uncertainty about the size and potential for this market, and the firm may well find itself with a lucrative investment.

To estimate the value of the second investment as an option, we begin by first identifying the underlying asset—the expansion project—and using the current estimate of expected value ($750 million) as the value of the underlying asset. Since the investment needed for the investment of $1 billion is the exercise price, this option is an out-of-the-money option. The two most problematic assumptions relate to the variance in the value of the underlying asset and the life of the option:

■ We estimated the average standard deviation of 35% in firm values of small, publicly traded, beverage companies in the United States, and assumed that this would be a good proxy for the standard deviation in the value of the expansion option.

■ We assumed that Ambev would have a five-year window to make its decision. We admit that this is an arbitrary constraint but, in the real world, it may be driven by any of the following:

    ■ Financing constraints (loans will come due)

    ■ Strategic prerogatives (you have to choose where your resources will be invested)

    ■ Personnel decisions (management has to be hired and put in place)

Based on these inputs, we had the following inputs to the option pricing model:

S = Present value of cash flows from expansion option today = $750

K = Exercise price = $1,000

t = 5 years

Standard deviation in value = 35%

We used a riskless rate of 5% and derived the expected upward and downward movements from the standard deviation:

$$u = 1.4032$$
$$d = 0.6968$$

The binomial tree is presented in Figure 29.2.

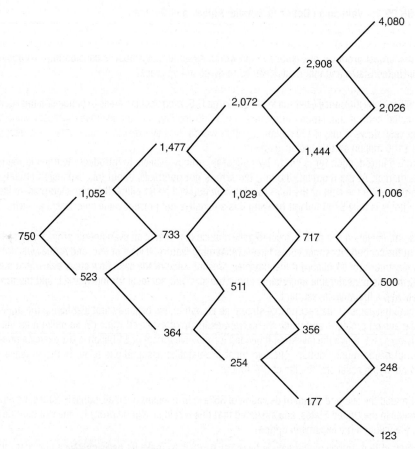

FIGURE 29.2   Binomial Tree—Ambev Expansion Option

Using the replicating portfolio framework described in Chapter 5, we estimate the value of the expansion option to be $203 million. This value can be added to the net present value of the original project under consideration.

$$\text{NPV of limited introduction} = -500 + 400 = -\$100 \text{ million}$$
$$\text{Value of option to expand} = \$203 \text{ million}$$
$$\text{NPV with option to expand} = -\$100 \text{ million} + \$203 \text{ million} = \$103 \text{ million}$$

Ambev should go ahead with the limited introduction, even though it has a negative net present value, because it acquires an option of much greater value as a consequence.

ESTIMATING VARIANCES FROM MONTE CARLO SIMULATIONS

It has been suggested a couple of times in the last two chapters that the variances to be used in real option pricing models be derived from simulations. A Monte Carlo simulation requires the following three steps:

1. You define probability distributions for each of the key inputs that underlie the cash flows, and the parameters of the distributions—the average and the standard deviation, if it is a normal distribution, for instance.
2. In each simulation, you draw one outcome from each distribution and estimate the present value of the cash flows based on these draws.
3. After repeated simulations, you should have a distribution of present values. The mean of this distribution should be the expected value of the project, and the standard deviation of the distribution can be used as the variance to value options on the project.

While the process of running these simulations is straightforward, and there are a number of software packages that exist that allow you to do this,[1] we would add the following notes of caution:

a. The most difficult step is estimating the probability distributions and parameters for the key variables. It is easier to do when a firm has had experience with similar projects in the past—a retail store considering a new store, for instance—than for a new product or a new market. If the distributions that feed into a simulation are random, the output, impressive though it might look on paper, is meaningless.
b. The standard deviation or variance that you want to use in option pricing models is a variance in value over time and not at a point in time. What is the difference, you might ask? Market testing, for instance, provides a distribution for the market potential today and reflects estimation uncertainty. The market itself will evolve over time, and it is the variance in that distribution that you would like to estimate.[2]

You should estimate the standard deviation in the value of the project—the sum of the present value of the cash flows—rather than the standard deviation in annual income or annual cash flows.

---

 expand.xls: **This spreadsheet allows you to estimate the value of the option to expand a project to cover new markets or new products, using the Black-Scholes model.**

---

[1] Crystal Ball and @Risk are two add-on packages to Excel that allow you to run simulations.
[2] You could, for instance, be fairly certain about the size of the market today—the variance would be low or even zero—but be uncertain about what the market will look like a year from now or three years from now. It is the latter variance that determines the value of the option.

Problems in Valuing the Option to Expand

The practical considerations associated with estimating the value of the option to expand are similar to those associated with valuing the option to delay. In most cases, firms with options to expand have no specific time horizon by which they have to make an expansion decision, making these open-ended options or, at best, options with arbitrary lives. Even in those cases where a life can be estimated for the option, neither the size nor the potential market for the product may be known, and estimating either can be problematic. To illustrate, consider the Ambev example discussed earlier. While we adopted a period of five years, at the end of which Ambev has to decide one way or another on its future expansion in United States, it is entirely possible that this time frame is not specified at the time the initial investment is made. Furthermore, we have assumed that both the cost and the present value of expansion are known at the time of the initial investment. In reality, the firm may not have good estimates for either input before opening the first store, since it does not have much information on the underlying market.

Extensions and Implications of Expansion Options

The option to expand can be used by firms to rationalize investing in projects that have negative net present values but provide significant opportunities to enter new markets or to sell new products. The option pricing approach adds rigor to this argument by estimating the value of these options, and it also provides insight into those occasions when they are most valuable. The option to expand is clearly more valuable for more volatile businesses with higher returns on projects (such as biotechnology or computer software), than it is for stable businesses with lower returns (such as automobile production). We will consider three cases where the expansion option may yield useful insights—strategic acquisitions, research and development expenses, and multistage projects.

Strategic Considerations in Acquisitions   In many acquisitions or investments, the acquiring firm believes that the transaction will give it competitive advantages in the future. These competitive advantages include:

- *Entry into a large or growing market.* An investment or acquisition may allow the firm to enter a large or potentially large market much sooner than it otherwise would have been able to do so. A good example of this is the acquisition of a Mexican retail firm by a U.S. firm, with the intent of expanding into the Mexican market.
- *Technological expertise.* In some cases, the acquisition is motivated by the desire to acquire a proprietary technology that will allow the acquirer to either expand its existing market or enter a new market.
- *Brand name.* Firms sometime pay large premiums over market price to acquire firms with valuable brand names, because they believe that these brand names can be used for expansion into new markets in the future.

While all these potential advantages may be used to justify large acquisition premiums, not all of them create valuable options. Even if these advantages can be viewed as valuable expansion options, the value has to be greater than the acquisition premium for stockholders to gain.

Research, Development, and Test Market Expenses   Firms that spend considerable amounts of money on research and development and test marketing are often stymied when they try to evaluate these expenses, since the payoffs are in terms of future investments. At the same time, there is the very real possibility that after the money has been spent, the products or projects may turn out not to be viable; consequently, the expenditure must be treated as a sunk cost. In fact, R&D has the characteristics of a call option—the amount spent on the R&D is the cost of the call option, and the projects or products that might emerge from it provide the payoffs on the options. If these products are viable (i.e., the present value of the cash inflows exceeds the needed investment), the payoff is the difference between the two.

Several logical implications emerge from this view of R&D. First, other things remaining equal, research expenditures should provide much higher value for firms that are in volatile businesses, since the variance in product or project cash flows is positively correlated with the value of the call option. Thus, Minnesota Mining and Manufacturing (3M), which expends a substantial amount on R&D on basic office products such as Post-it notes, should receive less option value for its research than does Amgen, whose research primarily concerns biotechnology products.[3] Second, the value of research and the optimal amount to be spent on research will change over time as businesses mature. The best example is the pharmaceutical industry: Pharmaceutical companies spent most of the 1980s investing substantial amounts in research and earning high returns on new products as health-care costs expanded. In the 1990s, however, as health-care costs started leveling off and the business matured, many of these companies found that they were not getting the same payoffs on research and started cutting back. Some companies moved research dollars from conventional drugs to biotechnology products, where uncertainty about future cash flows remains high.

Multistage Projects/Investments   When entering new businesses or taking new investments, firms sometimes have the option to move in stages. While doing so may reduce potential upside, it also protects the firm against downside risk, by allowing it at each stage to gauge demand and decide whether to go on to the next stage. In other words, a standard project can be recast as a series of options to expand, with each option being dependent on the previous one. There are two propositions that follow:

1. Some projects that are unattractive on a full-investment basis may be value-creating if the firm can invest in stages.
2. Some projects that look attractive on a full-investment basis may become even more attractive if taken in stages.

The gain in value from the options created by multistage investments has to be weighed against the cost. Taking investments in stages may allow competitors who decide to enter the market on a full scale to capture the market. It may also lead to higher costs at each stage, since the firm is not taking full advantage of economies of scale.

---

[3] This statement assumes that the quality of research is the same at both firms, though the research is in different businesses, and that the only difference is in the volatility of the underlying businesses.

Several implications emerge from viewing this choice between multistage and one-time investments in an option framework. The projects where the gains will be largest from making the investment in multiple stages include:

▪ *Projects where there are significant barriers to entry to competitors entering the market and taking advantage of delays in full-scale production.* Thus, a firm with a patent on a product or other legal protection against competition pays a much smaller price for starting small and expanding as it learns more about the market.

▪ *Projects where there is uncertainty about the size of the market and the eventual success of the project.* Here, starting small and expanding in stages allows the firm to reduce its losses if the product does not sell as well as anticipated, and to learn more about the market at each stage. This information can be useful in both product design and marketing in subsequent stages.

▪ *Projects where there is a substantial investment needed in infrastructure and high operating leverage (fixed costs).* Since the savings from doing a project in multiple stages can be traced to the investments needed at each stage, the benefit is likely to be greater in firms where those costs are large. Capital-intensive projects as well as projects that require large initial marketing expenses (a new brand-name product for a consumer product company), for example, will gain more from the options created by investing in the projects in multiple stages.

WHEN ARE EXPANSION OPTIONS VALUABLE?

While the argument that some or many investments have valuable strategic or expansion options embedded in them has great allure, there is a danger that this argument can be used to justify poor investments. In fact, acquirers have long justified huge premiums on acquisitions on synergistic and strategic grounds. We need to be more rigorous in our measurement of the value of real options and in our use of real options as justification for paying high prices or making poor investments.

SEQUENTIAL AND COMPOUND OPTIONS: SOME THOUGHTS

A compound option is an option on an option. A simple example would be a call option on a small company that has only one asset—a patent. Last chapter, we argued that a patent could be viewed as an option, and thus the call option on the company becomes a compound option. You can also have a sequence of options where the value of each option is dependent on whether the previous option is exercised. For instance, a five-stage project has sequential options. Whether you reach the fifth stage is obviously a function of whether you make it through the first four stages; the value of the fifth option in the sequence is determined by what happens to the first four options.

Needless to say, option pricing becomes more complicated when you have sequential and compound options. There are two choices. One is to value these options as simple options and accept the fact that the value that you obtain will be an approximation. The other is to modify the option pricing model to allow for the

---

special characteristics of these options. While we do not consider these models in this book, you can modify both the Black-Scholes and binomial models to allow them to price compound and sequential options.

Quantitative Estimation

When real options are used to justify a decision, the justification has to be in more than qualitative terms. In other words, managers who argue for investing in a project with poor returns, or paying a premium on an acquisition on the basis of the real options generated by this investment, should be required to value these real options and show that the economic benefits exceed the costs. There will be two arguments made against this requirement. The first is that real options cannot be easily valued, since the inputs are difficult to obtain and often noisy. The second is that the inputs to option pricing models can be easily manipulated to back up whatever the conclusion might be. While both arguments have some basis, an estimate is better than no estimate at all, and the process of trying to estimate the value of a real option is, in fact, the first step to understanding what drives its value.

Tests for Expansion Option to Have Value

Not all investments have options embedded in them, and not all options, even if they do exist, have significant value. To assess whether an investment creates valuable options that need to be analyzed and valued, we need to answer three key questions.

1. *Is the first investment a prerequisite for the later investment/expansion? If not, how necessary is the first investment for the later investment/expansion?* Consider our earlier analysis of the value of a patent or the value of an undeveloped oil reserve as options. A firm cannot generate patents without investing in research or paying another firm for the patents, and it cannot get rights to an undeveloped oil reserve without spending on exploration, bidding on it at a government auction, or buying it from another oil company. Clearly, the initial investment here (spending on R&D, bidding at the auction) is required for the firm to have the second investment. Now consider the Ambev investment in a limited introduction and the option to expand into the U.S. market later. The initial investment provides Ambev with information about market potential, without which presumably it is unwilling to expand into the larger market. Unlike the patent and undeveloped reserves examples, the initial investment is not a prerequisite for the second, though management might view it as such. The connection gets even weaker, and the option value lower, when we look at one firm acquiring another to have the option to be able to enter a large market. Acquiring a social media company to have a foothold in the social media market, or buying a Chinese brewery to preserve the option to enter the Chinese beer market, would be examples of less defensible options.

2. *Does the firm have an exclusive right to the later investment/expansion? If not, does the initial investment provide the firm with significant competitive advantages on subsequent investments?* The value of the option ultimately derives not from the

cash flows generated by the second and subsequent investments, but from the excess returns generated by these cash flows. The greater the potential for excess returns on the second investment, the greater the value of the expansion option in the first investment. The potential for excess returns is closely tied to how much of a competitive advantage the first investment provides the firm with, when it takes subsequent investments. At one extreme, again, consider investing in research and development to acquire a patent. The patent gives the firm that owns it the exclusive rights to produce that product, and if the market potential is large, the right to the excess returns from the project. At the other extreme, the firm might get no competitive advantages on subsequent investments, in which case, it is questionable as to whether there can be any excess returns on these investments. In reality, most investments will fall in the continuum between these two extremes, with greater competitive advantages being associated with higher excess returns and larger option values.

3. *Are the competitive advantages sustainable?* In a competitive marketplace, excess returns attract competitors, and competition drives down excess returns. The more sustainable the competitive advantages possessed by a firm, the greater will be the value of the options embedded in the initial investment. The sustainability of competitive advantages is a function of two forces. The first is the nature of the competition; with other things remaining equal, competitive advantages fade much more quickly in sectors where there are aggressive competitors. The second is the nature of the competitive advantage. If the resource controlled by the firm is finite and scarce (as is the case with natural resource reserves and vacant land), the competitive advantage is likely to be sustainable for longer periods. Alternatively, if the competitive advantage comes from being the first mover in a market or from having technological expertise, it will come under assault far sooner. The most direct way of reflecting this competitive advantage in the value of the option is to estimate the period of competitive advantage, and only the excess returns earned over this period count toward the value of the option.

If the answer is yes to all three questions, then the option to expand can be valuable. Applying the last two tests to the Ambev expansion option, you can see the potential problems. While Ambev is the largest producer of Guarana in the world, it does not have exclusivity on the product. If the initial introduction proves successful, it is entirely possible that Coke and Pepsi could produce their own versions of Guarana for the national market. If this occurs, Ambev will have expended $100 million of its funds to provide market information to its competitors. Thus, if Ambev gets no competitive advantage in the expansion market because of its initial investment, the option to expand ceases to have value and cannot be used to justify the initial investment. Now consider two intermediate scenarios: If Ambev gets a lead time on the expansion investment because of its initial investment, you could build in higher cash flows for that lead time and a fading off to lower cash flows thereafter. This will lower the present value of the cash flows for the expansion and the value of the option. A simpler adjustment would be to cap the present value of the cash flows, the argument being that competition will restrict how large the net present value can become, and value the option with the cap. For instance, if you assume that the present value of the cash flows from the expansion option cannot exceed $2 billion, the value of the expansion option drops to $142 million.[4]

VALUING A FIRM WITH THE OPTION TO EXPAND

Is there an option to expand embedded in some firms that can lead to these firms to trade at a premium over their discounted cash flow values? At least in theory, there is a rationale for making this argument for a small, high-growth firm in a large and evolving market. The discounted cash flow valuation is based on expected cash flows and expected growth, and these expectations should reflect the probability that the firm could be hugely successful (or a huge failure). What the expectations might fail to consider is that, in the event of success, the firm could invest more, add new products, or expand into new markets, and augment this success. This is the real option that is creating the additional value.

Relationship to Discounted Cash Flow Valuation

If the value of this option to expand is estimated, the value of a firm can be written as the sum of two components—a discounted cash flow value based on expected cash flows and a value associated with the option to expand:

Value of firm = Discounted cash flow value + Option to expand

The option pricing approach adds rigor to this argument by estimating the value of the option to expand, and it also provides insight into those occasions when it is most valuable. In general, the option to expand is clearly more valuable for more volatile businesses with higher returns on projects and greater barriers to competitive entry (such as new technology), than in stable businesses with lower returns (such as housing, utilities, or automobile production).

Again, though, you must be careful not to double-count the value of the option. If you use a higher growth rate than would be justified, based on expectations because of the option to expand, you have already counted the value of the option in the discounted cash flow valuation. Adding an additional component to reflect the value of the option would be double-counting.

---

[4] You can value the capped call by valuing the expansion option twice in the Black-Scholes model, once with a strike price of $1,000 (yielding the original expansion option value of $218 million), and once with the strike price of $2,000 (yield an option value of $76 million). The difference between the two is the value of the expansion option with a cap on the present value. You could also value it explicitly in the binomial by setting the value to $2,000 whenever it exceeds that number in the binomial tree.

Inputs for Valuing Expansion Option

To value a firm with the option to expand, you have to begin by defining the market that the firm has the option to enter, and then specifying the competitive advantages that you believe will give it some degree of exclusivity to make this entry. Once you are convinced that there is this exclusivity, you should then estimate the expected cash flows you would get if you entered the market today and the cost of entering that market. Presumably, the costs will exceed the expected cash flows, or you would have entered the market already. The cost of entering the market will become the exercise price of the option, and the expected cash flows from entering the market today will become the value of the underlying asset.

To estimate the variance in the value, you can either run simulations on how the market will evolve over time, or use the variances of publicly traded firms that service that market today and assume that this variance is a good proxy for the volatility in the underlying market. You also have to specify a period by which you have to make the decision of whether to enter the market; this will become the life of the option. You may tie this assumption to the assumptions you made about competitive advantages. For instance, if you have the exclusive license to enter a market for the next 10 years, you will use 10 years as your option life.

ILLUSTRATION 29.2:   Valuing the Option to Expand: Secure Mail

Secure Mail is a young software company specializing in security software. Assume that you have completed a conventional discounted cash flow valuation of the company and estimated a value of $111.54 million for the firm. However, there is the possibility that the company could use the customer base that it developed for the antivirus software and the technology on which the software is based to create a database software program sometime in the next five years, and you have collected the following information on the potential:

- It will cost Secure Mail about $500 million to develop a new database program if it decides to do it today.
- Based on the information that Secure Mail has right now on the market for a database program, the company can expect to generate about $40 million a year in after-tax cash flows for 10 years. The cost of capital for private companies that provide database software is 12%.
- The annualized standard deviation in firm value at publicly traded database companies is 50%.
- The five-year Treasury bond rate is 3%.

To value the expansion option, we used the information to derive the option inputs:

$$S = \text{Value of underlying asset}$$
$$= \text{PV of expected cash flows from entering database market}$$
$$= \frac{40\left(1 - \frac{1}{1.12^{10}}\right)}{0.12} = \$226 \text{ million}$$

$$K = \text{Exercise price} = \text{Cost of entering the database software market} = \$500 \text{ million}$$
$$t = \text{Life of the option} = \text{Period over which expansion opportunity exists} = 5 \text{ years}$$
$$\sigma = \text{Standard deviation of underlying asset} = 50\%$$
$$r = \text{Riskless rate} = 3\%$$

Inputting these numbers into the Black-Scholes model, we obtain the following[5]:

$$\text{Value of call} = S\,N(d1) - K\,e^{-rt}N(d2)$$
$$= 226(0.4932) - 500\,e^{-(.03)(5)}(0.1282) = \$56.30 \text{ million}$$

Note that the numbers would not justify developing the database program today—the present value of the expected cash flows ($226 million) is well below the cost. However, Secure Mail has two factors in its favor. The first is that it can refine its assessments of the market, based on how its antivirus program performs. The second is that it can adapt the database program, based on the information it collects, to increase the potential market and cash flows.

If we accept this value for the expansion option, we should add it to the value that we derived for Secure Mail earlier in the intrinsic valuation of $111.54 million. We would justify the use of the option pricing model in this case, by arguing that Secure Mail derives its exclusivity from its proprietary technology and access to customer lists (from its antivirus program).

---

 expand.xls: This spreadsheet allows you to estimate the value of the option to expand an investment or project.

VALUING THE OPTIONALITY IN USERS AND DATA

In the last two decades, a combination of access to the internet and the ubiquity of connected devices (e.g., smartphones, tablets, etc.) has given rise to two forces that have driven business and markets. The first is that millions, and sometimes tens of millions of users/subscribers/customers congregated on platforms delivering a variety of services, ranging from search engines (Google/Alphabet) to social media (Facebook/Meta) to entertainment (Netflix) to retail (Amazon). The second is that these companies collected data on their user behavior and choices, sometimes voluntarily provided and sometimes not, which they put to good use. The heady mix of millions of users and big data was used as justification for huge market capitalization, and while some of the argument was in terms of intrinsic value (higher earnings and growth), some of it was based on the promise and potential of unspecified benefits from the users and data (i.e., their optionality).

The Optionality in Users

In an earlier chapter, we estimated the intrinsic value of a user and subscriber and argued that this value comes from the standard drivers—the expected tenure of a user on the platform and the expected cash flows that the company generated from the user/subscriber

---

[5] The values that we derive for d1 and d2 are as follows:

$$d1 = \frac{\ln\left(\frac{226}{500}\right) + \left(0.03 + \frac{0.50^2}{2}\right)5}{0.50\sqrt{5}} - 0.0171$$

$$d2 = 0.0171 - 0.50\sqrt{5} = -1.1351$$

during that tenure. That approach can be used to value a subscriber to Netflix, an Amazon prime member, or even a Facebook user. To understand why you may still need to bring in optionality into the discussion, consider a company like Meta, which has close to three billion people on its multiple platforms (Facebook, Instagram, WhatsApp). Assume that you value Meta based on its advertising revenues, which remain their primary form of monetizing users currently, and estimate an intrinsic value of $500 per share, close to the current market price (in June 2024). While the firm looks fairly valued on an intrinsic value basis, there is the possibility that Meta may find other ways of generating revenues (entertainment, retail, gaming) from its user base, and while those possibilities may not be viable today, they could be in the future. In effect, you have made an optionality argument, which will justify paying a premium over intrinsic value, and convert the stock from fairly valued to undervalued.

Clearly, we are opening a Pandora's box with this argument, since it will then be used to pay premiums for any company that has large user/subscriber platforms, and those premiums will not be capped at reasonable numbers. While it may be premature to attach option pricing inputs and derive an actual value for the platform option, it is not premature to consider the following factors in determining whether a premium should exist, and if so, whether it should be large or small. Figure 29.3 shows the drivers of the option value in a platform.

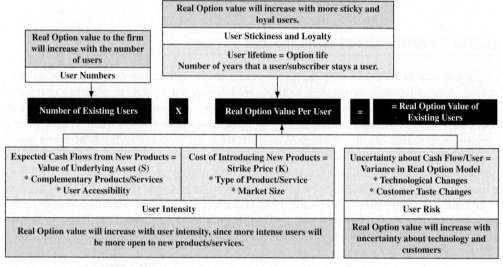

FIGURE 29.3   Optionality in Platforms – Value Drivers

The value of a real option comes from exclusivity, and to the extent that you have sticky intense users, you have a customer base that you can use to experiment with other products and services, whose value scales up with the number of uses. The value of optionality from a user base will be greatest at firms with lots of sticky, intense users in businesses where the future is unpredictable because of changes in product/service technology and customer tastes.

To understand how a real options argument will play out with a user-based company, contrast the Snapchat and Meta user platforms. While Snapchat has millions of users, the users tend to be less sticky and intense, and thus less likely to be open to add-on products and services that the company may offer. Meta users spend significantly more tie on its platform and are likely to be more to entertainment or retail products and services that the company may offer. With Amazon Prime, the potential upside of having 150 million Prime members, who have developed a loyalty to Amazon based upon numerous past interactions with it, at the company's beck and call, is the equivalent of having an army to back Amazon's disruption platform in almost any business it chooses to target, from Paypal in payment processing to CVS in prescription drugs. In contrast, we would argue that the Netflix model has less potential upside, in terms of other products and services that the company can sell subscribers, and thus less optionality.

The Optionality in Data

In 2017, MoviePass introduced an almost comically bad business model, where in return for paying ten dollars a month, subscribers could see as many movies as they wanted at the theaters of their choice. Its management justified the model by arguing that it would not only draw in millions of users, but also that the company could collect information from their users on movie responses and preference that could be monetized. That promise never delivered and the business model folded, but through the decade, there were hundreds of companies that used the promise of Big Data to command hefty market pricing. In many cases, the argument was that data collected today would find an unspecified use some time in the future, with significant economic benefits (i.e., an optionality argument).

We are believers in data, but we are skeptical about the Big Data value claims, because most of those claims are on flimsy grounds. In fact, there are three requirements that we would look for to attach high value to data:

1. *The data must be exclusive:* For data to have value, you have to some degree of exclusivity in access to that data or a proprietary edge on processing that data. It is one of the reasons that investors have been unable, for the most part, to convert increased access to financial data into investing profits. The data collected by Netflix on what their subscribers watch or stop watching is clearly exclusive, but the data collected by Bird Scooters on location is close to worthless, since it is available to dozens of entities.

2. *The data must be actionable:* To convert data to profits, you need to be able to find a way to monetize whatever data edge you have acquired. For companies that offer products and services, this will take the form of modifying existing products/services or coming up with new products/services to what you have learned from the data. Data that is abstract, where it is difficult to even think of ways to monetize that data, should be viewed as less valuable than data that is concrete and offers pathways to monetization, even if those pathways are not viable today.

3. *The data resolves (some) uncertainty:* In keeping with the principle that options derive their value from uncertainty, data that is collected in a space where there is significant uncertainty about outcomes or behavior is more valuable than data that is collected in spaces where there is less deviation from the norm.

Using this checklist to assess Big Data claims will make you more discriminating in assessing the value of data.

VALUE OF FINANCIAL FLEXIBILITY

When making financial decisions, managers consider the effects of such decisions on their capacity to make new investments or meet unanticipated contingencies in future periods. Practically, this translates into firms maintaining excess debt capacity or larger cash balances than are warranted by current needs in order to meet unexpected future requirements. While maintaining this financing flexibility has value to firms, it also has a cost; the large cash balances might earn below-market returns, and excess debt capacity implies that the firm is giving up some value and has a higher cost of capital.

Determinants of the Value of Financial Flexibility

One reason that a firm maintains large cash balances and excess debt capacity is to have the future option to take unexpected projects with high returns. To value financial flexibility as an option, assume that a firm has expectations about how much it will need to reinvest in future periods, based on its own history and current conditions in the industry. Assume also that a firm has expectations about how much it can raise from internal funds and its normal access to capital markets in future periods. There is uncertainty about future reinvestment needs; for simplicity, we will assume that the capacity to generate funds is known with certainty to the firm. The advantage (and value) of having excess debt capacity or large cash balances is that the firm can meet any reinvestment needs, in excess of funds available, using its debt capacity. The payoff from these projects, however, comes from the excess returns the firm expects to make on them. To value financial flexibility on an annualized basis, therefore, we will use the measures listed in Table 29.1.

TABLE 29.1   Inputs to Option Valuation: Financing Flexibility

Input to Model	Measure	Estimation Approach
S	Expected annual reinvestment needs as percent of firm value	Use historical average of (Net cap ex + Change in noncash working capital)/ Market value of firm
K	Annual reinvestment needs as percent of firm value that can be raised without financing flexibility	If firm does not want to or cannot use external financing:(Net income − Dividend + Depreciation)/Market value of firm
		If firm uses external capital (bank debt, bonds, or equity) regularly: (Net income + Depreciation + Net external financing)/ Market value of firm
σ^s	Variance in reinvestment needs	Variance in the reinvestment as percent of firm value (using historical data)
t	1 year	To get an annual estimate of the value of flexibility

ILLUSTRATION 29.3: Valuing Financial Flexibility at the Home Depot in 1999

The Home Depot is a giant retail chain that sells home improvement products, primarily in the United States. This firm traditionally has not been a heavy user of debt and has also grown at an extraordinary rate over the past decade. To estimate the value of financial flexibility for the Home Depot, we began by estimating reinvestments as a percent of firm value from 1989 to 1998 in the Table 29.2:

TABLE 29.2 Reinvestment Needs at Home Depot

Year	Reinvestment Needs	Firm Value	Reinvestment as % of Value	In(Reinvestment Needs)
1989	$ 175	$ 2,758	6.35%	−2.7574751
1990	$ 374	$ 3,815	9.80%	−2.3224401
1991	$ 427	$ 5,137	8.31%	−2.4874405
1992	$ 456	$ 7,148	6.38%	−2.7520951
1993	$ 927	$ 9,239	10.03%	−2.2992354
1994	$1,176	$12,477	9.43%	−2.3617681
1995	$1,344	$15,470	8.69%	−2.4432524
1996	$1,086	$19,535	5.56%	−2.8897065
1997	$1,589	$24,156	6.58%	−2.7214279
1998	$1,817	$30,219	6.01%	−2.8112841

Average reinvestment needs as % of firm value $= 7.71\%$
Standard deviation in In(Reinvestment needs) $= 22.36\%$

We followed up by estimating internal funds as a percent of firm value, using the sum of net income and depreciation as a measure of internal funds, in Table 29.3:

TABLE 29.3 Earnings, Value, and Internal Funds

Year	Net Income	Depreciation	Firm Value	Internal funds/Value
1989	$ 112	$ 21	$ 2,758	4.82%
1990	$ 163	$ 34	$ 3,815	5.16%
1991	$ 249	$ 52	$ 5,137	5.86%
1992	$ 363	$ 70	$ 7,148	6.06%
1993	$ 457	$ 90	$ 9,239	5.92%
1994	$ 605	$130	$12,477	5.89%
1995	$ 732	$181	$15,470	5.90%
1996	$ 938	$232	$19,535	5.99%
1997	$1,160	$283	$24,156	5.97%
1998	$1,614	$373	$30,219	6.58%

Internal funds, on average, were 5.82% of firm value between 1989 and 1998. Since the firm uses almost no external debt, the firm made up the difference between its reinvestment needs (7.71%) and internal fund generation (5.82%) by issuing equity. We will assume, looking forward, that Home Depot will no longer issue new equity.

The Home Depot's current debt ratio is 4.55%, and its current cost of capital is 9.51%. Using the cost of capital framework developed in Chapter 15, we estimated its optimal debt ratio to be 20%, and its cost of capital at that debt level is 9.17%. Finally, Home Depot in 1998 earned a return on capital of 16.37%, and we will assume that this is the expected return on new projects as well.

S = Expected reinvestment needs as percent of firm value = 7.71%

K = Reinvestment needs that can be financed without flexibility = 5.82%

t = 1 year

σ^2 = Variance in ln(Net capital expenditures) = $(.2237)^2$ = .05

With a risk-free rate of 6%, the option value that we estimate using these inputs is .02277. We then convert this option value into a measure of value over time by multiplying the value by the annual excess return, and then assuming that the firm forgoes this excess return forever[6]:

$$\text{Value of flexibility} = 02277 \times \frac{\text{Return on capital} - \text{Cost of capital}}{\text{Cost of capital}}$$

$$= .02277 \times (.1637 - .0951)/.0951 = 1.6425\%$$

On an annual basis, the flexibility generated by the excess debt capacity is worth 1.6425% of firm value at the Home Depot, which is well in excess of the savings (9.51% − 9.17% = 0.34%) in the cost of capital that would be accomplished, if it used up the excess debt capacity.

   The one final consideration here is that this estimate does not consider the fact that Home Depot does not have unlimited financial flexibility. In fact, assume that excess debt capacity of the Home Depot (which is 15.45%, the difference between the optimal debt ratio and the current debt ratio) is the upside limit on financial flexibility. We can value the effect of this limit by valuing a call with the same parameters as the call described earlier, but with a strike price of 21.27% (15.45% + 5.82%). In this case, the effect of imposing this constraint on the value of flexibility is negligible.

---

 finflex.xls: **This spreadsheet allows you to estimate the value of financial flexibility as an option.**

Implications of Financial Flexibility Option

Looking at financial flexibility as an option yields valuable insights on when financial flexibility is most valuable. Using the approach developed earlier, for instance, we would argue that:

■ Other things remaining equal, firms operating in businesses where projects earn substantially higher returns than their hurdle rates should value flexibility more than those that operate in stable businesses where excess returns are small. This would imply that firms such as Microsoft and Nvidia, which earn large excess returns on their projects, can use the need for financial flexibility as justification for holding large cash balances and maintaining excess debt capacity.

■ Since a firm's ability to fund these reinvestment needs is determined by its capacity to generate internal funds, other things remaining equal, financial flexibility should be worth less to firms with large and stable earnings as a percent of firm value. Firms that have small or negative earnings, and therefore a much lower capacity to generate internal funds, will value flexibility more.

---

[6] We are assuming that the project that a firm is unable to take because it lacks financial flexibility is lost forever, and that the excess returns on this project would also have lasted forever. Both assumptions are strong and may result in overstatement of the lost value.

■ Firms with limited internal funds can still get away with little or no financial flexibility if they can tap external markets for capital—bank debt, bonds, and new equity issues. Other things remaining equal, the greater the capacity (and the willingness) of a firm to raise funds from external capital markets, the less should be the value of flexibility. This may explain why private or small firms, which have far less access to capital, will value financial flexibility more than larger, publicly traded firms. The existence of corporate bond markets can also make a difference in how much flexibility is valued. In markets where firms cannot issue bonds and have to depend entirely on banks for financing, there is less access to capital and a greater need to maintain financial flexibility. In the Home Depot example, a willingness to tap external funds—debt or equity—would reduce the value of flexibility substantially.

■ The need for and the value of flexibility is a function of how uncertain a firm is about future reinvestment needs. Firms with predictable reinvestment needs should value flexibility less than firms in businesses whose reinvestment needs are volatile on a period-to-period basis.

In our analysis of Home Depot, we considered the firm's gross debt ratio, which cannot be less than 0 percent. If we consider a firm's net debt ratio (gross debt minus cash), we see it is entirely possible for a firm to have a negative net debt ratio. Extending the financing flexibility argument, you could argue that in extreme circumstances—low or negative internal cash flows and no access to capital markets—firms not only will not use their debt capacity (thus driving the gross debt ratio to zero) but will accumulate cash. This may explain why many emerging market firms and young technology firms use no debt and accumulate large cash balances.

THE OPTION TO ABANDON

When investing in new projects, firms worry about the risk that the investment will not pay off, and that actual cash flows will not measure up to expectations. Having the option to abandon a project that does not pay off can be valuable, especially on projects with a significant potential for losses. This section examines the value of the option to abandon and its determinants.

Payoff on the Option to Abandon

The option pricing approach provides a general way of estimating and building in the value of abandonment. To illustrate, assume that V is the remaining value on a project if it continues to the end of its life, and L is the liquidation or abandonment value for the same project at the same point in time. If the project has a remaining life of n years, the value of continuing the project can be compared to the liquidation (abandonment) value. If the value from continuing is higher, the project should be continued; if the value of abandonment is higher, the holder of the abandonment option could consider abandoning the project. The payoffs can be written as:

$$\text{Payoff from owning abandonment option} = 0 \quad \text{if } V \geq L$$
$$= L - V \quad \text{if } V < L$$

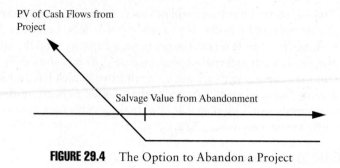

FIGURE 29.4   The Option to Abandon a Project

These payoffs are graphed in Figure 29.4, as a function of the expected stock price. Unlike the prior two cases, the option to abandon takes on the characteristics of a put option.

ILLUSTRATION 29.4:   Valuing an Option to Abandon: Airbus and Lear Aircraft

Assume that Lear Aircraft is interested in building a small passenger plane and that it approaches Airbus with a proposal for a joint venture. Each firm will invest $500 million in the joint venture and produce the planes. The investment is expected to have a 30-year life. Airbus works through a traditional investment analysis and concludes that its share of the present value of the expected cash flows would be only $480 million. The net present value of the project would, therefore, be negative, and Airbus would not want to be part of this joint venture.

On rejection of the joint venture, Lear approaches Airbus with a sweetener, offering to buy out Airbus's 50% share of the joint venture any time over the next five years for $400 million. This is less than what Airbus will invest initially, but it puts a floor on its losses, and thus gives Airbus an abandonment option. To value this option to Airbus, note that the inputs are as follows:

S = Present value of the share of cash flows from the investment today = $480 million

K = Abandonment value = $400 million

t = Period for which abandonment option holds = 5 years

To estimate the variance, assume that Airbus employs a Monte Carlo simulation on the project analysis and estimates a standard deviation in project value of 25%. Finally, note that since the project is a finite-life project, the present value will decline over time, because there will be fewer years of cash flow left. For simplicity, we will assume that this will be proportional to the time left on the project:

Cost of delay (y) = 1/Remaining life of the project = 1/30 = 3.33%

Inputting these values into the Black-Scholes model and using a 5% riskless rate, we value the put option as follows:

$$\text{Value of abandonment option} = 400\exp^{(-0.05)(5)}(1 - 0.5776)$$
$$-480\exp^{(-0.033)(5)}(1 - 0.7748)$$
$$= \$40.09 \text{ million}$$

Since this is greater than the negative net present value of the investment, Airbus should enter into this joint venture. On the other hand, Lear needs to be able to generate a positive net present value of at least $40.09 million to compensate for giving up this option.[7]

---

 abandon.xls: **This spreadsheet allows you to estimate the value of the option to abandon an investment.**

Problems in Valuing the Option to Abandon

Illustration 29.4 assumed, rather unrealistically, that the abandonment value was clearly specified and did not change during the life of the project. This may be true in some very specific cases, in which an abandonment option is built into the contract. More often, however, the firm has the option to abandon, and the salvage value from abandonment can only be estimated. Further, the abandonment value may change over the life of the project, making it difficult to apply traditional option pricing techniques. Finally, it is entirely possible that abandoning a project may not bring in a liquidation value but may create costs instead; a manufacturing firm may have to pay severance to its workers, for instance. In such cases, it would not make sense to abandon unless the cash flows on the project are even more negative.

Extensions and Implications of Abandonment Options

The fact that the option to abandon has value provides a rationale for firms to build the operating flexibility to scale back or terminate projects if they do not measure up to expectations. It also indicates that firms, which try to generate more revenues by offering their customers the option to walk away from commitments, will have to weigh the higher revenues against the cost of the options that have been granted to these customers.

Escape Clauses in Contracts The first and most direct way of creating an abandonment option is to build operating flexibility contractually with other parties that are involved in a project. Thus, contracts with suppliers may be written on an annual basis rather than be long term, and employees may be hired on a temporary basis rather than permanently. The physical plant used for a project may be leased on a short-term basis rather than bought, and the financial investment may be made in stages rather than as an initial lump sum. While there is a cost to building in this flexibility, the gains may be much larger, especially in volatile businesses.

Customer Incentives On the other side of the transaction, offering abandonment options to customers and partners in joint ventures can have a negative impact on value. As an example, assume that a firm that sells its products on multiyear contracts offers customers the option to cancel the contract at any time. While this may increase sales, there is likely to be a substantial cost. In the event of a recession, customers that are unable to meet their obligations are likely to cancel their contracts. Any benefits gained by the initial sale

---

[7] The binomial model yields a value of $46.44 million for this option.

(obtained by offering the inducement of cancellation by the buyer) may be offset by the cost of the option provided to customers.

RECONCILING NET PRESENT VALUE AND REAL OPTION VALUATIONS

Why does an investment sometimes have higher value when you value it using real-option approaches than with traditional discounted cash flow models? The answer lies in the flexibility that firms have to change the way they invest in and run a project, based on what they observe in the market. Thus, an oil company will not produce the same amount of oil, or drill as many new wells, if oil prices go to $15 a barrel as it would if oil prices would go up to $95 a barrel.

In traditional net present value, we consider the expected actions and the cash flow consequences of those actions to estimate the value of an investment. If there is a potential for further investments, expansion, or abandonment down the road, all you can do is consider the probabilities of such actions and build them into your cash flows. Analysts often allow for flexibility by using decision trees and mapping out the optimal path, given each outcome. You can then estimate the value of a project today, using the probabilities of each branch and estimating the present value of the cash flows from each branch.

This decision tree does bear a significant resemblance to the binomial tree approach that we use to value real options, but there are two differences. The first is that the probabilities of the outcomes are not used directly to value the real option, and the second is that you have only two branches at each node in the binomial tree. Notwithstanding this, you might wonder why the two approaches will yield different values for the project. The answer is surprisingly simple. It lies in the discount rate assumptions we make to compute the value. In the real - options approach, you use a replicating portfolio to compute value. In the decision tree, you used the cost of capital for the project as the discount rate all through the process. If the exposure to market risk, which is what determines the cost of capital, changes at each node, you can argue that using the same cost of capital all the way through is incorrect, and that you should be modifying the discount rate as you move through time. If you do, you will obtain the same value with both approaches. The real options approach does allow for far more complexity and is simpler to employ with continuous distributions (as opposed to the discrete outcomes that we assume in decision trees). We will return to examine decision trees and other probabilistic approaches in Chapter 33.

CONCLUSION

This chapter considered two options that are embedded in many investments—the option to expand an investment, and the option to abandon it. When a firm has an option to expand an investment, the value of this expansion option may sometimes allow it to override the fact that the initial investment has a negative net present value. Extending this concept to firm valuation, you may sometimes add a premium to the value obtained from a discounted cash flow valuation for a firm that has the potential to enter new markets or create new products. This expansion option has maximum value when the firm has the exclusive right to make these investments, and the value decreases as the competitive advantages enjoyed by the firm decline.

The option to abandon refers to the right that firms often possess to walk away from poor investments. To the extent that this reduces the firm's exposure to the worst outcomes, it can make the difference between investing in a new project and not investing.

QUESTIONS AND SHORT PROBLEMS

In the problems following, use an equity risk premium of 5.5 percent if none is specified.

1. NBC has the rights to televise the Winter Olympics in two years, and is trying to estimate the value of these rights for possible sale to another network. NBC expects it to cost $40 million (in present value terms) to televise the Olympics, and based on current assessments, expects to have a Nielsen rating of 15 for the games. Each rating point is expected to yield net revenue of $2 million to NBC (in present value terms). There is substantial variability in this estimate, and the standard deviation in the expected net revenues is 30%. The riskless rate is 5%.
   a. What is the net present value of these rights, based on current assessments?
   b. Estimate the value of these rights for sale to another network.
2. You are analyzing Skates Inc., a firm that manufactures skateboards. The firm is currently unlevered and has a cost of equity of 12%. You estimate that Skates would have a cost of capital of 11% at its optimal debt ratio of 40%. The management, however, insists that it will not borrow the money because of the value of maintaining financial flexibility and has provided you with the following information:
   - Over the past 10 years, reinvestment (net capital expenditures + working capital investments) has amounted to 10% of firm value, on an annual basis. The standard deviation in this reinvestment has been 0.30.
   - The firm has traditionally used only internal funding (net income + depreciation) to meet these needs, and these have amounted to 6% of firm value.
   - In the most recent year, the firm earned $180 million in net income on a book value of equity of $1 billion, and it expects to earn these excess returns on new investments in the future.
   - The riskless rate is 5%.

   a. Estimate the value of financial flexibility as a percent of firm value on an annual basis.
   b. Based on (a), would you recommend that Skates use its excess debt capacity?
3. Disney is considering entering into a joint venture to build condominiums in Vail, Colorado, with a local real estate developer. The development is expected to cost $1 billion overall and, based on Disney's estimate of the cash flows, generate $900 million in present value cash flows over 25 years. Disney will have a 40% share of the joint venture (requiring it to put up $400 million of the initial investment and entitling it to 40% of the cash flows), but it will have the right to sell its share of the venture back to the developer for $300 million anytime over the next five years. (The project life is 25 years.)
   a. If the standard deviation in real estate values in Vail is 30% and the riskless rate is 5%, estimate the value of the abandonment option to Disney.
   b. Would you advise Disney to enter into the joint venture?
   c. If you were advising the developer, how much would he need to generate in present value cash flows from the investment to make this a good investment?

4. Quality Wireless is considering making an investment in China. While it is known that the investment will cost $1 billion and generate only $800 million in cash flows (in present value terms), the proponents of expansion are arguing that the potential market is huge and that Quality should go ahead with its investment.
   a. Under what conditions will the expansion potential have option value?
   b. Assume now that there is an option value to expansion that exactly offsets the negative net present value on the initial investment. If the cost of the subsequent expansion in five years is $2.5 billion, what is your current estimate of the present value of the cash flows from expansion? (You can assume that the standard deviation in the present value of the cash flows is 25% and that the riskless rate is 6%.)

5. Reliable Machinery Inc. is considering expanding its operations in Thailand. The initial analysis of the project yields the following results:
   ■ The project is expected to generate $85 million in after-tax cash flows every year for the next 10 years.
   ■ The initial investment in the project is expected to be $750 million.
   ■ The cost of capital for the project is 12%.

6. If the project generates much higher cash flows than anticipated, you will have the exclusive right for the next 10 years (from a manufacturing license) to expand operations into the rest of Southeast Asia. A current analysis suggests the following about the expansion opportunity:
   ■ The expansion will cost $2 billion (in current dollars).
   ■ The expansion is expected to generate $150 million in after-tax cash flows each year for 15 years. There is substantial uncertainty about these cash flows, and the standard deviation in the present value is 40%.
   ■ The cost of capital for this investment is expected to be 12% as well. The risk-free rate is 6.5%.
   a. Estimate the net present value of the initial investment.
   b. Estimate the value of the expansion option.

CHAPTER 30

Valuing Equity in Distressed Firms

Chapter 22 examined how discounted cash flow models could be adapted to value firms with negative earnings. Most of the solutions estimated the expected cash flows into the future and assumed that an improvement in margins or earnings would result in positive cash flows and firm value. In the special case where the firm has substantial amounts of debt, we argued that there is a very real possibility of defaulting on the debt and going bankrupt. In these cases, discounted cash flow valuation will tell you that equity is worth nothing. This chapter looks at firms with negative earnings, significant assets in place, and substantial debt. We argue that the equity investors in this firm, given limited liability, have the option to liquidate the firm and pay off the debt. This call option on the underlying firm can add value to equity, especially when there is significant uncertainty about the value of the assets.

EQUITY IN HIGHLY LEVERED DISTRESSED FIRMS

In most publicly traded firms, equity has two features. The first is that the equity investors run the firm and can choose to liquidate its assets and pay off other claim holders at any time. The second is that the liability of equity investors in some private firms and almost all publicly traded firms is restricted to their equity investments in these firms. This combination of the option to liquidate and limited liability enables equity to have the features of a call option. In firms with substantial liabilities and negative earnings, the option value of equity may be in excess of the discounted cash flow value.

Payoff on Equity as an Option

The equity in a firm is a residual claim, that is, equity holders lay claim to all cash flows left after other financial claimholders (debt, preferred stock, etc.) have been satisfied. If a firm is liquidated, the same principle applies; equity investors receive the cash that is left in the firm after all outstanding debt and other financial claims have been paid off. With limited liability, if the value of the firm is less than the value of the outstanding debt, equity investors cannot lose more than their investment in the firm. The payoff to equity investors on liquidation can, therefore, be written as:

$$\text{Payoff to equity on liquidation} = V - D \quad \text{if } V > D$$
$$= 0 \quad \text{if } V \leq D$$

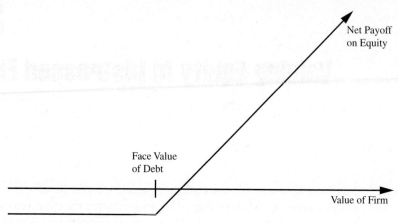

FIGURE 30.1 Payoff on Equity as Option on a Firm

where V = Liquidation value of the firm

D = Face value of the outstanding debt and other nonequity claims

Equity can, thus, be viewed as a call option on the firm, where exercising the option requires that the firm be liquidated and the face value of the debt (which corresponds to the exercise price) be paid off. The firm is the underlying asset, and the option expires when the debt comes due. The payoffs are shown in Figure 30.1.

IMPORTANCE OF LIMITED LIABILITY

The argument that equity is a call option holds only if equity has limited liability—that is, the most that an equity investor can lose is what he or she has invested in a firm. This is clearly the case in publicly traded companies. In private companies, however, the owners often have unlimited liability. If these firms get into financial trouble and are unable to make their debt payments, the owner's personal assets can be put at risk. You should not value equity as a call option in these cases.

ILLUSTRATION 30.1: Valuing Equity as an Option

Assume that you are valuing the equity in a firm whose assets are currently valued at $100 million; the standard deviation in this asset value is 40%. The face value of debt is $80 million. (It is zero coupon debt with 10 years left to maturity.) The 10-year Treasury bond rate is 10%. We can value equity as a call option on the firm, using the following inputs for the option pricing model:

Value of the underlying asset = S = Value of the firm = $100 million
Exercise price = K = Face value of outstanding debt = $80 million

Life of the option = t = Life of zero – coupon debt = 10 years
Variance in the value of the underlying asset = σ^2 = Variance in firm value = 0.16
Riskless rate = r = Treasury bond rate corresponding to option life = 10%

Based on these inputs, the Black-Scholes model provides the following value for the call:

$$d1 = 1.5994 \quad N(d1) = 0.9451$$
$$d2 = 0.3345 \quad N(d2) = 0.6310$$
$$\text{Value of the call} = 100(0.9451) - 80 \ \exp^{(-0.10)(10)}(0.6310) = \$75.94 \text{ million}$$

Since the call value represents the value of equity and the firm value is $100 million, the estimated value of the outstanding debt is:

$$\text{Value of the outstanding debt} = \$100 - \$75.94 = \$24.06 \text{ million}$$

The debt is a 10-year zero coupon bond, and the market interest rate on the bond is:

$$\text{Interest rate on debt} = (\$80/\$24.06)^{1/10} - 1 = 12.77\%$$

Thus, the default spread on this bond should be 2.77%.

OPTIONALITY IN VALUATION: A CORPORATE LIFE CYCLE PERSPECTIVE

In the last few chapters, we have looked at real options as a source of value for firms, starting with the option to delay in Chapter 28, with applications in valuing patents and natural resource reserves, moving on to the option to expand in Chapter 29, and how it can add to the value of some firms, and closing up with the option to liquidate, and why that option can make equity in deeply distressed firms more valuable. As we looked at these options, we also noted how easily they can be used, especially in their generalized versions, to justify the unjustifiable. In this section, we will use the corporate life structure perspective that we have used in earlier chapters to explain which options are more likely to come into play in each section of the life cycle

Real Options across the Corporate Life Cycle

The corporate life cycle, where we look at firms from start-up to decline and death, provides a lens through which we can trace not just the aging of firm, but also how the challenges in valuation change. That structure can help in understanding where the real options to delay, expand, abandon, and liquidate come into play in valuation, as can be seen in Figure 30.2.

As you can see, equity as an option is most likely to come into play in the later stages of the life cycle, and only with declining or mature firms that have accumulated large amounts of debt. In the absence of debt, with declining firms, you are more likely to see the option to abandon be more prevalent, as firms divest or sell businesses because their continuing value (from earnings and cash flows) is less than their divestiture value.

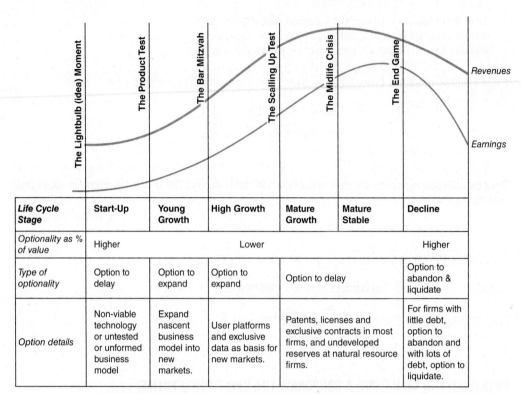

Life Cycle Stage	Start-Up	Young Growth	High Growth	Mature Growth	Mature Stable	Decline
Optionality as % *of value*	Higher		Lower			Higher
Type of optionality	Option to delay	Option to expand	Option to expand	Option to delay		Option to abandon & liquidate
Option details	Non-viable technology or untested or unformed business model	Expand nascent business model into new markets.	User platforms and exclusive data as basis for new markets.	Patents, licenses and exclusive contracts in most firms, and undeveloped reserves at natural resource firms.		For firms with little debt, option to abandon and with lots of debt, option to liquidate.

FIGURE 30.2   Optionality across the Corporate Life Cycle

Distressed Equity Screening

While it may seem outlandish that equity in a deeply distressed firm can have significant value, that value comes from three forces: a business with extended losses from operations, a disproportionately large debt load (of mostly longer-term debt) and volatility in operating results. To find companies that meet the criteria for viewing distressed equity as a (liquidation) option, we started by defining the following screens to capture them:

1. *Money losing:* We looked at net income in the last ten years and chose companies that had losses in at least four of those years. In addition, we looked at the most recent year's financials, and picked companies that were losing money.
2. *Large debt load:* As we saw in Chapter 3, there are multiple measures of debt load, but since we wanted to relate debt to the company's operating cash flows, we used total debt (including leases) as a multiple of EBITDA as a proxy. We would have liked to add a screen for debt maturity, focusing on companies with longer-term debt, but many of the companies in our data did not have this as a reported data item.
3. *Volatility in business:* To measure business risk, we considered a market-based risk measure in standard deviation in stock prices, as well as one based upon operating metrics in a coefficient of variation in operation income over the last ten years.

Running these screens on all 6,415 publicly traded U.S. companies at the start of 2024, we arrived at a list of 560 firms that have optionality in their equity, albeit to different degrees.

Looking across sectors, there are some sectors where you see these companies are overrepresented, and others where very few make the cut. The three sectors where you do see more distressed equity candidates are airlines, hotels and casinos, and real estate. What do they have in common? In addition to carrying significant amounts of debt, these firms tend to have assets that have significant liquidation value, with real estate in particular appealing to a broad cross-section of buyers. Note that there are sectors like biotechnology where there are large numbers of firms that are money-losing, but very few of them carry the debt load that would make the liquidation option come into play.

In sectors with little debt and/or healthy earnings, equity in every company continues to have an option (to liquidate) value, but that value is so far below the value of the company as an operating business that it does not come into play.

IMPLICATIONS OF VIEWING EQUITY AS AN OPTION

When the equity in a firm takes on the characteristics of a call option, you have to change the way you think about its value and what determines its value. In this section, we will consider a number of potential implications for equity investors and bondholders in the firm.

When Will Equity Be Worthless?

In a discounted cash flow valuation, we argue that equity is worthless if what you own (the value of the assets) is less than what you owe. The first implication of viewing equity as a call option is that equity will have value, even if the value of the assets falls well below the face value of the outstanding debt. While the firm will be viewed as troubled by investors, accountants, and analysts, its equity is not worthless. In fact, just as deep out-of-the-money traded options command value because of the possibility that the value of the underlying asset may increase above the strike price in the remaining lifetime of the option, equity commands value because of the time premium on the option (the time until the bonds mature and come due) and the possibility that the value of the assets may increase above the face value of the bonds before they come due.

ILLUSTRATION 30.2: Firm Value and Equity Value

Revisiting the preceding example, assume that the value of the firm drops to $50 million, below the face value of the outstanding debt ($80 million). Assume that all the other inputs remain unchanged. The parameters of equity as a call option are as follows:

Value of the underlying asset = S = Value of the firm = $50 million
Exercise price = K = Face value of outstanding debt = $80 million
Life of the option = t = Life of zero – coupon debt = 10 years
Variance in the value of the underlying asset = σ^2 = Variance in firm value = 0.16
Riskless rate = r = Treasury bond rate corresponding to option life = 10%

Based on these inputs, the Black-Scholes model provides the following value for the call:

$$d1 = 1.0515 \quad N(d1) = 0.8534$$
$$d2 = -0.2135 \; N(d2) = 0.4155$$

Value of the call (equity) $= 50(0.8534) - 80 \; \exp^{(-0.10)(10)}(0.4155) = \$30.44$ million

Value of the bond $= \$50 - \$30.44 = \$19.56$ million

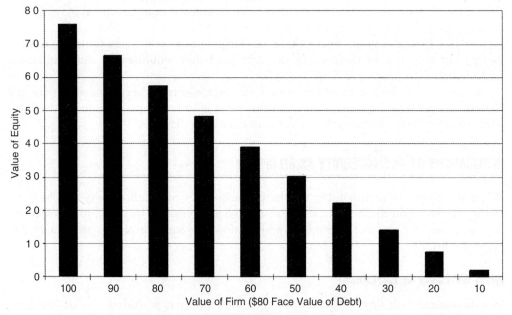

FIGURE 30.3   Value of Equity as Firm Value Changes

As you can see, the equity in this firm retains value, because of the option characteristics of equity. In fact, equity continues to have value in this example, even if the value of the assets drops to $10 million, as shown in Figure 30.3.

Risk and Equity Value

In traditional discounted cash flow valuation, higher risk almost always translates into lower value for equity investors. When equity takes on the characteristics of a call option, you should not expect this relationship to continue to hold. Risk can become your ally, when you are an equity investor in a troubled firm. In essence, you have little to lose and much to gain from swings in firm value.

ILLUSTRATION 30.3:   Equity Value and Volatility

Let us revisit the valuation in Illustration 30.1. The value of the equity is a function of the standard deviation in firm value, which we assumed to be 40%. If we change this estimate, holding all else constant, the value of the equity will increase as evidenced in Figure 30.4.

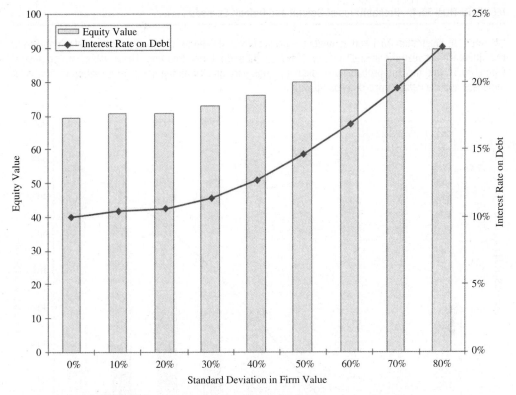

FIGURE 30.4 Equity Value and Standard Deviation in Firm Value

Note that the value of equity increases, if we hold firm value constant, as the standard deviation increases. The interest rate on debt also increases, as the standard deviation increases.

Probability of Default and Default Spreads

One of the more interesting pieces of output from the option pricing model is the risk-neutral probability of default that you can obtain for the firm. In the Black-Scholes model, you can estimate this value from N(d2), which is the risk-neutral probability that S > K, which in this model is the probability that the value of the assets will exceed the face value of the debt:

$$\text{Risk-neutral probability of default} = 1 - N(d2)$$

In addition, the interest rate from the debt allows us to estimate the appropriate default spread to charge on bonds.

You can see the potential in applying this model to bank loan portfolios to extract both the probability of default and to measure whether you are charging an interest rate that is high enough on the debt. In fact, there are commercial services that use sophisticated option pricing models to estimate both values for firms.

ILLUSTRATION 30.4:   Probabilities of Default and Default Spreads

We return to Illustration 30.1 and estimate the probability of default as $1 - N(d2)$ and the default spread as the difference between the interest rate on a firm's debt and the risk-free rate. These values are graphed in Figure 30.5. Note that the probability of default climbs very quickly as the standard deviation in firm value increases and the default spread keeps up with it.

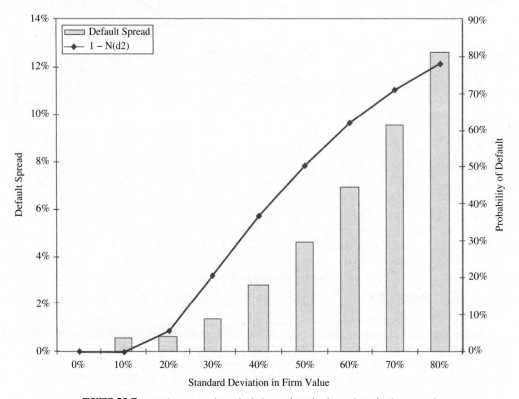

FIGURE 30.5   Risk-Neutral Probability of Default and Default Spread

As the value of the firm decreases, relative to debt due, both the likelihood of default and the default spread increase unsurprisingly. In practice, this firm, if rated by a bond ratings agency like S&P or Moody's, would see its ratings slide as firm value dropped, and the default spreads on its bonds rise. The option pricing approach provides a different way of estimating these spreads.

ESTIMATING THE VALUE OF EQUITY AS AN OPTION

The examples we have used thus far to illustrate the application of option pricing to value equity have included some simplifying assumptions. Among them are the following:

■ There are only two claimholders in the firm—debt and equity.
■ There is only one issue of debt outstanding, and it can be retired at face value.

■ The debt has a zero coupon and no special features (convertibility, put clauses, etc.).
■ The value of the assets of the firm and the variance in that value can be estimated. In liquidation, we assume that you will get the value of the assets as the liquidation proceeds.

Each of these assumptions is made for a reason. First, restricting the claimholders to just debt and equity makes the problem more tractable; introducing other claimholders such as preferred stock makes it more difficult to arrive at a result, albeit not impossible. Second, by assuming only one zero coupon debt issue that can be retired at face value any time prior to maturity, we align the features of the debt more closely to the features of the strike price on a standard option. Third, if the debt is coupon debt, or more than one debt issue is outstanding, the equity investors can be forced to exercise (liquidate the firm) at these earlier coupon dates, if they do not have the cash flows to meet their coupon obligations.

Finally, knowing the value of the firm assets in liquidation and the variance in that value makes the option pricing possible, but it also raises an interesting question about the usefulness of option pricing in equity valuation. If the bonds of the firm are publicly traded, the market value of the debt can be subtracted from the value of the firm to obtain the value of equity much more directly. The option pricing approach does have its advantages, however. Specifically, when the debt of a firm is not publicly traded, option pricing theory can provide an estimate of value for the equity in the firm. Even when the debt is publicly traded, the bonds may not be correctly valued, and the option pricing framework can be useful in evaluating the values of debt and equity. Finally, the value of the firm may be different from the liquidation value of the assets; the former also incorporate the expected value of growth potential.

Inputs for Valuing Equity as an Option

Because most firms do not fall into the neat framework just developed (such as having only one zero coupon bond outstanding), some compromises are needed to use this model in valuation.

Value of the Assets of the Firm   The liquidation value of the assets of the firm can be obtained in one of four ways. In the first, we cumulate the market values of outstanding debt and equity, assuming that all debt and equity are traded, to obtain firm value, and we assume this approximate liquidation value. The option pricing model then reallocates the firm value between debt and equity. This approach, while simple, is internally inconsistent. We start with one set of market values for debt and equity and, using the option pricing model, end up with entirely different values for each. We are also assuming that the going concern value of the firm is equal to what you would get if you liquidated its assets.

In the second, we estimate the value of the assets of the firm by discounting expected cash flows at the cost of capital. The one consideration that we need to keep in mind is that the value of the firm in an option pricing model should be the value obtained on liquidation. This may be less than the total firm value, which includes expected future growth potential, and it may also be reduced to reflect the cost of liquidation. If we estimate the firm value using a discounted cash flow model, this would suggest that only existing investments should be considered while estimating firm value.[1]

In the third approach, we estimate a multiple of revenues by looking at healthy mature firms (with little or no growth potential) in the same business, and then apply this multiple to the revenues of the firm you are valuing. Implicitly, we are assuming that a potential buyer, in the event of liquidation, will pay this value.

Variance in Firm Value   We can obtain the variance in firm value directly if both stocks and bonds in the firm are traded. Defining σ_e^2 as the variance in the stock price, σ_d^2 as the variance in the bond price, w_e as the market-value weight of equity, and w_d as the market-value weight of debt, we can write the variance in firm value as[2]:

$$\sigma_{firm}^2 = w_e^2 \sigma_e^2 + w_d^2 \sigma_d^2 + 2 w_e w_d \rho_{ed} \sigma_e \sigma_d$$

where ρ_{ed} is the correlation between the stock and bond prices. When the bonds of the firm are not traded, we can use the variance of similarly rated bonds as the estimate of σ_d^2 and the correlation between similarly rated bonds, and the firm's stock as the estimate of ρ_{ed}.

When companies get into financial trouble, this approach can yield misleading results as both its stock prices and its bond prices become more volatile. An alternative that often yields more reliable estimates is to use the average variance in firm value for other firms in the sector. Thus, the value of equity in a deeply troubled steel company can be estimated using the average variance in firm value of all traded steel companies.

---

 optvar.xls: This dataset on the web summarizes standard deviations in equity and firm value, by industry, for firms in the United States.

Maturity of the Debt   Most firms have more than one debt issue on their books, and much of the debt comes with coupons. Since the option pricing model enables only one input for the time to expiration, we must convert these multiple bonds issues and coupon payments into one equivalent zero coupon bond.

- One solution, which considers both the coupon payments and the maturity of the bonds, is to estimate the duration of each debt issue and calculate a face-value–weighted average of the durations of the different issues. This value-weighted duration is then used as a measure of the time to expiration of the option.
- An approximation is to use the face-value–weighted maturity of the debt coming for the maturity of the zero-coupon bond in the option pricing model.

---

[1] Technically, this can be done by putting the firm into stable growth and valuing it as a stable growth firm, where reinvestments are used to either preserve or augment existing assets.
[2] This is an extension of the variance formula for a two-asset portfolio.

Face Value of Debt When a distressed firm has multiple debt issues outstanding, you have three choices when it comes to what you use as the face value of debt:

1. You could add up the principal due on all of the debt of the firm, and then consider it to be the face value of the hypothetical zero coupon bond that you assume that your firm has issued. The limitation of this approach is that it will understate what the firm will truly have to pay out over the life of the debt, since there will be coupon payments and interest payments during the period.
2. At the other extreme, you could add the expected interest and coupon payments that will come due on the debt to the principal payments, to come up with a cumulated face value of debt. Since the interest payments occur in the near years and the principal payments are due only when the debt comes due, you are mixing cash flows up at different points in time when you do this. This is, however, the simplest approach to dealing with intermediate interest payments coming due.
3. You can consider only the principal due on the debt as the face value of the debt, and the interest payments each year, specified as a percent of firm value, can take the place of the dividend yield in the option pricing model. In effect, each year that the firm remains in existence, you would expect to see the value of the firm decline by the expected payments on the debt.

ILLUSTRATION 30.5: Valuing Equity as an Option: Eurotunnel in 1997

Eurotunnel was the firm that was created to build and ultimately profit from the tunnel under the English Channel linking England and France. The tunnel was readied for operations in the early 1990s but was not a commercial success, reporting significant losses each year after opening. In early 1998, Eurotunnel had a book value of equity of −£117 million, and in 1997, the firm had reported earnings before interest and taxes of −£3.45 million and net income of −£611 million on revenues of £456 million. By any measure, it was a firm in financial trouble.

Much of the financing for the tunnel had come from debt, and at the end of 1997, the Eurotunnel had debt obligations in excess of £8,000 million, raised from a variety of bond issues and bank debt. Adding the expected interest payments and coupon payments onto the debt brings the total obligations of the firm up to £8,865 million. Table 30.1 summarizes the outstanding debt at the firm, with our estimates of the expected duration for each class of debt:

TABLE 30.1 Debt Breakdown by Duration

Debt Type	Face Value (Including Cumulated Coupons)	Duration (Years)
Short term	£ 935	0.50
10 year	£2,435	6.7
20year	£3,555	12.6
Longer	£1,940	18.2
Total	**£8,865 mil**	**10.93**

The firm's only significant asset is its ownership of the tunnel, and we estimated the value of this asset from its expected cash flows and the appropriate cost of capital. The assumptions were as follows:

- Revenues will grow 10% a year for five years and 3% thereafter.
- The direct operating expenses, which were 72% of revenues in 1997, will drop to 60% of revenues by 2002 in linear increments and stay at that level. (This does not include depreciation.)

■ In the most recent year, capital expenditures were $45 million and depreciation amounted to $137 million. Capital spending and depreciation will grow 3% a year for the next five years. Beyond year 5, capital expenditures will offset depreciation.

■ There are no working capital requirements.

■ The debt ratio, which was 95.35% at the end of 1997, will drop to 70% by 2002. The cost of debt is 10% for the next five years and 8% after that.

■ The beta for the stock will be 2.00 for the next five years and drop to 0.80 thereafter (as the leverage decreases).

The long-term bond rate at the time of the valuation was 6% and the risk premium was 5.5%. Based on these assumptions, we estimated the cash flows in the Table 30.2:

TABLE 30.2   Expected Cash Flows to the Firm

	1	2	3	4	5	Term. year
Revenues	$ 501.60	$551.76	$606.94	$667.63	$ 734.39	$756.42
− COGS	$ 361.15	$380.71	$400.58	$420.61	$ 440.64	$453.85
− Depreciation	$ 141.11	$145.34	$149.70	$154.19	$ 158.82	$163.59
EBIT	−$ 0.66	$ 25.70	$ 56.65	$ 92.83	$ 134.94	$138.98
− EBIT × t	$ 0.00	$ 9.00	$ 19.83	$ 32.49	$ 47.23	$ 48.64
EBIT(1 − t)	−$ 0.66	$ 16.71	$ 36.83	$ 60.34	$ 87.71	$ 90.34
+ Depreciation	$ 141.11	$145.34	$149.70	$154.19	$ 158.82	$163.59
− Capital spending	$ 46.35	$ 47.74	$ 49.17	$ 50.65	$ 52.17	$163.59
− Δ working capital	$ 0.00	$ 0.00	$ 0.00	$ 0.00	$ 0.00	$ 0.00
Free CF to firm	$ 94.10	$114.31	$137.36	$163.89	$ 194.36	$ 90.34
Terminal value					$2,402.66	
Present value	$ 87.95	$ 99.86	$112.16	$125.08	$1,852.67	
Value of firm	$2,277.73					

The value of the assets of the firm is £2,278 million.

     The final input we estimated was the standard deviation in firm value. Since there are no directly comparable firms, we estimated the standard deviations in Eurotunnel stock and debt using the data over the previous years:[3]

$$\text{Standard deviation in Eurotunnel stock price} = 41\%$$

$$\text{Standard deviation in Eurotunnel bond price} = 17\%$$

We also estimated a correlation of 0.50 between Eurotunnel stock and bond prices, and the average market debt-to-capital ratio during the two-year period was 85%. Combining these inputs, we estimated the standard deviation in firm value to be:

$$\sigma^2_{\text{firm}} = 0.15^2 \times 0.41^2 + 0.85^2 \times 0.17^2 + 2 \times 0.15 \times 0.85 \times 0.5 \times 0.41 \times 0.17 = 0.0335$$

In summary, the inputs to the option pricing model were as follows:

Value of the underlying asset = S = Value of the firm = £2,312 million
Exercise price = K = Face value of outstanding debt = £8,865 million
Life of the option = t = Weighted average duration of debt = 10.93 years

---

[3]We used the natural log of stock prices to compute the standard deviations.

Variance in the value of the underlying asset $= \sigma^2 =$ Variance in firm value $= 0.0335$
Riskless rate $= r =$ Treasury bond rate corresponding to option life $= 6\%$

Based on these inputs, we estimate the following value for the call:

$$d1 = -0.8582 \quad N(d1) = 0.1955$$
$$d2 = -1.4637 \quad N(d2) = 0.0717$$

Value of the call $= 2,278(0.1955) - 8,865\ \exp^{(-0.06)(10.93)}(0.0717) = £116$ million

Eurotunnel's equity was trading at £150 million in 1997.

The option pricing framework, in addition to yielding a value for Eurotunnel equity, also yields some valuable insight into the drivers of value for this equity. While it is certainly important that the firm try to bring costs under control and increase operating margins, the two most critical variables determining equity value are the duration of the debt and the variance in firm value. Any action that increases or decreases the debt duration will have a positive or negative effect on equity value. For instance, when the French government put pressure on the bankers who had lent money to Eurotunnel to ease restrictions and allow the firm more time to repay its debt, equity investors benefited as their options became more long term. Similarly, an action that increases the volatility of expected firm value will increase the value of the option.

ILLUSTRATION 30.6: Valuing Equity as an Option: Jet India in 2013

Jet India was an Indian airline that generated ₹9,417 million rupees in EBITDA on revenues of ₹188,410 million. However, after depreciation and amortization of ₹9,300 million and interest expenses of ₹10,160 million, the company reported a small operating income of ₹123.50 million and a net loss of ₹7,800 million. As a continuously money-losing enterprise, the company's book equity had declined to −₹18,280 million rupees, and there was little light at the end of the tunnel.

The interest expenses were due on total debt of ₹114,272 million, with an average duration of approximately 4.5 years, and the threat of bankruptcy loomed large. In perhaps the only good news in the story, the Indian airline market was booming, with existing players and new entrants trying to capture the growth.

Since the pathways to finding a positive equity value in an intrinsic valuation were limited, we valued equity in Jet India as an option, with the following inputs:

- Based upon the EBITDA of ₹9,417 million rupees, and applying a multiple of 6.5 to that value, based upon pricing of publicly traded airlines in India, we estimated a pricing for Jet India's assets:

$$\text{Pricing of Jet India assets} = 9,417 \times 6.5 = ₹61,211 \text{ million}$$

- We used the debt outstanding of ₹114,272 million as the strike price of the option, and its duration of 4.5 years stood in for the option maturity.

- We used the average variance of 0.0826 in firm value of publicly traded airlines in India as our proxy for variation in asset value over time in the option pricing model.

The inputs to the option pricing model are listed here:

Value of the underlying asset $= S =$ Value of the firm $= ₹61,211$ million
Exercise price $= K =$ Face value of outstanding debt $= ₹114,272$ million
Life of the option $= t =$ Weighted average duration of debt $= 4.5$ years
Variance in the value of underlying asset $= \sigma^2$ Variance in firm value $= 0.0826$
Riskless rate $= r =$ Riskless rate corresponding to option life $= 8\%$

Based on these inputs, we estimate the following value for the call:

$$d1 = -0.1291 \quad N(d1) = 0.4487$$
$$d2 = -0.7384 \quad N(d2) = 0.2301$$
$$\text{Value of the call} = 61,211\,(0.4487) - 8,865\,\exp(-\,0.08)(4.5)(0.2301) = ₹9,113 \text{ million}$$

Jet India's equity is worth ₹9.1 billion in 2013.

 equity.xls: **This spreadsheet allows you to estimate the value the equity in a troubled firm as an option.**

VULTURE INVESTING AND OPTION PRICING

Vulture investing refers to an investment strategy of buying the securities of firms that are in severe financial distress. In a sense, you are investing in deep out-of-the-money options and hoping that some of these options pay off handsomely. Using the option pricing framework allows us to draw some conclusions about when and how this strategy can pay off:

- As with any portfolio of deep out-of-the-money options, you should expect a considerable proportion of the portfolio to end up worthless. The relatively few investments that do pay off, however, should earn huge returns, and you could still end up with a portfolio with impressive returns.

- You should direct your equity investments to equity in deeply troubled firms in volatile sectors. Risk is your ally when you invest in options, and the equity in these firms should be worth more than equity in deeply troubled stable sectors.

- If you are buying equity in deeply troubled firms, you should direct your investments toward troubled firms with longer-term debt rather than shorter-term debt. As the life of the option increases, you will see the value of the option also increase.

- If you are investing in debt issued by financially troubled firms, you cannot be a passive bondholder. You have to take an active role in the management and obtain an equity stake in the companies you invest in, perhaps by making the debt convertible.

DISTRESSED EQUITY AS AN OPTION: CONSEQUENCES FOR DECISION-MAKING

Option pricing theory can be applied to illustrate the conflict between stockholders and bondholders when it comes to investment analysis and conglomerate mergers. This section argues that decisions that make stockholders better off are not necessarily value maximizing for the firm and can hurt bondholders.

The Conflict between Bondholders and Stockholders

Stockholders and bondholders have different incentives and cash flow claims, and this can lead to agency problems, whereby stockholders expropriate wealth from bondholders. That conflict of interest can manifest itself in a number of ways. For instance, stockholders have an incentive to invest in riskier projects than bondholders, and to pay more out in dividends than bondholders would like them to. The conflict between bondholders and stockholders can be illustrated dramatically using the option pricing methodology developed in the previous section.

Investing in Risky Projects

Since equity is a call option on the value of the firm, other things remaining equal, an increase in the variance in the firm's value will lead to an increase in the value of equity. It is, therefore, conceivable that stockholders can invest in risky projects with negative net present values, which, while making them better off, may make the bonds and the firm less valuable. To illustrate, consider the firm in Illustration 30.1 with a value of assets of $100 million, a face value of zero coupon 10-year debt of $80 million, and a standard deviation in the value of the firm of 40 percent, valued in the earlier illustration. The equity and debt in this firm were valued as follows:

$$\text{Value of equity} = \$75.94 \text{ million}$$
$$\text{Value of debt} = \$24.06 \text{ million}$$
$$\text{Value of firm} = \$100 \text{ million}$$

Now assume that the stockholders have the opportunity to invest in a project with a net present value of −$2 million; the project is a very risky one that will push up the standard deviation in firm value to 50 percent. The equity as a call option can then be valued using the following inputs:

Value of the underlying asset = S = Value of the firm = $100 million − $2 million = $98 million (the value of the firm is lowered because of the negative net present value project)
Exercise price = K = Face value of outstanding debt = $80 million
Life of the option = t = Life of zero − coupon debt = 10 years
Variance in the value of the underlying asset = σ^2 = Variance in firm value = 0.25
Riskless rate = r = Treasury bond rate corresponding to option life = 10%

Based on these inputs, the Black-Scholes model provides the following value for the equity and debt in this firm:

$$\text{Value of equity} = \$77.71$$
$$\text{Value of debt} = \$20.29$$
$$\text{Value of firm} = \$98.00$$

The value of equity rises from $75.94 million to $77.71 million, even though the firm value declines by $2 million. The increase in equity value comes at the expense of bondholders, who find their wealth decline from $24.06 million to $20.29 million.

Conglomerate Mergers

Bondholders and stockholders may also be affected differently by conglomerate mergers, where the variance in earnings and cash flows of the combined firm can be expected to decline, because the merging firms have earning streams that are not perfectly correlated. In these mergers, the value of the combined equity in the firm will decrease after the merger because of the decline in variance; consequently, bondholders will gain. Stockholders can reclaim some or all this lost wealth by utilizing their higher debt capacity and issuing new debt. To illustrate, suppose you are provided with the following information on two firms, Lube & Auto (auto service) and Gianni Cosmetics (a cosmetics manufacturer) that hope to merge.

	Lube & Auto	Gianni Cosmetics
Value of the firm	$100 million	$150 million
Face value of debt	$80 million	$50 million (zero coupon debt)
Maturity of debt	10 years	10 years
Standard deviation in firm value	40%	50%

The correlation between firm cash flows is 0.4. The 10-year bond rate is 10%.

We calculate the variance in the value of the firm after the acquisition as follows:

$$\text{Variance in combined firm value} = w_1^2\sigma_1^2 + w_2^2\sigma_2^2 + 2w_1w_2\rho_{12}\sigma_1\sigma_2$$
$$= (0.4)^2(0.16) + (0.6)^2(0.25)$$
$$+ 2(0.4)(0.6)(0.4)(0.4)(0.5)$$
$$= 0.154$$

We estimate the values of equity and debt in the individual firms and the combined firm using the option pricing model:

	Lube & Auto	Gianni Cosmetics	Combined Firm
Value of equity in the firm	$ 75.94	$134.48	$207.58
Value of debt in the firm	$ 24.06	$ 15.52	$ 42.42
Value of the firm	$100.00	$150.00	$250.00

The combined value of the equity prior to the merger is $210.42 million; it declines to $207.58 million after that. The wealth of the bondholders increases by an equal amount. There is a transfer of wealth from stockholders to bondholders because of the merger. Thus, conglomerate mergers that are not followed by increases in leverage are likely to result in a wealth transfer from stockholders to bondholders.

IS EQUITY NOT A CALL OPTION IN EVERY FIRM?

Looking at the framework employed in this chapter, you are probably wondering why equity in every firm cannot be viewed as a call option and why, therefore, we should not add a premium to discounted cash flow values for all firms. It is true that equity is a call option in every firm, but in most firms the value of the firm as a going concern will be greater than the value you obtain from a liquidation option. Consider, for instance, a high-growth firm with very little assets in place and a high proportion of value from growth potential. If this firm liquidates, it will get the value of its assets in place; this will become the value of the underlying asset in the option pricing model and determine the value of equity as a call option on the firm. This value will be much lower than the value you would obtain if you valued the firm as a going concern and considered the cash flows from expected growth. For some mature firms that derive most of their value from assets in place and substantial debt, the equity value as a call option on liquidation can be the higher value. For other firms, though, the equity value as a going concern will be greater.

CONCLUSION

The value of equity in deeply troubled firms—firms with negative earnings and high leverage—can be viewed as a call option. The option rests in the hands of equity investors, who can choose to liquidate the firm and claim the difference between firm value and debt outstanding. With limited liability, they do not have to make up the difference if firm value falls below the value of the outstanding debt. The equity will retain value even when the value of the assets of the firm is lower than the debt outstanding, because of the time premium on the option.

QUESTIONS AND SHORT PROBLEMS

In the problems following, use an equity risk premium of 5.5 percent if none is specified.

1. Designate the following statements as true or false:
   a. Equity can be viewed as an option because equity investors have limited liability (limited to their equity investment in the firm).
      True ____   False ____
   b. Equity investors will sometimes take bad projects (with negative net present value) because they can add to the value of the firm.
      True ____   False ____
   c. Investing in a good project (with positive NPV)—which is less risky than the average risk of the firm—can negatively impact equity investors.
      True ____   False ____
   d. The value of equity in a firm is an increasing function of the duration of the debt in the firm (i.e., equity will be more valuable in a firm with longer-term debt than in an otherwise similar firm with short-term debt).
      True ____   False ____
2. XYZ Corporation has $500 million in zero coupon debt outstanding, due in five years. The firm had earnings before interest and taxes of $40 million in the most recent year (the tax rate is 40%). These earnings are expected to grow 5% a year in perpetuity, and the firm paid no dividends. The firm had a return on capital of 12% and a cost of capital of 10%. The annualized standard deviation in firm values of comparable firms is 12.5%. The five-year bond rate is 5%.
   a. Estimate the value of the firm.
   b. Estimate the value of equity, using an option pricing model.
   c. Estimate the market value of debt and the appropriate interest rate on the debt.

3. McCaw Cellular Communications reported earnings before interest and taxes of $850 million in 1993, with a depreciation allowance of $400 million and capital expenditures of $550 million in that year; the working capital requirements were negligible. The earnings before interest and taxes and net cap ex are expected to grow 20% a year for the next five years. The cost of capital is 10% and the return on capital is expected to be 15% in perpetuity after year 5; the growth rate in perpetuity is 5%. The firm has $10 billion in debt outstanding with the following characteristics:

Duration	Debt
1 year	$2 billion
2 years	$4 billion
5 years	$4 billion

The annualized standard deviation in the firm's stock price is 35%, while the annualized standard deviation in the traded bonds is 15%. The correlation between stock and bond prices has been 0.5, and the average debt ratio over the past few years has been 60%. The three-year bond rate is 5%, and the tax rate is 40%.
   1. Estimate the value of the firm.
   2. Estimate the value of the equity.
   3. The stock was trading at $30, and there were 210 million shares outstanding in January 1994. Estimate the implied standard deviation in firm value.
   4. Estimate the market value of the debt.
4. You have been asked to analyze the value of equity in a company that has the following features:
   ▧ The earnings before interest and taxes are $25 million, and the corporate tax rate is 40%.
   ▧ The earnings are expected to grow 4% a year in perpetuity, and the return on capital is 10%. The cost of capital of comparable firms is 9%.
   ▧ The firm has two types of debt outstanding—two-year zero coupon bonds with a face value of $250 million and bank debt with 10 years to maturity with a face value of $250 million. (The duration of this debt is four years.)
   ▧ The firm is in two businesses—food processing and auto repair. The average standard deviation in firm value for firms in food processing is 25%, whereas the standard deviation for firms in auto repair is 40%. The correlation between the businesses is 0.5.
   ▧ The riskless rate is 7%.
   Use the option pricing model to value equity as an option.
5. You are valuing the equity in a firm with $800 million (face value) in debt with an average duration of six years and assets with an estimated value of $400 million. The standard deviation in asset value is 30%. With these inputs (and a riskless rate of 6%) we obtain the following values (approximately) for d1 and d2:

$$d1 = -0.15 \quad d2 = -0.90$$

Estimate the default spread (over and above the risk-free rate) that you would charge for the debt in this firm.

CHAPTER 31

Value Enhancement:
A Discounted Cash Flow
Valuation Framework

In much of this book, we have taken on the role of a passive investor valuing going concerns. In this chapter, we switch roles and look at valuation from the perspective of an investor who can make a difference in the way a company is run, and hence, its value. Our focus is, therefore, on how actions taken by managers and owners can change the value of a firm.

We will use the discounted cash flow framework developed in earlier parts of the book to explore the requirements for an action to be value creating, and then go on to examine the different ways in which a firm can create value. In the process, we also examine the role that marketing decisions, production decisions, and strategic decisions all have in value creation.

VALUE-CREATING AND VALUE-NEUTRAL ACTIONS

The value of a firm is the present value of the expected cash flows from both assets in place and future growth, discounted at the cost of capital. For an action to create value, it has to do one or more of the following:

- Increase the cash flows generated by existing investments.
- Increase the expected growth rate in earnings while generating excess returns.
- Increase the length of the high growth period.
- Reduce the cost of capital that is applied to discount the cash flows.

Conversely, an action that does not affect any of the above cannot affect value.

While this might seem obvious, a number of value-neutral actions taken by firms receive disproportionate attention from both managers and analysts. Consider four examples:

1. Stock dividends and stock splits change the number of units of equity in a firm but do not affect cash flows, growth, or value. These actions can have price effects, though, because they alter investors' perceptions of the future of the company.

2. Accounting changes in inventory valuation and depreciation methods, that are restricted to the reporting statements and do not affect tax calculations, have no effect on cash flows, growth, or value. In recent years, firms have spent an increasing amount of time on the management and smoothing of earnings, and seem to believe that there is a value payoff to doing this.

3. When making acquisitions, firms often try to structure the deals in such a way that they can minimize negative effects on earnings in future periods. Prior to accounting changes barring the practice, many U.S. companies used pooling to account for acquisitions, in which the acquiring firm was allowed to pool assets and not show the premium paid as goodwill. To qualify for this practice, firms would often pay premiums and restructure deals to qualify for pooling, even though there was no impact on cash flow.

4. Over the years, firms have tried to garner favorable attention by changing their corporate names and logos to reflect market fads. In the late 1990s, for instance, at the peak of the technology boom, adding ".com" to a company's name was a common exercise.

Some would take issue with this proposition about what creates value. When a stock splits or a firm renames itself, they would argue, the stock price often goes up significantly.[1] While this may be true, we would emphasize that it is value, and not price, that we claim is unaffected by these actions.

While paying stock dividends, splitting stock, adding ".com" to a corporate name in 1999 or AI to a company's business description in 2024 are value-neutral actions, they can still be useful tools for a firm that perceives itself to be undervalued by the market. These actions can change market perceptions about growth or cash flows, and thus, act as signals to financial markets. By increasing trading volume and liquidity, they may provide a side benefit to investors and affect the stock price. Finally, in some cases, cosmetic actions can lead to changes in operations, and thus, ultimately affect cash flow and value.

WAYS OF INCREASING VALUE

The value of a firm can be increased by increasing cash flows from assets in place, by increasing expected growth (while preserving excess returns) and the length of the growth period, and by reducing the cost of capital. In reality, however, none of these is easily accomplished, and they are likely to reflect all the qualitative factors that financial analysts are often accused of ignoring in valuation. This section will consider how actions taken by a firm on a variety of fronts—marketing, strategic, and financial—can have an effect on value.

Increase Cash Flows from Existing Investments

The first place to look for value is in the firm's existing assets. These assets represent investments the firm has already made, and they generate the current operating income for the firm. To the extent that these investments earn less than their cost of capital or are earning less than they could if optimally managed, there is potential for value creation.

---

[1] This is backed up empirically. Stock prices do tend to increase, on average, when stocks are split.

Poor Investments: Keep, Divest, or Liquidate   Most firms have some investments that earn less than the cost of capital used to fund them and sometimes even lose money. At first sight, it would seem obvious that investments that do not earn their cost of capital should be either liquidated or divested. If, in fact, the firm could get back the original capital on liquidation, this statement would be true. In most cases, though, there are three different measures of value for an existing investment that we need to consider before making this judgment.

The first is the continuing value, and it reflects the present value of the expected cash flows from continuing the investment through the end of its life. The second is the liquidation or salvage value, which is the net cash flow that the firm would receive if it terminated the project today. Finally, there is the divestiture value, which is the price that will be paid by the highest bidder for this investment.

Whether a firm should continue with an existing project, liquidate the project, or sell it to someone else, will depend on which of the three values is highest. If the continuing value is the highest, the firm should continue with the project to the end of the project life, even though it might be earning less than the cost of capital. If the liquidation or divestiture value is higher than the continuing value, there is potential for an increase in value from liquidation or divestiture. The value increment can then be summarized:

If liquidation is optimal:

$$\text{Expected value increase} = \text{Liquidation value} - \text{Continuing value}$$

If divestiture is optimal:

$$\text{Expected value increase} = \text{Divestiture value} - \text{Continuing value}$$

How does a divestiture affect a firm's value? To answer this question, we compare the price received on the divestiture to the present value of the expected cash flows that the firm would have received from the divested assets. There are three possible scenarios:

1. If the divestiture value is equal to the present value of the expected cash flows, the divestitures will have no effect on the divesting firm's value.
2. If the divestiture value is greater than the present value of the expected cash flows, the value of the firm will increase on the divestiture.
3. If the divestiture value is less than the present value of the expected cash flows, the value of the firm will decrease on the divestiture.

The divesting firm receives cash in return for the assets and can choose to retain the cash and invest it in marketable securities, invest the cash in other assets or new investments, or return the cash to stockholders in the form of dividends or stock buybacks. These actions, in turn, can have a secondary effect on value.

ILLUSTRATION 31.1: Potential for Value Creation from Divestiture: Boeing in 1998

While it is difficult to make judgments about individual investments that firms might have and their capacity to generate continuing value, you can make some observations about the potential for value creation from divestitures and liquidation by looking at the cost of capital of and return on capital earned by different divisions of a firm. For instance, Boeing earned a return on invested capital of 5.82% in 1998, while its cost of capital was 9.18%. Breaking down Boeing's return by division, we obtain the numbers in the following table:

	Commercial Aircraft	Information, Space, and Defense	Firm
Operating income	$ 75	$1,576	$ 1,651
Capital invested	$18,673	$9,721	$28,394
After-tax ROIC	0.40%	16.21%	5.82%

At Boeing's annual meeting in 1999, Phil Condit, Boeing's CEO, was candid in admitting that 35% of Boeing's capital was in investments that earned less than the cost of capital. He revealed little, however, about whether it would be feasible to liquidate or divest these investments[2] and get more than continuing value from such actions.

Assume that Boeing is interested in selling its information, space, and defense systems division, and that it has found a potential buyer who is willing to pay $11 billion for the division. The division reported cash flows before debt payments but after-reinvestment needs and taxes of $393 million in the most recent year, and the cash flows are expected to grow 5% a year in the long term. The cost of capital for the division is 9%, a little lower than the cost of capital for the entire firm. The division, as a continuing part of Boeing, can be valued as follows:

$$\text{Value of division} = \$393(1.05)/(.09 - .05) = \$10,316 \text{ million}$$

With the divestiture value of $11 billion, the net effect of the divestiture will be an increase in Boeing's value of $684 million.

$$\text{Net effect on Boeing's value} = \text{Divestiture value} - \text{Continuing value}$$
$$= \$11,000 \text{ million} - \$10,316 \text{ million}$$
$$= \$684 \text{ million}$$

Improve Operating Efficiency   A firm's operating efficiency determines its operating margin, and thus, its operating income; more efficient firms have higher operating margins, other things remaining equal, than less efficient firms in the same business. If a firm can increase its operating margin on existing assets, it will generate additional value. There are a number of indicators of the potential to increase margins, but one of the more useful is how much a firm's operating margin deviates from its industry. When a firm's operating margins are well below those of the industry average, there is the possibility (though not a guarantee) of value potential from improving efficiency.

In most firms, the first step in value enhancement takes the form of cost cutting and layoffs. These actions are value enhancing only if the resources that are pruned do not contribute sufficiently either to current operating income or to future growth. Companies can easily show increases in current operating income by cutting back on expenditures, such as research and training, but they may sacrifice future growth in doing so.

---

[2] In 1999, Lockheed, Boeing's leading competitor in the sector, announced plans to divest itself of approximately 15% of its assets as a remedy for its poor stock price performance.

REASONS FOR DIVESTITURES

Why would a firm sell assets or a division? There are at least three reasons. The first is that the divested assets may have a higher value to the buyer of these assets. For assets to have a higher value, they have to either generate higher cash flows for the buyer or result in lower risk (leading to a lower discount rate). The higher cash flows can occur because the buyer is more efficient at utilizing the assets, or because the buyer finds synergies with its existing businesses. The lower discount rate may reflect the fact that the owners of the buying firm are more diversified than the owners of the firm selling the assets. In either case, both sides can gain from the divestiture and share in the increased value.

The second reason for divestitures is less value-driven and more a result of the immediate cash flow needs of the divesting firm. Firms that find themselves unable to meet their current operating or financial expenses may have to sell assets to raise cash. For instance, many leveraged acquisitions in the 1980s were followed by divestitures of assets. The cash generated from these divestitures was used to retire and service debt.

The third reason for divestitures relates to the assets not sold by the firm, rather than the divested assets. In some cases, a firm may find the cash flows and values of its core businesses affected by the fact that it has diversified into unrelated businesses. This lack of focus can be remedied by selling assets or businesses that are peripheral to the main business of a firm.

ILLUSTRATION 31.2: Operating Margin Comparisons

In 2000, Marks and Spencer, the U.K. retailer, had substantial operating problems that depressed profits and value. Figure 31.1 compares the after-tax operating margins at Marks and Spencer in 2000, with the average

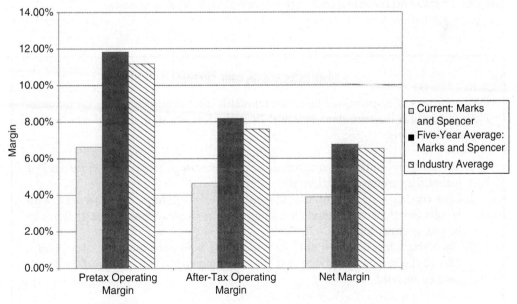

FIGURE 31.1   Marks and Spencer: Margin Comparisons

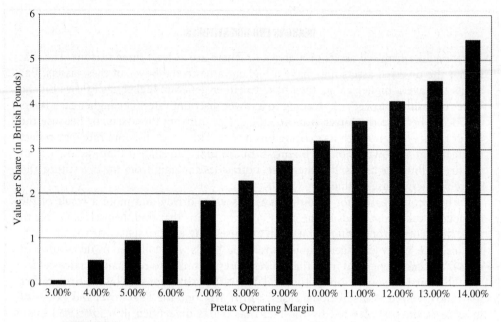

FIGURE 31.2 Operating Margin and Value per Share: Marks and Spencer

after-tax margin earned by the firm over the previous five years, and the average after-tax margin in 2000 for other firms in the sector.

Marks and Spencer's margins in 2000 lagged both its own historical levels and the average for the sector. We estimated the effect on value per share at Marks and Spencer of improvements in the operating margin from the current level. Figure 31.2 summarizes the effect of these changes.

While it is not surprising that the value per share is sensitive to changes in the operating margin, you can see that the decline in operating margins from historical levels to the current one has had a significant impact on value. Any value enhancement plan for the firm, therefore, must be centered on improving operating margins, even if it means not just scaling back revenue growth plans, or reducing revenues.

SOME THOUGHTS ON COST CUTTING

Cost cutting is often promised by firms, especially after acquisitions or new management comes into the firm, but seldom delivered. Here are some general conclusions about cost cutting:

1. The greater the absolute magnitude of the cost cuts promised, the more likely it is that they will not be delivered.
2. Cost cutting is never painless; not only is the economic cost associated with layoffs (severance pay) large, but there is an associated loss of morale that can be just as expensive.
3. The initial phases of cost cuts go much more smoothly than the later phases. Part of the reason for this is that the easy cost cuts come first, and the tough ones come later.

4. It is far more difficult to separate those costs that do not generate benefits for the firm from those that do than it seems at the outset, especially if we think of benefits in the long term.

5. Cost cutting that is promised in the abstract is less likely to happen than cost cutting that is described in detail. An example would be a bank merger where the branches that will be closed after the merger are specified as opposed to one where the bank just specified that economies of scale will lower costs.

From a valuation perspective, you should first evaluate the credibility of the management that is making the cost cutting claims, and even if you believe the managers you should allow for phasing in the cost cuts over time; the larger the firm and the bigger the cost cuts, the longer it will take to cut costs.

Reduce the Tax Burden   The value of a firm is the present value of its after-tax cash flows. Thus, any action that can reduce the tax burden on a firm for a given level of operating income will increase value. Although there are some aspects of the tax code that offer no flexibility to the firm, the tax rate can be reduced over time by doing any or all of the following:

- Multinational firms that generate earnings in different markets may be able to move income from high-tax locations to low-tax or no-tax locations. For instance, the prices that divisions of these firms charge each other for intracompany sales (transfer prices) can allow profits to be shifted from one part of the firm to another.[3]
- A firm may be able to acquire net operating losses that can be used to shield future income. In fact, this might be why a profitable firm acquires an unprofitable one.
- A firm can use risk management to reduce the average tax rate paid on income over time, because the marginal tax rate on income tends to rise, in most tax systems, as income increases. By using risk management to smooth income over time, firms can make their incomes more stable and reduce their exposure to the highest marginal tax rates.[4] This is especially the case when a firm faces windfall or supernormal profit taxes.

ILLUSTRATION 31.3:   Tax Rates and Value

In Illustration 15.1, we valued Telesp, the Brazilian telecom company, at 25,902 million Brazilian reals, using a tax rate of 30% in the valuation. This tax rate was used as the effective tax rate on income and the marginal tax rate to compute the after-tax cost of debt.

To the extent that Telesp may be able to reduce its tax rate, it will be able to increase the value of its operating assets. In Figure 31.3, the valuation of the operating assets is computed for Telesp under two scenarios. In the first, we change both the effective tax rate (used to compute after-tax income), and the marginal

---

[3]Taxes are only one aspect of transfer pricing. Brickley, Smith, and Zimmerman (1995) look at the broader issue of how to best set transfer prices.

[4]Stulz (1996) makes this argument for risk management. He also presents other ways in which risk management can be value enhancing.

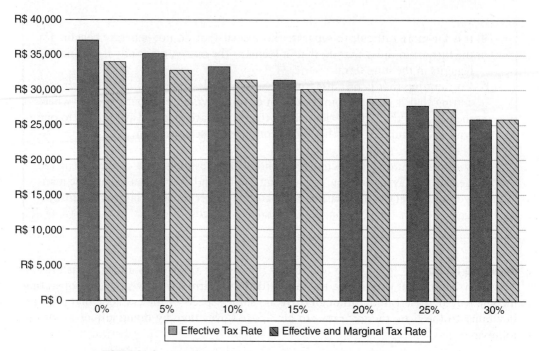

FIGURE 31.3   Tax Rate and Operating Asset Value—Telesp

tax rate (to compute the after-tax cost of debt). In the second, we change only the effective tax rate but leave the marginal tax rate at 30%.

The value of Telesp increases as tax rates decrease under both scenarios. However, the increase in value is greater if Telesp reduces its effective tax rate, while keeping its marginal tax rate intact. That allows Telesp to increase its after-tax cash flows, while keeping the tax benefits of debt unaffected.

Reduce Net Capital Expenditures on Existing Investments   The net capital expenditure is the difference between capital expenditures and depreciation, and, as a cash outflow, it reduces the free cash flow to the firm. Part of the net capital expenditure is designed to generate future growth, but part is to maintain existing assets. If a firm can reduce its net capital expenditure on existing assets, it will increase value. During short periods, the capital expenditures can even be lower than depreciation for those assets, creating a cash inflow from net capital expenditures.

There is generally a trade-off between capital maintenance expenditures and the life of existing assets. A firm that does not make any capital expenditures on its assets will generate much higher after-tax cash flows from these assets, but the assets will have a far shorter life. At the other extreme, a firm that reinvests all the cash flows it gets from depreciation into capital maintenance may be able to extend the life of its assets in place significantly. Firms often ignore this trade-off when they embark on cost cutting and reduce or eliminate capital maintenance expenditures. Although these actions increase current cash flows from existing assets, the firm might lose value as it depletes these assets at a faster rate.

Reduce Noncash Working Capital   The noncash working capital in a firm is the difference between noncash current assets, generally inventory and accounts receivable, and the nondebt portion of current liabilities, generally accounts payable. Money invested in noncash working capital is tied up and cannot be used elsewhere; thus, increases in noncash working capital are cash outflows, whereas decreases are cash inflows. For retailers and service firms, noncash working capital may be a much larger drain on cash flows than traditional capital expenditures.

The path to value creation seems simple. Reducing noncash working capital as a percentage of revenues should increase cash flows and, therefore, value. This assumes, however, that there are no negative consequences from cutting back working capital investments. Firms generally maintain inventory and provide credit because it allows them to sell more. If cutting back on one or both causes lost sales, the net effect on value may be negative.

Technology has helped companies in their efforts to rein in noncash working capital, helping them not only track inventory but also customer purchases and behavior. Using value chain management, firms like Walmart have found innovative ways of reducing working capital investments and boosting cash flows in the process.

ILLUSTRATION 31.4: Noncash Working Capital and Operating Asset Value

Angelos Stores is a publicly traded retail company in stable growth. In the most recent period, the firm reported after-tax operating income of $10 million on revenues of $200 million, capital expenditures of $5 million, depreciation of $3 million, and total noncash working capital of $40 million. Assume that the firm is in stable growth, growing 3% a year, with a cost of capital of 10%, and that all the inputs grow at the same rate:

$$\text{Expected change in noncash working capital next year} = \text{(Noncash WC as \% of revenues)}$$
$$\text{(Change in revenues)}$$
$$= (40/200)(200 \times .03)$$
$$= \$1.2 \text{ million}$$

$$\text{Expected free cash flow to firm (FCFF) next year} = \text{EBIT}(1 - t) - \text{(Capital expenditures} - \text{Depreciation)}$$
$$- \text{Change in noncash WC}$$
$$= 10(1.03) - (5 - 3)(1.03) - \$1.2 = \$7.04 \text{ million}$$

$$\text{Value of firm} = \frac{\text{Expected FCFF next year}}{\text{(Cost of capital} - \text{Expected growth rate)}}$$
$$= \frac{\$7.04}{(.10 - .03)} = \$100.57 \text{ million}$$

Note that a significant portion of the reinvestment comes from noncash working capital being 20% of revenues.

Now assume that the firm is able to reduce its noncash working capital from 20% of revenues to 10% of revenues. The first effect is an immediate positive cash flow as working capital declines from $40 million (20% of revenue) to $20 million (10% of revenues). The second impact is a continuing one, with higher expected FCFF each year:

$$\text{Expected FCFF next year} = \text{EBIT}(1 - t)(1 + g) - \text{(Capital expenditures}$$
$$- \text{Depreciation)}(1 + g) - \text{Change in noncash WC}$$
$$= 10(1.03) - (5 - 3)(1.03) - 20(.03) = \$7.64 \text{ million}$$

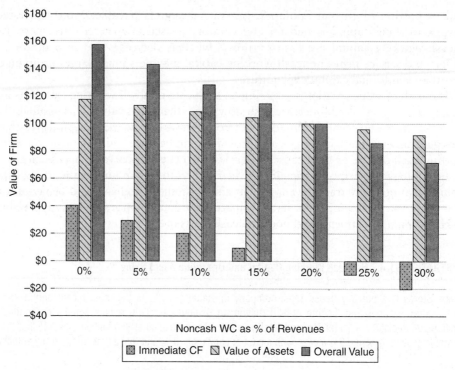

FIGURE 31.4   Noncash WC and Value

$$\text{Value of firm} = \frac{\text{Expected FCFF next year}}{(\text{Cost of capital} - \text{Expected growth rate})} + \text{One time cashflow from decline in WC}$$

$$= \frac{\$7.64}{(.10 - .03)} + \$20$$

$$= \$129.14 \text{ million}$$

Figure 31.4 summarizes the effect on value of changing noncash working capital as a percent of revenues, assuming (unrealistically) that it has no effect on revenues or growth.

 cfbasics.xls: This dataset on the web summarizes operating margins, tax rates, and noncash working capital as a percent of revenues by industry group for the United States.

Increase Expected Growth

A firm with low current cash flows can still have high value, if it is able to grow quickly while earning more than its cost of capital. For profitable firms, the growth will be defined in terms of earnings, but for money-losing firms, you have to consider the nexus of revenue growth and higher margins.

Profitable Firms   Higher growth arises from either increases in reinvestment or a higher return on capital. It does not always translate into higher value, though, since higher growth can be offset by changes elsewhere in the valuation. Thus, higher reinvestment rates usually result in higher expected growth but at the expense of lower cash flows, because reinvestment reduces the free cash flows. Higher returns on capital also cause expected growth to increase, but value can still go down if the new investments are in riskier businesses and there is a more than proportionate increase in the cost of capital.

The trade-off from increasing the reinvestment rate is listed in Table 31.1. The positive effect of reinvesting more, higher growth, has to be compared to the negative effect of reinvesting more, the drop in free cash flows.

We could work through the entire valuation and determine whether the present value of the additional cash flows created by higher growth is greater than the present value of the actual reinvestments made, in cash flow terms. There is, however, a far simpler test to determine the effect on value. Note that the net present value of a project measures the value added by the project to overall firm value, and that the net present value is positive only if the internal rate of return on the project exceeds the cost of capital. If we assume that the accounting return on capital on a project is a reasonable estimate for the internal rate of return, then increasing the reinvestment rate will increase value, if and only if, the return on capital is greater than the cost of capital. If the return on capital is less than the cost of capital, the positive effects of growth will be less than the negative effects of making the reinvestment.

Note that the return on capital that we are talking about is the marginal return on capital (i.e., the return on capital earned on the actual reinvestment), rather than the average return on capital. Given that firms tend to accept their most attractive investment first and their less attractive investments later, the average returns on capital will tend to be greater than the marginal returns on capital. Thus, a firm with a return on capital of 18 percent and a cost of capital of 12 percent may really be earning only 11 percent on its marginal projects. In addition, the marginal return on capital will be much lower if the increase in the reinvestment rate is substantial. Thus, you must be cautious about assuming large increases in the reinvestment rate while keeping the current return on capital constant.

A firm that can increase its return on capital while keeping the cost of capital fixed will increase its value. The increase in growth will increase value, and there are generally no offsetting effects. If, however, the increase in return on capital comes from the firm entering new businesses that are far riskier than its existing business, there might be an increase in the cost of capital that offsets the increase in growth. The general rule for value creation remains simple, however. As long as the projects, no matter how risky they are, have a marginal return on capital that exceeds their cost of capital, they will create value.

Using the comparison between return on capital and cost of capital, a firm that earns a return on capital that is less than its cost of capital can get an increase in value by accepting higher return investments, but it would get an even greater increase in value by not investing at all and returning the cash to the owners of the business. Liquidation or partial liquidation might be the most value-enhancing strategy for firms trapped in businesses where it is impossible to earn the cost of capital.

TABLE 31.1 Trade-Off on Reinvestment Rate

Negative Effects	Positive Effects
Reduces free cash flow to firm:	Increases expected growth:
FCFF = EBIT(1 − Tax rate)	Expected growth = Reinvestment rate ×
(1 − Reinvestment rate)	Return on capital

ILLUSTRATION 31.5: Reinvestment Rates, Return on Capital, and Value—Contrasting Boeing and the Home Depot in 1998

In 1998, Boeing earned a return on capital of 6.59% and had a reinvestment rate of 65.98%. If you assume a cost of capital of 9.17% for the firm, you would value the equity in the firm at $13.14 a share. In the same year, the Home Depot had a return on capital of 16.38%, a reinvestment rate of 88.62%, and a cost of capital of 9.51%, resulting in a value per share of $42.55.

	Boeing	The Home Depot
Cost of capital	9.17%	9.51%
Return on capital	6.59%	16.38%
Reinvestment rate	65.98%	88.62%
Expected growth rate	4.35%	14.51%
Value per share	$13.14	$42.55

If the Home Depot could increase its reinvestment rates without affecting its returns on capital, the effect on value will be positive, because it is earning excess returns. For Boeing, the effect of increasing the reinvestment rate at the current return on capital will be negative, since the firm's return on capital is less than its cost of capital. Figure 31.5 summarizes the impact on the value of equity of changing the reinvestment rate at both firms, keeping the cost of capital.

To illustrate, we reduced the reinvestment rate at Boeing from 65.98% to 45.98% and examined the percentage effect on value of equity; the change was +4.49%. The effect of a similar change at the Home Depot was negative. The effects of changes in the reinvestment rate were dramatic at the Home Depot because the high growth period lasts 10 years.

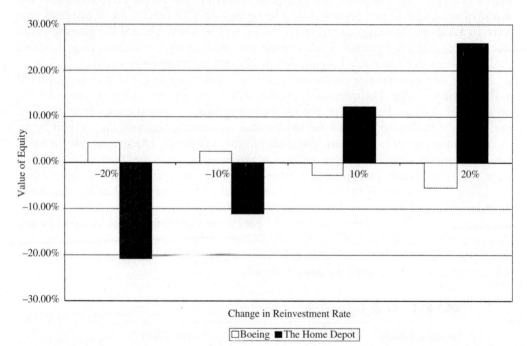

Change in Reinvestment Rate

☐ Boeing ■ The Home Depot

FIGURE 31.5 Effect of Changes in the Reinvestment Rate on the Value of Equity

fundgrEB.xls: This dataset on the web summarizes returns on capital and reinvestment rates by industry group for the United States.

Negative Earnings Firms For young firms with negative earnings, expected future cash flows are derived from assumptions made about three variables—the expected growth rate in revenues, the target operating margin, and the sales-to-capital ratio. The first two variables determine the operating earnings in future years, and the last variable determines reinvestment needs. Figure 31.6 summarizes the impact of each of these variables on the cash flows.

Other things remaining equal, the expected cash flows in future years will be higher if any of the three variables—revenue growth, target margins, and sales-to-capital ratios—increase. Increasing revenue growth and target margins will increase operating earnings, while increasing the sales-to-capital ratio will reduce reinvestment needs.

In reality, though, firms have to make a trade-off between higher revenue growth and higher margins. When firms increase prices for their products, they improve operating margins but reduce revenue growth. Michael Porter, one of the leading thinkers in corporate strategy, suggests that when it comes to pricing strategy, there are two basic routes a firm can take. It can choose to be a volume leader, reducing prices and hoping to increase revenues sufficiently to compensate for the lower margins. For this strategy to work, the firm needs a cost advantage over its competitors to prevent pricing wars that may make all firms in the industry worse off. Alternatively, it can attempt to be a price leader, increasing prices and hoping that the effect on volume will be smaller than the increased margins. The extent to which revenue growth will drop depends on how elastic the demand for the product is, and how competitive the overall product market is. The net effect will determine value (Porter 1980).

While a higher sales-to-capital ratio reduces reinvestment needs and increases cash flow, there are both internal and external constraints on the process. As the sales-to-capital ratio increases, the return on capital on the firm in future years will also increase. If the return on capital substantially exceeds the cost of capital, new competitors will enter the market, making it more difficult to sustain the expected operating margins and revenue growth.

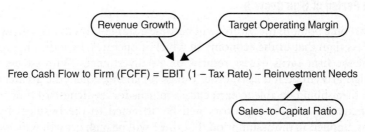

FIGURE 31.6 Determinants of Growth

LESS IS MORE: THE VALUE OF LESS GROWTH

In some cases, the best path to value creation comes from scaling back rather than increasing growth. To see why, consider the proposition that growth creates value only if the return on capital earned on new investments exceeds the cost of capital in funding those investments. Also consider the fact that in 2023, about 60% of all global companies generated composite returns on capital that were lower than their costs of capital. While this underperformance can be attributed to macroeconomic factors or temporary problems at some of these firms, it also reflects the fact that many of these firms were either in decline or in businesses where it is difficult, if not impossible, to generate excess returns.

There are lots of reasons why firms in the latter group continue on the value destructive path of investing increasing amounts in bad businesses. Some consider growth at any cost to be good and are aided and abetted by equity research analysts who share that impression. Others are driven by inertia, continuing patterns of investment that they adopted in earlier periods, when investment opportunities were lucrative and plentiful. Still others have overconfident managers who are convinced that they can change an entire business.

Whatever the reasons, value enhancement at firms that grow through bad enhancements is simple. Ceasing to make new investments will drive down growth and increase value at the same time. To illustrate, assume that a firm with a 10% cost of capital generates $10 million in after-tax operating income. Assume further that it is reinvesting 50% of that income in projects that generate a 6% return on capital. Using the resultant growth rate of 3%, we can estimate a value for the firm:

Value of firm (status quo) = 10(1.03)(1 − .50)/(.10 − .03) = $73.57 million

If this firm stopped reinvesting, its growth rate and reinvestment rate would drop to zero, and its value would increase to $100 million

Value of firm (restructured) = 10/.10 = $100 million

While the existing management at these firms may be reluctant to give up on growth, they are favored targets for activist investors.

Lengthen the Period of High Growth

Every firm, at some point in the future, will become a stable-growth firm, growing at a rate equal to or less than that of the economy in which it operates. In addition, growth creates value only if the firm earns excess returns on its investments. With excess returns, the longer the high-growth period lasts, other things remaining equal, the greater the value of the firm. No firm should be able to earn excess returns for any length of time in a competitive product market, since competitors will be attracted to the business by the excess returns. Thus, implicit in the assumption that there will be high growth with excess returns is the assumption that there also exist some barriers to entry that prevent competing firms from entering the market and eliminating the excess returns that prevail.

One way firms can increase value is by increasing existing barriers to entry and erecting new ones. Another way to express this idea is that companies earning excess returns have significant competitive advantages. Nurturing these advantages can increase value.

Brand-Name Advantage   As we noted earlier in the book, the inputs to the traditional discounted cash flow valuation incorporate the effects of brand name. In particular, firms with more valuable brand names are either able to charge higher prices than the competition for the same products (leading to higher margins), or sell more than the competitors at the same price (leading to higher turnover ratios). They usually have higher returns on capital and greater value than their competitors in the industry.

Creating a brand name is a difficult and expensive process that may take years to achieve, but firms can often build on existing brand names and make them valuable. Brand management and advertising can, thus, contribute to value creation. Consider the extraordinary success that Coca-Cola has had in increasing and sustaining its market value over a long time period. Some attribute its success to its high return on equity or capital, yet these returns are not the cause of its success but the consequence of it. The high returns can be traced to the company's relentless focus on making its brand name more valuable globally. Conversely, the managers of a firm who take over a valuable brand name and then dissipate its value, will reduce the value of the firm substantially. The near-death experience of Apple Computer in 1996 and 1997, and the travails of Quaker Oats after the Snapple acquisition suggest that managers can quickly squander the advantage that comes from valuable brand names.

Patents, Licenses, and Other Legal Protection   The second competitive advantage that companies can possess is a legal one. Firms may enjoy exclusive rights to produce and market a product because they own the patent rights on the product, as is often the case in the pharmaceutical industry. Alternatively, firms may have exclusive licensing rights or monopoly rights to service a market.

The key to value enhancement is not just to preserve but to increase any competitive advantages that the firm possesses. If the competitive advantage comes from its existing patents, the firm has to work at developing new patents that allow it to maintain this advantage over time. While spending more money on research and development (R&D) is clearly one way, the efficiency of reinvestment also applies here. The companies that have the greatest increases in value are not necessarily those that spend the most on R&D, but those that have the most productive R&D departments not only in generating patents but also in converting patents into commercial products.

The competitive advantage from exclusive licensing or a legal monopoly is a mixed blessing and may not lead to value enhancement. When a firm is granted these rights by another entity, say the government, that entity usually preserves the right to control the prices charged and margins earned through regulation. In the United States, for instance, much of the regulation of power and phone utilities was driven by the objective of ensuring that these firms did not earn excess returns. In these circumstances, firms may gain in value by giving up their legal monopolies, if they get pricing freedom in return. We could argue that this has already occurred, in great part, in the telecommunications businesses, and will occur in the future in other regulated businesses. In the aftermath of deregulation, the firms that retain competitive advantages will gain value at the expense of others in the business.

Networking Benefits   Over the course of this book, and especially in the chapter on valuing young firms, we noted the potential for network benefits in some businesses and how they can affect their values. In particular, network benefits refer to the possibility that as a firm gains a larger share of the market, it becomes easier for it to grow, rather than more difficult, because of the nature of the business. This has come into play especially in technology, where both customers seek out the largest players in a market, because that is where the other customers reside. Thus, if you want to have only one ride-sharing app on your phone, you will probably pick the dominant ride-sharing companies, since that is where the cars and drivers are most easily accessible, or if you want to list your apartment for vacation rentals, you will use Airbnb, since that is where most renters look.

While the notion of networking benefits has existed for a long time, it was Jeff Bezos at Amazon who pushed it to the forefront early in Amazon's life, as he used the flywheel to illustrate his plans to grow the company's presence in retail (in Figure 31.7).

In effect, Bezos believed that as more customers shopped on Amazon, more sellers would list on its platform, and that the lower cost structure from scale could be used to lower prices, to attract even more customers.

Just as a caution, we have learned that the flywheel has its limits, even in companies where it makes logical sense to use, and especially so when there is no customer exclusivity. Thus, in ridesharing, where customers can have multiple ride-sharing apps on their phone, the benefits of the flywheel accrued to ridesharing customers, and not to the companies providing the service.

Switching Costs   There are some businesses where neither brand name nor a patent provides adequate protection against competition. Products have short life cycles, competition is fierce, and customers develop little loyalty to companies or products. This describes the computer software business in the 1980s, and it still applies to a significant portion of that business today. How, then, did Microsoft succeed so well in establishing its presence in the market? Although many would attribute its success entirely to its ownership of the operating system needed to run the software, there is another reason.

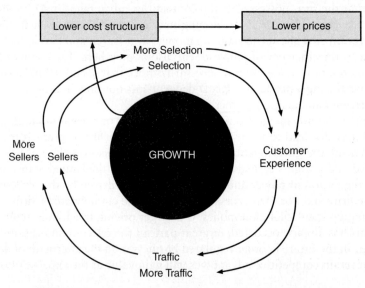

FIGURE 31.7   The Amazon Flywheel (Networking Benefits)

Microsoft recognized earlier than most firms that the most significant barrier to entry into the software business is the cost to the end user of switching from its products to those of a competitor. In fact, Microsoft Excel, early in its life, had to overcome the obstacle that most users were working with Lotus spreadsheets and did not want to bear the switching cost. Microsoft made it easy for end users to switch to its products (by allowing Excel to open Lotus spreadsheets, for instance), and it made it more and more expensive for them to switch to a competitor by creating Microsoft Office as a suite. Thus, a user who has Microsoft Office installed on his or her system and who wants to try to switch from Microsoft Word to WordPerfect has to overcome multiple barriers: Will the conversion work well on the hundreds of Word files that exist already? Will the user still be able to cut and paste from Microsoft Excel and PowerPoint into WordPerfect documents? The end result, of course, is that it becomes very difficult for competitors that do not have Microsoft's resources to compete with it in this arena.

There are a number of other businesses where the switching cost concept can be used to augment an argument for value enhancement or debunk it. For instance, there are many who argue that the valuations of social media companies such as Twitter and Facebook reflect their first-mover advantage—that is, the fact that they are pioneers in the online business. However, the switching costs in social media seem to be minimal, and these companies have to come up with a way of increasing switching costs if they want to earn high returns in the future. No wonder, both platforms encourage users to increase their friends and follower bases, making it more difficult to leave.

Cost Advantages   There are several ways in which firms can establish a cost advantage over their competitors and use it as a barrier to entry:

- In businesses where scale can be used to reduce costs, economies of scale can give bigger firms advantages over smaller firms. This is the advantage, for instance, that Walmart has used to gain market share at the expense of its smaller and often local competitors.
- Owning or having exclusive rights to a distribution system can provide firms with a cost advantage over its competitors. For instance, American Airlines' ownership of the Sabre airline reservation system gave it an early advantage over its competitors in attracting customers.
- Having access to lower-cost labor or resources can also provide cost advantages. Thus, a nonunionized company with a lower-cost labor force has an advantage over its unionized competitors, as do natural resource companies with access to reserves that are less expensive to exploit.

These cost advantages will influence value in one of two ways: The firm with the cost advantage may charge the same price as its competitors but have a much higher operating margin. Or the firm may charge lower prices than its competitors and have a much higher capital turnover ratio. In fact, the net effect of increasing margins or turnover ratios (or both) will increase the return on capital, and through it expected growth.

The cost advantage of economies of scale can create high capital requirements that prevent new firms from entering the business. In businesses such as aerospace and automobiles, the competition is almost entirely among existing competitors. The absence of new competitors may allow these firms to maintain above-normal returns, though the competition between existing firms will constrain the magnitude of these returns.

Measuring the Moat   Assessing competitive advantages and incorporating them into value and investing has always been part of prudent value investing, and as Warren Buffett said, "What we're trying to find is a business that, for one reason or another—it can be because it's the low-cost producer in some area, it can be because it has a natural franchise because of surface capabilities, it could be because of its position in the consumers' mind, it can be because of a technological advantage, or any kind of reason at all, that it has this moat around it".

That said, and notwithstanding the fact that there is an entire business discipline, known as corporate strategy, dedicated to the study of competitive advantages or moats, attempts to capture their strength and sustainability have generally fallen short. In valuation, the strength of the moat determines excess returns, which in turn drive the value of growth, and the sustainability captures how long you can deliver these excess returns. In Table 31.2, we have tried to capture these effects.

LEAD TIMES FROM COMPETITIVE ADVANTAGES

A key question that we often face when looking at the effects of a competitive advantage on value is how long a competitive advantage lasts. This is a difficult question to answer because there are a number of firm-specific factors, but there are few interesting studies in corporate strategy that try to address the issue. Levin et al. (1987) estimate, for instance, that it takes between three and five years to duplicate a patented product or process, and between one and three years to duplicate an unpatented product or process. The same study found that patenting is often much less effective at preventing imitation than moving quickly down the learning curve and creating sales and service networks. For example, Intel was able to maintain its competitive advantage even as its computer chips were being cloned by Advanced Micro Devices (AMD) by using the lead time it had to move quickly to the next-generation chips.

TABLE 31.2   Competitive Advantages (Moats) at Companies

		Type of Competitive Advantage (Moat)				
		Brand Name	Switching Costs	Network Benefit	Cost Advantages	Legal Protection
Moat Width	Wide	Top brand	Infinite	Global	Permanent	Full
	Narrow	Name brand	High	Local	Temporary	Partial
	No Moat	Generic	None	None	None	None
Place in story		Margins	Customer Retention	Market Share	Profit Margins	Pricing Power

Reduce the Cost of Financing

The cost of capital for a firm is a composite cost of debt and equity financing. The cash flows generated over time are discounted to the present at the cost of capital. Holding the cash flows constant, reducing the cost of capital will increase the value of the firm. This section will explore the ways in which a firm may reduce its cost of capital, or more generally, increase its firm value by changing both financing mix and type.

Change Operating Risk The operating risk of a firm is a direct function of the kinds of products or services it provides, and the degree to which these products or services are discretionary to the customer. The more discretionary they are, the greater the operating risk faced by the firm. Both the cost of equity and cost of debt of a firm are affected by the operating risk of the business or businesses in which it operates. In the case of equity, only that portion of the operating risk that is not diversifiable will affect value.

Firms can reduce their operating risk by making their products and services less discretionary to their customers. Advertising clearly plays a role, but finding new uses for a product or service is another way. Reducing operating risk will result in a lowered unlevered beta (cost of equity) and a lower cost of debt default risk (cost of debt).

Reduce Operating Leverage The operating leverage of a firm measures the proportion of its costs that are fixed. Other things remaining equal, the greater the proportion of the costs of a firm that are fixed, the more volatile its earnings will be, and the higher its cost of capital. Reducing the proportion of the costs that are fixed will make firms much less risky and reduce their cost of capital. Firms can reduce their fixed costs by using outside contractors for some services; if the business does not measure up, the firm is not stuck with the costs of providing this service. They can also tie expenses to revenues; for instance, tying wages paid to revenues made will reduce the proportion of costs that are fixed.

This basic idea of tying expenses to revenues is often described as making the cost structure more flexible. A more flexible cost structure influences three inputs in a valuation. It leads to a lower unlevered beta (due to the lower operating leverage), reduces the cost of debt (because of the reduction in default risk), and increases the optimal debt ratio. All three reduce the cost of capital and increase firm value.

Change the Financing Mix A third way to reduce the cost of capital is to change the mix of debt and equity used to finance the firm. As we argued in Chapter 15, debt is always cheaper than equity, partly because lenders bear less risk, and partly because of the tax advantage associated with debt. This benefit has to be weighed off against the additional risk of bankruptcy created by the borrowing; this higher risk increases both the beta for equity and the cost of borrowing. The net effect will determine whether the cost of capital will increase or decrease as the firm takes on more debt.

Note, however, that firm value will increase as the cost of capital decreases, if and only if, the operating cash flows are unaffected by the higher debt ratio. If, as the debt ratio increases, the riskiness of the firm increases, and this, in turn, affects the firm's operations and cash flows, the firm value may decrease even as cost of capital declines. If this is the case, the objective function when designing the financing mix for a firm has to be restated in terms of firm value maximization rather than cost of capital minimization.

wacc.xls: **This dataset on the web summarizes debt ratios and costs of capital by industry group for the United States.**

Change Financing Type   A fundamental principle in corporate finance is that the financing of a firm should be designed to ensure, as far as possible, that the cash flows on debt match as closely as possible the cash flows on the asset. By matching cash flows on debt to cash flows on the asset, a firm reduces its risk of default and increases its capacity to carry debt, which, in turn, reduces its cost of capital, and increases value.

Firms that mismatch cash flows on debt and cash flows on assets (by using short-term debt to finance long-term assets, debt in one currency to finance assets with cash flows in a different currency, or floating-rate debt to finance assets whose cash flows tend to be adversely impacted by higher inflation) will have higher default risk, higher costs of capital, and lower firm value. Firms can use derivatives and swaps to reduce these mismatches and, in the process, increase firm value. Alternatively, they can replace their existing debt with debt that is more closely matched to their assets. Finally, they can use innovative securities that allow them to pattern cash flows on debt-to-cash flows on investments. The use of catastrophe bonds by insurance companies and commodity bonds by natural resource firms are good examples.

WHAT ABOUT MILLER-MODIGLIANI?

One of corporate finance's best-known and most enduring propositions—the Miller-Modigliani theorem—argues that the value of a firm is independent of its capital structure. In other words, changing your financing mix should have no effect on your firm value. How would we reconcile our arguments in this section with the Miller-Modigliani theorem? Note that the original version of the theorem was derived for a world with no taxes and default. With these assumptions, debt creates no tax advantages and no bankruptcy costs, and does not affect value. In a world with taxes and default risk, you are much more likely to have to make trade-offs, and debt can increase value, decrease value, or leave it unaffected, depending on how the trade-offs play out.

VALUE ENHANCEMENT CHAIN

We can categorize the range of actions firms can take to increase value in several ways. One is in terms of whether they affect cash flows from assets in place, growth, the cost of capital, or the length of the growth period. There are two other levels at which we can distinguish between actions that create value:

1. *Does an action create a value trade-off or is it a pure value creator?* Very few actions increase value without any qualifications. Among these are the divestitures of assets when the divestiture value exceeds the continuing value, and the elimination of dead-weight costs that contribute nothing to the firm's earnings or future growth. Most actions have both positive and negative effects on value, and it is the net effect that

determines whether these actions are value enhancing. In some cases, the trade-off is largely internal, and the odds are much better for value creation. An example is a firm changing its mix of debt and equity to reduce the cost of capital. In other cases, however, the net effect on value will be a function of how competitors react to a firm's actions. As an example, reducing prices to increase revenues may not work as a value enhancement measure if competitors react and cut prices as well.

2. *How quickly do actions pay off?* Some actions generate an immediate increase in value. Among these are divestitures and cost cutting. Many actions, however, are designed to create value in the long term. Thus, building up a respected brand name clearly creates value in the long term but is unlikely to affect value today.

Table 31.3 summarizes a value enhancement chain, where actions that create value are categorized both on how quickly they create value and on how much control the firm has over the value creation. The first column, "Quick Fixes", lists actions in which the firm has considerable control over the outcome, and the benefit in terms of value creation is

TABLE 31.3   The Value Enhancement Chain

	Quick Fixes	Odds on	Long Term
Assets in Place	• Divest assets/projects with Divestiture Value > Continuing Value. • Terminate projects with Liquidation Value > Continuing Value. • Eliminate operating expenses that generate no current revenues and no growth. • Tax advantage of tax minimization strategies	• Reduce net working capital requirements, by reducing inventory and accounts receivable, or by increasing accounts payable. • Reduce capital maintenance expenditures on assets in place.	• Change pricing strategy to maximize the product of profit margins and turnover ratio. • Move to more efficient technology for operations to reduce expense and improve margins.
Expected Growth	• Eliminate new capital expenditures that are expected to earn less than the cost of capital.	• Increase reinvestment rate or marginal return on capital or both in firm's existing markets.	• Increase reinvestment rate or marginal return on capital or both in new markets.
Length of High Growth Period	• If any of the firm's products or services can be patented and protected, do so.	• Use economies of scale or cost advantages to create higher return on capital. • Build on networking benefits, if any.	• Build up brand name • Increase the cost of switching from product and reduce cost of switching to it.
Cost of Financing	• Use swaps and derivatives to match debt more closely to firm's assets. • Recapitalize to move the firm towards its optimal debt ratio.	• Change financing type and use innovative securities to reflect the types of assets being financed • Use the optimal financing mix to finance new investments. • Make cost structure more flexible to reduce operating leverage.	• Reduce the operating risk of the firm, by making products less discretionary to customers.

immediate. The second column, "Odds On", includes actions that are likely to create value in the near or medium term, and where the firm continues to exercise significant control over the outcome. The third column includes actions designed to create value in the long term. This is where the major strategic initiatives of the firm show up.

ILLUSTRATION 31.6:   Value Enhancement at SAP—May 2005

SAP is a business software manufacturing company headquartered in Germany. It has a well-deserved reputation for good management, especially when it comes to new investments; it reinvested 57.42% of its after-tax operating income back into the company and generated a return on capital of 19.93% in 2004. On both dimensions, it did considerably better than its peer group. The management is, however, extremely conservative when it comes to the use of debt and has a debt ratio of 1.4%; its resulting cost of capital is 8.68%. In Figure 31.8, we value the company assuming that it will continue its current investment policy (maintaining its reinvestment rate and return on capital from 2004 for the next five years) and its conservative financing policy. The value per share that we arrive at is 106.12 euros.

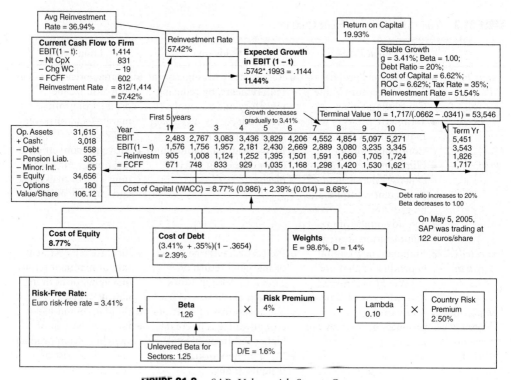

FIGURE 31.8   SAP: Value with Status Quo

How much can SAP afford to borrow? To answer this question, we estimate the cost of capital for SAP in Table 31.4, at debt ratios ranging from 0 to 90%.[5]

At a 30% debt ratio, the cost of capital is minimized at 7.95%; it is about 0.73% lower than the current cost of capital.

---

[5]The process of computing the cost of equity and debt at different debt ratios is described in detail in my book, *Applied Corporate Finance* (John Wiley & Sons, 4th ed., 2014).

TABLE 31.4   Cost of Capital and Debt Ratios: SAP

Debt	Beta	Cost of Equity	Bond Rating	Cost of debt (pretax)	Tax rate	Cost of debt (after-tax)	WACC
0%	1.25	8.72%	AAA	3.76%	36.54%	2.39%	8.72%
10%	1.34	9.09%	AAA	3.76%	36.54%	2.39%	8.42%
20%	1.45	9.56%	A	4.26%	36.54%	2.70%	8.19%
30%	1.59	10.16%	A–	4.41%	36.54%	2.80%	7.95%
40%	1.78	10.96%	CCC	11.41%	36.54%	7.24%	9.47%
50%	2.22	12.85%	C	15.41%	22.08%	12.01%	12.43%
60%	2.78	15.21%	C	15.41%	18.40%	12.58%	13.63%
70%	3.70	19.15%	C	15.41%	15.77%	12.98%	14.83%
80%	5.55	27.01%	C	15.41%	13.80%	13.28%	16.03%
90%	11.11	50.62%	C	15.41%	12.26%	13.52%	17.23%

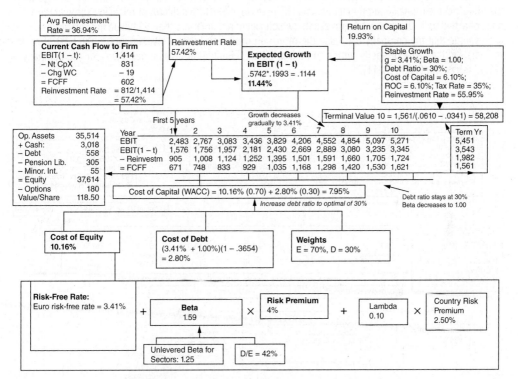

FIGURE 31.9   SAP: Value with Changed Financing

If we assume that the only thing we change at SAP is the financing mix, and we move the firm to its optimal debt ratio of 30% (and the resulting lower cost of capital), the value of SAP as a company will increase. In Figure 31.9, we show the restructured valuation of SAP with this change and arrive at a value of 118.50 euros per share. The value of control in the case of SAP is a relatively paltry 12.4 euros per share or about 12% of equity value.

ILLUSTRATION 31.7:   The Value of Changing Management—Blockbuster in April 2005

In April 2005, Carl Icahn shocked the management at Blockbuster, the video rental company, by contesting the management slate for seats on the board of directors. He based his challenge on the argument that Blockbuster was poorly managed and run, and could be worth more with significant management changes. While incumbent management contested him on this issue, Icahn was able to get enough stockholder support to get his representatives elected to the board.

Looking at Blockbuster's 2004 financial statements, there is a clear basis for stockholder dissatisfaction with the company. The company's revenues have stagnated, going from $5,566 million in 2002, to $5,912 million in 2003, to $6,054 million in 2004. Even more ominously, the company's operating income has dropped from $468.20 million in 2002 to $251.20 million in 2004, as competition has increased both from online rentals (Netflix) and from discount retailers (Walmart). The company earned a return on capital of 4.06% on its existing assets in 2004, while its cost of capital was 6.17%. Even if we assume that the return on capital on new investments will gradually increase to the cost of capital level over the next five years, we arrive at a value for the equity of $955 million and a value per share of only $5.13 (shown in Figure 31.10).

So, how would we restructure Blockbuster? The first and most important component is increasing the returns on existing assets to at least the cost of capital of 6.17%. This will require either generating more operating income (pretax operating income has to increase to $381.76 million), or releasing some of the existing capital tied up in the poorest return assets (which would require more than $1 billion in divestitures). If we also assume that the company can raise the return on capital on its new investments to the cost of capital immediately, the value of equity jumps to $2.323 billion, resulting in a value per share for the company is $12.47 (shown in Figure 31.11).

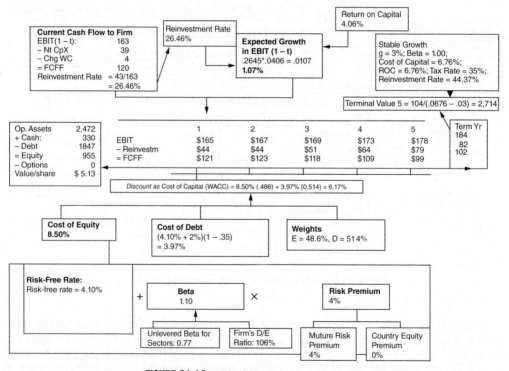

FIGURE 31.10   Blockbuster: Status Quo

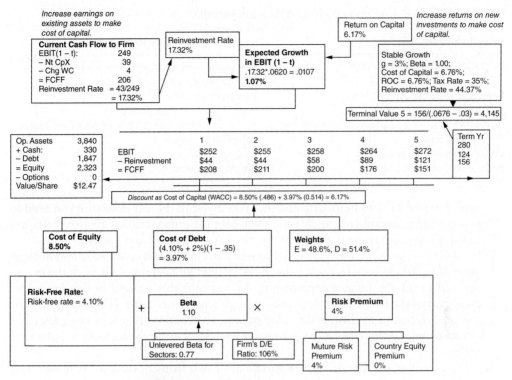

FIGURE 31.11   Blockbuster: Restructured

It is worth noting that Blockbuster has two classes of shares—118 million class A shares with one voting right per share, and 63 million class B shares with two voting rights per share. At the time of this analysis, both class A shares were trading at a price of $9.50 per share.

 valenh.xls: This spreadsheet allows you to estimate the approximate effect that changing the way a firm is run has on its value.

CLOSING THOUGHTS ON VALUE ENHANCEMENT

Almost all firms claim to be interested in value enhancement, but very few are able to increase value consistently. If value enhancement is as simple as it is made out to be in this chapter, you might wonder why this is so. There are four basic propositions you need to consider in the context of value enhancement:

1. *Value enhancement is hard work, takes time, and may make life uncomfortable for existing managers.* There are no magic bullets that increase value painlessly. Increasing cash flows requires hard decisions on layoffs and cost cutting, and in some cases, admitting past mistakes. Increasing the reinvestment rate will require that you analyze

TABLE 31.5 Value Enhancement Actions: Who Is Responsible?

Value-Enhancing Action	Primary Responsibility
Increasing operating efficiency	Operating managers and personnel, from shop-floor stewards to factory managers
Reducing working capital needs	Inventory personnel; credit personnel
Increasing revenue growth	Sales and marketing personnel
Increasing return on capital/reinvestment rate	Strategic teams, with help from financial analysts
Build brand name	Advertising personnel
Other competitive advantages	Strategic analysts
Reduce cost of financing	Finance department

new investments with more care and that you invest in the infrastructure you need to manage these investments. Increasing your debt ratio may also create new pressures to make interest payments and to deal with ratings agencies and banks.

2. *For a firm to enhance value, all its component parts need to buy into the value enhancement plan.* You cannot increase value by edict, and you cannot do it from the executive offices (or the finance department). As you probably noticed in the discussion, every part of the firm has a role to play in increasing value. Table 31.5 summarizes the role of each part of the firm in the value enhancement actions that have been described in this chapter. Departments have to cooperate for value enhancement to become a reality.

3. *Value enhancement has to be firm-specific.* No two firms in trouble share the same problems, and using a cookbook approach seldom works in value enhancement. You have to begin by diagnosing the specific problems faced by the firm you are analyzing and tailor a response to these problems. Thus, the value enhancement plan you would devise for a mature firm with cost overruns will be very different from the plan you would devise for a young firm that has a product that no longer meets market needs.

4. *Price enhancement may not always follow value enhancement.* This is perhaps the most disappointing aspect of value enhancement. A firm that takes all the right actions may not necessarily be rewarded immediately by financial markets. In some cases, markets may even punish such firms because of the effects of these actions on reported earnings. In the long term, markets most likely will recognize value-enhancing actions and reward them, but the manager who took these actions may not be around to share in the rewards.

CONCLUSION

Value enhancement is clearly on the minds of many managers today. Building on the discounted cash flow principles developed in the preceding chapter, the value of a firm can be increased by changing one of the four primary inputs into value: the cash flows from assets in place, the expected growth rate during the high-growth period, the length of the high-growth period, and the cost of capital. Conversely, actions that do not change any of these variables cannot create value. Cash flows from assets in place can be increased by cost cutting and more efficient operations, as well as by lowering taxes paid on income and reducing investment needs (capital maintenance and noncash working capital investments). Expected growth can be increased by increasing the reinvestment rate or the return on capital but increases in the reinvestment rate will generate value only if the return on capital exceeds the cost of capital. High growth, at least the value-creating kind, can be made to last longer by generating new competitive advantages or augmenting existing ones. Finally, the cost of capital can be lowered by moving toward an optimal debt ratio, using debt that is more suited for the assets being financed and by reducing market risk.

QUESTIONS AND SHORT PROBLEMS

In the problems following, use an equity risk premium of 5.5 percent if none is specified.

1. Marion Manufacturing, a steel company, announces that it will be taking a major restructuring charge that will lower earnings this year by $500 million. Assume that the charge is not tax deductible and has no effects on operations.
   a. What will the effect of this charge be on the value of the firm?
   b. When the firm announces the charge, what effect would you expect it to have on the stock price? Is your answer consistent with your response to question (a)?
2. Universal Health Care (UHC) is a company whose stock price has declined by 40% in the past year. In the current year, UHC earned $300 million in pretax operating income on revenues of $10 billion. The new CEO of the firm has proposed cost-cutting measures she anticipates will save the firm $100 million in expenses, without any effect on revenues. Assume the firm is growing at a stable rate of 5% a year and that its cost of capital is 10%; neither number is expected to change as a consequence of the cost cutting. The firm's tax rate is 40%. (You can assume that the firm reinvests $100 million each year and that this reinvestment will not change as the firm cuts costs.)
   a. What effect will cost cutting have on value?
   b. What effect will the cost cutting have on value if the expected growth rate drops to 4.5% as a consequence? (Some of the costs cut were designed to generate future growth.)
3. Atlantic Cruise Lines operates cruise ships and is headquartered in Florida. The firm had $100 million in pretax operating income in the current year, of which it reinvested $25 million. The firm expects its operating income to grow 4% in perpetuity and expects to maintain its existing reinvestment rate. Atlantic has a capital structure composed of 60% of equity and 40% of debt. Its cost of equity is 12% and it has a pretax cost of borrowing of 8%. The firm currently faces a tax rate of 40%.
   a. Estimate the value of the firm.
   b. Assume now that Atlantic Cruise Lines will move its headquarters to the Cayman Islands. If its tax rate drops to 0% as a consequence, estimate the effect on value of the shift.
4. Furniture Depot is a retail chain selling furniture and appliances. The firm has after-tax operating income of $250 million in the current year on revenues of $5 billion. The firm also has noncash working capital of $1 billion. The net capital expenditure this year is $100 million, and they expect revenues, operating income, and net capital expenditures to grow 5% a year forever. The firm's cost of capital is 9%.
   a. Assume that noncash working capital remains at the existing percent of revenues, estimate the value of the firm.
   b. Assume now that the firm is able to reduce its noncash working capital requirement by 50%. Estimate the effect on value of this change.

    c. If as a consequence of this noncash working capital change, earnings growth declines to 4.75%, what would the effect on value be of the drop in noncash working capital?

5. General Systems is a firm that manufactures personal computers. As a top manager in the firm, you are considering changes in the way the firm is run. Currently, the firm has after-tax operating income of $50 million on capital invested of $250 million (at the beginning of the year). The firm also reinvests $25 million in net capital expenditures and working capital.
    a. Estimate the expected growth rate in earnings, given the firm's current return on capital and reinvestment rate.
    b. Holding the return on capital constant, what would happen to the expected growth rate if the firm increased its reinvestment rate to 80%?
    c. What would the effect on growth be if, as the reinvestment rate increases to 80%, the return on capital on investments drops by 5%? (For instance, if the return on capital is currently 18%, it will drop to 13%.)

6. Compaq Computer has seen its stock price decline from $45 to $24. The firm is expected to reinvest 50% of its expected after-tax operating income of $2 billion in new investments and expects to earn a return on capital of 10.69%. The firm is all equity financed and has a cost of equity of 11.5%.
    a. What is the firm's expected growth rate, assuming that it maintains its existing reinvestment rate and return on capital?
    b. Assuming that this growth is perpetual, what is the value of the firm?
    c. How much value is being created or destroyed by the firm's new investments?

7. Referring to problem 6, now assume that Compaq's optimal debt ratio is 20%. Its cost of equity will increase to 12.5%, and its after-tax cost of debt will be 4.5% at the optimal debt ratio.
    a. What is the firm's expected growth rate, assuming it maintains its existing reinvestment rate and return on capital?
    b. Assuming this growth is perpetual, what is the value of the firm?
    c. How much value is being created or destroyed by the firm's new investments?

8. Coca-Cola is considered to have one of the most valuable brand names in the world. The firm has an after-tax operating margin of 20% on revenues of $25 billion. The capital invested in the firm is $10 billion. In addition, Coca-Cola reinvests 50% of its after-tax operating earnings.
    a. Estimate the expected growth in operating earnings, assuming Coca-Cola can sustain these values for the foreseeable future.
    b. Assume generic soft drink manufacturers have after-tax operating margins of only 7.5%. If Coca-Cola maintains its existing reinvestment rate but loses its brand name value, estimate the expected growth rate in operating earning. (You can assume that with the loss in brand name value Coca-Cola's operating margins would drop to 7.5% as well.)

9. BioMask Genetics is a biotechnology firm with only one patent to its name. The after-tax operating earnings in the current year are $10 million, and the firm has no reinvestment needs. The patent will expire in three years, and the firm will have a 15% growth rate in earnings during that period. After year 3, operating earnings are expected to remain constant forever. The firm's management is considering an advertising plan designed to build up the brand name of its patented product. The advertising campaign will cost $50 million (pretax) a year over the next three years; the firm's

tax rate is 40%. The firm believes this campaign will allow it to maintain a 15% growth rate for 10 years, as the brand name compensates for the loss of the patent protection. After year 10, the operating earnings are expected to remain constant forever. The firm has a cost of capital of 10%.

a. Estimate the value of the firm assuming it does not embark on the advertising campaign.

b. Estimate the value of the firm with the advertising campaign.

c. Assume there is no guarantee the growth rate will last 10 years as a result of the campaign. What would the probability of success need to be for the campaign to be financially viable?

10. Sunmask is a cosmetics firm that has seen its stock price fall and its earnings decline in the past year. You have been hired as the new CEO of the company, and a careful analysis of Sunmask's current financials reveals the following:

   ■ The firm currently has after-tax operating earnings of $300 million on revenues of $10 billion, and a capital turnover ratio (sales–book value of capital) of 2.5.

   ■ The firm is expected to reinvest 60% of its after-tax operating income.

   ■ The firm is all equity financed and has a cost of capital of 10%.

   a. Estimate the value of the firm, assuming existing policies continue forever. (Returns on capital and reinvestment rates remain constant forever as well.)

   b. Assume that you can increase operating margins from 3% to 5% without affecting the capital turnover ratio, that you can lower the reinvestment rate to 40%, and that the cost of capital will become 9% if you shift to your optimal debt ratio. How much would your firm's value increase if you were able to make these changes?

CHAPTER 32

Value Enhancement: Economic Value Added, Cash Flow Return on Investment, and Other Tools

The discounted cash flow model provides for a rich and thorough analysis of all the different ways in which a firm can increase value, but it can become complex as the number of inputs increases. It is also difficult to tie management compensation systems to a discounted cash flow model, since many of the inputs need to be estimated and can be manipulated to yield the results management wants.

If we assume that markets are efficient, we can replace the unobservable value from the discounted cash flow model with the observed market price and reward or punish managers based on the performance of the stock. Thus, a firm whose stock price has gone up is viewed as having created value, whereas one whose stock price has fallen has destroyed value. Compensation systems based on the stock price, including stock grants and warrants, have become a standard component of most management compensation packages.

While market prices have the advantage of being up-to-date and observable, they are also noisy. Even if markets are efficient, stock prices tend to fluctuate around the true value, and markets sometimes do make mistakes. Thus, a firm may see its stock price go up and its top management rewarded, even as value is destroyed. Conversely, the managers of a firm may be penalized as its stock price drops, even though the managers may have taken actions that increase firm value. The other problem with stock prices as the basis for compensation is that they are available only for the entire firm. Thus, stock prices cannot be used to analyze the managers of individual divisions of a firm, or for their relative performance.

In the past decade, while firms have become more focused on value creation, they have remained suspicious of financial markets. While they might understand the notion of discounted cash flow value, they are unwilling to tie compensation to a value that is based on dozens of estimates. In this environment, new mechanisms for measuring value that are simple to estimate and use, do not depend too heavily on market movements, and do not require a lot of estimation to find a ready market. While the mechanisms are too numerous to list, we focus on two in this chapter that encapsulate most of the other approaches.

1. *Economic value added (EVA)*, which measures the dollar surplus value created by a firm on its existing investment.
2. *Cash flow return on investment (CFROI)*, which measures the percentage return made by a firm on its existing investments.

This chapter looks at how each is related to discounted cash flow valuation. It also looks at the conditions under which firms using these approaches to judge performance and evaluate managers may end up making decisions that destroy value rather than create it.

ECONOMIC VALUE ADDED

The economic value added (EVA) mechanism is a measure of the dollar surplus value created by an investment or a portfolio of investments. It is computed as the product of the excess return made on an investment or investments and the capital invested in that investment or investments.

$$
\begin{aligned}
\text{Economic value added} &= (\text{Return on capital invested} - \text{Cost of capital}) \\
&\quad \times (\text{Capital invested}) \\
&= \text{After-tax operating income} - (\text{Cost of capital} \\
&\quad \times \text{Capital invested})
\end{aligned}
$$

This section begins by looking at the measurement of economic value added, then considers its links to discounted cash flow valuation, and closes with a discussion of its limitations as a value enhancement tool.

Calculating EVA

The definition of EVA outlines three basic inputs we need for its computation—the return on capital earned on investments, the cost of capital for those investments, and the capital invested in them. In measuring each of these, we will make many of the same adjustments that were discussed in the context of discounted cash flow valuation.

How much capital is invested in existing assets? One obvious answer is to use the market value of the firm, but market value includes capital invested not just in assets in place but in expected future growth.[1]

Since we want to evaluate the quality of assets in place, we need a measure of the capital invested in just these assets. Given the difficulty of estimating the value of assets in place, it is not surprising that we turn to the book value of capital as a proxy for the capital invested in assets in place. The book value, however, is a number that reflects not just the accounting choices made in the current period, but also accounting decisions made over time on how to depreciate assets, value inventory, and deal with acquisitions. At the minimum, the three adjustments we made to capital invested in the discounted cash flow valuation—converting operating leases into debt, capitalizing R&D expenses, and eliminating the effect of one-time or cosmetic charges—have to be made when computing EVA as well. The older the firm, the more extensive the adjustments that have to be made to the book value of capital to get to a reasonable estimate of the market value of capital invested

---

[1] As an illustration, computing the return on capital at NVidia or Microsoft in 2024, using the market value of the firm, instead of book value, results in a low return on capital. It would be a mistake to view this as a sign of poor investments on the part of the firm's managers.

in assets in place. Since this requires that we know and take into account every accounting decision over time, there are cases where the book value of capital is too flawed to be fixable. Here, it is best to estimate the capital invested from the ground up, starting with the assets owned by the firm, estimating the market value of these assets (perhaps to the best potential buyers), and cumulating this market value.

To evaluate the return on this invested capital, we need an estimate of the after-tax operating income earned by the firm on these investments. Again, the accounting measure of operating income has to be adjusted for operating leases, R&D expenses, and one-time charges to compute the return on capital.

The third and final component needed to estimate the economic value added is the cost of capital. In keeping with our arguments both in the investment analysis and the discounted cash flow valuation sections, the cost of capital should be estimated based on the market values of debt and equity in the firm, rather than book value. There is no contradiction between using book value for purposes of estimating capital invested and using market value for estimating cost of capital, since a firm has to earn more than its market value cost of capital to generate value. From a practical standpoint, using the book value cost of capital will tend to understate cost of capital for most firms, and will understate it more for more highly levered firms than for lightly levered firms. Understating the cost of capital will lead to overstating the economic value added.

EVA COMPUTATION IN PRACTICE

During the 1990s, EVA was promoted most heavily by Stern Stewart, a New York–based consulting firm. The firm's founders, Joel Stern and Bennett Stewart, became the foremost evangelists for the measure. Their success spawned a whole host of imitators from other consulting firms, all of which were variants on the excess return measure.

In the process of applying this measure to real firms, Stern Stewart found that it had to modify accounting measures of earnings and capital to get more realistic estimates of surplus value. In his 1991 book, *The Quest for Value*, Bennett Stewart mentions some of the adjustments that should be made to capital invested, including adjusting for goodwill (recorded and unrecorded). He also suggests adjustments that need to be made to operating income, including the conversion of operating leases into financial expenses.

Many firms that adopted EVA during this period also based management compensation on measured EVA. Consequently, how it was defined and measured became a matter of significant concern to managers at every level.

Economic Value Added, Net Present Value, and Discounted Cash Flow Valuation

One of the foundations of investment analysis in traditional corporate finance is the net present value rule. The net present value (NPV) of a project, which reflects the present value of expected cash flows on a project, netted against any investment needs, is a measure of dollar surplus value on the project. Thus, investing in projects with positive net present value will increase the value of the firm, while investing in projects with negative net present value will reduce value. Economic value added is a simple extension of the net present value rule. The net present value of the project is the present value of the economic value added by that project over its life.[2]

$$NPV = \sum_{t=1}^{t=n} \frac{EVA_t}{(1 + k_c)^t}$$

where EVA_t is the economic value added by the project in year t, and the project has a life of n years.

This connection between economic value added and NPV allows us to link the value of a firm to the economic value added by that firm. To see this, let us begin with a simple formulation of firm value in terms of the value of assets in place and expected future growth:

Firm value = Value of assets in place + Value of expected future growth

Note that in a discounted cash flow model, the values of both assets in place and expected future growth can be written in terms of the net present value created by each component:

$$\text{Value of firm} = \text{Capital Invested}_{\text{Assets in place}} + NPV_{\text{Assets in place}} + \sum_{t=1}^{t=\infty} NPV_{\text{future projects, t}}$$

Substituting the economic value-added version of net present value into this equation, we get:

$$\text{Firm value} = \text{Capital Invested}_{\text{Assets in place}} + \sum_{t=1}^{t=\infty} \frac{EVA_{t,\text{ Assets in place}}}{(1 + k_c)^t}$$

$$+ \sum_{t=1}^{t=\infty} \frac{EVA_{t,\text{ Future projects}}}{(1 + k_c)^t}$$

Thus, the value of a firm can be written as the sum of three components: the capital invested in assets in place, the present value of the economic value added by these assets, and the expected present value of the economic value that will be added by future investments.

ILLUSTRATION 32.1:   Discounted Cash Flow Value and Economic Value Added

Consider a firm that has existing assets in which it has capital invested of $100 million. Assume these additional facts about the firm:

- The after-tax operating income on assets in place is $15 million. This return on capital of 15% is expected to be sustained in the future, and the company has a cost of capital of 10%.
- At the beginning of each of the next five years, the firm is expected to make new investments of $10 million each. These investments are also expected to earn 15% as a return on capital, and the cost of capital is expected to remain 10%.

---

[2]This is true, though, only if the expected present value of the cash flows from depreciation is assumed to be equal to the present value of the salvage of the capital invested in the project. A proof of this equality can be found in my paper on value enhancement in the *Contemporary Finance Digest* in 1999.

■ After year 5, the company will continue to make investments, and earnings will grow 5% a year, but the new investments will have a return on capital of only 10%, which is also the cost of capital.

■ All assets and investments are expected to have infinite lives.[3] Thus, the assets in place and the investments made in the first five years will make 15% a year in perpetuity, with no growth.

This firm can be valued using an economic value-added approach, as follows:

Capital invested in assets in place	$100.00
+ EVA from assets in place $= (.15 - .10)(100)/.10 =$	$ 50.00
+ PV of EVA from new investments in year 1 $= [(.15 - .10)(10)/.10] =$	$ 5.00
+ PV of EVA from new investments in year 2 $= [(.15 - .10)(10)/.10]/1.1 =$	$ 4.55
+ PV of EVA from new investments in year 3 $= [(.15 - .10)(10)/.10]/1.1^2 =$	$ 4.13
+ PV of EVA from new investments in year 4 $= [(.15 - .10)(10)/.10]/1.1^3 =$	$ 3.76
+ PV of EVA from new investments in year 5 $= [(.15 - .10)(10)/.10]/1.1^4 =$	$ 3.42
Value of firm	$170.85

Note that the present values are computed assuming that the cash flows on investments are perpetuities, and that the investments are made at the beginning of each year. In addition, the value of the economic value added by the investments made in future years is discounted to today, using the cost of capital. To illustrate, the present value of the economic value added by investments made at the beginning of year 2 is discounted back one year. The value of the firm, which is $170.85 million, can be written using the earlier equation as follows:

$$\text{Firm value} = \text{Capital Invested}_{\text{Assets in place}} + \sum_{t=1}^{t=\infty} \frac{\text{EVA}_{t,\text{Assets in place}}}{(1 + k_c)^t}$$

$$+ \sum_{t=1}^{t=\infty} \frac{\text{EVA}_{t,\text{Future projects}}}{(1 + k_c)^t}$$

$$= \$100 \text{ million} + \$50 \text{ million} + \$20.85 \text{ million}$$

The value of existing assets is, therefore, $150 million, and the value of future growth opportunities is $20.85 million.

Another way of presenting these results is in terms of market value added (MVA), at least in an efficient market. The market value added, in this case, is the difference between the firm value of $170.85 million and the capital invested of $100 million, which yields $70.85 million. This value will be positive only if the return on capital is greater than the cost of capital and will be an increasing function of the spread between the two numbers. The number will be negative if the return on capital is less than the cost of capital.

Note that although the firm continues to grow operating income and makes new investments after the fifth year, these marginal investments create no additional value because they earn the cost of capital. A direct implication is that it is not growth that creates value, but growth in conjunction with excess returns. This provides a perspective, albeit not an unfamiliar one, on the quality of growth. A firm can be increasing its operating income at a healthy rate, but if it is doing so by investing large amounts at or below the cost of capital, it will not be creating value and may actually be destroying it.

This firm could also have been valued using a discounted cash flow valuation, with free cash flows to the firm discounted at the cost of capital. Table 32.1 shows expected free cash flows and the firm value, using the cost of capital of 10% as the discount rate.

---

[3] Note that this assumption is purely for convenience, since it makes the net present value easier to compute. This also allows us to assume the depreciation is offset by capital maintenance expenditures.

TABLE 32.1 Expected FCFF and Value

	0	1	2	3	4	5	Terminal Year
EBIT(1 − t) from assets in place	$ 0.00	$15.00	$15.00	$15.00	$15.00	$ 15.00	
EBIT(1 − t) from investments—Year 1		$ 1.50	$ 1.50	$ 1.50	$ 1.50	$ 1.50	
EBIT(1 − t) from investments— Year 2			$ 1.50	$ 1.50	$ 1.50	$ 1.50	
EBIT(1 − t) from investments— Year 3				$ 1.50	$ 1.50	$ 1.50	
EBIT(1 − t) from investments— Year 4					$ 1.50	$ 1.50	
EBIT(1 − t) from investments— Year 5						$ 1.50	
Total EBIT(1 − t)		$16.50	$18.00	$19.50	$21.00	$ 22.50	$23.63
− Net capital expenditures	$ 10.00	$10.00	$10.00	$10.00	$10.00	$ 11.25	$11.81
FCFF		$ 6.50	$ 8.00	$ 9.50	$11.00	$ 11.25	$11.81
PV of FCFF	−$ 10	$ 5.91	$ 6.61	$ 7.14	$ 7.51	$ 6.99	
Terminal value						$236.25	
PV of terminal value						$146.69	
Value of firm	$170.85						
Return on capital	15%	15%	15%	15%	15%	15%	10%
Cost of capital	10%	10%	10%	10%	10%	10%	10%

In looking at this valuation, note the following:

▧ The capital expenditures occur at the beginning of each year, and thus, are shown in the previous year. The investment of $10 million in year 1 is shown in period 0, the year 2 investment in year 1, and so on.

▧ In year 5, the net investment needed to sustain growth is computed by using two assumptions—that growth in operating income would be 5% a year beyond year 5, and that the return on capital on new investments starting in year 6 (which is shown in year 5) would be 10%.

$$\text{Net investment}_5 = \left[EBIT_6(1 - t) - EBIT_5(1 - t)\right]/ROC_6 = (\$23.625 - \$22.50)/.10 = \$11.25 \text{ million}$$

The value of the firm obtained by discounting free cash flows to the firm at the cost of capital is $170.85, which is identical to the value obtained using the economic value added approach.

ILLUSTRATION 32.2: An EVA Valuation of Lululemon in 2011

Lululemon is a Canadian apparel company, specializing in exercise and leisure clothes. To illustrate the equivalence of FCFF and EVA valuations, we will begin with a discounted cash flow valuation of the company, using the following inputs, in Table 32.2:

TABLE 32.2 Valuation Inputs—Lululemon

Length	High Growth Phase Next 10 years	Stable Growth Phase After 10 (forever)
Growth inputs		
– Reinvestment rate	50.00%	30.00%
– Return on capital	35.00%	10.00%
– Expected growth rate	17.50%	3.00%
Cost of capital inputs		
– Beta	1.40	1.10
– Cost of debt	NA	5.00%
– Debt ratio	0.00%	20.00%
–Cost of capital	10.50%	7.80%
General information		
–Tax rate	40%	40%

The risk-free rate was 3.5% and the equity risk premium was estimated to be 5%. During the transition period, we adjust the growth rate, reinvestment rate and cost of capital in linear increments from high growth levels to stable growth values. With these inputs, we can estimate the free cash flows to the firm in Table 32.3:

TABLE 32.3 Cost of Capital—Lululemon

Year	EBIT(1 – t)	Expected Growth Rate	Reinvestment Rate	FCFF	Cost of Capital	Cumulated WACC	PV
Base	$106,756		50.00%	$ 53,378			
1	$125,438	17.50%	50.00%	$ 62,719	10.50%	1.1050	$ 56,759.20
2	$147,389	17.50%	50.00%	$ 73,695	10.50%	1.2210	$ 60,354.80
3	$173,183	17.50%	50.00%	$ 86,591	10.50%	1.3492	$ 64,178.19
4	$203,490	17.50%	50.00%	$101,745	10.50%	1.4909	$ 68,243.77
5	$239,100	17.50%	50.00%	$119,550	10.50%	1.6474	$ 72,566.91
6	$274,009	14.60%	46.00%	$147,965	9.98%	1.8118	$ 81,665.09
7	$306,068	11.70%	42.00%	$177,519	9.45%	1.9830	$ 89,518.51
8	$333,002	8.80%	38.00%	$206,461	8.91%	2.1597	$ 95,596.60
9	$352,649	5.90%	34.00%	$232,748	8.36%	2.3402	$ 99,454.60
10	$363,228	3.00%	30.00%	$254,260	7.80%	2.5228	$100,785.36
Sum							$789,123.02

The sum of the present value of the cash flows over the growth period is $789.123 million. The terminal value is estimated based on the cash flow in the terminal year and the cost of capital of 7.80%.

$$\text{Terminal value} = \frac{EBIT_{10}(1 - \text{tax rate})(1 + g)(1 - \text{Reinvestment rate})}{(\text{Cost of capital} - \text{Stable growth rate})}$$

$$= \frac{363{,}228(1.03)(1 - .30)}{(.078 - 0.03)} = \$5{,}455{,}994$$

The discounted cash flow estimate of the value of the operating assets in Lululemon is shown here:

$$\text{Value of operating assets} = \text{PV of FCFF during high growth} + \frac{\text{Terminal value}}{\text{Cumulated WACC}_{10}}$$

$$= \$789{,}123 + \frac{\$5{,}455{,}994}{2.5228} = \$2{,}951{,}809$$

In the following table, we estimate the EVA for Lululemon each year for the next 10 years, and the present value of the EVA. To make these estimates, we begin with the current capital invested in the firm of $353,394 (in thousands), and then add the reinvestment each year to obtain the capital invested at the start of the next year, in Table 32.4:

TABLE 32.4 EVA and Present Value—Lululemon

Year	Invested Capital at Start	Reinvestment	Return on Capital	Cost of Capital	EVA	Cumulated WACC	PV
1	$ 358,394	$ 62,719	35.00%	10.50%	$ 87,806	1.1050	$ 79,463
2	$ 421,113	$ 73,695	35.00%	10.50%	$103,173	1.2210	$ 84,497
3	$ 494,807	$ 86,591	35.00%	10.50%	$121,228	1.3492	$ 89,849
4	$ 581,399	$101,745	35.00%	10.50%	$142,443	1.4909	$ 95,541
5	$ 683,144	$119,550	35.00%	10.50%	$167,370	1.6474	$101,594
6	$ 802,694	$126,044	34.14%	9.98%	$193,906	1.8118	$107,021
7	$ 928,738	$128,549	32.96%	9.45%	$218,313	1.9830	$110,090
8	$1,057,286	$126,541	31.50%	8.91%	$238,810	2.1597	$110,575
9	$1,183,827	$119,901	29.79%	8.36%	$253,691	2.3402	$108,403
10	$1,303,728	$108,969	27.86%	7.80%	$261,538	2.5228	$103,670
Sum							$990,704

The sum of the present values of the EVA for the high growth period is $990,704 (in thousands). At the end of year 10, the firm continues to earn excess returns (albeit at a slower pace), with a return on capital of 10% in perpetuity and a cost of capital of 7.80%. We compute the present value of the EVA after year 10 as follows:

$$\text{PV of EVA after year 10} = \frac{EBIT_{10}(1 - \text{tax rate})(1 + g) - \text{Capital invested}_{10} \times \text{Stable Cost of capital}}{(\text{Cost of capital} - \text{Stable growth rate})}$$

$$= \frac{363{,}228 (1.03) - 3{,}741{,}253 \times 0.078}{(0.078 - 0.03)}$$

$$= \$1{,}714{,}741$$

The total EVA can be computed by adding the present value of the terminal EVA to the present value of EVA over the next 10 years:

$$PV \text{ of } EVA = PV \text{ of } EVA \text{ during high growth} + \frac{\text{Terminal value of EVA}}{\text{Cumulated WACC}_{10}}$$

$$= \$990,704 + \frac{\$1,714,741}{2.5228} = \$1,670,405 \text{ (in thousands)}$$

Note that the capital invested in the terminal EVA computation is an imputed capital invested based on the expected after-tax operating income in the terminal year and the assumed ROC of 10%:

$$\text{Imputed capital invested in year 10} = \frac{EBIT_{10} \ (1 - t)(1 + g)}{\text{Stable ROIC}}$$

$$= \frac{363,228 \ (1.03)}{.10}$$

$$= \$3,741,253$$

If we had not made this adjustment, the capital invested at the start of year 11 would have been only $1,412,696 (in thousands):

$$\text{DCF capital invested} = \text{Capital invested}_{10} + \text{Reinvestment}_{10}$$

$$= \$1,303,728 + \$108,969 = \$1,412,696$$

The final component of value captures the present value of this change in capital invested:

$$\text{Change in capital invested at end of year 10} = \text{Imputed capital invested} - \text{DCF capital invested}$$

$$= \$3,741,253 - \$1,412,696 = \$2,328,557$$

$$PV \text{ of change in capital invested} = \frac{\$2,328,557}{2.5228} = \$923,010$$

The total value of the firm (in thousands) can then be computed as follows:

Capital invested in assets in place	$ 358,394
PV of EVA from assets in place	$1,670,405
PV of change in capital invested	$ 923,010
Value of operating assets	$2,951,809

This is identical to the value from the discounted cash flow model. If you find the adjustment of capital invested in year 10 to be an awkward one, it is worth recognizing that this is an implicit result of an excess return model, where excess returns abruptly change in the terminal year.

 fcffeva.xls: **This spreadsheet allows you to convert a discounted cash flow valuation into an EVA valuation, and vice versa.**

EVA and Firm Value: Potential Conflicts

Assume that a firm adopts economic value added as its measure of value and decides to judge managers on their capacity to generate greater than expected economic value added. What is the potential for abuse? Is it possible for a manager to deliver greater than expected economic value added while destroying firm value at the same time? If so, how can we protect stockholders against these practices?

To answer these questions, let us go back to the earlier equation where we decomposed firm value into capital invested, the present value of economic value added by assets in place, and the present value of economic value added by future growth.

$$\text{Firm value} = \text{Capital Invested}_{\text{Assets in place}} + \sum_{t=1}^{t=\infty} \frac{\text{EVA}_{t, \text{ Assets in place}}}{(1 + k_c)^t}$$
$$+ \sum_{t=1}^{t=\infty} \frac{\text{EVA}_{t, \text{ Future projects}}}{(1 + k_c)^t}$$

EVA VALUATION VERSUS DCF VALUATION: WHEN THEY WILL DISAGREE

To get the same value from discounted cash flow and EVA valuations, you have to ensure that the following conditions hold:

- The after-tax operating income that you use to estimate free cash flows to the firm should be equal to the after-tax operating income you use to compute economic value added. Thus, if you decide to adjust the operating income for operating leases and research and development expenses when doing discounted cash flow valuation, you have to adjust it for computing EVA as well.

- The growth rate you use to estimate after-tax operating income in future periods should be estimated from fundamentals when doing discounted cash flow valuation. In other words, it should be set to:

$$\text{Growth rate} = \text{Reinvestment rate} \times \text{Return on capital}$$

- If growth is an exogenous input into a DCF model and the relationship between growth rates, reinvestment, and return on capital outlined just does not hold, you will get different values from DCF and EVA valuations.

- The capital invested that is used to compute EVA in future periods should be estimated by adding the reinvestment in each period to the capital invested at the beginning of the period. The EVA in each period should be computed as follows:

$$\text{EVA}_t - \text{After tax operating income}_t - \text{Cost of capital} \times \text{Capital invested}_t$$

- You have to make consistent assumptions about terminal value in your discounted cash flow and EVA valuations. In the special case, where the return on capital on all investments—existing and new—is equal to the cost of capital after your terminal year, this is simple to do. The terminal value will be equal to your capital invested at the beginning of your terminal year. In the more general case, you will have to ensure that the capital invested at the beginning of your terminal year is consistent with your assumption about return on capital in perpetuity. In other words, if your after-tax operating income in your terminal year is $1.2 billion, and you are assuming a return on capital of 10 percent in perpetuity, you will have to set your capital invested at the beginning of your terminal year to be $12 billion.

The Capital Invested Game The first two terms in the preceding equation, the capital invested and the present value of economic value added by these investments, are both sensitive to the measurement of capital invested. If capital invested is reduced, keeping the operating income constant, the first term in the equation will drop, but the present value of economic value added will increase proportionately. To illustrate, consider the firm valued in Illustration 32.1. Assume that the capital invested is estimated to be $50 million rather than $100 million, and that the operating income on these investments stays at $15 million. This will increase the return on capital on existing assets to 30 percent. The assumptions about future investments remain unchanged. The firm value can then be written as shown in Table 32.5.

The value of the firm is unchanged, but more of it is redistributed to the economic value-added component. When managers are judged on the economic value added, there will be strong incentives to reduce the capital invested, at least as measured for EVA computations.

There are some actions managers can take to reduce capital invested that truly create value. Thus, in the example, if the reduction in capital invested came from closing a plant that does not (and is not expected to) generate any operating income, the cash flow generated by liquidating the plant's assets will increase value, but only because the plant closing releases cash. Some actions, however, are purely cosmetic in terms of their effects on capital invested, and thus, do not create and may even destroy value. For instance, firms can take one-time restructuring charges that reduce capital or lease assets, rather than buy them because the capital impact of leasing may be smaller.

To illustrate the potential destructiveness of these actions, assume that the managers of the firm in Illustration 32.1 are able to replace half their assets with leased assets. Assume further that the estimated capital invested in these leased assets is only $40 million, which is lower than the capital invested in the replaced assets of $50 million. In addition, assume that the action actually reduces the adjusted annual operating income from these assets from $15 million to $14.8 million. The value of the firm can now be written in Table 32.6. Note that the firm value declines by $2 million, but the economic value-added increases by $8 million.

TABLE 32.5 EVA Valuation of Firm: EVA and Assets in Place

Capital invested in assets in place	$ 50.00
+ EVA from assets in place = $(.30 - .10)(50)/.10$	$100.00
+ PV of EVA from new investments in year 1 = $[(.15 - .10)(10)/.10]$	$ 5.00
+ PV of EVA from new investments in year 2 = $[(.15 - .10)(10)/.10]/1.1$	$ 4.55
+ PV of EVA from new investments in year 3 = $[(.15 - .10)(10)/.10]/1.1^2$	$ 4.13
+ PV of EVA from new investments in year 4 = $[(.15 - .10)(10)/.10]/1.1^3$	$ 3.76
+ PV of EVA from new investments in year 5 = $[(.15 - .10)(10)/.10]/1.1^4$	$ 3.42
Value of firm	$170.85

TABLE 32.6   Value Reduction with Higher EVA

Capital invested in assets in place	$ 90.00
+ EVA from assets in place = $(.1644 - .10)(90)/.10$	$ 58.00
+ PV of EVA from new investments in year 1 = $[(.15 - .10)(10)/.10]$	$ 5.00
+ PV of EVA from new investments in year 2 = $[(.15 - .10)(10)/.10]/1.1$	$ 4.55
+ PV of EVA from new investments in year 3 = $[(.15 - .10)(10)/.10]/1.1^2$	$ 4.13
+ PV of EVA from new investments in year 4 = $[(.15 - .10)(10)/.10]/1.1^3$	$ 3.76
+ PV of EVA from new investments in year 5 = $[(.15 - .10)(10)/.10]/1.1^4$	$ 3.42
Value of firm	$168.85

When economic value added is estimated for divisions, the capital invested at the divisional level is a function of a number of allocation decisions made by the firm, with the allocation based on prespecified criteria (such as revenues or number of employees). While we would like these rules to be objective and unbiased, they are often subjective and over-allocate capital to some divisions and underallocate it to others. If this misallocation were purely random, we could accept it as an error and use changes in economic value added to measure success. Given the natural competition that exists among divisions in a firm for the marginal investment dollar, however, these allocations are also likely to reflect the power of individual divisions to influence the process. Thus, the economic value added will be overestimated for those divisions that are underallocated capital, and underestimated for divisions that are overallocated capital.

The Future Growth Game   The value of a firm is the value of its existing assets and the value of its future growth prospects. When managers are judged on the basis of economic value added in the current year, or on year-to-year changes, the economic value added that is being measured is just that from assets in place. Thus, managers may trade off the economic value added from future growth for higher economic value added from assets in place.

Again, this point can be illustrated simply using the firm in Illustration 32.1. The firm earned a return on capital of 15 percent on both assets in place and future investments. Assume that there are actions the firm can take to increase the return on capital on assets in place to 16 percent, but that these actions reduce the return on capital on future investments to 12 percent. The value of this firm can then be estimated in Table 32.7.

Note that the value of the firm has decreased, but the economic value added in year 1 is higher now than it was before. The economic value added at this firm for each of the next five years is graphed in Figure 32.1 for both the original firm and this one. The growth trade-off, while leading to a lower firm value, results in economic value added in each of the first three years that is larger than it would have been without the trade-off.

Compensation mechanisms based on EVA are sometimes designed to punish managers who give up future growth for current EVA. Managers are partly compensated based on the economic value added this year, but another part is held back in a compensation bank and is available to the manager only after a period (say three or four years). There are significant limitations with these approaches. First, the limited tenure that managers have with firms implies that this measure can at best look at economic value added only over the next three or four years. The real costs of the growth trade-off are unlikely to show up until much later. Second, these approaches are really designed to punish managers who increase economic value added in the current period, while reducing economic

TABLE 32.7 Trading Off Future Growth for Higher EVA

Capital invested in assets in place	$100.00
+ EVA from assets in place = (.16 − .10)(100)/.10	$ 60.00
+ PV of EVA from new investments in year 1 = [(.12 − .10)(10)/.10]	$ 2.00
+ PV of EVA from new investments in year 2 = [(.12 − .10)(10)/.10]/1.1	$ 1.82
+ PV of EVA from new investments in year 3 = [(.12 − .10)(10)/.10]/1.1^2	$ 1.65
+ PV of EVA from new investments in year 4 = [(.12 − .10)(10)/.10]/1.1^3	$ 1.50
+ PV of EVA from new investments in year 5 = [(.12 − .10)(10)/.10]/1.1^4	$ 1.37
Value of firm	$168.34

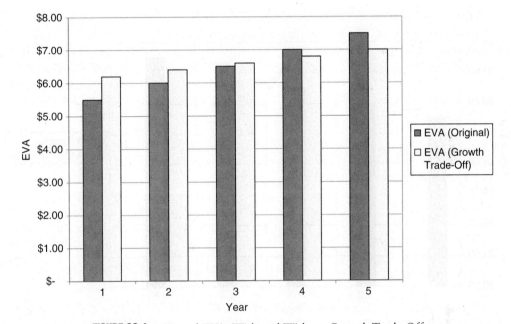

FIGURE 32.1 Annual EVA: With and Without Growth Trade-Off

value added in future periods. In the more subtle case, where the economic value added continues to increase but at a rate lower than it otherwise would have, it is difficult to devise a punishment for managers who trade off future growth. In the preceding example, for instance, the economic value added with the growth trade-off increases over time. The increases are smaller than they would have been without the trade-off, but that number would not have been observed, anyway.

The Risk-Shifting Game   The value of a firm is the sum of the capital invested and the present value of the economic value added. The latter term is, therefore, a function not just of the dollar economic value added but also of the cost of capital. A firm can invest in projects to increase its economic value added but still end up with a lower value if these investments increase its operating risk and cost of capital.

Again, using the firm in Illustration 32.1, assume that the firm is able to increase its return on capital on both assets in place and future investments from 15 percent to 16.25 percent, and from 10 percent to 11 percent after year 5. Simultaneously, assume that the cost of capital increases to 11 percent. The economic value added in each year for the next five years is contrasted with the original economic value added in each year in Figure 32.2.

While the economic value added in each year is higher with the high-risk strategy, the value of the firm is shown in Table 32.8. Note that the risk effect dominates the higher excess dollar returns, and the value of the firm decreases.

This risk shifting can be dangerous for firms that adopt economic value added based on just year-to-year EVA values. When managers are judged based on year-to-year economic value-added changes, there will be a tendency to shift into riskier investments. This tendency will be exaggerated if the measured cost of capital does not reflect the changes in risk or lags it.[4]

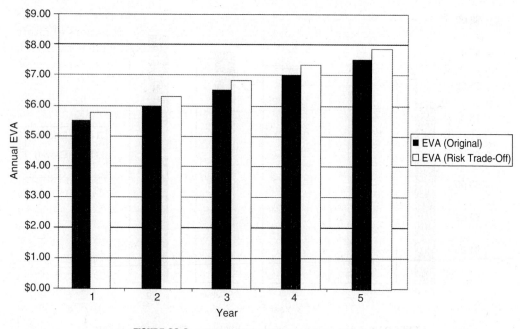

FIGURE 32.2   EVA: Higher Risk and Return

TABLE 32.8   EVA with High-Risk Strategy

Capital invested in assets in place	$100.00
+ EVA from assets in place = (.1625 − .11) (100)/.11	$ 47.73
+ PV of EVA from investments in year 1 = [(.1625 − .11)(10)/.11]	$ 4.77
+ PV of EVA from investments in year 2 = [(.1625 − .10)(10)/.11]/1.11	$ 4.30
+ PV of EVA from investments in year 3 = [(.1625 − .11)(10)/.11]/1.11²	$ 3.87
+ PV of EVA from investments in year 4 = [(.1625 − .11)(10)/.11]/1.11³	$ 3.49
+ PV of EVA from investments in year 5 = [(.1625 − .11)(10)/.11]/1.11⁴	$ 3.14
Value of firm	$167.31

[4]In fact, beta estimates that are based on historical returns will lag changes in risk. With a five-year return estimation period, for instance, the lag might be as long as three years, and the full effect will not show up for five years after the change.

In closing, economic value added is an approach skewed toward assets in place and away from future growth. It should not be surprising, therefore, that when economic value added is computed at the divisional level of a firm, the higher-growth divisions end up with the lowest economic value added, and in some cases, with negative economic value added. Again, while these divisional managers may still be judged based on changes in economic value added from year to year, the temptation at the firm level to reduce or eliminate capital invested in these divisions will be strong, since it will make the firm's overall economic value-added look much better.

EVA and Market Value   Will increasing economic value-added cause market value to increase? While an increase in economic value added will generally lead to an increase in firm value, barring the growth and risk games described earlier, it may or may not increase the stock price. This is so because the market value has built into it expectations of future economic value added. Thus, a firm like Apple is priced on the assumption that it will earn large and increasing economic value added over time. Whether a firm's market value increases or decreases on the announcement of higher economic value added will depend, in large part, on what the expected change in economic value added was. For mature firms, where the market might have expected no increase or even a decrease in economic value added, the announcement of an increase will be good news and cause the market value to increase. For firms that are perceived to have good growth opportunities and are expected to report an increase in economic value added, the market value will decline if the announced increase in economic value added does not measure up to expectations. This should be no surprise to investors, who have recognized this phenomenon with earnings per share for decades; the earnings announcements of firms are judged against expectations, and the earnings surprise is what drives prices.

Finally, it is unlikely that there will be much correlation between actual changes in economic value added at young growth firms and changes in market value. The market value is based on expectations of economic value added in future periods, and investors expect an economic value added that grows substantially each year. Thus, if the economic value-added increases but by less than expected, you could see its market value drop on the report.

We would, therefore, not expect any correlation between the magnitude of the economic value added and stock returns, or even between the change in economic value added and stock returns. Stocks that report the biggest increases in economic value added should not necessarily earn high returns for their stockholders.[5] These priors are confirmed by a study done by Richard Bernstein at Merrill Lynch, who examined the relationship between EVA and stock returns, and concluded that:

> ▪ A portfolio of the 50 firms that had the highest absolute levels[6] of economic value added earned an annual return on 12.9% between February 1987 and February 1997, while the S&P index returned 13.1% a year over the same period.

---

[5]A 1997 study by Kramer and Pushner found that differences in net operating profit after taxes (NOPAT) explained differences in market value better than differences in EVA. O'Byrne (1996), however, finds that changes in EVA explain more than 55 percent of changes in market value over five-year periods.

[6]See Quantitative Viewpoint, Merrill Lynch, December 19, 1997.

■ A portfolio of the 50 firms that had the highest growth rates[7] in economic value added over the previous year earned an annual return of 12.8% over the same time period, again underperforming the S&P 500.

EVA FOR HIGH-GROWTH FIRMS

The fact that the value of a firm is a function of the capital invested in assets in place, the present value of economic value added by those assets, and the economic value added by future investments points to some of the dangers of using it as a measure of success or failure for high-growth and especially high-growth technology firms. In particular, there are three problems:

1. We have already noted many of the problems associated with how accountants measure capital invested at technology firms. Given the centrality of capital invested to economic value added, these problems have a much bigger effect when firms use EVA than when you use discounted cash flow valuation.
2. When 80 to 90 percent of your value comes from future growth potential, the risks of managers trading off future growth for current EVA are magnified. It is also very difficult to monitor these trade-offs at young firms.
3. The constant change that these firms go through also makes them much better candidates for risk shifting. In this case, the negative effect (of a higher discount rate) can more than offset the positive effect of a higher economic value added.

 EVA.xls: This dataset on the web summarizes economic value added by industry group for the United States.

Equity Economic Value Added

Whereas EVA is usually calculated using total capital, it can easily be modified to be an equity measure:

$$\text{Equity EVA} = (\text{Return on equity} - \text{Cost of equity})(\text{Equity invested in project or firm})$$
$$= \text{Net income} - \text{Cost of equity} \times \text{Equity invested}$$

Again, a firm that earns a positive equity EVA is creating value for its stockholders, whereas a firm with a negative equity EVA is destroying value for its stockholders.

Why might a firm use this measure rather than the traditional measure? Chapter 21, when looking at financial service firms, noted that defining debt (and therefore, capital)

---

[7]See Quantitative Viewpoint, Merrill Lynch, February 3, 1998.

can open you open to measurement problems, since so much of the firm could potentially be categorized as debt. Consequently, it was argued that financial service firms should be valued using equity valuation models and multiples. Extending that argument to economic value added holds that equity EVA is a much better measure of performance for financial service firms than the traditional EVA measure.

It must be added that much or all of the issues raised in the context of the traditional EVA measure affect the equity EVA measure as well. Banks and insurance companies can play the capital invested, growth, and risk games to increase equity EVA just as other firms can with traditional EVA.

CASH FLOW RETURN ON INVESTMENT

The cash flow return on investment (CFROI) for a firm is the internal rate of return on existing investments, based on real (as opposed to nominal) cash flows. Generally, it should be compared to the real cost of capital to make judgments about the quality of these investments.

Calculating CFROI

The cash flow return on investment for a firm is calculated using four inputs. The first is the gross investment (GI) the firm has in its existing assets, obtained by adding back cumulated depreciation and inflation adjustments to the book value. The second input is the gross cash flow (GCF) earned in the current year on that asset, which is usually defined as the sum of the after-tax operating income of a firm and the noncash charges against earnings, such as depreciation and amortization. The third input is the expected life of the assets (n) in place at the time of the original investment, which varies from sector to sector but reflects the earning life of the investments in question. The expected salvage value (SV) of the assets at the end of this life, in current dollars, is the final input. This is usually assumed to be the portion of the initial investment, such as land and building, that is not depreciable, adjusted to current dollar terms. The CFROI is the internal rate of return of these cash flows (i.e., the discount rate that makes the net present value of the gross cash flows and salvage value equal to the gross investment), and it can thus be viewed as a composite internal rate of return in current dollar terms.

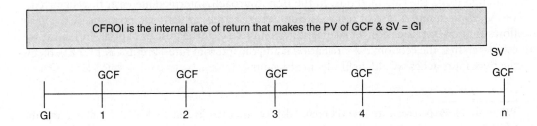

where n is the life of the asset at the time of the original purchase.

An alternative formulation of the CFROI allows for setting aside an annuity to cover the expected replacement cost of the asset at the end of the project life. This annuity is called the economic depreciation, and is computed as follows:

$$\text{Economic depreciation} = \frac{\text{Replacement cost in current dollars } (k_c)}{(1 + k_c)^n - 1}$$

where n is the expected life of the asset, k_c is the cost of capital, and the expected replacement cost of the asset is defined in current dollar terms to be the difference between the gross investment and the salvage value. The CFROI for a firm or a division can then be written as follows:

$$\text{CFROI} = \frac{\text{Gross cash flow} - \text{Economic depreciation}}{\text{Gross investment}}$$

For instance, assume that you have existing assets with a gross investment, of $2,431 million, a gross cash flow of $390 million, an expected salvage value (in today's dollar terms) of $607.8 million, and a life of 10 years.

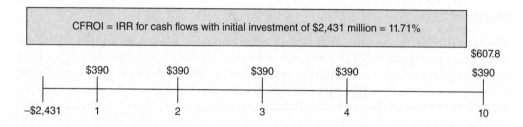

The conventional measure of CFROI is 11.71 percent, and the real cost of capital is 8 percent. The estimate using the alternative approach is computed as follows:

$$\text{Economic depreciation} = \frac{(2,431 \text{ million} - 607.8 \text{ million})(.08)}{1.08^{10} - 1} = \$125.86 \text{ million}$$

$$\text{CFROI} = \frac{(390.00 - 125.86)}{2431.00}$$

$$= 10.87\%$$

The difference in the reinvestment rate assumption accounts for the difference in CFROI estimated using the two methods. In the first approach, intermediate cash flows get reinvested at the internal rate of return, while in the second, at least the portions of the cash flows that are set aside for replacement get reinvested at the cost of capital. In fact, if we estimated that the economic depreciation using the internal rate of return is 11.71 percent, the two approaches would yield identical results.[8]

---

[8]With an 11.71 percent rate, the economic depreciation works out to $105.37 million, and the CFROI to 11.71 percent.

Cash Flow Return on Investment, Internal Rate of Return, and Discounted Cash Flow Value

If net present value provides the genesis for the economic value-added approach to value enhancement, the internal rate of return is the basis for the CFROI approach. In investment analysis, the internal rate of return on a project is computed using the initial investment on the project and all cash flows over the project's life:

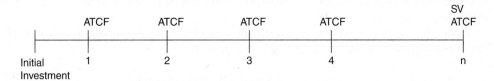

where the ATCF is the after-tax cash flow on the project, and SV is the expected salvage value of the project assets. This analysis can be done entirely either in nominal terms, in which case the internal rate of return is a nominal IRR and is compared to the nominal cost of capital, or in real terms, in which case it is a real IRR and is compared to the real cost of capital.

At first sight, the CFROI seems to do the same thing. It uses the gross investment in the project (in current dollars) as the equivalent of the initial investment, assumes that the gross current-dollar cash flow is maintained over the project life and computes a real internal rate of return. There are, however, some significant differences.

The internal rate of return does not require the after-tax cash flows to be constant over a project's life, even in real terms. The CFROI approach assumes that real cash flows on assets do not change over time. This may be a reasonable assumption for investments in mature sectors but will understate project returns if there is real growth. In these cases, the CFROI approach has to be modified to allow for growth.

The second difference is that the internal rate of return on a project or asset is based on incremental future cash flows. It does not consider cash flows that have occurred already, since these are viewed as "sunk". The CFROI, on the other hand, tries to reconstruct a project or asset, using both cash flows that have occurred already and cash flows that are yet to occur. To illustrate, consider the project described in the previous section. At the time of the original investment, assuming that the inputs for initial investment, after-tax cash flows, and salvage value are unchanged, both the internal rate of return and the CFROI of this project would have been 11.71 percent. The CFROI is, however, being computed three years into the project life and remains at 11.71 percent since none of the original inputs have changed. The IRR of this project will change, though. It will now be based on the current market value of the asset, the expected cash flows over the remaining life of the asset, and a life of seven years. Thus, if the market value of the asset has increased to $2.5 billion, the internal rate of return on this project would be computed to be only 6.80 percent.

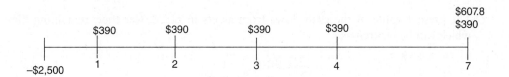

Given the real cost of capital of 8 percent, this would mean that the CFROI is greater than the cost of capital, while the internal rate of return is lower. Why is there a difference between the two measures, and what are the implications? The reason for the difference is that IRR is based entirely on expected future cash flows, whereas the CFROI is not. A CFROI that exceeds the cost of capital is viewed as a sign that a firm is deploying its assets well. If the IRR is less than the cost of capital, that interpretation is false, because the owners of the firm would be better off selling the asset and getting the market value for it rather than continuing its operation.

To link the cash flow return on investment with firm value, let us begin with a simple discounted cash flow model for a firm in stable growth:

$$\text{Firm value} = \frac{\text{Expected FCFF next year}}{(k_c - \text{Stable growth rate})}$$

where FCFF is the expected free cash flow to the firm, k_c is the cost of capital, and g_n is the stable growth rate. Note that this can be rewritten, approximately, in terms of the CFROI as follows:

$$\text{Firm value} = \frac{(\text{CFROI} \times \text{GI} - \text{DA})(1 - t) - (\text{CX} - \text{DA}) - \Delta\text{Working capital}}{(k_c - \text{Stable growth rate})}$$

where CFROI is the cash flow return on investment, GI is the gross investment, DA is the depreciation and amortization, CX is the capital expenditure and ΔWC is the change in working capital. To illustrate, consider a firm with a CFROI of 30%, a gross investment of $100 million, capital expenditures of $15 million, depreciation of $10 million, and no working capital requirements. If we assume a 10 percent cost of capital, a 40-percent tax rate, and a 5-percent stable growth rate, it would be valued as follows:

$$\text{Firm value} = \frac{(.30 \times 100 - 10)(1 - .4) - (15 - 10) - 0}{(.10 - .05)} = \$140 \text{ million}$$

More important than the mechanics, however, is the fact that firm value, while a function of the CFROI, is also a function of the other variables in the equation—the gross investment, the tax rate, the growth rate, the cost of capital, and the firm's reinvestment needs.

Again, sophisticated users of CFROI do recognize the fact that value comes from the CFROI not just on assets in place but also on future investments. In fact, Holt Associates, one of CFROI's leading proponents, allows for a fade factor in CFROI, where the current CFROI fades toward the real cost of capital over time. The fade factor is estimated empirically by looking at firms in different CFROI classes and tracking them over time. Thus, a firm that has a current CFROI of 20 percent, and real cost of capital of 8 percent will be projected to have lower CFROI over time. The value of the firm, in this more complex format, can then be written as a sum of the following:

■ The present value of the cash flows from assets in place over their remaining life, which can be written as:

$$\sum_{t=1}^{t=n} \frac{\text{CFROI}_{aip} \times \text{GI}_{aip}}{(1 + k_c)^t}$$

where $CFROI_{aip}$ is the CFROI on assets in place, GI_{aip} is the gross investment in assets in place, and k_c is the real cost of capital.

▨ The present value of the excess cash flows from future investments, which can be written in real terms as

$$\sum_{t=1}^{t=\infty} \frac{CFROI_{t,NI} \times \Delta GI_t}{(1 + k_c)^t} - \Delta GI_t$$

where $CFROI_{t,NI}$ is the CFROI on new investments made in year t, and ΔGI_t is the new investment made in year t. Note that if $CFROI_{t,NI} = k_c$, this present value is equal to zero.

Thus, a firm's value will depend on the CFROI it earns on assets in place, and both the abruptness and the speed with which this CFROI fades toward the cost of capital. A firm can, therefore, potentially increase its value by doing either of the following:

▨ Increasing the CFROI from assets in place for a given gross investment.
▨ Reducing the speed at which the CFROI fades toward the real cost of capital.

Note that this is no different from our earlier analysis of firm value in the discounted cash flow approach in Chapter 31, in terms of cash flows from existing investments (increase current CFROI), the length of the high growth period (reduce fade speed), and the growth rate during the growth period (keep excess returns from falling as steeply).

 cfroi.xls: This spreadsheet allows you to estimate the cash flow return on investment for a firm or project.

CFROI and Firm Value: Potential Conflicts

The relationship between CFROI and firm value is less intuitive than the relationship between EVA and firm value, partly because it is a percentage return. Notwithstanding this fundamental weakness, managers can take actions that increase CFROI while reducing firm value.

▨ *Reduce gross investment.* If the gross investment in existing assets is reduced, the CFROI may be increased. Since it is the product of CFROI and gross investment that determines value, it is possible for a firm to increase CFROI and end up with a lower value.

▨ *Sacrifice future growth.* CFROI, even more than EVA, is focused on existing assets and does not look at future growth. To the extent that managers increase CFROI at the expense of future growth, the value can decrease while CFROI goes up.

▨ *Risk trade off.* While the CFROI is compared to the real cost of capital to pass judgment on whether a firm is creating or destroying value, it represents only a partial correction for risk. The value of a firm is still the present value of expected future cash flows. Thus, a firm can increase its spread between the CFROI and cost of capital but still end up losing value if the present value effect of having a higher cost of capital dominates the higher CFROI.

In general, then, an increase in CFROI does not, by itself, indicate that the firm value has increased, since it might have come at the expense of lower growth and/or higher risk.

CFROI INNOVATIONS: THE FADE FACTOR AND IMPLIED COST OF CAPITAL

The biggest contribution made by practitioners who use CFROI has been the work that they have done on how returns on capital fade over time toward the cost of capital. Madden (1998) makes the argument that not only is this phenomenon widespread, but it is at least partially predictable. He presents evidence done by Holt Associates, a leading proponent of CFROI, which sorted the largest 1,000 firms by CFROI from highest to lowest and tracked them over time to find a convergence toward an average. It should be noted that this book has used fade factors, without referring to them as such, in the chapters on discounted cash flow valuation. The fade to a lower return on capital occurred either precipitously in the terminal year or over a transition period.

To compute the cost of capital, CFROI practitioners look to the market instead of the risk and return models that we have used to compute DCF value. Using the current market values of stocks and their estimates of expected aggregate cash flows, they compute internal rates of return that they use as the cost of capital in analysis. Chapter 7 used a very similar approach to estimate an implied risk premium, though this premium was used as an input into traditional risk and return models.

CFROI and Market Value

There is a relationship between CFROI and market value. Firms with high CFROI generally have high market value. This is not surprising, since it mirrors what we noted earlier about economic value added. However, it is *changes* in market value that create returns, not market value per se. When it comes to market value changes, the relationship between CFROI and value changes tends to be much weaker. Since market values reflect expectations, there is no reason to believe that firms that have high CFROI will earn excess returns.

The relationship between changes in CFROI and excess returns is more intriguing. To the extent that any increase in CFROI is viewed as a positive surprise, firms with the biggest increases in CFROI should earn excess returns. In reality, however, the actual change in CFROI has to be measured against expectations; if CFROI increases, but less than expected, the market value should drop; if CFROI drops but by less than expected, the market value should increase.

A POSTSCRIPT ON VALUE ENHANCEMENT

The value of a firm has three components. The first is its capacity to generate cash flows from existing assets, with higher cash flows translating into higher value. The second is its willingness to reinvest to create future growth, and the quality of these reinvestments.

Other things remaining equal, firms that reinvest well and earn significant excess returns on these investments will have higher value. The final component of value is the cost of capital, with higher costs or capital resulting in lower firm values. To create value, then, a firm has to:

- Generate higher cash flows from existing assets, without affecting its growth prospects or its risk profile.
- Reinvest more and with higher excess returns, without increasing the riskiness of its assets.
- Reduce the cost of financing its assets in place or future growth, without lowering the returns made on these investments.

All value enhancement measures are variants on these simple themes. Whether these approaches measure dollar excess returns, as does economic value added, or percentage excess returns like CFROI, they have acquired followers because they seem simpler and less subjective than discounted cash flow valuation. This simplicity comes at a cost, since these approaches make subtle assumptions about other components of value that are often not visible or not recognized by many users. Approaches that emphasize economic value added and reward managers for increasing the same often assume that increases in economic value added are not being delivered at the expense of future growth or by increasing risk. Practitioners who judge performance based on the cash flow return on investment make similar assumptions.

Is there something of value in the new value enhancement measures? Absolutely, but only in the larger context of valuation. One of the inputs we need for traditional valuation models is the return on capital (to get expected growth). Making the adjustments to operating income suggested by those who use economic value added and augmenting it with a cash flow return, with CFROI, may help us come up with a better estimate of this number. The terminal value computation in traditional valuation models, where small changes in assumptions can lead to large changes in value, becomes much more tractable if we think in terms of excess returns on investments rather than just growth and discount rates. Finally, the empirical evidence that has been collected by practitioners who use CFROI on fade factors can be invaluable in traditional valuation models, where practitioners sometimes make the mistake of assuming that current returns will continue forever.

CONCLUSION

This chapter considers two widely used value enhancement measures. Economic value-added measures the dollar excess return on existing assets. The cash flow return on investment is the internal rate of return on existing assets, based on the original investment in these assets and the expected future cash flows. While both approaches can lead to conclusions consistent with traditional discounted cash flow valuation, their simplicity comes at a cost. Managers can take advantage of measurement limitations in both approaches to make their firms look better with either approach while reducing firm value. In particular, they can trade off less growth in the future for higher economic value added today and shift to riskier investments.

As we look at various approaches to value enhancement, we should consider a few facts. The first is that no value enhancement mechanism will work at generating value unless there is a commitment on the part of managers to making value maximization their primary objective. If managers put other goals first, then no value-enhancement mechanism will work. Conversely, if managers truly care about value maximization, they can make almost any mechanism work in their favor. The second is that, while it is sensible to connect whatever value enhancement measure we have chosen to management compensation, there is a downside. Managers, over time, will tend to focus their attention on making themselves look better on that measure, even if that can be accomplished only by reducing firm value. Finally, there are no magic bullets that create value. Value creation is hard work in competitive markets and almost involves a trade-off between costs and benefits. Everyone has a role in value creation, and it certainly is not the sole domain of financial analysts. In fact, the value created by financial engineers is smaller and less significant than the value created by good strategic, marketing, production, or personnel decisions.

QUESTIONS AND SHORT PROBLEMS

In the problems following, use an equity risk premium of 5.5 percent if none is specified.

1. Everlast Batteries Inc. has hired you as a consultant. The firm had after-tax operating earnings in 1998 of $180 million and net income of $100 million, and it paid a dividend of $50 million. The book value of equity at the end of 1998 was $1.25 billion, and the book value of debt was $350 million. The firm raised $50 million of new debt during 1998. The market value of equity at the end of 1998 was twice the book value of equity, and the market value of debt was the same as the book value of debt. The firm has a cost of equity of 12% and an after-tax cost of debt of 5%.
   a. Estimate the return on capital earned by Everlast Batteries.
   b. Estimate the cost of capital earned by Everlast Batteries.
   c. Estimate the economic value added by Everlast Batteries.

2. Assume, in the preceding problem, that Everlast Batteries is in stable growth, and that it expects its economic value added to grow at 5% a year forever.
   a. Estimate the value of the firm.
   b. How much of this value comes from excess returns?
   c. What is the market value added (MVA) of this firm?
   How would your answers to (a), (b), and (c) change if you were told that there would be no economic value added after year 5?

3. Stereo City is a retailer of stereos and televisions. The firm has operating income of $150 million, after operating lease expenses of $50 million. The firm has operating lease commitments for the next five years and beyond:

Year	Operating Lease Commitment
1	55
2	60
3	60
4	55
5	50
Years 6–15	40 each year

The book value of equity is $1 billion, and the firm has no debt outstanding. The firm has a cost of equity of 11% and a pretax cost of borrowing of 6%. The tax rate is 40%.

    a. Estimate the capital invested in the firm, before and after adjusting for operating leases.

    b. Estimate the return on capital, before and after adjusting for operating leases.

    c. Estimate the economic value added, before and after adjusting for operating leases. (The market value of equity is $2 billion.)

4. Sevilla Chemicals earned $1 billion in after-tax operating income on capital invested of $5 billion last year. The firm's cost of equity is 12%, its debt-to-capital ratio is 25%, and the after-tax cost of debt is 4.5%.

    a. Estimate the economic value added by Sevilla Chemicals last year.

    b. Assume now that the entire chemical industry earned $40 billion after taxes on capital invested of $180 billion, and that the cost of capital for the industry is 10%. Estimate the economic value added by the entire industry.

    c. Based on economic value added, how did Sevilla do relative to the industry?

5. Jeeves Software is a small software firm in high growth. The firm is all equity financed. In the current year, the firm earned $20 million in after-tax operating income on capital invested of $60 million. The firm's cost of equity is 15%.

    a. Assume that the firm will be able to grow its economic value added 15% a year for the next five years, and that there will be no excess returns after year 5. Estimate the value of the firm. How much of this value comes from the EVA, and how much from capital invested?

    b. Now, assume the firm is able to reduce its capital invested this year by $20 million by selling its assets and leasing them back. Assuming operating income and cost of capital do not change as a result of the sale-lease back, estimate the value of the firm now. How much of the value of the firm now comes from EVA, and how much from capital invested?

6. Healthy Foods is a company that produces canned soups made without preservatives. The firm has assets that have a book value of $100 million. The assets are five years old and have depreciated $50 million over that period. In addition, the inflation rate over those five years has averaged 2% a year. The assets are currently earning $15 million in after-tax operating income. They have a remaining life of 10 years, and the depreciation each year is expected to be $5 million. At the end of these 10 years, the assets will have an expected salvage value, in current dollars, of $50 million.

    a. Estimate the CFROI of Healthy Foods, using the conventional CFROI approach.

    b. Estimate the CFROI of Healthy Foods, using the economic depreciation approach.

    c. If Healthy Foods has a cost of capital in nominal terms of 10% and the expected inflation rate is 2%, evaluate whether Healthy Foods' existing investments are value-creating or value-destroying.

CHAPTER 33

Probabilistic Approaches in Valuation: Scenario Analysis, Decision Trees, and Simulations

Through much of this book, we have focused on discounted cash flow and relative valuation approaches to valuation. Notwithstanding their popularity, these approaches share a common theme. The riskiness of an asset is encapsulated in one number—a higher discount rate, lower cash flows, or a discount to value—and the computation almost requires us to make assumptions (often unrealistic) about the nature of risk.

In this chapter, we consider a different and potentially more informative way of assessing the value of an investment. Rather than compute an expected value for an asset that tries to capture in one number all of the different possible outcomes, we could provide information on what the value of the asset will be under each outcome or at least a subset of outcomes. We will begin this section by looking at the simplest version, which is an analysis of an asset's value under three scenarios—a best case, the most likely case, and worst case—and then extend the discussion to look at scenario analysis more generally. We move on to examine the use of decision trees as a more complete approach to dealing with sequential risk. We will close the chapter by evaluating Monte Carlo simulations, the most complete approach to assessing risk across the spectrum.

SCENARIO ANALYSIS

The expected cash flows that we use to value risky assets can be estimated in one of two ways. They can represent a probability-weighted average of cash flows under all possible scenarios, or they can be the cash flows under the most likely scenario. While the former is the more precise measure, it is seldom used, simply because it requires far more information to compile. In both cases, there are other scenarios where the cash flows will be different from expectations: higher than expected in some, and lower than expected in others. In scenario analysis, we estimate expected cash flows and asset values under various scenarios, with the intent of getting a better sense of the effect of risk on value. In this section, we first consider an extreme version of scenario analysis where we consider the value in the best-case and the worst-case scenarios, and then a more generalized version of scenario analysis.

Best Case/Worst Case

With risky assets, the actual cash flow can be very different from expectations. At the limits, we can estimate the cash flows if everything works to perfection—a best-case scenario—and if nothing does—a worst-case scenario. In practice, there are two ways in which this analysis can be structured. In the first, each input into asset value is set to its best- (or worst-) possible outcome, and the cash flows are estimated with those values. Thus, when valuing a firm, you may set the revenue growth rate and operating margin at the highest possible level while setting the discount rate at its lowest level and computing the value as the best-case scenario. The problem with this approach is that it may not be feasible; after all, to get high revenue growth, the firm may have to lower prices and accept lower margins. In the second, the best possible scenario is defined in terms of what is feasible, while allowing for the relationship between the inputs. Thus, instead of assuming that revenue growth and margins will both be maximized, we choose that combination of growth and margin that is feasible and yields the maximum value. While this approach is more realistic, it does require more work to put into practice.

How useful is best-case/worst-case analysis? There are two ways in which the results from this analysis can be useful to decision-makers. First, the difference between the best-case and worst-case value can be used as a measure of risk on an asset; the range in value (scaled to size) should be higher for riskier investments. Second, investors who are concerned about the potential spill-over effects on their portfolio of an investment going bad may be able to gauge the effects by looking at the worst-case outcome on that investment.

In general, though, best-case/worse-case analyses are not very informative. After all, there should be no surprise in knowing that an asset will be worth a lot in the best case, and not very much in the worst case. Thus, an equity research analyst who uses this approach to value a stock, priced at $50 may arrive at values of $80 for the best case, and $10 for the worst case; with a range that large, it will be difficult to make a judgment on whether the stock is a good investment.

Multiple-Scenario Analysis

Scenario analysis does not have to be restricted to the best and worst cases. In its most general form, the value of a risky asset can be computed under a number of different scenarios, varying the assumptions about both macroeconomic and asset-specific variables.

Steps in Scenario Analysis   While the concept of sensitivity analysis is a simple one, it has four critical components:

1. The first is the determination of which factors the scenarios will be built around. These factors can range from the state of the economy for an automobile firm considering a new plant, to the response of competitors for a consumer product firm introducing a new product, to the behavior of regulatory authorities for a regulated company considering a new product or service. In general, you should focus on the two or three most critical factors that will determine the value of the asset and build scenarios around these factors.
2. The second component determines the number of scenarios to analyze for each factor. While more scenarios may be more realistic than fewer, it becomes more difficult to

collect information and differentiate between the scenarios in terms of asset cash flows. Thus, estimating cash flows under each scenario will be easier if you lay out five scenarios, for instance, than if you lay out 15 scenarios. The question of how many scenarios to consider will depend then upon how different the scenarios are, and how well you can forecast cash flows under each scenario.

3. The third component is the estimation of asset cash flows, discount rates and value under each scenario. It is to ease the estimation at this step that you focus on only two or three critical factors and build relatively few scenarios for each factor.

4. The final component is the assignment of probabilities to each scenario. For some scenarios, involving macroeconomic factors, such as exchange rates, interest rates, and overall economic growth, you can draw on the expertise of services that forecast these variables. For other scenarios, involving either the sector or competitors, you have to draw on your knowledge about the industry. Note, though, that this makes sense only if the scenarios cover the full spectrum of possibilities. If the scenarios represent only a subset of the possible outcomes on an investment, the probabilities will not add up to 1.

The output from a scenario analysis can be presented as values under each scenario and as an expected value across scenarios (if the probabilities can be estimated in the fourth step). If the scenarios are incomplete, the expected value cannot be computed.

This quantitative view of scenario analysis will be challenged by strategists, who have traditionally viewed scenario analysis as a qualitative exercise whose primary benefit is to broaden the thinking of decision-makers. As one strategist put it, scenario analysis is about devising "plausible future narratives" rather than probable outcomes; in other words, there are benefits to considering scenarios that have a very low probability of occurring. The benefit of the exercise is that it forces you to consider views of what may unfold that differ from the base case view.

Use in Valuation and Decision Making   How useful is scenario analysis in value assessment and decision-making? The answer, as with all tools, depends on how it is used. The most valuable information from a scenario analysis is the range of values across different scenarios, which provides a snapshot of the riskiness of the asset; riskier assets will have values that vary more across scenarios, and safer assets will have manifest more stability. In addition, scenario analysis can be useful in determining the inputs into an analysis that have the most effect on value. There is another advantage to doing scenario analysis: To the extent that value is much lower under some scenarios than others, investors can try to find ways to hedge against those scenarios' occurring.

If nothing else, the process of thinking through scenarios is a useful exercise in examining how the competition will react under different macroeconomic environments and what can be done to minimize the effect of downside risk and maximize the effect of potential upside on the value of a risky asset.

Issues   Multiple-scenario analysis provides more information than a best-case/worst-case analysis by providing asset values under each of the specified scenarios. It does, however, have its own set of problems:

■ *Garbage in, garbage out.* The key to doing scenario analysis well is the setting up of the scenarios and the estimation of cash flows under each one. Not only do the outlined scenarios have to be realistic, but they also have to try to cover the spectrum of possibilities. Once the scenarios have been laid out, the cash flows and value have to be estimated under each one; this trade-off has to be considered when determining how many scenarios to run.

■ *Continuous risk.* Scenario analysis is best suited for dealing with risk that takes the form of discrete outcomes. When the outcomes can take on any of a very large number of potential values or the risk is continuous, it becomes more difficult to set up scenarios.

■ *Double counting of risk.* As with the best-case/worst-case analysis, there is the danger that decision-makers will double-count risk when they do scenario analysis. Thus, an analyst may decide to reject the investment, even though it looks undervalued, because it looks significantly overvalued under at least one scenario. Since the expected value is already risk-adjusted, this would represent a double-counting of potentially the same risk or risk that should not be a factor in the decision in the first place (because it is diversifiable).

ILLUSTRATION 33.1:   Valuing a Company Facing the Threat of Nationalization

While the global threat of nationalization has diminished over the past few decades, there remain parts of the world where investors remain wary that firms might be expropriated or nationalized by a government. Analysts who attempt to incorporate the risk of nationalization into the expected cash flows or discount rates find very quickly that it is difficult to do so. Discount rates, in particular, are blunt instruments that do not lend themselves easily to the consideration of discrete risks (such as nationalization, distress, or regulatory change).

As an alternative, consider a very simple scenario analysis where you value the firm under two scenarios: as a going concern where the owners of the business keep the cash flows, and under nationalization, where the proceeds to the owners are not commensurate with fair value. The expected value for the firm will be a weighted average of the two estimates.

To move from abstractions, assume that you are valuing a Venezuelan company that expects to generate $10 million in after-tax operating income next year and grow 3% a year, in U.S. dollar terms, in perpetuity. Assume also that this firm generates a 20% return on capital (the book value of capital invested is $50 million) and faces a 12% cost of capital, with the latter including a country risk component for the macroeconomic (but not nationalization) risk. To value the firm as a going concern, we use the expected cash flows and cost of capital to arrive at a value of $94.44 million for the operating assets of the firm:

$$\text{Reinvestment rate} = g/\text{ROC} = 3\%/20\% = 15\%$$

$$\text{Value of operating assets}_{\text{Going concern}} = \frac{\text{EBIT}(1-t)\left(1 - \dfrac{g}{\text{ROIC}}\right)}{(\text{Cost of capital} - g)}$$

$$= \frac{\$10(1-.15)}{(.12-.03)} = \$94.44 \text{ million}$$

Now assume that you believe that there is a likelihood that the firm will be nationalized, and that the government will pay only the book value of operating assets to the owners of nationalized companies. The proceeds from nationalization can be estimated as follows:

$$\text{Value of operating assets}_{\text{Nationalization}} = \text{Book value} = \$50 \text{ million}$$

Bringing in a probability of nationalization (25%) allows us to estimate the expected value for the operating assets:

$$\text{Expected value} = \text{Value of operating assets}_{\text{going concern}} \times (1 - \text{Probability of nationalization})$$
$$+ \text{Value of operating assets}_{\text{nationalization}} \times (\text{Probability of nationalization})$$
$$= \$94.44(.75) + \$50(.25)$$
$$= \$83.33 \text{ million}$$

Note that expected value will decrease as the likelihood of nationalization increases, and the proceeds from nationalization decreases.

ILLUSTRATION 33.2:   Valuing a Regulated Company with Shifting Regulatory Risk

Scenario analysis becomes more complicated and potentially more useful as the number of scenarios increases and uncertainty magnifies. To illustrate, assume that you were valuing Wells Fargo, one of the largest commercial banks in the United States, in early 2009. The banking crisis of 2008 not only had wreaked havoc on the profitability of banks but had also increased the likelihood that regulatory authorities would tighten regulatory capital rules, requiring banks to set aside more capital to cover potential losses from their operations.

To see the impact of the crisis, Table 33.1 following lists key financial variables for Wells Fargo from 2001 to 2008:

TABLE 33.1   Key Financial Variables—2001–2008

Year	2008	2007	2006	2005	2004	2003	2002	2001	Average: 01–07
Dividends	$ 5,751	$ 3,955	$ 3,641	$ 3,375	$ 3,150	$ 2,527	$ 1,873	$ 1,710	
Net Income	$ 2,842	$ 8,057	$ 8,482	$ 7,671	$ 7,014	$ 6,202	$ 5,434	$ 3,423	
Book Equity	$47,628	$45,876	$40,660	$37,866	$34,469	$30,319	$27,214	$26,488	
Growth Rate	−64.73%	−5.01%	10.57%	9.37%	13.09%	14.13%	58.75%	−14.98%	12.28%
Payout ratio	202.36%	49.09%	42.93%	44.00%	44.91%	40.74%	34.47%	49.96%	43.73%
ROE	5.97%	17.56%	20.86%	20.26%	20.35%	20.46%	19.97%	12.92%	18.91%

Note that while dividends increased in 2008, net income and return on equity dropped precipitously. In early 2009, here were some key questions that an analyst would have faced in valuing Wells Fargo:

▧ What should you use as your base year values for earnings, dividends, and return on investment? In other words, could you assume that 2008 is an aberration and go back to normalized values that reflect the average from 2001 to 2007?

▧ Historically, banks have had a beta close to 1, which would have given Wells Fargo a cost of equity of about 9 percent in February 2009 (T-bond rate = 3%; ERP = 6%). Given that the crisis has shed new light on the hidden risks in banks, would you continue to use this beta in the valuation?

Rather than try to come up with a composite value for Wells Fargo across all possible scenarios, we developed three scenarios:

1. *Quick bounce back to normalcy (10% probability).* This was the most optimistic scenario, in which we assumed that the crisis would pass quickly, that regulatory capital ratios would not be changed, and that the return on equity and beta would revert back quickly to precrisis levels (beta = 1, ROE = 18.91%).
2. *Slow bounce back to normalcy (60% probability).* This is a more pessimistic (and more realistic) scenario, in which the crisis does fade slowly but is accompanied by increased regulatory capital requirements (which will lower return on equity to 15%) and higher volatility for banks (which will raise the cost of equity to 10%).
3. *New world order (30-percent probability).* This is the most pessimistic of the scenarios, where the crisis drags on and regulatory capital changes are draconian, with return on equity dropping to 12% and the cost of equity rising to 11%.

Using the return on equity and cost of equity as the levers in a dividend discount model, we were able to derive the value of equity:

$$\text{Value of equity} = \frac{\text{Expected dividends}_{\text{next year}}}{(\text{Cost of equity} - \text{Growth rate})}$$

$$= \frac{\text{Book Equity}_{\text{Base}} \times \text{ROE} \times \left(1 - \frac{g}{\text{ROE}}\right)}{(\text{Cost of equity} - \text{Growth rate})}$$

Assuming that Wells Fargo is in stable growth, growing 3% a year, we can estimate the value of equity as a function of the expected ROE and cost of equity. The following table summarizes the estimates for the aggregate value of equity (using $47,628 million as the base book equity) in Wells Fargo under all three scenarios:

Scenario	Probability	Net Income	ROE	Cost of equity	Value of equity
Quick bounce back to normalcy	10%	$9,006.45	18.91%	9%	$126,294
Slow bounce back to normalcy	60%	$7,144.20	15.00%	10%	$ 81,648
New world order	30%	$5,715.36	12.00%	11%	$ 53,582
Expected value = 0.10 ($126,294) + 0.60($81,648) + 0.30($53,582) =					$ 77,693

At its market capitalization of $66.643 billion in early 2009, Wells Fargo looks undervalued, but the valuation is sensitive to the probabilities attached to the three scenarios.

DECISION TREES

In some cases, risk is not only discrete but sequential. In other words, for the asset to have value, it must pass through a series of tests, with failure at any point potentially translating into a complete loss of value. This is the case, for instance, with a pharmaceutical drug that is just being tested for commercial use. The three-stage Food and Drug Administration (FDA) approval process lays out the hurdles that have to be passed for this drug to be commercially sold, and failure at any of the three stages dooms the drug's chances. When valuing a large pharmaceutical company with a portfolio of drugs, the risk that a drug will not make it through the process will be averaged out across the portfolio of drugs in the pipeline, thus allowing us to use conventional discounted cash flow models. In contrast, if you are valuing a small biotechnology company with only one drug making its way through the approval process, the value rests entirely on the sequential risk process. Decision trees allow us not only to consider the risk in stages but also to devise the right response to outcomes at each stage.

Steps in Decision Tree Analysis

The first step in understanding decision trees is to distinguish between root nodes, decision nodes, event nodes, and end nodes.

▨ The root node represents the start of the decision tree, where a decision-maker can be faced with a decision choice or an uncertain outcome. The objective of the exercise is to evaluate what a risky investment is worth at this node.

▨ Event nodes represent the possible outcomes on a risky gamble; whether a drug passes the first stage of the FDA approval process is a good example. We must figure out the possible outcomes and the probabilities of the outcomes occurring, based on the information we have available today.

▨ Decision nodes represent choices that can be made by the decision-maker—to expand from a test market to a national market after a test market's outcome is known.

▨ End nodes usually represent the final outcomes of earlier risky outcomes and decisions made in response.

Consider a very simple example. You are offered a choice where you can either take a certain amount ($20) or partake in a gamble where you can win $50, with a probability 50 percent, or $10 with probability 50 percent. The decision tree for this offered gamble is shown in Figure 33.1.

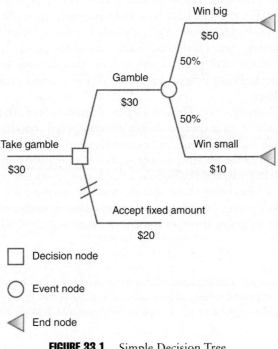

FIGURE 33.1 Simple Decision Tree

Note the key elements in the decision tree. First, only the event nodes represent uncertain outcomes and have probabilities attached to them. Second, the decision node represents a choice. On a pure expected value basis, the gamble is better (with an expected value of $30) than the guaranteed amount of $20; the double slash on the latter branch indicates that it would not be selected. While this example may be simplistic, the elements of building a decision tree it contains.

Step 1: Divide analysis into risk phases. The key to developing a decision tree is outlining the phases of risk that you will be exposed to in the future. In some cases, such as the FDA approval process, this will be easy to do since there are only two outcomes—the drug gets approved to move on to the next phase, or it does not. In other cases, it will be more difficult. For instance, a test market of a new consumer product can yield hundreds of potential outcomes; here, you will have to create discrete categories for the success of the test market.

Step 2: In each phase, estimate the probabilities of the outcomes. Once the phases of risk have been outlined and the outcomes at each phase are defined, the probabilities of the outcomes have to be computed. In addition to the obvious requirement that the probabilities across outcomes have to sum up to one, you will also have to consider whether the probabilities of outcomes in 1 phase can be affected by outcomes in earlier phases. For example, how does the probability of a successful national product introduction change when the test market outcome is only average?

Step 3: Define decision points. Embedded in the decision tree will be decision points where you will get to determine what your best course of action will be, based on observing the outcomes at earlier stages, and expectations of what will occur in the future. With the test market example, for instance, you will get to determine, at the end of the test market whether you want to conduct a second test market, abandon the product or move directly to a national product introduction.

Step 4: Compute cash flows/value at end nodes. The next step in the decision-tree process is estimating what the final cash flow and value outcomes will be at each end node. In some cases, such as abandonment of a test market product, this will be easy to do and will represent the money spent on the test marketing of the product. In other cases, such as a national launch of the same product, this will be more difficult to do because you will have to estimate expected cash flows over the life of the product and discount these cash flows to arrive at value.

Step 5: Folding back the tree. The last step in a decision-tree analysis is termed "folding back the tree", where the expected values are computed working backward through the tree. If the node is a chance node, the expected value is computed as the probability-weighted average of all of the possible outcomes. If it is a decision node, the expected value is computed for each branch, and the highest value is chosen (as the optimal decision). The process culminates in an expected value for the asset or investment today.[1]

There are two key pieces of output that emerge from a decision tree. The first is the expected value today of going through the entire decision tree. This expected value will

---

[1] There is a significant body of literature examining the assumptions that have to hold for this folding back process to yield consistent values. In particular, if a decision tree is used to portray concurrent risks, the risks should be independent of each other. See Sarin and Wakker (1994).

incorporate the potential upside and downside from risk, and the actions that you will take along the way in response to this risk. In effect, this is analogous to the risk-adjusted value that we talked about in the last chapter. The second is the range of values at the end nodes, which should encapsulate the potential risk in the investment.

ILLUSTRATION 33.3:   Decision Tree Valuation—Valuing a Young Pharmaceutical Company

To illustrate the steps involved in developing a decision tree, let us value a small biotechnology company, with only one product: a pharmaceutical drug for treating type 1 diabetes, that has gone through preclinical testing and is about to enter phase 1 of the FDA approval process.[2] Assume that you are provided with the additional information on each of the three phases:

1. Phase 1 is expected to cost $50 million and will involve 100 volunteers to determine safety and dosage; it is expected to last one year. There is a 70% chance that the drug will successfully complete the first phase.
2. In phase 2, the drug will be tested on 250 volunteers for effectiveness in treating diabetes over a two-year period. This phase will cost $100 million, and the drug will have to show a statistically significant impact on the disease to move on to the next phase. There is a 30% chance that the drug will prove successful in treating type 1 diabetes, but there is a 10% chance that it will be successful in treating both type 1 and type 2 diabetes and a 10% chance that it will succeed only in treating type 2 diabetes.
3. In phase 3, the testing will expand to 4,000 volunteers to determine the long-term consequences of taking the drug. If the drug is tested on only either type 1 or type 2 diabetes patients, this phase will last four years and cost $250 million; there is an 80% chance of success. If it is tested on both types, the phase will last four years and cost $300 million; there is a 75% chance of success.

If the drug passes through all three phases, the costs of developing the drug and the annual cash flows are provided as follows:

Disease Treatment	Cost of Development	Annual Cash Flow
Type 1 diabetes only	$500 million	$300 million for 15 years
Type 2 diabetes only	$500 million	$125 million for 15 years
Type 1 and 2 diabetes	$600 million	$400 million for 15 years

Assume that the cost of capital for the firm is 10%.

We now have the information to draw the decision tree for this drug. We will first draw the tree in Figure 33.2, specifying the phases, the cash flows at each phase, and the probabilities.

The decision tree shows the probabilities of success at each phase and the additional cash flow or marginal cash flow associated with each step. Since it takes time to go through the phases, there is a time value effect that has to be built into the expected cash flows for each path. We introduce the time value effect and compute the cumulative present value (today) of cash flows from each path, using the 10% cost of capital as the discount rate, in Figure 33.3.

---

[2] In type 1 diabetes, the pancreas does not produce insulin. The patients include young children and the disease is unrelated to diet and activity; they have to receive insulin to survive. In type 2 diabetes, the pancreas produces insufficient insulin. The disease manifests itself in older people, and can sometimes be controlled by changing lifestyle and diet.

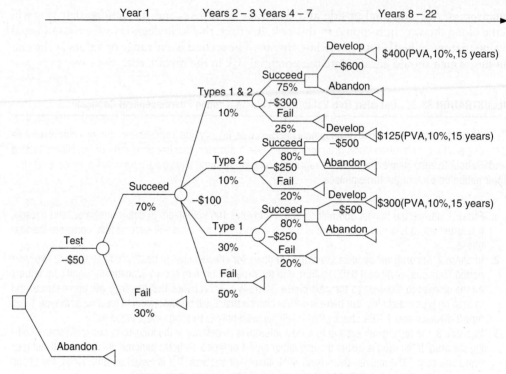

FIGURE 33.2　Decision Tree for Drug Development

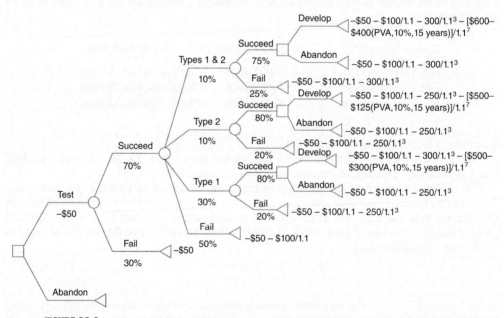

FIGURE 33.3　Present Value of Cash Flows at End Nodes: Drug Development Tree

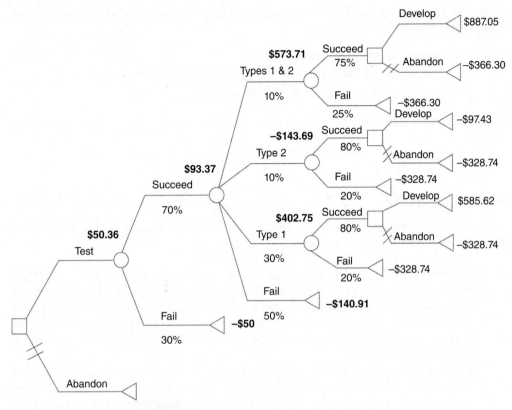

FIGURE 33.4   Drug Decision Tree Folded Back

Note that the present values of the cash flows from development after the third phase get discounted back an additional seven years (to reflect the time it takes to get through three phases). In the last step in the process, we compute the expected values by working backwards through the tree and estimating the optimal action in each decision phase in Figure 33.4.

The expected value of the drug today, given the uncertainty over its success, is $50.36 million. Since it is the only product for the biotechnology company, it is also the value for the company assuming that it does not have the capacity to develop new products. This value reflects all of the possibilities that can unfold over time, and shows the choices at each decision branch that are suboptimal, and thus, should be rejected. The decision tree also provides a range of outcomes, with the worst outcome being failure in phase 3 of the drug as a treatment for both type 1 and type 2 diabetes (−$366.30 million in today's dollars), to the best-case outcome of approval and development of the drug as treatment for both types of diabetes ($887.05 million in today's dollars).

There is one element in the last set of branches that may seem puzzling. Note that the present value of developing the drug as a treatment for just type 2 diabetes is negative (−$97.43 million). Why would the company still develop the drug? Because the alternative of abandoning the drug at the late stage in the process has an even more negative net present value (−$328.74 million). Another way to see this is to look at the marginal effect of developing the drug just for type 2 diabetes. Once the firm has expended the resources to take the firm through all three phases of testing, the testing cost becomes a sunk cost, and is not a factor in the decision.[3] The marginal cash flows from developing the drug after phase 3 yield a positive net present value of $451 million (in year 7 cash flows):

Present value of developing drug to treat
Type 2 diabetes in year 7 $= -500 + 125$ (PV of annuity, 10%, 15 years)
$= \$451$ million

Folding back the decision tree allows you to see what the value of the drug/company is at each phase in the process.

Use in Decision Making

There are several benefits that accrue from using decision trees, and it is surprising that they are not used more often in analysis.

- *Dynamic response to risk.* By linking actions and choices to outcomes of uncertain events, decision trees encourage you to consider how you should act under different circumstances. As a consequence, you will be prepared for whatever outcome may arise rather than be surprised by it. In the example in the preceding section, for instance, you will be ready with a plan of action, no matter what the outcome of phase 3 happens to be.
- *Value of information.* Decision trees provide a useful perspective on the value of information in decision-making. While it is not as obvious in the drug development example, it can be seen clearly when you consider whether to test market a product before commercially developing it. By test-marketing a product, you acquire more information on the chances of eventual success. You can measure the expected value of this improved information in a decision tree and compare it to the test marketing cost.
- *Risk management.* Since decision trees provide a picture of how cash flows unfold over time, they are useful in deciding what risks should be protected against and the benefits of doing so. Consider a decision tree on an asset where the worst-case scenario unfolds if the dollar is weak against the euro. Since you can hedge against this risk, the cost of hedging the risk can be compared to the loss in cash flows in the worst-case scenario.

In summary, decision trees provide a flexible and powerful approach for dealing with risk that occurs in phases, with decisions in each phase depending upon outcomes in the previous one. In addition to providing you with measures of risk exposure, they also force you to think through how you will react to both adverse and positive outcomes that may occur at each phase.

---

[3] It would be more accurate to consider only the costs of the first two phases as sunk, since by the end of phase 2 the firm knows that the drug is effective only against type 2 diabetes. Even if we consider only the costs of the first two phases as sunk, it still makes sense on an expected value basis to continue to phase 3.

Issues

There are some types of risk that decision trees are capable of handling, and others that they are not. In particular, decision trees are best suited for risk that is sequential; the FDA process where approval occurs in phases is a good example. Risks that affect an asset concurrently cannot be easily modeled in a decision tree.[4]

As with scenario analysis, decision trees generally look at risk in terms of discrete outcomes. Again, this is not a problem with the FDA approval process where there are only two outcomes—success or failure. There is a much wider range of outcomes with most other risks, and you have to create discrete categories for the outcomes to stay within the decision-tree framework. For instance, when looking at a market test, you may conclude that selling more than 100,000 units in a test market qualifies as a great success, between 60,000 and 100,000 units as an average outcome, and below 60,000 as a failure.

Assuming risk is sequential and can be categorized into discrete boxes, you are faced with estimation questions to which there may be no easy answers. In particular, you have to estimate the cash flow under each outcome and the associated probability. With the drug development example, you had to estimate the cost and the probability of success of each phase. The advantage that you have when it comes to these estimates is that you can draw on empirical data on how frequently drugs that enter each phase make it to the next one and historical costs associated with drug testing. To the extent that there may be wide differences across different phase 1 drugs in terms of success—some may be longer shots than others—there can still be errors that creep into decision trees.

The expected value of a decision tree is heavily dependent upon the assumption that you will stay disciplined at the decision points in the tree. In other words, if the optimal decision is to abandon if a test market fails and the expected value is computed, based on this assumption, the integrity of the process and the expected value will quickly fall apart, if you decide to overlook the market testing failure and go with a full launch of the product anyway.

Risk-Adjusted Value and Decision Trees

Are decision trees an alternative or an addendum to discounted cash flow valuation? The question is an interesting one because there are some analysts who believe that decision trees, by factoring in the possibility of good and bad outcomes, are already risk adjusted. In fact, they go on to make the claim that the right discount rate to use estimating present value in decision trees is the risk-free rate; using a risk-adjusted discount rate, they argue, would be double-counting the risk. Barring a few exceptional circumstances, they are incorrect in their reasoning.

- *Expected values are not risk adjusted.* Consider decision trees, where you estimate expected cash flows by looking at the possible outcomes and their probabilities of occurrence. The probability-weighted expected value that you obtain is not risk adjusted. The only rationale that can be offered for using a risk-free rate is that the risk embedded in the uncertain outcomes is asset-specific and will be diversified

---

[4]If you choose to model such risks in a decision tree, they have to be independent of each other. In other words, the sequencing should not matter.

away, in which case the risk-adjusted discount rate would be the risk-free rate. In the FDA drug development example, for instance, this may be offered as the rationale for why you would use the risk-free rate to discount cash flows for the first seven years, when the only risk you face is drug approval risk. After year 7, though, the risk is likely to contain a market element, and the risk-adjusted rate will be higher than the risk-free rate.

◼ *Double counting of risk.* You do have to be careful about making sure that you don't double-count for risk in decision trees by using risk-adjusted discount rates that are set high to reflect the possibility of failure at the earlier phases. One common example of this phenomenon is venture capital pricing. In Chapter 23, we noted that venture capitalists often value young start-up companies by estimating an exit value, based on projected earnings and a multiple of those earnings in the future, and then discounting the exit value at a target rate of return. Using this approach, for instance, the value today for a firm that is losing money currently but is expected to make $10 million in 5 years (when the earnings multiple at which it will be taken public is estimated to be 40) can be computed as follows (if the target rate is 35 percent):

Value of the firm in 5 years $= $ Earnings in year $5 \times PE = 10 \times 40 = \$400$ million
Value of firm today $= \$400/1.35^5 = \$89.20$ million

Note, however, that the target rate is set at a high level (35 percent) because of the probability that this young firm will not survive. In fact, you could frame this as a simple decision tree in Figure 33.5.

Assume that r is the correct discount rate, based on the business risk that the venture capitalist faces on this venture. Going back to the numeric example, assume that this discount rate would have been 15 percent for this venture. You can solve for the implied probability of failure, embedded in the venture capitalist's estimate of value of $89.20 million:

$$\text{Estimated value} = \$89.20 = \frac{\$400}{1.15^5} \text{ (p)}$$

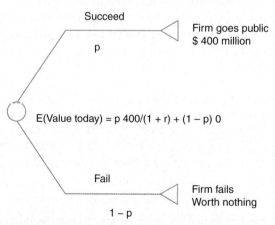

FIGURE 33.5 Decision Tree for Start-Up Firm

Solving for p, the probability of success at 44.85 percent. With this estimate of probability in the decision tree, you would have arrived at the same value as the venture capitalist, assuming that you use the right discount rate. Using the target rate of 35 percent as the discount rate in a decision tree would lead to a drastically lower value, because risk would have been counted twice. Using the same reasoning, you can see why using a high discount rate in assessing the value of a biotechnology drug in a decision tree will undervalue the drug, especially if the discount rate already reflects the probability that the drug will not make it to commercial production. If the risk of the approval process is drug-specific and thus diversifiable, this would suggest that discount rates should be moderate in decision tree analysis, even for products with very high likelihoods of not making it through the early stages in the process.

If the right discount rate to use in a decision tree should reflect the business risk looking forward, it is not only possible but likely that discount rates will be different at different points in the tree. For instance, extraordinary success at the test-market stage may yield more predictable cash flows than an average test market outcome; this would lead you to use a lower discount rate to value the former, and a higher discount rate to value the latter. In the drug development example, it is possible that the expected cash flows, if the drug works for both types of diabetes, will be more stable than if is a treatment for only one type. It would follow that a discount rate of 8 percent may be the right one for the first set of cash flows, whereas a 12-percent discount rate may be more appropriate for the second.

Reviewing the discussion, decision trees are not alternatives to risk-adjusted valuation. Instead, they can be viewed as a different way of adjusting for discrete risk that may be difficult to bring into expected cash flows or into risk-adjusted discount rates.

SIMULATIONS

If scenario analysis and decision trees are techniques that help us to assess the effects of discrete risk, simulations provide a way of examining the consequences of continuous risk. To the extent that most risks that we face in the real world can generate hundreds of possible outcomes, a simulation will give us a fuller picture of the risk in an asset or investment.

Steps in Simulation

Unlike scenario analysis, where we look at the values under discrete scenarios, simulations allow for more flexibility in how we deal with uncertainty. In its classic form, distributions of values are estimated for each parameter in the valuation (growth, market share, operating margin, beta, etc.). In each simulation, we draw one outcome from each distribution to generate a unique set of cash flows and value. Across a large number of simulations, we can derive a distribution for the value of investment, or an asset that will reflect the underlying uncertainty we face in estimating the inputs to the valuation. The steps associated with running a simulation are as follows:

1. *Determine probabilistic variables:* In any analysis, there are potentially dozens of inputs, some of which are predictable and some of which are not. Unlike scenario analysis and decision trees, where the number of variables that are changed and the potential outcomes have to be few in number, there is no constraint on how many

variables can be allowed to vary in a simulation. At least in theory, we can define probability distributions for each and every input in a valuation. The reality, though, is that this will be time consuming and may not provide much of a payoff, especially for inputs that have only marginal impact on value. Consequently, it makes sense to focus attention on a few variables that have a significant impact on value.

2. *Define probability distributions for these variables:* This is a key and the most difficult step in the analysis. Generically, there are three ways in which you can go about defining probability distributions:

    i. *Historical data:* For variables that have a long history and reliable data over that history, it is possible to use the historical data to develop distributions. Assume, for instance, that you are trying to develop a distribution of expected changes in the long-term Treasury bond rate (to use as an input in investment analysis). You could use the histogram in Figure 33.6, based on the annual changes in Treasury bond rates every year from 1928 to 2023, as the distribution for future changes. Implicit in this approach is the assumption that there have been no structural shifts in the market that will render the historical data unreliable.

    ii. *Cross-sectional data:* In some cases, you may be able to substitute data on differences in a specific variable across existing investments that are similar to the investment being analyzed. Assume that you are valuing an apparel firm and are

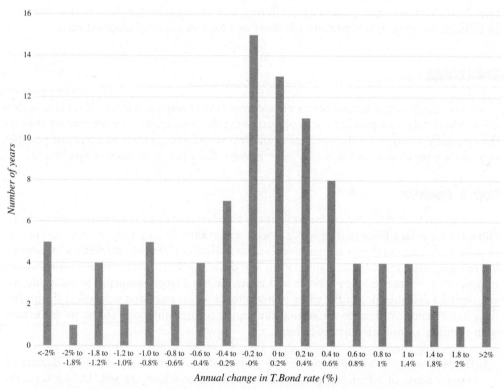

Annual change in T.Bond rate (%)

FIGURE 33.6 One-Year Change in U.S. 10-Year Treasury-Rate

concerned about the volatility in operating margins. Figure 33.7 provides a distribution of pretax operating margins across apparel companies in 2023.

In a simulation, you could either use this distribution directly or find a standardized statistical distribution that is close in terms of characteristics. Note, though, that if you use this distribution, you are in effect assuming that the underlying distribution of margins is the same across software firms.

iii. *Statistical distribution and parameters*: For most variables that you are trying to forecast, the historical and cross-sectional data will be insufficient or unreliable. In these cases, you have to pick a statistical distribution that best captures the variability in the input and estimate the parameters for that distribution. Thus, you may conclude that operating margins for software companies will be distributed uniformly, with a minimum of 0 percent and a maximum of 35 percent, and that revenue growth is normally distributed with an expected value of 15 percent and a standard deviation of 10 percent. Many simulation packages available for personal computers now provide a rich array of distributions, but picking the right distribution and the parameters for the distribution remains difficult for two reasons.

The first is that few inputs that we see in practice meet the stringent requirements that statistical distributions demand; revenue growth, for instance, cannot really be normally distributed because the lowest value it can take on is −100 percent. Consequently, you have to settle for statistical distributions that are close

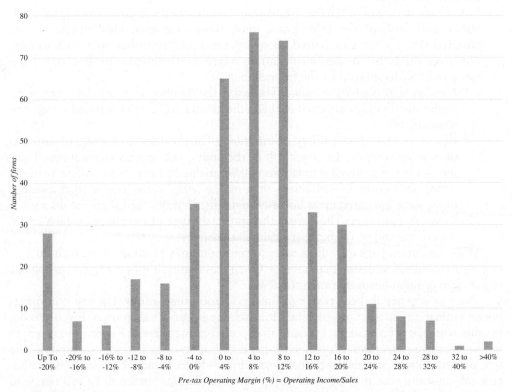

FIGURE 33.7 Pre-Tax Operating Margins: Global Apparel/Footwear firms in January 2024

enough to the real distribution that the resulting errors will not wreak havoc on your conclusion. The second is that the parameters still need to be estimated once the distribution is picked. For this, you can draw on historical or cross-sectional data; for the revenue growth input, you can look at revenue growth in prior years or revenue growth rate differences across peer group companies. The caveats about structural shifts making historical data unreliable and peer group companies not being truly comparable continue to apply.

In summary, the probability distributions will be discrete for some inputs and continuous for others and be based on historical data for some and statistical distributions for others.

3. *Check for correlation across variables:* While it is tempting to jump to running simulations right after the distributions have been specified, it is important that you check for correlations across variables. Assume, for instance, that you are developing probability distributions for both interest rates and inflation. While both inputs may be critical in determining value, they are likely to be correlated with each other; high inflation is usually accompanied by high interest rates. When there is strong correlation, positive or negative, across inputs, you have two choices. One is to pick create a composite input that captures the correlated variables. With interest rates and inflation, a real interest rate (difference between nominal interest rate and inflation) may be the simulated variable. The other is to build the correlation explicitly into the simulation; this requires more sophisticated simulation packages and adds more detail to the estimation process.

4. *Run the simulation:* For the first simulation, you draw one outcome from each distribution and compute the value based upon those outcomes. This process can be repeated as many times as desired, though the marginal contribution of each simulation drops off as the number of simulations increases. The number of simulations you run should be determined by the following:

  ▪ *Number of probabilistic inputs:* The larger the number of inputs that have probability distributions attached to them, the greater will be the required number of simulations.

  ▪ *Characteristics of probability distributions:* The greater the diversity of distributions in an analysis, the larger will be the number of required simulations. Thus, the number of required simulations will be smaller in a simulation where all of the inputs have normal distributions than in one where some have normal distributions, some are based upon historical data distributions, and some are discrete.

  ▪ *Range of outcomes:* The greater the potential range of outcomes on each input, the greater will be the number of simulations.

Most simulation packages allow users to run thousands of simulations, with little or no cost attached to increasing that number. Given that reality, it is better to err on the side of too many simulations rather than too few.

There have generally been two impediments to good simulations. The first is informational: estimating distributions of values for each input into a valuation is difficult to do. In other words, it is far easier to estimate an expected growth rate of 8 percent in revenues for the next five years than it is to specify the distribution of expected growth rates—the type of distribution, parameters of that distribution—for revenues. The second is computational; until the advent of personal computers, simulations tended to be too time and resource intensive for the typical analyst. Both these constraints have eased in recent years and simulations have become more feasible.

ILLUSTRATION 33.4:   Valuing Exxon Mobil—Monte Carlo Simulation

In Chapter 22, we valued Exxon Mobil, the integrated oil company in 2009. In Figure 33.8, we reproduce the graph Exxon's operating income as a function of the average oil price each year from 1985 to 2008.

Also in Chapter 22, we regressed the operating income of Exxon Mobil against the oil price per barrel to arrive at the following:

$$\text{Operating income} = -6{,}395 + 911.32 \text{ (Average oil price) } R_2 = 90.2\%$$

$$(2.950) \ (14.59)$$

Exxon Mobil's operating income increases about $9.11 billion for every $10 increase in the price per barrel of oil, and 90% of the variation in Exxon's earnings over time comes from movements in oil prices.[5]

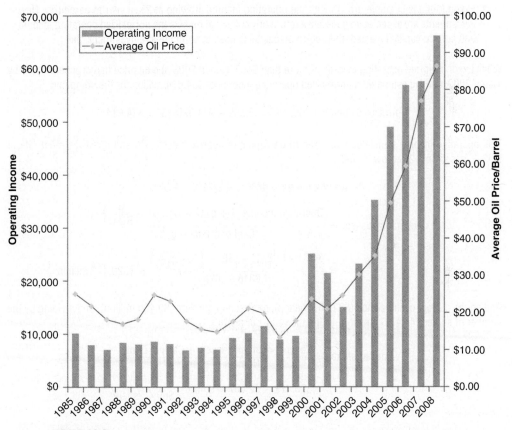

FIGURE 33.8   Operating Income versus Oil Prices for Exxon Mobil: 1985–2008

---

[5]The relationship is very strong at Exxon because it has been a large and stable firm for decades. It is likely that the relationship between earnings and oil prices will be weaker at smaller, evolving oil companies.

In Chapter 22, we made the following assumptions to estimate an equity value for Exxon in March 2009:

■ We estimated a bottom-up beta of 0.90 for Exxon Mobil, and then used the Treasury bond rate of 2.5% and an equity risk premium of 6.5% to estimate the cost of equity.

$$\text{Cost of equity} = 2.5\% + 0.90(6.5\%) = 8.35\%$$

■ Exxon has $9.4 billion of debt outstanding and a market capitalization of $320.4 billion (4941.63 million shares, trading at $64.83/share), resulting in a debt ratio of 2.85%. As an AAA-rated company, its cost of debt is expected to be 3.75%, reflecting a default spread of 1.25% over the risk-free rate. Using a marginal tax rate of 38%(rather than the effective tax rate) and Exxon's debt to capital ratio of 2.85%, we estimated a cost of capital of 8.18% for the firm:

$$\text{Cost of capital} = 8.35\% \,(.9715) + 3.75\% \,(1 - .38)(.0285) = 8.18\%$$

■ Exxon Mobil is in stable growth with the operating income growing at 2% a year in perpetuity. New investments are expected to generate a return on capital that reflects the normalized operating income and current capital invested; this return on capital is used to compute a reinvestment rate.

While Exxon reported operating income of more than $60 billion in 2008, the oil price had dropped to $45 by March 2009, and we estimated a normalized operating income of $34,614 million for the company:

$$\text{Normalized operating income} = -6,395 + 911.32(\$45) = \$34,614$$

This operating income translates into a return on capital of approximately 21% and a reinvestment rate of 9.52%, based on a 2% growth rate.[6]

$$\text{Reinvestment rate} = g/ROC = 2/21\% = 9.52\%$$

$$\text{Value of operating assets} = \frac{\text{Operating income } (1 + g) \,(1 - t) - \left(1 - \dfrac{g}{ROIC}\right)}{(\text{Cost of capital} - g)}$$

$$= \frac{34,614(1.02) \,(1 - .38) - \left(1 - \dfrac{2\%}{21\%}\right)}{(.0818 - .02)} = \$320,472 \text{ million}$$

Adding the current cash balance ($32,007 million), subtracting out debt ($9,400 million), and dividing by the number of shares (4,941.63 million) yields the value per share.

$$\text{Value per share} = \frac{\text{Value of operating assets} + \text{Cash} - \text{Debt}}{\text{Number of shares}}$$

$$= \frac{320,472 + 32,007 - 9,400}{4941.63} = \$69.43/\text{share}$$

---

[6]To compute the return on capital, we aggregated the book value of equity ($126,044 million), the book value of debt ($9,566 million), and netted out cash ($33,981 million) from the end of 2007, to arrive at an invested capital value of $101,629 million. The return on capital is computed as follows:

$$\text{Return on invested capital} = \frac{34,614 \,(1 - .38)}{101.629} = 21.1\%$$

At the prevailing stock price of $64.83, the stock looked slightly undervalued. However, that reflected the assumption that the current oil price (of $45 per barrel) is the normalized price.

Since the value per share is so dependent on the oil price, it would make more sense to allow the oil price to vary, and then value the company as a function of this price, and simulations can help flesh out the numbers:

Step 1: *Determine the probability distribution for the oil prices:* We used historical data on oil prices, adjusted for inflation, to both define the distribution and estimate its parameters. Figure 33.9 summarizes the distribution.

> Note that oil prices can vary from about $8 a barrel at the minimum to more than $120 a barrel. While we have used the current price of $45 as the mean of the distribution, we could have inserted an oil view into the distribution by choosing a higher or lower mean value.[7]

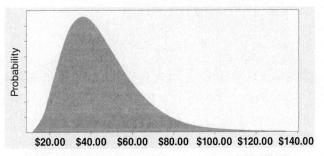

FIGURE 33.9   Oil Price Distribution—Historical data

Step 2: *Link the operating results to commodity price:* To link the operating income to commodity prices, we used the regression results from earlier in the illustration:

$$\text{Operating income} = -6{,}395 + 911.32 \text{ (Average oil price) } R_2 = 90.2\%$$

$$(2.950) \quad (14.59)$$

> As we noted in the earlier section, the regression approach works well for Exxon but may not for smaller, more volatile commodity companies.

Step 3: *Estimate the value as a function of the operating results.* As the operating income changes, there are two levels at which the value of the firm is affected. The first is that lower operating income, other things remaining equal, lowers the free cash flow, and reduces value. The second is that the return on capital is recomputed, holding the capital invested fixed, as the operating income changes. As operating income declines, the return on capital drops, and the firm will have to reinvest more to sustain the stable growth rate of 2 percent. While we could also have allowed the cost of capital and the growth rate to vary, we feel comfortable with both numbers and have left them fixed.

Step 4: *Develop a distribution for the value:* We ran 10,000 simulations, letting the oil price vary and valuing the firm and equity value per share in each simulation. The results are summarized in Figure 33.10.

---

[7]We used thirty years of historical data on oil prices, adjusted for inflation, to create an empirical distribution. We then chose the statistical distribution that seemed to provide the closest fit (lognormal) and chose parameter values that yielded numbers closest to the historical data.

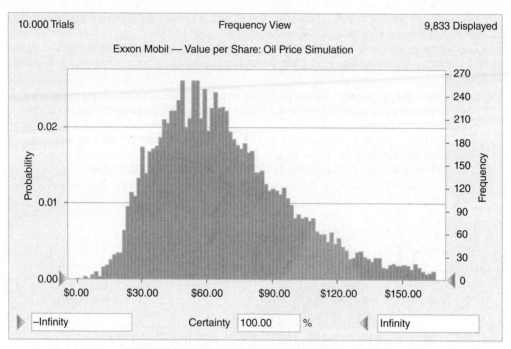

FIGURE 33.10 Exxon Mobil—Oil Price Simulation

The average value per share across the simulations was $69.59, with a minimum value of $2.25 and a maximum value of $324.42; there is, however, a greater than 50% chance that the value per share will be less than $64.83 (the current stock price). Put differently, this approach yields not only the value per share for the company but also the likelihood that the firm is really undervalued (less than 50%). That information can feed into the investment decision.

Use in Decision Making

A well-done simulation provides us with more than just an expected value for an asset or investment:

■ *Better input estimation.* In an ideal simulation, analysts will examine both the historical and cross-sectional data on each input variable before making a judgment on what distribution to use and the parameters of the distribution. In the process, they may be able to avoid the sloppiness that is associated with the use of point estimates; many discounted cash flow valuations are based upon expected growth rates that are obtained from managers or analysts, often with no basis in fact.

■ *It yields a distribution for expected value rather than a point estimate.* Consider the valuation of Exxon Mobil that we completed in the last illustration. In addition to reporting an expected value of $69.59/share, we also estimated a standard deviation in that value and a breakdown of the values by percentile. The distribution reinforces the obvious but important point that valuation models yield estimates of value for risky assets that are imprecise and explains why different analysts valuing the same asset may arrive at different estimates of value.

Note that there are two claims about simulations that we are unwilling to make. The first is that simulations yield better estimates of expected value than conventional risk-adjusted value models. In fact, the expected values from simulations should be fairly close to the expected value that we would obtain using the expected values for each of the inputs (rather than the entire distribution). The second is that simulations, by providing estimates of the expected value and the distribution in that value, lead to better decisions. This may not always be the case since the benefits that decision-makers obtain by getting a fuller picture of the uncertainty in value in a risky asset may be more than offset by misuse of that risk measure. As we will argue later in this chapter, it is all too common for risk to be double-counted in simulations, and for decisions to be based on the wrong type of risk.

MARGIN OF SAFETY AND SIMULATION

The margin of safety (MOS) is a measure used widely by value investors to control risk in investing. Here is how it works. A conservative value investor will require that a stock be priced more than X percent (10,15, or 20 percent) below the value before he or she buys it; the margin of safety is the X percent. While intuitive, the margin of safety is not an alternative to traditional risk measures, since you need to estimate the value of a stock first, before you can use the margin of safety. It is, however, a way in which you can bring your uncertainty and risk aversion into the decision process, with the margin of safety increasing as both increase. In practice, though, the margin of safety is often arbitrarily set and can vary widely across investors and investments.

A well-run simulation can be used to set margins of safety, since it provides information on the estimation error in value. For instance, assume that your margin of safety is 20 percent and that you are looking at Exxon Mobil in early 2009. In the Exxon Mobil simulation, for instance, where the expected value is $69.59 per share, adding this requirement would require that the stock be trading at less than $45 per share (separated by 20% or 2,000 outcomes from the expected value of $69.59), for it to be a stock that you would buy. Obviously, increasing (decreasing) the margin of safety would give you a lower (or higher) price threshold. Furthermore, the margin of safety will be greater for firms where you are more uncertain about the future than for firms where you feel more confident in your inputs.

Simulations with Constraints

There is a second use for simulations, and that is when you have a constraint that, if violated, creates very large costs for the firm and perhaps even causes its demise. You can examine the likelihood that the constraint will be violated, given the firm's current characteristics, and the implications for value. In this section, we will look at some of these constraints.

Book Value Constraints   The book value of equity is an accounting construct and, by itself, means little. Firms like Google and Apple trade at market values that are several times their book values. At the other extreme, there are firms that trade well below book value. In fact, there are several hundred firms in the United States, some with significant market values, that have negative book values for equity. There are two types of restrictions on book value of equity that may affect value.

1. *Regulatory capital restrictions.* Financial service firms, such as banks and insurance companies, are required to maintain book equity as a fraction of loans or other assets at or above a floor ratio specified by the authorities. Firms that violate these capital constraints can be taken over by the regulatory authorities and will have to cease operating. Not surprisingly, financial service firms not only keep a close eye on their book value of equity (and the related ratios) but are also conscious of the possibility that the risk in their investments or positions can manifest itself as a drop in book equity. In fact, value at risk (VAR), a risk measurement device used by many financial service firms, represents the efforts to understand the potential risks in their investments and to be ready for the possibility of a catastrophic outcome, though the probability of it occurring might be very small. By simulating the values of their investments under a variety of scenarios, investors can identify not only the possibility of a bank falling below the regulatory ratios but also the valuation consequences, which can range from loss of all equity value, as a worst case, to dilution from new equity capital issues, as a best case.

2. *Negative book value for equity.* As noted, there are hundreds of firms in the United States with negative book values of equity that survive its occurrence and have high market values for equity. There are some countries where a negative book value of equity can create substantial costs for the firm and its investors. For instance, companies with negative book values of equity in parts of Europe are required to raise fresh equity capital to bring their book values above zero. In some countries in Asia, companies that have negative book values of equity are barred from paying dividends. Even in the United States, lenders to firms can have loan covenants that enable them to gain at least partial control of a firm if its book value of equity turns negative. As with regulatory capital restrictions, investors can use simulations to assess the probability of a negative book value for equity and to capture the consequences for value.

Debt Constraints   In discounted cash flow valuation, the value of the firm is computed as a going concern, by discounting expected cash flows at a risk-adjusted discount rate. Deducting debt from this estimate yields equity value. The possibility and potential costs of not being able to meet debt payments is considered only peripherally in the discount rate. In reality, the costs of not meeting contractual obligations can be substantial. In fact, these costs are generally categorized as indirect bankruptcy costs, and could include the loss of customers, tighter supplier credit, and higher employee turnover. The perception that a firm is in trouble can lead to further trouble. By allowing investors to compare the value of a business to its outstanding claims in all possible scenarios (rather than just the most likely one), simulations allow them to not only quantify the likelihood of distress but also build the cost of indirect bankruptcy costs into valuation. In effect, you can explicitly model the effect of distress on expected cash flows and discount rates.

Issues   The use of simulations in investment analysis was first suggested in an article by David Hertz in the *Harvard Business Review*.[8] He argued that using probability distributions for input variables, rather than single best estimates, would yield more informative output. In the example that he provided in the paper, he used simulations to

---

[8]Hertz (1964) has a classic paper on the use of probabilistic approaches in decision-making.

compare the distributions of returns of two investments; the investment with the higher expected return also had a higher chance of losing money (which was viewed as an indicator of its riskiness). In the aftermath, there were several analysts who jumped on the simulation bandwagon, with mixed results. In recent years, there has been a resurgence in interest in simulations as a tool for risk assessment, especially in the context of derivatives. There are several key issues, though, that we have to deal when using simulations in risk assessment:

- *Garbage in, garbage out.* For simulations to have value, the distributions chosen for the inputs should be based on analysis and data, rather than guesswork. It is worth noting that simulations yield great-looking output, even when the inputs are random. Unsuspecting decision-makers may, therefore, be getting meaningless pictures of the risk in an investment. It is also worth noting that simulations require more than a passing knowledge of statistical distributions and their characteristics; analysts who do not know the difference between normal and uniform distributions should not be doing simulations.
- *Real data may not fit distributions.* The problem with the real world is that the data seldom fits the stringent requirements of statistical distributions. Using a probability distribution that bears little resemblance to the true distribution underlying an input variable will yield misleading results.
- *Nonstationary distributions.* Even when the data fits a statistical distribution or where historical data distributions are available, shifts in the market structure can lead to shifts in the distribution as well. In some cases, this can change the form of the distribution, and in others it can change the parameters of the distribution. Thus, the mean and variance estimated from historical data for an input that is normally distributed may change for the next period. What we would really like to use in simulations, but seldom can assess, are forward-looking probability distributions.
- *Changing correlation across inputs.* Earlier in this chapter, we noted that correlation across input variables can be modeled into simulations. However, this works only if the correlations remain stable and predictable. To the extent that correlations between input variables change over time, it becomes far more difficult to model them.

Risk-Adjusted Value and Simulations

In our discussion of decision trees, we referred to the common misconception that decision trees are risk adjusted because they consider the likelihood of adverse events. The same misconception is prevalent in simulations, where the argument is that the cash flows from simulations are somehow risk adjusted because of the use of probability distributions, and that the risk-free rate should be used in discounting these cash flows. With one exception, this argument does not make sense. Looking across simulations, the cash flows that we obtain are expected cash flows and are not risk adjusted. Consequently, we should be discounting these cash flows at a risk-adjusted rate.

The exception occurs when you use the standard deviation in values from a simulation as a measure of investment or asset risk and make decisions based on that. In this case, using a risk-adjusted discount rate will result in a double-counting of risk. Consider a simple example. Assume that you are trying to choose between two assets, both of which you have valued using simulations and risk-adjusted discount rates. The following table summarizes your findings.

Asset	Risk-Adjusted: Discount Rate	Simulation: Expected Value	Simulation: Standard Deviation
A	12%	$100	15%
B	15%	$100	21%

Note that you view asset B to be riskier and have used a higher discount rate to compute value. If you now proceed to reject asset B, because the standard deviation is higher across the simulated values, you would be penalizing it twice. You can redo the simulations using the risk-free rate as the discount rate for both assets, but a note of caution needs to be introduced. If we then base our choice between these assets on the standard deviation in simulated values, we are assuming that all risk matters in investment choice, rather than only the risk that cannot be diversified away. Put another way, we may end up rejecting an asset because it has a high standard deviation in simulated values, even though adding that asset to a portfolio may result in little additional risk (because much of its risk can be diversified away).

This is not to suggest that simulations are not useful to us in understanding risk. Looking at the variance of the simulated values around the expected value provides a visual reminder that we are estimating value in an uncertain environment. It is also conceivable that we can use it as a decision tool in portfolio management in choosing between two stocks that are equally undervalued but have different value distributions. The stock with the less volatile value distribution may be considered a better investment than another stock with a more volatile value distribution.

AN OVERALL ASSESSMENT OF PROBABILISTIC RISK-ASSESSMENT APPROACHES

Now that we have looked at scenario analysis, decision trees, and simulations, we can consider not only when each one is appropriate but also how these approaches complement or replace risk-adjusted value approaches.

Comparing the Approaches

Assuming that you decide to use a probabilistic approach to assess risk and could choose among scenario analysis, decision trees, and simulations, which one should you pick? The answer will depend upon how you plan to use the output and what types of risk you are facing:

■ *Selective versus full risk analysis.* In the best-case/worst-case scenario analysis, we look at only three scenarios (the best case, the most likely case, and the worst case) and ignore all other scenarios. Even when we consider multiple scenarios, we will not have a complete assessment of all possible outcomes from risky investments or assets. With decision trees and simulations, we attempt to consider all possible outcomes. In decision trees, we try to accomplish this by converting continuous risk into a manageable set of possible outcomes. With simulations, we can use distributions to capture all possible outcomes. Put in terms of probability, the sum of the probabilities of the scenarios we examine in scenario analysis can be less than 1, whereas the sum of the probabilities of outcomes in decision trees and simulations has to equal 1. As a consequence, we can compute expected values across outcomes in the latter, using the probabilities as weights, and these expected values are comparable to the single-estimate risk-adjusted values that we talked about in the preceding chapter.

- *Discrete versus continuous risk.* As noted earlier, scenario analysis and decision trees are generally built around discrete outcomes in risky events, whereas simulations are better suited for continuous risks. Focusing on just scenario analysis and decision trees, the latter are better suited for sequential risks, since risk is considered in phases, whereas the former is easier to use when risks occur concurrently.
- *Correlation across risks.* If the various risks that an investment is exposed to are correlated, simulations allow for explicitly modeling these correlations (assuming that you can estimate and forecast them). In scenario analysis, we can deal with correlations subjectively by creating scenarios that allow for them; the high (low) interest rate scenario will also include slower (higher) economic growth. Correlated risks are difficult to model in decision trees.

Table 33.2 summarizes the relationship between risk type and the probabilistic approach used.

Finally, the quality of the information will be a factor in your choice of approach. Since simulations are heavily dependent upon being able to assess probability distributions and parameters, they work best in cases where there is substantial historical and cross-sectional data available that can be used to make these assessments. With decision trees, you need estimates of the probabilities of the outcomes at each chance node, making them best suited for risks where these risks can be assessed, either using past data or population characteristics. Thus, it should come as no surprise that when confronted with new and unpredictable risks, analysts continue to fall back on scenario analysis, notwithstanding its slapdash and subjective ways of dealing with risk.

Complement or Replacement for Risk-Adjusted Value

As we noted in our discussion of both decision trees and simulations, these approaches can be used as either complements to or substitutes for risk-adjusted value. Scenario analysis, on the other hand, will always be a complement to risk-adjusted value, since it does not look at the full spectrum of possible outcomes.

TABLE 33.2   Risk Type and Probabilistic Approaches

Discrete/Continuous	Correlated/Independent	Sequential/Concurrent	Risk Approach
Discrete	Independent	Sequential	Decision tree
Discrete	Correlated	Concurrent	Scenario analysis
Continuous	Either	Either	Simulations

When any of these approaches are used as complements to risk-adjusted value, the caveats that we offered earlier in the chapter continue to apply and bear repeating. All of these approaches use expected rather than risk-adjusted cash flows and the discount rate that is used should be a risk-adjusted discount rate; the risk-free rate cannot be used to discount expected cash flows. In all three approaches, though, we still preserve the flexibility to change the risk-adjusted discount rate for different outcomes. Since all of these approaches will also provide a range for estimated value and a measure of variability (in terms of value at the end nodes in a decision tree or as a standard deviation in value in a simulation), it is important that we do not double-count for risk. In other words, it is patently unfair to risky investments to discount their cash flows back at a risk-adjusted rate (in simulations and decision trees) and to then reject them because the variability in value is high.

Both simulations and decision trees can be used as alternatives to risk-adjusted valuation, but there are constraints on the process. The first is that the cash flows will be discounted back at a risk-free rate to arrive at value. The second is that we now use the measure of variability in values that we obtain in both these approaches as a measure of risk in the investment. Comparing two assets with the same expected value (obtained with riskless rates as discount rates) from a simulation, we will pick the one with the lower variability in simulated values as the better investment. If we do this, we are assuming that all of the risks that we have built into the simulation are relevant for the investment decision. In effect, we are ignoring the line drawn between risks that could have been diversified away in a portfolio and asset-specific risk, on which much of modern finance is built. For investors considering investing all of their wealth in one asset, this should be reasonable. For a portfolio manager comparing two risky stocks that they are considering adding to a diversified portfolio, it can yield misleading results; the rejected stock with the higher variance in simulated values may be uncorrelated with the other investments in the portfolio, and thus, have little marginal risk.

The use of probabilistic approaches has become more common with the surge in data availability and computing power. It is not uncommon now to see a capital-budgeting analysis, with a 20–30 scenarios, or a Monte Carlo simulation attached to an equity valuation.

CONCLUSION

Estimating the risk-adjusted value for a risky asset or investment may seem like an exercise in futility. After all, the value is a function of the assumptions that we make about how the risk will unfold in the future. With probabilistic approaches to valuation, we estimate not only an expected value but also get a sense of the range of possible outcomes for value, across good and bad scenarios.

- In the most extreme form of scenario analysis, you look at the value in the best-case and worst-case scenarios and contrast them with the expected value. In its more general form, you estimate the value under a small number of likely scenarios, ranging from optimistic to pessimistic.
- Decision trees are designed for sequential and discrete risks, where the risk in an investment is considered in phases, and the risk in each phase is captured in the possible outcomes and the probabilities that they will occur. A decision tree provides a complete assessment of risk and can be used to determine the optimal courses of action at each phase and an expected value for an asset today.

▓ Simulations provide the most complete assessments of risk since they are based on probability distributions for each input (rather than just discrete outcomes). The output from a simulation takes the form of an expected value across simulations and a distribution for the simulated values.

With all three approaches, the keys are to avoid double-counting risk (by using a risk-adjusted discount rate and considering the variability in estimated value as a risk measure) or making decisions based on the wrong types of risk.

QUESTIONS AND SHORT PROBLEMS

In the problems following, use an equity risk premium of 5.5 percent if none if specified.

1. You have estimated the value per share for Littlefield Inc., a transportation company, under three scenarios: $5/share under the worst-case scenario, $30/share under the best-case scenario, and $18/share under the most likely scenario. If the stock is trading at $15, would you buy the stock? Why or why not?

2. You are analyzing Delta Enterprises, a small publicly traded company with $50 million of debt outstanding, and 25 million shares, trading at $10/share. The firm generated $40 million in after-tax cash flows last year, and you estimate that these cash flows will grow 2% a year in perpetuity, and that the cost of capital for the firm is 12%.
   a. Estimate the value per share for the firm, assuming it has no cash balance.
   b. Now assume that you find out that a significant portion of the firm's revenues come from one customer, and that there is a 20-percent chance that this contract will be lost next year. Assuming that a lost contract will result in a 50% drop in the after-tax cash flows, estimate the value per share today. (You can assume that the growth rate and cost of capital will be unaffected).

3. You are valuing Signet Bank during a period of substantial uncertainty about future regulatory rules. Signet Bank generated $100 million in net income last year on a book value of equity of $1 billion, and paid out $70 million in dividends. While you expect Signet to be a stable growth company, you envision the following regulatory scenarios for the future:
   ▓ *Status quo*—no changes in regulatory rules (40% probability): Signet will continue to generate its current return on equity in perpetuity and maintain its existing dividend payout ratio.
   ▓ *Regulatory easing*—lower regulatory capital ratios (25-percent probability): Signet will be able to generate a return on equity of 12 percent on future investments, while maintaining its stable growth rate (at status quo levels).
   ▓ *Regulatory tightening*—higher regulatory capital ratios (35-percent probability): Signet will see its return on equity drop to 9%, while maintaining its stable growth rate (at status quo levels).
   a. Estimate the value of equity in Signet Bank under each scenario. (You can leave current net income unchanged under all scenarios.)
   b. Given the probabilities of each scenario unfolding, estimate the value of equity in Signet Bank today.

4. Sigma Energy is an alternative energy company that produces solar energy panels. The company is expected to generate $50 million in after-tax operating income in the next year, but its prospects for future growth are dependent upon the level of oil prices and access to low-cost (and subsidized) government financing. You have outlined the following scenarios (with consequences for growth (g), return on invested capital [ROC] and cost of capital [r]):

	Government Subsidies Continue	Government Subsdies end
Oil prices > $100/barrel (30% probability)	g = 4%, ROC = 12%, r = 8%	g = 4%, ROC = 12%, r = 10%
Oil prices between $60 and $100/barrel (50% probability)	g = 3%, ROC = 10%, r = 8%	g = 3%, ROC = 10%, r = 10%
Oil prices < $60/barrel (20% probability)	g = 2%, ROC = 8%, r = 8%	g = 2%, ROC = 8%, r = 10%

   a. Estimate the value of the firm under each scenario. (You can leave the after-tax operating income for next year unchanged at $50 million under all the scenarios.)
   b. If the probability that the government will end subsidies is 40%, estimate the value of the firm across the scenarios.
5. Chavez Enterprises is a small Venezuelan company. The firm is profitable and is expected to generate 120 million bolivars in after-tax operating income next year on capital invested (book value) of 600 million bolivars. You have estimated a cost of capital of 12% for the firm and expect it to grow 4 percent a year in perpetuity.
   a. Estimate the value of the firm today.
   b. Now assume that you are concerned that the firm may be nationalized. If nationalization occurs, you will be paid book value for the assets. Assuming a 30% probability for nationalization, estimate the value of the firm today.
6. Loral Drugs is a biotechnology firm that is working on a new drug to treat insomnia. The drug is working its way through the FDA approval process, and is expected to generate $150 million in after-tax cash flows each year for 15 years, once it is approved. There are two more hurdles that the drug has to cross before approval:
   ▪ A small sample test on laboratory animals that will take a year to complete and is expected to cost $100 million (to be spent today); there is an 80-percent chance that it will succeed.
   ▪ If the lab animal test succeeds, it will be followed by a study on human subjects that will take two additional years to complete and cost $250 million (to be spent at the end of year 1); there is a 60-percent chance that this study will yield favorable results.
   The cost of capital for biotechnology firms is 10%.
   a. Outline the decision tree for the insomnia drug.
   b. Estimate the expected value of the drug to the company today.
7. You are a venture capitalist who is interested in investing $50 million in Friends Online, a social media company. The business will take three years to become operational (during which period it will generate no positive cash flows), and once

operational, it will generate $27 million in after-tax cash flows, growing 3% in perpetuity. The cost of capital for established social media companies is 12%, but there is a 60-percent chance that the business will not survive (in which case, it will have no assets of value to liquidate).

a. Estimate the value of Friends Online, once it is operational.

b. Given the likelihood of failure, estimate the proportion of equity in Friends Online you would demand today in return for your $50 million investment. (You can assume that Friends Online has no debt or cash.)

c. Estimate the target return you would demand over the next three years, with the risk of failure incorporated into the return.

To solve the next two problems, you will need access to a simulation program like Crystal Ball or @Risk.

8. You are valuing Stedman Inc., a chemical firm in stable growth (growing 3 percent a year), that is expected to generate $100 million in after-tax operating income next year. You have estimated the following:

▪ The return on invested capital on new investments is normally distributed, with an expected value of 15%, with a standard deviation of 3%.

▪ The cost of capital for the firm is 10%, uniformly distributed, with a minimum value of 8% and a maximum value of 12%.

The firm has $500 million in debt outstanding and a cash balance of $200 million. Develop a distribution of simulated values for Stedman Inc.

9. Simon Gold is a mature gold-mining firm that has mines that are expected to generate 100,000 ounces of gold every year for the next 25 years; at the end of that period, the mines will be exhausted and will be worth nothing. The company has fixed costs of $100 million that are expected to remain unchanged over the next 25 years and no variable costs. The cost of capital for gold mining companies is 8%.

a. If the current gold price is $1,500 an ounce and is expected to remain unchanged for the next 25 years, estimate the value of Simon Gold.

b. Now assume that you believe that gold prices will be normally distributed with an expected value of $1,500 an ounce and a standard deviation of $200 an ounce. Develop a distribution of simulated values for Simon Gold.

10. You are a portfolio manager and have analysts who have used Monte Carlo simulations to find 10 undervalued companies, listed here:

Company	Price	Expected Deviation	Standard Undervalued	% time Value	Lowest Value	Highest Value
A	$ 8.00	$ 10.00	$ 1.00	80%	$ 7.00	$ 13.00
B	$ 12.00	$ 13.50	$ 0.50	75%	$10.00	$ 16.00
C	$ 15.00	$ 20.00	$ 5	50%	$ 4.00	$ 50.00
D	$ 9.00	$ 10.00	$ 0.20	85%	$ 8.50	$ 13.00
E	$ 50.00	$ 80.00	$10.00	80%	$40.00	$150.00
F	$ 22.00	$ 25.00	$ 1.00	88%	$18.00	$ 28.00
G	$ 3.00	$ 5.00	$ 0.50	70%	$ 2.50	$ 6.00
H	$150.00	$200.00	$30.00	60%	$40.00	$500.00
I	$ 35.00	$ 70.00	$20.00	65%	$ 0.00	$200.00
J	$ 80.00	$100.00	$ 5.00	90%	$70.00	$115.00

a. Purely on an expected value basis, rank these companies (from best to worst investments).
b. If you wanted to incorporate the uncertainty in the estimates into your ranking, how would the rankings change?
c. If you were worried about downside risk (because you are highly levered), how would you incorporate that risk into your rankings?
d. Under what conditions might you incorporate the highest value into your ranking process?

CHAPTER 34

Overview and Conclusion

The problem in valuation is not that there are not enough models to value an asset, it is that there are too many. Choosing the right model to use in valuation is as critical to arriving at a reasonable value as understanding how to use the model. This chapter attempts to provide an overview of the valuation and pricing models introduced in this book, and a general framework that can be used to pick the right model for any task.

CHOICES IN VALUATION MODELS

In the broadest possible terms, firms or assets can be valued in one of four ways: asset-based valuation approaches where you estimate what the assets owned by a firm are worth currently, intrinsic valuation approaches that discount cash flows to arrive at a value of equity or the firm, pricing approaches that base how much to pay for an asset based on how comparable assets are priced, and option pricing approaches that use contingent claim valuation. Within each of these approaches, there are further choices that help determine the final value.

There are at least two ways in which you can value a firm using asset-based valuation techniques. One is liquidation value, where you consider what the market will be willing to pay for assets if the assets were liquidated today. The other is replacement cost, where you evaluate how much it would cost you to replicate or replace the assets that a firm has in place today.

In the context of discounted cash flow valuation, cash flows to equity can be discounted at the cost of equity to arrive at a value of equity, or cash flows to the firm can be discounted at the cost of capital to arrive at the value for the firm. The cash flows to equity themselves can be defined in the strictest sense as dividends, or in a more expansive sense as free cash flows to equity. These models can be further categorized on the basis of assumptions about growth into stable-growth, two-stage, three-stage and n-stage models. Finally, the measurement of earnings and cash flows may be modified to match the special characteristics of the firm/asset—current earnings for firms/assets that have normal earnings, or normalized earnings for firms/assets whose current earnings may be distorted either by temporary factors or cyclical effects.

In the context of multiples, you can use either equity or firm value as your measure of value and relate it to a number of firm-specific variables—earnings, book value, and sales. The multiples themselves can be estimated by using comparable firms in the same business or from cross-sectional regressions that use the broader universe. For other assets, such as real estate, the price can similarly be expressed as a function of gross income or per square foot of space. Here the comparables would be other properties in the same locale with similar characteristics.

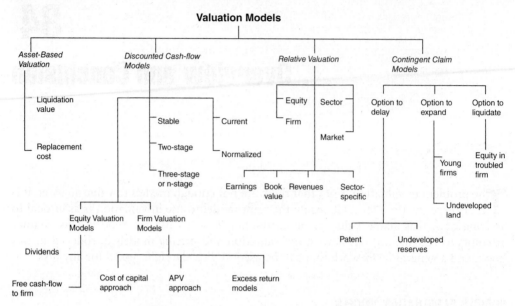

FIGURE 34.1 The Choices in Valuation Models

Contingent claim models can also be used in a variety of scenarios. When you consider the option that a firm has to delay making investment decisions, you can value a patent or an undeveloped natural resource reserve as an option. The option to expand may make young firms with potentially large markets trade at a premium on their discounted cash flow values. Finally, equity investors may derive value from the option to liquidate troubled firms with substantial debt. (See Figure 34.1.)

WHICH APPROACH SHOULD YOU USE?

The values that you obtain from the four approaches can be very different, and deciding which one to use can be a critical step. This judgment, however, will depend on several factors, some of which relate to the business being valued but many of which relate to you as the analyst.

Asset or Business Characteristics

The approach you use to value a business will depend on how marketable its assets are, whether it generates cash flows, and how unique it is in terms of its operations.

Marketability of Assets   Liquidation valuation and replacement cost valuation are easiest to do for firms that have assets that are separable and marketable. (See Figure 34.2.) For instance, you can estimate the liquidation value for a real estate company because its properties can be sold individually, and you can estimate the value of each property easily. The same can be said about a closed-end mutual fund. At the other extreme, consider a brand-name consumer product like Proctor and Gamble. Its assets are not only intangible but difficult to separate out. For instance, you cannot separate the razor business easily from the shaving cream business, and brand-name value is inherent in both businesses.

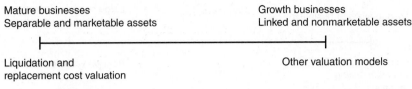

FIGURE 34.2   Asset Marketability and Valuation Approaches

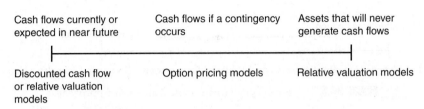

FIGURE 34.3   Cash Flows and Valuation Approaches

You can also use this same analysis to see why the liquidation or replacement cost value of a high-growth business may bear little resemblance to true value. Unlike assets in place, growth assets cannot be easily identified or sold.

Cash-Flow-Generating Capacity   You can categorize assets into three groups based on their capacity to generate cash flows: assets that are either generating cash flows currently or are expected to do so in the near future, assets that are not generating cash flows currently but could in the future in the event of a contingency, and assets that will never generate cash flows. (See Figure 34.3.)

1. The first group includes most publicly traded companies, and these firms can be valued using discounted cash flow models. Note that a distinction is not drawn between negative and positive cash flows, and young start-up companies that generate negative cash flow can still be valued using discounted cash flow models.
2. The second group includes assets such as drug patents, promising (but not viable) technology, undeveloped oil or mining reserves, and undeveloped land. These assets may generate no cash flows currently and could generate large cash flows in the future but only under certain conditions—if the FDA approves the drug patent, if the technology becomes commercially viable, if oil prices and commercial property values go up. While you could estimate expected values using discounted cash flow models by assigning probabilities to these events, you will understate the value of the assets if you do so. You should value these assets using option pricing models.
3. Assets that are never expected to generate cash flows include your primary residence, a baseball card collection, or fine art. These assets can only be valued using pricing or relative valuation models.

Uniqueness (or Presence of Comparables)   In a market where thousands of stocks are traded and tens of thousands of assets are bought and sold every day, it may be difficult to visualize an asset or business that is so unique that you cannot find comparable assets. On a continuum, though, some assets and businesses are part of a large group of similar assets, with no or very small differences across the assets. (See Figure 34.4.) These assets are tailor-made for pricing, since assembling comparable assets (businesses) and controlling for differences is

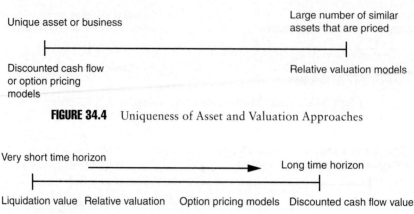

FIGURE 34.4   Uniqueness of Asset and Valuation Approaches

FIGURE 34.5   Investor Time Horizon and Valuation Approaches

simple. The further you move from this ideal, the less reliable is pricing. For businesses that are truly unique, discounted cash flow valuation will yield much better estimates of value.

Analyst Characteristics and Beliefs

The valuation approach that you choose to use will depend on your time horizon, the reason that you are doing the valuation in the first place, and what you think about markets—whether they are efficient, and if they are not, what form the inefficiency takes.

Time Horizon   At one extreme, in discounted cash flow valuation, you consider a firm as a going concern that may last into perpetuity. At the other extreme, with liquidation valuation, you are estimating value on the assumption that the firm will cease operations today. With pricing and contingent claim valuation, you take an intermediate position between the two. (See Figure 34.5.) Not surprisingly then, you should be using discounted cash flow valuation if you have a long time horizon, and pricing if you have a shorter time horizon. This may explain why discounted cash flow valuation is more prevalent when valuing a firm for an acquisition, and pricing is more common in equity research and portfolio management.

Reason for Doing the Valuation   Analysts value businesses for a number of reasons, and the valuation approach used will vary depending on the reason. (See Figure 34.6.) If you are an equity research analyst following steel companies, your job description is simple. You are asked to find the most under- and overvalued companies in the sector, and not take a stand on whether the sector overall is under- or overvalued. You can see why multiples would be your weapon of choice when valuing companies. This effect is likely to be exaggerated if the way you are judged and rewarded is on a relative basis (i.e., your recommendations are compared to those made by other steel company analysts). But if you are an individual investor setting money aside for retirement or a private businessperson valuing a business for purchase, you may want to estimate intrinsic value. Consequently, discounted cash flow valuation is likely to be more appropriate for your needs.

Beliefs about Markets   Embedded in each approach are assumptions about markets and how they work or fail to work. (See Figure 34.7.) With discounted cash flow valuation, you are assuming that market prices deviate from intrinsic value, but that they correct themselves over long periods. With pricing, you are assuming that markets are on average right, and

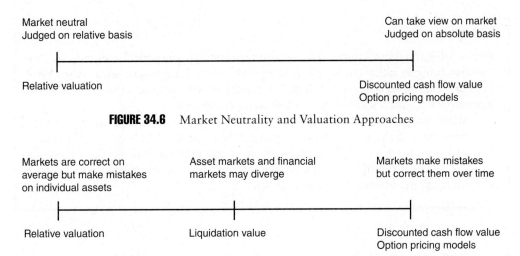

FIGURE 34.6   Market Neutrality and Valuation Approaches

FIGURE 34.7   Views on Market and Valuation Approaches

that while individual firms in a sector or market may be mispriced, the sector or overall market is fairly priced. With asset-based valuation models, you are assuming that the markets for real and financial assets can deviate and that you can take advantage of these differences. Finally, with option pricing models, you are assuming that markets are not very efficient at assessing the value of flexibility that firms have, and that option pricing models will, therefore, give you an advantage. In each and every one of these cases, though, you are assuming that markets will eventually recognize their mistakes and correct them.

CHOOSING THE RIGHT INTRINSIC VALUATION MODEL

The model used in valuation should be tailored to match the characteristics of the asset being valued. The unfortunate truth is that time and resources are wasted trying to make assets fit a prespecified valuation model, either because it is considered to be the best model or because not enough thought goes into the process of model choice. There is no one best model. The appropriate model to use in a particular setting will depend on a number of the characteristics of the asset or firm being valued.

BRIDGING THE PHILOSOPHICAL DIVIDE

Philosophically, there is a big gap between discounted cash flow valuation and pricing. In discounted cash flow valuation, we take a long-term perspective, evaluate a firm's fundamentals in detail, and try to estimate a firm's intrinsic value. In pricing, we assume that the market is right on average and estimate the pricing of a firm by looking at how similar firms are priced. There is utility in both approaches, and it would be useful if we could borrow the best features of pricing while doing discounted cash flow valuation, or vice versa.

Assume that your instincts lead you to discounted cash flow valuation, but that you are expected, as an analyst, to be market-neutral. You can stay market-neutral

(continued)

(continued)

market (described in Chapter 7) to estimate the cost of equity for the valuation. You can also bring in information about comparable firm margins and betas when estimating fundamentals for your firm. Your estimate of intrinsic value will then be market-neutral and include information about comparables.

Alternatively, assume that you prefer pricing. Your analysis can carry the rigor of a discounted cash flow valuation if you can bring in the details of the fundamentals into your comparisons. The chapters on pricing attempted to do this by noting the link between multiples and fundamentals, and also by examining how best to control for these differences in the analysis.

Choosing a Cash Flow to Discount

With consistent assumptions about growth and leverage, you should get the same value for your equity using the firm approach (where you value the firm and subtract outstanding debt) and the equity approach (where you value equity directly). If this is the case, you might wonder why you would pick one approach over the other. The answer is purely pragmatic. For firms that have stable leverage (i.e., they have debt ratios that are not expected to change during the period of the valuation), there is little to choose between the models in terms of the inputs needed for valuation. You use a debt ratio to estimate free cash flows to equity in the equity valuation model, and to estimate the cost of capital in the firm valuation model. Under these circumstances, you should stay with the model that you are more intuitively comfortable with.

For firms that have unstable leverage (i.e., they have too much or too little debt and want to move toward their optimal or target debt ratio during the period of the valuation), the firm valuation approach is much simpler to use, because it does not require cash flow projections from interest and principal payments, and is much less sensitive to errors in estimating leverage changes. The calculation of the cost of capital requires an estimate of the debt ratio, but the cost of capital itself does not change as much as a consequence of changing leverage as does the cash flow to equity. If you prefer to work with assumptions about dollar debt rather than debt ratios, you can switch to the adjusted present value approach.

In valuing equity, you can discount dividends or free cash flows to equity. You should consider using the dividend discount model under the following circumstances:

- You cannot estimate cash flows with any degree of precision either because you have insufficient or contradictory information about debt payments and reinvestments or because you have trouble defining what comprises debt. This was the rationale for using dividend discount models for valuing financial service firms in Chapter 21.
- There are significant restrictions on stock buybacks and other forms of cash return, and you have little or no control over what the management of a firm does with the cash. In this case, the only cash flows you can expect to get from your equity investment are the dividends that managers choose to pay out.

In all other cases, you will get much more realistic estimates of a firm's value using the free cash flow to equity, which may be greater than or lower than the dividend.

Excess Return or Total Cash Flow

In Chapter 32, we looked at excess return models, where rather than value a business based upon total cash flows, you break cash flows down into cash flows that cover the cost of capital and excess returns (cash flows earned above or below the cost of capital), and then value each stream separately. While we also noted that both approaches should yield the same value for a business, with consistent assumptions, excess return models are dependent on being able to estimate the returns that the business makes on its invested capital (return on invested capital) or on equity (return on equity).

Without rehashing arguments already made in this book, measuring accounting returns requires us to be able to estimate capital invested in existing assets/projects and earnings that are reflective of the earnings power of the assets. Those conditions are most likely to be met in mature businesses with stable earnings streams and where accounting decisions (on restructuring charges, write-offs) and financial decisions (on stock buybacks) have not skewed book values. That effectively narrows the scope for excess return models.

Should You Use Current or Normalized Earnings?

Most valuations begin with the current financial statements of the firm and use the reported earnings in those statements as the base for projections. There are some firms, though, where you may not be able to do this, either because the firm's earnings are negative, or because these earnings are abnormally high or low (a firm's earnings are abnormal if they do not fit in with the firm's own history of earnings).

When earnings are negative or abnormal, you can sometimes replace current earnings with a normalized value, estimated by looking at the company's history or industry averages, and value the firm based on these normalized earnings. This is the easiest route to follow if the causes for the negative or abnormal earnings are temporary or transitory, as in the following cases:

- A cyclical firm will generally report depressed earnings during an economic downturn and high earnings during an economic boom. Neither may capture properly the true earnings potential of the firm.
- A firm may report abnormally low earnings in a period during which it takes an extraordinary charge.
- A firm in the process of restructuring may report low earnings during the restructuring period as the changes made to improve firm performance are put into effect.

The presumption here is that earnings will quickly bounce back to normal levels and that little will be lost by assuming that this will occur immediately.

For some firms, though, the negative or low earnings may reflect factors that are unlikely to disappear quickly. There are at least three groups of firms where the negative earnings are likely to be a long-term phenomenon and may even threaten the firm's survival:

1. *Firms with long-term operating, strategic, or financial problems* can have extended periods of negative or low earnings. If you replace current earnings with normalized earnings and value these firms, you will overvalue them.
   - If a firm seems to be in imminent danger of default, the only models that are likely to provide meaningful measures of value are the option pricing model (if financial leverage is high) or a model based on liquidation value.

■ If the firm is troubled but unlikely to go bankrupt, you will have to nurse it back to financial health. In practical terms, you will have to adjust the operating margins over time to healthier levels and value the firm based on its expected cash flows.

2. *An infrastructure firm* may report negative earnings in its initial periods of growth, not because it is unhealthy, but because the investments it has made take time to pay off. The cash flows to the firm and equity are often also negative, because the capital expenditure needs for this type of firm tend to be disproportionately large relative to depreciation. For these firms to have value, capital expenditure has to drop once the infrastructure investments have been made, and operating margins have to improve. The net result will be positive cash flows in future years and a value for the firm today.

3. *Young start-up companies* often report negative earnings early in their life cycles, as they concentrate on turning interesting ideas into commercial products. To value such companies, you have to assume a combination of high revenue growth and improving operating margins over time.

Growth Patterns

In general, when valuing a firm, you can assume that your firm is already in stable growth, assume a period of constant high growth and then drop the growth rate to stable growth (two-stage growth), or allow for a transition phase to get to stable growth (three-stage or n-stage models). There are several factors you should consider in making this judgment.

Growth Momentum　　The choice of growth pattern will be influenced by the level of current growth in earnings and revenues. You can categorize firms, based on growth in recent periods, into three groups:

1. Stable-growth firms report earnings and revenues growing at or below the nominal growth rate in the economy that they operate in. Note that this growth rate can even be negative.

2. Moderate-growth firms report earnings and revenues growing at a rate moderately higher than the nominal growth rate in the economy; as a rule of thumb, consider any growth rate within 8–10 percent of the growth rate of the economy as a moderate growth rate.

3. High-growth firms report revenues growing at a rate much higher than the nominal growth rate in the economy, though their profit margins may still be negative.

For firms growing at the stable rate, the steady state models that assume constant growth provide good estimates of value. For firms growing at a moderate rate, the two-stage discounted cash flow model should provide enough flexibility in terms of capturing changes in the underlying characteristics of the firm, while a three-stage or n-stage model may be needed to capture the longer transitions to stable growth that are inherent in high-growth-rate firms.

Source of Growth (Barriers to Entry)　　The higher expected growth for a firm can come from either general competitive advantages acquired over time such as a brand name, reduced costs of production (from economies of scale), or specific advantages that are the result of legal barriers to entry—licenses or product patents. The former are likely to erode over time as new competitors enter the marketplace, while the latter are more likely to disappear abruptly when the legal barriers to entry are removed. The expected growth rate for a firm that has specific sources of growth is likely to follow the two-stage process where growth is high for a certain period (for instance, the period of the patent) and drops abruptly to a stable rate after that. The expected growth rate for a firm that has general sources of growth is more likely to decline gradually over time as new competitors come in. The speed with which this competitive advantage is expected to be lost is a function of several factors, including:

- *Nature of the competitive advantage.* Some competitive advantages, such as brand name in consumer products, seem to be more difficult to overcome and consequently are likely to generate growth for longer periods. Other competitive advantages, such as a first-mover advantage, seem to erode much faster.
- *Competence of the firm's management.* More competent management will be able to slow, though not stop, the loss of competitive advantage over time by creating strategies that find new markets in which to exploit the firm's current competitive advantage, and that attempt to find new sources of competitive advantage.
- *Ease of entry into the firm's business.* The greater the barriers to industry in entering the firm's business, because of either capital requirements or technological factors, the slower will be the loss of competitive advantage.

These factors are summarized and presented in Figure 34.8, with the appropriate discounted cash flow model indicated for each combination of the factors.

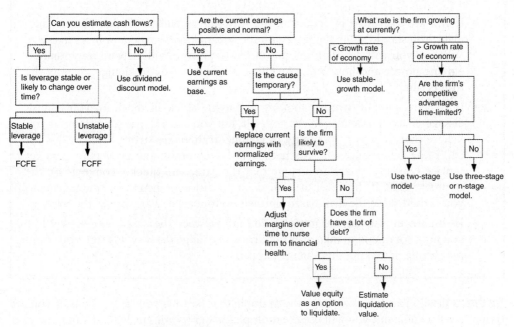

FIGURE 34.8 Discounted Cash Flow Models

CHOOSING THE RIGHT PRICING MODEL

Many analysts choose to value assets using pricing models. In making this choice, two basic questions have to be answered: Which multiple will be used in the valuation? Will this multiple be arrived at using the sector or the entire market?

Which Multiple Should I Use?

The chapters on multiples presented a variety of multiples. Some were based on earnings, some on book value, and some on revenues. For some multiples, current values were used, and for others forward or forecast values were used. Since the values you obtain are likely to be different using different multiples, deciding which multiple to use can make a big difference to your estimate of value. There are three ways you can answer this question: One is to adopt the cynical view that you should use the multiple that reflects your biases; the second is to value your firm with different multiples and try to use all of the values that you obtain; and the third is to pick the best multiple and base your valuation on it.

STATUS QUO VERSUS OPTIMAL MANAGEMENT

The chapters on valuing acquisitions and troubled firms noted that the value of a firm can be substantially higher if you assume that it is optimally run than if it is run by incumbent management. A question that you are often faced with in valuation is whether you should value the firm with incumbent management or with the optimal management. The answer is simple in some cases and complicated in others:

- If you are interested in acquiring the firm and intend to change the management, you should value the firm with the optimal management policies in place. Whether you will pay that amount in the acquisition will depend on your bargaining power and how long you think it will take you to change the way the firm is run.

- If you are a small investor looking at buying stock in the firm, you cannot change incumbent management yourself, but you can still pay a premium if you believe that there is a possibility of change. If there are strong mechanisms for corporate governance—hostile takeovers are common and poor managers get replaced quickly—you can assume that the value will quickly converge on the optimal value. If, however, it is difficult to dislodge incumbent management, you should value the firm based on their continued stewardship of the firm.

- If you are an institutional investor, you fall between these two extremes. While you may not intend to take over the firm and change the way it is run, you could play a role in making this change happen.

The Cynical View   You can always use the multiple that best fits your story. Thus, if you are trying to sell a company, you will use the multiple that gives you the highest value for your company. If you are buying the same company, you will choose the multiple that yields the lowest value. While this clearly crosses the line from analysis into manipulation, it is a more common practice than you might realize. Even if you never plan to employ this practice, you should consider ways in which you can protect yourself from being victimized by it. First, you have to recognize that conceding the choice of multiple and comparables to an analyst is the equivalent of letting him or her write the rules of the game. You should play an active role in deciding which multiple should be used to value a company and what firms will be viewed as comparable firms. Second, when presented with a value based on one multiple, you should always check to see what the value would have been if an alternative multiple had been used.

The Bludgeon View   You can always value a company using a dozen or more multiples, and then use all of the values, different though you might be, in your final recommendation. There are three ways in which you can present the final estimate of value. The first is in terms of a range of values, with the lowest value that you obtained from a multiple being the lower end of the range, and the highest value being the upper limit. The problem with this approach is that the range is usually so large that it becomes useless for any kind of decision-making. The second approach is a simple average of the values obtained from the different multiples. While this approach has the virtue of simplicity, it gives equal weight to the values from each multiple even though some multiples may yield more precise answers than others. The third approach is a weighted average, with the weight on each value reflecting the precision of the estimate. This weight can either be a subjective one or be a statistical measure—you can, for instance, use the standard error on a prediction from a regression.

The Best Multiple   While we realize that you might be reluctant to throw away any information, the best estimates of value are usually obtained by using the one multiple that is best suited for your firm. There are three ways in which you can find this multiple:

1. *Fundamentals approach.* You should consider using the variable that is most highly correlated with your firm's value. For instance, current earnings and value are much more highly correlated in consumer product companies than in young technology companies. Using price-earnings ratios makes more sense for the former than for the latter.
2. *Statistical approach.* You could run regressions of each multiple against the fundamentals that we determined affected the value of the multiple in earlier chapters, and use the R-squared of the regression as a measure of how well that multiple works in the sector. The multiple with the highest R-squared is the multiple that you can best explain using fundamentals and should be the multiple you use to value companies in that sector.
3. *Conventional multiple approach.* Over time, you usually see a specific multiple become the most widely used one for a specific sector. For instance, price-to-book ratios are the most used multiple to analyze financial service companies.

Table 34.1 summarizes the most widely used multiples by sector. In an ideal world, you should see all three approaches converge—the fundamental that best explains value should also have the highest R-squared and be the conventional multiple used in the sector. In fact, when the multiple in use conventionally does not reflect fundamentals, which can happen if the sector is in transition or evolving, you will get misleading estimates of value.

TABLE 34.1 Most Widely Used Multiples by Sector

Sector	Multiple Used	Rationale/Comments
Cyclical manufacturing High tech, high growth	PE, relative PE PEG	Often with normalized earnings. Big differences in growth across firms make it difficult to compare PE ratios.
High growth/negative earnings Infrastructure	EV/Sales, EV/ EBITDA	Assume future margins will be positive. Firms in sector have losses in early years, and reported earnings can vary depending on depreciation method.
REIT	P/CF	Restrictions on investment policy and large depreciation charges make cash flows better measure than equity earnings.
Financial services Retailing	PBV PS VS	Book value often marked to market. If leverage is similar across firms. If leverage is different.

Market or Sector Pricing

In most relative valuations, you value a firm relative to other firms in the industry in which the firm operates, and attempt to answer a simple question: Given how other firms in the business (sector) are priced by the market, is this firm under- or overpriced? Within this approach, you can define comparable firms either narrowly, as being firms that not only operate in the business in which your firm operates but also look like your firm in terms of size or market served, or broadly, in which case you will have far more comparable firms. If you are attempting to control for differences across firms subjectively, you should stick with the narrower group. But if you plan to control for differences statistically—with a regression, for instance—you should go with the broader definition.

The chapters on relative valuation presented an alternative approach to relative valuation, where firms were valued relative to the entire market. When you do this, you are not only using a much larger universe of questions but asking a different question: Given how other firms in the market are priced, is this firm under- or overvalued? A firm can be under-valued relative to its sector but overvalued relative to the market if the entire sector is mispriced.

The approach you use to relative valuation will depend again on what your task is defined to be. If you want to stay narrowly focused on your sector and make judgments on which stocks are under- or overvalued, you should stick with sector-based relative valuation. If you have more leeway and are trying to find under- or overvalued stocks across the market, you should look at the second approach—perhaps in addition to the first one.

WHEN SHOULD YOU USE THE OPTION PRICING MODELS?

The chapters on applying option pricing models to valuation presented a number of scenarios where option pricing may yield a premium on traditional discounted cash flow valuation. You should keep in mind the following general propositions when using option pricing models:

■ *Use the real options sparingly.* Restrict your use of options to where they make the biggest difference in valuation. In general, options will affect value the most at smaller firms that derive the bulk of their value from assets that resemble options. Therefore, valuing patents as options to estimate firm value makes more sense for a small biotechnology firm than it does for a drug giant like Merck. While Merck may have dozens of patents, it derives much of its value from a portfolio of developed drugs and the cash flows they generate.

■ *Opportunities are not always options.* You should be careful not to mistake opportunities for options. Analysts often see a firm with growth potential and assume that there must be valuable options embedded in the firm. For opportunities to become valuable options, you need some degree of exclusivity for the firm in question; this can come from legal restrictions on competition or a significant competitive edge.

■ *Do not double-count options.* All too often, analysts incorporate the effect of options on fundamentals and on company value, and then proceed to add on premiums to reflect the same options. Consider, for instance, the undeveloped oil reserves owned by an oil company. While it is legitimate to value these reserves as options, you should not add this value to a discounted cash flow valuation of the company if your expected growth rate in the valuation is set higher because of the firm's undeveloped reserves.

CAN A FIRM BE UNDERVALUED AND OVERPRICED AT THE SAME TIME?

If you value a firm using both discounted cash flow and pricing models, you may very well get different answers using the two: The firm may be undervalued using relative valuation models but overvalued using discounted cash flow models. What do we make of these differences, and why do they occur? If a firm is overvalued using a discounted cash flow model and undervalued using relative valuation, it is usually an indication that the sector is overvalued relative to its fundamentals. For instance, in March 2000, we valued Amazon at $30 a share using a discounted cash flow model, when it was trading at $70 a share, it was clearly overvalued. At the same time, a comparison of Amazon to other dot-com firms suggested that it was undervalued relative to these firms.

   If a firm is undervalued using a discounted cash flow model and overvalued using relative valuation, it indicates that the sector is undervalued. By March 2001, Amazon's stock price had dropped to $15, but the values of all Internet stocks had dropped by almost 90 percent. In March 2001 a discounted cash flow valuation suggested that Amazon was undervalued, but a relative valuation indicated that it was now overvalued relative to the sector.

   As an investor, you can use both discounted cash flow and relative valuation to decide how much to pay for a company. Optimally, you would like to buy companies that are undervalued and underpriced. That way, you benefit from market corrections both across time (which is the way you make money in discounted cash flow valuation) and across companies.

CONCLUSION

The analyst faced with the task of valuing a firm/asset or its equity has to choose among three different approaches—discounted cash flow valuation, relative valuation, and option pricing models—and within each approach, between different models. This choice will be driven largely by the characteristics of the firm/asset being valued—the level of its earnings, its growth potential, the sources of earnings growth, the stability of its leverage, and its dividend policy. Matching the valuation model to the asset or firm being valued is as important a part of valuation as understanding the models and having the right inputs.

Once you decide to go with one or another of these approaches, you have further choices to make—whether to use equity or firm valuation in the context of discounted cash flow valuation, which multiple you should use to value firms or equity, and what type of option is embedded in a firm.

References

Aboody, D., & Lev, B. (1998). The value relevance of intangibles: The case of software capitalization. *Journal of Accounting Research*, 36, 161–191.

Alexander, S. S. (1964). Price movements in speculative markets: Trends or random walks? In: *The Random Character of Stock Market Prices* (ed. P. Cootner), 338–372. Cambridge, MA: MIT Press.

Altman, E. I. (1968). Financial ratios, discriminant analysis and the prediction of corporate bankruptcy. *Journal of Finance*, 23, 589–609.

Altman, E. I., & Kishore, V. (2000). *The default experience of U.S. bonds,* [Working paper]. New York University.

Amram, M., & Kulantilaka, N. (1998). *Real Options: Managing Strategic Investments in an Uncertain World*. New York: Oxford University Press.

Arbel, A., & Strebel, P. J. (1983). Pay attention to neglected stocks. *Journal of Porfolio Management*, 9, 37–42.

Arnott, R. D. (1985). The use and misuse of consensus earnings. *Journal of Portfolio Management*, 11, 18–27.

Avellaneda, M., & Lawrence, P. (2000). *Quantitative Modeling of Derivative Securities*, New York: Chapman & Hall.

Ball, C. A., & Torous, W. N. (1983). A simplified jump process for common stock returns. *Journal of Financial and Quantitative Analysis*, 18, 53–65.

Banz, R. (1981). The relationship between return and market value of common stocks. *Journal of Financial Economics*, 9, 3–18.

Barclay, M. J., Smith, C. W., & Watts R. L. (1995). The determinants of corporate leverage and dividend policies. *Journal of Applied Corporate Finance*, 7(4), 4–19.

Basu, S. (1977). The investment performance of common stocks in relation to their price-earnings: A test of the efficient market hypothesis. *Journal of Finance*, 32, 663–682.

Basu, S. (1983). The relationship between earnings yield, market value and return for NYSE common stocks: Further evidence. *Journal of Financial Economics*, 12, 129–156.

Bathke, A. W., Jr., & Lorek, K. S. (1984). The relationship between time-series models and the security market's expectation of quarterly earnings. *Accounting Review*, 59, 163–176.

Beaver, W. H., Kettler, P., & Scholes, M. (1970). The association between market determined and accounting determined risk measures. *Accounting Review*, 45(4), 654–682.

Beckers, S. (1981). A note on estimating the parameters of the diffusion–jump process model of stock returns. *Journal of Financial and Quantitative Analysis*, 16, 127–140.

Bernstein, L. A., & Siegel, J. G. (1979). The concept of earnings quality. *Financial Analysts Journal*, 35, 72–75.

Bernstein, P. (1992). *Capital Ideas*. New York: Free Press.

Bernstein, P. (1996). *Against the Gods*. New York: John Wiley & Sons.

Bernstein, R. (1995). *Style Investing*. New York: John Wiley & Sons.

Bernstein, R. (1997a, December 19). EVA and market returns. *Quantitative Viewpoint*, Merrill Lynch.

Bernstein, R. (1997b, February 3). EVA and market returns. *Quantitative Viewpoint*, Merrill Lynch.

Bethke, W. M., & Boyd, S. E. (1983). Should dividend discount models be yield-tilted? *Journal of Portfolio Management*, 9, 23–27.

Bhide, A. (1989). The causes and consequences of hostile takeovers. *Journal of Applied Corporate Finance, 2,* 36–59.

Bhide, A. (1993). Reversing corporate diversification. In: *The New Corporate Finance–Where Theory Meets Practice* (ed. D. H. Chew Jr.). New York: McGraw-Hill.

Black, F., & Scholes, M. (1972). The valuation of option contracts and a test of market efficiency. *Journal of Finance, 27,* 399–417.

Blume, M. (1979). Betas and their regression tendencies: Some further evidence. *Journal of Finance, 34*(1), 265–267.

Booth, L. (1999). Estimating the equity risk premium and equity costs: New way of looking at old data. *Journal of Applied Corporate Finance, 12*(1), 100–112.

Box, G., & Jenkins, G. (1976). *Time Series Analysis: Forecasting and Control.* Oakland, CA: Holden-Day.

Bradley, M., Desai, A., & Kim, E. H. (1983). The rationale behind interfirm tender offers. *Journal of Financial Economics, 11,* 183–206.

Bradley, M., Desai, A., & Kim, E. H. (1988). Synergistic gains from corporate acquisitions and their division between the stockholders of target and acquiring firms. *Journal of Financial Economics, 21,* 3–40.

Brennan, M. J. (1970). Taxes, market valuation and corporation financial policy. *National Tax Journal, 23,* 417–427.

Brennan, M. J., & Schwartz, E. S. (1985). Evaluating natural resource investments. *Journal of Business, 58,* 135–158.

Brickley, J., Smith, C., & Zimmerman, J. (1995). The economics of organizational architecture. *Journal of Applied Corporate Finance, 8,* 19–31.

Brickley, J., Smith, C., & Zimmerman, J. (1995). Transfer pricing and the control of internal corporate transactions. *Journal of Applied Corporate Finance, 8*(2), 60–67.

Brown, L. D., & Rozeff, M. S. (1979). Univariate time series models of quarterly accounting earnings per share: A proposed model. *Journal of Accounting Research, 17,* 178–189.

Brown, L. D., & Rozeff, M. S. (1980). Analysts can forecast accurately! *Journal of Portfolio Management, 6,* 31–34.

Brown, S. J., & Warner, J. B. (1980). Measuring security price performance. *Journal of Financial Economics, 8*(3), 205–258.

Brown, S. J., & Warner, J. B. (1985). Using daily stock returns: The case of event studies. *Journal of Financial Economics, 14*(1), 3–31.

Bruner, R. F. (2005). *Deals from Hell: M&A Lessons that Rise above the Ashes.* Hoboken, NJ: John Wiley.

Bruner, R. F., Eades, K. M., Harris, R. S., et al. (1998). Best practices in estimating the cost of capital: Survey and synthesis. *Financial Practice and Education, 8,* 13–28.

Bruner, R. F., Eades, K. M., Harris, R. S., et al. (1998). Best practices in estimating the cost of capital: Survey and synthesis. *Financial Practice and Education, 8,* 14–28.

Buffett, W. E., & Cunningham, L. A. (2001). *The Essays of Warren Buffett: Lessons of Corporate America.* Minneapolis, MN: Cunningham Group.

Capaul, C., Rowley, I., & Sharpe, W. F. (1993). International value and growth stock returns. *Financial Analysts Journal, 49,* 27–36.

Carhart, M. M. (1997). On the persistence of mutual fund performance. *Journal of Finance, 52,* 57–82.

Carpenter, J. (1998). The exercise and valuation of executive stock options. *Journal of Financial Economics, 48,* 127–158.

Chambers, A. E., & Penman, S. H. (1984). Timeliness of reporting and the stock price reaction to earnings announcements. *Journal of Accounting Research, 22,* 21–47.

Chan, K. C., Karolyi, G. A., & Stulz, R. M. (1992). Global financial markets and the risk premium on U.S. equity. *Journal of Financial Economics, 32,* 132–167.

Chan, L. K., Hamao, Y., & Lakonishok, J. (1991). Fundamentals and stock returns in Japan. *Journal of Finance, 46,* 1739–1789.

Chan, S. H., Martin, J., & Kensinger, J. (1990). Corporate research and development expenditures and share value. *Journal of Financial Economics, 26,* 255–276.

Chen, N., Roll, R., & Ross, S. A. (1986). Economic forces and the stock market. *Journal of Business, 59,* 383–404.

Choi, F. D. S., & Levich, R. M. (1990). *The Capital Market Effects of International Accounting Diversity.* New York: Dow Jones–Irwin.

Clemons, E. K., Barnett, S., & Lanier, J. (2005, September 22). Fortune favors the forward-thinking. *Financial Times Special Reports/Mastering Risk.*

Collins, W., & Hopwood, W. (1980). A multivariate analysis of annual earnings forecasts generated from quarterly forecasts of financial analysts and univariate time series models. *Journal of Accounting Research, 20,* 390–406.

Conrad, J. (1989). The price effect of option introduction. *Journal of Finance, 44,* 487–498.

Cootner, P. H. (1961). Common elements in futures markets for commodities and bonds. *American Economic Review, 51*(2), 173–183.

Cootner, P. H. (1962). Stock prices: Random versus systematic changes. *Industrial Management Review, 3,* 24–45.

Copeland, T. E., & Antikarov, V. (2001). *Real Options: A Practitioners Guide.* New York: Texere.

Copeland, T. E., Koller, T., & Murrin, J. (1999). *Valuation: Measuring and Managing the Value of Companies.* New York: John Wiley & Sons.

Cottle, S., Murray, R., & Bloch, F. (1988). *Security Analysis.* New York: McGraw-Hill.

Cox, J. C., & Ross, S. A. (1976). The valuation of options for alternative stochastic processes. *Journal of Financial Economics, 3,* 145–166.

Cox, J. C., & Rubinstein, M. (1985). *Options Markets.* Upper Saddle River, NJ: Prentice Hall.

Cox, J. C., Ross S. A., & Rubinstein, M. (1979). Option pricing: A simplified approach. *Journal of Financial Economics, 7,* 229–264.

Cragg, J. G., & Malkiel, B. G. (1968). The consensus and accuracy of predictions of the growth of corporate earnings. *Journal of Finance, 23,* 67–84.

Crichfield, T., Dyckman, T., & Lakonishok J. (1978). An evaluation of security analysts forecasts. *Accounting Review, 53,* 651–668.

Cuny, C. C., & Jorion, P. (1995). Valuing executive stock options with endogenous departure. *Journal of Accounting and Economics, 20,* 193–205.

Damodaran, A. (1989). The weekend effect in information releases: a study of earnings and dividend announcements. *Review of Financial Studies, 2,* 607–623.

Damodaran, A. (1994). *Damodaran on Valuation.* New York: John Wiley & Sons.

Damodaran, A. (1999). *Dealing with cash, marketable securities and cross holdings.* www.stern .nyu.edu/&adamodar/New_Home_Page/papers.html.

Damodaran, A. (1999). *Estimating the equity risk premium.* www.stern.nyu.edu/&adamodar/New _Home_Page/papers.html.

Damodaran, A. (1999). *The treatment of operating leases.* www.stern.nyu.edu/&adamodar/New_ Home_Page/papers.html.

Damodaran, A. (1999). *The treatment of R&D.* www.stern.nyu.edu/&adamodar/New_Home_Page /papers.html.

Damodaran, A. (1999). Value enhancement: Back to the future. *Contemporary Finance Digest, 3,* 2–47.

Damodaran, A. (2001). *Choosing the right valuation model.* www.stern.nyu.edu/adamodar/New Home Page/papers.html.

Damodaran, A. (2001). *Corporate Finance: Theory and Practice, Second Edition.* New York: John Wiley & Sons.

Damodaran, A. (2001). *Dealing with negative earnings.* www.stern.nyu.edu/&adamodar/New_ Home_Page/papers.html.

Damodaran, A. (2001). *It's all relative: First principles of relative valuation.* www.stern.nyu.edu/& adamodar/New_Home_Page/papers.html.

Damodaran, A. (2001). *The Dark Side of Valuation.* Upper Saddle River, NJ: Prentice Hall.

Damodaran, A. (2017). *Narrative and Numbers.* Hoboken, NJ: John Wiley & Sons

Dann, L. Y., & DeAngelo, H. (1983). Standstill agreements, privately negotiated stock repurchases, and the market for corporate control. *Journal of Financial Economics*, *11*, 275–300.

Dann, L. Y., & DeAngelo, H. (1988). Corporate financial policy and corporate control: A study of defensive adjustments in asset and ownership structure. *Journal of Financial Economics*, *20*, 87–128.

Davis, D., & Lee, K. (1997). A practical approach to capital structure for banks. *Journal of Applied Corporate Finance*, *10*(1), 33–43.

DeAngelo, H., & Rice, E. M. (1983). Antitakeover charter amendments and stockholder wealth. *Journal of Financial Economics*, *11*, 329–360.

DeAngelo, H., DeAngelo, L., & Rice, E. M. (1984). Going private: The effects of a change in corporate ownership structure. *Midland Corporate Finance Journal*, *2*, 35–43.

DeBondt, W. F. M., & Thaler, R. (1985). Does the stock market overreact? *Journal of Finance*, *40*, 793–805.

DeBondt, W. F. M., & Thaler, R. (1987). Further evidence on investor overreaction and stock market seasonality. *Journal of Finance*, *42*, 557–581.

Deng, Z., & Lev, B. (1998). *The valuation of acquired R&D.* [Working paper]. New York University.

Denis, D. J., & Denis, D. K. (1993). Leveraged recaps in the curbing of corporate overinvestment. *Journal of Applied Corporate Finance*, *6*(1) 60–71.

Dimson, E. (1979). Risk measurement when shares are subject to infrequent trading. *Journal of Financial Economics*, *7*(2), 197–226.

Dimson, E., & Marsh, P. R. (1984). An analysis of brokers' and analysts' unpublished forecasts of UK stock returns. *Journal of Finance*, *39*, 1257–1292.

Dimson, E., & Marsh, P. R. (1986). Event studies and the size effect: The case of UK press recommendations. *Journal of Financial Economics*, *17*, 113–142.

Dimson, E., & Marsh, P. R. (2001). Murphy's law and market anomalies. *Journal of Portfolio Management*, *25*, 53–69.

Dimson, E., Marsh, P., & Staunton, M. (2010). Credit Suisse Global Investment Returns Yearbook 2010. Credit Suisse Research Institute.

Dubofsky, P., & Varadarajan, P. R. (1987). Diversification and measures of performance: Additional empirical evidence. *Academy of Management Journal*, *30*, 597–608.

Ehrbar, A. (1998). *EVA: The Real Key to Creating Wealth.* New York: John Wiley & Sons.

Elton, E., Gruber, M. J., & Mei, J. (1994). Cost of capital using arbitrage pricing theory: A case study of nine New York utilities. *Financial Markets, Institutions and Instruments*, *3*, 46–73.

Elton, E. J., & Gruber, M. J. (1995). *Modern Portfolio Theory and Investment Management.* New York: John Wiley & Sons.

Estep, T. (1985). A new method for valuing common stocks. *Financial Analysts Journal*, *41*, 26, 27, 30–33.

Estep, T. (1987). Security analysis and stock selection: Turning financial information into return forecasts. *Financial Analysts Journal*, *43*, 34–43.

Fama, E. F. (1965). The behavior of stock market prices. *Journal of Business*, *38*, 34–105.

Fama, E. F. (1970). Efficient capital markets: A review of theory and empirical work. *Journal of Finance*, *25*, 383–417.

Fama, E. F., & Blume, M. (1966). Filter rules and stock market trading profits. *Journal of Business*, *39*, 226–241.

Fama, E. F., & French, K. R. (1988). Permanent and temporary components of stock prices. *Journal of Political Economy*, *96*, 246–273.

Fama, E. F., & French, K. R. (1992). The cross-section of expected returns. *Journal of Finance*, *47*, 427–466.

Fama, E. F., & French, K. R. (2010). Luck versus Skill in the cross-section of mutual fund Returns. *The Journal of Finance, 65*, 1915–1947.

Fama, E. F., & Schwert, G. W. (1977). Asset returns and inflation. *Journal of Financial Economics, 5*, 115–146.

Fang, H., & Lai, T.-Y. (1997). Co-kurtosis and capital asset pricing. *Financial Review, 32*, 293–307.

Foster, G. (1977). Quarterly accounting data: Time series properties and predictive ability results. *Accounting Review, 52*, 1–31.

Fried, D., & Givoly, D. (1982). Financial analysts forecasts of earnings: A better surrogate for earnings expectations. *Journal of Accounting and Economics, 4*, 85–107.

Fruhan, W. E. (1979). *Financial Strategy: Studies in the Creation, Transfer and Destruction of Shareholder Value.* Homewood, IL: Irwin.

Fruhan, W. E., Kester, W. C., Mason, S. P., et al. (1992). *Congoleum: Case Problems in Finance.* Homestead, IL: Irwin.

Fuller, R. J., & Hsia, C. (1984). A simplified common stock valuation model. *Financial Analysts Journal, 40*, 49–56.

Fuller, R. J., Huberts, L. C., & Levinson M. (1992). It's not higgledy-piggledy growth! *Journal of Portfolio Management, 18*, 38–46.

Gabaix, X., Gopikrishnan, P., Plerou, V. et al. (2003). A theory of power law distributions in financial market fluctuations. *Nature, 423*, 267–270.

Gaughan, P. A. (1999). *Mergers, Acquisitions and Corporate Restructurings.* New York: John Wiley & Sons.

Geske, R. (1979). The valuation of compound options. *Journal of Finance, 7*, 63–82.

Gibbons, M. R., & Hess, P. (1981). Day of the week effects and asset returns. *Journal of Business, 54*, 579–596.

Givoly, D., & Lakonishok, J. (1984). The quality of analysts' forecasts of earnings. *Financial Analysts Journal, 40*, 40–47.

Godfrey, S., & Espinosa, R. (1996). A practical approach to calculating the cost of equity for investments in emerging markets. *Journal of Applied Corporate Finance, 9*(3), 80–81.

Goodman, D. A., & Peavy III, J. W. (1983). Industry relative price-earnings ratios as indicators of investment returns. *Financial Analysts Journal, 39*, 60–66.

Gordon, M. (1962). *The Investment, Financing and Valuation of the Corporation.* Homewood, IL: Irwin.

Graham, B. (2006). *The Intelligent Investor: The Definitive Book on Value Investing.* HarperBusiness.

Graham, B., Dodd, D. L., & Cottle, S. (1962). *Security Analysis, Fourth Edition.* New York: McGraw-Hill.

Graham, J. (1996). Debt and the marginal tax rate. *Journal of Financial Economics, 41*, 41–73.

Graham, J. R. (1996). Proxies for the corporate marginal tax rate. *Journal of Financial Economics, 42*(2), 187–221.

Graham, J. R. (2000). How big are the tax benefits of debt? *Journal of Finance, 55*(5), 1901–1941.

Grant, R. M. (1998). *Contemporary Strategy Analysis.* Malden, MA: Blackwell.

Griffin, P. A. (1977). The time series Behavior of quarterly earnings. *Journal of Accounting Research, 15*, (Spring), 71–83.

Gultekin, M. N., & Gultekin, B. N. (1983). Stock market seasonality: International evidence. *Journal of Financial Economics, 12*, 469–481.

Hamada, R. S. (1972). The effect of the firm's capital structure on the systematic risk of common stocks. *Journal of Finance, 27*, 435–452.

Haugen, R. (1997). *Modern Investment Theory.* Upper Saddle River, NJ: Prentice Hall.

Haugen, R. A. (1990). *Modern Investment Theory.* Englewood Cliffs, NJ: Prentice Hall.

Haugen, R. A., & Lakonishok, J. (1988). *The Incredible January Effect.* Homewood, IL: Dow Jones–Irwin.

Hawkins, E. H., Chamberlin, S. C., & Daniel W. E. (1984). Earnings expectations and security prices. *Financial Analysts Journal*, 40, 24–27, 30–38, 74.

Healy, P. M., Palepu, K. G., & Ruback, R. S. (1992). Does corporate performance improve after mergers? *Journal of Financial Economics*, 31, 135–176.

Hertz, D. (1964). Risk analysis in capital investment. *Harvard Business Review*.

Hong, H., Kaplan, R. S., & Mandelkar, G. (1978). Pooling vs. purchase: The effects of accounting for mergers on stock prices. *Accounting Review*, 53(1), 31–47.

Hooke, J. C. (2001). *Security Analysis on Wall Street*. New York: John Wiley & Sons.

Hull, J. C. (1995). *Introduction to Futures and Options Markets*. Upper Saddle River, NJ: Prentice Hall.

Hull, J. C. (1999). *Options, Futures and Other Derivatives*. Upper Saddle River, NJ: Prentice Hall.

Ibbotson, R. G., & Brinson, G. P. (1993). *Global Investing*. New York: McGraw-Hill.

Ibbotson, R. G., & Brinson, G. P. (1996). *Global Investing*. New York: McGraw-Hill.

Indro, D. C., & Lee, W. Y. (1997). Biases in arithmetic and geometric averages as estimates of long-run expected returns and risk premium. *Financial Management*, 26, 81–90.

Inselbag, I., & Kaufold, H. (1997). Two DCF approaches and valuing companies under alternative financing strategies. *Journal of Applied Corporate Finance*, 10(1), 115–122.

Itami, H. (1987). *Mobilizing Invisible Assets*. Cambridge, MA: Harvard University Press.

Jacobs, B. I., & Levy, K. N. (1988). Disentangling equity return irregularities: New insights and investment opportunities. *Financial Analysts Journal*, 44, 18–44.

Jacobs, B. I., & Levy, K. N. (1988). On the value of "value". *Financial Analysts Journal*, 44, 47–62.

Jacobs, B. I., & Levy, K. N. (1988a). Disentangling equity return irregularities: New insights and investment opportunities. *Financial Analysts Journal*, 44, 18–44.

Jacobs, B. I., & Levy, K. N. (1988b). On the value of "value". *Financial Analysts Journal*, 44, 47–62.

Jaffe, J. (1974). Special information and insider trading. *Journal of Business*, 47, 410–428.

Jarrell, G. A., Brickley, J. A., & Netter, J. M. (1988). The market for corporate control: The empirical evidence since 1980. *Journal of Economic Perspectives*, 2, 49–68.

Jarrow, R. A., & Rosenfeld, E. R. (1984). Jump risks and the intertemporal capital asset pricing model. *Journal of Business*, 57, 337–351.

Jegadeesh, N., & Titman, S. (1993). Returns to buying winners and selling losers: Implications for stock market efficiency. *Journal of Finance*, 48(1), 65–91.

Jegadeesh, N., & Titman, S. (2001). Profitability of momentum strategies: An evaluation of alternative explanations. *Journal of Finance*, 56(2): 699–720.

Jennergren, L. P. (1975). Filter tests of Swedish share prices. In: *International Capital Markets* (ed. E. J. Elton & M. J. Gruber), 55–67. New York: North-Holland.

Jennergren, L. P., & Korsvold, P. E. (1974). Price formation in the Norwegian and Swedish stock markets–Some random walk tests. *Swedish Journal of Economics*, 76, 171–185.

Jensen, M. (1968). The performance of mutual funds in the period 1945–64. *Journal of Finance*, 2, 389–416.

Jensen, M., & Bennington, G. A. (1970). Random walks and technical theories, some additional evidence. *Journal of Finance*, 25, 469–482.

Jensen, M. C. (1969). Risk, the pricing of capital assets, and the evaluation of investment portfolios. *Journal of Business*, 42, 167–247.

Jensen, M. C. (1986). Agency costs of free cash flow, corporate finance, and takeovers. *American Economic Review*, 76, 323–329.

Jensen, M. C. (1986). Agency costs of free cashflow, corporate finance and takeovers. *American Economic Review*, 76, 323–329.

Jensen, M. C., & Ruback, R. S. (1983). The market for corporate control. *Journal of Financial Economics*, 11, 5–50.

Kaplan, R. S., & Roll, R. (1972). Investor evaluation of accounting information: Some empirical evidence. *Journal of Business*, 45, 225–257.

Kaplan, S., & Weisbach, M. S. (1992). The success of acquisitions: The evidence from divestitures. *Journal of Finance, 47,* 107–138.

Kaplan, S. N. (1989). Campeau's acquisition of federated: Value destroyed or value added? *Journal of Financial Economics, 25,* 191–212.

Karpoff, J. M., & Malatesta, P. H. (1990). The wealth effects of second-generation state takeover legislation. *Journal of Financial Economics, 25,* 291–322.

Keim, D. (1983). Size related anomalies and stock return seasonality: Further empirical evidence. *Journal of Financial Economics, 12,* 13–32.

Kim, S. H., Crick, T., & Kim, S. H. (1986). Do executives practice what academics preach? *Management Accounting, 68,* 49–52.

Kisor, Jr, M., & Whitbeck, V. S. (1963). A new tool in investment decision-making. *Financial Analysts Journal, 19,* 55–62.

Knaup, A. E. (2005). Survival and longevity in the business employment dynamics data. *Monthly Labor Review,* 128(59): 50–56.

Knaup, A. E., & Piazza, M. C. (2007, September). Business employment dynamics data: Survival and longevity. *Monthly Labor Review, 130,* 3–10.

KPMG. (1999). *Unlocking Shareholder Value: The Keys to Success.* New York: KPMG Global Research Report.

Krallinger, J. C. (1997). *Mergers and Acquisitions: Managing the Transaction.* New York: eMcGraw-Hill.

Kramer, J. R., & Pushner, G. (1997). An empirical analysis of economic value added as a proxy for market value added. *Financial Practice and Education, 7,* 41–49.

Kraus, A., & Litzenberger, R. H. (1976). Skewness preference and the valuation of risk assets. *Journal of Finance, 31,* 1085–1100.

Lang, L. H. P., Stulz, R. M., & Walkling, R. A. (1991). A test of the free cash flow hypothesis: The case of bidder returns. *Journal of Financial Economics, 29,* 315–335.

Lease, R. C., McConnell, J. J., & Mikkelson, W. H. (1983). The market value of control in publicly-traded corporations. *Journal of Financial Economics, 11,* 439–471.

Leibowitz, M. L., & Kogelman, S. (1992). Franchise value and the growth process. *Financial Analysts Journal, 48,* 53–62.

Levin, R. C., Klevorick, A. K., Nelson, R. R. et al. (1987). Appropriating the returns from industrial research and development. *Brookings Paper on Economic Activity.*

Levy, H., & Lerman, Z. (1985). Testing P/E ratio filters with stochastic dominance. *Journal of Portfolio Management, 11,* 31–40.

Lewellen, W. G. (1971). A pure financial rationale for the conglomerate merger. *Journal of Finance, 26,* 521–537.

Lindenberg, E., & Ross, M. P. (1999). To purchase or to pool: does it matter? *Journal of Applied Corporate Finance, 12,* 32–47.

Linn, S., & McConnell, J. J. (1983). An empirical investigation of the impact of anti-takeover amendments on common stock prices. *Journal of Financial Economics, 11,* 361–399.

Lintner, J. (1965). The valuation of risk assets and the selection of risky investments in stock portfolios and capital budgets. *Review of Economics and Statistics, 47,* 13–37.

Little, I. M. D. (1960). *Higgledy Piggledy Growth.* Oxford: Institute of Statistics.

Litzenberger, R. H., & Ramaswamy, K. (1979). The effect of personal taxes and dividends on capital asset prices: Theory and empirical evidence. *Journal of Financial Economics, 7,* 163–196.

Longstaff, F. A. (1995). How much can marketability affect security values? *Journal of Finance, 50,* 1767–1774.

Mackie-Mason, J. (1990). Do taxes affect corporate financing decisions? *Journal of Finance, 45,* 1471–1494.

Madden, B. L. (1998). *CFROI Cash Flow Return on Investment Valuation: A Total System Approach to Valuing a Firm.* Woburn, MA: Butterworth-Heinemann.

Maher, J. M. (1976). Discounts for lack of marketability for closely held business interests. *Tax Magazine*, *1*, 562–571.

Malmendier, U., Moretti, E., & Peters, F. S. (2018). Winning by losing: Evidence on the long-run effects of mergers. *The Review of Financial Studies*, *31*, 3212–3264.

Mandelbrot, B. (1961). The variation of certain speculative prices. *Journal of Business*, *34*, 394–419.

Mandelbrot, B., & Hudson, R. L. (2004). *The (mis)Behavior of Markets: A Fractal View of Risk, Ruin and Reward*. New York: Basic Books.

Markowitz, H. M. (1991). Foundations of portfolio theory. *Journal of Finance*, *46*(2), 469–478.

Mauboussin, M. (1998). Get real. Boston: Credit Suisse First Boston.

Mauboussin, M., & Johnson, P. (1997). Competitive advantage period: The neglected value driver. *Financial Management*, *26*(2), 67–74.

McConnell, J. J., & Muscarella, C. J. (1985). Corporate capital expenditure decisions and the market value of the firm. *Journal of Financial Economics*, *14*, 399–422.

Mei, J., & Moses, M. (2001). *Art as an investment and the underperformance of masterpieces: evidence from 1875–2000*. [Working paper]. New York University.

Merton, R. C. (1973). The theory of rational option pricing. *Bell Journal of Economics*, *4*(1), 141–183.

Merton, R. C. (1976). Option pricing when the underlying stock returns are discontinuous. *Journal of Financial Economics*, *3*, 125–144.

Michaely, R., & Womack, K. L. (1999). Conflict of interest and the credibility of underwriter analyst recommendations. *Review of Financial Studies*, *12*, 653–686.

Michel, A., & Shaked, I. (1984). Does business diversification affect performance? *Financial Management*, *13*, 5–14.

Miller, M. (1977). Debt and taxes. *Journal of Finance*, *32*, 261–275.

Mitchell, M. L., & Lehn, K. (1990). Do bad bidders make good targets? *Journal of Applied Corporate Finance*, *3*, 60–69.

Modigliani, F., & Miller, M. (1958). The cost of capital, corporation finance and the theory of investment. *American Economic Review*, *48*, 261–297.

Moeller, S. B., Schlingemann, F. P., and Stulz, R. M. (2004). Firm size and gains from acquisitions. *Journal of Financial Economics*, *73*, 201–228.

Moroney, R. E. (1973). Most courts overvalue closely held stocks. *Tax Magazine*, *1*, 144–155.

Myers, S. C. (1976). Determinants of corporate borrowing. *Journal of Financial Economics*, *5*, 147–175.

Myers, S. C., & Majluf, N. S. (1984). Corporate financing and investment decisions when firms have information that investors do not have. *Journal of Financial Economics*, *13*, 187–221.

Nail, L. A., Megginson, W. L., & Maquieira, C. (1998). Wealth creation versus wealth redistributions in pure stock-for-stock mergers. *Journal of Financial Economics*, *48*, 3–33.

Nichols, D. C., & Wahlen, J. M. (2004). How do earnings numbers relate to stock returns? A review of classic accounting research with updated numbers. *Accounting Horizons*, *18*, 263–286.

Niederhoffer, V., & Osborne, M. F. M. (1966). Market making and reversal on the stock exchange. *Journal of the American Statistical Association*, *61*, 891–916.

O'Brien, P. (1988). Analysts' forecasts as earnings expectations. *Journal of Accounting and Economics*, *10*, 53–83.

O'Byrne, S. F. (1996). EVA and market value. *Journal of Applied Corporate Finance*, *9*(1), 116–125.

O'Byrne, S. F., & Young, S. D. (2000). *EVA and Value-based Management*. New York: McGraw-Hill.

Opler, T., Saron, M., & Titman, S. (1997). Designing capital structure to create stockholder value. *Journal of Applied Corporate Finance*, *10*, 21–32.

Palepu, K. G. (1986). Predicting takeover targets: A methodological and empirical analysis. *Journal of Accounting and Economics*, *8*(1), 3–35.

Palepu, K. G. (1990). Consequences of leveraged buyouts. *Journal of Financial Economics, 26,* 247–262.

Parrino, J. D., & Harris, R. S. Takeovers, management replacement and post-acquisition operating performance: Some evidence from the 1980s. *Journal of Applied Corporate Finance, 11,* 88–97.

Peters, D. J. (1991). Valuing a growth stock. *Journal of Portfolio Management, 17,* 49–51.

Peters, E. E. (1991). *Chaos and Order in the Capital Markets.* New York: John Wiley & Sons.

Pettit, J. (1999). Corporate capital costs: a practitioner's guide. *Journal of Applied Corporate Finance, 12*(1), 113–120.

Pinegar, J. M., & Wilbricht, L. (1989). What managers think of capital structure theory: A survey. *Financial Management, 18*(4), 82–91.

Porter, M. E. (1980). *Competitive Strategy: Techniques for Analyzing Industries and Competitors.* New York: Free Press.

Pradhuman, S. (2000). *Small Cap Dynamics.* Princeton, NJ: Bloomberg Press.

Praetz, P. D. (1972). The distribution of share price changes. *Journal of Business, 45*(1), 49–55.

Pratt, S., Reilly, R. F., & Schweihs, R. P. (2000). *Valuing a Business: The Analysis and Appraisal of Closely Held Companies.* New York: McGraw-Hill.

Press, S. J. (1967). A compound events model for security prices. *Journal of Business, 40*(3), 317–335.

Randall, D., & Ertel, C. (2005, September 15). Moving beyond the official future. *Financial Times Special Reports/Mastering Risk.*

Rappaport, A. (1998). *Creating Shareholder Value.* New York: Free Press.

Reinganum, M. R. (1983). The anomalous stock market behavior of small firms in January: Empirical tests for tax-loss effects. *Journal of Financial Economics, 12,* 89–104.

Rendleman, R. J., Jones, C. P., & Latané, H. A. (1982). Empirical anomalies based on unexpected earnings and the importance of risk adjustments. *Journal of Financial Economics, 10,* 269–287.

Richards, R. M., & Martin, J. D. (1979). Revisions in earnings forecasts: How much response? *Journal of Portfolio Management, 5,* 47–52.

Ritter, J., & Chopra, N. (1989). Portfolio rebalancing and the turn of the year effect. *Journal of Finance, 44,* 149–166.

Roll, R. (1983). Vas ist das? *Journal of Portfolio Management, 9,* 18–28.

Roll, R. (1984). A simple implicit measure of the bid-ask spread in an efficient market. *Journal of Finance, 39,* 1127–1139.

Roll, R. (1986). The hubris hypothesis of corporate takeovers. *Journal of Business, 59,* 197–216.

Rosenberg, B., & Guy, J. (1976). Beta and investment fundamentals; Beta and investment fundamentals–II. *Financial Analysts Journal, 32*(3), 60–72; *32*(4), 62–70.

Rosenberg, B., & Guy, J. (1995). Prediction of beta from investment fundamentals. *Financial Analysts Journal, 51*(1), 101–112.

Rosenberg, B., & Marathe, V. (1979). Tests of capital asset pricing hypotheses. *Research in Finance, 1,* 115–124.

Rosenberg, B., Reid, K., & Lanstein, R. (1985). Persuasive evidence of market inefficiency. *Journal of Portfolio Management, 11,* 9–17.

Ross, S. A. (1976). The arbitrage theory of capital asset pricing. *Journal of Economic Theory, 13*(3), 341–360.

Sarin, R., & Wakker, P. (1994). Folding back in decision tree analysis. *Management Science, 40,* 625–628.

Schipper, K., & Smith, A. (1983). Effects of recontracting on shareholder wealth: The case of voluntary spin-offs. *Journal of Financial Economics, 12,* 437–468.

Schipper, K., & Smith, A. (1986). A comparison of equity carve-outs and seasoned equity offerings: Share price effects and corporate restructuring. *Journal of Financial Economics, 15,* 153–186.

Scholes, M., & Williams, J. T. (1977). Estimating betas from nonsynchronous data. *Journal of Financial Economics, 5*(3), 309–327.

Senchack Jr, A. J., & Martin, J. D. (1987). The relative performance of the PSR and PER investment strategies. *Financial Analysts Journal, 43*, 46–56.

Seyhun, H. N. (1986). Insiders' profits, costs of trading and market efficiency. *Journal of Financial Economics, 16*, 189–212.

Seyhun, H. N. (1998). *Investment Intelligence from Insider Trading*. Cambridge, MA: MIT Press.

Shapiro, A. (1985). Corporate strategy and the capital budgeting decision. *Midland Corporate Finance Journal, 3*, 22–36.

Shapiro, A. (1989). *Modern Corporate Finance*. New York: Macmillan.

Sharpe, W. F. (1964). Capital asset prices: A theory of market equilibrium under conditions of risk. *Journal of Finance, 19*, 425–442.

Shiller, R. (1999). *Irrational Exuberance*. Princeton, NJ: Princeton University Press.

Siegel, D., Smith, J., & Paddock J. (1993). Valuing offshore oil properties with option pricing models. In: *The New Corporate Finance*, (ed. D. H. Chew Jr.). New York: McGraw-Hill.

Siegel, J. (2007). *Stocks for the Very Long Run: The Definitive Guide to Investment Strategies*. New York: McGraw-Hill.

Silber, W. L. (1991). Discounts on restricted stock: The impact of illiquidity on stock prices. *Financial Analysts Journal, 47*, 60–64.

Sirower, M. L. (1996). *The Synergy Trap*. New York: Simon & Schuster.

Smith, A. J. (1990). Corporate ownership structure and performance: The case of management buyouts. *Journal of Financial Economics, 27*, 143–164.

Smith, C. W. (1986). Investment banking and the capital acquisition process. *Journal of Financial Economics, 15*, 3–29.

Sorensen, E. H., & Williamson, D. A. (1985). Some evidence on the value of the dividend discount model. *Financial Analysts Journal, 41*, 60–69.

Stapleton, R. C. (1985). A note on default risk, leverage and the MM theorem. *Journal of Financial Economics, 2*, 377–381.

Stewart, G. B. (1991). *The Quest for Value*. New York: HarperBusiness.

Stickney, C. P. (1993). *Financial Statement Analysis*. Fort Worth, TX: Dryden Press.

Stocks, bonds, bills and inflation (1999). Chicago: Ibbotson Associates.

Stulz, R. (1996). Does the cost of capital differ across countries? An agency perspective. *European Financial Management, 2*, 11–22.

Stulz, R. (1996). Rethinking risk management. *Journal of Applied Corporate Finance, 9*(3), 8–24.

Stulz, R. M. (1999). Globalization, corporate finance, and the cost of capital. *Journal of Applied Corporate Finance, 12*(1), 8–25.

Sunder, S. (1973). Relationship between accounting changes and stock prices: problems of measurement and some empirical evidence. In: *Empirical Research in Accounting: Selected Studies*, 1–45. Toronto: Lexington.

Sunder, S. (1975). Stock price and risk related accounting changes in inventory valuation. *Accounting Review, 50*, 305–315.

Titman, S. (1984). The effect of capital structure on a firm's liquidation decision. *Journal of Financial Economics, 13*, 137–151.

Vander Weide, J. H., & Carleton, W. T. (1988). Investor growth expectations: Analysts vs. history. *Journal of Portfolio Management, 14*, 78–83.

Varadarajan, P. R., & Ramanujam, V. (1987). Diversification and performance: A reexamination using a new two-dimensional conceptualization of diversity in firms. *Academy of Management Journal, 30*, 369–380.

Warner, J. N. (1977). Bankruptcy costs: Some evidence. *Journal of Finance, 32*, 337–347.

Watts, R. (1975). *The time series behavior of quarterly earnings*. [Working paper]. University of Newcastle.

Weston, J. F., & Copeland, T. E. (1992). *Managerial Finance, Ninth Edition*. Orlando, FL: Harcourt Brace Jovanovich.

Weston, J. F., Chung, K. S., & Siu, J. A. (1998). *Takeovers, Restructuring and Corporate Governance*. New York: Simon & Schuster.

White, G. I., Sondhi, A., & Fried, D. (1997). *The Analysis and Use of Financial Statements*. New York: John Wiley & Sons.

Wilcox, J. W. (1984). The P/B-ROE valuation model. *Financial Analysts Journal, 40*, 58–66.

Williams, J. R. (1998). *GAAP Guide*. New York: Harcourt Brace.

Womack, K. (1996). Do brokerage analysts' recommendations have investment value? *Journal of Finance, 51*, 137–167.

Woodruff, C. S., & Senchack Jr, A. J. (1988). Intradaily price-volume adjustments of NYSE stocks to unexpected earnings. *Journal of Finance, 43*(2), 467–491.

Woolridge, R. (1993). Competitive decline and corporate restructuring. In: *The New Corporate Finance*, (ed. D. H. Chew Jr.), New York: McGraw-Hill.

Index